QUANTITATIVE METHODS FOR BUSINESS DECISIONS

With Cases

FIFTH EDITION

LAWRENCE L. LAPIN
San Jose State University

Harcourt Brace Jovanovich, Publishers
and its subsidiary, Academic Press

San Diego   New York   Chicago   Austin   Washington, D.C.
London   Sydney   Tokyo   Toronto

ISBN: 0-15-574331-7

Library of Congress Catalog Card Number: 90-83124

Printed in the United States of America

Preface

M y goal in writing *Quantitative Methods for Business Decisions* has been to provide a complete and modern treatment of basic management science methodology. The book is written for college students who have only an algebra background. Even more important, it is designed to provide a feeling for the variety and power of management science tools, to alleviate apprehension of the subject, and to enable students to recognize on-the-job situations in which management science methodology can be successfully employed.

The book has been thoroughly class-tested many times in a variety of different courses, which has resulted in the culling, revising, and grading of the problem material. In general, the problems are broken into several distinct parts to make the student's job easier and to permit the instructor added flexibility in making assignments. As an added bonus, brief answers to selected problems are provided in the back of the book, so that students can check their own work. Questions for each end-of-chapter case appear with the case, and the cases themselves have been upgraded for this edition.

The Fifth Edition provides a streamlined topical sequence that minimizes jumping back and forth. This revision has several major improvements in topical coverage that make the book easier to use, more flexible, more comprehensive, and more relevant than previous editions. As the tinted areas in the diagram on the next page indicate, the overall design of the book is modular to provide maximum flexibility for adaptation to the requirements of a particular course. All or portions of any part of these subject groupings may be used in constructing a one- or two-quarter or a one- or two-semester quantitative methods course. For example, Chapters 2–4 may be bypassed by students who have had a prior course in statistics or by instructors who teach a purely deterministic course (a viable possibility with this book). The specific sequencing constraints to be followed are also shown in the diagram.

In today's computerized environment, the optimal focus in teaching quantitative methods places less emphasis on hand computations with algorithms and more emphasis on concepts. To this end, the Fifth Edition includes several major improvements. Most chapters now end with sections describing computer applications. That placement eliminates any dependency on a particular computer or software package (and computer details may be easily skipped). The tilt toward the computer is a very gradual one, and this new edition will remain familiar to and comfortable for instructors who have taught out of prior ones.

The book's companion software package, *QuickQuant*, has also been improved. This program is now available in two editions. PC Version 2.0 for the IBM PC works on all compatible computers that have the MS-DOS capability. The new MacIntosh Version 2.0 duplicates the program features for MacIntosh Pluses, SEs, and IIs. This totally *optional* package is available to all users of this textbook. Menu-driven and user-friendly,

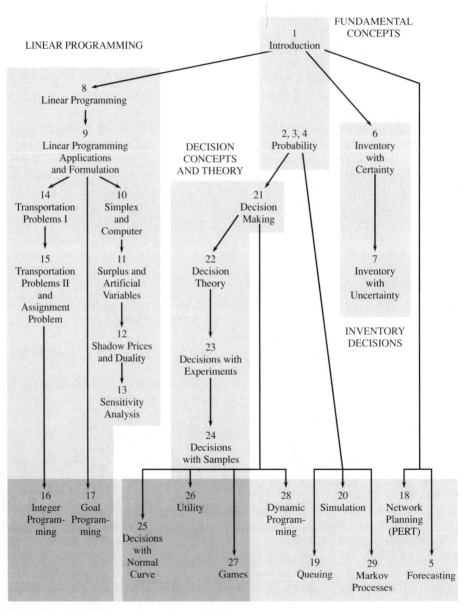

SPECIAL TOPICS

QuickQuant will do the messy computations for most procedures described in the book, giving instructors and students added freedom to explore new topics and applications. A detailed description of the new features of *QuickQuant* Version 2.0 is given in the Guide to *QuickQuant* at the end of this book.

A thorough discussion of the many changes made in the Fifth Edition is contained in the Synopsis in the following section. Some changes were motivated by my desire to improve the rigor of the book, while at the same time reducing hand-computational demands and giving better explanations in those areas where my own students had difficulties. My actual experience as owner of retail stores motivated certain changes to the presentation of inventory analysis. The availability of *QuickQuant* has freed me from previous computational constraints that had limited this book's scope. This increased freedom is reflected in new topical coverage and in improved presentations of original topics. Many new problems have been added to this edition, with some new cases and improvements to the existing ones.

This book is more intuitive than most. Discussions devoted to difficult topics therefore may be longer than those in some other books. Explanations are richly illustrated with relevant and interesting examples to provide more meaningful and *easier* learning experiences than those of briefer books. Chapter 10 thoroughly describes in nonmathematical terms the underlying rationale of the simplex method, so that the student can learn why—as well as how—this method works. More advanced concepts, such as artificial variables, are grouped in a second chapter (Chapter 11). Chapter 18 discusses network planning (PERT or CPM) in a broad context, including management implications, milestone and activity scheduling, time–cost trade-off, and (in an appendix to the chapter) probabilistic aspects. Chapter 20 introduces Monte Carlo simulation as a simple substitute for the stopwatch observation of an actual system operation. Highly intuitive decision trees are used extensively throughout to explain a variety of concepts.

The book also highlights the limitations and pitfalls associated with various mathematical models and algorithms. For example, some basic models, such as the EOQ model used in inventory decisions and the simple queuing formulas, are based on assumptions that rarely apply in real life. Wherever practical, alternative approaches such as Monte Carlo simulation are indicated and fully described. Traditional probabilistic PERT assumptions are accompanied by a critical analysis of their applicability. The severe limitations on the use of Markovian decision models are also noted.

The Instructor's Manual contains specific recommendations for various course designs, teaching suggestions, and detailed solutions to the nearly 600 problems and the end-of-chapter cases in the text. Also available is a testbook which contains a set of about 200 solved problems of slight to moderate difficulty. A comprehensive bibliography is included in the back of the book for students who wish to pursue a particular topic in greater detail.

I wish to thank my colleagues who were instrumental in helping me shape the manuscript: Gerry Gunn, Central Washington University; Ke T. Hsia, California State University, Los Angeles; and James E. Storbeck, Ohio State University. I also wish to acknowledge the valuable assistance of my students, and to extend special mention to Janet Anaya, who helped find errors and assisted in preparing the Instructor's Manual.

LAWRENCE L. LAPIN

Synopsis of Major Changes to the Fifth Edition

This Fifth Edition has been improved in many ways. Some of the key changes are summarized below.

A More Coherent Probability Segment One major change has been to move sampling discussions from Chapter 2 to Chapter 3, where probability distributions are introduced. This facilitates the new and simplified introduction to probability trees which appears with the basic material. Another shift brings the subjective probability chapter near the front of the book, as Chapter 4, so that it directly follows the two early probability chapters. Users can more easily introduce subjective cumulative probability distributions, their discrete approximations, and judgmental normal curves without having to wade through decision analysis. And the decision analysis itself should be easier to learn, since all probability preliminaries take place in a single sequence.

Expanded Forecasting Coverage Many additions have been made to the discussion of forecasting in Chapter 5. The chapter now has a more integrated organization, with improved notation and a new seasonal exponential smoothing model. The causal models have been enhanced to include nonlinear trend curves. Regression analysis is more thoroughly presented and completely incorporates standard computer output.

New Inventory Topics A major overhaul has been made of the coverage of inventory analysis in Chapters 6 and 7. The lost sales model has been added when demand is uncertain. This change recognizes that retailers typically experience lost sales when shortages arise, while the backordering model (still in the book) merely approximates their experience. The notation has been improved to better distinguish the various shortage penalties and the holding costs for multiple-period versus single-period models. Also included is a discussion of a service level model, with a corresponding imputed shortage penalty.

Revamped Linear Programming The linear programming segment has been improved in several ways. The LP introduction in Chapter 8 contains a new section that justifies the graphical method steps and discusses pitfalls from taking shortcuts. Chapter 8 now includes graphical explanations of unbounded and infeasible problems. This addition streamlines the later simplex discussions in Chapters 10 and 11, where greater prominence has been given to computerized evaluations. The presentation of the simplex algorithm has been improved by adding a new section that explains the meaning of the exchange coefficients and other elements of the simplex tableau. Chapter 10 has a new short symbolic section showing all simplex steps, where z_j and $c_j - z_j$ are introduced as alternative labels for sacrifice and improvement values. Chapter 11 now contains a section on alternative solution methods that includes a brief discussion of Karmarker's algorithm. The presentation of the dual linear program in Chapter 12 has been made more realistic through the inclusion of unrestricted dual variables. Complete rules are given for passing from a non-standard primal to its dual.

Modified LP Extensions   The presentation of special transportation method applications in Chapter 15 has been simplified and resequenced, with bounded cells, sources, and destinations placed at the chapter's end. The discussion of integer programming in Chapter 16 has been streamlined by eliminating redundant coverage of the assignment problem (retained as a transportation method application) and by simplifying the presentation of the branch-and-bound method. A graphical problem has been added to introduce this method. Coverage of goal programming in Chapter 17 has been simplified and strengthened. The simpler presentation begins with a graphical portrayal of multiple goals. The omnibus objective function is made more intuitive through the use of natural coefficients as a substitute for arbitrary weights. New to this edition is an alternative procedure, pre-emptive goal programming, which avoids entirely the omnibus objective by instead solving a succession of linear programs—each incorporating higher priority goals as constraints.

Improved Decision Analysis   Many improvements have been made to the decision analysis chapter group. A more general and systematic treatment is given in Chapter 22 to risk premiums and certainty equivalents. The discussion of decision making with experimental information is now enriched in Chapter 23 with the introduction of EVEI and ENGE concepts. That change helps students digest the Bayesian statistics in Chapter 24, where EVSI and ENGS are introduced. Chapter 24 has been totally rewritten in an attempt to sort out these concepts, to improve the discussion of the economic issues in sampling, and to integrate computer evaluations. A brief segment has been added to Chapter 26 graphically showing the relationships among attitude toward risk, expected values, certainty equivalents, and risk premiums. The notion of negative risk premium is also discussed in this chapter in conjunction with risk seeking attitude.

Greater Computer Thrust   The still optional use of the computer has been expanded to virtually every computationally intensive topic in this book. Many of the above changes are reflected in the *QuickQuant* package. A detailed summary of new features in Version 2.0 can be found in the Guide to *QuickQuant* at the back of this book. Every major *QuickQuant* application is illustrated within the related chapters. A substantial number of computer exercises have been added to the problems and cases.

Contents

1

Introduction to Quantitative Methods for Decision Making

$\mathbb{A}$ quiet revolution has taken place in managerial decision making over the past three decades—a revolution that is due largely to the successful implementation of *quantitative methods* and the widespread use of computers. The list of the types of business problems that these procedures can be employed to solve grows daily, and examples of successful applications can be found in every functional area—from marketing to production, from finance to personnel—and in all major industries. Indeed, quantitative methods can be applied to decision making in general and can be used by individuals or groups, in education, in the professions, and in every type of organization, including governments and nonprofit foundations.

1-1 Quantitative Methods: A Continuing Story of Success

A few short case histories will demonstrate how useful quantitative methods have been in solving a variety of actual problems.

■ **Managing Research and Development** In the late 1950s, the U.S. Navy was faced with the monumental task of equipping its nuclear submarine fleet with Polaris ballistic missiles. A quantitative method called PERT (Program Evaluation and Review Technique) was used to establish schedules and to coordinate and control the efforts of hundreds of contractors.

■ **Determining the Number of Bank Tellers** Banks often use quantitative analysis to decide how many tellers are needed at various times during the week, so employee workloads can be balanced and so customers spend a tolerable amount of time waiting in line.

■ **Locating Warehouses** A chemical company that produces fertilizers and pesticides employed quantitative methods to determine where to locate its warehouses. The resulting sites minimized the combined annual cost of transportation, storage, and handling.

■ **Designing an Oil-Tanker Port Facility** An international oil company committed several hundred million dollars to the construction of a port facility in the Persian Gulf to service oil tankers. Alternative designs were constructed and run "on paper" for a number of years to determine a statistical pattern for future profits. Through this computer simulation, the design was selected that provided the greatest rate of return on invested capital at an acceptable level of risk.

■ **Deployment of Fire Fighting Companies** A study was conducted in New York City to determine how many fire companies the city needed, where they should be located, and how they should be dispatched to alarms.* A simulation of the new adaptive procedure indicated that faster response times could be achieved and workloads could be substantially lowered at the same time. Total annual savings to the city exceeded $5 million per year.

■ **Investing in Satellite Communications Systems** Satellites have become an increasingly important element in worldwide communications. In 1971, the RCA Corporation decided to enter the satellite business for the private sector.† Various types of quantitative methods in many different areas of application were employed to evaluate the various alternatives and to recommend the optimal strategy.

■ **Planning Political Campaign Strategies** One interesting application of quantitative methods occurred during a U.S. senatorial race. By using quantitative methods to

---

* Ignall, E. J. et al., "Improving the Deployment of New York City Fire Companies," *Interfaces* (February 1975), pp. 48–61.
† Nigam, A. K., "Analysis for a Satellite Communications System," *Interfaces* (February 1975), pp. 37–47.

identify the important characteristics of small geographical units throughout the state, one candidate was able to concentrate campaign expenditures on the few that would be most profitable.

1-2 Management Science and Operations Research

This book is concerned largely with the specific techniques used in the cases just described and similar situations. These quantitative methods can be broadly categorized as techniques of **management science**—a field melding portions of business, economics, statistics, mathematics, and other disciplines into a pragmatic effort to help managers make decisions. As an area of study, these quantitative methods are often identified as **operations research**. Regardless of the label used, the techniques of management science and operations research are concerned with selecting the best alternative course of action whenever mathematics can be helpful in reaching a decision. Many problem situations can be structured so that the possible choices can be ranked on a numerical scale. Common rankings are *profit* or *cost*. In such cases, an **optimal solution** is the one that yields the maximum profit or minimum cost. Other yardsticks may apply in some applications, so that an optimal solution might be the most effective alternative in terms of time, reliability, or one of many kinds of measures. The particular quantitative method for finding the best solution is sometimes called a **mathematical optimization procedure**.

The beginnings of operations research can be traced to World War II, when the United States and Great Britain employed mathematicians and physicists to analyze military operations. After the war, many of those involved in military operations research retained their interest in analyzing decision making in peacetime endeavors and developed new techniques that could be directly applied to business problems. The availability of digital computers allowed these techniques to be applied quickly to large-scale optimization problems.

1-3 Procedures and Applications

Operations research is concerned with using available resources to find optimal courses of action. The field is primarily functional in nature, so that interdisciplinary teams (which sometimes include such disparate persons as historians, sociologists, and psychologists) are often used to attack decision-making problems. In this book, we will view operations research in terms of the tools historically associated with it, as these tools are applied to managerial decision making.

Operations-research methods have been cataloged by type of application and procedure. One of the earliest applications—the analysis of **waiting lines**—predates modern operations research by several decades and has given rise to an area of mathematics referred to as **queuing theory**. It has been used in a variety of operational decisions and in helping to design facilities. Successful applications range from determining the number of supermarket checkout counters, to deciding the size of a parking lot. Quantitative methods have also been developed in the areas of **inventory control** and

equipment replacement. Businesses have subsequently saved annual costs amounting to billions of dollars just by improving their inventory management.

The most well-known operations-research procedure is **linear programming**—a mathematical optimization tool that has been used to solve a tremendous variety of decision-making problems requiring the allocation of scarce resources. Linear programming is used in oil refineries to determine how gasolines should be blended and in similar applications throughout the chemical industry. Linear programming is also used to determine how goods should be transported.

Related resource-allocation methods include the more general **mathematical programming**, which extends beyond linear programming to a much wider class of problem situations. For decisions that must be made at several successive points in time, such as budgetary investment decisions, **dynamic programming** may be used. Another important tool, mentioned earlier, is PERT; the Polaris program experience shows that this technique has proved useful in controlling large, long-run projects. The list of operations-research procedures and applications is still growing.

Although the two fields are often confused and their borders may overlap, management science is somewhat broader in concept than operations research. Management science encompasses a variety of quantitative methods from older disciplines, especially economics, statistics, and industrial engineering, as well as from newer ones, such as cybernetics, systems analysis, organization theory, and computer and information sciences. Management science relies heavily on **statistical decision theory**—itself an amalgam of statistics, economics, and psychology. The concepts of **game theory**, which is the province of mathematicians and economists, are also included in management science. Both management science and operations research use elements of the stochastic processes employed in **probability theory**; important applications to business problems may be expressed as **Markov processes**. Another powerful tool—**Monte Carlo simulation** (used in the oil-tanker port facility study described earlier)—is essentially a form of statistical sampling that is usually carried out on a computer.

1-4 Models and Decision Making

Every decision-making situation involves **alternatives**. Quantitative methods are used to select the alternative that best satisfies the decision maker's goals. Identifying the possible alternatives and goals is an important task. Once the alternatives are identified, a problem can be quantitatively analyzed by comparing the alternatives in terms of how well they meet the decision maker's objectives. We have already noted that various yardsticks are used for comparison; the classical gauge in business is *profit* or *cost*, although we will encounter other measures as well.

The Mathematical Model: Parameters and Variables

The first step in applying quantitative methods is generally to express the problem mathematically. Such a formulation is called a **mathematical model**. All mathematical models consist of **variables** and constant terms, which are sometimes referred to as **parameters**. The variables and parameters are usually linked together by algebraic expressions that reflect the decision maker's goals and any special limitations on the kinds of alternatives to be considered.

As an example, we will consider a simple inventory problem where the decision maker's goal is to determine the quantity of items to order periodically so that total operating cost is minimized. A simple mathematical model takes the form

Total annual cost = Ordering cost + Holding cost + Procurement cost

and the objective can be expressed as

$$\text{Minimize:} \quad \text{Total annual cost} = \left(\frac{A}{Q}\right)k + hc\left(\frac{Q}{2}\right) + Ac$$

where Q is the order quantity and the single decision variable for this particular problem. The variable Q can assume many different alternative values, such as 0, 1, 2, 3,..., 100, 101,.... The parameters are

A = Annual number of items demanded

k = Cost of placing an order

h = Annual cost per dollar value for holding items in inventory

c = Unit cost of procuring an item

These parameters may be set at any levels that apply to a given situation, so that the same model applies regardless of the levels established for the parameters. This particular model will be explained in further detail in Chapter 5.

Constraints and Feasible Solutions

Sometimes a mathematical model incorporates **constraints** that place special limitations on the problem variables. These constraints are often expressed algebraically. For example, suppose that the storage facilities can accommodate only 300 units at a time. This constraint could be expressed as

$$Q \le 300$$

which would then become an integral part of the model formulation. This restriction disallows any order quantity greater than 300, such as $Q = 350$ units. In effect, this constraint separates the alternatives into two groups: **feasible solutions** (values of Q not exceeding 300 units) and **infeasible solutions** (values of Q exceeding 300 units).

Optimal Solutions

Quantitative methods are also employed to solve the problem by finding the value of the variable that meets the requirements of the mathematical model. For our inventory model, we must find the optimal value for the variable Q. Here, the **optimal solution** can be found from

$$Q = \sqrt{\frac{2Ak}{hc}}$$

which is derived from mathematical analysis. To illustrate, suppose that each order costs $4 to place, the annual demand is 1,000 units, it costs $.20 per year for each dollar value of items held in inventory, and these items may be procured from the supplier for $1 each. Substituting the values $k = 4$, $A = 1,000$, $h = .20$, and $c = 1$ into the above expression, the minimum-cost order quantity is

$$Q = \sqrt{\frac{2(1000)4}{.20(1)}} = \sqrt{40,000} = 200 \text{ units}$$

Algorithms and Model Types

The solution procedure we just used to solve our inventory problem is an example of an **algorithm**. Algorithms are often simple formulas, but they can also be complex and involve a series of required steps. Sometimes a mathematical model will exhibit certain undesirable features or be so complex or large that it is impractical to arrive at a solution by mathematical reasoning alone. In such cases, it may be impossible to construct an algorithm that results in a truly optimal solution. In such instances, it is still possible to apply quantitative methods to reach a reasonably satisfactory problem solution.

In this book, we will consider two basic classes of models. The simplest model, like the inventory order-quantity model, involves no uncertainty. These models contain certain (known and fixed) constants throughout their formulation and are referred to as **deterministic models**. It is more difficult to solve problems that involve one or more uncertain quantities. In these cases, probability must be considered and **stochastic models** may be used.

1-5 The Importance of Studying Quantitative Methods

The purpose of this book is not to make you an expert in quantitative methods. Its goal is to familiarize you with the important tools of quantitative methods and to expose you to a variety of successful applications. No great skill in mathematics is required.

Three main advantages can be gained from exposure to quantitative methods. First, it should increase your confidence as a decision maker, largely because you will see how vast and varied the problems are that can be solved through the application of quantitative methods. Second, a study of quantitative methods creates problem-solving skills that will be extremely helpful when you encounter an unsolved problem, whether or not you are directly responsible for finding the answer. A final advantage will be your ability to cope with decisions, as a manager, as an employee, or in your personal life.

Some knowledge of quantitative methods is especially crucial to the modern manager. An effective manager must make good choices, and the ability to know where, when, and how to use quantitative methods to make optimal decisions gives managers a definite advantage. This doesn't mean that an effective manager must be mathematically skilled or must personally develop models and solutions. There are a tremendous number of opportunities for the layman to do exactly that, but experts can be hired to perform the more demanding tasks. However, it is important to know enough about this subject to guide those high-powered analysts (who too often stray into a mathematical "never-never land"). As a bare minimum, any exposure to quantitative methods will teach future managers to ask the right questions and to recognize when outside help may be useful.

2

Probability
Concepts

$\mathbb{P}$robability plays a special role in all our lives, because we use it to measure uncertainty. We are continually faced with decisions that lead to uncertain outcomes, and we rely on probability to help us choose our course of action. In business, probability is a pivotal factor in most significant decisions. A department store buyer will order large quantities of a new style that is predicted to sell well. A company will introduce a new product when the chance of its success seems high enough to outweigh the possibility of losses due to its failure. A new college graduate is hired when the probability for satisfactory performance is judged to be sufficiently high.

A **probability** is a numerical value that measures the uncertainty that a particular event will occur. The probability for an event ordinarily represents the *proportion of times under identical circumstances that the event can be expected to occur*. Such a long-run frequency of occurrence is referred to as an **objective probability**. In tossing a fair coin, the probability for obtaining a head is 1/2. This can be verified after tossing the coin many times and observing that a head appears about half of the time. However, a probability value is often subjective; that is, it is determined solely on the basis of personal judgment. **Subjective probabilities** are expressed for events that have no meaningful long-run frequency of occurrence. For example, an oil wildcatter may express his uncertainty about the presence of oil beneath a candidate drilling site in terms of a probability value such as 1/2. One attempt will be made at drilling on that site; since no two sites are identical, there are no other situations like the present one from which the frequency of oil strikes can be determined.

Several mathematicians initially studied probability more than 300 years ago in connection with gambling problems. Probability theory has since evolved into one of the most elegant and useful branches of mathematics. Today, devices ordinarily associated with gambling, such as dice and playing cards, are useful in illustrating how to find probabilities.

2-1 The Language of Probability: Basic Concepts

Statisticians refer to an uncertain outcome as an **event**. There are two common outcomes associated with a coin toss: the two events "head" and "tail." An event is the result of a **random experiment**. For example, the event "head" is the result of a coin toss, which is the random experiment. Tomorrow's weather, your statistics class, an oil wildcatter's drilling venture, and the introduction of a new product are all random experiments.

Elementary Events and the Sample Space

The first step to take in any probability evaluation is to identify the relevant events of the random experiment in detail. The simplest possible outcomes of a random experiment are called **elementary events**. Imagine a deck of 52 playing cards. You thoroughly shuffle the cards; then you cut the deck and remove the top card. Each card that you can draw is an elementary event. Since there are 52 cards in a deck, there will be 52 elementary events, as shown in Figure 2-1.

The complete collection of elementary events is called the **sample space**. Although often pictured, like the sample space in Figure 2-1, a sample space for drawing one card can also be represented as a list:

$$\text{Sample space} = \{ \heartsuit K, \ \heartsuit Q, \ldots, \ \heartsuit 3, \ \heartsuit 2, \ \heartsuit A, \ \diamondsuit K, \ldots, \ \spadesuit A \}$$

For a coin toss the sample space can be listed as

$$\text{Sample space} = \{\text{head, tail}\}$$

A random experiment can result in many different elementary events. You must decide what you're looking for. If you are interested in the *side showing*, a coin toss has just the two element events "head" and "tail." But suppose you are interested instead in the *number of times a coin spins* before it comes to rest. The coin may not spin at all, or it may keep spinning for a very long time. Therefore, the sample space for the coin toss would have all the integers as elementary events.

$$\text{Sample space} = \{0, 1, 2, 3, 4, \ldots\}$$

FIGURE 2-1

Sample space for the card randomly selected from a deck of 52 playing cards.

SUIT

DENOMINATION	Spades (black)	Hearts (red)	Clubs (black)	Diamonds (red)
King	♠ K ●	♥ K ●	♣ K ●	♦ K ●
Queen	♠ Q ●	♥ Q ●	♣ Q ●	♦ Q ●
Jack	♠ J ●	♥ J ●	♣ J ●	♦ J ●
10	♠ 10 ●	♥ 10 ●	♣ 10 ●	♦ 10 ●
9	♠ 9 ●	♥ 9 ●	♣ 9 ●	♦ 9 ●
8	♠ 8 ●	♥ 8 ●	♣ 8 ●	♦ 8 ●
7	♠ 7 ●	♥ 7 ●	♣ 7 ●	♦ 7 ●
6	♠ 6 ●	♥ 6 ●	♣ 6 ●	♦ 6 ●
5	♠ 5 ●	♥ 5 ●	♣ 5 ●	♦ 5 ●
4	♠ 4 ●	♥ 4 ●	♣ 4 ●	♦ 4 ●
3	♠ 3 ●	♥ 3 ●	♣ 3 ●	♦ 3 ●
Deuce	♠ 2 ●	♥ 2 ●	♣ 2 ●	♦ 2 ●
Ace	♠ A ●	♥ A ●	♣ A ●	♦ A ●

SAMPLE SPACE

EXAMPLE ▬▬▬▬▬▬▬▬▬▬▬▬▬▬▬▬▬▬▬▬▬▬▬▬

Tossing Three Coins

Charlie Brown has a penny, a nickel, and a dime, all of which he plans to toss at the same time. Since all three coins will land at the same time—making one outcome—each outcome, or elementary event, is a different combination of the sides of the coins that will be showing. To impress his friends, Charlie Brown lists the sample space (Figure 2-2). In the list, H stands for a head, T for a tail, and the subscripts p, n, and d for the respective coins. Thus, if Charlie Brown tosses his three coins and gets heads with the penny and the nickel and a tail with the dime, he would represent this event as $H_p H_n T_d$.

FIGURE 2-2

Sample space for tossing three coins.

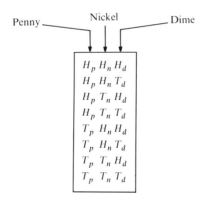

Composite Events and Event Sets

In finding probabilities you will ordinarily be interested in more complex outcomes than individual elementary events. You can represent such results conveniently as *groupings* of elementary events, or **composite events**.

Composite Event	*Elementary Events in Event Set*
King =	$\{\heartsuit K, \diamond K, \clubsuit K, \spadesuit K\}$
Heart =	$\{\heartsuit K, \heartsuit Q, \heartsuit J, \heartsuit 10, \heartsuit 9, \heartsuit 8, \heartsuit 7, \heartsuit 6, \heartsuit 5, \heartsuit 4, \heartsuit 3, \heartsuit 2, \heartsuit A\}$
Dime is a head =	$\{H_p H_n H_d, H_p T_n H_d, T_p H_n H_d, T_p T_n H_d\}$

Each *composite event will occur if any one of its elementary events occurs*. The collections of elementary events given on the right are partial listings of the elementary events of the whole sample space (for example, all 52 playing cards of a deck). Such collections are called **event sets**.

An event set may contain a single element, as with

$$\text{Queen of hearts} = \{\heartsuit Q\}$$

or (as in the above example)

$$\text{All heads} = \{H_p H_n H_d\}$$

When an event set contains no elements, the outcome is an **impossible event**.

$$\text{Impossible event} = \{\ \} \quad \text{or} \quad \varnothing$$

(The empty braces indicate that there are no elements in the set.) Such an event set is called a **null set**. An example of an impossible event is "queen" when all of the face cards have been removed from the deck.

Basic Definitions of Probability

The probability for an event may be defined as the **long-run frequency** at which the event will occur in a series of identical random experiments.

The Count-and-Divide Method   When the elementary events are **equally likely**, a probability (Pr) can be found by counting and dividing.
When the sample space consists of elementary events that are equally likely, then

$$\text{Pr[event]} = \frac{\text{Number of elementary events in the event set}}{\text{Total number of equally likely elementary events}}$$

The count-and-divide method applies to the preceding examples, as shown here.

$$\text{Pr[head]} = \frac{1}{2} \qquad \text{(single coin)}$$

$$\text{Pr[king]} = \frac{4}{52} = \frac{1}{13}$$

$$\text{Pr[heart]} = \frac{13}{52} = \frac{1}{4}$$

$$\text{Pr[dime is a head]} = \frac{4}{8} = \frac{1}{2} \qquad \text{(three coins)}$$

EXAMPLE ▰▰▰▰▰▰▰▰▰▰▰▰▰▰▰▰▰▰▰▰▰▰▰▰▰▰▰▰▰▰▰▰▰

Categories for Scholarship Students

The business students who hold scholarships at State University are represented by a biological symbol in Figure 2-3. You will select one student from this group at random, so Figure 2-3 represents the sample space. To find the probability that the student you select will be a woman, count the number of women and divide by the number of students. There are 32 women out of 72 scholarship students. Thus,

$$\text{Pr[woman]} = \frac{32}{72}$$

Similarly, there are 16 accounting majors, so the probability that the selected student's major is accounting is

$$\text{Pr[accounting]} = \frac{16}{72}$$

FIGURE 2-3
Sample space for business scholarship students.

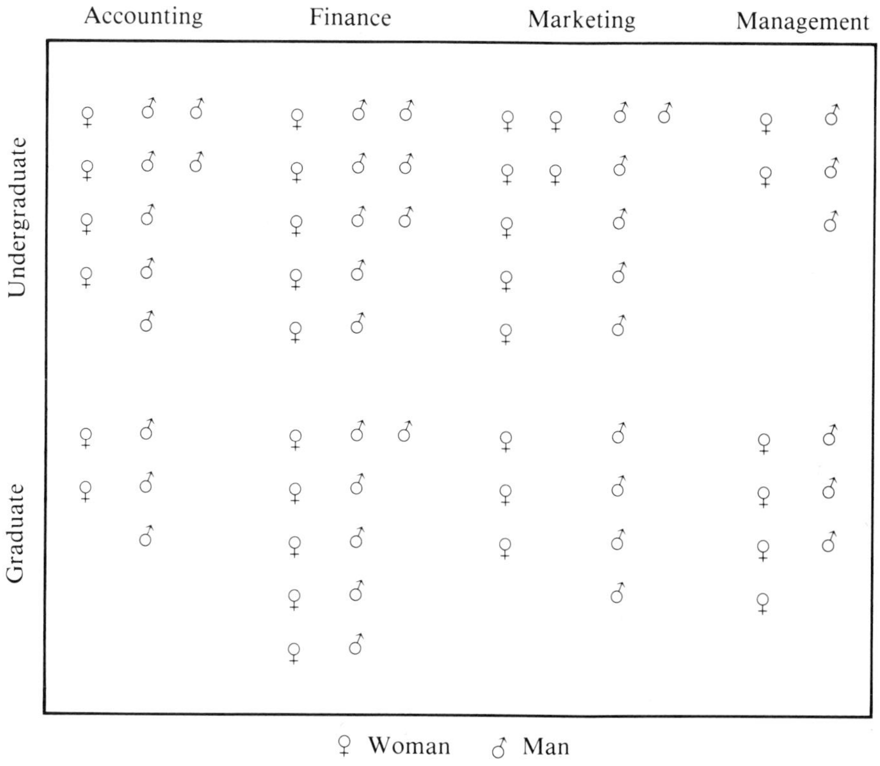

And, there are 30 graduate students, so that

$$Pr[graduate] = \frac{30}{72}$$

Probability Estimates   Remember that the count-and-divide method applies only if the elementary events are *equally likely*. What if, for example, a lopsided coin is tossed? The probability for an event in such a random experiment is still a long-run frequency, but it can only be *estimated* from the actual results experienced by repeating the experiment many times.

Certain and Impossible Events

An event's probability is a fraction or decimal between 0 and 1. You can see this by looking at two extreme probabilities. Since an **impossible event** *never* occurs,

$$Pr[impossible\ event] = 0$$

Similarly, a **certain event** (for example, "the selected card has a suit") will *always* occur.

$$\text{Pr[certain event]} = 1$$

All other probabilities will lie between these two extremes.

Objective and Subjective Probabilities

All probability values considered so far apply to *repeatable* random experiments. Quantities obtained from repeatable experiments are called **objective probabilities**. Many important uncertain business events arise from nonrepeatable circumstances. Consider next year's sales of a product, the yearly high of the Dow-Jones Average, or your final grade in statistics. Any probabilities given to such events must be based solely on *judgment*. Since people often disagree on the values, these numbers are called **subjective probabilities**. Chapter 4 describes various procedures for determining subjective probabilities.

2-2 Compound Events and Event Relationships

It is sometimes helpful to treat an uncertain outcome as a **compound event** that can be expressed in terms of two or more **compound events**. One reason for this is that the component event probabilities are often given values or are easier to calculate first. You can then use these given or easily calculated values to arrive at the probability for a more complex outcome.

There are several types of compound events.

FIGURE 2-4
The union of three component events.

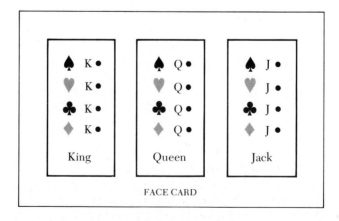

Face card = King *or* queen *or* jack

FIGURE 2-5

Intersection of two event sets for tossing three coins.

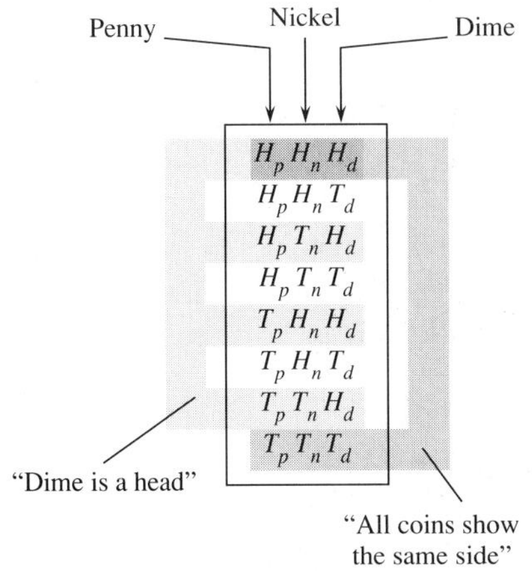

$$H_p H_n H_d$$
$$H_p H_n T_d$$
$$H_p T_n H_d$$
$$H_p T_n T_d$$
$$T_p H_n H_d$$
$$T_p H_n T_d$$
$$T_p T_n H_d$$
$$T_p T_n T_d$$

"Dime is a head"

"All coins show
the same side"

The Union—Several Events Grouped Together

One type of compound event is created by the **union** of the sets of two or more component events. This type is illustrated in Figure 2-4, where the compound event "face card" is the union of the component events "king," "queen," and "jack." *The union of several sets is a set having as its elements the elements of those sets being joined.* You can conveniently summarize this by the logical connective *or*.

Face card = King *or* queen *or* jack

The Intersection—Joint Events

Another type of compound event is created by the **intersection** of the sets of two or more component events. Figure 2-5 shows the intersection of the two events "dime is a head" and "all coins show the same side." The result is an event set having the single elementary event $H_p H_n H_d$. *The intersection of several sets is a set having as its elements just those elements common to all the sets.* You can represent this relationship by the logical connective *and*.

"Dime is a head" *and* "All coins show the same side" $= \{H_p H_n H_d\}$

A compound event formed by the intersection of several component events is often referred to as a **joint event**.

Do not confuse union and intersection. Refer to Figure 2-6, which illustrates the random selection of a scholarship student with the characteristics "finance major" and

FIGURE 2-6

Union and intersection of two event sets for business scholarship students.

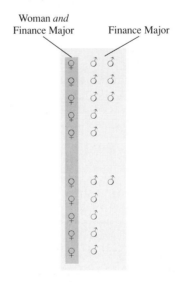

"undergraduate." These two characteristics are the component events. Any student included in the shaded areas is an elementary event in the *union* of the two component events, "undergraduate *or* finance major," and in finding probabilities each elementary event is counted just once. The *intersection* of the two component events, "undergraduate *and* finance major," is represented by the darker area, which includes only those students defined by *both* event sets.

FIGURE 2-7

Subset for business scholarship students.

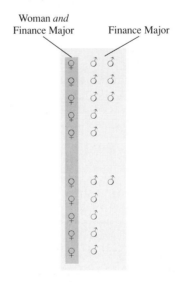

FIGURE 2-8

Empty set for intersection of two event sets.

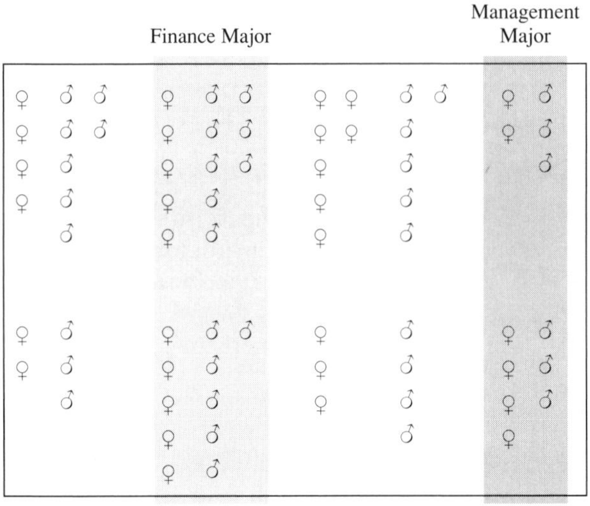

Finance Major *and* Management Major = {   }

A commonly encountered case is shown in Figure 2-7 for the student selection events "woman" and "finance major." The event set for the intersection of these two component events (represented by the darker area) lies totally *within* that of "finance major." Here the elements of "woman *and* finance major" constitute a **subset** of the event set "finance major."

Mutually Exclusive Events

Two events *A* and *B* are **mutually exclusive** if the occurrence of one precludes the other, so that *A and B* is impossible. For example, in drawing only one playing card, you cannot get both the events "king" and "queen." These events are mutually exclusive because a card has only one denomination.

$$\Pr[\text{king } and \text{ queen}] = 0$$

The intersection of mutually exclusive events is an empty set ({ } or $\emptyset$), as illustrated in Figure 2-8 for "finance major" and "management major." (State University does not allow double majors.)

EXAMPLE ██

Rainfall, Bankruptcy, and Profit

Next year's annual rainfall for San Francisco is an uncertain quantity that may range from as low as 10 inches or less to as high as 40 inches or more. Any level of precipitation between these extremes is a possible event. But because there will be only one rainfall level, all the possibilities are mutually exclusive events.

The events "bankruptcy" and "profit" may result from the current year's operation of a firm. These events are *not* mutually exclusive, since it is possible for a business to make a profit and yet also be forced into bankruptcy by the claims of impatient creditors.

Collectively Exhaustive Events

Events that include the entire sample space are **collectively exhaustive**. When considered as separate events, the four possible majors for the selected scholarship student are collectively exhaustive, since every student is included.

> accounting major   marketing major
>
> finance major   management major

Although this group of events is also mutually exclusive, this need not be true for a group of collectively exhaustive events. Consider the events

> woman   undergraduate   man

These events are collectively exhaustive because they include all the students, but they are not mutually exclusive because the undergraduates also belong to the groups "woman" and "man."

The union of collectively exhaustive events is a certain event and has a probability of 1. For example,

$$\Pr[\text{woman } or \text{ undergraduate } or \text{ man}] = 1$$

Complementary Events (Opposites)

When a pair of events are both mutually exclusive and collectively exhaustive they are **complementary events**, or *opposites*. Looking at Figure 2-9, you can see that the student selection events "undergraduate" and "graduate" are complementary.

The word "not" is used to denote an event's complement.

> Event   Complement
>
> A not A

Independent and Dependent Events

Two events A and B are **statistically independent** if the probability for A will be the same value when B occurs, when B does not occur, or when nothing is known about the occurrence of B. In tossing three coins (look back at Figure 2-2), the events H_p and H_n are

FIGURE 2-9

Complementary events for business scholarship students.

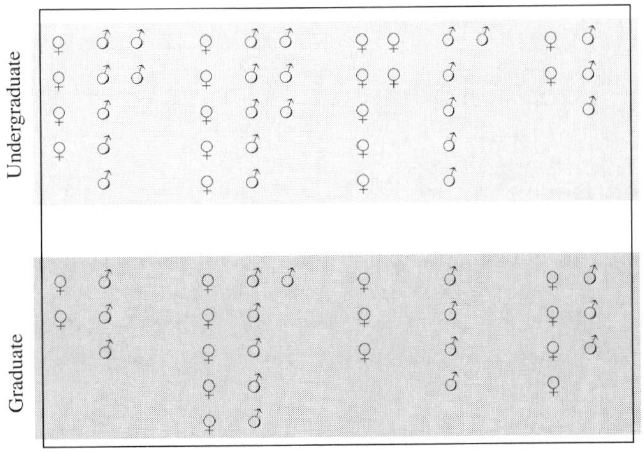

statistically independent because the showing side obtained with one coin will not be influenced in any way by the showing side for the other. Each individual event has a probability of 1/2 regardless of whether or not the other occurs.

Such is not the case for the experiment of randomly selecting a person from the business scholarship students at State University. Consider the events "graduate" and "woman." The probability for "woman" does not have the same value when the event "graduate" occurs as when some other event, such as "all students" occurs.

$$\Pr[\text{woman}] = \frac{32}{72} = .444 \qquad \text{(all students considered)}$$

$$\Pr[\text{woman}] = \frac{14}{30} = .467 \qquad \text{(graduate students considered)}$$

Thus, the events "graduate" and "woman" are **dependent**.

Our concern is with a *statistical* dependence or independence between two events. These are special relationships that can be established by comparing probabilities under various conditions. Statistical independence is concerned with event *frequencies* rather than cause-and-effect or timing. (Do you think two possible mutually exclusive events can ever be independent?)*

The characteristics or variate values of successive units selected during sampling are usually dependent events. Independence and dependence are important considerations in deductive statistics. These concepts apply generally to decision making under uncertainty whenever predictive information is used to revise probabilities. Consider petroleum

---

* The answer is no, since the probability for either one is zero if the other is known to occur.

exploration, where a seismic survey is often used to help find oil. Obviously, the probability for oil is higher when a seismic survey is favorable than when a survey is unfavorable. The events "oil" and "favorable seismic" are dependent events.

2-3 Probabilities for Compound Events

The Count-and-Divide Method

Consider the event sets "finance major" and "undergraduate" shown in Figure 2-6 for a randomly selected scholarship student. The probability that the chosen person is either a finance major or an undergraduate is found by counting the elementary events in the union of the two event sets (53) and then dividing by the size of the sample space (72).

$$\text{Pr[finance major } or \text{ undergraduate]} = \frac{53}{72}$$

Similarly, the **joint probability**—the probability for a joint event, or intersection—that the selected student is *both* a finance major and an undergraduate is

$$\text{Pr[finance major } and \text{ undergraduate]} = \frac{13}{72}$$

Here, the intersection of the two component event sets has 13 elementary events out of the entire sample space of 72.

The count-and-divide method can be used only when each elementary event is equally likely and the number of events is known. Other methods can be used to find compound event probabilities from known probabilities for the components.

The Addition Law—Probabilities for Unions

When two or more mutually exclusive events are combined by means of union (*or*), the probability for the compound event may be found by adding together the probabilities for the component events. This is the **addition law for mutually exclusive events**

$$\text{Pr}[A \text{ } or \text{ } B \text{ } or \text{ } C] = \text{Pr}[A] + \text{Pr}[B] + \text{Pr}[C]$$

EXAMPLE ▆▆▆▆▆▆▆▆▆▆▆▆▆▆▆▆▆▆▆▆▆▆▆▆▆▆▆▆▆▆▆

Reasons for Denial of Credit

The credit manager for the Hide-Away Safe Company has several reasons for denying credit to buyers: (1) low income, (2) poor repayment history, (3) high debts, and (4) no collateral. Records of past transactions list just one of these as the primary reason for denial of credit. If you assume that past frequencies will apply in the future, you have the following probabilities that the next credit application will be rejected for each primary reason.

$$Pr[\text{low income}] = .15$$

$$Pr[\text{poor repayment}] = .20$$

$$Pr[\text{high debts}] = .25$$

$$Pr[\text{no collateral}] = .40$$

Reasons (3) and (4) apply to what are called "balance sheet deficiencies." To find the probability that a balance sheet deficiency will be the reason for the next credit denial, you can apply the addition law.

$$Pr[\text{balance sheet}] = Pr[\text{high debts } or \text{ no collateral}]$$

$$= Pr[\text{high debts}] + Pr[\text{no collateral}]$$

$$= .25 + .40 = .65$$

The Addition Law and Collectively Exhaustive Events   If a collection of events is collectively exhaustive as well as mutually exclusive, then their union will be a certainty, so that

$$Pr[A \text{ or } B \text{ or } C] = Pr[A] + Pr[B] + Pr[C] = 1$$

EXAMPLE

The Number of Sample Defectives

Soft-Where-House takes a sample of its program diskettes every hour to determine the quality of its final product. If only 10% of the diskettes are defective, then the following probabilities apply for the number of defectives in a sample of 5 diskettes.

NUMBER OF DEFECTIVES	PROBABILITY
0	.5905
1	.3280
2	.0729
3	.0081
4	.0005
5	.0000
	1.0000

The events for "number defective" are mutually exclusive and collectively exhaustive, and their probabilities add up to 1.

Application to Complementary Events

When two events are complementary (opposite), their probabilities add up to 1. Thus,

$$Pr[A] = 1 - Pr[\text{not } A]$$

This is helpful when you want to know an event's probability, but the probability for its complementary event is easier to find. If you want to find the probability for "at least 1" defective diskette in the above example, you can use the addition law and add together the probabilities for "exactly 1," "exactly 2," and so on. But you can find the answer faster if you recognize that "at least 1" is the opposite of "exactly 0." The above example gives the probability for "0 defective" as .5905, so that

$$Pr[\text{at least 1 defective}] = 1 - Pr[\text{exactly 0 defective}]$$

$$= 1 - .5905 = .4095$$

General Addition Law

When the component events are *not* mutually exclusive, you should use the **general addition law**

$$Pr[A \text{ or } B] = Pr[A] + Pr[B] - Pr[A \text{ and}.B]$$

For example, consider the selection of playing cards that are either "ace" or "heart." (The event sets for these outcomes are given in Figure 2-10.) You can use the general addition law to find

$$Pr[\text{ace } or \text{ heart}] = Pr[\text{ace}] + Pr[\text{heart}] - Pr[\text{ace } and \text{ heart}]$$

$$= \frac{4}{52} + \frac{13}{52} - \frac{1}{52} = \frac{16}{52}$$

Since the events "ace" and "heart" are not mutually exclusive (both include the ace of hearts as a possible elementary event), it is necessary to subtract the joint probability for "ace *and* heart." This way the event "ace of hearts" is not counted twice.

The Multiplication Law—Joint Probabilities

If you want to find the probability that two or more events occur jointly (that is, intersect), you will sometimes find it convenient to use the **multiplication law for independent events**

$$Pr[A \text{ and } B] = Pr[A] \times Pr[B]$$

To illustrate, consider once more the events "ace" and "heart." The joint probability for these independent events can be found from the multiplication law.

FIGURE 2-10

The union of events "ace" and "heart" is the entire shaded area.

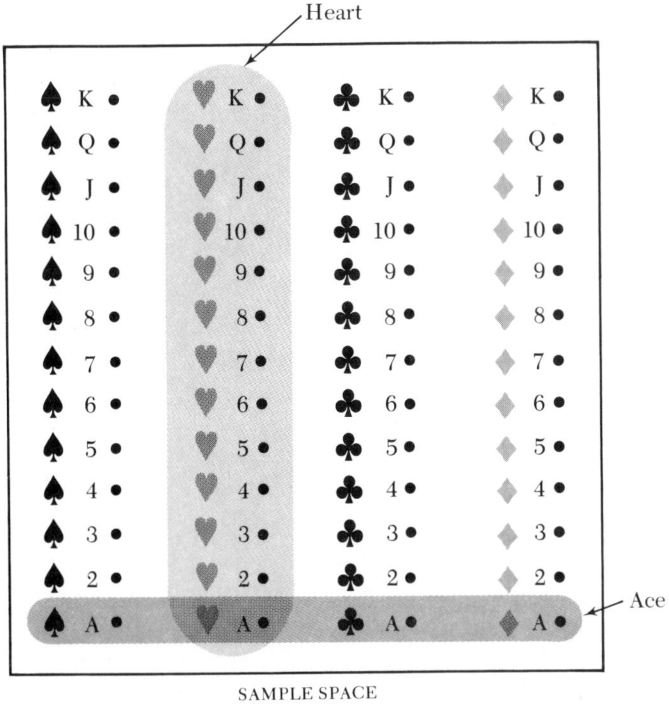

SAMPLE SPACE

$$\Pr[\text{ace } and \text{ heart}] = \Pr[\text{ace}] \times \Pr[\text{heart}]$$

$$= \frac{4}{52} \times \frac{13}{52} = \frac{1}{52}$$

The multiplication law is not usually applied when the answer may be obtained more easily by counting and dividing. (There is 1 "ace *and* heart" out of a total of 52 cards.) In the following example the multiplication law is essential to finding the answer.

EXAMPLE ▪▬▬▬▬▬▬▬▬▬▬▬▬▬▬▬▬▬▬▬▬▬

Busy Computer Teleports

Giant Enterprises has a central computer connected to district offices in a telecommunications network. At any given moment there is a 20% chance that all teleports are busy and incoming messages must be placed on hold. Messages are sent out frequently by any particular office, so that the teleports at successive inquiries have *independent* status, much like two coin tosses.

We will let B_1 represent the event that an office's first message of the day encounters a busy signal, B_2 likewise for the second message, and so on. For any individual query the probabilities for a busy signal are $Pr[B_1] = .20$ and $Pr[B_2] = .20$. The joint probability that the first two messages encounter busy signals is

$$Pr[B_1 \ and \ B_2] = Pr[B_1] \times Pr[B_2]$$
$$= .20 \times .20 = .04$$

The multiplication law applies to the joint occurrence of any number of independent component events. Thus, the joint probability that the first three queries encounter a busy computer system is

$$Pr[B_1 \ and \ B_2 \ and \ B_3] = Pr[B_1] \times Pr[B_2] \times Pr[B_3]$$
$$= .20 \times .20 \times .20 = .008$$

and the joint probability that five successive busy signals will be encountered is

$$(.20)^5 = .00032$$

The probability that the first query reaches the computer directly (D_1) is

$$Pr[D_1] = 1 - Pr[B_1] = 1 - .20 = .80$$

Thus, the joint probability that the first message is connected directly and the two after encounter a busy signal is

$$Pr[D_1 \ and \ B_2 \ and \ B_3] = Pr[D_1] \times Pr[B_2] \times Pr[B_3]$$
$$= .80 \times .20 \times .20 = .032$$

2-4 Conditional Probability and the Joint Probability Table

A probability value for an event computed under the assumption that some other event is going to occur is a **conditional probability**. The weather provides some examples. Consider the events "rain" and "cloudy," for which the following might be true.

$$Pr[rain \mid cloudy] = .70$$

This equation is read, "The probability that there will be rain *given* that it is cloudy is .70." The event "rain" is listed first, and .70 is the probability for this event. The second event, which appears after the vertical bar, is the **given event**, "cloudy." This event establishes the condition under which .70 applies. Given some other event, "rain" could have a different probability. For example,

$$Pr[rain \mid low \ pressure] = .30$$

In either case, the probability for rain is conditional because it assumes that another event—"cloudy" or "low pressure"—is going to occur. Should no conditions be stipulated for the weather, we might have the value

$$Pr[rain] = .20$$

which is an **unconditional probability**.

Computing Conditional Probabilities

Count-and-Divide Method   The condition, or given event, eliminates extraneous possibilities that would need to be accounted for in establishing unconditional probabilities. For example, consider a randomly selected playing card. You can see that

$$Pr[jack \,|\, face\ card] = \frac{4}{12} = \frac{1}{3}$$

since there are only 12 face cards and just 4 of these are jacks. The condition of "face card" effectively reduces the sample space to just 12 cards, and the count-and-divide method can then be applied to the smaller, or restricted, sample space. Without the condition, you would have to consider the entire sample space, so that

$$Pr[jack] = \frac{4}{52} = \frac{1}{13}$$

As another example, consider the student selection experiment in Figure 2-6 (page 16). You can find the probability for "finance major given undergraduate" by observing that the condition "undergraduate" eliminates all graduate students. Therefore, the 42 students in the event set "undergraduate" are the restricted sample space. Of those 42 students, 13 are finance majors, so that

$$Pr[finance \,|\, undergraduate] = \frac{13}{42}$$

Conditional Probability Identity   If the necessary probability values are known, you may find it helpful to use the **conditional probability identity**

$$Pr[A \,|\, B] = \frac{Pr[A\ and\ B]}{Pr[B]}$$

This equation states that the conditional probability for an event can be found by dividing the joint probability for the two events (if it is known) by the unconditional probability for the given event (if that value is also known).

We can see from Figure 2-6 that

$$Pr[finance\ and\ undergraduate] = \frac{13}{72}$$

and that

$$Pr[\text{undergraduate}] = \frac{42}{72}$$

Thus, the conditional probability for "finance" given "undergraduate" is

$$Pr[\text{finance} \mid \text{undergraduate}] = \frac{Pr[\text{finance } and \text{ undergraduate}]}{Pr[\text{undergraduate}]}$$

$$= \frac{13/72}{42/72} = \frac{13}{42}$$

In this case, the conditional probability identity is a more roundabout method than counting and dividing to find the probability. However, the identity will often be useful when the count-and-divide method cannot be used.

Note: The conditional probability identity only works when the probability values are available to plug into the formula.

EXAMPLE

Finding Probabilities for Sample Defectives

The receiving department of Soft-Where-House is sample testing a small shipment of high velocity recording heads. Suppose that out of the 10 heads in the shipment, 2 are defective (*D*) and the rest are satisfactory (*S*). (Of course, the inspector does not know this fact.) Two heads, represented by the subscripts 1 and 2, are randomly selected one at a time and tested just once.

You can see that

$$Pr[D_1] = \frac{2}{10}$$

and given that the first head is defective, only 1 defective is among the 9 remaining heads, so that

$$Pr[D_2 \mid D_1] = \frac{1}{9}$$

Should the first head instead be satisfactory, then 2 defectives are left in the remaining 9, and

$$Pr[D_2 \mid S_1] = \frac{2}{9}$$

You cannot use the conditional probability identity here since you do not know the values for $Pr[D_1 \text{ and } D_2]$ or $Pr[S_1 \text{ and } D_2]$.

Comparing Conditional and Unconditional Probabilities

Remember that two events are *independent* if the probability for one is unaffected by the occurrence of the other.

1. *A* and *B* are *independent* events whenever

$$\Pr[A] = \Pr[A \mid B]$$

2. *A* and *B* are *dependent* events whenever

$$\Pr[A] \neq \Pr[A \mid B]$$

Note: To establish that two events are independent or dependent, you need only to compare the unconditional probability for one event to its conditional probability given the other event.

To better understand this point, think again of playing cards. The events "ace" and "heart" are independent, since

$$\Pr[\text{ace}] = \frac{4}{52} = \frac{1}{13} = \Pr[\text{ace} \mid \text{heart}]$$

And the events "ace" and "face card" are dependent, since

$$\Pr[\text{ace}] = \frac{4}{52} \neq \frac{1}{3} = \Pr[\text{ace} \mid \text{face card}]$$

The Joint Probability Table

The following table shows the number of State University scholarship students (example on page 12) classified in terms of sex (man, woman) and level (undergraduate, graduate).

	LEVEL		
SEX	*Undergraduate*	*Graduate*	*Total*
Man	24	16	40
Woman	18	14	32
Total	42	30	72

By dividing the number of students in each category by the total number of students, you get the following **joint probability table**.

	LEVEL		
SEX	Undergraduate (U)	Graduate (G)	Marginal Probability
Man (M)	24/72	16/72	40/72
Woman (W)	18/72	14/72	32/72
Marginal Probability	42/72	30/72	1

You can read the *joint probabilities* for various combinations of sex and level events directly from this table. For example, the probability that the selected student will be both a man and an undergraduate ($\Pr[M \ and \ U]$) is 24/72, and the probability for a woman graduate student ($\Pr[W \ and \ G]$) is 14/72.

Marginal Probabilities   The values in the margins of the table are referred to as **marginal probabilities**. Each represents the probability for the event listed at the head of its row or column. Thus, $\Pr[M] = 40/72$ and $\Pr[U] = 42/72$ may be read directly from the table. Notice that each marginal probability is equal to the sum of the joint probabilities in its row or column.

Computing Conditional Probabilities from the Joint Probability Table   Once you have found the entries in the joint probability table, you can figure various conditional probabilities. For example, the probability that a randomly selected scholarship student is a "man" given that he is a "graduate" is

$$\Pr[M \mid G] = \frac{\Pr[M \ and \ G]}{\Pr[G]} = \frac{16/72}{30/72} = \frac{16}{30} = .533$$

You may reverse the events to obtain the conditional probability for "graduate given man."

$$\Pr[G \mid M] = \frac{\Pr[M \ and \ G]}{\Pr[M]} = \frac{16/72}{40/72} = \frac{16}{40} = .400$$

Although the numerators in these two probability calculations are the same, different divisors apply in the two cases because the uncertain and given events are reversed.

2-5 The General Multiplication Law and Probability Trees

The General Multiplication Law

The multiplication law given on page 22 to find joint probabilities applies only to *independent* events. To determine joint probabilities when the components are dependent events, you must use the **general multiplication law**

$$\Pr[A \ and \ B] = \Pr[A] \times \Pr[B \,|\, A]$$

and

$$\Pr[A \ and \ B] = \Pr[B] \times \Pr[A \,|\, B]$$

As you can see, these equations use both conditional and unconditional probabilities.
    To illustrate, consider the following experience of an accountant. She has established that 60% of all accounts receivable involve incorrect remittances (I), and that 10% of those involve partial payments (P). This history may be expressed in terms of the following probabilities.

$$\Pr[I] = .60$$

$$\Pr[P \,|\, I] = .10$$

The multiplication law provides the probability that a particular remittance will be both incorrect and a partial payment.

$$\Pr[I \ and \ P] = \Pr[I] \times \Pr[P \,|\, I]$$

$$= .60 \times .10$$

$$= .06$$

Thus, 6% of all remittances for accounts receivable will fall into the two categories. (You can verify the result in terms of percentages: 10% of 60% is 6%.)

ILLUSTRATION
Oil Wildcatting with a Seismic Survey

    The owner of the Petroleum Entrepreneurship is a wildcatter who judges that there is a 30% chance of oil (O) beneath his leasehold on Fossil Ridges, with complementary chances that the site is dry (D). That is, the following unconditional probabilities apply.

$$\Pr[O] = .30 \quad and \quad \Pr[D] = 1 - .30 = .70$$

The wildcatter has the option of drilling now or ordering a seismic survey. Such a test is 90% reliable in predicting favorable (F) when there is actually oil, but only 70% reliable in providing an unfavorable (U) forecast when a site is dry. Stated more precisely,

$$\Pr[F \,|\, O] = .90 \quad and \quad \Pr[U \,|\, D] = .70$$

The general multiplication law may be used to establish the joint probability that Fossil Ridges does indeed contain oil and that the seismic survey will be favorable.

$$\Pr[O \ and \ F] = \Pr[O] \times \Pr[F \,|\, O]$$

$$= .30 \times .90 = .27$$

Similarly, the joint probability for a dry site and an unfavorable seismic survey is

$$\Pr[D \text{ and } U] = \Pr[D] \times \Pr[U|D]$$
$$= .70 \times .70 = .49$$

Constructing a Joint Probability Table Using the Multiplication Law

Section 2-4 discussed the construction of a joint probability table for a random experiment when there is sufficient information to apply the count-and-divide method. However, we may construct a joint probability table even when that method will not work. To do this, combine the general multiplication law with the addition law for mutually exclusive events and then use the property of complementary events.

Consider Table 2-1—the joint probability table constructed for the preceding oil wildcatting illustration. Recall the joint probabilities established earlier.

$$\Pr[O \text{ and } F] = .27 \quad \text{and} \quad \Pr[D \text{ and } U] = .49$$

They have been placed (in boldface type) in their respective positions in Table 2-1. The geology event marginal probabilities

$$\Pr[O] = .30 \quad \text{and} \quad \Pr[D] = .70$$

have also been positioned in the table in boldface. Using this information, the rest of the table entries were determined. The joint probability for "oil" *and* "unfavorable," .03, is determined by subtracting the joint probability for "oil" *and* "favorable," .27, from the marginal probability for "oil," which is .30. The joint probability for "dry" *and* "favorable," .21, represents the difference between the marginal probability for "dry," .70, and the joint probability for "dry" *and* "unfavorable," .49. The marginal probabilities of .48 for a favorable seismic survey and .52 for an unfavorable survey are determined by summing the joint probabilities in each column.

TABLE 2-1
Joint Probability Table for Oil Wildcatting with a Seismic Survey.

	SURVEY RESULT		
GEOLOGY	Favorable (F)	Unfavorable (U)	Marginal Probability
Oil(O)	.27	.03	.30
Dry(D)	.21	.49	.70
Marginal Probability	.48	.52	1.00

Multiplication Law for Several Events

The general multiplication law can be expanded to apply to situations involving more than two component events. For three events,

$$Pr[A \text{ and } B \text{ and } C] = Pr[A] \times Pr[B|A] \times Pr[C|A \text{ and } B]$$

All terms except the first are conditional probabilities, with the preceding events assumed as given events. There may be any number of component events.

To illustrate, in a particular industry it has been found that 80% of all new firms survive (S) past one year. Of those, 40% close (C) within the second year, half due to bankruptcy (B) and the rest for a number of other reasons. This experience provides the following probabilities for a start-up.

$$Pr[S] = .80$$

$$Pr[C|S] = .40$$

$$Pr[B|S \text{ and } C] = .50$$

The multiplication law provides the joint probability that a particular new firm will survive the first year, close during the second, and then go bankrupt.

$$Pr[S \text{ and } C \text{ and } B] = Pr[S] \times Pr[C|S] \times Pr[B|S \text{ and } C]$$

$$= .80 \times .40 \times .50$$

$$= .16$$

EXAMPLE

The Matching Birthday Problem

Consider the probability that there is at least one matching birthday (day and month) among a group of persons.

It will be simplest to find the probability of the complementary event—no matches—by using the general multiplication law. Envision each member of a group of size n being asked in succession to state his or her birthday. We conveniently define our events as follows.

A_i = the ith person queried does not share a birthday with the previous $i - 1$ persons

Then $Pr[\text{no match}] = Pr[A_1 \text{ and } A_2 \text{ and } \dots \text{ and } A_{n-1} \text{ and } A_n]$, which is the probability of the event that no person shares a birthday with the preceding persons. For simplicity, assume all dates to be equally likely and ignore leap year. Thus

$$Pr[A_1] = \frac{365}{365} \qquad Pr[A_2|A_1] = \frac{364}{365} \qquad Pr[A_3|A_1 \text{ and } A_2] = \frac{363}{365}$$

TABLE 2-2
Probabilities for at Least One Matching Birthday

GROUP SIZE	Pr[no matches]	Pr[at least one match]
3	.992	.008
7	.943	.057
10	.883	.117
15	.748	.252
23	.493	.507
40	.109	.891
50	.030	.970
60	.006	.994

so that the nth person cannot have a birthday on the previously cited $n - 1$ dates, $365 - (n - 1) = 365 - n + 1$ days are allowable for his or her birthday. Therefore, we may apply the multiplication law to obtain

$$\text{Pr[no matches]} = \frac{365}{365} \times \frac{364}{365} \times \frac{363}{365} \times \cdots \times \frac{365 - n + 1}{365}$$

The probability for at least one match may be found from

$$\text{Pr[at least one match]} = 1 - \text{Pr[no matches]}$$

One interesting issue is finding the size of the group for which the probability exceeds 1/2 that there is at least one match. Knowing this number, you can amaze your less knowledgeable friends and perhaps win a few bets. The "magical" group size turns out to be 23.

Why such a low group size? If it were physically possible to list all the ways (triples, sextuples, septuples, and so forth) in which 23 birthdays can match (there are several million, and for each a tremendous number of date possibilites), an intuitive appreciation as to why could be attained. Table 2-2 shows the matching probabilities for several group sizes. Note that for groups above 60 there is almost certain to be at least one match.

The Probability Tree Diagram

Business decision makers find the joint probability table cumbersome at times. They prefer to organize their probability calculations using a **probability tree**. The probability tree diagram for the preceding oil wildcatting illustration is shown in Figure 2-11. There, each event is represented as a **branch** in one or more **event forks**. This representation is especially convenient when events occur at different times or stages.

In probability trees, time moves from left to right. Since the geology events precede the seismic events, the branches for oil (O) and dry (D) appear in the event fork on the

FIGURE 2-11

Probability tree diagram for oil wildcatting with a seismic survey.

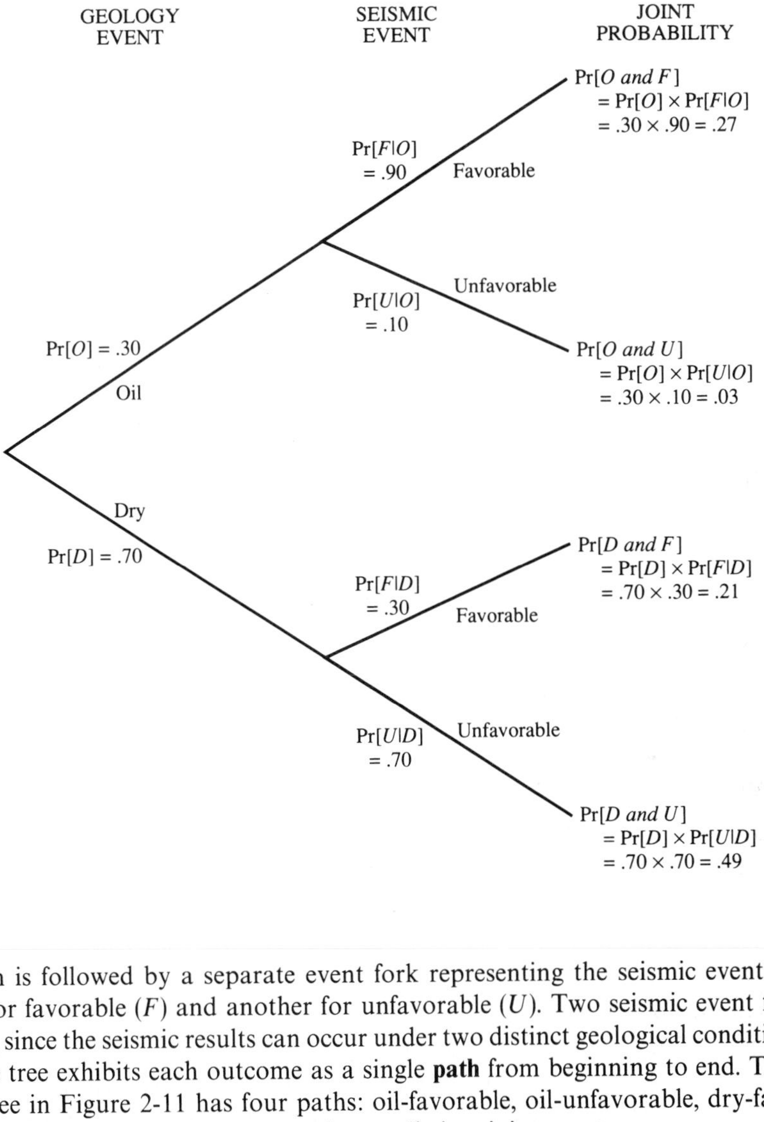

left. Each is followed by a separate event fork representing the seismic events, with a branch for favorable (F) and another for unfavorable (U). Two seismic event forks are required, since the seismic results can occur under two distinct geological conditions. The complete tree exhibits each outcome as a single **path** from beginning to end. The probability tree in Figure 2-11 has four paths: oil-favorable, oil-unfavorable, dry-favorable, dry-unfavorable. Each path corresponds to a distinct joint event.

The probabilities for each event are placed alongside its branch. The values listed in the left fork, $\Pr[O] = .30$ and $\Pr[D] = .70$, are unconditional since that event fork has no predecessor. Probabilities for later stage events will all be *conditional* probabilities, with the branch or subpath leading to the branching point signifying the given events. The top seismic event fork lists the probabilities $\Pr[F \mid O] = .90$ for favorable and $\Pr[U \mid O] = .10$ for unfavorable. Since that fork is preceded by the oil (O) branch, both conditional probabilities involve O as the given event. A *completely different* set of conditional probabilities, $\Pr[F\,|\,D] = .30$ and $\Pr[U\,|\,D] = .70$, apply in the bottom event fork; that branching point is preceded by the dry (D) branch, so that D is the given event.

The events emanating from a single branching point are mutually exclusive and collectively exhaustive, so that exactly one must occur. All the probabilities on branches within the same fork must therefore sum to 1.

The probability tree is very convenient for determining joint probabilities. A joint event is represented by a path through the tree, and its probability is determined by multiplying together all the individual branch probabilities for its path. For instance, the topmost path represents the outcome sequence oil-favorable. The corresponding joint probability is

$$\Pr[O \ and \ F] = \Pr[O] \times \Pr[F\,|\,O]$$
$$= .30(.90)$$
$$= .27$$

All of the joint probabilities for the oil wildcatter are listed in Figure 2-11 at the terminus of the respective event path. Notice that these sum to 1. That is because the joint events themselves are mutually exclusive and collectively exhaustive.

2-6 Revising Probabilities Using Bayes' Theorem

You may find it valuable to apply the probability revision procedures originally proposed by the Reverend Thomas Bayes over 200 years ago. These involve changing an initial set of probability values in accordance with a particular experimental finding.

Prior Probabilities

You often hear a weather forecast such as, "For tomorrow there is a 50% chance of rain." You may even occasionally come up with your own chance percentage, or **prior probability**, for rain the next day. The adjective *prior* means that the probability value is temporary and may change, depending on what further information develops. There are two classes of prior probabilities.

1. **Subjective probabilities:** The value 50% for rain is a subjective probability, since another forecaster may disagree, believing perhaps that there is instead a 40% chance of rain. This subjectivity exists because the underlying random experiment (tomorrow's weather, in this case) is strictly nonrepeatable. Similar uncertainties are common in business. Consider one-shot events such as a new product's reception in the marketplace, a company's sales, or the state of the economy.

2. **Objective probabilites:** A prior probability can be an objective value, reflecting the long-run frequency at which the event would occur in repeated random experiments. Such probabilities are encountered in sampling experiments when the population has known frequencies for various characteristics.

Posterior Probabilities

If you decide there is a .50 prior probability for rain, you might go to bed planning to dress "for the weather" when you arise. But in the morning you might first look outside at the cloud cover. If it is solid and black, you might revise your probability for rain upward to a value like .90; if the clouds are patchy, you might instead reduce that probability to a number like .20, choosing to leave your umbrella at home. Such a revised value is called a **posterior probability**.

Posterior probabilities are *conditional* probabilities of the form

$$\Pr[\text{event} \,|\, \text{result}]$$

The given event is the **result** of an experiment (in the preceding, looking at the sky) upon which the revised probability is based. Thomas Bayes proposed a formal mechanism for finding posterior probabilities by merging prior judgment with empirical results. In doing this, you encounter a third type of probability.

Conditional Result Probabilities

Suppose that for an entire year you keep records of a weather forecaster's predictions and the actual next day's weather. Assume that this weatherperson makes one of two forecasts: (1) rain likely and (2) rain unlikely. You may consider your viewing of the 11 P.M. TV weather broadcast as an experiment having those two *results*. Suppose that 60% of the days when rain actually occurred were preceded by an 11 P.M. forecast in which rain was predicted "likely." Suppose further that 80% of the days when no rain fell were preceded by an "unlikely" forecast. Assuming that this pattern continues into the future, the conditional probability is .60 that the forecast will be "likely" given that rain follows and .80 that it will be "unlikely" given that no rain follows. These numbers are referred to as **conditional result probabilities**. They provide a measure of the reliability of predictive information.

Bayes' Theorem

Using the concepts of prior and conditional result probabilities, Bayes arrived at a theorem for determining posterior probabilities.

Bayes' Theorem The posterior probability for event E for a particular result R of an empirical investigation can be found from

$$\Pr[E \,|\, R] = \frac{\Pr[E]\Pr[R \,|\, E]}{\Pr[E]\Pr[R \,|\, E] + \Pr[\text{not } E]\Pr[R \,|\, \text{not } E]}$$

Here E stands for "event" and R stands for "result." The prior probability for the main event of interest E is *specified in advance* as $\Pr[E]$, with $\Pr[\text{not } E] = 1 - \Pr[E]$. The conditional result probabilities must also be stipulated before making calculations.

You can apply Bayes' theorem to the weather illustration to find the posterior probability that it will rain (E) given a likely forecast (R). The prior probability is

$$\Pr[\text{rain}] = .50$$

and the conditional result probabilities are

$$\Pr[\text{likely}\,|\,\text{rain}] = .60$$

$$\Pr[\text{likely}\,|\,\text{no rain}] = 1 - \Pr[\text{unlikely}\,|\,\text{no rain}] = 1 - .80 = .20$$

Plugging these values into Bayes' theorem, you find

$\Pr[\text{rain}\,|\,\text{likely}]$

$$= \frac{\Pr[\text{rain}] \times \Pr[\text{likely}\,|\,\text{rain}]}{\Pr[\text{rain}] \times \Pr[\text{likely}\,|\,\text{rain}] + \Pr[\text{no rain}] \times \Pr[\text{likely}\,|\,\text{no rain}]}$$

$$= \frac{.50(.60)}{.50(.60) + (1 - .50)(.20)} = \frac{.30}{.30 + .10} = .75$$

A similar calculation provides the posterior probability for rain (E) given an unlikely forecast (different R). The following conditional result probabilities apply.

$$\Pr[\text{unlikely}\,|\,\text{rain}] = 1 - .60 = .40$$

$$\Pr[\text{unlikely}\,|\,\text{no rain}] = .80$$

You find that

$\Pr[\text{rain}\,|\,\text{unlikely}]$

$$= \frac{\Pr[\text{rain}] \times \Pr[\text{unlikely}\,|\,\text{rain}]}{\Pr[\text{rain}] \times \Pr[\text{unlikely}\,|\,\text{rain}] + \Pr[\text{no rain}] \times \Pr[\text{unlikely}\,|\,\text{no rain}]}$$

$$= \frac{.50(.40)}{.50(.40) + (1 - .50)(.80)} = \frac{.20}{.20 + .40} = .333$$

Notice how the posterior probability for rain *increases* to .75 from the prior level of .50 given a likely forecast. This is what we should expect with any reliable experimental result. Similarly the posterior probability for rain *decreases* from .50 to .33 given an unlikely forecast.

EXAMPLE ■■

Posterior Probabilities for Oil Wildcatting with a Seismic Survey

Based on 20 years of wildcatting experience, Lucky Luke assigns a prior probability of .20 for oil (O) beneath Crockpot Dome. Thus,

$$\Pr[O] = .20 \quad \text{and} \quad \Pr[\text{not } O] = 1 - .20 = .80$$

Luke has decided to order a seismic survey. A petroleum engineering consultant has rated this particular test as 90% reliable in confirming oil (C) when there is actually oil, but only 70% reliable in denying oil (D) when a site has no oil. These figures establish the conditional result probabilities.

$$\Pr[C|O] = .90 \quad \text{and} \quad \Pr[D|\text{not } O] = .70$$

Suppose that the seismic survey confirms the presence of oil. Luke's posterior probability for oil would then be

$$\Pr[O|C] = \frac{\Pr[O] \times \Pr[C|O]}{\Pr[O] \times \Pr[C|O] + \Pr[\text{not } O] \times \Pr[C|\text{not } O]}$$

$$= \frac{.20(.90)}{.20(.90) + .80(1 - .70)} = \frac{.18}{.18 + .24}$$

$$= .429$$

If you assume instead that the seismic survey denies any oil beneath Crockpot Dome, Luke's posterior probability for oil would be different.

$$\Pr[O|D] = \frac{\Pr[O] \times \Pr[D|O]}{\Pr[O] \times \Pr[D|O] + \Pr[\text{not } O] \times \Pr[D|\text{not } O]}$$

$$= \frac{.20(1 - .90)}{.20(1 - .90) + .80(.70)} = \frac{.02}{.02 + .56}$$

$$= .034$$

Notice how a positive experimental result raises the oil probability above its prior level, while a negative result lowers the oil probability below its initial value.

- Remember that a prior probability $\Pr[E]$ is a *given* value and is an *unconditional* probability.
- The posterior probability $\Pr[E|R]$ must be *computed*. This is a *conditional* probability.
- Do not confuse the posterior probability with the conditional result probabilities $\Pr[R|E]$ and $\Pr[R|\text{not } E]$. Here E and not E are the given events and are therefore listed last. Conditional result probabilities are *specified in advance*.

Posterior Probabilities Computed from the Joint Probability Table

The fraction used in expressing Bayes' theorem is really nothing more than a detailed rephrasing of the conditional probability identity (page 25).

$$\Pr[E|R] = \frac{\Pr[E \text{ and } R]}{\Pr[R]}$$

At times, rather than use Bayes' theorem, you may find it easier to first construct a joint probability table and then apply the above identity to find posterior probabilities.

To understand this, continue with the weather illustration. You can construct the following joint probability table using the data originally given.

MAIN EVENT	RESULT (forecast)		Marginal Probability
	Likely	Unlikely	
Rain	.30	.20	.50
No Rain	.10	.40	.50
Marginal Probability	.40	.60	1.00

The marginal probabilities for "rain" and "no rain" were given as the prior probability values. You find the joint probability for "rain" and "likely" by using the general multiplication law (page 29).

$$\text{Pr}[\text{rain } and \text{ likely}] = \text{Pr}[\text{rain}] \times \text{Pr}[\text{likely} | \text{rain}]$$
$$= .50(.60) = .30$$

Subtracting this value from the marginal probability for the first row (.50), you get the second joint probability of .20. You can likewise find the joint probability for "no rain" and "unlikely."

$$\text{Pr}[\text{no rain } and \text{ unlikely}] = \text{Pr}[\text{no rain}] \times \text{Pr}[\text{unlikely} | \text{no rain}]$$
$$= .50(.80) = .40$$

Now, you find the missing joint probability in the second row by subtracting .40 from the marginal probability for the row (.50). Finally, the marginal probabilities for the columns are found by adding together the joint probabilities in each column.

To find the posterior probability for rain given a likely weather forecast, you substitute the appropriate values into the identity directly from the joint probability table.

$$\text{Pr}[\text{rain} | \text{likely}] = \frac{\text{Pr}[\text{rain } and \text{ likely}]}{\text{Pr}[\text{likely}]} = \frac{.30}{.40} = .75$$

Likewise, the posterior probability for rain given an unlikely forecast is

$$\text{Pr}[\text{rain} | \text{unlikely}] = \frac{\text{Pr}[\text{rain } and \text{ unlikely}]}{\text{Pr}[\text{unlikely}]} = \frac{.20}{.60} = .333$$

CASE

The Three Marketeers

Dar Tan Yun, president of the Three Marketeers, has formed a consumer test panel to help devise a marketing strategy for a line of microwavable gourmet meals. The panel would be responsible for choosing promotions, formulating advertising copy, and selecting advertising media.

Table 2-3 shows a partial breakdown of the 25 panel members. Dar believes that they are a microcosm of the target market. If true, the probability that a potential customer has various characteristics should coincide with the probability that a randomly selected panel member has them also.

TABLE 2-3
Demographic Breakdown of Three Marketeers Consumer Test Panel

NAME	MARITAL STATUS	LEVEL OF EDUCATION	HOME	SIBLING STATUS	CHILDREN AT HOME
Ruth Baird	married	high school	renter	firstborn	yes
Ann Schultz	unmarried	some college	renter	youngest	no
Mark Maris	unmarried	bachelor's	renter	firstborn	no
Tom Steel	married	some college	owner	youngest	yes
Bill Adamson	unmarried	master's	renter	only child	yes
Pete Gonzales	unmarried	bachelor's	renter	middle	no
Morris Chin	married	high school	owner	middle	yes
Heidi Gravitz	married	bachelor's	owner	middle	no
Todd Fullmer	unmarried	bachelor's	renter	firstborn	yes
Scott Meadows	unmarried	master's	owner	youngest	no
Harvey Abramovitz	married	bachelor's	owner	firstborn	yes
Andy Pilsner	unmarried	some college	renter	youngest	no
Ann Goldberg	unmarried	some college	renter	only child	yes
Mike O'Hara	married	bachelor's	renter	youngest	yes
Larry Ellington	married	high school	owner	only child	no
Dick Senn	unmarried	bachelor's	renter	firstborn	no
Tom Sellers	married	bachelor's	renter	middle	no
Jack Beringer	unmarried	high school	owner	middle	no
Don McKinsey	unmarried	bachelor's	renter	only child	no
Sally Deerwalker	married	some college	owner	firstborn	yes
Ingrid Folsom	married	bachelor's	owner	only child	yes
Gloria Gravenstein	married	high school	owner	middle	yes
Marsha Markovich	unmarried	some college	renter	middle	yes
Ursula Hernandes	unmarried	bachelor's	renter	only child	no
Tom Fujimoto	unmarried	bachelor's	renter	youngest	no

Questions

1. Various two-way joint probability tables might be constructed for the characteristics of a randomly selected panel member.
   (a) Including a person's sex as a main feature, how many different joint
       probability tables may be constructed using the demographic groupings in
       Table 2-3?
   (b) Construct the following joint probability tables.
       (1) marital status versus education
       (2) education versus home
       (3) home versus sibling status
       (4) sex versus marital status
       (5) marital status versus children at home
       (6) sibling status versus education
   (c) Using your answers to (b), identify any event pairs that are statistically
       independent.
   (d) What might you conclude regarding the incidence of independence among
       demographic characteristics in target markets?

2. Determine the following conditional probabilities for a randomly selected panel
   member.
   (a) Pr[bachelor's | married]   (e) Pr[firstborn | owner]
   (b) Pr[married | bachelor's]   (f) Pr[owner | firstborn]
   (c) Pr[renter | master's]   (g) Pr[unmarried | no children at home]
   (d) Pr[master's | renter]   (h) Pr[no children at home | unmarried]

3. A recent survey showed that 20% of the subscribers to the *Rising Loafer* are
   college graduates. Another 10% of the subscribers have master's degrees, and
   only 5% never went beyond high school. Determine the probability that a
   randomly selected panel member who reads this magazine (a) owns his or her
   home; (b) is married.

4. Half of the subscribers to *Foodaholics NewScooper* have no siblings. Of these,
   10% are the firstborn, and 30% are the youngest child. Determine the probability
   that a panel member who subscribes to this newsletter (a) is a homeowner; (b) has
   a master's degree.

5. Half of all the people in the target market eat oatmeal. Of these, 30% of the
   females prefer that dried fruit be added to the premix, whereas only 20% of the
   men do. Assuming that the same percentages apply to the panel members,
   determine the probability that a panel member will (a) eat oatmeal; (b) prefer
   dried fruit in their oatmeal.

6. Crunchy-Munchy is a new snack food. Of the children living with a married
   parent, only 20% will eat the snack. And of the children living with a single
   parent, 40% will eat it. Crunchy-Munchy will be marketed if at least 5% of all
   potential buyers have a child at home who would eat it. Assuming that the panel
   matches the market, should Crunchy-Munchy be marketed?

PROBLEMS

2-1   Determine the following probabilities.
  (a) A man chosen randomly from a group of ten men is a lawyer; the group contains two lawyers.
  (b) A particular name will be drawn out of 10,000 persons in a registry.
  (c) A head will be obtained on one toss each of a dime and a penny. (First determine the sample space.)
  (d) A number greater than 2 will be the value of the showing face from the toss of a six-sided die.

2-2   In a special study an accountant found the following history for 850 receivables: (a) 119 were paid early, (b) 340 were settled on time, (c) 221 were paid late, and (d) 170 were uncollectible. Assume that this experience is representative of the future. Estimate the probabilities that a particular receivable will fall into each of the four categories.

2-3   The following table shows the number of panelists in each category of a Wee Tees consumer test panel.

OCCUPATION	FAMILY INCOME			Total
	Low	Medium	High	
Homemaker	8	26	6	40
Blue-collar Worker	16	40	14	70
White-collar Worker	6	62	12	80
Professional	0	2	8	10
Total	30	130	40	200

  One person is selected at random.
  (a) Find the probability that the selected person will fall into the following occupations.
      (1) homemaker   (3) white-collar worker
      (2) blue-collar worker   (4) professional
  (b) Find the probability that the selected person's family income is (1) low; (2) medium; (3) high.
  (c) Find the probability that the selected person will be classified as the following.
      (1) a white-collar worker with a high income
      (2) a homemaker with a low income
      (3) a professional with a medium income

2-4   You are asked to toss a pair of six-sided dice, one red and one green. Each side of a die cube has a different number of dots, 1 through 6.
  (a) List the possible sums of the number of dots on the two showing sides.
  (b) For each possible sum, list the corresponding elementary events and determine the sum's probability. (Identify your elementary events using a convenient code, such as 2R-5G for 2 dots showing on the red die and 5 on the green.)

2-5   Refer to the random experiment in Figure 2-3 for a business student selected at random. Use the count-and-divide method to find the probability that the selected student will be classified as the following.
   (a) a finance major
   (b) a graduate *and* a woman
   (c) a man *and* a marketing major
   (d) either a man *or* a woman
   (e) not an accounting major
   (f) a graduate in marketing

2-6   There are 100 employees at GizMo Corporation: 40 women and 60 men. Of these, 15 of the women and 35 of the men are married. One employee is selected at random.
   (a) Find the probabilities of the following outcomes.
      (1) man
      (2) married man
      (3) woman
      (4) married woman
      (5) married
      (6) unmarried man
      (7) unmarried
      (8) unmarried woman
   (b) Using your answers to (a), apply the addition law to find the probabilities of the following results.
      (1) woman *or* unmarried
      (2) man *or* married
      (3) woman *or* married
      (4) man *or* unmarried

2-7   The following probabilities have been obtained for the lead-time demand for barrels of Boll Toll pesticide.

NUMBER OF BARRELS	PROBABILITY
0	.3
1	.2
2	.1
3	.1
4	.1
5	.1
6	.1
7 or more	0
Total	1.0

Determine the probability for the following number of barrels.
   (a) fewer than 4 barrels
   (b) between 2 and 6 barrels, inclusively
   (c) at least 1 barrel
   (d) between 2 and 4 barrels, inclusively
   (e) at the most, 2 barrels

2-8   In conducting a check, an auditor randomly selects 5 accounts receivable out of 10 that are listed as outstanding. Only 4 of the 10 accounts are in error. The following probabilities have been obtained for the number of accounts having incorrect balances.

NUMBER OF INCORRECT ACCOUNTS	PROBABILITY
0	1/42
1	10/42
2	20/42
3	10/42
4	1/42

Determine the probability for the following number of incorrect balances.
(a) at least 2   (c) 1 or more   (e) fewer than 4
(b) at most 3   (d) greater than 2   (f) 4 or fewer

2-9   The Ourman-Friday Employment Agency specializes in clerical and data processing help. Candidates are classified in terms of primary skills and years of experience. The skills are bookkeeping, VDT, and clerical. (We will assume that no candidate is proficient in more than one.) Experience categories are less than one year, one to three years, and more than three years. There are 100 persons currently on file, and their skills and experience are summarized in the following table.

EXPERIENCE	Bookkeeping	VDT	Clerical	Total
	SKILL			
Less than One Year	15	5	30	50
One to Three Years	5	10	5	20
More than Three Years	5	15	10	30
Total	25	30	45	100

One person's file is selected at random. Find the probability that the selected person will fall into each of the following categories.
(a) bookkeeping   (d) one to three years of experience
(b) less than one year of experience   (e) clerical
(c) VDT   (f) more than three years of experience

2-10 Refer to Problem 2-9.
(a) Assume the selected person has less than one year of experience. What is the probability that his or her skill is bookkeeping?
(b) Does the bookkeeping probability in (a) differ from the one you found in Problem 2-9? Are bookkeeping and less than one year of experience statistically independent events?
(c) Find Pr[bookkeeping *and* less than one year of experience]. Can the multiplication law given in this chapter be used to determine this probability?

2-11 Refer to Problem 2-9.
(a) Use the addition law to determine the probabilities for the following component events.
(1) bookkeeping *or* VDT
(2) clerical *or* VDT
(3) less than one year of experience *or* more than three years of experience
(b) Use the count-and-divide method to determine the probabilities for the following component events.
(1) bookkeeping *or* less than one year of experience
(2) VDT *or* more than three years of experience
(3) clerical *or* one to three years of experience

2-12 The statistics students at Adams College are 60% male. Exactly 20% of the men and 20% of the women are married. Use the multiplication law to find the probability that a randomly selected student will be classified as the following.
(a) man *and* married   (c) woman *and* married
(b) man *and* unmarried   (d) woman *and* unmarried

2-13   Refer to the consumer test panelists in Problem 2-3. One panelist is selected at random.
(a) Construct a joint probability table for occupation versus family income events.
(b) Find the following probabilities.
   (1) Pr[homemaker *and* high]   (3) Pr[blue-collar *and* low]
   (2) Pr[white-collar *and* low]   (4) Pr[professional *and* high]
(c) Find the following probabilities.
   (1) Pr[high│homemaker]   (3) Pr[blue-collar│low]
   (2) Pr[white-collar│high]   (4) Pr[professional│low]

2-14   A State University business scholarship student is randomly selected. Figure 2-3 summarizes the sample space. Let U and G denote level; M and W, sex; A, accounting major; and F, finance major.
(a) Find the following probabilities by applying the count-and-divide method to the elementary events given in Figure 2-3.

(1)	(2)	(3)	(4)	(5)	(6)
$Pr[U]$	$Pr[F]$	$Pr[W]$	$Pr[G]$	$Pr[M]$	$Pr[W]$
$Pr[W\|U]$	$Pr[U\|F]$	$Pr[A\|W]$	$Pr[M\|G]$	$Pr[F\|M]$	$Pr[U\|W]$

(b) Apply the multiplication law to each pair of probabilities in (a) to find the following joint probabilities.
   (1) $Pr[U$ *and* $W]$ (3) $Pr[W$ *and* $A]$ (5) $Pr[M$ *and* $F]$
   (2) $Pr[F$ *and* $U]$ (4) $Pr[G$ *and* $M]$ (6) $Pr[W$ *and* $U]$

2-15   The probability is .95 that a GizMo Corporation traveling sales representative will have no automobile accidents in a year. Assuming that accident frequencies in successive years are independent events, find the probability that a particular driver (a) goes 5 straight years with no accident; (b) has at least 1 accident in 5 years.

2-16   The general manager of the Gotham City Hellcats is evaluating an employment screening test for the front office clerical staff. During this experiment all new clerical employees are given the test. Seventy percent pass the test; the rest fail. At a later time, it is determined whether the new clerks are satisfactory or unsatisfactory. Historically, 80% of all clerical hires have been found to be satisfactory, and 75% of the satisfactory clerks in the program have passed the screening test.
   Consider the events applicable to a new clerk in the experiment.
(a) From the given information, find the following values.
   (1) Pr[pass]   (2) Pr[satisfactory]   (3) Pr[pass│satisfactory]
(b) Using your answers to (a), find Pr[pass *and* satisfactory].
(c) Construct the joint probability table for test results versus employee performance events.
(d) Using your answers to (c), determine the following conditional probabilities.
   (1) Pr[fail│unsatisfactory]   (5) Pr[satisfactory│pass]
   (2) Pr[fail│satisfactory]   (6) Pr[unsatisfactory│pass]
   (3) Pr[pass│unsatisfactory]   (7) Pr[satisfactory│fail]
   (4) Pr[unsatisfactory│fail]
(e) Using your answers to (d), find the following percentages.
   (1) failing clerks who prove to be unsatisfactory employees
   (2) passing clerks who prove to be satisfactory employees.
(f) Government guidelines are that a proper screening test must provide at least 20% for (1) in (e) and at least 60% for (2). Does this test meet those guidelines?

2-17   A new family with two children of different ages has moved into the neighborhood. Suppose that it is equally likely that either child is a boy or girl, so that the following situations are equally likely.

YOUNGEST	OLDEST	
boy	boy	(B, B)
boy	girl	(B, G)
girl	boy	(G, B)
girl	girl	(G, G)

(a) Find Pr[at least one girl].
(b) If you know there is at least one girl, what is the conditional probability that the family has exactly one boy?
(c) Given that at least one child is a girl, what is the conditional probability that the other child is a girl?

2-18 Waysafe Markets employs two groups of 100 test shoppers to audit store performance. One person is selected at random from each group.

(a) Group A is 50% men and 50% women; 70% of the members are married, and just as many men as women are married. Thus, any two sex and marital status events are independent. Construct a joint probability table by first finding the marginal probabilities and then using the multiplication law to obtain the joint probabilities, which in this case may be expressed as the products of the two respective marginal probabilities.
(b) Group B is also 50% men and 50% women, and 70% of the members are married. However, only 60% of the men are married, whereas 80% of the women are married. Thus, any two sex and marital status events are dependent. This means that the product of the respective marginal probabilities does not equal the corresponding joint probability. Construct a joint probability table using the count-and-divide method.

2-19 A winery superintendent accepts or rejects truckloads of grapes after performing tests on a few sample bunches. She rejects 15% of all the truckloads she inspects. Thus far, she has rejected 95% of all bad truckloads inspected, and 10% of all truckloads have ultimately proved to be bad.

(a) Using this experience as a basis, find the values of the following probabilities regarding the outcome of any particular truckload.
(1) Pr[reject]   (2) Pr[bad]   (3) Pr[reject | bad]
(b) Apply the multiplication law to the appropriate values you found in (a) to find Pr[reject *and* bad].
(c) Construct a joint probability table showing the joint and marginal probabilities for the superintendent's actions (accept or reject) and the quality (good or bad) of the grapes in a truckload.

2-20 Refer to the winery superintendent's situation in Problem 2-19 and to your answers.

(a) What percentage of all good shipments get rejected?
(b) Construct a probability tree diagram representing the disposition of a truckload of grapes. Represent the quality of the grapes (good, bad) in the first fork and the superintendent's actions (accept, reject) as forks in the second stage. Enter all branch probabilities onto your tree and then apply the multiplication law to establish the joint probability for each quality-act combination.

2-21   An experiment is conducted using three boxes, each containing a mixture of 10 (R)ed and (W)hite marbles. The three boxes have the following compositions.

BOX A	BOX B	BOX C
6 R	4 R	7 R
4 W	6 W	3 W

Two marbles are selected at random. The first is selected from Box A. If it is red, the second marble is to be taken from Box B; if the first marble is white, the second marble is to be taken from Box C. Use R_1 and W_1 to represent the color of the first marble and R_2 and W_2 to represent the color of the second marble.

(a) Find the following probabilities.
   (1) $\Pr[R_1]$ (3) $\Pr[R_2|R_1]$ (5) $\Pr[W_2|R_1]$
   (2) $\Pr[W_1]$ (4) $\Pr[R_2|W_1]$ (6) $\Pr[W_2|W_1]$
(b) Apply the multiplication law to your answers to (a) to determine the following joint probabilities.
   (1) $\Pr[R_1 \text{ and } R_2]$ (3) $\Pr[W_1 \text{ and } R_2]$
   (2) $\Pr[R_1 \text{ and } W_2]$ (4) $\Pr[W_1 \text{ and } W_2]$
(c) Determine the following probabilities.
   (1) one red and one white marble will be chosen
   (2) either two red or two white marbles will be chosen

2-22   Felina Wild is an oil wildcatter who decides that the probability for striking gas (G) is .40. Felina orders a seismic survey that confirms (C) gas with a probability of .85 in known gas fields and denies (D) gas with a probability of .60 when there is no gas.
(a) Determine (1) $\Pr[G \text{ and } C]$ and (2) $\Pr[\text{no } G \text{ and } D]$.
(b) Construct the joint probability table for geology and survey events.

2-23   Refer to Problem 2-22. Construct a probability tree diagram. Determine the joint probability for each geology and seismic outcome.

2-24   A new movie "Star Struck" has a prior probability for success of .20. Ruth Grist is going to review the film. She has liked 70% of all the successful films and has disliked 80% of all the unsuccessful films she has reviewed. Find the posterior probability that "Star Struck" will be a success if (a) Grist likes it; (b) Grist dislikes it.

2-25   One student is selected at random from the sample space in Figure 2-3.
(a) What is the prior probability that the student is a man (M)?
(b) Suppose that the student's major is known. What is the posterior probability that a man is selected given that the student is a finance major (F)?

2-26   Wendy Storm makes a daily television forecast indicating the probability that it will rain tomorrow. On one particular evening, she announces an 80% chance of rain (E) the next day. The manager of the city golf courses has established a policy that he will water the greens only if the probability for rain is less than 90%. Using the local TV forecast as his prior probability, the manager also relies on his mother-in-law's rheumatism. Historically, she gets a rheumatic pain (R) on 90% of all days that are followed by rain, but she also experiences rheumatic pain on 20% of the days that are not followed by rain. The following probabilities therefore apply.

$$\Pr[E] = .80 \qquad \Pr[R|E] = .90 \qquad \Pr[R|\text{not } E] = .20$$

(a) Assuming that the golf course manager's mother-in-law is currently receiving rheumatic signals (R), find the posterior probability that it will rain (E) tomorrow. Should the manager water the greens?

(b) If the manager's mother-in-law does not feel any rheumatic pain, what is the posterior probability for rain (E) tomorrow?

2-27 Felix Wilde has assigned a probability of .50 to striking oil on his property. He orders a seismic survey that has proved to be only 80% reliable in the past. Given oil, it predicts favorably 80% of the time; given no oil, it augurs unfavorably with a frequency of .8.

(a) Given a favorable seismic result, what is the probability for oil?

(b) Given an unfavorable seismic result, what is the probability for oil?

2-28 A marketing researcher wishes to determine whether, given a certain response to a question, a randomly selected person will choose NuScents when next purchasing deodorant. The question is designed to reveal whether or not the selected person recalls the name NuScents — an event we will denote by R. Previous testing has established that 99% of the people who bought NuScents previously recalled the name and that only 10% of the people who did not buy NuScents recalled this particular brand name. Since NuScents has cornered 30% of the deodorant market, the researcher chooses .30 as the prior probability that the person selected will buy NuScents. Denoting this event B gives us the following probabilities.

$$\Pr[B] = .30 \qquad \Pr[R \mid B] = .99 \qquad \Pr[R \mid \text{not } B] = .10$$

(a) If the person who is selected remembers NuScents, what is the posterior probability that NuScents will be purchased next?

(b) If the person who is selected does *not* remember NuScents, what is the posterior probability that NuScents will be purchased next?

2-29 Comp-u-Quik is evaluating an employment screening test for possible inclusion in clerical services hiring decisions. Presently, only 50% of the persons hired for these positions perform satisfactorily. The test itself has been evaluated by outside consultants, who have given it an upside reliability of 90% (90% of all satisfactory employees will pass the test) and a downside reliability of only 80% (80% of all unsatisfactory employees will fail the test). One clerical applicant (acceptable in all other screening activities) is chosen at random. Find the following probabilities.

(a) The prior probability for satisfactory on-the-job performance if the applicant is hired.

(b) The posterior probability for satisfactory on-the-job performance if the applicant passes the screening test.

(c) The posterior probability for satisfactory on-the-job performance if the applicant is hired after failing the screening test.

CHAPTER

3

Probability Distributions, Expected Value, and Sampling

$\mathcal{C}$hapter 2 provided us with the fundamental concepts of probability. We are now ready to study some of the tools that are used to analyze business decisions when uncertainty is present. The outcomes of business decisions are often numerical, and the result to be achieved is usually expressed as a variable. Because the particular value is uncertain and determined by chance, we call it a **random variable**. The probabilities assigned to each possible value of this variable constitute a **probability distribution**.

For instance, alternative locations for a new plant can be compared in terms of profitability, which can be viewed as a random variable with a probability distribution. But to rank the attractiveness of each candidate plant site, we must obtain a single profit figure for each site. We will see how the expected level of profitability can be determined for each alternative by using the respective probability distribution to arrive at an "average" figure. The average level of a random variable is referred to as its **expected value**.

In this chapter, we will discuss random variables, probability distributions, and expected value. We will examine four specific probability distributions: the *binomial distribution*, which is one of the most commonly encountered distributions; the *normal distribution*, which is the most important distribution when sample information is used to help analyze decisions; the *Poisson distribution*, applicable to the number of events occurring randomly over time; and the *exponential distribution*, which provides probabilities for the time between events.

3-1 Random Variables and Probability Distributions

A variable whose level is determined by chance is called a **random variable**. When a specific outcome is uncertain, it is treated as a variable. The random variable assumes actual numerical value only *after* all relevant outcomes are known. Many different kinds of random variables can be generated by a single situation.

The Probability Distribution

The relationship between the values of a random variable and their probabilities is summarized by the **probability distribution**. Many probability distributions can be expressed in terms of a table. Table 3-1 lists the possible rates of return from operating a new piece of equipment. Notice that the probabilities sum to 1. When there are too many possibilities to list conveniently in a table, an algebraic expression is used to describe the probability distribution.

TABLE 3-1
Probability Distribution for the
Rate of Return

POSSIBLE RATE OF RETURN	PROBABILITY
10%	.05
11	.10
12	.15
13	.17
14	.12
15	.08
16	.09
17	.06
18	.05
19	.05
20	.04
21	.04
Total	1.00

Finding the Probability Distribution

A probability distribution can be established by applying the probability concepts and procedures found in Chapter 2. The following example shows how to create a probability distribution using the multiplication and addition laws.

EXAMPLE ■■■■■■■■■■■■■■■■■■■■■■■■■■■■■■■■■■■■

Amount Paid for a Personal Computer

Quant Jacques wishes to buy a personal computer made by VBM (Very Big Machines). From past purchases, VBM has established the following breakdown for the percentage of times that a particular component is selected for a system.

COMPUTER AND MEMORY	PRINTER	MONITOR
30%—250K ($1500)	50%—Matrix ($500)	60%—Monochrome ($200)
70%—500K ($2000)	50%—Laser ($1000)	40%—Color ($400)

Assuming that Quant selects the three components independently and that the probability for each choice agrees with the percentages given in the table, what is the probability distribution for his total system cost?

Begin by listing all the possible combinations. You can determine the probability for each by using the multiplication law.

COMPUTER AND MEMORY	PRINTER	MONITOR	COST	PROBABILITY
250K	Matrix	Monochrome	1,500 + 500 + 200 = $2,200	.3(.5)(.6) = .09
250K	Matrix	Color	1,500 + 500 + 400 = 2,400	.3(.5)(.4) = .06
250K	Laser	Monochrome	1,500 + 1,000 + 200 = 2,700	.3(.5)(.6) = .09
250K	Laser	Color	1,500 + 1,000 + 400 = 2,900	.3(.5)(.4) = .06
500K	Matrix	Monochrome	2,000 + 500 + 200 = 2,700	.7(.5)(.6) = .21
500K	Matrix	Color	2,000 + 500 + 400 = 2,900	.7(.5)(.4) = .14
500K	Laser	Monochrome	2,000 + 1,000 + 200 = 3,200	.7(.5)(.6) = .21
500K	Laser	Color	2,000 + 1,000 + 400 = 3,400	.7(.5)(.4) = .14

List the possible costs, applying the addition law as needed, to construct the probability distribution table.

COST	PROBABILITY
$2,200	.09
2,400	.06
2,700	.09 + .21 = .30
2,900	.06 + .14 = .20
3,200	.21
3,400	.14
	1.00

Probability Trees and Sampling

Especially important to quantitative decision making are probability distributions that summarize the potential results from sampling. Sampling ordinarily involves multiple observations, and, therefore, the probability calculations can be complicated. Probability trees are helpful in organizing those computations.

To illustrate, consider a shipment of 100 printed circuit (PC) boards received by a computer manufacturer. Each board is either defective (D) or good (G). The decision to accept or reject the shipment will be based on a sample of three boards selected at random. The inspector has no way of knowing ahead of time how many defective boards there are. Let's assume that there are exactly 5 defective boards and 95 good boards.

The probability tree in Figure 3-1 summarizes the essential information. The first observation is represented by the two branches in the event fork farthest to the left. We use the abbreviation D_1 to denote the event "the first board is defective" and G_1 to denote the event "the first board is good." The subscripts help to distinguish the results from different observations. Each branch for the first observation leads to a separate event fork for the second. Both forks for the second observation have a D_2 and G_2 branch. Together, the initial observations create four distinct circumstances under which the third observation might occur, and each of these is represented by a separate fork that has a D_3 and G_3 branch.

The probabilities for each branch are determined using the count-and-divide method, according to the number of defective and good boards remaining up to that point in the tree. The initial fork has probabilities

$$\Pr[D_1] = \frac{5}{100} \quad \text{and} \quad \Pr[G_1] = \frac{95}{100}$$

Because the quality mix of the remaining items varies at the second stage, the probabilities for D_2 and G_2 differ in the two event forks for that observation. The values shown are *conditional probabilities*. The top set applies when D_1 has occurred, when there are only 4 defective boards and 95 good boards remaining. With 99 boards available for

FIGURE 3-1

Probability tree diagram for selecting a sample of three PC Boards without replacement.

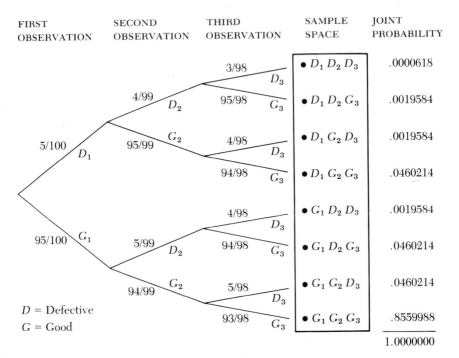

testing, the count-and-divide procedure provides

$$\Pr[D_2|D_1] = \frac{4}{99} \quad \text{and} \quad \Pr[G_2|D_1] = \frac{95}{99}$$

Likewise, the lower second stage fork involves

$$\Pr[D_2|G_1] = \frac{5}{99} \quad \text{and} \quad \Pr[G_2|G_1] = \frac{94}{99}$$

since, at that point—with 1 good board removed—the tree indicates that 5 defective and 94 good boards remain.

The forks for the third stage involve probabilities reflecting the respective histories of defective and good for the previously tested items. The fork at the top right is preceded by D_1 and D_2 branches, so that the following conditional probabilities appear.

$$\Pr[D_3|D_1 \text{ and } D_2] = \frac{3}{98} \quad \text{and} \quad \Pr[G_3|D_1 \text{ and } D_2] = \frac{95}{98}$$

It is easy to verify the remaining third stage probabilities.

Each path through the tree in Figure 3-1 corresponds to a distinct outcome, and is summarized in the sample space listed in the box beside the tree. The probability for these elementary events is determined by multiplying together the branch probabilities on its respective path. For instance, to determine the second elementary event probability we have

$$Pr[D_1 D_2 G_3] = \frac{5}{100} \times \frac{4}{99} \times \frac{95}{98} = .0019584$$

We are actually applying the multiplication law for several joint events.

$$Pr[D_1 \text{ and } D_2 \text{ and } G_3] = Pr[D_1] \times Pr[D_2 | D_1] \times Pr[G_3 | D_1 \text{ and } D_2]$$

By itself, the probability tree is too detailed to help the inspector decide how to dispose of a particular shipment. However, she would find useful the probability distribution for the number of defectives R provided in Table 3-2. The table probabilities were determined using the information in the last two columns of Figure 3-1 and then applying the addition law for mutually exclusive events.

Using the values in Table 3-2, the inspector can determine the probability that the shipment would contain more than 1 defective.

$$Pr[R > 1] = Pr[R = 2] + Pr[R = 3]$$

$$= .0058752 + .0000618$$

$$= .0059370$$

TABLE 3-2
Probability Distribution for the Number of Defective PC Boards
When Three Sample Items Are Inspected without Replacement

NUMBER OF DEFECTIVES r	CORRESPONDING ELEMENTARY EVENTS	ELEMENTARY EVENT PROBABILITY	PROBABILITY $Pr[R = r]$
0	$G_1 G_2 G_3$	.8559988	.8559988
1	$D_1 G_2 G_3$	.0460214	.1380642
	$G_1 D_2 G_3$	.0460214	
	$G_1 G_2 D_3$	.0460214	
		.1380642	
2	$D_1 D_2 G_3$	.0019584	.0058752
	$D_1 G_2 D_3$	.0019584	
	$G_1 D_2 D_3$	.0019584	
		.0058752	
3	$D_1 D_2 D_3$	.0000618	.0000618
			1.0000000

FIGURE 3-2

Probability tree for selecting a sample of three PC Boards with replacement.

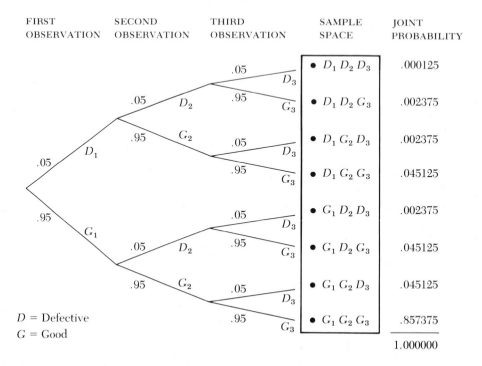

FIRST OBSERVATION	SECOND OBSERVATION	THIRD OBSERVATION	SAMPLE SPACE	JOINT PROBABILITY
			• $D_1 D_2 D_3$	.000125
			• $D_1 D_2 G_3$	.002375
			• $D_1 G_2 D_3$	.002375
			• $D_1 G_2 G_3$	.045125
			• $G_1 D_2 D_3$	.002375
			• $G_1 D_2 G_3$	.045125
			• $G_1 G_2 D_3$	.045125
			• $G_1 G_2 G_3$	.857375

D = Defective
G = Good

1.000000

If she rejects shipments having more than 1 defective item, less than 1% of similar shipments would be unacceptable.

Independent Sample Observations   The preceding illustration involves **sampling without replacement**, since the inspected sample units are set aside. Although it seems inherently wasteful (and even impossible when testing destroys the items), some inspection schemes replace the items in the original population, allowing them the same chance of being selected for each subsequent observation as the other items. Such a procedure is called **sampling with replacement**. As we shall see, sampling with replacement simplifies the probability calculations.

Figure 3-2 shows the probability tree diagram that would apply if the inspector sampled with replacement. Notice that all the D branches have identical probabilities of .05, and, similarly, the probabilities for the G branches are all .95. Since sampled items are replaced, the probabilities for later quality events must be unaffected by what happens earlier. In effect, successive quality events are *statistically independent*. Independence between successive sample observations arises naturally when sampling from a continuing production line, when replacement or nonreplacement would yield identical probabilities due to the theoretically infinite population size.

The probability distribution for the number of defectives found using sampling with replacement is given in Table 3-3. The probabilities are obtained in the same manner as

TABLE 3-3
Probability Distributions for the Number of
Defective PC Boards

NUMBER OF DEFECTIVES r	Pr[R = r] FOR SAMPLING	
	without Replacement	*with Replacement*
0	.8559988	.857375
1	.1380642	.135375
2	.0058752	.007125
3	.0000618	.000125
	1.0000000	1.000000

before. To help compare the two procedures, the two sets of probabilities are given side by side.

The two sets of values are very close. As noted earlier, the probabilities computed for sampling without replacement involve cumbersome calculations, and they are often *approximated* using the cleanly computed values that strictly apply for sampling with replacement. The computations for both types of similar distributions can be streamlined. When there is replacement—or, more generally, when successive observations are independent—the *binomial distribution* (described in Section 3-3) applies. Using sampling without replacement in finite populations, a second distribution, the *hypergeometric distribution* theoretically applies.

3-2 Expected Value

When business decisions are made under uncertain conditions, a different random variable with its own probability distribution is usually arrived at for each possible choice. In comparing alternative budget decisions, a company president may be faced with a variety of choices with different rate-of-return probability distributions similar to the one in Table 3-1. It is hard to compare several tables. To facilitate the choice, each probability distribution is often summarized by a single "average" value. These summary numbers can then be used to rank the various alternatives.

This average can be computed directly from the probability distribution. The resulting figure, called the **expected value** of the random variable, is found by multiplying every possible value by its probability and summing all the products. The expected value is therefore a weighted average, with the probabilities serving as weights. Table 3-4 shows the calculation of the expected value for the number of dots obtained in tossing a six-sided die.

The Meaning of Expected Value

The expected value has many uses. In a gambling game, it tells us what our long-run average losses per play will be. Sophisticated gamblers know that slot machines pay

TABLE 3-4
Calculation of the Expected Value for a Die Toss

NUMBER OF DOTS	PROBABILITY	NUMBER × PROBABILITY
1	1/6	1/6
2	1/6	2/6
3	1/6	3/6
4	1/6	4/6
5	1/6	5/6
6	1/6	6/6
	1	21/6 = 3.5

Expected value = 3.5 dots

poorly in relation to the actual odds and that the average loss per play is less in roulette or dice games. In the early 1960s, the mathematician Edward Thorp caused quite a stir when he demonstrated that various betting strategies could be applied in playing the card game blackjack to produce positive expected winnings.*

Roulette provides another example. The winnings from betting $1 on the 7 slot have the following probability distribution.

WINNINGS	PROBABILITY
+$35	1/38
− $1	37/38

Applying the probability weights, the expected value is

$$(+\$35)(1/38) + (-\$1)(37/38) = -\$2/38 = -\$.053$$

The expected winnings from a single roulette gamble is a loss of 5.3 cents. This means that the gambler who keeps making $1 bets indefinitely will lose an average of 5.3 cents on each bet. Of course, an individual gamble will show either a gain of $35 or a loss of $1. But *on the average* the gambler will win $35 in only 1 out of every 38 gambles and will lose $1 in 37 out of every 38 gambles.

Note that in both illustrations, the expected values of the random variables themselves are not outcomes of the uncertain situation. It is impossible for 3.5 dots to show; the outcome must be a whole number (1, 2, 3, 4, 5, or 6). The roulette player will

---

* See Edward Thorp, *Beat the Dealer*, 2nd ed. (New York: Random House, 1966). Unlike other gambling games, bets in blackjack can be placed when the odds are in the player's favor, because the card deck may not be reshuffled after each stage of play. By significantly raising their bets at these times, players will make a profit on the average.

TABLE 3-5

Calculation of the Expected Value for the Rate of Return

POSSIBLE RATE OF RETURN	PROBABILITY	RATE × PROBABILITY
10%	.05	.50%
11	.10	1.10
12	.15	1.80
13	.17	2.21
14	.12	1.68
15	.08	1.20
16	.09	1.44
17	.06	1.02
18	.05	.90
19	.05	.95
20	.04	.80
21	.04	.84
	1.00	14.44%

Expected rate of return = 14.44%

always be dealing in whole dollars. In either case, the expected value is only an average result. Although it is possible to obtain the expected value in some random experiments, there is no reason why the expected outcome should be a possible result in a single circumstance.

Because any decision that involves uncertainty may be viewed as a gambling situation, knowing the expected value can help us choose among alternative actions. But unlike a casino game, practical business decisions must often be made regarding nonrepeatable situations, such as the sales response to an advertising budget. In such cases, there is only one opportunity to "play." Here, uncertainty must be measured in terms of *subjective* probabilities. An expected value may still be calculated, but in these situations it represents an average of the decision maker's *convictions* about the outcomes. This is illustrated in Table 3-5, where the expected rate of return is calculated for the equipment discussed in Section 3-1.

What does a 14.44% expected rate of return mean? In this instance, the future conditions that will produce a particular percentage return are not repeatable, and the given probabilities really express the decision maker's convictions that the respective percentages will result. Thus, the expected value calculated from these subjective probabilities expresses the decision maker's "average conviction" as to what the return will be.

The Variance of a Random Variable

The expected value measures the *central tendency* of a probability distribution. A second type of measure—*dispersion or variability*–summarizes the degree to which the

TABLE 3-6
Calculation of the Variance for a Die Toss

NUMBER OF DOTS	DEVIATION: NUMBER -3.5	$(\text{NUMBER} -3.5)^2$	PROBABILITY	$(\text{NUMBER} -3.5)^2$ × PROBABILITY
1	-2.5	6.25	1/6	6.25/6
2	-1.5	2.25	1/6	2.25/6
3	$-.5$	.25	1/6	.25/6
4	.5	.25	1/6	.25/6
5	1.5	2.25	1/6	2.25/6
6	2.5	6.25	1/6	6.25/6
				17.50/6

Variance = 17.50/6 = 2.917

possible random-variable values differ among themselves. To determine the dispersion, we use the **variance**, which expresses the average of the squared deviations of the individual values from their expected value or mean. This is analogous to a statistical variance. The variance for the number of dots obtained from a die toss is calculated in Table 3-6.

Because the variance expresses dispersion in terms of original units squared (squared dots for a die), its square root is often used to measure dispersion. The resulting value is called the **standard deviation**. The standard deviation for the die toss outcome is

$$\sqrt{2.917} = 1.71 \text{ dots}$$

Both the expected value, or mean, and the variance can be useful in evaluating outcomes that are random variables. In making investment decisions, the variance is often used as a measure of risk. In analyzing stock portfolios, for example, each possible security combination may be portrayed in two dimensions: expected return and variance in returns.* The concept of variance is very important when decisions are made based on sample information. Later in this chapter, we will see how the normal distribution can be characterized in terms of two parameters—the mean and the variance (or standard deviation).

3-3 The Binomial Distribution

In making decisions under uncertain conditions it is often necessary to use sample data. We are presently concerned with samples obtained from *qualitative* populations, so that each observation results in one of two complementary outcomes, such as liking or disliking a new package design. Here, we will discuss the **binomial distribution**, which is concerned with the *number of outcomes* in a particular category.

---

* See Harry M. Markowitz, *Portfolio Selection: Efficient Diversification of Investments* (New Haven: Yale University Press, 1959).

A Coin Tossing Illustration

An evenly balanced coin is tossed fairly five times. The corresponding probability tree diagram appears in Figure 3-3, where the sample space is also listed. Our initial problem is to find the probability for obtaining exactly two heads. Since each of the 32 outcomes is equally likely, the basic definition of probability allows us to find the answer by counting the number of elementary events involving two heads and dividing this result by the total number of equally likely elementary events. The sample space contains 32 elementary events, and Figure 3-3 shows that 10 of these are two-head outcomes. Thus, we can determine that

$$\Pr[\text{exactly two heads}] = \frac{10}{32}$$

As we saw in Chapter 2, it is impractical to list all possible outcomes unless there are only a few. For instance, if 10 tosses were to be considered, the list would contain 1,024 (2^{10}) entries. Before discussing a procedure to simplify finding such probabilities, it will be helpful to relate coin tossing to a similar class of situations.

The Bernoulli Process

A sequence of coin tosses is one example of a **Bernoulli process**. A great many circumstances fall into the same category: All involve a series of situations (such as tosses of a coin), which are referred to as **trials**. For each trial, *there are only two possible complementary outcomes*, such as head or tail. Usually one outcome is referred to as a *success*; the other, as a *failure*.

Examples include giving birth to a single child in a maternity hospital, where each birth is a trial resulting in a boy or a girl; canning a vegetable, where each trial is a full can that is slightly overweight or underweight (cans of precisely correct weight are so improbable that we can ignore them); and transcribing numerical data, where each completed data block is a trial that will either contain errors or be correct. In all cases, only two opposite trial outcomes are considered.

What further distinguishes these situations as Bernoulli processes is that the *success probability remains constant* from trial to trial. The probability for obtaining a head is the same, regardless of which toss is considered; this is also true of the probability for delivering a boy for any successive birth in a maternity hospital, picking up an overweight can of vegetables, and receiving a correct data block each time. (The last condition would not hold if the operator tires over time; then the probability would be larger for an earlier block being correct than a later block would be.)

A final characteristic of a Bernoulli process is that *successive trial outcomes must be independent events*. Like a fairly tossed coin, the probability for obtaining a success (head) must be independent of what occurred in previous trials (tosses). The births in a *single family* may violate this requirement if the parents use medical techniques to have a second child of the opposite sex of their first child. Or a data operator's errors may occur in batches due to fatigue, so that once an error is made it is more likely to be followed by another.

FIGURE 3-3
Probability tree diagram for five coin tosses.

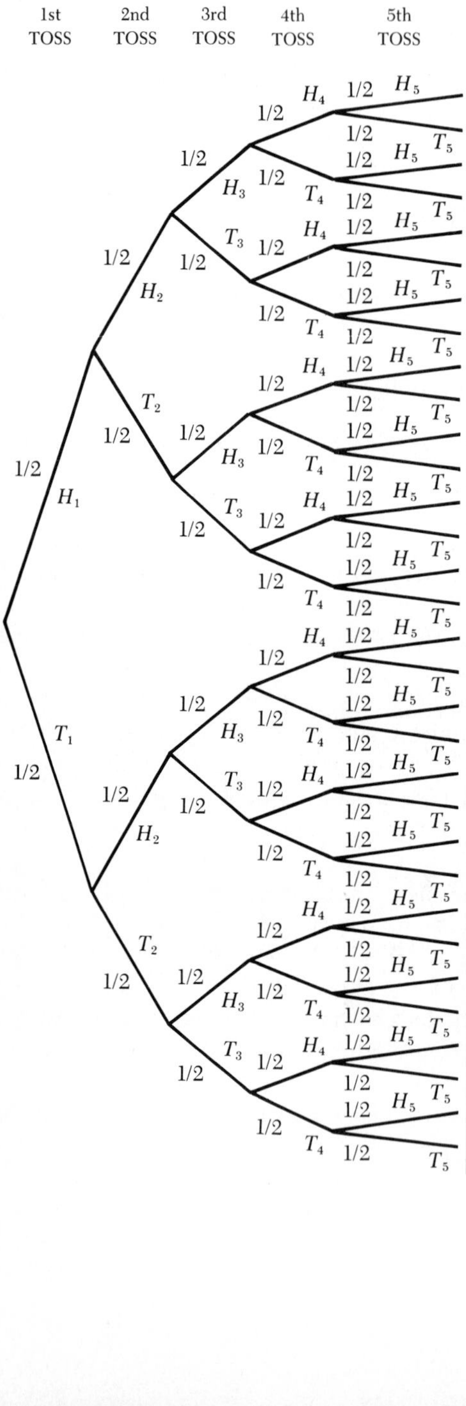

SAMPLE SPACE	PROBABILITY	NO. OF HEADS	0	1	2	3	4	5
▪$(H_1H_2H_3H_4H_5)$	1/32	5						*
▪$(H_1H_2H_3H_4T_5)$	1/32	4					*	
▪$(H_1H_2H_3T_4H_5)$	1/32	4					*	
▪$(H_1H_2H_3T_4T_5)$	1/32	3				*		
▪$(H_1H_2T_3H_4H_5)$	1/32	4					*	
▪$(H_1H_2T_3H_4T_5)$	1/32	3				*		
▪$(H_1H_2T_3T_4H_5)$	1/32	3				*		
▪$(H_1H_2T_3T_4T_5)$	1/32	2			*			
▪$(H_1T_2H_3H_4H_5)$	1/32	4					*	
▪$(H_1T_2H_3H_4T_5)$	1/32	3				*		
▪$(H_1T_2H_3T_4H_5)$	1/32	3				*		
▪$(H_1T_2H_3T_4T_5)$	1/32	2			*			
▪$(H_1T_2T_3H_4H_5)$	1/32	3				*		
▪$(H_1T_2T_3H_4T_5)$	1/32	2			*			
▪$(H_1T_2T_3T_4H_5)$	1/32	2			*			
▪$(H_1T_2T_3T_4T_5)$	1/32	1		*				
▪$(T_1H_2H_3H_4H_5)$	1/32	4					*	
▪$(T_1H_2H_3H_4T_5)$	1/32	3				*		
▪$(T_1H_2H_3T_4H_5)$	1/32	3				*		
▪$(T_1H_2H_3T_4T_5)$	1/32	2			*			
▪$(T_1H_2T_3H_4H_5)$	1/32	3				*		
▪$(T_1H_2T_3H_4T_5)$	1/32	2			*			
▪$(T_1H_2T_3T_4H_5)$	1/32	2			*			
▪$(T_1H_2T_3T_4T_5)$	1/32	1		*				
▪$(T_1T_2H_3H_4H_5)$	1/32	3				*		
▪$(T_1T_2H_3H_4T_5)$	1/32	2			*			
▪$(T_1T_2H_3T_4H_5)$	1/32	2			*			
▪$(T_1T_2H_3T_4T_5)$	1/32	1		*				
▪$(T_1T_2T_3H_4H_5)$	1/32	2			*			
▪$(T_1T_2T_3H_4T_5)$	1/32	1		*				
▪$(T_1T_2T_3T_4H_5)$	1/32	1		*				
▪$(T_1T_2T_3T_4T_5)$	1/32	0	*					

Totals 32/32   1 5 10 10 5 1

Sampling to determine the impact of advertising, voter preference, or response to drug treatment can all be classified as Bernoulli processes. To preserve the requirements of independence and constant probability for success, we must sample with replacement, thereby allowing each person the same chance of being selected each time and perhaps of being selected more than once. In each case, the probability for a trial success would be the proportion of persons in the respective population who would provide the desired response.

The Number of Combinations

Now we will derive an algebraic expression for computing binomial probabilities. Looking at Figure 3-3 again, we see that 10 elementary events involve exactly two heads.

$$
\begin{array}{lll}
H_1 H_2 T_3 T_4 T_5 & T_1 H_2 H_3 T_4 T_5 & T_1 T_2 H_3 H_4 T_5 \\
H_1 T_2 H_3 T_4 T_5 & T_1 H_2 T_3 H_4 T_5 & T_1 T_2 H_3 T_4 H_5 \\
H_1 T_2 T_3 H_4 T_5 & T_1 H_2 T_3 T_4 H_5 & T_1 T_2 T_3 H_4 H_5 \\
H_1 T_2 T_3 T_4 H_5 & &
\end{array}
$$

Each of these outcomes represents one path of branches in the probability tree. They differ only in terms of which particular two tosses are heads.

If we want to find out the number of two-head outcomes without constructing an entire probability tree we can determine how many different ways there are to pick the two tosses to be heads from the total of five. It will help if each toss is represented by a fork.

FIRST	SECOND	THIRD	FOURTH	FIFTH
TOSS	TOSS	TOSS	TOSS	TOSS

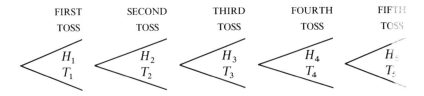

We want to save one branch from each fork. Two of the branches saved will be H's; three will be T's. Our problem is to determine how many ways there are to pick two H branches to save from the five.

If we pick the H branches one at a time, we have 5 possibilities for the first choice. No matter which H branch is chosen first, 4 H branch possibilities remain for the second choice. Multiplying the possibilities gives

$$5 \times 4 = 20$$

This answer is twice as large as it should be because the order of selection is considered. But we do not care whether an $H_3 H_5$ resulted from H_3 being the first or the second choice, so we divide by 2 to avoid accounting for order of selection.

$$\frac{5 \times 4}{2} = 10$$

This calculation can be used to find the number of **combinations** of items for a variety of situations. It will be helpful if we reexpress this fraction in the equivalent form

$$\frac{5 \times 4}{2} = \frac{5 \times 4}{2 \times 1} = \frac{5 \times 4 \times 3 \times 2 \times 1}{2 \times 1 \times 3 \times 2 \times 1} = 10$$

Multiplying both the numerator and the denominator of the middle fraction by 3, then by 2, and finally by 1 leaves the result unchanged. The final fraction contains factorial terms. A **factorial** is the product of successive integer values ending with 1. Such a product is denoted by placing an exclamation point after the highest number.

$$2! = 2 \times 1 \qquad (=2)$$

$$3! = 3 \times 2 \times 1 \qquad (=6)$$

$$5! = 5 \times 4 \times 3 \times 2 \times 1 \qquad (=120)$$

We define

$$1! = 1$$

$$0! = 1$$

In factorial notation, the number of two-head sequences in five coin tosses is

$$\frac{5 \times 4 \times 3 \times 2 \times 1}{2 \times 1 \times 3 \times 2 \times 1} = \frac{5!}{2!3!} = 10$$

This result suggests the general procedure for finding the

Number of Combinations   The number of combinations of r objects taken from n objects may be determined from

$$\frac{n!}{r!(n-r)!}$$

In our illustration, there are $n = 5$ tosses and we are considering exactly $r = 2$ heads occurring in those tosses. Thus, the number of two-head sequence combinations is

$$\frac{5!}{2!(5-2)!} = \frac{5!}{2!3!} = 10$$

The Binomial Formula

When the trial outcomes result from a Bernoulli process, the number of successes is a random variable with a binomial distribution. The following expression, referred to as the **binomial formula**, can then be used to find the probability values.

$$\Pr[\text{successes} = r] = \frac{n!}{r!(n-r)!} P^r (1-P)^{n-r}$$

where n = number of trials achieved

P = trial success probability

$r = 0, 1, \ldots, n$

We place an exclamation point after the quantity to denote factorial notation. A 5 factorial is

$$5! = 5 \times 4 \times 3 \times 2 \times 1 = 120$$

In general

$$n! = n \times (n-1) \times (n-2) \times \cdots \times 2 \times 1$$

with the following defined values

$$0! = 1$$

$$1! = 1$$

The binomial formula can be used to determine the probability found earlier for obtaining successes $= 2$ heads in $n = 5$ tosses of a fair coin. In this case, $P = \Pr[\text{head}] = 1/2$ and $1 - P = \Pr[\text{tail}] = 1/2$, so that

$$\Pr[\text{successes} = 2] = \frac{5!}{2!(5-2)!} \left(\frac{1}{2}\right)^2 \left(1 - \frac{1}{2}\right)^{5-2} = \frac{5!}{2!3!} \left(\frac{1}{2}\right)^2 \left(\frac{1}{2}\right)^3$$

$$= 10\left(\frac{1}{2}\right)^5 = \frac{10}{32}$$

The factorial terms in this product provide the number of outcomes involving exactly 2 heads, which is equal to 10 and represents the number of combinations of 2 particular tosses that may result in heads out of a total of 5 tosses. The product containing 1/2 represents the probability for obtaining any one of the 10 two-head sequences represented by the end positions in the probability tree diagram in Figure 3-3. Each of these positions is reached by traversing a particular path of 2 head and $5 - 2 = 3$ tail branches. Each of these probabilities can be obtained by applying the multiplication law. Since a two-head result can occur in any one of 10 equally likely ways, the addition law of probability tells us to add 10 of the identical terms together or, more simply, to multiply by 10.

The entire binomial distribution corresponding to the number of heads resulting from $n = 5$ fair coin tosses appears in Table 3-7. There the probability values are found by applying the binomial formula to all possible r values.

We have already noted that different Bernoulli processes will have different probability values. But the number of successes resulting from each process is a random variable belonging to the binomial family. Note that the probabilities for all possible values of r depend on the value of P. Different sizes of n will result in a larger or smaller number of possible r values and will also affect each probability value.

TABLE 3-7

**Binomial Distribution for the Number of Heads
Obtained in Five Coin Tosses**

POSSIBLE NUMBER OF HEADS r	$\Pr[\text{heads} = r]$
0	$\dfrac{5!}{0!5!}\left(\dfrac{1}{2}\right)^{0}\left(\dfrac{1}{2}\right)^{5} = \dfrac{1}{32} = .03125$
1	$\dfrac{5!}{1!4!}\left(\dfrac{1}{2}\right)^{1}\left(\dfrac{1}{2}\right)^{4} = \dfrac{5}{32} = .15625$
2	$\dfrac{5!}{2!3!}\left(\dfrac{1}{2}\right)^{2}\left(\dfrac{1}{2}\right)^{3} = \dfrac{10}{32} = .31250$
3	$\dfrac{5!}{3!2!}\left(\dfrac{1}{2}\right)^{3}\left(\dfrac{1}{2}\right)^{2} = \dfrac{10}{32} = .31250$
4	$\dfrac{5!}{4!1!}\left(\dfrac{1}{2}\right)^{4}\left(\dfrac{1}{2}\right)^{1} = \dfrac{5}{32} = .15625$
5	$\dfrac{5!}{5!0!}\left(\dfrac{1}{2}\right)^{5}\left(\dfrac{1}{2}\right)^{0} = \dfrac{1}{32} = .03125$
	1.00000

Cumulative Probabilities

Using the binomial formula to calculate probabilities can be tedious and time consuming. Imagine the effort it would take to determine the probability for 17 successes in $n = 58$ trials when $P = .13$. We can simply find the probabilities we need from a table, but most tables provide only **cumulative probabilities**.

To illustrate this concept, consider the binomial probabilities in Table 3-8 provided for the number of aircraft departure delays at a major airport for $n = 10$ departing flights on different dates. We will assume that a Bernoulli process applies and that the probability that any particular flight will be delayed is $P = .4$. The cumulative probabilities, which appear in column (3), were obtained by adding all the preceding entries for the values in column (2). Thus,

$$\Pr[\text{successes} \le 0] = \Pr[\text{successes} = 0] = .0060$$

and

$$\Pr[\text{successes} \le 1] = \Pr[\text{successes} = 0] + \Pr[\text{successes} = 1]$$

$$= .0060 + .0404 = .0464$$

and

$$\Pr[\text{successes} \le 2] = \Pr[\text{successes} = 0] + \Pr[\text{successes} = 1] + \Pr[\text{successes} = 2]$$

$$= .0060 + .0404 + .1209 = .1673$$

TABLE 3-8
**Cumulative Probability Distribution for the Number of
Aircraft Departure Delays**

(1) NUMBER OF SUCCESSES (delays) r	(2) Pr[successes $= r$]	(3) CUMULATIVE PROBABILITIES Pr[successes $\leq r$]
0	.0060	.0060
1	.0404	.0464
2	.1209	.1673
3	.2150	.3823
4	.2508	.6331
5	.2007	.8338
6	.1114	.9452
7	.0425	.9877
8	.0106	.9983
9	.0016	.9999
10	.0001	1.0000
	1.0000	

The sign $\leq$ means "less than or equal to," so that [successes ≤ 2] means either exactly 0, 1, or 2 successes. Table 3-8 is constructed cumulatively from the individual probability values, so that the values obtained constitute the **cumulative probability distribution** for the number of successes.

The individual probabilities are graphed as spikes in Figure 3-4(a). (No spike appears for 10 successes, since the probability for this outcome is too low to show.) The cumulative probability distribution appears in Figure 3-4(b). The cumulative probability value corresponding to any particular number is obtained from the *highest point* on the "stairway" directly above. For instance, the cumulative probability for 5 or fewer delays is .8338 (not .6331, which is associated with the lower "step"). Notice that the size of each step in (b) is the same as the height of the respective spike of the individual probability in (a). The underlying probability distribution may be obtained from the cumulative probability distribution by finding these step sizes. For example, to find the probability that there will be exactly 5 departure delays, we find the difference

$$\Pr[\text{successes} = 5] = \Pr[\text{successes} \leq 5] - \Pr[\text{successes} \leq 4]$$
$$= .8338 - .6331 = .2007$$

Using Binomial Probability Tables

Appendix Table A provides the cumulative binomial probability values for various sizes of n (with separate tabulations for several P values). It is possible to use this table to compute probabilities for the number of successes in a variety of situations. To illustrate, suppose we wish to find probabilities regarding the number of $n = 100$ readers who will

FIGURE 3-4

(a) Binomial probability distribution and (b) cumulative probability distribution function for the number of successes from a Bernoulli process (n = 10 and P = .4).

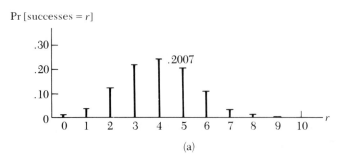

(a)

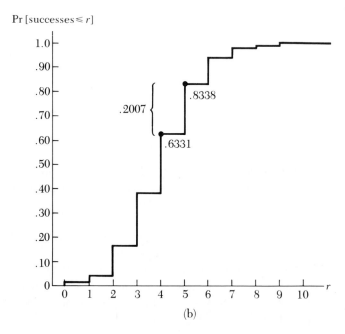

(b)

remember an aspirin advertisement that appears on the back cover of *Time*. We assume that $P = .30$ is the underlying proportion of all readers who will remember the ad. Use the portion of Appendix Table A that begins at $n = 100$.

1. **To obtain a result less than or equal to a particular value.**   The probability that 40 or fewer persons in the sample will remember the ad is a cumulative probability value that can be read directly from the table when $r = 40$ successes.

$$\Pr[\text{successes} \le 40] = .9875$$

2. **To obtain a result exactly equal to a single value.**   Recall that cumulative probabilities represent the sum of individual probability values and are portrayed graphically as a stairway (see Figure 3-4). A single-value probability may be obtained by determining the size of the step between two neighboring cumulative probabilities. For example, the probability that exactly 32 of the readers will remember the ad is

$$\text{Pr[successes} = 32] = \text{Pr[successes} \leq 32] - \text{Pr[successes} \leq 31]$$

$$= .7107 - .6331$$

$$= .0776$$

3. **To obtain a result strictly less than some value.**   The probability that fewer than 30 successes are achieved is the same as the probability that exactly 29 or less successes are obtained, or

$$\text{Pr[successes} < 30] = \text{Pr[successes} \leq 29] = .4623$$

4. **To obtain a result greater than or equal to some value.**   To find the probability that at least 20 of the readers will remember the ad, we look up the cumulative probability that 19 or less will remember and subtract this value from 1.

$$\text{Pr[successes} \geq 20] = 1 - \text{Pr[successes} \leq 19]$$

$$= 1 - .0089 = .9911$$

5. **To obtain a result that lies between two values.**   Suppose we want to find the probability that the number of successes will lie somewhere between 25 and 35, inclusively. Thus, we want to determine

$$\text{Pr}[25 \leq \text{successes} \leq 35]$$

In this case, we obtain the difference between two cumulative probabilities.

$$\text{Pr[successes} \leq 35] - \text{Pr[successes} \leq 24] = .8839 - .1136 = .7703$$

The Mean and Variance of the Binomial Distribution

The expected number of successes can be determined from probabilities obtained by using the binomial formula or a binomial distribution table for a particular n and P. Instead of multiplying these probabilities, by the respective number of successes and summing the products, however, a special feature of the binomial distribution enables us to arrive at the answer quickly. The following expression provides the expected number of successes.

$$\text{Expected successes} = nP$$

Thus, the expected number of aircraft delays when $n = 10$ and $P = .4$ is $10(.4) = 4$.

A similar expression provides the variance and the standard deviation.

$$\text{Variance} = nP(1 - P)$$

$$\text{Standard deviation} = \sqrt{nP(1 - P)}$$

In our aircraft delay example, the variance is $10(.4)(1 - .4) = 2.4$ and the standard deviation is $\sqrt{2.4} = 1.55$.

3-4 The Normal Distribution

The **normal distribution** plays a central role in sampling. It is used to describe frequency patterns for a great many phenomena, including the physical characteristics of both things and people, and is often used to express the probability distribution for times needed to complete work tasks, such as a bank teller's transaction or the installation of an automobile bumper.

The normal distribution applies to *continuous random variables*, such as times, weights, and diameters measured on a continuous scale. It is usually described in terms of a bell-shaped curve, as shown in Figure 3-5. There, x represents the possible values of the random variable, and the height of the curve represents the relative frequency at which the corresponding values occur. A particular normal distribution is specified by only two parameters: the *mean* μ (Greek lowercase *mu*) and the *standard deviation* σ (Greek lowercase *sigma*).* The location or center of the corresponding normal curve is

FIGURE 3-5
Frequency curve for the normal distribution.

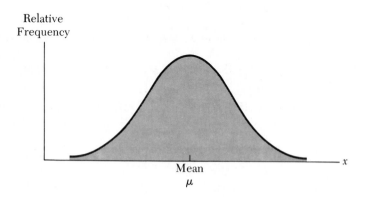

----

* Mathematically, this curve is called a *probability density function,* and its height may be determined from

$$f(x) = \frac{1}{\sqrt{2\pi\sigma^2}} e^{-[(x-\mu)^2/2\sigma^2]}$$

where $\pi = 3.1416$ and e is the base of natural logarithms (2.7183).

FIGURE 3-6
Three normal distributions graphed on a common axis.

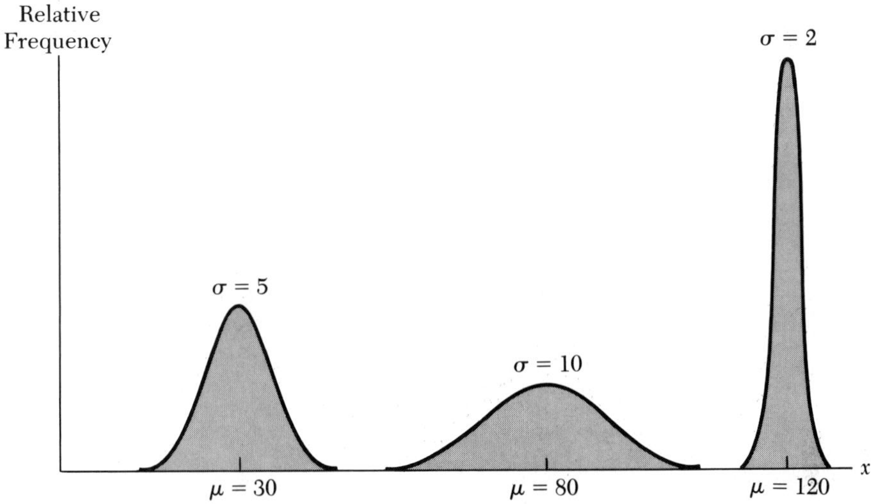

determined by the mean, and its shape is established by the standard deviation. Figure 3-6 shows the curves for three different normal distributions.

Because the height of the normal curve above any point expresses its relative frequency, or proportional occurrence, the total area beneath the normal curve is 1. We can find the probabilities for various values of a normally distributed random variable by determining the *areas* under the applicable portions of its normal curve. These areas correspond to the proportion of times that the particular range of values will occur when identical conditions are repeated.

The areas under the normal curve are tied to the distance separating the points of interest from the mean. For example, the Stanford-Binet IQ test was designed so that the scores of persons taking it have a mean of $\mu = 100$ and a standard deviation of $\sigma = 16$. A feature of every normal curve is that about 68% of the values will fall within ± 1 standard deviation from the mean. Thus, 68% of all people who take the Stanford-Binet test should achieve IQ scores within the range $\mu \pm 1\sigma$, or 100 ± 16, and their IQs should fall between 84 and 116. Likewise, about 95.5% of the test scores will fall within $\mu \pm 2\sigma$, or $100 \pm 2(16)$, reflecting IQs between 68 and 132. Approximately 99.7% of all scores should fall within $\mu \pm 3\sigma$, so that the IQs of practically all people lie between $100 - 3(16) = 52$ and $100 + 3(16) = 148$. Of course, higher or lower scores are possible; but, like geniuses, the extremes are rare. Theoretically, the tails of the normal curve never touch the axis, so that there is always some area, and hence probability, for any extreme set of values.

Finding Areas under the Normal Curve

Before we can obtain the probability values of normally distributed random variables, we must find the appropriate area lying under the normal curve by using Appendix Table B.

FIGURE 3-7

Determining the area under a normal curve.

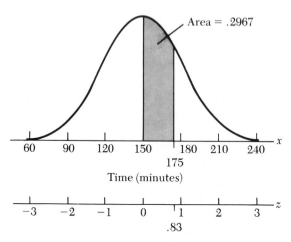

Number of Standard Deviations above Mean ($\sigma = 30$)

How would you find the desired areas for the time a particular typesetter takes to compose 500 lines of standard type? We will assume that the population of times is normally distributed, with a mean of $\mu = 150$ minutes and a standard deviation of $\sigma = 30$ minutes. The time it takes to set any given 500 lines, such as the next 500 to be composed, represents a randomly selected time from this population.

The probability that it takes between 150 and 175 minutes to set 500 lines is represented by the shaded area under the normal curve in Figure 3-7. We know that the area beneath the normal curve between the mean and a certain point depends only on the number of standard deviations separating the two points. We see that 175 minutes is equivalent to a distance above the mean of .83 standard deviation. This figure is determined by observing that 175 minutes minus the mean of 150 minutes is equal to 25 minutes. Since the standard deviation is 30 minutes, 25 minutes is only $25/30 = .83$ of the standard deviation.

Appendix Table B has been constructed for the **standard normal curve**, which provides the area between the mean and a point above the mean at some specified distance measured in standard deviations. Because this distance will vary, it is treated as a variable and denoted by z. Sometimes the value of z is referred to as a *normal deviate*. The distance z that separates a possible normal random variable value x from its mean can be determined from the following expression for the *normal deviate*.

$$z = \frac{x - \mu}{\sigma}$$

A negative value will be obtained for z when x is smaller than μ.

The first column of Appendix Table B lists values of z to the first decimal place. The second decimal place value is located at the head of one of the remaining 10 columns. The area under the curve between the mean and z standard deviations is found at the intersection of the correct row and column. For example, when $x = .83$, we find the area of .2967 by reading the entry in the .8 row and the .03 column. The area under the normal curve for a completion time between 150 and 175 minutes is .2967, which represents the probability that it will take this long to set the next 500 lines of print.

Although Table B provides areas only between the mean and some point above it, we can also use this table to find areas encountered in other common probability situations, such as those shown in Figure 3-8. Each of these areas is described here.

(a) Area between the Mean and Some Point Lying below the Mean   To find the probability that the completion time lies between 125 and 150 minutes, first we must calculate the normal deviate.

$$z = \frac{125 - 150}{30} = -.83$$

Here, z is negative because 125 is a point lying below the mean. Since the normal curve is symmetrical about the mean, this area must be the same as it would be for a positive value of z of the same magnitude (in this case .2967, as before). It is therefore unnecessary to tabulate areas for negative values of z. The area between the mean and a point lying below it will be equal to the area between the mean and a point the same distance above it.

(b) Area to the Left of a Value above the Mean   To find the probability that 500 lines can be set in 185 minutes or less, we must find the entire shaded area below 185. Here, we must consider the lower half of the normal curve separately. Since the entire area of the normal curve is 1, the area under the half to the left of 150 must be .5. The area of 150 and 185 is found from Table B, with $z = (185 - 150)/30 = 1.17$, to be .3790. The entire shaded portion is the sum of the two areas, or $.5000 + .3790 = .8790$.

(c) Area in Upper Tail   To find the probability that the number of minutes required exceeds 195, first we must find the area between the mean and 195. The normal deviate is $z = (195 - 150)/30 = 1.50$; the area from Table B is .4332. Since the area under the upper half of the normal curve is .5, we find the desired area above 195 by subtracting the unwanted portion, or $.5000 - .4332 = .0668$.

(d) Area in Lower Tail   To find the probability that it will take 90 minutes or less to set the type, we follow two steps similar to those taken in **(c)**. First, we find the area between 90 and 150. Using $z = (90 - 150)/30 = -2.00$, we obtain .4772 from Table B. Subtracting this value from .5 yields $.5000 - .4772 = .0228$.

(e) Area to the Right of a Value below the Mean   To find the probability that the completion time will be equal to or greater than 85 minutes, the area between 85 and the mean is added to the area to the right of the mean, which is .5. Here, we calculate $z = (85 - 150)/30 = -2.17$. Adding the area from Table B (.4850) to .5, gives us a combined area of $.4850 + .5000 = .9850$.

FIGURE 3-8

Various areas under the normal curve, where x = completion time in minutes and z = standard deviations.

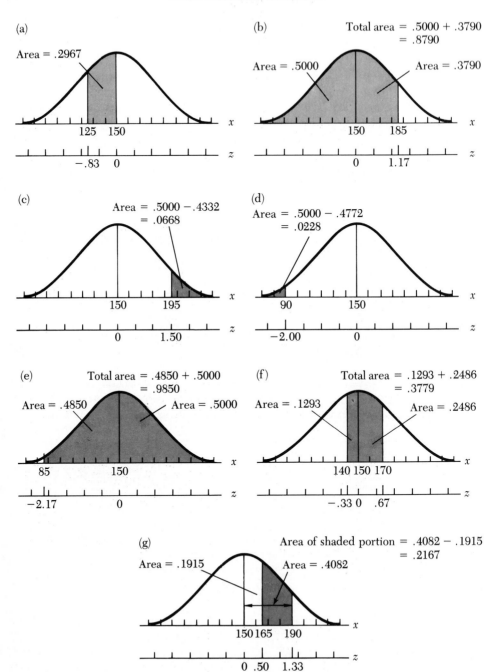

(f) Area under Portion Overlapping the Mean   To find the probability that it will take between 140 and 170 minutes to set the 500 lines, we simply add the portion of the shaded area that lies below the mean to the portion above it. The respective normal deviates are $z = (140 - 150)/30 = -.33$ and $z = (170 - 150)/30 = .67$. From Table B, the lower area is .1293 and the upper area is .2486, so that the combined area is .1293 + .2486 = .3779.

(g) Area between Two Values Lying above or below the Mean   To find the probability that the composition time is between 165 and 190 minutes, first we must determine the areas between the mean and each of these two values. The respective normal deviates are $z = (165 - 150)/30 = .50$ and $z = (190 - 150)/30 = 1.33$. From Table B, the area between the mean and 190 is .4082, and the area between the mean and 165 is .1915. Thus, the shaded area is found by subtracting the smaller area from the larger one, or .4082 - .1915 = .2167.

The normal curve represents values that lie on a continuous scale, such as height, weight, and time. The probability that a specific value, such as 129.40 minutes, will occur is 0 (the area under the normal curve covering a single point is 0). Thus, in finding a probability, it does not matter whether we use a "strict" inequality, such as the composition time is "less than" ($<$) 129.40 minutes, or an ordinary inequality, such as the time is "less than or equal to" ($\leq$) 129.40 minutes. Using $z = (129.40 - 150)/30 = -.69$, the area is the same in either case, or .5000 - .2549 = .2451.

The Standard Normal Random Variable

The area under any normal curve can be found by using the standard normal curve. This curve provides the probability distribution for the **standard normal random variable**. In our typesetting illustration, we essentially transformed the original random variable X, the time required to set 500 lines, into the standard normal random variable whenever we used Appendix Table B to find areas. This transformation can be accomplished physically by shifting the center of the curve and then stretching or contracting it. To shift the original curve so that its center lies above the point $x = 0$, we subtract μ from each point on the x axis. Then the repositioned curve may be stretched or squeezed until the scale on the horizontal axis matches the scale for the standard normal distribution. If all the values of the random variable are divided by its standard deviation, the transformed curve will have the same shape as the standard normal curve in Figure 3-9. The net effect will always be the same, no matter what the values of μ and σ are. The horizontal scale may be either expanded or contracted. Fortunately, we do not need to physically transform the original random variable X into the standard normal random variable, because we can manipulate the possible values of X algebraically.

As an example, suppose the Sunflower Vegetable Oil Company supplies its customers from barrels that contain about 100 gallons apiece. The current stock of barrels fluctuates in carrying capacity, having a mean of $\mu = 100$ gallons and a standard deviation of $\sigma = .6$ gallon. Letting X represent the capacity of any particular barrel selected at random from barrels ready for shipment to a certain customer, we can determine the

FIGURE 3-9

Illustration of the linear transformation of normal random variables into the standard normal distribution.

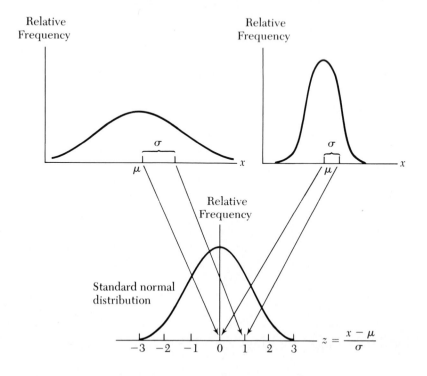

probability that $X \leq 99$ gallons. The normal deviate is

$$z = \frac{99 - 100}{.6} = -1.67$$

Thus, the applicable area under the normal curve lies 1.67 standard deviations below the mean. From Appendix Table B, the area under the standard normal curve between 0 and $z = 1.67$ is .4525. Because the normal curve is symmetrical, the area between $z = -1.67$ and 0 is also .4525. We wish to obtain the lower tail area, so we subtract .4525 from .5, yielding

$$Pr[X \leq 99] = .5000 - .4525$$

$$= .0475$$

This tells us that about 5% of all barrels shipped will contain 99 gallons or less. To avoid possible ill will, management has decided to replace Sunflower's present barrels with a more uniform variety having a mean of $\mu = 100$ gallons and a standard deviation of $\sigma = .25$ gallon. The probability that a chosen new barrel will have a capacity of 99 gallons or less is

$$z = \frac{99 - 100}{.25} = -4.00$$

$$\Pr[X \le 99] = .5000 - .49997 = .00003$$

Thus, on the average, a barrel containing 99 gallons or less will be shipped fewer than 3 times out of 100,000.

The Normal Distribution and Sampling

In several applications of quantitative methods, we use sample information to facilitate the final choice. Frequently, the value of the *sample mean* is the pivotal factor in making such a decision. It is therefore important to be able to compute probabilities for the possible values of the sample mean for a given situation. The normal distribution plays a critical role in establishing these probabilities.

We use a special symbol $\bar{X}$ to represent the **sample mean**, which is calculated from

$$\bar{X} = \frac{X_1 + X_2 + \cdots + X_n}{n}$$

This expression indicates that $\bar{X}$ is the arithmetic average of the n sample observations taken from a population or universe. We presume that the sample is selected randomly. Because the actual value of $\bar{X}$ cannot be known until after the sample has been selected, the sample mean must be treated like any other random variable until that time. The expected value of $\bar{X}$ is the mean μ of the population from which the sample is taken. The standard deviation σ of that population partly determines the variability in the possible levels of $\bar{X}$.

The Central Limit Theorem of Statistics   Probabilities for the value of $\bar{X}$ may be closely approximated from the normal curve when the sample size is large. This normal curve has a mean of μ and a standard deviation of $\sigma_{\bar{x}} = \sigma/\sqrt{n}$, reflecting the fact that $\bar{X}$ should exhibit less variability and cluster more tightly about its expected value μ than any single random observation. Thus, the normal curve can be a valuable analytical tool in a tremendous variety of decision-making situations involving samples.

To illustrate, suppose that you are asked to estimate the mean income of persons in various professions. You are to determine this by taking a random sample of persons from each group and finding the mean income $\bar{X}$.

Consider surgeons and teachers. You are interested in the population mean income μ for each group. These are unknowns, but the following "ballpark" guesses apply for the respective standard deviations.

Teachers	Surgeons
$\sigma = \$2,000$	$\sigma = \$25,000$

Income data ordinarily provide population frequency curves that are positively skewed, as shown in Figure 3-10. Even though the particular shapes are not known,

FIGURE 3-10

How the size of σ affects $\sigma_{\bar{x}}$ and thus reliability of $\bar{X}$. (Scales are approximate.)

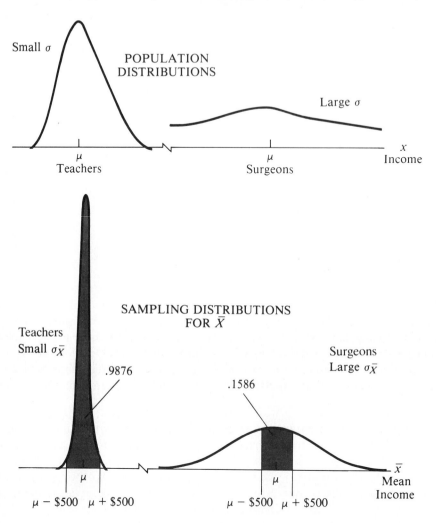

the central limit theorem allows you to use normal distributions in finding probabilities for $\bar{X}$.

Suppose that you take samples of size $n = 100$ from each population. The following standard deviations apply for $\bar{X}$.

$$\text{Teachers} \qquad\qquad \text{Surgeons}$$

$$\sigma_{\bar{x}} = \frac{\$2,000}{\sqrt{100}} \qquad\qquad \sigma_{\bar{x}} = \frac{\$25,000}{\sqrt{100}}$$

$$= \$200 \qquad\qquad\quad = \$2,500$$

You now decide that you want to find the probability that $\bar{X}$ lies within $\pm\$500$ of the population mean of each group. Find the normal deviates, substituting $500 for $(\bar{x} - \mu)$ in the equation $z = (\bar{x} - \mu)/\sigma_{\bar{x}}$. Then read the areas from Appendix Table B. Since you wish to obtain a value that is both above and below the means ($\pm\$500$), you must multiply each tabled area by 2.

<table>
<tr><td align="center">Teachers</td><td align="center">Surgeons</td></tr>
<tr><td>$z = \dfrac{\$500}{\$200} = 2.50$</td><td>$z = \dfrac{\$500}{\$2,500} = .20$</td></tr>
<tr><td>$\Pr[-\$500 \le \bar{X} - \mu \le +\$500]$</td><td>$\Pr[-\$500 \le \bar{X} - \mu \le +\$500]$</td></tr>
<tr><td>$= 2(.4938) = .9876$</td><td>$= 2(.0793) = .1586$</td></tr>
</table>

As reflected by the shaded areas under the bottom curves in Figure 3-10, there is a higher probability that $\bar{X}$ will be close to its target with teachers than with surgeons. This is because the smaller standard deviation for that more homogeneous income group provides a smaller standard error for $\bar{X}$.

3-5 Poisson and Exponential Distributions

Two other probability distributions play very important roles in management-science applications. One of these—the **Poisson distribution**—provides probabilities for the number of events that may occur over time. A related distribution—the **exponential distribution**—provides probabilities for the times between events. Both of these distributions are used extensively in queuing (waiting-line) analysis, where the events of interest are customer *arrivals* to the service facility being evaluated. Both distributions apply to situations in which events occur randomly over time.

As an illustration, consider cars arriving at a toll booth. Figure 3-11 illustrates this concept. Each dot represents a car and is positioned so that its horizontal distance from the origin (at 9:00 A.M.) indicates when it arrives at the booth. Such a graph could be constructed from an aerial photograph taken at 9:00 A.M. of the two miles of highway leading to the booth. Assuming that all cars are traveling at the speed limit, we could then directly translate each car's distance from the booth into its arrival time. Notice that the dots in Figure 3-11 are scattered with no apparent pattern, as if placed there at random.

FIGURE 3-11
Random arrival times of cars at a toll booth.

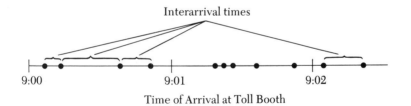

Time of Arrival at Toll Booth

The Poisson Process

Even though the cars arrive randomly over time, much detailed information can be gleaned from one key characteristic of the arrival stream (of which our graph is only a small sample). Seemingly without pattern, such an arrival stream is an example of a *Poisson process*, named after the eighteenth-century mathematician and physicist Siméon Poisson. It is the randomness of this pattern that provides the basis for the information it yields. What distinguishes one arrival stream from another—and the only thing that can make any two Poisson processes differ—is the **mean arrival rate**. This parameter, denoted by λ (lowercase Greek *lambda*), tells us the mean number of arrivals occurring per minute (or some other unit of time, such as per second or per hour). A busy toll booth may experience an arrival rate of $\lambda = 100$ cars per minute, whereas an out-of-the way booth may register a rate of $\lambda = 1/2$ car per minute.

A Poisson process must meet the following conditions.

1. A Poisson process has *no memory*. The number of events occurring in one interval of time is *independent* of what happened in previous time periods.

2. The process rate λ *must remain constant* for the entire time period being considered.

3. It is extremely *rare for more than one event to occur* during a short interval of time. The shorter the duration of the interval, the rarer the occurrence of two or more events becomes. And the probability that exactly one event will occur in such an interval is approximately λ times its duration.

The Poisson process provides two very important probability distributions: the *exponential distribution*, which provides probabilities for the times between arrivals and, because time is the random variable, is *continuous* (like the normal distribution); and the *Poisson distribution*, which provides probabilities for the number of arrivals in any specific interval of time. The Poisson distribution is *discrete* (like the binomial distribution), since the number of cars arriving in any particular unit of time must be a whole number. As we will see, *both the exponential and the Poisson distributions express the same process in different ways.*

The Exponential Distribution

The gaps between the dots in Figure 3-11 represent the interarrival times, or the times between successive arrivals of cars. The exponential distribution is concerned with the *size* of the gap, measured in units of time, that separates successive cars. Although the dots are scattered randomly over time, the relative frequency of interarrival times of various sizes is predictable. Suppose that the cars arriving at the toll booth are observed for several minutes and that the time of each car's arrival is noted. These data would provide a histogram similar to the one in Figure 3-12(a), which approximates the shape of the underlying frequency curve in Figure 3-12(b), the height of which may be determined for any interarrival time t from the expression

$$f(t) = \lambda e^{-\lambda t}$$

FIGURE 3-12
The exponential distribution for the interarrival times of cars at a toll booth.

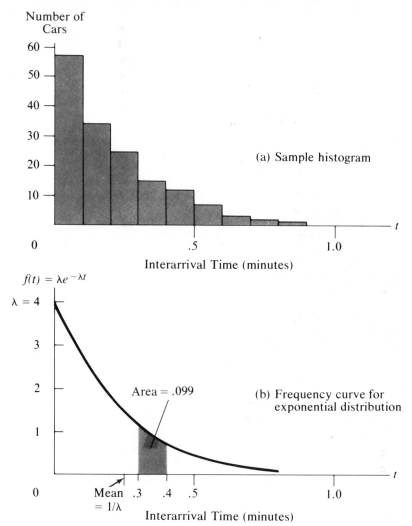

(a) Sample histogram

(b) Frequency curve for exponential distribution

$f(t) = \lambda e^{-\lambda t}$

Area = .099

Mean = $1/\lambda$

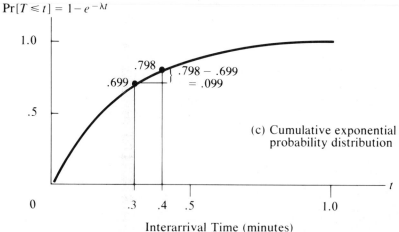

$\Pr[T \le t] = 1 - e^{-\lambda t}$

.798

.699

.798 − .699 = .099

(c) Cumulative exponential probability distribution

Interarrival Time (minutes)

This is the probability density function for the exponential distribution and is based on the constant e, which is equal to 2.7183 and serves as the base for natural logarithms. The particular distribution applicable to a specific situation depends only on the level of λ. In our toll booth illustration, the mean arrival rate is $\lambda = 4$ cars per minute. Notice that the frequency curve intersects the vertical axis at a height of $\lambda = 4$ in Figure 3-12(b). The mean and the standard deviation of the exponential distribution are identical and may be expressed in terms of λ as

$$\text{Mean} = 1/\lambda$$

$$\text{Standard deviation} = 1/\lambda$$

Also notice that the mean time between arrivals is the reciprocal of the mean rate of arrivals. Thus, if $\lambda = 4$ *cars per minute*, then the mean time between arrivals is $1/\lambda = 1/4 = .25$ *minutes per car*. Another feature of the exponential distribution is that *shorter durations are more likely than longer ones*, so that the curve in Figure 3-12(b) decreases in height and the slope becomes less pronounced as t becomes larger. The tail of the exponential curve, like the tails of the normal curve, never touches the horizontal axis, indicating that there is no limit to how large the interarrival time t can conceivably be.

As is true of the normal curve, probabilities for the exponential random variable can be found by determining the area under the frequency curve. The cumulative probability that the time T between two successive arrivals is t or less may be obtained from

$$\Pr[T \le t] = 1 - e^{-\lambda t}$$

Figure 3-12(c) shows the applicable cumulative probability graph when $\lambda = 4$. Appendix Table D may be used to find values for $e^{-\lambda t}$.

For example, using $\lambda = 4$ cars per minute, we find that the probability that the interarrival time between any two cars is $t = .4$ minute or less is

$$\Pr[T \le .4] = 1 - e^{-4(.4)} = 1 - e^{-1.6}$$

$$= 1 - .202$$

$$= .798$$

The probability that the time is $t = .3$ minute or less is

$$\Pr[T \le .3] = 1 - e^{-4(.3)} = 1 - e^{-1.2}$$

$$= 1 - .301$$

$$= .699$$

The difference in the above two values is

$$\Pr[.3 \le T \le .4] = .798 - .699$$

$$= .099$$

which provides the area under the exponential frequency curve in Figure 3-12(b) between the interarrival times of .3 and .4 minute.

The Poisson Distribution

The Poisson distribution expresses the probabilities for the number of arrivals in any given time period, such as the 1 minute between 9:08 and 9:09, the 5 minutes between 9:09 and 9:14, or the 1 hour between 10 A.M. and 11 A.M. Letting X represent the actual number of arrivals in a period of duration t, we can compute the probability that X is equal to one of the possible levels x from

$$\Pr[X = x] = \frac{e^{-\lambda t}(\lambda t)^x}{x!}$$

where

$$x = 0, 1, 2, \ldots$$

Continuing with our illustration, consider any 1-minute interval, so that $t = 1$ minute. Again, given $\lambda = 4$ cars per minute, we find that $\lambda t = 4$ cars. Appendix Table D provides $e^{-4} = .018316$. The probability that exactly 2 cars will arrive is therefore

$$\Pr[X = 2] = \frac{e^{-4}(4)^2}{2!}$$

$$= \frac{.018316(4)^2}{2}$$

$$= .1465$$

The probability values for other numbers of cars are calculated in Table 3-9. Notice that the probabilities for arrivals between 0 and 14 sum to only .9999, reflecting the fact that the number of arrivals might be 15, 16, or some larger number, but that these unlisted quantities would have miniscule probabilities that round to zero at four decimal places. Indeed, the Poisson distribution assigns some small probability to any integer value, no matter how large.

The Poisson distribution is completely specified by the process rate λ and the period of duration t. Its mean and variance are identical and are expressed in terms of the parameters

$$\text{Mean} = \lambda t$$

$$\text{Variance} = \lambda t$$

(Here, the mean is equal to the variance, rather than the standard deviation.) In this example, $\lambda = 4$ cars are expected to arrive in any given minute, and the variance in the number of arrivals is also 4. And because results for any two time periods are independent, the number of arrivals in any given minute has no effect on the probabilities for arrivals

TABLE 3-9

Poisson Probability Distribution for the Number of Arrivals at a Toll Booth in 1 Minute ($\lambda = 4$, $t = 1$)

NUMBER OF ARRIVALS x	PROBABILITY $Pr[X = x]$
0	.0183
1	.0733
2	.1465
3	.1953
4	.1953
5	.1563
6	.1042
7	.0596
8	.0297
9	.0133
10	.0053
11	.0019
12	.0006
13	.0002
14	.0001
	.9999

in the next minute. Thus, if 14 or more cars arrive between 9:05 and 9:06, (a rare event when $\lambda = 4$), the probability for the reoccurrence of that event between 9:06 and 9:07 remains unchanged.

Using Poisson Probability Tables

Like binomial probabilities, computing Poisson probabilities by hand can be an onerous chore. Cumulative values of the Poisson probabilities are computed in Appendix Table E for levels of λt ranging from 1 to 20. A table of individual probability terms is not provided because, like the binomial probabilities, the Poisson probabilities can be easily obtained from the respective cumulative values.

The table provides values of $Pr[X \leq x]$. For example, to find the cumulative probability values of the number of cars arriving at a toll booth during an interval of $t = 10$ minutes when the arrival rate is $\lambda = 2$ per minute, we consult Appendix Table E where $\lambda t = 2(10) = 20$.

The probability that the number of arriving cars is ≤ 15 is

$$Pr[X \leq 15] = .1565$$

whereas the probability that ≤ 20 cars will arrive during the 10-minute interval is

$$\Pr[X \leq 20] = .5591$$

As with the cumulative binomial table, it is possible to obtain the individual term, the $>$, $<$, $\geq$, and interval Poisson probability values from Appendix Table E. For example, the probability that exactly 15 cars will arrive in 10 minutes is

$$\Pr[X = 15] = \Pr[X \leq 15] - \Pr[X \leq 14] = .1565 - .1049 = .0516$$

Similarly, we can obtain the probability that the number of cars arriving lies between two values. Thus, the probability that between 16 and 20 cars will arrive in 10 minutes is

$$\Pr[16 \leq X \leq 20] = \Pr[X \leq 20] - \Pr[X \leq 15] = .5591 - .1565 = .4026$$

And the probability that >20 cars will arrive is

$$\Pr[X > 20] = 1 - \Pr[X \leq 20] = 1 - .5591 = .4409$$

Other Instances of Poisson Processes

The Poisson process is used in queuing analysis mainly to represent arrivals. As we will see, this process can also be used to represent completions of customer service when the server is busy. A multitude of applications other than queuing exist. The Poisson distribution can be used to represent inventory demands, for example. The exponential distribution can also apply to times between equipment failures and be used in reliability analyses of alternative engineering designs. A Poisson process may even be appropriate in some rather bizarre instances; historically, it fits well to the number of U.S. Supreme Court vacancies in any year, deaths of Prussian recruits kicked by horses, and the very rare Lake Zurich freezes.

Although our present application of the Poisson process treats events that occur randomly over *time*, the respective probability distributions may apply when time is not a factor. The Poisson process may appropriately characterize events that occur in *space* as well. If we consider the locations of objects spread randomly over a space (such as misspelled names in a telephone directory) to be events, then encountering objects while the space (in this case, the pages of the directory) is searched may also be viewed as a Poisson process. This particular application has proved fruitful in quality control and in such esoteric areas as developing radar search techniques, establishing tactics for ships transiting minefields, and hunting for submarines. Here, λ represents the mean number of events *per unit distance* (such as an inch), *area* (a square mile), or *space* (a cubic centimeter). More generally, λ may be the mean number of a particular kind of event per observation made of the phenomena in question. Thus, λ could be 3 errors per page or 5 bad debts per 1,000 installment contracts. The "durations" would be analogous—the space searched, the number of pages scanned, the number of contracts written, and so on.

FIGURE 3-13
Probability menu for *QuickQuant*.

```
                    - QuickQuant -
  CHOICES FOR COMPUTING PROBABILITIES OR EXPECTED VALUES


    1. Binomial Distribution.

    2. Poisson Distribution.

    3. Hypergeometric Distribution.

    4. Normal Distribution.

    5. Exponential Distribution.

    6. Compute Expected Value, Variance, and Standard Deviation.
          --for Supplied Probability Distribution.

    7. FINISHED--Return to Main Menu.
```

FIGURE 3-14
QuickQuant report of the binomial probabilities for a quality control investigation.

```
================================================================================
                           QuickQuant Report
                 BINOMIAL PROBABILITY DISTRIBUTION
--------------------------------------------------------------------------------
PROBLEM: Quality Control                                Date: 11-10-1989
                                                               Larry


    Pr[ R <= 0 ] = 0.048668       Pr[ R < 0 ] = 0.000000

    Pr[ 0 <= R <= 7 ] = 0.988742

    Pr[ 0 <= R < 7 ] = 0.967631

    Pr[ 0 < R <= 7 ] = 0.940074

    Pr[ 0 < R < 7 ] = 0.918963

    Pr[ R >= 7 ] = 0.032369        Pr[ R > 7 ] = 0.011258

    Number of trials n = 200   Trial success probability P = .015
```

Number of Successes r	Probability Pr[R=r]	Cumulative Probability Pr[R<=r]
0	0.048668	0.048668
1	0.148229	0.196897
2	0.224600	0.421497
3	0.225740	0.647237
4	0.169305	0.816542
5	0.101068	0.917610
6	0.050021	0.967631
7	0.021111	0.988742

3-6 Computer-Assisted Probability Evaluations

Computation of probabilities for binomial and Poisson probabilities can be quite challenging by hand. Although the tabled values will simplify this task considerably, no table can have all the possible parameter levels. For example, suppose that a shipment of items is assumed to have proportion $P = .037$ defective and that a sample of 13 items will be inspected. Appendix Table A will not be helpful in finding the probability that the sample contains between 2 and 5 defectives. Or, suppose that supermarket checkout counter arrivals occur at a mean rate of 3.24 per minute; Appendix Table E cannot provide the probability that exactly 3 customers arrive between 12:05 and 12:06.

QuickQuant, the software package available to the users of this book, may considerably ease the task of finding probabilities. This computer program is available in both IBM PC and MacIntosh versions. The probability segment (accessible from the main menu or by booting the probability file) provides the main menu shown in Figure 3-13. *QuickQuant* will compute probabilities for five distributions and will also provide expected value calculations for a user-supplied probability distribution.

Figure 3-14 is an example of *QuickQuant* output of the binomial probabilities for a

FIGURE 3-15

***QuickQuant* report of the hypergeometric probabilities for a quality control investigation.**

```
=================================================================================
                              QuickQuant Report
                    HYPERGEOMETRIC PROBABILITY DISTRIBUTION
---------------------------------------------------------------------------------
PROBLEM: Quality Control                                      Date: 11-10-1989
                                                                        Larry


          Pr[ R <= 0 ] = 0.034263        Pr[ R < 0 ] = 0.000000

          Pr[ 0 <= R <= 7 ] = 0.996046

          Pr[ 0 <= R < 7 ] = 0.982712

          Pr[ 0 < R <= 7 ] = 0.961783

          Pr[ 0 < R < 7 ] = 0.948449

          Pr[ R >= 7 ] = 0.017288        Pr[ R > 7 ] = 0.003954

          Parameters: n = 200   P = .015   N =  1000

                    Number of                    Cumulative
                    Successes    Probability     Probability
                        r          Pr[R=r]         Pr[R<=r]
                    -----------------------------------------
                        0         0.034263         0.034263
                        1         0.130774         0.165037
                        2         0.231472         0.396509
                        3         0.252035         0.648544
                        4         0.188786         0.837330
                        5         0.103044         0.940374
                        6         0.042338         0.982712
                        7         0.013334         0.996046

---------------------------------------------------------------------------------
```

FIGURE 3-16

QuickQuant report of the Poisson probabilities for the number of car arrivals at a toll booth.

```
================================================================================
                            QuickQuant Report
                    POISSON PROBABILITY DISTRIBUTION
--------------------------------------------------------------------------------
PROBLEM: Toll Crossing                                       Date: 11-10-1989
                                                                       Larry


        Pr[ X <= 0 ] = 0.011109        Pr[ X < 0 ] = 0.000000

        Pr[ 0 <= X <= 8 ] = 0.959743

        Pr[ 0 <= X < 8 ] = 0.913414

        Pr[ 0 < X <= 8 ] = 0.948634

        Pr[ 0 < X < 8 ] = 0.902305

        Pr[ X >= 8 ] = 0.086586         Pr[ X > 8 ] = 0.040257

        Mean rate lambda = 1.5  Duration t = 3

                Number of                   Cumulative
                 Events        Probability  Probability
                   x            Pr[X=x]      Pr[X<=x]
                ----------------------------------------
                   0            0.011109     0.011109
                   1            0.049990     0.061099
                   2            0.112479     0.173578
                   3            0.168718     0.342296
                   4            0.189808     0.532104
                   5            0.170827     0.702931
                   6            0.128120     0.831051
                   7            0.082363     0.913414
                   8            0.046329     0.959743

--------------------------------------------------------------------------------
```


FIGURE 3-17

QuickQuant report of the expected value results using supplied probability distribution for personal computer cost.

```
================================================================================
                            QuickQuant Report
              EXPECTED VALUE, VARIANCE AND STANDARD DEVIATION
--------------------------------------------------------------------------------
PROBLEM: Personal Computer Cost                              Date: 11-10-1989
                                                                Quant Jacques


                    Value         Probability
                    ---------------------------
                   2200.0000       0.090000
                   2400.0000       0.060000
                   2700.0000       0.300000
                   2900.0000       0.200000
                   3200.0000       0.210000
                   3400.0000       0.140000


                Expected value = 2880
                Variance =   124600
                Standard deviation = 352.9872

--------------------------------------------------------------------------------
```

quality control investigation using a sample of size $n = 200$ when the proportion defective (trial success probability) is $P = .015$. (These parameters are not tabled in the back of the book.) The user may request probabilities for a limited range of possible outcomes; various probabilities are given here over the range from 0 to 7 defectives. Hypergeometric probabilities using these same parameters (with population size $N = 1,000$) are shown in Figure 3-15. Figure 3-16 shows the *QuickQuant* output of the Poisson probabilities applicable at a toll booth with $t = 3$ minutes when $\lambda = 1.5$ cars arrive on the average during each minute (a combination of parameters not tabled). The number of events are specified to be from 0 to 7. Figure 3-17 shows the *QuickQuant* report of the expected value results for the personal computer cost probability distribution given in Section 3-1.

CASE

AlphaComp

AlphaComp is a specialized microcomputer manufacturer. Mark Wun, the head of procurement and quality assurance, needs to refine company policy regarding the disposal of shipments. To begin, Mark investigates two microcircuit chips: the customized-logic Z-1020 and the A-19, for harddrive controllers. The Z-1020 chips are shipped from a sole supplier in lots of 1,000 chips each. The A-19 chips are sent from a different source in lots of 50.

Mark contemplates two actions for all the microcircuit chip shipments: (1) accept the shipment and install all the chips untested or (2) reject the shipment, testing all the chips, eliminating the defective ones before installation. Accepting a shipment can be very costly, since defective chips will be identified in later system testing and will have to be removed from assembled computers. The late replacement cost is estimated to be $25 for defective Z-1020's and $100 for defective A-19's. Individual testing costs for a Z-1020 chip and an A-19 chip are $2.00 and $4.00, respectively. But, all of the chips in a rejected lot must be tested, so that the decision to reject a shipment is not necessarily cheaper. The suppliers will replace, for free, all the defective chips, whether or not they have first been installed.

Mark's current acceptance sampling plan for Z-1020 shipments is based on a sample of $n = 5$ chips randomly selected *without replacement*. If the number of sample defectives is 0, the Z-1020 shipment is accepted; otherwise, the shipment is rejected. A similar plan is used for shipments of A-19 chips, but a smaller sample of size $n = 3$ is selected. As for the Z-1020 chips, an A-19 shipment is accepted only when 0 defectives are found.

Questions

1. Two levels are possible for the proportion of defective chips found in a Z-1020 shipment: (1) $P = .05$ and (2) $P = .10$.

(a) For each assumed level of P above, use the binomial distribution to determine the approximate probabilities for the number of defective chips found in a sample of Z-1020's.

(b) For each level of P, determine the probability that a Z-1020 shipment will be accepted.

(c) For each level of P, determine the probability that a Z-1020 shipment will be rejected.

2. Two levels are possible for the proportion of defective chips found in an A-19 shipment: (1) $P = .10$ and (2) $P = .20$.

(a) For each assumed level of P above, determine the probability distribution for the number of defective chips found in a sample of A-19's. (*Hint:* The binomial distribution cannot be used. To start, construct for each case a probability tree diagram similar to Figure 3-1.)

(b) For each level of P, determine the probability that an A-19 shipment will be accepted.

(c) For each level of P, determine the probability that an A-19 shipment will be rejected.

3. Find the breakeven level for the proportion of defectives P found in a shipment of (a) Z-1020's and (b) A-19's. This will be the level for P at which the net cost for accepting a shipment is equal to that for rejecting. (For simplicity, ignore the cost of the sample.)

4. There is a 50% chance that the Z-1020 supplier will send shipments containing either exactly 5% or exactly 10% defectives. Mark has no way of knowing how many defectives a particular shipment contains. Calculate the expected cost for (a) accepting and (b) rejecting every shipment without the benefit of any sample evidence.

5. For a Z-1020 shipment, Mark wants to determine the expected cost of, first, conducting the sampling study and then using the sample results to determine a final action.

(a) Refer to the probability results from Question 1 and assume that the two levels for P are equally likely. Find the missing values in the following table.

PROPORTION DEFECTIVE	SAMPLE RESULT	JOINT PROBABILITY
$\Pr[P = .05] = \underline{\quad}$	$\Pr[\text{Accept } (R = 0) \mid P = .05] = \underline{\quad}$	$\Pr[P = .05 \text{ and Accept}] = \underline{\quad}$
$\Pr[P = .05] = \underline{\quad}$	$\Pr[\text{Reject } (R > 0) \mid P = .05] = \underline{\quad}$	$\Pr[P = .05 \text{ and Reject}] = \underline{\quad}$
$\Pr[P = .10] = \underline{\quad}$	$\Pr[\text{Accept } (R = 0) \mid P = .10] = \underline{\quad}$	$\Pr[P = .10 \text{ and Accept}] = \underline{\quad}$
$\Pr[P = .10] = \underline{\quad}$	$\Pr[\text{Reject } (R > 0) \mid P = .10] = \underline{\quad}$	$\Pr[P = .10 \text{ and Reject}] = \underline{\quad}$

(b) Determine the expected cost of, first, conducting a sampling studying and then using the results to determine whether to accept or reject a Z-1020 shipment. Find the missing values in the following table. Include the cost of the sample.

PROPORTION DEFECTIVE	SAMPLE RESULT	TOTAL COST	JOINT PROBABILITY	COST × PROBABILITY
$P = .05$	Accept $(R = 0)$	——	——	——
$P = .05$	Reject $(R > 0)$	——	——	——
$P = .10$	Accept $(R = 0)$	——	——	——
$P = .10$	Reject $(R > 0)$	——	——	——
			Expected sampling cost =	——

(c) Does sampling provide a lower expected cost than either of the two actions in Question 4?

6. Suppose that Mark raises the acceptance number from 0 to 1 sample defective for shipments of Z-1020 chips. Repeat Questions 5(a) and 5(b). Determine, separately, the joint probabilities and costs for $R = 0$ and $R = 1$ sample defectives. In the cases where sample defectives are found, the total cost must reflect the amount saved as a result of not having to remove the defective chips found before installation.

7. Suppose that Mark increases the sample size of Z-1020's to $n = 10$. Repeat Question 1(a).

8. Suppose that when $n = 10$ Mark would modify further his sampling scheme by raising the acceptance number to 2 sample defectives. Using the analogous ground rules given in Question 6, repeat Questions 5(a) and 5(b).

9. Refer to your answers to Questions 4–8. What might you conclude Mark should do before finalizing his choices of acceptance sampling plans?

CASE

New Guernsey Toll Authority

The operations manager for the New Guernsey Toll Authority uses probability to make a variety of assessments. She is presently concerned with expanding the toll plaza of the Silver Slate Bridge.

Provision must be made for the nuisance of vehicles whose drivers left their money at home. These cars must be diverted to the central office while all cars are held at their respective toll stations until the way is clear, causing nerve-wracking delays for commuters. Past records show that on the average 1 driver out of 500 has no money to pay the toll. A Bernoulli process approximates the toll-paying capabilities of successive vehicles.

Traffic intensity varies with time of day and day of week. The following situations are to be used in the manager's evaluations.

	(1) WEEKDAY A.M. RUSH	(2) WEEKDAY P.M. RUSH	(3) SATURDAY AFTERNOON	(4) SUNDAY MORNING
Cars per minute	100	120	50	20

In each of the above cases, a Poisson process may be assumed.

One unusual feature uncovered in past studies is that the mean time to collect a toll and the corresponding standard deviation both decrease as the traffic becomes heavier. The following data apply.

	(1) WEEKDAY A.M. RUSH	(2) WEEKDAY P.M. RUSH	(3) SATURDAY AFTERNOON	(4) SUNDAY MORNING
Mean (seconds)	12	10	15	16
Standard deviation	3	2	4	4

A normal distribution is assumed to apply for individual collection times.

Questions

1. Determine, for each of the major time periods, the probability that in any given six seconds (one-tenth of a minute) the following number of cars will arrrive.
   (a) 0   (b) 1   (c) 2   (d) 3   (e) 4   (f) 5 or more
2. Determine, for each of the major time periods, the probability that the time between the next two successive arriving cars will be
   (a) ≤3 seconds (.05 minute).
   (b) between 1.2 and 2.4 seconds (.02 and .04 minute).
   (c) >1.8 seconds (.03 minute).
3. Determine, for each of the major time periods, the probability that the time to collect the toll for a particular car is
   (a) less than 10 seconds.   (b) between 7 and 15 seconds.
   (c) longer than 12 seconds.

PROBLEMS

3-1   A silver dollar is tossed three times. Use the binomial formula to determine the probability distribution for the number of heads. Then, calculate the expected number of heads.

3-2   In roulette there are 38 slots, of which 18 are red, 18 are black, and 2 are green. A player may bet on red or on black, in which case he will win if the ball drops into a slot of matching color.

(Every bettor loses if the ball drops into a green slot.) Determine the probability distribution for the winnings of a player who places a $1 bet on the red field. Then, calculate the expected winnings and state the meaning of your answer in words.

3-3   In canasta, points are assigned to cards in the following manner: red three = 100; joker = 50; ace or deuce = 20; 8 through king = 10; 4 through 7 and black three = 5 points. A canasta deck is composed of two decks of ordinary playing cards, each containing 52 cards and 2 jokers. Determine the probability distribution for the point value of the first card dealt from a shuffled canasta deck.

3-4   A pair of six-sided dice, one red and one green, are tossed. The sides of each die cube exhibit the values 1 through 6.
(a) List the elementary events in the sample space.
(b) List the possible sums of the dots showing on the upturned faces of the two cubes.
(c) For each answer to (b), indicate the elementary events that correspond to each possible sum value. Then, determine the probability for each sum.

3-5   Shirley Smart has assigned the following probabilities for her final grades.

	A	B	C
Statistics	.2	.8	0
Finance	0	.4	.6
Accounting	.5	.5	0
Marketing	0	.2	.8

(a) List all possible elementary events for Shirley's grades. Assuming independence between courses, apply the multiplication law to determine the probability for each elementary event.
(b) Assume that the following grade points are assigned.

$$A = 4 \qquad B = 3 \qquad C = 2$$

Determine Shirley's total grade points for each elementary event identified in (a). Then, for each possibility, compute her grade point average (GPA). Finally, construct a table summarizing her probability distribution for GPA.

3-6   Of the precision rods in a lot of 50, 10% are known to be out-of-tolerance. Three rods are randomly selected, one at a time, and measured. Each rod in turn is returned to the lot and given the same chance of being selected as the unmeasured items. Construct a probability tree diagram for this situation. Then, find the following probabilities describing the final results of the sampling procedure.
(a) No out-of-tolerance items are selected.
(b) All the items selected are out-of-tolerance.
(c) Exactly one rod in the sample is out-of-tolerance.

3-7   Repeat Problem 3-6 if the successively measured items are not replaced.

3-8   The Centralia plant of DanDee Assemblers experiences power failures with a probability of .10 during any given month. Assume that power events in successive months are independent. Find the probability that there will be (a) no power failures during a 3-month span of time;

(b) exactly 1 month involving a power failure during the next 4 months; (c) at least 1 power failure during the next 5 months.

3-9   Ty Kune wishes to buy a stock to hold for one year in anticipation of capital gain. The choice has been narrowed down to High-Volatility Engineering and Stability Power. Both stocks currently sell for $100 per share and yield $5 dividends. The following probability distributions for next year's price have been judgmentally assessed for each stock.

HIGH-VOLATILITY ENGINEERING		STABILITY POWER	
Price	Probability	Price	Probability
$ 25	.05	$ 95	.10
50	.07	100	.25
75	.10	105	.50
100	.05	110	.15
125	.10		1.00
150	.15		
175	.12		
200	.10		
225	.12		
250	.14		
	1.00		

(a) Determine the expected price of a share of each stock.
(b) Should the investor select the stock with the highest expected value? Explain your answer.

3-10   The point spread for tossing two fair dice is the difference between the number of dots showing on the upturned faces. Determine the probability distribution for this random variable.

3-11   The following probability distribution table has been obtained for the number of persons arriving at Original Joe's during any specified minute between 8 and 9 P.M.

PERSONS	PROBABILITY
0	.4
1	.3
2	.2
3	.1
	1.0

Calculate the expected value and the variance for the number of persons arriving between 8:30 and 8:31 P.M.

3-12   Can each of the following situations be classified as a Bernoulli process? If not, state why.
(a) Childbirths in a hospital, the relevant events being the sex of each newborn child.

(b) The outcomes of successive rolls of a die, considering only the events "odd" and "even."

(c) A crooked gambler has rigged a roulette wheel so that whenever the player loses, a mechanism is released that gives the player better odds; when a player wins, the chance of winning on the next spin is somewhat smaller than before. Consider the outcomes of successive spins.

(d) The measuring mechanism on a paint mixer that determines how much dye to squirt into the mixture occasionally violates the required tolerances. The mechanism is highly reliable when it is new, but with use it continually wears, becoming less accurate. Consider the outcomes (within or not within tolerance) of successive mixings.

(e) A machine produces items that are sometimes too heavy or too wide to be used. The events of interest express the quality of each successive item in terms of both weight and width.

3-13 A nervous numismatist tosses an evenly balanced double-eagle $20 gold piece seven times.
(a) Use the binomial formula to determine the probabilities for obtaining (1) exactly 2 heads, (2) exactly 4 heads, (3) no tails, and (4) exactly 3 tails
(b) What do you notice about your answers to (2) and (4)? Why is this so?

3-14 Suppose that the proportion of product users favoring NuScents is $P = .70$. A random sample of $n = 5$ users is selected. Use the binomial formula to determine the probabilities for the following number of users favoring NuScents.
(a) exactly 5   (b) none   (c) exactly 3

3-15 Peppermint Patty randomly selects n wafers from a production process that yields 5% defectives. What is the expected number of defectives when (a) $n = 5$, (b) $n = 10$, and (c) $n = 100$?

3-16 Refer to probability values in Table 3-7 (page 64). Construct the cumulative probability distribution table for the number of heads.

3-17 A fair coin is tossed 20 times in succession. Using Appendix Table A, determine the probabilities for the following number of heads obtained.
(a) less than or equal to 8   (d) greater than or equal to 12
(b) equal to 10   (e) greater than 13
(c) less than 15   (f) between 8 and 14, inclusively

3-18 Bugoff Chemical Company's policy is that five sample vials be drawn from the final stage of a chemical process at random times over a four-hour period. If one or more vials (20% or more) contain impurities, all the settling tanks are cleaned. Find the probability that the tanks will have to be cleaned when the process is so clean that the following probabilities for a dirty vial apply.
(a) $P = .01$ (b) $P = .05$ (c) $P = .20$ (d) $P = .50$
(*Hint:* Use the fact that Pr[at least 1 dirty vial] $= 1 - $ Pr[no dirty vials].)

3-19 A process produces defective parts at the rate of .05. If a random sample of five items is selected, what is the probability that at least 80% of the sample will be defective?

3-20 You are handed a penny with Lincoln's beard filed off. There is now a 60% chance of a head on each toss. If the coin is tossed 20 times, find the probabilities for obtaining the following number of heads.
(a) less than or equal to 8   (d) greater than or equal to 12
(b) equal to 9   (e) greater than 13
(c) less than 15   (f) between 8 and 14, inclusively

3-21   Procrastinator Pete marks an examination consisting of 50-true-or-false questions by tossing a coin. Assuming that one-half of the correct answers should be marked true, find the probability that Pete will pass the examination by marking at least 60% of the answers correctly.

3-22   Errors in the measurement of the height of a weather satellite above a ground station are normally distributed with a mean of $\mu = 0$ and a standard deviation of $\sigma = 1$ mile. These errors will be negative if the measured altitude is too low and positive if the altitude is too high. Find the probability that for the next orbit the error will fall in the following ranges.
(a) between 0 and $+1.55$ miles   (e) -1.25 miles or less
(b) between -2.45 and 0 miles   (f) greater than -1.25 miles
(c) $+.75$ miles or less   (g) between $+.10$ and $+.60$ miles
(d) greater than $+.75$ miles   (h) between $+1$ and $+2$ miles

3-23   The lifetimes of Spinex floppy disks are normally distributed, with a mean of $\mu = 1,000$ hours and a standard deviation of $\sigma = 100$ hours. Find the probability for each of the following lifetime outcomes for one drive unit.
(a) between 1,000 and 1,150 hours   (e) 870 hours or less
(b) between 950 and 1,000 hours   (f) longer than 780 hours
(c) 930 hours or less   (g) between 700 and 1,200 hours
(d) more than 1,250 hours   (h) between 750 and 850 hours

3-24   Assume that Elegant Clutter's accounts receivable have a mean time to payment of $\mu = 45$ days and that the standard deviation is $\sigma = 10$ days. Find the probability that the mean of a sample of 100 payment times will lie between 43 and 47 days.

3-25   Creative Robotics recommends that machine shops shut down an automatic lathe for corrective maintenance whenever a sample of the parts it produces has an average diameter greater than 2.01 inches or smaller than 1.99 inches. The lathe is designed to produce parts with a mean diameter of 2.00 inches, and the sample averages have a standard deviation of .005 inches. Assume that the normal distribution applies.
(a) What is the probability that the lathe is shut down when operating as designed, with $\mu = 2.00$ inches?
(b) If the lathe begins to produce parts that on the average are too wide, with $\mu = 2.02$ inches, what is the probability that the lathe will continue to operate?
(c) If an adjustment error causes the lathe to produce parts that on the average are too narrow, with $\mu = 1.99$ inches, what is the probability that the lathe will be stopped?

3-26   Marketing Metrics Associates takes a random sample of size $n = 100$ job applicants from a population of screening test scores having a mean of $\mu = 70$ and a standard deviation of $\sigma = 15$.
(a) Find the probability that the sample mean will lie in the following ranges.
    (1) below 74   (2) between 68 and 72   (3) above 73
(b) The test is revised whenever the sample mean score falls outside the 67 through 73 range. Find the probability that the test will *not* be revised when the following apply.
    (1) $\mu = 69$ (2) $\mu = 70$ (3) $\mu = 71.5$

3-27   The controller mechanism filling jars of Skater Aid is adjusted whenever a mean of 25 sample jars is more than $\frac{1}{2}$ ounce under or over the intended mean of 32 ounces. The filling process has a standard deviation of 1 ounce per jar.
(a) What is the probability that the controller will be adjusted when it is operating as intended?

(b) What is the probability that the controller will be adjusted when it overfills each jar by an average of 1 ounce?

3-28 On Tuesday mornings, customers arrive at the Central Valley National Bank at a rate of $\lambda = 1$ per minute. What is the probability that the time between the next two successive arrivals will be (a) shorter than 1 minute; (b) longer than 5 minutes; (c) between 2 and 5 minutes?

3-29 During the late Friday rush at the Central Bank in Problem 3-28, an average of $\lambda = 5$ customers arrive per minute. What is the probability that no customers will arrive during a specified 1-minute interval?

3-30 Soap Opera Updates receives calls between 9 and 10 A.M. during weekdays at the rate of $\lambda = 3$ per minute. Find the probabilities that the number of calls received in any interval of
(a) $t = 2$ minutes will be equal to 3.　　(c) $t = 1.5$ minutes will be equal to 4.
(b) $t = 1$ minute will be equal to zero.　　(d) $t = 1$ minute will be at least 1.

3-31 In each of the following situations, use Appendix Table E to find the probabilities that the stated number of events occur. Assume a Poisson process with $\lambda = 8$ per hour when the following durations are considered.
(a) $t = 2$ hours; 10 or fewer events　　(c) $t = 1$ hour; exactly 3 events
(b) $t = 1.5$ hours; 6 or more events　　(d) $t = .125$ hour; between 1 and 5 events

3-32 Sally Strokes commits typing errors at a rate of .01 per word. Assuming that a Poisson process applies, use Appendix Table E to find the probabilities for each of the following numbers of errors made in a 500-word letter.
(a) exactly 5　　(c) more than 10
(b) zero　　　　(d) between 3 and 7

C H A P T E R

Assessing Probabilities through Judgment

Although probability concepts have been extensively used in earlier chapters, little discussion has been devoted to **subjective probabilities**. Subjective probabilities are applicable to nonrepeatable circumstances, such as introducing a new product or drilling a wildcat oil well, and must be arrived at through *judgment*. This is in contrast to the long-run frequencies used to establish **objective probabilities**, which are valid only when elements of repeatability are present. Because so many business decisions involve one-shot situations that never recur exactly, there is a strong need for subjective probabilities when analyzing decision making under uncertainty. In this chapter, we will examine the procedures for translating judgment into the subjective probability values that are required when implementing Bayesian analysis to help solve decision problems in the real world.

4-1 Probabilities Obtained from History

Historical experience can be a convenient starting point for assigning probabilities. To calculate the historical frequency of an event, we need to know only two things: the number of times the event has occurred in the past and the number of opportunities when it could have occurred. This is how fire insurance underwriters obtain probabilities for determining the expected claim sizes that are used to establish policy charges. With tens of thousands of buildings involved, *the event frequencies themselves define the probabilities*, because in the traditional sense, probability fundamentally expresses long-run frequency of occurrence.

There are inherent difficulties in using historical frequencies as probabilities. One is the limited extent of history—the available data may only provide a crude frequency estimate. Unless the number of similar past circumstances is large, statistical estimates of event frequencies can be unreliable. Past history may be suitable for setting fire insurance rates. But past frequencies cannot be wholly adequate—indeed, are unavailable—to determine the probability distributions for a great many variables encountered in business, such as the demand for a new product.

Another serious difficulty is that conditions change over time. The recent experience of automobile casualty insurance firms serves as an example of how changing conditions can make historical frequencies unsuitable for obtaining probabilities. Car insurers, who have consistently complained about losing money on collision and comprehensive coverage, have found that past experience has proved to be a poor predictor of future levels of damage claims. This is due not to sampling error, which is virtually nonexistent because the data obtained constitute a census, but rather to changing circumstances. Cars are becoming less and less sturdy, so that minor impacts that would hardly have dented an older car can seriously damage a new one. Repair costs have also been rising in a pronounced inflationary spiral. More cars are sharing roads that are not increasing at the same rate, and driving habits are changing accordingly, affecting the accident rate. Automobile thefts have also been increasing as the result of new social pressures.

Using historical frequencies to estimate the probabilities for future automobile insurance claims may be compared to tossing a die, some side of which is shaved before each toss. We do not know which side has been shaved or by how much. Under these circumstances, we can never obtain a reasonable probability distribution for the respective sides from historical frequencies alone.

4-2 Subjective Probabilities

To apply basic decision-making models based on expected values, we must employ probabilities. Past history can sometimes provide probability values that fit into the mold of long-run frequencies. But the applicability of such data is limited to events with a rich history, such as insurance claims. And even when they are available, these data can be misleading, owing to the forces of change.

In many business decisions, the only recourse is to use subjective probabilities, which are not tied to a long-run frequency of occurrence, because so many decisions involve one-shot situations that may be characterized by essentially nonrepeatable uncertainties. Good *judgment* may be the only method available to transform such uncertainties into a set of probabilities for the various events involved.

We have seen that decision making under uncertainty is analogous to gambling. However, unlike card games, lotteries, dice, or roulette, most real life gambles can be analyzed only with the help of subjective probabilities, which reflect the decision-maker's judgment and experience. How do we obtain a subjective probability?

Betting Odds

Subjective probabilities can be considered betting odds; that is, they can be treated just like the probabilities that the decision maker would desire in a lottery situation of his or her own design in which the payoffs are identical in every respect to the possible payoffs from the actual decision being evaluated. For example, suppose that a contractor assigns a subjective probability of .5 to the event of winning a contract that will increase profits by $50,000 and that losing the contract will cost $10,000. This contractor ought to be indifferent between preparing a bid for the contract and gambling on a coin toss where a head provides a $50,000 win and a tail results in a $10,000 loss. The subjective probability for winning the contract can therefore be transformed directly into an "objective" .5 probability of obtaining a head from a coin toss. Assuming indifference between the real life gamble and a hypothetical coin toss, we can then substitute the latter into the decision analysis.

One practical benefit of substituting a hypothetical gamble for an actual uncertainty is that subjective probabilities can be used in conjunction with the traditional long-run frequencies of occurrence. In effect, apples and oranges may be mixed, permitting wider acceptance of decision-theory analysis. More significantly, a hypothetical gamble or lottery can provide a convenient means of obtaining the subjective probability value itself. Consider the following example.

Substituting a Hypothetical Lottery for the Real Gamble

A project engineer must choose between two technologies in designing a prototype sonar system. She may use Doppler shift or acoustic ranging. If the Doppler shift is used, time becomes a crucial factor. To analyze this decision, the engineer must determine the probability for completing the project on time. If she is late, the project will be canceled and she will be out of a job. But if she is early or on time, her contract will be extended for two more years. The event fork of concern appears in Figure 4-1(a).

Suppose that the engineer considers the hypothetical lottery shown in Figure 4-1(b), in which one marble is to be randomly selected from a box of 100. Some marbles are labeled *E* (for early); the rest are marked *L* (for late). In this hypothetical gamble, selecting an *E* marble will result in an extended contract, but drawing an *L* marble will result in a canceled contract. Our engineer can determine the mix of *L* and *E* marbles. She is asked what mixture will make her *indifferent* between letting her future be decided by trying the Doppler shift design or by selecting a marble from the box.

Suppose that the engineer determines that 70 *E* marbles and 30 *L* marbles would make her indifferent. This means that the probability for selecting an *E* marble is .70. This value can be considered the engineer's **judgmental assessment** that the project will be early or on time if the Doppler shift is used. Thus, our decision maker can let .70 represent the probability for being early or on time in analyzing her decision and place .70 on the early event branch of the fork in Figure 4-1(a).

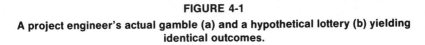

FIGURE 4-1

A project engineer's actual gamble (a) and a hypothetical lottery (b) yielding identical outcomes.

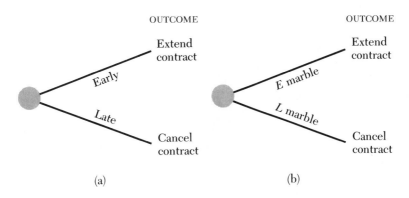

Arriving at subjective probabilities by substituting the real life gamble for an equally preferred lottery is a useful procedure when the number of possible events is small. But this method can be quite cumbersome when the situation involves more than a handful of events. In business applications, we are often faced with variables, such as product demand, which can be measured on many possible levels. It is best to use an entire *probability distribution* to represent such uncertain quantities.

Subjective Probability Distributions

We have seen that probability distributions can be divided into two categories. *Discrete probability distributions* apply to variables, such as the demand for cars, that must be a whole number. *Continuous probability distributions* represent variables, such as time, that can be expressed on a continuous scale and measured to any degree of precision desired. When the number of possibilities is great, discrete variables are often treated as if they are approximately continuous. For this reason, we focus on finding continuous probability distributions.

Next we will consider using judgment to determine the normal distribution, which constitutes perhaps the most common distribution family encountered in business decision making with continuous variables. We will then discuss the more general problem of establishing a probability distribution for *any* uncertain quantity.

4-3 Determining a Normal Curve Judgmentally

The normal distribution plays an important role in decision making. This is largely due to the fact that the probabilities for sample means can usually be characterized by a normal curve. But the normal curve can be applied in many situations other than sampling. The frequency patterns of physical measurements often approximate the normal curve. This feature makes it especially important in production applications, where natural fluctuations in size, density, concentration, and other factors cause individual units to vary according to the normal distribution. Test scores used to determine personal aptitude or achievement are also often characterized by the normal curve. Questions of facility design as it relates to waiting lines in manufacturing, retailing, or data-processing situations must take into account the time needed to produce units, service customers, or complete jobs; these service times are often normally distributed.

Since the normal distribution is prevalent in such a broad spectrum of decision-making situations, we will give it special emphasis in this chapter. We have seen that any normal distribution is uniquely defined in terms of two parameters—the mean μ and the standard deviation σ. Except in the rare circumstances when these parameters are known precisely, it is impossible to measure their values directly without expensive sampling procedures. It may be more convenient to exercise judgment in determining μ and σ. With these two quantities, we can specify the entire normal distribution. (In fact, it may be optimal not to take samples at all—a question that we will consider in Chapter 24. Often sampling itself is impossible because no population currently exists from which observations can be taken.)

Finding the Mean

The mean of the subjective normal curve for any quantity X believed to have a normal distribution can be established by selecting the **midpoint** of all possible values. *The subjective mean μ is that point judged to have a 50–50 chance for any value X to lie at or above it versus below it.* This value is actually the **median level**, since it is just as likely that X will fall below or above the identified point. Because the normal curve is symmetrical, this central value must also equal the mean.

For example, suppose that an engineer is evaluating a new teleprocessing terminal design to determine if a prototype should be fabricated. Based on the physical characteristics of the unit compared to existing equipment of similar scope, the engineer concludes that messages could be printed at a rate of between 30 and 70 lines per second, depending on the type of message. Because the unit has never been built, the true rate X for a typical message is uncertain. The engineer assumes that this quantity is normally distributed, because similar data in related applications have been found to fit well to the normal curve.

To determine the mean printing rate, the engineer is asked to establish a level such that it is equally likely for X to fall above or below it. This decision can be phrased in terms of a coin toss: "Suppose that you had to find a middle value such that it would be difficult for you to choose whether the actual printing rate X lies above or below it. If your professional reputation depended on being correct and you had to make a prediction for X, you would be willing to select one side or the other of that value by tossing a coin. Where would your midpoint lie?" After some thought the engineer might reply, "I think it is a coin-tossing proposition that the printing rate experienced in actual testing may fall above or below 50 lines per second." This establishes the desired midpoint and therefore the mean of the subjective probability distribution, so that $\mu = 50$ lines per second.

Relating the judgmental evaluation to coin tossing makes the problem easy for a person who is not used to dealing with probability. The 50–50 gamble is the easiest to envision. We may extend this concept to finding the standard deviation as well. *The subjective standard deviation σ can be found by establishing a middle range of values centered at μ such that X is judged to have an equal chance of lying inside or outside that interval.* To see how this works, let's review some properties of the normal curve.

Finding the Standard Deviation

In Chapter 3, we saw that the area under the normal curve between any two points is established by the distances separating each point from the mean, which are expressed in units of standard deviation. This standardized distance can be represented by a value of the normal deviate z, where for any particular point x, the corresponding normal deviate can be computed from

$$z = \frac{x - \mu}{\sigma}$$

We seek two possible values of X that are equally distant from μ such that the area between them is .50. This means that the area between μ and the upper limit must be one-half this value, or .25. From the normal curve areas in Appendix Table B, the normal deviate value of $z = .67$ provides the closest area, .2486. We use $z = .67$ to find σ.

Figure 4-2 illustrates the underlying principles involved. The area between μ and $\mu + .67\sigma$ is about .25, so that the area in the interval $\mu \pm .67\sigma$ is about .50. If we know the distance separating the upper limit $\mu + .67\sigma$ and the mean μ, or the **half-width** of the interval, we determine the corresponding value of σ by setting .67σ equal to that distance.

FIGURE 4-2
Finding the standard deviation of a subjective normal distribution.

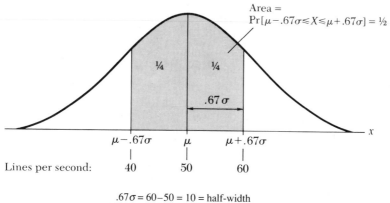

$$.67\sigma = \text{Upper limit} - \mu$$

Dividing both sides by .67, we obtain the expression for the **judgmental standard deviation**.

$$\sigma = \frac{\text{Upper limit} - \mu}{.67} = \frac{\text{Half-width}}{.67}$$

Thus, to find σ, we need to establish only the width of the middle range (covered by the shaded area in Figure 4-2). This quantity is sometimes called the **interquartile range**. This evaluation is tantamount to establishing the half-width such that there is a 50–50 chance that any particular value of X will fall within μ plus or minus this quantity.

The engineer in our example is now asked to establish the half-width of the central interval. This problem might be formulated: "Select the range of values centered at $\mu = 50$ lines per second so that the actual printing rate will be just as likely to fall inside or outside of it. To find the interval, determine an amount such that μ plus or minus that quantity establishes the range." The engineer might respond: "I would guess that ± 10 lines per second is suitable for this purpose. This means that it is a coin-tossing proposition that the actual printing rate will fall somewhere between $50 - 10 = 40$ and $50 + 10 = 60$ lines per second." This establishes the half-width of 10 lines per second for the middle range, and we calculate the standard deviation to be

$$\sigma = \frac{10}{.67} = 14.9 \text{ lines per second}$$

The subjective probability distribution for the actual printing time of the proposed terminal is now specified. Combining this with economic data, the decision maker can then apply decision-theory concepts to evaluate various alternatives regarding the manufacturing or marketing of the proposed unit.

4-4 The Judgmental Probability Distribution: The Interview Method

The procedure we have just examined is a limited one. Although the normal distribution is very common, it is the exception. We will now consider how judgment can be exercised to determine probability distributions. Our procedure applies to any variable with a large number of possible values, such as product demand.

A natural and fairly simple procedure for obtaining a probability distribution judgmentally is to use cumulative probabilities. By posing a series of 50–50 gambles, it is quite simple to make a judgmental determination of the cumulative probability distribution for a random variable. Each response provides a point that can be plotted on a graph; a smoothed curve can then be drawn through the points. This curve completely specifies the underlying probability distribution. The following illustration shows how this procedure may be carried out.

The president of a food manufacturing concern wishes to obtain the probability distribution for the demand for a new snack product. This will be used to help the president decide whether or not to market the product. A statistical analyst asks the president a series of questions to obtain answers that will be used to formulate later questions. The interview follows.*

Q. What do you think the largest and smallest possible levels of demand are?

A. Certainly demand will exceed 500,000 units. But I would set an upper limit of 3,000,000 units. I don't think that under the most favorable circumstances we could sell more than this amount.

Q. Okay, we have determined the range of possible demand. Now I want you to tell me what level of demand divides the possibilities into two equally likely ranges. For example, do you think demand will be just as likely to fall above 2,000,000 as below?

A. No. I'd rather pick 1,500,000 units as the 50–50 point.

Q. Very good. Now let's consider the demand levels below 1,500,000. If demand were to fall somewhere between 500,000 and 1,500,000 units, would you bet that it lies above or below 1,000,000?

A. Above. I would say that a demand of 1,250,000 units would be a realistic dividing point.

Q. We will use that amount as our 50–50 point. Let's do the same thing for the upper range of demand.

A. If I were to pick a number, I would choose 2,000,000 units. I feel that demand is just as likely to fall into the 1.5 to 2 million range as into the 2 to 3 million range.

Q. Excellent. We're making good progress. To get a finer fix on the points obtained so far, I now want you to tell me whether you think demand is just as likely to fall between 1.25 and 2 million units as it is to fall outside that range.

A. No. I think it is more likely to fall inside. I suppose this means I am being inconsistent.

Q. Yes, it does. Let's remedy this. Do you think that we ought to raise the 1,250,000 dividing point or lower the 2 million unit figure?

A. Lower the 2 million figure to 1.9 million.

Q. Let's check to see if this disturbs our other answers. Do you think that 1,500,000 splits demand over the range from 1,250,000 to 1,900,000 into two equally likely regions?

A. Yes, I am satisfied that it does.

Q. Just a few more questions. Suppose demand is above 1,900,000. What level splits this demand range into two equally likely regions?

A. I'd say 2,200,000.

Q. Good. Now if demand is between 2,200,000 and 3,000,000, where would you split?

A. I would guess that 2,450,000 units would be the 50–50 point.

Q. How about when demand is below 1,250,000?

A. Try 1,100,000 units.

Q. And when demand is between 500,000 and 1,100,000 units?

A. I think demand is far more likely to be close to the higher figure. I would bet on 950,000 units.

---

* This procedure was inspired by Howard Raiffa, *Decision Analysis: Introductory Lectures on Choices Under Uncertainty* (Reading, Mass.: Addison-Wesley, 1968).

TABLE 4-1

**Judgmental Assessment of
Fractiles for Snack
Food Demand**

FRACTILE	AMOUNT
0	500,000
.0625	950,000
.125	1,100,000
.25	1,250,000
.50	1,500,000
.75	1,900,000
.875	2,200,000
.9375	2,450,000
1.000	3,000,000

Table 4-1 shows the information obtained from this interview. The initial decision to divide demand at 1,500,000 units makes this level the 50% point or median. Since .5 has been judged the probability that demand will be below 1,500,000, we will refer to this as the .5 *fractile*. This means that the probability is .5 that the actual demand will be 1,500,000 units *or less*. Our decision maker has chosen to divide the range from 500,000 to 1,500,000 units at a demand level of 1,250,000. Believing that the chance of demand falling into this range is .5, the president has judged the chance that demand will be at or below 1,250,000 units to be $.5(.5) = .25$; thus, we refer to 1,250,000 units as the .25 fractile. This establishes a .25 probability that demand will be less than or equal to 1,250,000. The median of the range from 1,500,000 to 3,000,000 units is 1,900,000, which becomes the .75 fractile, since the probability is $.5 + .5(.5) = .75$ that demand will fall somewhere below 1,900,000 units. The analyst has proceeded to find the medians of the regions by working outward from previously determined 50% points. Thus, the .125 fractile of 1,100,000 units is the median demand for possible levels below the .25 fractile (1,250,000 units), which had to be determined first. The median of demands above 1,900,000 units is the .875 fractile of 2,200,000 units. Similarly, the median of the demands below 1,100,000 is the .0625 fractile of 950,000 units, whereas the median demand level above 2,200,000 is the .9375 fractile of 2,450,000.

The fractiles and the corresponding demands are plotted as points in Figure 4-3. The vertical axis represents the cumulative probability for demand. A curve has been smoothed through these points, which serves as an approximation of the cumulative probability distribution for the first-year demand for the snack product. The curve has an S shape; its slope increases initially and then decreases over higher levels of demand. The slope changes most rapidly for large and small demands, so that more points in these regions provide greater accuracy. This is why we work outward from the median in assessing the demand fractiles.

This example illustrates how we can obtain a very detailed measurement of judgment by posing a few 50–50 gambles. As a rule of thumb, the seven fractile values ranging from .0625 to .9375 in Table 4-1 are adequate for this purpose. Little can be gained from obtaining more fractiles, since further gambles might result in a lumpy curve and would

FIGURE 4-3
Cumulative probability distribution for a new snack product.

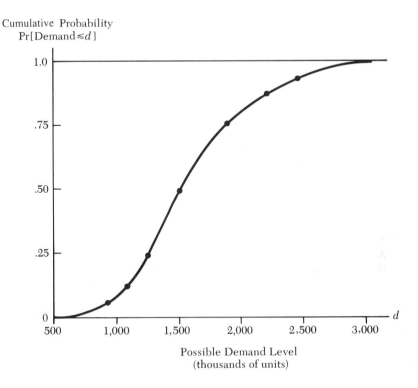

Cumulative Probability
Pr[Demand≤d]

Possible Demand Level
(thousands of units)

probably not alter the basic shape anyway. Besides, there is no reason to "gild the lily" or to try the decision maker's patience. A curve obtained by following this procedure provides about as accurate a judgmental assessment as is humanly possible.

Common Shapes of Subjective Probability Curves

Ordinarily, subjective probability distributions obtained by judgmental assessment provide S-shaped graphs that are elongated at either the top or the bottom. Such graphs represent underlying probability distributions that are skewed to the left or to the right, as the corresponding frequency curves in Figure 4-4(a) and (b) show. Although **skewed distributions** are most common for business and economic variables, a symmetrical distribution, shown in Figure 4-4(c), is also possible.

Lumpy cumulative probability graphs with two stacked S-shaped curves, like the one in Figure 4-4(d), are to be avoided. The corresponding frequency curve has the two-humped shape that typifies a **bimodal distribution**. Such distributions reflect some underlying nonhomogeneous influence that operates differently for the lower-valued possibilities than it does for the higher-valued possibilities. The bimodal distribution is

FIGURE 4-4
Possible shapes of subjective probability distributions.

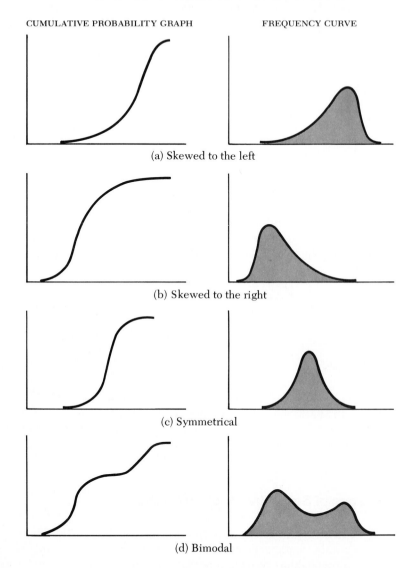

CUMULATIVE PROBABILITY GRAPH   FREQUENCY CURVE

(a) Skewed to the left

(b) Skewed to the right

(c) Symmetrical

(d) Bimodal

epitomized by combining the heights of men and women. In statistics, it is more meaningful to portray male and female heights in terms of two separate curves.

Similarly, if such a result occurs in assessing subjective probability distributions,
some identifiable factor in the decision maker's mind might explain the bimodality. A
good example would be determining the demand for automobiles in the next model year.
If there is a possibility of an oil embargo, as in 1973–74, or an energy crisis, as in 1978–80,
the assessment should be broken down into greater detail: (1) Find a subjective probability
for a gasoline shortage; (2) determine the subjective probability distribution for auto-

mobile demand assuming a shortage occurs; and (3) establish a second separate distribution for demand given that no shortage occurs.

If there is no identifiable explanation, lumpiness in the cumulative probability graph can be due to inconsistencies in expressing judgment, which may be resolved by moving one or more points to the left or right and posing again the succeeding 50–50 gambles. One easy consistency check is to see if there is actually a 50–50 chance of the factor under consideration falling inside or outside the interquartile range, from the .25 fractile (1,250,000 units in our example) to the .75 fractile (1,900,000 units). If the decision maker judges the inside to be more likely, then the middle range should be narrowed, either by raising the .25 fractile (perhaps to 1,300,000 units) or by reducing the .75 fractile (perhaps to 1,800,000 units). Conversely, if the outside is more likely, then one of the fractiles should be changed in the opposite direction.

Approximating the Subjective Probability Distribution

It is difficult to employ the cumulative S curve directly in decision analysis, where expected values must be determined. Expected values are ordinarily calculated from a table that lists the possible variable values and their probabilities. To obtain such a table,

FIGURE 4-5
Approximating the cumulative probability distribution using 10 intervals.

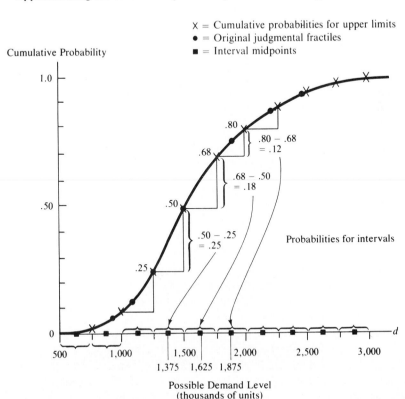

Possible Demand Level
(thousands of units)

it is necessary to approximate the cumulative probability curve by the method shown in Figure 4-5.

Each possible variable value is represented by an interval. A fairly accurate approximation is obtained with 10 intervals of equal width. The probabilities for each interval are shown as the step sizes at the upper limit for the respective interval. The probabilities for individual intervals are determined by the difference between successive cumulative probability values. All values in an interval are represented by a typical value. For this purpose, the midpoint is used.

To see how this is done, suppose that the decision maker now wishes to establish subjective probabilities for intervals of demand from 500,000 to 3,000,000 units in increments of 250,000. Table 4-2 shows how these demand probabilities have been obtained by reading values (marked by X's) from the cumulative probability curve in Figure 4-5. The resulting probability distribution can be used in further evaluations. From it, the approximate expected demand is computed to be 1,587,500 units.

The interval probabilities can be used to plot the histogram for demand shown in Figure 4-6. The height of .25 for the bar covering the interval from 1,250,000 to 1,500,000

FIGURE 4-6

The frequency curve and the individual interval probabilities for snack food demand.

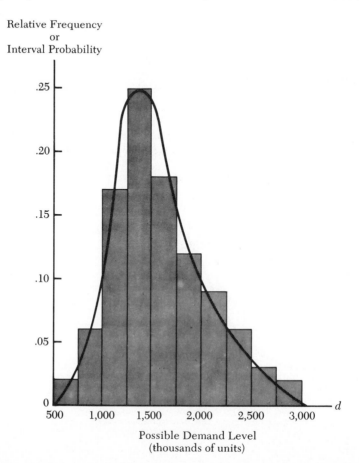

TABLE 4-2
Subjective Demand Probabilities and Approximating the Expected Demand

(1) DEMAND INTERVAL (thousands)	(2) INTERVAL MIDPOINT (thousands)	(3) PROBABILITY FOR DEMANDS AT OR BELOW UPPER LIMIT (obtained from curve)	(4) PROBABILITY FOR DEMAND INTERVAL	(5) DEMAND × PROBABILITY (2) × (4)
500– 750	625	.02	.02	12.50
750–1,000	875	.08	.06	52.50
1,000–1,250	1,125	.25	.17	191.25
1,250–1,500	1,375	.50	.25	343.75
1,500–1,750	1,625	.68	.18	292.50
1,750–2,000	1,875	.80	.12	225.00
2,000–2,250	2,125	.89	.09	191.25
2,250–2,500	2,375	.95	.06	142.50
2,500–2,750	2,625	.98	.03	78.75
2,750–3,000	2,875	1.00	.02	57.50

Approximate expected demand = 1,587.50

units represents the probability that demand will fall somewhere between these amounts. Superimposed onto this histogram is a smoothed curve representing the judgmental frequency curve for demand. Note that the curve is positively skewed.

4-5 Finding a Probability Distribution from Actual/Forecast Ratios

The interview method is most suitable for use on a one-time basis when uncertain circumstances are involved that may never be encountered again. When judgmental forecasts of a single value are made more often, they provide a history that can be used to determine the underlying probability distribution.

TABLE 4-3
Judgment Forecasts and Actual/Forecast Ratios of Blitz Beer Weekly Sales (in barrels)

ACTUAL	FORECAST	ACTUAL/FORECAST
1,133	1,200	.94
1,422	1,150	1.24
1,288	1,300	.99
1,317	1,370	.96
1,080	1,410	.77
1,344	1,580	.85
1,506	1,650	.91
1,752	1,650	1.06
1,924	1,750	1.10
1,783	2,000	.89

We will illustrate this procedure with an example involving weekly sales forecasts for Blitz Beer made by the company's sales manager. The relevant data over a 10-month period are provided in Table 4-3. We will assume that the forecasts have been made solely from judgment. The actual sales values are divided by the respective forecast sale figures to provide **actual/forecast ratios**.

Actual sales of Blitz Beer for the first week were 1,133 barrels. The manager had forecast 1,200 barrels. Thus,

$$\frac{\text{Actual sales}}{\text{Forecast sales}} = \frac{1,133}{1,200} = .94 \qquad \text{(actual/forecast ratio)}$$

The sales manager's forecasting record is summarized in the cumulative probability graph in Figure 4-7. To plot this, the actual/forecast ratios are arranged in increasing value. There are 10 ratios, so each ratio is assigned a probability of 1/10. Thus, a .10 step in cumulative probability occurs at each value. A smoothed curve is then drawn freehand through the resulting cumulative probability stairway. This curve can be combined with the sales manager's next forecast to obtain the cumulative probability distribution for beer

FIGURE 4-7

Subjective probability distribution for Blitz Beer sales based on actual/forecast ratios.

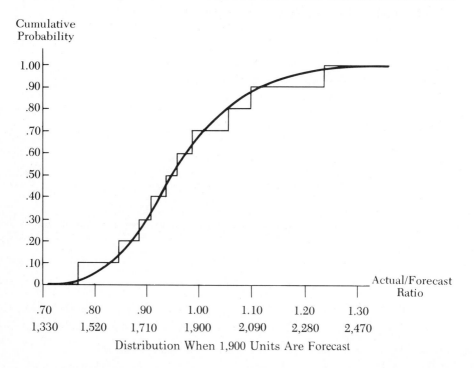

Distribution When 1,900 Units Are Forecast

sales for that week. For instance, to find the probability distribution when the sales forecast is 1,900 barrels, the actual/forecast ratios on the horizontal axis are multiplied by 1,900.

4-6 Additional Remarks

We have seen that probability values for decision making may sometimes be obtained from past history, but that past history is of limited use in business situations and may not exist at all for nonrepeatable circumstances. We have emphasized the direct assessment of a decision maker's judgment rather than traditional statistical techniques. But it should be noted that traditional techniques also rely heavily on judgmental inputs (usually of an indirect nature).

It is not necessary for a decision maker to obtain subjective probabilities personally. Such judgments can be delegated. For example, the chairman of General Motors might rely on various officers within the corporation to determine some or all of the probabilities to be used in analyzing a decision. After all, this is an area in which expert opinion should be relied on whenever possible. Exercising judgment to find subjective probabilities is similar to assessing attitudes toward decision outcomes. Chapter 26 shows how such attitudes may be summarized by a utility curve. It is dangerous for any decision maker to delegate the assessment of attitudes to others. Attitudes are highly personal and express unique tastes, whereas judgment can be shared. (The collective assessment of attitudes is prohibited by the axioms of utility theory. However, there is no reason why a committee cannot determine the subjective probabilities to be used.)

CASE

The Permian Plunge

Rod Shafter is a geologist who has formed a series of limited partnerships engaging in wildcat drilling for oil and gas. While evaluating a leasehold site in the Permian Basin of West Texas, Shafter employed Cal Crunch as a consultant. Crunch was to provide numbers useful for deciding whether or not the partnership should take the plunge and sink a wildcat shaft there.

The initial uncertainty pertains to whether or not a proper structural environment for fossil fuels exists beneath the site. Given the proper structure, there is some probability that the site will contain gas only, oil only, a combination of oil and gas, or neither. Shafter does not feel comfortable about arriving at the correct values for these probabilities. Crunch reassures him that satisfactory numbers can be "pulled out of thin air" using a box of marbles as a prop.

Even if there is oil or gas, Rod is uncertain about the recoverable quantities. Crunch plans to show him how to determine subjective probability distributions for each case. He plans to achieve this by conducting an interview that will "quantify Shafter's judgments."

Questions

1. With Cal's help, Rod arrives at the following probabilities.

$$Pr[\text{structure}] = .40$$

$$Pr[\text{oil only} \mid \text{structure}] = .10$$

$$Pr[\text{gas only} \mid \text{structure}] = .05$$

$$Pr[\text{oil } and \text{ gas} \mid \text{structure}] = .20$$

$$Pr[\text{neither} \mid \text{structure}] = .65$$

Determine the probability that the site contains the following. (Structure must be present in order for oil or gas to have formed.)
(a) oil only   (b) gas only   (c) oil and gas   (d) neither

2. Gas is measured in units of thousand cubic feet (mcf). Rod estimates that given gas (with or without oil), there is a 50–50 chance that the field contains 100 million mcf of recoverable gas reserves. He judges that should the quantity be higher than 100 million mcf, there is an even chance that reserves will be at or below 150 million mcf; should it be lower than 100 million, there is a 50–50 chance that the field will yield at or below 75 million mcf. Above 150 million the median level is 250 million mcf, while below 75 million mcf the median is 60 million mcf. Should there be more than 250 million mcf, it is "even money" that the level of reserves will lie above or below 400 million mcf, and should there be less than 60 million mcf, it is even money again that reserves will be at or below 50 million mcf. Assuming some gas, it is virtually certain that the field will contain more than 25 million mcf and less than 750 million mcf.
   (a) Construct a graph showing the cumulative probability distribution.
   (b) Starting at 0 as the lower limit and using 8 intervals each at a width of 100 million mcf, construct a table approximating the cumulative probability distribution.
   (c) Using your answer to (b), compute the expected level of gas reserves.

3. Oil is measured in barrels. Rod estimates that given oil (with or without gas), there is a 50–50 chance that the field contains 300,000 recoverable barrels of oil. He judges that should the quantity be higher than that level, there is an even chance that reserves are at or below 400,000 barrels; should it be lower than 300,000, there is a 50–50 chance that the field will yield at or below 250,000 barrels. Above 400,000 barrels the median level is 550,000 barrels, while below 250,000 the median is 220,000 barrels. Should there be more than 550,000 barrels, it is even money that the level of reserves will lie above or below 750,000 barrels, and should there be less than 220,000 barrels, it is even money again that reserves will be at or below 200,000 barrels. Assuming some oil, it is virtually certain that the field will contain more than 100,000 and less than 1,000,000 barrels of oil.

(a) Construct a graph showing the cumulative probability distribution.
(b) Starting at 50,000 barrels as the lower limit and using 10 intervals each at a width of 100,000 barrels, construct a table approximating the cumulative probability distribution.
(c) Using your answer to (b), compute the expected level of oil reserves.

PROBLEMS

4-1   Discuss whether historical frequencies are meaningful in estimating the probabilities for each of the following cases.
(a) the first-year salary levels of business school graduates
(b) the faces obtained by tossing an asymmetrical die
(c) the deaths during the next year of people in various age, health, sex, and occupational categories

4-2   Use your judgment to assess probabilities for the following events.
(a) The New York Yankees will play in and win the next World Series.
(b) If you are presently single, you will marry within one year. If you are presently married, your spouse will change jobs within one year.
(c) You will replace one of your present automobiles in the coming year.

4-3   Use your judgment to assess the probability that you will receive an A on your next examination. Imagine that your instructor will let you obtain your grade by lottery, so that 100 slips of paper (some labeled A; the rest, not A) will be put into a hat and mixed. You will draw one of these slips at random, and the letter obtained will be the grade you receive. How many A slips must there be to make you indifferent between letting your grade be determined by lottery or by earning it?

4-4   An automobile production manager believes that the time it takes to install a new car bumper is normally distributed. He has established that it is a 50–50 proposition that this task will take more than 60 seconds and that it is "even money" that the required time for any particular car will be between 45 and 75 seconds.
(a) Calculate the mean and the standard deviation of the subjective probability distribution.
(b) Find the probabilities that the installation for a particular car will take
 (1) between 50 and 70 seconds.
 (2) less than 25 seconds.
 (3) more than 1 minute.
 (4) between 20 and 90 seconds.

4-5   The yield of an active ingredient from a chemical process is assumed to be normally distributed. The 50–50 point is 30 grams per liter. The interquartile range (middle 50%) spans 4 grams per liter.
(a) Calculate the mean and the standard deviation of the subjective probability distribution.
(b) Find the probability that the yield falls (1) below 29 grams; (2) between 28.5 and 30.5 grams; (3) above 31.5 grams.

4-6   The dean of The Dover School of Business is assessing the probability distribution for next term's grade point average (GPA) for the entire school. It is "even money" that the GPA will fall at or below 2.75. The dean assigns a 50–50 probability that the low side will be at or below 2.70 and that the high side will be at or above 2.80. If the GPA is lower than 2.70, it is a coin-tossing proposition that it will fall at or below 2.60; similarly, the odds are even that the GPA will fall at or above 2.95, given that it lies above 2.80. Find the subjective probability that the GPA will lie within the following limits.

(a) 2.60 and 2.95   (c) 2.60 and 2.75
(b) 2.70 and 2.80   (d) 2.75 and 2.95

4-7 Establish your own subjective probability distribution for the heights of adult males residing within 50 miles of your campus. Use the normal curve that you obtain to establish the probabilities that a randomly chosen man is (a) less than 6′2″; (b) taller than 5′6″; (c) taller than your father.

4-8 Consider the cumulative probability distribution in Figure 4-8 to determine the following probabilities.

(a) $\Pr[D > 500]$ (c) $\Pr[D \geq 300]$
(b) $\Pr[D \leq 150]$ (d) $\Pr[200 \leq D \leq 800]$

FIGURE 4-8
Cumulative probability distribution for demand.

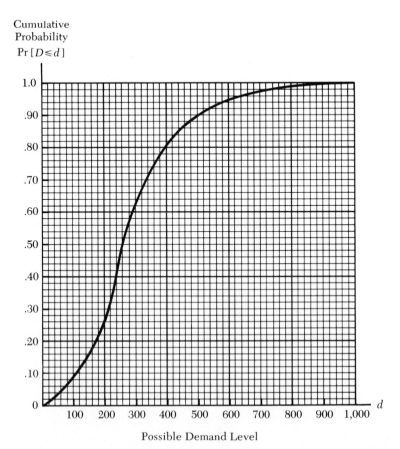

Possible Demand Level

4-9   Consider the cumulative probability distribution in Figure 4-8 to determine the following fractiles.

(a) .10   (b) .50   (c) .125   (d) .75   (e) .37

4-10   The following fractiles apply to the subjective probability distribution for the demand for a new product.

FRACTILE	QUANTITY
.0625	10,000
.125	25,000
.25	35,000
.50	40,000
.75	45,000
.875	55,000
.9375	75,000

Determine the probabilities that demand will fall within the following limits.

(a) 10,000 to 40,000   (c) 25,000 to 55,000
(b) 35,000 to 75,000   (d) 25,000 to 45,000

4-11   Willy B. Rich is a real estate investor who has established the following judgmental results regarding the rate of return on a proposed project. No value less than -20% or greater than 50% is possible.

RATE OF RETURN	50–50 POINT
all	15%
below 15%	7
above 15%	20
below 7%	3
above 20%	24
below 3%	−4
above 24%	28

(a) Complete the following table for the investor.

FRACTILE	RATE OF RETURN
0	
.0625	
.125	
.25	
.50	
.75	
.875	
.9375	
1.000	

(b) Plot the cumulative probability distribution for the investor's rate of return.

(c) From your graph, find the investor's subjective probability that the rate of return is between 20% and 40%.

4-12 Envision your income during the first full calendar year after graduation. Establish your own subjective probability distribution for the adjusted gross income figure that you will report to the IRS. (If applicable, include your spouse's earnings, interest, dividends, and other income.) If your graph has an unusual shape, try to eliminate any inconsistencies or to identify the nonhomogeneous factors (such as pregnancy, unemployment, or divorce) that might explain the shape. Remember, you are the expert about yourself.

4-13 Consider the total size of the U.S. car market (passenger cars sold—both imported and domestic) from October of the current year to the following October. Establish your subjective probability distribution for this quantity, and plot the results on a cumulative probability graph.

4-14 Consider the cumulative probability distribution for demand in Figure 4-8. Construct the approximate probability distribution for demand, using five intervals in increments of 200. Select the midpoints of these intervals as representative values, and determine the approximate expected demand.

4-15 The following approximation has been obtained for the subjective probability distribution for water wheelies demand.

DEMAND D	PROBABILITY
1,000	.08
2,000	.18
3,000	.36
4,000	.18
5,000	.10
6,000	.04
7,000	.03
8,000	.02
9,000	.01

(a) Determine the expected demand.

(b) Suppose that the profit for each level of demand is determined by

$$\text{Profit} = \begin{cases} -\$500 + .3D & \text{if } D \leq 5{,}000 \\ \$1{,}000 & \text{if } D > 5{,}000 \end{cases}$$

Calculate the expected profit.

4-16 The following sales data apply to Deuce Hardware (in thousands of dollars).

ACTUAL	FORECAST	ACTUAL	FORECAST
550	600	650	700
490	550	700	690
610	560	680	700
580	600	780	750
620	650	800	850

(a) Compute the actual/forecast ratios. Plot the cumulative probability graph, and then sketch a smoothed curve through the stairway.

(b) Suppose that the sales forecast for next year is 1,000 thousand dollars. Read from your curve the subjective probability that sales will fall at or below (1) 920; (2) 970; (3) 1,100.

4-17   A sports writer has forecast the Gotham City Hellcats' seasonal batting average for a 10-year period. The following values apply.

ACTUAL	FORECAST	ACTUAL	FORECAST
.273	.250	.350	.278
.332	.315	.364	.340
.366	.320	.359	.355
.307	.365	.331	.360
.318	.330	.388	.373

(a) Compute the actual/forecast ratios. Plot the cumulative probability graph and then sketch a smoothed curve through the stairway.

(b) Suppose that the forecast batting average is .350 for the next baseball season. Read from your graph the subjective probability that the Hellcats' batting average will be (1) ≤.300; (2) ≤.360; (3) ≤.375.

5

Forecasting

Forecasting the future is a fundamental aspect of business decision making. *Future sales* is the most important variable in business forecasts. *Unit sales* establish levels for most business activities—from purchasing and production to marketing—and knowledge about sales is a prerequisite to the budgetary and planning process.

A variety of quantitative techniques have been developed to forecast future values. The underlying models can be classified into three broad categories.

1. **Forecasting Using Past Data** The historical patterns of a variable are identified and projected into the future. These patterns are obtained through extrapolation from time-series data.

2. **Forecasting Using Causal Models** A relationship is found between the unknown variable and one or more other known variables. The values of the known variables are then used to predict the value of the variable of interest.

3. **Forecasting Using Judgment** Quantitative representations are used to express judgments in terms of subjective probabilities. These methods can incorporate the forecaster's actual "batting average" and may provide a way to express collective judgments.

In Chapter 5, we will survey the forecasting methods commonly used in each of these three categories.

5-1 Forecasting Using Past Data: Time-Series Analysis

A **time series** is a numerical sequence in which individual values are generated at regular intervals of time. The goal of **time-series analysis** is to identify the swings and fluctuations of a time series and then to sort them into various categories by the arithmetic manipulation of the numerical values obtained.

Several models can be used to characterize time series. The classical model used by economists provides the clearest explanation of the following four components of time-series variation and how they relate to each other.

1. Secular trend (T_t)
2. Cyclical movement (C_t)
3. Seasonal fluctuation (S_t)
4. Irregular variation (I_t)

These components can be related to the forecast variable by mathematical equations. The forecast variable is denoted by the symbol Y_t, where the subscript t refers to a period of time. Examples of Y_t are annual sales, passenger miles flown by domestic airlines, and acre-feet of water supplied to a city.

The Classical Time-Series Model

The classical time-series model originally used by economists combines the four components of time-series variation in the equation

$$Y_t = T_t \times C_t \times S_t \times I_t$$

This equation states that factors associated with each of these components can be multiplied together to provide the value of the forecast variable.

This model can be explained by means of a hypothetical time series—the sales Y_t of stereo speakers by the Speak E-Z Company. Figure 5-1 shows how the final time series (bottom graph) might be obtained by combining the four components. But only a hypothetical time series can be synthesized from the assumed characteristics of the four components. In actual applications, we may not know anything about T_t, C_t, S_t, or I_t. Usually, we begin with the raw time-series data and reverse the procedure, sifting the data to sort out and identify the components.

Forecasting with Time Series

Three major approaches are used in arriving at forecasts using past data. **Exponential smoothing** averages past time-series values in a systematic fashion. The resulting smoothed values are created using one of several averaging processes that agree with the

FIGURE 5-1
Complete time series for Speak E-Z sales, using individual components.

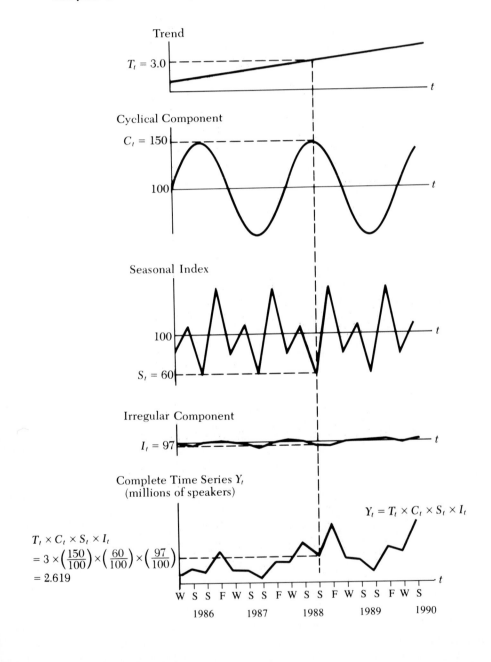

underlying nature of the data. Section 5-2 describes three popular procedures, each utilizing a set of parameters. Those parameters may be fine-tuned to the historical time series in order to achieve a best fit. In the following sections, we will encounter the second approach. There, **decomposition methods** are applied in isolating one or more time-series components. In Section 5-3, a trend line is found that may be used in making forecasts. Section 5-6 describes a second decomposition method that uncovers seasonal indexes for making forecasts. A third family of time-series analyses involve **autoregressive methods**; unfortunately, space limitations do not allow this book to provide a detailed discussion of these.

5-2 Exponential Smoothing

Exponential smoothing is a popular forecasting procedure that offers two basic advantages: It simplifies forecasting calculations, and its data-storage requirements are small. Exponential smoothing produces self-correcting forecasts with built-in adjustments that regulate forecast values by increasing or decreasing them in the opposite direction of earlier errors, much like a thermostat.

Single-Parameter Exponential Smoothing

The basic exponential-smoothing procedure provides the next period's forecast directly from the current period's actual and forecast values. This is summarized by the expression

$$F_{t+1} = \alpha Y_t + (1 - \alpha)F_t$$

where t is the current time period, F_{t+1} and F_t are the forecast values for the next period and the current period, respectively, and Y_t is the current actual value. α (the lowercase Greek letter *alpha*) is the **smoothing constant**—a chosen value lying between 0 and 1. Since only one smoothing constant is used, we refer to this procedure as **single-parameter exponential smoothing**.

To illustrate, we will suppose that actual sales of Blitz Beer in period 10 (October 19X1) were $Y_{10} = 5,240$ barrels and that $F_{10} = 5,061.6$ had been forecast earlier for this period. Using a smoothing constant of $\alpha = .20$, the forecast for period 11 (November 19X1) sales can be calculated as

$$F_{11} = .20 Y_{10} + (1 - .20)F_{10}$$
$$= .20(5,240) + .80(5,061.6) = 5,097.3 \text{ barrels}$$

Elementary exponential smoothing is extremely simple, because only one number—last period's forecast—must be saved. But, in essence, the entire time series is embodied

TABLE 5-1

Forecast of Blitz Beer Sales by Single-Parameter Exponential Smoothing ($\alpha = .20$)

MONTH	PERIOD t	ACTUAL SALES Y_t	FORECAST SALES F_t	ERROR $Y_t - F_t$	ERROR^2 $(Y_t - F_t)^2$
January 19X1	1	4,890	—	—	—
February	2	4,910	4,890.0	20.0	400.00
March	3	4,970	4,894.0	76.0	5,776.00
April	4	5,010	4,909.2	101.8	10,160.64
May	5	5,060	4,929.4	130.6	17,056.36
June	6	5,100	4,955.5	144.5	20,880.25
July	7	5,050	4,984.4	65.6	4,303.36
August	8	5,170	4,997.5	172.5	29,756.25
September	9	5,180	5,032.0	148.0	21,904.00
October	10	5,240	5,061.6	178.4	31,826.56
November	11	5,220	5,097.3	122.7	15,055.29
December	12	5,280	5,121.8	158.2	25,027.24
January 19X2	13	5,330	5,153.5	176.5	31,152.25
February	14	5,380	5,188.8	191.2	36,557.44
March	15	5,440	5,227.0	213.0	45,369.00
April	16	5,460	5,269.6	190.4	36,252.16
May	17	5,520	5,307.7	212.3	45,071.29
June	18	5,490	5,350.2	139.8	19,544.04
July	19	5,550	5,378.1	171.9	29,549.61
August	20	5,600	5,412.5	187.5	35,156.25
September	21	—	5,450.0	—	—
					460,797.99

MSE $= 460,797.99/19 = 24,252.53$

in that forecast. If we express F_t in terms of the preceding actual Y_{t-1} and forecast F_{t-1} values, then the equivalent expression for next period's forecast is

$$F_{t+1} = \alpha Y_t + \alpha(1 - \alpha)Y_{t-1} + (1 - \alpha)^2 F_{t-1}$$

Continuing this for several earlier periods shows us that all preceding Y's are reflected in the current forecast. The name for this procedure is derived from the successive weights α, $\alpha(1 - \alpha)$, $\alpha(1 - \alpha)^2$, $\alpha(1 - \alpha)^3,\ldots$, which *decrease exponentially*. Thus, the more current the actual value of the time series is, the greater its weight is. Progressively less forecasting weight is assigned to older Y's, and the oldest Y's are eventually wiped out. The forecasting procedure can be modified at any time by changing the value of α.

Table 5-1 provides the actual and forecast Blitz Beer sales for 20 periods when $\alpha = .20$. There, the actual sales figure for period 1 has been used for the initial forecast for period 2. (Eventually, the same F's will be achieved in later time periods, regardless of the initial value.)

FIGURE 5-2

Single-parameter exponential smoothing results for Blitz Beer sales ($\alpha = .20$).

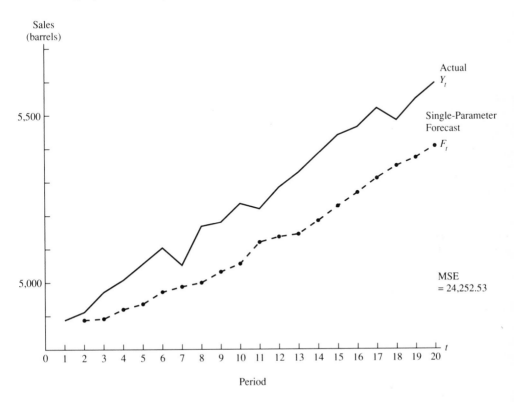

The actual and forecast values may be compared in the plot provided in Figure 5-2. Notice that the forecast values deviate considerably from the actual values. This reflects a poorness of fit in using this particular model and level for α. The overall forecasting quality may be assessed in terms of the forecasting errors.

Forecasting Errors

The errors in a forecasting procedure are determined by subtracting the forecasts from their respective actual values,

$$\varepsilon_t = Y_t - F_t$$

α should be set at a level that minimizes these errors. Often several separate sets of forecasts are required to "tune" the smoothing constant to past data. Large α levels assign more weight to current values, whereas small α levels emphasize past data. By trial and error, an optimal level can be found for α that minimizes *variability* in forecasting errors.

For any set of actual and forecast values, the **mean squared error**, denoted as MSE, is used to summarize this variability. The following expression is used to compute the **mean squared error**.

$$MSE = \frac{\sum (Y_t - F_t)^2}{n - m}$$

where n denotes the number of time periods and m is the number of smoothing parameters. A value of $MSE = 24{,}252.53$ applies to the Blitz Beer data in Table 5-1.

Two-Parameter Exponential Smoothing

The forecast sales found earlier for Blitz Beer are smaller than (lag behind) the actual sales. Whenever there is a pronounced upward trend in actual data (here, increasing sales), forecasts resulting from the single-parameter exponential smoothing will be consistently low.

TABLE 5-2
Forecast of Blitz Beer Sales by Two-Parameter Exponential Smoothing ($\alpha = .20$ and $\gamma = .30$)

MONTH	PERIOD t	ACTUAL SALES Y_t	TREND T_t	TREND SLOPE b_t	FORECAST SALES F_t	ERROR $Y_t - F_t$	ERROR^2 $(Y_t - F_t)^2$
January 19X1	1	4,890	—	—	—	—	—
February	2	4,910	4,890	20.0	—	—	—
March	3	4,970	4,922	23.6	4,910.0	60.0	3,600.00
April	4	5,010	4,958	27.3	4,945.6	64.4	4,147.36
May	5	5,060	5,000	31.7	4,985.3	74.7	5,580.09
June	6	5,100	5,045	35.7	5,031.7	68.3	4,664.89
July	7	5,050	5,075	34.0	5,080.7	−30.7	942.49
August	8	5,170	5,121	37.6	5,109.0	61.0	3,721.00
September	9	5,180	5,163	38.9	5,158.6	21.4	457.96
October	10	5,240	5,210	41.3	5,201.9	38.1	1,451.61
November	11	5,220	5,245	39.4	5,251.3	−31.3	979.69
December	12	5,280	5,283	39.0	5,284.4	−4.4	19.36
January 19X2	13	5,330	5,324	39.6	5,322.0	8.0	64.00
February	14	5,380	5,367	40.6	5,363.6	16.4	268.96
March	15	5,440	5,414	42.5	5,407.6	32.4	1,049.76
April	16	5,460	5,457	42.7	5,456.5	3.5	12.25
May	17	5,520	5,504	44.0	5,499.7	20.3	,412.09
June	18	5,490	5,536	40.4	5,548.0	−58.0	3,364.00
July	19	5,550	5,571	38.8	5,576.4	−26.4	696.96
August	20	5,600	5,608	38.3	5,609.8	−9.8	96.04
September	21	—	—	—	5,646.3	—	—
							31,528.51

$$MSE = 31{,}528.51/18 = 1{,}751.58$$

Two-parameter exponential smoothing eliminates such a lag by explicitly accounting for trend by using a second smoothing constant for the slope of the line. A total of three equations are employed.

$$T_t = \alpha Y_t + (1 - \alpha)(T_{t-1} + b_{t-1}) \qquad \text{(smooth the data to get trend)}$$

$$b_t = \gamma(T_t - T_{t-1}) + (1 - \gamma)b_{t-1} \qquad \text{(smooth the slope in trend)}$$

$$F_{t+1} = T_t + b_t \qquad \text{(forecast)}$$

Here, T_t represents the smoothed value for period t. This quantity conveys the underlying *trend* in the data. The difference between the current and the prior trend values provides the current slope in trend: $T_t - T_{t-1}$. The second equation contains the **slope-smoothing constant** γ (the lowercase Greek letter *gamma*), which is used to obtain smoothed-trend line slopes, represented by b_t. The third equation provides the forecast.

Table 5-2 lists the forecasts of Blitz Beer sales when $\alpha = .20$ and $\gamma = .30$. (The initial trend value of $T_2 = 4,890$ is the actual sales for period 1. The first slope value of $b_2 = 20$ is the difference in actual sales for periods 1 and 2.) The actual and forecast values are plotted in Figure 5-3.

FIGURE 5-3
Two-parameter exponential smoothing results for Blitz Beer sales ($\alpha = .20$, $\gamma = .30$).

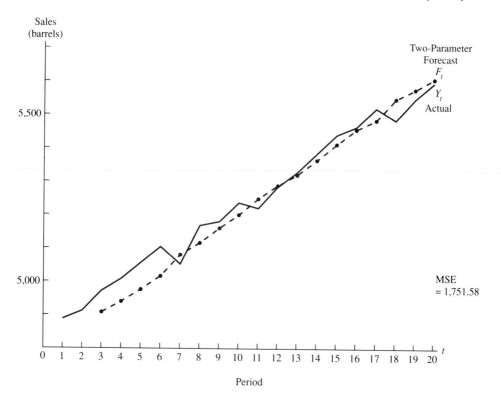

As an illustration, to forecast period 8 sales, first we obtain the smoothed-data value or trend for period 7.

$$T_7 = .20Y_7 + (1 - .20)(T_6 + b_6)$$
$$= .20(5,050) + .80(5,045 + 35.7)$$
$$= 5,075 \text{ barrels}$$

Then we compute the smoothed slope in trend for period 7.

$$b_7 = .30(T_7 - T_6) + (1 - .30)b_6$$
$$= .30(5,075 - 5,045) + .70(35.7)$$
$$= 34.0$$

which indicates that sales were increasing at a rate of 34.0 barrels per period at that time. The forecast for period 8 is the sum of the preceding period's trend and slope values.

$$F_8 = T_7 + b_7 = 5,075 + 34.0 = 5,109.0 \text{ barrels}$$

The forecasts that result from this procedure are close to the actual sales values. The current trend itself is readjusted for each period to coincide with the latest growth in the raw data.

Notice, in Figure 5-3, how closely the forecasts from two-parameter smoothing lie to the actual sales figures. When the underlying time series exhibits a pronounced trend, two-parameter exponential smoothing will ordinarily provide better forecasts than those made with a single parameter. The MSE will then be smaller, as is the case with the two sets of Blitz Beer forecasts.

$$MSE = 24,252.53 \quad \text{(single parameter)}$$
$$MSE = 1,751.58 \quad \text{(two parameters)}$$

MSE can also be used to gauge how well different levels for α and γ provide forecasts that fit past time-series data.

Computer Applications

Computer assistance is an obvious advantage when performing exponential smoothing. It is helpful for tuning the model (by adjusting the smoothing constants) to the historical data and obtaining a best fit. Figure 5-4 shows a portion of the output from a *QuickQuant* computer run using the Blitz Beer sales data given in Table 5-2.

One of the *QuickQuant* menu choices automatically begins a search for the best α and β. It does this by creating a set of F_t's with each possible combination of levels for those parameters, starting with $\alpha = .10$ and $\gamma = .10$, in progressive increments of .10. The program computes the MSE for each forecast set; the results are shown in Figure 5-4.

FIGURE 5-4

Portion of *QuickQuant* report showing the first phase of a search for best-fitting parameters using the Blitz Beer sales data.

```
=======================================================================
                        QuickQuant Report
                     EXPONENTIAL SMOOTHING
-----------------------------------------------------------------------
PROBLEM: Blitz Beer                                   Date: 11-21-1989
                                                            Larry
                     SEARCH FOR BEST PARAMETERS

           Gamma=0.10 Gamma=0.20 Gamma=0.30 Gamma=0.40 Gamma=0.50
Alpha=0.10   8140.87   4891.873   3427.701   2766.366   2434.934
Alpha=0.20   3075.782   2055.964   1734.615   1599.486   1542.31
Alpha=0.30   1971.414   1560.42    1463.607   1458.581   1499.135
Alpha=0.40   1623.855   1436.939   1427.561   1470.52    1534.033
Alpha=0.50   1503.583   1422.656   1454.751   1517.956   1591.366
Alpha=0.60   1479.104   1458.943   1517.594   1598.094   1687.502
Alpha=0.70   1509.432   1531.623   1613.768   1714.244   1824.319
Alpha=0.80   1582.039   1640.486   1748.534   1874.428   2011.89
Alpha=0.90   1697.211   1793.912   1936.158   2099.747   2281.261
Alpha=1.00   1863.988   2009.151   2203.035   2429.167   2689.538

           Gamma=0.60 Gamma=0.70 Gamma=0.80 Gamma=0.90 Gamma=1.00
Alpha=0.10   2228.51    2072.009   1945.874   1849.493   1784.782
Alpha=0.20   1538.044   1572.496   1633.844   1713.081   1802.744
Alpha=0.30   1564.219   1638.937   1711.793   1775.053   1825.436
Alpha=0.40   1602.4     1667.67    1728.09    1785.916   1845.341
Alpha=0.50   1667.626   1745.934   1828.363   1917.52    2015.101
Alpha=0.60   1782.754   1883.996   1991.667   2105.222   2222.8
Alpha=0.70   1941.794   2065.819   2195.351   2329.097   2466.139
Alpha=0.80   2159.347   2316.534   2484.032   2663.544   2858.41
Alpha=0.90   2481.789   2704.748   2955.869   3243.667   3580.059
Alpha=1.00   2991.96    3349.016   3779.019   4307.892   4972.222

   Best Fit:    Alpha =0.50 Gamma =0.20 MSE = 1422.656
-----------------------------------------------------------------------
```

There, the lowest MSE is found to be 1,422.656, when $\alpha = .50$ and $\gamma = .20$. Those parameter settings give a preliminary best fit.

During the optional second *QuickQuant* pass, a finer search is performed in the vicinity of these parameter levels, using increments of .01; the results are shown in the top portion of Figure 5-5. The second search yields the final best fit. The MSE is found to be 1,418.864, when $\alpha = .45$ and $\gamma = .23$. The bottom portion of Figure 5-5 shows the detailed forecast information using these parameters.

QuickQuant allows the user to specify the α and γ levels, skipping the search for best fit. Notice the entry in the last row. There, we find a forecast value of $F_{21} = 5,631.82$ for the upcoming time period.

QuickQuant will also perform all the calculations for single-parameter exponential smoothing and for the three-parameter procedure, to be discussed next.

Seasonal Exponential Smoothing with Three Parameters

The two exponential-smoothing procedures described thus far ignore any seasonal aspects. Consider the quarterly sales data for Stationer's Supply, plotted in Figure 5-6. A

FIGURE 5-5

Portion of *QuickQuant* report showing the final phase of search for best-fitting parameters using the Blitz Beer sales data.

```
====================================================================================
                             QuickQuant Report
                          EXPONENTIAL SMOOTHING
------------------------------------------------------------------------------------
PROBLEM: Blitz Beer                                      Date: 11-21-1989
                                                                    Larry
                         SEARCH FOR BEST PARAMETERS

             Gamma=0.15 Gamma=0.16 Gamma=0.17 Gamma=0.18 Gamma=0.19
Alpha=0.45    1451.587   1442.04    1434.55    1428.817   1424.558
Alpha=0.46    1447.068   1438.404   1431.703   1426.659   1423.044
Alpha=0.47    1443.379   1435.522   1429.548   1425.182   1422.191
Alpha=0.48    1440.433   1433.354   1428.084   1424.349   1421.906
Alpha=0.49    1438.194   1431.839   1427.23    1424.085   1422.194
Alpha=0.50    1436.606   1430.959   1426.96    1424.374   1423.002
Alpha=0.51    1435.653   1430.653   1427.252   1425.201   1424.305
Alpha=0.52    1435.289   1430.913   1428.066   1426.521   1426.096
Alpha=0.53    1435.487   1431.699   1429.385   1428.333   1428.357
Alpha=0.54    1436.211   1432.981   1431.183   1430.59    1431.031


             Gamma=0.20 Gamma=0.21 Gamma=0.22 Gamma=0.23 Gamma=0.24
Alpha=0.45    1421.593   1419.744   1418.875   1418.864   1419.613
Alpha=0.46    1420.681   1419.363   1418.995   1419.44    1420.604
Alpha=0.47    1420.357   1419.563   1419.653   1420.531   1422.1
Alpha=0.48    1420.612   1420.291   1420.826   1422.109   1424.046
Alpha=0.49    1421.387   1421.523   1422.472   1424.145   1426.457
Alpha=0.50    1422.656   1423.224   1424.574   1426.616   1429.269
Alpha=0.51    1424.415   1425.394   1427.124   1429.52    1432.487
Alpha=0.52    1426.635   1427.998   1430.087   1432.823   1436.119
Alpha=0.53    1429.286   1431.038   1433.465   1436.526   1440.114
Alpha=0.54    1432.369   1434.463   1437.245   1440.599   1444.494

        Best Fit:   Alpha =0.45 Gamma =0.23 MSE = 1418.864

              SMOOTHED DATA WITH BEST PARAMETERS

            Alpha =0.45      Gamma =0.23      MSE = 1418.864
```

Period t	Actual Yt	Trend Tt	Slope bt	Forecast Ft	Error Yt−Ft
1	4890.00	--	--	--	--
2	4910.00	4890.00	20.00	--	--
3	4970.00	4937.00	26.21	4910.00	60.00
4	5010.00	4984.27	31.05	4963.21	46.79
5	5060.00	5035.42	35.68	5015.32	44.68
6	5100.00	5084.11	38.67	5071.10	28.90
7	5050.00	5090.03	31.14	5122.77	−72.77
8	5170.00	5143.14	36.19	5121.16	48.84
9	5180.00	5179.63	36.26	5179.33	0.67
10	5240.00	5226.74	38.76	5215.89	24.11
11	5220.00	5245.02	34.05	5265.50	−45.50
12	5280.00	5279.49	34.14	5279.07	0.93
13	5330.00	5321.00	35.84	5313.63	16.37
14	5380.00	5367.26	38.23	5356.83	23.17
15	5440.00	5421.02	41.81	5405.49	34.51
16	5460.00	5461.56	41.51	5462.83	−2.83
17	5520.00	5510.69	43.27	5503.07	16.93
18	5490.00	5525.17	36.65	5553.95	−63.95
19	5550.00	5556.50	35.42	5561.82	−11.82
20	5600.00	5595.56	36.26	5591.93	8.07
21	--	--	--	5631.82	--

FIGURE 5-6
Actual quarterly sales data for Stationer's Supply.

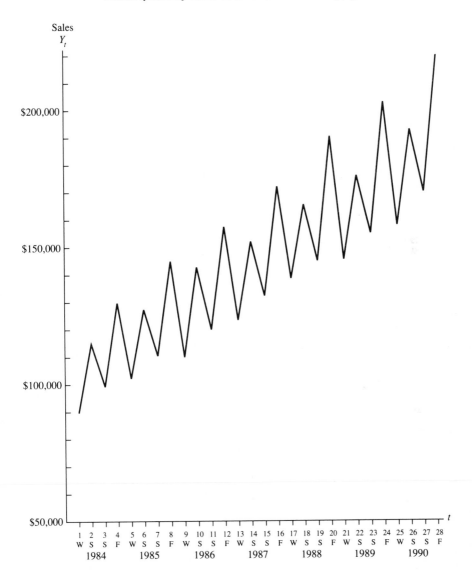

retail outlet, Stationer's Supply has historically experienced two busy periods, Spring and Fall, interspersed with the more quiet Summer and Winter quarters. The results show a very pronounced seasonal pattern that gives a saw-toothed effect to the time series.

Seasonal exponential smoothing makes forecasts by isolating the trend and seasonal time-series components as separate smoothed series. The underlying model extends the two-parameter procedure, incorporating the **seasonal smoothing constant** β (Greek lowercase letter *beta*) as the third parameter. The following four equations apply.

$$T_t = \alpha\left(\frac{Y_t}{S_{t-p}}\right) + (1-\alpha)(T_{t-1} + b_{t-1}) \qquad \text{(smooth the data to get trend)}$$

$$b_t = \gamma(T_t - T_{t-1}) + (1-\gamma)b_{t-1} \qquad \text{(smooth the slope in trend)}$$

$$S_t = \beta\left(\frac{Y_t}{T_t}\right) + (1-\beta)S_{t-p} \qquad \text{(smooth the seasonal factor)}$$

$$F_{t+1} = (T_t + b_t)S_{t-p+1} \qquad \text{(forecast)}$$

The first equation smooths the past data to obtain the trend. In doing this, the current value Y_t is first *deseasonalized*.

$$\frac{Y_t}{S_{t-p}}$$

This is accomplished by dividing the actual by the latest applicable seasonal factor, S_{t-p}. The $t-p$ subscript signifies that the seasonal factor is taken from p periods earlier. The letter p denotes the number of periods during a major period. There would be $p = 4$ *quarters* in a year, $p = 12$ *months* in a year, and $p = 7$ *days* in a week. For Stationer's Supply, the data are quarterly, and $p = 4$, so that the current Spring sales is divided by the S applicable for the preceding Spring, and so on.

The second equation smooths the slope in trend, just as in the previous model. The third equation smooths the seasonal factor. The current portion of the seasonal factor is defined by the following ratio.

$$\frac{Y_t}{T_t}$$

The above ratio receives a weight β and is added to $1-\beta$ times the prior matching seasonal factor value.

The final equation creates a new deseasonalized projection, adding the prior period's trend and the latest slope in trend. That quantity is multiplied by the latest applicable known seasonal factor S_{t-p} (*not* S_t) to give the forecast value.

Table 5-3 shows the detailed summary obtained from applying the above to the Stationer's Supply sales data, with $\alpha = .4$, $\gamma = .5$, and $\beta = .7$. We will use period 20 to illustrate the calculations with the seasonal model.

Taking, as the current period, $t = 20$ (Fall 1988) and all available data from that and the prior periods, we will determine the forecast for period 21 (Winter 1989). The first step is to compute the smoothed values for trend and slope in trend, averaging current values with those of period 19.

$$T_{20} = .40\left(\frac{Y_{20}}{S_{16}}\right) + (1-.40)(T_{19} + b_{19})$$

$$= .40\left(\frac{\$190,400}{1.09}\right) + .60(\$169,823.34 + \$3,376.46)$$

$$= \$173,810.45$$

$$b_{20} = .50(T_{20} - T_{19}) + (1 - .50)b_{19}$$
$$= .50(\$173,810.45 - \$169,823.34) + .50(\$3,376.46)$$
$$= \$3,681.79$$

Notice that $S_{16} = 1.09$ (Fall 1987) is used as the divisor to find T_{20}, not S_{20} (which cannot be available until T_{20} has been computed). The seasonal factor for period 20 is computed with the above, however, since it will be needed to make future-period calculations.

TABLE 5-3
Seasonal Exponential Smoothing Results for Stationer's Supply ($\alpha = .4$, $\gamma = .5$, $\beta = .7$).

QUARTER	t	ACTUAL Y_t	TREND T_t	SLOPE b_t	SEASONAL S_t	FORECAST F_t	ERROR $Y_t - F_t$
1984 W	1	90,640	—	—	—	—	—
S	2	115,540	90,640.00	24,900.00	1.27	—	—
S	3	99,190	109,000.00	21,630.00	.91	—	—
F	4	128,800	129,898.00	21,264.00	.99	—	—
1985 W	5	102,350	131,637.20	11,501.60	.78	—	—
S	6	127,440	125,873.46	2,868.93	1.09	182,460.92	−55,020.92
S	7	112,530	126,709.17	1,852.32	.89	117,155.58	−4,625.58
F	8	145,080	135,663.61	5,403.38	1.05	127,474.79	17,605.21
1986 W	9	110,490	141,482.77	5,611.27	.78	109,681.81	808.20
S	10	143,000	140,679.34	2,403.92	1.04	160,498.08	−17,498.08
S	11	119,700	139,367.03	545.81	.87	128,011.98	−8,311.98
F	12	157,760	144,273.64	2,726.21	1.08	146,355.97	11,404.03
1987 W	13	123,710	151,647.84	5,050.21	.81	114,647.37	9,062.63
S	14	153,360	153,066.75	3,234.56	1.01	162,791.25	−9,431.25
S	15	131,950	154,474.06	2,320.93	.86	135,922.52	−3,972.52
F	16	173,160	158,254.92	3,050.90	1.09	169,220.94	3,939.06
1988 W	17	135,900	164,310.22	4,553.10	.82	129,853.54	6,046.46
S	18	164,780	166,383.72	3,313.30	1.00	171,059.64	−6,279.64
S	19	146,010	169,823.34	3,376.46	.86	145,738.78	271.22
F	20	190,400	173,810.45	3,681.79	1.09	188,736.47	1,663.53
1989 W	21	145,070	177,220.66	3,545.99	.82	145,627.08	−557.08
S	22	175,960	179,044.81	2,685.08	.99	180,252.36	−4,292.36
S	23	155,480	181,397.27	2,518.76	.86	156,194.73	−714.73
F	24	202,960	184,576.81	2,849.16	1.10	201,153.27	1,806.73
1990 W	25	157,500	189,364.59	3,818.47	.83	153,529.97	3,970.03
S	26	192,240	193,811.88	4,132.88	.99	190,688.30	1,551.70
S	27	168,330	197,257.61	3,789.30	.85	169,803.64	−1,473.64
F	28	218,960	200,407.03	3,469.36	1.09	220,716.22	−1,756.22
1991 W	29	—	—	—	—	168,800.52	—
S	30	—	—	—	—	205,365.31	—
S	31	—	—	—	—	180,182.80	—
F	32	—	—	—	—	234,460.20	—

$$S_{20} = .70\left(\frac{Y_{20}}{T_{20}}\right) + (1 - .70)S_{16}$$

$$= .70\left(\frac{\$190,400}{\$173,810.45}\right) + .30(1.09)$$

$$= 1.09$$

Finally, the forecast is made for period 21.

$$F_{21} = (T_{20} + b_{20})S_{17}$$

$$= (\$173,810.45 + \$3,681.79)(1.09)$$

$$= \$145,627.08$$

The complete set of forecast values are plotted alongside the actual sales figures in Figure 5-7. Notice that the F_t's become close to the Y_t values only after the process has settled down, after three full years of data have been incorporated. This slowness in attaining forecasting accuracy is mainly due to poor starting values. Rather than rely on guesswork, the illustrated procedure uses the actual Y_1 as the first T_2 (which appears to be quite low in relation to the later T's). That in turn distorts the initial seasonal values. (Although *QuickQuant* does not employ them, a quicker start might be achieved by making good guesses for the starting S's.) As with any exponential-smoothing process, earlier inaccuracies eventually wash out.

When applying the seasonal model, forecasts may be found for the entire seasonal cycle using the following expression.

$$F_{t+m} = (T_t + b_t m)S_{t-p+m}$$

The above was used to obtain the last set of four Stationer's Supply forecast values, shown in Figure 5-7 and at the bottom of Table 5-3.

Fine-Tuning Exponential-Smoothing Parameters

With computer assistance, it is practicable to fine-tune the parameters to the historical data, thereby achieving a best fit (minimum *MSE*). Generally, the following applies to any parameter.

The fine-tuning of parameters to past data does indeed provide a best historical fit. But, there are no guarantees that the parameters thereby obtained will continue to fit the actual data well. And, should the historical fit result in a parameter that is very close to 0 or to 1, it

FIGURE 5-7
Actual and quarterly sales data for Stationer's Supply ($\alpha = .4$, $\gamma = .5$, $\beta = .7$).

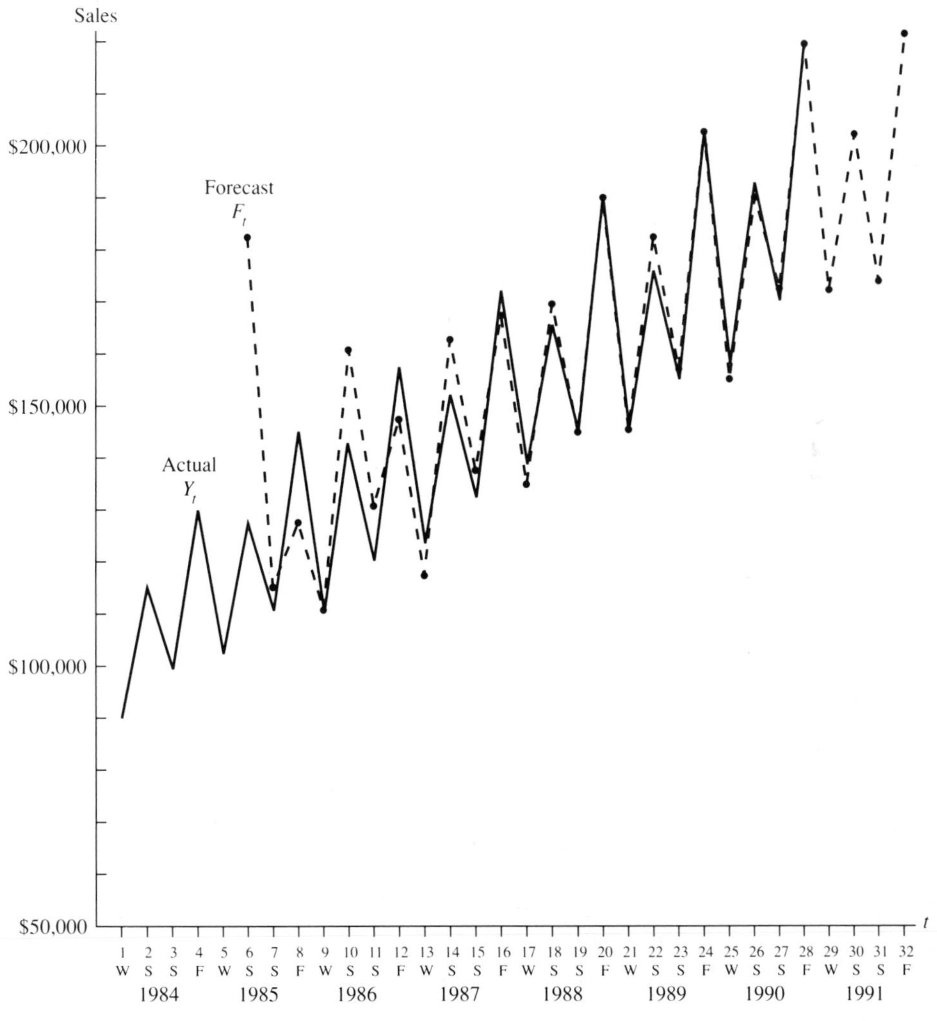

may be wise to choose a less extreme number that sacrifices past *MSE* for greater future stability or responsiveness.

Figure 5-8 shows the results of using different β levels with the Stationer's Supply data (all with the same α and γ as before). Each *MSE* value was obtained with a separate *QuickQuant* run. Notice that *MSE* declines steadily as β is increased, but the curve flattens out around $\beta = .7$. That number appears to be a good compromise for future forecasts of Stationer's Supply sales, allowing for both stability and responsiveness to a seasonal pattern that will likely prevail with little change. Using that β, the other parameters were fine-tuned. Figure 5-9 shows a portion of the *QuickQuant* report obtained.

FIGURE 5-8

Relationship between MSE and level for β using Stationer's Supply data ($\alpha = .40$, $\gamma = .50$).

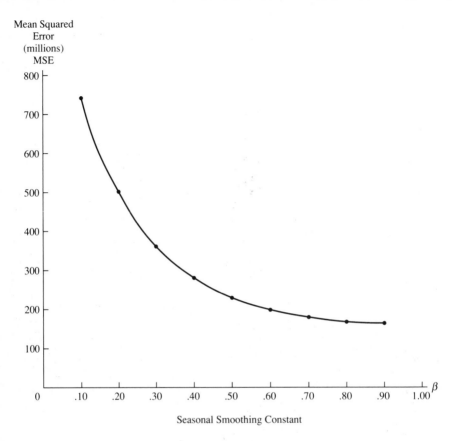

Further Exponential-Smoothing Procedures

A wide variety of exponential-smoothing procedures are available. One popular group employs *adaptive response*, involving changes to one or more smoothing constants as conditions change from one period to the next. More elaborate procedures explicitly allow for nonlinear trend. The references in the back of this book list sources for more information on these and other exponential-smoothing procedures.

5-3 Forecasting Trend Using Regression

The secular trend component T_t of a time series may be the most valuable variable in making forecasts. Trend analysis focuses on finding the appropriate trend line or curve that provides the best fit to the historical scatter of Y_t over time.

FIGURE 5-9

Portion of *QuickQuant* report for Stationer's Supply data, using parameters
$\alpha = .42$, $\gamma = .67$, and $\beta = .7$.

```
=============================================================================
                          QuickQuant Report
                        EXPONENTIAL SMOOTHING
-----------------------------------------------------------------------------
PROBLEM: Stationer's Supply                          Date: 11-24-1989
                                                                    Larry

  Best Fit (Using Beta =0.70) Alpha =0.42 Gamma =0.67 MSE = 1.683232E+08

                    SMOOTHED DATA WITH BEST PARAMETERS

        Alpha =0.42        Gamma =0.67       Beta =0.70     MSE = 1.683232E+08
```

Period t	Actual Yt	Trend Tt.	Slope bt	Seasonal St	Forecast Ft	Error Yt−Ft
1	90640.00	--	--	--	--	--
2	115540.00	90640.00	24900.00	1.27	--	--
3	99190.00	108673.00	20299.11	0.91	--	--
4	128800.00	128899.83	20250.68	1.00	--	--
5	102350.00	129494.31	7081.02	0.79	--	--
6	127440.00	121203.38	-3218.19	1.12	174094.38	-46654.38
7	112530.00	120212.53	-1725.87	0.93	107689.59	4840.41
8	145080.00	129703.09	5789.14	1.08	118394.91	26685.09
9	110490.00	137298.61	6999.41	0.80	107090.66	3399.34
10	143000.00	137392.98	2373.04	1.06	161387.66	-18387.66
11	119700.00	135175.55	-702.58	0.90	129854.63	-10154.63
12	157760.00	139189.27	2457.34	1.12	145601.42	12158.58
13	123710.00	147067.55	6089.37	0.83	113378.81	10331.20
14	153360.00	149362.34	3547.01	1.04	162973.81	-9613.81
15	131950.00	150360.97	1839.59	0.88	137402.25	-5452.25
16	173160.00	153314.63	2586.01	1.13	170193.91	2966.09
17	135900.00	159277.73	4848.67	0.85	129234.62	6665.38
18	164780.00	161869.59	3336.61	1.02	170357.38	-5577.38
19	146010.00	165201.52	3333.47	0.88	146019.86	-9.86
20	190400.00	168765.05	3487.61	1.13	189783.17	616.83
21	145070.00	171931.78	3272.62	0.84	145716.30	-646.30
22	175960.00	173791.39	2325.90	1.02	179405.00	-3445.00
23	155480.00	176032.00	2268.76	0.88	155659.53	-179.53
24	202960.00	179014.16	2746.73	1.13	201044.73	1915.27
25	157500.00	183759.22	4085.61	0.85	153482.34	4017.66
26	192240.00	188424.98	4474.32	1.02	190836.69	1403.31
27	168330.00	191909.34	3811.04	0.88	170412.25	-2082.25
28	218960.00	194764.34	3170.49	1.13	221536.58	-2576.58
29	--	--	--	--	168896.92	--
30	--	--	--	--	204916.47	--
31	--	--	--	--	179562.70	--
32	--	--	--	--	233695.00	--

Describing Trend

In the hypothetical time series for stereo speaker demand that was discussed in Section 5-1, secular trend was represented by a straight line. A straight-line trend assumes that Y_t changes at a constant rate.

Most time series do not involve long-term behavior that changes constantly over time. In business or economic situations, a variable will usually increase or decline at a rate

FIGURE 5-10
Basic shapes of common trend curves.

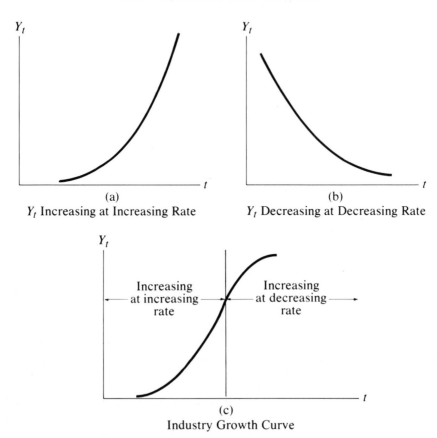

(a)
Y_t Increasing at Increasing Rate

(b)
Y_t Decreasing at Decreasing Rate

(c)
Industry Growth Curve

that itself changes from period to period. Some basic shapes of nonlinear trend curves frequently encountered are provided in Figure 5-10. For example, consider the movement in GNP levels over a prolonged period. The GNP for the United States has increased by more in the recent past than it did following World War II, so that the trend is represented best by a curve with increasing and positive slope as in Figure 5-10(a). In absolute terms, the U.S. GNP has been increasing in recent times at an increasing rate.*

Diagram (b) in Figure 5-10 shows the trend for a time series that decreases at a decreasing rate. The level of activity for a declining industry may sometimes be represented by such a curve. The decline is initially dramatic but becomes more gradual

---

* The *percentage* rate of *growth* in real GNP has been more or less constant at about 3%, even though the absolute rate of increase in GNP has been rising. Percentage growth rate is expressed relative to the current position and works like compound interest paid by a bank. The original savings account balance will increase at an increasing rate, so that the shape in diagram (a) applies over time, even though the percentage rate of interest or growth remains constant.

with time. An example of such a trend is the number of railroad passengers carried in the United States each year during the past four decades.

The long-range growth of a firm or an industry may sometimes be explained in terms of a trend having the shape shown in Figure 5-10(c). Here, output increases at an increasing rate when innovative products are brought onto the market to satisfy emerging needs. As the industry matures, rapid growth is replaced by a period of gradual increases; product sales still increase, but at a decreasing rate. Ultimately, sales peak and a period of stagnation begins. Such S-shaped curves are therefore called **growth curves**. Two growth curves frequently encountered in statistics are the logistic and the Gompertz.

The particular shape to portray the trend of a specific time series is selected partly by studying the scatter of the data on a graph. The choice should be a basic shape that not only seems to fit the historical data closely but also coincides with good judgment about how it should be related to future data. There are no rules to tell us which shape must be used. Judgment and experience play the dominant role, so that fitting a trend curve to make forecasts is as much an art as a science.

Determining Linear Trend Using Regression

Time series covering a small number of years usually may be fitted by a straight line. This involves finding the following **regression equation**.

$$\hat{Y}(X) = a + bX$$

Here, Y represents the **dependent variable** (the variable being forecast) of the time series, and X represents the **independent variable** (the time period). We use X instead of t, because it is simpler to express time relative to a base period. The values a and b in this expression are referred to as **estimated regression coefficients**. It is traditional to place a caret over the letter Y, using $\hat{Y}$ (Y-hat) to denote the predicted or forecast value for Y.

The regression coefficients are calculated from the equations

$$b = \frac{\Sigma XY - n\bar{X}\bar{Y}}{\Sigma X^2 - n\bar{X}^2}.$$

$$a = \bar{Y} - b\bar{X}$$

where $\bar{Y}$ and $\bar{X}$ are the respective mean values.

ILLUSTRATION
Trend in Civilian Employment

We will illustrate this procedure using the total level of civilian employment in the United States from 1978 through 1987. The time-series data are provided in the first two columns of Table 5-4. The results are $b = 1.68$ and $a = 95.35$, so that the trend equation is $\hat{Y}(X) = 95.35 + 1.68X$ with $X = 0$ at 1978.

TABLE 5-4

Computations for Fitting Trend Line to Employment Data

YEAR	YEAR IN TRANSFORMED UNITS X	TOTAL CIVILIAN EMPLOYMENT (millions) Y	XY	x^2
1978	0	96.1	0	0
1979	1	98.8	98.8	1
1980	2	99.3	198.6	4
1981	3	100.4	301.2	9
1982	4	99.5	398.0	16
1983	5	100.8	504.0	25
1984	6	105.0	630.0	36
1985	7	107.2	750.4	49
1986	8	109.6	876.8	64
1987	9	112.4	1,011.6	81
	$\overline{45}$ $= \Sigma X$	$\overline{1,029.1}$ $= \Sigma Y$	$\overline{4,769.4}$ $= \Sigma XY$	$\overline{285}$ $= \Sigma x^2$

$$n = 10 \qquad \bar{X} = 4.5 \qquad \bar{Y} = 102.91$$

$$b = \frac{\Sigma XY - n\bar{X}\bar{Y}}{\Sigma X^2 - n\bar{X}^2} = \frac{4,769.4 - 10(4.5)(102.91)}{285 - 10(4.5)^2} = 1.68$$

$$a = \bar{Y} - b\bar{X} = 102.91 - 1.68(4.5) = 95.35$$

$$\hat{Y}(X) = 95.35 + 1.68X \quad (X = 0 \text{ at } 1978)$$

Source: *Economic Report of the President*, 1989.

This equation indicates that the trend value for 1978 is an employment level of 95.35 million and that Y_t increases by 1.68 million per year. Because we have transformed the calendar years, it is important to indicate the base year: $X = 0$ at 1978. The trend line and time series obtained are plotted in Figure 5-11.

The trend line may be used to project the level of employment for 1988. We must use $X = 20$, because this year is $X = 1998 - 1978 = 20$ periods beyond the base year. From the trend equation, we project employment for 1998 as

$$\hat{Y}(X) = 95.35 + 1.68(20)$$

$$= 128.95 \text{ million}$$

The projected trend line is shown in Figure 5-11 as the portion of the line extending beyond the time periods actually observed. It is emphasized that the estimate of 128.95 million is an *extrapolation*; its validity depends on the assumption that the ensuing ten

FIGURE 5-11
Actual data and trend line for U.S. civilian employment.

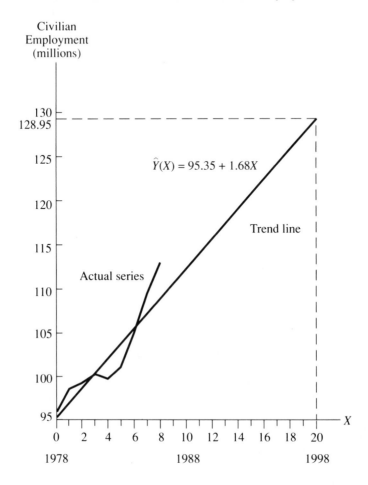

years has exhibited growth similar to that existing in the past. The assumption of linearity is perhaps a poor one to use here, for the labor force grows in the same manner as the population, which for the United States has been nonlinear. Had more past years been used, a curve with slope increasing over time would have provided a closer fit to the actual time-series data. Even then, good judgment would be an essential element.

Forecasting Sales Using a Trend Line

In business decision making, sales must often be forecast for planning purposes. Figure 5-12 shows the trend line for BriDent toothpaste using the data in Table 5-5.

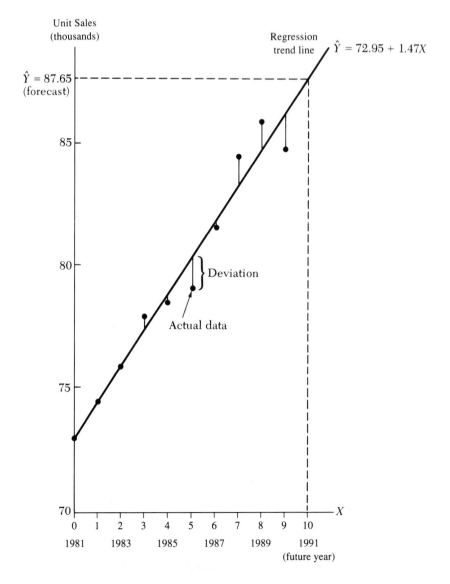

FIGURE 5-12
Regression line for trend in unit sales of BriDent toothpaste.

The regression coefficients are calculated as

$$b = \frac{3{,}701.2 - 10(4.5)(79.56)}{285 - 10(4.5)^2} = 1.47$$

$$\bar{X} = 45/10 = 4.5 \quad \text{and} \quad \bar{Y} = 795.6/10 = 79.56$$

$$a = 79.56 - 1.47(4.5) = 72.95$$

TABLE 5-5
Computations for Fitting Trend Line to BriDent Toothpaste Sales

YEAR	YEAR IN TRANSFORMED UNITS X	UNIT SALES (thousands) Y	XY	X^2
1981	0	72.9	0	0
1982	1	74.4	74.4	1
1983	2	75.9	151.8	4
1984	3	77.9	233.7	9
1985	4	78.6	314.4	16
1986	5	79.1	395.5	25
1987	6	81.7	490.2	36
1988	7	84.4	590.8	49
1989	8	85.9	687.2	64
1990	9	84.8	763.2	81
	$45 = \sum X$	$795.6 = \sum Y$	$3,701.2 = \sum XY$	$285 = \sum X^2$

The regression equation for the trend line in BriDent toothpaste sales (in thousands) is therefore

$$\hat{Y} = 72.95 + 1.47X \qquad (X = 0 \text{ for } 1981)$$

This equation indicates that for 1981 the trend value is sales of 72.95 thousand units and that Y_t increases by 1.47 thousand per year. Because the calendar years have been transformed, it is important to indicate the base year: $X = 0$ for 1981.

We can forecast BriDent sales for 1991 on the basis of the trend line. To do this, we must use $X = 10$, because this year is $X = 1991 - 1981 = 10$ periods beyond the base year. From the trend equation, we can project that 1991 BriDent sales will be

$$\hat{Y} = 72.95 + 1.47(10) = 87.65 \text{ thousand}$$

Nonlinear Trend: Exponential Trend Curve

For many time series, a straight line provides a poor fit to the data. A straight line assumes that Y_t increases (or decreases) by a constant amount each year. This assumption is not valid for most time series, where Y_t may change at either an increasing or decreasing rate.

ILLUSTRATION
Airlines Take Away Railroad Passengers

Figure 5-13 shows the time series for domestic airline fare-paying passengers from 1946 to 1969. Here, the number of passengers has increased at an increasing rate over time.

FIGURE 5-13
Airline and railroad passenger data.

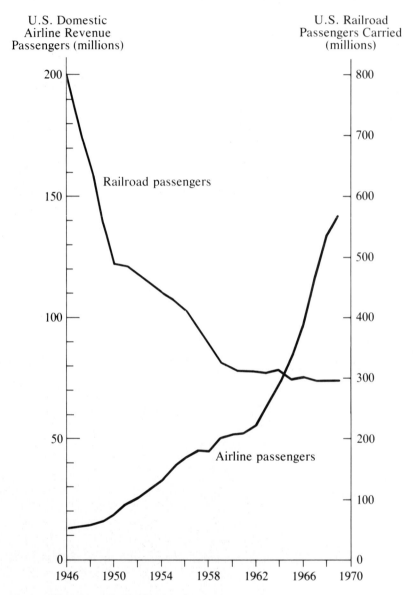

This is contrasted with the number of railroad passengers carried, also shown, for which the trend is decreasing but at a seemingly decreasing rate.

Part of the railroad passenger drop may be explained by a preference for airplane travel and part by wider use of the automobile. Few passenger trains run over long distances in the United States, and these have been declining so very fast that the government now runs railroad passenger service. The leveling-off at around 300 million passengers may be attributed to the growing significance of commuters, who now comprise a high proportion of rail passengers.

Either of these time series may be fitted by a J-shaped or exponential curve. For the airline passenger data, the equation would be of the form

$$\hat{Y}(X) = ab^X$$

where b is a constant (always positive) raised to the power of the number of time periods beyond the base year, and a is a constant multiple. The railroad passenger series has a negative exponential shape, so that the appropriate equation is

$$\hat{Y}(X) = ab^{-X}$$

where the minus sign before the X is used because $\hat{Y}(X)$ decreases for increasing X.

The advantage of using an exponential curve for fitting a trend is evident when taking the logarithm of both sides of $\hat{Y}(X) = ab^X$. When an exponential trend curve is converted in this manner, we have the equation for the **logarithmic trend line**.

$$\log \hat{Y}(X) = \log a + X \log b$$

This equation has the form of a straight line using $\log \hat{Y}(X)$ for the values on the vertical scale, with intercept of $\log a$ and slope of $\log b$.

Figure 5-14(a) shows the graph of the exponential trend curve $\hat{Y}(X) = 5(7)^X$, so that $a = 5$ and $b = 7$. We have

$$\log \hat{Y}(X) = \log 5 + X \log 7$$

$$= .6990 + .8451X$$

The logarithm values are obtained from Appendix Table G. The logarithmic trend line in Figure 5-14(b) is drawn with $\log \hat{Y}(X)$ as the dependent variable, so that the vertical axis is expressed in $\log Y$ units. Both the exponential trend curve and the corresponding logarithmic trend line provide the same information, and values of $\hat{Y}(X)$ may be obtained from the value for $\log \hat{Y}(X)$, and vice versa.

This suggests the possibility of fitting historical time-series data to an exponential trend curve, using the method of least squares to first find the logarithmic trend line. This may be accomplished by taking the logarithm of the observed time-series values Y, determining the regression coefficients $\log a$ and $\log b$. For this purpose, we modify the earlier equations for a and b, obtaining the **logarithmic regression coefficients**.

$$\log b = \frac{\sum X \log Y - \bar{X} \sum \log Y}{\sum X^2 - n\bar{X}^2}$$

$$\log a = \frac{\sum \log Y}{n} - \bar{X} \log b$$

These expressions replace a, b, and Y values by $\log a$, $\log b$, and $\log Y$.

FIGURE 5-14

Graphs of the exponential curve and corresponding logarithmic trend line.

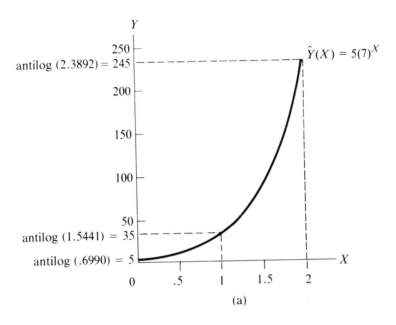

(a)

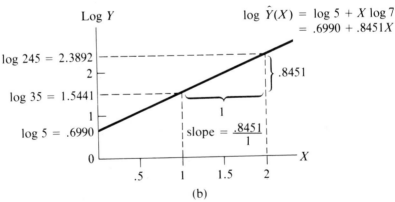

(b)

The procedure is illustrated by the calculations in Table 5-6 using more current airline passenger data. The logarithmic regression coefficients are

$$\log b = \frac{637.161 - 11.5(52.73077)}{4,324 - 24(11.5)^2} = .0267$$

$$\log a = (52.73077)/24 - 11.5(.0267) = 1.8901$$

The logarithmic trend line has the equation

$$\log \hat{Y}(X) = 1.8901 + .0267X$$

TABLE 5-6
Computations for Fitting Exponential Trend Curve to Airline Passenger Data

YEAR	YEARS BEYOND BASE PERIOD X	REVENUE PASSENGER ORIGIN (millions) Y	log Y	X log Y	X^2
1964	0	60.5	1.781755	0	0
1965	1	69.9	1.844477	1.844477	1
1966	2	79.4	1.899820	3.799641	4
1967	3	97.2	1.987666	5.962999	9
1968	4	118.8	2.074817	8.299266	16
1969	5	126.3	2.101404	10.50702	25
1970	6	122.9	2.089552	12.53731	36
1971	7	124.3	2.094471	14.66130	49
1972	8	136.6	2.135451	17.08360	64
1973	9	144.8	2.160769	19.44692	81
1974	10	148.0	2.170262	21.70262	100
1975	11	147.4	2.168497	23.85347	121
1976	12	160.5	2.205475	26.46570	144
1977	13	172.2	2.236033	29.06843	169
1978	14	196.1	2.292477	32.09469	196
1979	15	211.6	2.325516	34.88274	225
1980	16	222.0	2.346353	37.54165	256
1981	17	205.4	2.312600	39.31421	289
1982	18	208.4	2.318898	41.74016	324
1983	19	223.7	2.349666	44.64365	361
1984	20	242.4	2.384533	47.69065	400
1985	21	268.4	2.428783	51.00443	441
1986	22	300.9	2.478422	54.52529	484
1987	23	349.2	2.543074	58.49070	529
	276	4,136.9	52.73077	637.16100	4,324
	$=\Sigma X = 276$		$=\Sigma$ log Y	$=\Sigma X$ log Y	$=\Sigma X^2$

$n = 24$ $\bar{X} = 11.5$

SOURCE: *Moody's Transportation Manual*, 1988.

The values for a and b may be found by taking the antilogs of the above coefficients.

$$a = \text{antilog}(1.8901) = 77.64$$
$$b = \text{antilog}(.0267) = 1.063$$

The equation for the exponential trend curve is then

$$\hat{Y}(X) = 77.64(1.063)^X \quad (X = 0 \text{ at } 1964)$$

In computing trend values, the equation form $\hat{Y}(X) = ab^X$ would not ordinarily be used. Instead, the log $\hat{Y}(X)$ values would be calculated from the fitted logarithmic trend line. The $\hat{Y}(X)$ values may be easily obtained from the antilogs of these. For example, to find the $\hat{Y}(X)$ for 1987, we have $X = 1987 - 1964 = 23$. Thus,

$$\log \hat{Y}(23) = 1.8901 + .0267(23) = 2.5042$$

$$\hat{Y}(23) = \text{antilog}(2.5042) = 319.3 \text{ million passengers}$$

The value is fairly close to the actual figure of 349.2 million passengers carried in 1987.

The trend curve and the original time series are shown in Figure 5-15. This graph has an *arithmetic* vertical scale. The time-series behavior in the early years is hardly noticeable, whereas the points in later years rise by progressively larger amounts. So as not to exaggerate the importance of the later data, exponential trend curves are sometimes graphed with a compressed vertical scale called the **semilogarithmic**. The ruling on such a

FIGURE 5-15

Exponential trend curve and original data for airline passengers.

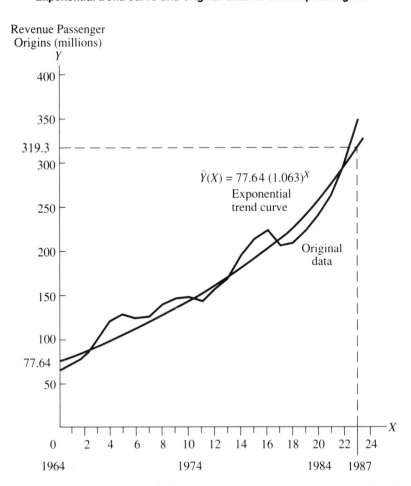

scale is made so that equal vertical distances correspond to values of Y that have increased by the same percentage. This is accomplished by spacing the scale marks at distances that correspond to the logarithm of their heights.

Figure 5-16 shows the airline passenger time series and trend plotted with a semilogarithmic vertical scale. The exponential trend curve plots as a straight line, indicating that the number of passengers grew at a constant percentage rate during the period shown. The value $b = 1.063$ indicates that this rate was .063, or 6.3%, per year.

Computer-Assisted Evaluations

The calculations for finding trend lines are tedious and error-prone when done by hand. The software package *QuickQuant*, will perform the necessary calculations for establishing regression coefficients.

QuickQuant will prove helpful when the trend relationship is best represented by a curve rather than a straight line. Equations may be found for a variety of nonlinear trend relationships using variable transformations followed by a computer-assisted regression.

FIGURE 5-16
Airline passenger data plotted on semilogarithmic graph paper.

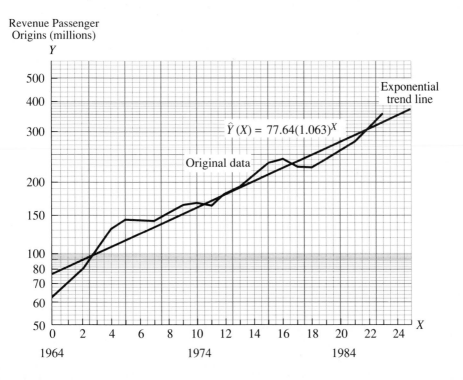

5-4 Forecasting Using Causal Models: Regression Analysis

Thus far, we have discussed forecasting procedures based only on extrapolations from time-series data, and until this point, our conclusions have been somewhat tenuous. Such forecasts—especially long-range ones—can be severely in error, because they are based on historical patterns that will not necessarily continue in the future. Often the cause for such patterns cannot even be identified.

Sometimes we can achieve more satisfactory forecasts by using a causal model that explains the dependent forecast variable in terms of the level for one or more predictor variables (rather than simply in terms of a period of time). Ideal predictors *lead* (have values that are determined in advance of) the main variable. Thus, a student's success at college might be predicted from his or her high school grade point average. Predictions of future growth in GNP might be based on today's prices, level of employment, and plant capacities. Or a product's sales forecast might be determined from its current share of the market and planned advertising expenditures.

Table 5-7 shows the observations of distances and transportation times for a sample of ten rail shipments made by an automobile parts supplier. These data will be used to arrive at predictions of transit times for future shipments.

TABLE 5-7
Sample Observations of Rail Distance and Transportation Times for Ten Shipments by a Parts Supplier

CUSTOMER	RAIL DISTANCE TO DESTINATION X	TRANSPORTATION TIME (days) Y
1. Muller Auto Supply	210	5
2. Taylor Ford	290	7
3. Auto Supply House	350	6
4. Parts 'n' Spares	480	11
5. Jones & Sons	490	8
6. A. Hausman	730	11
7. Des Moines Parts	780	12
8. Pete's Parts	850	8
9. Smith Dodge	920	15
10. Gulf Distributors	1,010	12

Using the values in Table 5-7, the means, intermediate sums of columns, sums of products, and sums of squares were computed. From these, we find the slope b for the estimated regression line.

$$b = \frac{\sum XY - n\bar{X}\bar{Y}}{\sum X^2 - n\bar{X}^2} = \frac{64,490 - 10(611.0)(9.5)}{4,451,500 - 10(611.0)^2}$$

$$= \frac{6,445}{718,290} = .00897$$

Substituting $b = .00897$, we obtain the intercept.

$$a = \bar{Y} - b\bar{X} = 9.500 - .00897(611.0)$$
$$= 9.500 - 5.481 = 4.019$$

Thus, we have determined the following equation for the estimated regression line graphed in Figure 5-17.

$$\hat{Y}(X) = 4.019 + .00897X$$

We may now use the above regression equation to predict the transportation time $\hat{Y}(X)$ for a shipment of known rail distance X from the parts supplier's plant. For instance,

FIGURE 5-17
Fitting the regression line to the parts supplier's data.

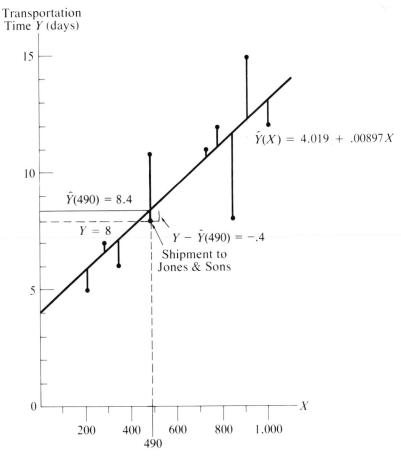

Rail Distance to Destination (miles)

when $X = 490$, we have

$$\hat{Y}(490) = 4.019 + .00897(490)$$

$$= 8.4 \text{ days}$$

Thus, the prediction for the transportation time to a customer 490 miles away is $\hat{Y}(490) = 8.4$ days.

The Least-Squares Criterion

The estimated regression coefficients a and b are chosen so that the following sum is minimized.

$$\sum [Y - \hat{Y}(X)]^2 = \sum [Y - a - bX]^2$$

The resulting regression line is fit to the data so that the sum of the *squares* of the *vertical deviations* separating the points from the line will be a minimum. Figure 5-17 shows how vertical deviations relate to their regression line in the scatter diagram for the parts supplier's data. The deviations are the lengths of the vertical lines that connect each point to the regression line.

To explain how this procedure may be interpreted, we investigate the shipment to Jones & Sons at a distance of $X = 490$ miles from the supplier's plant. Our data show that $Y = 8$ days were required for the shipment to arrive. This transportation time is represented on the graph by the vertical distance to the corresponding data point along the dashed line from the X axis at $X = 490$. The predicted or estimated transportation time for the *next* shipment to Jones & Sons equals the vertical distance all the way up to the regression line, a total of $\hat{Y}(X) = \hat{Y}(490) = 8.4$ days. The difference between the observed transportation time, $Y = 8$ days, and the predicted value for Y is the deviation $Y - \hat{Y}(X) = Y - \hat{Y}(490) = 8 - 8.4 = -.4$ days. This is represented by the vertical line segment connecting the point to the regression line. The vertical deviation represents the amount of *error associated with using the regression line to predict* a future shipment's transportation time. We want to find the values of a and b that will minimize the sum of the squares of these vertical deviations (or prediction errors).

One reason for minimizing the sum of the *squared* vertical deviations is that some of the deviations are negative and others are positive. For any set of data, a great many lines can be drawn for which the sum of the unsquared deviations is zero, but most of these lines would fit the data poorly.

Regression analysis employs inferential statistics in reaching conclusions from the observed values, which are themselves ordinarily sample data. Thus, a and b are only *estimates* of the true regression parameters, and the computed values may deviate from the true levels. In order to use statistical methodology in qualifying these estimates, certain assumptions must be made regarding the nature of the X-Y relationship. Among these is the assumption that the variability in Y's is constant, unaffected by the level for X. Another assumption is that the levels for X are nonrandom. Further assumptions of statistical regression analysis—and the associated pitfalls—will be discussed shortly.

Regression Variation and Residuals

Figure 5-18 shows the regression line found earlier for the parts supplier's original transportation times. Suppose the parts supplier predicts how long the next order will take to ship without using that line. That sample mean would then give a suitable estimate, providing the following

$$\bar{Y} = 9.5 \text{ days} \qquad \text{(prediction without regression)}$$

The above estimate ignores how far the shipment will go. Suppose that this shipment goes to Smith Dodge, for which the distance is known to be $X = 920$ miles. This information allows the supplier to make a better forecast,

$$\hat{Y}(920) = 12.3 \text{ days} \qquad \text{(prediction using regression line)}$$

FIGURE 5-18
Illustration of total, explained, and unexplained variation in Y.

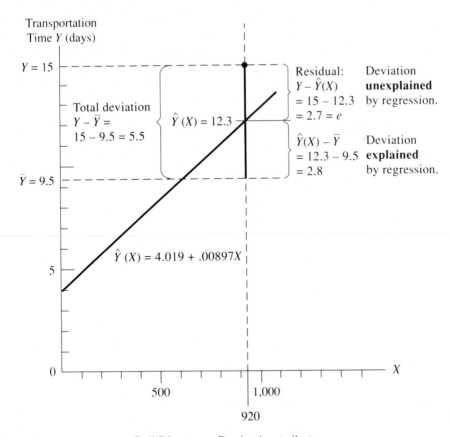

Rail Distance to Destination (miles)

Although the actual time of the next shipment to Smith Dodge is uncertain, it can be represented by the time originally observed in the sample,

$$Y = 15.0 \text{ days} \qquad \text{(observed time)}$$

The first prediction falls wide of the mark, providing a **total deviation** of $Y - \bar{Y} = 15.0 - 9.5 = 5.5$ days, none of which can be explained. The second prediction is better since it yields a smaller prediction error of $Y - \hat{Y}(X) = 15.0 - 12.3 = 2.7$ days. By using the regression line, the total error is reduced by the amount $\hat{Y}(X) - \bar{Y} = 12.3 - 9.5 = 2.8$ days. Thus, part of the total error may be attributed to using the regression line, so that $\hat{Y}(X) - \bar{Y} = 2.8$ days is the **explained deviation**. The remaining portion of the error is due to unidentifiable causes, so that $Y - \hat{Y}(X) = 2.7$ days is an **unexplained deviation**. The total deviation of the observed Y may then be expressed as

$$[Y - \bar{Y}] = [\hat{Y}(X) - \bar{Y}] + [Y - \hat{Y}(X)]$$

Stated in words, we have

$$\text{Total deviation} = \text{Explained deviation} + \text{Unexplained deviation}$$

The unexplained deviations are often referred to as the **residuals** and are defined by the differences

$$e_i = Y_i - \hat{Y}(X_i)$$

By squaring the above deviations and then summing, we extend the relationship to the entire collection of observations.

$$
\begin{array}{ccccc}
\text{Total} & & \text{Explained} & & \text{Unexplained} \\
\text{variation} & = & \text{variation} & + & \text{variation}
\end{array}
$$

$$\sum [Y - \bar{Y}]^2 = \sum [\hat{Y}(X) - \bar{Y}]^2 + \sum [Y - \hat{Y}(X)]^2$$

$$
\begin{array}{ccccc}
SSTO & = & SSR & + & SSE
\end{array}
$$

The total variation expresses the amount that the individual Y's deviate from their mean Y without regard to the regression relationship. The result is referred to as the **total sum of squares**.

$$SSTO = \sum [Y - \bar{Y}]^2$$

As shown in Figure 5-18, the distance between Y and the regression line at X explains a portion of the deviation in the observed Y from its mean $\bar{Y}$. The explained variation summarizes the collective squared distances between the regression line $\hat{Y}(X)$ and the sample mean $\bar{Y}$. This is expressed by the **regression sum of squares**.

$$SSR = \sum [\hat{Y}(X) - \bar{Y}]^2$$

The final component of total variation involves the residuals and measures the overall observed error in the sample. This is the **error sum of squares**.

$$SSE = \sum [Y - \hat{Y}(X)]^2$$

The method of least squares selects the regression coefficients a and b, so that the above quantity is minimized. The above term expresses the collective dispersion in Y about the regression line. The regression line leaves those deviations *unexplained*.

The Coefficient of Determination and Correlation Coefficient

Rearranging the terms, the identity

$$\frac{\text{Explained}}{\text{variation}} = \frac{\text{Total}}{\text{variation}} - \frac{\text{Unexplained}}{\text{variation}}$$

$$SSR \quad = \quad SSTO \quad - \quad SSE$$

is used to construct a useful index. Dividing the explained variation by the total variation provides the **sample coefficient of determination**. The following expression applies.

$$r^2 = \frac{\text{Explained variation}}{\text{Total variation}} = \frac{SSTO - SSE}{SSTO} = \frac{\sum [Y - \bar{Y}]^2 - \sum [Y - \hat{Y}(X)]^2}{\sum [Y - \bar{Y}]^2}$$

An equivalent expression is

$$r^2 = \frac{\text{Explained variation}}{\text{Total variation}} = 1 - \frac{\sum [Y - \hat{Y}(X)]^2}{\sum [Y - \bar{Y}]^2}$$

The sample coefficient of determination expresses the proportion of the total variation in Y explained by the regression line.

The coefficient of determination for the parts supplier's data is $r^2 = .64$, indicating that the regression line explains 64% of the variation in transportation time.

A related index is the **sample correlation coefficient** r. The following relationship applies.

$$\text{Coefficient of determination} = (\text{Correlation coefficient})^2$$

The sign for r may be positive (when the slope of the regression line is positive, and $b > 0$) or negative (when $b < 0$). For the parts supplier illustration, the sample correlation coefficient is

$$r = \sqrt{.64} = +.80$$

The above relationship provides another perspective on how the coefficient of determination measures the strength of association between X and Y. In the special case when all the data points fall directly on the regression line, so that there is a perfect correlation and $r = +1$ or $r = -1$, all of the variation in Y is explained and r must then be equal to one. At the other extreme, a horizontal regression line is obtained when X and Y exhibit zero correlation, so that all of the variation in Y is unexplained and r^2 must then be equal to zero.

Forecasting Accuracy in Regression Analysis

We have seen that the mean squared error MSE may be used to compare two sets of forecasts in terms of how well they fit the actual data. In regression evaluations the MSE is computed from

$$MSE = \frac{\sum [Y - \hat{Y}]^2}{n - m} = \frac{\sum e^2}{n - m}$$

where n denotes the number of observations (data points) and m represents the number of variables used.

Table 5-8 shows the MSE calculations for the parts supplier's illustration. There, a value of $MSE = 4.084$ applies to the data. Because the quantity is in units of squared days, it is common to take the square root, giving the same information in original units.

$$\sqrt{MSE} = \sqrt{4.084} = 2.02 \text{ days}$$

TABLE 5-8
MSE Calculations for the Parts Supplier's Data

CUSTOMER	RAIL DISTANCE TO DESTINATION X	TRANSPORTATION TIME (days) Y	PREDICTED TIME FROM REGRESSION LINE $\hat{Y}(X) = 4.019 + .00897X$	ERROR OR RESIDUAL $e = Y - \hat{Y}(X)$	SQUARED ERROR $e^2 = [Y - \hat{Y}(X)]^2$
1	210	5	5.9027	− .9027	.8149
2	290	7	6.6203	.3797	.1442
3	350	6	7.1585	−1.1585	1.3421
4	480	11	8.3246	2.6754	7.1578
5	490	8	8.4143	− .4143	.1716
6	730	11	10.5671	.4329	.1874
7	780	12	11.0156	.9844	.9690
8	850	8	11.6435	−3.6435	13.2751
9	920	15	12.2714	2.7286	7.4453
10	1,010	12	13.0787	−1.0787	1.1636
					32.6710

$$MSE = \frac{32.6710}{10 - 2} = 4.084$$

The above calculation gives easier-to-use values that are smaller in size. This quantity is often referred to as the **standard error of the estimate**.

Under the theoretical assumptions of the regression model, *MSE* is a statistical estimator of the variance for the probability distribution in residuals that might be obtained when they are computed using the true regression line.

A second mean square is employed in regression analysis. The **regression mean square** is found from

$$MSR = \frac{SSR}{m-1}$$

The above quantity may be used in conjunction with *MSE* to perform a key statistical test. That test is based on the statistic

$$F = \frac{MSR}{MSE}$$

which allows analysts to find the probability that the observed regression line could have been obtained when the true regression coefficient for the independent variable(s) is (are) in fact zero.

Multiple Regression Analysis

Predictions made from a regression line relating Y to a single independent variable are categorized as **simple regression analysis**. The procedure may be extended, so that Y is related simultaneously to several independent predictors. The resulting predictions involve **multiple regression analysis**. Multiple regression can dramatically improve forecasting accuracy.

The sample data in Table 5-9 may be used to predict the sales for retail outlets of the Deuce Hardware chain. In doing this, two possible independent predictor variables are available for each store, floorspace X_1 and monthly advertising expenditures X_2. A simple regression using only X_1 as the predictor provides the following equation.

$$\hat{Y}(X_1) = 3{,}895 + 6.66X_1$$

We will now consider how an expanded multiple regression using *both* X_1 and X_2 as predictors might provide improved sales predictions.

The essential advantage of considering two or more independent variables is that it permits greater use of available information. For example, a regression line that expresses a new store's sales in terms of the population of the city it serves should yield a poorer sales forecast than an equation that also considers median income, number of nearby competitors, and the local unemployment rate. A plant manager ought to predict more precisely the cost of processing a new order if he considers, in addition to the size of the order, the total volume of orders, his current staffing levels, and the production capacity of available equipment. A marketing manager ought to gauge more finely the sales

TABLE 5-9

**Sales, Floorspace, and Advertising Expenditure Data
for Deuce Hardware Store**

STORE	MONTHLY SALES Y	FLOORSPACE (square feet) X_1	MONTHLY ADVERTISING EXPENDITURE X_2
1	$20,100	3,050	$350
2	14,900	1,300	980
3	16,800	1,890	830
4	9,100	1,750	760
5	15,500	1,010	930
6	26,700	2,690	770
7	34,600	4,210	440
8	7,200	1,950	570
9	21,800	2,830	310
10	23,400	2,030	920

response to a magazine advertisement if she considers, in addition to the magazine's circulation, the demographical features of its readers, such as median age, median income, and proportion of urban readers.

Linear multiple regression analysis involves two or more independent variables. In the case of two independent variables, denoted by X_1 and X_2, the **estimated multiple regression equation** is

$$\hat{Y} = a + b_1 X_1 + b_2 X_2$$

Here, two independent variables and one dependent variable, or a total of three variables, are considered. The sample data will consist of three values for each sample unit observed, so that a scatter diagram of these observations will be three dimensional.

To explain how multiple regression data can be portrayed in three dimensions, we will draw an analogy using the walls and floor of a room. Letting a corner of the room represent the case when all three variables have a value of zero, the data points may be represented by suspending marbles in space at various distances from the floor and the two walls. A marble's height above the floor can be the value of Y for that observation. Its distance along the wall on the right then measures the observed value of X_1, and its distance along the wall on the left expresses the observed value of X_2. Figure 5-19 is a pictorial representation of a three-dimensional scatter for a hypothetical set of data.

The regression equation corresponds to a plane. This plane must be slanted in such a way that it provides the best least-squares fit to the sample data. The three-dimensional surface that results is the **regression plane**. Slanting this plane can be compared to determining how to position a pane of glass through the suspended marbles so that its incline approximates the incline of the pattern of the scatter. As with the regression line, a, b_1, and b_2 are chosen in such a way that the vertical deviations between the actual values and the regression plane are minimized.

FIGURE 5-19
A regression plane for multiple regression using three variables.

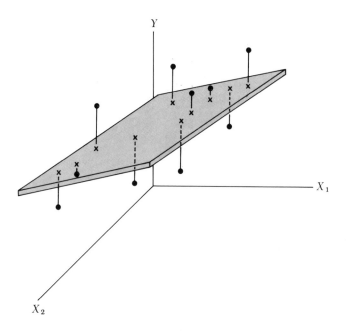

To illustrate, we will consider our Deuce Hardware data again. Monthly sales Y can now be predicted using floorspace X_1 and daily advertising expenditure X_2 as a set of independent variables. A computer solution provides the following values (rounded).

$$a = -22{,}979$$

$$b_1 = 11.42$$

$$b_2 = 23.41$$

The values of a, b_1, and b_2 provide the estimated multiple regression equation

$$\hat{Y} = -22{,}979 + 11.42X_1 + 23.41X_2$$

which can be used to forecast the sales of a particular store. Suppose a new store is to be built that will have 2,500 square feet of floorspace and spend $750 a month on advertising. The forecast sales level is then

$$\hat{Y} = -\$22{,}979 + 11.42(2{,}500) + 23.41(750)$$

$$= \$23{,}129$$

The above results were obtained using *QuickQuant*. A detailed printout is shown in Figure 5-20. In addition to a, b_1, and b_2, the report provides the mean and standard deviation for Y, X_1, and X_2. Also given are various sample correlation coefficients. The

FIGURE 5-20

QuickQuant printout for a multiple regression run, using the Deuce Hardware Store data.

```
=============================================================================
                             QuickQuant Report
                            REGRESSION ANALYSIS
-----------------------------------------------------------------------------
PROBLEM: Deuce Hardware Store                           Date: 03-08-1990
                                                              Larry

                            PROBLEM DATA
          ------------------------------------------------
                  : VARIABLE
                  :    1        2        3
          Obs.  : Flrspace  Advert.   Sales
          ------------------------------------------------
             1 :   3050       350      20100
             2 :   1300       980      14900
             3 :   1890       830      16800
             4 :   1750       760       9100
             5 :   1010       930      15500
             6 :   2690       770      26700
             7 :   4210       440      34600
             8 :   1950       570       7200
             9 :   2820       310      21800
            10 :   2030       920      23400
          ------------------------------------------------
          Total:  22700      6860     190100
          Mean :   2270       686      19010
          S.Dev:  940.1064  249.9422  8179.981
          ------------------------------------------------


                         REGRESSION RESULTS

Vari-              Regression              Standard   Correlation
able    Name       Coefficient   Mean     Deviation   X vs. Y       t       Prob.
-------------------------------------------------------------------------------------
X1 Flrspace        11.38221      2270     940.1064    .765592    4.944583  .0010
X2 Advert.         23.24029       686     249.9422   -.2893151   2.684153  .0240
Y3 Sales                        19010     8179.981

Intercept:  -22770.44    Coeff. of Det.:   .7960476    F Statistic:  13.66
Number Observ.:   10     St. Error Est.:  4188.793          Prob.:   .0079

-------------------------------------------------------------------------------------
```

sample coefficient of determination for this problem is $r^2 = .798$ and the mean squared error is $MSE = 13,780,000$.

The F statistic is computed to be 13.83. Directly below that quantity in the printout is the probability, .0079, that such a regression result could have been obtained when the true regression coefficients are both zero. Further data, shown in the last columns of the table, provide computed t values and analogous probabilities for the individual regression coefficients.

Comparison of Simple and Multiple Regression

Table 5-10 shows the Deuce Hardware sales forecasts made by applying both simple and multiple regression to the actual data. Note that multiple regression provides greater

TABLE 5-10

Comparison of Forecasting Errors Using Simple and Multiple Regression

			SIMPLE REGRESSION		MULTIPLE REGRESSION	
ACTUAL DATA			Forecast	Error	Forecast	Error
X_1	X_2	Y	$\hat{Y}$	$Y - \hat{Y}$	$\hat{Y}$	$Y - \hat{Y}$
3,050	350	20,100	24,195	−4,095	20,036	64
1,300	980	14,900	12,547	2,353	14,809	91
1,890	830	16,800	16,474	326	18,032	−1,232
1,750	760	9,100	15,542	−6,442	14,795	−5,695
1,010	930	15,500	10,617	4,883	10,327	5,173
2,690	770	26,700	21,799	4,901	25,760	940
4,210	440	34,600	31,915	2,685	35,386	−786
1,950	570	7,200	16,874	−9,673	12,629	−5,429
2,830	310	21,800	22,731	−931	16,588	5,213
2,030	920	23,400	17,406	5,994	21,738	1,663
			$MSE = 31,170,000$		$MSE = 13,780,000$	

accuracy, because the forecasting errors tend to the smaller when this procedure is used. Including the second predictor variable (advertising expenditure) allows us to "explain" more variation in sales Y.

QuickQuant can accommodate multiple regressions in higher dimensions, so that as many as 10 or 15 independent X's might be used in making predictions. It is not clear whether including more variables generally reduces forecasting error. In some cases, adding independent variables can even confuse the analysis. Independent variables must be chosen with care and must have some rational basis for affecting Y.

Special Problems in Causal Regression Analysis

In order for probability to be used in qualifying regression results, certain assumptions must apply. In addition to those mentioned earlier, a key theoretical requirement is that the residual values (error terms) be normally distributed with mean zero and constant variance (regardless of the level for X). When those ideal conditions do not apply, the price paid is wrongful probabilities.

Time-series data may present special difficulties arising from a **serial correlation** between observations made in successive time periods. A serial correlation or **autocorrelation** exists whenever there is a tendency for similar values to follow the earlier number. For example, the following successive monthly seasonally adjusted unemployment rates show a serial correlation.

7.3 7.4 7.6 7.5 7.3 7.1 7.0 6.9 6.9 7.1 7.2 7.3

Notice that each successive monthly rate lies close to the preceding level, reflecting the inertia in the economy.

Multiple regression presents additional challenges. A potential problem can arise when two independent variables are highly correlated. For example, consider retail sales and foot traffic or magazine advertising revenue and number of pages. In a three-variable situation, such a relationship would provide sample data that are scattered closely about a single line lying inside the least-squares regression plane. Although the estimated regression equation can be found with no special difficulty when X_1 and X_2 are highly correlated, a second set of sample observations may result in drastically different regression coefficients, even when the second line of scatter is nearly identical to the first one. Because many different regression planes can contain the same line, the regression exhibits **multicollinearity**. Including a third independent variable might eliminate the problem created by the multicollinearity.

Further Considerations

We have barely scratched the surface of regression analysis. For example, we have entirely avoided an examination of nonlinear relationships. Forecasts made from the regression line or plane can be qualified in a statistical sense by means of confidence intervals. The procedures involved, however, are based on formidable theoretical assumptions that are too complex to discuss here. Regression analysis is often accompanied by **correlation analysis**, where the major concern is how strongly the variables are related. Advanced techniques, such as **stepwise multiple regression**, help determine not only the regression equation but also the particular predictor variables it is best to include. An area of statistics and economics called **econometrics** considers causal models in great depth and wide breadth. References dealing with this topic are provided in the bibliography.

5-5 Polynomial Regression

We have seen that nonlinear relationships may portray trend more accurately. Nonlinearities exist in causal relationships and one way to accommodate nonlinearity is to use a logarithmic transformation. That approach can be useful when the Y's tend to increase with greater levels for X. But logarithms are not suitable for all nonlinear relationships.

Multiple regression procedures may be adapted by applying the least-squares criterion to obtain curves of an appropriate shape. The resulting regression equations are called **polynomials**. The functions express the dependent variable as a combination of the independent variable X raised to various powers. Here, we may extend the least-squares method to establish polynomial regression equations in the following forms.

$$\hat{Y} = a + b_1 X + b_2 X^2 \qquad \text{(parabola)}$$

$$\hat{Y} = a + b_1 X + b_2 X^2 + b_3 X^3 \qquad \text{(third-degree polynomial)}$$

(Although higher-degree polynomials can be accommodated in a regression analysis, in business applications, we do not ordinarily encounter data for which those polynomials are appropriate.)

The type of curve selected to best fit the data depends on the form of the scatter diagram, but there may be a previously established basis for selecting a particular shape.

Consider the curve shown in Figure 5-21 for an assembly line experiment, where the data points represent productivity index Y obtained for various assembly line speeds X. The data suggest the parabolic curve plotted on the graph. This type of curve best fits the data given in Table 5-11 for a multiple regression using $X_1 = X$ and $X_2 = X^2$ as the dependent variables. The estimated regression equation assumes the form

$$\hat{Y} = 13.4 + 265.5X - 267.3X^2$$

At slow or fast levels of line speed, we see that productivity is very low. Maximum productivity occurs at a level of around .50 mph. A **parabola** is the proper form to use when the underlying curve is everywhere convex or everywhere concave in shape, achieving a readily identifiable maximum or minimum level.

The second type of curve form is the **third-degree polynomial**. It is the proper form to use when an *inflection point* is present in the underlying shape. The plotted data points are best fitted by a curve that shows a progression from concave to convex, or vice versa. Such

FIGURE 5-21
Regression parabola for the assembly line experiment.

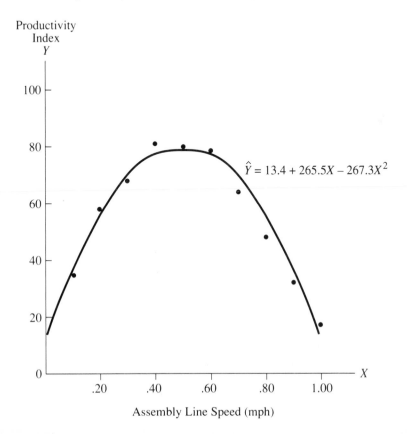

TABLE 5-11

Sample Data for the Assembly Line Experiment

PRODUCTIVITY INDEX Y	LINE SPEED (miles per hour) $X_1 = X$	$X_2 = X^2$
77	.60	.3600
81	.40	.1600
35	.10	.0100
80	.50	.2500
64	.75	.5625
48	.80	.6400
32	.90	.8100
68	.30	.0900
57	.20	.0400
17	1.00	1.0000

a curve will have a slope that steadily increases before it decreases, or that steadily decreases before it increases.

In Figure 5-22, the total cost Y of production for a plant is plotted against the volume X. As suggested by the data in the figure, this economic production function assumes the form of a common shape. Here, data points have been obtained for the various levels of production activity in the plant. The curve best fits the data given in Table 5-12 for a multiple regression using $X_1 = X$, $X_2 = X^2$, and $X_3 = X^3$ as the independent variables.

TABLE 5-12

Sample Data for the Production Function

TOTAL COST Y	PRODUCTION QUANTITY $X_1 = X$	$X_2 = X^2$	$X_3 = X^3$
$ 5,680	100	10,000	1,000,000
9,200	185	34,225	6,331,625
14,100	350	122,500	42,875,000
14,800	390	152,100	59,319,000
22,900	520	270,400	140,608,000
19,800	490	240,100	117,649,000
26,100	550	302,500	166,375,000
39,600	640	409,600	262,144,000
11,300	250	62,500	15,625,000
14,500	370	136,900	50,653,000
46,200	670	448,900	300,763,000
62,100	690	476,100	328,509,000
81,300	720	518,400	373,248,000
16,000	440	193,600	85,184,000
12,800	320	102,400	32,768,000

FIGURE 5-22
Third-degree polynomial regression for the production function of a plant.

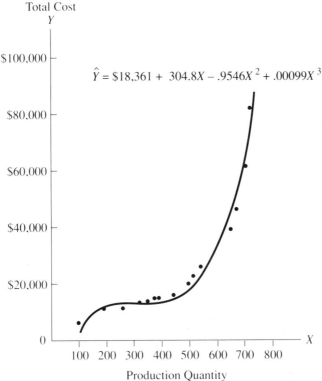

The estimated regression equation is

$$\hat{Y} = -\$18{,}361 + 304.8X - .9546X^2 + .00099X^3$$

At low levels of production activity, this function reflects *decreasing marginal cost* (slope) as greater volumes of production are achieved. But a point is reached at around 400 units where all factors are operating most efficiently and greater volume can only be achieved at a disproportionately higher cost. There the plant reaches its maximum level of economic productivity, after which the increase in volume reduces incremental efficiency and the curve shows increasing marginal cost at an increasing rate.

5-6 Forecasting Using Seasonal Indexes

In this section, we will examine a procedure for isolating seasonal fluctuations in time-series data. Identifying seasonal patterns is a necessary first step in short-range planning. The management of a firm whose business drops in May is not alarmed if it is only the beginning of an annual seasonal trough. Likewise, government economists recognize that the consumer price index will rise or fall in certain months solely due to the influence of seasonal factors, such as changing varieties of produce on the market. To monitor the performance of a business or an economy, it is useful to "deseasonalize" time-series data to determine whether a current drop or rise is greater than normal.

Ratio-to-Moving-Average Method

The **ratio-to-moving-average method** is widely used to isolate seasonal fluctuations. Beginning with the actual time series, the trend and cyclical elements are isolated together in what is referred to as a "smoothed" time series. The isolation of the long-term elements is accomplished by means of **four-quarter moving averages**.

In the context of the classical time-series model, the ratio-to-moving-average method is summarized by the expression

$$\frac{Y_t}{\text{Moving average}} = \frac{T_t \times C_t \times S_t \times I_t}{T_t \times C_t} = S_t \times I_t$$

The moving average provides both trend and cycle, so that $T_t \times C_t$ is obtained for each time period. Dividing Y_t by the moving average is therefore equivalent to canceling the $T_t \times C_t$ terms from the multiplicative model, so that only the seasonal and irregular components, expressed by $S_t \times I_t$, remain.

The procedure is carried out in a number of steps. First, the first four successive values in the original time series are summed. That total is divided by 4 to get the first four-quarter moving average, which represents one complete year. These computations are repeated, except the initial quarter is dropped and the fifth is added, so that the second four-quarter average also represents a full year. The process is continued until you have run out of new quarters. The final step is to center the data by computing for each period the **centered moving average**. This is accomplished by averaging each successive pair of four-quarter averages.

To illustrate the procedure, Table 5-13 provides data for Haskin-Dobbins ice cream sales (in thousands of gallons). The first four-quarter average is found by adding the actual sales for the quarters of 1986 and dividing by 4.

$$\frac{5,100 + 9,800 + 15,200 + 11,300}{4} = 10,350$$

This value corresponds to that point in time when the Spring 1986 quarter ends and the Summer 1986 quarter begins—midnight, June 30, 1986.

The second four-quarter average is found by dropping sales for Winter 1986 and including the figure for Winter 1987.

$$\frac{9,800 + 15,200 + 11,300 + 6,100}{4} = 10,600$$

TABLE 5-13
Time-Series for Haskin-Dobbins Data

(1)	(2)	(3) FOUR-QUARTER MOVING AVERAGE	(4) CENTERED MOVING AVERAGE	(5) ORIGINAL AS A PERCENTAGE OF MOVING AVERAGE	(6) SEASONAL INDEX
QUARTER	SALES				
1986					
Winter	5,100				53.58
Spring	9,800				101.04
		10,350			
Summer	15,200		10,475	145.11	144.97
		10,600			
Fall	11,300		10,913	103.55	100.40
		11,225			
1987					
Winter	6,100		11,625	52.47	53.58
		12,025			
Spring	12,300		12,263	100.30	101.04
		12,500			
Summer	18,400		12,638	145.59	144.97
		12,775			
Fall	13,200		13,000	101.54	100.40
		13,225			
1988					
Winter	7,200		13,513	53.28	53.58
		13,800			
Spring	14,100		14,000	100.71	101.04
		14,200			
Summer	20,700		14,375	144.00	144.97
		14,550			
Fall	14,800		14,850	99.66	100.40
		15,150			
1989					
Winter	8,600		15,575	55.22	53.58
		16,000			
Spring	16,500		16,213	101.77	101.04
		16,425			
Summer	24,100		16,575	145.40	144.97
		16,725			
Fall	16,500		17,088	96.56	100.40
		17,450			
1990					
Winter	9,800		18,113	54.10	53.58
		18,775			
Spring	19,400		18,988	102.17	101.04
		19,200			
Summer	29,400				144.97
Fall	18,200				100.40

As before, this value applies to the point in time separating Summer 1986 from Fall 1986—midnight, September 30. Since the values apply between quarters, the column of four-quarter averages is positioned one-half line off the rest of the table.

Column (4) contains the centered moving averages. The first of these is found by averaging the first two four-quarter averages.

$$\frac{10,350 + 10,600}{2} = 10,475$$

This value applies to the midpoint of Summer 1986, coinciding in time with the original data.

The irregular component must be removed before a final set of seasonal indexes can be obtained. This is accomplished by first finding for each season the *median* percentage of moving average for the applicable quarters. (Although the mean could be used, the median is preferred because it is less affected by unusually large or small values.) Then the median percentages are adjusted so that the final indexes average to 100% for the entire year.

The first **percentage of moving average** is computed for Summer 1986 by dividing the original sales level of 15,200 by that quarter's centered moving average of 10,475. This is then multiplied by 100.

$$\frac{15,200}{10,475} \times 100 = 145.11$$

Sales for Summer 1986 were thus 145.11% of the trend and cyclical components.

Table 5-14 shows all the percentages of moving averages.

There are four percentages for each quarter, with the median obtained by averaging the middle-sized two. The sum of the medians is 400.79. To obtain indexes that sum to 400% (and that average to 100% throughout the year), each median is multiplied by 400/400.79. These seasonal indexes provide the S_t values for ice cream sales.

When the original time series is given by months, the general procedures illustrated for quarterly data can also be applied. A year's worth of successive monthly figures is averaged to provide twelve-month moving averages. Each successive pair of these is then averaged to obtain the **twelve-month centered moving average**. The indexes must sum to 1,200%.

TABLE 5-14
Calculation of Seasonal Indexes for Haskin-Dobbins Sales

		QUARTER			
YEAR		Winter	Spring	Summer	Fall
1986				145.11	103.55
1987		52.47	100.30	145.59	101.54
1988		53.28	100.71	144.00	99.66
1989		55.22	101.77	145.40	96.56
1990		54.10	102.17		
	Median	53.69	101.24	145.26	100.60

Sum of medians = 400.79

$$\text{Seasonal index} = \text{Median} \times \frac{400}{400.79}$$

		53.58	101.04	144.97	100.40

Making the Forecast

Seasonal indexes are useful in making short-term forecasts. First, a trend over the annual period is determined, and then seasonal adjustments are made for each period within the year. For example, suppose that the managers of a department store who wish to forecast monthly sales for 1991 determine the following trend equation:

$$\hat{Y} = 1,025,000 + 50,000X$$

where X is in months and $X = 0$ for January 15, 1991. Calculations of the monthly forecasts for department store sales are provided in Table 5-15. The 12 monthly seasonal indexes appear in column (3), and the monthly sales trend levels are calculated in column (4) from the managers' trend equation. For January, the trend value of $1,025,000 is multiplied by 56.7% to obtain the forecast sales of $581,175. The sales forecasts for all 12 months are listed in column (5).

Computer-Assisted Evaluations

The computations for finding seasonal indexes and deseasonalizing the time-series data are tedious. Computer assistance would be helpful. As with the trend line, a personal computer software package like *QuickQuant* may be used to do all of these calculations.

TABLE 5-15
Calculations of the Monthly Forecasts for Department Store Sales

(1) MONTH	(2) X	(3) SEASONAL INDEX	(4) MONTHLY SALES TREND LEVEL $\hat{Y}$	(5) MONTHLY SALES FORECAST [(3) × (4)] ÷ 100
January	0	56.7	$1,025,000	$ 581,175
February	1	64.5	1,075,000	693,375
March	2	62.1	1,125,000	698,625
April	3	99.9	1,175,000	1,173,825
May	4	83.6	1,225,000	1,024,100
June	5	67.4	1,275,000	859,350
July	6	58.2	1,325,000	771,150
August	7	100.1	1,375,000	1,376,375
September	8	110.6	1,425,000	1,576,050
October	9	137.7	1,475,000	2,031,075
November	10	167.3	1,525,000	2,551,325
December	11	191.9	1,575,000	3,022,425
		1,200.0		

5-7 Forecasting Using Judgment

The third major forecasting technique is based on judgment. In a sense, all forecasting involves some judgment, even when data are extensively analyzed. But we can use judgment to make forecasts even when no data at all are available.

Until now, all of the forecasting methods we have discussed involve *point forecasts*; that is, they provide future predictions in the form of specific numerical values. Such forecasts are almost certain to be in error. The actual data will inevitably differ in some way from the forecasts; at best, the forecasts will be slightly above or below the actual values. It may therefore be more realistic to predict a *range of values*. An even better method might be to include future uncertainty by treating it as a random variable with a *probability distribution*. A detailed discussion of three methods for finding judgmental probability distributions was given in Chapter 4.

In one popular prediction procedure called **Delphi forecasting**, individual judgments regarding future events are combined to express a collective opinion. Delphi forecasting has been successfully employed in predicting technological breakthroughs and scientific advancements. It has also been used to forecast long-range sales and profits.

Another judgmental application, **scenario projection**, is often employed in government and military planning. Here, detailed circumstances are used as stage settings to provide background for a future analysis that simulates reality. **Industrial** and **world dynamics** operate in the same vein. In these procedures, mathematical models are employed to make long-range predictions and to simulate future conditions.

There are many other types of forecasting methods too numerous to mention here. More detailed discussions of forecasting methods can be found in some of the references in the bibliography.

CASE

BugOff Chemical Company

The following sales data (thousands of gallons) apply to the pesticide Malabug.

	QUARTER				
YEAR	Winter	Spring	Summer	Fall	Total
1985	18	80	30	22	150
1986	24	105	54	27	210
1987	33	141	48	38	260
1988	40	150	75	45	310
1989	35	180	55	50	320
1990	48	205	70	57	380

For planning purposes, management wants to make detailed forecasts of 1991 quarterly sales. Management also wants to make short-range and long-range annual forecasts.

The total national production of the interchangeable technical base products has been determined by an industry trade association. The following data (thousands of gallons) have been provided.

YEAR	PRODUCTION QUANTITY	YEAR	PRDOUCTION QUANTITY
1981	587	1986	1,639
1982	648	1987	2,059
1983	815	1988	2,655
1984	1,050	1989	3,050
1985	1,359	1990	3,546

For budgeting and planning, the BugOff comptroller wishes to determine a relationship for predicting the direct processing cost per gallon of Malabug. For the 5 past runs, the following data have been obtained.

DIRECT COST PER GALLON	TECHNICAL BASE (gallons)	RAW STOCK (gallons)
$9.82	500	1,000
9.14	1,000	500
8.75	700	800
9.24	400	1,100
8.33	350	1,150

Questions

1. Determine the seasonal indexes for the Malabug sales data.
2. Deseasonalized sales values for any given quarter may be found by dividing actual sales by the seasonal index. Determine for each quarter the deseasonalized Malabug sales values.
3. Determine the regression trend line for annual Malabug sales. Use your regression line to predict sales for (a) 1991, (b) 1995, and (c) 2000.
4. Using your above forecast for 1991 sales, apply the seasonal indexes from Question 1 to make Malabug sales forecasts for each quarter in 1991.

5. An alternative procedure is to use seasonal exponential smoothing. Determine Bugoff's forecast Malabug quarterly sales for 1991 using $\alpha = .5$, $\gamma = .5$, and $\beta = .5$. Compute the MSE?

6. Compare your answers to questions 4 and 5. Which procedure do you prefer? Explain.

7. Exponential smoothing may be used to forecast future production levels of the technical base. For the following smoothing parameters, use the actual data to determine the forecast values. Compute the MSE. Which set appears to best fit the actual data?
   (a) $\alpha = .20$; $\gamma = .40$
   (b) $\alpha = .30$; $\gamma = .30$

8. BugOff management assumes that its 40% share of the technical market will be maintained. Using the better set of parameters from Question 4, forecast the 1991 industry production quantity. From that quantity, determine BugOff's forecast technical chemical sales for 1991.

9. Find the regression equation for predicting direct cost per gallon of Malabug for a batch having a known volume of technical base and raw stock. Then, estimate the direct cost per gallon for the following production runs.

	TECHNICAL BASE (gallons)	RAW STOCK (gallons)
(a)	1,000	1,000
(b)	500	750
(c)	750	500
(d)	400	600

PROBLEMS

5-1   Managers of the Variety Galore Store wish to forecast its sales for the next calendar year. The following components have been determined by the store accountant.

QUARTER t	TREND T_t	CYCLICAL COMPONENT C_t	SEASONAL INDEX S_t
Winter	$100,000	90	80
Spring	110,000	110	70
Summer	121,000	100	100
Fall	133,100	90	150

Use the multiplicative time-series model to determine the forecasts of sales Y_t for each quarter.

5-2   The sales data for Humpty Dumpty Toys, Inc., have been analyzed, and the trend, cyclical, seasonal, and irregular components have been determined for operations during the preceding four quarters. Supply the missing values in the following table, assuming that the time-series components are multiplicative.

QUARTER t	TREND T_t	CYCLICAL COMPONENT (percentage) C_t	SEASONAL INDEX (percentage) S_t	IRREGULAR COMPONENT (percentage) I_t	SALES Y_t
Winter	$1,000,000	107	50	101	—————
Spring	1,100,000	105	70	—	$ 820,000
Summer	1,200,000	105	—	98	987,840
Fall	1,300,000	—	200	97	2,622,880

5-3   Tuti-Fruti Yogurt's seasonally adjusted quarterly sales data (thousands of gallons) are given below.

PERIOD	SALES	PERIOD	SALES
1	2	9	12
2	3	10	14
3	5	11	15
4	7	12	17
5	6	13	18
6	8	14	22
7	9	15	24
8	10	16	27

(a) Use single-parameter exponential smoothing with $\alpha = .20$ to forecast sales levels.
(b) Compute the mean squared error.

5-4   Repeat Problem 5-3. Use $\alpha = .50$.

5-5   Refer to the Tuti-Fruti data in Problem 5-3.
(a) Use two-parameter exponential smoothing with $\alpha = .40$ and $\gamma = .10$ to forecast sales levels.
(b) Compute the mean squared error.

5-6   Big Mountain Power serves a region in which the following amounts of annual electricity usage (millions of kilowatt-hours) have been recorded.

YEAR	CONSUMPTION	YEAR	CONSUMPTION
1981	205	1986	241
1982	206	1987	267
1983	223	1988	268
1984	231	1989	277
1985	234	1990	290

(a) Plot the time-series data on graph paper.
(b) Use single-parameter exponential smoothing with $\alpha = .20$ to forecast values for each past year. Then, compute the MSE and find the forecast usage for 1991.
(c) Repeat (b), using two-parameter exponential smoothing with $\alpha = .30$ and $\gamma = .20$.
(d) Which forecast appears better? Explain.

5-7   Garment Suspenders recorded the following quarterly sales data (millions of dollars).

	1986	1987	1988	1989	1990
Winter	3.9	7.8	12.9	13.9	13.5
Spring	6.1	10.6	15.2	14.4	18.2
Summer	4.3	6.9	10.3	10.2	14.2
Fall	10.8	13.5	18.7	17.3	20.7

(a) Plot the time-series data on graph paper.
(b) Use three-parameter seasonal exponential smoothing with $\alpha = .3$, $\gamma = .2$, and $\beta = .4$ to forecast sales levels for the past quarters.
(c) Determine quarterly sales forecasts for 1991.

5-8   In arranging for short-term credit with its bank, the Make-Wave Corporation must project its cash needs on a monthly basis. Management wishes to use the following historical data to project monthly cash requirements (hundreds of thousands of dollars).

	1986	1987	1988	1989	1990
January	2.7	2.9	3.5	2.5	4.2
February	5.4	6.4	7.3	8.1	9.6
March	9.3	10.1	11.3	7.9	12.4
April	2.4	4.1	3.8	5.2	6.2
May	6.1	7.8	8.1	9.2	8.7
June	7.3	7.4	6.9	8.1	8.3
July	6.5	5.5	6.5	7.6	6.6
August	9.7	9.6	8.9	9.3	9.8
September	13.4	13.5	14.3	15.8	16.3
October	10.6	10.7	11.5	12.6	13.4
November	5.1	4.8	6.5	7.2	6.9
December	3.4	2.8	3.9	4.1	6.1

(a) Plot the time-series data on graph paper.
(b) Use three-parameter seasonal exponential smoothing with $\alpha = .2$, $\gamma = .1$, $\beta = .3$ to forecast cash requirements for past months.
(c) Determine forecast monthly requirements for 1991.

5-9   Refer to the data provided in Problem 5-6.

(a) Using the method of least squares, determine the equation for the estimated regression line $\hat{Y}(X) = a + bX$, with X in years and $X = 0$ in 1981. Plot this line on your graph.

(b) What is the forecast consumption for 1991?

5-10 McFadden's has experienced the following annual sales.

YEAR	SALES	YEAR	SALES
1979	$18 million	1985	$ 82 million
1980	28	1986	89
1981	26	1987	108
1982	43	1988	121
1983	55	1989	155
1984	54		

(a) Plot the time-series data on graph paper.

(b) Would a straight line provide a suitable summary of the trend in sales? Explain.

5-11 Refer to the data provided in Problem 5-10.

(a) Representing sales by Y, use least-squares regression of $\log Y$ on X, where X is in years and $X = 0$ at 1979, to find the logarithmic trend line, $\log \hat{Y}(X) = \log a + X \log b$.

(b) Determine the exponential trend equation $\hat{Y}(X) = ab^X$.

(c) What is the annual percentage growth in sales indicated by the trend equation found in (b)?

(d) Using the trend equation from (a), what is the projected sales level for 1994?

5-12 A statistician for the Civil Aeronautics Board wishes to determine the equation relating destination distance to freight charge for a standard-sized crate. The following data were obtained for a random sample of 10 freight invoices.

DISTANCE (hundreds of miles)	CHARGE (to nearest dollar)
14	68
23	105
9	40
17	79
10	81
22	95
5	31
12	72
6	45
16	93

(a) Plot the scatter diagram for the data.

(b) Using the method of least squares, determine the equation for the estimated regression line. Then, plot the regression line on your scatter diagram.

5-13 The manufacturer of Spinex floppy disks wishes to conduct a regression analysis to estimate the average lifetime (hours) at various drive-unit tracking forces X (grams). The regression equation $\hat{Y}(X) = 1,300 - 200X$ has been obtained for a sample of $n = 100$ disks that were run at various tracking forces until they were worn out. Find the forecast lifetimes when (a) $X = 1$ gram, (b) $X = 2$ grams, and (c) $X = 3$ grams.

5-14 The Old Ivy College admissions director relies on high school GPA X_1 and IQ scores X_2 to predict college GPA Y. The following regression equation applies.

$$\hat{Y} = .5 + .8X_1 + .003X_2$$

Forecast the college GPA for each of the following students.

	HIGH SCHOOL GPA X_1	IQ SCORE X_2
(a)	2.9	123
(b)	3.0	118
(c)	2.7	105
(d)	3.5	136

5-15 Megaphonetrics uses special machines to press recording grooves onto blank disks from a die. Each die lasts for about 1,000 pressings. Due to the time constraints inherent in the record business, it is sometimes necessary to use several pressing machines simultaneously. Because each machine requires an expensive die disk and many production runs are completed before the useful lifetime of each die disk is exhausted, this increases production costs. For $n = 100$ production runs, the total manufacturing cost Y (thousands of dollars) has been determined for the number of pressings made X_1 (thousands) and the number of die disks required X_2. The following regression equation applies.

$$\hat{Y} = 1.082 + 1.2X_1 + .553X_2$$

Forecast the cost $\hat{Y}$ of each of the following production runs.

RUN	NUMBER OF PRESSINGS (thousands)	NUMBER OF DIE DISKS
(a)	15	5
(b)	20	3
(c)	15	4
(d)	100	10

5-16 The following percentage of moving average values have been obtained for the sales of High Tower Publications.

	QUARTER			
YEAR	Winter	Spring	Summer	Fall
1984	—	—	156	111
1985	49	92	137	109
1986	53	93	148	108
1987	52	91	162	104
1988	51	89	153	110
1989	51	90	151	112
1990	48	88		

Determine the seasonal index for each quarter.

5-17 Refer to the data provided in Problem 5-7.
(a) Determine the four-quarter moving averages.
(b) Calculate the percentages of moving average values and determine the seasonal indexes.

5-18 Refer to the data provided in Problem 5-8.
(a) Using 12-month moving averages, determine the seasonal index for each month by means of the ratio-to-moving-average method.
(b) Make-Wave's cash needs for the coming year are forecast to be $1 million per month on the average. Using the seasonal indexes you calculated in (a), estimate the cash requirements for each month.

5-19 *Computer exercise.* Telesat Corporation obtained the following message volumes (thousands) relayed on successive days by a new communications satellite.

DAY	VOL.	DAY	VOL.	DAY	VOL.	DAY	VOL.	DAY	VOL.
1	990	11	1038	21	1064	31	1088	41	1112
2	998	12	1041	22	1069	32	1093	42	1107
3	876	13	1039	23	1071	33	1099	43	1115
4	1014	14	1042	24	1069	34	1101	44	1118
5	1009	15	1045	25	1073	35	1098	45	1119
6	1017	16	1040	26	1074	36	1104	46	1123
7	1023	17	1052	27	1076	37	1103	47	1121
8	1015	18	1057	28	1078	38	1106	48	1123
9	1028	19	1063	29	1079	39	1108	49	1124
10	1035	20	1061	30	1080	40	1110	50	1125

Using two-parameter exponential smoothing to forecast message volumes. Compute the mean squared error for each of the following cases.
(a) $\alpha = .10; \gamma = .10$
(b) $\alpha = .10; \gamma = .20$
(c) $\alpha = .10; \gamma = .30$

(d) $\alpha = .20; \gamma = .10$

(e) Which of the above parameter levels provides the best fit to the actual data? Find, to the nearest .01, the best-fitting levels for α and γ.

5-20 *Computer exercise.* Refer to the data provided in Problem 5-8. Use three-parameter seasonal exponential smoothing to determine the optimal levels for α and γ (to the nearest .01) and associated *MSE* when (a) $\beta = .2$, (b) $\beta = .5$, (c) $\beta = .7$, and (d) $\beta = .9$.

5-21 *Computer exercise.* Restaurant sales predictions are to be made from a regression equation based on total floorspace and number of employees. The following data have been obtained for a sample of $n = 5$ restaurants.

SALES (thousands of dollars) Y	FLOORSPACE (thousands of square feet) X_1	NUMBER OF EMPLOYEES X_2
20	10	15
15	5	8
10	10	12
5	3	7
10	2	10

Construct and calculate the multiple regression equation for these data.

5-22 *Computer exercise.* A systems programmer for InfoSoft wishes to predict run times of payroll programs run on a particular software-hardware configuration. The following data have been obtained for 20 runs.

RUN TIME (minutes) Y	REQUIRED MEMORY (thousands of bytes) X_1	AMOUNT OF OUTPUT (thousands of lines) X_2	AMOUNT OF INPUT (thousands of lines) X_3
11.3	24	10	5
8.7	8	6	5
5.5	14	8	2
7.4	35	6	2
9.1	11	9	4
6.1	23	4	3
15.2	24	11	11
18.2	110	9	3
5.0	20	5	2
22.7	75	21	9
15.9	28	13	9
4.0	20	4	1
10.2	19	4	7
11.9	74	13	2

RUN TIME (minutes) Y	REQUIRED MEMORY (thousands of bytes) X_1	AMOUNT OF OUTPUT (thousands of lines) X_2	AMOUNT OF INPUT (thousands of lines) X_3
6.8	7	4	5
14.0	26	8	5
10.2	37	9	4
6.4	16	3	2
5.9	21	3	3
25.5	96	22	7

(a) Using required memory and amount of output as the independent variables and run time as the dependent variable, determine the estimated multiple regression equation.

(b) Forecast the run times for the following jobs.

	MEMORY	OUTPUT	INPUT
(1)	100	10	5
(2)	50	5	5
(3)	20	8	2
(4)	30	5	10

5-23 *Computer exercise.* Refer to the data provided in Problem 5-22. Determine the estimated multiple regression equation. Include the amount of input X_3 as a third predictor.

5-24 *Computer exercise.* The Druid's Drayage truck dispatcher wishes to predict how many driver hours it will take to deliver less-than-truckload shipments over any one of a number of routes. Using four independent variables, he has collected the following 20 sample observations.

DRIVER TIME (hours) Y	DISTANCE (miles) X_1	INITIAL LOAD (tons) X_2	DELIVERIES X_3	SPEED (mph) X_4
3.0	90	1.5	1	50
7.2	150	3.7	3	35
4.5	65	4.9	3	42
4.3	74	2.6	5	37
6.4	60	3.1	8	40
3.1	70	1.9	2	45
7.0	120	4.7	5	48
5.2	48	3.4	4	29

(continues)

DRIVER TIME (hours) Y	DISTANCE (miles) X_1	INITIAL LOAD (tons) X_2	DELIVERIES X_3	SPEED (mph) X_4
5.4	125	4.1	3	43
9.2	156	3.4	7	40
5.9	121	2.9	4	46
6.1	98	3.0	6	42
5.5	91	4.5	6	53
5.0	65	4.0	7	42
7.3	74	4.0	8	37
4.7	83	3.6	5	39
4.5	44	2.7	3	48
1.9	33	1.9	1	29
4.2	106	2.0	2	46
4.4	73	3.0	3	37

(a) Determine the estimated multiple regression equation.

(b) Forecast driver time for the following trips.

	DISTANCE	LOAD	DELIVERIES	SPEED
(1)	100	2	5	40
(2)	50	3	8	50
(3)	60	2	2	45
(4)	70	3	5	45

5-25 The following sample data have been obtained by an Agragroup staff agronomist who is working to develop new grain hybrids.

YIELD (bushels per acre) Y	RAINFALL (inches) X
25	37
48	11
123	14
62	44
107	15
119	21
63	33
91	12
152	22
98	29
126	23

(a) Plot the scatter diagram for the data.
(b) Which form, a parabola or third-degree polynomial, appears to best fit the data? Select whichever curve shape seems to provide an appropriate explanation of the underlying relationship.
(c) Using the method of least squares, determine the estimated regression equation for the curve form selected in (b).
(d) Sketch the shape of the regression curve on your scatter diagram.
(e) At around what level of rainfall does maximum crop yield occur?
(f) Using your answer to (c), calculate the predicted crop yield when the level of rainfall is 30 inches.

5-26 A chemical engineer for GetGo provided the following fuel consumption data for sample test car runs.

FUEL CONSUMPTION (mpg) Y	SPEED (mph) X
28.9	56
30.2	34
29.3	32
23.8	59
29.5	25
29.5	40
27.3	22
29.8	47
26.3	57
28.6	21
29.9	28
28.8	52

(a)–(d) Repeat problem 5-25 using the above data.
(e) At what speed does optimal fuel consumption occur?
(f) Using your answer to (c), calculate the predicted miles per gallon when the speed is 35 miles per hour.

CHAPTER 6

Inventory Decisions with Certain Factors

One area of business decision making in which quantitative methods have played a highly successful role in achieving cost savings is the area of inventory control. A primary reason for this success story is that inventory represents such a vast segment of total economic activity. In the United States alone, hundreds of billions of dollars are invested in inventory. Due to the sheer size of inventory investments, even minor improvements in controlling inventory can create large savings.

Two phenomena have contributed to improvements in controlling inventory. One has been the application of mathematical models and optimization techniques to achieve efficiencies. In Chapter 6, we will focus on these quantitative methods. A second source of savings has been the development of the digital computer with improved information processing and retrieval capabilities. Managers in complex organizations now have immediate access to all kinds of information relevant to inventory that was once impossible to obtain quickly. The closing of this information gap has dramatically reduced the need to maintain inventory. Many inventory systems are automated to the extent that even orders to replenish stock are issued by computer.

The central problem we face in making any decision involving physical storage is finding an efficient **inventory policy**. A key element in establishing such a policy is to determine how many items should be stocked periodically and when replenishment should occur. It is convenient to refer to the number of items to be stocked as the **order quantity** and to the level of inventory when the requisition is made as the **order point**. For example, a family might always purchase two gallons of milk (the order quantity) and repurchase milk only when all of it has been drunk (so that the order point is zero).

Our objective is to determine optimal inventory policies. In this chapter, we will consider the basic structure of inventory decisions and present some of the models that are applicable when all factors are certain. These models will serve to explain the essential concepts that are common to more advanced models. In Chapter 7, we will consider inventory decisions made under uncertainty.

6-1 Factors Influencing Inventory Policy

The usual long-run objective of an inventory policy is to maximize profits or to minimize costs. In the simpler situations we will encounter in this chapter, these two goals coincide. The desired end result is ordinarily achieved by minimizing the average inventory cost over a short period of time, such as one year. Our initial models will all be based on minimizing *annual* cost.

Inventory Cost Components

In typical business situations, the various costs considered in evaluating inventory systems are as follows.

1. Ordering and procurement costs for items to be stocked
2. Holding or carrying costs
3. Shortage costs

Inventory ordering and procurement costs represent all expenses incurred in ordering or manufacturing items, including not only the acquisition costs but also the costs of transporting, collecting and sorting, and placing the items in storage. Also included in this category are any managerial and clerical costs associated with placing an order. These costs often vary with the size of the order; for example, this occurs when products are priced with quantity discounts. Ordering and procurement costs are of two kinds: (1) a fixed portion for each order that is independent of the number of items stocked, and (2) a variable portion for each order that is dependent on the number of items stocked. We will refer to the *fixed* portion as the *ordering costs* and to the *variable* portion as the *procurement costs.*

Inventory holding or carrying costs are the expenses incurred during the storage of items. This includes physical costs—the most common being the operation of warehouse facilities—as well as the costs of insurance and property taxes. Other cost components might be expenses arising from pilferage, spoilage, and obsolescence. A very important portion of inventory holding costs is the **opportunity cost** of those funds invested in inventory that might have been used profitably elsewhere. All such costs depend on *how many* items are stored and for *how long*. Such costs can be 20–25% of the value of the items held in inventory.

Inventory shortage costs occur whenever there is a demand for items that are not currently in stock. For items that are usually backordered, such as a new car of a particular color with special options, shortage costs may have only a fixed component — the extra paperwork and managerial expenses incurred in processing the order. For shortages of more mundane items, such as a particular brand of paint, an additional variable cost component that depends on the *duration* of the shortage must be considered. This cost is due largely to the potential loss of customer goodwill that may be expected to increase in proportion to the length of the delay; such a decline in goodwill might be reflected in the loss of future business. In extreme cases of convenience products, such as cigarettes, or necessities, such as gasoline, there is no backordering at all. Under these circumstances, a shortage results in the loss of a sale. The minimum cost of a lost sale is the marginal profit that the item would have earned, but it may be larger due to the loss of goodwill.

In evaluating an inventory policy, some or all these three types of costs might be considered. But it is very important that only **relevant costs** be used. These involve only those expenses that are in some way affected by the inventory policies themselves. Certain legitimate accounting costs may therefore be ignored. For instance, the rent on a warehouse would not be included as a carrying cost if the same facility were to be used regardless of the number of items stocked. Instead, the rent would be considered properly as an overhead item, like the company president's salary. No proration of overhead items should be reflected in the inventory costs, unless these items somehow differ from policy to policy. But certain nonaccounting costs, such as the opportunity cost of invested capital and the loss of customer goodwill, are definitely relevant and should be incorporated into the evaluation.

The Nature of Demand and Supply

In a typical business situation, demand occurs erratically. The demand for most items also occurs discretely; that is, a few items are demanded at a time. In this chapter, demand is assumed to occur *continuously* (as if each item is a cubic foot of natural gas fed into a heater that is always lighted — either from a pilot light or by the main flame) and *at the same rate over time* (as if the gas heater is always on full flame). As long as demand is predictable, such a simplifying assumption makes little difference in the inventory costs or in the particular policy that minimizes cost.

But one element does matter. Demand typically occurs *randomly* over time, so that the overall level is generally uncertain. In this chapter, however, we will consider only cases in which the demand is *certain* and known in advance. These cases will prepare us for the discussion in Chapter 7, where uncertainty in demand will be explicitly considered.

How items are supplied is another important element in establishing inventory policies. Generally, this is handled in one of two ways. From the retailer's or the wholesaler's point of view, the only question is how long does it take to fill an order. This is the *lead time* that it will take to receive the units ordered. Like demand, lead time is often uncertain. Here, we will only consider *constant* lead times. This greatly simplifies the analysis and allows us to analyze most problems without explicitly considering the lead time at all, as if inventories were instantaneously replenished. In Chapter 7, we will consider how the choice of policy is affected by uncertain lead times.

The method of supply differs for the manufacturer who must produce items for later sale. Here, replenishment cannot be instantaneous. Instead items must be added to the inventory at a rate equal to the speed at which they are produced.

6-2 The Economic Order Quantity (EOQ) Model

The simplest inventory model involves one type of item that has a known and constant demand and that is resupplied instantaneously. No backordering of items is allowed. The problem objective is to select an inventory policy—that is, to choose the order quantity (which in turn establishes the time when an order must be placed)—in such a way that the annual inventory cost is minimized.

The Mathematical Model

The following parameters are used to establish a mathematical model for this problem.

k = Fixed cost per order

A = Annual number of items demanded

c = Unit cost of procuring an item

h = Annual cost per dollar value of holding items in inventory

T = Time between orders

The objective is to choose the number of items to order

$$Q = \text{Order quantity}$$

such that

Total annual cost = Ordering cost + Holding cost + Procurement cost

is minimized.

The features of this inventory system are illustrated in Figure 6-1, where the inventory level is plotted against calendar time. This graph will help to explain the development of the mathematical model. Figure 6-1 tells us that Q items are replenished periodically, at which time a new **inventory cycle** begins and an old one ends. Each cycle has a duration of T years (some fraction of one year), which is determined by the order quantity Q. The

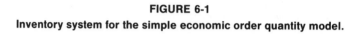

FIGURE 6-1

Inventory system for the simple economic order quantity model.

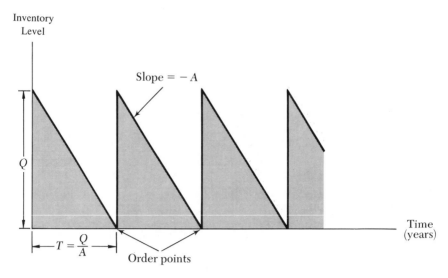

length of time is equal to the proportion of the annual demand consumed in one inventory cycle, or

$$T = \frac{Q}{A}$$

The items are depleted at the rate of A units per year, so that the slanted line segments, each with a slope of $-A$, indicate the level of inventory at any given point in time. The saw-tooth effect of the graph represents the sequence of inventory depletions and replenishments of successive inventory cycles. Because it costs something to hold items in inventory, there is no advantage to restocking until the inventory is zero. Thus, each inventory cycle can be pictured as a triangle of height Q and base T, with a new cycle or triangle beginning at the order point, where the leg of the preceding triangle touches the time axis.

To find a mathematical expression for the problem objective, we begin with the first cost component, the **annual ordering cost**, which is based on how many orders are placed each year. The number of annual orders depends on two factors: (1) the annual number of items demanded A, and (2) the order quantity Q. It follows that

$$\text{Number of annual orders} = \frac{A}{Q}$$

Multiplying this equation by the cost per order k, we obtain

$$\text{Annual ordering cost} = \left(\frac{A}{Q}\right)k$$

The second cost component, the **annual holding cost**, is based on the number of items placed in inventory and the duration they are held in inventory. Individually, some items will be sold immediately; others will be held until the inventory is restocked. However, we need to concern ourselves only with an average value. Since the inventory level in any cycle ranges from Q downward to zero and there is a constant rate of depletion, we have, for any cycle,

$$\text{Average inventory} = \frac{Q}{2}$$

This same quantity applies from cycle to cycle and therefore represents the *average inventory level* throughout the entire operating life of the inventory system.

It is realistic to base the holding cost on the value of the items held. This is certainly true of the opportunity cost of the invested capital and applies to other costs, such as insurance and property taxes, as well. (Physical storage costs are usually highly correlated with an item's value, too.) Here, we base the value of an item on its procurement cost. The cost of holding an item in inventory for one year is therefore the product of the annual holding cost per dollar h and the unit procurement cost c, or

$$\text{Annual holding cost of one item} = hc$$

We can now determine the annual holding cost of all the items involved by multiplying the above cost by the average inventory, or

$$\text{Annual holding cost} = hc\left(\frac{Q}{2}\right)$$

There is another way of looking at this annual cost component that will prove useful in discussing later models. Consider the *single-cycle holding cost*, which can be related to the area of one of the triangles in Figure 6-1. The single-cycle holding cost represents the average item-time (product years) for one inventory cycle, or

$$\text{Triangle area} = \frac{1}{2}\text{base} \times \text{Height}$$

$$= \frac{1}{2}TQ$$

$$= \frac{1}{2}\left(\frac{Q}{A}\right)Q = \frac{Q^2}{2A}$$

The holding cost of a single cycle is the product of hc and this area, or $hc(Q^2/2A)$. Since there are A/Q inventory cycles in one year, the annual holding cost can be obtained by multiplying the single-cycle value by A/Q. Canceling terms yields $hc(Q/2)$, which is the expression we obtained earlier for the annual holding cost.

For the entire year, A items will be demanded, so that

$$\text{Annual procurement cost} = Ac$$

Adding together the three cost components, we find that

$$\text{Total annual cost} = \left(\frac{A}{Q}\right)k + hc\left(\frac{Q}{2}\right) + Ac$$

The problem objective is to select the value Q that minimizes this total annual cost.

However, we need to consider only relevant costs (which differ, depending on the inventory policy). We can therefore ignore the procurement cost Ac, since that expense will arise regardless of the value of Q. Equivalently, the objective for our simple inventory model is to

$$\text{Minimize } TC = \left(\frac{A}{Q}\right)k + hc\left(\frac{Q}{2}\right)$$

where TC is the **total annual relevant cost**.

Finding the Optimal Solution

The TC equation is a mathematical expression that we refer to as the **objective function**. The value of TC depends on the order quantity Q. The TC expression is plotted in Figure 6-2, where the vertical axis indicates the annual cost and the horizontal axis represents the order quantity Q. The total annual relevant cost has two components: (1) annual ordering cost and, (2) annual holding cost. Each of these components is also plotted in Figure 6-2. Since TC is the sum of ordering and holding costs, the height of the TC curve at any level of Q is the sum of the respective heights of the ordering-cost curve and the holding-cost line.

The annual ordering-cost curve has the geometric shape of a hyperbola. Recall that the cost of each order is an amount k, regardless of how many items are requested each time. Thus, very low levels of Q will involve a great number of orders throughout the year, and ordering costs will be huge. As Q becomes larger, fewer orders are required and the annual ordering cost declines as we move to the right on the ordering-cost curve. The annual holding cost is plotted as a straight line because this component is a constant multiple of the average inventory level. This line begins at the origin with zero holding cost at $Q = 0$, where no inventory is held. Each item is sold as demanded, so that the holding-cost line rises with constant slope as Q increases. This is because progressively larger order quantities raise the average inventory level, causing holding costs to rise proportionately.

The **optimal solution** to the objective function occurs at the point where total annual relevant cost is minimized. We denote the optimal order quantity by Q^*. This level

FIGURE 6-2

Graphical representation of inventory cost components.

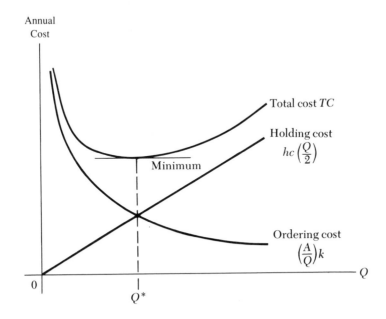

corresponds to the *minimum-cost point* on the TC curve, where its slope is zero. The slope equation for a curve may be determined by using mathematical procedures. Once the equation for the slope has been found, it can be set equal to zero and algebraically solved to determine the corresponding order quantity.[†]

The equation for the **optimal order quantity** is

$$Q^* = \sqrt{\frac{2Ak}{hc}}$$

which is sometimes called the **economic order quantity**. This equation is often referred to as the *Wilson formula*, in honor of the man who first proposed it. Once Q^* has been

---

[†] To do this, we employ calculus. The first derivative of the objective function $TC(Q)$ is obtained and set equal to zero.

$$\frac{dTC(Q)}{dQ} = -\frac{A}{Q^2}k + \frac{hc}{2} = 0$$

Because $TC(Q)$ is convex from below, if we solve for Q, the minimum cost occurs when

$$Q = \sqrt{\frac{2Ak}{hc}}$$

obtained, the corresponding reorder time is automatically determined to be

$$T^* = \frac{Q^*}{A}$$

and a complete optimal inventory policy is thereby obtained which tells how much should be ordered and when each order should be placed. The total annual relevant cost of this policy can be determined by substituting the value of Q^* for Q in the TC equation.

Referring again to Figure 6-2, we can see that Q^* happens to be the order quantity at which holding cost is equal to ordering cost. The Wilson formula can be verified by setting the respective component cost equations equal to each other and algebraically solving for Q. Study of the Q^* formula allows us to draw some interesting conclusions. The economic (optimal) order quantity increases with the square root of the annual demand A instead of becoming proportional to it. Also, it is inversely proportional to the square root of the unit procurement cost c, indicating that all else being equal, fewer expensive items should be ordered than would be the case for cheaper items. Thus, the various **parameters** k, A, c and h really serve to determine the optimal inventory policy, and widely different results may be obtained for different levels of these constants.

ILLUSTRATION
A Liquor Store Owner's Inventory Decision

Suppose that a liquor store sells 5,200 cases of beer each year. For simplicity, we will assume that the beer is sold at a constant rate throughout the year. The net cost of each case to the store is $2. The wholesale supplier charges $10 for each delivery, regardless of how many cases have been ordered, and delivery always occurs the day after the order is placed. The owner's only working capital is tied up in inventory, and these funds have been borrowed from the local bank at a simple annual interest rate of 10%. In addition, the owner must pay a state franchise tax of 5% of the annual inventory value, and another 5% for theft insurance. All other operating costs are either fixed in nature or do not depend on the amounts of beer ordered.

The owner wishes to evaluate the present procedure of ordering 100 cases each week and to establish a better inventory policy that will minimize the annual costs of doing business in beer. The following constants apply.

$k = \$10$ per order

$A = 5,200$ cases per year

$c = \$2$ per case

$h = \$.20$ annual cost per dollar value of beer held in inventory

The present policy of ordering every week involves an order quantity of

$$Q = \frac{5,200}{52} = 100 \text{ cases}$$

The total annual relevant cost of this policy is

$$TC = \left(\frac{A}{Q}\right)k + hc\left(\frac{Q}{2}\right)$$

$$= \left(\frac{5,200}{100}\right)10 + .20(2)\left(\frac{100}{2}\right)$$

$$= 520 + 20$$

$$= 540 \text{ dollars per year}$$

Note that the annual ordering cost of $520 is much larger than the annual $20 holding cost. These two cost components should be the same to achieve an optimal inventory policy.

To establish the optimal inventory policy, first we use the Wilson formula to determine the economic order quantity.

$$Q^* = \sqrt{\frac{2Ak}{hc}}$$

$$= \sqrt{\frac{2(5,200)10}{.20(2)}}$$

$$= \sqrt{260,000}$$

$$= 509.9, \text{ or } 510 \text{ cases of beer}$$

The optimal time between orders is

$$T^* = \frac{510}{5,200}$$

$$= .098 \text{ years}$$

which can be converted to once every $365(.098) = 35.8$ or 36 days. The optimal inventory policy is therefore to order 510 cases of beer every 36 days. The resulting total annual relevant cost is

$$TC = \left(\frac{5,200}{510}\right)10 + .20(2)\left(\frac{510}{2}\right)$$

$$= 101.96 + 102.00$$

$$= 203.96 \text{ dollars per year}$$

(The two cost components differ by $.04 because we rounded the value of Q^* to the nearest whole number.) Thus, more than $300 in annual beer costs alone can be saved by switching to the optimal inventory policy.

The Effect of Parameter Values on the Solution

To show how greatly the solution depends on the parameter values, we will consider the retail store's inventory policy for fine domestic wine. Suppose that only 1,000 cases of this wine are sold annually at a net cost of $20 per case. The liquor store is located in San Francisco, and the owner—who prides himself on the caliber of his product—makes periodic trips through the Napa Valley to pick up orders at various wineries. He always rents a large truck and travels a fixed route; the cost is a flat $100 per trip. The holding costs are the same as they are for beer. Thus,

$k = \$100$ per order

$A = 1,000$ cases per year

$c = \$20$ per case

$h = \$.20$ annual cost per dollar value of wine held in inventory

The optimal inventory policy (again, assuming a known, constant demand rate and a predictable lead time for inventory replenishment) is

$$Q^* = \sqrt{\frac{2(1,000)100}{.20(20)}} = \sqrt{50,000}$$

$$= 223.6, \text{ or } 224 \text{ cases of wine}$$

$$T^* = \frac{224}{1,000} = .224 \text{ years, or approximately 82 days}$$

The total annual relevant cost is

$$TC = \left(\frac{1,000}{224}\right)100 + .20(20)\left(\frac{224}{2}\right)$$

$$= 894.43 \text{ dollars per year}$$

Notice the difference between the results for wine and beer.

Some Limitations of the Model

Applying economic order quantity analysis to two different items is only valid under special conditions. Here, we must assume that beer and wine have independent demands and that the storage capacity is sufficient to handle any contemplated quantities of each product. If beer and wine must compete for limited space or if there is a constraint on the amount of working capital that can be tied up in inventories, then the products must be analyzed jointly and the mathematics can become quite complicated.

6-3 Optimal Inventory Policy with Backordering

The simple inventory model we have just described assumes that backordering is not possible. We will now consider how items can be sold even after the inventory has been exhausted. Such a situation could apply when buying automobile tires, for example; a retailer might not have the exact size in current stock but might be willing to place a special order to satisfy a customer. An inventory system that permits backordering is summarized in Figure 6-3. As before, Q represents the order quantity. Since sales may be made even after the on-hand inventory reaches the zero level, it may be desirable to use part of each successive order to fill backordered items. The **order level** is represented by S; this quantity is the on-hand inventory position at the beginning of each inventory cycle. The optimal inventory policy must specify the values of both Q and S that minimize total annual cost.

The New Model

We will now assume that a shortage cost applies and that, like a holding cost, this cost depends on how many items are short and on the amount of time that each shortage lasts.

FIGURE 6-3

Inventory system for the economic order quantity model when backordering is allowed.

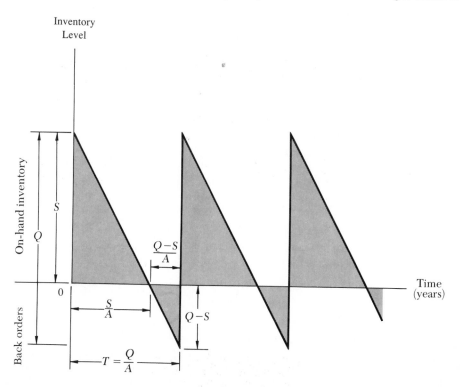

Such a **shortage penalty**, represented by p, arises largely from loss of goodwill. The inventory models of this chapter are all expressed on an *annual* basis, and p is the cost of being short one item for an *entire year*. (An additional fixed shortage penalty that is based only on the number of items short is sometimes applied, but for simplicity, that second penalty is not included here.)

Thus, we may now express total annual relevant cost as

$$TC = \text{Ordering cost} + \text{Holding cost} + \text{Shortage cost}$$

The total annual relevant cost may be expressed as

$$TC = \left(\frac{A}{Q}\right)k + \frac{hcS^2}{2Q} + \frac{p(Q - S)^2}{2Q}$$

The problem objective is to find the values of Q and S that minimize TC. The following expressions may be used to calculate the optimal values.[†]

$$Q^* = \sqrt{\frac{2Ak}{hc}}\sqrt{\frac{p + hc}{p}}$$

$$S^* = \sqrt{\frac{2Ak}{hc}}\sqrt{\frac{p}{p + hc}}$$

The time between orders is

$$T^* = \frac{Q^*}{A}$$

Returning to our earlier example, beer is a convenience product that cannot be backordered (customers will always buy it elsewhere rather than wait). However, wine customers are connoisseurs who are willing to order out-of-stock items. Nevertheless, the store owner will incur some penalty if there is a shortage of wine.

Suppose that each day that a customer must wait for a favorite wine costs the store a penny per case; this means that the annual penalty is $p = \$3.65$ per case. Using the same constants for wine as before ($k = \$100$, $A = 1,000$, $c = \$20$, and $h = \$.20$), we establish the optimal inventory policy.

$$Q^* = \sqrt{\frac{2(1,000)100}{.20(20)}}\sqrt{\frac{3.65 + .20(20)}{3.65}} = 324$$

$$S^* = \sqrt{\frac{2(1,000)100}{.20(20)}}\sqrt{\frac{3.65}{3.65 + .20(20)}} = 154$$

[†] It can be established that the function $TC(Q, S)$ is convex over the ranges being considered. These equations are derived by setting the partial derivatives with respect to Q and S equal to zero and solving them algebraically.

and

$$T^* = \frac{324}{1,000} = .324 \text{ years, or approximately } 118 \text{ days}$$

The optimal inventory policy is to order 324 cases of wine every 118 days. Only 154 of these cases will be stored in inventory; the remaining $Q^* - S^* = 170$ cases will be used to satisfy outstanding backorders. The total annual relevant cost of this policy is

$$TC = \left(\frac{1,000}{324}\right)100 + \frac{.20(20)(154)^2}{2(324)} + \frac{3.65(170)^2}{2(324)}$$

$$= 617.82 \text{ dollars per year}$$

Note that this cost is smaller than the optimal cost of $894.43 when no backordering was allowed. This is because fewer orders are placed when backordering is permitted, so that the average on-hand inventory level is lower. Although shortage costs now exist, these costs are lower than the combined cost reduction for ordering and holding items.

Shortage Penalty Considerations

Implementation of the preceding model may be hampered because of difficulties in establishing a value for the shortage penalty p. It must be emphasized that the model assumes that shortage costs vary only with time, as shown in Figure 6-4(a). Furthermore, an item's shortage penalty is an *annualized* amount, so that, when the actual shortage lasts just a month, week, or day, the experienced shortage cost must be converted.

$$p = 12 \times \text{ one month's shortage cost}$$

$$p = 52 \times \text{ one week's shortage cost}$$

$$p = 365 \times \text{ one day's shortage cost}$$

Such a cost may arise from the loss of goodwill (reduced future business) with the shorted customer, who may become increasingly disenchanted as the waiting times become longer.

The given model allows no *fixed* shortage-cost component. A retailer may experience such a one-shot cost, p_S, as shown in Figure 6-4(b). That cost element may reflect the added labor of logging in backorders, removing items on arrival, storing them, and notifying customers. Included in p_S would be any immediate goodwill impact that does not depend on the duration of shortage. And, if the stockout period is very short, the fixed component may be dominant. In Chapter 7, we will consider models that explicitly incorporate p_S. (For those models, it will be the negligible time-based component p that is left out.)

Loss of goodwill is hard to quantify accurately. Often only a ballpark figure can be established for p. That amount may be used to find Q^* and could result in acceptable inventory evaluations, since Q may be *insensitive* over a wide range of levels for p.

FIGURE 6-4

Shortage penalty considerations showing (a) how penalty relates to length of shortage and (b) the presence of a fixed penalty p_s.

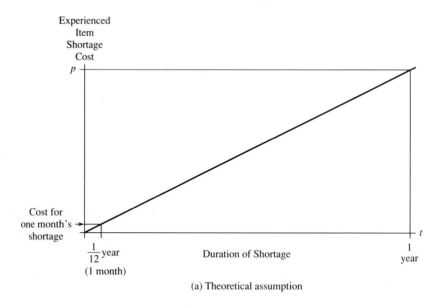

(a) Theoretical assumption

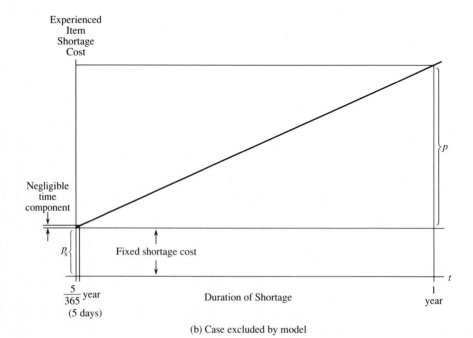

(b) Case excluded by model

FIGURE 6-5

Effect of *p* on order quantity and order levels for the wine ordering illustration.

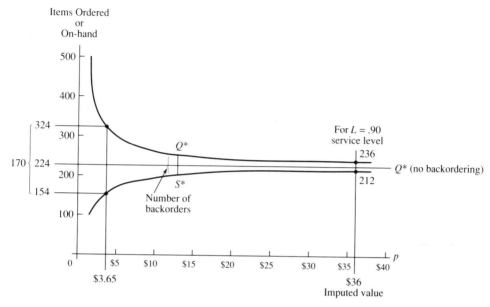

In Figure 6-5, the optimal item quantities are plotted for various levels of p. Notice that beyond \$5 the level for p has a minor effect on Q^* and S^*.

6-4 Establishing Inventory Policies Based on Service Level

An alternative approach for establishing an inventory policy is based on achieving a desired **service level**. A common measure of service level in inventory evaluations is the *proportion of demand met on time*. Using the **service level proportion** L, the order quantity and service level are chosen, so that

$$\frac{Q^* - S^*}{Q^*} = 1 - L \quad \text{or} \quad Q^* - S^* = (1 - L)Q^*$$

It follows that

$$LQ^* = S^*$$

Using the individual expressions for Q^* and S^*, the above may be reexpressed as

$$L\sqrt{\frac{2Ak}{hc}}\sqrt{\frac{p+hc}{p}} = \sqrt{\frac{2Ak}{hc}}\sqrt{\frac{p}{p+hc}}$$

from which an expression for the *imputed* shortage penalty is found:

$$p = \frac{hcL}{1-L}$$

To illustrate, we continue with the wine ordering example. Suppose that the retailer wishes to provide a service level in which 90% of the customer demand is filled on time (so that shortages occur just 10% of the time). Thus, $L = .90$. Using the same parameters as before, we have

$$p = \frac{.20(20)(.90)}{1-.90} = 36$$

The corresponding optimal quantities are

$$Q^* = \sqrt{\frac{2(1,000)100}{.20(20)}}\sqrt{\frac{36+4}{36}} = 223.6\sqrt{1.11}$$

$$= 235.7, \quad \text{or} \quad 236$$

and

$$S^* = \sqrt{\frac{2(1,000)100}{.20(20)}}\sqrt{\frac{36}{36+4}} = 223.6\sqrt{.90}$$

$$= 212.1, \quad \text{or} \quad 212$$

The above quantities are much closer together than those obtained from the backordering model using $p = 3.65$. We see that a higher level of service corresponds to using a greater p.

6-5 Inventory Policy for Lost Sales

As we have already noted, items like convenience products cannot be backordered. When a demand for such an item cannot be met from on-hand inventory, a sale is lost. It is possible to extend the model we have developed with backordering to accommodate this special case. However, a complete analysis of the case of lost sales is merely a mathematical exercise. If an inventory system is to be in operation at all, it can be shown that the basic economic order quantity model should be used, so that no shortages leading to lost sales should be allowed as long as demand is predictable.

Remember that in this chapter we have been dealing with certain, constant demand and predictable lead time for replenishment. We know that many successful retail establishments occasionally run out of convenience items like cigarettes and lose some sales. But these businesses are faced with *uncertain* demand. Stores would never run out of convenience items if demand could be predicted precisely and lead time never varied.

In Chapter 7, we will consider inventory policy when uncertainty leads to unplanned shortages, and how to make evaluations when those shortages result either in backorders or in lost sales.

6-6 Economic Production-Quantity Model

In the models presented thus far, orders have been filled instantaneously. Identical results are obtained when the lead time is constant, so that all items arrive at some future date that is fixed when the order is placed. We will now consider the special case encountered when a manufacturer can supply demanded items either from inventory or from current production. Since production itself requires some time, the replenishment of inventory items is not instantaneous. We assume that production, like demand, occurs at some known and constant rate. The **annual production rate**, in items per year, is denoted by B. We further assume that no backorders are allowed and that the production rate exceeds the demand rate, or $B > A$.

Figure 6-6 illustrates such an inventory system. Each inventory cycle consists of two phases, depending on whether or not production is occurring. The **production phase** is represented by the upward-sloping triangle on the left. Although the total amount produced is Q, a portion of the items produced is siphoned off to customers before it can

FIGURE 6-6

The production and inventory system when items are produced at a uniform rate.

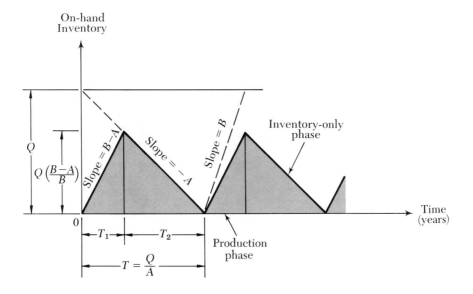

be stored, so that the maximum inventory buildup is

$$\text{Maximum inventory} = Q\left(\frac{B-A}{B}\right)$$

at which point production stops. The net accumulation of on-hand inventory occurs at the rate of $B - A$ units; the duration of the production phase is T_1. The **demand-only phase**, represented by the downward-sloping triangle, then begins. During this stage, all demands are filled from inventory until the stock is totally depleted; the duration of the demand-only phase is T_2. The respective phase durations are

$$T_1 = \frac{Q}{B}$$

$$T_2 = T - T_1 = \frac{Q}{A} - \frac{Q}{B}$$

$$= Q\left(\frac{B-A}{AB}\right)$$

In place of the usual ordering cost k, we now substitute the *fixed* cost of making a production run. This quantity is referred to as a **set-up cost** or a **start-up cost**. The **variable production cost** per item is denoted as c. The total annual relevant cost is

$$TC = \left(\frac{A}{Q}\right)k + hc\left(\frac{Q}{2}\right)\left(\frac{B-A}{B}\right)$$

which differs only slightly from this cost in the simple EOQ model. The minimum-cost production (order) quantity, often referred to as the **economic production quantity**, is found from

$$Q^* = \sqrt{\frac{2Ak}{hc}}\sqrt{\frac{B}{B-A}}$$

To illustrate, consider a manufacturer whose product demand is $A = 100,000$ units per year. Assume that the product can be produced at the rate of $B = 200,000$ units per year. Each production run costs $k = \$5,000$ to set up, and the variable production cost of each item is $c = \$10$. The annual cost per dollar value of holding items in inventory is $h = \$.20$.

The optimal production run is of size

$$Q^* = \sqrt{\frac{2(100,000)5,000}{.20(10)}}\sqrt{\frac{200,000}{200,000 - 100,000}}$$

$$= 31,623 \text{ items}$$

and each production run lasts

$$T_1^* = \frac{Q^*}{B} = \frac{31,623}{200,000} = .158 \text{ years, or approximately 58 days}$$

A new production run occurs every

$$T^* = \frac{Q^*}{A} = \frac{31,623}{100,000} = .316 \text{ years, or approximately 115 days}$$

The total annual relevant cost of this production plan is

$$TC = \left(\frac{100,000}{31,623}\right)5,000 + .20(10)\left(\frac{31,623}{2}\right)\left(\frac{200,000 - 100,000}{200,000}\right)$$

$$= 15,811 + 15,812$$

$$= 31,623 \text{ dollars per year}$$

6-7 Additional Remarks

The EOQ (economic order quantity) models discussed in this chapter have been purposely simplified. More complex models are available. For instance, a second shortage penalty that does not depend on the duration of a backorder is sometimes included in more general representations. The models described here can be expanded to include several different types of items. These more advanced models consider constraints that might reflect limitations on storage space or on the dollar investment in inventory. Slight extensions of the basic EOQ models also permit the treatment of quantity discounts.

Perhaps the greatest deficiency of the simple EOQ models is that they do not reflect that uncertainties exist. Few real-life inventory systems are based on predictable, constant demands. Yet the models presented in this chapter set the stage for our examination of inventory policy formulation under uncertainty in Chapter 7. There, we will see that the basic Wilson formula can often provide a solution that is very close to optimal, even though many of the assumptions on which it is based are not strictly true.

6-8 Computer-Assisted Inventory Evaluations

Computer assistance would be helpful for inventory evaluations in several ways. As noted, a computer may be used for maintaining data bases, so that each transaction is incorporated. In large-scale operations, those data make workable a perpetual inventory system, which needs to be monitored continuously so that the number of items on hand can always be known.

FIGURE 6-7

***QuickQuant* report for the wine ordering illustration when backordering is allowed.**

```
=============================================================================
                            QuickQuant Report
    INVENTORY ANALYSIS--ECONOMIC ORDER QUANTITY MODEL WITH BACKORDERING
-----------------------------------------------------------------------------
PROBLEM: Wine Ordering                              Date: 12-10-1989
                                                              Larry

      Parameter Values:
           Fixed Cost per Order: k = 100
           Annual Number of Items Demanded: A = 1000
           Unit Cost of Procuring an Item: c = 20
           Annual Holding Cost per Dollar Value: h = .2
           Annual Cost of Being Short One Item: p = 3.65

      Optimal Values:
           Economic Order Quantity: Q = 323.7198
           Economic Order Level: S = 154.4546
           Time Between Orders (year): T = .3237198
           Total Annual Relevant Cost: TC = 617.8182

-----------------------------------------------------------------------------
```

Even for the simple models of the present chapter, the necessary calculations can be a chore. The computer program, *QuickQuant*, may be used to simplify this chore. Figure 6-7 shows the *QuickQuant* report for the wine ordering illustration using $p = \$3.65$ with the backordering model.

CASE

Ingrid's Hallmark Shop I

Ingrid's Hallmark Shop is a card and gift store specializing in Hallmark cards and related items. A substantial portion of the business is with allied gift items for non-Hallmark suppliers and with toys. Altogether there are several hundred different products in this group that are ordered throughout the year.

One item demanded with some regularity is balloons, usually sold inflated with helium at the time of purchase. The balloons come in a variety of shapes and styles. It generally takes Ingrid two hours to place a balloon order, to track it, and to eventually pay the supplier. Her average cost per ballon is $.50, plus about $.25 for the helium, string and clamps.

Before taxes, Ingrid's Hallmark Shop has been netting about 20% on invested capital. The physical costs of storing merchandise are fixed. The store volume is too small to take advantage of any significant supplier quantity discounts.

Ingrid has no evidence regarding what shortage penalty applies when the store runs out of a particular balloon. She wishes to achieve a 95% service level, so that no particular balloon is out of stock more than 5% of the time.

Ingrid estimates that her shop will sell between 1,500 and 2,000 balloons in the coming year.

Questions

1. Comment on the suitability of using an EOQ model to determine how many balloons to order, and how often.

2. Remember, costs for inventory decisions may be assigned differently than those of traditional accounting. Discuss why it would not be appropriate to include the costs of the supplies—string, clamps, and helium—as part of the procurement cost for balloons.

3. Ingrid values her time at $10 per hour.
   (a) Establish values for (1) the unit procurement cost, (2) the ordering cost, and (3) the annual cost of holding a dollar's value in inventory.
   (b) State any assumptions you must make.

4. Refer to the parameters found in Question 3. Determine the optimal order quantity, assuming that no shortages are permitted and that annual demand is for (a) 1,500, (b) 1,600, (c) 1,700, (d) 1,800, (e) 1,900, and (f) 2,000 units.

5. Assuming backorders are taken, with an annual shortage penalty of $10 per balloon, determine the EOQ and order level when annual demand is 2,000 balloons.

6. Assume, instead, a 95% service level.
   (a) Compute the value of p that would be imputed from that policy you found in (a).
   (b) Determine the EOQ and order level when annual demand is 2,000 balloons.

7. The EOQ models described in this chapter are based on a single product.
   (a) Comment on the suitability of lumping together different balloon topics and designs, treating all as a single item.
   (b) What do you suggest for Ingrid?

PROBLEMS

6-1   Compu-Fast is a retailer that sells 1,000 personal computer disk drives per year. The units cost $400 each, and its costs $2,000 to place an order with the supplier. The annual cost per dollar value of holding items in inventory is $.25.
   (a) Determine the economic disk-drive order quantity.
   (b) How often should orders be placed?

6-2   Albers, Crumbly, and Itch sells mosquito repellents all over the world. Demand for the Malabug brand is 10,000 bottles per year. The African supplier charges AC&I $2 per bottle,

and the fixed cost of placing an order for Malabug is $100. AC&I targets a 15% annual rate of return on working-capital funds. The physical storage cost of Malabug is fixed.
(a) Determine the optimal order quantity and inventory cycle duration for Malabug.
(b) How many orders should be placed each year?
(c) Compute the total annual relevant inventory cost of Malabug.
(d) Suppose, for managerial convenience, that AC&I orders 2,500 bottles of Malabug each quarter.
    (1) Compute the total annual relevant inventory cost.
    (2) Is this sum larger or smaller than the amount in (c)? Explain.

6-3   Mini Stock is a car parts wholesaler that supplies 20 batteries to various service stations on each weekday. Batteries are purchased from the manufacturer in lots of 100 for $1,000 per lot. Multiple and fractional lots can be ordered at any time, and all orders are filled the next day. Each order placed with the manufacturer incurs a $50 handling charge and a $200 per-lot freight charge. The incremental cost is $.50 per year to store a battery in inventory. Mini Stock finances inventory investments by paying its holding company $1\frac{1}{2}$% monthly for borrowed funds.
(a) Determine the values of k, A, c, and h.
(b) How many batteries should be ordered, and how often should orders be placed to minimize total annual inventory cost?

6-4   Suppose that the store in Problem 6-2 can backorder Malabug when it is out of stock. But since most customers are simply itching to go backpacking and may have to delay their departure to wait to purchase the repellent, there is a penalty of $10 per year in lost goodwill for every bottle short.
(a) Determine the optimal order quantity, inventory level, and time between orders. What proportion of the time is Malabug out of stock?
(b) Compute the total annual relevant inventory cost of the policy you found in (a). Is this cost larger or smaller than your answer to Problem 6-2(c)? Do you think the same conclusion would be reached if the annual shortage penalty were $1,000 per bottle?

6-5   Paul Bunyan's Lumber Company periodically buys 10-penny size nails. The supplier will deliver any quantity of a particular order size for a charge of $1 plus $.20 per pound. It costs the store $.15 per dollar value of inventory items stored for one year. A total of 600 pounds of 10-penny nails are sold each year.
(a) How many pounds of nails should be ordered, and how often should orders be placed to minimize total annual inventory cost?
(b) Suppose that Paul Bunyan's has patient customers who will backorder 10-penny nails when they are out of stock. The annual cost of each pound of nails short is $.01.
    (1) Determine the optimal order quantity.
    (2) How many nails will have been backordered when each new shipment arrives?

6-6   Wheeling Wire Works, the manufacturer of the nails in Problem 6-5, makes them at an annual rate of 400 tons, even though only 300 tons are demanded per year. The unit cost of manufacturing is $100 per ton, and it costs an additional $30 to set up a production run. The annual holding cost of the nails is $.20 per dollar value.
(a) Determine the optimal number of tons that should be manufactured in a single production run. How often should the nails be produced? How long will a production run last?
(b) Compute Wheeling's total annual relevant inventory and production cost using the optimal policy you found in (a).

6-7   DanDee Assemblers buys SX-3 printed circuit boards for $10 each. Annual demand is 1,000 boards. No shortages are permitted. It costs DanDee $500 to process an order. The annual holding cost per dollar value is unknown.

(a) Suppose that $Q = 100$ boards are ordered. What imputed value is necessary for h in order for that policy to be optimal?

(b) Suppose that h is $.25. Determine the optimal order quantity and relevant inventory cost.

6-8   The Getco headquarters office buys 1,000 boxes of computer paper every two months at a cost of $5 per box. Paper usage is uniform and constant over time. The cost of placing an order with the supplier is $50. Assume that the present inventory policy is optimal, so that it minimizes annual paper inventory cost.

(a) How many boxes will be demanded in one year?

(b) What annual cost per dollar value of holding items in inventory is implicit under the present policy?

6-9   Suppose that it costs the office in Problem 6-8 $2 to hold a box of paper in inventory for one year.

(a) Determine the annual cost per dollar value of holding items in inventory.

(b) Suppose that the policy of ordering 1,000 boxes every two months must be reevaluated because shortages are now allowed. Assume an annual penalty of $10 per box short.

(1) Determine the optimal order quantity and inventory level.

(2) How often should orders be placed?

(c) Suppose, instead, that shortages are allowed only 5% of the time.

(1) Determine the optimal order quantity, order level, and imputed shortage penalty.

(2) Compute the corresponding total annual relevant inventory cost.

6-10   WysiWyg Systems lives up to its name. They provide word processing software for which *what you see* on the screen *is what you get* when printed. Company programs are distributed on floppy diskettes. Usage averages 500 disks per day, and the production schedule runs 300 days per year. WysiWyg currently earns 40% on invested capital. Each diskette order costs $100 to initiate and track, and the vendor supplies diskettes for $.35 each. Freight charges amount to $.05 per disk.

(a) Assuming that no shortages are permitted, determine the optimal order quantity and total annual relevant inventory cost.

(b) Actual WysiWyg company policy is to allow shortages no more than 1% of the time. Suppose that this policy is extended to floppies.

(1) Determine the optimal order quantity, order level, and imputed shortage penalty.

(2) Compute the corresponding total annual relevant inventory cost.

6-11   The manufacturer of Snail Hail, a garden mollusk pesticide, distributes its product from a plant warehouse. The plant has the capacity to produce 1,000 tons per year at a variable cost of $100 per ton. However, only 200 tons of Snail Hail are sold annually. The cost of setting up a production run is $2,000. The net cost of holding the highly volatile Snail Hail in inventory is $.40 per dollar value per year.

(a) Determine the economic production quantity.

(b) How long is each inventory cycle?

(c) How long will a production run last?

6-12   AlphaComp buys memory chips from overseas for $5 each. It costs $200 to place an order with the supplier. Annual demand is 100,000 units, and the company earns 30% on invested capital.

(a) Assuming that no shortages are allowed, determine the optimal order quantity.

(b) Suppose that some shortages do occur, so that 100 chips are backordered per inventory cycle. For Q^*, AlphaComp uses the answer you found in (a) plus half this amount.

    (1) Determine the order level for this policy.

    (2) Determine the implied service level percentage.

    (3) Compute the imputed shortage penalty.

6-13 *Quantity discounts.* Refer to Problem 6-5. Suppose that Paul Bunyan's Lumber Company buys 10-penny nails according to the following price schedule.

	QUANTITY (pounds)	PRICE PER POUND
(1)	0–200	$.20
(2)	201–500	.19
(3)	over 500	.18

Assume that no shortages are allowed.

(a) Determine the economic order quantity and the corresponding total annual inventory cost (including total procurement cost) for each price.

(b) Indicate, for each price level, whether the optimal order quantity you found in (a) is feasible, so that the quantity agrees with the price schedule. If it is not feasible, replace Q^* for that price by the price break quantity and recompute total annual cost.

(c) The overall optimal order quantity will be feasible and have the minimum total annual cost. Which of the three order quantities found in (a) is optimal?

6-14 Ace Widgets Supply distributes two products—Regular and Deluxe widgets—throughout the Midwest. The demand for the two items are independent; a total of 2,000 Regular and 4,000 Deluxe items are sold every year. The Regular items cost Ace $10 each; the Deluxe models cost twice as much. Ace's annual holding cost is $.25 for each dollar invested in inventory. The ordering cost is $100 per batch for each item. The Regular item may be ordered only when a Deluxe order is placed, but Regular widgets may be ordered less frequently than Deluxe widgets.

(a) Determine the optimal order quantity and the total annual relevant inventory cost for each item.

(b) Assume that a maximum of $10,000 may be invested in inventory at any given time. Are the quantities you found in (a) still possible?

(c) Ace's warehouse can store a maximum of only 1,000 items. Are the quantities you found in (a) still possible?

(d) Suppose that the Regular and the Deluxe models must be ordered at the same time and that each order costs $200. Treat combinations of 1 Regular and 2 Deluxe units as a single item.

    (1) Determine the economic order quantity and the corresponding total annual relevant cost.

    (2) Is this procedure less costly than the one in (a)? Explain.

6-15 Mrs. Moo's is a self-sufficient dairy; all feed grasses are grown on the premises. To rejuvenate the grass and trigger growth, periodic fertilizing is necessary. The dairy herd eats full-grown grass at the rate of 5,000 acres per year. Each fertilizing costs $100 to set up and requires $50 worth of chemicals per acre to create full growth. It takes a fertilized acre one-tenth of a year to reach maturity. There are 1,000 acres of grassland at Mrs. Moo's. The dairy finances its chemical purchases through the local bank at a 10% annual interest rate.

(a) Determine the number of acres that should be fertilized in each application. How often should fertilization take place? How many applications should be made each year?

(b) Do you think that it is totally satisfactory to apply the EOQ model to this problem? Explain.

6-16 The Coin-Op is a vending machine operator that must establish a policy for periodically restocking its candy machines and collecting the coins deposited by customers. The total labor cost of restocking a machine is $7, most of which is due to travel time. Each machine can hold quite a lot of candy, so the machines do not need to be filled to capacity. All machines are identical, and each satisfies a demand of 5,000 candy bars per year. Candy bars cost $.10 each and are sold for $.25. The firm's annual opportunity cost of working capital is 20%. A significant aspect in establishing a policy is that all those quarters are uselessly locked up in coin boxes, so that the quicker retrieval of these funds translates directly into smaller working-capital requirements.

(a) Determine the values of c and h. (Assume that the same cost of working capital applies to the value of the candy and to the value of the coins. Also assume that the average inventory of candy bars is the same as the average inventory of quarters.)

(b) Determine the restocking quantity that minimizes total annual cost. How often should the machines be restocked?

CHAPTER

7

Inventory Decisions with Uncertain Factors

ost inventory decisions must be made under uncertain conditions, so that one or more quantities must be represented by random variables having probability distributions. Real-world demands are usually not constant and uniform, and probabilities should be used to represent them. Mathematical models involving probability are often referred to as **stochastic models**. In situations that do not involve uncertainty, such as those discussed in Chapter 6, the analytical procedures employ **deterministic models**.

Deterministic models are limited in scope and may be applied only approximately to most real-world decision-making problems. They do, however, provide points of departure for developing more realistic methods of analysis. It is easier to cope with uncertainty when an analytical framework has already been established by means of deterministic models. But making the leap from certainty into the world of uncertainty presents new difficulties.

Inventory models involving probability are generally based on expected values. The optimal inventory policy is found by considering *expected* profits or costs, so that the best we can do is to maximize or minimize long-run "average" profits or costs. Thus, even an optimal policy may lead to a range of outcomes from poor to excellent. The actual result is determined largely by luck. Such a lack of determinism on the part of the decision maker is an unavoidable burden we face whenever we attempt to cope with uncertainty.

7-1 A Simple Inventory Decision: The *Playboy* Problem

To set the stage for analyzing inventory decisions from explicit mathematical models, we identify the alternative inventory policies and use them, together with uncertain demand events, to construct a payoff table. Applying probability values for each possible demand level, we then choose the inventory policy that provides the best expected payoff. At this point, the optimal decision is indicated.

The Nature of Uncertain Demand

As an illustration, consider the problem a small drugstore faces in trying to determine how many copies of various magazines to order. In particular, the drugstore owner wants to estimate how many copies of the October issue of *Playboy* to stock. Assume that past demand has provided a history of customer interest in this product and that the owner knows the frequencies of the various demand levels, which serve to establish probabilities for demand in future months.

Demand is a totally distinct notion from *sales*. A retailer can only sell a product if it is in stock or if a customer is willing to order and wait for it. *Playboy* is not an item that customers will order (except by subscription); if they do not see it on the shelf, no sale can be made. Yet, the desire to buy a copy of *Playboy* is a demand. Thus, we may define the **demand** for an item as the *intent to buy* it. Such a demand results in either a sale or the loss of a potential sale (when the item is not in stock).

Suppose that the drugstore owner has determined the following probability distribution for the demand for the October issue of *Playboy*.

COPIES DEMANDED	PROBABILITY
$D = 20$	.2
$D = 21$	.4
$D = 22$	.3
$D = 23$	.1

Alternative order quantities must be considered. Obviously, *Playboy* is a profitable item to include on the magazine rack, so the owner will not want to stock less than the minimum demand (if any issues are stocked at all, which is another question entirely). Also, there is no advantage to stocking more than the maximum demand.

TABLE 7-1

Payoff Table for the *Playboy* Problem

DEMAND EVENT	ORDER QUANTITY ACT			
	Q = 20	Q = 21	Q = 22	Q = 23
D = 20	$18.00	$16.60	$15.20	$13.80
D = 21	18.00	18.90	17.50	16.10
D = 22	18.00	18.90	19.80	18.40
D = 23	18.00	18.90	19.80	20.70

Maximizing Expected Profit

Playboy is purchased directly from the local distributor at an assumed price of $2.10 and sells for $3.00 per copy. Unsold copies are returned at the end of the month for a $.70 credit. We assume the drugstore owner's goal is to maximize profit, so that the **payoff table** in Table 7-1 applies. In calculating the profits for each act and event combination, we assume that whenever Q is greater than D, that $Q - D$ unsold *Playboys* will be returned for the $.70 credit. Also, when Q is smaller than D, we assume that the excess demand is not filled and the disappointed customer must buy the October *Playboy* elsewhere. No penalty is considered for being short.

We assume that the owner will choose the value of Q that maximizes expected profit. Table 7-2 shows the calculations involved. The optimal order quantity is $Q = 21$ *Playboys*.

TABLE 7-2

Expected Payoffs for the *Playboy* Problem

DEMAND EVENT	PROBABILITY	PROFIT × PROBABILITY			
		Q = 20	Q = 21	Q = 22	Q = 23
D = 20	.2	$3.60	$3.32	$3.04	$2.76
D = 21	.4	7.20	7.56	7.00	6.44
D = 22	.3	5.40	5.67	5.94	5.52
D = 23	.1	1.80	1.89	1.98	1.07
	Expected profits	$18.00	$18.44	$17.96	$16.79
			Maximum		

7-2 Marginal Analysis: The Newsboy Problem

The *Playboy* problem typifies inventory policy decisions when the demand for a product is uncertain and its lifetime is limited, so that a single time period applies. Such a perishable product is epitomized by the daily newspaper, which has an effective demand lasting only one day. A news vendor has one opportunity to decide how many copies of today's *Wall*

Street Journal to stock. An entire class of inventory decisions of identical structure is referred to as the **newsboy problem**.

It is convenient to develop a mathematical model to solve this type of problem. Although analysis using a payoff table or a decision tree is effective for small-scale problems like our *Playboy* example, a large number of alternatives or possible events makes these procedures impractical.

The Mathematical Model

In its simplest form, the objective of the newsboy problem is to decide how many items Q should be stocked at the beginning of the inventory cycle. The uncertain demand D expresses the number of items that customers will require during this period. Two types of outcomes may occur. If demand is less than or equal to the order quantity, sales will equal the quantity demanded; if demand is greater than the initial stock, sales will equal the order quantity.

$$\text{Sales} = \begin{cases} D & \text{if } D \leq Q \\ Q & \text{if } D > Q \end{cases}$$

Four cost elements are considered.

$c =$ Unit procurement cost

$h_E =$ Additional cost of each item held at the *end* of the inventory cycle

$p_S =$ Penalty for each item short (loss of goodwill)

$p_R =$ Selling price

Single-period inventory decisions usually involve a short cycle, and none of the above parameters are time based. Here, we use subscripts to expand the notation from Chapter 6. In this model, the holding cost applies only at the *end* of the inventory cycle, and h_E has the subscript E to distinguish this usage of holding cost from that in previous inventory models. Likewise, instead of one shortage penalty p, there are now two, p_S and p_R. We will assume that there is no fixed ordering cost. The unit holding cost ordinarily represents the disposal cost of the unsold items in the ending inventory. If these items have any further limited economic use, h_E represents the unit disposal cost minus the salvage value (so that h_E may be negative). The shortage cost has two components for each item demanded beyond the quantity stocked. These are the values p_S and p_R for the loss of customer goodwill. Including p_R reflects the *lost revenue* from missing a sale; the reason for this is explained in the following discussion.

As we did in the *Playboy* problem, we will assume that the news vendor's objective is to maximize expected profit or to minimize expected cost for the inventory period. This may be achieved only when revenue is assumed to be independent of inventory policy, which is not strictly true when the potential for lost sales exists. For example, if the news vendor pays $c = \$.20$ for each paper and sells it for $p_R = \$.23$, then the revenue consists of $\$.23$ times the demand minus $\$.20$ times the unfilled demand if shortages arise. We may ignore the former, since it is unaffected by inventory policy. But the latter is the revenue lost due to shortages and must be treated as a cost of unfilled demand. The full $.23 (not just the $.03 gross profit) must therefore be included in the shortage penalty, along with any other amounts identified in that category, such as the loss of goodwill. Here, we assume that each paper short costs an average of two cents in future profits, so that $p_S = \$.02$. Should there be no loss of goodwill ($p_S = 0$), the shortage penalty would consist only of lost revenue. The revenue lost due to shortages would be identical to the out-of-pocket cost the news vendor would incur if shortages had to be filled by purchasing papers from another dealer at the full $.23 retail price.

To obtain the expected cost, we will assume that probabilities $\Pr[D = d]$ for possible levels of demand d are available in tabular form. (It is convenient to use capital D to denote the actual but unknown demand and lowercase d to represent any one of the many possible demands.) For an order quantity of Q when demand is d, the total cost is

$$TC = cQ + \begin{cases} h_E(Q - d) & \text{if } d \le Q & \text{(holding cost)} \\ (p_S + p_R)(d - Q) & \text{if } d > Q & \text{(shortage cost)} \end{cases}$$

cQ is the total procurement cost. Note that this applies to the ordered quantity Q and not to the demand. The unit holding cost h_E applies only to the surplus items procured beyond the amount demanded, represented by the difference $Q - d$. The shortage penalty $p_S + p_R$ applies only to the deficit in available items below the actual demand, which is denoted by the quantity $d - Q$. The **total expected cost** TEC is found by applying the appropriate probability weights and summing over all possibilities, or

$$TEC(Q) = cQ + \sum_{d=0}^{Q} h_E(Q - d)\Pr[D = d] + \sum_{d > Q} (p_S + p_R)(d - Q)\Pr[D = d]$$

Note that the total expected cost depends on what value of Q is chosen.

Finding the Optimal Solution through Marginal Analysis

To facilitate our explanation of how to find the optimal order quantity that minimizes total expected cost, we will develop the news vendor's problem. We already know that the unit procurement cost is $c = \$.20$, the goodwill cost is $p_S = \$.02$ per paper short, and the selling price is $p_R = \$.23$. Although reprocessors sometimes buy unsold newspapers, the cyclical demand for paper salvage is down and they are not buying now. Unsold papers must be hauled to the dump at a cost of $h_E = \$.01$ each. The probability distribution in Table 7-3 is assumed to apply for daily demand. This table provides the cumulative probabilities for demand and the calculation of expected demand, which is equal to 49.50 papers.

The optimal solution could be obtained by calculating a payoff table with 11 events (one for each possible demand) and 11 order quantity acts. Using cost as the payoff measure, we could then find the expected cost of each value of Q by multiplying the respective column values by the probabilities for d and summing. The optimal Q would have the smallest expected cost. However, it is simpler to follow another approach called **marginal analysis**.

Marginal analysis is based on *convexity*—a mathematical property of expressions of the form $TEC(Q)$. In principle, any mathematical expression is convex when its value

TABLE 7-3
Probability Distribution Data for the Newsboy Problem

(1) POSSIBLE DEMAND d	(2) PROBABILITY $\Pr[D = d]$	(3) CUMULATIVE PROBABILITY $\Pr[D \leq d]$	(4) DEMAND × PROBABILITY
45	.05	.05	2.25
46	.06	.11	2.76
47	.09	.20	4.23
48	.12	.32	5.76
49	.17	.49	8.33
50	.20	.69	10.00
51	.12	.81	6.12
52	.08	.89	4.16
53	.06	.95	3.18
54	.04	.99	2.16
55	.01	1.00	.55
	1.00		Expected demand = 49.50

decreases steadily at a progressively slower rate for increasing levels of the independent variable until a minimum is achieved, after which values of the expression increase steadily at an increasing rate. This means that $TEC(Q)$ achieves its minimum value at the lowest level of Q that is followed by an increase in total expected cost. This feature is illustrated in Figure 7-1.

We can find the smallest order quantity that is followed by an increase in total expected cost by considering all of the differences between successive TEC's.

$$\text{Difference} = TEC(Q + 1) - TEC(Q)$$

The smallest Q having a non-negative difference is optimal.

A mathematical analysis shows that the successive total cost difference[†] is

$$\text{Difference} = c + h_E \Pr[D \leq Q] - (p_S + p_R)(1 - \Pr[D \leq Q])$$

[†] The difference in *holding costs only* is

$$\sum_{d=0}^{Q+1} h_E[(Q + 1) - d] \Pr[D = d] - \sum_{d=0}^{Q} h_E(Q - d) \Pr[D = d] = h_E \Pr[D \leq Q]$$

Likewise, the difference in *shortage costs only* is

$$\sum_{d > Q+1} (p_S + p_R)[d - (Q + 1)] \Pr[D = d] - \sum_{d > Q} (p_S + p_R)(d - Q) \Pr[D = d]$$
$$= -(p_S + p_R)(1 - \Pr[D \leq Q])$$

Combining these results with the fact that ordering $Q + 1$ items involves one unit of further procurement (an expenditure of c) gives us the above expression.

FIGURE 7-1

The convexity principle in marginal analysis.

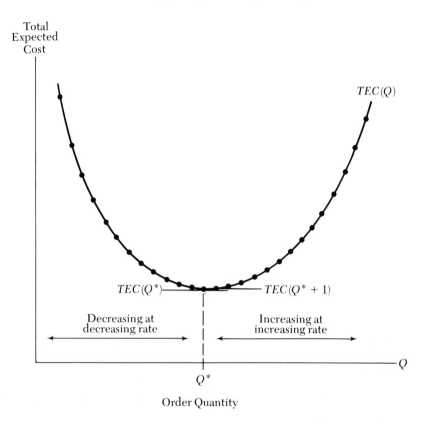

Order Quantity

which must be greater than or equal to zero. Notice that this expression involves only the unit cost constants and the cumulative probability that demand falls at or below the order quantity. The condition for the optimal order quantity is established by setting the total expected cost difference greater than or equal to zero and rearranging terms.

The **optimal order quantity** Q^* is the smallest possible demand such that

$$\Pr[D \leq Q^*] \geq \frac{p_S + p_R - c}{p_S + p_R + h_E}$$

This tells us that we need to calculate only the above ratio, using the constants given for the problem, and establish the cumulative probability for demand. The smallest demand with a cumulative probability that exceeds this ratio is equal to the order quantity that minimizes total expected cost.

Returning to the news vendor example, we calculate the ratio

$$\frac{p_S + p_R - c}{p_S + p_R + h_E} = \frac{.02 + .23 - .20}{.02 + .23 + .01} = .192$$

TABLE 7-4

Total Expected Cost Calculation for the News Vendor's Optimal Inventory Policy ($Q^* = 47$)

POSSIBLE DEMAND d	PROBABILITY $\Pr[D = d]$	HOLDING COST $.01(47 - d)$	SHORTAGE COST $(.02 + .23)(d - 47)$	COST × PROBABILITY
45	.05	$.02	—	$.0010
46	.06	.01	—	.0006
47	.09	0	—	0
48	.12	—	$ .25	.0300
49	.17	—	.50	.0850
50	.20	—	.75	.1500
51	.12	—	1.00	.1200
52	.08	—	1.25	.1000
53	.06	—	1.50	.0900
54	.04	—	1.75	.0700
55	.01	—	2.00	.0200
	1.00			$.6666

$$cQ = \$.20(47) = \$9.40$$

$$TEC(47) = \$9.40 + \$.6666 = \$10.0666$$

From column (3) of Table 7-3, we see that the smallest cumulative demand probability that exceeds this value is .20, which applies when the demand is for 47 papers. Thus, $Q^* = 47$, and the news vendor will minimize expected cost by stocking exactly 47 papers. The total expected cost of this inventory policy is calculated in Table 7-4 to be $TEC(47) = \$10.0666$. Notice that this optimal order quantity is less than the expected demand of 49.50. Depending on the values for c, h_E, p_S, and p_R, Q^* may lie above or below the expected demand.

The Impact of Cost Elements on Total Expected Cost

The shortage penalty ($p_S + p_R$) is perhaps the most elusive cost element in inventory decisions because it is difficult to quantify the loss of goodwill. For this reason, it may be desirable to analyze the inventory decision for a range of levels of ($p_S + p_R$). Such optional additional work is referred to as **sensitivity analysis**, because it tells us just how sensitive the optimal solution is to variations in the value assumed for the parameter constant. Table 7-5 shows the total expected costs for the newsboy problem when ($p_S + p_R$) is .25, .30, .35, .40, or .45, with $c = .20$ and $h_E = .01$. Notice that within each row, at each level of Q, the TEC's increase as ($p_S + p_R$) increases (except in the last row, where Q is equal to the maximum possible demand and shortages are impossible). This is because a greater shortage penalty may only increase total inventory cost.

It is interesting to see how Q^* changes as ($p_S + p_R$) is increased. When ($p_S + p_R$) is raised from .25 to .30, the optimal order quantity jumps from $Q^* = 47$ to $Q^* = 49$ and remains at that level through ($p_S + p_R$) = .40. At ($p_S + p_R$) = .45, the optimal order

TABLE 7-5

Total Expected Costs for the Newsboy Problem at Several Levels
for the Combined Shortage Penalty Components

ORDER QUANTITY Q	TOTAL EXPECTED COST $TEC(Q)$				
	$p_S + p_R = .25$	$p_S + p_R = .30$	$p_S + p_R = .35$	$p_S + p_R = .40$	$p_S + p_R = .45$
45	$10.1250	$10.3500	$10.5750	$10.8000	$11.0250
46	10.0880	10.2655	10.4430	10.6205	10.7980
47	10.0666*	10.1996	10.3326	10.4656	10.5986
48	10.0686	10.1616	10.2546	10.3476	10.4406
49	10.1018	10.1608*	10.2198*	10.2788*	10.3378
50	10.1792	10.2127	10.2462	10.2797	10.3132*
51	10.3086	10.3266	10.3446	10.3626	10.3806
52	10.4692	10.4777	10.4862	10.4947	10.5032
53	10.6506	10.6536	10.6566	10.6596	10.6626
54	10.8476	10.8481	10.8486	10.8491	10.8496
55	11.0550	11.0550	11.0550	11.0550	11.0550
$\dfrac{p_S + p_R - c}{p_S + p_R + h_E}$	.192	.323	.417	.488	.543
Q^*	47	49	49	49	50

quantity jumps again to $Q^* = 50$. Thus, we can see that when shortage penalties are more severe, larger order quantities (larger levels of Q^*) are required to minimize total expected costs.

Similar conclusions may be drawn about the other cost parameters. In general, TEC will increase as either c or h_E increases, but the relationship to Q^* will differ. Since the optimal order quantity is determined by the ratio $(p_S + p_R - c)/(p_S + p_R + h_E)$ and the cumulative probability for demand, Q^* increases as the ratio increases. Thus, holding $(p_S + p_R)$ and h_E fixed, a reduction in c will make the numerator larger and increase Q^*, whereas the reverse is true for an increase in c. This reflects the fact that a smaller procurement cost makes it less painful to hold unsold items. Increasing the level of h_E will increase the denominator, thereby reducing the ratio, and lowering the level of Q^*, whereas a reduction in h_E will increase Q^*. Thus, everything else being equal, the more expensive it is to dispose of unsold items, the lower the order quantity should be.

7-3 Continuous Probability Distribution For Demand: The Christmas Tree Problem

When the number of possible demands is large—as it would be when hundreds or thousands of units are sold daily—it is usually convenient to use a continuous approximation for the demand probability distribution. The single-period models discussed thus far may be adapted to continuous probability distributions. As was true for the discrete probabilities applicable in these earlier models, the order level depends only on the cumulative probability for demand. However, there is one change: Q^* is chosen, so that the ratio is exactly equal to the cumulative probability that demand lies at or below that level. When demand is a continuous random variable, the **optimal order quantity** Q^* is that level of possible demand where

$$\Pr[D \leq Q^*] = \frac{p_S + p_R - c}{p_S + p_R + h_E}$$

Suppose that the demand for Christmas trees experienced by a particular Gotham City seller is approximately normally distributed with a mean of $\mu = 2,000$ trees and a standard deviation of $\sigma = 500$ trees. The trees sell for an average of $9 and cost $3 each. The loss of goodwill arising from shortages is judged to be $1 per tree short. The city license requires that all unsold trees be converted into mulch pulp, which is donated to the Gotham City Parks Department; the cost of pulverization averages $.50 per tree. The seller has already committed funds to any fixed costs involved. How many trees should be ordered from Canadian suppliers to minimize inventory costs (and thereby maximize profits)?

The applicable cost constants (in dollars) are

$$c = 3 \qquad h_E = .50 \qquad p_S = 1 \qquad p_R = 9$$

The following ratio applies.

$$\frac{p_S + p_R - c}{p_S + p_R + h_E} = \frac{1 + 9 - 3}{1 + 9 + .50} = .67$$

This ratio establishes the cumulative demand probability that determines Q^*, or

$$\Pr[D \leq Q^*] = .67$$

Figure 7-2 helps to explain how the value of Q^* is obtained. The shaded area under the normal curve for Christmas tree demand is equal to the cumulative probability of .67. The portion of this area that is above the mean is equal to .17, which corresponds to a normal deviate value of $z = .44$ (see Appendix Table B). This expresses the number of standard deviations that Q^* lies beyond the mean, so that

$$Q^* = \mu + z\sigma$$

Substituting $\mu = 2,000$ and $\sigma = 500$ trees into this equation, we obtain

$$Q^* = 2,000 + .44(500) = 2,220 \text{ trees}$$

The Gotham City seller should order 2,220 Christmas trees.

FIGURE 7-2

The normal curve used to establish Q*.

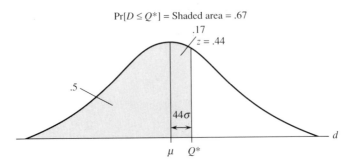

$\Pr[D \le Q^*] = $ Shaded area $ = .67$

Christmas Tree Demand

Computing the Total Expected Cost

The determination of total expected cost *TEC* when demand has a continuous normal distribution may be accomplished in the same way as before. That involves creating a table listing a few representative demands *d*. The probability for each possible demand is the area under the normal curve for the interval centered at *d*, as illustrated in Figure 7-3. There, we see that each *d* has a holding cost, shown as the height of the line in (a), or a shortage cost in (b), depending on which side of *Q* demand happens to fall. Each applicable cost is multiplied by the applicable probability, with *cQ* then added to the sum of those products to obtain *TEC*.

The expected value thereby obtained is only *approximately* correct, with the accuracy improving with the number of *d* levels considered. Fortunately, we may avoid those cumbersome calculations by using values from an Appendix table constructed especially for this purpose. The following expression may then be used.

$$
TEC(Q) = cQ + \begin{cases} (h_E + p_S + p_R)\sigma L\left(\dfrac{Q - \mu}{\sigma}\right) + h_E(Q - \mu) & \text{if } Q \ge \mu \\[3ex] (h_E + p_S + p_R)\sigma L\left(\dfrac{\mu - Q}{\sigma}\right) + (p_S + p_R)(\mu - Q) & \text{if } Q < \mu \end{cases}
$$

$L(x)$ is the **normal loss function**, the values for which apply to the *distance* x separating μ and Q (measured in standard deviation units).[†] These values are listed in Appendix Table C.

[†] This function is ordinarily used in calculating expected opportunity losses, which accounts for its name. These applications will be discussed in Chapter 25.

FIGURE 7-3

How expected cost calculations may be approximated when demand is normally distributed.

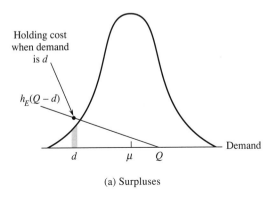

Holding cost
when demand
is d

$h_E(Q - d)$

Demand

d μ Q

(a) Surpluses

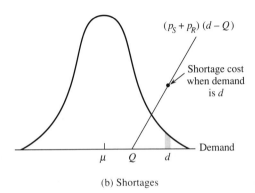

$(p_S + p_R)(d - Q)$

Shortage cost
when demand
is d

Demand

μ Q d

(b) Shortages

For the Christmas tree problem the total expected cost may be computed using the above expression with an optimal policy of $Q^* = 2{,}220$ trees. We use the $Q \geq \mu$ case.

$$TEC(2{,}220) = \$3(2{,}220) + (.50 + 1 + 9)(500)L\left(\frac{2{,}220 - 2{,}000}{500}\right) + .50(2{,}220 - 2{,}000)$$

$$= \$6{,}660 + 5{,}250L(.44) + 110$$

Appendix Table C provides the value $L(.44) = .2169$, so that

$$TEC(2{,}220) = \$6{,}660 + 5{,}250(.2169) + 110 = \$7{,}909$$

7-4 Multi-Period Inventory Policies

Until this point, we have discussed only single-period inventory problems. These models generally apply to perishable items that may be ordered only once and that may not be held in inventory to satisfy demands occurring in another period. It is far more common, however, to encounter the problem of establishing an inventory policy for items that may be stored over several time periods and that may be reordered with considerable flexibility.

We began our initial discussion of inventory decisions in Chapter 6 with what we may now refer to as **multi-period inventory policies**. At this point, we must begin to cope with uncertainties. The two major uncertain variables encountered in inventory decisions are **demand** and **lead time** required to fill orders.

The mathematical procedures for analyzing multi-period inventory decisions under uncertainty fall into two categories. *Continuous review models* assume that a continuous monitorship of inventory positions takes place, so that decision rules regarding replenishment are based on the current inventory position. These models give rise to (r, Q) policies, and orders are triggered whenever the current inventory position falls below the **reorder point** r, at which point Q items are ordered.

Figure 7-4 illustrates the behavior of an inventory system when demand and lead time are uncertain. Notice that inventory depletion occurs erratically due to the varying intensities of demand. Orders are placed whenever the inventory position falls below r. But continued variations in demand and unpredictable lead times cause shortages to occur in some periods and not in others. This erratic behavior results in varying cycle durations and beginning inventory positions.

The other category of multi-period inventory decisions involves *periodic review models.* These models apply when circumstances permit a physical count of the inventory items to be made only once every week, month, quarter, or year. In such inventory systems, the current inventory position remains unknown between inventory tallies. Periodic

FIGURE 7-4
Inventory system using (r, Q) policy with uncertain demand and lead time.

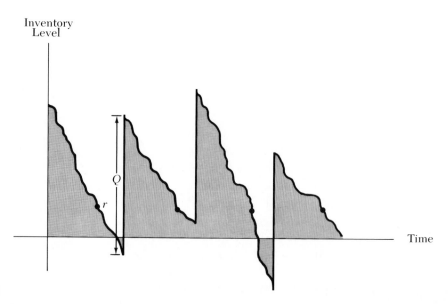

review models differ considerably from the (r, Q) type of model that we will consider in this chapter.

Here, we will present two simple continuous review models that may be employed to find the optimal multi-period inventory policy. Our models are only approximately correct, although the solutions they provide are usually as adequate as more complex formulations. We will consider two cases: (1) short items are *backordered* and (2) *sales are lost* due to shortages.

The EOQ Model for Uncertain Demand

Because several time periods are involved in a multi-period inventory decision, we will return to the problem objective we established in Chapter 6 of minimizing total annual relevant cost. Since demand and lead time are now uncertain, we minimize *expected cost*, which is the sum of the following expected values.

Annual ordering cost

Annual holding cost

Annual shortage cost

Although demand is no longer presumed to be certain, we will assume that the mean annual demand rate applies uniformly over time. We use the symbol

$$A = \text{Mean annual demand rate}$$

(The *mean* demand rate is constant, but demand may vary from period to period.) If Q items are ordered each time at a cost of k per order, it follows that

$$\text{Expected annual ordering cost} = \left(\frac{A}{Q}\right)k$$

which was true for the earlier models described in Chapter 6.

The actual demand D over any interval of time is uncertain and must be specified in terms of a probability distribution. Instead of focusing on some fixed calendar period like a day, week, or month, our model will consider the level of demand during the lead time for filling an order. For this purpose, we will employ the probability distribution for **lead-time demand**, which we will distinguish from the earlier single-period distributions by a subscript L.

$$\text{Probability for } d \text{ units demanded in lead time} = \text{Pr}_L[D = d]$$

This distribution reflects two uncertainties: one regarding the demand itself and one surrounding the duration of the lead time. Our model will focus on the expected value of D.

$$\mu = \text{Mean lead-time demand}$$

There are two major cases considered in inventory evaluations. These are based on how shortages are handled.

1. **Backordering** occurs when items are out of stock. Any demand occurring during this time will be filled when the outstanding order arrives. A shortage penalty applies that includes the added cost of processing plus any cost assigned to the loss of customer goodwill.
2. **Lost sales** arise from any demand occurring while items are out of stock. The shortage penalty reflects the seller's gross profit (margin) for the missing items that would otherwise have been sold, plus the cost of the diminished goodwill that results from the shortage.

The two cases have very similar models. We begin with a detailed discussion of the backordering case.

Inventory Model with Backordering

This model is appropriate whenever items are ordinarily backordered. For example, it applies to printed computer forms or similar items that have no substitutes. There may be a special cost for processing a backorder, and there may be some loss of goodwill that could impact future business with the shorted customer.

Each inventory cycle begins when an order arrives. Stock is then depleted until it falls below the reorder point r, which is assumed to exceed μ, and a new order is placed. Continued depletion occurs until the order arrives. Any items short are then provided from the incoming shipment. The expected level of inventory just before the order arrives is $r - \mu$, so that the subsequent cycle begins with an expected inventory of $Q + r - \mu$ items. Because the mean rate of depletion is uniform, the average inventory level during a cycle must be the average of these quantities. Thus,

$$\text{Expected average cycle inventory} = \frac{1}{2}[(Q + r - \mu) + r - \mu]$$

$$= \frac{Q}{2} + r - \mu$$

As we did in the EOQ models described in Chapter 6, we let h represent the *annual* cost per *dollar value* of holding items in inventory. From this, it follows that

$$\text{Expected annual holding cost} = hc\left[\frac{Q}{2} + r - \mu\right] \quad \text{(with backordering)}$$

The most complicated part of the EOQ models for uncertain demand involves the shortage cost component. That cost depends on the number of shortages in each cycle, which is a random variable due to the uncertain lead-time demand. Since items are only backordered when lead-time demand exceeds the reorder point r, we may determine the

expected number of shortages per inventory cycle

$$B(r) = \sum_{d > r} (d - r) \Pr_L[D = d]$$

In the backordering case, all shortages will eventually be filled, and $B(r)$ may then be viewed as the expected number of backorders. Multiplying $B(r)$ by the expected number of cycles per year A/Q and the penalty p_S for each item short, we obtain

$$\text{Expected annual shortage cost} = p_S \left(\frac{A}{Q}\right) B(r) \quad \text{(with backordering)}$$

In keeping with the single-cycle models employed in this chapter, we let p_S represent the cost of each item short, regardless of how long it is backordered. This parameter therefore differs from its counterpart in the backordering model we examined in Chapter 6, where the penalty applied to the duration of the shortage as well. Since backordering occurs, no lost sales revenue is included in p_S.

The **total annual expected cost** may be expressed as

$$TEC(r, Q) = \left(\frac{A}{Q}\right)k + hc\left[\frac{Q}{2} + r - \mu\right] + p_S\left(\frac{A}{Q}\right)B(r) \quad \text{(with backordering)}$$

Our objective is to find the values of Q and r that minimize this expression.

The following procedure permits us to determine the optimal levels of these variables.

1. For a given order quantity Q, the **optimal reorder point** r^* is the *smallest* quantity having a cumulative lead-time demand probability such that

$$\Pr_L[D \leq r^*] \geq 1 - \frac{hcQ}{p_S A} \quad \text{(with backordering)}$$

2. For a given reorder point r, the **optimal order quantity** Q^* is found from

$$Q^* = \sqrt{\frac{2A[k + p_S B(r)]}{hc}} \quad \text{(with backordering)}$$

To solve for either r or Q, the value of the other variable must be known. Before we may begin, a seed value must be obtained for one of these variables. This value is then used to determine the level of the second variable, which in turn is used to refine the value of the first variable. This procedure continues—using the last Q to obtain the next r and that r to obtain the next Q—until no values change.

A good starting or seed value may be obtained by using the Wilson formula from Chapter 6 for the economic order quantity when no backordering is allowed.

$$Q_1 = \sqrt{\frac{2Ak}{hc}}$$

The subscript 1 simply indicates that this is the first attempt to determine the value of the order quantity.

ILLUSTRATION
Ordering Typewriter Ribbons

Suppose that a stationery store stocks carbon typewriter ribbons. The demand and lead time are uncertain, but historical experience indicates that the lead-time demand distribution in Table 7-6 applies. The mean annual demand is 1,500 ribbons per year; the cost of placing an order is $5; each ribbon has a wholesale price of $1.50; the store finances its working capital through bank loans at a rate of 12% per annum; and the store incurs an estimated penalty in future profits of $.50 for each ribbon short and backordered. Thus, the following parameters apply.

$$A = 1,500 \text{ items per year}$$

$$k = \$5 \text{ per order}$$

$$c = \$1.50 \text{ per item}$$

$$h = \$.12 \text{ per dollar value per year}$$

$$p_S = \$.50 \text{ per unit short (no matter how long)}$$

The mean lead-time demand is computed in Table 7-6, where $\mu = 4$.
   The starting value for the order quantity is

$$Q_1 = \sqrt{\frac{2(1,500)5}{.12(1.5)}} = 289$$

TABLE 7-6
Lead-Time Demand Probability Distribution for Carbon Typewriter Ribbons

POSSIBLE DEMAND d	PROBABILITY $Pr_L[D = d]$	DEMAND × PROBABILITY	CUMULATIVE PROBABILITY $Pr_L[D \leq d]$
0	.01	0	.01
1	.07	.07	.08
2	.16	.32	.24
3	.20	.60	.44
4	.19	.76	.63
5	.16	.80	.79
6	.10	.60	.89
7	.06	.42	.95
8	.03	.24	.98
9	.01	.09	.99
10	.01	.10	1.00
	1.00	$\mu = 4.00$	

The following steps permit us to determine the optimal levels of Q and r.

1. Using the value $Q = 289$, we compute

$$1 - \frac{hcQ}{p_s A} = 1 - \frac{.12(1.5)289}{.5(1,500)} = .93$$

The smallest cumulative lead-time demand probability greater than or equal to this value in Table 7-6 is

$$\Pr_L[D \leq 7] = .95$$

so that the optimal reorder point is $r* = 7$ ribbons.

2. Using $r = 7$, we first evaluate the corresponding expected number of backorders per cycle $B(r) = B(7)$. This quantity is computed as follows.

DEMAND d	PROBABILITY $\Pr_L[D = d]$	DIFFERENCE $d - r = d - 7$	DIFFERENCE $\times$ PROBABILITY
8	.03	1	.03
9	.01	2	.02
10	.01	3	.03
			$B(7) = .08$

Substituting $B(7) = .08$ into the expression for $Q*$ gives us

$$Q* = \sqrt{\frac{2(1,500)[5 + .5(.08)]}{.12(1.5)}} = 290$$

Since this result differs from the initial value of $Q = 289$, we must continue the procedure with a second *iteration*.

1. (*Second iteration.*) We use $Q = 290$ to recompute the reorder point. First, we find

$$1 - \frac{hcQ}{p_s A} = 1 - \frac{.12(1.5)290}{.5(1,500)} = .93$$

which is identical to the cumulative probability indicated for $r* = 7$ found before. The reorder point does not change, so that no step 2 calculations are required.

Thus, the values in the optimal (r, Q) policy are

$$r* = 7 \quad \text{and} \quad Q* = 290$$

so that $Q^* = 290$ ribbons should be ordered whenever the current inventory falls below $r^* = 7$. The total annual expected cost of this policy is

$$TEC = \left(\frac{1{,}500}{290}\right)5 + .12(1.5)\left[\frac{290}{2} + 7 - 4\right] + .50\left(\frac{1{,}500}{290}\right)(.08)$$

$$= 25.86 + 26.64 + .21$$

$$= 52.71 \text{ dollars}$$

Notice that the Wilson formula for the simple inventory model provides an order quantity of $Q_1 = 289$, which is very close to the final optimal solution of $Q^* = 290$. Although the starting and final values will not always be so close (this depends on the various parameter values and on the lead-time demand distribution), this illustration shows that sometimes the simple inventory model works quite well—even though it assumes that demand is certain and constant.

The expected inventory on-hand when an order arrives is called the **safety stock**. This is the difference between the reorder point and mean lead time, or

$$\text{Safety stock} = r - \mu$$

In this illustration, the safety stock is $7 - 4 = 3$ ribbons. On the average, when the optimal $(7, 290)$ policy is employed, 3 ribbons will be on hand when any order arrives.

Safety stock as computed above may be *negative*, so that there may be, on the average, some backorders outstanding whenever a shipment arrives. Certain combinations of levels for the problem parameters may bring about such a solution.

Inventory Model with Lost Sales

This model is appropriate whenever it is impossible to backorder items or when customers will simply find another source of supply. Many convenience items, such as cigarettes, should be evaluated in terms of lost sales. Immediate necessities fall into this category.

This case is easiest to describe in terms of how it differs from backordering. The expected average inventory level will be the same as in backordering, except that the expected shortage $B(r)$ must be added back (since any short items will not be sold). Thus, the expected annual holding cost becomes

$$\text{Expected annual holding cost} = hc\left[\frac{Q}{2} + r - \mu + B(r)\right] \quad \text{(with lost sales)}$$

The shortage penalty is more elaborate than before. In addition to the penalty p_S (reflected here primarily as the value of lost goodwill arising from a shortage), we must account for the gross profit on the lost sale. We denote the lost revenue per short item by p_R (selling price), so that the lost gross profit is computed by subtracting the item procurement cost c. The following applies.

$$\text{Expected shortage penalty per item} = \text{Loss of goodwill} + \text{Lost profit}$$

$$= p_S + (p_R - c)$$

Multiplying the above by the expected size of shortage $B(r)$, we obtain the expected shortage cost per inventory cycle. When the resulting quantity is multiplied by the number of orders, the expected annual shortage cost is obtained. Using A/Q to *approximate* that quantity, we have

$$\text{Expected annual shortage cost} = [p_S + (p_R - c)]\left(\frac{A}{Q}\right)B(r) \quad \text{(with lost sales)}$$

The expected relevant inventory cost is determined in a way similar to the backordering case. The holding and shortage cost components reflect the above adjustments. A further modification must be made in the number of orders, reduced in this model by the annual level of lost sales. That reduction is accomplished by replacing annual *demand* A by the annual *sales* A', from which all lost sales have been removed. Thus, we have

$$TEC(r, Q) = \left(\frac{A'}{Q}\right)k + hc\left[\frac{Q}{2} + r - \mu + B(r)\right] + [p_S + (p_R - c)]\left(\frac{A'}{Q}\right)B(r)$$

(with lost sales)

using $A' = A(1 - B(r)/Q)$.

The same iterative approach is used here as with backordering. Different expressions are used for finding r and Q. The following steps apply, using Q_1 (as before) as the seed value.

1. For a given order quantity Q, the **optimal reorder point** r^* is the smallest quantity having a cumulative lead-time demand probability such that

$$\Pr_L[D \le r^*] \ge \frac{[p_S + (p_R - c)]A}{hcQ + [p_S + (p_R - c)]A} \quad \text{(with lost sales)}$$

2. For a given reorder point r, the **optimal order quantity** Q^* is found from

$$Q^* = \sqrt{\frac{2A[k + (p_S + [p_R - c])B(r)]}{hc}} \quad \text{(with lost sales)}$$

ILLUSTRATION
Ordering Floppy Diskettes

The stationery store in the preceding illustration is able to backorder typewriter ribbons, since customers are willing to suffer a slight delay in getting those items when out of stock. But the users of 3.5″ floppy diskettes are not so patient. Those customers will go elsewhere to purchase their floppies during stockouts. Not only is the markup on the sale lost, but some amount of future business (not just for floppies) may be lost after these customers locate a new source of supply for the missing items. Each floppy short is estimated to cost an average of $.10 in future profits. The following parameters apply.

$$A = 5{,}000 \text{ items per year}$$

$$k = \$20 \text{ per order}$$

$$c = \$.45 \text{ per item}$$

$$h = \$.12 \text{ per dollar value per year}$$

$$p_S = \$.10 \text{ per item short}$$

$$p_R = \$.90 \text{ per item}$$

The lead-time demand probability distribution for floppy diskettes is given in Table 7-7, where $\mu = 123.4$.

The starting value for the order quantity is

$$Q_1 = \sqrt{\frac{2(5{,}000)20}{.12(.45)}} = 1{,}925$$

The following steps permit us to determine the optimal levels of Q and r.

1. Using the value $Q = 1{,}925$, we compute the ratio

$$\frac{[p_S + (p_R - c)]A}{hcQ + [p_S + (p_R - c)]A} = \frac{[.10 + (.90 - .45)]5{,}000}{.12(.45)(1{,}925) + [.10 + (.90 - .45)]5{,}000}$$

$$= .964$$

The smallest cumulative lead-time demand probability greater than or equal to this value in Table 7-7 is

$$\Pr_L[D \le 160] = .97$$

so that the optimal reorder point is $r^* = 160$ floppy diskettes.

2. Using $r = 160$, we first evaluate the corresponding expected number of items short per inventory cycle $B(r) = B(160)$. This quantity is computed as follows.

DEMAND d	PROBABILITY $\Pr_L[D = d]$	DIFFERENCE $d - 160$	DIFFERENCE × PROBABILITY
170	.02	10	.2
180	.01	20	.2
			$B(160) = .4$

Substituting $B(160) = .4$ into the expression for Q^* gives us

$$Q^* = \sqrt{\frac{2A[k + (p_S + [p_R - c])B(r)]}{hc}} = \sqrt{\frac{2(5{,}000)[20 + (.10 + [.90 - .45])(.4)]}{.12(.45)}}$$

$$= 1{,}935$$

TABLE 7-7

Lead-Time Demand Probability Distribution for Floppy Diskettes

POSSIBLE DEMAND d	PROBABILITY $Pr_L[D = d]$	DEMAND × PROBABILITY	CUMULATIVE PROBABILITY $Pr_L[D \le d]$
90	.05	4.5	.05
100	.12	12.0	.17
110	.17	18.7	.34
120	.22	26.4	.56
130	.19	24.7	.75
140	.14	19.6	.89
150	.05	7.5	.94
160	.03	4.8	.97
170	.02	3.4	.99
180	.01	1.8	1.00
	1.00	$\mu = 123.4$	

Since this result differs from the initial value of $Q = 1,925$, we must continue the procedure with a second iteration.

1. *(Second iteration.)* We use $Q = 1,935$ to recompute the reorder point. First, we find the ratio

$$\frac{[.10 + (.90 - .45)]5,000}{.12(.45)(1,935) + [.10 + (.90 - .45)]5,000} = .963$$

which yields the identical cumulative demand probability found before, and $r^* = 160$.

The reorder point does not change. Thus, no step 2 is required, and the values in the optimal (r, Q) policy are

$$r^* = 160 \quad \text{and} \quad Q^* = 1,935$$

so that $Q^* = 1,935$ diskettes should be ordered whenever the current inventory falls below $r^* = 160$. The expected annual diskette sales is

$$A' = (1 - B(r)/Q)A = (1 - .4/1,935)(5,000) = 4,999$$

(with only 1 diskette shortage expected per year). The total annual expected cost of this policy is

$$TEC = \left(\frac{4,999}{1,935}\right)20 + .12(.45)\left[\frac{1,935}{2} + 160 - 123.4 + .4\right]$$

$$+ [.10 + (.90 - .45)]\left(\frac{4,999}{1,935}\right)(.4)$$

$$= 51.67 + 54.24 + .57 = 106.48 \text{ dollars}$$

7-5 The EOQ Models for Normally Distributed Demand

When large inventory systems are comprised of many units or when a product such as gasoline is sold in divisible quantities, it is convenient to represent lead-time demand with a continuous probability distribution. Only slight modifications are required to use the preceding model to find the optimal (r, Q) policy when lead time is normally distributed.

The primary change is the way in which the expected number of shortages $B(r)$ is computed. This is somewhat complicated due to the nature of continuous random variables. Figure 7-5 suggests how the expected demand may be computed by approximating the normal curve for lead-time demand. As with the previous model involving normal curves (page 216), this may be accomplished by a simple computation using a tabled value. The following expression applies.

$$B(r) = \begin{cases} \sigma L\left(\dfrac{r - \mu}{\sigma}\right) & \text{if } r \geq \mu \\ \mu - r + \sigma L\left(\dfrac{\mu - r}{\sigma}\right) & \text{if } r < \mu \end{cases}$$

where

$$\mu = \text{Mean lead-time demand}$$
$$\sigma = \text{Standard deviation in lead-time demand}$$

L is the normal loss function, and its values are listed in Appendix Table C.

The Backordering Case

The following example shows how the EOQ model with backordering is applied when lead-time demand is normally distributed.

ILLUSTRATION
A Gasoline Refinery

The normal demand model may be illustrated with an example of how to find the optimal inventory policy for unleaded gasoline at an oil refinery. Due to the varying availability of crude oil and other petroleum processing requirements, the starting time for processing a batch of unleaded gasoline is unpredictable. The lead time is the period from the point that an order is issued until the unleaded gasoline product begins to flow into the holding tanks. We will assume that the demand while this is happening is normally distributed with a mean of $\mu = 200{,}000$ liters and a standard deviation of $\sigma = 20{,}000$ liters. When the unleaded tanks are empty, trucks scheduled to deliver that fuel are dispatched with other gasolines, and the unleaded customers receive their backorders later via a special delivery.

FIGURE 7-5

Suggested approximation for finding expected shortage when lead-time demand is normally distributed.

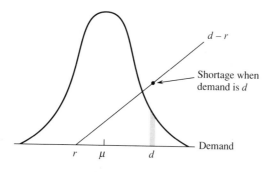

(a) Negative safety stock ($r < \mu$)

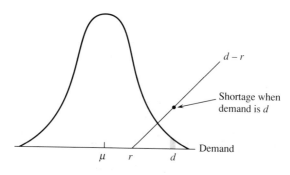

(b) Positive safety stock ($r \geq \mu$)

The mean annual demand rate for unleaded fuel from this refinery is $A = 40$ million liters per year. The fixed cost of a production run is $k = \$1,000$, and the wholesale value of this gasoline is $c = \$.40$ per liter. The annual opportunity cost per dollar value of funds tied up in inventory is $h = \$.20$. From the refinery's point of view, the only shortage cost for backordering fuel is the expense of the special delivery, which exceeds regular costs by $p_S = \$.05$ per liter. (For simplicity, we will assume that the production rate is so much greater than the inventory depletion rate that the savings in holding costs while simultaneously filling and emptying the holding tanks are too small to be significant.)

First Iteration   The starting value for the order quantity is

$$Q_1 = \sqrt{\frac{2(40,000,000)(1,000)}{.20(.40)}} = 1,000,000 \text{ liters}$$

The following steps permit us to determine the optimal levels of Q and r.

1. Using the value of $Q = 1,000,000$, we compute

$$1 - \frac{hcQ}{p_s A} = 1 - \frac{.20(.40)(1,000,000)}{.05(40,000,000)} = .96$$

The optimal reorder point r^* is the lead-time demand with a cumulative probability *equal* to this result (since the distribution is continuous). This corresponds to a **normal deviate** z for the area under the standard normal curve. We choose the normal deviate with the area between the mean and z that is closest to $.96 - .5 = .46$. Reading Appendix Table B in reverse, we obtain $z = 1.75$. This means that the reorder point r^* lies $z = 1.75$ standard deviations above the mean lead-time demand. Thus,

$$r^* = \mu + z\sigma$$
$$= 200,000 + 1.75(20,000)$$
$$= 235,000 \text{ liters}$$

2. This figure is then used to calculate Q^*. This requires computing the expected number of backorders in an inventory cycle $B(r)$. For $r = 235,000$ liters,

$$B(235,000) = (20,000)L\left(\frac{235,000 - 200,000}{20,000}\right)$$
$$= (20,000)L(1.75)$$

From Appendix Table C, we find that $L(1.75) = .01617$, so that

$$B(235,000) = (20,000)(.01617) = 323.4$$

Substituting this value and the other parameter values into the equation for Q^* gives us the improved order quantity value

$$Q^* = \sqrt{\frac{2(40,000,000)[1,000 + .05(323.4)]}{.20(.40)}} = 1,008,050 \text{ liters}$$

Since this result differs from the initial value of $Q = 1,000,000$, a second iteration is required.

Second Iteration   Returning to step 1, we use the improved order quantity to recompute the reorder point. First, we find

$$1 - \frac{hcQ}{p_s A} = 1 - \frac{.20(.40)(1,008,050)}{.05(40,000,000)} = .9597$$

The closest normal deviate corresponding to .9597 is $z = 1.75$, which is identical to the normal deviate in the first iteration. *No further steps are required,* since the value of r^*, and therefore of Q^*, do not change.

The optimal policy is

$$Q^* = 1,008,050 \text{ liters}$$

$$r^* = 235,000 \text{ liters}$$

The total annual expected cost of this policy is

$$TEC = \left(\frac{40,000,000}{1,008,050}\right) 1,000 + .20(.40)\left[\frac{1,008,050}{2} + 235,000 - 200,000\right]$$

$$+ .05\left(\frac{40,000,000}{1,008,050}\right) 323.4$$

$$= 39,680.57 + 43,122 + 641.63$$

$$= 83,444.20 \text{ dollars}$$

Negative Safety-Stock Policies

In the preceding illustration, r was always greater than μ. That need not be the case. For example, suppose that the BugOff Chemical Company experiences the following parameters for its Bug-a-Cider technical pesticide base.

$$A = 1,000 \text{ gallons per year}$$

$$k = \$600 \text{ per cycle}$$

$$c = \$50 \text{ per gallon}$$

$$h = \$.50 \text{ per dollar held one year}$$

$$p_s = \$10 \text{ per gallon short}$$

$$\mu = 50 \text{ gallon lead-time demand}$$

$$\sigma = 9 \text{ gallons}$$

First Iteration   The starting value for the order quantity is

$$Q_1 = \sqrt{\frac{2(1,000)600}{.50(50)}} = 219$$

The following steps permit us to determine the optimal levels of Q and r.

1. Using the value of $Q = 219$, we compute

$$1 - \frac{hcQ}{p_s A} = 1 - \frac{.50(50)219}{10(1,000)} = .4525$$

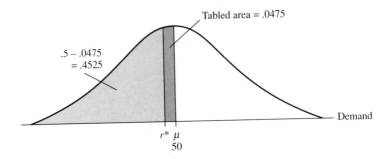

This value corresponds to a cumulative probability lying in the *lower tail* of the lead-time demand normal curve. To find the tabled area, the cumulative probability must be *subtracted* from .5, giving us $.5 - .4525 = .0475$. This corresponds to the closest normal deviate value $z = -.12$. (The negative sign applies because the indicated cumulative probability is a lower-tailed area.)

The optimal reorder point when $Q = 219$ is

$$r^* = \mu + z\sigma$$

$$= 50 + (-.12)9$$

$$= 48.9, \text{ or } 49$$

2. Using the expression applicable when $r < \mu$, the above will result in the following expected number of backorders in an inventory cycle $B(r)$.

$$B(49) = 50 - 49 + 9L\left(\frac{50 - 49}{9}\right)$$

$$= 1 + 9L(.11) = 1 + 9(.3464) = 4.1176$$

Using $r = 49$, the optimal order quantity is

$$Q^* = \sqrt{\frac{2(1,000)[600 + 10(4.1176)]}{.50(50)}} = 226.48, \text{ or } 226$$

Second Iteration   Returning to step 1, we use $Q = 226$ to recompute the reorder point. First, we find

$$1 - \frac{.50(50)226}{10(1,000)} = .4350$$

As before, the area under the lead-time demand normal curve lies in the lower tail. For a tabled area of $.5 - .4350 = .0650$, the nearest normal deviate is $z = -.16$, and the optimal reorder point is

$$r^* = 50 + (-.16)9 = 48.56, \text{ or } 49$$

No further steps are required, since the value of r^*, and therefore of Q^*, do not change.

The optimal policy is

$$r^* = 49 \text{ gallons}$$

$$Q^* = 226 \text{ gallons}$$

The Lost Sales Case

The following example shows how the EOQ model with lost sales is applied.

ILLUSTRATION
A Gasoline Service Station

Although the refinery in our earlier illustration may backorder those demands arising during stockout, the service stations may not do the same. The drivers that need unleaded gasoline will simply drive away, searching until they find a gas station that has the needed fuel. Demands arising during stockout become *lost sales*.

We assume that Roger's Sentinel Station experiences an annual demand of $A = 500,000$ gallons for unleaded gasoline. The lead-time demand is assumed to be normally distributed with mean $\mu = 1,000$ gallons and standard deviation $\sigma = 50$ gallons. Deliveries to Roger's involve a tanking charge averaging $k = \$100$, and fuel costs of $c = \$1.48$ per gallon. Roger's net proceeds average to $p_R = \$1.75$ per gallon. Some of the customers who leave with unfilled tanks are lost permanently. Roger estimates that he loses $p_S = \$.25$ in future profits for every gallon short. Roger presently earns 19% on his invested capital, so that $h = \$.19$ applies to each dollar's worth of inventory tied up for one year.

First Iteration   The starting value for the order quantity is

$$Q_1 = \sqrt{\frac{2(500,000)100}{.19(1.48)}} = 18,858 \text{ gallons}$$

The following steps permit us to determine the optimal levels of Q and r.

1. Using the value $Q = 18,858$, we compute

$$\frac{[p_S + (p_R - c)]A}{hcQ + [p_S + (p_R - c)]A} = \frac{[.25 + (1.75 - 1.48)]500,000}{.19(1.48)18,858 + [.25 + (1.75 - 1.48)]500,000}$$

$$= .9800$$

The above value corresponds to a nearest tabled normal deviate of $z = 2.05$. Thus, the optimal reorder point is

$$r^* = \mu + z\sigma$$

$$= 1,000 + 2.05(50)$$

$$= 1,103 \text{ gallons}$$

2. This figure is then used to calculate Q^*. This requires computing the expected number of gallons short per inventory cycle $B(r)$. For $r = 1,103$ gallons,

$$B(1,103) = 50L\left(\frac{1,103 - 1,000}{50}\right)$$

$$= 50L(2.05) = 50(.007418)$$

$$= .371 \text{ gallons}$$

Substituting this value and the other parameter values into the equation for Q^*, on page 225 we obtain the improved EOQ value

$$Q^* = \sqrt{\frac{2(500,000)[100 + (.25 + [1.75 - 1.48])(.371)]}{.19(1.48)}} = 18,876$$

Since this result differs from the starting value of $Q = 18,858$, a second iteration is required.

Second Iteration   Returning to step 1, use $Q = 18,876$ to recompute the reorder point. First, we find

$$\frac{[p_S + (p_R - c)]A}{hcQ + [p_S + (p_R - c)]A} = \frac{[.25 + (1.75 - 1.48)]500,000}{.19(1.48)18,876 + [.25 + (1.75 - 1.48)]500,000}$$

$$= .9800$$

Since the above ratio is unchanged from before, z remains the same. The subsequent r^* and Q^* will also not change.

The optimal policy is

$$r^* = 1,103 \text{ gallons}$$

$$Q^* = 18,876 \text{ gallons}$$

7-6 Analytic and Numerical Solution Methods

Methods for analyzing multi-period inventory decisions can be quite complex. These methods may be divided into two categories. **Analytic methods** solve the model mathematically, giving precise answers that lead to truly optimal inventory policies. All of the procedures we have described thus far are analytic methods. Unfortunately, we have found that the problem situations to which a particular mathematical model may be applied are severely limited. Often, the representation of the inventory system itself must be simplified or slightly changed to make an existing model fit the situation. This may lead to decidedly inferior solutions despite the mathematical perfection of the analytic method.

To avoid this pitfall, complex inventory systems are often evaluated by **numerical**

methods. Strict optimization is not the goal of a numerical method; instead, a reasonably good inventory policy is sought. A numerical solution may be obtained essentially by a "trial-and-error" process or by making suitable approximations. Two types of numerical methods are primarily employed. One of these methods embodies **heuristic procedures** and might be called an "optimal-seeking" approach. Under such a policy, a starting solution is obtained and successively improved through minor modifications until further improvements are hard to make.

When uncertainty is present, **Monte Carlo simulation** is a very satisfactory numerical solution procedure. (Chapter 20 is devoted entirely to this topic.) Usually performed with the assistance of a digital computer, Monte Carlo simulation evaluates alternatives "on paper" through exhaustive trial-and-error operations. Various combinations of (r, Q) policies may be evaluated by applying each one to an inventory decision over a very long time frame of, say, 100 years. The (r, Q) policy that yields the minimum average cost is then chosen for actual use. Simulation may be used to tackle highly complex problems that are too intractable to solve realistically any other way.

7-7 Computer-Assisted Inventory Evaluations

Computation of reorder points and order quantities is both time consuming and error prone when done by hand. This is one area where computer assistance is especially valuable.

QuickQuant, the software package available to users of this textbook, has a segment for performing the necessary calculations for inventory evaluations. The program will find economic order quantities for the models of Chapter 6 as well as their multi-period counterparts described in the present chapter. It will also provide order quantities for the

FIGURE 7-6

QuickQuant **report for the service station inventory decision for unleaded gasoline.**

```
=================================================================================
                              QuickQuant Report
    MULTI-PERIOD EOQ MODEL (Lost Sales)--NORMALLY DISTR. LEAD-TIME DEMAND
---------------------------------------------------------------------------------
PROBLEM: Roger's Sentinel Station                          Date: 03-05-1990
                                                                    Larry

        Parameter Values:
            Mean Lead-Time Demand: mu = 1000
            Std. Deviation for Lead-Time Demand: sigma = 50
            Fixed Cost per Order: k = 100
            Annual Demand Rate: A = 500000
            Unit Cost of Procuring an Item: c = 1.48
            Annual Holding Cost per Dollar Value: h = .19
            Shortage Cost per Unit: pS = .25
            Selling Price per Unit: pR = 1.75

        Optimal Values:
            Optimal Order Quantity: Q = 18876
            Optimal Reorder Point: r = 1103
            Total Expected Cost: TEC = 5336.818

---------------------------------------------------------------------------------
```

single-period problems of the newsboy and Christmas tree variety. Figure 7-6 shows the computer printout for a *QuickQuant* run for the gasoline service station illustration.

CASE

Ingrid's Hallmark Shop II

Ingrid's Hallmark Shop is a retail store specializing in "social expression" products, such as greeting cards, stationery, albums, and party goods. The social expression industry is noted for its seasonal volatility—an average December day outselling an average August day by ten to one.

Christmas merchandise must be ordered many months in advance. It is impossible to reorder most items once the selling season begins. Consider Ingrid's decision regarding how many angel ornaments to order. She believes that there is equally likely demand for any quantity between 16 and 25 items, inclusive. Her cost (including freight) is $5.50, and the ornaments retail for $10. Unsold angels will be disposed of during the half-off sale after Christmas.

Everyday merchandise never goes on sale, so there is less concern about over-ordering. Hallmark Cards has a systematic program, where certain items are reordered automatically. This is achieved when a store employee pulls a "ticket" that is sent to Hallmark. It then takes about two weeks for the requested merchandise to arrive. Tickets are to be pulled only when store stock for that item falls below the reorder point. The order quantities and reorder points have been established for retailers in various size categories. For example, a "Happy Birthday—Wife" counter card is assumed to have a lead-time demand in small stores of one card every two days—on the average—and total lead-time demand is equally likely to fall between 6 and 10 cards, inclusively.

Ingrid's son, Daniel, wants to establish order quantities and reorder points for both seasonal and everyday items.

Questions

1. Determine the optimal number of angels for Ingrid to order.
2. Why isn't Ingrid concerned with the reorder point for angels?
3. An average of 3 minutes of clerk time is spent in activities associated with pulling a ticket. Each clerk costs $5 per hour. Determine the optimal order quantity for the "Happy Birthday—Wife" counter card costing $.50 and selling for $1.00. You may assume the shortage penalty to be a minuscule $.05 per card, reflecting a high degree of product substitutability. Assume also that the annual holding cost is $.20 per dollar and that all lead-time demands from 5 to 10 are equally likely. Determine, also, the optimal reorder point, assuming lost sales for out-of-stock cards.

4. A typical Hallmark store has several hundred different counter cards. Lower-priced cards are shipped presealed in packets of 10 or 12. Dealers may arrange for shipments of 1, 2, or 3 packets per design. Suppose you were the store manager. Discuss how you might implement the policy found in Question 3. Do you think any compromises would be necessary?

PROBLEMS

7-1 Clark Kent's aunt sells *Daily Planets* from a stand for $.10 each. The following probability distribution for demand applies.

COPIES	PROBABILITY
31	.05
32	.11
33	.18
34	.21
35	.17
36	.13
37	.10
38	.05

She pays $.05 for each paper. Unsold papers are thrown away at no further cost to Ms. Kent. How many copies should she stock in order to maximize her expected profit?

7-2 The Green Thumb roadside fruit and vegetable stand must order its cherries from a nearby orchard before they are picked. The following probability distribution for seasonal cherry demand applies.

POSSIBLE DEMAND	PROBABILITY
$D = 100$ boxes	.15
$D = 150$	.20
$D = 200$	.30
$D = 250$	.20
$D = 300$	.15

Green Thumb buys its cherries for $2 a box and sells them for $3 a box. Unsold, over-ripe cherries are picked up for disposal by a hog farmer, who charges $.10 for each box. Green Thumb must determine how many boxes to order so that expected profit is maximized.
(a) Construct the payoff table.
(b) Determine which quantity of cherries should be ordered.

7-3 Refer to problem 7-2.
  (a) Construct the cumulative probability distribution for Green Thumb's cherry demand.
  (b) Use the newsboy problem approach to determine the optimal number of cherries to order to minimize total expected cost.

7-4 Personalized Printing Company must decide how many Christmas gift calendars should be made this season. All unsold calendars will be purchased by schools for $.10. Each calendar costs $.50 and ordinarily sells for $1. Loss of goodwill for shortages is $.05 per calendar. The following probability distribution for demand applies.

DEMAND	PROBABILITY
2,000	.05
3,000	.20
4,000	.25
5,000	.30
6,000	.20

How many calendars should be made?

7-5 The demand for Halloween pumpkins at The Black Cat's Patch is normally distributed with a mean of 1,000 and a standard deviation of 200. Each pumpkin costs $.50 and sells for $.90. Unsold pumpkins are disposed of at a cost of $.10 each. How many items should be stocked?

7-6 A news vendor must decide how many copies of the *Berkeley Barb* he should leave in a sidewalk stand. Each paper sells for $.50 and costs a quarter. Unsold papers are then converted into fireplace logs, giving them a nickel in value. The news vendor believes that any quantity between 51 and 70 papers, inclusively, is equally likely to be demanded. There is no goodwill lost due to unfilled demands.
  (a) How many *Berkeley Barbs* should be placed to minimize total expected daily cost?
  (b) What is the total expected daily cost of the optimal inventory policy?
  (c) What is the news vendor's maximum expected daily profit from selling *Berkeley Barbs*?

7-7 A baker must decide how many dozen donuts to bake. Leftovers are ordinarily sold the next day, but she is closing her shop today to take a vacation. The following probability distribution for daily demand applies.

DOZEN DONUTS	PROBABILITY
5	.10
10	.15
15	.30
20	.20
25	.15
30	.10

Donuts cost $.50 per dozen to make, and they sell for $1 per dozen. Before closing the shop, the baker plans to throw away any unsold donuts. How many donuts should be baked?

7-8 The captain of a tramp steamer picks up a load of cocoa beans whenever he travels to West Africa. He always sells them to a candymaker in Rotterdam for twice what he paid for them. The candymaker buys only what she needs, and the captain must dispose of any excess beans at less than cost to a cocoa dealer who also resides in Rotterdam. The present African price is 2 guilders per kilogram, and the Dutch cocoa dealer buys the beans for 1.50 guilders per kilogram. The following probability distribution for the candymaker's demand applies.

DEMAND	PROBABILITY
100 kg	.05
200	.12
300	.18
400	.25
500	.22
600	.09
700	.09

How many kilograms of cocoa beans should the captain take on?

7-9 Horatio Dull is a college professor who supplements his paltry salary each year by selling Christmas trees—a venture that has been immensely successful in the past. He must order his trees in October for delivery in early December. His net cost for each tree is $5, and the trees sell for an average of $15. On those occasions when there have been unsold trees, Horatio has managed to dispose of every excess tree on Christmas Eve for a price of $0.50. Having built up a loyal clientele, Dull values any goodwill lost for each tree short at $20. Demand for his trees has been established as approximately normally distributed, with a mean of $\mu = 5{,}000$ trees and a standard deviation of $\sigma = 1{,}000$. How many trees should Professor Dull order to minimize total expected cost?

7-10 The annual demand for Water Wheelies is 5,000. Due to uncertain deliveries and customer requirements, the following distribution for lead-time demand applies.

ITEMS	PROBABILITY
20	.05
25	.10
30	.30
35	.25
40	.25
45	.05

(a) Determine the mean value and the cumulative probability distribution for lead-time demand.

(b) Each Water Wheelie costs $100 and the ordering charge is $500, regardless of the quantity ordered. Assuming an annual holding cost of $.20 and a goodwill loss of $5 per item short, determine the optimal reorder point and order quantity when backordering occurs.

7-11 Miller's Mothballs are stocked by a pesticide supply house. The annual demand is 1,000 boxes. Due to uncertain deliveries and customer requirements, the following distribution for lead-time demand applies.

BOXES	PROBABILITY
11	.10
12	.25
13	.30
14	.20
15	.15

(a) Determine the mean value and the cumulative probability distribution for lead-time demand.

(b) Each box of mothballs costs $10, and the ordering charge is $10, regardless of the quantity ordered. Assume an annual holding cost of $.20 per dollar value and a goodwill loss of $1 per box short.

(1) Determine the optimal reorder point and order quantity when backordering occurs.

(2) What is the total annual expected cost?

7-12 Refer to Problem 7-10. Assume that no backordering is possible. Using the same parameters, and a $120 selling price, determine the optimal reorder point and order quantity.

7-13 Refer to Problem 7-11. Assume that no backordering is possible. Use the same parameters and a $13 selling price.

(a) Determine the optimal reorder point and order quantity.

(b) Compute the total annual expected cost.

7-14 Sylvester's Bootery caters to customers who cannot obtain the more specialized shoe sizes anywhere else. An optimal policy is sought for stocking size $8\frac{1}{2}$ EEE men's wingtip shoes, which cost Sylvester $20 a pair. The manufacturer charges a flat $10 for each size and style that is special ordered, regardless of quantity. When it is out of stock, all customers will backorder this shoe. But they will usually reheel and resole their present shoes while waiting, so Sylvester loses some amount of future profits, which he estimates to be $5 for each pair short. He finances his inventory with a bank loan at a 10% annual interest rate. The following distribution for lead-time demand applies.

DEMAND	PROBABILITY
5	.1
6	.2
7	.3
8	.2
9	.1
10	.1

Sylvester sells an average of 100 size $8\frac{1}{2}$ EEE pairs of wingtip shoes each year.

(a) Determine the mean lead-time demand.
(b) Determine the optimal reorder point and order quantity, assuming backordering.
(c) What is the safety stock level?
(d) Determine the expected annual inventory cost for this particular shoe.

7-15 The cost data given in Problem 7-14 apply for Sylvester's size 10 AA shoes, which are rarer. An average of only 50 pairs of these shoes are sold per year. The following distribution for lead-time demand applies.

DEMAND	PROBABILITY
8	.05
9	.13
10	.21
11	.36
12	.11
13	.07
14	.04
15	.03

Answer (a)–(d) in Problem 7-14 for this shoe.

7-16 Refer to the oil refinery illustration on pages 228–31. Suppose that the refinery experiences identical costs for its leaded or regular gasoline, which has a mean annual demand of 100 million liters and a normally distributed lead-time demand of 500,000 liters with a standard deviation of 100,000 liters. Determine the optimal reorder point and order quantity.

7-17 Buster Black is contemplating mail-order shoe business for super sizes. He will contract with a manufacturer in Italy to make shoes. For each size, the supplier charges Buster $500 per order as a set-up charge, plus $25 per pair (including shipping, taxes, and handling). Buster will receive $35 per pair after selling expenses. No backordering is possible and no goodwill is lost from shortages. Expected annual demand is 100 pairs of size 18D shoes per year. A 20% annual rate of return is assumed on Buster's invested capital. The following distribution for lead-time demand applies.

DEMAND	PROBABILITY
4	.08
5	.12
6	.21
7	.29
8	.19
9	.11
	1.00

(a) Determine the applicable inventory parameters and expected demand.
(b) Determine the optimal reorder point and order quantity.
(c) What is the safety stock level?

7-18 Refer to the BugOff Chemical illustration on pages 231–33. A related product is Caterpillar Chiller, having an expected annual demand of 2,000 gallons and a direct manufacturing cost of $30 per gallon. The product is sold for $35, and lost goodwill costs $3 per gallon short. The same set-up and holding cost apply. No backordering is allowed, and the lead-time demand is normally distributed with a mean of 60 gallons and a standard deviation of 12. Determine the optimal reorder point and order quantity.

7-19 Refer to Roger's Sentinel Station illustration on pages 233–34. Suppose that Roger has a mean annual demand of 100,000 gallons of leaded regular gasoline. A separate tanking charge of $50 applies to this fuel, which costs Roger $.85 per gallon and yields him revenue of $1.07 per gallon. The lead-time demand is normally distributed with a mean of 500 gallons and a standard deviation of 100. Assume no appreciable loss of goodwill arising from shortages and that the same $.19 holding cost applies.
(a) Determine the optimal reorder point and order quantity.
(b) Compute the total annual expected cost.

7-20 A chemical manufacturer periodically formulates batches of SX-100. There is a set-up cost of $500 for each production run, and the variable cost is $5 per gallon. Each dollar invested in inventory costs $.20 per year, and each backordered gallon represents a loss of $.25. Annual demand is for 100,000 gallons. Assume that the lead-time demand is normally distributed, with a mean of $\mu = 5,000$ gallons and a standard deviation of $\sigma = 1,000$ gallons. Determine the optimal reorder point and order (production) quantity.

7-21 The Bugoff Chemical Company periodically formulates batches of Ant-Can't pesticide. There is a set-up cost of $1,000 for each production run, and the variable cost is $10 per pound. Each dollar invested in inventory costs $.25 per year, and each backordered pound of Ant-Can't represents a loss of $2.00. Annual demand is 500,000 pounds. Assume that the lead-time demand is normally distributed, with a mean of $\mu = 10,000$ pounds and a standard deviation of $\sigma = 1,000$ pounds. Determine the optimal reorder point and order (production) quantity.

7-22 *Computer exercise.* Refer to the Roger's Sentinel Station illustration on pages 233–34. Apply the backordering model with $p_S = .25 + (1.75 - 1.48) = .52$.
(a) Determine the optimal reorder point and order quantity.
(b) Compare your above answers to the solution on page 234. What may you conclude regarding the use of the backordering model to approximate the lost-sales case?

7-23 *Computer exercise.* Refer to the typewriter ribbon illustration on pages 222–24. Suppose that the shortage penalty p_S for the ribbons is unknown.
(a) Determine the optimal inventory policy when (1) $p_S = \$1.00$, (2) $p_S = \$2.00$, and (3) $p_S = \$3.00$.
(b) What may you conclude regarding the relationship between safety stock and p_S for this problem?

Linear Programming

In Chapter 8, we will consider perhaps the most successful quantitative procedure currently used to facilitate the process of making business decisions. The collection of tools referred to as **linear programming** has a wide variety of applications. It is used by oil companies to determine the best mixture of ingredients for blending gasoline. It has successfully served in the development of optimal schedules for transportation, production, and construction. And, it has been applied in such diverse areas as finance and advertising. Without doubt, linear programming has had the widest impact of all modern quantitative methods. Billions of dollars in annual cost savings have been attributed to it alone.

What is linear programming? The use of the word "programming" here should not be confused with the written instructions to a computer called "programs." In the present context, we speak of programming as a form of planning that involves the economic allocation of scarce resources to meet all of the basic requirements. Thus, *programming establishes a plan that efficiently applies all factors toward the achievement of the desired objective.* For example, a linear program will tell a refinery manager the precise number of gallons of various petroleum distillates to use in blending a batch of gasoline with a certain octane rating. Moreover, the plan will achieve this in such a way that costs are minimized and the ultimate automobile exhaust meets environmental pollution limits.

By linear programming we mean that the ultimate plan is obtained by employing a mathematical procedure that involves *linear relationships*; that is, the entire problem may be expressed in terms of straight lines, planes, or analogous geometrical figures. There can be no curved surfaces in any graphical representation of the problem. The mathematical model expressing the problem relates all requirements and management's goals by means of algebraic expressions representing straight lines.

Although we will be restricted to linear situations in this textbook, similar allocation models and procedures exist for more general relationships. Quadratic, convex, and stochastic programming are included under the umbrella of mathematical programming. Each approach is similar to linear programming but involves mathematics beyond the scope of this text. In Chapter 16, linear procedures will be extended to **integer programming**. Problems involving multiple objectives are evaluated in Chapter 17 using **goal programming**. A further procedure, **dynamic programming**, involves planning decisions over time; this topic will be discussed in Chapter 28.

8-1 The Redwood Furniture Problem

The Redwood Furniture Company manufactures tables and chairs as part of its line of patio furniture. Table 8-1 shows the resources consumed and the unit profits for each product. For simplicity, we will assume that only two resources are consumed in manufacturing the patio furniture: wood (300 board feet in inventory), and labor (110 hours available). The owner wishes to determine how many tables and chairs should be made to maximize the total profits for patio furniture.

Linear programming is not essential to establishing such a production plan. After all, it is a recent technique that has been used widely for only the last 40 years, and people have been making furniture for several thousand years. Without any knowledge of linear programming, the owner may decide to make as many chairs as possible, since chairs are more profitable than tables. Altogether, there is enough labor to produce exactly 11 chairs, and the owner's profit would be $88. But this plan would leave 80 board feet of wood unused. Would it be more profitable for the owner to make some tables and fewer chairs? If so, how many of each item should be produced? Which brings us back to where we began. Linear programming will tell the owner of Redwood Furniture the exact number of tables and chairs that will *maximize profit*.

TABLE 8-1
Data Obtained for the Redwood Furniture Problem

RESOURCE	UNIT REQUIREMENTS		Amount Available
	Table	Chair	
Wood (board feet)	30	20	300
Labor (hours)	5	10	110
Unit profit	$6	$8	

8-2 Formulating the Linear Program

Defining the Variables

We begin by treating the number of tables and the number of chairs as unknown quantities, or **variables**. We then express the problem algebraically, using the following symbols.

$$X_T = \text{Number of tables made}$$
$$X_C = \text{Number of chairs made}$$

Our usual convention is to represent a problem's essential variables in terms of X, with subscripts taken directly from the variable's description. Thus, using X_T ("X sub T") to represent the number of tables, where T is the first letter in the word "table," eases our task of abstracting the problem to a *mathematical model*. Occasionally, letters other than X and numbers are used to represent subscripts.

Expressing the Constraints

Each resource places limitations on the values of X_T and X_C. In the case of wood, any production plan must meet the following requirement.

Wood for tables + Wood for chairs ≤ Available wood

This **constraint** tells us that the amount of wood used cannot exceed the amount of wood that is available. Note that this constraint does not require that every single foot of wood be used, but only that we do not use more wood than there is. This is why we use the "less than or equal to" symbol ≤. It would be less flexible, and therefore less desirable, to be unduly restrictive and require the use of all wood, which is what using = in this constraint would indicate.

The wood constraint is referred to as an **inequality**. It is convenient to express this inequality in terms of the quantity variables for tables and chairs in the following equivalent form.

$$30X_T + 20X_C \leq 300 \quad \text{(wood)}$$

The first term on the left side $(30X_T)$ expresses the total amount of wood to be used in the manufacture of tables and is found by multiplying the 30 board feet of wood required for each table by the number of tables X_T. Similarly, since each chair requires 20 board feet, $20X_C$ represents the total amount of wood that will be used in the manufacture of chairs.

An analogous constraint pertains to the labor resource.

$$5X_T + 10X_C \leq 110 \quad \text{(labor)}$$

As before, this simply says that the total quantity of labor expended on either tables or chairs cannot exceed the 110 units available. Together, these two constraint inequalities establish limits for the values of X_T and X_C.

The Objective Function

The profit objective may also be stated algebraically. Denoting total profit by P, we relate this to the variables by

$$P = 6X_T + 8X_C$$

since total profit consists of the profit derived by selling tables at $6 each plus the profit derived by selling chairs at $8 each. Thus, $6X_T$ is the profit for making and selling tables, and $8X_C$ is the corresponding profit for making chairs. Remember that the owner wants to achieve the greatest possible profit, or to maximize P. We may incorporate this objective directly into the mathematical model by writing the profit equation as

$$\text{Maximize} \quad P = 6X_T + 8X_C \quad \text{(objective)}$$

In this form, the profit expression provides the **objective function**.

Before proceeding, we should note that there are two fundamental types of objective functions, depending on the goal. Instead of maximizing profit, in some problems our goal is to minimize cost. In such situations, the objective function would take the form "minimize C," where C represents the unknown cost variable.

Not all linear programming applications involve cost or profit objectives. A marketing manager may want to maximize *sales*, an advertiser may desire to maximize *exposure* to potential buyers, and an investor may want to maximize *rate of return*. Similarly, a project manager may want to minimize *time* needed to finish, while a freight dispatcher may want to minimize *delays*. For simplicity, we will still use the letter P to express the level of the objective function for all maximization problems and the letter C when minimizing.

The Complete Mathematical Model

We are now ready to incorporate all of these expressions into a single mathematical model, which will prescribe exactly what is to be done within the resource limitations. The model itself, referred to as a **linear program**, is

$$\text{Letting} \quad X_T = \text{Number of tables made}$$

$$X_C = \text{Number of chairs made}$$

$$\text{Maximize} \quad P = 6X_T + 8X_C \quad \text{(objective)}$$

$$\text{Subject to} \quad 30X_T + 20X_C \leq 300 \quad \text{(wood)}$$

$$5X_T + 10X_C \leq 110 \quad \text{(labor)}$$

$$\text{where} \quad X_T, X_C \geq 0 \quad \text{(non-negativity)}$$

This linear program identifies the variables and specifies the problem objective, subject to the constraints that limit what may be done.

The Non-Negativity Conditions

The linear program includes further limitations that we have not previously encountered. The **non-negativity conditions** state that the variables cannot assume negative values. Although a negative quantity of tables or chairs makes no sense at all, without these prescriptions it would be mathematically possible to obtain a solution such as $(X_T = -10, X_C = 16)$ with a profit of \$68. Obviously, this solution is impossible, because it implies the absurdity of disassembling 10 tables, retrieving all the wood and labor used to manufacture them, and channeling both of the "saved" resources into the production of more chairs than could have been made with the original wood and labor!

8-3 Solving Linear Programs

A linear program is only a mathematical *formulation*. It merely sets up the problem. We still do not know how many tables and chairs should be made. This answer is provided by the **solution** to the linear program.

Several different approaches or **algorithms** may be used to solve this problem. In this book, we will consider a variety of algorithms for solving linear programs. For simple linear problems, the easiest procedure is the **graphical method**.

We begin by constructing a graph that represents the linear program in two dimensions—one for the number of tables X_T, and the other for the number of chairs X_C. We use a ruler to make a heavy horizontal line for the X_T axis and a heavy vertical line for the X_C axis on a piece of graph paper, as shown in Figure 8-1. For convenience, we place tick marks every five squares along the respective axes and label these in increments of 5, starting at 0 in each case. Any point in this two-dimensional space corresponds to a production quantity combination or plan for tables and chairs.

The **origin** is the point where the two axes cross and may be represented in terms of its coordinates along the respective axes $(X_T = 0, X_C = 0)$. The coordinates for point $A(X_T = 2, X_C = 12)$ represent its distance of 2 units along the X_T axis and its height of of 12 units along the X_C axis. This same point represents a production plan for 2 tables and 12 chairs.

Plotting Constraint Lines

Our next step is to plot the constraints on the graph. Begin with the wood constraint, which we expressed as

$$30X_T + 20X_C \leq 300 \quad \text{(wood)}$$

Temporarily, consider the special case where the left side of this expression (wood used) is precisely equal to the right side (wood available), which provides the wood *equation*

$$30X_T + 20X_C = 300 \quad \text{(wood)}$$

FIGURE 8-1

Linear programming axes constructed on graph paper.

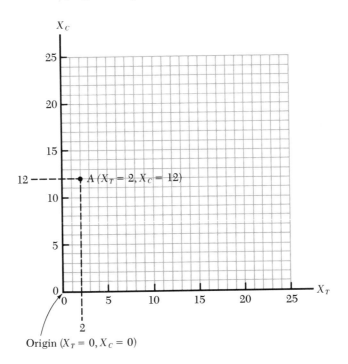

When plotted on our graph, this equality is linear. It is therefore referred to as the wood **constraint line**. All points falling on this line represent combinations of table and chair quantities that consume the exact amount of wood that is available.

In constructing the wood constraint line, we apply the geometrical principle that any line may be defined by two points. These may then be connected by positioning a straightedge beside both points and drawing the connecting line.

Generally, it is simplest to locate the two points where the line cuts the respective axes. First, consider the X_T axis. The intersection point on the horizontal axis is called the **horizontal intercept**. Since it has no vertical height, one of its coordinates is $X_C = 0$. Plugging this value of X_C into the wood equation gives us

$$30X_T + 20(0) = 300$$

Since $20 \times 0 = 0$, we may ignore the second term on the left, so that we have

$$30X_T = 300$$

Dividing both sides of this equation by 30, we obtain

$$X_T = 300/30 = 10$$

FIGURE 8-2

Plotting the wood constraint line for the Redwood Furniture problem.

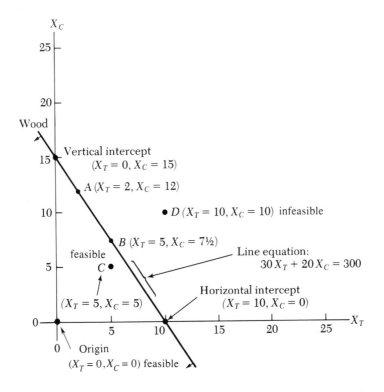

Thus, the remaining coordinate for the horizontal intercept is $X_T = 10$. In a similar way, we obtain the **vertical intercept** by setting $X_T = 0$ and solving the wood equation for X_C.

$$30(0) + 20X_C = 300$$

$$X_C = 300/20 = 15$$

We then plot these intercepts in Figure 8-2 and draw the wood constraint line to connect them. (For clarity, the grid squares have been omitted in this figure.)

The wood constraint line represents all possible production plans that call for the consumption of the entire 300 board feet of available wood. This is true for the vertical intercept ($X_T = 0$, $X_C = 15$), which corresponds to 0 tables and 15 chairs, and for the horizontal intercept ($X_T = 10$, $X_C = 0$), which corresponds to 10 tables and 0 chairs. For any other point on the wood constraint line, such as point A ($X_T = 2$, $X_C = 12$) or point B ($X_T = 5$, $X_C = 7\frac{1}{2}$), exactly 300 board feet of wood are used. Note that *it is possible to have fractional quantities in linear programming*; coordinates do not have to be whole numbers.

Finding the Valid Side of the Constraint Line

Of course, the original wood constraint does not require us to use all of the available wood. We must reconsider the inequality ≤ that we temporarily discarded so that we could work with the wood equation. Actually, an inequality relationship may be incorporated in a linear graph. Any inequality allows all of the points that fall on one side of the constraint line to be valid. But which side is the valid side?

A simple check is to evaluate a point that does not fall on the line itself. If that point satisfies the constraint, then all points on the same side of the line are valid; if it does not, then all points on the other side of the line are valid. The simplest point to evaluate is the origin. If $(X_T = 0, X_C = 0)$ satisfies the original wood constraint, then every point on the same side of the wood line will also satisfy it. To check this, plug the origin's coordinates into the original wood inequality, so that

$$30(0) + 20(0) \leq 300$$

Thus,

$$0 \leq 300$$

which is a true statement. Now we know that the origin is valid and that all points lying on the same side—below and to the left of the line—apply. We indicate the valid side by attaching small arrows to the constraint line, as shown in Figure 8-2. (Keep in mind that the origin happens to be valid for this particular constraint. In a different situation, the origin may not satisfy the constraint and the opposite side of the line would be the valid side.)

To show that other points on the same side of the line in Figure 8-2 satisfy the constraint, consider the point C $(X_T = 5, X_C = 5)$. This production plan consumes $30(5) + 20(5) = 250$ board feet of wood, which is less than the available 300 board feet. Point C is a valid point. However, point D $(X_T = 10, X_C = 10)$, which lies above the wood line, is *infeasible*, since it would consume $30(10) + 20(10) = 500$ board feet of wood, which is more than the existing amount of 300 board feet.

The Feasible Solution Region

The entire procedure that we followed to determine the wood constraint must now be duplicated for the labor constraint. The labor equation (again ignoring the ≤) is

$$5X_T + 10X_C = 110 \quad \text{(labor)}$$

The horizontal intercept is $X_T = 110/5 = 22$, and the vertical intercept is $X_C = 110/10 = 11$. The labor line and the wood line are plotted on the same graph in Figure 8-3. The valid side of the labor line includes the origin (doing nothing meets the labor constraint).

Any workable production plan must simultaneously satisfy these wood and labor constraints. Any such plan is called a **feasible solution**. The feasible solutions correspond

FIGURE 8-3

A complete graph of the Redwood Furniture problem constraints, showing the feasible solution region.

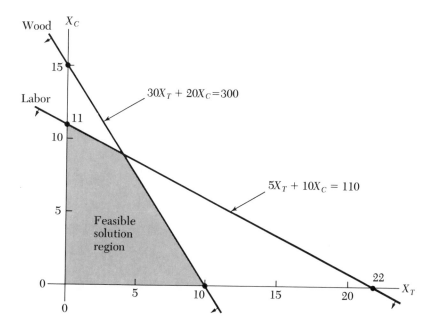

to the points that lie on the valid sides of both constraint lines, or within the shaded area in Figure 8-3, which is called the **feasible solution region**. Since the non-negativity conditions do not permit negative levels of either X_T or X_C, the feasible solution region is bounded not only by the two constraint lines but also by the vertical and horizontal axes.

The Most Attractive Corner

The Redwood Furniture Company can produce the number of tables and chairs that corresponds to any point in the feasible solution region, since all of these solutions are possible. However, the owner's objective is to maximize total profit, as expressed by the equation

$$P = 6X_T + 8X_C$$

To complete the graphical solution method, we must therefore incorporate profit in our graph.

Because P itself is unknown, various values of profit must be considered. If $P = 48$, for example, the objective function may be written as

$$48 = 6X_T + 8X_C$$

FIGURE 8-4

Finding the direction of increasing profit and the most attractive corner for the Redwood Furniture problem.

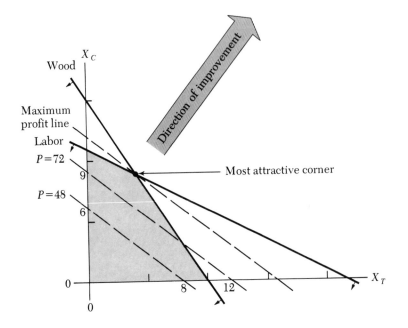

which we recognize as the equation for a straight line. This *profit line* has intercepts of $X_T = 48/6 = 8$ and $X_C = 48/8 = 6$ and is plotted in Figure 8-4 as a dashed line to distinguish it from the constraint lines found earlier. Of course, we can plot a similar line for any other value of P, such as 47, 49 or 53. We chose $P = 48$ because it is evenly divisible by both unit profits, so that the $P = 48$ profit line is easy to construct.

Each point that lies on the $P = 48$ profit line and that also lies inside the feasible solution region corresponds to a production plan yielding a profit of exactly $48. But we need to know if we can do better and, if so, what the best possible profit is. Let's see what happens if we consider a larger profit, such as $P = 72$ (again a value that is evenly divisible by $6 and $8). The corresponding profit line has been plotted as a second dashed line in Figure 8-4. Notice that the $P = 72$ profit line lies above the $P = 48$ profit line. All feasible points on the $P = 72$ profit line will yield the larger profit of $72.

Note that these two profit lines are *parallel*. This is characteristic of any linear program and of any value of P. This property of parallel profit lines is all that we need to know to find the maximum profit. Together, the two profit lines in our graph indicate the **direction of improvement** shown by the large arrow in Figure 8-4.

Now, we may begin to put the solution to our problem together. We still do not know the maximum P, but we do know that as larger possible values of P are considered, the profit lines we plot will be parallel to the first two lines and will lie above them. But there is a limit to how large P can become, because we are only interested in determining the maximum profit that can be achieved by a feasible production plan. By positioning a straightedge parallel to the original two profit lines in Figure 8-4 and sliding it in the direction of increasing profit, we see by a visual inspection of the graph that the highest allowable profit line must just touch the corner of the feasible solution region where the wood and labor constraint lines intersect. Any higher profit line will lie outside the feasible solution region. We refer to the highest allowable point as the **most attractive corner**. A third dashed profit line passes through this corner in Figure 8-4. We must now determine what value of P this *maximum profit line* represents.

Finding the Optimal Solution

The most attractive corner provides us with the production plan that will yield the maximum possible profit. We refer to this plan as the **optimal solution**. Mathematically, the coordinates of the most attractive corner are determined by simultaneously solving the wood and labor equations with two unknowns.

$$30X_T + 20X_C = 300 \quad \text{(wood)}$$
$$5X_T + 10X_C = 110 \quad \text{(labor)}$$

The simplest procedure is to use the method of elimination. We do this by subtracting a multiple of one equation from the other equation in such a way that one of the variables has a coefficient of 0 in the resulting equation difference. The value of the remaining unknown may then be found directly. We can eliminate X_C from the equation difference if we multiply the labor equation by 2 and subtract the result from the wood equation.

$$30X_T + 20X_C = 300 \quad \text{(wood)}$$
$$\underline{-2(5X_T + 10X_C = 110) \quad \text{(labor)}}$$
$$20X_T + 0X_C = 80$$

Thus,
$$X_T = 80/20 = 4 \text{ tables}$$

Substituting this value into either of the constraint equations, we solve for the value of X_C. Using the wood equation,

$$30(4) + 20X_C = 300$$
$$20X_C = 300 - 30(4) = 300 - 120 = 180$$
so that
$$X_C = 180/20 = 9 \text{ chairs}$$

The optimal solution to the Redwood Furniture linear program is therefore

$$X_T = 4 \text{ tables}$$
$$X_C = 9 \text{ chairs}$$

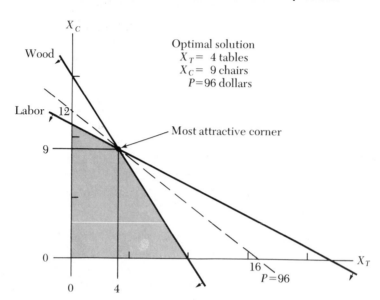

FIGURE 8-5

The optimal solution to the Redwood Furniture problem.

and the profit obtained is calculated by substituting these numbers into the objective function.

$$P = 6(4) + 8(9) = 96 \text{ dollars}$$

Figure 8-5 illustrates the profit line that corresponds to $P = 96$. Notice that this line touches the most attractive corner, confirming our earlier conclusion that the profit line that passes through this point will represent the maximum profit.

8-4 Cost Minimization: A Feed-Mix Problem

We will now consider a simplified problem that may be faced by a seed packager—determining the number of pounds of two types of seeds that should be mixed to formulate the wheat portion of a batch of wild birdseed. Table 8-2 shows the nutritional content of two seed types—buckwheat and sunflower wheat—along with the minimum required pounds of fat and protein. In addition, there is a maximum limit of 1,500 pounds of roughage. Unlimited quantities of either seed type can be purchased at the costs indicated. The packager's goal is to minimize the total cost of satisfying the nutritional requirements of the birdseed mix.

The linear program for this problem may be formulated as follows.

Letting X_B = Pounds of buckwheat in mixture

X_S = Pounds of sunflower wheat in mixture

$$\text{Minimize} \quad C = .18X_B + .10X_S \quad \text{(objective)}$$

$$\text{Subject to} \quad .04X_B + .06X_S \geq \quad 480 \quad \text{(fat)}$$

$$.12X_B + .10X_S \geq 1{,}200 \quad \text{(protein)}$$

$$.10X_B + .15X_S \leq 1{,}500 \quad \text{(roughage)}$$

$$\text{where} \quad X_B, X_S \geq \quad 0$$

The fat and protein constraints are represented by $\geq$ (greater than or equal to) inequalities because minimum quantities of each have been established, and the total pounds of fat or protein (provided on the left sides of the respective inequalities) must be at least as large as these quantities. The roughage constraint is a $\leq$ (less than or equal to) inequality, since total mixture roughage (again represented on the left side) cannot exceed 1,500 pounds.

Figure 8-6 is a graphical representation of the feed-mix problem. Notice that the valid sides of the fat and protein constraints are opposite to the origin side (0 pounds of both seed types will satisfy neither constraint). Cost lines for $C = 1{,}800$ and $C = 900$ dollars have been plotted. (Even though the $C = 900$ cost line lies outside the feasible solution region, the direction of decreasing cost is readily determined.) The most attractive corner occurs at the intersection of the protein and roughage constraint lines.

Solving the protein and roughage equations simultaneously, we determine the optimal solution.

$$.12X_B + .10X_S = 1{,}200 \quad \text{(protein)}$$

$$-\tfrac{2}{3}(.10X_B + .15X_S = 1{,}500) \quad \text{(roughage)}$$

$$\overline{.053333X_B + \quad 0X_S = \quad 200}$$

$$X_B = 200/.053333 = 3{,}750 \ \text{ pounds}$$

Plugging the value of X_B into the protein equation, we then find the value of X_S.

$$.12(3{,}750) + .10X_S = 1{,}200$$

$$.10X_S = 1{,}200 - .12(3{,}750) = 1{,}200 - 450 = 750$$

$$X_S = 750/.10 = 7{,}500 \ \text{pounds}$$

TABLE 8-2
Data Obtained for the Feed-Mix Problem

NUTRITIONAL ITEM	PROPORTIONAL CONTENT		Total Requirement
	Buckwheat	Sunflower Wheat	
Fat	.04	.06	$\geq \quad$ 480 lb
Protein	.12	.10	$\geq 1{,}200$
Roughage	.10	.15	$\leq 1{,}500$
Cost per pound	$.18	$.10	

FIGURE 8-6
The graphical solution to the feed-mix problem.

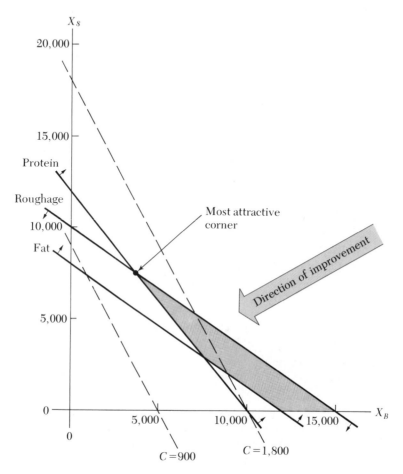

The optimal solution to the feed-mix problem is therefore

$$X_B = 3,750 \text{ pounds}$$
$$X_S = 7,500 \text{ pounds}$$

and the minimum cost is

$$C = .18(3,750) + .10(7,500) = 1,425 \text{ dollars}$$

8-5 Graphical Solution Procedure—Steps and Rationale

Although the graphical solution procedure just illustrated only works for two-variable problems that may be plotted in two dimensions, this method will be helpful in presenting the concepts common to solving larger linear programs. Before proceeding, let's examine a formal summary of the graphical solution procedure.

Since beginners to linear programming often do not immediately grasp the implications of certain steps, they tend to take shortcuts that often lead to wrong solutions. An appreciation of the rationale for each step in the solution procedure may help prevent those blunders.

Summary of the Graphical Solution Procedure

The steps in solving a linear program may now be summarized.

1. **Formulate the linear program.**   A proper formulation begins with a definition of the variables that clearly describes how the symbols apply. The rest is algebraic calculation. First, the objective function (maximize P or minimize C) is stated in an equation, followed by the expressions for the constraints. No formulation is complete without a final statement of non-negativity conditions, if they apply.

2. **Construct a graph and plot the constraint lines.**   Ordinarily, this involves locating two points and connecting them. The points are usually the horizontal and vertical intercepts found from each constraint equation. But we will see that for certain constraints, a different pair of points must be found to draw these lines.

3. **Determine the valid side for each inequality constraint.**   The simplest approach is to see whether the origin (the point of "doing nothing") satisfies the constraint by plugging its coordinates $(0, 0)$ into the inequality. If it does, then all points on the origin's side of the line are valid, and the rest are infeasible. If the origin does not satisfy the constraint, then the valid points lie on the side of the line that is opposite the origin. The *two exceptions* to this rule of thumb will be discussed shortly.

4. **Identify the feasible solution region.**   This region will be indicated by the group of points on the graph that are valid for all constraints collectively. These points correspond to feasible plans. Ordinarily, the feasible solution region is a contiguous area lying in the positive quadrant, since the non-negativity conditions preclude negative variable values.

5. **Plot two objective function lines and determine the direction of improvement.**   When profit maximization is the goal, two P lines will tell us the direction of increasing P. Two lines are necessary because the direction cannot always be predicted from a single line. The two P lines do not have to intersect the feasible solution region to indicate the direction of increasing P. When the goal is to minimize cost, two C lines are plotted. In this case, the direction of improvement is a decrease in C.

6. **Find the most attractive corner by visual inspection.**   This corner will be the last point in the feasible solution region touched by the P or C line that is formed by sliding a straightedge in the direction of improvement while holding it parallel to the two original objective lines.

7. **Determine the optimal solution by algebraically calculating coordinates of the most attractive corner.**   The optimal solution is often represented by the intersection of two constraint lines. However, it might also be denoted by the coordinates of a corner point formed by the horizontal or vertical intercept of one constraint equation. When this is

the case, the algebraic calculations have already been performed and the optimal solution may be read directly from the coordinates shown on the graph without error.

8. **Determine the value of the objective function for the optimal solution.**   This is found by substituting the optimal variable values into the P or C equation. No solution is complete until the maximum value of P or the minimum value of C is stated.

Rationale for Procedure and Practical Suggestions

The following comment is common from students encountering linear programming for the first time.

> "I don't know what the fuss is. I just solved the two equations, getting the same answer, and I *didn't even construct a graph!*"

Of course, the Redwood Furniture problem has been kept simple on purpose. And, for that problem, many shortcuts could have been taken in reaching the correct solution. But, there is a reason for every step, and shortcuts may lead to wrong answers.

The Graph Guarantees Feasibility of Solution   Figure 8-7 shows a graph for a similar production problem involving *six* constraints. Including those on the axes, there are 26 possible points of intersection, any of which may contain the solutions. Which pair of equations should we solve simultaneously?

Without the graph, we would fly blind, perhaps picking one of the 17 *infeasible* intersection points.

Plot Objective Lines to Avoid Picking a Non-Optimal Point   Another comment commonly heard among beginners is

> "Yeah, I drew the graph. But why do we need to draw P lines? Solving for the intersection point, I got the correct answer. Isn't the maximum profit always where the two constraint lines cross?"

The above objection may apply only to problems with two binding constraints. (Why?)

Consider the graph in Figure 8-8. By raising the chair profit, the P lines become flatter. The most attractive corner is point A when profit is $15 per chair (leaving table unit profit unchanged). Or, lowering the chair profit results in steeper P lines. Point B is the most attractive corner when the chair profit is only $3 (and table profit is held fixed). In either case, point C is *not* a most attractive corner.

Find the Most Attractive Corner by Rolling Your Pencil in the Direction of Improvement   *Two P* lines are helpful in isolating the most attractive corner visually. The two lines must be parallel, and the direction of improvement is toward the line having the better objective (higher P, lower C). The second line is optional, but safest if the objective function involves a negative coefficient for one of the variables. (In those cases, the direction of improvement may be down, up, right, or left, depending on the form of the

FIGURE 8-7
Possible points of intersection for a typical linear program.

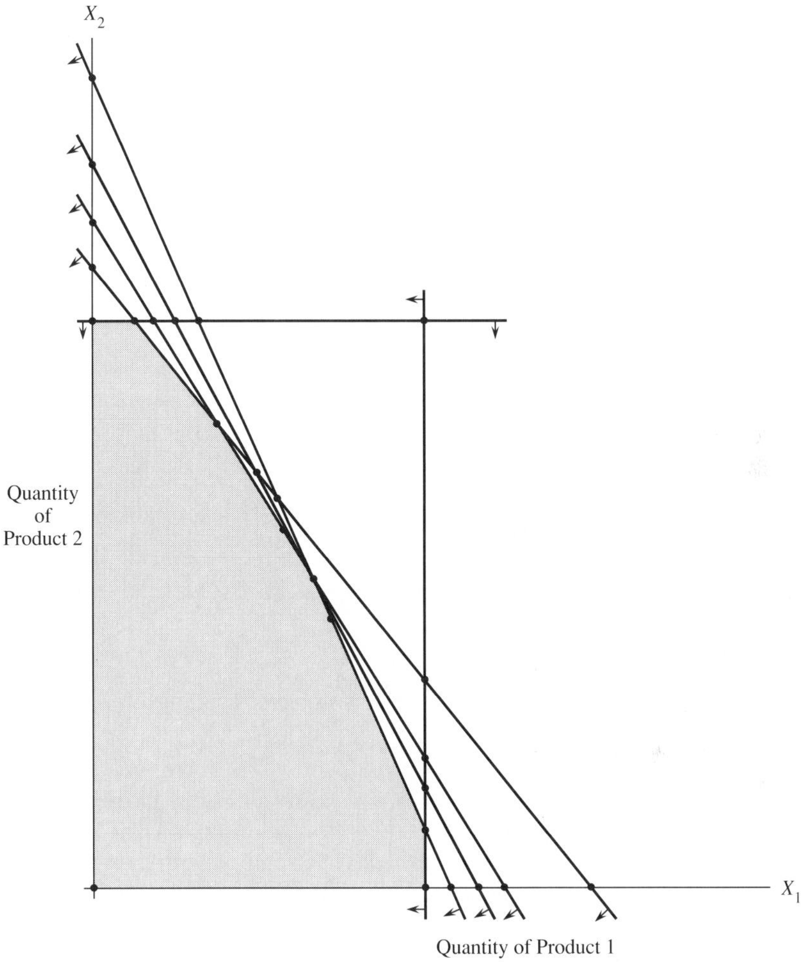

X_2
Quantity of Product 2
X_1
Quantity of Product 1

objective function.) Once the direction of improvement is determined, place your pencil at any spot on the graph and set it parallel to the plotted line; it lies on top of an imaginary P line (C line) that is either better or worse. As you roll the pencil in the direction of improvement, it describes progressively better lines. The most attractive corner is the *last* feasible point your pencil rolls past.

If it looks like two points may be the most attractive corners, then a separate algebraic evaluation should be made of each. That point having the best P or C is the most attractive one. *There may be a tie.*

Skipping the Algebra May Lead to Inaccuracies The graph itself minimizes only the more glaring errors. But it is, by itself, not foolproof. To illustrate, suppose that one

FIGURE 8-8

Illustration of how the most attractive corner and solution may shift as objective coefficients change.

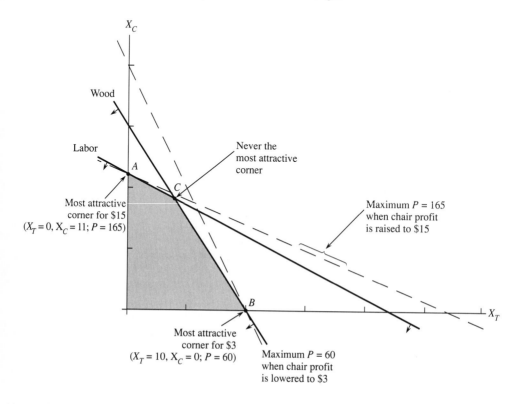

extra hour of labor becomes available, so that we change the right-hand side of the labor constraint to 111. The graph in Figure 8-5 will change slightly, with a tiny upward shift in the labor line. Visually, it will still look like $X_T = 4$ and $X_C = 9$ is the solution. That is not the case. The solution becomes

$$X_T = 3.90$$

$$X_C = 9.15$$

$$P = 96.60 \quad (111 \text{ labor hours})$$

(Verify this to your satisfaction.)

The graph provides the same essential information as before, showing that the most attractive corner is where the labor and wood lines cross. *The purpose of the most attractive corner is to identify which algebra problem to solve* (here, the simultaneous solution of the wood and labor equations).

Linear Programs Do Not Require Integer Solutions   Notice that the modified problem's optimal solution involves variable values that are not integers. Linear programming does not require that solutions be integer values. (But integers may nevertheless be a legitimate requirement. In those cases, a related procedure, called *integer programming* would apply. This topic will be discussed in Chapter 16.)

8-6 Special Problems in Constructing Lines

Earlier, we indicated that most constraint lines may be constructed by connecting the horizontal and vertical intercepts. Even though we generally restrict solutions to the positive quadrant, there is no reason why one of these intercepts cannot be negative. Consider the line

$$-5X_1 + 3X_2 = 15$$

which is graphed as line A in Figure 8-9. Notice that the horizontal intercept is *negative*.

$$X_1 = 15/-5 = -3$$

The equation for line B in Figure 8-9 is

$$X_1 - 2X_2 = 0$$

FIGURE 8-9
Examples of special types of lines.

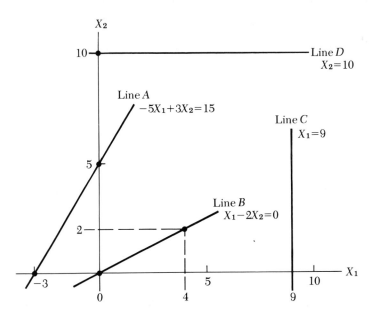

Both the vertical and horizontal intercepts for this equation occur at the *origin*. Since the intercept method yields a single point in this case, a second point must be found. The choice of this second point is arbitrary. We can plug the value of $X_2 = 2$ into the equation to obtain the other coordinate.

$$X_1 - 2(2) = 0$$
$$X_1 = 0 - [-2(2)] = 0 - (-4) = 4$$

Connecting the origin with the point $(X_1 = 4, X_2 = 2)$ will then give us the required line.

A third type of line has only one intercept. These lines are either horizontal or vertical and have equations of the form

$$X_1 = 9 \quad \text{(line } C\text{)}$$
$$X_2 = 10 \quad \text{(line } D\text{)}$$

where only one variable appears in the equation. For $X_1 = 9$, the value of X_1 is restricted to exactly 9, regardless of the value of X_2, which may be any quantity whatsoever. This relationship is illustrated in Figure 8-9 by line C, a vertical line perpendicular to the X_1 axis and parallel to the X_2 axis. For the equation $X_2 = 10$, line D is plotted as a horizontal line perpendicular to the X_2 axis at a height of 10 units. For that matter, the axes themselves may be represented in terms of the equations $X_2 = 0$ (for the horizontal axis) and $X_1 = 0$ (for the vertical axis).

8-7 Mixture Constraints

A line that passes through the origin generally applies to a special type of restriction called a **mixture constraint**. Such a constraint arises in manufacturing applications when some products must be made in a fixed ratio to other products. The Redwood Furniture problem can be modified slightly to incorporate a mixture constraint.

Ordinarily, Redwood's tables and chairs are sold in sets of 4 chairs and 1 table. However, there is an occasional need for extra chairs. Thus, Redwood wishes to make at least 4 chairs for every table, which means that the number of chairs must be at least as large as the number of tables multiplied by 4. This adds a further mixture constraint to the problem of the form

$$4 \times \text{Number of tables} \leq \text{Number of chairs}$$

Expressed in terms of the variable symbols used in the previous Redwood problem, this constraint tells us that

$$4X_T \leq X_C \quad \text{(mixture)}$$

For convenience, all variables are usually collected on the left side of the inequality. Subtracting X_C from both sides, we obtain

$$4X_T - X_C \leq 0 \quad \text{(mixture)}$$

Temporarily ignoring the inequality gives us the following equation for the mixture constraint line.

$$4X_T - X_C = 0 \quad \text{(mixture)}$$

The above is the expression for a line that passes through the origin.

The graph for the expanded Redwood Furniture problem is provided in Figure 8-10. (The original wood and labor constraints are replotted here.) The mixture constraint line is found by connecting the origin with the point $(X_T = 3, X_C = 12)$, since when 3 tables are made, $3 \times 4 = 12$ chairs must be produced.

Finding the valid side of the mixture constraint line is a little complicated. Since the line passes through the origin, we cannot use the origin for this purpose. Instead, we must evaluate some point that does not lie on the line. Any such point will do, so we choose $(X_T = 10, X_C = 15)$. Substituting these coordinates into the mixture inequality gives us

$$4(10) - 15 \le 0$$

$$25 \le 0$$

which is certainly not true. Thus, the valid side of the mixture constraint line lies opposite this point.

The feasible solution region obtained by including the mixture constraint is smaller than the feasible solution region for the original Redwood Furniture problem in Figure 8-3. (Additional constraints ordinarily reduce the number of possible solutions.

FIGURE 8-10

The graphical solution to the Redwood Furniture problem expanded to include a mixture constraint.

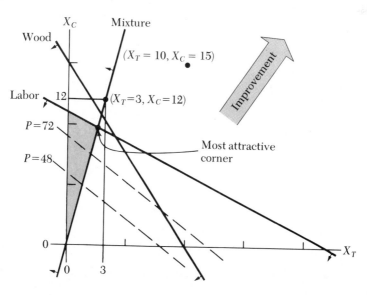

Why?) Visual inspection indicates that the most attractive corner for this new linear program lies at the intersection of the mixture and labor constraint lines. The simultaneous solution of these equations provides the optimal solution.

$$X_T = 22/9 \ = 2\tfrac{4}{9} \text{ tables}$$

$$X_C = 88/9 \ = 9\tfrac{7}{9} \text{ chairs}$$

$$P = 836/9 = 92\tfrac{8}{9} \text{ dollars}$$

Remember that linear programming may produce fractional solutions. We can view the extra $\tfrac{4}{9}$ table and $\tfrac{7}{9}$ chair as work-in-progress inventory items.

One interesting feature of this solution is that there is leftover wood. The total amount of wood consumed is

$$30(22/9) + 20(88/9) = 268\tfrac{8}{9} \text{ board feet}$$

leaving $300 - 268\tfrac{8}{9} = 31\tfrac{1}{9}$ board feet of wood in inventory. The unused portion of an inventoried resource is called *slack*. We will explore the concept of slack extensively in Chapter 10.

8-8 Equality Constraints

Thus far, all of the constraints we have encountered have been expressed as inequalities. As we have seen, inequalities produce valid points that lie to one side of a bisected plane. Under some circumstances, however, constraints may take the form of a strict equality. They are then called **equality constraints**. For example, suppose that Redwood Furniture sells all of its tables and chairs only in sets and that *exactly* 4 chairs are required for each table. The basic constraint would have no $<$ inequality in it and would be expressed directly by the equation for the line

$$4X_T - X_C = 0 \quad \text{(revised mixture)}$$

Figure 8-11 is a graph of the linear program that reflects this further amendment. Notice that *there is no valid side of the mixture line*: Valid points must lie exactly on the line. The feasible solution region consists of that *line segment* of the mixture constraint that also satisfies the remaining resource constraints. In general, when there is one equality constraint, the feasible points will lie on a line segment, but there are no other basic changes in the linear programming steps.

When there is more than one equality constraint, the procedure becomes ridiculously simple. Suppose that Redwood wishes to produce 2 tables because exactly this number can be sold. In this case, the **quantity constraint** would be

$$X_T = 2 \quad \text{(table quantity)}$$

Figure 8-12 is a graph of this more restricted linear program. The constraint is plotted as a vertical line intersecting the X_T axis at 2. Notice that the *feasible solution region consists of*

FIGURE 8-11

The graphical solution to the Redwood Furniture problem amended to incorporate an equality mixture constraint.

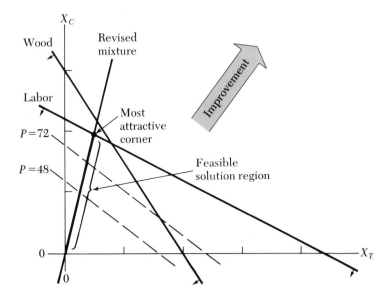

FIGURE 8-12

The graphical solution to the Redwood Furniture problem restricted by two equality constraints.

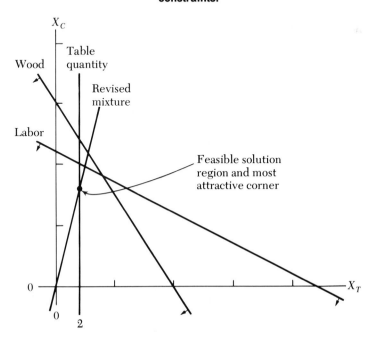

the single point where the two equality constraints intersect. The most attractive corner is the same point! In this case, the optimal solution is $X_T = 2$ tables and $X_C = 8$ chairs, with a profit of $P = 76$ dollars.

8-9 Multiple Optimal Solutions

Until now, we have examined linear programs with unique optimal solutions corresponding to the most attractive corner. Although the solution to a linear program is generally represented by a corner point of the feasible solution region, more than one corner can be equally most attractive. As an example, consider the following linear program.

$$\text{Maximize} \quad P = 10X_1 + 12X_2 \quad \text{(objective)}$$

$$\text{Subject to} \qquad 5X_1 + 6X_2 \leq 60 \quad \text{(resource } A\text{)}$$

$$8X_1 + 4X_2 \leq 72 \quad \text{(resource } B\text{)}$$

$$3X_1 + 5X_2 \leq 45 \quad \text{(resource } C\text{)}$$

$$\text{where} \qquad X_1, X_2 \geq 0$$

This problem is graphed in Figure 8-13. Visual inspection indicates that there are two candidates for the most attractive corner: the intersection of the A and C lines at point (1) or the intersection of the A and B lines at point (2). To resolve this potential ambiguity, we must determine which point is the last one touched by the highest P line. A visual analysis is not precise enough, because if we slide a straightedge in the direction of increasing P, it is impossible to make a distinction between the two corner points. Alternatively, we can simultaneously solve the respective equation pairs for both points and choose the one with the greatest P. Doing this, we obtain

	(1)	(2)
	$X_1 = 4\frac{2}{7}$	$X_1 = 6\frac{6}{7}$
	$X_2 = 6\frac{3}{7}$	$X_2 = 4\frac{2}{7}$
	$P = 120$	$P = 120$

which both yield the same profit. This means that both points are equally attractive, and we have *two most attractive corners*. Thus, both of these solutions are optimal, and the maximum profit is $P = 120$.

Why did we obtain two most attractive corners? The answer is because *the objective function line is parallel to one of the constraint lines*, so that the maximum P line must coincide with that constraint. This can be verified visually in Figure 8-13, where the $P = 30$ and $P = 60$ profit lines are parallel to the resource A constraint line. It is possible to prove mathematically that all P lines are parallel to that line by comparing their equations.

$$P = 10X_1 + 12X_2 \quad \text{(objective)}$$

$$5X_1 + 6X_2 = 60 \quad \text{(resource } A\text{)}$$

FIGURE 8-13
The graphical solution to a problem having multiple optimal solutions.

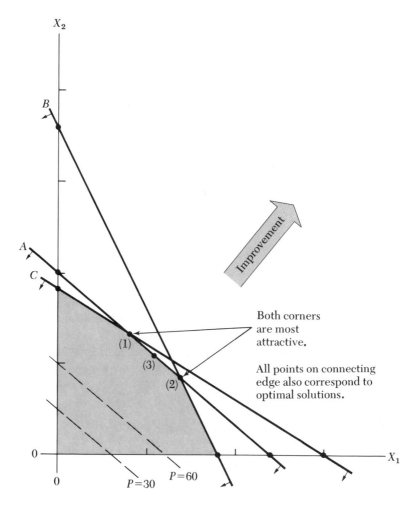

Notice that the coefficients of the variables in the resource equation exhibit a constant ratio to the respective coefficients in the P equation. The X_1 terms are 10 and 5, so that the ratio is $10/5 = 2$; this same ratio result $12/6 = 2$ applies to X_2. Thus, the coefficients in the P equation are exactly *twice* the value of the coefficients in the resource A equation. Whenever all of the coefficients in one equation are the same multiple of their counterparts in another equation, the two lines must be parallel.

Whenever more than one corner provides the optimal solution, all points on the connecting edge will also correspond to optimal solutions. For example, consider point (3), which is midway on the optimal edge in Figure 8-13, with coordinates ($X_1 = 5\frac{4}{7}$, $X_2 = 5\frac{5}{14}$). The maximum profit for this solution is also

$$P = 10(5\tfrac{4}{7}) + 12(5\tfrac{5}{14}) = 120$$

Any other point on the *most attractive edge* will also represent an optimal solution with a profit of $P = 120$, reflecting the fact that the maximum P line must coincide with this edge.

8-10 Infeasible Problems

Thus far, we have encountered only problems that have solutions. It is possible, however, for constraints to be so restrictive that no solution exists. Such a linear program is called an **infeasible problem**. Consider the following linear program.

$$\text{Maximize} \quad P = 6X_1 + 4X_2$$

$$\text{Subject to} \quad X_1 + X_2 \le 5$$

$$X_2 \ge 8$$

$$\text{where} \quad X_1, X_2 \ge 0$$

This problem is graphed in Figure 8-14. Notice that there is no feasible solution region, since the constraints are mutually incompatible.

Ordinarily, an infeasible problem indicates that a mistake has been made in the initial formulation. The remedy is to check the constraint expressions to verify that they properly reflect the problem. One number may have been miscopied or assigned the wrong sign; or perhaps a $\le$ should really be a $\ge$. Once the mistake has been remedied, the corrected linear program can be solved again. It is more perplexing when the formulation properly reflects the problem, indicating that the problem in itself represents contradictory requirements. Then unless the impasse is resolved, the decision maker will never be able to solve the problem. (No kind of answer—not even a poor one—is possible for an infeasible problem.)

FIGURE 8-14
Graph for the infeasible problem.

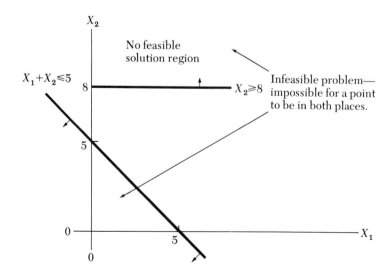

8-11 Unbounded Problems

Another category of linear programs yields ridiculous solutions that place no effective limit on one or more variables. Thus, any level of profit is possible—even a profit level of trillions of dollars, or more. Such a linear program is called an **unbounded problem**. As an example consider the following linear program.

$$\text{Maximize} \quad P = 3X_1 + 6X_2$$
$$\text{Subject to} \quad 3X_1 + 4X_2 \geq 12$$
$$-2X_1 + X_2 \leq 4$$
$$\text{where} \quad X_1, X_2 \geq 0$$

The graph of this linear program in Figure 8-15 shows that the feasible solution region lies open and becomes wider in the direction of improvement. There is no most attractive corner, and P can be as large as we want it to be. No matter how large a P is chosen, larger and larger P lines can be drawn through the feasible solution region. In essence, P can be infinite.

In the real world, no economic situations are literally unbounded. Thus, when a linear program turns out to be unbounded, some essential restriction (plant capacity, initial

FIGURE 8-15
Graph for the unbounded problem.

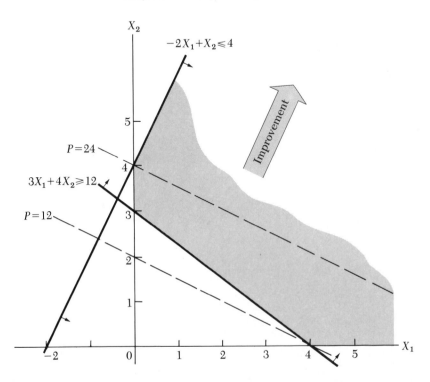

inventory level, and so on) has been left out of the formulation. Once the missing constraint is determined, the properly formulated linear program should result in a realistic solution.

8-12 Linear Programming Applications and Solution Procedures

Linear programming has been very successful in a variety of business applications. Chapter 9 describes in detail how linear programming can help a portfolio manager select securities. Also described there is a product distribution application, where shipments of skis are scheduled. The range of linear programming applications is a wide one. Chapter 9 shows how it may be used to select advertising media and to blend liquids. It may even be helpful in personnel decisions, indicating the optimal assignments of worker to jobs.

In this chapter, we have considered the essential features of linear programming. But we have only scratched the surface of this subject. By nature, the graphical solution method is limited to problems that contain two variables, since our graphs can only represent two dimensions. It would be possible for us to extend this analysis to three variables, using three-dimensional graphs, but to do so would be cumbersome. When four or more variables are involved, entirely different algorithms must be used. In Chapter 10, we will consider the most generally used solution procedure in linear programming—the **simplex method**. In later chapters, more efficient special-purpose algorithms will be described.

CASE

Cee's Candy Company

Cee's Candy Company mixes its Rainbow Box from two basic confections—chocolates and pastels. To meet its packaging requirements and to reflect changing ingredient costs, the company runs a linear program periodically to determine the number of pounds of each type of candy to put into the mix. The costs and requirements for a one-pound box are provided below.

ITEM	PROPORTION OF CANDY WEIGHT		Minimum Mix Requirement
	Chocolates	*Pastels*	
Nuts	.15	.05	.10 lb
Soft centers	.50	1.00	.60
Hard centers	.50	0.00	.20
Cost per pound	$4.00	$1.00	

For example, in each pound of chocolate candy 15% of the contents consists of nuts, 50% of the pieces have soft centers, and 50% have hard centers. These percentages do not add to 100% because nuts are included in some candies of both types (hard and soft centers). The total weight restriction guarantees that boxes contain at least 1 pound of candy.

A batch of chocolate-coated candies is to be made using the same cream base. The chef wishes to determine how many pounds to make of the creamy fudge and Burgundy cherry. Each pound of these candies requires the following amounts of ingredients.

ITEM	FLAVOR		Amount Available
	Creamy Fudge	Burgundy Cherry	
Pecans	.5 oz	.3 oz	500 oz
Chocolate	2.0 oz	2.0 oz	3,000 oz
Vanilla	3 ml	1 ml	2,400 ml
Cherries	0	24	28,000

All other ingredients are in plentiful supply. Each pound of Burgundy cherry contributes $1.00 to overhead and profit, while the creamy fudge brings $2.00. The total weight of the cherry candy must be at least half that of the fudge.

Questions

1. Consider the problem of deciding how much of each candy type to put into a Rainbow Box.
   (a) Formulate Cee's linear program and then solve it graphically to determine the optimal weights of chocolates and pastels to put in a Rainbow Box. Assume that each box must contain *exactly* 1 pound.
   (b) Suppose that the total weight restriction is relaxed, so that *at least* 1 pound of candy must be included in each box. Find the new most attractive corner and the optimal solution.

2. Formulate Cee's second linear program regarding the number of candy types to make. Determine the optimal number of pounds to make of the two types.

PROBLEMS

8-1   Labeling the horizontal axis X_1 and the vertical axis X_2, plot the following lines on a graph.
(a) $X_1 + X_2 = 5$ (d) $X_1 = 12$
(b) $2X_1 + 3X_2 = 18$ (e) $X_2 = 9$
(c) $-3X_1 + 6X_2 = 24$ (f) $X_1 - 2X_2 = 0$

8-2 Solve each of the following equation pairs simultaneously.

(a) $X_1 + X_2 = 10$ (c) $8X_1 + 7X_2 = 10$
$\quad X_1 - X_2 = 5$ $\quad 4X_1 + 5X_2 = 8$
(b) $2X_1 + 3X_2 = 6$ (d) $4X_1 + 4X_2 = 12$
$\quad\quad X_2 = 1$ $\quad 5X_1 + 3X_2 = 6$

8-3 Use the graphical procedure to determine the optimal solution to the following linear program.

$$\text{Maximize} \quad P = 5X_A + 6X_B$$

$$\text{Subject to} \quad 3X_A + 2X_B \leq 12 \quad \text{(labor)}$$

$$2X_A + 3X_B \leq 12 \quad \text{(materials)}$$

$$\text{where} \quad X_A, X_B \geq 0$$

8-4 Use the graphical procedure to determine the optimal solution to the following linear program.

$$\text{Minimize} \quad C = .5X_A + .3X_B$$

$$\text{Subject to} \quad X_A + 2X_B \geq 10 \quad \text{(protein)}$$

$$X_A + X_B \geq 8 \quad \text{(fiber)}$$

$$\text{where} \quad X_A, X_B \geq 0$$

8-5 Solve the following linear program graphically.

$$\text{Maximize} \quad P = 4X_1 + 7X_2$$

$$\text{Subject to} \quad X_1 + X_2 \leq 5 \quad \text{(labor)}$$

$$2X_1 + 3X_2 \leq 12 \quad \text{(machine time)}$$

$$X_1 \leq 4 \quad \text{(finishing time)}$$

$$X_2 \leq 3 \quad \text{(assembly time)}$$

$$\text{where} \quad X_1, X_2 \geq 0$$

8-6 Use the graphical procedure to determine the optimal solution to the following linear program.

$$\text{Maximize} \quad P = 2X_1 - 3X_2$$

$$\text{Subject to} \quad 4X_1 + 5X_2 \leq 40 \quad \text{(resource } A\text{)}$$

$$2X_1 + 6X_2 \leq 24 \quad \text{(resource } B\text{)}$$

$$3X_1 - 3X_2 \geq 6 \quad \text{(mixture)}$$

$$X_1 \geq 4 \quad \text{(demand)}$$

$$\text{where} \quad X_1, X_2 \geq 0$$

8-7 Solve the following linear program graphically.

Minimize $C = 3X_1 - 2X_2$

Subject to $5X_1 + 5X_2 \geq 25$ (restriction A)

$2X_1 \qquad\quad \leq 20$ (resource B)

$X_2 \leq\ 3$ (resource C)

$3X_1 + 9X_2 \leq 36$ (resource D)

where $X_1, X_2 \geq\ 0$

8-8 Consider the following linear program.

Maximize $P = 2X_1 + 4X_2$

Subject to $4X_1 + 8X_2 \leq 48$ (resource)

$8X_1 + 4X_2 \geq 48$ (requirement)

$X_2 \leq\ 5$ (limitation)

where $X_1, X_2 \geq\ 0$

(a) Plot the constraint lines on a graph. Then, determine the feasible solution region and plot two profit lines. Indicate the direction of increasing profit.
(b) How many attractive corners are there? Find the optimal solution that corresponds to each corner you find.
(c) Plot point ($X_1 = 8, X_2 = 2$) on your graph. What profit level corresponds to this point? What can you conclude about this point?

8-9 Consider the following problem.

Maximize $P = 2X_1$

Subject to $X_1 + X_2 \leq 5$ (resource)

$X_2 \geq 6$ (demand)

where $X_1, X_2 \geq 0$

Attempt to solve it graphically and briefly state any difficulties you encounter.

8-10 Consider the following linear program.

Maximize $P = 10X_1 + 15X_2$

Subject to $5X_1 +\ 6X_2 \geq 30$ (mixture)

$-7X_1 +\ 6X_2 \leq 42$ (resource)

$X_2 \leq 10$ (limitation)

where $X_1, X_2 \geq\ 0$

(a) Attempt to solve this problem using the graphical procedure.
(b) Do you notice anything unusual? Explain.

(c) The following constraint was missing.

$$X_1 \le 10 \quad \text{(quantity)}$$

Find the optimal solution to the corrected problem.

8-11   Consider the following linear program.

$$\text{Minimize} \quad C = 3X_A + 1X_B$$

$$\text{Subject to} \qquad X_A + X_B \ge 2 \quad \text{(mixture)}$$

$$X_A + 2X_B \le 5 \quad \text{(resource)}$$

$$X_B \ge 3 \quad \text{(quantity)}$$

$$\text{where} \qquad X_A, X_B \ge 0$$

(a) Attempt to solve this problem using the graphical procedure.
(b) Do you notice anything unusual? Explain.
(c) The righthand side of the quantity (third) constraint should have been 1. Find the optimal solution to the corrected problem.

8-12   Ace Widgets makes two models of its ubiquitous product—regular and deluxe. Both models are assembled from an identical frame. The regular model differs from the deluxe model only in terms of the finish work, which takes 5 hours of labor on the regular version and 8 hours on the deluxe model. In planning the current month's production, Ace's foreman finds that only 12 frames and 80 hours of finishing labor are available. The supply of all other required materials and labor is unlimited. Any number of widgets can be sold at a profit: $10 per regular widget, and $15 per deluxe widget. The foreman wants to produce quantities of the two models that will maximize company profits.
(a) Formulate the foreman's problem as a linear program.
(b) Solve the linear program graphically.

8-13   The marketing manager of Hops Brewery must determine how many television spots and magazine ads to purchase within an advertising budget of $100,000. Each spot is expected to increase sales by 30,000 cans, whereas each magazine ad will account for 100,000 cans in sales. Hops' gross profit on sales is $.10 per can. One television spot costs $2,000; each magazine ad requires an expenditure of $5,000. To have a balanced marketing program, the advertising budget must involve no more than $70,000 in magazine ads and no more than $50,000 in television spots.
(a) Determine the net increase in beer profits for each television spot and magazine ad (that reflects their respective costs).
(b) Assuming that Hops' management wishes to maximize the net increase in beer profits, formulate the marketing manager's decision as a linear program.
(c) Solve the linear program graphically.

8-14   Mildred's Tool and Die shop must provide exactly 10 experimental bits to a pneumatic drill company. The bits can be shaped either by forging or by machining. Both procedures involve a final milling stage, but the forged bits require more milling because they are not as smooth initially. In either case, only one bit can be shaped at a time using either process, and the order must be filled within two working days. The following table summarizes the restrictions.

	HOURS PER ITEM		Total Hours
PROCESS	Forged	Machined	Available
Forging	3	—	15
Machining	—	2	16
Milling	2	4/3	16
Unit profit	$12	$9	

(a) Assuming that the proprietor, Ms. Mildred Riveter, wishes to maximize profits, formulate a linear program specifying the number of bits that should be shaped using each process in order to maximize total profits.

(b) Solve this problem graphically.

8-15 Tubby Tucker is on a very strict diet and is allowed a bonus on Saturday night if he remains on his diet throughout the week. The bonus must contain less than 200 mg sodium (Na) and no more than 60 g carbohydrate (CHO). Tubby wants to consume as many calories as he can within these constraints. He has selected apple pie a la mode, for which the following data apply.

	Calories	Na	CHO
Piece of pie	100	120	15
Scoop of ice cream	140	40	15

(a) Formulate Tubby's decision as a linear program and then solve it graphically.

(b) How much pie and ice cream will Tubby eat?

Linear Programming Applications and Problem Formulation

Linear programming is perhaps the most successful quantitative method, as evidenced by its widespread use at virtually all levels of business and in every major industry. It is well accepted and is used in most functional areas—particularly finance, management, marketing, and production. Linear programming has an excellent track record for achieving operational efficiencies and cost savings. In this chapter, we will examine a variety of linear programming applications. The problem descriptions will also illustrate a variety of ways to formulate linear programs.

9-1 Production Application: Product-Mix Selection

Production planning is an extensive area of linear programming application. A detailed schedule of which items to make and what quantities of each item to produce falls into the broad category of **product-mix selection**. Such a detailed listing is one type of production plan that linear programming can generate in such a way that the most profitable mix is found for a given set of constraints. This may be done in such a way that the customer demand for each product is met. All resources used in manufacturing—raw materials, labor, supplies, and facilities—can be explicitly accounted for to ensure that limitations are satisfied by a feasible production plan that employs these resources most efficiently. Special interrelationships between two or more products—for example, the requirement that at least four chairs must be manufactured for each table—may also be reflected as constraints in the linear program.

Microcircuit Production Plan

The plant superintendent for a custom microcircuit manufacturer must decide how many modules to assemble of five different sizes. The following variables are defined.

$$X_E = \text{Number of extra-large modules to assemble}$$

$$X_L = \text{Number of large modules to assemble}$$

$$X_R = \text{Number of regular modules to assemble}$$

$$X_S = \text{Number of small modules to assemble}$$

$$X_M = \text{Number of miniature modules to assemble}$$

Each module is mounted on a printed circuit board, which has been cut to size from available stock of large sheets. All modules contain varying quantities of two component chips, type A and type B, supplies of which are limited. There is also a limited number of assembly time hours.

All other needed materials (such as solder and photographic etching chemicals), additional components (such as connectors), and other categories of labor (such as that for etching, coating, and finishing) are in plentiful supply. *Linear program constraints are needed only for those limited resources that might be potential bottlenecks.* Not all production factors need to be reflected in the linear program's *constraints.*

The Objective Function

However, everything must be reflected in the *objective* by incorporating *costs* of all labor, freight, and component materials. By subtracting a per-unit total of all direct charges from unit revenue, the unit *profit* of each final product is determined. These unit profits have been determined for each module, and the following objective function applies.

$$\text{Maximize} \quad P = 58X_E + 43X_L + 25X_R + 17X_S + 28X_M$$

Resource Availability Constraints

A 25-square-inch printed circuit board is needed for the extra-large modules. The areas are 15, 10, 5, and 1 square inches for the large, regular, small, and miniature modules, respectively. Altogether, there are 50,000 square inches of available material. The following constraint applies.

$$25X_E + 15X_L + 10X_R + 5X_S + 1X_M \leq 50,000 \quad \text{(P.C. board availability)}$$

The following numbers of component chips are needed in the various module units.

MODULE	TYPE A	TYPE B
Extra-large	28	52
Large	24	48
Regular	18	40
Small	12	60
Miniature	5	75

There are 10,000 type A chips and 25,000 type B chips available. The following availability constraints apply.

$$28X_E + 24X_L + 18X_R + 12X_S + 5X_M \leq 10,000 \quad (A \text{ availability})$$
$$52X_E + 48X_L + 40X_R + 60X_S + 75X_M \leq 25,000 \quad (B \text{ availability})$$

The assembly times are 1.50, 1.25, 1.00, .75, and 1.50 hours for the extra-large, large, regular, small, and miniature modules, respectively. There are 2,000 hours available in the present production cycle. The following constraint applies.

$$1.50X_E + 1.25X_L + 1.00X_R + .75X_S + 1.50X_M \leq 2,000 \quad \text{(assembly time)}$$

Quantity Constraints

There are orders on hand for 200 regular modules and for 100 small modules. These minimum quantities must be produced. The following two constraints apply.

$$X_R \geq 200 \quad \text{(regular quantity)}$$
$$X_S \geq 100 \quad \text{(small quantity)}$$

Mixture Constraints

The large and extra-large modules are usually ordered in groups, with, on the average, at least 2 large modules ordered for every extra-large one. Wanting to keep enough large units on hand, the superintendent obtains the following constraint.

Form (1) $2X_E \leq X_L$ (oversized mixture)

The preceding formula says that the number of large modules must be at least two times the number of extra-large. (The coefficient 2 goes with X_E, not with X_L, which must be the greater quantity.)

The preceding statement is mathematically equivalent to the following:

Form (2) $X_L \geq 2X_E$ (oversized mixture)

which reverses the direction of the inequality and lists the variables in reverse sequence. Other mathematically equivalent forms could be used.

$$X_E \leq .5X_L \quad \text{and} \quad .5X_L \geq X_E$$

(Found from (1) and (2) by dividing both sides of the inequality by 2.)

A similar constraint applies to the miniature modules. These cannot exceed half the combined total of all other module types. This constraint is formulated as follows.

(1) $X_M \leq .50(X_E + X_L + X_R + X_S)$ (miniature mixture)

The above may be rewritten in the following form.

(2) $.50(X_E + X_L + X_R + X_S) \geq X_M$ (miniature mixture)

Non-Negativity Conditions

Mathematically, the linear program is incomplete without stating the non-negativity conditions. These are essential. This statement is achieved by the following,

where $X_E, X_L, X_R, X_S, X_M \geq 0$

When there are many variables in a linear program, a statement to the effect that "all variables are non-negative" would be sufficient.

The Complete Linear Program

The following complete linear program has been formulated.

Letting X_E, X_L, X_R, X_S, and X_M denote the respective number of extra-large, large, regular, small, and miniature modules to assemble, the objective is to

Maximize $P = 58X_E + 43X_L + 25X_R + 17X_S + 28X_M$

Subject to

$$25X_E + 15X_L + 10X_R + 5X_S + 1X_M \le 50{,}000 \quad \text{(P.C. board)}$$

$$28X_E + 24X_L + 18X_R + 12X_S + 5X_M \le 10{,}000 \quad (A \text{ avail.})$$

$$52X_E + 48X_L + 40X_R + 60X_S + 75X_M \le 25{,}000 \quad (B \text{ avail.})$$

$$1.50X_E + 1.25X_L + 1.00X_R + .75X_S + 1.50X_M \le 2{,}000 \quad \text{(assy. time)}$$

$$X_R \ge 200 \quad \text{(reg. quant.)}$$

$$X_S \ge 100 \quad \text{(small quant.)}$$

$$2X_E \le X_L \quad \text{(ovsz. mix.)}$$

$$X_M \le .50(X_E + X_L + X_R + X_S) \quad \text{(min. mix.)}$$

where

$$X_E, X_L, X_R, X_S, X_M \ge 0$$

The Problem Solution

Applying the methods of Chapters 10 and 11, the following solution is obtained.

$$X_E = 67.54 \qquad X_S = 100.00$$

$$X_L = 135.08 \qquad X_M = 13.39$$

$$X_R = 200.00$$

$$P = 16{,}800.64 \text{ dollars}$$

Remember that linear programs allow for fractional solutions. If fractional results would not be permitted, the problem must be solved instead as an *integer program*. (Procedures for doing this are described in Chapter 16.)

9-2 Formulating Constraints and the Standardized Format

Any of the constraint forms in the above problem mathematically expresses the correct requirement. The hardest part is getting the "first draft" for the constraint, which may then be rearranged later.

Steps in Arriving at a Correct Mathematical Constraint

The following optional steps may be used in mathematically expressing a constraint.

1. **Identify the constraint from the problem description.** For example, consider again the first mixture constraint for the oversized modules. The passage in the description

providing this constraint is

"... at least 2 large modules ordered for every extra-large one..."

2. **Paraphrase the original descriptive wording in a form suitable for introducing symbols.** One such rewording would be

"The number of large modules must be at least (greater than or equal to) twice (2 times) the number of extra-large modules."

The parenthetical portions more precisely express in mathematical terms the preceding verbal concept.

3. **Position the variables, fitting them into the reworded phrase.**   This step provides that

$$X_L \text{ must be greater than or equal to } 2X_E$$

This makes it easy to accomplish the fourth step.

4. **Substitute mathematical symbols.**   Doing this, we achieve the constraint

$$X_L \geq 2X_E \quad \text{or} \quad 2X_E \leq X_L$$

Of course, it is not necessary to slavishly go through all of these steps, many of which may be skipped entirely for most constraints. But it is important to realize that formulating linear programs is basically an exercise in translating English into the language of mathematics. Like mastery of any new language, skill in doing this comes with practice.

Although not required by the mathematics of linear programming, it is desirable to identify each constraint by a short parenthetical description, as done in the above example. These descriptions will prove helpful when introducing auxiliary variables during the solution. (The procedures for doing this are described in Chapters 10 and 11.)

The Standardized Format

Eventually it will be necessary to rearrange the constraints in **standardized format**. Such refinements are needed in preparing input data for computer solution or in setting up a linear program for solution using the simplex method (to be described in Chapter 10). The basic requirements of this arrangement are listed below.

1. **All variables should be listed in a single row on the left-hand side of the expression.** Thus, the first version of the oversize module quantity constraint is expressed as

$$2X_E - X_L \leq 0$$

and the second version has the standardized format

$$-2X_E + X_L \geq 0$$

The preceding constraints must still be fixed in accordance with requirements 3 and 4 below.

2. **The sequence of the variables should be in the same order as that used in defining the original list of variables.** As the preceding statements show, X_E is positioned before X_L, because that was the order in which they were listed originally.

3. **Each variable receives its own numerical coefficient.** Thus, the first form of the miniature module mixture constraint, originally given as

$$X_M \leq .50(X_E + X_L + X_R + X_S)$$

would end up with all terms collected on the left and the .50 appearing as the coefficient for each individual X that was inside the original parentheses.

$$-.50X_E - .50X_L - .50X_R - .50X_S + 1X_M \leq 0$$

The first four variables are collected on the left-hand side and appear in the original list sequence, each with coefficient $-.50$. A one now appears as the coefficient for X_M.

Notice that the right-hand side now has a zero. The direction of any inequality constraint having a zero on the right-hand side may be reversed by changing the signs of all variable coefficients. As we shall see, it is advantageous to express such constraints in the ≤ 0 form rather than as ≥ 0.

4. **A zero coefficient appears in front of those variables which do not apply in the represented constraint.** Thus, the first version of the oversized module mixture constraint would appear as

$$2X_E - 1X_L + 0X_R + 0X_S + 0X_M \leq 0$$

And, the quantity constraint for regular modules would appear as

$$0X_E + 0X_L + 1X_R + 0X_S + 0X_M \geq 200$$

This last step preserves a space for each variable in every constraint. This becomes useful when constraints are algebraically manipulated in the process of solution.

The following is the complete standardized format formulation of the linear program in Section 9-1.

Letting X_E, X_L, X_R, X_S, and X_M denote the respective number of extra-large, large, regular, small, and miniature modules to assemble, the objective is to

Maximize $P = 58X_E + 43X_L + 25X_R + 17X_S + 28X_M$

Subject to $25X_E + 15X_L + 10X_R + 5X_S + 1X_M \leq 50{,}000$ (P.C. board)

$28X_E + 24X_L + 18X_R + 12X_S + 5X_M \leq 10{,}000$ (A avail.)

$52X_E + 48X_L + 40X_R + 60X_S + 75X_M \leq 25{,}000$ (B avail.)

$$1.50X_E + 1.25X_L + 1.00X_R + .75X_S + 1.50X_M \leq 2{,}000 \quad \text{(assy. time)}$$
$$0X_E + \quad 0X_L + \quad 1X_R + \quad 0X_S + \quad 0X_M \geq \quad 200 \quad \text{(reg. quan.)}$$
$$0X_E + \quad 0X_L + \quad 0X_R + \quad 1X_S + \quad 0X_M \geq \quad 100 \quad \text{(sm. quan.)}$$
$$2X_E - \quad 1X_L + \quad 0X_R + \quad 0X_S + \quad 0X_M \leq \quad 0 \quad \text{(ovsz. mix.)}$$
$$-.50X_E - \ .50X_L - \ .50X_R - .50X_S + \quad 1X_M \leq \quad 0 \quad \text{(min. mix.)}$$

where
$$X_E, X_L, X_R, X_S, X_M \geq \quad 0$$

9-3 Finance Application: Portfolio Selection

Portfolio managers use linear programming and its extensions to determine what investments to make.

Bond Portfolio Selection Problem

An income portfolio is to be made up of bonds from six different corporations. The manager must choose the amounts to invest in each security, amounts which may be expressed as

$$X_i = \text{Dollar investment in company } i \text{ bonds}$$

Here, i represents any one of the six companies: A, B, C, D, E, or F. The objective is to choose the values of the X's that will maximize total interest income. The following yields apply.

BOND	CURRENT INTEREST YIELD
A	8.5%
B	9.0
C	10.0
D	9.5
E	8.5
F	9.0

The objective function may be expressed as

$$\text{Maximize} \quad P = .085X_A + .090X_B + .100X_C + .095X_D + .085X_E + .090X_F$$

The initial portfolio investment will be $100,000, so that the individual bond purchases must sum to this amount.

$$X_A + X_B + X_C + X_D + X_E + X_F = 100{,}000 \quad \text{(funds)}$$

It is usually wise to diversify investments. Public investment funds are often diversified because limitations are placed on the proportion of the portfolio that may be applied to any particular issue. We will assume that our manager cannot place more than 25% of the invested funds in any single bond. The diversification constraint that applies to bond A is therefore

$$X_A \le 25,000 \quad \text{(diversification limit for bond } A)$$

Identical constraints are applicable to X_B, X_C, X_D, X_E, and X_F.
The following redemption dates and bond ratings apply.

BOND	SCHEDULED REDEMPTION	QUALITY RATING
A	1996	Excellent
B	2005	Very good
C	1992	Fair
D	1993	Good
E	1997	Excellent
F	2000	Very good

Investment policy is that at least one-half of the funds be placed in longer maturity (post 1995) issues. This requirement provides the maturity constraint

$$X_A + X_B + X_E + X_F \ge 50,000 \quad \text{(maturity)}$$

It is also investment policy that no more than 30% of all funds be placed in bonds rated in categories lower than "very good." This requirement is represented by the quality constraint

$$X_C + X_D \le 30,000 \quad \text{(quality)}$$

Non-negativity conditions ordinarily apply to the variables in portfolio selection,

$$\text{where} \quad X_A, X_B, X_C, X_D, X_E, X_F \ge 0$$

The Problem Solution

The preceding linear program involves six variables. The graphical methods of Chapter 8 *will not work*. In Chapter 10 an algebraic procedure, called the simplex method, is introduced for solving linear programs having three or more variables. That procedure provides the following solution.

$$X_A = 20,000 \qquad X_D = 5,000$$
$$X_B = 25,000 \qquad X_E = 0$$
$$X_C = 25,000 \qquad X_F = 25,000$$
$$P = 9,175$$

Notice that none of bond E is purchased—a plausible result considering its low yield of 8.5%. But more money must be invested in bond F at 9% than in bond D at 9.5%. This is largely due to maturity and quality differences. Collectively, several linear programming constraints may provide surprising—even perplexing—results. Linear programming has been used extensively by many mutual funds and other large financial institutions to facilitate portfolio selections.

9-4 Management Application: Shipment Scheduling

A large category of linear programs arises from the need to control distribution costs. A typical problem is faced by a multiplant manufacturer who must schedule shipments to several regional warehouses. When the number of sources and destinations is great, linear programming solutions may involve a great number of unobvious shipping assignments. Cost savings in transportation may be huge. Many companies of moderate size have saved millions of dollars in freight charges by using linear programming to schedule shipments.

Ski Distribution Problem

Consider the operations of a sporting goods company that makes skis in three plants throughout the world. The plants supply four company-owned warehouses that distribute the skis directly to ski shops. Depending on which mode is cheaper, the product is air-freighted or trucked from the plants to the warehouses. Table 9-1 provides the various point-to-point costs of shipping a pair of skis. The monthly capacities of the plants in terms of the number of pairs of skis that can be made are

PLANT	CAPACITY
Juarez	100
Seoul	300
Tel Aviv	200
Total	600

and warehouse demand requirements for next month are

WAREHOUSE	DEMAND
Frankfurt	150
New York	100
Phoenix	200
Yokohama	150
Total	600

TABLE 9-1

The Shipping Costs per Pair of Skis

FROM PLANT	TO WAREHOUSE			
	Frankfurt	New York	Phoenix	Yokohama
Juarez	$19	$ 7	$ 3	$21
Seoul	15	21	18	6
Tel Aviv	11	14	15	22

To determine how many pairs of skis should be shipped from each plant to the various warehouses, the shipping schedule shown in Table 9-2 is constructed. The numbers of pairs of skis sent via each route are unknown and are represented as variables by the letter X with the appropriate subscripts. In general, we will adopt the convention

$$X_{ij} = \text{Quantity of skis shipped from plant } i \text{ to warehouse } j$$

where each possible i or j may be represented by a number $(1, 2, 3, 4, \ldots)$ or a letter $(A, B, C, D, \ldots)$ corresponding to the identity of the respective plant or warehouse.

The X's are to be chosen so that total shipping cost is minimized. The total cost over each route is the shipping cost per pair of skis multiplied by the quantity shipped. From Juarez to Frankfurt, this cost would be $19X_{JF}$. Summing the values from all routes, our problem objective is to

$$\text{Minimize} \quad C = \quad 19X_{JF} + 7X_{JN} + 3X_{JP} + 21X_{JY}$$
$$+ 15X_{SF} + 21X_{SN} + 18X_{SP} + 6X_{SY}$$
$$+ 11X_{TF} + 14X_{TN} + 15X_{TP} + 22X_{TY}$$

The problem involves two kinds of constraints. One set applies to the plants and specifies that *the total number of units shipped from each plant must equal that plant's*

TABLE 9-2

The Shipment Schedule for Skis

FROM PLANT	TO WAREHOUSE				Plant Capacity
	F	N	P	Y	
J	X_{JF}	X_{JN}	X_{JP} -	X_{JY}	100
S	X_{SF}	X_{SN}	X_{SP}	X_{SY}	300
T	X_{TF}	X_{TN}	X_{TP}	X_{TY}	200
Warehouse Demand	150	100	200	150	600

capacity. The three plant capacity constraints for this problem are

$$X_{JF} + X_{JN} + X_{JP} + X_{JY} = 100 \quad \text{(Juarez capacity)}$$

$$X_{SF} + X_{SN} + X_{SP} + X_{SY} = 300 \quad \text{(Seoul capacity)}$$

$$X_{TF} + X_{TN} + X_{TP} + X_{TY} = 200 \quad \text{(Tel Aviv capacity)}$$

Analogously, every warehouse must meet a second set of constraints, so that *the total number of units shipped to each warehouse must equal that warehouse's demand.* The four warehouse demand constraints for our problem are expressed explicitly as

$$X_{JF} + X_{SF} + X_{TF} = 150 \quad \text{(Frankfurt demand)}$$

$$X_{JN} + X_{SN} + X_{TN} = 100 \quad \text{(New York demand)}$$

$$X_{JP} + X_{SP} + X_{TP} = 200 \quad \text{(Phoenix demand)}$$

$$X_{JY} + X_{SY} + X_{TY} = 150 \quad \text{(Yokohama demand)}$$

Finally, we include the non-negativity conditions,

$$\text{where} \quad \text{all } X_{ij}\text{'s} \geq 0$$

The Problem Solution

Our example illustrates a class of linear programming situations that are referred to as **transportation problems**. In Chapter 14, we will learn how such problems are solved using the **transportation method**. The optimal solution to this problem (which will be discussed in detail in Chapter 14) is

$$X_{JF} = 0 \qquad X_{JN} = 0 \qquad X_{JP} = 100 \qquad X_{JY} = 0$$

$$X_{SF} = 50 \qquad X_{SN} = 0 \qquad X_{SP} = 100 \qquad X_{SY} = 150$$

$$X_{TF} = 100 \qquad X_{TN} = 100 \qquad X_{TP} = 0 \qquad X_{TY} = 0$$

$$C = 6{,}250$$

This solution provides the most economical plan. Some of the results are obvious— for example, that Seoul (Korea) supply Yokohama (Japan) but not New York. It seems a little odd that Seoul supplies Phoenix, but its demand outstrips Juarez's capacity and the Korean supplier must take up the slack.

9-5 Marketing Application: Budgeting Advertising Expenditures

Linear programming may be employed in establishing advertising budgets to designate a firm's level of expenditures for each media, such as television, radio, billboards, and magazines. Linear programming may even be used to determine how much space or time should be allocated to each medium, as the following example illustrates.

Real Reels Problem

The owner of Real Reels, a fishing equipment manufacturing company, wishes to determine how many quarter-page ads to place in *Playboy*, *True*, and *Esquire*. The following variables apply.

$$X_P = \text{Number of ads in } Playboy$$

$$X_T = \text{Number of ads in } True$$

$$X_E = \text{Number of ads in } Esquire$$

The goal is to maximize total product exposure to significant buyers of expensive fishing gear. Exposure in any particular magazine is the number of ads placed multiplied by the number of significant buyers. The following data apply.

	Playboy	True	Esquire
Readers	10 million	6 million	4 million
Significant buyers	10%	15%	7%
Cost per ad	$10,000	$5,000	$6,000

The exposure for a *Playboy* ad is .10 × 10,000,000 = 1,000,000. It will be convenient to express everything in millions. Letting P represent total exposure, the objective function is to

$$\text{Maximize} \quad P = 1X_P + .9X_T + .28X_E$$

Real has budgeted a maximum of $100,000 for the ads. The owner has already determined that no more than 5 ads should be placed in *True* and that at least 2 ads apiece should be placed in *Playboy* and *Esquire*. The problem constraints are

$$10,000X_P + 5,000X_T + 6,000X_E \leq 100,000 \quad \text{(budget)}$$
$$1X_T \leq 5 \quad \text{(maximum } True \text{ ads)}$$
$$1X_P \geq 2 \quad \text{(minimum } Playboy \text{ ads)}$$
$$1X_E \geq 2 \quad \text{(minimum } Esquire \text{ ads)}$$
$$\text{where} \quad X_P, X_T, X_E \geq 0$$

The Problem Solution

Using the procedures of Chapters 10 and 11, the optimal solution to this problem is found to be

$$X_P = 6.3 \qquad X_T = 5 \qquad X_E = 2$$

$$P = 11.36 \text{ million}$$

Notice that this solution involves a fractional amount for the *Playboy* ads. Remember that linear programming permits this. Fractional solutions may not be troublesome when quantities are large. In Chapter 16, we will examine **integer programming**, where variables are restricted to whole numbers.

Further Advertising Considerations

The above example only partially illustrates the power of linear programming in advertising decision making. Many more magazines and media types may be considered simultaneously and several time periods may even be incorporated in a linear programming problem. Various demographic characteristics in the target audiences, such as reader ages and earnings, may also be included. Constraints may result in more or less emphasis on certain groups of people. Advertising problems involving thousands of variables with hundreds of constraints have been solved by using the linear programming approach.

9-6 Management Application: Assigning Personnel

Linear programming is widely used to assign workers to specific jobs. Such linear programs fall into the broad class of **assignment problems**. These are discussed in detail in Chapter 15.

Mildred's Tool and Die Shop Problem

Mildred Riveter runs a small machine shop, where each worker operates different pieces of equipment at varying skill levels. The following average times apply to each item processed by the shop.

INDIVIDUAL	TIME REQUIRED TO COMPLETE ONE JOB		
	Drilling	*Grinding*	*Lathe*
Ann	5 min	10 min	10 min
Bud	10	5	15
Chuck	15	15	10

Management wishes to assign operators to jobs so that the total time required to process one item is minimized.

As in shipment scheduling, it is convenient to designate the variables with double subscripts. In this case,

$$X_{ij} = \text{Fraction of time individual } i \text{ is assigned to job } j$$

Notice that we have $3 \times 3 = 9$ variables (the number of individuals multiplied by the number of jobs). The objective function is to

$$
\begin{aligned}
\text{Minimize} \quad C = \quad & 5X_{AD} + 10X_{AG} + 10X_{AL} \\
& + 10X_{BD} + 5X_{BG} + 15X_{BL} \\
& + 15X_{CD} + 15X_{CG} + 10X_{CL}
\end{aligned}
$$

One set of constraints applies to the availability of the operators, thereby ensuring that every individual is fully occupied.

$$
\begin{aligned}
X_{AD} + X_{AG} + X_{AL} &= 1 \quad \text{(Ann's availability)} \\
X_{BD} + X_{BG} + X_{BL} &= 1 \quad \text{(Bud's availability)} \\
X_{CD} + X_{CG} + X_{CL} &= 1 \quad \text{(Chuck's availability)}
\end{aligned}
$$

Another set of constraints applies to the jobs, each of which requires a complete assignment.

$$
\begin{aligned}
X_{AD} + X_{BD} + X_{CD} &= 1 \quad \text{(drill-press requirement)} \\
X_{AG} + X_{BG} + X_{CG} &= 1 \quad \text{(grinder requirement)} \\
X_{AL} + X_{BL} + X_{CL} &= 1 \quad \text{(lathe requirement)}
\end{aligned}
$$

Of course, non-negativity is a condition for all variables.

The Problem Solution

Chapter 15 discusses how to solve assignment problems. The optimal solution to this problem is

$$
\begin{aligned}
X_{AD} &= 1 & X_{CL} &= 1 \\
X_{BG} &= 1 & \text{all other } X\text{'s} &= 0 \\
& & C &= 20
\end{aligned}
$$

9-7 Production Application: Liquid Blending

Many products, from toothpaste to gasoline, are blended from a variety of raw ingredients. The processes involved are often highly flexible because these products must meet various restrictions, such as limited ingredient availability and minimum product demand. Managers may apply linear programming to determine the particular blend of ingredients that will meet all constraints and still maximize total profit.

Linear programming is used extensively by oil and chemical companies to solve **liquid blending problems**. Managers at many large oil refineries routinely employ linear programs in operational planning. One refinery makes a daily computer run to solve a linear program that indicates the day's gasoline blending plan. Shifts in ingredient availabilities and costs and slight variations in ingredient composition require frequent planning, and linear programming has proved to be a very valuable tool in accomplishing this task.

A Scent-Mixing Problem

An aftershave and a cologne are both made of essentially the same three active ingredients: oil, rinse, and stabilizer. As with assignment and transportation problems, it is convenient to define the variables using double subscript notation, so that

$$X_{ij} = \text{Volume (liters) of ingredient } i \text{ used in blending product } j$$

The letters O, R, and S will be used to denote the respective ingredients; A and C, the products.

We will begin this particular formulation by defining the constraints that pertain to liquid availabilities (in liters).

$$X_{OA} + X_{OC} \leq 2,000 \quad \text{(available oil)}$$

$$X_{RA} + X_{RC} \leq 500 \quad \text{(available rinse)}$$

$$X_{SA} + X_{SC} \leq 1,000 \quad \text{(available stabilizer)}$$

The left-hand sides of these inequalities represent the total quantities of the respective ingredients actually used; the right-hand sides indicate the current inventory levels.

A second set of constraints pertains to volume (quantity) requirements for the final products.

$$X_{OA} + X_{RA} + X_{SA} \geq 1,500 \quad \text{(aftershave volume)}$$

$$X_{OC} + X_{RC} + X_{SC} \geq 500 \quad \text{(cologne volume)}$$

Here, the left-hand sides represent the total volumes of active liquid ingredients in the present production run of the respective products, and the right-hand sides indicate the minimum volumes required to meet the product demands.

A final set of constraints pertains to the proportional content of the ingredients in each product. For example, at least 30% of the volume of cologne must be emulsions. The oil is 50% emulsions, the rinse is 100%, and the stabilizer is only 10%. The emulsion requirement may therefore be summarized as

$$\frac{.50X_{OC} + 1.00X_{RC} + .10X_{SC}}{X_{OC} + X_{RC} + X_{SC}} \geq .30 \quad \text{(emulsions in cologne)}$$

where the numerator expresses the total emulsion volume of the cologne ingredients and the denominator indicates the total volume of the cologne. This ratio must be at least .30.

A similar restriction applies to the aftershave, which must contain at least 20% evaporative agents. The rinse is 25% evaporatives, the stabilizer is 50%, and the oil contains none. The evaporative requirement is summarized as

$$\frac{.25X_{RA} + .50X_{SA}}{X_{OA} + X_{RA} + X_{SA}} \geq .20 \quad \text{(evaporatives in aftershave)}$$

These two proportional content constraints are ordinarily rearranged by multiplying both sides of the inequality by the denominator, canceling, and then collecting X terms on the left-hand side.

$$.20X_{OC} + .70X_{RC} - .20X_{SC} \geq 0 \quad \text{(emulsions in cologne)}$$

$$-.20X_{OA} + .05X_{RA} + .30X_{SA} \geq 0 \quad \text{(evaporatives in aftershave)}$$

Of course, all X's must be non-negative. The objective is to maximize total profit. We begin to express this by considering total sales. The value per liter of active ingredients is $10 for aftershave and $20 for cologne. This gives us total sales of

$$10(X_{OA} + X_{RA} + X_{SA}) + 20(X_{OC} + X_{RC} + X_{SC})$$

Ingredient costs are $2 per liter of oil, $30 per liter of rinse, and $4 per liter of stabilizer. Total cost is therefore expressed as

$$2(X_{OA} + X_{OC}) + 30(X_{RA} + X_{RC}) + 4(X_{SA} + X_{SC})$$

By subtracting total cost from total revenue and collecting and rearranging terms, we obtain the objective function

$$\text{Maximize} \quad P = 8X_{OA} - 20X_{RA} + 6X_{SA} + 18X_{OC} - 10X_{RC} + 16X_{SC}$$

In standardized format, the objective function and constraints for this problem are provided below.

Maximize P

$$= 8X_{OA} - 20X_{RA} + 6X_{SA} + 18X_{OC} - 10X_{RC} + 16X_{SC}$$

Subject to

$1X_{OA} +$	$0X_{RA} +$	$0X_{SA} +$	$1X_{OC} +$	$0X_{RC} +$	$0X_{SC} \leq 2{,}000$	(avail. oil)
$0X_{OA} +$	$1X_{RA} +$	$0X_{SA} +$	$0X_{OC} +$	$1X_{RC} +$	$0X_{SC} \leq 500$	(avail. rinse)
$0X_{OA} +$	$0X_{RA} +$	$1X_{SA} +$	$0X_{OC} +$	$0X_{RC} +$	$1X_{SC} \leq 1{,}000$	(avail. stab.)
$1X_{OA} +$	$1X_{RA} +$	$1X_{SA} +$	$0X_{OC} +$	$0X_{RC} +$	$0X_{SC} \geq 1{,}500$	(afshv. vol.)

$$0X_{OA} + \quad 0X_{RA} + \quad 0X_{SA} + \quad 1X_{OC} + \quad 1X_{RC} + \quad 1X_{SC} \geq \quad 500 \quad \text{(col. vol.)}$$

$$0X_{OA} + \quad 0X_{RA} + \quad 0X_{SA} + .20X_{OC} + .70X_{RC} - .20X_{SC} \geq \quad 0 \quad \text{(emul. col.)}$$

$$-.20X_{OA} + .05X_{RA} + .30X_{SA} + \quad 0X_{OC} + \quad 0X_{RC} + \quad 0X_{SC} \geq \quad 0 \quad \text{(evap. afshv.)}$$

where $\qquad\qquad\qquad\qquad\qquad\qquad\qquad\qquad$ all X's $\geq \quad 0$

The Problem Solution

Applying the methods of Chapters 10 and 11, the optimal solution to this problem is found to be

$$X_{OA} = \quad 220 \qquad X_{OC} = 1{,}780$$

$$X_{RA} = \quad 280 \qquad X_{RC} = \quad 0$$

$$X_{SA} = 1{,}000 \qquad X_{SC} = \quad 0$$

$$P = 34{,}200$$

The product manager would find the preceding solution a bit disconcerting, because it indicates that the cologne must consist of nothing but oil. Of course, the overall problem has been simplified, and only a few essential requirements are shown. However, an important step in any linear programming application is to examine the results to see if they make sense. An unreasonable solution could result from a missing requirement or an improperly formulated constraint.

Special Considerations in Defining Variables

Perhaps the most challenging part of the linear program formulation is properly defining the variables and separating variables from their constraints. Liquid blending problems are particularly troublesome to beginners. Keep in mind that the X's are what the decision maker wants to find. In the present illustration, the question is: How much of each available ingredient (oil, rinse, and stabilizer) is to go into each final product (cologne and aftershave)? There is a separate variable for each ingredient-product combination, and it makes sense to have the OA, RA, SA, OC, RC, and SC variable designations.

In determining what is a variable (and to be decided) and what is a secondary quantity, keep in mind that the latter will ordinarily occur in *fixed proportion* to another unknown quantity to be decided. For example, the amount of *wood* used by Redwood Furniture in making tables is *not* what is to be decided (even though the amount is not known). Exactly 30 board feet will be used in making each table (the variable). Once the number of tables and chairs has been determined, of course, the amount of wood and labor going into each product can be readily determined. Wood and labor are not variables, and there are not separate WT and WC or LT and LC variables. Wood and labor are not blended, with finished furniture emerging from a melting pot.

Although also unknown, the level of emulsions in cologne or aftershave is *not* a variable, but rather a secondary quantity that is automatically fixed once values have been determined for the X's defined earlier.

Keep your list of variables as short as possible. Although in the scent-melting problem the total amounts to be used of oil, rinse, and stabilizer are unknowns and equal to the following

$$\text{Total volume of oil} = X_{OA} + X_{OC}$$

$$\text{Total volume of rinse} = X_{RA} + X_{RC}$$

$$\text{Total volume of stabilizer} = X_{SA} + X_{SC}$$

It only "muddies the water" to have additional separate O, R, and S variables for the totals. If a constraint involves a specification on the total amount of oil, the variable *sum* $X_{OA} + X_{OC}$ should be used whenever the total oil is needed.

A similar conclusion may be made regarding the amount of final product.

$$\text{Total volume of aftershave} = X_{OA} + X_{RA} + X_{SA}$$

$$\text{Total volume of cologne} = X_{OC} + X_{RC} + X_{SC}$$

There should be no separate A and C variables. Use the *sum* of the double-subscripted X's whenever expressing the total amount of a final product.

9-8 Production Application: The Diet Problem

An important linear programming application is the **diet problem**. In this problem, quantities are selected for various ingredients used in mixing a final product so that minimum nutritional requirements are met while at the same time minimizing costs.

TABLE 9-3
Trail-Mix Delight Dietetic Requirements

NUTRIENTS	NUTRITIONAL VALUE OF INGREDIENTS PER KILOGRAM					Minimum Requirement
	Dried Currants	Roasted Peanuts	Roasted Walnuts	Pumpkin Kernels	Dried Milk	
Calories	540	5,720	6,540	5,530	4,990	3,000 cal.
Protein	20	270	150	290	260	56 g.
Iron	10	30	20	110	10	10 mg.
Vitamin A	230	0	300	700	9,200	1,000 μg
Thiamin	.5	2.5	4.8	2.4	2.9	1.4 mg.
Riboflavin	.5	2.6	1.3	1.9	12.1	1.6 mg.
Niacin	3	170	12	24	7	18 mg.
Calcium	600	720	830	510	9,120	800 mg.
Ascorbic Acid	2,000	10	30	0	90	60 μg RE
Cost per kilogram	$1.50	$2.50	$4.00	$1.00	$1.50	

SOURCE: Louise Bullock

Trail-Mix Delight Decision

Yosemite Ann's supplies hikers with a variety of provisions. One of these is Trail-Mix Delight, a one kilogram package made up of natural ingredients. Each package provides the hiker with the complete nutritional requirements for one day, in accordance with the requirements given in Table 9-3.

All ingredients are readily available from local suppliers, so that there are no quantity limitations. Yosemite Ann wants to determine the weight of the various ingredients that will be mixed together to give exactly one kilogram of the product. She defines the following variables.

X_C = Weight of dried currants in a one-kilogram package

X_P = Weight of roasted peanuts in a one-kilogram package

X_W = Weight of roasted walnuts in a one-kilogram package

X_K = Weight of pumpkin kernels in a one-kilogram package

X_M = Weight of dried milk in a one-kilogram package

These quantities are to be selected in such a way that total ingredient cost is minimized. Yosemite's objective function is to

$$\text{Minimize} \quad C = 1.50X_C + 2.50X_P + 4.00X_W + 1.00X_K + 1.50X_M$$

Diet problems usually involve a constraint for the total weight of the final product, which is the sum of the ingredient weights.

$$X_C + X_P + X_W + X_K + X_M = 1 \quad \text{(total weight)}$$

The above constraint is essential, since there is no other way to guarantee that a kilogram of ingredients will be put into the one-kilogram package.

Each nutritional requirement provides a separate constraint, as shown in Table 9-4.

TABLE 9-4
Constraints for Yosemite Ann's Trail-Mix Delight Linear Program

$540X_C + 5{,}720X_P + 6{,}540X_W + 5{,}530X_K + 4{,}990X_M \geq 3{,}000$ (calories)

$20X_C + 270X_P + 150X_W + 290X_K + 260X_M \geq 56$ (protein)

$10X_C + 30X_P + 20X_W + 110X_K + 10X_M \geq 10$ (iron)

$230X_C + 0X_P + 300X_W + 700X_K + 9{,}200X_M \geq 1{,}000$ (vitamin A)

$.5X_C + 2.5X_P + 4.8X_W + 2.4X_K + 2.9X_M \geq 1.4$ (thiamin)

$.5X_C + 2.6X_P + 1.3X_W + 1.9X_K + 12.1X_M \geq 1.6$ (riboflavin)

$3X_C + 170X_P + 12X_W + 24X_K + 7X_M \geq 18$ (niacin)

$600X_C + 720X_P + 830X_W + 510X_K + 9{,}120X_M \geq 800$ (calcium)

$2{,}000X_C + 10X_P + 30X_W + 0X_K + 90X_M \geq 60$ (asc. acid)

Of course, the non-negativity conditions are assumed to apply.

It does not matter that the units vary from constraint to constraint. (Indeed, as we have seen, one constraint might be in board feet, another in hours of labor, and so on.) In linear programming, it is only essential that the same units are used on the left and the right side within each constraint.

The Problem Solution

Applying the methods of Chapters 10 and 11, the optimal solution to this problem is

$$X_C = .0283 \qquad X_P = .9348$$
$$X_W = 0 \qquad X_K = .0369$$
$$X_M = 0$$
$$C = 1.0326$$

Yosemite Ann found the results extremely unsatisfactory, because no nuts were included in the solution.

Fearing that nobody would buy the insipid, but nutritional, mix, she decided to add two constraints guaranteeing that at least 10% of the total weight be peanuts and 10% be walnuts. The following two constraints were added to the earlier problem.

$$0X_C + 1X_P + 0X_W + 0X_K + 0X_M \geq .10 \quad \text{(peanuts)}$$
$$0X_C + 0X_P + 1X_W + 0X_K + 0X_M \geq .10 \quad \text{(walnuts)}$$

The following solution was obtained to the expanded linear program.

$$X_C = .0258 \qquad X_P = .7246$$
$$X_W = .1000 \qquad X_K = .0497$$
$$X_M = .1000$$
$$C = 1.4877$$

CASE

Shale–Bituminous Processors

Shale–Bituminous Processors use gasification and pressurization to make low-sulfur and high-sulfur crude oil. The two processes require different mixtures of coal and shale solids. A batch processed by gasification requires an input of 1 ton of coal and 2 tons of shale to yield 100 gallons of low-sulfur crude and 200 gallons of high-sulfur crude. Under pressurization, each batch requires 2 tons of coal and 1 ton of shale to provide 150 gallons of low-sulfur crude and 100 gallons of high-sulfur crude.

The refinery manager wishes to determine how many batches should be converted to crude oil under each process to maximize total profits when supplying an order for exactly 10,000 gallons of low-sulfur and 5,000 gallons of high-sulfur crudes. Available tonnages for filling this order are 100 tons of coal and 150 tons of shale. The costs of the solids per ton are $20 for coal and $25 for shale. The processor receives $.50 per gallon for low-sulfur crude and $.30 for high-sulfur crude.

Questions

1. If 10 batches are processed under gasification and 20 batches are processed under pressurization, determine how many
    (a) tons of coal are used.
    (b) tons of shale are used.
    (c) gallons of low-sulfur crude are produced.
    (d) gallons of high-sulfur crude are produced.

2. Determine the profit per batch converted under each process.

3. Formulate the processor's problem as a linear program.

4. Try to solve the linear program in Question 3 graphically. What conclusion do you reach?

5. Suppose that the refinery manager persuades the customer to take all of the ordered high-sulfur crude and half of the low-sulfur crude now. Reformulate the linear program and solve it graphically.

PROBLEMS

The following problems all involve too many variables to be solved graphically and are to be *formulated only*. Standardized formats are optional.

9-1   Rott Irony manufactures four types of light fixtures. A fancy lamp yields a profit of $100, takes 10 hours of labor and 2 hours of machine time, and requires 10 ft^2 of sheet metal. An ornate lamp yields a profit of $150, takes 8 hours of labor and 3 hours of machine time, and requires 20 ft^2 of metal. The plain and rococo lamps each yield a $200 profit and involve 1 hour of machine time. However, the rococo lamp requires 20 hours of labor and 30 ft^2 of metal, and the plain lamp requires 10 hours of labor and 15 ft^2 of metal. Rott must produce at least twice as many plain lamps as rococo ones. Only 1,000 hours of labor and 200 hours of machine time are available, and 5,000 ft^2 of sheet metal are in inventory. Rott wishes to determine how many of each type of lamp to make to maximize total profits. Formulate this problem as a linear program.

9-2 You have been given the assigment of scheduling the production of Hoopla Hoops. There are four basic models, with the following resource usages.

| | MODEL | | | | |
RESOURCE	A	B	C	D	Available
Plastic	5	6	6	7	100 ft
Beads	10	12	15	15	500 oz
Nylon	4	5	5	0	600 ft
Teflon	0	2	3	4	200 gal
Labor	.5	.4	.5	.8	300 hrs

The number of model A's cannot exceed the combined total of the other models. Hoopla must make at least 50 model B and 20 model D hoops.

Hoopla wants to determine the number of models of each type that should be made in order to maximize total profit. The unit profits are $2 for models A and C, $1.50 for model B, and $2.50 for model D. Formulate Hoopla's problem as a linear program.

9-3 The Myrtlewood Box Company manufactures small, medium, and large boxes. Wood usages are 4, 8, and 16 board feet for the respective products. Assembly time requirements are 1, 2, and 3 hours, respectively. Only 500 board feet of wood and 200 hours of assembly time are presently available. All boxes produced will be sold for the following unit profits: small, $10; medium, $15; and large, $30. How many boxes of each type should Myrtlewood produce? Formulate this problem as a linear program.

9-4 Quicker Oats must determine how much of its $200,000 advertising and promotional budget should be spent in the following mediums: television, radio, magazines, and prize promotion. Each dollar spent on television advertising increases sales $10; both radio and magazine ads result in half that return, and prize promotion returns $20 in sales for each dollar invested. Television advertising cannot exceed half of the total budget, and total radio advertising must be at least 20% of total TV advertising. At least $20,000 must be spent on magazine ads, and no more than $25,000 may be spent on the prize promotion. Management's objective is to maximize the total increase in Quicker's sales volume. Formulate the decision as a linear program.

9-5 CompuQuick must determine which of its computer facilities should process client company payrolls. Based on the complexity and size of the payroll and on processing speed, data-transmission requirements, and volumes of input and output, the following costs apply.

| | COMPANY PAYROLL | | |
FACILITY	Blitz Beer	WaySafe Markets	Quicker Oats
Arizona	$500	$750	$400
California	600	500	300
Illinois	700	600	300

Each facility has the capacity to process only one payroll. CompuQuick wishes to minimize its total data-processing costs. Formulate this problem as a linear program, using double subscripts in defining your variables.

9-6 A trust officer for the Million Bank wishes to invest in the following bonds.

BOND	YIELD	MATURITY	RISK	TAX-FREE
A	8%	Long	High	Yes
B	9	Short	Low	No
C	9	Long	High	No
D	10	Short	Low	No
E	9	Short	High	Yes

She will use a linear program to find the dollar investment in each bond that will maximize total interest income.

(a) Define the variables that apply and then express her linear programming objective in terms of these.

(b) Express each of the following linear programming constraints using the variables defined in (a).

  (1) Exactly $100,000 will be invested altogether.
  (2) At least $50,000 must be placed in short maturity bonds.
  (3) No more than $30,000 may be invested in high-risk issues.
  (4) At least $25,000 must be placed in tax-free issues.
  (5) Total funds invested in low-risk bonds must be less than or equal to total funds placed in long-maturity issues.
  (6) The interest income derived from tax-free bonds must be at least one-fourth of the total income.

9-7 Ima Hogg wishes to determine the quantity of ingredients to use in making each pound of sausage at a minimum cost. The available ingredients and their costs are provided in the following table.

POUND OF INGREDIENT	COST	PROTEIN	FAT	WATER
Hog bellies	$.30	3 oz	5 oz	6 oz
Tripe	.20	5	3	4
Beef	.70	4	2	5
Pork	.60	3	4	9
Chicken	.45	3	3	4

Ima must meet the specified weight exactly, and there are further restrictions. Not more than 10% of the sausage weight can be composed of hog bellies and tripe, chicken cannot exceed 25% of the total content, and at least 30% of the sausage must consist of beef. In addition, a minimum of 3 ounces of protein must be present in each pound of sausage. Furthermore, each pound of sausage may contain a maximum of 4 ounces of fat and must contain a maximum of 8 ounces of water. Formulate the decision as a linear program.

9-8 The BugOff Chemical Company manufactures three pesticides—Ant-Can't, Boll-Toll, and Caterpillar-Chiller—at respective profits of $5, $6, and $7 per gallon. BugOff must decide what quantities of each pesticide to produce. Regardless of brand, each gallon requires 100 milligrams (.1 gram) of catalyst. Every gallon of Ant-Can't and Caterpillar-Chiller requires 1/10 gallon of malathion, and each gallon of Boll-Toll and Caterpillar-Chiller must contain 2/10 gallon of parathion. Seasonal requirements dictate that the quantity of Ant-Can't may exceed the quantity of Boll-Toll by no more than 500 gallons. The available ingredients are 1,000 grams of catalyst, 1,000 gallons of malathion, and 2,000 gallons of parathion. BugOff wishes to produce the most profitable quantities of each pesticide. Formulate this problem as a linear program.

9-9 Willy B. Rich wishes to invest $100,000 of current receipts in order to maximize total annual interest income. He has narrowed his choices to a municipal bond yielding 6%, an industrial bond yielding 8%, Treasury bills at 10%, and certificates of deposit (CDs) at 9%. For safety, at least one-half of the funds must be placed in bonds. For liquidity, at least 25% of the funds must be invested in CDs. Due to volatile Fed policies, no more than 20% of the portfolio can be in Treasury bills. Tax-sheltering considerations dictate that at least 30% of the investment must be in municipal bonds. Formulate this problem as a linear program.

9-10 Refer to the scent-mixing problem described in Section 9-7. Formulate each of the following constraints in a form suitable for incorporation into the original linear program.
(a) The proportion of alcohol in cologne cannot exceed 50% of the total volume. The oil contains no alcohol, but the rinse is 50% alcohol and the stabilizer is 20% alcohol.
(b) The volume of skin-bracing agents in the aftershave cannot exceed 30%. These agents comprise 10% of the oil, 20% of the rinse, and 20% of the stabilizer.

9-11 Druids' Drayage hauls rock from two quarries to three tombstone masons. The manager, H. Priest, wishes to minimize total shipping costs in such a way that every quarry operates precisely at full capacity and each mason receives exactly the number of stones demanded. The unit shipping costs and quantity requirements for tombstones are provided in the following table.

FROM QUARRY	TO MASON			Quarry Capacity
	Cedrick	Dunstan	Eldred	
Abinger	£10	£ 15	£ 8	100
Barnesly	12	9	10	200
Mason Demand	50	150	100	300

A linear program may be used to establish a shipping schedule that indicates how many tombstones should be supplied from each quarry to the various masons. A quarry can service any number of masons, and any mason can receive shipments from one or more quarries. Formulate this problem as a linear program, using variables defined with double subscripts.

9-12 All-American Meat Processors is mixing the ingredients for a batch of German and Italian sausages. The following cuts are to be used.

MEAT	COST PER POUND	AVAILABLE QUANTITY (lbs)
Beef rib	$1.00	200
Beef shank	1.50	500
Beef tongue	1.00	700
Pork	.90	1,000
Lamb	1.20	800

All-American wants to determine the minimum cost mixture that will provide at least 500 pounds of German sausage and 300 pounds of Italian. This must be done so that at least 60% of the German sausage is beef and at least 80% of the Italian sausage is beef. Furthermore, the German sausage can contain no more than 10% lamb, while the Italian sausage cannot have more than 20% pork. Using double-subscripted variables throughout, formulate All-American's problem as a linear program.

9-13 ChipMont manufactures silicon wafer circuits for use in microprocessors. Computer makers presently buy ChipMont's entire production of the following types of silicon chips: central processing unit (CPU), integrated circuit, and core memory. The following data apply.

ITEM	CHIP TYPES			Available Maximums
	CPU	Integrated	Memory	
Silicon	.005	.02	.01	10,000 sheets
Sorting labor	.2	.5	.1	200,000 minutes
Chemical wash	.10	.40	.15	400,000 hours
Profit per wafer	$.25	$.40	$.15	

ChipMont must decide how many of each chip to manufacture. The number of integrated circuits must be at least as large as the combined total for the other two types of wafers.
(a) Formulate ChipMont's decision as a linear program.
(b) One possible production plan is to make 50,000 CPU's, 300,000 integrated circuits, and 200,000 core memories. Place these quantities in each of your linear programming constraints to verify that this plan is feasible. Then, find the corresponding profit.

9-14 Channel Zee blends two fragrance bases, Mystery and Anomaly, which are used by perfume makers worldwide. The ingredients include gland extract, spice oil, and brandy. Channel wants to use linear programming in determining what volume of each ingredient to mix in one batch each of the final products. This will be done in order to maximize total profit. Costs per liter are: gland, $5,000; spice, $100; and brandy, $10. Mystery sells for $200 per liter and Anomaly for $300.
(a) Define the variables that apply and then express the linear programming objective in terms of these.
(b) The following proportions of ingredient volumes contain agents for fixing perfumes.

INGREDIENT	PRESERVING	ACCENTUATING	STABILIZING
Gland extract	.01	.20	.01
Spice oil	.10	.02	.05
Brandy	.20	.01	.01

Express each of the following constraints using the variables defined in (a).

(1) Preserving agents in the Mystery batch must be at least 10% of the total volume for that product.

(2) Accentuating agents cannot exceed 15% of the total Anomaly volume.

(3) Stabilizing agents must be at least 2% of the total Mystery volume.

(4) Stabilizing agents cannot exceed 3% of the total Anomaly volume.

(5) The preserving agents in Mystery must occupy at least twice the volume of the accentuating agents.

(6) The stabilizing agents in Anomaly cannot exceed one-tenth the volume of the preserving agents.

9-15 Conformity Systems has three employees, a clerk, a typist, and a stenographer. Each employee will be assigned exactly one of the following tasks: filing, bookkeeping, or report preparation. The manager wishes to assign workers to jobs so that total cost is minimized. The costs for each possible employee–job assignment are provided in the following table.

EMPLOYEE	JOB		
	Filing	Bookkeeping	Reports
Clerk	$20	$25	$35
Typist	25	20	30
Stenographer	30	25	25

Treating each possible employee–job assignment as a separate variable, formulate this problem as a linear program.

9-16 Blitz Beer has allotted $10,000 for radio advertising in Gotham City and must determine the placement of spot ads that will maximize increased sales. Top-40 stations attract a heavier beer-drinking audience than golden-oldie stations do, but top-40 stations also charge more for each spot. The following data apply.

STATION	COST PER SPOT	SALES INCREASE PER SPOT	SPOTS AVAILABLE	FORMAT
KBAT	$100	$300	30	Top-40
WJOK	50	120	Unlimited	Golden-oldie
WROB	75	150	Unlimited	Golden-oldie
KPOW	150	400	40	Top-40

At least 25% of the spots must be placed with golden-oldie stations. Formulate Blitz's problem as a linear program.

9-17 Geo-Pet is the managing partner in a variety of oil-exploration ventures. It must decide its level of dollar investment in the five ventures described in the following table.

JOINT VENTURE	EXPECTED RETURN	MINIMUM INVESTMENT	PRIMARY PRODUCT
Athabasca Tar Sands (Canada)	100%	$100,000	Crude
Kern County (U.S.)	30	None	Crude
Louisiana Miocene Trend (U.S.)	50	50,000	Gas
Persian Gulf (Arabia)	150	None	Crude
West Texas (U.S.)	75	100,000	Gas

Geo-Pet wishes to maximize its expected rate of return on a maximum total investment of $700,000 and still meet the dollar minimums given here. At least $300,000 must be placed in gas-producing investments, and no more than one-half of the total amount can be invested outside the United States. Formulate this problem as a linear program.

9-18 Ace Widgets manufactures products in plant A at a cost of $10 each and products in plant B at a cost of $11 each. The products are shipped to warehouses at a cost of $.01 per mile. The following distances apply.

	DISTANCE TO		
FROM	C	D	E
A	100	200	300
B	200	100	200

Plant A can manufacture 1,000 units; plant B has the capacity to manufacture only 500 units. Warehouse demands are 500 units for each. Ace Widgets must determine a manufacturing and shipping schedule that will meet these exact limitations at the least total cost. Formulate Ace's problem as a linear program.

9-19 Backpackers' Budget Shoppe is concocting a package to sell under the label "Hiker's Daily Dried Gruel." Designed only with nutritional value and ease of preparation in mind, each kilogram of the mix must meet the nutritional requirements provided in the following table.

NUTRIENT	NUTRITIONAL VALUE OF INGREDIENT PER KILOGRAM					Minimum Requirement
	Corn Meal	Beans	Spinach	Peanuts	Milk	
Calories	4,000	3,000	250	2,000	2,000	2,500
Protein	100	200	25	100	100	75 g
Iron	12	100	30	8	2	12 g
Vitamin A	4,000	1,000	50,000	5,000	13,000	5,000 units
Thiamine	2	6	1.5	1.5	1	2 mg
Riboflavin	1	5	3	1	6	3 ng
Niacin	12	25	8	80	3	20 mg
Ascorbic acid	0	0	500	0	15	100 mg
Cost per kilogram	$.50	$.75	$1.25	$.75	$1.50	

Formulate a linear program that determines the minimum-cost ingredient weights that satisfy these nutritional requirements.

10

Solving Linear Programs I: Simplex and the Computer

$\mathbb{W}$e are now ready to tackle linear programs that are impossible to solve by the graphical method because they contain too many variables to plot on a two-dimensional graph. An algebraic procedure—the **simplex method**—works on all linear programs, regardless of the number of variables. With the aid of a digital computer, the simplex method may be used to solve problems with thousands of variables and ten times that number of constraints. Indeed, without the simplex method, linear programming would be little more than a mathematical curiosity that could describe problems algebraically but could not solve any problem that had more than two or three variables.

The word simplex was *not* formed by adding the ubiquitous suffix *-ex* to the word simple (as in Kleenex and Memorex). *Simplex* is a legitimate term in the language of mathematics that represents the simplest object in an *n*-dimensional space connecting $n + 1$ points. In one dimension, a simplex is a line segment connecting two points. In two dimensions, a simplex is a triangle formed by joining three points. A three-dimensional simplex is a four-sided pyramid having just four corners. Such geometrical objects, extended to higher dimensions, are used to explain how and why the simplex method works. Although the procedure itself is quite simple to master, the mathematical arguments justifying this procedure are fairly complex.

Even though its underlying concepts are geometrical, the simplex algorithm itself is fundamentally an algebraic procedure. George B. Dantzig developed the algorithm after World War II and, with other mathematicians, has since extended and expanded it in a variety of ways. Like the graphical method, the simplex algorithm finds the most attractive corner of the feasible solution region, thereby solving the linear program. Ordinarily, the region itself exists in a higher dimensional space that may be imagined but not pictured. An underlying theoretical concept of the simplex method is that *any problem having a solution at all must have an optimal solution that corresponds to a corner point.*

This means that we need to evaluate only the corner points. Although finding and evaluating corners would seem to be child's play, remember that they are not pictured, so we cannot see them. Furthermore, the number of corners associated with even a moderately large linear program may be huge. For example, solving a 10-product planning problem with 10 resource constraints would involve nearly 200,000 corners. In our lifetimes, the biggest, fastest computer could not evaluate the trillions and trillions of corners in a problem just 10 times that size. A second feature of the simplex method incorporates a reliable search through the formidable thicket of corners to rapidly find the most attractive one. Based on *economic analysis*, this searching procedure is so efficient that only about 20 corners are evaluated in the 10-product case just mentioned.

In conclusion, the simplex method embodies geometry, but it combines algebra with economic principles to solve linear programs. Simplex is really an odyssey in *n*-dimensional space where you visit a few corner points on a multifaceted "gem stone" you cannot see. Each time you stop, you perform a small analysis to find out where you should stop next; your journey ends at the most attractive corner.

10-1 Basic Simplex Concepts

To introduce the simplex method, we will continue our Redwood Furniture problem, using the data repeated in Table 10-1. As before, X_T and X_C represent the number of tables and chairs. The following linear program applies.

TABLE 10-1
Data Obtained for the Redwood Furniture Problem

RESOURCE	UNIT REQUIREMENTS		Amount Available
	Table	Chair	
Wood (board feet)	30	20	300
Labor (hours)	5	10	110
Unit profit	$6	$8	

$$\text{Maximize} \quad P = 6X_T + 8X_C \quad \text{(objective)}$$
$$\text{Subject to} \quad 30X_T + 20X_C \le 300 \quad \text{(wood)}$$
$$5X_T + 10X_C \le 110 \quad \text{(labor)}$$
$$\text{where} \quad X_T, X_C \ge 0$$

Slack Variables

We will now solve this problem algebraically. Our first step is to acknowledge the existence of *slack*, which represents unused resources. We define the following **slack variables**.

$$S_W = \text{Amount of unused wood}$$
$$S_L = \text{Amount of unused labor}$$

The letter S is traditionally used for this type of auxiliary variable. (The original problem variables X_T and X_C are sometimes called *main variables* to distinguish them from the slacks.) Each slack variable is incorporated into the original constraints. In the case of wood, we may equivalently express the constraint as

Wood used in tables or chairs + Unused wood = Available wood

By adding the quantities of wood on the left side, this constraint tells us "what we use plus what we don't use must equal what we start with." The meaning of the constraint is the same as before. Stated algebraically, our revised wood constraint is

$$30X_T + 20X_C + S_W = 300 \quad \text{(wood)}$$

which is equivalent to the original expression. Adding the slack variable converts an inequality into an equality. The S_W term bridges the gap, taking up the slack between the less than ($<$) and the equal ($=$) signs.

In the same way, we may convert the labor constraint into the following equality.

$$5X_T + 10X_C + S_L = 110 \quad \text{(labor)}$$

Notice that the unused wood S_W appears only in the wood constraint equation and that the unused labor S_L appears only in the labor constraint equation.

Slack variables have a two-fold purpose. First, and most importantly, adding the slack variables allows us to convert inequalities into equalities, thereby converting the linear program into a form that is amenable to algebraic solution. It is mathematically easier to analyze equalities than inequalities. Second, slack variables permit us to make a more comprehensive economic interpretation of a solution than would otherwise be possible.

Expressing the Linear Program in Terms of Slacks

Incorporating the slack variables into the entire linear program formulation, we have

$$\text{Maximize} \quad P = 6X_T + 8X_C + 0S_W + 0S_L \quad \text{(objective)}$$

$$\text{Subject to} \quad 30X_T + 20X_C + 1S_W + 0S_L = 300 \quad \text{(wood)}$$

$$5X_T + 10X_C + 0S_W + 1S_L = 110 \quad \text{(labor)}$$

$$\text{where} \quad X_T, X_C, S_W, S_L \geq 0$$

S_W and S_L appear in the objective equation with coefficients of zero, reflecting the fact that unused resources contribute nothing to profit (or to cost) but remain assets in inventory. The non-negativity conditions apply to S_W and S_L as well as to X_T and X_C. Slack variables cannot be negative. (If they were, it would mean that more of the resource than was originally available could be consumed, which would remove the limitation of the original constraint.)

For later convenience, S_W and S_L appear in their respective constraint equations with coefficients of 1. S_L also has a coefficient of zero in the wood constraint, and S_W similarly appears with a coefficient of zero in the labor constraint. This in no way distorts the original relationships, since a term appearing with a coefficient of zero is mathematically equivalent to being absent. This arrangement merely makes it easier for us to keep track of the problem.

Algebraic Solution

The feasible solution region to the new problem cannot be graphed, because we now have four variables and our problem is four-dimensional. Our algebraic system contains two constraint equations with four unknowns.

$$30X_T + 20X_C + 1S_W + 0S_L = 300$$

$$5X_T + 10X_C + 0S_W + 1S_L = 110$$

We learned how to solve two equations with two unknowns in Chapter 8 when we found the coordinates for the most attractive corner. But here *we have more unknowns than equations.* How do we find the solution?

Let's take a slight detour and consider the problem of finding values for x and y that satisfy the equation

$$2x + 4y = 12$$

Here, we must solve one equation with two unknowns. We recognize that this equation represents a line in the xy plane; we can even graph it. But here we are faced with essentially the same dilemma presented in the preceding linear program.

What's the answer? The line itself is the answer! But what are the x and y values? An infinite number of pairs of x and y values satisfy the equation, each pair being the coordinates of some point on the line.

To find any one solution, we must fix the value of x or y and then solve for the other variable. For example, if we

$$\text{set } x = 3$$

then, we have

$$2(3) + 4y = 12$$

$$4y = 12 - 2(3) = 12 - 6 = 6$$

and

$$y = \tfrac{6}{4} = 1\tfrac{1}{2}$$

Thus, $(x = 3, y = 1\tfrac{1}{2})$ is one pair of coordinates. For any other arbitrary value of x, we can obtain a unique y. Likewise, for any arbitrary value of y, we can find a unique x. These ambiguous solutions are the best we can achieve.

Continuing with our detour, consider the equations

$$2x + 4y + 3z = 12$$

$$3x + 2y + 1z = 6$$

Here again, we have more unknowns than equations. In a three-dimensional graph, each equation represents a plane and the solution is the intersection of the planes. (Imagine two sheets of paper held at different angles and crossed.) The solution is a line again! As before, we can only obtain numerical values of x, y, and z that satisfy both equations by arbitrarily establishing the value of one variable and then solving for the others. For example, if we

$$\text{set } y = 1$$

then, we have

$$2x + 4(1) + 3z = 12 \quad \text{or} \quad 2x + 3z = 8$$

$$3x + 2(1) + 1z = 6 \quad \text{or} \quad 3x + 1z = 4$$

and, solving for x and z, we obtain

$$x = \tfrac{4}{7} \qquad y = 1 \qquad z = 2\tfrac{2}{7}$$

From our detour, we may draw the following conclusion: *Whenever the number of variables exceeds the number of equations, the values of the extra variables must be arbitrarily set.*

The Basic Variable Mix

In our Redwood Furniture problem, there are two more variables than equations. The values of these extra variables must be fixed before the equations can be solved

TABLE 10-2
Possible Basic Variable-Mix Combinations and Their Algebraic Solutions for the Redwood Furniture Problem

CORNER POINT	BASIC VARIABLE MIX (free variables)	NONBASIC VARIABLES (arbitrarily set at 0)	ALGEBRAIC SOLUTION				
			X_T	X_C	S_W	S_L	P
A	$S_W\ S_L$	$X_T\ X_C$	0	0	300	110	$ 0
B	$S_W\ X_C$	$X_T\ S_L$	0	11	80	0	88
C	$S_L\ X_T$	$X_C\ S_W$	10	0	0	60	60
D	$X_T\ X_C$	$S_W\ S_L$	4	9	0	0	96
E	$S_L\ X_C$	$S_W\ X_T$	0	15	0	−40	Infeasible
F	$S_W\ X_T$	$S_L\ X_C$	22	0	−360	0	Infeasible

algebraically. Part of our problem is deciding which variables are assigned arbitrary values and which variables are "free" to be solved for algebraically. We must also determine what arbitrary values to use.

We will refer to the variables that must be solved for algebraically as the **basic variable mix**. As we have seen, their values can be found only after the other variables have been fixed at some arbitrary level. The fixed-value variables are identified as not being in the basic mix. Table 10-2 shows all of the possible combinations of basic and nonbasic variables for the Redwood Furniture problem. In each of the six cases, two complementary pairs of variables are involved.

We have noted that an essential feature of simplex is to evaluate corner points only. *Such a corner point is the algebraic solution to the constraint equations when the nonbasic variables have been arbitrarily set at 0.* This fact considerably simplifies finding solutions and allows us to greatly streamline the overall simplex method.

Each of the six basic mix pairs in Table 10-2 for the Redwood Furniture problem provides a different **corner point solution**. All of these corner points are graphed in Figure 10-1. The solutions for corner points *A*, *B*, *C*, and *D* follow.

Corner Point A   Set $X_T = 0, X_C = 0$

$$30(0) + 20(0) + 1S_W + 0S_L = 300$$
$$5(0) + 10(0) + 0S_W + 1S_L = 110$$

getting

$$1S_W\qquad\quad = 300$$
$$1S_L = 110$$

Solution $X_T = 0, X_C = 0, S_W = 300, S_L = 110$

Profit $P = 6(0) + 8(0) + 0(300) + 0(110) = 0$

Corner Point B   Set $X_T = 0, S_L = 0$

$$30(0) + 20X_C + 1S_W + 0(0) = 300$$
$$5(0) + 10X_C + 0S_W + 1(0) = 110$$

FIGURE 10-1
Possible corner points for the Redwood Furniture problem.

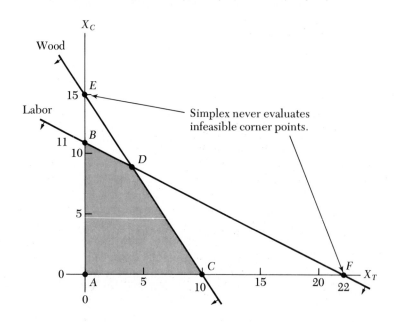

getting
$$20X_C + 1S_W = 300$$
$$10X_C = 110$$

Solution $X_T = 0$, $X_C = 11$, $S_W = 80$, $S_L = 0$

Profit $P = 6(0) + 8(11) + 0(80) + 0(0) = 88$

Corner Point C   Set $X_C = 0$, $S_W = 0$

$$30X_T + 20(0) + 1(0) + 0S_L = 300$$
$$5X_T + 10(0) + 0(0) + 1S_L = 110$$

getting
$$30X_T = 300$$
$$5X_T + 1S_L = 110$$

Solution $X_T = 10$, $X_C = 0$, $S_W = 0$, $S_L = 60$

Profit $P = 6(10) + 8(0) + 0(0) + 0(60) = 60$

Corner Point D   Set $S_W = 0$, $S_L = 0$

$$30X_T + 20X_C + 1(0) + 0(0) = 300$$
$$5X_T + 10X_C + 0(0) + 1(0) = 110$$

getting

$$30X_T + 20X_C = 300$$

$$5X_T + 10X_C = 110$$

Solution $X_T = 4$, $X_C = 9$, $S_W = 0$, $S_L = 0$

Profit $P = 6(4) + 8(9) + 0(0) + 0(0) = 96$

Only corner points A, B, C, and D are feasible. Point E is infeasible because it violates the labor constraint (the algebraic solution leads to a negative quantity for S_L), and point F is infeasible because it violates the wood constraint.

Before we continue, let's put our current example into its proper context. We are only illustrating the *concepts* of the simplex method here. We have not yet described the algorithm steps. Furthermore, it is never necessary to perform all of these calculations to solve a simple problem for which a graphical solution can be achieved. Resolving the Redwood Furniture problem algebraically here just makes it easier for us to understand what is happening. Ordinarily, *simplex will only be used when there are too many main variables in the original inequality formulation to be depicted on a graph.* In Figure 10-1, points on the constraint line represent zero slack for that particular resource; a feasible point off the line has an amount of positive slack that cannot be directly read from the graph.

Although the Redwood Furniture problem has been graphed in Figure 10-1, the augmented problem incorporating slacks S_W and S_L is *four-dimensional*. The feasible solution region is a polyhedron in that space. Thus, simplex evaluates the corners of a geometrical surface which cannot be pictured on an ordinary graph. Figure 10-1 only shows *projections* of that higher dimensional region onto the two-dimensional X_T-X_C plane.

Before describing the simplex algorithm in detail, a few more points will prove helpful. Suppose that we can identify all of the corner points in a linear program (as we did in Table 10-2). Then why can't we simply evaluate all of the feasible corner points algebraically and pick the one with the largest P? In our example, the most attractive corner is point D, with a profit of $96. After all, no graph is needed to list all of the combinations of basic mixes, and we know that each basic mix pair must correspond to a particular corner.

There are two reasons why we do not follow this procedure. First, as we noted earlier, the number of corners can be astronomical for a moderately sized problem, and even if we want to, it may be impossible to consider them all. Second, each corner point evaluation requires a lengthy algebraic solution. To obtain each corner point solution for a 10-constraint linear program, 10 equations with 10 unknowns must be solved—a horrendous task without some simplifying procedure. Simplex eliminates both of these difficulties.

10-2 The Simplex Method

Simplex ordinarily begins at the corner that represents "doing nothing," where the basic variable mix is composed only of slack variables. It then moves to the neighboring corner point that improves the solution at the greatest rate. It continues to move progressively from neighboring corner to neighboring corner, making the greatest possible improvement in the solution on each successive move. When no more improvements can be made in the solution, the most attractive corner has been found. As we have noted, this method usually results in evaluating only a tiny fraction of all of the corner points in a linear program; a huge number of corner points are simply skipped. Simplex also reduces the task of algebraically solving for the unknowns at a corner point to a few simple arithmetic steps.

The Simplex Tableau

For convenience, we will again express the latest Redwood Furniture linear program.

$$\text{Maximize}\quad P = 6X_T + 8X_C + 0S_W + 0S_L \quad \text{(objective)}$$

$$\text{Subject to}\quad 30X_T + 20X_C + 1S_W + 0S_L = 300 \quad \text{(wood)}$$

$$5X_T + 10X_C + 0S_W + 1S_L = 110 \quad \text{(labor)}$$

$$\text{where}\quad X_T, X_C, S_W, S_L \geq 0 \quad \text{(non-negativity)}$$

All of this information is incorporated into Figure 10-2, which is referred to as a **simplex tableau**. Along the top of the central portion of the tableau, we list the problem variables in their original order of appearance in the formulated constraint equations. In the top margin, we list the corresponding per-unit profits for the objective equation. The first row in the body of the tableau consists of the coefficients in the first constraint equation in their original order of appearance; the numbers in the second row are reproduced from the second constraint equation. In essence, these two rows supply the same information that the original equations provide; *they are streamlined and equivalent versions of the original constraint equations.*

The basic mix column of the tableau lists the slack variables S_W and S_L; we will solve for these variables. All variables that are not listed in this column are categorized as nonbasic variables and are assumed to be arbitrarily fixed at zero. Thus, X_T and X_C are presently set at zero. The solution column lists the values of the basic variables: $S_W = 300$

FIGURE 10-2
Simplex tableau for the Redwood Furniture problem.

UNIT PROFIT		6	8	0	0	
	Basic Mix	X_T	X_C	S_W	S_L	Sol.
	S_W	30	20	1	0	300
	S_L	5	10	0	1	110

and $S_L = 110$. This tells us that all of the available wood and labor are unused. The amounts are precisely what would be left from the original equations after zeroing out X_T and X_C.

$$30(0) + 20(0) + 1S_W + 0S_L = 300 \quad \text{or} \quad S_W = 300$$
$$5(0) + 10(0) + 0S_W + 1S_L = 110 \quad \text{or} \quad S_L = 110$$

The rows of the simplex tableau simultaneously provide us with two pieces of information.

1. Each row is written in a new form that preserves the original constraint equation.
2. The rows indicate the basic variable mix for the corner point being evaluated. The basic variable values appear in the solution column; all nonbasic variables are assumed to have a value of zero.

The values in the body of the tableau represent the original constraint coefficients and are sometimes referred to as **exchange coefficients**, because they indicate how many units of the variable listed on the left must be given up to accommodate a unit increase in the variable listed at the top of the tableau. Thus, the value 30 in the S_W row and the X_T column indicates that 30 board feet of unused wood may be exchanged for one table. We can also see that exactly 20 units of wood must be provided to produce one chair. Similarly, 5 hours of unused labor must be given up to produce one table, and 10 hours must be given up to produce one chair. These are the same figures we used at the outset in Table 10-1. The exchange coefficients are 0 or 1 for the mix variables and are not very meaningful. They indicate, for example, that 1 board foot of unused wood may be traded for 1 more board foot and that no unused wood is required to accommodate more unused labor.

The simplex tableau for the Redwood Furniture problem is expanded in Figure 10-3. In the left margin, we list the per-unit profits for the basic variables. For the slack variables S_W and S_L, per-unit profits are zero. Below the heavy rule are two special rows where

FIGURE 10-3
An expanded simplex tableau for the Redwood Furniture problem.

UNIT PROFIT		6	8	0	0		
	Basic Mix	X_T	X_C	S_W	S_L	Sol.	
0	S_W	30	20	1	0	300	Exchange
0	S_L	5	10	0	1	110	coefficients
	Sac.	0	0	0	0	0	←— Current P
	Imp.	6	8	0	0	—	

economic data are compiled that tell us which corner point to evaluate next. Values in the **sacrifice row** tell us what we will lose in per-unit profits by making a change. The **improvement row** indicates the per-unit change in profits that will result from making that same change.

The sacrifice entry for each column is determined by making the following computation.

$$\text{Unit sacrifice} = \text{Unit profit column} \times \text{Exchange coefficient column}$$

The result of this calculation is a **vector product**, because the terms in the unit profit and exchange coefficient columns constitute **vectors**. First, each pair of values is multiplied together; then the sum of these products is obtained. For example, in the X_T column, we have

UNIT PROFIT COLUMN	$\times$	X_T COLUMN	
0	$\times$	30	$= 0$
0	$\times$	5	$= 0$
		Sacrifice for X_T	$= 0$

The first product (0×30) is the unit profit of unused wood multiplied by the amount needed to make one table; this is the reduction in unused wood profit required to produce one table. The second product (0×5) is the unused labor profit that must be given up to make that table. Together, these products constitute the profit that must be sacrificed by the mix variables to accommodate a unit increase in tables.

This computation can also be made for the solution column. The entry obtained, which is $P = 0$ in Figure 10-3, is the current value of the objective function.

Since the unit profit column for the current basic mix (the slack variables) consists of zeros, all of the sacrifice terms result in product sums of zero. This concept seems obvious now—we give up no profit to make tables or chairs if the unused resource has no profit to begin with—but it will prove crucial later.

The entries in the improvement row are found by subtracting each sacrifice term from the corresponding unit profit listed at the top of the tableau.

$$\text{Unit improvement} = \text{Unit profit} - \text{Unit sacrifice}$$

In the tableau in Figure 10-3, all of the improvement terms are identical to the unit profits, since all the sacrifices are zero.

Summary of the Simplex Method

Before we examine the simplex algorithm, it will be helpful to summarize the required steps in the simplex method.

1. **Formulate the linear program in standardized format.** Add slack variables to the problem, eliminating any inequality constraints. Construct the initial simplex tableau, using slack variables in the starting basic variable mix.

2. **Find the sacrifice and improvement rows.**

3. **Apply the entry criterion.** Find the current nonbasic variable that increasing from zero will improve the objective at the greatest rate, breaking any ties arbitrarily. This variable is the **entering variable**. Mark the top of its column with an arrow pointing down. If no improvement can be found, the optimal solution is represented by the present tableau.

4. **Apply the exit criterion.** Use the current tableau's exchange coefficient values from the column of the entering variable to calculate the following **exchange ratio** for each row.

$$\frac{\text{Solution value}}{\text{Exchange coefficient}}$$

Ignoring ratios with zero or negative denominators, find the smallest *non-negative* exchange ratio,* again breaking ties arbitrarily. The basic variable for the row of this ratio is the **exiting variable**. Mark this variable's row with an arrow pointing left.

5. **Construct a new simplex tableau.** Replace the basic mix label of the exiting variable with that of the entering variable. All other basic variable mix labels remain the same. Also, change the unit profit (unit cost) column value to correspond to the newly entered basic variable. Then recompute the row values to obtain a new set of exchange coefficients applicable to each basic variable. (This procedure is illustrated in the Redwood Furniture example.)

6. **Go back to step 2.**

Thus far in our Redwood Furniture example, we have completed steps 1 and 2. We must now determine the **entering variable** through economic analysis by applying the **entry criterion** in step 3. In our profit-maximization problem, we accomplish this by finding the largest positive value in the improvement row. Referring to Figure 10-4, we can see that 8 in the X_C column is the largest per-unit improvement. This means that we can improve the current solution by $8 per unit for each chair made. Increasing the value of the X_C variable from zero (remember, X_C is a nonbasic variable and all such variables equal zero) to some positive quantity is the best change to make. (Another change—increasing tables—has a smaller per-unit improvement of only $6.) Thus, X_C is the entering variable. We indicate this on the simplex tableau by placing a small arrow pointing downward just to the right of the X_C column. In step 4, we find the **exiting variable**. As the name implies, one variable will enter the basic mix and replace another, which *exits* from the basic mix and assumes a nonbasic status. Such an exchange of variables is referred to as a **pivot operation**. Simplex involves a sequence of such pivots. In

---

* A divisor of zero results in an infinitely large ratio (and is treated as such, even when the numerator is 0, too). If all divisors are zero or negative, the problem is **unbounded**. This special case is discussed on pages 269–70.

FIGURE 10-4

Simplex tableau showing the entering and exiting variables and the pivot element.

UNIT PROFIT		6	8	0	0		
	Basic Mix	X_T	X_C	S_W	S_L	Sol.	Exchange ratios:
0	S_W	30	20	1	0	300	300/20 = 15
0	S_L ←	5	(10)	0	1	110	110/10 = 11*
	Sac.	0	0	0	0	0	* Smallest non-negative ratio
	Imp.	6	8	0	0	—	

Greatest per-unit improvement

each case, the pivot identifies the next corner point to be evaluated. The current basic mix differs by only one variable from the subsequent basic mix created by the pivot. The two corresponding corners are often called *neighbors.*

At this point, we want to increase our entering variable X_C as much as possible from zero. Dividing the solution value by the corresponding exchange coefficient in the X_C column, we obtain

$$300/20 = 15 \quad \text{for the } S_W \text{ row}$$

$$110/10 = 11 \quad \text{for the } S_L \text{ row}$$

These **exchange ratios** tell us how many chairs Redwood can make by trading away all of the current level of the respective basic variable. By trading 300 board feet of unused wood, Redwood can produce 15 chairs, because one chair can be exchanged at the rate of 20 board feet. Likewise, by trading all 110 hours of unused labor at an exchange rate of 10 hours per chair, Redwood can produce 11 chairs.

The **exit criterion** requires that we find the smallest ratio; here, it is 11. This value limits the number of chairs that can result from the exchange. It is impossible to make more than 11 chairs because all of the available labor will be used to produce that quantity. The exiting variable is therefore S_L, so that X_C will replace S_L in the basic mix. S_W will remain in the basic mix, since labor will be depleted before wood and some unused wood will still remain once the exchange is made. We indicate that unused labor exits the basic mix by placing a small arrow pointing toward the S_L in Figure 10-4.

The circled value in the X_C column and the S_L row is called the **pivot element**. This value is used to evaluate the new corner point represented by exchanging X_C and S_L. The evaluation is achieved by means of a *new* simplex tableau.

Constructing the New Simplex Tableau

We must construct a new simplex tableau that provides the solution values for the new corner point. Each mix-variable row must also represent an equation, and together these equations must preserve the underlying constraint relationships. We begin with the following constraint equations.

$$30X_T + 20X_C + 1S_W + 0S_L = 300 \quad \text{(old } S_W \text{ row)}$$

$$5X_T + 10X_C + 0S_W + 1S_L = 110 \quad \text{(old } S_L \text{ row)}$$

Set at zero

Since X_C is to replace S_L, we want to transform the second equation so that X_C will have a coefficient of 1. Dividing both sides of the second equation by 10 gives us

$$\left(\frac{5}{10}\right)X_T + \left(\frac{10}{10}\right)X_C + \left(\frac{0}{10}\right)S_W + \left(\frac{1}{10}\right)S_L = \frac{110}{10}$$

and provides us with the equivalent expression

$$\tfrac{1}{2}X_T + 1X_C + 0S_W + \tfrac{1}{10}S_L = 11 \quad \text{(new } X_C \text{ row)}$$

which we will refer to as the new X_C row. If the latest nonbasic variables, X_T and S_L, are set at zero, this equation directly provides the solution $X_C = 11$.

Now consider the following two equations.

$$30X_T + 20X_C + 1S_W + 0S_L = 300 \quad \text{(old } S_W \text{ row)}$$

$$\tfrac{1}{2}X_T + 1X_C + 0S_W + \tfrac{1}{10}S_L = 11 \quad \text{(new } X_C \text{ row)}$$

The variable X_C can be eliminated from the first equation, so that X_C will appear in only one equation. Then $X_C = 11$ is a solution value that satisfies both equations. Subtracting 20 times the second equation from the first, we obtain

$$30X_T + 20X_C + 1S_W + 0S_L = 300$$

$$\underline{-20(\tfrac{1}{2}X_T + 1X_C + 0S_W + \tfrac{1}{10}S_L = 11)}$$

$$20X_T + 0X_C + 1S_W - 2S_L = 80 \quad \text{(new } S_W \text{ row)}$$

We will refer to the equation for this difference as the new S_W row, since it provides the solution $S_W = 80$ when the nonbasic variables are set at zero ($X_T = 0$, $S_L = 0$). This reflects the fact that when 11 chairs—each requiring 20 board feet of wood— are made, exactly $300 - 11(20) = 80$ board feet will remain unused.

Our two new constraint equations are then

$$20X_T + 0X_C + 1S_W - 2S_L = 80 \quad \text{(new } S_W \text{ row)}$$

$$\tfrac{1}{2}X_T + 1X_C + 0S_W + \tfrac{1}{10}S_L = 11 \quad \text{(new } X_C \text{ row)}$$

Set at zero

Since we obtained each equation by dividing both sides of an original constraint equation by a constant or by subtracting equal amounts from both sides of an original constraint equation, the two new equations preserve the problem constraints.

FIGURE 10-5

Constructing the new simplex tableau for the Redwood Furniture problem.

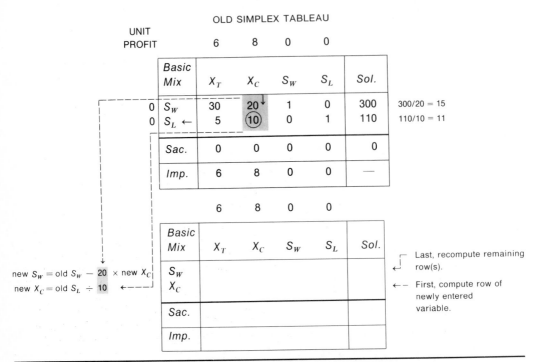

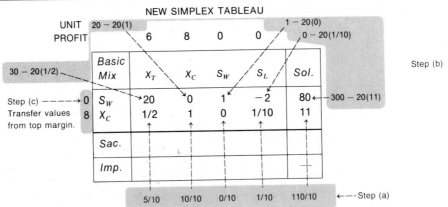

The beauty of the simplex method is that we do not have to perform all of these steps to obtain these new equations. We can work directly from the previous tableau to determine the values for the new tableau. The following procedure summarizes **the steps for obtaining new rows.**

a. Divide all values in the row of the exiting variable by the pivot element. (Such calculations can be easily made in your head.) Place the answers in the *same position* in the new tableau. Label this row with the symbol of the newly entered variable.

b. To obtain each of the remaining rows, find the value in that row in the old tableau that is also in the pivot element column. Then, multiply the first number in the new row found in step (a) by this quantity and *subtract* that product from the old value in the first position. The result is the first term in the new row. Repeat this process for all positions in the new row, including the solution position. Then, repeat this process for all the remaining rows until the tableau is complete. The basic variables for these rows will be the same as they were in the old tableau.

c. Place the appropriate unit profits (costs) for the mix variables in the left margin.

Applying this procedure to the simplex tableau in Figure 10-4 results in the bottom tableau provided in Figure 10-5 for the Redwood Furniture problem. Every term in the new X_C row is found by dividing the respective old S_L row value by 10 (the pivot element). The new S_W row values are found by successively subtracting from the old S_W row the product of 20 (the old S_W row value in the pivot element column) multiplied by the new X_C row value for that column position. Notice that the new tableau is exactly what we would obtain if we transferred the coefficients from the equations on page 317. Also notice that this procedure yields *column* values for each mix variable with a 1 where the basic variable's row and column intersect and a *zero* everywhere else. This feature ensures that the underlying equations will provide solution values when the nonbasic variables are zeroed out.

Finding the Optimal Solution

We have now completed the final simplex step 5 for the Redwood Furniture problem. At this point, according to the procedure, we return to step 2 and begin a new iteration with a new tableau and basic variable mix. Each iteration repeats the earlier ones, using new values.

We must also find the per-unit sacrifice and improvement values for the new simplex tableau, which is given in Figure 10-6. But before we perform the calculations to obtain these values, let's assess the exchange coefficients in the X_T column. The value in the S_W row is 20, which indicates that Redwood must give up a net amount of 20 board feet of

FIGURE 10-6
Completed second simplex tableau.

UNIT PROFIT		6	8	0	0	
	Basic Mix	X_T	X_C	S_W	S_L	Sol.
0	S_W	20	0	1	-2	80
8	X_C	1/2	1	0	1/10	11
	Sac.	4	8	0	8/10	88 ← Current P
	Imp.	2	0	0	-8/10	—

unused wood to make one table—not the 30 board feet specified in the original problem statement. Where are the missing 10 board feet? The second number in that column, 1/2, tells us that Redwood must also relinquish one-half of a chair to produce one table. This happens because some labor currently being spent on chairs must be diverted to that table. That one-half chair returns 5 hours of labor as well as the missing 10 board feet of wood to Redwood.

The exchange coefficients in the S_L column tell a similar story. To increase S_L by one unit—that is, to increase unused labor by one hour—we must trade $-2S_W$. In other words, if one hour of labor is *taken away* (which is what increasing unused resource means), Redwood must give up -2 board feet of unused wood; that is, Redwood gets back $+2$ board feet of unused wood (so that it uses 2 feet less than before). The net changes in unused resources correspond to the requirements for a fraction of a chair (1/10, to be exact) that must be relinquished if S_L is increased by one hour (remember, it takes 10 hours to make a whole chair). This is why the second exchange coefficient in the X_C row is 1/10.

The per-unit profits for S_W and X_C are \$0 and \$8. The per-unit sacrifice for X_T is therefore

UNIT PROFIT	×	EXCHANGE COEFFICIENT	
0	×	20	= 0
8	×	1/2	= 4
		Sacrifice for X_T	= 4

This represents the \$4 profit forgone by giving up the 1/2 chair to accommodate one table. For S_L, we obtain

UNIT PROFIT	×	EXCHANGE COEFFICIENT	
0	×	−2	= 0
8	×	1/10	= 8/10
		Sacrifice for S_L	= 8/10

which is the \$8/10 profit (one-tenth of \$8) lost by giving up the 1/10 of a chair that cannot be made if unused labor is increased by one hour. The value computed in the solution column is

$$0 \times 80 = 0$$
$$8 \times 11 = 88$$
$$\overline{ 88}$$

which is the \$88 profit represented by the current basic variable mix solution.

The solution for the new basic variable mix may be read directly from Figure 10-6 as

$$X_T = 0 \qquad S_W = 80$$

$$X_C = 11 \qquad S_L = 0$$

$$P = 88$$

X_T and S_L are not in the basic variable mix and must therefore be zero. Figure 10-7 summarizes our current situation. We have now reached a second corner of the feasible solution region that must be evaluated further. For this purpose, we must determine the possible per-unit profit improvements from increasing each of the nonbasic variables.

The values in the per-unit improvement row of the latest simplex tableau, shown again as the top tableau in Figure 10-8, are found by subtracting the sacrifice values from the profits listed in the top margin. We can see that only one value is positive (the 2 in the X_T column). This indicates that increasing X_T will result in a net increase in profits of $2 per unit. Redwood does not receive the full profit of $6 on each table, because for every table made, we must "steal" back resources that could be used to make one-half a chair, thereby losing $4 of chair profit. Thus, Redwood receives a profit of only $6 − $4 = $2 per table.

Our entering variable is X_T. According to the exit criterion, we see that the smallest exchange ratio applies to S_W, which limits table production more (Redwood would run

FIGURE 10-7

Graphical illustration of successive corners evaluated in simplex.

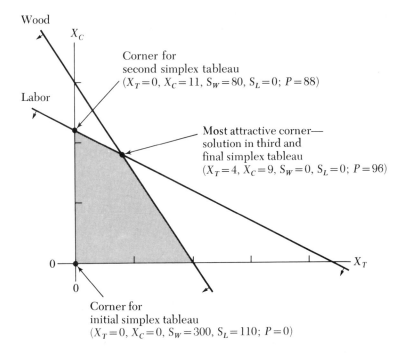

Wood

X_C

Corner for
second simplex tableau
$(X_T=0, X_C=11, S_W=80, S_L=0; P=88)$

Labor

Most attractive corner—
solution in third and
final simplex tableau
$(X_T=4, X_C=9, S_W=0, S_L=0; P=96)$

X_T

0

0

Corner for
initial simplex tableau
$(X_T=0, X_C=0, S_W=300, S_L=110; P=0)$

FIGURE 10-8

Constructing the third simplex tableau from the second tableau for the Redwood Furniture problem.

UNIT PROFIT		6	8	0	0		
	Basic Mix	X_T	X_C	S_W	S_L	Sol.	Exchange ratios:
0	$S_W \leftarrow$	(20)↓	0	1	−2	80	80/20 = 4*
8	X_C	1/2	1	0	1/10	11	11/(1/2) = 22
	Sac.	4	8	0	8/10	88	*Smallest non-negative ratio
	Imp.	2	0	0	−8/10	—	

[old S_W ÷ 20]	6	X_T	1	0	1/20	−1/10	4
[old X_C − 1/2 new X_T]	8	X_C	0	1	−1/40	3/20	9
		Sac.	6	8	1/10	6/10	96
		Imp.	0	0	−1/10	−6/10	—

No per-unit improvement is positive;
no further improvement is possible.

out of unused wood before giving back all chairs). This exchange will result in 4 tables and no unused wood, so that the exiting variable is S_W. The present pivot element occurs where the S_W row and X_T column intersect and has a value of 20.

The new (third) simplex tableau, constructed by transforming the second tableau, appears as the bottom tableau in Figure 10-8. This tableau provides the solution

$$X_T = 4 \qquad S_W = 0$$
$$X_C = 9 \qquad S_L = 0$$
$$P = 96$$

which we know (from our earlier graphical analysis in Chapter 8) is the optimal solution. Simplex tells us that this must be the stopping point, since none of the per-unit improvement row values is positive. No further improvement is possible.

10-3 The Computational Aspects of Simplex

The only real thinking involved in solving a linear programming problem occurs during the formulation phase. Once the initial tableau has been satisfactorily completed, the rest is simple arithmetic. However, simplex calculations require a substantial amount of time.

They are particularly onerous when we must determine the new tableau's exchange coefficients, since fractions such as 5/3, 2/17, and 23/31 often occur. It may be helpful to keep computations in fractional form throughout the process to avoid errors due to rounding. Making side calculations on scratch paper, with the aid of a calculator, can be helpful.

For example, suppose that we must subtract $4/7 \times 6/21$ from 5. We perform the calculation

$$5 - \left(\frac{4}{7}\right)\left(\frac{6}{21}\right) = 5 - \frac{24}{147}$$

and convert the difference to fractions that have the same denominator.

$$5\left(\frac{147}{147}\right) - \frac{24}{147} = \frac{735 - 24}{147} = \frac{711}{147}$$

We then attempt to reduce the resulting fraction to the form with the lowest common denominator by dividing 711 by factors that comprise the denominator (21, 7, and 3) to see if a whole number results. In this case, $711/3 = 237$ exactly, and we obtain the more elementary fraction 237/49. Although this is equal to 4 and 41/49, it is preferable to enter the basic fraction 237/49 in the new tableau.

It is easy to make errors in arithmetic when performing simplex computations by hand. Unfortunately, just one mistake can ruin every calculation that follows. These checks may be made to catch obvious errors:

1. The solution column values can never be negative. If one value is negative, an error has been made somewhere, and no further steps should be taken until it has been corrected.

2. The basic variable columns should contain a single 1 in the proper row and a zero everywhere else, except the sacrifice row.

3. The new P or C should be at least as good as the preceding one. If it is not, an error has been made.

4. If any set of solution values violates the original problem's constraints, an error has been made.

Hand computation is not only error-prone, but it is also quite time consuming. A good arithmetician could spend a day or two solving a 10-row, 20-column simplex problem by hand. The same person would require more than a week to find the answer to a simplex problem represented by a tableau with twice as many rows and columns. Such large problems are best solved with the assistance of a computer. The details of how this is done are described in Section 10-7.

10-4 Applying Simplex When Graphing Is Impossible

Simplex was developed to solve realistic problems that ordinarily have too many variables to be solved graphically. We illustrate this with the following linear program, which involves five main variables and two constraints.

Maximize $\quad P = 5X_1 + 4X_2 + 4X_3 + 1X_4 + 2X_5$

Subject to $\qquad 1X_1 + 2X_2 \qquad\qquad\quad + 4X_5 \le 30$ (resource A)

$\qquad\qquad\qquad 4X_1 \qquad + 8X_3 + 5X_4 \qquad\quad \le 40$ (resource B)

where $\qquad\qquad\qquad\qquad\qquad\qquad$ all X's $\ge\ 0$

As slack variables, we use S_A and S_B to denote the unused quantities of the respective resources. In presimplex equation form, this linear program may be expressed as

Maximize $\quad P = 5X_1 + 4X_2 + 4X_3 + 1X_4 + 2X_5 + 0S_A + 0S_B$

Subject to $\qquad 1X_1 + 2X_2 + 0X_3 + 0X_4 + 4X_5 + 1S_A + 0S_B = 30$ (resource A)

$\qquad\qquad 4X_1 + 0X_2 + 8X_3 + 5X_4 + 0X_5 + 0S_A + 1S_B = 40$ (resource B)

where $\qquad\qquad\qquad\qquad\qquad\qquad$ all variables ≥ 0

Figure 10-9 summarizes the entire simplex procedure. The first tableau involves a starting solution of "doing nothing," and the slack variables are in the starting basic

FIGURE 10-9

Simplex tableaus for a linear programming problem that cannot be graphed.

UNIT PROFIT		5	4	4	1	2	0	0		
	Basic Mix	X_1	X_2	X_3	X_4	X_5	S_A	S_B	Sol.	
0	S_A	1↓	2	0	0	4	1	0	30	30/1 = 30
0	S_B←	④	0	8	5	0	0	1	40	40/4 = 10*
	Sac.	0	0	0	0	0	0	0	0	
	Imp.	5	4	4	1	2	0	0	—	

[old S_A − 1 new X_1] 0 | S_A←

		X_1	X_2	X_3	X_4	X_5	S_A	S_B	Sol.	
0	S_A←	0	②↓	−2	−5/4	4	1	−1/4	20	20/2 = 10*
5	X_1	1	0	2	5/4	0	0	1/4	10	10/0 (ignore)
	Sac.	5	0	10	25/4	0	0	5/4	50	
	Imp.	0	4	−6	−21/4	2	0	−5/4	—	

[old S_A − 1 new X_1]
[old S_B ÷ 4]

		X_1	X_2	X_3	X_4	X_5	S_A	S_B	Sol.
4	X_2	0	1	−1	−5/8	2	1/2	−1/8	10
5	X_1	1	0	2	5/4	0	0	1/4	10
	Sac.	5	4	6	15/4	8	2	3/4	90
	Imp.	0	0	−2	−11/4	−6	−2	−3/4	—

[old S_A ÷ 2]
[old X_1 − 0 new X_2]

variable mix. The entering variable is X_1 (because it has the greatest per-unit improvement of 5), which replaces the exiting variable S_B (because it has the smaller exchange ratio of 10).

The values in the second tableau are calculated first by dividing the old S_B row entries from the first tableau by 4 (the pivot element in the first tableau). This results in the new X_1 row. Because the old S_A row has a 1 in the entering column, we can calculate the new S_A row values by subtracting 1 multiplied by the new X_1 row values from the old S_A row values.

The entering variable for the second tableau is X_2. This replaces the exiting variable S_A. (The exchange ratio of 10/0 found for the X_1 row is ignored because the divisor is zero.)

The new X_2 values in the third tableau are found by dividing the old S_A values from the second tableau by 2 (the pivot element found there). The new X_1 row values are the same as the X_1 row values in the second tableau because there is a zero in the X_1 position of the entering variable column.

No improvement is possible from the third tableau, and the following solution is obtained.

$$X_1 = 10 \qquad X_4 = 0 \qquad S_A = 0$$
$$X_2 = 10 \qquad X_5 = 0 \qquad S_B = 0$$
$$X_3 = 0$$
$$P = 90$$

10-5 Shortcuts in Constructing Simplex Tableaus

A variety of shortcuts may be taken when making simplex computations. The following rules of thumb always apply.

1. In constructing the new tableau from the old tableau, only the columns for the nonbasic and exiting variables change. The columns for any remaining basic variable may therefore be incorporated directly into the new tableau.

2. To simplify calculations, wherever a zero is found in the pivot *column*, that *row* in the body of the tableau is repeated in the next tableau without change. Wherever a zero is found in the pivot *row*, that *column* in the body of the tableau is repeated in the next tableau without change.

3. The newly entered basic variable's column will contain a zero everywhere, except that a 1 will appear in the same position as the pivot element in the preceding tableau and the per-unit profit or cost for this variable will appear in the sacrifice row.

10-6 Special Simplex Considerations

We have just described the simplex algorithm in detail. The same steps are followed regardless of the number of variables or constraints involved. But we must consider several further aspects before our discussion is complete.

Like the graphical technique, the simplex method may be applied to either profit-maximization or cost-minimization problems. Only a slight procedural modification is required when minimizing C. Costs are substituted for profits. As we will see in Chapter 11, we must reinterpret the improvement row of the simplex tableau to coincide with this change in the problem objective, which will cause a minor change in the application of the entry criterion.

All of the simplex constraints we have encountered in this chapter involve the ≤ (less than or equal to) constraint, which is the natural orientation when considering resource limitations. Sometimes it is necessary to manipulate a constraint expression to obtain the proper orientation. For example, suppose that a mixture requirement for Redwood Furniture is that a minimum of 4 chairs be made for each table, so that the number of chairs must be ≥ (greater than or equal to) 4 times the number of tables. Algebraically, this requirement is

$$X_C \geq 4X_T \quad \text{(mixture)}$$

If we subtract $4X_T$ from both sides of this constraint, we obtain an inequality that has the wrong orientation.

$$X_C - 4X_T \geq 0 \quad \text{(wrong orientation)}$$

By changing all signs, the direction of the inequality can be reversed, giving us a mathematically equivalent expression that has the proper orientation.

$$-X_C + 4X_T \leq 0 \quad \text{(proper orientation)}$$

It is not always possible to reverse inequality orientations this way without creating difficulties. (If the constant term were not zero, then this type of change would result in a negative right-hand side, which simplex cannot handle.) Chapter 11 tells how to deal with constraints of the ≥ or = form.

10-7 Solving Linear Programs with a Computer

The computational difficulties in simplex would preclude the use of linear programming in many applications if it were not for digital computers. The computer eliminates the errors that are so inevitable in hand calculations and completes these calculations much more quickly. Today, it is routine to use a computer to solve problems that involve thousands of variables and constraints. In business, a linear program is rarely completely solved by hand. In modern linear programming applications, the human element is concentrated on the conceptual areas of problem formulation.

Solving Linear Programs with QuickQuant

The *QuickQuant* software package available to users of this book has a segment for solving linear programs. The program is *user friendly*, with screen-prompt questions guiding all necessary choices and inputs. The program allows you to go back and fix your selections before it continues into the next phase.

This approach is especially helpful in translating the linear programming expressions into computer input. *QuickQuant* does this by displaying on the screen the objective function and constraints with blank spaces for you to fill in. *QuickQuant* gives you the chance to make corrections to all or a portion of the completed expressions before proceeding to solve the linear program.

You will have the opportunity to save the problem input data on a disk in case you want to run it again. You may then modify the saved problem with minimal keyboard data entry. *QuickQuant* will let you change any constants and expressions to the current problem or one created earlier and saved on disk. You may also expand existing problems by incorporating additional variables or constraints.

Complete operating instructions for making runs with *QuickQuant* are provided in the Appendix at the end of this book.

ILLUSTRATION
A Production Decision

To illustrate, consider a production planner wishing to decide the quantities to produce of five models of widgets.

QuickQuant begins processing a linear program with the following prompts on the screen. The user response is shown in boldface.

```
What is the name of your problem?   Widget Product
Specify the objective:
    Maximize P or Minimize C--Enter p or c:?   p
```

```
      Specifications for Linear Programming Problems
   1. The maximum number of constraints is 40.
   2. The maximum number of main variables is 40.
```

```
SPECIFY THE NUMBER OF VARIABLES FOR YOUR PROBLEM:
```

```
      Do not include slacks, surpluses, or artificials.
      QuickQuant automatically creates these auxiliary variables.
      (Up to 50 auxiliary variables can be accommodated.)
```

```
--How many?   5
SPECIFY THE NUMBER OF CONSTRAINTS FOR YOUR PROBLEM:
```

```
      Non-negativity conditions are automatically included.
```

```
--How many?   5

Supply names (up to four characters) for each of your variables:
    What is the name of variable number 1 ?   XC
    What is the name of variable number 2 ?   XR
    What is the name of variable number 3 ?   XD
    What is the name of variable number 4 ?   XS
    What is the name of variable number 5 ?   XE
```

The top of the monitor screen looks like the following before the objective coefficients are entered.

```
Type needed values where highlighted. ENTER or ARROW keys move highlighter.
Entries become permanent when highlighter moves. BACKSPACE erases mistakes
in unfinished entries. You can skip any spot or go back and retype entries.
DO NOT USE COMMAS. NEW SCREENS appear as needed. Press HOME when finished.
```

```
Objective Function for: Widget Product

Maximize P =

    +_____ XC  +_____ XR  +_____ XD  +_____ XS
    +_____ XE
```

The above is the *template* for the objective function. *QuickQuant* waits until the user supplies all the entries and verifies them before displaying a second template for the constraints. After the objective has been completely entered, the monitor screen looks like the following:

```
Type needed values where highlighted. ENTER or ARROW keys move highlighter.
Entries become permanent when highlighter moves. BACKSPACE erases mistakes
in unfinished entries. You can skip any spot or go back and retype entries.
DO NOT USE COMMAS. NEW SCREENS appear as needed. Press HOME when finished.
```

```
Constraints for: Widget Product

                                        Enter < for , > for , or =.

C1: +_____ XC  +_____ XR  +_____ XD  +_____ XS   ↓
    +_____ XE                                         __ _____

C2: +_____ XC  +_____ XR  +_____ XD  +_____ XS
    +_____ XE                                         __ _____

C3: +_____ XC  +_____ XR  +_____ XD  +_____ XS
    +_____ XE                                         __ _____

C4: +_____ XC  +_____ XR  +_____ XD  +_____ XS
    +_____ XE                                         __ _____

C5: +_____ XC  +_____ XR  +_____ XD  +_____ XS
    +_____ XE                                         __ _____
```

Notice that the type of constraint gets stipulated at this time. Just before typing the right-hand side value, you will enter an $=$ sign if the constraint is an equality. If it is an inequality, you will enter into the respective blank spot either a $<$ sign or a $>$ sign.

The completed linear program is displayed on the monitor screen as follows.

```
Problem: Widget Production
Maximize P =
        + 30 XC      + 40 XR      + 45 XD      + 50 XS
        + 60 XE
```

```
Subject to:
  C1:        + 3 XC        + 3 XR        + 4 XD        + 4 XS
             + 2 XE                                              ≤  500

  C2:        + 20 XC       + 15 XR       + 25 XD       + 30 XS
             + 30 XE                                             ≤ 3000

  C3:        + 50 XC       + 45 XR       + 40 XD       + 60 XS
             + 65 XE                                             ≤ 7000

  C4:        + 5 XC        + 8 XR        + 7 XD        + 7 XS
             + 8 XE                                              ≤ 1000

  C5:        + 12 XC       + 12 XR       + 15 XD       + 10 XS
             + 15 XE                                             ≤ 1500
```

INSPECT this formulation in detail. Note the locations of errors. You may
make corrections by selecting option 3 when you get back to the menu.
Press any key to continue.

You will have the option of printing the above report onto hard copy.

It is not necessary to enter any information regarding slack variables. All required auxiliary variables are created automatically by *QuickQuant* in accordance with the type of constraint entered. In the present illustration, the program assigns the five slack variables needed. These are designated as S1, S2, S3, S4, and S5, numbered to correspond to the sequence in which the constraints were entered.

At the user's option, *QuickQuant* will display on screen each simplex tableau. These may be skipped if only a final report is required. The screen for the first simplex tableau in the illustration is shown in Figure 10-10. Notice that the entire tableau does not fit onto the screen in Figure 10-10(a). The tableau itself functions as a *window,* and the missing portions may be brought onto the screen by hitting the appropriate arrow keys; the missing columns for the first tableau appear on the screen in Figure 10-10(b). Each successive tableau is brought to the screen by pressing the Home key with a PC or clicking the mouse with a MacIntosh. The final simplex tableau is provided in Figure 10-11. (Users may obtain hard printed copy of selected tableau segments by performing a *screen dump*—accomplished on the PC by depressing the shift key while hitting the PrtSc key.)

A variety of final reports may be brought to the screen. The solution to the illustrated problem, as it would appear on the monitor screen, is shown below.

Original Variable	Value	Slack/Surplus Variable	Value
XC	0.00000	S1	62.50002
XR	62.50000	S2	0.00000
XD	0.00000	S3	0.00000
XS	56.25000	S4	6.25000
XE	12.50001	S5	0.00000

Objective Value: P = 6062.50000

Any output report may also be saved on a file or printed on hard copy.

FIGURE 10-10

QuickQuant screens showing the initial simplex tableau for the widget product illustration.

PROBLEM: Widget Production   Iteration: 1

UNIT P,C	30	40	45	50	60	
Basic	**1**	**2**	**3**	**4**	**5**	
Mix	XC	XR	XD	XS	XE	Solution
0 1S1	3	3	4	4	2	500
0 2S2 ←20		15	25	30	30	3000
0 3S3	50	45	40	60	65	7000
0 4S4	5	8	7	7	8	1000
0 5S5	12	12	15	10	15	1500
6						
7						
8						
9						
Sac.	0	0	0	0	0	0
Imp.	30	40	45	50	60	--

HOME key gets next iteration. ARROW keys move window. END skips to end.

(a) First five columns of tableau

PROBLEM: Widget Production   Iteration: 1

UNIT P,C	0	0	0	0	0	
Basic	**6**	**7**	**8**	**9**	**10**	
Mix	S1	S2	S3	S4	S5	Solution
0 1S1	1	0	0	0	0	500
0 2S2 ←0		1	0	0	0	3000
0 3S3	0	0	1	0	0	7000
0 4S4	0	0	0	1	0	1000
0 5S5	0	0	0	0	1	1500
6						
7						
8						
9						
Sac.	0	0	0	0	0	0
Imp.	0	0	0	0	0	--

HOME key gets next iteration. ARROW keys move window. END skips to end.

(b) Last five columns of tableau

FIGURE 10-11

QuickQuant screens showing the final simplex tableau for the widget product illustration.

PROBLEM: Widget Production   Iteration: 4

UNIT P,C		30	40	45	50	60	
	Basic	1	2	3	4	5	
	Mix	XC	XR	XD	XS	XE	Solution
0	1S1	.2500013	0	11.25	0	0	62.50002
60	2XE	.2500005	0	4.249999	0	1	12.50001
50	3XS	.1249997	0	-2.375	1	0	56.25
0	4S4	-2.541666	0	6.291666	0	0	6.25
40	5XR	.583333	1	-2.083333	0	0	62.5
	6						
	7						
	8						
	9						
	Sac.	44.58334	40	52.91665	50	60	6062.5
	Imp.	-14.58334	0	-7.916649	0	0	--

FINISHED. ARROW keys move window. Hit HOME key to get final report.

(a) First five columns of tableau

PROBLEM: Widget Production   Iteration: 4

UNIT P,C		0	0	0	0	0	
	Basic	6	7	8	9	10	
	Mix	S1	S2	S3	S4	S5	Solution
0	1S1	1	.525	-.475	0	.875	62.50002
60	2XE	0	.225	-.175	0	.375	12.50001
50	3XS	0	-.0875	.1125	0	-.3125	56.25
0	4S4	0	.4791667	-.3875	1	.1875001	6.25
40	5XR	0	-.2083333	.125	0	-.125	62.5
	6						
	7						
	8						
	9						
	Sac.	0	.791666	.125	0	1.875	6062.5
	Imp.	0	-.791666	-.125	0	-1.875	--

FINISHED. ARROW keys move window. Hit HOME key to get final report.

(b) Last five columns of tableau

10-8 A Symbolic Representation of the Simplex Method

It is helpful to use symbols to reinforce the simplex method concepts. Consider a profit-maximization problem that has five variables and three constraints. Including the slack variables among the X's, the formulation may be expressed as

$$\text{Maximize}\quad P = c_1 X_1 + c_2 X_2 + c_3 X_3 + c_4 X_4 + c_5 X_5$$

$$\text{Subject to}\quad e_{11} X_1 + e_{12} X_2 + e_{13} X_3 + e_{14} X_4 + e_{15} X_5 = b_1 \quad \text{(constraint 1)}$$

$$e_{21} X_1 + e_{22} X_2 + e_{23} X_3 + e_{24} X_4 + e_{25} X_5 = b_2 \quad \text{(constraint 2)}$$

$$e_{31} X_1 + e_{32} X_2 + e_{33} X_3 + e_{34} X_4 + e_{35} X_5 = b_3 \quad \text{(constraint 3)}$$

where

$$X_1, X_2, X_3, X_4, X_5 \geq 0$$

There is a separate c_j for each variable X_j. These are the **objective coefficients**. In a maximization problem, the c_j's are the unit profits (contributions), and, in a minimization problem, they are the unit costs. There is one exchange coefficient e_{ij} for each row-column position. The b_i's are right-hand sides of the respective constraints; these must always be *non-negative*.

All problem information is represented in the following simplex tableau.

c_j		c_1	c_2	c_3	c_4	c_5	
	Basic Mix	X_1	X_2	X_3	X_4	X_5	Sol.
c_{k_1}	X_{k_1}	e_{k_11}	e_{k_12}	e_{k_13}	e_{k_14}	e_{k_15}	b_{k_1}
c_{k_2}	X_{k_2}	e_{k_21}	e_{k_22}	e_{k_23}	e_{k_24}	e_{k_25}	b_{k_2}
c_{k_3}	X_{k_3}	e_{k_31}	e_{k_32}	e_{k_33}	e_{k_34}	e_{k_35}	b_{k_3}
	Sac.	z_1	z_2	z_3	z_4	z_5	P or Z
	Imp.	$c_1 - z_1$	$c_2 - z_2$	$c_3 - z_3$	$c_4 - z_4$	$c_5 - z_5$	—

The simplex method associates one variable with each row, and every column corresponds permanently to a particular variable. The variable-to-row assignments shift with the iterations. We use X_{k_1} to denote the basic mix variable in row 1, and subscripts k_2 and k_3 to represent the basic variable for row 2 and row 3. This subscripting is also reflected above with the e's and b's. In the beginning, the e's and b's match the original problem formulation. But as simplex progresses, their values *and interpretations* change. Throughout, the exchange coefficients have the following meaning.

$$e_{k_ij} = \text{Amount by which the basic mix variable for row } k_i \text{ must}$$
$$\textit{decrease} \text{ in exchange for a one-unit increase in the level for } X_j$$

The exchange coefficients in the basic variable's own column must be a unit column vector with a 1 in the intersection of that variable's row and column and a zero everywhere else in its column. The b_{k_i}'s represent the current solution values for the X_{k_i}'s. (When simplex starts with slack variables as the basic mix, the solution values are the original right-hand sides. The starting solution represents full slack for all constraints.)

Step 2 of the simplex method first determines the sacrifice values z_j for every column. These are the vector products of the c_{k_i} column and $e_{k_i j}$ column.

$$z_j = \begin{pmatrix} c_{k_1} \\ c_{k_2} \\ c_{k_3} \end{pmatrix} \times \begin{pmatrix} e_{k_1 j} \\ e_{k_2 j} \\ e_{k_3 j} \end{pmatrix} \quad \text{(sacrifice)}$$

The above multiplies each exchange coefficient by the objective coefficient for the respective basic variable. This signifies the change or *sacrifice* in current objective value (profit, cost) associated with a one-unit increase in variable X_j. Subtracting that sacrifice from the objective coefficient c_j for X_j provides the net change or *improvement* in profit or cost.

$$c_j - z_j \quad \text{(improvement)}$$

The *entering variable* is that X_j with the most favorable improvement value. Simplex stops if none of the X_j's yield a better objective value. (Ties are broken arbitrarily). We use X_N (New) to denote the entering variable.

The *exiting variable* is found by computing for each row the exchange ratio, obtained by dividing each solution value by the respective exchange coefficient in the column of the entering variable.

$$\frac{b_{k_i}}{e_{k_i N}}$$

The above represents the maximum reduction in basic variable X_{k_i} that may be achieved by a total exchange of it for X_N. The exchange ratios are not computed for rows where $e_{k_i N}$ is ≤ 0. The exiting variable X_L (Leaving) is the basic mix variable for which the above is minimum (and non-negative).

After determining the entering and exiting variable, the simplex tableau is transformed. This involves first determining the newly entered variable's row.

a. Divide all the terms in the X_L row by the *pivot element* e_{LN}, getting the new X_N row.

Then, eliminate X_N from all other rows. To do this, subtract, from the old X_{k_i} row, that multiple times the X_N row, leaving 0 as the new value for $e_{k_i N}$.

b. For all other rows, the the new values are computed, one column position at a time, from

$$\text{New } k_i = \text{Old } k_i - (\text{old } e_{k_i N}) \times (\text{new } X_N \text{ row})$$

The old $e_{k_i N}$ terms are taken from the respective row, in the entering variable's column, of the old tableau.

10-9 Interpreting the Simplex Tableau

Every number in any simplex tableau has an economic interpretation. To illustrate, consider the following linear program involving the manufacture of four types of headphones, the quantities of which are denoted as X_1, X_2, X_3, and X_4.

$$\text{Maximize} \quad P = 20X_1 + 23X_2 + 27X_3 + 19X_4$$

$$\text{Subject to} \quad 5X_1 + 6X_2 + 6.5X_3 + 4.5X_4 \le 1{,}000 \quad \text{(labor)}$$
$$1X_1 + 1X_2 + 1X_3 + 1X_4 \le 500 \quad \text{(connectors)}$$
$$1X_1 + 1X_2 + 1X_3 - 1X_4 \le 0 \quad \text{(mix)}$$
$$0X_1 + 1X_2 + 1X_3 + 0X_4 \le 500 \quad \text{(switches)}$$
$$1X_1 + 1X_2 + 1X_3 + 0X_4 \le 400 \quad \text{(pads)}$$

$$\text{where} \quad X_1, X_2, X_3, X_4 \ge 0$$

Figure 10-12 shows the third simplex tableau, where S_L, S_C, S_M, S_S, and S_P are the slack variables for the respective constraints.

Consider the entries in the X_1 column. There, all values summarize the impact of a one-unit increase in X_1. The first entry is $-.136$, which indicates that increasing X_1 from its current level of 0 to 1 will decrease X_4 by $-.136$, so that raising X_1 will actually cause an increase in the level of X_4 by .136. (The negative sign reverses the effect.) The next exchange coefficient is .273, which states that increasing X_1 by one unit will decrease unused connectors by .273. That same increase will cause a decrease in the level of X_3 by .864. Because the signs are negative, the $-.864$ for S_S and the -5.82 for S_P indicate

FIGURE 10-12
Third simplex tableau for the headphones problem.

UNIT PROFIT		20	23	27	19	0	0	0	0	0	
	Basic Mix	X_1	X_2	X_3	X_4	S_L	S_C	S_M	S_S	S_P	Sol.
19	X_4	−.136	−.045	0	1	.091	0	−.591	0	0	90.91
0	S_C	.273	.091	0	0	−.182	1	.182	0	0	318.18
27	X_3	.864	.955	1	0	.091	0	.409	0	0	90.91
0	S_S	−.864	.045	0	0	−.091	0	−.409	1	0	409.09
0	S_P	−5.82	−3.27	0	0	−1.45	0	−2.54	0	1	1,045.45
	Sac.	20.72	24.91	27	19	4.18	0	−.182	0	0	4,181.82
	Imp.	−.72	−1.91	0	0	−4.18	0	.182	0	0	—

that both slack variables will *increase* with X_1, unused switches by .864 and unused pads by 5.82.

The sacrifice value of 20.72 indicates that a one-unit increase in X_1 will reduce the current solution's profit by $20.72. That amount is based on the above changes, with the respective unit profits multiplied by the exchange coefficients in the X_1 column. Since X_1 will bring a profit of $20 a unit, the net effect of the one-unit change would be a $.72 net reduction of profit, as indicated by the $-.72$ in the improvement row. Raising X_1 worsens the situation, and that variable will not be selected as the entering variable.

CASE

Swatville Sluggers I

Swatville Sluggers is a small manufacturer of custom baseball bats. The obscure company is unfamiliar to the general public because it sells exclusively to professional baseball teams, mainly minor league clubs. Swatville sells its entire production at pre-negotiated prices, and the availability of essential resources— especially wood—dictates the final quantities in each monthly production run.

Sluggers are handmade from high-quality 3-by-3-inch blocks of hard wood. They come in six models, depending on length. The owner, George Herman "Sultan" Swat, wants to set the quantities for March production. The following data apply for that month.

RESOURCE	LENGTH (inches)						Available Quantity
	30	32	34	36	38	40	
Lathe time	10	10	11	11	12	12	5,000 min
Finishing time	25	27	29	31	33	35	8,000 min
Boxes	1	1	1	1	1	1	500
Stain	2	2	2	3	3	3	1,000 oz
Varnish	5	5	6	6	7	7	2,000 oz

In addition to the above, after allowing for scrap, only 10,000 inches of wood blocks are on hand. Numerous other materials are needed and further functions must be performed in making the bats, but the quantities are so ample and capacities so high that they place no practical limitations on production.

Further restrictions are: (1) the number of 34″ bats cannot exceed the combined total of 30″ and 32″ models; (2) the number of 38″ bats cannot exceed the combined total of the 32″ and 34″ varieties; and (3) the number of 30″ bats must be less than or equal to the total number of 36″ and 38″ lengths.

The following costs apply.

Wood cost per inch	$.08
Lathe cost per minute	.05
Finishing cost per minute	.02
Box cost	.50
Stain cost per ounce	.30
Varnish cost per ounce	.25

The selling prices are $21 for 30" and 32" bats, $22 for the 34" and 36" versions, and $25 for the 38" and 40" lengths. Other direct costs are $2 per bat, regardless of model.

In previous months, production quantities have been established by trial and error. Swat's nephew, Babe, has just completed a course in linear programming. He will use it to help his uncle maximize profit.

Questions

1. Formulate Swat's decision problem as a linear program.
2. Letting S_W, S_L, S_F, S_B, S_S, S_V, S_1, S_2, and S_3 denote the respective slack variables, the following intermediate simplex tableau applies.

UNIT
PROFIT

Basic Mix	X_{30}	X_{32}	X_{34}	X_{36}	X_{38}	X_{40}	S_W	S_L	S_F	S_B	S_S	S_V	S_1	S_2	S_3	Sol.
S_W	102	142	0	36	0	40	1	0	0	0	0	0	−72	−38	0	10,000
S_L	33	45	0	11	0	12	0	1	0	0	0	0	−23	−12	0	5,000
S_F	87	122	0	31	0	35	0	0	1	0	0	0	−62	−33	0	8,000
S_B	3	4	0	1	0	1	0	0	0	1	0	0	−2	−1	0	500
S_S	7	10	0	3	0	3	0	0	0	0	1	0	−5	−3	0	1,000
S_V	18	25	0	6	0	7	0	0	0	0	0	1	−13	−7	0	2,000
X_{34}	−1	−1	1	0	0	0	0	0	0	0	0	0	1	0	0	0
X_{38}	−1	−2	0	0	1	0	0	0	0	0	0	0	1	1	0	0
S_3	0	−2	0	−1	0	0	0	0	0	0	0	0	1	1	1	0
Sac.																
Imp.																

(a) If the level of X_{30} is increased by one unit, what will be the reduction in (1) unused wood, (2) unused lathe time, and (3) unused stain?

(b) If the level of X_{36} is increased by one unit, what will be the reduction in (1) unused finishing time (2) unused varnish, and (3) unused boxes?

3. Complete the unit profit row and column. Then, complete the entries for the sacrifice and improvement rows. Identify the entering and exiting variables.

4. How many bats of the various types should Swatville manufacture? (Solve using a computer.)

PROBLEMS

10-1 Express the following linear programming constraints in equation form, using an appropriate slack variable.
(a) $2X_1 + 3X_2 \leq 12$ (wood)
(b) $4X_A + 2X_B \leq 20$ (labor)
(c) $3X_1 - 2X_2 \leq 3$ (byproduct)
(d) $X_1 + 2X_2 + 3X_3 \leq 100$ (machine time)

10-2 Reformulate the following linear program, incorporating the slack variables S_A, S_B, and S_C into the respective constraints. The modified objective equation will include the slack variables, and each constraint will be represented by an equation instead of an inequality. Then, construct the initial simplex tableau only. Position all marginal values and label all rows and columns, but do not compute the sacrifice and improvement values.

$$\text{Maximize} \quad P = 20X_1 + 40X_2 + 60X_3$$

$$\text{Subject to} \quad 2X_1 + 3X_2 \qquad\qquad \leq 20 \quad \text{(resource } A\text{)}$$

$$4X_2 + 5X_3 \leq 30 \quad \text{(resource } B\text{)}$$

$$X_1 + 2X_2 + X_3 \leq 50 \quad \text{(resource } C\text{)}$$

$$\text{where} \qquad X_1, X_2, X_3 \geq 0$$

10-3 Consider the following simplex tableau.

UNIT PROFIT		5	7	9	7	8	
	Basic Mix	X_1	X_2	X_3	X_4	X_5	Sol.
9	X_3	-2	0	1	2	1	6
7	X_2	3	1	0	-3	2	3
	Sac.						
	Imp.						—

(a) Complete the sacrifice and improvement rows.
(b) Find the entering variable and the exiting variable and identify the pivot element.

10-4   Consider the following simplex tableau.

UNIT PROFIT		5	3	4	5	0	
	Basic Mix	X_1	X_2	X_3	X_4	X_5	Sol.
5	X_4	−2	0	0	1	0	1.5
4	X_3	1	0	1	0	−1	2.5
3	X_2	3	1	0	0	2	3.0
	Sac.	3	3	4	5	2	26.5
	Imp.	2	0	0	0	−2	—

The entering variable is X_1 and the exiting variable is X_2. Construct the next simplex tableau.

10-5   Consider the following simplex tableau.

UNIT PROFIT		3	2	1	0	0	
	Basic Mix	X_1	X_2	X_3	X_4	X_5	Sol.
0	X_4	0	2	1	1	0	10
0	X_5	0	−3	2	0	1	15
3	X_1	1	1	0	0	0	20
	Sac.						
	Imp.						—

(a) Complete the sacrifice and improvement rows.
(b) Find the entering and exiting variables and identify the pivot element.
(c) Construct the next simplex tableau.

10-6   For the linear program

$$\text{Maximize}\quad P = 100X_1 + 200X_2 + 150X_3$$

$$\text{Subject to}\quad 5X_1 + 20X_2 + 30X_3 \le 60 \quad \text{(resource } A\text{)}$$

$$10X_1 + 20X_2 + 50X_3 \le 100 \quad \text{(resource } B\text{)}$$

$$\text{where}\quad X_1, X_2, X_3 \ge 0$$

the following final simplex tableau applies, where S_A and S_B are the slack variables for the first and second constraints, respectively.

UNIT PROFIT		100	200	150	0	0	
	Basic Mix	X_1	X_2	X_3	S_A	S_B	Sol.
100 X_1		1	0	4	$-1/5$	1/5	8
200 X_2		0	1	1/2	1/10	$-1/20$	1
	Sac.	100	200	500	0	10	1,000
	Imp.	0	0	-350	0	-10	—

Use the data provided in this tableau to determine the optimal values of all five variables and the maximum possible profit.

10-7 Consider the following simplex tableau.

UNIT PROFIT		10	20	30	15	5	0	0	0	0	0	
	Basic Mix	X_1	X_2	X_3	X_4	X_5	S_1	S_2	S_3	S_4	S_5	Sol.
	S_1	2	3	0	0	4	1	2	0	4	0	0
	X_3	-1	.2	1	0	.5	0	5	0	$-.5$	0	10
	S_3	13	4	0	0	1	0	20	1	0	0	24
	X_4	.5	-2	0	1	-1	0	0	0	5	0	4
	S_5	4	3	0	0	2	0	$-.4$	0	2	1	50
	Sac.											
	Imp.											

(a) Complete the sacrifice and improvement rows.
(b) Identify the entering and exiting variables.

10-8 Consider the following simplex tableau. The entering variable is X_A and the exiting variable is S_3. Construct the new rows in the main portion of the subsequent tableau.

Basic Mix	X_A	X_B	X_C	S_1	S_2	S_3	Sol.
S_1	-1	0	0	1	.5	0	0
S_3	5	4	0	0	.4	1	10
X_C	2	.5	1	0	2	0	24

10-9 Consider the following linear program.

$$\text{Maximize} \quad P = 2X_1 + 3X_2$$

$$\begin{aligned}
\text{Subject to} \qquad & 3X_1 + 2X_2 \leq 6 \quad \text{(resource } A) \\
& X_1 \qquad\quad \leq 5 \quad \text{(resource } B) \\
& X_2 \leq 4 \quad \text{(resource } C)
\end{aligned}$$

$$\text{where} \qquad X_1, X_2 \geq 0$$

(a) Solve this problem graphically.
(b) Reformulate this problem in an equation form that is suitable for the simplex method.
(c) Solve the problem again using the simplex procedure.

10-10 Consider the third simplex tableau given for the headphones problem in Figure 10-12.
(a) Suppose that there is a one-unit increase in the level of X_2. Indicate the resulting amount of increase or decrease in the levels of the basic variables.
(b) Suppose that the slack in the mix constraint is raised by one unit. Indicate the resulting amount of increase or decrease in the levels of the basic variables.

10-11 The following simplex tableau applies to a problem where five products (A, B, C, D, and E) are being made using five resources (1, 2, 3, 4, and 5). The unused quantity of resource i is denoted as S_i.

UNIT PROFIT	5	6	7	8	8	0	0	0	0	0	
Basic Mix	X_A	X_B	X_C	X_D	X_E	S_1	S_2	S_3	S_4	S_5	Sol.
S_1	.5	5	0	0	.5	1	.2	0	2	0	10
X_C	−1	.1	1	0	4	0	4	0	1	0	8
S_3	10	2	0	0	1	0	0	1	−.5	0	15
X_D	.5	−2	0	1	−2	0	1	0	4	0	4
S_5	4	−1	0	0	1	0	−.5	0	1	1	100
Sac.											
Imp.											

(a) Suppose that there is a one-unit increase in X_B. Indicate for each resource whether the currently indicated unused amount would increase, decrease, or remain unchanged. If there would be a change, by what amount would it be?
(b) Suppose that there is a one-unit increase in X_B. Indicate for each of the other products whether the currently indicated amount to be made would increase, decrease, or remain unchanged. If there would be a change, by what amount would it be?
(c) Complete the unit profit column and the sacrifice and improvement rows. Then, identify the entering and exiting variables.

10-12 Consider the following linear program.

$$\text{Maximize} \quad P = 5X_A + 6X_B$$

$$\text{Subject to} \quad 3X_A + 2X_B \leq 12 \quad \text{(resource 1)}$$

$$2X_A + 3X_B \leq 12 \quad \text{(resource 2)}$$

$$\text{where} \quad X_A, X_B \geq 0$$

(a) Solve this problem graphically.
(b) Reformulate this problem in equation form that is suitable for the simplex method.
(c) Solve the problem again using the simplex procedure.

10-13 The manager of Ace Widgets must decide how many regular and deluxe models to produce. It requires 5 hours of finishing labor and 1 frame to produce the regular model and 8 hours and 1 frame to produce the deluxe widget. Only 12 frames and 80 hours of labor are available. The unit profits are $10 for the regular model and $15 for the deluxe widget.
(a) Formulate the linear program for this problem and solve it graphically.
(b) Reformulate the problem in an equation form that is suitable for the simplex method.
(c) Solve the problem again using the simplex procedure.

10-14 Reconsider the Hops Brewery advertising decision in Problem 8-13 (page 274), where no more than the budgeted $100,000 is to be spent on television spots (costing $2,000 each) and magazine ads (costing $5,000 each). The net profit to Hops is $1,000 per television spot and $5,000 per magazine ad. Maximum allowable expenditures are $50,000 for television spots and $70,0000 for magazine ads.
(a) Formulate the linear program for this problem and solve it graphically.
(b) Reformulate the problem in an equation form that is suitable for the simplex method.
(c) Solve the problem again using the simplex procedure.

10-15 The following linear program applies for the Piney Woods Furniture Company, which makes tables (T), chairs (C), and bookcases (B).

$$\text{Maximize} \quad P = 20X_T + 15X_C + 15X_B$$

$$\text{Subject to} \quad 10X_T + 3X_C + 10X_B \leq 100 \quad \text{(wood)}$$

$$5X_T + 5X_C + 5X_B \leq 60 \quad \text{(labor)}$$

$$\text{where} \quad X_T, X_C, X_B \geq 0$$

Apply the simplex method to determine how many of each item should be made.

10-16 Sammy Love sells three types of candied apples on the street corner—butterscotch, cinnamon, and peppermint. In making today's batch, Sammy is limited only by the amounts of sugar and gelatin, since all other ingredients are in good supply. Each butterscotch apple requires 1 cup of sugar; each cinnamon or peppermint apple requires $\frac{1}{2}$ cup of sugar. Cinnamon apples require 2 ounces of gelatin; peppermint apples, 1 ounce; and butterscotch apples, none. Only 200 cups of sugar and 100 ounces of gelatin are available.

Sammy makes a profit of $.10 on each butterscotch apple, $.15 on each cinnamon apple, and $.20 on each pepermint apple. He always sells his entire stock.
(a) Formulate Sammy's linear program.
(b) Identify any slack variables required to solve this problem using the simplex method.
(c) Apply the simplex method to determine how many candied apples of each type Sammy should make.

10-17 Refer to Problem 9-3 (page 298). Apply the simplex method to determine how many boxes of each type Myrtlewood should manufacture.

10-18 Refer to Problem 9-1 (page 297). Apply the simplex method to determine how many lamps of each type Rott Irony should manufacture. (*Hint:* Make sure all of the constraints are of the $\leq$ form before introducing the slack variables.)

10-19 Refer to Problem 9-8 (page 300). Apply the simplex method to determine what quantities of the respective pesticides the Bugoff Chemical Co. should produce. (*Hint:* Make sure all of the constraints are of the $\leq$ form before introducing the slack variables.)

10-20 Refer to Problem 9-13 (page 301). Apply the simplex method to determine how many silicon chips of each type ChipMont should manufacture. (*Hint:* Make sure all of the constraints are of the $\leq$ form before introducing the slack variables.)

10-21 *Computer exercise.* Le Petite Fromagerie makes 10 varieties of cheese. Letting X_i denote the number of pounds to be made of variety i, the following linear program applies.

Maximize

$$P = 2.00X_1 + 2.50X_2 + 1.75X_3 + 1.50X_4 + 2.05X_5$$
$$+ 2.85X_6 + 2.90X_7 + 3.15X_8 + 2.70X_9 + 1.95X_{10}$$

Subject to

$$.5X_1 + .6X_2 + .4X_3 + .9X_4 + .8X_5$$
$$+ .7X_6 + .6X_7 + .5X_8 + .5X_9 + .7X_{10} \leq 1,000 \quad \text{(gallons of milk)}$$

$$2X_1 + 3X_2 + 1X_3 + 4X_4 + 3X_5$$
$$+ 2X_6 + 9X_7 + 4X_8 + 3X_9 + 1X_{10} \leq 10,000 \quad \text{(storage cake-weeks)}$$

$$1X_1 + 1X_2 + 1X_3 + 1X_4 + 1X_5$$
$$+ 1X_6 + 1X_7 + 1X_8 + 1X_9 + 1X_{10} \leq 2,000 \quad \text{(molds)}$$

$$2X_1 + 3X_2 + 1X_3 + 2X_4 + 3X_5$$
$$+ 2X_6 + 1X_7 + 1X_8 + 2X_9 + 2X_{10} \leq 3,000 \quad \text{(culture packs)}$$

$$.5X_1 + .6X_2 + .7X_3 + .5X_4 + .6X_5$$
$$+ .5X_6 + .4X_7 + .3X_8 + .3X_9 + .2X_{10} \leq 1,500 \quad \text{(salt ounces)}$$

$$2X_1 + 1X_2 + 2X_3 + 1X_4 + 2X_5$$
$$+ 1X_6 + 1X_7 + 2X_8 + 2X_9 + 1X_{10} \leq 3,000 \quad \text{(gauze sheets)}$$

$$0X_1 + 0X_2 - 1X_3 + 0X_4 + 0X_5$$
$$+ 0X_6 + 0X_7 + 1X_8 + 0X_9 + 0X_{10} \leq 0 \quad \text{(product mix 1)}$$

$$-1X_1 + 0X_2 + 1X_3 + 0X_4 + 0X_5$$
$$+ 0X_6 + 0X_7 + 0X_8 + 0X_9 + 0X_{10} \leq 0 \quad \text{(product mix 2)}$$

$$0X_1 + 0X_2 + 0X_3 + 0X_4 + 0X_5$$
$$+ 1X_6 + 1X_7 + 1X_8 + 1X_9 + 1X_{10} \leq 1,000 \quad \text{(group limitation)}$$

where $\qquad\qquad$ all X's $\geq$ 0

(a) How many pounds should be made of each type of cheese? What is the corresponding maximum profit?

(b) Indicate the unused amount of each resource.

10-22 *Computer exercise.* Hoopla Hoops must decide how to allocate magazine advertising funds for water wheelies. This is to be done so that total exposure, based on circulation, is maximized. No more than $100,000 will be spent. The following data apply for one-page ads in various publications.

MAGAZINE	COST PER AD (thousands)	CIRCULATION (millions)	MAXIMUM PLACEMENTS	TYPE OF READERSHIP
1. Tiger Club	2.0	1.5	10	Teen
2. Rocky	2.5	1.4	2	Teen
3. Spider Glider	1.5	.7	10	Youth
4. Toy Fans	1.0	.8	3	Youth
5. Mr. T's	2.0	1.1	2	Teen
6. Hideaway	2.0	1.5	5	General
7. Micky Club	.8	.3	4	Youth
8. Sport Rods	1.2	.9	6	General
9. Go Cars	3.0	2.1	7	Youth
10. Two-4-8	1.8	1.9	5	Youth
11. Up We Go	1.5	1.4	5	Teen
12. Fan Times	1.5	1.6	4	Teen
13. Fan Fare	3.0	2.0	2	Teen
14. UpBeat	2.0	1.6	2	General
15. Comic Craze	.8	.9	3	Youth

The total number of teen market ads must be no greater than the number of youth placements. Also, the number of general ads must be less than or equal to half the combined total of youth and teen placements. Finally, no more than $40,000 may be placed in teen-oriented media.

Determine the optimal number of ads to be placed in each of the above magazines.

Solving Linear Programs II: Surplus and Artificial Variables

The applications of linear programming we described in Chapter 10 were limited to profit-maximization problems with constraints of the $\leq$ form. We are now ready to consider more general problems with constraints involving $\geq$ or $=$ relations. These applications will require us to use some new auxiliary variables that play an analogous role to the slack variable we have already encountered. By including cost-minimization problems in this chapter, we will also expand the scope of the problems that can be solved using the simplex method. Chapter 11 concludes with a discussion of the special difficulties encountered in linear programming.

11-1 Surplus and Artificial Variables: The Big-M Method

Suppose that we slightly modify our original Redwood Furniture problem to include a third product—benches—and that we represent the quantity of benches by the variable X_B. This increases the number of dimensions for the problem beyond our capability to draw a simple graph, thereby making the use of the simplex method essential. Suppose that each bench requires 25 board feet of wood and 7 hours of labor and is sold for a profit of $7. To further complicate the problem, we will assume that at least 2 benches must be made to satisfy outstanding orders, which creates a third quantity constraint. The basic linear program is

$$\text{Maximize} \quad P = 6X_T + 8X_C + 7X_B \quad \text{(objective)}$$

$$\text{Subject to} \quad 30X_T + 20X_C + 25X_B \leq 300 \quad \text{(wood)}$$

$$5X_T + 10X_C + 7X_B \leq 110 \quad \text{(labor)}$$

$$X_B \geq 2 \quad \text{(quantity)}$$

$$\text{where} \quad X_T, X_C, X_B \geq 0$$

The new quantity constraint must be converted into an equality. This presents a special problem, because the inequality points to the right. Since the value on the left can be larger than the minimum requirement of 2 benches, we can express any extra quantity beyond 2 as *surplus* benches. Thus, the quantity constraint can be equivalently stated

$$\text{Number of benches} - \text{Surplus benches} = 2$$

Or, if we let S_Q represent the surplus benches beyond the minimum quantity requirement, this constraint becomes

$$X_B - S_Q = 2 \quad \text{(quantity)}$$

We refer to S_Q as a **surplus variable**. Surplus variables are analogous to slack variables, in that they allow us to express linear programs in the equation form required by simplex. Surplus variables also have an economic connotation. Like any simplex variable, S_Q must be non-negative. (A negative surplus has no meaning here.)

Our quantity constraint has one further inadequacy. Zeroing out X_B leaves us with $0 - S_Q = 2$, or $S_Q = -2$, so that S_Q would begin as a negative value, which is not allowed. Thus, our quantity constraint cannot serve as a starting simplex row in its present form, and S_Q cannot be part of the *initial* basic mix. In fact, *surplus variables can never be in the initial basic mix.*

To begin the simplex procedure, we introduce the **artificial variable**—a quantity that has no meaningful economic interpretation. It is merely a temporary expedient. We generally use the letter a, with an appropriate subscript, to identify this type of variable. In our problem, a_Q will represent the artificial variable. This is added to the left side of the quantity constraint equation, providing

$$X_B - S_Q + a_Q = 2 \quad \text{(quantity)}$$

This expression in no way distorts the underlying production requirement *as long as a_Q ultimately assumes a value of zero.* To guarantee that $a_Q = 0$ (so that it is not in the final basic mix), we must make it highly unprofitable to do otherwise. We therefore assign a very large negative per-unit profit to a_Q. For this purpose, we use the letter M (for mammoth) to represent a huge number and assign a per-unit profit of $-M$ to a_Q.

Employing the slack variables S_W and S_L as before and noting that, like slacks, surplus variables contribute nothing to profit (or cost), we obtain the expanded linear program in a form suitable for beginning the simplex procedure.

Maximize $P = 6X_T + 8X_C + 7X_B + 0S_W + 0S_L + 0S_Q - Ma_Q$ (objective)

Subject to $30X_T + 20X_C + 25X_B + 1S_W + 0S_L + 0S_Q + 0a_Q = 300$ (wood)

$5X_T + 10X_C + 7X_B + 0S_W + 1S_L + 0S_Q + 0a_Q = 110$ (labor)

$0X_T + 0X_C + 1X_B + 0S_W + 0S_L - 1S_Q + 1a_Q = 2$ (quantity)

where $X_T, X_C, X_B, S_W, S_L, S_Q, a_Q \geq 0$

As before, we list all variables in all equations. Those variables not in the original constraint equations appear with coefficients of zero.

The initial simplex tableau for this problem is provided in Figure 11-1. The basic mix consists of the slack variables and the artificial variable. Notice that the columns of these variables contain a 1 in their row and zeros elsewhere. The initial solution is $X_T = X_C = X_B = S_Q = 0$, $S_W = 300$, $S_L = 110$, $a_Q = 2$, and $P = -2M$ (a very poor profit indeed). Also notice that the sacrifice and improvement rows contain M terms.

The entering variable is X_B, since it shows the largest profit improvement of $7 + M$ dollars per unit. The exit criterion indicates that a maximum of 2 units of X_B can be traded in the variable mix for a_Q, the exiting variable. The remaining iterations of the simplex method are provided in Figure 11-2.

The optimal solution obtained from the final simplex tableau is

$$X_T = 0 \qquad\qquad S_W = 0$$
$$X_C = 65/11 \qquad\quad S_L = 0$$
$$X_B = 80/11 \qquad\quad S_Q = 58/11$$
$$P = 1{,}080/11 = 98.18 \text{ dollars}$$

FIGURE 11-1
Initial simplex tableau for the slightly modified Redwood Furniture problem.

UNIT PROFIT		6	8	7	0	0	0	−M		
	Basic Mix	X_T	X_C	X_B	S_W	S_L	S_Q	a_Q	Sol.	
0	S_W	30	20	25↓	1	0	0	0	300	300/25 = 12
0	S_L	5	10	7	0	1	0	0	110	110/7 = 15.71
−M	a_Q ←	0	0	①	0	0	−1	1	2	2/1 = 2*
	Sac.	0	0	−M	0	0	M	−M	−2M	
	Imp.	6	8	7 + M	0	0	−M	0	—	

FIGURE 11-2

Simplex tableaus for the remaining iterations of the expanded Redwood Furniture problem.

	UNIT PROFIT		6	8	7	0	0	0	-M		
		Basic Mix	X_T	X_C	X_B	S_W	S_L	S_Q	a_Q	Sol.	
[old S_W -25 new X_B]	0	S_W	30	20↓	0	1	0	25	-25	250	250/20 = 12.5
[old S_L -7 new X_B]	0	S_L ←	5	⑩	0	0	1	7	-7	96	96/10 = 9.6*
[old a_Q ÷ 1]	7	X_B	0	0	1	0	0	-1	1	2	2/0 = ∞
		Sac.	0	0	7	0	0	-7	7	14	
		Imp.	6	8	0	0	0	7	-M-7	—	

		Basic Mix	X_T	X_C	X_B	S_W	S_L	S_Q	a_Q	Sol.	
[old S_W -20 new X_C]	0	S_W ←	㉒↓	0	0	1	-2	11	-11	58	58/20 = 2.9*
[old S_L ÷ 10]	8	X_C	1/2	1	0	0	1/10	7/10	-7/10	9.6	9.6/(1/2) = 19.2
[old X_B -0 new X_C]	7	X_B	0	0	1	0	0	-1	1	2	2/0 = ∞
		Sac.	4	8	7	0	.8	-1.4	1.4	90.8	
		Imp.	2	0	0	0	-.8	1.4	-M-1.4	—	

		Basic Mix	X_T	X_C	X_B	S_W	S_L	S_Q	a_Q	Sol.	
[old S_W ÷ 20]	6	X_T ←	1	0	0	1/20	-1/10	⑪/20↓	-11/20	2.9	2.9/(11/20) = 5.27*
[old X_C -(1/2) new X_T]	8	X_C	0	1	0	-1/40	3/20	17/40	-17/40	8.15	8.15/(17/40) = 19.18
[old X_B -0 new X_T]	7	X_B	0	0	1	0	0	-1	1	2	2/-1 = -2
		Sac.	6	8	7	.1	.6	-.3	.3	96.6	
		Imp.	0	0	0	-.1	-.6	.3	-M-.3	—	

		Basic Mix	X_T	X_C	X_B	S_W	S_L	S_Q	a_Q	Sol.	
[old X_T ÷ 11/20]	0	S_Q	20/11	0	0	1/11	-2/11	1	-1	58/11	
[old X_C -(17/40) new S_Q]	8	X_C	-17/22	1	0	-7/110	5/22	0	0	65/11	
[old X_B -(-1) new S_Q]	7	X_B	20/11	0	1	1/11	-2/11	0	0	80/11	
		Sac.	72/11	8	7	7/55	6/11	0	0	1,080/11	
		Imp.	-6/11	0	0	-7/55	-6/11	0	-M	—	

Notice that when benches are included in Redwood's product line, it is no longer most profitable to make tables. We can also see that the surplus variable has a value greater than zero, indicating that $S_Q = X_B - 2 = 58/11$ benches should be produced beyond the minimum level of 2. Finally, notice that the artificial variable is not in the final basic mix and has a value of zero. Since a_Q has no economic meaning, we ordinarily do not include it when we report the optimal solution.

As a general rule, a *separate surplus variable should be used for every* ≥ *constraint, and each of these constraints must also have its own artificial variable.* The respective basic variable in the initial simplex tableau must always be that artificial variable introduced into the constraint equation for that row. An artificial variable must also ordinarily be used when there is an *equality constraint* in the first formulation, as might be the case if Redwood were forced to make *exactly* 1 table for every 4 chairs. Since such a constraint begins in the form of an equality (=), neither a surplus nor a slack variable is required but an artificial variable is needed to begin the simplex procedure.

11-2 A Summary of the Simplex Formulation Requirements

We have seen that under various conditions the simplex procedure requires slack, surplus, or artificial variables in addition to the main problem variables. A summary of the simplex formulation requirements is provided in Table 11-1.

TABLE 11-1
A Summary of the Simplex Formulation Requirements

TYPE OF CONSTRAINT	CONSTRAINT RELATIONSHIP	EXTRA VARIABLES NEEDED FOR SIMPLEX	OBJECTIVE COEFFICIENT		INITIAL VARIABLE MIX
			Max. P	*Min. C*	
Resource or maximum requirement	≤	Slack (added)	0	0	Yes
		No artificial	—	—	—
Quantity or minimum requirement	≥	Surplus (subtracted)	0	0	No
		Artificial (added)	$-M$	$+M$	Yes
Mixture or exact requirement	=	No slack or surplus	—	—	—
		Artificial (added)	$-M$	$+M$	Yes

Cost-minimization problems are handled somewhat differently by simplex. This is due to reversing the objective from maximization.

1. Coefficients of artificial variables are $+M$ (positive instead of negative).
2. The entering variable is the one in whose column lies the greatest absolute value of *negative* improvement quantities.

11-3 **Computer Solution**

As a practical matter, linear programs involving a variety of constraint types will ordinarily be solved with computer assistance. The big-M method is rarely carried through by hand any more.

To illustrate, consider a further expansion of the Redwood Furniture problem. There are three table sizes—small (X_{TS}), regular (X_{TR}), and large (X_{TL}), two chair styles—standard (X_{CS}) and armed (X_{CA}), and two bookcases sizes—short (X_{BS}) and tall (X_{BT}). Greater resource quantities are available, and machine shop time is now in short supply. There are minimum quantities for each product group, and there are mixture constraints that must be met exactly.

For tables the requirement is that the number of small tables be equal to the combined total of regular and large ones.

$$X_{TS} = X_{TR} + X_{TL} \quad \text{or} \quad X_{TS} - X_{TR} - X_{TL} = 0$$

For chairs, the number of regulars must be exactly four times the number of armed ones, while an equal number of bookcases must be made of the two types.

Table 11-2 summarizes production requirements.

TABLE 11-2
Data Obtained for the Expanded Redwood Furniture Problem

	VARIABLE							
CONSTRAINT	(1) X_{TS}	(2) X_{TR}	(3) X_{TL}	(4) X_{CS}	(5) X_{CA}	(6) X_{BS}	(7) X_{BT}	Available Quantity
(1) Wood	20	30	40	15	25	20	30	$\leq 3,000$
(2) Labor	4	5	6	8	12	6	8	$\leq 1,100$
(3) Machine time	2	2	2	3	3	2	2	≤ 250
(4) Quantity, tables	1	1	1					≥ 30
(5) Quantity, chairs				1	1			≥ 20
(6) Quantity, bookcases						1	1	≥ 20
(7) Mix, tables	1	-1	-1					$= 0$
(8) Mix, chairs				1	-4			$= 0$
(9) Mix, bookcases						1	-1	$= 0$
Unit Profit	$5	$6	$7	$6	$10	$8	$6	

TABLE 11-3

Variables for the Expanded Redwood Furniture Problem

VARIABLE	REFERENCE SYMBOL	TYPE
XTS	X_{TS}	Main
XTR	X_{TR}	Main
XTL	X_{TL}	Main
XCS	X_{CS}	Main
XCA	X_{CA}	Main
XBS	X_{BS}	Main
XBT	X_{BT}	Main
S1	S_W	Slack for 1
S2	S_L	Slack for 2
S3	S_M	Slack for 3
S4	S_{QT}	Surplus for 4
S5	S_{QC}	Surplus for 5
S6	S_{QB}	Surplus for 6
a4	a_{QT}	Artificial for 4
a5	a_{QC}	Artificial for 5
a6	a_{QB}	Artificial for 6
a7	a_{MT}	Artificial for 7
a8	a_{MC}	Artificial for 8
a9	$a_M{}^B$	Artificial for 9

QuickQuant Computer Solution

In response to queries regarding the problem structure, *QuickQuant* internally designates variables $X1$ through $X7$ as the main variables. It creates 3 slack variables, 3 surplus variables, and 6 artificial variables. These variables will apply to the constraints according to the sequence in which they are entered. Table 11-3 lists the designations that apply.

The objective function and constraint data are entered, one expression at a time. No separate entries are needed for the auxiliary variables. These are placed automatically, according to the nature of the constraint ($\leq$, $\geq$, or $=$). *QuickQuant* provides the following solution to the expanded Redwood Furniture problem.

```
Original                     Slack/Surplus
Variable    Value            Variable          Value

  XTS      15.00000             S1           135.00000
  XTR       0.00000             S2           319.00000
  XTL      15.00000             S3             0.00000
  XCS      16.00000             S4             0.00000
  XCA       4.00000             S5             0.00000
  XBS      32.50000             S6            45.00000
  XBT      32.50000

Objective Value:    P = 771.00000
```

11-4 Cost-Minimization Problems

The Persian Sausage Problem

Suppose that a meat packer must determine the quantities of ingredients that should be used in making 100 pounds of Persian sausage. Table 11-4 provides the pertinent labeling requirements and cost data.

We will assume that spices and casings add an insignificant amount to the total sausage weight and that unlimited quantities of the main ingredients are available at the indicated costs. The total ingredient weight must equal 100 pounds. If we represent the number of pounds of beef by X_B, chicken by X_C, and lamb by X_L, the following linear program formulation applies.

$$
\begin{aligned}
\text{Minimize} \quad C = \quad & 1X_B + .5X_C + .7X_L \quad \text{(objective)} \\
\text{Subject to} \quad & .20X_B + .15X_C + .25X_L \leq 24 \quad \text{(fat)} \\
& .20X_B + .15X_C + .15X_L \geq 12 \quad \text{(protein)} \\
& .60X_B + .70X_C + .60X_L \leq 64 \quad \text{(water)} \\
& 1X_L \geq 30 \quad \text{(ingredient)} \\
& 1X_B + 1X_C + 1X_L = 100 \quad \text{(total weight)} \\
\text{where} \quad & X_B, X_C, X_L \geq 0 \quad \text{(non-negativity)}
\end{aligned}
$$

An inspection of this program indicates that we must include two slack variables for the fat and water constraints and two surplus variables for the protein and ingredient constraints. These are respectively denoted by S_F, S_W, S_P, and S_I. Since they involve surplus variables, the protein and ingredient constraints must include the artificial variables a_P and a_I. Finally, we include an artificial variable a_T for the equality constraint for total weight.

TABLE 11-4
Labeling Requirements and Cost Data for the
Persian Sausage Problem

| | PERCENTAGE OF WEIGHT | | | |
LABEL CATEGORY	Beef	Chicken	Lamb	Required Percentage
Fat	20	15	25	$\leq 24\%$
Protein	20	15	15	$\geq 12\%$
Water	60	70	60	$\leq 64\%$
Percentage of total weight	Any	Any	$\geq 30\%$	
Cost per pound	$1.00	$.50	$.70	

The pre-simplex formulation of this linear program is

Minimize

$$C = 1X_B + .5X_C + .7X_L + 0S_F + 0S_P + 0S_W + 0S_I + Ma_P + Ma_I + Ma_T$$

Subject to

$$.20X_B + .15X_C + .25X_L + 1S_F + 0S_P + 0S_W + 0S_I + 0a_P + 0a_I + 0a_T = 24$$
$$.20X_B + .15X_C + .15X_L + 0S_F - 1S_P + 0S_W + 0S_I + 1a_P + 0a_I + 0a_T = 12$$
$$.60X_B + .70X_C + .60X_L + 0S_F + 0S_P + 1S_W + 0S_I + 0a_P + 0a_I + 0a_T = 64$$
$$0X_B + 0X_C + 1X_L + 0S_F + 0S_P + 0S_W - 1S_I + 0a_P + 1a_I + 0a_T = 30$$
$$1X_B + 1X_C + 1X_L + 0S_F + 0S_P + 0S_W + 0S_I + 0a_P + 0a_I + 1a_T = 100$$

where   all variables $\geq$ 0

Handling these artificial variables differs in one way from the handling of these variables in profit-maximization problems. In the objective function, a_P, a_I, and a_T have positive unit costs of $+M$, making them terribly costly (and ensuring that these variables leave the basic variable mix early).

The final simplex tableau is provided in Figure 11-3. The optimal solution is

$$X_B = 0 \qquad S_F = 3$$
$$X_C = 40 \qquad S_I = 30$$
$$X_L = 60 \qquad S_P = 3$$
$$S_W = 0$$
$$C = 62 \text{ dollars}$$

FIGURE 11-3
Final simplex tableau for the Persian sausage problem.

UNIT COST		1	.5	.7	0	0	0	0	M	M	M	
	Basic Mix	X_B	X_C	X_L	S_F	S_P	S_W	S_I	a_P	a_I	a_T	Sol.
0	S_F	−.05	0	0	1	0	1	0	0	0	−.85	3
0	S_I	1	0	0	0	.0	−10	1	0	−1	7	30
.5	X_C	0	1	0	0	0	10	0	0	0	−6	40
.7	X_L	1	0	1	0	0	−10	0	0	0	7	60
0	S_P	−.05	0	0	0	1	0	0	−1	0	.15	3
	Sac.	.7	.5	.7	0	0	−2	0	0	0	1.9	62
	Imp.	.3	0	0	0	0	2	0	M		M − 1.9 + M	—

Thus, no beef should be used in the Persian sausage, and the main ingredients should consist of 40 pounds of chicken and 60 pounds of lamb. The sausage will contain 3 pounds less fat than the maximum allowable amount, and 3 pounds of extra protein above the minimum requirement. Also, 30 pounds of lamb above the minimum required level of 30 pounds will be included.

11-5 Special Problems in Linear Programming

At this point, we have substantially covered the simplex method. Only a few special problem areas remain to be discussed. First, we will consider two types of problems that have no practical solutions. Then we will describe the procedure to follow when there may be several optimal solutions (most attractive corners). Finally, we will consider two technical difficulties that are inherent in the simplex procedure.

Infeasible Problems

In Chapter 8, we encountered the following *infeasible problem.*

$$\text{Maximize} \quad P = 6X_1 + 4X_2$$
$$\text{Subject to} \quad X_1 + X_2 \leq 5$$
$$X_2 \geq 8$$
$$\text{where} \quad X_1, X_2 \geq 0$$

It is not so easy to recognize that a problem is infeasible when several variables and constraints are involved. Fortunately, we can determine whether or not a problem is feasible when we begin to apply the simplex method. Figure 11-4 shows the simplex tableaus for this infeasible problem using S_1 as the slack for the first constraint, S_2 as the surplus for the second, and a as the artificial variable. The final tableau includes the artificial variable in the basic mix, with a value of $a = 3$. We know that this makes no economic sense. *If one or more artificial variables remain with positive value in the final basic variable mix, the linear program must be infeasible.*

Unbounded Problems

In Chapter 8, the following linear program was established to be *unbounded.*

$$\text{Maximize} \quad P = 3X_1 + 6X_2$$
$$\text{Subject to} \quad 3X_1 + 4X_2 \geq 12$$
$$-2X_1 + X_2 \leq 4$$
$$\text{where} \quad X_1, X_2 \geq 0$$

FIGURE 11-4

Simplex tableaus for the infeasible problem.

UNIT PROFIT		6	4	0	0	-M	
	Basic Mix	X_1	X_2	S_1	S_2	a	Sol.
0	$S_1 \leftarrow$	1	①↓	1	0	0	5
-M	a	0	1	0	-1	1	8
	Sac.	0	-M	0	M	-M	-8M
	Imp.	6	4 + M	0	-M	0	—
4	X_2	1	1	1	0	0	5
-M	a	-1	0	-1	-1	1	3
	Sac.	4 + M	4	4 + M	M	-M	20 - 3M
	Imp.	2 - M	0	-4 - M	-M	0	—

Recall that an unbounded problem can have any level for the objective. (In two dimensions, there are feasible solutions but no most attractive corner.)

As in the case of infeasible problems, simplex can identify the unbounded problem for us. Figure 11-5 shows the simplex iterations for this unbounded problem, using S_1 and a as the surplus and artificial variables for the first constraint and S_2 as the slack variable for the second. In the third tableau, X_1 is the entering variable. Notice that no exiting variable can be found there, since no value in the X_1 column is positive. In essence, there is no limit on the quantity X_1; it can replace either X_2 or S_1 in the variable mix at any level desired.

Whenever the exit criterion fails, the linear program is unbounded. *A linear programming problem is unbounded whenever none of the values in the entering variable's column is positive*, so that *there is no exiting variable*.

Ties for the Optimal Solution

In Chapter 8, we saw that whenever a most attractive corner lies on an edge parallel to the objective function, there is another equally attractive corner at the opposite end of that edge. All points on this edge correspond to optimal solutions.

In the higher dimensional problems encountered when simplex is used, similar ties for the most attractive corner apply. The simplex procedure can be used to evaluate every most attractive corner, finding all **ties** for the optimal solution. Such ties occur when the objective function coefficients are in constant ratio to the respective coefficients in the expression for one constraint (or some constraint that might result when two or more

FIGURE 11-5

Simplex tableaus for the unbounded problem.

UNIT PROFIT		3	6	0	0	-M	
	Basic Mix	X_1	X_2	S_1	S_2	a	Sol.
-M	a ←	3	④↓	-1	0	1	12
0	S_2	-2	1	0	1	0	4
	Sac.	-3M	-4M	M	0	-M	-12M
	Imp.	3 + 3M	6 + 4M	-M	0	0	—
6	X_2	.75	1	- .25↓	0	.25	3
0	S_2 ←	-2.75	0	⑤.25	1	-.25	1
	Sac.	4.5	6	-1.5	0	1.5	18
	Imp.	-1.5	0	1.5	0	-M - 1.5	—
6	X_2	-2↓	1	0	1	0	4
0	S_1	-11	0	1	4	-1	4
	Sac.	-12	6	0	6	0	24
	Imp.	15	0	0	-6	-M	—

There is no exiting variable.

constraint equations are combined). Under some circumstances, there can be more than two most attractive corners, permitting a multitude of ties to occur. But there will ordinarily be no ties at all.

Suppose that we must amend our Persian sausage problem slightly because beef now costs $.70 per pound instead of $1. The top tableau in Figure 11-6 corresponds to the final simplex tableau in Figure 11-3. (For simplicity, the artificial variable columns have been removed.) The optimal solution obtained from the first tableau is

$$X_B = 0 \qquad S_F = 3$$
$$X_C = 40 \qquad S_P = 3$$
$$X_L = 60 \qquad S_W = 0$$
$$S_I = 30$$
$$C = 62 \text{ dollars}$$

FIGURE 11-6

A further simplex iteration to find the tying optimal solution to the Persian sausage problem.

UNIT COST		.7	.5	.7	0	0	0	0	
	Basic Mix	X_B	X_C	X_L	S_F	S_P	S_W	S_I	Sol.
0	S_F	− .05↓	0	0	1	0	1	0	3
0	S_I ←	①	0	0	0	0	− 10	1	30
.5	X_C	0	1	0	0	0	10	0	40
.7	X_L	1	0	1	0	0	− 10	0	60
0	S_P	− .05	0	0	0	1	0	0	3
	Sac.	.7	.5	.7	0	0	− 2	0	62
	Imp.	0	0	0	0	0	2	0	—
0	S_F	0	0	0	1	0	.5	.05	4.5
.7	X_B	1	0	0	0	0	− 10	1	30
.5	X_C	0	1	0	0	0	10	0	40
.7	X_L	0	0	1	0	0	0	− 1	30
0	S_P	0	0	0	0	1	− .5	.05	4.5
	Sac.	.7	.5	.7	0	0	− 2	0	62
	Imp.	0	0	0	0	0	2	0	—

which is identical to our prior optimal solution to the Persian sausage problem, except that a *zero improvement* exists for the nonbasic variable X_B. This indicates that if some beef were used, so that X_B became part of the basic mix, there would be no change in total cost. In effect, a *simplex pivot* treating X_B as the entering variable would produce a new solution also having a cost of $C = 62$ dollars. In other words, a tie would exist for the optimal solution.

Now suppose that we carry out one more iteration, treating X_B (beef) as the entering variable. In Figure 11-6, we can see that S_I (surplus ingredient lamb) exits, and the solution is provided by the second tableau, where

$$X_B = 30 \qquad S_F = 4.5$$
$$X_C = 40 \qquad S_P = 4.5$$
$$X_L = 30 \qquad S_W = 0$$
$$S_I = 0$$
$$C = 62 \text{ dollars}$$

This solution is tied with the first optimal solution. In general, a *tie for optimal solution exists whenever a nonbasic variable exhibits zero per-unit improvement in the final simplex*

TABLE 11-5
Finding an Optimal Solution Lying on an Edge

VARIABLE	VALUES FOR TYING OPTIMAL CORNER		OPTIMAL EDGE POINT (40% first + 60% second)
	First	Second	
X_B	0	30	$0 + 18 = 18$
X_C	40	40	$16 + 24 = 40$
X_L	60	30	$24 + 18 = 42$
S_F	3	4.5	$1.2 + 2.7 = 3.9$
S_P	3	4.5	$1.2 + 2.7 = 3.9$
S_W	0	0	$0 + 0 = 0$
S_I	30	0	$12 + 0 = 12$
C	62	62	62

tableau. This is true whether that variable is a main, slack, or surplus variable. The tying solution can be found by a further simplex pivot that treats this variable as the entering variable. (This feature is also present in the second tableau for S_I, which tells us that we could then enter S_I and exit X_B, bringing us back to where we started. The process is reversible.) Once an optimal solution has been found, it is a simple matter to employ further pivots successively to find all of the tying solutions.

We have found two optimal corner point solutions. Any feasible linear combination of these solutions (any point on the connecting edge) will also be optimal. Whenever a fixed percentage of all the values of one corner is added to the complementary percentage of all the values of the other corner, such a combination will result. For example, Table 11-5 shows the optimal edge point when 40% of the first corner is combined with 60% of the second corner.

Redundant Constraints and Degeneracy

When the constraints of some linear programs are considered collectively, one or more of the problem constraints may be **redundant**. Ordinarily, no problem is caused by including a redundant constraint in a linear programming problem, although the simplex computations can be shortened if obviously redundant constraints are eliminated beforehand. For example, the second constraint provided below is less restrictive than the first one and is not needed.

$$2X_1 + 3X_2 \leq 6$$

$$2X_1 + 3X_2 \leq 7$$

It is often difficult to determine in advance whether a redundancy exists, however. Under some circumstances, simplex may therefore yield a *tie for the exiting variable*. The rules of simplex permit any tie (whether it is for an entering or an exiting variable) to be broken arbitrarily. But when this happens during the exit phase, the new tableau contains a zero value in the solution column, indicating that the variable for that row could lie outside the basic mix. In effect, a redundancy is present somewhere in the problem.

Whenever there is a zero in the solution column, the linear program is said to be **degenerate**. This is normally of no practical consequence. But on very rare occasions, degeneracy may cause the simplex procedure to *cycle* indefinitely, repeating an identical sequence of pivots and never reaching a conclusion. If this ever happens, the remedy is simple: Return to the tableau where the tie occurred, make the other variable the exiting variable, and proceed from there.

Variables That Are Unrestricted as to Sign

Simplex requires that every variable be non-negative. However, certain real-world problems involve variables that can be either positive or negative. In a security investment problem, for example, the number of shares of a particular stock might be represented by a long position (a positive quantity), a short position (a negative quantity), or no shares (zero). Oil refining provides another example. Some byproducts can be created in one stage and consumed in a later one—in varying amounts in both cases. Thus, the net amount of the resulting byproduct could be either positive (more is created than is consumed) or negative (more is consumed than is created). In both applications *the sign of the variable is* **unrestricted**.

Simplex still requires non-negativity, even when it is applied to such a problem. One way to accommodate the non-negativity condition is to represent the unrestricted variable by the difference between two separate non-negative variables. For example,

	SECURITY INVESTMENT	OIL REFINING
Unrestricted	X_P = Position in stock	X_B = Net change in byproduct
New non-negative variables	X_L = Shares held long	X_C = Byproduct created
	X_S = Shares shorted	X_U = Byproduct consumed
	$X_P = X_L - X_S$	$X_B = X_C - X_U$

The difference $X_L - X_S$ (or $X_C - X_U$) can be substituted everywhere X_P (or X_B) appears, and the respective linear programs will contain only non-negative variables. If the solution to the investment problem provides $X_L = 0$, $X_S = 100$, then $X_P = 0 - 100 = -100$. If the solution to the oil refining problem is with $X_C = 10,000$, $X_U = 11,000$, then $X_B = 10,000 - 11,000 = -1,000$.

11-6 Finding a Better Solution Procedure

For nearly all linear programs encountered in practical applications, the simplex method is guaranteed to eventually reach the optimal solution (if one exists). For very large problems, involving tens of thousands of variables and constraints, a very large and fast main-frame computer must be used. But some problems are too huge to be solved within a reasonable amount of time, even using the fastest of computers.

More efficient variant forms of simplex have been employed with computers. That may considerably reduce the amount of computer time needed to solve large problems. Special purpose algorithms, based on the simplex concepts, are efficiently applied to problems having particular structures. One such procedure, the **transportation method**, is presented in Chapter 14 for solving linear programs involving distribution.

But in spite of the simplex method's attractive properties, even using the best of today's large computers, some problems are still too big to be solved with that procedure. Alternative approaches have been developed for solving large linear programs. One successful procedure, developed in the early 1980s by N. Karmarker, avoids simplex's tortuous journey from corner to corner. Karmarker's algorithm instead uses geometrical transformations, allowing large shortcuts to be made by jumping through the solution space. This algorithm involves fewer iterations than simplex requires. But each step is far more complex, so that its overall advantage appears to occur only for the very largest of linear programs.

CASE

Horrible Harry's

Horrible Harry's is a chain of 47 self-service gas stations served by a small refinery and mixing plant. Each day's product requirements are met by blending feedstocks on hand at midnight. The volumes vary daily, depending on the previous day's refinery output and on bulk receipts.

The entire operation is run by the owner, Harry Oldaker. Although dozens of chemicals and byproducts are generated by the refinery, Harry's major concern is the retail distribution of gasoline products.

On a particular Tuesday there are sufficient volumes of leaded and unleaded regular gasolines at the stations. Only the two hybrid petroleum products—gasohol and petrolmeth—will be shipped that day. Both products are blended from 90-octane unleaded gasoline. Ethyl alcohol, the only additive to gasohol, cannot exceed 10% of the final product's volume. Petrolmeth may contain both ethyl and methyl alcohols, but these combined ingredients must not exceed 30% of the final product's volume. The octane ratings are 120 for ethyl alcohol and 110 for methyl alcohol. Final product octane ratings must equal the average octane ratings for the ingredients by volume. Gasohol must have an octane rating of at least 91, and petrolmeth must have a rating of at least 93.

There are 20,000 gallons of gasoline presently available for blending, at a cost of $1.00 per gallon. Up to 5,000 gallons of methyl alcohol can be acquired for $.50 per gallon, and 3,000 gallons of ethyl alcohol are available at $1.50 per gallon. The demands are at least 10,000 gallons for gasohol and 5,000 gallons for petrolmeth.

Until now Harry has determined product blends by trial and error. A new staff analyst says that she can save a considerable amount of money by using linear programming to establish a minimum-cost blending formulation. Harry is a bit skeptical, but he offers her the challenge to do better than the following.

> 9,000 gallons of unleaded gas to gasohol
> 1,000 gallons of ethyl alcohol to gasohol
> 3,500 gallons of unleaded gas to petrolmeth
> 1,500 gallons of methyl alcohol to petrolmeth

$$Cost = \$14,750$$

If the analyst can save a significant amount, she will use linear programming for all future blending decisions.

Questions

1. Formulate Horrible Harry's decision problem as a linear program.

2. Run your linear program on a computer to determine the optimal volumes to be blended. How much lower is the cost of the optimal solution than that of Harry's original plan?

PROBLEMS

11-1 Refer to Hoopla Hoops product-mix decision in Problem 9-2 (page 298).
    (a) Formulate the linear program in standardized form.
    (b) Reexpress the above formulation in equation form, positioning all necessary auxiliary variables that would be used in solving Hoopla's production scheduling problem using the simplex method. Then, make a list defining each auxiliary variable with a verbal description.
    (c) Construct the *first* simplex tableau only. *Do not compute* values for the sacrifice and improvement rows, and *do not* construct any subsequent simplex tableaus.

11-2 Refer to All-American Meat Processors' decision in Problem 9-12 (page 301).
    (a) Formulate the linear program in standardized form.
    (b) Reexpress the above formulation in equation form, positioning all necessary auxiliary variables that would be used in solving All-American's sausage ingredient selection problem using the simplex method. Then, make a list defining each auxiliary variable with a verbal description.
    (c) Construct the initial simplex tableau only. *Do not compute* values for the sacrifice and improvement rows, and *do not* construct any subsequent simplex tableaus.

11-3 Consider the following linear program.

$$\text{Maximize} \quad P = 5X_1 + 6X_2$$

$$\text{Subject to} \qquad 3X_1 + 4X_2 \le 12 \quad \text{(resource)}$$
$$2X_1 + 6X_2 \ge 12 \quad \text{(mixture)}$$
$$\text{where} \qquad X_1, X_2 \ge 0$$

(a) Solve this problem graphically.
(b) Reformulate this problem in an equation form that is suitable for the simplex method.
(c) Solve the problem again using the simplex procedure.

11-4   Consider the following linear program.

$$\text{Maximize} \quad P = 2X_1 - 3X_2$$
$$\text{Subject to} \qquad 4X_1 + 5X_2 \le 40 \quad \text{(resource } A\text{)}$$
$$2X_1 - 6X_2 \le 24 \quad \text{(resource } B\text{)}$$
$$3X_1 - 3X_2 \ge 6 \quad \text{(mixture)}$$
$$X_1 \qquad \ge 4 \quad \text{(quantity)}$$
$$\text{where} \qquad X_1, X_2 \ge 0$$

(a) Solve this problem graphically.
(b) Reformulate this problem in an equation form that is suitable for the simplex method.
(c) Solve the problem again using the simplex procedure.

11-5   Consider the following linear program.

$$\text{Minimize} \quad C = .5X_A + .3X_B$$
$$\text{Subject to} \qquad X_A + 2X_B \ge 10 \quad \text{(restriction } Y\text{)}$$
$$2X_A + X_B \ge 8 \quad \text{(restriction } Z\text{)}$$
$$\text{where} \qquad X_A, X_B \ge 0$$

(a) Solve this problem graphically.
(b) Reformulate this problem in an equation form that is suitable for the simplex method.
(c) Solve the problem again using the simplex procedure.

11-6   For each of the following linear programs, an intermediate or final simplex tableau is presented. In each case, state whether the simplex method indicates (1) an optimal solution, (2) an unbounded problem, (3) an infeasible problem, (4) that further steps are required (in which case, find the entering and exiting variables), or (5) that a tie exists for the optimal solution and that the final tableau provides just one optimal solution.

(a)   Maximize $P = 14X_1 + 18X_2 + 16X_3 + 80X_4$
$$\text{Subject to} \qquad 4\tfrac{1}{2}X_1 + 8\tfrac{1}{2}X_2 + 6X_3 + 20X_4 \le 6{,}000 \quad \text{(resource } A\text{)}$$
$$X_1 + X_2 + 4X_3 + 40X_4 \le 4{,}000 \quad \text{(resource } B\text{)}$$
$$\text{where} \qquad \text{all } X\text{'s} \ge 0$$

UNIT PROFIT		14	18	16	80	0	0	
	Basic Mix	X_1	X_2	X_3	X_4	S	S_B	Sol.
14	X_1	1	2	1	0	1/4	−1/8	1,000
80	X_4	0	−1/40	3/40	1	−1/160	9/320	75
	Sac.	14	26	20	80	3	1/2	20,000
	Imp.	0	−8	−4	0	−3	−1/2	—

(b)

Maximize $P = 2X_1 + 2X_2$

Subject to $X_1 + X_2 \geq 3$ (limitation)

$X_1 + X_2 \leq 2$ (resource)

where $X_1, X_2 \geq 0$

UNIT PROFIT		2	2	0	0	−M	
	Basic Mix	X_1	X_2	S_L	S_R	a	Sol.
−M	a	0	0	−1	−1	1	1
2	X_1	1	1	0	1	0	2
	Sac.	2	2	M	$M+2$	−M	$4-M$
	Imp.	0	0	−M	$-M-2$	0	—

(c)

Maximize $P = X_1 + X_2$

Subject to $2X_1 + 2X_2 \leq 4$ (resource A)

$X_1 \qquad\quad \leq 3$ (resource B)

where $X_1, X_2 \geq 0$

UNIT PROFIT		1	1	0	0	
	Basic Mix	X_1	X_2	S_A	S_B	Sol.
1	X_2	1	1	1/2	0	2
0	S_B	1	0	0	1	3
	Sac.	1	1	1/2	0	2
	Imp.	0	0	−1/2	0	—

(d)

$$\text{Maximize} \quad P = \quad 5X_1 + 6X_2$$

$$\text{Subject to} \quad -4X_1 + 2X_2 \le 12 \quad \text{(resource } A\text{)}$$

$$-4X_1 + 3X_2 \le 12 \quad \text{(resource } B\text{)}$$

$$\text{where} \quad X_1, X_2 \ge 0$$

UNIT PROFIT		5	6	0	0	
	Basic Mix	X_1	X_2	S_A	S_B	Sol.
0	S_A	$-4/3$	0	1	$-2/3$	4
6	X_2	$-4/3$	1	0	1/3	4
	Sac.	-8	6	0	2	24
	Imp.	13	0	0	-2	—

(e)

$$\text{Minimize} \quad C = 40X_1 + 60X_2$$

$$\text{Subject to} \quad 3X_1 + 3X_2 \ge 3 \quad \text{(restriction } A\text{)}$$

$$2X_1 + 3X_2 \ge 4 \quad \text{(restriction } B\text{)}$$

$$\text{where} \quad X_1, X_2 \ge 0$$

UNIT COST		40	60	0	0	M	M	
	Basic Mix	X_1	X_2	S_A	S_B	a_A	a_B	Sol.
60	X_2	2/3	1	$-1/3$	0	1/3	0	1
M	a_B	1	0	1	-1	-1	1	1
	Sac.	$40 + M$	60	$-20 + M$	$-M$	$20 - M$	M	$60 + M$
	Imp.	$-M$	0	$20 - M$	M	$-20 + 2M$	0	—

11-7 The simplex method has been attempted on various forms of the headphone manufacturing problem (originally formulated on page 334). For each version of that maximization problem, a simplex tableau is provided. In each case that follows, indicate the appropriate circumstance as explained in (1)–(5) at the beginning of Problem 11–6.

(a)

UNIT PROFIT

		20	23	27	19	0	0	0	0	0	
	Basic Mix	X_1	X_2	X_3	X_4	S_L	S_C	S_M	S_S	S_P	Sol.
0	S_L	−1.5	−.5	0	11	1	0	−6.5	0	0	1,000
0	S_C	0	0	0	2	0	1	−1	0	0	500
27	X_3	1	1	1	−1	0	0	1	0	0	0
0	S_S	−1	0	0	1	0	0	−1	1	0	500
0	S_P	−8	−4	0	16	0	0	−12	0	1	2,500
	Sac.	27	27	27	−27	0	0	27	0	0	0
	Imp.	−7	−4	0	46	0	0	−27	0	0	—

(b)

UNIT PROFIT

		20	23	27	19	0	0	0	0	0	
	Basic Mix	X_1	X_2	X_3	X_4	S_L	S_C	S_M	S_S	S_P	Sol.
19	X_4	1.111	1.333	1.444	1	.222	0	0	0	0	222.22
0	S_C	−.111	−.333	−.444	0	−.222	1	0	0	0	277.78
0	S_M	2.111	2.333	2.444	0	.222	0	1	0	0	222.22
0	S_S	0	1	1	0	0	0	0	1	0	500
0	S_P	−.444	2.667	6.222	0	−.889	0	0	0	1	1,611.11
	Sac.	21.11	25.33	27.44	19	4.22	0	0	0	0	4,222.22
	Imp.	−1.11	−2.33	−.44	0	−4.22	0	0	0	0	—

(c)

UNIT PROFIT

		21.21	23.11	27.51	18.69	0	0	0	0	0	
	Basic Mix	X_1	X_2	X_3	X_4	S_L	S_C	S_M	S_S	S_P	Sol.
18.69	X_4	−.136	−.045	0	1	.091	0	−.591	0	0	90.91
0	S_C	.273	.091	0	0	−.182	1	.182	0	0	318.18
27.51	X_3	.864	.955	1	0	.091	0	.409	0	0	90.91
0	S_S	−.864	.045	0	0	−.091	0	−.409	1	0	409.09
0	S_P	−5.82	−3.27	0	0	−1.45	0	−2.55	0	1	1,045.46
	Sac.	21.21	25.41	27.51	18.69	4.2	0	.21	0	0	4,200
	Imp.	0	−2.30	0	0	−4.2	0	−.21	0	0	—

(d)

UNIT PROFIT		21.21	23.11	27.51	18.69	0	0	0	0	−M	
	Basic Mix	X_1	X_2	X_3	X_4	S_L	S_M	S_S	S_P	a	Sol.
18.69	X_4	1.111	1.333	1.444	1	.222	0	0	0	0	222.22
−M	a	−.111	−.333	−.444	0	−.222	0	0	0	1	277.78
0	S_M	2.111	2.333	2.444	0	.222	1	0	0	0	222.22
0	S_S	0	1	1	0	0	0	1	0	0	500
0	S_P	−4.44	2.667	6.222	0	−.889	0	0	1	0	1,611.11
	Sac.	.11M +20.8	.3M +24.9	.4M +27.0	18.69	.2M +4.5	0	0	0	−M +0	277.78M +4,153.3
	Imp.	−.11M +.6	−.3M −1.8	−.4M +.5	0	−.2M −4.5	0	0	0	0	—

(e)

UNIT PROFIT		10	15	20	25	0	0	−M	−M	
	Basic Mix	X_1	X_2	X_3	X_4	S_1	S_3	a_1	a_2	Sol.
25	X_4	−.136	−.045	0	1	−.091	−.591	.091	0	90.91
−M	a_2	0	0	0	0	0	−1	0	1	500
20	X_3	.864	.955	1	0	−.091	.409	.091	·0	90.91
	Sac.	13.86	17.95	20	25	−4.09	M −6.59	4.09	−M +0	4,200
	Imp.	−3.86	−2.95	0	0	4.09	−M +6.59	−M −4.09	0	—

11-8 For the following linear program,

$$\text{Maximize} \quad P = 6X_1 + 10X_2 + 2X_3$$

$$\text{Subject to} \quad 2X_1 + 4X_2 + 3X_3 \leq 40 \quad \text{(resource } A\text{)}$$

$$X_1 + X_2 \qquad \leq 10 \quad \text{(resource } B\text{)}$$

$$2X_2 + X_3 \leq 12 \quad \text{(resource } C\text{)}$$

$$\text{where} \qquad X_1, X_2, X_3 \geq 0$$

the slack variables are S_A, S_B, and S_C. The final simplex tableau is provided on the following page.

UNIT PROFIT		6	10	2	0	0	0	
	Basic Mix	X_1	X_2	X_3	S_A	S_B	S_C	Sol.
0	S_A	0	0	2	1	-2	-1	8
6	X_1	1	0	-1/2	0	1	-1/2	4
10	X_2	0	1	1/2	0	0	1/2	6
	Sac.	6	10	2	0	6	2	84
	Imp.	0	0	0	0	-6	-2	—

A tie exists for the optimal solution.
(a) Identify the values of the solution variables. Then, determine the tying optimal solution and provide the corresponding variable values.
(b) Determine the optimal edge-point solution lying halfway between the two tying optimal corner points.

11-9 For the following linear program,

$$\text{Maximize} \quad P = 5X_1 + 2X_2 + 10X_3$$

$$\text{Subject to} \qquad X_1 \quad - \quad X_3 \leq 10 \quad \text{(resource } A\text{)}$$

$$X_2 - \quad X_3 \geq 10 \quad \text{(limitation } B\text{)}$$

$$\text{where} \qquad X_1, X_2, X_3 \geq 0$$

the extra variables are S_A (slack), S_B (surplus), and a (artificial). Consider the intermediate simplex tableau provided below.

UNIT PROFIT		5	2	10	0	0	-M	
	Basic Mix	X_1	X_2	X_3	S_A	S_B	a	Sol.
5	X_1	1	0	-1	1	0	0	10
2	X_2	0	1	-1	0	-1	1	10
	Sac.	5	2	-7	5	-2	2	70
	Imp.	0	0	17	-5	2	-M-2	—

(a) Identify the entering variable. Then, determine the exiting variable. Do you notice anything unusual? Indicate your finding.
(b) The following constraint was missing from the earlier formulation.

$$X_1 + X_2 + X_3 \leq 10 \quad \text{(resource } C\text{)}$$

Use the simplex method to solve the new linear program from the beginning.

11-10 For the following linear program,

$$\text{Maximize} \quad P = 20X_1 + 10X_2 + 2X_3$$

$$\text{Subject to} \qquad 2X_1 + \quad X_2 + \ X_3 \le \ 9 \quad \text{(resource } A)$$

$$X_1 + \quad X_2 \qquad\quad \ge 10 \quad \text{(limitation } B)$$

$$\text{where} \qquad\qquad X_1, X_2, X_3 \ge \ 0$$

the extra variables are S_A (slack), S_B (surplus), and a (artificial). The final simplex tableau is provided below.

UNIT PROFIT		20	10	2	0	0	−M	
	Basic Mix	X_1	X_2	X_3	S_A	S_B	a	Sol.
10	X_2	2	1	1	1	0	0	9
−M	a	−1	0	−1	−1	−1	1	1
	Sac.	20 + M	10	10 + M	10 + M	M	−M	90 − M
	Imp.	−M	0	−8 − M	−10 − M	−M	0	—

(a) What does the solution you obtained from this tableau tell you about the problem?

(b) Suppose this is corrected by changing the limitation level for B from 10 to 4. Using the simplex method, start from the beginning and find the optimal solution to this revised problem.

11-11 *Computer exercise.* Refer to your answer to Problem 11-1(a).

(a) A Hoopla analyst attempted to solve this problem on a computer. What conclusion did she reach?

(b) The analyst found additional sources of supply for certain raw materials. She increased the available amounts to the following levels: 400 units of plastic and 700 units of beads. She also received permission to reduce the minimum quantity for model B to 20 units. Solve her modified linear program to determine how many units of each model Hoopla should make.

11-12 *Computer exercise.* Refer to your answer to Problem 11-2(a). Solve this problem on a computer to determine what quantities of the various ingredients All-American should use for each sausage type.

11-13 *Computer exercise.* Refer to Problem 9-4 (page 298). Solve this problem on a computer to determine how much Quicker Oats should spend on each advertising and promotional activity.

11-14 *Computer exercise.* Refer to Problem 9-6 (page 299). Solve this problem on a computer to determine how much Million Bank should invest in each bond. Assume that constraints (1)–(6) all apply.

11-15 *Computer exercise.* Refer to Problem 9-9 (page 300). Solve this problem on a computer to determine how much Willy B. Rich should invest in each financial instrument.

11-16 *Computer exercise.* Refer to Problem 9-7 (page 299). Solve this problem on a computer to determine the optimal solution for the sausage ingredient problem.

11-17 *Computer exercise.* Refer to Problem 9-16 (page 302). Solve this problem on a computer to determine the number of spot ads Blitz Beer should place with each radio station.

11-18 *Computer exercise.* Refer to Problem 9-14 (page 301). Solve this problem on a computer to determine the optimal blending schedule for Channel Zee's product. Assume that constraints (1)–(6) all apply.

11-19 *Computer exercise.* Refer to Problem 9-17 (page 302). Solve this problem on a computer to determine Geo-Pet's optimal dollar investment levels in the proposed ventures.

11-20 *Computer exercise.* Grubby Stakes Mining Company is establishing a production plan for the current week at its Bonstock Lode, which has three main veins of varying characteristics. The net yields per ton for each of the veins is provided below.

	MINING VEINS		
ORE	*Eastern*	*Northern*	*Tom's Lucky*
Gold	.2 oz	.3 oz	.4 oz
Silver	30 oz	20 oz	30 oz
Copper	50 lb	20 lb	25 lb

Gold presently sells for $150 per ounce, silver sells for $5 per ounce, and copper sells for $2 per pound. Eastern is the most accessible vein, requiring 1 man-hour per ton of ore; Northern and Tom's Lucky veins are more remote and require 2 man-hours per ton. Only 300 man-hours are available, and all labor costs are fixed. At least 100 tons must be mined from the Northern vein this week, so that it can be reshored next week; there are no tonnage limitations for the other tunnels. The company must also yield at least 5,000 pounds of copper to meet contractual commitments.

(a) Formulate Grubby's linear program to determine how many tons must be mined from each vein to maximize total revenue.

(b) Find the optimal solution.

11-21 *Computer exercise.* The Flying Chef supplies in-flight dinners to airlines. On a particular run, the passengers are given their choice of beef, chicken, or fish entrees. The owner must decide how many meals of each type to prepare in order to minimize total cost. Historically, 55% of all passengers prefer beef, 30% prefer chicken, and 15% prefer fish. However, to compensate for varying tastes from flight to flight, the number of meals provided must be as great as the above percentages of total passengers. On the current flight, there are 200 passengers and 300 meals must be provided. Airline policy states that at least one-half the extra meals on any given flight must be beef. Costs are $2 for each beef entree, $1.50 for chicken, and $1 for fish.

(a) Formulate the linear program for this problem.

(b) Solve this problem.

(c) How many meals of each type should be provided?

11-22   *Computer exercise.*   Morrie's Thrift Shoppe sells three kinds of suits: used, seconds (rejects

from large clothing manufacturers), and Hong Kong specials. Morrie is buying his stock for the coming season. The used suits yield an average profit of $30 per suit, each second nets $20, and the Hong Kong suits are the most profitable at $50 each. Since Morrie has a 100% markup policy, the preceding figures also represent his wholesale costs. Morrie can spend no more than $10,000 this year. To maintain his "quality" image, not more than one-fourth of his suits can be used suits. Morrie does not wish to be too exotic, so the Hong Kong suits must not outnumber the used and second suits combined. To maintain his factory contacts, Morrie must buy at least 100 seconds each year.

Morrie always sells his entire inventory every year, and he wishes to maximize his total suit profits.

(a) Formulate this problem as a linear program.

(b) Identify any necessary slack and surplus variables separately and solve the problem.

12

Shadow Prices and Duality in Linear Programming

$\mathbb{W}$e have seen how linear programming may be used to solve a variety of profit-maximization or cost-minimization problems. The variables in these applications are generally unknown quantities, such as number of tables, pounds of beef, or dollars spent on television advertising. In production-planning applications, the problem is to determine how much of each product type should be made. An entirely different way to represent the production decision as a linear program will be presented in this chapter.

We know that a linear program actually tells us how scarce resources should be allocated to maximize profits. Now suppose that our primary concern is to determine the most efficient application of the production resources themselves. The focus is on *resources*, rather than on products. Only indirectly related to their accounting costs, each of these has a **shadow price** that reflects the true impact of scarcity. To find these amounts we may look at a wholly different expression of the underlying problem. In effect, we must "cross through the looking glass" into a special mathematical environment that essentially mirrors our ordinary one. In this new linear programming environment, problems are formulated differently but have equivalent solutions. Every ordinary problem has its doppelgänger, which we refer to as the **dual linear program** or, for short, the **dual**.

12-1 Shadow Prices and Opportunity Costs

Let's explore the resource orientation by again evaluating the original Redwood Furniture problem used in earlier chapters. Table 12-1 shows in greater detail than before the essential information regarding that problem. Management must decide the number of tables and chairs to be made that will maximize total profit while not exceeding the available quantities of labor and wood. The unit profits for each item of furniture are determined by subtracting the costs of all resources used. Notice that not all resources appear in the original linear program, just the ones in scarce supply.

Letting X_T and X_C denote the number of tables and chairs to be made, the following linear program applies.

$$\text{Maximize} \quad P = 6X_T + 8X_C$$

$$\text{Subject to} \quad 30X_T + 20X_C \leq 300 \quad \text{(wood)}$$

$$5X_T + 10X_C \leq 110 \quad \text{(labor)}$$

$$\text{where} \quad X_T, X_C \geq 0$$

Denoting by S_W and S_L the slack variables (unused quantities) of wood and labor, the above linear program was solved in Chapter 10. The final simplex tableau in Figure 12-1 was obtained.

The Effect of Raising Unused Resource Quantities

Recall that the improvement row provides the net change in the objective value that would result from a one-unit increase in the variable listed at the top of the tableau. Figure 12-1 thus indicates that increasing S_W by one board foot (from its optimal level of zero) will change P by $-\$1/10$. That is, raising the amount of unused wood by one board foot will decrease P by $\$.10$, the profit dropping from $\$96.00$ to $\$95.90$. And, an increase in unused wood has the same effect as reducing the original amount of available wood (all of

TABLE 12-1
Data Obtained for the Original Redwood Furniture Problem

RESOURCE	Unit Cost	EACH TABLE		EACH CHAIR		Available Quantity
		Amount Required	Product Cost	Amount Required	Product Cost	
Wood	$1/ft	30 ft	$ 30	20 ft	$ 20	300 ft
Labor	$10/hr	5 hrs	50	10 hrs	100	110 hrs
Others	Various	Lots	120	Lots	100	Plentiful
Total cost			$200		$220	
Selling price			$206		$228	
Profit			$6		$8	

FIGURE 12-1

Final simplex tableau for the original Redwood Furniture linear program.

UNIT PROFIT		6	8	0	0	
	Basic Mix	X_T	X_C	S_W	S_L	Sol.
6	X_T	1	0	1/20	−1/10	4
8	X_C	0	1	−1/40	3/20	9
	Sac.	6	8	1/10	6/10	96
	Imp.	0	0	−1/10	−6/10	—

Each unit increase in S_W will change profit by −$1/10.

Each unit increase in S_L will change profit by −$6/10.

which is being used in the above solution). Thus, the net effect of reducing available wood one unit (from 300 board feet to 299 board feet) will be a $.10 reduction in profit.

Figure 12-1 provides a similar interpretation for labor. The improvement value is −6/10 under the S_L column. Thus, increasing S_L from the zero level by one hour changes P by −$6/10. The effect of reducing available labor would therefore be a *decrease* in profit of $.60 for each hour taken away from production.

The Effect of Increasing Available Resource Quantities

If removing one board foot from the used to the unused category will reduce P by $.10 and doing the same for one hour of labor results in a $.60 profit reduction, then how will profit be affected by a one-unit *increase* in each resource?

It seems plausible that more available wood would result in a $.10 *increase* in P for each additional board foot, while more labor would *raise* P by $.60 for each additional hour made available. We can see why this must be so.

Refer to the graphical solution to the Redwood Furniture problem, shown in Figure 12-2. There we can see that increasing the amount of available wood to 301 board feet results in a rightward shift of the wood line, making the feasible solution region wider than before. The intersection of the new wood line with the labor line provides the new most attractive corner, which shifts to the right and downward. This indicates that more tables and fewer chairs should be made than before. To determine the optimal solution exactly, we can simultaneously solve the new wood and original labor constraint equations

$$30X_T + 20X_C = 301 \quad \text{(new wood)}$$

$$5X_T + 10X_C = 110 \quad \text{(original labor)}$$

FIGURE 12-2

The graphical interpretation of the dual variable for the cost of wood.

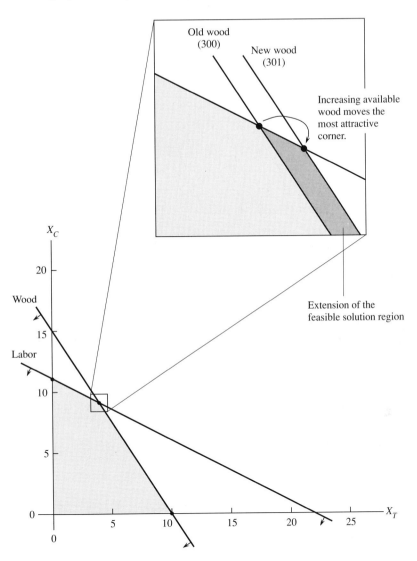

which yields

$$X_T = 4.05$$
$$X_C = 8.975$$

The resulting profit is

$$P = 6(4.05) + 8(8.975)$$
$$= 96.10 \text{ dollars}$$

which is exactly $.10 larger than the maximum profit when only 300 board feet of wood are available.

A similar finding applies to a one-hour increase in available labor. The optimal solution to that linear program may be determined by simultaneously solving the original wood equation and the new labor equation

$$30X_T + 20X_C = 300 \quad \text{(original labor)}$$
$$5X_T + 10X_C = 111 \quad \text{(new labor)}$$

which yields

$$X_T = 3.90$$
$$X_C = 9.15$$

The resulting profit is

$$P = 6(3.90) + 8(9.15)$$
$$= 96.60 \text{ dollars}$$

which is exactly $.60 larger than the maximum profit when only 110 hours of labor are available.

Opportunity Costs

We may refer to the $.10 increase in P resulting from an additional board foot of wood as the **opportunity cost** per unit, since there is opportunity to earn that much more profit by having more wood. Do not confuse this amount with the accounting cost of the wood (given as $1.00 in Table 12-1). The opportunity cost reflects the net effect of the additional board foot, and the usual $1.00 supply cost still applies for the material, which of course could not be obtained for free. Likewise, an additional hour of labor has an opportunity cost of $.60. This is the added profit that would result, even after paying the worker $10 in wages and benefits.

Shadow Prices

The amounts $.10 for wood and $.60 for labor are sometimes referred to as the **shadow prices** for the resources. In effect, the decision maker would improve total profit by paying a premium for wood and labor not exceeding the shadow price. For example, if more wood could be obtained by making a special trip to the mill, at an added cost under $.10 per board foot, then Redwood should do so. Likewise, Redwood would be better off coaxing workers to give more hours as long as the company does not have to pay more than $.60 per hour (beyond the standard $10) as the incentive.

The shadow prices apply to each resource individually, and any change in the available quantity of one resource can bring about changes in the shadow prices of the others. Also, each shadow price is only valid over a limited range of resource levels. Chapter 13 considers how such limits are established.

The Dual Linear Program

From an economic viewpoint, the production decision brings about optimal allocation of resources. This may be achieved by minimizing the opportunity costs (shadow prices) for all scarce resources used in production. From a mathematical viewpoint, this is the result that would be achieved by solving a second linear program, called the *dual*.

In one sense, the original or **primal linear program** is concerned only with operational types of production decisions—determining what quantities of each product should be produced in a given time period. But the dual variables can point out areas that affect longer range decisions. For example, a host of constraints in manufacturing that arise from limited equipment availability or physical size pertain to capacities. The dual linear program for a production-planning decision establishes the opportunity cost of each extra hour of machine time or additional square foot of plant space. The solution to a tactical production problem can therefore provide attractive alternatives to consider in the strategical areas of capital investment. The dual values can indicate critical points where expansion may prove very profitable.

12-2 The Dual Linear Program

The opportunity costs associated with wood and labor depend on how these factors are employed in production. These amounts are variables that will change as the production quantities are themselves shifted. We want to express a linear program that finds levels of the opportunity cost variables that reflect the resources' true worth in accomplishing an underlying production plan. The linear programming objective is to assign these values, so that we

> Minimize C = Total resource opportunity cost
>
>   = Total oppor. cost of wood + Total oppor. cost of labor

This is to be achieved in such a way that the end products—tables and chairs—are never more profitable than the opportunity cost of the resources used to produce them. Each *product* has a constraint of the form

> Opportunity cost of resources per item $\geq$ Profit per item

Such a requirement might seem peculiar at first. After all, how can any production plan be efficient if costs exceed profits? But remember that we are talking about a special kind of cost that *we set ourselves*—not the wholesale price of lumber or the labor wage scale. Our variables are not accounting costs and have nothing to do with payments to lumber mills or to workers. (Those costs are already reflected in the $6 per table and $8 per chair profit figures.)

Let's express our dual linear program in terms of the variables

$$U_W = \text{Wood cost per board foot}$$

$$U_L = \text{Labor cost per hour}$$

Although any letter would suffice, our use of U's to designate the dual variables is traditional. The total resource costs may then be expressed as

Total opportunity cost of wood

= Board feet available × Opportunity cost per board foot

= $300U_W$

Total opportunity cost of labor

= Hours available × Opportunity cost per hour

= $110U_L$

The objective function may then be expressed as

$$\text{Minimize} \quad C = 300U_W + 110U_L \quad \text{(objective)}$$

Table 12-1 tells us that each table requires 30 board feet of wood and 5 hours of labor. In terms of the unknown cost variables,

$$30U_W = \text{Opportunity cost of wood per table}$$

$$5U_L = \text{Opportunity cost of labor per table}$$

so that

$$30U_W + 5U_L = \text{Opportunity cost of resources per table}$$

The table constraint

Opportunity cost of resources per table ≥ Profit per table

is then

$$30U_W + 5U_L \geq 6 \quad \text{(table)}$$

Likewise, since a chair requires 20 board feet of wood and 10 hours of labor, the chair constraint is

Opportunity cost of resources per chair ≥ Profit per chair

$$20U_W + 10U_L \geq 8 \quad \text{(chair)}$$

Since the worth of a resource can never be negative, non-negativity conditions apply to U_W and U_L.

The Primal and the Dual

Before we solve the dual and interpret it further let's see how it directly relates to the original Redwood Furniture problem, for which the variables were quantities of tables and chairs. The original linear program is called the **primal** to distinguish it from its dual. The primal and the dual linear programs for the Redwood Furniture problem are outlined in Table 12-2.

Notice that the two programs are arranged similarly. The exchange coefficients of the two problems arranged as matrices are

$$
\begin{array}{cc}
\text{PRIMAL} & \text{DUAL} \\[4pt]
\begin{pmatrix} 30 & 20 \\ 5 & 10 \end{pmatrix} & \begin{pmatrix} 30 & 5 \\ 20 & 10 \end{pmatrix}
\end{array}
$$

Note that the rows of the dual coefficients are the columns of the primal coefficients and that the columns of the dual are the rows of the primal. We refer to one matrix as the *transpose* of the other. The coefficients of the objective of the primal linear program appear as the right-hand sides of the dual constraints, and the right-hand sides of the primal constraints provide the objective coefficients for the dual. In effect, the position of every constraint in the dual is exactly what we would obtain by rotating the primal 90° counterclockwise when the P equation is written last and then resequencing the inequalities.

The objective of the primal problem is to maximize P. The objective of the dual is the opposite—to minimize C. The primal constraints are $\le$ inequalities; the dual constraints are $\ge$ inequalities. One linear program is the transpose of the other with totally opposite objective and constraint orientations. (In effect, the primal itself is the "dual" of the dual.)

A fundamental fact of linear programming is that for any feasible respective solutions to the dual and primal

$$C \ge P$$

TABLE 12-2
Primal and Dual Linear Programs for the Redwood Furniture Problem

PRIMAL PROGRAM	DUAL PROGRAM
X_T = Number of tables	U_W = Wood oppor. cost per board foot
X_C = Number of chairs	U_L = Labor oppor. cost per hour
Maximize	Minimize
$P = 6X_T + 8X_C$	$C = 300U_W + 110U_L$
Subject to	Subject to
$30X_T + 20X_C \le 300$ (wood)	$30U_W + 5U_L \ge 6$ (table)
$5X_T + 10X_C \le 110$ (labor)	$20U_W + 10U_L \ge 8$ (chair)
where $X_T, X_C \ge 0$	where $U_W, U_L \ge 0$

Further, the objective value in both problems is identical for the respective optimal solutions. Thus,

$$\text{Minimum } C = \text{Maximum } P$$

so that the smallest possible cost is equal to the maximum possible profit. We will learn the importance of this feature later.

Solving the Dual Graphically

The dual linear program for the Redwood Furniture problem is solved graphically in Figure 12-3. Since the most attractive corner lies at the intersection of the table and chair

FIGURE 12-3
The graphical solution to the dual for the Redwood Furniture problem.

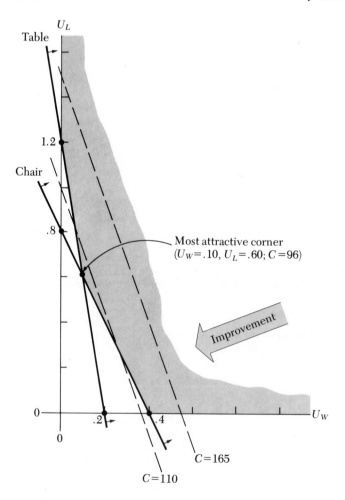

constraint lines, the simultaneous solution of these equations provides

$$U_W = \$.10 \text{ per board foot}$$
$$U_L = \$.60 \text{ per hour}$$

and the minimum value of the objective function is

$$C = 300(.10) + 110(.60)$$
$$= 96 \text{ dollars}$$

This is the figure that we originally obtained in Chapter 8 for the maximum profit of the primal linear program.

12-3 Solving the Dual Linear Program with Simplex

Like any other linear program, the dual can be solved using simplex. The surplus variables are

$$U_T = \text{Surplus table opportunity cost beyond unit profit}$$
$$U_C = \text{Surplus chair opportunity cost beyond unit profit}$$

for the table and chair constraints, respectively. (Two artificial variables are also required in the basic variable mix.)

The final simplex tableaus for the dual and for the primal are shown in Figure 12-4 (where, for clarity, the artificial variable columns have been removed).

The final primal improvement row gives us the optimal values of the dual variables with their signs reversed. The optimal dual surplus variable values can be found in the same per-unit improvement row under X_T and X_C.

This illustrates an amazing fact. *Whenever simplex is used to solve the primal linear program, it simultaneously provides the solution to the dual.* Indeed, the simplex solution to the dual provides the optimal primal values as well. Looking at the per-unit improvement row in the dual tableau, we find a 4 under U_T and a 9 under U_C. These happen to be the optimal number of tables and chairs for the primal. Likewise, the zero improvements under U_W and U_L are the optimal values of the primal slacks for wood and labor, which have values of $S_W = 0$ and $S_L = 0$.

As a matter of fact, *the primal and the dual final simplex tableaus contain exactly the same information.* The same exchange coefficients for the nonbasic variable columns are present in each tableau with reversed signs and in transposed positions (the columns of one are the rows of the other), reflecting the same kind of transposition in the initial formulations. This means that simplex can be used to solve either the dual or the primal linear programming problem first. Only a small amount of extra work is required to construct the final tableau to the other problem.

FIGURE 12-4

Final primal and dual simplex tableaus for the Redwood Furniture problem.

FINAL PRIMAL TABLEAU

UNIT PROFIT		6	8	0	0		
	Basic Mix	X_T	X_C	S_W	S_L	Sol.	
6	X_T	1	0	1/20	$-1/10$	4	Nonbasic:
8	X_C	0	1	$-1/40$	3/20	9	$S_W = 0$
							$S_L = 0$
	Sac.	6	8	1/10	6/10	96	
	Imp.	0	0	$-1/10$	$-6/10$	—	
		$-U_T$	$-U_C$	$-U_W$	$-U_L$		

FINAL DUAL TABLEAU

OBJECTIVE COEFFICIENT		300	110	0	0		
	Basic Mix	U_W	U_L	U_T	U_C	Sol.	
300	U_W	1	0	$-1/20$	1/40	.10	Nonbasic:
110	U_L	0	1	1/10	$-3/20$	.60	$U_T = 0$
							$U_C = 0$
	Sac.	300	110	-4	-9	96	
	Imp.	0	0	4	9	—	
		S_W	S_L	X_T	X_C		

12-4 Complementary Slackness

We have carefully chosen the variable subscripts in the Redwood Furniture problem so that it is immediately apparent what each variable represents. We have accomplished this by using the first letter in the word for the respective item as the subscript. Table 12-3 summarizes the optimal solution values for the primal and dual programs.

One interesting feature is that the product of the optimal primal and dual variables is zero for each item.

$$X_T U_T = \quad 4 \times 0 = 0$$

$$X_C U_C = \quad 9 \times 0 = 0$$

$$S_W U_W = 0 \times .10 = 0$$

$$S_L U_L = 0 \times .60 = 0$$

This result illustrates the **principle of complementary slackness**.

TABLE 12-3

Correspondence between Primal and Dual Solutions

ITEM	VARIABLE TYPE	
	Primal Quantity	Dual Cost
Product	Main	Surplus
Table	$X_T = 4$ (tables)	$U_T = 0$ ($/table)
Chair	$X_C = 9$ (chairs)	$U_C = 0$ ($/chair)
Resource	Slack	Main
Wood	$S_W = 0$ (board feet)	$U_W = .10$ ($/board foot)
Labor	$S_L = 0$ (hours)	$U_L = .60$ ($/hour)

As its name implies, complementary slackness relates the optimal value of slack or surplus variables to their counterpart main variables in the opposite problem. If one primal constraint involves positive slack, so that the constraint is *not binding* on the optimal solution, then all of the underlying resource is not being used and must have an opportunity cost of zero (having more of the resource will not improve profits). But if that constraint has zero slack, so that it is *binding*, then all of the resource is being used and should have a positive opportunity cost (more of the resource will improve profit by allowing greater production). Since resources are represented by slack variables in the primal and by main cost variables in the dual, this principle states that the following must hold for every resource.

$$\text{Primal slack} \times \text{Dual main} = 0$$

A similar argument applies for each product made. When no items are produced, this implies that the resources necessary to make these items can be better employed elsewhere; that is, the opportunity cost of those resources exceeds the unit profit of that product, so that there is surplus product opportunity cost. But if some of the product is made, then the opportunity costs of its resources must equal its unit profit (the resources are just as valuable when they are employed this way as they would be if they were used any other way), so that the surplus product cost is zero. Production quantities are primal main variables, and surplus product costs are dual surplus variables. Complementary slackness therefore indicates that for every product item

$$\text{Primal main} \times \text{Dual surplus} = 0$$

An important value of the complementary slackness principle is that it adds further meaning to duality. But it has practical application in linear programming algorithms other than simplex. For certain types of problems, these solution procedures are faster and more efficient than simplex. Complementary slackness can also be helpful in obtaining the primal linear programming solution when only the dual solution is known.

12-5 Evaluating New Variables Using the Dual

Suppose that Redwood Furniture is considering the manufacture of two additional products—benches and planter boxes. We will assume that the benches yield a per-unit profit of $7 and the planter boxes yield a per-unit profit of only $2. We will further assume that a bench requires 25 board feet of wood and 7 hours of labor and a planter box only consumes 10 board feet of wood and 2 hours of labor.

We can use the dual values we found earlier for wood and labor to determine if it is even worthwhile to consider these new products. For the benches, the opportunity cost of the resources used is

$$\text{Opportunity cost of one bench} = 25U_W + 7U_L$$
$$= 25(\$.10) + 7(\$.60) = \$6.70$$

This means that resources currently earning $6.70 in profits with tables and chairs must be diverted from those products in order to make one bench. Since that amount is less than the profit of $7 per bench, benches should be made. A similar calculation shows that each planter box consumes resources at an opportunity cost of $2.20, which exceeds the per-unit profit of $2.00. Planter boxes should therefore not be made, since the resources that would be consumed to produce them can be used more profitably elsewhere.

12-6 Solving the Primal from the Dual

The above analysis does not tell us how many benches to make. To determine this, we must solve the expanded linear program. Letting X_B represent the unknown quantity of benches to be produced, the primal linear program is

$$\text{Maximize} \quad P = \quad 6X_T + \quad 8X_C + \quad 7X_B$$

Subject to

$$U_W: \qquad 30X_T + 20X_C + 25X_B \leq 300 \quad \text{(wood)}$$
$$U_L: \qquad 5X_T + 10X_C + \quad 7X_B \leq 110 \quad \text{(labor)}$$

where $\qquad\qquad X_T, X_C, X_B \geq \quad 0$

Since this program has three main variables, simplex is required. However, the dual for this problem has only two main variables and can be solved graphically. (Since the original linear program is expanded, the previous values $U_W = .10$ and $U_L = .60$ no longer apply.) The dual for the expanded problem is

$$\text{Minimize} \quad C = 300U_W + 110U_L$$

Subject to
$$30U_W + \quad 5U_L \geq 6 \quad \text{(table)}$$
$$20U_W + \quad 10U_L \geq 8 \quad \text{(chair)}$$
$$25U_W + \quad 7U_L \geq 7 \quad \text{(bench)}$$

where $\qquad\qquad U_W, U_L \geq 0$

This dual is solved graphically in Figure 12-5. The optimal solution is represented by the intersection of the bench and chair lines. The simultaneous solution of the respective constraint equations yields

$$U_W = \frac{7}{55} \quad \text{and} \quad U_L = \frac{30}{55}$$

with a cost of

$$C = 300\left(\frac{7}{55}\right) + 110\left(\frac{30}{55}\right) = \frac{1,080}{11}$$

The dual constraints may be expressed in equation form by including surplus variables for the three constraints. Denoting by U_T, U_C, and U_B the respective surplus opportunity costs of the resources used to make one table, one chair, and one bench, the equations are

$$30U_W + \ 5U_L - 1U_T + 0U_C + 0U_B = 6 \quad \text{(table)}$$
$$20U_W + 10U_L + 0U_T - 1U_C + 0U_B = 8 \quad \text{(chair)}$$
$$25U_W + \ 7U_L + 0U_T + 0U_C - 1U_B = 7 \quad \text{(bench)}$$

FIGURE 12-5
The graphical solution to the dual for the expanded Redwood Furniture problem.

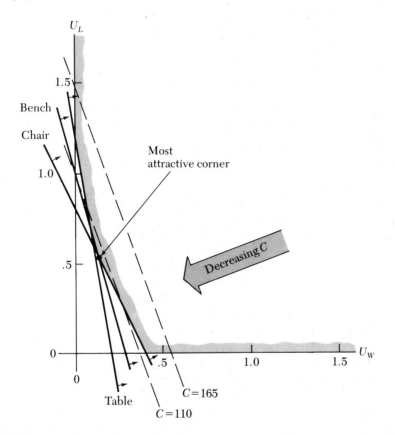

Plugging the optimal values found from the graphical solution into the table equation and solving for U_T, the following value is obtained.

$$U_T = 30\left(\frac{7}{55}\right) + 5\left(\frac{30}{55}\right) - 6 = \frac{30}{55}$$

Similarly, it follows that

$$U_C = 0 \quad \text{and} \quad U_B = 0$$

Consider, again, the original primal problem. If the slack variables are included in the original constraints, these may be expressed in equation form as

$$30X_T + 20X_C + 25X_B + 1S_W + 0S_L = 300 \quad \text{(wood)}$$
$$5X_T + 10X_C + 7X_B + 0S_W + 1S_L = 110 \quad \text{(labor)}$$

The above cannot be solved directly since there are 5 variables and only 2 equations. But knowledge gleaned from the dual will allow us to eliminate the three "extra" variables. By the principle of complementary slackness, it follows that

$$X_T = 0 \quad \text{since } U_T > 0$$
$$X_C \geq 0 \quad \text{since } U_C = 0$$
$$X_B \geq 0 \quad \text{since } U_B = 0$$
$$S_W = 0 \quad \text{since } U_W > 0$$
$$S_L = 0 \quad \text{since } U_L > 0$$

Thus, the three "extra" primal variables are X_T, S_W, and S_L. These may be zeroed out of the equations, leaving

$$30(0) + 20X_C + 25X_B + 1(0) + 0(0) = 300$$
$$5(0) + 10X_C + 7X_B + 0(0) + 1(0) = 110$$

providing

$$20X_C + 25X_B = 300$$
$$10X_C + 7X_B = 110$$

The simultaneous solution is thus $X_C = 65/11$ and $X_B = 80/11$. The solution to the primal problem is

$$X_T = 0 \text{ tables}$$
$$X_C = 65/11 \text{ chairs}$$
$$X_B = 80/11 \text{ benches}$$

and the maximum profit is

$$P = 6(0) + 8\left(\frac{65}{11}\right) + 7\left(\frac{80}{11}\right) = \frac{1,080}{11}$$

which is identical to the minimum C found for the dual.

12-7 Dual for a Generalized Linear Program

The examples of the dual presented thus far involve production type problems where all constraints pertain to resource availabilities. In a more general context, each constraint in the primal corresponds to a dual variable, even if the constraint involves a non-resource restriction, such as quantity or mixture requirements. In general, for the kth primal constraint in a profit-maximization problem, the dual variable is defined as

$U_k =$ Opportunity cost per one-unit increase in the
right-hand side of constraint k

Now, suppose that we revive the requirement that there be at least 4 chairs for every table. This states that

$$X_C \geq 4X_T$$

Rearranging the terms, the above may be equivalently expressed as

$$U_M: \qquad 4X_T - X_C \leq 0 \quad \text{(mixture)}$$

Denoting by U_M the dual variable that corresponds,

$U_M =$ Opportunity cost per one-unit increase (beyond 0)
in the allowable mixture combination

If the optimal dual solution were to yield $U_M = .50$, then profit would increase by \$.50 if the allowable difference were raised by 1, so that $4X_T - X_C = 1$. An extra one-fourth of a table would improve profitability by that amount.

The examples of the dual encountered thus far involve a linear program having a *regular form*, in which, for a maximization primal, all the constraints are of the $\leq$ type. But linear programs may have a more general form, with constraints of the $\geq$ and $=$ types, as well as $\leq$'s. The dual linear program corresponding to such a problem will have non-standard features.

To illustrate, consider the further expansion of the Redwood Furniture problem, now involving quantity variables for three table models—small (X_{TS}), regular (X_{TR}), and large (X_{TL}); two chair types—standard (X_{CS}) and armed (X_{CA}); and two bookcase sizes—short (X_{BS}) and tall (X_{BT}). Figure 12-6 shows how the primal and dual relate in the more general

FIGURE 12-6

FIGURE 12-6

Relationship between the general primal linear program and its dual for the expanded Redwood Furniture problem.

PRODUCT

	Obj. Coeff.	Main Var.	Sign	Obj. Coeff.: Main Variable: Sign:	Small Tables 5 X_{TS} +	Regular Tables 6 X_{TR} +	Large Tables 7 X_{TL} +	Standard Chairs 6 X_{CS} +	Armed Chairs 10 X_{CA} +	Short Bkcases. 8 X_{BS} +	Tall Bkcases. 6 X_{BT} +	Type	PRIMAL (Max. P) Right-hand Side	
R	3,000	U_W	+	Wood	20	30	40	15	25	20	30	≤	3,000	R
E	1,100	U_L	+	Labor	4	5	6	8	12	6	8	≤	1,100	E
Q	250	U_M	+	Machine Time	2	2	2	3	3	2	2	≤	250	Q
U	30	U_{QT}	–	Qty. Tables	1	1	1					≥	30	U
I	20	U_{QC}	–	Qty. Chairs				1	1			≥	20	I
R	20	U_{QB}	–	Qty. Bkcases.						1	1	≥	20	R
E	0	U_{MT}	±	Mix, Tables	1	–1	–1					=	0	E
M	0	U_{MC}	±	Mix, Chairs				1	–4			=	0	M
E	0	U_{MB}	±	Mix, Bkcases.						1	–1	=	0	E
N														N
T														T
	DUAL (Min. C)			Constr. Type: Right-hand Side:	≥ 5	≥ 6	≥ 7	≥ 6	≥ 10	≥ 8	≥ 6			

PRODUCT

context. The need for special treatment occurs with the ≥ and = constraint types. The orientation of those requirements gives rise to counterpart dual variables which might be *negative*, so that the usual non-negativity conditions only partially reign.

Consider the quantity requirement for tables. There must be at least 30 tables altogether, and the following applies.

$$U_{QT}: \qquad 1X_{TS} + 1X_{TR} + 1X_{TL} \geq 30 \quad \text{(quantity, tables)}$$

The dual linear program has a variable, denoted by U_{QT}, for this requirement. This variable may be defined as follows.

$$U_{QT} = \text{Opportunity cost per one-unit increase in the} \\ \text{minimum table quantity}$$

Raising the right-hand side from 30 to 31 will reduce production scheduling freedom. Such diminished flexibility cannot increase profitability, so that P would at best remain unchanged and might actually *decrease* when the right-hand side is 31 tables. (This is the opposite effect to raising the right-hand side in the wood constraint from 3,000 to 3,001, which would make production more flexible and which would either *increase* profit or leave it unchanged.)

Thus, U_{QT} cannot be positive (but may be zero). The dual linear program will have the requirement

$$U_{QT} \leq 0$$

Such a **non-positivity condition** applies for any dual variable that corresponds to a $\geq$ restriction in the primal *maximization* problem.* In the expanded Redwood Furniture problem, $\geq$ constraints also occur for the chair and bookcase quantity constraints, since each has a *minimum* requirement. The corresponding dual variables are U_{QC} and U_{QB}, for which the following must hold.

$$U_{QC} \leq 0 \quad \text{and} \quad U_{QB} \leq 0$$

The impact on P of a right-hand side change for a strict equality ($=$) constraint is not so clear-cut. Consider, from Figure 12-6, the mixture constraint for tables.

$$U_{MT}: \qquad 1X_{TS} - 1X_{TR} - 1X_{TL} = 0 \quad \text{(mix, tables)}$$

This stipulates that a mix of tables be met such that the number of small tables is *exactly* equal to the total number of the other two types. The dual variable is

$$U_{MT} = \text{Opportunity cost per one-unit increase (beyond 0)}$$
$$\text{in the table mix}$$

Raising the allowable difference to 1 could increase P, decrease P, or leave P unchanged. That determination cannot be made until the dual linear program has been solved. For now, we can only state that U_{MT} is *unrestricted as to sign*. Defining analogously the dual variables for the remaining constraints, the complete formulated dual is as follows.

Minimize $\quad C$

$$= 3{,}000U_W + 1{,}100U_L + 250U_M + 30U_{QT} + 20U_{QC} + 20U_{QB} + 0U_{MT} + 0U_{MC} + 0U_{MB}$$

Subject to

$20U_W + 4U_L + 2U_M + 1U_{QT}$	$+1U_{MT}$	≥ 5	(small tables)
$30U_W + 5U_L + 2U_M + 1U_{QT}$	$-1U_{MT}$	≥ 6	(reg. tables)
$40U_W + 6U_L + 2U_M + 1U_{QT}$	$-1U_{MT}$	≥ 7	(large tables)
$15U_W + 8U_L + 3U_M \quad +1U_{QC}$	$+1U_{MC}$	≥ 6	(stand. chairs)
$25U_W + 12U_L + 3U_M \quad +1U_{QC}$	$-4U_{MC}$	≥ 10	(armed chairs)
$20U_W + 6U_L + 2U_M \qquad\quad +1U_{QB}$	$+1U_{MB}$	≥ 8	(sh. bkcases.)
$30U_W + 8U_L + 2U_M \qquad\quad +1U_{QB}$	$-1U_{MB}$	≥ 6	(tall bkcases.)

where
$$U_W, U_L, U_M \geq 0 \quad \text{(non-neg.)}$$
$$U_{QT}, U_{QC}, U_{QB} \leq 0 \quad \text{(non-pos.)}$$

And U_{MT}, U_{MC}, and U_{MB} are unrestricted as to sign.

---

* As we shall see shortly, the usual non-negativity is the case for a $\geq$ restriction when the primal is to minimize C.

FIGURE 12-7

Summary of the formulation requirements for passing from the primal to the dual.

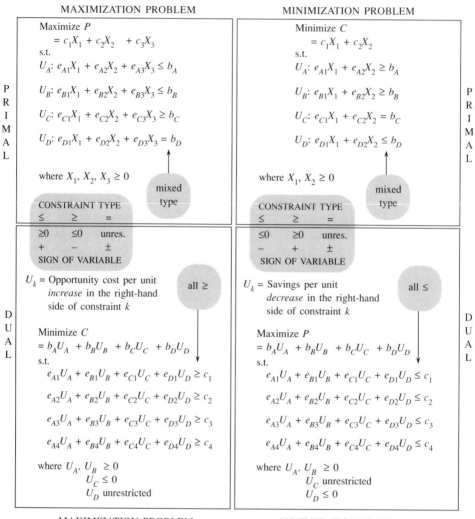

Figure 12-7 summarizes the formulation requirements for obtaining the dual. (Section 12-9 describes in detail the case when the primal is a minimization problem.)

Solving the Dual for the Generalized Case

The optimal solution to the dual may be obtained by using simplex to solve the primal problem. The optimal U's may then be read from the improvement row entry in the corresponding column. Consider the *QuickQuant* screen in Figure 12-8 that shows the final iteration for the expanded Redwood Furniture problem. As before, the U values appear in the improvement row with opposite signs. The U's for $\geq$ and $=$ constraints are read from the corresponding primal *artificial* variable columns, ignoring the M terms.

Recall that the dual variables indicate how much profit will rise per one-unit *increase* in the right-hand side of the corresponding primal constraint. Since the dual solutions are $U_W = 0$ and $U_L = 0$ for wood and labor, no additional wood or labor will improve the final profit. The result $U_M = 3.5$ for machine time shows that increased machine time would improve profit by $3.50 per hour obtained beyond what is currently available.

The dual variables for $\geq$ constraints will be zero or negative. The result $U_{QT} = -1$, applicable to the table quantity restriction, indicates that profit would be reduced by $1.00 for each increase in the total number of tables required; the reverse effect applies for a reduction in the minimum number of tables. For example, reducing the table demand from 30 to 25 (an "increase" of -5 tables) will change profit by $(-\$1.00) \times (-5) = +\$5.00$. Similarly, the result $U_{QC} = -3.7$ expresses a potential worsening of profit by $3.70 per one-unit increase in the minimum number of chairs; conversely, reducing the required number of chairs will improve profit by that amount. The value $U_{QB} = 0$ signifies that increasing (or reducing) the minimum for bookcases will have no effect on profit.

The interpretation of the dual for $=$ constraints is similar to the above. But the solution values can be positive or negative. Consider the table mix requirement, for which $U_{MT} = -1.0$. Raising the right-hand side of the primal constraint from 0 to 1, so that the allowable difference in table quantities becomes

$$X_{TS} - X_{TR} - X_{TL} = 1$$

will reduce the optimal P by $1.00. (And, lowering the right-hand side to -1 will increase P by $1.00.) A similar finding applies to the chair mix, for which $U_{MC} = -.8$, with P decreasing or increasing by $.80 for each rise or fall in the chair difference. For bookcases, the result $U_{MB} = 1.0$ is positive, so that raising the mix difference from 0 to 1 will improve profit by $1.00.

Solving the Dual Directly

Although the solution to the dual appears in the final simplex tableau when the primal is solved, a direct solution may involve computation efficiencies. Unfortunately, when the dual involves a mixture of non-negativity and non-positivity conditions, plus unrestricted variables, the simplex algorithm (as described in this book) cannot be used. That obstacle can be overcome by first reexpressing the primal in a regular form, so that the dual will have non-negative variables only. That is a cumbersome task, and it can be tricky to properly translate the simplex solution.

FIGURE 12-8

Annotated composite *QuickQuant* screen showing the final simplex tableau for the expanded Redwood Furniture problem.

			1	2	3	4	5	6	7	8	9
PROBLEM: Redwood Furniture (Expanded)										S_N	S_L
UNIT P,C			5	6	7	6	10	8	6	0	0
	Basic		1	2	3	4	5	6	7	8	9
	Mix		XTS	XTR	XTL	XCS	XCA	XBS	XBT	S1	S2
0	S1		0	-10	0	0	0	0	0	1	0
0	S2		0	-1	0	0	0	0	0	0	1
0	S6		0	0	0	0	0	0	0	0	0
7	XTL		0	1	1	0	0	0	0	0	0
10	XCA		0	0	0	0	1	0	0	0	0
6	XBT		0	0	0	0	0	0	1	0	0
5	XTS		1	0	0	0	0	0	0	0	0
6	XCS		0	0	0	1	0	0	0	0	0
8	XBS		0	0	0	0	0	1	0	0	0
	Sac.		5	7	7	6	10	8	6	0	0
	Imp.		0	-1	0	0	0	0	0	0	0

$U_N = 0$ $U_L = 0$

These columns provide dual surplus (slack) variable values.

12-8 Computer Applications and the Dual

When large linear programs are solved on a computer, the solution to the dual is often provided as part of the standard output. It is therefore not usually necessary to actually examine the improvement row of the final simplex tableau.

QuickQuant provided the following solution to this expanded Redwood Furniture problem.

Original Variable	Value	Slack/Surplus Variable	Value
XTS	15.00000	S1	135.00000
XTR	0.00000	S2	319.00000
XTL	15.00000	S3	0.00000
XCS	16.00000	S4	0.00000
XCA	4.00000	S5	0.00000
XBS	32.50000	S6	45.00000
XBT	32.50000		

Objective Value: P = 771.00000

QuickQuant provides the dual solution from the simplex tableau. A portion of the report for the expanded Redwood Furniture problem is given on the following page.

FIGURE 12-8 (*continued*)

S_M	S_{QT}	S_{QC}	S_{QB}	a_{QT}	a_{QC}	a_{QB}	a_{MT}	a_{MC}	a_{MB}	
0	0	0	0	-M	-M	-M	-M	-M	-M	
10	**11**	**12**	**13**	**14**	**15**	**16**	**17**	**18**	**19**	
S3	S4	S5	S6	a4	a5	a6	a7	a8	a9	Solution
-12.5	5	-20.5	0	-5	20.5	0	10	2	5	135
-3.5	-2	-1.7	0	2	1.7	0	1	.8000002	1	319
.5	1	1.5	1	-1	-1.5	-1	0	0	0	45
0	-.5	0	0	.5	0	0	-.5	0	0	15
0	0	-.2	0	0	.2	0	0	-.2	0	4
.25	.5	.75	0	-.5	-.75	0	0	0	-.5	32.5
0	-.5	0	0	.5	0	0	.5	0	0	15
0	0	-.8	0	0	.8	0	0	.2	0	16
.25	.5	.75	0	-.5	-.75	0	0	0	.5	32.5
3.5	1	3.7	0	-1	-3.7	0	-1	-.8000001	1	771
				-1M	-1M	-1M	-1M	-1M	-1M	
-3.5	-1	-3.7	0	1	3.7	0	1	.8000001	-1	--

$U_M = 3.5$ — Use artificial columns — $U_{QT} = -1$ $U_{QC} = -3.7$ $U_{QB} = 0$ $U_{MT} = -1$ $U_{MC} = -.80$ $U_{MB} = 1$

Note: Dual variable values appear in improvement row within column of slack or artificial variable, with signs reversed.
Ignore the M term.

Constraint Number	Type	Auxiliary Variable	Value of Dual Variable	
1	$\leq$	S1=135.00000	0.00000	(**wood**)
2	$\leq$	S2=319.00000	0.00000	(**labor**)
3	$\leq$	S3= 0.00000	3.50000	(**mach. t.**)
4	$\geq$	S4= 0.00000	-1.00000	(**qty. tab.**)
5	$\geq$	S5= 0.00000	-3.70000	(**qty. ch.**)
6	$\geq$	S6= 45.00000	0.00000	(**qty. bk.**)
7	=	a7= 0.00000	-1.00000	(**mix tab.**)
8	=	a8= 0.00000	- .80000	(**mix ch.**)
9	=	a9= 0.00000	1.00000	(**mix bk.**)

12-9 Dual for a Cost-Minimization Primal

The dual linear program can be found for a cost-minimization primal. The standard form of the dual is reversed to reflect the opposite orientation. The variables are defined differently.

$$U_k = \text{Savings per one-unit } \textit{reduction} \text{ in right-hand side of constraint } k$$

Feed-Mix Problem

To see how to find and use the dual for a cost-minimization problem, consider the wild birdseed problem originally presented in Chapter 8. Letting X_B and X_S denote the pounds of buckwheat and sunflower wheat to be included in the final mix, the primal linear program is as follows.

$$\text{Minimize} \quad C = .18X_B + .10X_S$$

Subject to

$$U_F: \qquad .04X_B + .06X_S \geq \quad 480 \quad \text{(fat)}$$

$$U_P: \qquad .12X_B + .10X_S \geq 1,200 \quad \text{(protein)}$$

$$U_R: \qquad .10X_B + .15X_S \leq 1,500 \quad \text{(roughage)}$$

$$\text{where} \qquad\qquad\qquad X_B, X_S \geq \quad 0$$

The dual linear program is found in the usual way, but the orientation is maximization and the inequalities are of the $\leq$ type.

$$\text{Maximize} \quad P = 480U_F + 1,200U_P + 1,500U_R$$

$$\text{Subject to} \qquad .04U_F + \quad .12U_P + \quad .10U_R \leq .18 \quad \text{(buckwheat)}$$

$$.06U_F + \quad .10U_P + \quad .15U_R \leq .10 \quad \text{(sunflower)}$$

$$\text{where} \qquad\qquad\qquad U_F, U_P \geq 0 \quad \text{and} \quad U_R \leq 0$$

The variables are defined as follows.

U_F = Savings resulting from a one-pound reduction in minimum fat quantity requirement

U_P = Savings resulting from a one-pound reduction in minimum protein quantity requirement

U_R = Savings resulting from a one-pound reduction in maximum roughage quantity requirement

The dual constraints express the requirement that the per-pound savings in the relaxation of requirements not exceed the cost per pound of the respective ingredient.
The solution to the dual is

$$U_F = 0$$

$$U_P = 2.125$$

$$U_R = -.75$$

$$C = 1,425 \text{ dollars}$$

which indicates that there would be no cost advantage to reducing the minimum fat requirement, but that lowering the minimum protein requirement by one pound would

FIGURE 12-9

Annotated composite *QuickQuant* screen showing the final simplex tableau for the feed-mix problem.

PROBLEM: Feed-Mix Problem		S_F	S_P	S_R	a_F	a_P	
UNIT P,C .18	.1	0	0	0	M	M	

	Basic	1	2	3	4	5	6	7	
	Mix	XB	XS	S1	S2	S3	a1	a2	Solution
.1	1 XS	0	1	0	12.5	15	0	-12.5	7500
.18	2 XB	1	0	0	-18.75	-12.5	0	18.75	3750.001
0	3 S1	0	0	1	0.56E-07	.4	-1	-.56E-07	120
	4								
	5								
	6								
	7								
	8								
	9								
	Sac.	.18	.1	0	-2.125	-.7499999	0	2.125	1425
	Imp.	0	0	0	2.125	.7499999	1M 0	1M -2.125	--

Read artificial columns. $U_R = -.75$ $U_F = 0$ $U_M = 2.125$

save \$2.125 in the overall batch cost. The value $U_R = -.75$ indicates that there would be a negative savings from reducing the maximum roughage content. This means that the cost savings would be \$.75 per *extra* pound that might be allowed for maximum roughage weight.

Notice that the *signs of the dual variables are reversed* from what they would be when the primal is a maximization problem. Refer to Figure 12-7 for a complete summary of the dual formulation requirements.

As with a maximization problem, the dual solution may be extracted from the improvement row of the final simplex tableau for the primal problem. Figure 12-9 shows the final screen for the feed-mix problem obtained using *QuickQuant*. There, the solution of the dual is annotated.

CASE

Swatville Sluggers II

Swatville Sluggers is a small manufacturer of baseball bats handmade from high quality 3-by-3-inch blocks of wood. The following linear programming data were entered into a computer to establish optimal April production quantities of the various sizes. (The subscripts refer to the bat length in inches.) The times are in minutes, and the volumes of stain and varnish are in ounces.

CONSTRAINT	SIZE OF BAT						Available Quantity
	X_{30}	X_{32}	X_{34}	X_{36}	X_{38}	X_{40}	
Wood	30	32	34	36	38	40	≤ 12,000
Lathe time	10	10	11	11	12	12	≤ 6,000
Finishing time	25	27	29	31	33	35	≤ 7,000
Boxes	1	1	1	1	1	1	≤ 1,000
Stain	2	2	2	3	3	3	≤ 1,500
Varnish	5	5	6	6	10	10	≤ 3,000
Restriction 1	−1	−1	1	0	0	0	≤ 0
Restriction 2	0	−1	−1	0	1	0	≤ 0
Restriction 3	1	0	0	−1	−1	0	≤ 0

The following cost data apply to the resources used in making bats.

Wood cost per inch	$.12
Lathe cost per minute	.06
Finishing cost per minute	.03
Box cost	.50
Stain cost per ounce	.25
Varnish cost per ounce	.20

The above costs differ from the March figures (in Chapter 10). The larger bats now get an extra coat of varnish, and the available quantities of the resources have changed. Also, the selling prices have been revised for April. These are $22 for 30″ and 32″ bats, $24 for 34″ and 36″ versions, and $28 for the 38″ and 40″ lengths. Other direct costs are now higher, $3 per bat, regardless of model.

   The owner, George Herman "Sultan" Swat, and his nephew, Babe, want to know where to expand supplies, inventories, and functional capacities. He would also like to know whether it would be profitable to add to the product mix.

Questions

1. Determine the unit profit for each bat. Then, formulate the primal linear program in regular form.

2. Formulate the dual linear program for Swat's decision problem.

3. Letting S_W, S_L, S_F, S_B, S_S, S_V, S_1, S_2, and S_3 denote the respective primal slack variables, the following final simplex tableau (with missing borders) applies.
   (a) State the solution to the primal linear program.
   (b) Complete the unit profit row and column. Then, compute the entries for the sacrifice and improvement rows.

(c) Determine, from your completed tableau, the optimal values for the dual main variables.
(d) What is the maximum premium that Swat would pay (beyond standard cost) for one more unit of (1) wood, (2) lathe time, and (3) finishing time?

Basic Mix	X_{30}	X_{12}	X_{34}	X_{36}	X_{38}	X_{40}	S_W	S_L	S_F	S_B	S_S	S_V	S_1	S_2	S_3	Sol.
S_W	0	.3448	0	.3448	0	−1.0345	1	0	−1.1724	0	0	0	0	0.0000	−.6897	3793.10
S_L	0	−.2414	0	−.2414	0	−1.2759	0	1	−.3793	0	0	0	0	0.0000	−.5172	3344.83
X_{30}	1	−.0230	0	−.3563	0	.4023	0	0	.0115	0	0	0	0	.3333	.7126	80.46
S_B	0	.0690	0	.0690	0	−.2069	0	0	−.0345	1	0	0	0	0.0000	−.1379	758.62
S_S	0	.1609	0	.4943	0	.1839	0	0	−.0805	0	1	0	0	−.3333	.0115	936.78
S_V	0	−.5172	0	−2.5172	0	1.5517	0	0	−.2414	0	0	1	0	−1.0000	1.0345	1310.34
X_{34}	0	.9770	1	.6437	0	.4023	0	0	.0115	0	0	0	0	−.6667	−.2874	80.46
X_{38}	0	−.0230	0	.6437	1	.4023	0	0	.0115	0	0	0	0	.3333	−.2874	80.46
S_1	0	−2.0000	0	−1.0000	0	0.0000	0	0	0.0000	0	0	0	1	1.0000	1.0000	0

4. Swatville has been offered a contract to manufacture the Corner Pounder. This bat is 39 inches long, will require 10 minutes of lathe time and 30 minutes of finishing time. No box is required, but the bat requires 4 ounces of stain and 8 ounces of varnish. Swatville will receive $23 for each bat made. Determine whether or not the contract should be accepted.

PROBLEMS

12-1 Formulate the dual for the following primal linear program and then solve it graphically.

$$\text{Maximize} \quad P = 12X_1 + 16X_2$$
$$\text{Subject to} \quad 4X_1 + 4X_2 \le 16 \quad (\text{resource } A)$$
$$6X_1 + 4X_2 \le 24 \quad (\text{resource } B)$$
$$\text{where} \quad X_1, X_2 \ge 0$$

12-2 Reconsider Ace Widgets' problem of deciding how many regular and deluxe models to produce. The regular model requires 5 hours of finishing labor and 1 frame. The deluxe version requires 8 hours and 1 frame. Only 12 frames and 80 hours of labor are available. The per-unit profits are $10 for the regular model and $15 for the deluxe version.
(a) Formulate the primal linear program and solve it graphically.
(b) Formulate the dual linear program. State in words the meaning of your dual variables.
(c) Solve the dual graphically.

12-3 Now suppose that Ace Widgets in Problem 12-2 makes a third product—the super widget—at a per-unit profit of $25. Each super widget requires 10 hours of labor and 1 frame.

(a) Formulate Ace's new primal linear program.
(b) Formulate the dual linear program and solve it graphically.
(c) Suppose that Ace can sell a fourth model—the cheap widget—at a per-unit profit of $6. This model requires 2 hours of labor and 1 frame. Should any cheap models be made?

12-4 For the following linear program,

$$\text{Maximize} \quad P = 100X_1 + 200X_2 + 150X_3$$

$$\text{Subject to} \qquad 5X_1 + 20X_2 + 30X_3 \le 60 \quad \text{(resource } A\text{)}$$

$$10X_1 + 20X_2 + 50X_3 \le 100 \quad \text{(resource } B\text{)}$$

$$\text{where} \qquad\qquad X_1, X_2, X_3 \ge 0$$

the following final simplex tableau applies, where S_A and S_B are the slack variables for the first and second constraints, respectively.

UNIT PROFIT		100	200	150	0	0	
	Basic Mix	X_1	X_2	X_3	S_A	S_B	Sol.
100	X_1	1	0	4	$-1/5$	1/5	8
200	X_2	0	1	1/2	1/10	$-1/20$	1
	Sac.	100	200	500	0	10	1,000
	Imp.	0	0	-350	0	-10	—

(a) Formulate the dual linear program.
(b) Determine the solution to the dual from this tableau.

12-5 The Piney Woods Furniture Company makes tables (T), chairs (C), and bookcases (B). The following linear program applies.

$$\text{Maximize} \quad P = 20X_T + 15X_C + 15X_B$$

$$\text{Subject to} \qquad 10X_T + 3X_C + 10X_B \le 100 \quad \text{(wood)}$$

$$5X_T + 5X_C + 5X_B \le 60 \quad \text{(labor)}$$

$$\text{where} \qquad\qquad X_T, X_C, X_B \ge 0$$

The dual linear program is

$$\text{Minimize} \quad C = 100U_W + 60U_L$$

$$\text{Subject to} \qquad 10U_W + 5U_L \ge 20 \quad \text{(table)}$$

$$3U_W + 5U_L \ge 15 \quad \text{(chair)}$$

$$10U_W + 5U_L \ge 15 \quad \text{(bookcase)}$$

$$\text{where} \qquad\qquad U_W, U_L \ge 0$$

and the solution to the dual is

$$U_W = \frac{5}{7} \qquad U_L = \frac{18}{7} \qquad C = \frac{1580}{7} \text{ dollars}$$

(a) What is the maximum premium that Piney Woods would pay for an additional unit of wood? For an additional unit of labor?
(b) Letting U_T, U_C, and U_B represent the dual surplus variables for the respective constraints, determine the optimal values of these variables.
(c) Letting S_W and S_L represent the primal slack variables, use the principle of complementary slackness to determine which primal main and slack variables have zero values. Then, determine the optimal solution to the primal linear program algebraically.
(d) Suppose that Piney Woods can sell desks at a per-unit profit of $50 and that each desk requires 30 board feet of wood and 10 hours of labor. Should any desks be made?

12-6 Pumpkin-Goblins must decide how many gallons of pumpkin (X_P) and licorice (X_L) ice cream to make for sale during Halloween week. All ingredients are in plentiful supply, except for artificial carbon black, vanilla extract, and orange food coloring. The following linear program applies.

$$\text{Maximize} \quad P = 2.00X_P + 1.50X_L$$

$$\begin{aligned} \text{Subject to} \qquad\qquad .50X_L &\le 1,000 \quad \text{(carbon black)} \\ .02X_P + .01X_L &\le \quad 25 \quad \text{(vanilla extract)} \\ .10X_P \qquad\quad &\le \quad 50 \quad \text{(orange food coloring)} \end{aligned}$$

$$\text{where} \qquad\qquad X_P, X_L \ge \quad 0$$

(a) Formulate the dual linear program.
(b) The solution to the primal linear program is $X_P = 250$, $X_L = 2,000$; $P = 3,500$. Assuming that these quantities are made, determine the amount of unused (slack) resource for each primal constraint.
(c) Identify the dual surplus variables. Then, apply the principle of complementary slackness to determine the optimal solution to the dual linear program you found in (a).

12-7 A brewery president wishes to develop a monthly production schedule that will maximize gross profits. He sells three products: light beer, dark beer, and malt liquor. The respective production quantities (in gallons) are denoted by X_L, X_D, and X_M. The president is faced with three constraints pertaining to the respective usages and availabilities of hops-handling capacity (bushels), fermentation space (cubic feet), and bottling time (hours). The corresponding slack variables are S_H, S_F, and S_B. The following final simplex tableau applies.

UNIT PROFIT		1	2	1.5	0	0	0	
	Basic Mix	X_L	X_D	X_M	S_H	S_F	S_B	Sol.
1	X_L	1	0	0	−3	1	.5	100,000
1.5	X_M	0	0	1	−.6	0	1	10,000
2	X_D	0	1	0	2	1	−.75	20,000
	Sac.	1	2	1.5	.1	3	.5	155,000
	Imp.	0	0	0	−.1	−3	−.5	—

(a) Determine the optimal production levels for the various products?
(b) For each constraint in the original primal problem, there is a variable in the dual problem with a minimization objective. Describe in words the meanings of these dual variables and indicate their respective values.
(c) A capital expansion is contemplated. The following incremental monthly costs of three alternatives are to be added to capacities.

> 1 bushel of hops-handling capacity, $.20
> 1 cubic foot of fermentation space, $1.00
> 1 hour of bottling time, $.10

Assuming that you can use the information in the final simplex tableau, what alternative investment would be most profitable if the capital expansion is very limited? Explain.

12-8   Refer to the bond portfolio selection problem in Section 9-3. Formulate the dual linear program and define all variables.

12-9   Refer to the Real Reels advertising decision problem in Section 9-5. Formulate the dual linear program and define all variables.

12-10   Refer to Yosemite Ann's final cost-minimization linear program for producing trail mix, described in Section 9-8. Formulate the dual linear program and define all variables.

12-11   Refer to Sammy Love's candied apple decision in Problem 10-16 (page 341).
(a) Formulate Sammy's linear program and separately identify any slack variables required to solve this problem using the simplex method.
(b) Formulate the dual linear program and separately identify any surplus variables required to solve this problem using the simplex method.
(c) Solve the dual *graphically*. What are the optimal values of the dual main variables? Of the dual surplus variables?
(d) What is the maximum premium that Sammy would pay for extra cups of sugar? For extra ounces of gelatin?
(e) Solve the primal linear program using only your answer to (c). How many candied apples of each type should Sammy make? What is his maximum profit? Which ingredients will not be totally used?

12-12   ChipMont manufactures three types of silicon chips for computers: central processing units (C), integrated circuits (I), and core memories (M). The following linear program applies.

$$\text{Maximize} \quad P = .25X_C + .40X_I + .15X_M$$

$$\text{Subject to} \quad .005X_C + .02X_I + .01X_M \le 10{,}000 \quad \text{(silicon sheets)}$$
$$.2X_C + .5X_I + .1X_M \le 200{,}000 \quad \text{(labor in minutes)}$$

$$\text{where} \quad X_C, X_I, X_M \ge 0$$

The dual linear program is

$$\text{Minimize} \quad C = 10{,}000U_S + 200{,}000U_L$$

$$\text{Subject to} \quad .005U_S + .2U_L \ge .25 \quad \text{(CPU's)}$$
$$.02U_S + .5U_L \ge .40 \quad \text{(integrated circuits)}$$
$$.01U_S + .1U_L \ge .15 \quad \text{(memories)}$$

$$\text{where} \quad U_S, U_L \ge 0$$

and the solution to the dual is

$$U_S = \frac{10}{3} \qquad U_L = \frac{7}{6} \qquad C = 800,000/3$$

(a) What is the maximum premium that ChipMont would pay for one additional silicon sheet? For one additional minute of labor?

(b) Letting U_C, U_I, and U_M represent the dual surplus variables for the respective constraints, determine the optimal values of these variables.

(c) Letting S_S and S_L represent the primal slack variables, use the principle of complementary slackness to determine which primal main and slack variables have nonzero values. Then, determine the optimal solution to the primal linear program algebraically.

(d) Suppose that ChipMont can manufacture an all-purpose video game chip at a profit of $1 per chip. If each game chip requires .01 silicon sheet and .4 minute of labor, should any game chips be made?

12-13 Rott Irony makes three fancy door hinges: Baltic, chic, and Gothic. All of the materials used in making these hinges are plentiful, except that only 100 ft^2 of brass plate are on hand and a maximum of 200 hours of handcrafting labor can be spared. A set of heavy Baltic hinges requires 2 ft^2 of brass plate; a set of chic or Gothic hinges requires 1 ft^2. Handcrafting takes 1 hour for a set of Baltic hinges, 3 hours for a set of chics, and $1\frac{1}{4}$ hours for a set of Gothics. Rott can sell the entire production run at a profit of $10 for a set of Baltic or Gothics and $15 for a set of chics.

(a) Formulate Rott's linear program and separately identify any slack variables required to solve this problem using the simplex method.

(b) Formulate the dual linear program and separately identify any surplus variables required to solve this problem using the simplex method.

(c) Solve the dual graphically. What are the optimal values of the dual main variables? Of the dual surplus variables?

(d) What is the maximum premium that Rott would pay for each extra square foot of brass plate? For each extra hour of handcrafting?

(e) Solve the primal linear program using only your answer to (c). How many sets of each type of hinge should Rott make? What will Rott's maximum profit be?

12-14 *Computer exercise.* Consider Willy B. Rich's investment decision originally described in Problem 9-9 (page 300).

(a) Formulate Willy's decision problem as a linear program.

(b) Formulate the dual linear program.

(c) Using a computer, solve the primal problem and determine the solution to the dual from the same computer run.

12-15 *Computer exercise.* Consider the Blitz Beer advertising decision originally described in Problem 9-16 (page 302).

(a) Formulate the decision problem as a linear program.

(b) Formulate the dual linear program.

(c) Using a computer, solve the primal problem and determine the solution to the dual from the same computer run.

12-16 *Computer exercise.* Consider the All-American Meat Processors' decision for mixing sausage batches, originally described in Problem 9-12 (page 301).

(a) Formulate the decision problem as a cost-minimization linear program.

(b) Formulate the dual linear program.

(c) Using a computer, solve the primal problem and determine the solution to the dual from the same computer run.

12-17 *Computer exercise.* Consider Le Petite Fromagerie's decision in Problem 10-21 (page 342).

   (a) Formulate the dual linear program.
   (b) Determine the solution to the dual.
   (c) For which resources would it be profitable to expand the available quantities?

12-18 *Computer exercise.* Consider the Hoopla Hoops advertising decision in Problem 10-22 (page 343).

   (a) Formulate the dual linear program.
   (b) Determine the solution to the dual.
   (c) How much will profit increase for each additional dollar added to the total funds available for advertising?
   (d) How much will profit increase for each additional dollar allowed beyond $40,000 for ads in teen media?

CHAPTER 13

Sensitivity Analysis in Linear Programming

No linear programming solution can be of a higher quality than the assumptions underlying the mathematical model itself. Often the basic parameters—unit profits or costs, exchange coefficients, requirement levels, and resource availabilities—are themselves only estimates or educated guesses. An unsureness about any of these parameters may cast doubt on the validity of the optimal solution itself. We can extend linear programming concepts to assess the effects of changes in the original parameter values. Such an extension is referred to as a **sensitivity analysis**.

The primary objective of sensitivity analysis is to determine exactly what effect minor variations in the assumed parameters have on the overall solution. When these variations make little difference, we say that the optimal solution is *insensitive* to a change in asssumptions. The degree of sensitivity can range from no change at all to a considerable shift in the optimal solution and will vary with the parameter considered and with the magnitude of change in its value.

Related to sensitivity analysis are questions about the form of the model itself. For example, we may wonder how our solution will change if we incorporate a new resource constraint. Or, we may wish to evaluate how our answer will change if a new candidate product is included in the production plan. In this chapter, we will see how much of the work we have already accomplished can be preserved when the original problem is amended.

13-1 Sensitivity Analysis for Right-hand Side Values

For the purpose of illustration, we will reconsider the wood and labor constraints of the Redwood Furniture problem. What will happen to the optimal solution if a strike at the lumber mills makes less wood available? How will the new production plan be amended if one of the cabinetmakers goes on sick leave? We will answer these questions using the final simplex solution in Figure 13-1 for our original linear program.

$$X_T = \text{Number of tables}$$

$$X_C = \text{Number of chairs}$$

$$\text{Maximize} \quad P = 6X_T + 8X_C$$

$$\text{Subject to} \quad 30X_T + 20X_C \le 300 \quad \text{(wood)}$$

$$5X_T + 10X_C \le 110 \quad \text{(labor)}$$

$$\text{where} \quad X_T, X_C \ge 0$$

Recall that the simplex procedure places us at the most attractive corner. A change in resource availability creates one of two effects. If the change is minor, the feasible solution region will expand or contract so that the most attractive corner is slightly repositioned and the basic variables simply assume different values. A major change may not only enlarge or reduce the feasible solution region, but it may also distort its basic shape to the extent that a new most attractive corner that is not analogous to the old one exists. Such a change creates a different optimal basic mix as well as new variable values.

The first question to be answered by sensitivity analysis is therefore: *Over what range of right-hand side values does the current basic mix apply?* Let's consider the amount of wood first. How small must the initial level of wood become before the simplex basic mix changes? To determine the level at which the basic mix will change, we only need to look at

FIGURE 13-1

The final simplex tableau for the Redwood Furniture problem.

UNIT PROFIT		6	8	0	0	
	Basic Mix	X_T	X_C	S_W	S_L	Sol.
6	X_T	1	0	1/20	−1/10	4
8	X_C	0	1	−1/40	3/20	9
	Sac.	6	8	1/10	6/10	96
	Imp.	0	0	−1/10	−6/10	—

our unused wood slack variable S_W. If S_W is increased, then there will be less wood available to produce tables and chairs, and the production plan must be amended accordingly.

By what amounts can available wood be reduced? This is the same as asking how much can we increase S_W? We answer a similar question every time we apply the *entry criterion* in a simplex pivot. Treating S_W like an entering variable in Figure 13-1, we can determine the maximum possible increase in unused wood before one of the mix variables, X_T or X_C, is reduced to zero and leaves the solution mix. An examination of the exchange coefficients for S_W shows that we must give up 1/20 of a table for each board foot of wood we increase S_W. This releases enough labor to make 1/40 of a chair more, since X_C has an exchange coefficient of $-1/40$ in the S_W column. As we enlarge S_W, Redwood will eventually run out of tables. Since the current optimal solution indicates that $X_T = 4$, we can trade all tables for 20 board feet of wood each, obtaining $4 \div 1/20 = 80$ board feet of unused wood. (Remember that Redwood cannot get back all of the 30 board feet required to produce each table, since it is profitable to divert some of this wood to making chairs.) Any increase in S_W smaller than 80 will still leave some wood for tables. This tells us that if the available wood is at least $300 - 80 = 220$ board feet, X_T will remain in the variable mix. If more than 80 board feet are removed Redwood cannot make any tables and will have to cut back on chairs as well.

Now, what happens if we increase the amount of available wood? How large an increase can occur and still permit Redwood to manufacture both tables and chairs? Again, we can answer this by looking at S_W. In effect, adding more wood is analogous to borrowing wood, or obtaining surplus wood. Viewing surplus as negative slack, we can reduce S_W to a negative level. (Remember that this cannot actually be done, since all variables must be non-negative. But let's pretend.) The interpretation of the exchange coefficients is reversed when an entering variable is decreased. The coefficients tell us that Redwood can *get back* 1/20 of a table and must get back $-1/40$ or give up 1/40 of a chair for each board-foot reduction in S_W. All 9 chairs can be exchanged for a deficit level of unused wood equal to $9 \div 1/40 = 360$ board feet. In other words, available wood can be increased up to 360 board feet beyond the original amount of 300 board feet, making the new total amount $300 + 360 = 660$, and it would still be more profitable for Redwood to make both tables and chairs. Any larger change would eliminate chairs from the production plan, so that X_C would be removed from the basic mix.

We can now see that the present basic mix will be optimal for all levels of available wood between the *lower limit* of 220 board feet and the *upper limit* of 660 board feet. This is verified graphically in Figure 13-2. Notice in Figure 13-2(a) that although the feasible solution region becomes narrower as the level of available wood is reduced, it maintains the same basic four-sided shape and that, until 220 board feet is reached, the most attractive corner is where the wood and labor constraint lines intersect. At 220 board feet and below, the feasible solution region is triangular and no tables are made while there is slack labor. In Figure 13-2(b), as the level of available wood is raised, the feasible region's shape remains the same and the intersection of the labor and wood constraint lines provides the most attractive corner until 660 board feet is reached. Thereafter, the region is triangular, formed only by the labor constraint line and the axes, no chairs are made, and there is slack wood.

FIGURE 13-2

Graphical illustrations of how the feasible solution region changes for various levels of available wood.

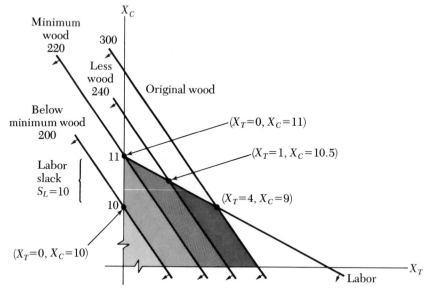

(a) Effect of lowering the wood level

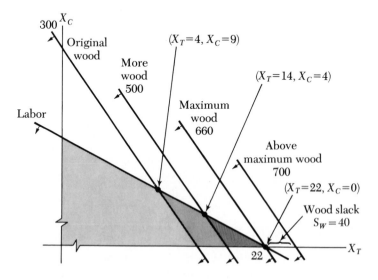

(b) Effect of raising the wood level

The Procedure When Slack Is Not in the Basic Mix

The Redwood Furniture final simplex tableau in Figure 13-1 shows no slacks in the basic mix. We can summarize the procedure for finding the range in right-hand side values over which the current basic mix will remain optimal. Using the final simplex tableau for the original problem, we treat the corresponding slack variable as if it were an entering variable and calculate the following exchange ratio for every row.

$$\text{Exchange ratio} = \frac{\text{Solution value}}{\text{Exchange coefficient in slack column}}$$

We then find the

$$\text{Lower limit} = \text{Original level} - \text{Smallest positive ratio}$$
$$\text{or } -\infty \quad \text{(if no ratio is positive)}$$

and the

$$\text{Upper limit} = \text{Original level} + \text{Smallest absolute value of negative ratios}$$
$$\text{or } \infty \quad \text{(if no ratio is negative)}$$

If there is an exchange coefficient of zero, then the exchange ratio for that row will be $+\infty$, even when the solution value is also zero. When only the solution value is zero, then the ratio is also zero, but it is treated as positive or negative (having the same sign as the exchange coefficient).

Table 13-1 shows how the range values are calculated for the right sides of the wood and labor constraints. Since Redwood's problem only has two simplex rows, only two

TABLE 13-1
Range Calculations for the Right-Hand Side Values

BASIC MIX	WOOD RANGE FOR SAME OPTIMAL BASIC MIX		
	Exchange Coefficient in S_W Column	Solution Column	Exchange Ratio
X_T	1/20	4	$4 \div (1/20) = 80$
X_C	$-1/40$	9	$9 \div (-1/40) = -360$
	Lower limit $= 300 - 80 = 220$ board feet		
	Upper limit $= 300 + 360 = 660$ board feet		

BASIC MIX	LABOR RANGE FOR SAME OPTIMAL BASIC MIX		
	Exchange Coefficient in S_L Column	Solution Column	Exchange Ratio
X_T	$-1/10$	4	$4 \div (-1/10) = -40$
X_C	3/20	9	$9 \div (3/20) = 60$
	Lower limit $= 110 - 60 = 50$ hours		
	Upper limit $= 110 + 40 = 150$ hours		

exchange ratios are calculated for each resource. We can see that X_T and X_C remain the optimal basic mix at any level of labor between 50 and 150 hours. (You can verify this graphically in a similar manner to the way we raised and lowered the level of wood in Figure 13-2.) *Each of the ranges we find in this manner applies only as long as the right-hand sides of all other constraint equations remain at their original levels.* Each range accommodates only one change at a time.

The Procedure for Slack in the Basic Mix

If the final simplex tableau has a slack variable in the basic mix, the applicable range for the corresponding right-hand side of the constraint must be determined differently. We have

Lower limit = Original level − Solution value of slack

Upper limit = ∞

The rationale for the lower limit is that not all of the available resource is used in the present optimal solution, so that we can eliminate some of the original resource and still have slack. Since the most slack we can eliminate is all of it, the reduction of the original right-hand side level by any larger amount would change the variable mix. The upper limit is even easier to understand. Since not all of the present level of resource is being used, raising that level can only raise the slack. No other change is possible, and the variable mix must remain exactly the same.

The Right-hand Sides of Other Types of Constraints

Thus far, we have considered only the ≤ constraint usually associated with resource limitations. However, the same principles apply to the ≥ and = constraints, which ordinarily pertain to minimum or exact requirements, respectively.

The surplus variable is the basis for determining the right-hand side limits of the ≥ constraint. The exchange ratios must be interpreted in the reserve manner, however, since the surplus variable is originally subtracted (rather than added, as the slack is).

When the surplus is not in the basic mix

Lower limit = Original level − Smallest absolute value of negative ratios
or −∞ (if no ratio is negative)

Upper limit = Original level + Smallest positive ratio
or ∞ (if no ratio is positive)

When the surplus is in the basic mix

Lower limit = −∞

Upper limit = Original level + Solution value of surplus

For the strict equality constraint, the starting simplex formulation must include an artificial variable. The artificial variable here is analogous to the slack variable in sensitivity analysis. Everything remains exactly the same, except that the case of the artificial variable being in the final basic mix never needs to be considered. Why? As a practical matter, the artificial variables for the equality constraints are the only artificials ever used in sensitivity analysis. *The columns of all other artificial variables are best eliminated before starting.*

Sensitivity analysis of the right-hand side of constraints can be applied to the most general linear programming form, regardless of whether the underlying problem is profit maximization or cost minimization. Next, we will consider how to obtain the solution when the right-hand side of the constraint changes.

13-2 Solving for a Right-hand Side Change

If the right-hand side of one of the constraints changes, we could find the optimal solution to the revised problem by beginning the simplex procedure all over again. However, with just a little work, we can find the answer by slightly modifying the original solution. As long as the new right-hand side (r.h.s.) falls between the limits just described, the following rule applies to the revised solution value.

Revised value = Original value + Exchange coefficient $\times$ Net r.h.s. change

The net right-hand side change is always found by subtracting the old level from the new one. For example, suppose that Redwood Furniture's wood supply is increased from 300 to 500 board feet. The revised production plan for tables and chairs would then be

$$X_T = 4 + (1/20)(500 - 300) \quad = 14 \text{ tables}$$
$$X_C = 9 + (-1/40)(500 - 300) = \quad 4 \text{ chairs}$$

where the exchange coefficients from the S_W column for slack wood in Figure 13-1 apply. The new profit would therefore be

$$P = 6(14) + 8(4) = 116 \text{ dollars}$$

Or suppose that the available labor is decreased to 80 hours instead. The revised solution would then be obtained by using the exchange coefficients for slack labor S_L.

$$X_T = 4 + (-1/10)(80 - 110) = \quad 7 \text{ tables}$$
$$X_C = 9 + (3/20)(80 - 110) \quad = 4.5 \text{ chairs}$$

The profit would be

$$P = 6(7) + 8(4.5) = 78 \text{ dollars}$$

If the slack variable for a constraint having a revised right-hand side is a basic variable, then any new level within the applicable range will only cause the slack variable to increase or decrease by the net change. All other variable values and the profit will remain unchanged.

Matters become more complex when changing a right-hand side value to a level outside the range for the present optimal basic mix. More elaborate sensitivity analysis can be used to solve such a changed problem. This analysis involves manipulating the original final simplex tableau and performing additional simplex pivots. Because this requires an extensive amount of work, it may be easier to solve the changed problem from scratch. Starting over again is also recommended when more than one constraint is revised.

Right-hand Side Changes for Other Types of Constraints

When the right-hand side of a strict equality constraint changes, the procedures are identical to those just described if we substitute the corresponding artifical variable for the slack. Analogous steps also apply to accommodating changes in the right-hand sides of ≥ constraints if we treat the corresponding surplus variable as we would a slack variable.

When the right-hand side of a ≥ constraint changes, the direction of change is reversed. (As we have seen before, this is because the surplus variable was originally subtracted on the left-hand side.) When the change falls within the prescribed limits, the following relationship applies whenever the surplus is not in the variable mix.

Revised value = Original value − Exchange coefficient × Net r.h.s. change

If the surplus is part of the variable mix, then it will simply increase or decrease by the amount of the change, and all the other variables and the profit will remain the same.

13-3 Sensitivity Analysis for Unit Profit

The other major area of sensitivity analysis arises from changes in unit profits. The underlying rationale is basically the same as it is for right-hand side analysis (which can be applied to the dual problem, in which the right sides are the primal unit profits). Like the foregoing analysis, the main consideration in evaluating changes in unit profits is finding *limits* over which the current basic mix applies.

Continuing with our original Redwood Furniture problem, let's see what happens if the profit per table is changed. As Figure 13-3(a) shows, an increase in table profit results in a new maximum P line. Increasing the profit per table from \$6 to \$10 yields a steeper profit line, but the most attractive corner remains the same. At a profit of \$15 per table, it is no longer attractive to make chairs, and the most attractive corner occurs where the wood line intersects the X_T axis; in effect, the resulting maximum P line is steeper than the wood constraint line. Figure 13-3(b) illustrates the reverse situation—when the unit table profit decreases. At a \$5 profit, the maximum P line is flatter than before, and the original corner remains most attractive. At a \$3 profit for each table, making tables is no longer attractive, and the most attractive corner occurs where the labor line intersects the X_C axis; the resulting maximum P line is flatter than the labor constraint line.

FIGURE 13-3

Graphical illustrations of how the most attractive corner (the optimal solution) changes with different unit profit levels for tables.

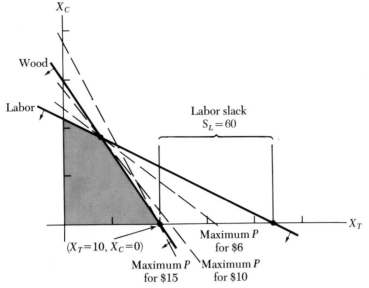

(a) Effect of raising the unit wood profit

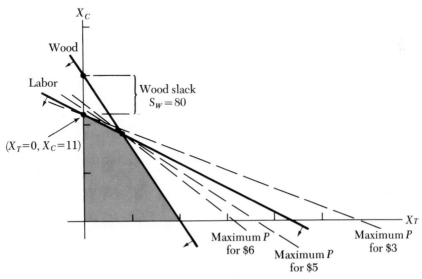

(b) Effect of lowering the unit wood profit

Figure 13-3 tells us that the same basic mix applies over a wide range of unit profits. Furthermore, exactly the same optimal variable values ($X_T = 4$, $X_C = 9$) apply over that range; only the level of P is affected. We may obtain the limits directly from the final simplex tableau given in Figure 13-4 for the original problem. When the main variable being evaluated is in the final mix, first we calculate the following **improvement ratios**.

$$\text{Improvement ratio} = \frac{\text{Per-unit improvement value}}{\text{Exchange coefficient in variable row}}$$

These ratios are found only for the values in the columns of the nonmix variables.

The numerator is the per-unit improvement in total profit associated with an increase in the variable for that column. The per-unit improvement for S_W is $-1/10$, which indicates that profit will be reduced by $\$.10$ for each additional board foot of unused wood. The denominator is the applicable exchange coefficient. In the X_T row and S_W column the exchange coefficient is $1/20$, which tells us that for every additional board foot of unused wood, we give up one-twentieth of a table. Dividing the profit lost from one more board foot of unused wood by the quantity of tables that must be sacrificed per board foot, we obtain our ratio for the X_T row and S_W column.

$$\frac{-1/10}{1/20} = -2 \text{ dollars}$$

This expresses the reduction in profit incurred by trading 1 table for 20 board feet of unused wood.

Now consider what happens if tables are sold at a lower price, so that they are less profitable. This should make the exchange of unused wood for a table less painful. If the profit per table is reduced by the $2 amount, to $6 - $2 = $4, then the unit sacrifice and

FIGURE 13-4
The final simplex tableau for the original Redwood Furniture problem.

		UNIT PROFIT				
		6	8	0	0	
	Basic Mix	X_T	X_C	S_W	S_L	Sol.
6	X_T	1	0	1/20	−1/10	4
8	X_C	0	1	−1/40	3/20	9
	Sac.	6	8	1/10	6/10	96
	Imp.	0	0	−1/10	−6/10	—

$$X_T \text{ improvement ratios:} \quad \frac{-1/10}{1/20} = -2 \qquad \frac{-6/10}{-1/10} = 6$$

improvement values of S_W will change to zero (verify this to your satisfaction). Trading tables for unused wood would not be harmful then. Any profit per table lower than $4 will make unused wood more attractive than any tables. In effect, a $2 drop in the profit per table establishes the lower limit of $4 for keeping X_T in the optimal basic mix. A similar argument can be made in terms of S_L to establish the upper limit of the profit per table.

The *unit-profit limits for a main variable in the basic mix* are calculated from

Lower profit limit = Original level − Smallest absolute value of negative ratios
             or −∞   (if no ratio is negative)

Upper profit limit = Original level + Smallest positive ratio
             or ∞   (if no ratio is positive)

where all the improvement ratios applicable to the variable being evaluated are used and entries in all nonmix variable columns (except artificals) are used. The improvement ratios for X_T and X_C are calculated in Figure 13-4 and provide the following limits.

	LOWER LIMIT	UPPER LIMIT
Profit per table	$6 − 2 = $4	$6 + 6 = $12
Profit per chair	$8 − 4 = $4	$8 + 4 = $12

(It is simply coincidence that an identical range applies for tables and chairs.) As is true of right-hand side ranges, the respective profit limits are valid only when all other unit profits are fixed at their original levels.

Thus, we have found that holding profit per chair at the original $8, the current optimal solution ($X_T = 4$, $X_C = 9$) will remain identical for any profit per table between $4 and $12. Only total profit itself can change, ranging from a low of $P = $4(4) + $8(9) = $88 to a high of $P = $12(4) + $8(9) = $120.

In performing a profit sensitivity analysis, the *artificial variable columns are ignored.* In effect, any exchange of quantities between basic variables and an artificial variable makes no sense, because the artificial variable itself has no economic interpretation. Thus, we would not compute ratios using the coefficients in the artificial columns.

As in right-hand side analysis, we treat zero or a positive quantity divided by zero as ∞ and a negative quantity divided by zero as −∞. Similarly, zero divided by −10 is included with the negative ratios (as the value zero) and zero divided by 100 yields a zero-valued positive ratio.

In the Redwood Furniture problem, only finite positive values are profit limits, but these limits can be negative or infinite. Under some circumstances, for example, a variable with a *negative* unit profit can remain in the optimal basic mix (for example, a "loss leader").

Profit Range When the Main Variable Is Not in the Mix

If the main variable being evaluated is not in the final basic mix, a somewhat different procedure must be employed. Since simplex has determined that this variable is unattractive, its unit profit can be lowered to any level without causing the optimal basic mix to change. But raising its unit profit to some level should make the variable attractive enough to enter the mix. This level is the one at which the value of the unit improvement (in the bottom row of the simplex tableau) will no longer be negative. The *unit-profit limits for a main variable not in the mix* are therefore

Lower profit limit $= -\infty$

$$\text{Upper profit limit} = \text{Original level} + \frac{\text{Absolute size of per-unit}}{\text{improvement value}}$$

Sensitivity Analysis for Unit Cost

The same sensitivity analysis procedures may be applied to a cost-minimization problem, where the objective coefficients are unit costs. When evaluating the unit cost of a main variable in the final optimal basic mix, the cost-limit calculations are identical to the profit analysis. If the main variable is not in the basic mix, the unit cost can be raised to any arbitrary level, and nothing will change. But the cost cannot be lowered by more than the per-unit improvement value without making it attractive to enter the basic mix. Thus, the *unit-cost limits for a variable not in the mix* are

Lower cost limit = Original level − Unit improvement value

Upper cost limit $= \infty$

13-4 Case Illustration: The Persian Sausage Problem

To help assimilate the various procedures for the variety of sensitivity analyses and problem revision situations that can be encountered, we will now consider a comprehensive case illustration. We will successively analyze and modify the Persian sausage problem from Chapter 11. The problem objective is to establish the ingredient weights for making a 100-pound batch of sausage subject to the requirements in Table 13-2.

TABLE 13-2
The Persian Sausage Requirements

LABEL CATEGORY	PERCENTAGE OF WEIGHT			Requirement Percentage
	Beef	Chicken	Lamb	
Fat	20%	15%	25%	≤24%
Protein	20	15	15	≥12%
Water and other	60	70	60	≤64%
Total weight (%)	Any	Any	≥30%	
Cost per pound	$1.00	$.50	$.70	

Included is the restriction that all ingredients must sum to 100 pounds. The linear program is specified below, where the main variables are pounds of beef X_B, chicken X_C, and lamb X_L.

$$\text{Minimize} \quad C = 1X_B + .5X_C + .7X_L$$

$$\text{Subject to} \quad .20X_B + .15X_C + .25X_L \leq 24 \quad \text{(fat)}$$

$$.20X_B + .15X_C + .15X_L \geq 12 \quad \text{(protein)}$$

$$.60X_B + .70X_C + .60X_L \leq 64 \quad \text{(water)}$$

$$1X_L \geq 30 \quad \text{(ingredient)}$$

$$1X_B + 1X_C + 1X_L = 100 \quad \text{(total weight)}$$

$$\text{where} \quad X_B, X_C, X_L \geq 0$$

In the final simplex tableau in Figure 13-5, S_F and S_W represent the slack weights for fat and water, S_P and S_I are surplus weights beyond the protein and ingredient minimums, and a_T is the artificial variable associated with the total weight requirement. (All other artificial variables originally used in conjunction with the $\geq$ constraints to begin the simplex procedure are no longer necessary and their columns do not appear in the table.)

The ranges for the respective right-hand sides of the original constraints are calculated in Table 13-3. Sample calculations of the new solutions for right-hand side changes inside the respective limits are provided in Table 13-4. Remember that the respective limits and the new solutions apply only as long as all other parameters are held constant at their original levels.

Continuing, we find the ranges in unit ingredient costs over which the present basic mix remains optimal. Table 13-5 shows how these cost limits are calculated. Each range applies only as long as all other parameters remain fixed. Remember that a change in unit cost will not change the variable values, as long as the new cost falls within the computed limits; only the total cost will change.

FIGURE 13-5
The final simplex tableau for the Persian sausage problem.

UNIT COST		1	.5	.7	0	0	0	0	M	
	Basic Mix	X_B	X_C	X_L	S_F	S_P	S_W	S_I	a_T	Sol.
0	S_F	−.05	0	0	1	0	1	0	−.85	3
0	S_I	1	0	0	0	0	−10	1	7	30
.5	X_C	0	1	0	0	0	10	0	−6	40
.7	X_L	1	0	1	0	0	−10	0	7	60
0	S_P	−.05	0	0	0	1	0	0	.15	3
	Sac.	.7	.5	.7	0	0	−2	0	1.9	62
	Imp.	.3	0	0	0	0	2	0	−1.9 + M	—

TABLE 13-3
Range Calculations for the Right-hand Sides

| BASIC MIX | SLACK, SURPLUS, OR ARTIFICIAL VARIABLE | | | | | |
| | NOT IN BASIC MIX | | IN BASIC MIX | | | |
	Solution/S_W	Solution/a_T	S_F	S_P	S_I	Solution
S_F	3	−3.53				3
S_I	−3	4.29				30
X_C	4	−6.67				40
X_L	−6	8.57				60
S_P		20.00				3
Smallest positive	3	4.29				
Smallest absolute negative	3	3.53				
Constraint type	≤ (water)	= (total)	≤ (fat)	≥ (protein)	≥ (ingredient)	
Original level	64	100	24	12	30	
Lower limit	64 − 3 = 61	100 − 4.29 = 95.71	24 − 3 = 21	−∞	−∞	
Upper limit	64 + 3 = 67	100 + 3.53 = 103.53	∞	12 + 3 = 15	30 + 30 = 60	

TABLE 13-4
Calculations for a Sample of the Right-hand Side Changes
within Their Respective Limits

| UNIT COST | BASIC MIX | SOLUTION FOR NEW RIGHT-HAND SIDES | | | | |
		Fat 25	Protein 5	Water 65	Ingredient 20	Total Weight 102
0	S_F	4	3	4	3	1.3
0	S_I	30	30	20	20	44
.5	X_C	40	40	50	40	28
.7	X_L	60	60	50	60	74
0	S_P	3	−4	3	3	3.3
	Total cost	$62	$62	$60	$62	$65.80
	Net r.h.s change	25 − 24 = 1	5 − 12 = −7	65 − 64 = 1	20 − 30 = −10	102 − 100 = 2

TABLE 13-5
Range Calculations for the Unit Ingredient Costs

MAIN VARIABLES IN MIX	NONMIX VARIABLES (not artificial)		SMALLEST RATIO	
	Improvement/X_B	Improvement/S_W	Positive	Absolute Negative
X_C	∞	.20	.20	none
X_L	.30	$-.20$	.30	.20
Improvement:	.30	2		

MAIN VARIABLES IN MIX	Original Level		LIMITS	
		Improvement	Lower Limit	Upper Limit
X_C	.50	0	$.50 - \infty = -\infty$	$.50 + .20 = .70$
X_L	.70	0	$.70 - .20 = .50$	$.70 + .30 = 1.00$
Main variable not in mix: X_B	1.00	.30	$1 - .30 = .70$	∞

TABLE 13-6
Data Obtained for Expanded Redwood Furniture Problem

CONSTRAINT	VARIABLE							Available Quantity
	(1) X_{TS}	(2) X_{TR}	(3) X_{TL}	(4) X_{CS}	(5) X_{CA}	(6) X_{BS}	(7) X_{BT}	
(1) Wood	20	30	40	15	25	20	30	$\leq 3,000$
(2) Labor	4	5	6	8	12	6	8	$\leq 1,100$
(3) Machine time	2	2	2	3	3	2	2	≤ 250
(4) Quantity, tables	1	1	1					≥ 30
(5) Quantity, chairs				1	1			≥ 20
(6) Quantity, bookcases						1	1	≥ 20
(7) Mix, tables	1	-1	-1					$= 0$
(8) Mix, chairs				1	-4			$= 0$
(9) Mix, bookcases						1	-1	$= 0$
Unit profit	$5	$6	$7	$6	$10	$8	$6	

13-5 Sensitivity Analysis with the Computer

When linear programs are solved on a computer, applicable ranges for profits and right-hand sides will ordinarily be provided as optional output. Consider, one more time, the data for the expanded Redwood Furniture problem summarized in Table 13-6. The computer solution to the primal was given in Chapter 11 (page 350). *QuickQuant* provided the following optional output.

Sensitivity Analysis--Right-hand Sides

Constraint Number	Lower Limit	Original Value	Upper Limit	
1	2865.00000	3000.00000	No Limit	(wood)
2	781.00000	1100.00000	No Limit	(labor)
3	160.00000	250.00000	260.80000	(mach. t.)
4	0.00000	30.00000	57.00000	(qty. tab.)
5	13.41000	20.00000	50.00000	(qty. ch.)
6	No Limit	20.00000	50.00000	(qty. bk.)
7	−13.50000	0.00000	30.00000	(mix tab.)
8	−67.50000	0.00000	20.00000	(mix ch.)
9	−27.00000	0.00000	65.00000	(mix bk.)

Sensitivity Analysis--Objective Function

Original Variable	Lower Limit	Original Value	Upper Limit
XTS	No Limit	5.00000	7.00000
XTR	No Limit	6.00000	7.00000
XTL	6.00000	7.00000	9.00000
XCS	No Limit	6.00000	10.61000
XCA	No Limit	10.00000	28.50000
XBS	−6.00000	8.00000	No Limit
XBT	−8.00000	6.00000	No Limit

CASE

Sound Shack

The Sound Shack, a chain of retail stereo stores, sells four private brand compact disk players: SS-4, SS-5, SS-6, and SS-8. The company-owned plant is planning next month's production. Depending on the model, a regular or a super laser is used. One of three cartridges is installed on any model: Ace, Bidwell, or Capstone. Only the lasers and cartridges, which are long lead-time items, constrain the quantities produced. All other components can be readily purchased from suppliers. In addition, there is a limitation due to the amount of assembly labor time available at the plant. Because it has been heavily backordered, at least 100 units of model SS-4 must be made.

The following linear program applies, where X_4, X_5, X_6, and X_8 represent the quantities of the various compact disk players to be made.

Maximize $P = 20X_4 + 25X_5 + 35X_6 + 45X_8$

Subject to

$$X_4 + X_5 + X_6 \leq 250 \quad \text{(regular laser)}$$
$$X_8 \leq 60 \quad \text{(super laser)}$$
$$X_4 \leq 120 \quad \text{(Ace cartridge)}$$
$$X_5 \leq 60 \quad \text{(Bidwell cartridge)}$$
$$X_6 + X_8 \leq 80 \quad \text{(Capstone cartridge)}$$
$$2X_4 + 3X_5 + 4X_6 + 6X_8 \leq 1,000 \quad \text{(labor)}$$
$$X_4 \geq 100 \quad \text{(quantity)}$$

where   all X's $\geq$ 0

It is assumed that all units produced will be sold and will yield the unit profits (in dollars) indicated in the program. Figure 13-6 shows the final simplex tableau that applies. The slack variables for the respective resource availability constraints are S_R, S_S, S_A, S_B, S_C, and S_L. S_Q represents the surplus production of the SS-4 model beyond the required minimum.

FIGURE 13-6

The final simplex tableau for the Sound Shack problem.

UNIT PROFIT		20	25	35	45	0	0	0	0	0	0	0	
	Basic Mix	X_4	X_5	X_6	X_8	S_R	S_S	S_A	S_B	S_C	S_L	S_Q	Sol.
0	S_R	0	0	0	0	1	1	-1	-1	-1	0	0	50
45	X_8	0	0	0	1	0	1	0	0	0	0	0	60
0	S_Q	0	0	0	0	0	0	1	0	0	0	1	20
25	X_5	0	1	0	0	0	0	0	1	0	0	0	60
35	X_6	0	0	1	0	0	-1	0	0	1	0	0	20
0	S_L	0	0	0	0	0	-2	-2	-3	-4	1	0	140
20	X_4	1	0	0	0	0	0	1	0	0	0	0	120
	Sac.	20	25	35	45	0	10	20	25	35	0	0	7,300
	Imp.	0	0	0	0	0	-10	-20	-25	-35	0	0	—

Questions

1. Determine the range for available Capstone cartridges over which the present variable mix remains optimal. Determine the new optimal solution if the supply of these cartridges is 110 instead of 80.

2. Returning to the original problem, determine the range for available Bidwell cartridges over which the present mix remains optimal. Determine the new optimal solution if the supply of these cartridges is 70 instead of 60.

3. Returning to the original problem, over what range in available labor does the present variable mix remain optimal? If available labor is lowered from 1,000 to 900 hours, what is the new optimal solution?

4. Returning to the original problem, over what range in the minimum quantity for model SS-4 does the present variable mix remain optimal? If the minimum quai-tity is raised from 100 to 110 SS-4 turntables, what is the new optimal solutio ι?

5. Determine the range for the SS-8 model profit over which the present optimal solution remains the same.

6. Suppose instead that the unit profit for the SS-4 is reduced to $10 and determine the new optimal solution.

PROBLEMS

13-1   The following linear program applies for the Piney Woods Furniture Company, which makes tables (T), chairs (C), and bookcases (B).

$$\text{Maximize} \quad P = 20X_T + 15X_C + 15X_B$$

$$\text{Subject to} \quad 10X_T + 3X_C + 10X_B \leq 100 \quad \text{(wood)}$$

$$5X_T + 5X_C + 5X_B \leq 60 \quad \text{(labor)}$$

$$\text{where} \quad X_T, X_C, X_B \geq 0$$

Using S_W and S_L as the respective slack variables for unused wood and labor, the final simplex tableau shown in Figure 13-7 applies.

FIGURE 13-7
The final simplex tableau for Problem 13-1.

UNIT PROFIT		20	15	15	0	0	
	Basic Mix	X_T	X_C	X_B	S_W	S_L	Sol.
20	X_T	1	0	1	1/7	-6/70	64/7
15	X_C	0	1	0	-1/7	2/7	20/7
	Sac.	20	15	20	5/7	18/7	1,580/7
	Imp.	0	0	-5	-5/7	-18/7	—

(a) Determine the range for available wood over which the present basic mix will remain optimal. Do the same for available labor.

(b) Find the new optimal solution when available wood is 90 board feet.

(c) Find the new optimal solution when available labor is 100 hours.

13-2 Refer to the data in Problem 13-1.

(a) Determine the ranges for unit profits over which the current solution will remain optimal.

(b) What is the total profit when each table yields a profit of $18?

(c) What is the total profit when each chair yields a profit of $10?

13-3 Computer manufacturers presently buy ChipMont's entire production of the following types of silicon chips: central processing units (C), integrated circuits (I), and core memories (M). The following linear program applies.

$$\text{Maximize} \quad P = .25X_C + .40X_I + .15X_M$$

$$\text{Subject to} \quad .005X_C + .02X_I + .01X_M \leq 10,000 \quad \text{(silicon sheets)}$$

$$.2X_C + .5X_I + .1X_M \leq 200,000 \quad \text{(labor in minutes)}$$

$$.10X_C + .40X_I + .15X_M \leq 400,000 \quad \text{(washing hours)}$$

$$X_C - X_I + X_M \leq 0 \quad \text{(quantity limitation)}$$

$$\text{where} \quad X_C, X_I, X_M \geq 0$$

Using S_S, S_L, S_W, and S_Q as the respective slack variables, the final simplex tableau shown in Figure 13-8 applies.

(a) Determine the range for available silicon sheets over which the present basic mix will remain optimal. Do the same for available labor and washing hours.

(b) Find the new optimal solution when 11,000 silicon sheets are available.

(c) Find the new optimal solution when 150,000 minutes of labor are available.

(d) Find the new optimal solution when 300,000 hours of washing time are available.

FIGURE 13-8
The final simplex tableau for Problem 13-3.

UNIT PROFIT		.25	.40	.15	0	0	0	0	
	Basic Mix	X_C	X_I	X_M	S_S	S_L	S_W	S_Q	Sol.
0	S_S	0	0	6/700	1	−25/700	0	15/7,000	20,000/7
.40	X_I	0	1	−1/7	0	10/7	0	−2/7	2,000,000/7
0	S_W	0	0	85/700	0	−5/7	1	3/70	1,800,000/7
.25	X_C	1	0	6/7	0	10/7	0	5/7	2,000,000/7
	Sac.	.25	.40	11/70	0	65/70	0	45/700	1,300,000/7
	Imp.	0	0	−5/700	0	−65/70	0	−45/700	

13-4   Refer to the data in Problem 13-3.
   (a) Determine the ranges for unit profits over which the current solution will remain optimal.
   (b) What is the total profit when each central processing unit yields a profit of $.30?
   (c) What is the total profit when each integrated circuit yields a profit of $.10?
   (d) What is the total profit when each core memory yields a profit of $.05?

13-5   For the following linear program,

$$\text{Maximize} \quad P = 10X_1 + 15X_2 + 20X_3$$

$$\begin{array}{llll}
\text{Subject to} & 2X_1 + 3X_2 + 4X_3 \le 100 & (\text{constraint } A) \\
& 4X_1 \quad\quad\; + 2X_3 \ge 50 & (\text{constraint } B) \\
& \quad -5X_2 + 5X_3 \ge 20 & (\text{constraint } C) \\
& X_1 + X_2 + X_3 = 20 & (\text{constraint } D) \\
\end{array}$$

$$\text{where} \quad X_1, X_2, X_3 \ge 0$$

the final simplex tableau in Figure 13-9 applies.
   (a) Determine the ranges for the right-hand sides over which the present basic mix remains optimal.
   (b) What is the optimal solution when the right-hand side for constraint A is raised to 200?
   (c) What is the optimal solution when the right-hand side for constraint B is raised to 60?

FIGURE 13-9
The final simplex tableau for Problem 13-5.

UNIT PROFIT		10	15	20	0	0	0	$-M$	
	Basic Mix	X_1	X_2	X_3	S_A	S_B	S_C	a_D	Sol.
10	X_1	1	-1	0	0	$-1/2$	0	-1	5
20	X_3	0	2	1	0	1/2	0	2	15
0	S_A	0	-3	0	1	-1	0	-6	30
0	S_C	0	15	0	0	5/2	1	10	55
	Sac.	10	30	20	0	5	0	30	350
	Imp.	0	-15	0	0	-5	0	$-M-30$	—

13-6   Refer to the data in Problem 13-5.
   (a) For each main variable, determine the range for unit profit over which the current solution remains optimal.
   (b) What is the total profit when the unit profit for X_1 is raised to $12?

13-7   *Computer exercise.* Consider the Blitz Beer advertising decision in Problem 9-16 (page 302).

(a) Find the optimal solution.
(b) Determine the limits over which the present basic mix remains optimal for the following limitations.
  (1) available funds
  (2) available spots on **KBAT**
  (3) available spots on **KPOW**
(c) Determine the limits over which the present solution remains optimal for the sales increase per spot on:
  (1) **KBAT**   (3) **WROB**
  (2) **WJOK**   (4) **KPOW**

13-8   *Computer exercise.*   Consider the sausage ingredient decision in Problem 9-7 (page 299).

(a) Find the optimal solution.
(b) Determine the limits over which the present basic mix remains optimal for the following limitations.
  (1) allowable chicken
  (2) minimum beef
  (3) minimum protein
  (4) maximum fat
(c) Determine the limits over which the present solution remains optimal for the cost of the following.
  (1) hog bellies   (3) beef
  (2) tripe   (4) chicken

13-9   *Computer exercise.*   Consider Le Petite Fromagerie's decision in Problem 10-21 (page 342).
(a) Find the optimal solution.
(b) Determine the limits over which the present basic mix remains optimal for the following resources.
  (1) milk   (3) molds
  (2) storage   (4) salt
(c) Determine the limits over which the present solution remains optimal for the unit profit of each type of cheese.

13-10   *Computer exercise.*   Consider the Hoopla Hoops advertising decision in Problem 10-22 (page 343).
(a) Find the optimal solution.
(b) Determine the limits over which the present basic mix remains optimal for the following limitations.
  (1) available funds
  (2) maximum teen placement expenditures
(c) Determine the limits over which the present solution remains optimal for the circulation of the following.
  (1) Tiger Club   (3) Spider Glider
  (2) Rocky   (4) Toy Fans

14

The Transportation Problem I

One of the most important and successful applications of quantitative analysis in solving business problems has been in the area of the physical distribution of products. Great cost savings have been achieved by the more efficient routing of freight from supply points to required destinations. In this chapter, we will consider the **transportation problem**, which serves as the framework for analyzing such decisions. The purpose of the transportation problem in its basic form is to minimize the total cost of shipping goods from plants to warehouse distribution centers in such a way that the needs of each warehouse are met and every factory operates within its capacity.

Ordinarily, it is convenient to express such a problem mathematically in terms of a linear program. Like any linear program, the transportation problem can be solved by the simplex algorithm. But simplex is a general procedure, and its universality has built-in limitations. The special structure of the transportation problem permits us to solve it by using a faster, more streamlined algorithm than simplex. In studying the transportation problem, we will therefore gain a new insight into quantitative analysis: *The judicious choice of the solution procedure itself can result in savings of both time and money.* This chapter illustrates another way to "skin a cat" that is better for certain kinds of cats. It is important to know that alternative procedures exist or can be developed to solve a variety of linear programming problems.

TABLE 14-1
The Shipping Costs per Pair of Skis

FROM PLANT	TO WAREHOUSE			
	Frankfurt	New York	Phoenix	Yokohama
Juarez	$19	$ 7	$ 3	$21
Seoul	15	21	18	6
Tel Aviv	11	14	15	22

The transportation problem establishes a convenient format that has been adapted to a variety of applications that do not involve the physical distribution of goods, to be discussed in Chapter 15. One of these applications that we will discuss there is the assignment problem, which is concerned with the efficient placement of specific individuals in particular jobs. In Chapter 15 we will also examine a production scheduling application.

14-1 A Ski Shipment Scheduling Illustration

In this section, we will return to the shipment scheduling application concerning the operation of the sporting goods company first discussed in Chapter 9. To review, the company makes skis in three plants throughout the world. The plants supply four company-owned warehouses that distribute the skis directly to ski shops. Depending on which mode is cheaper, the product is air-freighted or trucked from the plants to the warehouses. Table 14-1 provides the various point-to-point shipping costs of shipping a pair of skis. The problem is to find how many pairs of skis should be shipped from each plant to the various warehouses to minimize total cost. This is accomplished by determining the quantities for the shipment schedule shown in Figure 14-1, where X_{ij} represents the quantity shipped from plant i to warehouse j.

FIGURE 14-1
The shipment schedule for skis.

FROM PLANT	TO WAREHOUSE				Plant Capacity
	F	N	P	Y	
J	X_{JF}	X_{JN}	X_{JP}	X_{JY}	100
S	X_{SF}	X_{SN}	X_{SP}	X_{SY}	300
T	X_{TF}	X_{TN}	X_{TP}	X_{TY}	200
Warehouse Demand	150	100	200	150	600

In Chapter 9, we formulated this problem as

$$\text{Minimize} \quad C = \quad 19X_{JF} + \quad 7X_{JN} + \quad 3X_{JP} + 21X_{JY}$$
$$+ 15X_{SF} + 21X_{SN} + 18X_{SP} + \quad 6X_{SY}$$
$$+ 11X_{TF} + 14X_{TN} + 15X_{TP} + 22X_{TY}$$

$$\text{Subject to} \quad X_{JF} + \quad X_{JN} + \quad X_{JP} + \quad X_{JY} = 100 \quad \text{(Juarez capacity)}$$
$$X_{SF} + \quad X_{SN} + \quad X_{SP} + \quad X_{SY} = 300 \quad \text{(Seoul capacity)}$$
$$X_{TF} + \quad X_{TN} + \quad X_{TP} + \quad X_{TY} = 200 \quad \text{(Tel Aviv capacity)}$$
$$X_{JF} + \quad X_{SF} + \quad X_{TF} = 150 \quad \text{(Frankfurt demand)}$$
$$X_{JN} + \quad X_{SN} + \quad X_{TN} = 100 \quad \text{(New York demand)}$$
$$X_{JP} + \quad X_{SP} + \quad X_{TP} = 200 \quad \text{(Phoenix demand)}$$
$$X_{JY} + \quad X_{SY} + \quad X_{TY} = 150 \quad \text{(Yokohama demand)}$$

$$\text{where} \quad \text{all } X\text{'s} \geq \quad 0$$

Special Requirements of Transportation Problems

The number of constraints is dictated by the number of plants (or rows in the shipment schedule) and the number of warehouses (or columns in the shipment schedule). Altogether, every transportation problem must have exactly the following number of equality constraints.

$$\text{Number of constraints} = \text{Number of rows} + \text{Number of columns}$$

As we can see in Figure 14-1, each X is represented exactly once in the capacity constraints and exactly once in the demand constraints. This can happen if and only if the total quantity shipped is exactly equal to the total quantity received: *Total plant capacity must equal total warehouse demand.* In our example, the capacities sum to 600, which is also the sum of the demands.

$$600 = 100 + 300 + 200 = 150 + 100 + 200 + 150$$

Later, we will see that this fact plays an important role in solving a transportation problem.

You may be wondering why each plant must produce exactly at its capacity and each warehouse must receive precisely its demand. Isn't that unrealistic? These requirements are needed to solve the problem by the most efficient means. Of course they are unrealistic, but we will see that it will always be possible to formulate any transportation problem in this manner, even when true demands and capacities are not in exact balance.

14-2 Getting Started: The Northwest Corner Rule

We solve the transportation problem in iterations proceeding from solution to solution much like we do in simplex. We begin with an initial solution that satisfies all constraints.

A convenient starting point is to apply the **northwest corner rule**. We begin with a blank shipment schedule, shown in Figure 14-2. Each plant-warehouse route is represented by a cell. For convenience, the unit shipping costs are placed in the upper right-hand corner of each cell. The central portion of the cell is reserved for the quantity to be shipped.

The northwest corner rule begins in the cell in the upper left-hand corner of the schedule. (On a map, this would be called the "northwest corner.") In this cell, we place the largest possible quantity that satisfies the capacity and demand constraints. This means that we look in the row and column margins of Figure 14-2 for the smallest demand or capacity applicable and write this number in the northwest corner cell. Further cell allocations are made by moving down or to the right in the direction of leftover demand or capacity and inserting the maximum feasible quantity at each step. We stop when the southeast corner has been allocated. The cell-to-cell movement in this procedure is analogous to the movement of chess pieces. Only horizontal and vertical movements, like those of the "rook," are allowed; no diagonal "bishop" moves are permitted.

The northwest corner solution for the ski distribution problem is provided in Figure 14-3. Our beginning corner receives an allocation of 100 pairs to be shipped from Juarez to Frankfurt. This is the largest possible number of pairs of skis that can be shipped over that route, since Juarez's capacity is 100 pairs; Frankfurt must receive 150 pairs, but we cannot ship more skis from Juarez that it can make. This leaves an unfilled demand of $150 - 100 = 50$ pairs for Frankfurt, so our next cell for skis shipped from Seoul to Frankfurt lies directly below. The largest possible allocation to that cell is 50 pairs, since the gap in Frankfurt's demand is exhausted before this warehouse takes up Seoul's capacity. This leaves us with an unused capacity for Seoul in the amount of $300 - 50 = 250$ pairs. We therefore move to the cell at the right, where we must allocate a shipment from Seoul to New York. There, we fill New York's total demand of 100, leaving $300 - 50 - 100 = 150$ pairs under capacity at Seoul. We move to the right again, where we allocate 150 pairs from Seoul to Phoenix. This does not exhaust that

FIGURE 14-2
A blank shipment schedule.

To From	F	N	P	Y	Capacity
J	19	7	3	21	100
S	15	21	18	6	300
T	11	14	15	22	200
Demand	150	100	200	150	600

FIGURE 14-3

The shipment schedule for the ski distribution problem found by the northwest corner rule.

From \ To	F	N	P	Y	Capacity
J	[19] (100)	[7]	[3]	[21]	100
S	[15] (50)----→	[21] (100)----→	[18] (150)	[6]	300
T	[11]	[14]	[15] (50)----→	[22] (150)	200
Demand	150	100	200	150	600

warehouse's demand, leaving $200 - 150 = 50$ pairs short at Phoenix. Moving down, we pick up 50 pairs from Tel Aviv to take care of Phoenix, and then move to the right, where we allocate the rest of Tel Aviv's capacity as a 150-pair shipment to Yokohama. At this point, all constraints are satisfied.

The solution in Figure 14-3 serves as the starting feasible solution. The cell entries are the values of the corresponding problem variables; empty cells correspond to zero quantities. The total cost of this shipment schedule is computed below to be $C = 11,500$ dollars.

QUANTITY	UNIT COST	ROUTE COST
$X_{JF} = 100$	$c_{JF} = 19$	$19 \times 100 = 1,900$
$X_{SF} = 50$	$c_{SF} = 15$	$15 \times 50 = 750$
$X_{SN} = 100$	$c_{SN} = 21$	$21 \times 100 = 2,100$
$X_{SP} = 150$	$c_{SP} = 18$	$18 \times 150 = 2,700$
$X_{TP} = 50$	$c_{TP} = 15$	$15 \times 50 = 750$
$X_{TY} = 150$	$c_{TY} = 22$	$22 \times 150 = 3,300$
		$C = \overline{11,500}$

14-3 Solving the Problem: The Transportation Method

We have just begun to solve this transportation problem. Our next task is to search for improvements. We could try the trial-and-error approach, reallocating cell values until it becomes hard to find improvements. Not only would this procedure be inefficient, but there is no guarantee that the optimal solution would be found. We would probably give up in frustration, not knowing if more improvements were possible. Instead, we will take a systematic approach to the problem.

The Simplex Analogy

First, we will recall some important features of simplex that apply equally well here. We know that any feasible bounded problem has at least one optimal solution that is a corner point. Remember that a **corner point** can be defined as the solution to the underlying constraints when all so-called nonbasic variables are fixed arbitrarily at zero. The free variables are called **basic variables**. Exactly the same principles apply to the transportation problem, which, after all, is just a special kind of linear program. The basic variables for any shipment-schedule solution correspond to the **nonempty cells** (cells containing a circled value); the **empty cells** represent the nonbasic variables.

The northwest corner rule provides us with a corner point solution. (Here, we are referring to a corner in the higher dimensional space and *not* to the cell in a corner of the shipment-schedule table.) As in simplex, we seek a neighboring corner to evaluate next, choosing the one that improves cost at the greatest rate. And, as in simplex, we reach this corner by means of a pivot procedure in which the *status* of the cells is exchanged: A currently nonempty cell becomes empty, and a presently empty cell receives a quantity allocation. The new nonempty cell is referred to as the **entering cell**, and the cell it replaces is called the **exiting cell**. Such an exchange will result in a cheaper shipment schedule. We continue this procedure until we reach a most attractive corner that cannot be improved on. This is the optimal solution.

Finding the Entering Cell: Row and Column Numbers

The entering cell is found through economic analysis, as it is in simplex. In the transportation problem, we evaluate every empty cell by determining the per-unit cost improvement associated with allocating one unit to that cell. Our procedure for doing this may seem roundabout at first, but it is really quite efficient.

We begin by assigning special values to each row and column of the current shipment schedule. The unit shipping cost for a cell is denoted by c_{ij}. The **row numbers** are represented by r_i, and the **column numbers** are represented by k_j. These values are calculated so that the following relationship holds.

$$\text{For nonempty cells:} \qquad c_{ij} = r_i + k_j$$

We begin by assigning zero as the row number for the first row. The pattern of the nonempty cells and their unit costs then dictate the values of the remaining row and column numbers. These are found algebraically by solving a sequence of equations, each with one unknown.

Returning to our ski distribution example, consider the present solution shown in Figure 14-4. The row and column numbers appear outside the shipment schedule in the respective margins. The letters indicate the *sequence* in which these values were obtained.

FIGURE 14-4

Row and column numbers for the initial solution to the ski distribution problem.

From \ To	F	N	P	Y	Capacity	
J	ⁱ⁹ ⓐ100	⁷	³	²¹	100	$r_J =$ 0 ⓐ
S	¹⁵ ⓐ50	²¹ ⓐ100 *	¹⁸ ⓐ150	⁶	300	$r_S = -4$ ⓒ
T	¹¹	¹⁴	¹⁵ ⓐ50	²² ⓐ150	200	$r_T = -7$ ⓔ
Demand	150	100	200	150	600	
	$k_F = 19$ ⓑ	$k_N = 25$ ⓖ	$k_P = 22$ ⓓ	$k_Y = 29$ ⓕ	* skipped cell	

The proper sequence is extremely important when computing the r and k values. A general rule in finding the row and column numbers is to work from the last number found, proceeding through a nonempty cell in its row or column that needs the opposite number. Then move to the row or column containing the newest number and repeat the procedure. Always use the newest r value to obtain the next k value, and vice versa. Continue this zigzagging process until there are no new nonempty cells needing a number. Occasionally, there will be more than one nonempty cell to choose from in making the next assignment. Break the tie by picking just one of them arbitrarily. Mark the skipped cells and return to them (in any order) after exhausting the chain of r and k assignments made by working from that cell where you broke the original tie.

The following detailed explanation tells how the row and column numbers were obtained for the ski distribution example.

ⓐ We begin with the first row. It always receives a zero row number. Thus, $r_J = 0$.

ⓑ Looking at row J, we see that there is one nonempty cell JF that does not yet have a column number. For this cell

$$c_{JF} = r_J + k_F$$

must hold. We know that $c_{JF} = 19$, and we have just found $r_J = 0$. Plugging these numbers into this equation, we obtain

$$19 = 0 + k_F$$

and we find that $k_F = 19$.

ⓒ There are no other nonempty cells in row J. We now look in column F for any nonempty cell that does not have a row number. SF does not. We know that

$$c_{SF} = r_S + k_F$$

Plugging $c_{SF} = 15$ and $k_F = 19$ into this equation gives us

$$15 = r_S + 19$$

which yields

$$r_S = 15 - 19 = -4$$

ⓓ There are no other nonempty cells in column F. We then search row S, where we see that both cell SN and cell SP do not yet have a column number. Cell SN is skipped and marked (*) for a later return. Working through cell SP, we plug $c_{SP} = 18$ and $r_S = -4$ into

$$c_{SP} = r_S + k_P$$

which yields

$$18 = -4 + k_P$$

so that $k_P = 18 - (-4) = 22$.

ⓔ We can see that column P contains nonempty cell TP, which has no row number. Plugging $c_{TP} = 15$ and $k_P = 22$ into

$$c_{TP} = r_T + k_P$$

we obtain

$$15 = r_T + 22$$

so that $r_T = 15 - 22 = -7$.

ⓕ One more nonempty cell, TY, remains in row T without a column number. Substituting $c_{TY} = 22$ and $r_T = -7$ into

$$c_{TY} = r_T + k_Y$$

gives us

$$22 = -7 + k_Y$$

and $k_Y = 22 - (-7) = 29$.

ⓖ Now only column N needs a number. Returning to cell SN, skipped earlier, we substitute $r_S = -4$ and $c_{SN} = 21$ into

$$c_{SN} = r_S + k_N$$

getting

$$21 = -4 + k_N$$

so that $k_N = 21 - (-4) = 25$.
All rows and columns now have their numbers.

With practice, you can make these computations very rapidly in your head without having to use scratch paper.

The r and k values obtained in this way are now used in conjunction with the present shipment schedule to find the entering cell. To do this, we calculate *for the empty cells only* the

Improvement difference: $c_{ij} - r_i - k_j$

This difference indicates the per-unit cost improvement that can be achieved by raising the shipment allocation in the corresponding cell from its present level of zero. *The empty cell with the greatest absolute negative improvement difference is the entering cell.*

Figure 14-5 shows how the entering cell is found for our example. There, the differences have been entered in the lower left-hand corners of each empty cell. For example, the improvement difference in cell JN is

$$c_{JN} - r_J - k_N = 7 - 0 - 25 = -18$$

This tells us that raising the quantity allocated to that cell will reduce costs by $18 per pair of skis. The other differences are calculated in the same way.

We can see that cells JP and SY in Figure 14-5 are tied for the greatest cost improvement at $19 per pair. We will break this tie arbitrarily and choose JP as the entering cell. Our next step is to determine just how much we can allocate to the cell.

FIGURE 14-5

Improvement values and the closed-loop path for the initial solution to the transportation problem.

To / From	F	N	P	Y	Capacity	
J	19 (100) (−) −18	7 −19	3 (+)	21 −8	100	$r_J = 0$
S	15 (50) (+)	15 (100)	18 (150) (−)	6 −19	300	$r_S = -4$
T	11 −1	14 −4	15 (50)	22 (150)	200	$r_T = -7$
Demand	150	100	200	150	600	

$k_F = 19$ $k_N = 25$ $k_P = 22$ $k_Y = 29$

Finding the New Solution: The Closed-Loop Path

We begin by placing a $(+)$ in cell JP to indicate that its allocation (the shipment from Juarez to Phoenix) will be increased from zero quantity. Whatever change we make must be *balanced*, so that the new quantities in row J and column P sum to the respective capacity of 100 for Juarez and demand of 200 for Phoenix. Thus, we must reduce cell JF by the amount of the change. We place a $(-)$ there to reflect this reduction. But if we reduce cell JF, we must make a compensating change in column F. Our rule is that *there can be only one increasing and one decreasing cell in any row or column. Except for the entering cell, all changes must involve nonempty cells.* Thus, we place a $(+)$ in cell SF, since it is the only nonempty cell in column F. This leaves us in row S, where a compensating $(-)$ change must be made. We can readily see that cell SN must be skipped because it is the only nonempty cell in its column, so we place the $(-)$ in cell SP. All of our changes now balance.

Connecting the $(+)$ and $(-)$ signs with line segments, we can see that they provide a **closed-loop path**. This path highlights the changes involved in reallocating the shipments. *For any entering cell, the closed-loop path is unique.* Its corners are alternating $(+)$ and $(-)$ cells, and only the entering cell is empty. *Only the corner cells on the path will be changed.* (Those cells that a line segment passes through are not involved.) We can find the closed-loop path by proceeding either clockwise or counter-clockwise and starting up, down, right, or left (but never moving diagonally). We proceed, turning at each new $(+)$ or $(-)$, until our path closes. If we reach an impasse, ending up in a cell where we cannot turn (because all other cells in its column or row are empty), then we backtrack to the last turning point and go the other way or move forward to another nonempty cell in the same row or column.

The closed-loop path verifies that we will indeed save \$19 by increasing the quantity allocated to cell JP. Tracing its trajectory counter-clockwise, we have

Change:	$(+)$	$(-)$	$(+)$	$(-)$
Cell:	JP	JF	SF	SP

Each unit shifted along this path will produce a cost increase in the $(+)$ cells and a cost reduction in the $(-)$ cells, so that the net unit cost change is

$$3 - 19 + 15 - 18 = -19$$

The fact that we obtain -19 by using the r and k values is not coincidental. (The $c_{ij} - r_i - k_j$ differences are analogous to the entries in the per-unit improvement row of a simplex tableau.)

We must now make our change in the shipment schedule. The shift in quantities will occur only in the cells at the corners of the closed-loop path. *The amount shifted each time is equal to the smallest quantity in the losing cells.* The smallest $(-)$ quantity is selected because all affected cells will change by plus or minus the same amount, and the resulting quantities cannot be negative. The smallest losing-cell shipment quantity occurs in cell JF, where 100 pairs can be taken away. The following changes are made.

CELL ON CLOSED-LOOP PATH	PRESENT QUANTITY	CHANGE	NEW QUANTITY
JP	(empty)	+100	100
JF	100	−100	(empty)
SF	50	+100	150
SP	150	−100	50

Since cell JF becomes empty, it is the *exiting cell*.

Figure 14-6 shows the new shipment schedule that results from the above allocations. The total cost savings is

$$100 \times 19 = 1{,}900 \text{ dollars}$$

so that the total route cost is now $C = 11{,}500 - 1{,}900 = 9{,}600$ dollars.

Our example involves rectangular closed-loop paths. But *closed-loop paths may assume unusual shapes*, such as Ľs, figure-8's, and even loops inside loops.

Further Iterations to Find the Optimal Solution

Now we begin again, using the new row and column numbers. Notice that except for $r_J = 0$, all of the r and k values in Figure 14-6 are different than before. This is because the

FIGURE 14-6

The second solution to the transportation problem.

$$C = 9{,}600$$

From \ To	F	N	P	Y	Capacity	
J	19	7	3 (100)	21	100	$r_J = 0$ ⓐ
	19	1		11		
S	15 (150)	21 (100) *	18 (50) (−)	6 (+) −19	300	$r_S = 15$ ⓒ
T	11	14 (50) (+) *	15 (150) (−)	22	200	$r_T = 12$ ⓕ
	−1	−4				
Demand	150	100	200	150	600	

$k_F = 0$ ⓓ $k_N = 6$ ⓔ $k_P = 3$ ⓑ $k_Y = 10$ ⓖ   * skipped cell

set of nonempty cells has changed. The sequence in which these numbers are obtained is different as well. There are no shortcuts; the r and k values must be recomputed from scratch for each new shipment schedule.

Next, we find the differences for the empty cells. We can see that cell SY is the entering cell, where costs are reduced by \$19 per unit (coincidentally, the same amount as before). The closed-loop path is indicated in Figure 14-6, and the smallest quantity in the losing cells is 50 pairs.

Figure 14-7 provides the next shipment schedule, where total cost has been reduced by $19 \times 50 = 950$ dollars to $C = 9{,}600 - 950 = 8{,}650$ dollars. Recomputing the row and column numbers and the empty-cell differences, we find that cell TN is the entering cell. Increasing its allocation will save \$23 per unit.

The smallest quantity in the losing cells is 100 pairs, which happens to be the same for cells SN and TY. Whenever there is a tie for the exiting cell, more than one cell will be reduced to zero. This presents a problem we have not encountered previously. Before we proceed, a few more observations must be made regarding the nature of our solution procedure.

The Required Number of Nonempty Cells

In our illustration, there have always been exactly six nonempty cells. All of the successive changes made in the shipment schedules guarantee this. This number is one less

FIGURE 14-7
The third solution to the transportation problem.

$$C = 8{,}650$$

To / From	F		N		P		Y		Capacity	
J		19		7	(100)	3		21	100	$r_J = $ 0 ⓐ
	0		−18				11			
S	(150)	15	(100)	21		18	(50)	6	300	$r_S = -4$ ⓔ
		*	(−)		19		(+)			
T		11		14	(100)	15	(100)	22	200	$r_T = $ 12 ⓒ
	−20		(+) −23				(−)			
Demand	150		100		200		150		600	

$k_F = 19$ ⓖ $k_N = 25$ ⓕ $k_P = 3$ ⓑ $k_Y = 10$ ⓓ   * skipped cell

than the number of rows and columns. In general

Number of nonempty cells = Number of rows + Number of columns − 1

This condition results from the fundamental linear programming solution procedure. To have a corner-point solution, there must be as many basic variables (here, nonempty cells) as there are nonredundant constraints in the formulation of the linear program.

Every transportation problem has as many constraints as there are rows and columns in the shipment schedule. But together these constraints are redundant, because when the constraints are combined with the underlying condition that total capacity must be equal to total demand, any one constraint can be eliminated without affecting the problem solution. Our illustration involves three plant-capacity requirements (rows) and four warehouse-demand limitations (columns), or seven constraints in all. But both total capacity and demand must equal 600. If we left out the Yokohama demand constraint, for example, the other six constraints combined with this condition would still ensure that the Yokohama warehouse received its required 150 pairs of skis. Only six constraints are nonredundant. This is why the number of nonempty cells is one less than the number of rows and columns in the shipment schedule.

If there were less than the necessary number of nonempty cells, it would be impossible to obtain a unique set of row and column numbers and, in some cases, to form closed-loop paths. (Too many nonempty cells cause similar problems.) This does not mean that our example cannot have a solution with only five nonzero cells, but it does mean that a total of six cells must be treated as nonempty.

Ties for the Exiting Cell

Whenever there is a tie for the exiting cell, both cells will lose all of their allocation and be reduced to zero. To meet the required number of nonempty cells, exactly one of these tying cells must thereafter be treated as nonempty. Referring to Figure 14-7, we can see that both cell SN and cell TY will be reduced to zero by reallocating 100 units along the closed-loop path. Either cell SN or cell TY must, however, continue to be treated as if it were nonempty. It does not matter which cell we choose, since ties can almost always be broken arbitrarily in linear programming.

Figure 14-8 provides the new shipment schedule. The cost savings are $23 \times 100 = 2,300$ dollars, and the new total cost is $C = 8,650 - 2,300 = 6,350$ dollars. We place a circled zero in cell TY and treat it as nonempty, even though the shipping quantity is zero.

We can see that increasing the allocation into cell TF will save \$20 per unit. However, one of the losing cells is TY, which involves a zero quantity. Shifting zero around the closed-loop path gives us the new schedule in Figure 14-9. The total cost for this schedule is exactly the same as before, but the zero shipping quantity now appears in cell TF. Although no quantities have changed, the new pattern for the nonempty cells is an improvement.

Determining the Optimal Solution

Cell SP in Figure 14-9 provides a \$1 cost improvement. The smallest quantity in the losing cells is 100 pairs in cell TP. Reallocating this amount along the closed-loop path, we

FIGURE 14-8

The fourth solution to the transportation problem.

$C = 6,350$

To \ From	F	N	P	Y	Capacity	
J	19 0	7 5	3 (100) 11	21	100	$r_J = $ 0 (a)
S	15 (150) (−) 23	21 19	18	6 (150) (+)	300	$r_S = -4$ (f)
T	11 −20 (+)	14 (100)	15 (100)	22 (0) (−) *	200	$r_T = 12$ (c)
Demand	150	100	200	150	600	

$k_F = 19$ (g) $k_N = 2$ (d) $k_P = 3$ (b) $k_Y = 10$ (e)   * skipped cell

FIGURE 14-9

The fifth solution to the transportation problem.

$C = 6,350$

To \ From	F	N	P	Y	Capacity	
J	19 20	7 5	3 (100)	21 31	100	$r_J = $ 0 (a)
S	15 (150) (−) 3	21	18 (+) −1	6 (150)	300	$r_S = 16$ (e)
T	11 (0) (+)	14 (100)	15 (100) (−) *	22 20	200	$r_T = 12$ (c)
Demand	150	100	200	150	600	

$k_F = -1$ (d) $k_N = 2$ (g) $k_P = 3$ (b) $k_Y = -10$ (f)   * skipped cell

FIGURE 14-10

The optimal solution to the transportation problem.

$C = 6,250$

From \ To	F	N	P	Y	Capacity	
J	19	7	3 ⟨100⟩	21	100	$r_J = 0$ ⓐ
	19	4		30		
S	15 ⟨50⟩	21	18 ⟨100⟩	6 ⟨150⟩	300	$r_S = 15$ ⓒ
		3		*		
T	11 ⟨100⟩	14 ⟨100⟩	15	22	200	$r_T = 11$ ⓔ
		1		20		
Demand	150	100	200	150	600	

$k_F = 0$ ⓓ $k_N = 3$ ⓕ $k_P = 3$ ⓑ $k_Y = -9$ ⓖ   * skipped cell

obtain the new shipment schedule in Figure 14-10, where the cost saving is $1 \times 100 = 100$ and $C = 6,350 - 100 = 6,250$ dollars.

The schedule in Figure 14-10 is optimal. No empty cells yield potential cost reductions, so that *further improvements are impossible.*

14-4 Northwest Corner Rule Difficulties

The northwest corner rule is used to find a starting solution to the transportation problem. Recall that its allocations progress rightward and downward, always to an adjacent cell, and that diagonal jumps are not allowed. In certain problem situations, the northwest corner rule leads us to a point where no further movement is possible. This difficulty is easily remedied by a slight modification of the rule.

Consider the shipment schedule in Figure 14-11. Applying the northwest corner rule, we place 100 units in cell AW. Moving in the direction of surplus capacity, we then allocate 150 units to cell AX. This exhausts the capacity of plant A, and the remaining 50 units of warehouse X demand are filled by plant B. At this point, an impasse is reached: No further allocation can be made in row B or column X, and no horizontal or vertical movement is possible. We could bend our rule by moving diagonally to cell CY and continuing from there. But by doing this, we would end up with one less nonempty cell than the transportation problem requires.

FIGURE 14-11

An impasse in getting started using the northwest corner rule.

From \ To	W	X	Y	Z	Capacity
A	(100)-------→(150)				250
B		(50)-------→No surplus capacity			50
C		No unfilled demand			150
D					50
E					400
F					100
Demand	100	200	300	400	1,000

To avoid that pitfall, we will move to the cell at the right or below anyway. *The direction we choose is arbitrary.* Suppose that we move down to cell *CX* and place a zero shipping quantity there. Cell *CX* will be treated as a nonempty cell, even though no shipment will be scheduled from plant *C* to warehouse *X*. We then proceed as before. Figure 14-12 shows the completed shipment schedule. Although this problem has only one, some problems may require two or more circled zeroes.

FIGURE 14-12

A northwest corner starting solution involving a zero shipping allocation.

From \ To	W	X	Y	Z	Capacity
A	(100)-------→(150)				250
B		(50)			50
C		(0)-------→(150)			150
D			(50)		50
E			(100)-------→(300)		400
F				(100)	100
Demand	100	200	300	400	1,000

In proceeding to solve the problem, one of three things can happen to cell CX: (1) it will not be a turning point on the closed-loop path and continue to have a zero shipping quantity; (2) it will be a gaining cell, receiving an allocation and joining the ranks of the other nonempty cells as a full-fledged member; or (3) it will be a losing cell, so that the zero will move to a presently empty cell location.

The northwest corner rule is concerned only with the positions of cells and ignores cost information. Although this makes it easy to understand and to apply, it usually provides a starting solution that is far from the optimal solution. The next section describes alternative starting procedures which consider the cell costs, enabling us to begin much closer to the optimum. For large problems, the faster start involves less overall work than the northwest corner rule.

14-5 Starting Procedures Based on Cost

Two starting solutions are popular in solving transportation problems. First to be described is the **cheapest cell method**. This is followed by a brief summary of the more elaborate **Vogel's approximation**.

Cheapest Cell Method

The cheapest cell method is very simple. The following steps apply.

1. Starting with a blank shipping schedule, find the cheapest (lowest cost) cell. Allocate the maximum possible quantity into that cell.

2. Cross out the column or row into which further quantity allocations are impossible. (In some cases, both a column and a row must be crossed out.)

3. Find the cheapest cell in the portions of the shipping schedule not yet crossed out. Place the maximum possible quantity into that cell.

4. Repeat steps 2 and 3 until only one or two cells remain which do not lie in a row or column already crossed out. Allocate into the remaining cell(s) whatever quantities will make a feasible schedule. The cell quantities obtained provide the *starting solution*.

In performing the above steps, ties may be broken arbitrarily.

We will illustrate this method on a new transportation problem in Figure 14-13, where the results of step 1 are shown. The cheapest cell is CK, with a unit shipping cost of $6. The maximum quantity allocation for that cell is 300 units, which equals both the capacity of C and the demand of K. Both row C and column K are crossed out, since neither can receive further quantity allocations. Step 3 indicates that the next allocation must go into cell AJ, with 100 units being the maximum allocation there. Going back to step 2, no further quantities can be placed into row A, which must be crossed out.

Figure 14-14 shows the resulting status of the shipping schedule. We see that a tie exists for cheapest remaining cell, either DH or DI, both at a cost of $9. The tie is broken arbitrarily with the selection of DH, which receives a maximum allocation of 100 units. This necessitates the removal of column H from further allocations.

FIGURE 14-13

Transportation schedule showing steps 1 and 2 of the cheapest cell method.

To From	H	I	J	K	Capacity
A	15	10	8	7	100
B	10	14	13	12	100
C	7	10	8	6 (300)	300
D	9	9	15	8	200
Demand	100	50	250	300	700

FIGURE 14-14

Transportation schedule showing the second iteration of the cheapest cell method.

To From	H	I	J	K	Capacity
A	15	10	8 (100)	7	100
B	10	14	13	12	100
C	7	10	8	6 (300)	300
D	9	9	15	8	200
Demand	100	50	250	300	700

FIGURE 14-15

Transportation schedule showing the third iteration of the cheapest cell method.

From \ To	H	I	J	K	Capacity
A	15	10	8 ⟨100⟩	7	100
B	10	14	13	12	100
C	7	10	8	6 ⟨300⟩	300
D	9 ⟨100⟩	9	15	8	200
Demand	100	50	250	300	700

Figure 14-15 shows the new quantities. There we see that cell DI is the cheapest remaining cell of those not yet crossed out. Cell DI can receive at most 50 units. Figure 14-16 shows the result of this allocation, with column I now crossed out.

Only two cells, BJ and DJ, remain uncrossed out. Both receive maximum quantities. Figure 14-17 shows the completed starting solution, with all the cross lines erased. The total cost is $C = 6,000$.

Positioning Circled Zeroes

Unlike the northwest corner rule, the cheapest cell method does *not guarantee* that exactly the required number of nonempty cells will be obtained. The present 4×4 problem requires exactly $4 + 4 - 1 = 7$ nonempty cells. Figure 14-17 shows that only six nonempty cells were obtained. One circled zero must therefore be included in the shipping schedule.

It is easiest to position the circled zeroes as we determine the row and column numbers. Figure 14-18 illustrates the procedure. We start with $r_A = 0$. From this and nonempty cell AJ, we obtain $k_J = 8$. We then work through cell BJ to get $r_B = 5$ and cell DJ to get $r_D = 7$. Proceeding in row D from that number, working through cell DI, $k_I = 2$ is obtained. Also in row D, working through cell DH, $k_H = 2$ is obtained.

An impasse is reached at this point, since column H has no other nonempty cells through which further row numbers could be found. This obstacle is surmounted by

FIGURE 14-16

Transportation schedule showing the fourth iteration of the cheapest cell method.

To From	H	I	J	K	Capacity
A	15	10	8 (100)	7	100
B	10	14	13	12	100
C	7	10	8	6 (300)	300
D	9 (100)	9 (50)	15	8	200
Demand	100	50	250	300	700

FIGURE 14-17

Transportation schedule showing the completed starting solution with the cheapest cell method.

To From	H	I	J	K	Capacity
A	15	10	8 (100)	7	100
B	10	14	13 (100)	12	100
C	7	10	8	6 (300)	300
D	9 (100)	9 (50)	15 (50)	8	200
Demand	100	50	250	300	700

FIGURE 14-18

Row and column numbers and positioning circled zero for the starting solution.

$$C = 6,000$$

From \ To	H	I	J	K	Capacity	
A	13	10	8	7	100	$r_A = 0$ ⓐ
	11	8	(100)	6		
B	10	14	13	12	100	$r_B = 5$ ⓒ
	3	7	(100)	6		
C	7	10	8	6	300	$r_C = 5$ ⓖ
	(−) (0)	3	(+) −5	(300)		
D	9	9	15	8	200	$r_D = 7$ ⓓ
	(+) (100)	(50)	(50) (−)	0		
Demand	100	50	250	300	700	

$k_H = 2$ ⓕ $k_I = 2$ ⓔ $k_J = 8$ ⓑ $k_K = 1$ ⓗ

identifying in column H those empty cells lying in rows needing numbers and placing in one of these a circled zero. There is only one such cell, CH. By placing a ⓪ into cell CH, it is then possible to get the value $r_C = 5$. From there, working through cell CK, the value $k_K = 1$ is found.

All row and column numbers are obtained, and there is precisely the correct number of nonempty cells. The basic steps of the original transportation method may now be continued until the optimal solution is found.

It is common for a starting solution to need more than one ⓪. Just add a ⓪ to the problem as each impasse is reached while assigning row and column numbers. If there is more than one empty cell where the ⓪ might be placed, pick the cheapest and break any ties arbitrarily.

Finding the Optimal Solution

Once a complete quantity assignment has been achieved (so that the number of nonempty cells is exactly equal to the number of rows plus the number of columns minus one) and a set of row and column numbers is found, the transportation method proceeds as before. The starting solution, with $C = \$6,000$, is shown in Figure 14-18. There the entering cell is found to be CJ, and the corresponding closed-loop path is identified. The

FIGURE 14-19
Intermediate step in the transportation method.

$$C = 6,000$$

From \ To	H	I	J	K	Capacity	
A	13	10	8 (100)	7	100	$r_A = 0$ ⓐ
	11	8	1			
B	10	14	13 (100)	12	100	$r_B = 5$ ⓒ
	3	7	1			
C	7	10	8 (0)	6 (300)	300	$r_C = 0$ ⓓ
	5	8	(+) ⋯ (−)			
D	9 (100)	9 (50)	15 (50) (−) ⋯ (+)	8	200	$r_D = 7$ ⓕ
			−5			
Demand	100	50	250	300	700	

$k_H = 2$ ⓗ $k_I = 2$ ⓖ $k_J = 8$ ⓑ $k_K = 6$ ⓔ

minimum quantity in the losing cells is 0, so that in the next iteration the ⓪ will be in a new spot.

Figure 14-19 shows the resulting solution. Although only the ⓪ has shifted and no other quantities have changed, with C remaining the same, the new pattern of non-empty cells allows for further improvement possibilities. We see that DK is the entering cell and DJ is the exiting cell. Fifty units are shifted along the closed-loop path at a cost savings of $250.

Figure 14-20 shows the resulting solution. There, BH is the entering cell and BJ is the exiting cell. (That cell ties with DH, but since the latter is cheaper, it receives a ⓪. Remember: only one cell can go blank.) This change results in a shifting of 100 units along the closed-loop path, at a cost savings of $200.

Figure 14-21 shows the resulting solution. There we see that no further improvement is possible, and an optimal solution is reached with a cost of $C = $5,550.

Vogel's Approximation

The more elaborate Vogel's approximation may sometimes provide better starting solutions than the above. This also involves crossing out rows and columns. The procedure shown on page 445 applies.

FIGURE 14-20
Intermediate step in the transportation method.

$C = 5,750$

To From	H	I	J	K	Capacity	
A	13	10	8 (100)	7	100	$r_A = 0$ ⓐ
B	6 10 (+)	3 14	1 13 (−) (100)	12	100	$r_B = 5$ ⓒ
C	−2 7	2 10	1 8 (+) (50)	6 (−) (250)	300	$r_C = 0$ ⓓ
D	0 9 (−) (100)	3 9 (50)	15 (+)	8 (50)	200	$r_D = 2$ ⓕ
Demand	100	50	250	300	700	

$k_H = 7$ ⓗ $k_I = 7$ ⓖ $k_J = 8$ ⓑ $k_K = 6$ ⓔ

FIGURE 14-21
The optimal shipment schedule.

$C = 5,550$

To From	H	I	J	K	Capacity	
A	13	10	8 (100)	7	100	$r_A = 0$ ⓐ
B	6 10 (100)	3 14	1 13	12	100	$r_B = 3$ ⓗ
C	4 7	2 10	3 8 (150)	6 (150)	300	$r_C = 0$ ⓒ
D	0 9 (0)	3 9 (50)	15	8 (150)	200	$r_D = 2$ ⓔ
Demand	100	50	250	300	700	

$k_H = 7$ ⓖ $k_I = 7$ ⓕ $k_J = 8$ ⓑ $k_K = 6$ ⓓ

1. Find for each uncrossed row and column the difference between the cheapest and the next cheapest uncrossed cell.

2. Identify that row or column having the greatest difference and place the maximum possible quantity in the cheapest uncrossed cell in that row or column.

3. Cross out any row or column that can receive no further quantities.

4. Repeat steps 1 through 3 until only one or two uncrossed cells remain. Place into those cells the quantities needed to make a feasible schedule.

Many users of the transportation method find Vogel's approximation too messy and not sufficiently better than the cheapest cell method to justify the extra effort.

14-6 Imbalanced Capacity and Demand: Dummy Rows and Columns

So far we have encountered only transportation problems for which the total demand exactly matches total capacity. There is no reason why a real-world distribution system must have this feature, which is only a requirement of the solution algorithm and not the linear program. In this section we will see how a problem for a distribution system having *imbalanced capacity and demand* may still be solved. This is accomplished by reexpressing the problem in a standard form through the creation of dummy rows or columns, resulting in an equivalent problem where total demand does equal total capacity.

We began our ski distribution example with total demand and total capacity in balance. Ordinarily, distribution systems are not so perfectly balanced. There is usually excess system capacity or more demand than can possibly be filled. In such cases, the shipment schedule must include an additional plant or warehouse to take up the slack. We refer to these fictional distribution points as **dummy sources** or **dummy destinations**.

Consider the following example, involving two plants and three warehouses.

PLANT CAPACITY		WAREHOUSE DEMAND	
A	500	W	250
B	300	X	400
	800	Y	300
			950

Total demand is for 950 units, which exceeds the total capacity of 800 units by 150 units. The shortage in total capacity is made up by including a dummy plant with a 150-unit capacity. Figure 14-22 provides the optimal shipment schedule for this expanded problem. All shipments from the dummy plant have zero cost, since they represent product items that are not being made and not being sent. Notice that 150 units from the dummy plant are allocated to warehouse X. This means that warehouse X is shorted 150 units. In effect, X is the most costly warehouse to service, so it receives less units than its demand.

FIGURE 14-22

The optimal shipment schedule for the problem requiring a dummy plant.

From \ To	W	X	Y	Capacity
A	(250) ⌐2	(250) ⌐4	⌐6	500
B	⌐3	⌐3	(300) ⌐1	300
Dummy	⌐0	(150) ⌐0	(0) ⌐0	150
Demand	250	400	300	950

Now, consider the following example.

PLANT CAPACITY	WAREHOUSE DEMAND
A 300	W 200
B 400	X 350
C 200	Y 250
900	800

Here, the total plant capacity of 900 units exceeds the total demand for 800 units by 100 units. The surplus capacity is handled by including a dummy warehouse with a demand equal to the difference of 100. Figure 14-23 provides the optimal solution to this problem. We use zero unit shipping costs to the dummy warehouse, reflecting the fact that allocations to those cells represent product items that are not being made and not being sent. We can see that 50 units apiece are allocated to the dummy warehouse from plant A and B. These amounts represent the unused surplus capacities of these plants. In terms of distribution costs, plants A and B are less efficient than plant C, operating at full capacity.

FIGURE 14-23

The optimal schedule for the problem requiring a dummy warehouse.

From \ To	W	X	Y	Dummy	Capacity
A	13	14	10 (250)	0 (50)	300
B	12	8 (350)	11	0 (50)	400
C	6 (200)	10	13	0 (0)	200
Demand	200	350	250	100	900

14-7 Advantages of the Transportation Method

The transportation method is easy to use and understand, and the shipment schedule can be manipulated without the need for symbols. The results are essentially nonmathematical, giving it wider acceptance than the more general linear program. The shipment schedule is in a ready-to-use format that needs no translation, and the transportation method expedites communications at all levels.

Earlier in this chapter, we indicated that a transportation problem could be solved using the simplex method described in Chapters 10 and 11. But the special structure of the transportation problem allows us to use a more limited algorithm that is tailor-made for it. At this point, you have worked with simplex enough to know what is required. Each iteration involves time-consuming computations, and one mistake can ruin everything! To really appreciate the transportation method, you have to work a few problems to see just how much easier and faster it is to use than simplex.

One main advantage of the transportation problem is that it involves only the main variables. Artificial variables are not required, as they are in simplex. After getting a starting solution, we are at least as far as we would be after eliminating the artificial variables in simplex—and the simplex procedure would require a minimum of iterations (tableaus) equal to the number of rows plus columns minus 1.

Although both procedures involve iterations, it is much easier to obtain a new table using the transportation method than it is to construct a new simplex tableau. The r and k

values can be found by simple arithmetic, and the improvement differences can be computed as fast as they can be written down. The pivot step is also much easier in the transportation problem. The most time-consuming step is copying a blank shipment schedule for each iteration—and even that time can be minimized by using a copier or carbon paper.

A final advantage of the transportation method is that it is not nearly as error-prone as simplex. A quick tally will indicate whether or not the shipment quantities sum to the respective row and column totals. A mistake in calculating the r and k values will only slow the process down. Such mistakes are not "fatal" errors, as they are in simplex.

Although the transportation method is more efficient than the general-purpose simplex algorithm, it is actually a variant form of simplex and is based on exactly the same concepts. The row and column numbers are really analogous to the dual variable values, and the $c_{ij} - r_i - k_j$ differences represent the values in the per-unit improvement row of the simplex tableau that would apply if the transportation problem had been solved that way instead.

14-8 Computer Solution to Transportation Problems

The transportation method is a procedure well suited to computer solution. It is not uncommon for a distribution problem to involve hundreds, even thousands, of sources and destinations. Such problems obviously cannot be solved by hand, and even problems as small as 10-by-10 would be difficult to solve by hand.

Solving Transportation Problems with *QuickQuant*

The *QuickQuant* software package available to users of this book has a segment for solving transportation problems. The program is *user friendly*, with screen-prompt questions guiding all necessary choices and inputs. The program allows you to go back and fix your selections before it continues into the next phase.

As with the more general linear programming application discussed in Chapters 10 and 11, *QuickQuant* begins with queries regarding the number of sources and destinations and the overall objective. A table then appears on the screen with blank spaces for you to fill in the problem data. *QuickQuant* gives you the chance to make corrections to all or a portion of the completed table before proceeding to solve the problem. Key segments from a *QuickQuant* session may be printed on hard copy.

You will have the opportunity to save the problem input data on a disk in case you want to run it again. You may then modify the saved problem with minimal keyboard data entry. *QuickQuant* will let you change any constants and expressions to the current problem or to one created earlier and saved on a disk. You may expand existing problems by incorporating additional sources and destinations.

Complete operating instructions for making runs with *QuickQuant* are provided in the Appendix at the end of this book.

ILLUSTRATION
A Distribution Decision

To illustrate, consider the medium-sized transportation problem faced by National Express in Table 14-2.

QuickQuant begins processing a transportation problem program with the following prompts on the screen. The user response is shown in boldface.

```
SPECIFY A NAME FOR YOUR TRANSPORTATION PROBLEM:
--What is it?   National Express

SPECIFY THE NUMBER OF SOURCES (ROWS):
--How many?   4

SPECIFY THE NUMBER OF DESTINATIONS (COLUMNS):
--How many?   15

Is your objective to maximize profit or to minimize cost (enter p or c)?   c
```

The monitor then displays the screen in Figure 14-24 while the objective coefficients are entered. In the shown screen, the unit cost for shipments from P2 to W3 is about to be entered. The cost matrix fills in as successive entries are made. Notice that only part of large problems, such as this, can fit onto a single screen. Additional columns and rows are brought onto the screen as needed to get all the required input data.

After displaying all of the entered data, *QuickQuant* will ask for any changes and will give you the opportunity to save your data onto a disk file. That would be helpful if you want to make a few changes to a problem created earlier. Should total demand not equal total capacity, *QuickQuant* automatically creates the needed dummy row or column.

The program starts the solutions procedure, with the user choosing either the northwest corner method or Vogel's approximation. It then displays the complete shipment schedule, including row numbers, column numbers, improvement differences, the entering cell, and the closed-loop path. A portion of the first northwest corner solution is shown in Figure 14-25 for the National Express problem.

Notice that only a portion of the shipment schedule fits onto the screen. *QuickQuant* allows you to examine the entire schedule by using the arrow keys to move the viewing

TABLE 14-2
National Express Transportion Problem

PLANT	W1	W2	W3	W4	W5	W6	W7	W8	W9	W10	W11	W12	W13	W14	W15	Cap.
						SHIPPING COST TO DESTINATIONS										
P1	5	6	7	5	4	13	16	7	8	13	16	4	11	10	9	2,700
P2	7	11	10	12	9	8	11	10	9	9	11	8	13	9	5	3,000
P3	9	8	9	9	7	10	12	11	12	14	13	10	11	10	11	2,000
P4	6	7	9	8	10	9	9	8	9	11	10	9	8	7	10	1,500
Dem.	500	900	800	200	500	400	500	700	800	800	900	600	700	500	400	9,200

FIGURE 14-24

***QuickQuant* screen showing the cost data input for National Express (MacIntosh version pictured).**

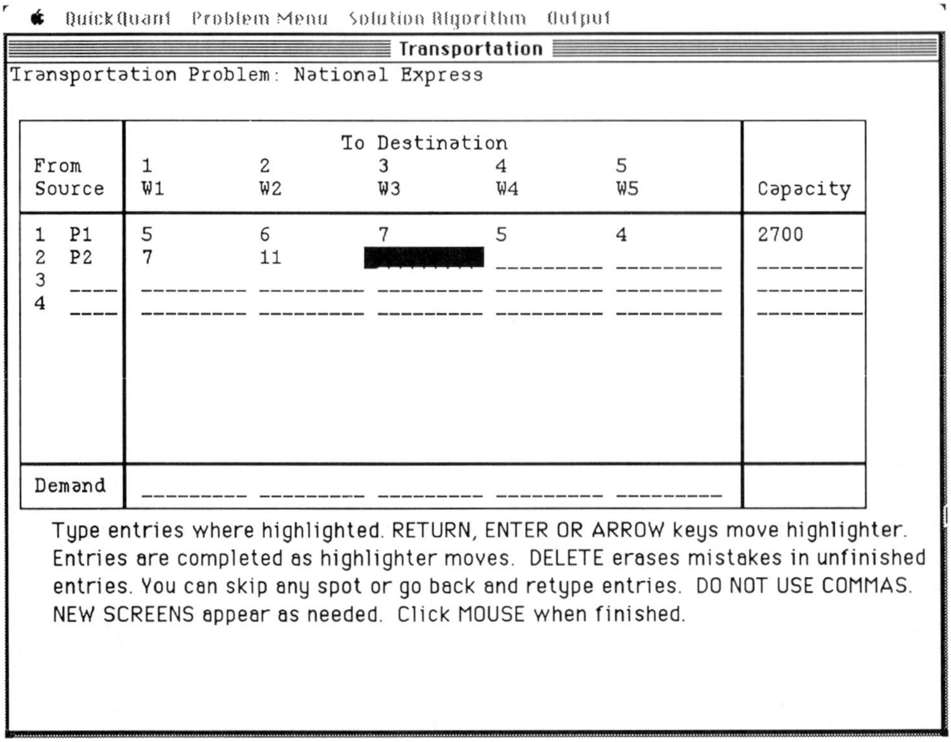

```
 ⌘  QuickQuant  Problem Menu  Solution Algorithm  Output
╔══════════════════════════ Transportation ══════════════════════════╗
Transportation Problem: National Express

                        To Destination
    From     1         2         3         4         5
    Source   W1        W2        W3        W4        W5        Capacity

    1  P1    5         6         7         5         4         2700
    2  P2    7         11        ▬▬▬▬▬▬   _____  _____  _____
    3  ____  _____  _____  _____  _____  _____  _____
    4  ____  _____  _____  _____  _____  _____  _____




    Demand   _____  _____  _____  _____  _____

    Type entries where highlighted. RETURN, ENTER OR ARROW keys move highlighter.
    Entries are completed as highlighter moves. DELETE erases mistakes in unfinished
    entries. You can skip any spot or go back and retype entries. DO NOT USE COMMAS.
    NEW SCREENS appear as needed. Click MOUSE when finished.
```

window to the portions of the matrix presently off the screen. At the user's option, *QuickQuant* will display on screen each shipment schedule. These may be skipped if only a final report is required. (Users may obtain hard printed copy of selected schedule segments by performing a *screen dump.*)

The final report for the National Express problem is given below.

Source	Destination	Quantity	Source	Destination	Quantity
P1	W1	500	P2	W11	800
P1	W4	200	P2	W15	400
P1	W5	500	P3	W2	900
P1	W8	700	P3	W3	800
P1	W9	200	P3	W7	300
P1	W12	600	P4	W7	200
P2	W6	400	P4	W11	100
P2	W9	600	P4	W13	700
P2	W10	800	P4	W14	500

Minimum cost is C = 70900

FIGURE 14-25

QuickQuant screen showing the first iteration of the National Express problem (MacIntosh version pictured).

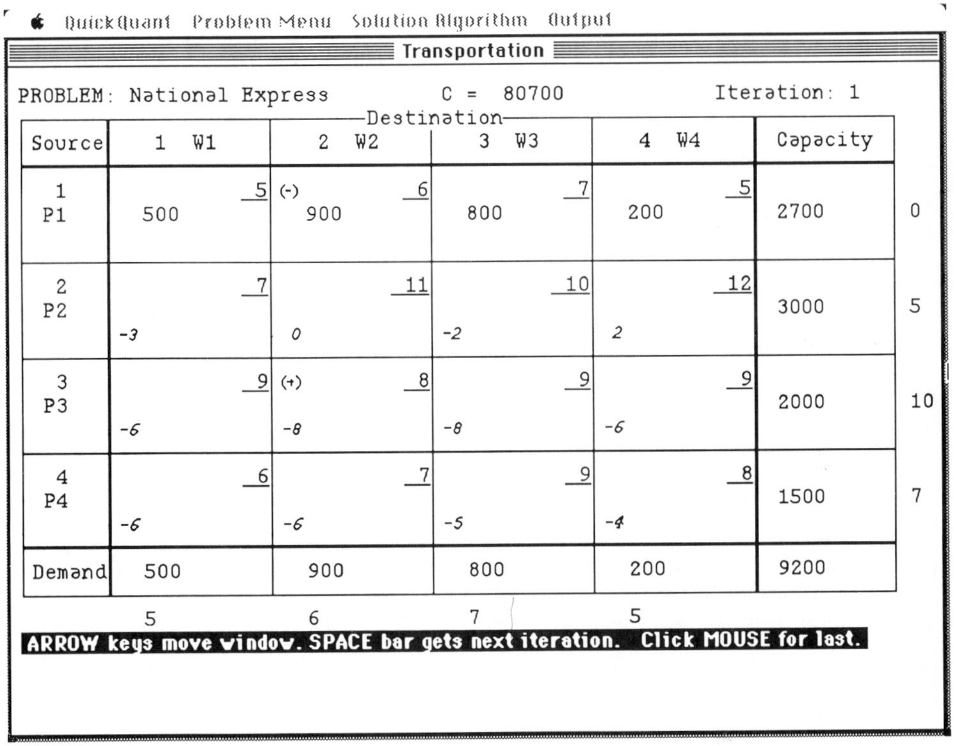

Data Editing

The hardest part of a computer solution is data input. For very large shipment schedules, the last problem solved may serve as a "template" for future problems. Only changes to the previous problem, such as revised costs for a particular route, increases in capacities, or reductions in demands, need to be reentered (overlayed) onto the data file created for the previous problem. The *QuickQuant* package allows users to take full advantage of such data editing. To save computer time, some programs even permit runs to begin using the last solution, adjusted to be feasible within the new constraints, as the starting solution to the new patched-up transportation problem.

CASE

Thread-Bare Fabrics

Every month Thread-Bare Fabrics schedules shipments from its mills worldwide to its distribution centers located near major markets. For the month of March, the following costs for air freight apply per bolt of fabric.

MILLS	DISTRIBUTION CENTERS							
	Los Angeles	Chicago	London	Mexico City	Manila	Rome	Tokyo	New York
Bahamas	2.00	2.00	3.00	3.00	7.00	4.00	7.00	1.00
Hong Kong	6.00	7.00	8.00	10.00	2.00	9.00	4.00	8.00
Korea	5.00	6.00	8.00	11.00	4.00	9.00	1.00	7.00
Nigeria	14.00	12.00	6.00	9.00	11.00	7.00	5.00	10.00
Venezuela	4.00	3.00	5.00	1.00	9.00	6.00	11.00	4.00

Thread-Bare makes three types of cloth: cotton, polyester, and silk. For March, the following demands apply for the various types.

TYPE	FABRIC DEMAND (bolts)							
	Los Angeles	Chicago	London	Mexico City	Manila	Rome	Tokyo	New York
Cotton	500	800	900	900	800	100	200	700
Polyester	1,000	2,000	3,000	1,500	400	700	900	2,500
Silk	100	100	200	50	400	200	700	200

Thread-Bare mills have varying capacities for producing the various types of cloth. The following quantities apply during March.

MILLS	PRODUCTION CAPACITY (bolts)		
	Cotton	Polyester	Silk
Bahamas	1,000	3,000	0
Hong Kong	2,000	2,500	1,000
Korea	1,000	3,500	500
Nigeria	2,000	0	0
Venezuela	1,000	2,000	0

Thread-Bare schedules production and shipments in such a way that the most costly customers are shorted when there is insufficient capacity and the least efficient plants operate at less than full capacity when capacity outstrips demand.

Questions

1. Find the optimal shipment schedule and its total transportation cost for (a) cotton, (b) polyester cloth, and (c) silk.
2. Suppose that Nigeria opens a silk-making department having a 1,000-bolt capacity. Find the new optimal shipment schedule and total cost for that fabric.
3. Suppose that the cotton demands for Manila and Mexico City increase by 10% each, while the polyester demands drop by 10% in New York and Chicago. Find the new optimal shipment schedules and total costs for (a) cotton and (b) polyester.

PROBLEMS

14-1 Use the northwest corner method to find the starting solution to the problem shown in Figure 14-26.

FIGURE 14-26
Blank shipment schedule for Problem 14-1.

$$C =$$

From \ To	H	I	J	K	Capacity
A	15	9	8	7	200
B	11	14	13	12	150
C	6	16	5	4	200
D	17	18	20	3	200
Demand	150	200	250	150	750

14-2 (*Continuation of Problem 14-1*): Use the cheapest cell method to find the starting solution to the problem.

FIGURE 14-27
Blank shipment schedule for Problem 14-3.

From \ To	A	B	C	D	Capacity	
P1	[11]	[12]	[6] (150)	[9]	150	$r_1 =$
P2	[14] (50)	[10]	[10]	[13]	50	$r_2 =$
P3	[17] (150)	[8] (0)	[15]	[11] (50)	200	$r_3 =$
P4	[15]	[12]	[13]	[10] (200)	200	$r_4 =$
P5	[17]	[8] (150)	[9] (100)	[11]	250	$r_5 =$
Demand	200	150	250	250	850	
	$k_A =$	$k_B =$	$k_C =$	$k_D =$		

14-3 The starting solution has been obtained for a transportation problem (see Figure 14-27). It is not optimal.
(a) Find a complete set of row and column numbers.
(b) Determine the improvement value for each empty cell.
(c) Identify the entering cell and indicate the closed-loop path.
(d) Construct the new shipment schedule and compute the new total cost.

14-4 Use the cheapest cell method to find the starting solution to the ski manufacturer's transportation problem in Figure 14-2.

14-5 Use Vogel's approximation to find the starting solution to the ski manufacturer's transportation problem in Figure 14-2.

14-6 A distribution system must meet the following requirements.

PLANT CAPACITY		WAREHOUSE DEMAND	
A	100	U	150
B	150	V	200
C	300	W	200

Unit shipping costs are

From \ To	U	V	W
A	$10	$ 7	$ 8
B	15	12	9
C	7	8	12

(a) Formulate this transportation problem as a linear program.
(b) Determine the optimal solution using the transportation method.

14-7 (*Continuation of Problem 14-6*): Suppose that a new plant D is opened that has a capacity of 200. It costs $8 per unit for this plant to service each warehouse. Use the transportation method to determine the shipment schedule that minimizes total transportation cost.

14-8 (*Continuation of Problem 14-6*): Suppose that a new warehouse X is opened that has a demand of 100. It costs $15 to ship each unit to this warehouse, regardless of the origin. Use the transportation method to determine the shipment schedule that minimizes total transportation cost.

14-9 Consider the intermediate shipment schedule shown in Figure 14-28 for a transportation problem. Determine the row and column numbers. Then, find the closed-loop path. (Remember, the closed-loop path is defined only by the turning points.) *Do not solve the problem further.* Indicate the new solution by crossing out the numbers that have changed and by adding the new shipment quantities to the revised cells.

14-10 Use the transportation method to determine the optimal tombstone shipment schedule for Druids' Drayage in Problem 9-11 (page 300).

14-11 (*Continuation of Problem 14-10*): An alternative (tying) optimal solution exists for a transportation problem whenever an empty cell in the final schedule has an improvement value of zero. Beginning with your final table in Problem 14-10, find the alternative optimal solution for shipping tombstones.

14-12 Use the transportation method to determine the optimal production and shipment schedule for Ace Widgets in Problem 9-18 (page 303).

14-13 *Computer exercise.* WaySafe Markets services eleven district warehouses from three regional centers. The following traffic volumes apply.

CENTER	W1	W2	W3	W4	W5	W6	W7	W8	W9	W10	W11	Center Capacity (kilotons)
C1	10	22	29	45	11	31	42	61	36	21	45	500
C2	25	35	17	38	9	17	65	45	42	5	41	750
C3	18	19	22	29	24	54	39	78	51	14	38	400
Warehouse Demand (kilotons)	112	85	138	146	77	89	101	215	53	49	153	

The average cost of moving goods from a center to a warehouse is $.50 per ton per mile. Find the optimal shipment schedule and its cost.

FIGURE 14-28
Intermediate shipment schedule for Problem 14-9.

To \ From	J	K	L	M	N	O	P	Capacity
A	2	10	8	8	5 (100)	6 (100)	7	200
B	21	15	14	24	7	14 (100)	9	100
C	10	8 (200)	8	14 (100)	10	9	9	300
D	10	11	11 (200)	10	14	16	10	200
E	3	3	2 (200)	8	1	4 (100)	5	300
F	9 (200)	11	12	8 (200)	9	8	7	400
G	12	11 (200)	10	11	13	10	11 (100)	300
H	10	8	12	17	10 (200)	12	10 (100)	300
Demand	200	400	400	300	300	300	200	2,100

14-14 *Computer exercise.* DanDee Assemblers ships parts from four manufacturing plants to 10
 assembly plants. The following data apply.

MANUFACTURING PLANT	COST FOR SHIPPING ONE POUND OF ITEMS										Manufacturing Capacity (thous. lbs.)
	A1	A2	A3	A4	A5	A6	A7	A8	A9	A10	
M1	$ 7	$11	$15	$ 8	$19	$12	$12	$6	$ 9	$10	155
M2	13	14	9	10	13	11	15	9	12	14	245
M3	8	9	12	20	10	5	4	8	15	12	325
M4	17	11	8	15	7	6	9	7	11	16	175
Assembly Demand (thous. lbs.)	75	155	120	130	75	95	115	55	145	95	

Find the optimal shipment schedule and its cost.

CHAPTER

15

Transportation Problems II: Special Applications and Assignment Problems

he **transportation problem** with its solution methods is one of the most widely used forms of linear programming. This chapter shows how the transportation method may be extended to a variety of distribution applications that do not have shipment schedules fitting the standard format encountered in Chapter 14.

The transportation problem is an important linear programming application because it applies to widely encountered distribution decisions. But its value is magnified when the transportation method solves a wider class of linear programming problems. It works on any problem formulated in the rectangular format of a shipment schedule, even when cell entries do not represent physical movement of items. In one manufacturing application, the sources and destinations represent points in time, so that the "transportation" problem yields a plan which gives the optimal production timing for filling demands at different periods. The **assignment problem** is another application fitting the transportation format, in which persons are sources to be assigned to job destinations.

15-1 The Transshipment Problem

The distribution systems encountered so far have just two sets of locations, one to ship and the other to receive. A more general problem is faced by manufacturers with three sets of locations: plants, warehouses, and customers. Warehouses in such systems both receive and transship a product. A distribution optimization for such a system falls into a special class of linear programs called the **transshipment problem**. Such a problem may be solved using the transportation method by including for each transshipment point (warehouse) a row and a column, with identical capacity and demand. Shipments may be allowed between transshipment points, although the respective cells may be made impossible when this is not allowed. Each transshipment point will have a zero-cost *dummy cell* representing the quantity it "ships" to itself; any entry into such a cell represents the amount by which that location operates below its capacity.

To illustrate, consider a single-plant manufacturer with four customers. The 1,000-unit capacity plant makes shipments directly to customers, C1, C2, C3, and C4, as shown in Figure 15-1. But by first making shipments at reduced bulk rates to a company warehouse, overall savings in freight costs are achieved. The warehouse has capacity to handle 500 units, and is represented in Figure 15-1 by both a column and row. The warehouse receives only 200 units from the plant, which are transshipped to C1. It operates 300 units below its capacity, as reflected by the entry in the dummy cell of the warehouse row and column.

FIGURE 15-1
The optimal shipping schedule for the transshipment problem.

$C = 7,700$

From \ To	C1	C2	C3	C4	Warehouse	Capacity
Plant	12	7 (300)	8 (300)	9 (200)	2 (200)	1,000
Warehouse	5 (200)	6	7	8	0 (300)	500
Demand	200	300	300	200	500	1,500

15-2 The Assignment Problem

An important managerial decision is personnel assignment. People vary so widely in their skill and competence levels that it is challenging to determine which workers are best suited to perform specific jobs. A classical application of the **assignment problem** is provided by a small machine shop, where individual machinists are assigned to particular machines or jobs. This must be done so that every worker is assigned to exactly one job and every job is assigned to a worker. The assignments must minimize the combined time or cost for completing all of the required jobs.

As we saw in Chapter 9, the linear programming approach is well suited to machine shop personnel assignments, because each task is well defined and the respective productivities (time required per item) of each worker can be accurately measured. Moreover, machine shop jobs require similar skills, so that workers can easily be shifted to new assignments. The types of personnel situations to which the assignment problem can be applied are limited. As a linear program, the assignment problem is encountered much less frequently than the transportation problem.

A Machine Shop Assignment Problem

We will expand the machine shop example described in Chapter 9 to include six individual machinists who are to be assigned to six jobs, each to be performed on a different type of machine. Each of the six tasks is to be completed successively on aluminum castings that will be shaped into a final product. Past records provide individual performance data for all six workers. Table 15-1 summarizes the average times (in minutes) that each worker takes to complete each job for one item.

Our objective is to assign the individuals to jobs in such a way that the total average labor time per item is minimized. The assignments are summarized in the assignment schedule in Figure 15-2. The unknown cell quantities are represented by the variables

$$X_{ij} = \text{Fraction of time individual } i \text{ is assigned to job } j$$

TABLE 15-1
Average Times (in minutes) for Machine Shop Assignments

INDIVIDUAL i \ JOB j	Drilling	Grinding	Lathe	Milling	Polishing	Routing
Ann	13	22	19	21	16	20
Bud	18	17	24	18	22	27
Chuck	20	22	23	24	17	31
Eduardo	14	19	13	30	23	22
Sam	21	14	17	25	15	23
Tom	17	23	18	20	16	24

FIGURE 15-2
The machine shop assignment schedule.

Job j / Individual i	D	G	L	M	P	R	Availability
A	13 X_{AD}	22 X_{AG}	19 X_{AL}	21 X_{AM}	16 X_{AP}	20 X_{AR}	1
B	18 X_{BD}	17 X_{BG}	24 X_{BL}	18 X_{BM}	22 X_{BP}	27 X_{BR}	1
C	20 X_{CD}	22 X_{CG}	23 X_{CL}	24 X_{CM}	17 X_{CP}	31 X_{CR}	1
E	14 X_{ED}	19 X_{EG}	13 X_{EL}	30 X_{EM}	23 X_{EP}	22 X_{ER}	1
S	21 X_{SD}	14 X_{SG}	17 X_{SL}	25 X_{SM}	15 X_{SP}	23 X_{SR}	1
T	17 X_{TD}	23 X_{TG}	18 X_{TL}	20 X_{TM}	16 X_{TP}	24 X_{TR}	1
Requirement	1	1	1	1	1	1	6

The marginal row and column totals are 1. Thus, every person must be fully occupied (so that the row X's sum to 1) and every job must be completely assigned (so that the column X's sum to 1). The average completion times for individual–job combinations serve the same function as the unit shipping costs in a transportation problem.

Solving the Assignment Problem

Assignment problems have all the structural elements of the transportation problem. Thus, the transportation method can be used to solve that class of problems as well.

Either the northwest corner method, the cheapest cell method, or Vogel's approximation may be used to find a starting solution. Figure 15-3 shows the initial assignment

FIGURE 15-3

Starting solution for the machine shop assignment problem using the transportation method.

Job j / i Individual	D	G	L	M	P	R	Availability	
A	13 ①	22	19	21	16	20	1	$r_A = 0$ ⓐ
B	18	17 ⓪	24	18 ①	22	27	1	$r_B = 8$ ⓖ
C	20	22	23	24	17 ⓪	31 ①	1	$r_C = 11$ ⓚ
E	14 ⓪	19	13 ①	30	23	22	1	$r_E = 1$ ⓒ
S	21	14 ①	17 ⓪	25	15	23	1	$r_S = 5$ ⓔ
T	17	23	18	20 ⓪	16 ①	24	1	$r_T = 10$ ⓘ
Requirement	1	1	1	1	1	1	6	

$k_D = 13$ ⓑ $k_G = 9$ ⓕ $k_L = 12$ ⓓ $k_M = 10$ ⓗ $k_P = 6$ ⓙ $k_R = 20$ ⓛ

using the cheapest cell method. Five ⓪ values are inserted in Figure 15-3 as the row and column numbers are determined.

Figure 15-4 shows the first iteration for solving the machine shop assignment problem using the transportation method. The row and column numbers we found in Figure 15-3 have been used to compute the empty cell differences. Cell *CD* is the entering cell, which has an improvement value of -10. The closed-loop path turns out to be a double figure-8. Notice that the losing cells all contain circled zeros. The maximum quantity to be reallocated along the closed-loop path is zero, and exactly one of the losing cells will go blank in the next solution. We break the tie by choosing the most expensive losing cell, and the circled zero from cell *CR* moves to cell *CD*. The total time savings is $10 \times 0 = 0$.

After several more iterations that involve only the movement of circled zeroes, we can establish that the present assignment of workers to jobs is in fact optimal. Actually, there is a tie for the optimal solution. Either of the following assignments will minimize total average time.

WORKER	OPTIMUM		ALTERNATIVE OPTIMUM	
	Job	*Time*	*Job*	*Time*
Ann	Drilling	13 min	Routing	20 min
Bud	Milling	18	Milling	18
Chuck	Polishing	17	Polishing	17
Eduardo	Lathe	13	Lathe	13
Sam	Grinding	14	Grinding	14
Tom	Routing	24	Drilling	17
		99 min		99 min

And any solution in which Ann and Tom split the drilling and routing jobs—say, spending one-half of their time on each job—would also be optimal.

FIGURE 15-4

The first iteration for solving the machine shop assignment problem using the transportation method.

i Individual \ Job *j*	*D*	*G*	*L*	*M*	*P*	*R*	Availability	
A	[13] ①	[22] 13	[19] 7	[21] 11	[16] 16	[20] 6	1	$r_A = 0$
B	[18] −3	[17] ⓪ (−)	[24] 4	[18] ① (+)	[22] 14	[27] 5	1	$r_B = 8$
C	[20] (+) −10	[22] −4	[23] −6	[24] −3	[17] ①	[31] ⓪ (−)	1	$r_C = 17$
E	[14] ⓪ (−)	[19] 9	[13] ① (+)	[30] 19	[23] 22	[22] 7	1	$r_E = 1$
S	[21] 3	[14] ① (+)	[17] ⓪ (−)	[25] 10	[15] 10	[23] 4	1	$r_S = 5$
T	[17] −6	[23] 4	[18] −4	[20] ⓪ (−)	[16] 6	[24] ① (+)	1	$r_T = 10$
Requirement	1	1	1	1	1	1	6	
	$k_D = 13$	$k_G = 9$	$k_L = 12$	$k_M = 10$	$k_P = 0$	$k_R = 14$		

15-3 Other Applications of the Transportation Problem

The scope of the transportation problem can be expanded to consider production costs as well as freight charges. For example, suppose that the three plants in the ski distribution illustration all operated at different unit costs—say, $60 for Juarez, $50 for Seoul, and $65 for Tel Aviv. Cost differentials are just as important in choosing which plants will service which warehouses as the physical distances separating the production and consumption centers. By adding 60 to row J costs, 50 to row S costs, and 65 to row T costs, the ski distribution transportation problem can be solved so that all distribution costs—instead of just the freight costs—can be optimized. Indeed, any formulation that does not reflect all cost differentials between plants is undesirable and generally leads to an inferior solution. (This revised problem will be left as an exercise.)

The transportation problem is so-named because it was originally used to determine shipment schedules in distribution systems. However, its basic source–destination structure makes it suitable for solving many other types of problems that do not involve the physical distribution of items. For example, this format can be used to establish a plant's production schedule for several time periods.

Transportation Method Used in Production Scheduling

As an illustration, we will suppose that the Juarez ski plant can actually operate at as much as 150% of its stated capacity during the August–November period by placing its work force on overtime. We will also assume that the company policy is to use this plant exclusively to service the Phoenix warehouse. Moreover, we will assume that Juarez can make up to 100 pairs of skis monthly at a cost of $60 per pair using regular labor; for an additional $20 per pair, Juarez can make 50 additional pairs of skis per month using overtime labor. Finally, we will assume that the factory can store extra skis for later distribution at a cost of $1 per pair per month.

Now, suppose that the following demands occur at the Phoenix warehouse.

August	100 pairs
September	150
October	200
November	100
	550 pairs

Figure 15-5 provides the optimal ski production schedule. There are eight "plants," each representing the month and type of production (R = regular, O = overtime). There are four "warehouses"—one for each monthly demand, plus one dummy warehouse (since total capacity exceeds total demand).

In constructing Figure 15-5, we have omitted the unit freight charge, since it is the same for all cells. Notice that it is impossible to satisfy an earlier demand from later production. For the sake of completeness, however, the cells representing these situations appear in the table. Such allocations receive a very large unit cost of M dollars. Any starting solution that involved such a cell would exit early. Also notice that each cell in the dummy column has a unit cost of zero.

FIGURE 15-5
The optimal ski production schedule.

From Month \ To Month	A	S	O	N	Dummy	Capacity
AR	60 (100)	61 (0)	62	63	0	100
AO	80	81 (50)	82	83	0 (0)	50
SR	M	60 (100)	61 (0)	62	0	100
SO	M	80	81 (50)	82	0	50
OR	M	M	60 (100)	61	0	100
OO	M	M	80 (50)	81	0	50
NR	M	M	M	60 (100)	0	100
NO	M	M	M	80 (0)	0 (50)	50
Demand	100	150	200	100	50	600

The transportation problem format may be used for certain production scheduling problems where the nature of the physical items themselves, not just the timing, is to be decided. This approach might be used in an assembly operation, where various components are joined together into final products. Supply constraints exist for the components, and these must be allocated to final products to meet demand constraints. All other production factors must be assumed in plentiful supply, so that there are no labor or machine time constraints, for example. (The coefficients of the X's must always be one, and all constraints must involve simple addition with the X's.)

Profit Maximization Problems

Assembly type production problems have an overall objective of maximizing profit rather than minimizing cost. The transportation method is easily adapted for that objective. The simplest approach would be to reverse the entry criterion, selecting as the entering cell the one having greatest *positive* difference $c_{ij} - r_i - k_j$. The northwest corner start would be identical. A faster start could be achieved by using a most-profitable-cell method, analogous to the cheapest cell method, in which the most profitable cell in the uncrossed out portion is given a maximum allocation at each step.

15-4 Solving Nonstandard Transportation Problems

The transportation method requires that total demand exactly match total capacity. There is no reason why a real-world distribution system must have this feature, which is only a requirement of the solution algorithm and not the linear program. In Chapter 14, we saw how the inclusion of a dummy source or destination can convert any transportation problem into the required standard form having balanced capacity and demand.

There are other nonstandard problem forms. Some of these arise from **impossible cells**. For example, a plant dispatcher might not be able to send items from one plant to a particular warehouse, perhaps because it is more than the allowed distance from the plant. A second group of nonstandard transportation problems involve **bounded cells**. These may arise because only single truckloads may be allowed to service remote locations, so that there is a maximum quantity allowed over a particular route, while a minimum quantity may be needed to justify sending a truck at all.

This section concludes with a group of nonstandard problems that arise from constraints on sources or destinations. A source may have a **bounded capacity**, so that the amount disbursed falls somewhere between lower and upper limits. This may be the case, for example, if a second production line could be added at any time. A related problem is one having **bounded demand**; for example, when a warehouse handles special customer orders that may vary widely.

Special Treatment of Cells

Cell constraints arise when, in addition to the usual non-negativity conditions, a particular source–destination combination has special restrictions that apply only to shipments along that route.

The Impossible Cell The transportation method requires that there be a completely rectangular shipment schedule. This means that there must be a position or cell for all combinations of sources and destinations, even if one of these represents a route that is impossible. The cell must be present, even if it is to receive no quantity. This may be accomplished by making the cell prohibitively costly, assigning it a cost of M. In a computer solution, an impossible cell is assigned a cost thousands or millions of times higher than regular cell costs. Such a cell would never be selected by a cost-based starting procedure, and would exit the shipping schedule soon after starting with any other procedure.

Upper Limit for Cell   Figure 15-6(a) shows the blank shipment schedule for a transportation problem where cell AJ has an upper bound of 50 units. All other cells in the problem are regular ones.

Figure 15-6(b) shows the amended problem, which was achieved by splitting column J into two columns. The new column, labeled $J2$, has a demand of 50 units. Any

FIGURE 15-6

Shipment schedules for the transportation problem when a cell has an *upper bound*. The original problem in (a) is expanded in (b) with the addition of a second column J2 and a revised demand for J.

From \ To	J	K	L	Capacity
A *(Upper cell bound of 50 units)*	2	4	9	150
B	8	5	9	150
C	4	11	3	350
Demand	180	270	200	650

(a) Original problem

$C = 2,490$

From \ To	J	J2	K	L	Capacity
A	M	2 (30)	4 (150)	9	150
B	8	8	5 (150)	9	150
C	4 (150)	4 (50)	11	3 (200)	350
Demand	$180 - 50 = 130$	50	270	200	650

(b) Amended problem with optimal solution

shipments out of A to J will appear as a quantity in this column. There are no restrictions as to which sources can ship into $J2$, and any quantity listed there is interpreted as actually going to destination J. The original cell AJ has been made impossible to guarantee that J receive at most 50 units from A. The other sources, B and C, must fulfill the remainder of J's demand. The original demand for column J is reduced by 50 units, so that the demands for J and $J2$ sum to the original demand for destination J.

The optimal solution provides only 30 units from A to J (shown in column $J2$). The remaining 150 units of J's demand will be filled by source C, with 130 units sent via column J and 20 units via column $J2$.

The following steps summarize this procedure. It can only be applied when the cell restriction does not violate existing demand and capacity constraints.

1. Bring total capacity and total demand into balance, incorporating a dummy row or column, as needed.
2. Add a new column that has the same costs as the original destination column containing the restricted cell.
3. The demand for the new column will equal the upper limit for the restricted cell.
4. Reduce the demand in the original column containing the restricted cell by the amount of the upper limit.
5. Make the original restricted cell impossible by giving it an arbitrarily high cost M.

Lower Limit for Cell   A related situation arises when a cell has a lower bound, as illustrated in Figure 15-7(a). There, cell HL must receive no fewer than 20 units, and all other cells are regular ones. Figure 15-7(b) shows the amended problem, which was achieved by splitting row H into two rows. A new row, labeled $H2$, is added. Any shipments from row $H2$ are interpreted as actually coming from the original source H. The $H2$ row has a capacity equal to the HL minimum of 20, and it may ship only to destination L, so that cells $H2$-M and $H2$-N are impossible. The original H row has its capacity reduced by 20, so that altogether the capacity of source H remains unchanged. Unlike the above case, cell HL is not impossible, reflecting that more than 20 units may be sent from H to L.

The solution shows that source H will send $80 + 20 = 100$ units to destination L, which exceeds the minimum by 80.

The following steps summarize this procedure. It can only be applied when the cell restriction does not violate existing demand and capacity constraints.

1. Bring total capacity and total demand into balance, incorporating a dummy row or column, as needed.
2. Add a new row with the cell for the restricted route having the original cost. All other cells in the new row must be impossible with arbitrarily large costs of M. (The original restricted cell is *not* made impossible.)
3. The capacity for the new row will equal the lower limit for the restricted cell.
4. Reduce the capacity in the original row containing the restricted cell by the amount of the lower limit.

FIGURE 15-7

Shipment schedules for the transportation problem when a cell has a *lower bound*. The original problem in (a) is expanded in (b) with the addition of a second row *H2* and a revised capacity for *H*.

From \ To	L	M	N	Capacity
H (Lower cell bound of 20 units)	2	8	9	100
I	4	7	6	200
J	7	2	3	300
Demand	300	100	200	600

(a) Original problem

$C = 1,800$

From \ To	L	M	N	Capacity
H	(80) 2	8	9	100 − 20 = 80
H2	(20) 2	M	M	20
I	(200) 4	7	6	200
J	(0) 7	(100) 2	(200) 3	300
Demand	300	100	200	600

(b) Amended problem with optimal solution

FIGURE 15-8

Shipment schedules for the transportation problem when a cell has *both* an upper and a lower bound. The original problem (a) is first expanded in (b) to reflect the upper bound. That problem is then expanded in (c) to reflect the lower bound.

From \ To	T	U	Capacity
R	[5]	[6]	50
S	[7]	[4]	150
Demand	100	100	200

Upper bound = 30 (established first)

Lower bound = 20

(a) Original problem

From \ To	T	T2	U	Capacity
R	[M]	[5]	[6]	50
S	[7]	[7]	[4]	150
Demand	100 − 30 = 70	30	100	200

Lower bound = 20

(b) Amended problem reflecting upper bound only of 30 for RT

C = 1,080

From \ To	T	T2	U	Capacity
R	[M]	[5] (10)	[6] (20)	50 − 20 = 30
R2	[M]	[5] (20)	[M]	20
S	[7] (70)	[7]	[4] (80)	150
Demand	70	30	100	200

(c) Final amended problem with optimal solution

Cell with Both Upper and Lower Bound   Whenever a cell has both an upper bound and a non-zero lower bound, the above two procedures may be applied sequentially. Consider the original shipment schedule in Figure 15-8(a) where cell RT has an upper bound of 30 units and a lower bound of 20 units. Initially ignoring the lower bound, the 30-unit upper bound is reflected in Figure 15-8(b). From that formulation, cell R-$T2$ will be restricted to a lower bound of 20 units. The final shipment is reflected in Figure 15-8(c). The optimal solution involves a total of 30 units shipped from R to T (R-$T2$ having 10 units and $R2$-$T2$ having 20 units).

Although the impossible cell designations will vary, an identical overall solution will be achieved if the lower bound is established as the first step.

Bounded Capacity

Consider a transportation problem where one source has a bounded capacity. To illustrate, consider a modification to the ski distribution problem originally described in Chapter 14. The optimal solution to that problem is shown in Figure 15-9.

Suppose that the Juarez plant (row J) could triple its capacity by adding a second or third shift and that the added lines can be shut down early if necessary. Thus, the modified problem involves a Juarez plant having capacity C_J such that

$$100 \le C_J \le 300$$

The original capacity of 100 must still be met; this quantity becomes a *lower bound*. The

FIGURE 15-9
The optimal solution to the original ski distribution problem.

$C = 6{,}250$

From \ To	F	N	P	Y	Capacity
J	19	7	3 (100)	21	100
S	15 (50)	21	18 (100)	6 (150)	300
T	11 (100)	14 (100)	15	22	200
Demand	150	100	200	150	600

upper bound is 300, achieved if the maximum additional skis were to be produced on added shifts.

Figure 15-10 shows how the original problem is modified through the creation of a new row for a *second* Juarez source, $J2$. All shipping costs are identical, and the new row has capacity equal to the difference in limits on C_J, $300 - 100 = 200$. The new source makes overall capacity exceed total demand, and a dummy warehouse must be created having the same demand as the new row's capacity.

Notice that the dummy cell in row J is impossible and has cost M. This will force Juarez to at least meet its capacity minimum. Remember that all shipments into a dummy cell represent product not made and not sent. Thus, we see that the Juarez plant should ship 100 pairs from the first shift's production plus another 200 pairs from second and third shifts (row $J2$). The dummy column has 150 pairs from Seoul (row S) and 50 from Tel Aviv (row T). These represent production diverted to the Juarez plant. Altogether, the resulting distribution cost is $3,850, a substantial savings from the original problem.

The above illustration shows how to apply the transportation method when the maximum total capacity exceeds total demand. If maximum total capacity is exactly equal to total demand, no extra row is needed. For instance, if New York demand had been 300 (instead of 100), no $J2$ row would be added, and the original J row with capacity 300 (the upper limit) would suffice. This is because all sources would then have to operate at full capacity in order to meet the 800 units demanded. Should the total demand exceed

FIGURE 15-10

The optimal shipping schedule for the ski distribution problem modified to have a plant with a bounded capacity.

$C = 3,850$

From \ To	F	N	P	Y	Dummy	Capacity
J	19	7	3 (100)	21	M	100
J2	19	7 (100)	3 (100)	21	0 (0)	200
S	15	21	18	6 (150)	0 (150)	300
T	11 (150)	14	15	22	0 (50)	200
Demand	150	100	200	150	200	800

maximum total capacity, a dummy source *row* would be needed. That would be the case if New York's demand were 400. But, again, no $J2$ row would be needed, and there would be no impossible cells.

When *QuickQuant* is used to solve a bounded capacity problem, the program automatically creates dummy rows or columns where needed. However, the costs of impossible cells must be increased from zero using the edit routine, selected from the main menu choice 3.

Bounded Demand

An analogous nonstandard problem will have a bounded demand for one of the destinations. To illustrate, consider, again, the ski distribution problem with no extra shifts contemplated at Juarez. Suppose that the demand D_F at Frankfurt (column F) may fall anywhere between 100 and 250 skis. Thus,

$$100 \leq D_F \leq 250$$

Figure 15-11 shows the optimal shipping schedule for this modified problem. The demand for column F is 100 in this changed problem. There is an added column, $F2$, representing any shipments into Frankfurt exceeding the minimum demand. This column has identical

FIGURE 15-11

The optimal shipping schedule for the ski distribution problem modified to have a warehouse with a bounded demand.

$C = 5,950$

From \ To	F	F2	N	P	Y	Capacity
J	19	19	7	3 (100)	21	100
S	15	15 (50)	21	18 (100)	6 (150)	300
T	11 (100)	11 (100)	14	15	22	200
Dummy	M	0	0 (100)	0 (0)	0	100
Demand	100	150	100	200	150	700

costs to the original column F and a demand equal to the maximum potential excess beyond the minimum, $250 - 100 = 150$. A dummy row has been created to bring total capacity up to total demand. The original column F can receive no shipments from the dummy source, and so a cell cost of M appears in that impossible cell.

Notice that the dummy cell in column N (New York) provides the entire demand for that warehouse, so that in effect New York receives no skis. It is less expensive to divert all of those items to $F2$ (Frankfurt's new demand). (If wiping out all ski shipments to New York were not allowed, the problem could be further amended so that there is a lower bound on shipments to that destination.)

The above illustration shows how to apply the transportation method when the maximum total demand exceeds total capacity. If maximum total demand is less than or equal to total capacity, no extra column is required. For instance, if Seoul capacity had been 450 (instead of 300), the original Frankfurt column with demand 250 (the upper limit) would suffice. This is because all demands would be met exactly. Should Seoul capacity be still higher, a dummy destination *column* would be needed (but no $F2$ column).

15-5 Additional Remarks

Some problem situations are so specially structured that a refinement of the transportation method itself provides an even more efficient solution procedure. Special purpose linear programming algorithms have been developed to solve assignment problems. One popular approach is the *Hungarian method*,* which is more streamlined than the more general transportation method. The assignment problem may also be treated as an *integer program* (to be described in Chapter 16) and solved using a procedure such as the *branch-and-bound method*. Another group of algorithms, based on the concepts of flows through networks, are often used in place of the transportation method to solve similar problems. Further discussion of these and other linear programming algorithms is beyond the scope of this book. Many of the references at the back of the book examine these procedures in detail.

CASE

Fast-Gro Fertilizer Company I

Fast-Gro Fertilizer Company currently operates in California with two plants, located in Red Bluff (annual capacity 1,500,000 tons) and Bakersfield (1,000,000 tons). Fast-Gro has two warehouses, each with a capacity of 500,000 tons, situated in Sacramento and Visalia. Each facility lies near the center of gravity of a local sales territory. The California market is divided into five more territories, each containing hundreds of individual customers.

---

* This method requires much trial and error, which may actually make it harder to apply to large problems.

TABLE 15-2

Mileage Data and Allowed Routes for the Fast-Gro Fertilizer Company

TERRITORY	DISTANCE									Demand (thous. tons)
	1	2	3	4	5	6	7	8	9	
1. Bakersfield (plant)	35	240	240	—	210	150	140	150	50	250
2. Imperial	—	10	—	—	—	—	—	—	—	300
3. Napa/North Coast	—	—	20	—	50	100	—	100	—	150
4. Red Bluff (plant)	—	—	120	30	110	240	—	200	280	200
5. Sacramento (whse.)	—	—	50	—	25	140	—	70	—	400
6. Salinas	—	—	100	—	—	15	—	80	160	400
7. San Bernardino	—	130	—	—	—	—	15	—	—	200
8. Turlock	—	—	100	—	—	80	—	25	—	150
9. Visalia (whse.)	—	—	—	—	—	160	—	95	20	300

Fast-Gro plants serve the warehouse function for the territory in which they are situated. Any warehouse may deliver to customers in neighboring territories, within geographical constraints. Table 15-2 provides the territory demands and the applicable distances. Blank entries indicate that no shipments are allowed over that route.

The numbers along the main diagonal represent average delivery distances from the central point to customers within the territory. For example, 10 miles is the average distance from the center to customers within the Imperial territory. That distance will be used as the miles to the Imperial customer group aggregation. A shipment from the Bakersfield plant to the customer group in that territory will go by truck over a distance of $240 + 10 = 250$ miles. A shipment to the Turlock customer group may be made directly from the Bakersfield plant, a truck distance of $150 + 25 = 175$ miles. The same Turlock customer group might instead receive shipments through the Visalia warehouse; those items would travel 50 miles by rail from Bakersfield to Visalia, then another $95 + 25 = 120$ miles by truck. (Since rail and truck routes differ, the total distances are not the same.)

Freight costs per ton-mile are $.02 by truck and $.01 by rail. Rail shipments are made only from a plant to a warehouse.

Questions

1. Construct a transportation problem matrix for Fast-Gro's distribution. Be sure to set up the schedule as a *transshipment* problem, so that each warehouse has both a row and a column. Warehouses may not ship to another warehouse, and the corresponding variables should be represented in the shipment schedule as *impossible cells*, as would forbidden routings. Those cells should each have an arbitrarily high cost M. As a final step, add a dummy row or column to make total demand equal total capacity.

2. Solve the above transportation problem and find the minimum transportation cost, using a computer if possible. If you solve it by hand, use the cheapest cell method or Vogel's approximation to start. Make no allocations to impossible cells, and proceed to determine the optimal solution.

3. Suppose that the warehouse capacities are increased to 750,000 tons each. Determine the new optimal shipment schedule and its total cost.

PROBLEMS

15-1 The Bugoff Chemical Company has three plants and four warehouses. The costs, capacities, and demands are given in the blank shipment schedule in Figure 15-12. Suppose that a Kansas City distribution center is added with a capacity of 2,000 units. The center will receive large shipments from plants and transship units to warehouses. The following transportation costs apply.

PLANT TO KANSAS CITY		KANSAS CITY TO WAREHOUSE	
Chicago	2	Boston	8
Memphis	2	Denver	3
New Orleans	1	Houston	5
		Phoenix	6

Find the minimum-cost solution.

FIGURE 15-12
Blank shipment schedule for Problem 15-1.

From \ To	Boston	Denver	Houston	Phoenix	Capacity
Chicago	13	4	6	11	1000
Memphis	10	5	3	9	800
New Orleans	12	7	2	8	700
Demand	500	750	800	450	2500

15-2 Refer to Problem 14-6 (page 454). Suppose that a hub center is added with a capacity of 300 units. The hub will receive large shipments from plants and transship units to warehouses. The following transportation costs apply.

PLANT TO HUB		HUB TO WAREHOUSE	
A	2	U	5
B	3	V	6
C	2	W	7

Find the minimum-cost solution.

15-3 An assignment schedule in Figure 15-13 has been obtained using a cost-based starting procedure. Use the transportation method to determine the optimal solution or to verify that the current solution is optimal.

FIGURE 15-13
Blank shipment schedule for Problem 15-2.

$C = 27$

Task *j* / Person *i*	V	W	X	Y	Z	Availability
A	6	17	7	13	5 (1)	1
B	15	2	8 (1)	19	25	1
C	9	14	18	1 (1)	12	1
D	3 (1)	16	4	24	23	1
E	21	10 (1)	20	11	22	1
Demand	1	1	1	1	1	5

15-4 Hans and Fritz, and their cousins Gert and Zelda, wish to divide their chores to minimize total combined working time and to maximize their playing time. Each is faster at certain daily chores. The following times apply.

	Chase Hippos	Pen Ostriches	Retrieve The Captain's Pipe	Scare Cannibals
Fritz	15 min	30 min	10 min	15 min
Hans	10	20	15	10
Gert	20	15	15	20
Zelda	10	20	10	15

Each brat must do one chore, and all chores must be done. Solve this assignment problem using the transportation method.

15-5 Use the transportation method to solve CompuQuick's assignment decision in Problem 9-5 (page 298).

15-6 Use the transportation method to solve Conformity Systems' assignment decision in Problem 9-15 (page 302).

15-7 The following costs apply to an assignment problem.

INDIVIDUAL i \ JOB j	J	K	L	M	N
A	3	17	5	21	13
B	10	4	14	24	7
C	10	15	26	8	20
D	23	6	9	19	25
E	11	18	27	12	22

Determine the optimal assignment.

15-8 A six-person team is entered in the World Greased-Pig Wrestling Championship. The following wrestler-task assignments, along with the average penalty points assessed in preliminary contest, are possible:

WRESTLER \ TASK	Grabbing	Holding	Identifying	Jerking	Kicking	Loading
Anastasia	0	18	7	2	21	14
Basil	9	1	15	24	31	6
Carlos	19	28	10	20	34	12
Daphne	4	16	16	3	13	32
Elsie	17	23	8	26	15	29
Fred	5	25	22	11	35	27

An assignment is to be made that will minimize the total average penalty points for the entire team. Determine the optimal assignment.

15-9 Suppose that the following demands apply instead for providing skis from the Juarez plant to the Phoenix warehouse in the problem discussed in Section 15-3.

August	25 pairs
September	175
October	150
November	150

Also, suppose that now the regular production cost is $50 per pair, the overtime premium is $25 per pair, and the storage cost is $5 per pair. Solve this problem using the transportation method to determine the optimal plan for ski production at the Juarez plant.

15-10 Love and Peace Leather Works creates products from exotic skins obtained by the owner on hunting trips. After each hunt, the skins are cut into strips to make purse straps, belts, plant hangers, and hatbands. These items are sold to The Skin Boutique at an agreed price. On the latest trip, our hunter has obtained the following numbers of strips: 30 rattlesnakes, 100 crocodiles, 50 armadillos, and 20 Gila monsters. Each strip is of equal size, and any one type of skin can be used for each final product. The Skin Boutique will buy up to 50 purse straps, 100 belts, 50 plant hangers, and 100 hatbands—regardless of the material used to make them. The prices yield the following profits to Love and Peace.

	PRODUCT			
SKIN	Purse Strap	Belt	Plant Hanger	Hatband
Rattlesnake	$ 5	$12	$ 5	$10
Crocodile	10	15	5	10
Armadillo	8	10	10	5
Gila monster	10	20	20	15

Solve this problem using the transportation method to determine how Love and Peace can maximize its profits.

15-11 Refer to Problem 15-1. For each of the following amendments, modify Figure 15-12 to construct a blank shipment schedule that expresses the transportation problem in standard form.
(a) New Orleans cannot ship to Boston, and Memphis cannot ship to Phoenix.
(b) At least 100 units must be shipped from Chicago to Boston.
(c) No more than 200 units may be shipped from New Orleans to Houston.

15-12 (*Continuation of Problem 15-11*): Find the optimal solution to the three amended versions of the BugOff Chemical problem.

15-13 Refer to the shipment schedule for the BugOff Chemical distribution decision in Problem 15-1. For each of the following amendments to Figure 15-12, set up a blank shipment schedule that expresses the transportation problem in standard form.
(a) Chicago has a lower limit of 900 and an upper limit of 1200 units.
(b) Phoenix has a lower limit of 300 and an upper limit of 500 units.

15-14 (*Continuation of Problem 15-13*): Find the optimal solution to the two amended versions of the BugOff Chemical problem.

15-15   A freight dispatcher must supply five stores with daily shipments from two warehouses. The following unit cost and quantity requirements apply.

From Warehouse \ To Store	J	K	L	M	N	Warehouse Loading Capacity
A	$5	$8	$6	$4	$13	1,000
B	6	9	4	5	6	500
Store Requirement	400	300	200	300	300	1,500

In addition, store N is so far from warehouse A that it is possible to send only one truckload per day from A to N. Up to 100 units can be carried in one trip.
(a) Construct the shipment schedule for this problem and find the northwest corner solution.
(b) Continue to solve the problem until you determine the optimal shipment schedule.

Integer Programming and the Branch-and-Bound Method

Integer programming is an extension of linear programming, with the additional restriction that the variables must be integers or whole numbers. In this chapter, we will investigate integer programs and focus on one solution technique that has been successfully used to solve them—the branch-and-bound method.

16-1 An Introduction to Integer Programming

We have seen that linear programs permit fractional solutions, which is satisfactory for most applications. In manufacturing, the completion of one-half or one-third of a unit might merely signify that the production period is ending with unfinished goods or some work-in-progress inventory. Even at the end of a production run, when no unfinished goods are held over, one-third of an item may be inconsequential when quantities are in the hundreds or thousands.

But there is a significant class of situations for which the solution values must be whole numbers or **integers**. For example, an airline might use a linear program to determine what aircraft to buy. A linear programming solution involving $5\frac{2}{3}$ Boeing 747's and $9\frac{3}{8}$ DC-10's would not be very meaningful. Furthermore, a rounded solution—with respective values of 6 and 9, in this case—may not even be feasible or may cost millions of dollars more than the truly optimal solution. Problems that may otherwise be solved by employing linear programming, except that there are integer restrictions on the variables involved, fall into the category of **integer programs**.

Difficulties in Solving Integer Programs

To the uninitiated, integer programs may appear to be easier to solve than linear programs. After all, linear programs usually have an infinite number of feasible solutions, and most integer programs should have a finite number of integer solutions. This is true. But procedures for solving linear programs such as simplex allow us to find the optimal solution by evaluating only a few corner points. We never have to enter the interior.

Simplex locates the treasure lying on one of the few mountain peaks on the edge of unexplored territory. Integer programming can require an extensive search of all corner and interior points. Even small integer programs with a handful of constraints and variables may have billions of feasible solutions. And no known procedure even approaches simplex in keeping the number of evaluations to a minimum. We must trudge through the rain forest until we trip over the prize.

Several algorithms can be used in solving integer programs. The most promising are the branch-and-bound techniques described in this chapter. New research is currently under way to find more effective ways to evaluate integer programs.

Graphical Solutions

As an example, consider the following integer program.

$$\text{Maximize} \quad P = 14X_1 + 16X_2$$
$$\text{Subject to} \quad 4X_1 + 3X_2 \leq 12 \quad (A)$$
$$6X_1 + 8X_2 \leq 24 \quad (B)$$

where X_1 and X_2 are non-negative integers

In place of the requirement that all X's ≥ 0, we specify that X_1 and X_2 must be non-negative integers.

It is convenient to begin by treating the problem as a linear program, which is solved graphically in Figure 16-1. If this solution involves only integer values, then it will be the solution to the integer program as well. But, we obtain

$$X_1 = 1\frac{5}{7} \qquad X_2 = 1\frac{5}{7}$$
$$P = 51\frac{3}{7}$$

which does not meet the integer specifications. It is tempting to round this solution off

FIGURE 16-1

Graphical solutions to a problem formulated as a linear program and as an integer program.

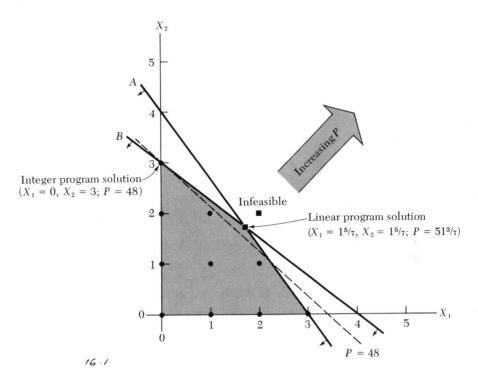

16·1

to ($X_1 = 2$, $X_2 = 2$), but our graph indicates that this is infeasible. The dots in Figure 16-1, which are sometimes referred to as **lattice points**, represent all of the integer solutions that lie within the feasible solution region of the linear program. The optimal integer solution is

$$X_1 = 0 \qquad X_2 = 3$$
$$P = 48$$

Notice that its lattice point is not even adjacent to the most attractive linear programming corner.

Enumeration and Cutting-Plane Solutions

How do we solve integer programs? The most difficult approach would be to evaluate every lattice point to determine its P value and whether or not it is feasible. But even for a modest problem with only a few variables, this task could take years!

Figure 16-1 suggests that there is another way. First, we can find a solution to the problem when it is formulated as a linear program (which, with luck, could contain integers). Notice that the optimal lattice point lies at the corner of the region obtained by cutting away the small triangle above the dashed line. This suggests a solution procedure that successively cuts down the feasible solution region until an integer-valued corner is found.

Cutting-plane methods, which are not limited to situations involving two variables, do just that. Each successive linear program is solved by simplex, and the feasible solution region for each linear program is smaller than its precursor. Eventually, one of the linear programs yields an all-integer solution.

Unfortunately, each cut can turn out to be a small whittling off a big log. Since even integer programs of modest size can involve thousands of iterations, the cutting-plane method could take even longer than complete enumeration. A more promising procedure called the **branch-and-bound method** will be described in the next section.

16-2 The Branch-and-Bound Method

The branch-and-bound method is an effective search procedure that involves solving a succession of carefully formulated linear programs. Each linear program shares the original program constraints, with new ones added in accordance with findings from previous solutions. The process begins with the original integer program solved as a *linear program (LP)*, so that some of the solution values will ordinarily involve fractional parts.

Solving a Succession of Linear Programs

This **parent linear program** provides essential information about the more restrictive integer program. In a profit-maximization problem, its optimal P establishes an **upper bound** on the level of P for the integer program. It is easy to understand why this must be so. Although the integer program shares all the restrictions of the LP, it must meet further limitations, so that its best P cannot be better than the maximum profit of the less restrictive LP.

The solution to the first parent linear program allows investigators to identify two potential **descendant linear programs** that share all of the parent problem's constraints. Each descendant has just one additional constraint. The new problems are selected by picking from the parent's solution one of the noninteger-valued variables, which becomes the **branching variable**. One descendant LP has the new restriction that this variable must lie at or below the largest integer not exceeding its solution value for the parent problem; the second limits that X to be greater than or equal to the next larger integer from its sibling's restriction. The two descendant LP's partition the feasible solution region of the parent. The respective optimal P's can at best be less than or equal to the maximum profit for the parent.

A tree portrayal may be used to keep track of the whole process. Each problem is represented by a node, followed by branches leading to the descendant LP's. As the tree gets bigger, more information becomes known about the solution to the original integer program.

The process of subdividing LP's continues until one solution is so restrictive that it *happens* (but is not forced) to end up with all integer values. This is a feasible solution to the original *integer* program, although it may not be optimal. The P for this first integer solution, called the **best-solution-so-far** establishes a **lower bound** on profit, which can be no worse. The tree may then be pruned, with LP's having P's worse than this lower bound eliminated from further consideration. Eventually, the tree becomes fully pruned, and the optimal solution is found.

ILLUSTRATION
A Profit-Maximization Problem

To illustrate the procedure, we will use a modified version of the original Redwood Furniture problem. The objective is to

$$\text{Maximize} \quad P = 6X_T + 8X_C$$

$$\text{Subject to} \quad 30X_T + 20X_C \leq 310 \quad \text{(wood)}$$

$$5X_T + 10X_C \leq 113 \quad \text{(labor)}$$

$$\text{where } X_T \text{ and } X_C \text{ are non-negative integers}$$

(The right-hand sides differ slightly from those in Chapter 8.)

Relaxing the integer requirements, the above gives rise to Problem 1, the first linear program. That problem is solved graphically using Figure 16-2. We obtain the following results.

FIGURE 16-2
Graphical solution to Problem 1.

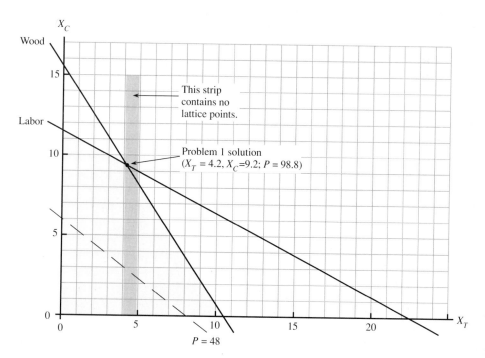

$$\text{Problem 1} \qquad X_T = 4.2 \qquad X_C = 9.2$$
$$P = 98.8$$

Since both X_T and X_C are nonintegers, either quantity may serve as the branching variable. We will arbitrarily choose X_T. The value $X_T = 4.2$ serves to determine a partition for the Problem 1 feasible solution region. Since no lattice points lie on the strip where X_T is >4 and also <5, all of those points may be eliminated from further consideration. The feasible solution region is partitioned to exclude that strip, with one part having the restriction that

$$X_T \le 4$$

and the other that

$$X_T \ge 5$$

Two descendant linear programs are thereby defined. Each incorporates the constraints of the parent problem, plus one of the above.

<table>
<tr><td colspan="2">Problem 2</td><td colspan="2">Problem 3</td></tr>
<tr><td>Maximize</td><td>$P = 6X_T + 8X_C$</td><td>Maximize</td><td>$P = 6X_T + 8X_C$</td></tr>
<tr><td>Subject to</td><td>$30X_T + 20X_C \le 310$</td><td>Subject to</td><td>$30X_T + 20X_C \le 310$</td></tr>
<tr><td></td><td>$5X_T + 10X_C \le 113$</td><td></td><td>$5X_T + 10X_C \le 113$</td></tr>
<tr><td></td><td>$X_T \le 4$</td><td></td><td>$X_T \ge 5$</td></tr>
<tr><td>where</td><td>$X_T, X_C \ge 0$</td><td>where</td><td>$X_T, X_C \ge 0$</td></tr>
</table>

FIGURE 16-3

Initial tree for the branch-and-bound method applied to the modified Redwood Furniture problem.

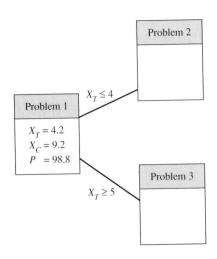

Figure 16-3 summarizes, on a tree diagram, the current situation. The further growth of the tree will depend on what solution values are obtained for these LP's.

Problems 2 and 3 are solved graphically using Figure 16-4. We obtain the following results.

$$Problem\ 2 \quad X_T = 4 \quad X_C = 9.3$$
$$P = 98.4$$
$$Problem\ 3 \quad X_T = 5 \quad X_C = 8$$
$$P = 94$$

Notice that both solutions yield worse P's than that of the parent. Remember that the parent's optimal P establishes an upper bound on the P's of its descendants.

We see that the solution to Problem 3 is 100% integer valued. That result is a solution to the original integer program and is the *best-solution-so-far*. The objective value $P = 94$ establishes a *lower bound* on the integer program's optimal profit. We can do no worse than this profit, but we may find an improvement.

The search for the optimal solution continues. A **branching point** must be found. This will always be the box for one of the evaluated linear programs not yet having descendants and which involves at least one noninteger solution value. Only Problem 2 falls into this

FIGURE 16-4

Graphical solutions to Problems 2 and 3.

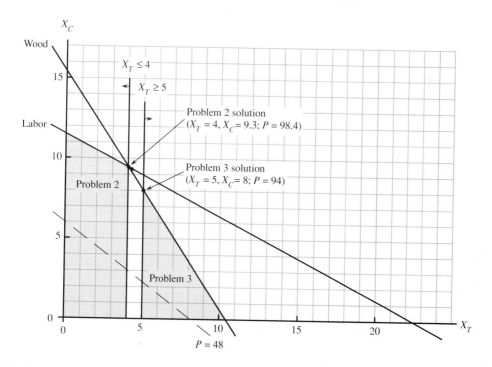

category, and the next branching takes place from there. Should there be a choice, *that candidate having the greatest P would be selected as the next branching point.*

The branching variable is X_C (the only noninteger valued variable in the Problem 2 solution). The descendant LP's involve the following constraints.

$$X_C \leq 9 \quad \text{and} \quad X_C \geq 10$$

Figure 16-5 shows the current tree. The new linear programs are

Problem 4		**Problem 5**	
Maximize	$P = 6X_T + 8X_C$	Maximize	$P = 6X_T + 8X_C$
Subject to	$30X_T + 20X_C \leq 310$	Subject to	$30X_T + 20X_C \leq 310$
	$5X_T + 10X_C \leq 113$		$5X_T + 10X_C \leq 113$
	$X_T \leq 4$		$X_T \leq 4$
	$X_C \leq 9$		$X_C \geq 10$
where	$X_T, X_C \geq 0$	where	$X_T, X_C \geq 0$

FIGURE 16-5

Continuation of the tree for the branch-and-bound method applied to the modified Redwood Furniture problem.

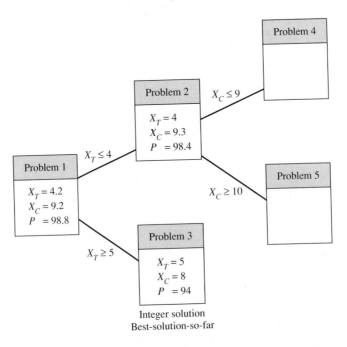

FIGURE 16-6

Graphical solutions to Problems 4 and 5.

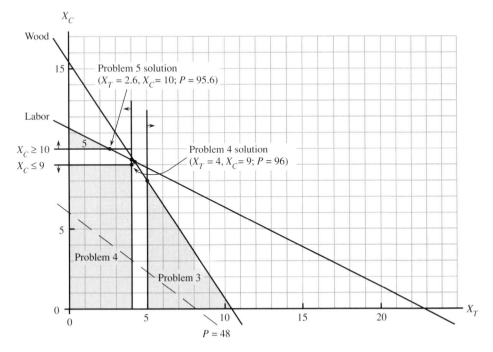

The above problems are solved graphically using Figure 16-6. We obtain the following results.

$$Problem\ 4 \qquad X_T = 4 \qquad X_C = 9$$
$$P = 96$$

$$Problem\ 5 \qquad X_T = 2.6 \qquad X_C = 10$$
$$P = 95.6$$

The solution to Problem 4 involves all integers. Since it's P exceeds that of the best-solution-so-far, it replaces Problem 3. That problem may be pruned from the tree, as shown in Figure 16-7. The new lower bound on profit is now 96. Since this amount exceeds $P = 95.6$ for Problem 5, that problem is also pruned from the tree. (None of the descendants of Problem 5 need to be investigated, since none will have a better P than 95.6.) Figure 16-7 indicates that there are no further branching points. The best-solution-so-far is optimal, and the solution to the original integer program is

$$X_T = 4 \qquad X_C = 9$$
$$P = 96$$

FIGURE 16-7

Pruned final tree for the branch-and-bound method applied to the modified Redwood Furniture problem.

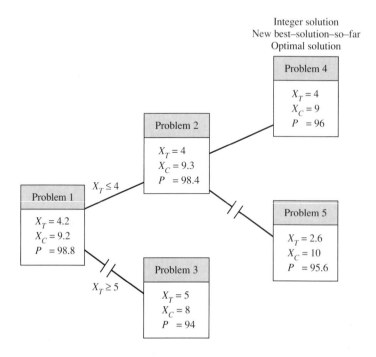

Solving Larger Problems

If a problem can be graphed, the branch-and-bound method is not needed at all. The solution can be obtained, as in Figure 16-1, by locating the feasible lattice point that has the best objective value. But by working a two-dimensional problem we can see why that method must still work for problems that cannot be graphed. In a three-variable problem, the linear programs must all be solved using simplex, and the only picture available is the tree. That tree can grow to be quite large before any pruning takes place.

Once three-pruning begins, the bounds get progressively tighter, providing a bi-directional pincer action that converges on the optimum. Unfortunately, that process can be agonizingly slow, and hundreds of LP's may have to be solved before uncovering the answer to a problem having a half-dozen variables. Computers are needed for even very small integer programs.

Cost-Minimization Problems

The branch-and-bound method works analogously for cost-minimization problems. The parent LP is obtained from the original problem by ignoring integer restrictions. The otpimal C to any parent problem establishes a **lower bound** on the C's of its descendants.

The C for the first integer solution establishes an **upper bound** on all remaining solutions, and any problem having a worse-cost solution may be pruned from the tree. The most promising branching point will be the non-parent linear program with the best C, which has some noninteger solution values.

ILLUSTRATION
A Cost-Minimization Problem

As an illustration, consider the following integer program.

$$\text{Minimize} \quad C = 4X_1 + 3X_2 + 5X_3$$
$$\text{Subject to} \quad 2X_1 - 2X_2 + 4X_3 \geq 7$$
$$2X_1 + 4X_2 - 2X_3 \geq 5$$

where X_1, X_2, and X_3 are non-negative integers

We will temporarily ignore the integer restriction and refer to the resulting linear program as Problem 1. The simplex method provides the following linear programming solution.

$$\text{Problem 1} \quad X_1 = 2\tfrac{5}{6} \quad X_2 = 0 \quad X_3 = \tfrac{1}{3}$$
$$C = 13$$

Since two of the variables have noninteger values, further steps are required to uncover the integer solution. As our branching variable, we may use X_1 or X_3, both of which have noninteger values. We arbitrarily choose X_1.

The solution provides $X_1 = 2\tfrac{5}{6}$, so that 2 is the highest integer not exceeding this value. Thus, the descendant linear programs include the original constraints, plus one of the following.

$$\text{Problem 2} \quad X_1 \leq 2$$
$$\text{Problem 3} \quad X_1 \geq 3$$

The respective solutions to these linear programs obtained using simplex are shown in Figure 16-8, which provides a tree summary of the entire procedure. Neither linear program has an integer solution, so further branching will be the next step.

Problem 3 has the smallest minimum cost of $C = 13\tfrac{1}{4}$, so it becomes the new parent linear program and the subset problems are partitioned from it. The only noninteger solution value is $X_3 = \tfrac{1}{4}$, which makes X_3 the branching variable. The following descendant linear programs are obtained by adding the respective constraint to the parent problem. Thus,

$$\text{Problem 4} \quad X_3 \leq 0 \quad \text{or} \quad X_3 = 0$$
$$\text{Problem 5} \quad X_3 \geq 1$$

FIGURE 16-8

The branch-and-bound method applied to a general integer program.

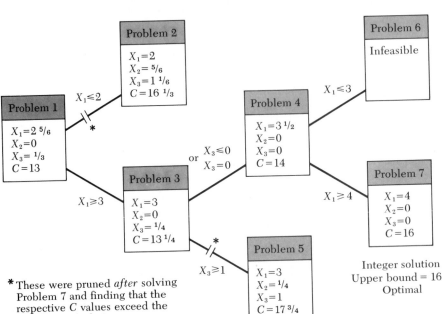

Both of these linear programs involve the original constraints and the restriction in Problem 3 that $X_1 \geq 3$.

The solutions are provided in Figure 16-8. Of all the non-parent LPs, Problem 4 has the smallest objective of $C = 14$. This linear program is then partitioned, again using X_1 as the branching variable. This time $L_1 = 3$, which is the largest integer $< 3\frac{1}{2}$ (the solution value). The descendants include the earlier constraints for Problem 4 plus one of the following.

$$\textit{Problem 6} \quad X_1 \leq 3$$

$$\textit{Problem 7} \quad X_1 \geq 4$$

In Problem 6, we include $X_1 \geq 3$ (the earlier constraint for Problem 3). This constraint together with the new constraint yields the restriction that $X_1 = 3$ exactly.

Problem 6 is infeasible. Problem 7 yields the following solution.

$$\textit{Problem 7} \quad X_1 = 4 \quad X_2 = 0 \quad X_3 = 0$$

$$C = 16$$

Since all of the variables have integer values, this is a solution to the original integer program. This is the best-solution-so-far. The objective establishes an upper bound of 16 on the C values of any further integer solutions to be evaluated.

Referring to Figure 16-8, we can see that Problems 2 and 5 remain childless. Since the respective C values (lower bounds) of these subsets exceed the upper bound of 16, these linear programs can be eliminated and the branches leading to them can be pruned. This leaves no non-parent LP's having noninteger solutions and our solution to Problem 7 is the optimal integer solution.

16-3 Computer Applications with Integer Programming

A small integer program evaluation may involve hundreds of separate linear programs, each of which must be solved using simplex. This is a job best done with computer assistance. Each separate linear program may be solved one at a time, as the tree branches are constructed by hand. A suitable program for this would be one having capability to store and retrieve the current linear program, which may then be slightly modified before the next iteration. It would be inefficient to have to enter all problem information from scratch each time.

The repetitive nature of integer programming iterations makes the entire process an attractive procedure to perform on a computer. An elaborate program can do the branching-and-bounding itself, using the preceding solution as the starting solution for the next iteration.

There are no guarantees that a solution will be found early. A large problem might seem interminable even when solved with the help of a computer. Indeed, the optimal solution may take too long or be too expensive to find. It would be wise to limit the number of iterations. The best-solution-so-far, which may be nearly as attractive as the elusive optimal solution, can then be used as the final solution.

Solving Integer Programs with *QuickQuant*

Chapters 10 and 11 describe how to use *QuickQuant* to solve linear programs. This software package, available to users of this textbook, can be used to solve any succession of linear programs, with constraints added and amended along the way. Thus, it may be employed in the branch-and-bound process.

But the number of descendant linear programs can be quite large—even for a problem of modest size. Solving one linear program at a time would be too time consuming, even with a computer. For this reason, *QuickQuant* has a separate module that will automatically solve integer programs using the branch-and-bound procedure. All you have to do is enter the data in the same fashion as a simple linear program. You must then wait a while as the program builds and prunes the solution tree (maintained internally, but not displayed). This could take dozens of iterations. *QuickQuant* will terminate the run after 300 iterations, providing the best-solution-so-far, if at that point any integer solution has yet been found.

The *QuickQuant* main menu will allow you to select the integer programming segment. Data input may be made by entering the requested choices and supplying that data requested by the screen prompts (see Chapter 10, page 327, for an example). You may save your input on file for later runs, and the output may be printed on line or stored on file to be printed later. Complete operating instructions are provided in the Appendix to this textbook.

To illustrate how *QuickQuant* works in solving integer programs, consider again the expanded Redwood Furniture problem summarized in Table 11-2, page 349. Using exactly the same input data as in the original linear program, the following report was obtained. (The printer types < and > for ≤ and ≥.)

Problem Number	Profit Upper Bound	Parent Problem	Branching Variable	Problem Status
1	771.000			
2	770.000	1	XBS (<32)	
3	Infeasible	1	XBS (>33)	
4	768.533	2	XTS (<15)	
5	769.000	2	XTS (>16)	
6	768.000	5	XBS (<31)	
7	Infeasible	5	XBS (>32)	
8	764.000	4	XCS (<16)	Integer
9	766.375	4	XCS (>17)	
10	766.533	6	XTS (<16)	
11	767.000	6	XTS (>17)	
12	766.000	11	XBS (<30)	
13	Infeasible	11	XBS (>31)	
14	762.000	10	XCS (<16)	Integer
15	764.375	10	XCS (>17)	
16	Infeasible	9	XCA (<4)	
17	752.500	9	XCA (>5)	
18	764.533	12	XTS (<17)	
19	765.000	12	XTS (>18)	
20	764.000	19	XBS (<29)	
21	Infeasible	19	XBS (>30)	
22	760.000	18	XCS (<16)	Integer
23	762.375	18	XCS (>17)	
24	Infeasible	15	XCA (<4)	
25	750.500	15	XCA (>5)	

This problem illustrates *profit maximization.* Notice that the P for each parent linear program establishes an *upper bound* on the P values of all descendent problems. The P for the best-solution-so-far establishes a *lower bound* on profit. Any problem having a P smaller than that lower bound is pruned from the evolving tree. The first such solution was not obtained for Redwood Furniture until Problem 8, the first linear program to have all integer values. It took 17 more problems to establish that Problem 8 is indeed optimal.

QuickQuant provides the following report for the large Redwood Furniture problem.

Original Variable	Value
XTS	15.00
XTR	0.00
XTL	15.00
XCS	16.00
XCA	4.00
XBS	32.00
XBT	32.00

Objective Value: P = 764

16-4 Integer Programming Applications

Integer programming has been applied to a wide variety of decision-making situations. Although it is not used as extensively as linear programming, integer programming is suited to almost as wide a range of applications. As we noted earlier, solving an integer programming problem requires a lot of computer time. Integer programming procedures are often used to solve problems involving a large number of variables, although computations are usually terminated before the optimal solution can be firmly established. The best-solution-so-far is then used in place of the optimal solution.

One popular application of integer programming is *facility location*. For instance, the problem of locating warehouses can be a significant decision for a manufacturer of bulky items, such as a chemical company. Hundreds of candidate cities could accommodate warehouses, but only a few cities will be chosen. These sites may be selected to minimize total distribution costs. If the warehouse locations were already fixed, the problem could be solved as a linear program, using the transportation method to determine the quantities to be shipped from source to destination. But when the warehouse locations are variables, an entire set of integer-valued, zero-one variables must be considered—one for each possible site. The fixed cost of operating a warehouse site applies only when a facility is built there. (Its variable is equal to *one*, and the fixed cost is charged in the objective function.) Otherwise, there is no fixed cost and the site variable has a value of *zero*.

The use of zero-one variables can be extended to other applications. Production runs usually involve fixed set-up costs, regardless of what quantities are eventually made. In any planning period, each product is assigned a zero-one variable indicating whether or not it will be produced in that period. The concepts encountered in warehouse location also apply to a variety of capital-budgeting decisions that involve not only physical facilities but also the introduction of new products and research and development projects, among others.

A fractional item may make no practical sense in a product-mix decision. A production run may be practical only in batches of a particular size—say, 1,000 items at a time. Integer requirements must be met in these cases.

CASE

Swatville Sluggers III

Swatville Sluggers is a small manufacturer of baseball bats. In evaluating earlier analyses of March and April production using linear programming, owner George Herman "Sultan" Swat is dissatisfied with the fractional values obtained. He suggested to his nephew, Babe, that those answers be rounded to the nearest whole numbers. Babe objects to that, stating that doing so would not necessarily be optimal and might even give an infeasible production plan.

Questions (*computer assisted*)

1. Refer to Swat's original March problem in Chapter 10 (page 335).
   (a) Round to the nearest integer values the linear programming solution found earlier. Determine the total profit of the rounded solution?
   (b) Solve the original problem as an integer program. Does this solution have a profit higher than that of the rounded solution?
2. Refer to Swat's original April problem in Chapter 12 (page 394). Repeat Question 1 (a) and (b).

CASE

Fast-Gro Fertilizer Company II

Fast-Gro Fertilizer Company currently operates in California with two plants, located in Red Bluff (annual capacity 1,500,000 tons) and Bakersfield (1,000,000 tons). Fast-Gro has two warehouses, each with a capacity of 500,000 tons, situated in Sacramento and Visalia. Each facility lies near the center of gravity of a local sales territory. The California market is divided into five more territories, each containing hundreds of individual customers.

A consultant studying the distribution system wants to determine if Fast-Gro might achieve significant cost reductions by increasing the number of warehouses, thereby taking advantage of inexpensive bulk rail shipments. All Fast-Gro warehouses would be identical to the present two, each of which can receive and deliver 500,000 tons annually at a fixed operating cost of $400,000 per site, exclusive of delivery costs. There will be no capital costs for opening warehouses, since they will be operating from leased premises. Any new warehouse would be located at the center of agricultural activity within one of the sales territories. For ease of analysis, all customers within a territory will be aggregated into a single customer group.

Fast-Gro plants serve the warehouse function for the territory in which they are situated. Any warehouse may deliver to customers in neighboring territories, within geographical constraints. The mileages between company facilities and customer groupings are given in the original Fast-Gro case in Chapter 15, where blank entries indicate that no shipments are allowed over that route. Freight costs per ton-mile are $.02 by truck and $.01 by rail. Rail shipments are made only from a plant to a warehouse.

Questions I

1. Formulate the linear program for scheduling Fast-Gro shipments under the present facility arrangement. This should be in the form of a *transshipment problem* with one source for each facility, a destination for each sales territory customer group, and one destination for each warehouse. Define your variables to coincide with a transportation problem matrix format. (Include a dummy plant or customer to make up any imbalance between total demand and total capacity.)

   Fast-Gro warehouses may not ship to another warehouse, and the corresponding variables would be represented in a shipment schedule as impossible cells, as would cells representing forbidden routings. To maintain a rectangular shipment schedule format, include variables for impossible cells in your formulation. These should appear in the objective equation with coefficient M.

2. Construct a transportation problem matrix for Fast-Gro's distribution, assuming that *no* new warehouses are built. Add a dummy row or column to make total demand equal total capacity.

3. Solve the above transportation problem and find the minimum transportation cost, using a computer if possible. If you solve the problem by hand, use the cheapest cell method or Vogel's approximation to start. Make no allocations to impossible cells, and proceed to determine the optimal solution.

4. Determine the total Fast-Gro distribution cost by adding to the transportation cost (from Question 3) the fixed operating costs of the two existing warehouses.

5. The Fast-Gro warehouse location decision is a *mixed integer program* that may be formulated by augmenting the linear program found in Question 1. This may be accomplished by first reformulating the linear program to include a warehouse candidate in each of the five remaining territories where Fast-Gro has no facility, with a row and column for each. Zero-one integer-valued variables, W_2, W_3, W_6, W_7, and W_8, may then be introduced for territories 2, 3, 6, 7, and 8. The value for any W will be 1 if the territory includes a warehouse and 0 if the territory does not include a warehouse.
   (a) What coefficient value should be used for the W's in the objective function?
   (b) Each W is like a switch that activates a transportation matrix row and column whenever the corresponding site has a warehouse. For the warehouse in territory 2, express (1) the demand constraint for its column and (2) the capacity constraint for its row. (For simplicity, ignore any dummy columns or rows.)

Questions II (computer assisted)

1. Construct a blank shipment schedule, with cell costs, for the expanded transportation problem when a warehouse is included at each candidate site.

2. A solution to a transportation problem with the above matrix can provide a solution to the mixed integer program itself. The fixed costs of those warehouses in operation must be added to the transportation costs to get the total distribution system cost. Possible solutions are distinguished by whichever combination of warehouses are opened or closed (not leased). An open warehouse has capacity and demand of 500,000; it is closed when its quantities are reduced to zero.

    Suppose that only the existing two warehouses plus the Imperial candidate are open. (So that the four rows and four columns for the other candidate warehouses have zero capacities and demands.) Enter the modified transportation matrix data into the computer and determine the optimal shipment schedule.

    Including the shipment costs and the warehouse operating costs, what is the total distribution system cost?

3. Add a second new warehouse at Salinas. (Reactivate the row and column for that warehouse by changing the capacity and demand from zero to 500,000.) Solve the transportation problem and find the total distribution system cost.

4. To solve the mixed integer program, $2^5 = 32$ possible combinations of new warehouse locations must be separately evaluated. The optimal solution will be the one having the lowest total distribution system cost. A new transportation problem must be solved for each combination, with the corresponding capacities and demands set at 500,000 if a location has a warehouse and at 0 otherwise. Determine that optimal solution.

PROBLEMS

16-1   Consider the following integer program.

$$\text{Maximize} \quad P = 3X_1 + 4X_2$$
$$\text{Subject to} \qquad X_1 + 2X_2 \leq 8$$
$$3X_1 + X_2 \leq 10$$

where X_1 and X_2 are non-negative integers

(a) Ignoring the integer constraints, solve this problem graphically as a linear program.

(b) Identify all of the lattice points on your graph that lie inside the feasible solution region of the linear program.

(c) Find the most profitable feasible lattice point and the optimal solution to the original integer program.

16-2 Solve the following integer program graphically.

$$\text{Maximize} \quad P = 3X_1 + 4X_2$$

$$\text{Subject to} \quad 6X_1 + 7X_2 \leq 84$$

$$2X_1 \quad\quad \geq 11$$

$$3X_2 \geq 14$$

where X_1 and X_2 are non-negative integers

16-3 Solve the following integer program graphically.

$$\text{Maximize} \quad P = 5X_1 + 7X_2$$

$$\text{Subject to} \quad 12X_1 + 7X_2 \leq 84$$

$$5X_1 + 7X_2 \geq 35$$

$$2X_2 \leq 7$$

where X_1 and X_2 are non-negative integers

16-4 Refer to Problem 8-12 (page 274). Assume that Ace Widgets must produce only whole items. Formulate the problem as an integer program and solve it graphically.

16-5 Apply the branch-and-bound method to solve the integer program in Problem 16-1. Do this by solving graphically a succession of linear programs. Summarize the procedure using a tree diagram.

16-6 Repeat Problem 16-5 using instead the integer program in Problem 16-2.

16-7 The solutions to several linear programs appearing in the table below have been obtained in the process of solving the following integer program.

$$\text{Minimize} \quad C = 5X_1 + 2X_2 + 3X_3$$

$$\text{Subject to} \quad 3X_1 - 2X_2 + 4X_3 \geq 8$$

$$3X_1 + 4X_2 - 2X_3 \geq 6$$

where X_1, X_2, and X_3 are non-negative integers

PROBLEM	LATEST BRANCHING VARIABLE	X_1	X_2	X_3	C	
1	none	$2\frac{2}{9}$	0	$\frac{1}{3}$	$12\frac{1}{9}$	
2	X_1	2	$\frac{1}{3}$	$\frac{2}{3}$	$12\frac{2}{3}$	
3	X_1	3	0	0	15	
4	X_2	—	—	—	—	(infeasible)
5	X_2	$1\frac{5}{9}$	1	$1\frac{1}{3}$	$13\frac{7}{9}$	
6	X_1	1	$1\frac{5}{6}$	$2\frac{1}{6}$	$15\frac{1}{6}$	
7	X_1	2	1	1	15	

Construct a tree diagram summarizing the problem solution. Indicate the optimal solution(s).

16-8   The solutions to several linear programs appearing in the table below have been obtained in the process of solving the following integer program.

$$\text{Maximize} \quad P = 3X_A + 5X_B + 4X_C$$

$$\text{Subject to} \quad 2X_A + 3X_B + 3X_C \le 13$$

$$5X_A + 4X_B + 5X_C \le 17$$

where X_A, X_B, X_C are non-negative integers

PROBLEM	LATEST BRANCHING VARIABLE	X_A	X_B	X_C	P	
1	none	0	4.25	0	21.25	
2	X_B	0	4	.2	20.8	
3	X_B	—	—	—	—	(infeasible)
4	X_C	.2	4	0	20.61	
5	X_C	0	3	1	19	
6	X_A	0	4	0	20	
7	X_A	1	3	0	18	

Construct a tree diagram summarizing the problem's solutions. Indicate the optimal solution(s).

16-9   *Computer exercise.*   Solve the following integer program.

$$\text{Minimize} \quad C = 2X_1 + 3X_2 + 4X_3$$

$$\text{Subject to} \quad 2X_1 - 3X_2 + 3X_3 \ge 7$$

$$-3X_1 + 2X_2 + 4X_3 \ge 5$$

where X_1, X_2, and X_3 are non-negative integers

16-10   *Computer exercise.*   Refer to Problem 10-15 (page 341). Determine the integer programming solution to the Piney Woods Furniture problem originally stated as a linear program.

16-11   *Computer exercise.*   Refer to the Real Reels advertising decision in Chapter 9 (page 288). Find the integer programming solution to this problem.

16-12   *Computer exercise.*   Refer to the microcircuit production decision of Chapter 9 (page 277). Find the integer programming solution to this problem.

C H A P T E R

17

Goal Programming

T he linear programming applications encountered so far in this book all involve a *single objective*. For those problems, maximizing profit or minimizing cost seems like a proper thing to do. But that approach can be a serious oversimplification when the decision maker has *multiple goals*. For example, a manufacturer may want not only to maximize profit, but also to increase share of market, to keep within a capital spending budget, to maintain a minimum cash reserve, and to achieve steady work force growth. All of these goals are important and should be incorporated into the process of selecting a solution.

Of course, it may not be possible to achieve all the goals absolutely. Consider the traditional investor dilemma, illustrated by Willy B. Rich, who makes his choice of stock with the two following objectives in mind.

Maximize return   and   Minimize risk

The market structures for securities make it impossible for an investor to achieve both goals. Although Willy expects High-Volatility Engineering to give a high dividend payout and to have substantial opportunity for appreciation, he feels so uncomfortable with the stock's potential for losing its market value that he buys Stability Power—a stock having lower expected returns but a lot less risk of losing its market value. That purchase decision achieves for Willy his *optimal balance* in attaining the conflicting goals.

The concepts of linear programming may be extended to achieve such an optimal balance in meeting multiple objectives. The procedure is aptly called **goal programming**. Like the investor, however, it may be impossible for decision makers to meet all of their goals. More realistically, the focus aims at achieving certain *targets* for each goal. The overall objective is to find that solution which collectively minimizes deviations from these targets.

17-1 Linear Programming and Multiple Objectives

To lay the foundation for a new method for accommodating multiple goals, we consider once more the familiar Redwood Furniture problem. There are now three main objectives that must be met to establish a production plan. These objectives are to

> Maximize *profit*
>
> Maximize *revenue* to maintain market share growth
>
> Maximize *training time* to increase work force productivity

Suppose that Redwood wants to achieve all of the above while still meeting the original constraints in establishing quantities of tables X_T and chairs X_C to produce. The following data apply.

	TABLE	CHAIR
Profit per unit	$ 6	$ 8
Revenue per unit	$50	$25
Training time per unit	1 hour	3 hours

The above data indicate that chairs actually generate higher profits with less revenue. Chairs are also richer in the amount of training time they provide.

The constraints are

$$30X_T + 20X_C \le 300 \quad \text{(wood)}$$

$$5X_T + 10X_C \le 110 \quad \text{(labor)}$$

$$\text{where } X_T, X_C \ge \quad 0$$

Standard linear programs have a single objective. The linear programming approach would treat this problem as three separate LP's, all sharing the same constraints, but each having just one of the following objectives.

> Objective 1   Maximize $P = 6X_T + 8X_C$ (profit)
>
> Objective 2   Maximize $R = 50X_T + 25X_C$ (revenue)
>
> Objective 3   Maximize $T = 1X_T + 3X_C$ (training)

The separate problems are solved graphically using Figure 17-1. We see that each LP has different optimal levels for the X's, with the respective solutions corresponding to different most attractive corners of the common feasible solution region.

As with Willy B. Rich's investment decisions, this problem illustrates in more detail that it is usually impractical to meet several objectives in an absolute sense through direct maximization or minimization. A more realistic set of multiple goals, however, can be accommodated by extending the linear programming approach.

FIGURE 17-1

Graphical solution to separate linear programs with different goals for the Redwood Furniture problem.

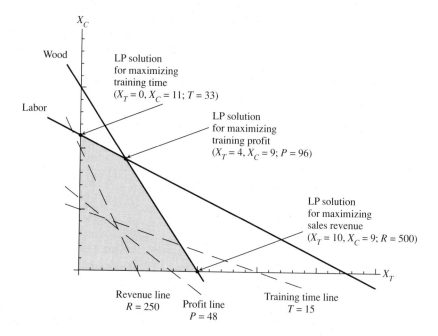

17-2 Linear Programming with Goal Targets

Redwood management establishes the following realistic **goal targets**.

Profit	$ 90
Sales revenue	$450
Achieved training time	30 hours

Using these targets, individual goals may be expressed as inequalities (or equations).

Goal 1	$6X_T + 8X_C \geq 90$	(profit)
Goal 2	$50X_T + 25X_C \geq 450$	(revenue)
Goal 3	$1X_T + 3X_C \geq 30$	(training)

Treating each goal separately, the above are plotted in Figure 17-2. There, each goal has its own line and valid side. The figure also shows the original resource constraints and feasible solution region bordered by the wood and labor lines. Notice that Goal 2 has no feasible points in common with the other goals, while there is a small overlapping region where both Goal 1 and Goal 3 are met. (Should a goal target be too high, there may be no feasible point satisfying that goal.)

FIGURE 17-2

Graphical representation of the goal program for the Redwood Furniture problem.

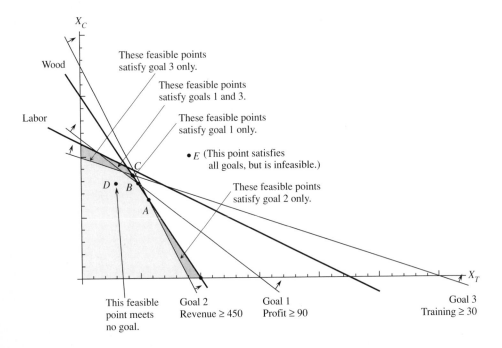

The graph in Figure 17-2 illustrates a further inadequacy in the straight linear programming approach. No matter what objective function is used, *there may be no feasible solution satisfying all goals.*

17-3 Goal Programming

Unlike standard linear programming, goal programming is flexible in accommodating multiple goals, allowing a trade-off to be made between them. This is accomplished by allowing some of the goals to be only partially met. An optimal balance between goals may be achieved in several ways.

Goal Deviations

What distinguishes the goal program from a simple linear program is that the goals are treated as *constraints* of a less rigid type than those encountered so far in this book. These special constraints permit goal attainment to be measured in terms of how the achieved levels deviate from their targets.

The amount of deviation from a target is itself treated as a *variable*. Thus, each goal will have its own **goal deviation**. These may be illustrated using the profit goal for the

Redwood Furniture problem. We let

Y_P = The amount by which profit deviates from the target level

This may be expressed in terms of the other elements in the problem as

$$Y_P = (6X_T + 8X_C) - 90 \quad \text{(profit)}$$

so that Y_P is the solution profit minus the target. Similarly, the goal deviations for the two other Redwood goals are

$$Y_R = (50X_T + 25X_C) - 450 \quad \text{(revenue)}$$
$$Y_T = (\ 1X_T + \ \ 3X_C) - \ \ 30 \quad \text{(training)}$$

Referring to Figure 17-2, we compute Y_P for points C (4.29, 8.57) and D (3, 8).

C: $Y_P = (6[4.29] + 8[8.57]) - 90 = 94.3 - 90 = +4.3$

D: $Y_P = (6[3] + 8[8]) - 90 = 82 - 90 = -8$

Notice that Y_P can be either positive or negative. It is *unrestricted as to sign*. As we shall see, the simplex method may be used to eventually solve the goal programming problem. That procedure requires that all variables be *non-negative*. We must therefore reexpress the goal deviations in an equivalent form suitable for simplex.

Goal Deviation Variables

Any unrestricted variable may be equivalently expressed as the difference between two non-negative quantities. For the profit goal deviation, we express this as

$$Y_P = Y_P^+ - Y_P^-$$

Only one of the right-hand side terms in the above expression can ever be non-zero. When Y_P is positive, Y_P^+ is equal to that goal deviation and is a positive quantity. And, when Y_P is negative, it will be equal to $-Y_P^-$, so that Y_P^- is itself also a positive quantity. The two component variables are referred to as **goal deviation variables**. All goal deviation variables must be *non-negative*.

Consider once more points C and D from Figure 17-2. The goal deviation variable values are as follows.

C: $Y_P = +4.3 = 4.3 - 0 = Y_P^+ - Y_P^-$, so that $Y_P^+ = 4.3$ and $Y_P^- = 0$

D: $Y_P = -8 = 0 - 8 = Y_P^+ - Y_P^-$, so that $Y_P^+ = 0$ and $Y_P^- = 8$

For the two remaining Redwood goals, the goal deviation variables are defined analogously.

$$Y_R = Y_R^+ - Y_R^-$$
$$Y_T = Y_T^+ - Y_T^-$$

The Goal Program

We are now ready to express the goal program for the Redwood Furniture problem. A goal program is a special linear program that ties all of the goals together through a set of **goal deviation constraints**, with one constraint for each goal.

For the Redwood Furniture problem the profit goal is represented by the following constraints.

$$\text{Goal 1} \qquad 6X_T + 8X_C - (Y_P^+ - Y_P^-) = 90 \quad \text{(profit)}$$

The remaining goal constraints are expressed analogously.

$$\text{Goal 2} \qquad 50X_T + 25X_C - (Y_R^+ - Y_R^-) = 450 \quad \text{(revenue)}$$

$$\text{Goal 3} \qquad 1X_T + 3X_C - (Y_T^+ - Y_T^-) = 30 \quad \text{(training)}$$

The goal program is a linear program having a single **omnibus objective function** involving non-zero coefficients for the goal-deviation variables only. The objective is to minimize the collective cost of the goal deviations.

It only costs Redwood $1 to fall a dollar below the profit target, so that the coefficient for Y_P^- is 1; since exceeding the profit target is desirable, the other goal deviation variable Y_P^+ will have a coefficient of 0. Redwood has found that falling below its revenue target diminishes future market share. The present value of lost earnings potential is judged to be $2 for each current dollar under the revenue target. (Revenues beyond target are assumed to have a negligible impact on future profitability.) Thus, the coefficient of Y_R^- is 2 per dollar of revenue, while the coefficient for Y_R^+ is 0. Finally, training time up to 30 hours will enhance future efficiencies. That is assumed to be worth $.50 per hour obtained. Beyond 30 hours the training effect would be unnoticeable. Thus, for Y_T^- the coefficient is .50 per hour, while for Y_T^+ it is 0.

Including the original resource constraints, we may finally express the complete goal program in terms of the following linear program.

Minimize

$$C = 0X_T + 0X_C + 0Y_P^+ + 1Y_P^- + 0Y_R^+ + 2Y_R^- + 0Y_T^+ + .5Y_T^-$$

Subject to

Regular Constraints

(wood):	$30X_T + 20X_C$	≤ 300
(labor):	$5X_T + 10X_C$	≤ 110

Goal Deviation Constraints

G1 (profit):	$6X_T + 8X_C - (Y_P^+ - Y_P^-)$		$= 90$
G2 (revenue):	$50X_T + 25X_C$	$- (Y_R^+ - Y_R^-)$	$= 450$
G3 (training):	$1X_T + 3X_C$	$- (Y_T^+ - Y_T^-)$	$= 30$

where   all variables ≥ 0

The above is a linear program with 8 main variables and 5 constraints. Simplex further requires slacks S_W for unused wood and S_L for unused labor. An artificial variable is required for each goal deviation equality constraint. The following solution is obtained.

$$X_T = 6 \qquad Y_P^+ = 0 \qquad Y_P^- = 6$$

$$X_C = 6 \qquad Y_R^+ = 0 \qquad Y_R^- = 0$$

$$S_W = 0 \qquad Y_T^+ = 0 \qquad Y_T^- = 6$$

$$S_L = 20$$

$$C = 9$$

The above solution corresponds to point A in Figure 17-2, where the revenue goal is exactly on target, and $Y_R^+ = Y_R^- = 0$. The profit lies $Y_P^- = 6$ dollars below target and the training time falls $Y_T^- = 6$ hours under target. Not all of the labor gets used, so that production falls below resource capacity, with only 6 tables and 6 chairs to be made. The cost of this solution is 9 dollars, the minimum possible, which establishes an optimal compromise among the three goals.

The Solution Depends on Levels for Objective Coefficients

The goal program solution depends on the objective coefficients used. Should the relative costs of the goal deviations change, a different solution may be obtained. For example, by increasing the coefficients for Y_P^- to 5 dollars and for Y_T^- to 1 dollar, the optimal solution is point B (5, 7.5) in Figure 17-2. That point then provides the best balance among goal deviations. Should the cost for Y_T^- be bumped up to 10 dollars per hour, point C (4.29, 8.57) becomes optimal.

Other Goal Forms

The Redwood Furniture problem involves only goals of the $\geq$ form, for which the targets are *minimums*. Goals may also take the $\leq$ form, so that the target is a *maximum*. For example, suppose that Redwood Furniture desires a working capital budget of $325. Tables involve direct costs of $44 each, while chairs involve an expenditure of $17. This goal may be expressed as

$$44X_T + 17X_C \leq 325 \quad \text{(budget)}$$

The goal program involves two goal deviation variables, denoted here as Y_B^+ and Y_B^-, so that the above gives rise to the following goal deviation constraint.

$$44X_T + 17X_C - (Y_B^+ - Y_B^-) = 325 \quad \text{(budget)}$$

Although the constraint has the same form as the original three, the objective must be to keep Y_B^+ small in order to avoid exceeding the budgetary limit; Y_B^- may be any amount without violating the goal. Thus, the omnibus objective function would have coefficients such as 1 for Y_B^+ and 0 for Y_B^-.

A third form involves goals that aim at targets that ought to be met *exactly*. For Redwood Furniture, such a goal may be to produce exactly 4 chairs for each table. This may be expressed as

$$4X_T - 1X_C = 0 \quad \text{(mixture)}$$

This goal involves two goal deviation variables Y_M^+ and Y_M^-, so that the following goal deviation constraint applies.

$$4X_T - 1X_C - (Y_M^+ - Y_M^-) = 0 \quad \text{(mixture)}$$

Both of the variables Y_M^+ and Y_M^- may have non-zero coefficients in the omnibus objective function.

Other Goal-Programming Approaches

Some goal programming applications have no natural costs for use as objective coefficients. Those problems can still be solved using *penalty points* arbitrarily chosen to coincide with the relative importance of the goals. The use of artificial objectives may be avoided by using **preemptive goal programming**, a procedure to be discussed in Section 17-5.

17-4 Goal Programming with Penalty Points

To show how penalty points may be used in goal programming, consider, again, the ChipMont custom chip manufacturer first encountered in Chapter 9. A decision has to be made about how many modules of the various sizes to assemble. These quantities are X_E (extra-large), X_L (large), X_R (regular), X_S (small), and X_M (miniature). Each module is mounted on a printed circuit board, which has been cut to size from available stock of large sheets. All modules contain varying quantities of two component chips, type A and type B, supplies of which are limited. There is also a limited number of assembly time hours. These restrictions are incorporated into a set of constraints to be described later.

ChipMont determined the unit profit of each final module, and these were used in Chapter 9 to formulate the original objective function.

$$\text{Maximize} \quad P = 58X_E + 43X_L + 25X_R + 17X_S + 28X_M$$

Although ChipMont still wants to achieve the above, the superintendent would be satisfied with any level of profit for the production period exceeding $15,000. He wishes to consider three other goals.

▪ To maintain present market share for the modules, each period's production must average at least 600 units overall.

- To cultivate a stable relationship with key suppliers of printed circuit boards, usage of this raw input should be limited to 10,000 square inches during any production period.
- Erratic shift scheduling should be avoided; that may be achieved by keeping total assembly hours at the historical average level of 700.

Applying the unit profits as coefficients, ChipMont's first goal may be reexpressed in terms of the X's as follows.

Goal 1 $58X_E + 43X_L + 25X_R + 17X_S + 28X_M \geq 15{,}000$

Analogously, the second goal is expressed as

Goal 2 $X_E + X_L + X_R + X_S + X_M \geq 600$

A 25-square-inch printed circuit board is needed for the extra-large modules. The areas for the others are 15, 10, 5, and 1 square inches for the large, regular, small, and miniature modules, respectively. Thus, ChipMont's third goal is

Goal 3 $25X_E + 15X_L + 10X_R + 5X_S + 1X_M \leq 10{,}000$

The assembly times are 1.50, 1.25, 1.00, .75, and 1.50 hours for the extra-large, large, regular, small, and miniature modules, respectively. The fourth goal is, thus, expressed as

Goal 4 $1.50X_E + 1.25X_L + 1.00X_R + .75X_S + 1.50X_M = 700$

Distinguishing Goals from Constraints

ChipMont may not be able to find a production plan that meets all the goals. For this reason, the solution is allowed to deviate from the targets for some or even all of the goals. This is the distinguishing feature between goals and constraints. *Constraints cannot be violated by any proposed solution.*

In Chapter 9, the following *constraint* was expressed for the availability of printed circuit boards.

$25X_E + 15X_L + 10X_R + 5X_S + 1X_M \leq 50{,}000$ (P.C. board)

The 50,000 square inches on the right-hand side represents the maximum availability of that input and includes material that would have to be procured from unreliable supplementary suppliers. The *constraint* allows printed circuit board usage to be any level below that maximum, such as 25,000 or 38,000 square inches. But those levels would conflict with Goal 3, with its 10,000-square-inch limitation. Nevertheless, ChipMont may find it advantageous to exceed that limit in order to reach an optimal balance with respect to its other goals.

The distinction between goal and constraint should become clearer if we consider a second ChipMont constraint, this one for assembly time.

$1.50X_E + 1.25X_L + 1.00X_R + .75X_S + 1.50X_M \leq 2{,}000$ (assembly time)

Compare this constraint to Goal 4, for which the right portion is 700 hours *exactly*. The above expresses ≤ 2,000 hours, placing an upper limit on available labor. The extra hours, 2,000 − 700 = 1,300, would be achieved by asking workers for overtime and by bringing temporaries into the plant. This is something that ChipMont does not want to do, with its Goal 4 stipulation that labor exactly match 700 hours available from the regular shifts. But it may be impossible to achieve the optimal levels for the other goals and keep labor usage at the 700-hour target level.

Assigning Weights to Goal Deviations

The ChipMont superintendent begins the process of assigning weights to the goal components by ranking his goals in terms of importance.

Goal 1	Minimum profit	Most important
Goal 4	Stable labor	
Goal 2	Maintain market share	
Goal 3	Reliable suppliers	Least important

He then decides that Goal 1 is as important as the remaining goals combined, and that he feels the middle two goals to be of equal importance and that both are twice as important as the last. Using a weight of 1 for the last goal, he arrives at the following preliminary penalty point assignments.

GOAL	PENALTY POINTS
1	5
4	2
2	2
3	1

Goals 1 and 2 are of the ≥ type, so that only negative deviations are to be avoided. Goal 3 is of the ≤ type, and for it, only positive deviations are harmful. Goal 4 is an = type, so that both deviations, positive and negative, are to be kept small. Assuming that the above weight should be split equally between these, the following table of weights applies.

GOAL i	TYPE	COMPONENT	
		Positive Y_i^+	Negative Y_i^-
1	≥	0	5
2	≥	0	2
3	≤	1	0
4	=	1	1

Letting Y_1^+, Y_1^-, Y_2^+, Y_2^-, Y_3^+, Y_3^-, Y_4^+, and Y_4^- denote the respective goal deviation variables, the following goal program is to be solved.

$$\text{Minimize} \quad C = 0Y_1^+ + 5Y_1^- + 0Y_2^+ + 2Y_2^- + 1Y_3^+ + 0Y_3^- + 1Y_4^+ + 1Y_4^-$$

Subject to the following original problem constraints:

$$
\begin{array}{llllllll}
25X_E + & 15X_L + & 10X_R + & 5X_S + & 1X_M & \leq & 50{,}000 & \text{(P.C. board)} \\
28X_E + & 24X_L + & 18X_R + & 12X_S + & 5X_M & \leq & 10{,}000 & \text{(A avail.)} \\
52X_E + & 48X_L + & 40X_R + & 60X_S + & 75X_M & \leq & 25{,}000 & \text{(B avail.)} \\
1.50X_E + & 1.25X_L + & 1.00X_R + & .75X_S + & 1.50X_M & \leq & 2{,}000 & \text{(assy. time)} \\
0X_E + & 0X_L + & 1X_R + & 0X_S + & 0X_M & \geq & 200 & \text{(reg. qt.)} \\
0X_E + & 0X_L + & 0X_R + & 1X_S + & 0X_M & \geq & 100 & \text{(small qt.)} \\
2X_E - & 1X_L + & 0X_R + & 0X_S + & 0X_M & \leq & 0 & \text{(ovsz. mix.)} \\
-.50X_E - & .50X_L - & .50X_R - & .50X_S + & 1X_M & \leq & 0 & \text{(min. mix.)}
\end{array}
$$

and subject to the following goal deviation constraints:

$$
\begin{array}{lllllll}
58X_E + & 43X_L + & 25X_R + & 17X_S + & 28X_M - (Y_1^+ - Y_1^-) = & 15{,}000 & \text{(Goal 1)} \\
1X_E + & 1X_L + & 1X_R + & 1X_S + & 1X_M - (Y_2^+ - Y_2^-) = & 600 & \text{(Goal 2)} \\
25X_E + & 15X_L + & 10X_R + & 5X_S + & 1X_M - (Y_3^+ - Y_3^-) = & 10{,}000 & \text{(Goal 3)} \\
1.50X_E + & 1.25X_L + & 1.00X_R + & .75X_S + & 1.50X_M - (Y_4^+ - Y_4^-) = & 700 & \text{(Goal 4)}
\end{array}
$$

where $\qquad$ all variables $\geq \quad 0$

The following solution is obtained for ChipMont's problem.

$$
\begin{array}{lll}
X_E = \ 27.82 & Y_1^+ = 0.00 & Y_1^- = \quad 0.00 \\
X_L = \ 55.63 & Y_2^+ = 0.00 & Y_2^- = \quad 44.82 \\
X_R = \ 371.33 & Y_3^+ = 0.00 & Y_3^- = 4{,}256.39 \\
X_S = \ 100.00 & Y_4^+ = 0.00 & Y_4^- = \quad 141.80 \\
X_M = \ \ \ 0.40 & &
\end{array}
$$

$$C = 231.446$$

The achieved results for each goal are given below.

Goal 1 Period profit (exactly on target):

$$58X_E + \quad 43X_L + \quad 25X_R + \ 17X_S + \quad 28X_M = 15{,}000.00$$

Goal 2   Total number of units (44.82) below target):

$$1X_E + \quad 1X_L + \quad 1X_R + \quad 1X_S + \quad 1X_M = \quad 555.18$$

Goal 3   Total P.C. board area (4,256.39 below target):

$$25X_E + \quad 15X_L + \quad 10X_R + \quad 5X_S + \quad 1X_M = \quad 5,743.61$$

Goal 4   Assembly hours used (141.80 below target):

$$1.50X_E + 1.25X_L + 1.00X_R + .75X_S + 1.50X_M = \quad 558.20$$

The above solution provides ChipMont with the $15,000 minimum level of profit and with nearly the minimum number of units produced. The plan also comes close to the exact goal of 700 assembly hours. It falls far short of the 10,000-square-inch maximum P.C. board area, meeting Goal 3 with a huge margin.

17-5 Preemptive Goal Programming

Some investigators find the artificial assignment of penalty points unappealing. An alternative procedure returns to solving individual linear programs. These are formulated and evaluated in succession, depending on the results obtained. The problems are based on a prioritization of goals. The first LP has, as its objective, to singly minimize the applicable goal deviation for the highest priority goal. As long as the higher priority goals are met completely, a further LP is solved. It will have the analogous objective applied to the remaining goal with highest priority, with an added constraint that the preceding goal deviation be kept at zero. The preemptive nature of the goals makes it unnecessary to minimize goal deviations for any goal with lower priority than one that cannot be completely met. The process therefore stops when the first LP solution is reached that has an optimal C greater than 0.

We will illustrate the procedure using the Redwood Furniture example. Two new goals mentioned earlier are not included. These are the budget goal and the mixture goal. The latter is a $\leq$ goal instead of an exact equality, stipulating that at least 4 chairs be made for each table. To avoid confusion, the goal numbers are assigned in accordance with relative importance, so that we now have

$$\text{Highest priority} \to \text{G1:} \quad 6X_T + \quad 8X_C \geq \quad 90 \quad \text{(profit)}$$
$$\text{G2:} \quad 4X_T - \quad 1X_C \leq \quad 0 \quad \text{(mixture)}$$
$$\text{G3:} \quad 44X_T + 17X_C \leq 325 \quad \text{(budget)}$$
$$\text{G4:} \quad 50X_T + 25X_C \geq 450 \quad \text{(revenue)}$$
$$\text{Lowest priority} \to \text{G5:} \quad 1X_T + \quad 3X_C \geq \quad 30 \quad \text{(training)}$$

We have as the

First LP:

Minimize $\quad C = Y_P^-$

Subject to

$$
\begin{array}{llll}
 & 30X_T + 20X_C & \leq 300 & \text{(wood)} \\
 & 5X_T + 10X_C & \leq 110 & \text{(labor)} \\
\text{G1:} & 6X_T + 8X_C - (Y_P^+ - Y_P^-) = 90 & & \text{(profit)} \\
\text{G2:} & 4X_T - 1X_C - (Y_M^+ - Y_M^-) = 0 & & \text{(mixture)} \\
\text{G3:} & 44X_T + 17X_C - (Y_B^+ - Y_B^-) = 325 & & \text{(budget)} \\
\text{G4:} & 50X_T + 25X_C - (Y_R^+ - Y_R^-) = 450 & & \text{(revenue)} \\
\text{G5:} & 1X_T + 3X_C - (Y_T^+ - Y_T^-) = 30 & & \text{(training)}
\end{array}
$$

where $\qquad\qquad$ all variables $\geq \quad 0$

The solution to the above is

$$
\begin{array}{lll}
X_T = 5 & Y_P^+ = 0 & Y_P^- = 0 \\
X_C = 7.5 & Y_M^+ = 12.5 & Y_M^- = 0 \\
S_W = 0 & Y_B^+ = 22.5 & Y_B^- = 0 \\
S_L = 10 & Y_R^+ = 0 & Y_R^- = 12.5 \\
 & Y_T^+ = 0 & Y_T^- = 2.5 \\
 & C = 0 &
\end{array}
$$

We see that the highest priority Goal 1 (profit) is met completely, so that $C = 0$. A second linear program must be solved.

The next linear program ensures that Goal 1 (profit) be met completely by incorporating the *constraint* $Y_P^- = 0$ into the preceding linear program. The objective is to minimize the applicable goal deviation variable for the next higher priority goal, which is now Goal 2 (mixture). But we must use Y_M^+ in the objective (not Y_M^-).

We have as the

Second LP:

Minimize $\quad C = Y_M^+$

Subject to

$$
\begin{array}{lll}
30X_T + 20X_C & \leq 300 & \text{(wood)} \\
5X_T + 10X_C & \leq 110 & \text{(labor)}
\end{array}
$$

$$G1: \quad 6X_T + 8X_C - (Y_P^+ - Y_P^-) = 90 \quad \text{(profit)}$$

$$G2: \quad 4X_T - 1X_C - (Y_M^+ - Y_M^-) = 0 \quad \text{(mixture)}$$

$$G3: \quad 44X_T + 17X_C - (Y_B^+ - Y_B^-) = 325 \quad \text{(budget)}$$

$$G4: \quad 50X_T + 25X_C - (Y_R^+ - Y_R^-) = 450 \quad \text{(revenue)}$$

$$G5: \quad 1X_T + 3X_C - (Y_T^+ - Y_T^-) = 30 \quad \text{(training)}$$

$$Y_P^- = 0 \quad \text{(priority 1)}$$

where   all variables $\geq$ 0

The solution to the above is

$$X_T = 2.44 \qquad Y_P^+ = 2.89 \qquad Y_P^- = 0$$

$$X_C = 9.78 \qquad Y_M^+ = 0 \qquad Y_M^- = 0$$

$$S_W = 31.11 \qquad Y_B^+ = 0 \qquad Y_B^- = 51.22$$

$$S_L = 0 \qquad Y_R^+ = 0 \qquad Y_R^- = 83.33$$

$$Y_T^+ = 1.78 \qquad Y_T^- = 0$$

$$C = 0$$

Again, we see that the highest priority remaining goal, the mixture, is met completely, with $C = 0$. A third linear program must be solved.

The next linear program ensures that Goal 2 (mixture) be met completely by incorporating the *constraint* $Y_M^+ = 0$ into the preceding linear program. The objective is to minimize the applicable goal deviation variable for the next higher priority goal, which is now Goal 3 (budget). The positive goal deviation Y_B^+ is to be minimized.

We have as the

Third LP:

Minimize $C = Y_B^+$

Subject to

$$30X_T + 20X_C \leq 300 \quad \text{(wood)}$$

$$5X_T + 10X_C \leq 110 \quad \text{(labor)}$$

$$G1: \quad 6X_T + 8X_C - (Y_P^+ - Y_P^-) = 90 \quad \text{(profit)}$$

$$G2: \quad 4X_T - 1X_C - (Y_M^+ - Y_M^-) = 0 \quad \text{(mixture)}$$

$$G3: \quad 44X_T + 17X_C - (Y_B^+ - Y_B^-) = 325 \quad \text{(budget)}$$

$$G4: \quad 50X_T + 25X_C - (Y_R^+ - Y_R^-) = 450 \quad \text{(revenue)}$$

$$G5: \quad 1X_T + 3X_C - (Y_T^+ - Y_T^-) = 30 \quad \text{(training)}$$

$$Y_P^- = 0 \quad \text{(priority 1)}$$

$$Y_M^+ = 0 \quad \text{(priority 2)}$$

where   all variables $\geq$ 0

The solution to the above is identical to the result for the second LP, and with $Y_B^+ = 0$ the budget constraint is met completely. A fourth LP must be solved. Its objective is to minimize for Goal 4 (revenue), Y_R^-, and include the new constraint $Y_B^+ = 0$.

We have as the

Fourth LP:

$$\text{Minimize} \quad C = Y_R^-$$

Subject to

$$30X_T + 20X_C \qquad\qquad \leq 300 \quad \text{(wood)}$$

$$5X_T + 10X_C \qquad\qquad \leq 110 \quad \text{(labor)}$$

G1: $\quad 6X_T + 8X_C - (Y_P^+ - Y_P^-) = 90 \quad \text{(profit)}$

G2: $\quad 4X_T - 1X_C - (Y_M^+ - Y_M^-) = 0 \quad \text{(mixture)}$

G3: $\quad 44X_T + 17X_C - (Y_B^+ - Y_B^-) = 325 \quad \text{(budget)}$

G4: $\quad 50X_T + 25X_C - (Y_R^+ - Y_R^-) = 450 \quad \text{(revenue)}$

G5: $\quad 1X_T + 3X_C - (Y_T^+ - Y_T^-) = 30 \quad \text{(training)}$

$$Y_P^- = 0 \quad \text{(priority 1)}$$

$$Y_M^+ = 0 \quad \text{(priority 2)}$$

$$Y_B^+ = 0 \quad \text{(priority 3)}$$

where $\qquad$ all variables ≥ 0

The solution to the above involves exactly the same quantities as in the preceding two LP's. But the objective is $C = 83.33$, reflecting the result that $Y_R^- = 83.33$, so that the solution falls below the revenue target. The revenue goal can only be met partially, and there is no need to consider further the lower priority goal (training). We have reached the solution to the preemptive goal program.

$$X_T = 2.44 \qquad Y_P^+ = 2.89 \qquad Y_P^- = 0$$

$$X_C = 9.78 \qquad Y_M^+ = 0 \qquad\quad Y_M^- = 0$$

$$S_W = 31.11 \qquad Y_B^+ = 0 \qquad\quad Y_B^- = 51.22$$

$$S_L = 0 \qquad\quad Y_R^+ = 0 \qquad\quad Y_R^- = 83.33$$

$$Y_T^+ = 1.78 \qquad Y_T^- = 0$$

$$C = 83.33$$

17-6 Goal Programming Applications

Because it is a relatively new procedure and quite specialized, the number of reported successes using goal programming is limited in comparison to older applications, such as transportation problems or integer programming. Nevertheless, goal programming is growing in importance and its usage in solving business decisions is expected to increase at a rapid rate.

The following examples of goal programming applications have been reported in the management science literature.

- St. Louis MO, private schools used goal programming to assign teachers to schools (*Interfaces*, August 1983).
- Truck Transport Corporation used goal programming in its facility location decisions (*Interfaces*, June 1982).
- The U.S. Navy used goal programming in manpower planning (*Management Science*, August 1980).
- Goal programming was used in conjunction with input-output analysis to organize an inventory system in a start-up company (*Interfaces*, September–October 1986).

17-7 Computer Solutions and Goal Programming

As with the linear programming applications in earlier chapters, computer assistance is desirable in solving goal programs. Since these are really linear programs with extra variables and constraints, it would be impractical to solve even small problems by hand.

Solving Goal Programs with *QuickQuant*

Chapters 10 and 11 describe how to use *QuickQuant* to solve linear programs. This user-friendly software package, available to users of this book, has a segment for solving goal programs. The *QuickQuant* main menu will allow you to select that segment.

The input differs somewhat from the basic linear programming in that the goals and weights are entered separately before the main constraints. *QuickQuant* automatically creates the goal deviation variables (Y's), organizes the goal deviation constraints, and automatically creates all needed auxiliary variables.

If you prefer, you may instead use the linear programming segment described in Chapter 10 to solve an already formulated goal program. In either case, data input may be made by entering the requested choices and supplying that data requested by the screen prompts. You may save your input on file for later runs, and the output may be printed on line or stored on file to be printed later. Complete operating instructions are provided in the Appendix to this book.

CASE

Swatville Sluggers IV

Swatville Sluggers is a small manufacturer of custom baseball bats. A complete set of details describing the monthly production requirements are given in Chapter 10 (page 335). The owner, George Herman "Sultan" Swat, wants to determine the quantities for March production.

Swat's nephew, Babe, has already evaluated that decision in terms of a linear program. Having learned of his uncle's multiple goals, Babe now wants to reconsider the problem.

The following goals are applicable to Swatville Sluggers.

Goal 1   Achieve a profit of at least $3,000.

Goal 2   Use no more than 4,000 hours of lathe time in order to allow for preventive maintenance scheduling.

Goal 3   Use exactly 7,500 hours of finishing time in order to level-out work force scheduling.

Goal 4   Use no more than 7,000 inches of wood to stabilize long-run inventories.

Babe chose to evaluate the problem using goal programming. On his own, Babe decided to assign weights to the various goals. He assigns zero weight (no penalty) to bettering the targets for Goals 1, 2, and 4. For Goal 3, Babe chose to give equal weight to falling below or above the target.

Questions

1. You have been called upon by Babe as a consultant to help him with the problem.
   (a) Formulate Babe's goal program assuming that Babe uses weights of .40 for Goal 1, .20 each for Goals 2 and 4, and .10 each for falling under or over the target for Goal 3.
   (b) *Computer exercise.* Solve Babe's goal program to find the optimal production plan.

2. Babe's uncle is not happy with the solution to Problem 1. He feels that not enough weight has been given to profit, which should be .60. He wants to reduce the weights for Goals 2 and 4 to .15 each and to reduce the weights for Goal 3 from .10 to .05 for each deviation direction.
   (a) Reformulate the objective function for Swat's revised goal program.
   (b) *Computer exercise.* Solve the revised goal program to find the optimal production plan.

3. *Computer exercise.* On seeing the results to the above, Swat decided that changing weights was ineffectual. He concluded that he should instead raise the Goal 1 target to a minimum profit of $4,000.

   Using the same weights as in Question 2, solve Swat's revised goal program.

PROBLEMS

17-1   Ace Widgets must determine how many regular and deluxe widgets to produce. Each regular widget requires 5 hours of labor, while 8 hours are needed to complete a deluxe widget; only 80 hours are available. Each unit requires exactly 1 frame, and there are just 12 frames available. The following information applies.

	REGULAR	DELUXE
Selling price	$30	$60
Unit cost	20	45
Unit profit	10	15

Find the optimal solution assuming that the objective is (a) to maximize profit and (b) to maximize sales revenue. (You may use graphical methods.)

17-2   Refer to the information given in Problem 17-1. The following goals must be met.

Goal 1   Sales revenue $\geq$ $500

Goal 2   Production cost $\leq$ $400 budget

Goal 3   Profit $\geq$ $140

Goal 4   At least as many regular widgets as deluxes must be made.

The cost of violating Goals 1–3 is $1 per dollar, while there is a $2 per unit violation of Goal 4.

(a) Formulate the decision as a goal program.

(b) Determine the value of each goal deviation variable under a production plan to make 4 regular and 7 deluxe widgets. What is the omnibus objective value under that plan?

17-3   *Computer exercise.*   Consider the decision in Problems 17-1 and 17-2. Solve the goal program.

17-4   Consider the ChipMont decision in Section 17-4. Suppose that management sets a minimum profit goal of $16,000, with a faster assembly process that takes only 1.00, .80, .70, .60, and 1.20 hours for the extra-large, large, regular, small, and miniature modules, respectively. Suppose, further, that total number of units should now be *exactly* 700, while the maximum desired total P.C. board area may be lowered to 8,000 square inches. The original Goal 2 penalty weight should now be split evenly for the positive and negative deviations. All other constants remain the same.

(a) Formulate the complete goal program.

(b) *Computer exercise.*   Solve the goal program.

17-5   Refer to Problem 9-16 (page 302). The following demographics apply to Blitz Beer's radio advertising linear program.

STATION	FEMALE LISTENERS	MALE LISTENERS	HIGH-INCOME LISTENERS	LOW-INCOME LISTENERS
KBAT	50,000	75,000	40,000	85,000
WJOK	15,000	10,000	20,000	5,000
WROB	23,000	19,000	5,000	37,000
KPOW	175,000	200,000	250,000	125,000

The above are averages. Each category has an exposure goal. Exposure is the sum of the products obtained by multiplying the number of listeners times the number of spots. The following goals apply.

Goal 1   Female exposure $\geq$ 1,000,000

Goal 2   Male exposure $\leq$ 500,000

Goal 3   High-income exposure $\geq$ 1,500,000

Goal 4   Low-income exposure $\leq$ 500,000

In achieving the above, all of the original constraints in Problem 9-16 must be satisfied. Violations of the above goals are equally serious, so that coefficients of 1 may be used on the applicable goal deviation variables in the omnibus objective function.

(a) Formulate this problem as a goal program.
(b) *Computer exercise.*   Find the optimal solution.

17-6   Refer to Problem 17-2 and to your answers. Assume that the goals are listed in decreasing priority; solve the formulated problem as a preemptive goal program.

17-7   Refer to Problem 17-5 and to your answers. Assume that the goals are listed in decreasing priority; solve the formulated problem as a preemptive goal program.

17-8   Consider the Real Reels advertising decision described in Chapter 9 (page 288). The following three goals must be met, in addition to the original constraints.

Goal 1   A minimum total exposure of 12 million buyers (penalty 5)

Goal 2   Total number of ads to be at least 15 (penalty 3)

Goal 3   Dollar expenditure in *Playboy* not to exceed $50,000 (penalty 2)

(a) Formulate Real Reels' goal program.
(b) *Computer exercise.*   Solve the goal program.

17-9   A mutual fund manager wishes to determine the level of future purchases to be made in the categories listed below.

	GROWTH	INCOME	NEW ISSUES	WARRANTS
Expected appreciation	15%	10%	20%	15%
Loss exposure	20%	5%	30%	40%
Avg. holding time (yrs.)	2	1	3	1
Brokerage cost	1%	5%	2%	5%

There is $1,000,000 to invest, and no more than half of the funds may be invested in any single category. The following goals must be met.

Goal 1   At least $140,000 in annualized price appreciation

Goal 2   Total potential loss exposure no greater than $200,000

Goal 3   Average portfolio holding time no greater than 1.5 years

Goal 4   Total brokerage cost not to exceed $15,000

The above goals are listed in decreasing priority. The manager uses penalty points of 5, 3, 2, and 1 for violating the respective goals.

(a) Formulate this problem as a goal program.
(b) *Computer exercise.*   Find the optimal solution.

17-10 Consider the portfolio selection problem in Chapter 9 (page 283). The following goals must be met, in addition to the original constraints.

Goal 1   A minimum return of $9,500 is desired (penalty 5)

Goal 2   The dollar investment in any particular bond should not be more than 20% of the total committed funds (six goals, each of penalty 1)

(a) Formulate the manager's goal program.
(b) *Computer exercise.*   Solve the goal program.

17-11 Consider the feed-mix problem described in Chapter 8 (page 254). The following four goals must be met, in addition to the original constraints.

Goal 1   A maximum total cost of $1,500 is desired (penalty 5)

Goal 2   Sunflower seeds must be at least 8,000 lbs. of the mixture bulk (penalty 3)

Goal 3   The protein level must be at least 1,300 (penalty 2)

Goal 4   The fat level must be at least 500 (penalty 1)

(a) Formulate the feed-mix decision as a goal program.
(b) *Computer exercise.*   Solve the goal program.

17-12 Consider the final version of Yosemite Ann's Trail-Mix Delight formulation problem described in Chapter 9 (page 296). Suppose that Yosemite has appearance goals that dried currants and roasted walnuts each be at least 15% of the total ingredient weight (Goals 1 and 2). She furthermore wants dried milk and pumpkin kernels combined not to exceed 50% of the total weight (Goal 3). All of this is to be done so that total cost does not exceed $2 per kilogram (Goal 4). These goals are not absolute, although the original constraints still apply and must all be satisfied. Yosemite assigns equal penalty weights to falling on the wrong side of each goal target.

(a) Formulate Yosemite Ann's goal program.
(b) *Computer exercise.*   Solve the goal program.

Network Planning with PERT

$\parallel$mportant applications of quantitative methods can be made in the area of *project management*, where a great deal of effort is aimed at a specific accomplishment. Such a program might be the construction of a dam, the development of a new aircraft, the implementation of a new computer system, or the introduction of a new product. All of these examples require management that is oriented toward directing and coordinating the activities of disparate organizations and people. Each project is fraught with uncertainties and takes a great deal of time to complete.

18-1 The Importance of Time in Planning

Time is often a paramount factor in selecting alternative ways of completing such projects. This is especially true of construction projects, which must generally be completed by the builder by the date the user plans to begin operating the facilities. A new headquarters building for a corporation illustrates the importance of timely completion.

Suppose that a company's present lease expires in June and that it is planning to move from New York to the San Francisco tower in July. The move itself requires planning to keep disruptions in company functions to a minimum. Hundreds of employees will also be selling their homes, buying new ones, and packing to move. If the new building is not ready for occupancy until October, either a temporary San Francisco headquarters will have to be found or all moving plans must be delayed. In either case, much bother and expense will result. The builder must therefore be given every incentive to finish the job in June. Such an incentive may involve a bonus of thousands of dollars per day for early completion, with a substantial penalty imposed on each day's delay.

The builder will want to finish the job as quickly as possible and will have every expectation of achieving an acceptable profit. This, too, requires a lot of planning. The efforts of dozens of subcontractors, who will be separately responsible for such components as air-conditioning excavation, glasswork, and carpeting, will have to be coordinated. Because the sequence of work is not very flexible (for instance, the framework must be completed before the plumbing or wiring can begin), this coordination must be achieved through the judicious *scheduling of activities.* All subcontractors must adhere to this overall schedule, since a delay on the part of any one of them could make the entire project late.

One procedure generally used to establish schedules for large projects is the **Program Evaluation and Review Technique**, usually referred to by the acronym **PERT**. This procedure may also be referred to as the **Critical Path Method**, or **CPM**. In addition to helping establish schedules, PERT can serve as a management tool for controlling the progress of any large project when timely completion is important.

PERT was developed in the late 1950s, when it came into extensive use in military research and development. Its first important application was in the Polaris program for the first submarine-launched ballistic missiles. PERT has been credited with saving several months in completion time compared with the expected results if more traditional procedures had been used. Since then, PERT and other project management tools have been adopted by the Defense Department for most large research and development efforts. PERT has also been adopted by the construction industry, and to a lesser extent it has been successfully employed in other types of industrial applications.

18-2 The Basic Concepts of PERT

PERT builds on a foundation of basic work groupings called **activities**. In construction, an activity is usually a function, such as excavating or installing plumbing, that is the responsibility of a single subcontractor. In the development of an aircraft, designing the landing gear may be one activity; that same component may involve several more activities in successive stages: testing materials, establishing final specifications, fabricating test gears, ground testing, and flight testing. Regardless of how the activities are identified, they have one feature in common: *Activities take time.* Usually, activities also consume resources in the form of labor, material, or money.

The number of activities to be identified will vary with the scope of the project. There may be only a handful of activities involved in building a house, but the construction of a nuclear power plant or an oil refinery may involve several thousand activities. One ballistic missile development program involved more than 2,000 activities at the top-management level, where the U.S. Air Force established schedules and directly monitored the progress of contractors. Several major contractors were responsible for separate systems of the missile, such as propulsion or guidance. Each organization had its own activities to control, so that each contractor monitored several thousand activities for internal PERT purposes. Altogether, tens of thousands of activities were involved in the development of this particular missile.

PERT involves structuring the various project activities in such a way that schedules are developed, alternative plans are investigated, and the project's status is continuously monitored. This is accomplished by employing a graphical procedure.

The PERT Network

The central focus of any PERT procedure is a logical representation of the project activities. This is accomplished by means of a **PERT network**, which graphically indicates the interrelationships between the activities in chronological order. Figure 18-1 provides the PERT network for constructing a small home. Each activity is represented by an *arrow*,* and each arrow is connected with another in such a way that the required sequence of activities is followed. Before a network can be constructed, all activities must

FIGURE 18-1
A PERT network for constructing a home.

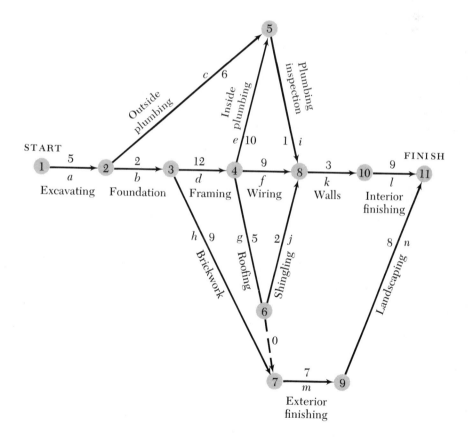

---

* CPM applications use a circle to represent an activity. Although graphically reversed, the basic concepts of either procedure are the same. See Appendix 18-2 (page 553) for further details.

be identified and the immediately preceding activities must be determined. The information is provided in Table 18-1 for the home construction illustration.

We see that the project starts with excavating, which is activity (*a*). The foundation (*b*)
and the outside plumbing (*c*) follow immediately. Both the framing (*d*) and the brickwork
(*h*) are preceded by the foundation (*b*), which must be completed before these activities can
begin. The basic principle underlying a PERT network is that certain activities must be
completed before others can begin, whereas some activities can be conducted simultaneously. The network must follow the basic chronological logic dictated by the characteristics of the project. In constructing a home, grading and excavation must be completed before the foundation can be poured. And the foundation must be present before
the framework can be installed. The network in Figure 18-1 has been purposely simplified, and some necessary details may be missing. It does *not* represent every house—
only a particular one.

Notice that the arrows for framing (*d*) and brickwork (*h*) activities begin at *circle* 3.
This circle constitutes that *point in time* when the foundation (activity *b*) is completed. The
PERT network for this project has 11 circles, which are called **events**. An event signals the
completion or the starting point of one or more activities. Although any arbitrary system
can be used, the events in this illustration have been numbered so that each activity arrow
begins with a lower-numbered event than the event number at the end of the arrow. This
system can be convenient when a PERT network is computerized, because each activity
can then be defined by a beginning and terminating event pair. The events themselves
consume neither time nor resources. They serve mainly as **project milestones** and provide
the logical "glue" that connects the various activities.

The activities in any neighboring collection exhibit one of two basic relationships
to each other. When activities must be completed in a strict sequence, they appear in a

TABLE 18-1
**Basic Data Used to Construct a PERT Network
for Building a Home**

	ACTIVITY	IMMEDIATELY PRECEDING ACTIVITY	EXPECTED COMPLETION TIME
(a)	Excavating	—	5 days
(b)	Pour foundation	a	2
(c)	Outside plumbing	a	6
(d)	Framing	b	12
(e)	Inside plumbing	d	10
(f)	Wiring	d	9
(g)	Roofing	d	5
(h)	Brickwork	b	9
(i)	Plumbing inspection	c, e	1
(j)	Shingling	g	2
(k)	Cover walls	f, i, j	3
(l)	Interior finishing	k	9
(m)	Exterior finishing	h, g	7
(n)	Landscaping	m	8

FIGURE 18-2
Activities in series.

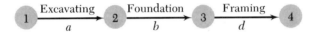

series, as shown in Figure 18-2. For example, excavating (*a*), pouring the foundation (*b*), and framing (*d*) must be performed in that order. The activity sequence *a-b-d* must be represented by a succession of arrows, each following the other, indicating that an activity cannot begin until the preceding activity has been completed. Such a sequence of activities forms a portion of a particular *path* through the network from start to finish. The sequence *a-b-d-f-k-l* in Figure 18-1 is one of several such paths.

Activities that may occur simultaneously can be stacked, as shown in Figure 18-3. Any such arrangement involves *parallel* activities. Conceivably, plumbers, electricians, and roofers could all work on the house on the same day. Because parallel activities may be of varying durations, it is not necessary that they actually occur simultaneously, but we allow for that possibility in our PERT network. If, for some reason, electricians and plumbers cannot work together (perhaps because quarters are cramped), then the present portrayal becomes unrealistic and the project network should be restructured to reflect a series arrangement between inside plumbing and wiring. *But activities should not be placed in series unless it is absolutely necessary.* Whenever two or more jobs may be done at the same time, this possibility should be reflected in the network—even if it has never been done that way before. This approach allows greater flexibility in planning and may actually shorten the project's duration.

Once the required activity sequence has been specified, the construction of the PERT network can begin. It is best to use a very large sheet of paper for this and to begin with a rough draft. The network can then be copied and some events can be repositioned to keep the number of crossing arrows small. In some applications, the PERT network is drawn in successive revised versions as new activities or interrelationships come to mind.

Computer routines have been written as an aid in arriving at a final graphical display. It may be impractical to have any pictorial representation at all of very large projects. (If

FIGURE 18-3
Activities in parallel.

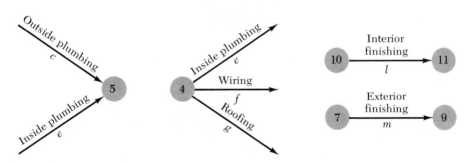

FIGURE 18-4

An incorrect network representation.

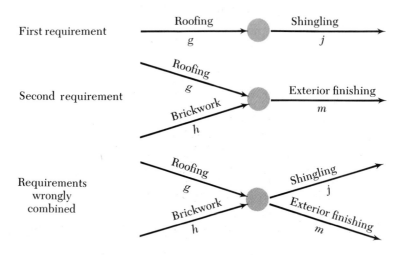

drawn, a PERT network with several thousand activities could completely cover the walls of a big room.) Such projects are usually processed entirely on a computer.

The arrow length and the duration of the corresponding activity are not related. In elaborate PERT systems, the network itself may be time-phased, so that *events* are positioned sequentially according to a master schedule (developed in an earlier PERT analysis) at distances from the start of one week (or day or month) to an inch or some other fixed interval. Although such graphical fine points can be helpful when communicating with managers, they are not essential to the successful application of PERT.

Dummy Activities

The broken arrow leading from event 6 to event 7 in Figure 18-1 is an example of a **dummy activity**. Such a portrayal is required to meet the underlying chronology of the work groupings without introducing spurious constraining relationships. The requirements in Table 18-1 indicate that shingling (j) is preceded by roofing (g) and that exterior finishing (m) is preceded by both brickwork (h) and roofing (g). All of these constraints are met by the network arrangement shown in Figure 18-4.

However, the final portion of Figure 18-4 is incorrect, since it improperly indicates that shingling (j) cannot start until brickwork (h) is completed (see Figure 18-5). No such

FIGURE 18-5

Spurious requirement induced by not employing a dummy activity.

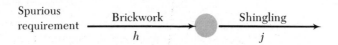

FIGURE 18-6
A correct network representation involving a dummy activity.

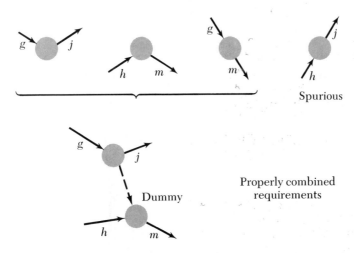

requirement exists, and there is no apparent reason why shingling cannot commence while the bricklayers are still working (this particular house does not have a fireplace protruding through the roof). This means that the X formed by the activities in the bottom portion of Figure 18-4 does not apply; only the first three portions shown in Figure 18-6 are correct.

The graphical dilemma is solved by using two events in place of one and letting the precedence of activity *g* before activity *m* be represented by a broken arrow pointing downward. The resulting dummy activity explicitly disallows the spurious constraint indicated earlier. A dummy activity is necessary only to preserve the interactivity logic; it consumes neither time nor resources.

Activity Completion Times

The duration of an activity is usually uncertain. It is impossible to predict the exact number of working days it will take to frame a house, although reliable estimates accurate to plus or minus a few days can be made. Much less precision can be expected in estimating how long a research effort or a series of tests will take.

In its most general form, PERT treats activity completion times as random variables, each having a distinct probability distribution. To further simplify the analysis, each variable is usually represented by a mean value called the *expected activity completion time*. The numbers appearing above the arrows in the PERT network in Figure 18-1 are the expected completion times for the various activities. For instance, framing (activity *d*) has a mean completion time of 12 days. After the job is done, the builder's records may show that it actually took 11.50 or 13.25 days to erect the frame. But before building begins, the actual time is an unknown future value, and the expected time of 12 days is a convenient number to use in planning.

18-3 An Analysis of the PERT Network

Thus far, we have seen what a PERT network represents and how such a network may be constructed. We will soon see how PERT may be used in project planning and control. A major advantage of PERT is that *the network provides a basis for establishing a compatible activity schedule that permits project completion in a minimum amount of time.* Additional PERT concepts will be discussed when the steps leading to a final schedule are described.

Keep in mind that much of the following discussion is essentially *deterministic*, since the expected activity times are treated as if they were the actual durations. Later in the chapter, we will investigate some of the implications of this approach.

The Earliest Possible Event Times

PERT analysis begins by focusing on events. Recall that an event is simply a point in time that represents either the completion of one activity or a group of parallel activities or the start of one or more activities. An event is therefore a milestone that must be reached by all activities that directly precede it before future activities can begin. For example, event 4 in the network for constructing a home, redrawn for convenience in Figure 18-7, must occur just after framing is finished and before inside plumbing, wiring, or roofing can begin.

Our first step is to find the *event times* when the respective events occur. If we want to schedule each activity so that it begins as soon as possible, the permissible starting time for a particular activity can be no later than the **earliest possible event time** for the event preceding that activity.

For convenience, we use the letters *TE* to represent the earliest possible event times that can be expected. We begin at the start of the project, designated as time zero (so that it can represent any calendar time desired, such as 8 A.M. on Friday, November 16, 1993). A *TE* value of 0 applies to event 1 in Figure 18-7. For ease of identification, each *TE* is placed in the *square* alongside its corresponding event. The *TE* for any event is based on the sum of the preceding event's *TE* plus the expected completion time for the connecting activity.

Figure 18-8 shows how to apply this principle. There, event 2 is connected to event 1 by excavating (activity *a*), which takes a mean of 5 days to complete. Thus, the *TE* for event 2 is $0 + 5 = 5$ days, and the earliest that event 2 can be expected to occur is at the *end* of the fifth working day of the project. Likewise, the *TE* for event 3 is obtained by adding the *TE* for event 2 to the 2-day expected completion time for the foundation (activity *b*, which connects events 2 and 3) to obtain $5 + 2 = 7$ days. At event 4, we add this time to the mean framing (activity *d*) time of 12 days to obtain a *TE* of $7 + 12 = 19$ days.

When two or more activities terminate at a single event, that event cannot occur until all those activities are completed. Thus, its *TE* is equal to the earliest point in time when the last activity is expected to be completed. Consider event 5, where both outside and inside plumbing (*c* and *e*) terminate. We find the respective expected numbers of working days for the earliest completion of these activities to be

$$5 + 6 = 11 \text{ days for outside plumbing } (c)$$

$$19 + 10 = 29 \text{ days for inside plumbing } (e)$$

FIGURE 18-7

A PERT network for constructing a home, showing the earliest possible event times (*TE*'s).

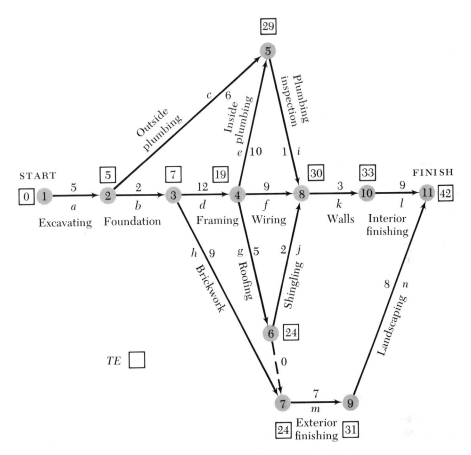

The largest sum of 29 days is required for inside plumbing (*e*), which is expected to be the last of the two activities to be completed. Thus, a *TE* of 29 is the earliest possible time for event 5. In general, the *TE* for an event must be the largest sum applicable to those activities that terminate there.

Now, consider event 8, where three activities terminate. The earliest possible completion times for these activities are

$$29 + 1 = 30 \text{ days for plumbing inspection } (i)$$

$$19 + 9 = 28 \text{ days for wiring } (f)$$

$$24 + 2 = 26 \text{ days for shingling } (j)$$

As before, the *TE* for event 8 must be the largest of these values, or 30.

TE values are found by making a *forward pass* through the network to establish the earliest possible times expected for the respective events. By adding successive activity

FIGURE 18-8
An illustration of how to find event *TE* values.

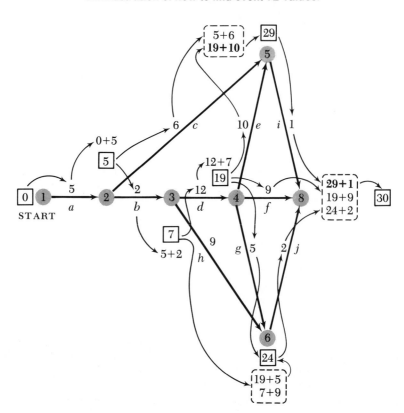

completion times together, we can see that an *event's earliest possible time (TE) is equal to the longest duration of all activity paths leading to it from the start.* For instance, paths *a-c* and *a-b-d-e* lead to event 5; the durations of these paths are

$$5 + 6 = 11 \text{ days for path } a\text{-}c$$

$$5 + 2 + 12 + 10 = 29 \text{ days for path } a\text{-}b\text{-}d\text{-}e$$

The longer duration path to event 5 takes 29 days—the same figure found for its *TE*. Likewise, there are four paths leading to event 8. The durations of these paths are

$$5 + 6 + 1 = 12 \text{ days for path } a\text{-}c\text{-}i$$

$$5 + 2 + 12 + 10 + 1 = 30 \text{ days for path } a\text{-}b\text{-}d\text{-}e\text{-}i$$

$$5 + 2 + 12 + 9 = 28 \text{ days for path } a\text{-}b\text{-}d\text{-}f$$

$$5 + 2 + 12 + 5 + 2 = 26 \text{ days for path } a\text{-}b\text{-}d\text{-}g\text{-}j$$

and the longest duration of 30 days is the *TE* for event 8.

The Critical Path

The path with the longest total time through the PERT network from start to finish is called the **critical path**. The shaded arrows in Figure 18-9 indicate this particular activity sequence for the home construction project, giving us

$$\text{Critical path} = a\text{-}b\text{-}d\text{-}e\text{-}i\text{-}k\text{-}l$$

The following table represents the succession of activities on the critical path.

	ACTIVITY SEQUENCE	EXPECTED COMPLETION TIME
	START	
(a)	Excavating	5 days
(b)	Pour foundation	2
(d)	Framing	12
(e)	Inside plumbing	10
(i)	Plumbing inspection	1
(k)	Cover walls	3
(l)	Interior finishing	9
	FINISH	Total 42 days

Because they compose the critical path, the tasks in this table are called **critical activities**.

The duration of the critical path is equal to the *TE* for the last event in the project, which is event 11 in our example. That final milestone can occur no sooner than 42 working days from the start. This is also the earliest time that all activities—and therefore the project itself—can be finished. Thus, *the duration of the critical path can serve as the expected completion time for the entire project.*

Although the critical path is *defined* by the particular activity sequence that takes the longest time, it is *sometimes identified* in terms of an event sequence. In our illustration,

$$\text{Critical path} = 1\text{-}2\text{-}3\text{-}4\text{-}5\text{-}8\text{-}10\text{-}11$$
$$\qquad\qquad\text{START} \qquad\qquad \text{FINISH}$$

Several activity sequences may tie for the longest amount of time in a PERT network. In such cases, each sequence will be a critical path. There is no reason why a project cannot have several critical paths.

The critical path has many ramifications. Before investigating these further, however, we will describe two additional preliminary PERT procedures.

Latest Allowable Event Times

By themselves, the earliest event times are insufficient to establish schedules because not all activities must start at the earliest opportunity. Many "harmless" or noncritical

FIGURE 18-9

A PERT network for constructing a home, showing the critical path, the earliest possible event times (*TE*'s), and the latest allowable event times (*TL*'s).

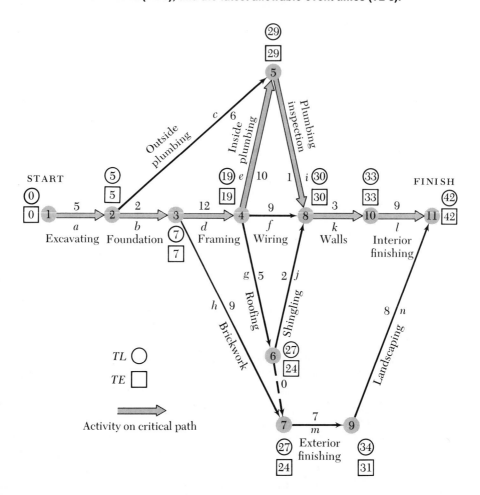

activities can actually be started later without delaying the entire project. A second set of numbers for the network events, called the **latest allowable event times**, serves to establish limits on the degree of scheduling flexibility.

The latest allowable event times, abbreviated *TL*, appear inside the *circles* beside the respective events in Figure 18-9. The *TL* value establishes the point in time by which an event must occur before an automatic delay can be expected in everything that follows, including the project itself.

For example, consider event 9, which follows exterior finishing (*m*). If this milestone does not occur before its latest allowable time of *TL* = 34 days, the project cannot be expected to be completed in the shortest possible duration of 42 working days. To see why this is so, suppose that event 9 does not occur until the end of the 36th working day. Since 8 more days are expected for landscaping, the project could then be expected to take 44 days to complete.

The TL and the TE values are determined similarly, but the TL values are computed in a *backward pass* through the network, and expected activity completion times are *subtracted*. Figure 18-10 illustrates this procedure. We start at the project finish, assigning the same number to the TL value of the last event that we obtained earlier for its TE value. Thus, event 11 is assigned a latest allowable time of $TL = 42$ days. Subtracting the 9 days for completing interior finishing (l), we obtain a TL of $42 - 9 = 33$ days for event 10. Repeating this step for event 8, we start with the TL we just found for event 10 and subtract the activity time of 3 for covering the walls (k)—the connecting activity—to obtain $33 - 3 = 30$ days, which is the TL for event 8.

FIGURE 18-10
An illustration of how to find event TL values.

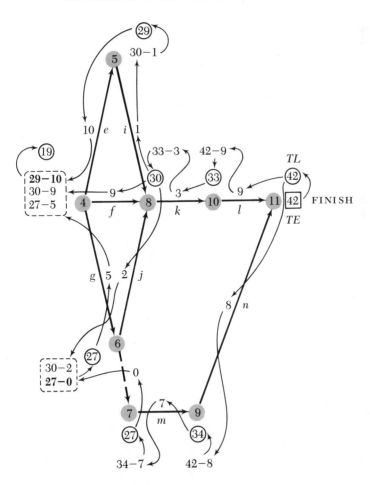

No special problems exist until an event is encountered that is the beginning point for more than one activity, so that two or more arrows point away from it. For example, event 4 signals the starting point for the three activities.

> (e)   Inside plumbing, ending at event 5
>
> (f)   Wiring, ending at event 8
>
> (g)   Roofing, ending at event 6

To determine the *TL* for event 4, we find the *smallest difference* between the *TL* for the terminating event and the activity time.

$$29 - 10 = 19 \text{ days for inside plumbing } (e)$$
$$30 - 9 = 21 \text{ days for wiring } (f)$$
$$27 - 5 = 22 \text{ days for roofing } (g)$$

Thus, the latest allowable time for event 4 is 19 days.

Like the *TE* values, each *TL* value is related to an activity sequence—the longest duration path from the event to the project finish. The durations of these paths equal the sum of the applicable activity times as well as the earliest *project* completion time minus the *TL* value. (In our example, the longest path leading from event 4 to the finish is expected to take $42 - 19 = 23$ days.)

The significance of the *TL* values in project scheduling will be discussed later. We will now examine the importance of the information that can be gleaned when the *TE* and *TL* values are considered together.

Event Slack Times: Finding the Critical Path

The *TE* value of an event establishes the earliest possible time within which it can be expected to occur; the *TL* value of that event is the latest allowable time that it can occur without causing expected delays in the entire project. The difference between these quantities tells the project manager how much leeway exists in achieving such an event. This duration, called the **event slack time**, is computed

$$\text{Event slack time} = TL - TE$$

As an example, consider event 9, which has a *TL* of 34 days and a *TE* of 31 days; its event slack time is therefore $34 - 31 = 3$ days. The slack times for the other home construction events are computed similarly. These slack times appear in the triangles beside the respective events in Figure 18-11.

The main advantage of event slack times in PERT analysis is that they help to identify the critical path. Although the *TE* for the terminal event tells us the length of the critical path, it can be hard to identify exactly which acts compose that path without some guideline. In a network of several hundred activities, there can be millions of distinct paths from start to finish, but there may be only one critical path. It would be an incredible waste

FIGURE 18-11

The complete PERT network for the home construction illustration.

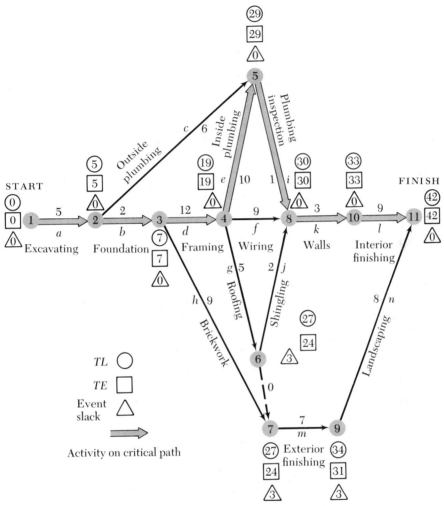

of time, money, and human resources to attempt to locate it by trial and error.

Because the critical path is the longest activity sequence from start to finish, it should be readily apparent that *all connecting events in the critical path must have zero slack times.* This limits our search to those paths connecting zero-slack events. In Figure 18-11, there are three such sequences.

1-2-5-8-10-11	(or, *a-c-i-k-l*)
1-2-3-4-5-8-10-11	(or, *a-b-d-e-i-k-l*)
1-2-3-4-8-10-11	(or, *a-b-d-f-k-l*)

Two of these paths are not critical because their activity times do not sum to the project duration of 42 days that we found earlier. The activity times in the first path sum to 24 days; in the last path, they total only 40 days. The middle sequence describes the critical path identified in the network in Figure 18-11.

18-4 Planning and Control Using the PERT Network

The PERT network information in Figure 18-11 can be used to establish project schedules and to aid in controlling activities so that delays can be avoided.

Activity Scheduling

Recall that the earliest possible event time *TE* sets a lower limit on when successive activities can be expected to start and that the latest allowable event time *TL* sets an upper limit on when preceding activities can end without causing expected delays in the project. Thus, considered together, the *TE* and *TL* values provide the basis for scheduling activities.

A schedule for an activity consists of a starting date and a completion date. The PERT network establishes limits for these dates. An activity can be expected to begin on any date between its **early starting time ES** and its **late starting time LS**. By adding the estimated activity completion time, these dates determine the **early finishing time EF** and the **late finishing time LF**.

An activity's early starting time is equal to the earliest possible time *TE* in which the immediately preceding event can be attained, or

$$ES = TE \text{ for preceding event}$$

By adding the expected activity completion time, represented by the letter *t*, we can then compute the early finishing time for each activity, or

$$EF = ES + t$$

The late finishing time for an activity is equal to the *TL* for the event at the point when it ends, or

$$LF = TL \text{ for succeeding event}$$

Subtracting the expected activity completion time, we calculate the late starting time as

$$LS = LF - t$$

Table 18-2 shows these quantities for the home construction illustration. Consider, for example, wiring (activity *f*). From Figure 18-11, we see that this activity is preceded by event 4 (with an earliest possible time of *TE* = 19) and succeeded by event 8 (with a latest

TABLE 18-2
Limits for Scheduling Home Construction Activities

ACTIVITY		t	STARTING TIMES		FINISHING TIMES	
			ES Preceding TE	LS $LF - t$	EF $ES + t$	LF Succeeding TL
(a)	Excavating	5	0	0	5	5
(b)	Pour foundation	2	5	5	7	7
(c)	Outside plumbing	6	5	23	11	29
(d)	Framing	12	7	7	19	19
(e)	Inside plumbing	10	19	19	29	29
(f)	Wiring	9	19	21	28	30
(g)	Roofing	5	19	22	24	27
(h)	Brickwork	9	7	18	16	27
(i)	Plumbing inspection	1	29	29	30	30
(j)	Shingling	2	24	28	26	30
(k)	Cover walls	3	30	30	33	33
(l)	Interior finishing	9	33	33	42	42
(m)	Exterior finishing	7	24	27	31	34
(n)	Landscaping	8	31	34	39	42

allowable time of $TL = 30$). Thus, the early starting time for wiring is $ES = 19$ days from the project start. Adding the expected completion time of $t = 9$ days for this activity, the early finishing time for wiring is $EF = 19 + 9 = 28$ days from time zero. The late finishing time for wiring is $LF = 30$ days, and the late starting time is $LS = 30 - 9 = 21$ days.

In scheduling the project, the builder can start wiring anytime between the early starting time of $ES = 19$ days and the late starting time of $LS = 21$ days. Thus, if the project is to start at 8 A.M. on Wednesday, August 1, 1993, wiring may be scheduled to begin sometime just after 19 working days, or at 8 A.M. on August 28 (the beginning of the 20th day) but not later than after 21 working days (8 A.M. on August 30). If the early starting time is chosen, wiring can be scheduled for completion at any time between the two corresponding finishing dates. But, if a late starting time is chosen, wiring must be scheduled for completion exactly at the late finishing time (the end of the 30th working day, or 5 P.M. on September 11—assuming that Labor Day is a working day).

Activity Slack Times

We have now identified the points in time that are associated with the activities themselves. These points provide another set of measures, called **activity slack times**, that are useful in project planning. Like their event counterparts discussed earlier, these values indicate how much leeway exists in completing an activity before project delays can be expected. For any particular activity, the activity slack time is computed from the difference between the late and early finishing times, or

$$\text{Activity slack time} = LF - EF$$

(The same results can be obtained from the difference $LS - ES$.)

TABLE 18-3
Activity Slack Times for the Home Construction
Illustration

	ACTIVITY	LF	EF	ACTIVITY SLACK TIME
		FINISHING TIME		
(a)	Excavating	5	5	0
(b)	Pour foundation	7	7	0
(c)	Outside plumbing	29	11	18
(d)	Framing	19	19	0
(e)	Inside plumbing	29	29	0
(f)	Wiring	30	28	2
(g)	Roofing	27	24	3
(h)	Brickwork	27	16	11
(i)	Plumbing inspection	30	30	0
(j)	Shingling	30	26	4
(k)	Cover walls	33	33	0
(l)	Interior finishing	42	42	0
(m)	Exterior finishing	34	31	3
(n)	Landscaping	42	39	3

The activity slack times for our home construction example are computed in Table 18-3. Notice that some activities have zero slack. A *critical path connects only zero-slack activities, and all such activities lie on at least one critical path.* Our example has only one critical path, *a-b-d-e-i-k-l.*

Although they are very similar, activity slack measures something different than event slack does, and one set of values cannot generally be computed directly from the other set.

Milestone Scheduling

Sometimes it is necessary to establish milestone schedules for project events rather than for activities. When PERT is applied to military development programs in which the Defense Department specifies important dates in contractual work statements, event scheduling is a convenient device. Although a PERT network may serve as a basis, the actual schedule times are negotiated between the government agency and the contractor. To avoid potential delays in meeting these dates, the contractor must schedule each finishing time for each activity so that it occurs no later than the applicable milestone date for the succeeding event.

An example from a major weapon system project demonstrates how important PERT planning is in establishing milestone schedule dates. One contractor was responsible for designing and building hardware, which was then to be tested by another contractor. The second contractor was scheduled to provide the U. S. Air Force with its testing results on a certain date. But the first contractor's schedule called for delivery of the necessary hardware *after* the testing had to be performed. This obvious inconsistency in contractor schedules went unnoticed for several months, until a PERT network was developed and its critical path was determined.

Managing with PERT

The preceding example illustrates an important feature of PERT: It can provide a structure for controlling the multitude of activities in a complex project. When separate organizations are responsible for work that must be done in small pieces over a long period of time at widely separated locations, good coordination of these efforts is a prerequisite for success. Strict adherence to mutually compatible schedules almost assures this. Although it is by no means a panacea, PERT accomplishes this function well.

Management through PERT does not stop with the publication of schedules. Remember, the PERT analysis we have examined so far is based on a single set of numbers—the *expected* activity completion times. The amount of time actually required for a particular activity is uncertain. Consider the framing of a house. Inclement weather, an accident on the job, poor workmanship, illness, or a variety of other circumstances might delay its completion. As we have seen in our home construction example, this particular activity is critical. A delay in framing will delay the project unless the lost time can be made up by speeding up the completion of one or more later activities on the critical path.

If the timely completion of the entire project is extremely important, the critical activities deserve special attention. This is an excellent application of the *management-by-exception principle*. Less attention should be paid to activities that are not on the critical path simply because small delays in completing them will not delay the entire project.

Again, it should be emphasized that the expected activity completion times themselves are only estimated values. If some activity that was not on the critical path were unduly delayed, the critical path from that point in time onward may actually shift and a new set of activities may become critical. Special managerial attention should therefore be given to the critical and near-critical (low slack time) activities.

18-5 Replanning and Adjustment with PERT

As just indicated, PERT involves much more than setting schedules. If situations that cause unusual delays are encountered, PERT must somehow accommodate them. Also, our discussions until now have focused on time to the exclusion of resources that might be consumed in completing a project. This is natural, since PERT is essentially a time-minimizing procedure. But a project manager should also be concerned with minimizing the *cost* of the resources being used.

The Time–Cost Trade-off

The expected activity completion times used in the basic PERT analysis are predicated on some assumed level of resource commitment. Labor is the dominant resource in most projects that lend themselves to PERT analysis, and management has the greatest flexibility and control over this resource. For instance, it is possible to shorten the time it takes to complete an activity by concentrating more labor on it. This can be accomplished in framing a house simply by using a larger crew of carpenters than originally planned.

Ordinarily, an activity can be shortened only by increasing its cost. For example, adding a third carpenter to the original two will shorten the work completion time but will not necessarily increase overall crew output by 50%, which can happen only if the work of the original two carpenters is less than optimal (from a productivity point of view). Beyond the optimal crew size, the marginal productivity of each extra worker decreases so that the total framing cost will be higher if three carpenters are employed. Another way to get the job done faster is to permit overtime work, but any overtime wage premium would also raise the total cost of completing the job.

Figure 18-12 shows how project completion time and cost are related by a curve. Each point on this **time–cost trade-off curve** corresponds to a possible project plan. Note the dilemma faced by a project manager: It is possible to reduce the duration of a project only

FIGURE 18-12
Time–cost trade-off curve for a project.

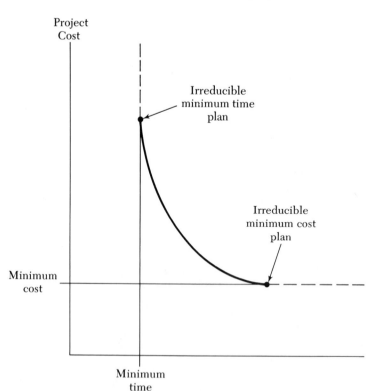

by increasing its cost and to reduce its cost only by increasing the duration of the project. Moreover, there are irreducible minimum plans with respect to time and cost. Only these plans and the ones lying in between, represented by the solid portion of the time–cost trade-off curve will ever be considered.

Unless time savings can be expressed in terms of a dollar return, quantitative analysis cannot identify the optimal point on the curve, because minimizing time and minimizing cost are competing objectives.

Regular and Crash Activity Plans

A good activity manager should be aware not only of how long a particular task may take under varying working conditions, but also of how much these various working arrangements should cost. When quantified, such information provides a graph such as the one shown in Figure 18-13, where two planning extremes determine a time–cost trade-off for an activity. The **crash activity plan** brings the expected activity completion time to its irreducible minimum, regardless of cost. At the other extreme, the **regular activity plan** involves the most efficient working arrangement in terms of resource use; it is the minimum-cost plan. Either of these plans, or one between them, may be chosen.

Table 18-4 provides some potential data for regular and crash activity plans for our home construction project. We can see that excavating (activity *a*) is expected to take 5

FIGURE 18-13
Time–cost trade-off line for an activity.

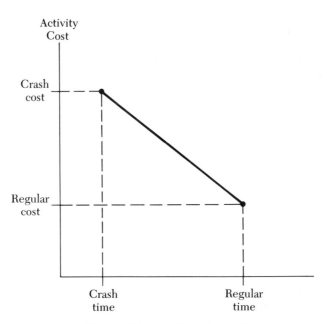

Expected Activity Completion Time

TABLE 18-4
Regular and Crash Programs for Constructing a Home

	ACTIVITY	EXPECTED ACTIVITY TIMES		DIRECT COST		ADDITIONAL COST PER DAY SAVED
		Regular	Crash	Regular	Crash	
(a)	Excavating	5 days	4 days	$1,000	$1,300	$300
(b)	Pour foundation	2	2	500	500	—
(c)	Outside plumbing	6	4	900	1,300	200
(d)	Framing	12	8	2,400	2,800	100
(e)	Inside plumbing	10	7	1,500	2,100	200
(f)	Wiring	9	6	1,800	2,250	150
(g)	Roofing	5	3	1,000	1,400	200
(h)	Brickwork	9	7	1,800	2,150	175
(i)	Plumbing inspection	1	1	50	50	—
(j)	Shingling	2	2	400	400	—
(k)	Cover walls	3	2	300	425	125
(l)	Interior finishing	9	8	1,500	1,725	225
(m)	Exterior finishing	7	5	1,200	1,650	225
(n)	Landscaping	8	4	2,000	2,100	25
				$16,350	$20,150	

days and to cost $1,000 in labor under the regular plan. On a crash basis, larger equipment can be rented to reduce the completion time of excavating by 1 day to a crash time of 4 days for a total direct crash cost of $1,300; the additional cost of shortening this activity's completion time is $300 per day reduced. Pouring the foundation (activity b) cannot be shortened. The expected regular time for outside plumbing (activity c) is 6 days and the regular cost is $900. But if the plumbers work overtime, an expected crash time of 4 days and a crash cost of $1,300 can be achieved; the added cost reflects the overtime pay, so that the crash program for outside plumbing costs $400 more and saves 2 days, and the daily cost of reducing that activity's completion time is $200. Altogether, the direct costs (nonmaterial) total $16,350 under the regular plans and $20,150 if all possible activities are crashed.

Constructing the Time–Cost Trade-off Curve

The time–cost trade-off curve can help the manager select a master plan for the project. To start, we consider the plan by which all activities are to be conducted on a regular basis, so that the first set of activity times in Table 18-4 apply. These times were used in the original PERT network constructed earlier. The final version of this network is repeated in Figure 18-14. This plan has a completion time of 42 days and total direct costs of $16,350.

Since the duration of the project is dictated by the longest activity sequence through the PERT network, it can only be shortened by reducing the completion times of activities on the critical path. For the initial plan, the critical path is a-b-d-e-i-k-l. As long as

FIGURE 18-14

A PERT network for the home construction illustration when all activities have regular expected completion times (plan 1).

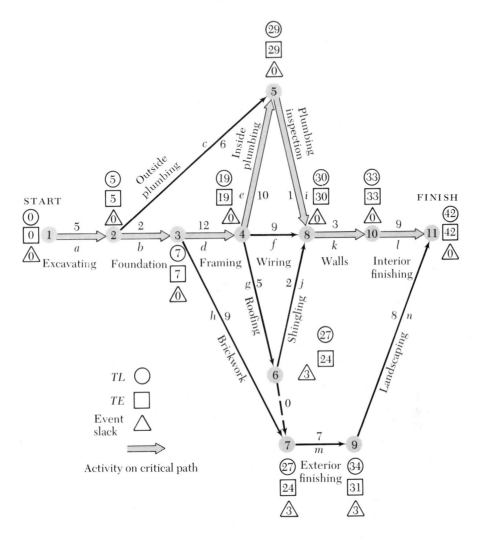

this path remains critical, any reduction in the expected completion time of one of the critical activities will reduce the project completion time by the same amount.

From the initial regular project plan, a succession of faster plans will be developed by crashing various activities in such a way that each new plan is the cheapest possible one for the indicated project completion time. Table 18-5 shows the plans that result.

The procedure is started by crashing the cheapest critical activity, which happens to be framing (activity d), since this increases the direct costs by the smallest amount (only $100 per day saved). A maximum reduction of 4 days is possible. This faster plan yields a project completion time of 38 days and a larger total direct cost of $16,750.

TABLE 18-5

**Potential Home Construction Project Plans, Listed in Increasing Order
of Additional Cost per Day Saved**

PROJECT PLAN	PROJECT COMPLETION TIME	TOTAL DIRECT COST	LAST ACTIVITY CRASHED	ADDITIONAL COST PER DAY SAVED	CRITICAL PATH
1	42 days	$16,350	None	—	a-b-d-e-i-k-l
2	38	16,750	d by 4 days	$100	a-b-d-e-i-k-l
3	37	16,875	k by 1 day	125	a-b-d-e-i-k-l
4	35	17,275	e by 2 days	200	a-b-d-e-i-k-l
					a-b-d-f-k-l
					a-b-d-g-m-n
5	34	17,525	l by 1 day	225	a-b-d-e-i-k-l
			n by 1 day	25	a-b-d-f-k-l
				250	a-b-d-g-m-n
6	33	17,825	a by 1 day	300	a-b-d-e-i-k-l
					a-b-d-f-k-l
					a-b-d-g-m-n
7	32	18,200	e by 1 day	200	a-b-d-e-i-k-l
			f by 1 day	150	a-b-d-f-k-l
			n by 1 day	25	a-b-d-g-m-n
				375	

The third plan is to crash activity k (walls), the next cheapest critical activity at $125, for a reduction of 1 day in completion time. This plan takes 37 days and costs $16,875.

The cheapest critical activity remaining to be crashed is inside plumbing (e), which costs $200 extra for each day's reduction. Although activity e can be crashed from 10 to 7 days to save 3 days, just 2 days of this reduced completion time will be felt by the project as a whole. This is because two other paths (a-b-d-f-k-l- and a-b-d-g-m-n) also become critical when the time for activity e is reduced by 2 days. Thus, the fourth plan incorporates a 2-day reduction (a partial crash) in the expected completion time for activity e to 8 days. This lowers the project time to 35 days and increases the cost to $17,275. This plan, reflecting all of the time changes made so far, has the PERT network shown in Figure 18-15. Each of the *three* critical paths takes 35 days. (If activity e were completely crashed all the way to 7 days, the project would still take 35 days, since that activity does not lie on the two new critical paths.)

The next time reduction is complicated by the fact that there are several critical paths. The durations of all three paths must be reduced in order to shorten the project further. This could be accomplished in a variety of ways. By trial and error, we can find the cheapest method. This is to crash interior finishing (l) and to partially crash landscaping (n), saving 1 day on each activity at a combined cost of $250. This fifth plan allows the project to be completed in 34 days at a cost of $17,525.

FIGURE 18-15
The PERT network for plan 4.

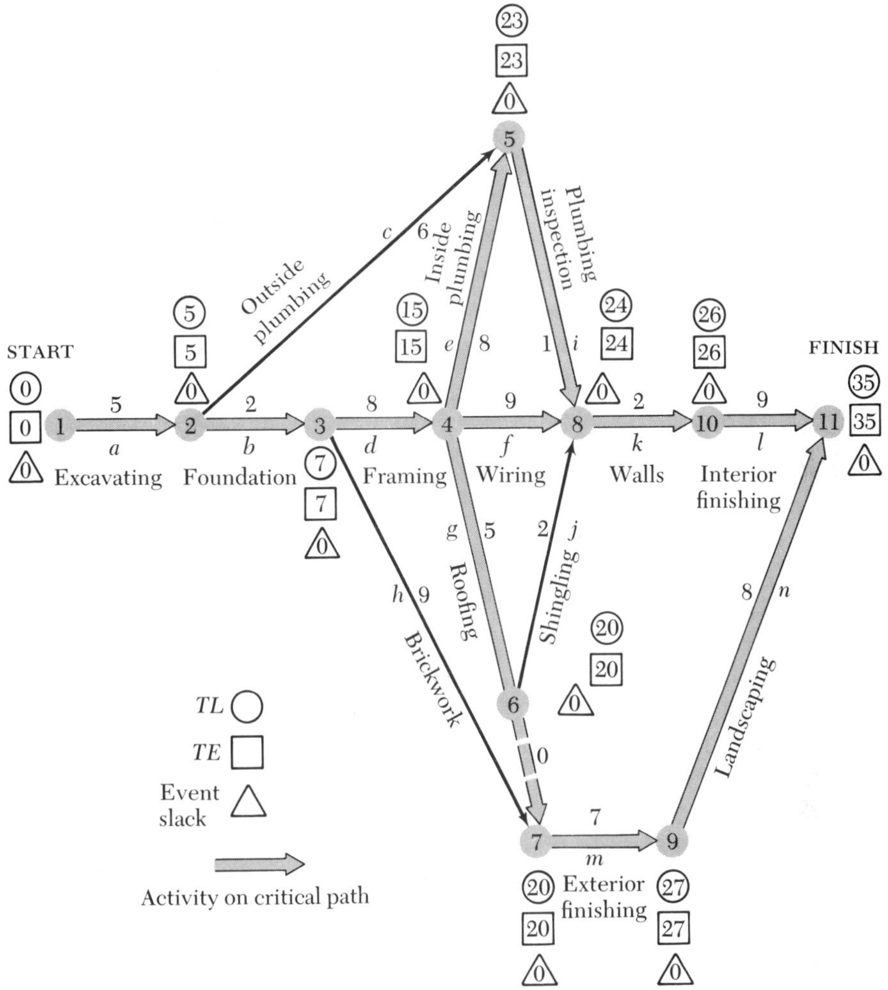

All three critical paths involve excavating (*a*). Crashing this activity is the next cheapest change, costing $300 for a 1-day reduction in completion time. This results in plan 6, which reduces the project completion time to 33 days and increases total direct costs to $17,825.

The seventh plan must involve a 1-day reduction in activity *e*, since this is the only activity remaining in the original critical path that has not been completely crashed. In the other two critical paths, a 1-day partial crash reduction combination for activities *f* and *n* provides the least costly change. Altogether, these time reductions raise total direct cost by $375 to $18,200 and reduce project completion time to 32 days. The PERT network for plan 7 is provided in Figure 18-16. No further time reductions are possible, because every

FIGURE 18-16
The PERT network for plan 7.

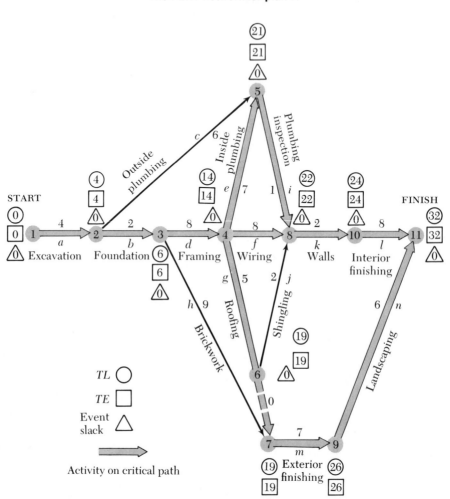

activity in the critical path *a-b-d-e-i-k-l* is completely crashed. Since that critical path cannot be shortened, any further crashing of critical activities will only increase total direct cost without providing a compensatory time savings for the project as a whole.

The procedure just outlined for finding each new plan is strictly a matter of trial and error. It will be helpful to begin with several blank copies of the basic PERT network. The project time for new plans should be reduced in *one-day increments* to avoid making large time reductions that might not be valid for the project as a whole due to the unnoticed emergence of new critical paths. (Two or more successive plans involving identical activity changes can be combined later.) For each new plan, start with a fresh network, change the activity times on the arrows, and recompute the *TE*, *TL*, and slack values. Then clearly mark the critical paths. As you go along, put an × on the arrows of those activities on your latest diagram that cannot be crashed further and cross the respective activities off your original list (like the one in Table 18-4). Ignoring earlier networks, study your latest diagram to find further time-reduction alternatives. Changes will become more complex as the number of critical paths grows. Fortunately, fewer possibilities are left to be considered after each new plan.

The time–cost trade-off curve for the home construction project appears in Figure 18-17. This curve provides the builder with a comprehensive summary of possible master plans and indicates the most efficient plan for successive reductions in project completion time. For example, if there is some advantage in shaving 5 days off the original completion time, then plan 3 should be adopted if the gain outweighs the added cost. (In-between plans are also possible, such as a 2-day reduction in expected project completion time by only partially crashing activity *d* by 2 days instead of the full 4 days possible.)

FIGURE 18-17
Time–cost trade-off curve for the home construction illustration.

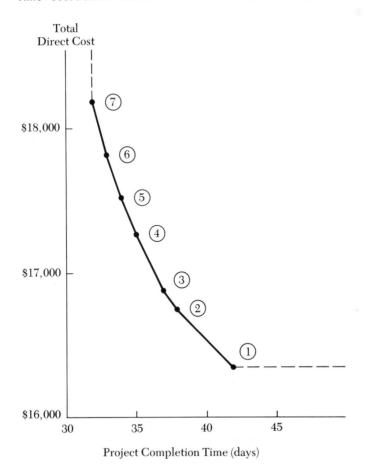

Project Completion Time (days)

Updating the PERT Network

Once a plan has been established, the appropriate schedules can be determined and the project can be started. PERT can still be used as the project progresses. The actual completion times of the early activities can deviate, perhaps considerably, from the expected values identified at the outset due to such factors as strikes, poor weather, illness, or chance. Or the expected completion times for some future activities may have to be revised in the light of new information. Or a subcontractor may simply not be able to start work on the scheduled date. Such discrepancies may necessitate revising the PERT network, because much of the earlier analysis is no longer applicable. For example, a delay of several days in the completion of the brickwork could effectively shift the critical path in our home construction example to a portion of the network never considered critical before.

When the project is well underway, PERT procedures are the same as before, except that completed activities will have actual rather than expected completion times. New time–cost trade-offs can be made (completed activities, of course, cannot be changed), and a new master plan can be developed that involves revised schedules.

The ability to update PERT networks is especially important in long projects with considerable uncertainties, such as those encountered in weapon system development. Such projects can take more than five years to complete and often involve major technological breakthroughs. In such cases, all of the activities cannot even be identified in detail before the project starts. Initial PERT planning often begins with educated guesses about the specific tasks that will be required three or four years into the project. As planning becomes more precise, the PERT network can grow and be based on more sophisticated time estimates. As the PERT network is modified, revised schedules reflecting current planning can be periodically published.

18-6 Additional Remarks

In this chapter, we have reviewed the essential concepts of PERT, but we have barely scratched the surface of this method of analysis. For instance, we have not considered how to deal explicitly with the uncertainties about activity completion times or how to obtain the expected values. Appendix 18-1 discusses a traditional procedure for probability analysis using PERT. A further treatment involving simulation will be presented in Chapter 20.

Although it may not readily appear to be so, the mathematical properties of PERT place it in an area of linear programming. Establishing TE values is a linear programming problem in which the objective is to minimize time. A whole class of linear programming problems involving network flows can be analyzed in a manner similar to the PERT network.

Large PERT systems are generally computerized. A variety of programs have been developed to perform various portions of PERT analysis. These programs often integrate PERT into the structure of broader management information systems. A precursor was the Defense Department's PERT/Cost System, which linked cost control and scheduling of activities. The success of that system was limited due to conflicts with contractors' internal accounting systems. But despite problems with some of the systems associated with PERT, its time-minimization and scheduling aspects are generally accepted as a very valuable management tool.

18-7 Computer Applications with PERT

Since their inception, network planning methods have been successfully employed with computer assistance. PERT has been employed on projects involving thousands of activities, each of which is represented on a common network. It would be impracticable to evaluate such networks by hand. Indeed, the network can be too big to physically diagram without papering the walls of a large room. Some computer systems, notably the Apple MacIntosh, will graphically portray the network on a screen window that can be moved to show the missing portions.

Large-scale implementations of PERT must incorporate the computer, with all details stored in a data base. These stored details include the estimated completion times for the activities and how the activities are logically connected. Also maintained in the data base are data for the various event times and scheduling information for events. The data base may be updated constantly as activities are completed, delayed, or accelerated. Additional activities may be added as they are identified.

Computers facilitate probabilistic evaluations (see Appendix 18-1). They are also useful in simulating alternative project activity arrangements (see Chapter 20).

PERT Network Evaluations with *QuickQuant*

The *QuickQuant* software package, available to users of this textbook, has a segment for evaluating PERT networks. The program is *user friendly*, with screen-prompt questions guiding all necessary choices and inputs. Complete operating instructions for this program are provided in the Appendix at the back of this textbook.

Data may be entered either in network form or in tabular form. In the latter case, *QuickQuant* will internally construct the PERT network. Due to graphics limitations, the current version of the program will not display the network itself on the screen. But it will provide on screen or hard copy the necessary information regarding the network, significantly easing the task of making the diagram.

A feature of *QuickQuant* is its data editing features that allow you not only to correct problem inputs, but to modify them for a slightly different case. *QuickQuant* allows you to save your problem data for later use.

Shown in Tables 18-6 and 18-7 are two output reports from a *QuickQuant* run for the home construction illustration described earlier. The first of these is an activity report that summarizes essential information for scheduling and monitoring the activities. The report shown in Table 18-6 may be used to construct a physical graph. However, it should be easier to begin the graph by using the event milestone report shown in Table 18-7.

TABLE 18-6
Activity Report from a *QuickQuant* Run for the Home Construction Illustration

ACTIVITY REPORT FOR Home-Building

Activity			Beg.	End.	Planning Times					
No.	Code	Name	Event	Event	Exp. t	ES	LS	EF	LF	Slack
1	a	Excav.	1	2	5	0	0	5	5	0
2	b	Found.	2	3	2	5	5	7	7	0
3	c	Outs Pl.	2	5	6	5	23	11	29	18
4	d	Framing	3	4	12	7	7	19	19	0
5	e	Ins Pl.	4	5	10	19	19	29	29	0
6	f	Wiring	4	8	9	19	21	28	30	2
7	g	Roofing	4	6	5	19	22	24	27	3
8	h	Brickw.	3	7	9	7	18	16	27	11
9	i	Pl Insp.	5	8	1	29	29	30	30	0
10	j	Shingl.	6	8	2	24	28	26	30	4
11	k	Walls	8	10	3	30	30	33	33	0
12	l	Int Fin.	10	11	9	33	33	42	42	0
13	m	Ext Fin.	7	9	7	24	27	31	34	3
14	n	Landsc.	9	11	8	31	34	39	42	3

Critical Path(s)	Expected Project Time
a-b-d-e-i-k-l	42

TABLE 18-7
Event Milestone Report from a *QuickQuant* Run for the Home Construction Illustration

EVENT MILESTONE REPORT FOR Home-Building

Event	Event Connections		Times			Activity Connections		
	Predecessors	Successors	TE	TL	Slack	End There	Begin There	
1 :	none	: 2 __ __ :	0	0	0	: none	: a	__ __
2 :	1 __ __ :	3 5 __ :	5	5	0	: a __ __ :	b	c __
3 :	2 __ __ :	4 7 __ :	7	7	0	: b __ __ :	d	h __
4 :	3 __ __ :	5 6 8 :	19	19	0	: d __ __ :	e	f g
5 :	2 4 __ :	8 __ __ :	29	29	0	: c e __ :	i	__ __
6 :	4 __ __ :	7 8 __ :	24	27	3	: g __ __ :	j	Dum __
7 :	3 6 __ :	9 __ __ :	24	27	3	: h Dum __ :	m	__ __
8 :	4 5 6 :	10 __ __ :	30	30	0	: f i j :	k	__ __
9 :	7 __ __ :	11 __ __ :	31	34	3	: m __ __ :	n	__ __
10 :	8 __ __ :	11 __ __ :	33	33	0	: k __ __ :	l	__ __
11 :	9 10 __ :	none :	42	42	0	: l n __ :	none	

Critical Path(s)	Expected Project Time
1-2-3-4-5-8-10-11	42

Appendix 18-1:
Traditional PERT Analysis with Three Time Estimates*

In the body of this chapter, we did not consider how we arrive at expected activity completion times. Although the techniques presented in Chapter 4 can be used for this purpose, in traditional PERT analysis, they are obtained from a special procedure that involves three time estimates.

$$a = \text{Optimistic time}$$

$$m = \text{Most likely time}$$

$$b = \text{Pessimistic time}$$

These estimates are fairly easy for activity line managers to provide.

The activity duration will almost certainly exceed the optimistic time a, and the actual completion time will almost certainly be below the pessimistic time b. The most likely time m is analogous to the *mode* in statistics. These three times estimates specify a particular continuous probability distribution that is a member of the **modified beta distribution**

FIGURE 18-18

Three basic shapes of frequency curves for the PERT modified beta distribution.

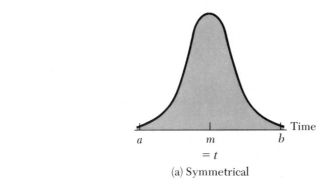

(a) Symmetrical

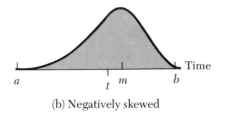

(b) Negatively skewed

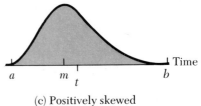

(c) Positively skewed

---

* This section is optional.

family. Such a distribution can be symmetrical or skewed (positively or negatively), depending on the relative positions of *a*, *m*, and *b*. The frequency curves for each case appear in Figure 18-18. The expected activity completion time may be computed from these three estimates.

$$t = \frac{a + 4m + b}{6}$$

The values calculated from this equation can then be used in the main PERT analysis. It may also be useful to know the variance in completion time, which is computed

$$\text{Variance} = \left(\frac{b - a}{6}\right)^2$$

Suppose that the expected regular activity completion times *t* for each activity used in the home construction example are obtained in this manner from the three time-estimate sets provided in Table 18-8.

Notice that the possible times for each activity vary considerably. Thus, any of the various events in the PERT network could occur at a wide variety of points in time, and the project completion time could be considerably shorter or longer than the 42 days originally anticipated.

As a result, the duration *T* of the original critical path *a-b-d-e-i-k-l* cannot be predicted precisely. We do know that its expected value, represented by μ, is the sum of the expected completion times for the component activities, or

$$\mu = 5 + 2 + 12 + 10 + 1 + 3 + 9 = 42 \text{ days}$$

TABLE 18-8

Three Time Estimates Used to Compute the Expected Values and Variances of Activity Completion Times for the Home Construction Illustration

ACTIVITY	OPTIMISTIC TIME *a*	MOST LIKELY TIME *m*	PESSIMISTIC TIME *b*	EXPECTED TIME $t = \frac{a + 4m + b}{6}$	VARIANCE $\left(\frac{b-a}{6}\right)^2$
a	3	5	7	5	.444
b	1	1.5	5	2	.444
c	4	5	12	6	1.778
d	8	10	24	12	7.111
e	7	10	13	10	1.000
f	5	9.5	11	9	1.000
g	3.5	5	6.5	5	.250
h	6	8	16	9	2.778
i	1	1	1	1	0
j	1	2	3	2	.111
k	1.5	3	4.5	3	.250
l	7	9	11	9	.444
m	6	6.5	10	7	.444
n	5	7.5	13	8	1.778

If we assume that the activity times are *independent*, we can closely approximate the complete probability distribution for the length T of this particular path. Its variance σ^2 is then the sum of the variances of the individual completion times for the critical activities, or

$$\sigma^2 = .444 + .444 + 7.111 + 1.000 + 0 + .250 + .444 = 9.693$$

And the standard deviation for T is

$$\sigma = \sqrt{9.693} = 3.11 \text{ days}$$

A general form of the central limit theorem, discussed in Chapter 3, indicates that T is approximately normally distributed with a mean of μ and a variance of σ. Thus, we can establish the probability that 50 days or less will be required to complete path *a-b-d-e-i-k-l* as

$$z = \frac{50 - 42}{3.11} = 2.57$$

$$\Pr[T \leq 50] = .5 + .4949 = .9949$$

and the probability that it will take more than 40 days as

$$z = \frac{40 - 42}{3.11} = -.64$$

$$\Pr[T > 40] = .5 + .2389 = .7389$$

There is one major fallacy in this analysis. *T is the duration for a particular path—not for the project itself*. This point has been widely misunderstood. There is a considerable chance that some path other than the one we identify as the critical path will actually take longer. Thus, $\mu = 42$ days is not really a measure of how long the *project* may be expected to take, and it can considerably understate the true value of the project's expected length.

A complete probability analysis of project completion time is beyond the scope of this book. In Chapter 20, Monte Carlo simulation will be used to estimate the mean project completion time.

Appendix 18-2: The CPM Network*

The PERT network in this chapter uses a different graphical representation than what is frequently used in some applications. The alternative portrayal is generally used in CPM (critical path method). *There, each activity is represented by a circle.* The circles are connected with arrows in accordance with the required logical sequence, forming a network like the one in Figure 18-19 for the home construction example. The expected

---

* This section is optional.

FIGURE 18-19

The CPM network for the home construction illustration.

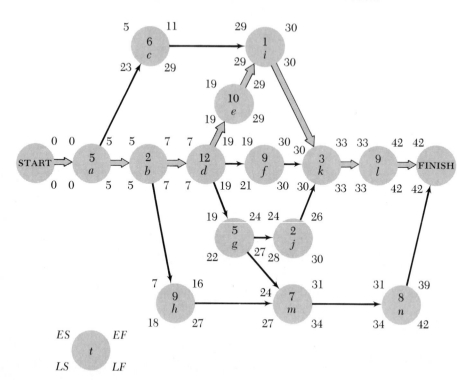

activity completion times appear inside the respective circles. (For convenience, circles are also used to represent the project's start and finish.)

The critical path is located by a similar procedure. First, a forward pass is made to obtain the *ES* and *EF* values. A value of zero is used for the start; the *ES* is the largest *EF* of immediately preceding activities. An activity's *ES* value represents the longest path of activities that must be completed before it can start. The *LF* and *LS* values are found in a backward pass. The *LS* used to begin this process is equal to the *ES* for finish; the *LF* is always the smallest *LS* of immediately succeeding activities. An activity's *LF* is the longest duration from its completion to finish. In doing the above, the following relationships are used.

$$EF = ES + t$$

$$LS = LF - t$$

$$\text{Activity slack} = LF - EF = LS - ES$$

The critical path is one connecting zero-slack activities.

One distinct disadvantage of the CPM-type network is that it is clumsy for identifying events, which makes it less desirable for milestone scheduling. Each divergence or convergence of arrows corresponds to the standard PERT network event. Earliest possible and latest allowable event times may be obtained from the following.

$$TE = \text{Largest } EF \text{ for preceding activity}$$

$$TL = \text{Smallest } LS \text{ for succeeding activity}$$

Another disadvantage of the CPM-type network is that it is harder to identify activities for computer processing; in standard PERT each activity can be defined in terms of predecessor and successor events. The main advantage of the CPM network is that it is easier to graph than the PERT network because dummy activities are not required.

CASE

A House with Seven Gables

Salem Daughters Construction Company has contracted with a Mr. Hawthorne to build a classic house having seven gables. The customer wants to complete the house as soon as possible, at a minimum cost. The preliminary data in Table 18-9 apply for the various activities.

TABLE 18-9
Data for the Construction Activities

	ACTIVITY	IMMEDIATELY PRECEDING ACTIVITY	EXPECTED COMPLETION TIME
(a)	Grade	—	3 days
(b)	Excavate	—	4
(c)	Basement	b	1
(d)	Foundation	a, c	2
(e)	Floor joists	d	3
(f)	Exterior plumbing	a, c	3
(g)	Floor	e, f	2
(h)	Power on	d	1
(i)	Walls	g	10
(j)	Wire	h, i	2
(k)	Com lines	j	1
(l)	Inside plumbing	i	5
(m)	Windows	l	2
(n)	Doors	l	2
(o)	Sheetrock	k, l	3
(p)	Interior trim	n, o	5
(q)	Exterior trim	n	4
(r)	Paint	m, p, q	3
(s)	Carpet	r	1
(t)	Buyer inspection	s	1

Samantha Salem believes that the data in Table 18-9 reflect optimal expenditures of labor and resources. The following cost estimates correspond.

ACTIVITY	COST	ACTIVITY	COST	ACTIVITY	COST	ACTIVITY	COST
a	$1,000	f	$ 500	k	$ 200	p	$8,000
b	2,500	g	3,000	l	1,500	q	3,000
c	4,400	h	500	m	2,300	r	3,000
d	5,500	i	4,000	n	1,000	s	5,000
e	2,000	j	2,300	o	3,200	t	0

The preceding includes the cost of materials supplied by subcontractors. Additional Salem materials costs are $51,000.

A few activities can be speeded up. By working on extended hours, carpenters can complete the walls in 8 days at a total cost of $4,500. Working at night, workers can complete the sheetrock in 2 days at a total of $3,500. For a premium of $700, the plumbing contractor can complete inside plumbing in 3 days. Using night lighting, crews can finish the excavation in 2 days at a total of $3,500 and complete the grading in 2 days for $1,600.

Questions

1. Construct a PERT network for the project, entering the expected activity completion times alongside the applicable arrows.

2. For each event, find the earliest possible, latest allowable, and slack times. Then, establish the critical path. How long is the project expected to take?

3. Determine a sequence of plans for Salem Daughters Construction Company, each plan representing a one-day savings in project completion time at a minimal increase in cost.

4. Salem has accepted an incentive clause which provides for a payment of $400 for each day saved from an anticipated 40-day duration until project completion. Which plan identified in Question 3 should be implemented? Specify which activities should be speeded up and by how many days. What is Salem's net project cost using the optimal plan?

PROBLEMS

18-1 Find the critical path for the PERT network in Figure 18-20.

FIGURE 18-20
The PERT network for Problem 18-1.

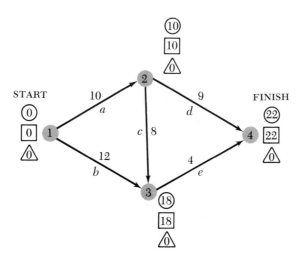

18-2 Copy the PERT network in Figure 18-21 on a piece of paper.
(a) Determine the *TE*, *TL*, and slack values for each event.
(b) Find the critical path(s). What project duration is indicated?
(c) Determine the *ES*, *EF*, *LS*, *LF*, and slack values for each activity.

FIGURE 18-21
The PERT network for Problem 18-2.

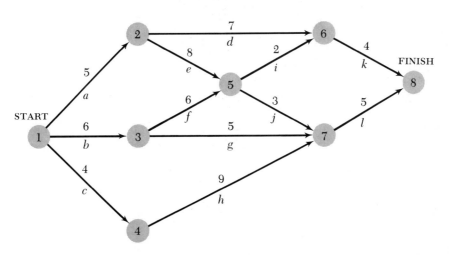

18-3 For the PERT network in Figure 18-22, determine (1) the earliest event completion times, (2) the latest allowable event completion times, (3) the event slack times, and (4) the critical path(s).

FIGURE 18-22
The PERT network for Problem 18-3.

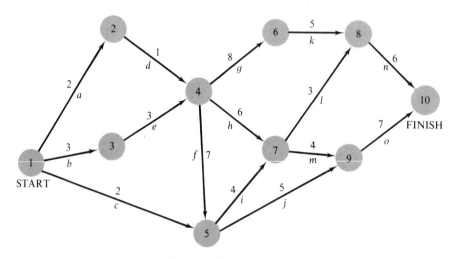

18-4 Table 18-10 contains a list of project activities and the sequencing requirements.
(a) Construct a PERT network for the project.
(b) Determine the *TE*, *TL*, and slack values for each event. Indicate these values on your diagram, using a square, circle, and triangle, respectively, for each event.
(c) Find the critical path(s).

TABLE 18-10
Data for Problem 18-4

ACTIVITY	IMMEDIATELY PRECEDING ACTIVITY	EXPECTED COMPLETION TIME
a	—	8 days
b	—	7
c	—	6
d	a	6
e	b	7
f	c	6
g	c	3
h	a	5
i	d, e, f	3
j	c	3
k	h, i, j	4

18-5 Table 18-11 contains a list of project activities and sequencing requirements.
(a) Construct a PERT network for the project.
(b) Find the critical path(s).

TABLE 18-11
Data for Problem 18-5

ACTIVITY	IMMEDIATELY PRECEDING ACTIVITY	EXPECTED COMPLETION TIME
a	—	2 days
b	—	3
c	—	2
d	b	4
e	a, b	3
f	b	2
g	f, c	5
h	g	4
i	f	3
j	i, d	2
k	j	1
l	e	6

18-6   Consider the PERT network in Figure 18-20, where the expected completion times are in eight hour working days. Assuming that the project will start at 8 A.M. on Monday, September 1, determine a set of mutually compatible schedule dates for starting and finishing each activity that will permit the projects to be completed in a minimum amount of time. (No work is to be done on weekends or holidays, and activities must start at 8 A.M. and end at 5 P.M. on the scheduled dates.)

18-7   Table 18-12 contains a list of project activities and sequencing requirements.
(a) Construct the PERT network for the project.
(b) Find the critical path. How long is the project expected to take?

TABLE 18-12
Data for Problem 18-7

ACTIVITY	IMMEDIATELY PRECEDING ACTIVITY	EXPECTED COMPLETION TIME
a	—	5 days
b	—	4
c	—	3
d	a	4
e	a, b	5
f	a, b	6
g	c	8
h	d, e	3
i	h	1
j	f, g	1
k	i	2
l	h, j	4

18-8   Consider the computer installation project network in Figure 18-23.

FIGURE 18-23
The PERT network for Problem 18-8.

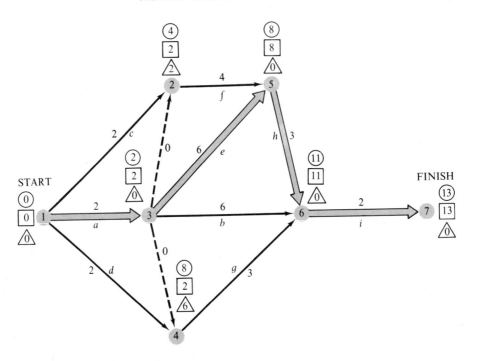

The following time and cost data apply.

| | TIME (weeks) | | COST | | ADDITIONAL |
ACTIVITY	Regular	Crash	Regular	Crash	COST/WEEK SAVED
a	2	1	$1,000	$2,000	$1,000
b	6	6	1,000	1,000	—
c	2	1	500	700	200
d	2	1	600	700	100
e	6	4	400	1,000	300
f	4	1	500	1,700	400
g	3	3	1,000	1,000	—
h	3	1	1,000	2,000	500
i	2	1	1,000	1,600	600

The following is a partially completed listing of the succession of plans for the time–cost trade-off. Complete the list, identifying each successive plan that will save one week in project completion time at the smallest increase in cost.

PROJECT PLAN	PROJECT COMPLETION TIME (weeks)	TOTAL DIRECT COST	LAST ACTIVITIES CRASHED	ADDITIONAL COST PER WEEK SAVED	CRITICAL PATHS
1	13	$7,000	none	—	a-e-h-i
2	12	7,300	e by 1 week	$300	a-e-h-i
3	11	7,600	e by 1 week	300	a-e-h-i
					c-f-h-i
					a-f-h-i

18-9   The following table provides information on a research project.

	EXPECTED TIME		DIRECT COST	
ACTIVITY	Regular	Crash	Regular	Crash
a	9 days	9 days	$500	$500
b	18	17	400	600
c	10	9	300	500
d	22	20	700	900
e	21	20	600	900

The PERT network is provided in Figure 18-24.
(a) Using regular times, find the critical path. How long is the project expected to take? How much will it cost?
(b) Determine the plans that the project manager should want to consider in making a time–cost trade-off. List these, beginning with the most lengthy duration plan and ending with the most costly plan. (Do not list plans that should not be considered at all.)
(c) Suppose that the project manager saves $150 in late penalties for each day that the project is completed ahead of regular time.
  (1) Which of the above plans would be used?
  (2) If he saves, instead, $300 per day, which of the above plans would be used?

FIGURE 18-24
The PERT network for Problem 18-9.

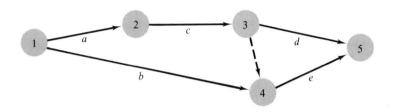

18-10   The following activities apply to the computerization of a company's accounting system, which is presently operated manually.

	ACTIVITY	EXPECTED COMPLETION TIME
(a)	Select computer	2 months
(b)	Assemble and install computer	6
(c)	Design data input forms	2
(d)	Design output report forms	2
(e)	Write main processing programs	6
(f)	Write input routines	4
(g)	Write output routines	3
(h)	Generate accounting data bank	3
(i)	Test and revise system	2

All of the program routines can be written independently before the computer is installed and can be debugged using computer time rented from another company. No programs or routines can be written until the particular computer model has been selected, although forms and reports can be designed while alternative computers are being evaluated. No input or output routines can be written until the corresponding forms have been designed. The main processing programs and input routines are required to establish the accounting data bank, which can be created on rental equipment. The final activity before implementation is complete is to test and revise the system.

(a) Construct a PERT network for converting the accounting system.
(b) What is the earliest time that the conversion can be finished assuming that the completion times are certain?
(c) Establish the early and late starting and finishing times for each activity. Which activities are critical?

18-11 Consider the PERT network in Figure 18-21. Suppose that the following regular and crash data apply.

ACTIVITY	EXPECTED TIME Regular	Crash	DIRECT COST Regular	Crash
a	5 days	4 days	$100	$ 120
b	6	4	200	260
c	4	4	300	300
d	7	5	500	580
e	8	6	700	800
f	6	5	500	560
g	5	5	400	400
h	9	8	950	1020
i	2	2	200	200
j	3	2	250	325
k	4	3	350	440
l	5	3	500	700

(a) Construct the time–cost trade-off curve for this project. (*Hint:* Before starting, make several copies of the PERT network, omitting the activity times; use a new network for each plan.)

(b) Suppose that the project manager values each day of the project completion time saved at $85. Which point on your curve is optimal? What direct cost and project completion time apply?

18-12 In publishing a textbook, the following simplified sequence of activities applies, as shown in Table 18-13.

(a) Construct the PERT network and find the critical path for this activity sequence. How long should the project take from start to finish?

(b) If the project is well managed, it is possible to produce a book in 18 months or less without crashing any activities. This contradicts your findings in (a). Discuss each of the following.

(1) How do you think publishers get the job done so quickly?

(2) Does this mean that PERT is not applicable to book publishing?

(3) Publishers usually require an author's complete manuscript before they begin to work on the book. In light of your answer to (2), suggest how PERT may be used to shorten the publication time of a book even further.

TABLE 18-13
Data for Problem 18-12

ACTIVITY		PRECEDING ACTIVITY	EXPECTED COMPLETION TIME
(a)	Write book	—	12 months
(b)	Design book	a	1
(c)	Edit manuscript	a	6
(d)	Check editing	c	2
(e)	Accept design	b	1
(f)	Copy edit	d, e	2
(g)	Prepare artwork	d, e	4
(h)	Accept and correct artwork	g	$\frac{1}{2}$
(i)	Set galleys	f	4
(j)	Check and correct galleys	i	1
(k)	Pull page proofs	h, j	2
(l)	Check and correct pages	k	1
(m)	Prepare index	k	1
(n)	Set and correct index	m	$\frac{1}{2}$
(o)	Check camera-ready copy	l, n	$\frac{1}{2}$
(p)	Print and bind book	o	1

18-13   *Computer exercise.*   The following activities apply to the research and development of a new pharmaceutical product.

ACTIVITY	PRECEDING ACTIVITY	EXPECTED COMPLETION TIME (weeks)	ACTIVITY	PRECEDING ACTIVITY	EXPECTED COMPLETION TIME (weeks)
a	—	6.3	v	l, mm	8.3
b	—	6.0	w	l, mm	13.1
c	—	2.9	x	t, u, v	8.1
d	—	8.5	y	t, u, v	4.2
e	—	3.8	z	t, u, v	5.9
f	a	5.9	aa	s, x	25.9
g	a	4.7	bb	y	13.3
h	b	6.3	cc	k, w, z	12.6
i	c	6.8	dd	y, aa	4.9
j	d	11.6	ee	y, aa	11.4
k	e	13.7	ff	y, aa	9.7
l	e, j	16.2	gg	bb, ff	9.1
m	e, j	7.9	hh	bb, ff	6.8
n	g, h, i	11.8	ii	ee, hh	5.7
p	f	11.6	jj	r, dd	14.3
q	f	4.1	kk	ii, jj	9.8
r	q	5.4	ll	cc, gg	2.5
s	q	4.1	mm	m, n, p	11.4
t	q	4.5	nn	ee, hh	9.2
u	mm	9.5			

(a) Obtain the activity report. From this, find (1) the critical path(s) and (2) the expected duration of that path.

(b) Obtain the event milestone report. From this, determine the event sequence taken by the critical path.

18-14   *(Continuation of Problem 18-13):* Suppose that a new activity, *pp*, expected to take 12 weeks is added to the project. The new activity is immediately preceded by activity *y* only, and it is an immediate predecessor only to activity *aa*. All other activity data remains exactly the same.

(a) Obtain the activity report. From this, find (1) the critical path(s) and (2) the expected duration of that path.

(b) Obtain the event milestone report. From this, determine the event sequence taken by the critical path.

18-15   *(Continuation of Problem 18-13):* Additional information has been obtained regarding expected completion times for the original activities in the project. The following now apply.

ACTIVITY	TIME
h	11.5
x	7.5
ee	18.0
jj	7.5

All original activity data remains exactly the same (with activity *pp* above not included).

(a) Obtain the activity report. From this, find (1) the critical path(s) and (2) the expected duration of that path.

(b) Obtain the event milestone report. From this, determine the event sequence taken by the critical path.

18-16 *Probability analysis.* Consider the PERT network in Figure 18-25. Suppose that the following probabilities (in parentheses) apply to the completion times for the various activities.

a	*b*	*c*	*d*	*e*
8(1)	$5(\frac{1}{2})$	$2(\frac{1}{2})$	$5(\frac{1}{4})$	$8(\frac{3}{4})$
	$6(\frac{1}{2})$	$3(\frac{1}{2})$	$6(\frac{3}{4})$	$9(\frac{1}{4})$

(a) Use these data to compute the expected activity completion times. Then, determine the critical path and its duration based on the expected values.

(b) What actual durations are possible for the critical path you found in (a)? Assuming that activity times are independent events, determine the probability for each duration.

(c) Repeat (b) for the other (noncritical) path.

(d) Use your answers to (b) and (c) and the multiplication law to construct the joint probability table for the durations of the two paths.

(e) From your joint probability table, identify the situations in which the "critical" path is actually of shorter duration than the "noncritical" path. What is the probability that any one of these situations will occur?

(f) Use your joint probability table to determine the probability distribution for the length of the longest path(s) from START TO FINISH. This distribution represents the *project* completion time. What is its expected value? Is this the same as the duration you found in (a)? Explain.

FIGURE 18-25
The PERT network for Problem 18-16.

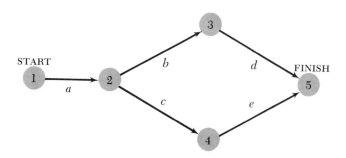

*18-17 PERT *with three time estimates.* Consider a small project that involves the following activities.

---

* This problem involves material in Appendix 18-1 to the chapter.

ACTIVITY	PRECEDING ACTIVITY	COMPLETION TIMES (days)		
		Optimistic	Most Likely	Pessimistic
a	—	5	6	7
b	—	4	5	18
c	a	4	15	20
d	b, c	3	4	5
e	a	16	17	18

(a) Determine the expected value and the variance of the completion time for each activity.
(b) Use the expected times from (a) to find the critical path.
(c) Assuming that the normal distribution applies, determine the probability that the critical path will take between 18 and 26 days to complete.

C H A P T E R

19

Waiting Lines (Queues)

Quantitative methods have been successfully applied to waiting line situations. Although it may seem that no one cares how long you have to wait in line to cash a check or to buy groceries, most businesses pay a great deal of attention to customer waiting times. Many large retail establishments have actually been designed to achieve an optimal balance between customer inconvenience and operational efficiency. This explains why a supermarket may have ten checkout counters, even though only two or three are in operation most of the time; during the Saturday afternoon rush hours, all of these counters may be open. Retailers do not dare to make their customers wait in line for long, because people value their time highly and would rather switch to a competing store than wait for service.

In management science or operations research, a waiting line is called a **queue**. As a field of study, **queuing theory** is one of the richest areas of operations research methodology. The number of models representing specific situations has grown steadily over the years, and new ones are being reported even now. Queuing theory is one of the earliest quantitative methods. Its origins were published in a 1909 paper by a Danish telephone engineer, A. K. Erlang, whose name is associated with a large class of probability distributions used in conjunction with mathematical queuing models. Since then, thousands of articles and numerous books have been written on the subject.

The usual objective of a queuing model is to determine how to provide service to customers in such a way that an efficient operation is achieved. Unlike the inventory or linear programming models encountered earlier in this book, a minimum-cost or a maximum-profit solution is not always sought. Rather, the aim of these models is to determine various characteristics of the queuing system, such as the mean waiting time and the mean length of the waiting line. These mean values may then be used in a later cost analysis. Or a targeted level of satisfactory customer service is established, and facilities and operations are planned to meet this goal.

To the uninitiated, it may seem that any waiting line is a sign of inefficiency and that good management should eliminate the nuisance of waiting entirely. This viewpoint probably results from the fact that we are all somebody's customers, but relatively few of us operate public establishments. If we reflect on this problem, we see that eliminating waiting lines entirely would be prohibitively costly for banks, stores, or gas stations. The main reason we have to wait in line at the bank is that customers arrive unpredictably (sometimes creating congestion) and seek a variety of services, each requiring a varying amount of a teller's time. Several times the usual number of tellers may be required to completely eliminate waiting lines, and many tellers would then be idle almost all the time. No bank has fewer tellers than are needed to service its customers within a reasonable time span, and these employees still spend many idle minutes. We rarely remember the days when we did not have to wait in a line at all!

19-1 Basic Queuing Situations

All queuing situations involve customer arrivals at a **service facility**, where some time may be spent waiting for and then receiving the desired service. We usually think of customers as people, but customers may also be objects, such as cars being repaired in a garage, unfinished items proceeding to the next stage of production, aircraft waiting to land, or jobs being processed on a computer. A service facility may be a single person, such as a barber or a hairdresser, or several persons, such as a surgical team. A server may also be a machine that dispenses candy bars, stamps parts, or processes data, or a complex entity, such as an airport runway or an oil refinery port facility.

Structures of Queuing Systems

The simplest queuing system involves a single-service facility that handles one customer at a time, so that any customer arriving while an earlier customer is being serviced must wait in line. Such a system is represented schematically in Figure 19-1. In this **single-server single-stage queue**, all the required services are performed before each customer leaves. The waiting line itself is not necessarily a physical string of customers, like the line that forms at a theater ticket window. The waiting line may simply be some

FIGURE 19-1
Schematic of a single-server single-stage queue.

Arrival stream   Customers   Service
                                      in queue   facility

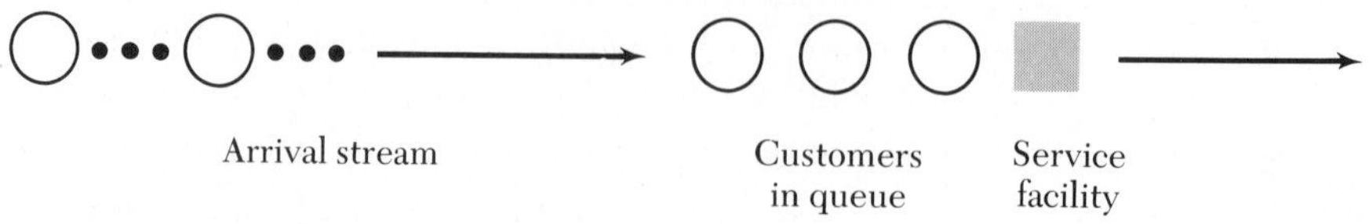

FIGURE 19-2

Schematic of a multiple-server single-stage queue.

identifiable grouping of customers whose sequence of service may or may not be designated (perhaps by a number, as is often the case in a retail store where physical lines are inconvenient). The customers do not even have to comingle physically. For example, several inquiries (customers) may stack up in a central computer system, even though they have been processed by remote terminals scattered across a huge geographical expanse, or planes attempting to land at New York's Kennedy Airport may be spread over tens of thousands of square miles of air space.

Somewhat more complicated is the queuing system depicted in Figure 19-2, which is a **multiple-server single-stage queue** with several service facilities. In the simplest case, each facility provides identical service, a single waiting line forms, and the leading customer proceeds to the first free server. Many banks employ such a system, where a single line feeds customers to the teller windows. Slightly different characteristics apply when arriving customers must select one server and wait in separate server lines, as is still the case when checking out of a large self-service market.

Another way of viewing queues is in terms of the number of service points or stages a customer must pass through before leaving the system. The simplest of these queuing systems is represented by the **single-server multiple-stage queue** shown in Figure 19-3. Before leaving the system, each customer must receive two or more kinds of service. This situation may arise when buying a bulky item, such as a tent, at a department store. First, you must wait for a clerk to begin processing your order; second, the clerk checks out your credit by telephoning a central office, which may also have to run quick credit checks on several other customers; finally, a third queue may form when you pick up your tent at the loading dock. Such a queue may also apply in manufacturing, where semifinished items await further processing at various stages of production.

The most complex queuing system is the **multiple-server multiple-stage queue** shown in Figure 19-4. Such a system may apply when getting a driver's license. You line up at one of several windows to pay the fee and to receive a written test; then you take the exam and wait for it to be graded; next, your eyes are examined; this is followed by a behind-the-wheel test administered by one of several possible examiners; finally, you may then wait to be photographed and to obtain a temporary license.

FIGURE 19-3

Schematic of a single-server multiple-stage queue.

FIGURE 19-4
Schematic of a multiple-server multiple-stage queue.

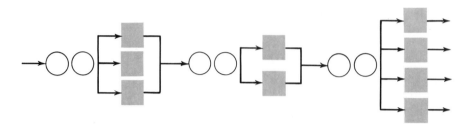

Queue Disciplines

An important aspect of any queuing situation is the *order* in which customers receive service. We refer to the manner of customer sequencing as the **queue discipline**. The mathematical models developed for essentially the same queuing structure may differ, depending on the discipline that applies.

The most common queue discipline is a physical **FIFO** (*first in, first out*) discipline, where customers receive service in the order of their arrival. Retail establishments and public service agencies usually employ this system. Indeed, FIFO has become almost a basic human right—like freedom of speech. In our generally calm modern society, few actions evoke as strong emotions as line cutting.* Many successful establishments rigidly enforce FIFO by issuing numbers to arriving customers. FIFO applies to all of the queuing models discussed in this chapter.

Much less common is the **LIFO** (*last in, first out*) discipline. There are some obvious circumstances, such as using elevators, in which LIFO may apply. In most cargo-handling situations, the last item loaded is the first one removed. The queuing aspects of these situations are not of great interest, but the following application of the LIFO discipline is well worth noting.

> Steel ingots arrive at a rolling-mill from open-hearth shops. They are still hot, but there are still temperature gradients within them. They must therefore be placed in reheating furnaces ("soaking pits") before being rolled into slabs or billets, as a more even heat distribution and a higher temperature are required by the rolling operation. If the soaking pits are full when the ingots arrive, they must wait .... While they wait, they become cooler. The longer they wait, the longer they must eventually remain in the soaking pits.*

To minimize energy costs the last (hottest) ingot in line should be the first one placed in a soaking pit, so that the LIFO discipline applies there.

Another interesting queue discipline is **SIRO** (*service in random order*). A theater refreshment counter during intermission is one of the most exasperating examples of SIRO. Perhaps the most important waiting line situation involving SIRO occurs at a

---

* Prior to Christmas 1973, a man was killed in an altercation that resulted when a family crowded into a line of people waiting to see Santa Claus.
* Lee, A. M. *Applied Queuing Theory* (New York: St. Martin's Press, 1966), p. 16.

telephone switchboard. The telephone call that arrives just after a free line is open is the one that is placed. We view this waiting line as comprising all of the calls that have encountered the "busy" signal. However, no record has been kept of these calls, so that there is no way to determine which call was placed first, and the only way for a call to connect is for the caller to redial it. The order of service may therefore be considered random. Modern telephone equipment places all calls on hold until they can be connected; in such systems, the FIFO discipline generally applies.

A variety of other queue disciplines exists. Situations in which customers have **priority** over others are very common. In a hospital emergency room, for example, the patients who have more serious problems are seen first. Computer systems often function according to priorities, so that the highest priority jobs are processed before all others, regardless of waiting times (and in elaborate systems, jobs may be automatically bumped into successively higher priorities the longer they wait). **Preemptive priority** queues arise when service on a lower priority customer is interrupted when a higher priority customer arrives. An example is the flat tire job at a service station; the attendant stops working on the tire when a higher priority gasoline customer arrives.

Arrival and Service Patterns

Arrival and service patterns are very important aspects of waiting line situations. Customers typically arrive at the queuing system randomly. Various probability distributions may be used to represent the time between arrivals; the most common of these is the **exponential distribution**, described in Chapter 3. Service time also usually varies (although it may be *constant*), and a variety of probability distributions may be used to characterize service patterns as well. Queuing models may differ considerably for various combinations of arrival and service patterns.

Queuing models usually assume that customers arrive singly, although some models do allow for the batching of arrivals. The latter type of model may apply when a cross-country bus stops at a roadside restaurant. Most models assume that the same interarrival time distribution applies to all customers throughout the period studied. Obviously, this cannot always be true, since busy periods arise in nearly all waiting line situations. Thus, a particular model may be appropriate only during peak hours, and another model may be required for slack periods. The service pattern is usually presumed to be independent of how customers arrive, which may not be strictly true for some types of service facilities. For example, a supermarket checker may work faster when several persons are waiting in line than when no one is.

19-2 The Single-Server Queuing Model with Exponential Service Times

Basic queuing models are concerned with the state of the system. Under various assumptions regarding the queue discipline and service, a probability distribution may be obtained for the number of customers in the system (either waiting or receiving service) at any future point in time. This probability information may then be used to derive certain useful results mathematically, such as the amount of time that a customer may expect to wait in line.

Our initial model represents the single-server single-stage queuing system. We assumed "first come, first served," so that the FIFO discipline applies. Arrivals are assumed to be a Poisson process, so that the arrivals are events that occur randomly over time and meet the other necessary conditions of that process. Thus, the interarrival times have an exponential distribution, and the number of customers arriving in any specified time interval has a Poisson distribution. Arrivals are assumed to occur at a **mean arrival rate** λ. Due to the resulting mathematical convenience, our basic model further assumes that *the service times are exponentially distributed.* The **mean service rate** (customers per minute, second, or hour) is represented by μ (lowercase Greek mu). It follows that the mean service time is $1/\mu$. Moreover, we assume that *the mean service rate must exceed the mean arrival rate,* or $\mu > \lambda$, so that the queuing system must have more than enough capacity to service all customers. (Without this last restriction, a queuing system would be unstable and the waiting line would grow indefinitely.)

Some Important Queuing Results

The queuing model provides the following important results.

1. **The probability distribution for the number of customers in the system**   This distribution is the basis for establishing all the other results listed here. It may also be useful in designing facilities that can physically hold waiting customers.

2. **The mean number of customers in the system**   This quantity accounts for the number of customers either waiting in line or receiving service. It is useful primarily as an intermediate device for finding the mean customer time spent in the system.

3. **The mean customer time spent in the system**   This is an average amount representing the total time spent by a customer in the system. When a cost may be associated with each unit of a customer's time, it may be used to make economic comparisons of alternative queuing systems.

4. **Mean number of customers waiting (length of line)**   This quantity is similar to the mean number of customers in the system, but only involves the customers who are actually waiting in line and not being serviced. Knowing the average number of customers waiting in line can help to establish the size of holding facilities, such as the size of hospital waiting rooms, and is also used in an intermediate step to establish the mean customer waiting time.

5. **The mean customer waiting time**   This is an average value that may be used to evaluate the quality of service. Like the mean customer time spent in the system, this quantity may sometimes be used in economic analysis, but it is unsatisfactory for this purpose if alternative queuing systems involve different service-time distributions.

6. **The server utilization factor**   This is the proportion of time that the server actually spends with customers—the time during which the server is busy. It provides an estimate of the expected amount of server idle time that may be devoted to secondary tasks not directly involved with service.

Although a discussion of them is beyond the scope of this book, other important results, such as complete probability distributions for a customer's waiting time and the duration of the server's busy period, may be obtained from queuing models.

Basic Queuing Formulas

Although many of the mathematical details are beyond the scope of this book, algebraic expressions have been derived for all of the results provided by the present queuing model. We express all results in terms of two parameters.

$$\lambda = \text{Mean customer arrival rate}$$

$$\mu = \text{Mean service rate}$$

We will begin with the probability distribution for the number of customers in the system. This distribution may be found by considering each possible number of customers either waiting or receiving service as a distinct *state* that may be entered by the arrival of a new customer or left by the completion of the leading customer's service. The schematic representation in Figure 19-5 will help to explain this process. Consider a barbershop with a single barber. There are two ways in which there may be exactly one customer in the shop. There may be no customers in the shop and then one arrives; or there may be two customers in the shop and the first customer's service is completed. These two cases are represented by the two arrows pointing to 1 in Figure 19-5—one at the top leaving 0 and one at the bottom leaving 2. Likewise, the barbershop can leave the one-customer state either by the arrival of a new customer or by finishing with the present one. Again, these possibilities are shown as two arrows leaving 1—the top one pointing to 2 and the bottom one to 0. This same feature is exhibited for any number of customers n in the system. Beside each arrow, the mean rate is indicated for the possible change in state—λ for an arrival and μ for a departure.

For any given instant of time, we define

$$P_n = \Pr[n \text{ customers in system}]$$

Under the assumption of exponentially distributed arrival and service times, the

FIGURE 19-5

Schematic of single-server queuing system states.

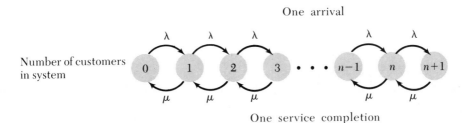

One arrival

Number of customers in system

One service completion

probability for leaving a state must be equal to the probability of entering that state, and, in short time intervals, movement is possible only between neighboring states (two to three customers, five to four, six to seven, and so on). There are two ways to enter and two ways to leave any state except zero, depending on the preceding number of customers and on whether a departure or an arrival occurs first. The probability for one movement (arrival or service completion) is approximately the product of the corresponding rate (λ or μ) with the duration of time considered between changes. These facts lead to the following *balance equations.*

$$\lambda P_0 = \mu P_1$$

$$\lambda P_1 + \mu P_1 = \lambda P_0 + \mu P_2$$

$$\lambda P_2 + \mu P_2 = \lambda P_1 + \mu P_3$$

A solution of the balance equations provides the result

$$P_n = \left(\frac{\lambda}{\mu}\right)^n P_0$$

for

$$n = 1, 2, 3, \ldots$$

implying that

$$P_0 = 1 - \frac{\lambda}{\mu}$$

These expressions may then be used to derive the remaining queuing formulas, which follow.

Mean Number of Customers in the System

$$L = \frac{\lambda}{\mu - \lambda}$$

Mean Customer Time Spent in the System

$$W = \frac{L}{\lambda} = \frac{1}{\mu - \lambda}$$

Mean Number of Customers Waiting (length of line)

$$L_q = \frac{\lambda^2}{\mu(\mu - \lambda)}$$

Mean Customer Waiting Time

$$W_q = \frac{L_q}{\lambda} = \frac{\lambda}{\mu(\mu - \lambda)}$$

We define the

Server Utilization Factor

$$\rho = \frac{\lambda}{\mu}$$

which is represented by ρ (lowercase Greek rho).

A Supply Room Example

Consider the queuing system involved in the operation of a central supply room for a large office. Employees pick up needed supplies there, just like customers who make purchases at a stationery store. An average of 25 employee customers withdraw supplies during each hour of normal operation. A full-time clerk is required to check persons out of central supply, primarily to assure proper accounting control of requisitioned items. Each requisition takes an average of 2 minutes, so the clerk may check out 30 customers per hour. We will assume that the pattern of arrivals at the checkout counter is a close approximation to a Poisson process and that the checkout times are exponentially distributed. Thus,

$$\lambda = 25 \text{ customers per hour}$$

$$\mu = 30 \text{ customers per hour}$$

The mean number of customers either waiting in line or being checked out is

$$L = \frac{\lambda}{\mu - \lambda} = \frac{25}{30 - 25} = 5 \text{ customers}$$

and the mean time spent by customers in the system is

$$W = \frac{1}{\mu - \lambda} = \frac{1}{30 - 25} = \frac{1}{5} \text{ hour}$$

or 12 minutes, which could also have been calculated $W = L/\lambda = 5/25 = 1/5$.
    The mean number of customers in the waiting line (or its length) is

$$L_q = \frac{\lambda^2}{\mu(\mu - \lambda)} = \frac{(25)^2}{30(30 - 25)} = \frac{25}{6} = 4\frac{1}{6} \text{ customers}$$

and the mean customer waiting time is

$$W_q = \frac{\lambda}{\mu(\mu - \lambda)} = \frac{25}{30(30 - 25)} = \frac{1}{6} \text{ hour}$$

or 10 minutes, which could also have been calculated $W_q = L_q/\lambda = (25/6) \div 25 = 1/6$.

The server utilization factor is

$$\rho = \frac{\lambda}{\mu} = \frac{25}{30} = \frac{5}{6}$$

so that the supply room clerk is busy five-sixths of the time.

A Queuing System Cost Analysis

These results may be used to determine the average daily cost of the waiting line situation. Suppose that the cost of the supply room clerk's labor is $5 per hour, whereas the unproductive time of employee customers is valued at an average hourly payroll figure of $7. The daily cost for the clerk is then

$$\$5 \times 8 = \$40$$

Each customer spends an average of $W = 1/5$ hour getting supplies and then checking out of the supply room, so that the average queuing cost per customer is

$$\$7 \times 1/5 = \$1.40$$

An average of $25 \times 8 = 200$ customers request supplies daily, so that the average daily queuing cost is

$$\$1.40 \times 200 = \$280$$

The average total daily cost of checking out of the supply room is therefore

$$\$280 \text{ (queuing cost)} + \$40 \text{ (clerk's cost)} = \$320$$

This amount does not include the time that each employee spends selecting supplies off the shelves—time that is independent of the queuing system itself, which encompasses only the checkout process.

Management should consider this daily cost figure highly excessive, especially since the average cost of the labor lost checking out of the supply room is seven times as great as the cost of the clerk. Two remedies are possible. The checkout process itself could be speeded up by hiring a faster clerk, by making the customers do some of the bookkeeping, or by partially automating the system. Or one or more extra clerks could be hired to assist the first clerk. The latter alternative would involve a *multiple-channel queue*, which will be described later in the chapter.

Now, we will consider a partially automated system that enables the clerk to double his service rate, so that $\mu = 60$ customers per hour. The mean customer time spent in the system then becomes

$$W = \frac{1}{\mu - \lambda} = \frac{1}{60 - 25} = \frac{1}{35} \text{ hour, or 1.7 minutes}$$

The faster service considerably reduces the average total daily cost of the labor lost in checking out to

$$200 \times \$7 \times 1/35 = \$40$$

Suppose that the special equipment and handling required for automation costs $50 per day in addition to the clerk's wages. The average total daily cost would then be

$$\$40 \text{ (queuing cost)} + \$50 \text{ (equipment cost)} + \$40 \text{ (clerk's cost)} = \$130$$

Partial automation would yield an average savings of $190 per day over manual operation with one clerk.

A Queuing System Probability Analysis

Management may also be concerned with the amount of traffic through the supply room. If too many people congregate there, it may become too attractive to persons wishing to socialize on company time. Using the partially automated system, the following probabilities apply for the number of persons being checked out.

$$P_0 = 1 - \frac{\lambda}{\mu} = 1 - \frac{25}{60} = \frac{7}{12} = .583$$

$$P_1 = \left(\frac{\lambda}{\mu}\right)^1 P_0 = \frac{25}{60}\left(\frac{7}{12}\right) = \frac{35}{144} = .243$$

$$P_2 = \left(\frac{\lambda}{\mu}\right)^2 P_0 = \left(\frac{25}{60}\right)^2\left(\frac{7}{12}\right) = \frac{175}{1728} = .101$$

TABLE 19-1

System State Probabilities for Number of Customers in Checkout Process ($\lambda = 25$, $\mu = 60$)

NUMBER OF CUSTOMERS n	P_n	CUMULATIVE PROBABILITY FOR $\leq n$	PROBABILITY FOR $> n$
0	.583	.583	.417
1	.243	.826	.174
2	.101	.927	.073
3	.042	.969	.031
4	.018	.987	.013
5	.007	.994	.006
6	.003	.997	.003
7	.001	.998	.002
8	.001	.999	.001
9	.000	.999	.001

Table 19-1 provides the system state probabilities for $n = 0$ through $n = 9$. We see from the table that there is less than a 10% chance that more than two persons will ever be checking out of the supply room at the same time.

19-3 Interpreting Queuing Formulas and Alternative Expressions

An interpretation of the basic queuing formulas may prove helpful at this point. We might view λ as a measurement of the "demand" for service and μ as an expression of the "capacity" of the service facility. The difference $\mu - \lambda$ then represents the "excess capacity" of the system to fill demand. Thus, the mean number of customers in the system is the ratio of demand to excess capacity, or

$$L = \frac{\text{Demand}}{\text{Excess capacity}} = \frac{\lambda}{\mu - \lambda}$$

When excess capacity is small in relation to demand, congestion is heavy and a large number of customers can be expected in the system. In the supply room operated manually by one clerk, demand is $\lambda = 25$ customers per hour, which is five times the excess capacity of $\mu - \lambda = 5$ customers per hour, so that $L = 5$ customers.

The mean customer time spent in the system may be determined by multiplying the mean time between customer arrivals $1/\lambda$ and the mean number of customers L, or

$$W = \left(\frac{1}{\lambda}\right)L = \frac{L}{\lambda}$$

When the supply room is operated manually with one clerk, we find an average of 5 customers in the system, who arrive once every $1/\lambda = 1/25$ hour. Each customer may therefore expect to spend $1/25 \times 5 = 1/5$ hour checking out of the supply room. (It may seem perplexing that to obtain W from L, we multiply by the mean time between arrivals $1/\lambda$ instead of the mean service time $1/\mu$. But remember that $L = 5$ is only a mean figure— not the actual number in the system, which at any given time may be more or less than 5. If it is known in advance that exactly 5 customers are in the system, then the fifth customer would indeed expect to spend $(1/\mu)(5) = (1/30)(5) = 1/6$ hour being checked out. But that result is not W, which applies only when the number of customers is unspecified.)

A customer's mean waiting time is simply the difference between the mean time that customer spends in the system and the mean service time for that customer, or

$$W_q = W - \frac{1}{\mu}$$

This is algebraically equivalent to $\lambda/[\mu(\mu - \lambda)]$. The mean customer waiting time is also equal to the product of the mean time between arrivals and the mean number of customers in the waiting line, or

$$W_q = \left(\frac{1}{\lambda}\right)L_q = \frac{L_q}{\lambda}$$

Multiplying both sides of this equation by λ, we obtain the expression for the mean number of customers in the waiting line.

$$L_q = \lambda W_q$$

We see that all of the queuing results may be obtained by beginning with L, which we may view as the ratio of "demand" (λ) to "excess capacity" ($\mu - \lambda$). We could start with W, L_q, or W_q instead and obtain the other results without memorizing all four basic formulas. And, some of the relationships described here apply to other queuing situations, where one result may be easier to obtain directly than the others. Alternative expressions for the queuing results using the server utilization factor are described below.

It is easy to see that when the checkout clerk operates the supply room manually, he will only be busy an average of 5 minutes out of every 6. In an eight hour day, the clerk will check out $8 \times 25 = 200$ customers. This will take an average of 2 minutes (1/30 hour), so that a total of 400 minutes will be spent checking out customers. Each working day is comprised of $60 \times 8 = 480$ minutes. The proportion of busy minutes is therefore $400/480 = 5/6$.

The expression for W_q may be obtained from the expression for W by multiplying by the server utilization factor, so that

$$W_q = \left(\frac{\lambda}{\mu}\right)W$$

This same fact applies to L_q and to L, so that

$$L_q = \left(\frac{\lambda}{\mu}\right)L$$

Thus, we see why the values of L_q and W_q, which do not consider that customer receiving service, are both smaller than L and W, which do. Since the clerk is only busy $\lambda/\mu = 5/6$ of the time under manual operation, L_q and W_q are only five-sixths as large as L and W. The expression for L_q may also be arrived at by subtracting the server utilization factor from the mean number of customers in the system.

$$L_q = L - \frac{\lambda}{\mu}$$

This is algebraically equivalent to $\lambda^2/[\mu(\mu - \lambda)]$. One rationale for this result is that L_q does not include the one customer who may be receiving service. Since the server is only busy λ/μ of the time, then on the average, we expect that fraction of a customer to be receiving service at any time. Thus, the fraction λ/μ of a customer must be subtracted to provide the expected number of customers who are waiting only.

19-4 The Multiple-Server Queuing Model

We now extend the basic queuing model for a one-service facility to the case of several facilities. We will assume that each facility is identical in all respects and that each is capable of performing service at the rate of μ customers per unit of time. As before, the pattern of arrivals is assumed to be a Poisson process and the service times are presumed to be exponentially distributed. The queuing formulas given here are based on the FIFO discipline, and we will assume that the customer at the head of the line proceeds to the first free server.

Queuing Formulas

The queuing formulas for a multiple-channel system are based on principles similar to those used for a single server, but a new parameter is needed to represent the number of channels.

$$S = \text{Number of service channels}$$

Figure 19-6 shows how movement occurs between customer states. As in the single-server model, the arrows represent changes and the quantity beside an arrow corresponds to the applicable rate for that particular change.

Notice that when all servers are not busy—that is, when the number of customers n is less than S—no customers are waiting in line and the combined rate of service is $n\mu$. For example, consider a bank that has 5 tellers, so that $S = 5$. When $n = 3$ customers are present, each is being served and the combined rate at which service is being performed is 3μ. For any increment of time, it is therefore three times as likely that service will be completed for any one of these three customers as a group as it is that service will be completed individually for any specific customer. When the number of customers is at least as large as the number of servers, so that $n \geq S$, all servers are busy and the combined

FIGURE 19-6
Schematic of multiple-server queuing system states.

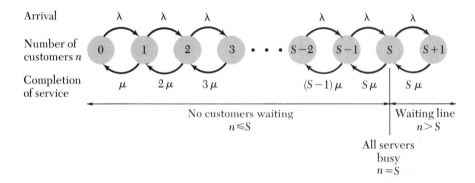

rate of service is $S\mu$. If the bank has $n = 7$ customers, then two customers are waiting in line and the combined service rate is 5μ. As in our earlier model, we assume that total service capacity must exceed customer requirements, so that $S\mu > \lambda$.

The queuing formulas that result with S service channels are a little more complex than those that apply to the single-channel case. When there are S service channels, queuing formulas are based on the following probabilities.

Probability that No Customers Are in the System

$$P_0 = 1 \Big/ \left[\sum_{n=0}^{S-1} \frac{(\lambda/\mu)^n}{n!} + \frac{(\lambda/\mu)^S}{S!} \left(\frac{1}{1 - \lambda/S\mu} \right) \right]$$

Probability that n Persons Are in the System

$$P_n = \begin{cases} \dfrac{(\lambda/\mu)^n}{n!} P_0 & \text{if } 0 \le n \le S \\[2ex] \dfrac{(\lambda/\mu)^n}{S!S^{n-S}} P_0 & \text{if } n \ge S \end{cases}$$

The remaining expressions, all based on first calculating L_q, follow.

Mean Number of Customers Waiting (length of line)

$$L_q = \frac{(\lambda/\mu)^S(\lambda/S\mu)}{S!(1 - \lambda/S\mu)^2} P_0$$

Mean Customer Waiting Time

$$W_q = \frac{L_q}{\lambda}$$

Mean Customer Time Spent in the System

$$W = W_q + \frac{1}{\mu}$$

Mean Number of Customers in the System

$$L = L_q + \frac{\lambda}{\mu}$$

Server Utilization Factor

$$\rho = \frac{\lambda}{S\mu}$$

Notice that the server utilization factor differs from that of a single-server system. In a multiple-server system, it is not possible to express the mean customer waiting time as the product of λ/μ and the mean customer time in the system. Thus,

$$W_q \neq \left(\frac{\lambda}{\mu}\right)W \quad \text{and} \quad L_q \neq \left(\frac{\lambda}{\mu}\right)L$$

One reason for this is that λ/μ does not represent the same thing in a multiple-server queuing system.

EXAMPLE

Two Copying Machines

A company is considering renting office copying machines. One alternative is to lease two model A machines that can make 100 copies per minute. However, because items must be manually placed on the machine to be copied, the effective copying rate is quite a bit slower. The actual machine time will also vary from user to user, depending on the number of copies required and the originals used. Based on the manufacturer's historical experience for offices with similar workloads, the total time per user is approximately exponentially distributed with a mean of 2 minutes per job. The effective service rate is therefore .5 jobs per minute. The demand for copying by company employees occurs at the rate of three jobs every 5 minutes, or an average of .6 jobs per minute. Historical experience shows that the need for copying occurs randomly over time and that a Poisson process applies to jobs arriving at the copying center. The parameters of this problem are

$$S = 2 \text{ service channels}$$

$$\mu = .5 \text{ jobs per minute}$$

$$\lambda = .6 \text{ jobs per minute}$$

The probability that no jobs are in the copying system is

$$P_0 = 1 \Big/ \left[\frac{(\lambda/\mu)^0}{0!} + \frac{(\lambda/\mu)^1}{1!} + \frac{(\lambda/\mu)^2}{2!}\left(\frac{1}{1 - \lambda/2\mu}\right)\right]$$

$$= 1 \Big/ \left[\frac{(.6/.5)^0}{0!} + \frac{(.6/.5)^1}{1!} + \frac{(.6/.5)^2}{2!}\left(\frac{1}{1 - .6/2(.5)}\right)\right]$$

$$= 1 \Big/ \left[1 + 1.2 + \frac{(1.2)^2}{2}\left(\frac{1}{1 - .6}\right)\right]$$

$$= 1/[1 + 1.2 + 1.8] = 1/4 = .25$$

The mean number of jobs waiting to be copied is therefore

$$L_q = \frac{(.6/.5)^2[.6/2(.5)]}{2![1 - .6/2(.5)]^2}(.25) = .68 \text{ job}$$

and the mean waiting time per job is

$$W_q = \frac{L_q}{\lambda} = \frac{.68}{.6} = 1.13 \text{ minutes}$$

The mean time each job spends in the copying center is

$$W = W_q + \frac{1}{\mu} = 1.13 + \frac{1}{.5} = 3.13 \text{ minutes}$$

and the mean number of jobs at the copying center at any given time is

$$L = L_q + \frac{\lambda}{\mu} = .68 + \frac{.6}{.5} = 1.88 \text{ jobs}$$

Management is concerned about the average hourly cost of operating two model A machines. Each job is personally processed by the user, whose average hourly payroll cost is $10. Machine rental is a straight $.05 per copy, and an average job involves 12 copies.

The average number of jobs per hour is

$$.6 \times 60 = 36 \text{ jobs}$$

and each employee using the machine spends an average of $W = 3.13$ minutes, or

$$\frac{3.13}{60} = .0522 \text{ hour}$$

in the copying center. The average hourly cost of the labor lost in making copies is therefore

$$\$10 \times 36 \times .0522 = \$18.79$$

The hourly rental cost for the two machines is

$$\$.05 \times 12 \times 36 = \$21.60$$

The total hourly average cost of operating two model A machines is therefore

$$\$18.79 \text{ (labor lost)} + \$21.60 \text{ (equipment rental)} = \$40.39$$

Two Servers Compared to One Server Who Is Twice as Fast

An interesting result arises from queuing theory. To the uninitiated, it may seem that one server who is twice as fast will produce results identical to two separate facilities, each servicing customers at the regular rate. *This is not true.* (If it were, we would not need a separate model for multiple-channel queues; the single-channel system with twice as large a value of μ could be used instead.)

Suppose that the effective service rate of the model T copying machine is twice as fast as that of the model A. If $\mu = 1$ job per minute, the single-server model provides a mean number of jobs waiting of

$$L_q = \frac{\lambda^2}{\mu(\mu - \lambda)} = \frac{(.6)^2}{1(1 - .6)} = .9 \text{ job} \quad \text{(one model } T\text{)}$$

which is more than three times as large as the comparable number when two model A machines are used. The mean waiting time per job using one model T would be

$$W_q = \frac{L_q}{\lambda} = \frac{.9}{.6} = 1.5 \text{ minutes} \quad \text{(one model } T\text{)}$$

which is considerably longer than before. Of course, the service rate of the model T is twice as fast, so the average time a job spends in the system is smaller than it would be if two model A machines were used, or

$$W = \frac{1}{\mu - \lambda} = \frac{1}{1 - .6} = 2.5 \text{ minutes} \quad \text{(one model } T\text{)}$$

This results in a smaller hourly lost labor cost of

$$\$10 \times 36 \times \frac{2.5}{60} = \$15.00$$

Even if the faster model T rents for a little more per copy than the slower model A does, it would still be cheaper for management to rent one model T instead of two model A machines.

19-5 A Model for Nonexponential Service Times

Some distribution other than the exponential—such as the normal distribution—could more appropriately represent the service pattern of a queuing system. Recall from Chapter 3 that a normal distribution is specified by two parameters—the mean and the standard deviation σ. A different queuing model applies when only the arrivals form a Poisson process, while the service times follow some other distribution. That model depends only on the standard deviation σ for service time and assumes no particular form for the distribution itself. The following equations apply.

$$P_0 = 1 - \lambda/\mu$$

$$L_q = \frac{\lambda^2\sigma^2 + (\lambda/\mu)^2}{2(1 - \lambda/\mu)} \qquad L = L_q + \frac{\lambda}{\mu}$$

$$W_q = \frac{L_q}{\lambda} \qquad\qquad W = W_q + \frac{1}{\mu}$$

The state probabilities are the same as in the earlier single-server model. Notice that L_q—and therefore all the other queuing results—depend on the standard deviation σ of the service-time distribution. L_q, L, W_q, and W all become larger as σ increases. Thus, greater variability in service time will result in longer lines and longer waiting times. This indicates that consistency in service times is very important to the overall quality of the service provided.

Recall from Chapter 3 that the exponential distribution has a mean and standard deviation that are both equal to $1/\mu$. The preceding equations provide identical results to the earlier ones when $\sigma = 1/\mu$. Should σ be larger or smaller, however, results will vary. Consider the following three cases applicable to the supply room example given earlier.

ORIGINAL VARIABILITY $(\sigma = 1/\mu = 1/30)$	LESS VARIABILITY $(\sigma = 1/60)$	GREATER VARIABILITY $(\sigma = 1/15)$
$L_q = 4.167$ customers	$L_q = \dfrac{(25)^2(1/60)^2 + (25/30)^2}{2(1 - 25/30)}$	$L_q = \dfrac{(25)^2(1/15)^2 + (25/30)^2}{2(1 - 25/30)}$
	$= 2.61$ customers	$= 10.42$ customers
$W_q = .167$ hr	$W_q = 2.61/25 = .10$ hr	$W_q = 10.42/25 = .42$ hr
$W = .20$ hr	$W = .10 + 1/30 = .133$ hr	$W = .42 + 1/30 = .453$ hr
Cost = \$320	Cost = 7(.133)200 + 40	Cost = 7(.453)200 + 40
	$= \$226$	$= \$674$

19-6 Additional Remarks

In this chapter, we have described only two queuing models in detail. Both models presume the FIFO discipline and exponential distributions for interarrival and service times. Many other queuing situations exist and have been studied in detail. Several additional queuing models are described in the appendix to this chapter.

Arrivals that occur *singly* over time often historically fit the Poisson distribution. It is inappropriate to use this distribution when customers arrive in groups—for example, when customers pick up their baggage after a flight. Generally, a Poisson process is of limited duration, so that the basic queuing formulas are really only applicable for short periods of time. As we have seen, a bank or a toll station will exhibit different characteristics at different times of the day or on different days of the week. Thus, a different value of λ may be appropriate for any particular period, and different mean waiting times and queuing results would apply to each.

For mathematical simplicity, the first two queuing models discussed in this chapter are based on exponential service times. Although the normal distribution or some other two-tailed, nonsymmetrical distribution could provide more realistic representations, the exponential distribution will often adequately represent service times. Thus, the basic queuing formulas may often yield satisfactory approximations to the actual results that would be derived using more accurate models.

As is true of certain other applications of quantitative methods, various mathematical queuing models have limited scope and often only approximate reality. This is due to the many simplifying assumptions that must ordinarily be made to accommodate the mathematical analysis. To avoid erroneous results, numerical solution procedures are often used instead of standard queuing formulas to evaluate complex queuing situations. One useful procedure—*Monte Carlo simulation*—will be discussed in Chapter 20.

19-7 Queuing Analysis with the Computer

The simple queuing models discussed in this chapter may be applied with a minimal amount of hand computation. Nevertheless, some of these calculations can be messy, so that you might delegate that computational work to the computer. *QuickQuant*, the software package available to users of this book, will compute the various queuing constants applicable to any specified arrival rate, service rate, and number of servers. It will also provide Poisson probabilities for the number of arrivals or service completions in a specified duration, exponential probabilities for the times between arrivals and service completions, and steady-state probabilities for the number of customers in the system.

FIGURE 19-7

QuickQuant **report showing the multiple-server queuing evaluation for the copying machine example.**

```
==============================================================================
                            QuickQuant Report
             BASIC QUEUING SYSTEM EVALUATION--MULTIPLE SERVERS
------------------------------------------------------------------------------
PROBLEM: Copying Machines                               Date: 02-10-1990
                                                                    Larry

        Parameter Values:
             Mean Customer Arrival Rate: lambda = .6
             Mean Customer Service Rate: mu = .5
             Number of Servers: S = 2

        Queuing Results:
             Mean Number of Customers in System: L = 1.875
             Mean Customer Time Spent in System: W = 3.125
             Mean Number of Customers Waiting
                         (Length of Line): Lq = .6750001
             Mean Customer Waiting Time: Wq = 1.125
             Server Utilization Factor: rho = .6

             Number in                      Cumulative
             System n    Probability Pn    Probability
             ------------------------------------------
                0            0.2500           0.2500
                1            0.3000           0.5500
                2            0.1800           0.7300
                3            0.1080           0.8380
                4            0.0648           0.9028
                5            0.0389           0.9417
                6            0.0233           0.9650
                7            0.0140           0.9790
                8            0.0084           0.9874
                9            0.0050           0.9924
               10            0.0030           0.9955
------------------------------------------------------------------------------
```

The main menu will lead to the applicable segment of *QuickQuant*, and the data input may be made by entering the requested choices and supplying that data requested by the screen prompts.

Figure 19-7 shows the *QuickQuant* report obtained for the copying machine example in Section 19-4. The probability listing can be as long as desired.

Appendix 19-1: Some Further Queuing Models*

A tremendous variety of queuing models exists. Each model applies to a particular situation in which any one or a combination of differences occurs in the underlying structure, queue discipline, or arrival or service pattern. This appendix provides three additional queuing models that are widely applicable. All of these models are based on the FIFO discipline and assume a Poisson process for arrivals. The first two models also assume that service times are exponentially distributed.

A Single-Server Model for a Finite Queue

Often the number of customers that a queuing system can handle at any given time is limited. For example, a hospital emergency room only has enough beds to accommodate a specific number of patients waiting to see the attending doctors, and any additional patients must be diverted to other hospitals. A waiting line of limited length is called a *finite queue*. A finite queue may arise due to a physical constraint, such as the emergency room. Or customers may simply give up when the waiting line becomes too long. In either case, a customer who is turned away does not return to the system. Systems involving finite queues differ from the queuing systems discussed in the chapter, where no limits were placed on the number of customers waiting for service. The underlying queuing formulas must be modified to reflect this structural difference. The resulting model may be expressed in terms of the constant

$$M = \text{Maximum number of customers in the system}$$

The probabilities for the number of customers in the system are

$$P_0 = \frac{1 - \lambda/\mu}{1 - (\lambda/\mu)^{M+1}}$$

$$P_n = (\lambda/\mu)^n P_0 \quad \text{for } 1 \le n \le M$$

The mean number of customers in the system is

$$L = \frac{\lambda/\mu}{1 - \lambda/\mu} - \frac{(M + 1)(\lambda/\mu)^{M+1}}{1 - (\lambda/\mu)^{M+1}}$$

---

* This section is optional.

The remaining queuing results may be found from this expression. The mean length of the waiting line is found by subtracting the proportion of time the server is busy, which is $1 - P_0$ here.

$$L_q = L - (1 - P_0)$$

The respective mean customer waiting times are

$$W_q = \frac{L_q}{\lambda(1 - P_M)} \qquad W = \frac{L}{\lambda(1 - P_M)}$$

A Single-Server Model for a Limited Population

A related queuing model arises when the customers arriving at the system represent a small population. Although this case resembles the model for a finite queue, here the potential customers (rather than the line itself) are limited. Such a situation may arise in a plant that contains several machines that need to be serviced when they break down. Each malfunctioning machine is treated as an arriving customer, and the breakdowns can be assumed to be a Poisson process. The model involves the constant

$$M = \text{Maximum number of customers that may need service}$$

The probabilities for the number of customers either waiting or receiving service are

$$P_0 = 1 \bigg/ \sum_{n=0}^{M} \left[\frac{M!}{(M-n)!} \left(\frac{\lambda}{\mu}\right)^n \right]$$

$$P_n = \frac{M!}{(M-n)!} \left(\frac{\lambda}{\mu}\right)^n P_0 \quad \text{for } 1 \leq n \leq M$$

The remaining results are

$$L_q = M - \frac{\lambda + \mu}{\lambda}(1 - P_0) \qquad L = L_q + (1 - P_0)$$

$$W_q = \frac{L_q}{\lambda(M - L)} \qquad W = \frac{L}{\lambda(M - L)}$$

A Single-Server Model with Constant Service Times

As a special case, suppose that service times are constant, so that it takes time $1/\mu$ to serve each customer. Since successive customers will all require the same amount of time, the variance is zero. Substituting $\sigma^2 = 0$ into the model in Section 19-5, we find

$$L_q = \frac{(\lambda/\mu)^2}{2(1 - \lambda/\mu)}$$

The results for L, W_q, and W may then be calculated as before, using this level for L_q.

CASE

Caledonia Bank

Peter McGregor is the operations manager for Caledonia Bank. He is establishing teller schedules for the Seventh Street Branch. The following data apply to the arrivals of customers at various times of the week.

PERIOD	DAILY AVERAGE NUMBER OF ARRIVALS
(1) Monday–Friday 10 A.M–12 P.M.	155
(2) Monday–Friday 12–1 P.M.	242
(3) Monday–Friday 1–3 P.M.	290
(4) Friday 3–6 P.M.	554

The bank opens at 10 A.M. and closes at 3 P.M., except for Friday, when it closes at 6 P.M. Past study shows that arrivals over each period constitute a Poisson process. The mean time to complete customer transactions is 2 minutes, and individual service times are approximated by an exponential distribution.

Tellers all work part time and cost $10 per bank hour. Past experience shows that a significant drop-off in clientele soon follows when customers are forced to experience lengthy waits.

McGregor also needs to decide whether or not to install an automatic teller machine (ATM). The equipment supplier claims that other banks experience a 30% diversion of regular business away from human tellers, plus a further 10% expansion in the previous level of overall client transactions (but all of the increase going to the ATM).

ATM business takes place on a 24-hour basis, although traffic is negligible between 11 P.M. and 6 A.M. During the busier hours, times between customer arrivals are assumed to be represented by a single exponential distribution.

The mean service time at an ATM is one-half minute, and again the exponential distribution serves as an adequate approximation. McGregor believes that once an ATM is installed, the human tellers would be left with a greater proportion of the more involved and lengthy transactions, raising the mean service time to 2.5 minutes.

Questions

1. Assume that Caledonia Bank uses human tellers only.
   (a) For each time period, determine the minimum number of tellers needed on station to service the customer stream.
   (b) Assume that the numbers of tellers in (a) are used. For each time period, determine the mean customer waiting time.

(c) For each time period, determine the mean customer waiting time when the number of tellers is one more than found in (a).

2. Past experience shows that the drop-off in clientele due to waiting translates into an expected net present value in lost future profits of $.10 per minute. For each time period, determine the average hourly queuing system costs, assuming that the bank uses (a) the minimum number of human tellers necessary to service the arriving customers and (b) one teller more than is found in (a) of Question 1.

3. Suppose that the ATM is installed and that customers themselves decide whether to use human tellers or to use the ATM, and that two queues form independently for each. Finally, assume that there is a 10% traffic increase generated by the ATM within each open time period, and that all of it is for the ATM. Determine, in each case, the mean customer arrival rate (a) at the human teller windows and (b) at the ATM. Then, find (c) the minimum number of human tellers required to be on station during each time period.

4. Determine, for Peter McGregor, the mean customer waiting time during each open time period for those customers who seek (a) human tellers and (b) access to the ATM. Assume that the number of human tellers used is one more than that found in (c) of Question 3.

5. The hourly cost of maintaining and operating the ATM is $5. Increased customer traffic results in additional bank profit estimated to be $.20 per transaction. Determine, for Peter McGregor, the net hourly queuing system cost, reflecting any profit increase, for operating with the ATM for periods (1)–(4). Use the mean waiting times from Question 4.

PROBLEMS

19-1 For each of the following single-server queuing systems, determine the values of L, W, L_q, W_q, and ρ.

(a)	(b)	(c)	(d)
$\lambda = 20$	$\lambda = 8$	$\lambda = 2$	$\lambda = .4$
$\mu = 25$	$\mu = 12$	$\mu = 5$	$\mu = .7$

19-2 Patrons arrive at the Dogpatch post office at the rate of 30 per hour. There is one clerk on duty, who takes an average of 1 minute to serve each customer. Service times are approximately exponential.

(a) Calculate the mean customer time (1) spent waiting in line and (2) spent receiving or waiting for service. Also, find the mean number of customers (3) in line and (4) receiving or waiting for service.

(b) Construct the probability distribution for the number of customers inside the post office (stopping at that n where the probability rounds to zero to two decimal places).

19-3 For each of the following waiting line situations, give at least one reason why the models provided in this chapter may be inappropriate for determining the mean customer waiting time.

(a) Telephone calls being placed through a manually operated switchboard

(b) Customers arriving at a restaurant for dinner

(c) Patients visiting a dermatologist, who sees patients only by appointment

(d) A bottling machine filling empties with ingredients

(e) Plant workers showing their badges to a security guard while passing through the corridor into the main building

19-4 Sammy Lee is the sole operator of a barbershop. Between noon and 6 P.M. on Saturday afternoons, 1 customer arrives every 15 minutes on the average. Sammy takes an average of 10 minutes to trim each customer. His little shop has chairs for only 2 waiting customers in addition to the customer getting a haircut.

(a) What is the probability that any particular customer will have to spend part of his waiting time standing up?

(b) What percentage of an average Saturday afternoon is Sammy busy? How many hours is he idle on an average Saturday afternoon?

19-5 Ace Airlines has one reservations clerk on duty at a time to handle information about flight times and make reservations. All calls to Ace Airlines are answered by an operator. If a caller requests information or reservations, the operator transfers the call to the reservations clerk. If the clerk is busy, the operator asks the caller to wait. When the clerk becomes free, the operator transfers the call of the person who has been waiting the longest. Assume that arrivals and services can be approximated by a Poisson process. Calls arrive at a rate of 10 per hour, and the reservations clerk can service a call in an average of 4 minutes.

(a) What is the average number of calls waiting to be connected to the reservations clerk?

(b) What is the average time that a caller must wait before reaching the reservations clerk?

(c) What is the average time it takes for a caller to complete a call?

19-6 Suppose that the management of Ace Airlines in Problem 19-5 is considering installing some visual display equipment and a new reservations system. One of the benefits of this system is that it will reduce the average time required to service a call from 4 to 3 minutes.

(a) Under the new system, what would be the average number of calls waiting to be connected?

(b) Under the new system, what would be the average waiting time for a caller?

(c) Suppose that instead of installing the new system, a second reservations clerk is added. Calls could then be referred to whichever clerk was free.

  (1) What would be the average number of calls waiting?

  (2) What would then be the average waiting time for a caller?

19-7 Mildred's Tool and Die Shop has a central tool cage manned by a single clerk, who takes an average of 5 minutes to check and carry parts to each machinist who requests them. The machinists arrive once every 8 minutes on the average. Times between arrivals and for service are assumed to both have exponential distributions. A machinist's time is valued at $15 per hour; a clerk's time is valued at $9 per hour. What are the average hourly queuing system costs associated with the tool cage operation?

19-8 Mildred wishes to improve the costs for the tool cage operation in Problem 19-7. Two alternatives are (1) use two clerks who are equally fast and (2) have a machinist instead of a clerk operate the tool cage. (Special knowledge enables the machinist to provide service twice as fast as the clerk.)

(a) Determine the mean machinist time spent checking out tools for both alternatives.

(b) Find the average hourly queuing system costs for both alternatives. Which one would be cheaper?

(c) Discuss any advantages of each alternative that cannot be measured by applying queuing models.

19-9   C. A. Gopher & Sons is to excavate a site from which 100,000 cubic yards of dirt must be removed. Gopher has the choice of using a scoop loader or a shovel crane. He has leased 10 trucks at $20 per hour. A scoop loader costs $40 per hour, and a shovel crane costs $60 per hour. Once work has been started, the trucks will arrive according to a Poisson process at a mean rate of $\lambda = 7$ trucks per hour. Truck-filling times are approximately exponentially distributed. A scoop loader can fill an average of 10 trucks per hour. The shovel crane is faster and is capable of filling 15 trucks per hour on the average. (For simplicity, we will assume that the truck arrival rate is the same, regardless of the equipment used.)

Since the number of truck arrivals required to excavate the site is fixed by the amount of dirt to be removed, the optimal choice of filling equipment will be the one that minimizes the combined average hourly costs of unproductive truck time plus the cost of the filling equipment. Determine the optimal choice.

19-10   The manager of a WaySafe market with 10 checkout counters wishes to determine how many counters to operate on Saturday morning. His decision will be determined in part by the costs assigned to each additional minute that a customer spends checking out of the store. In a special experiment in obsolete stores about to be closed, customers were forced to wait in line for an abnormally long time. The study concluded that an average of $.05 in future profits is lost for every minute that a customer spends waiting.

Assume that WaySafe customer arrivals at the checkout area are approximated by a Poisson process with a mean rate of $\lambda = 2$ per minute, that each attendant can check out customers at a mean rate of .5 per minute, and that the service time is exponentially distributed.

(a) What is the minimum number of checkers required for the service capacity to *exceed* the demand for service? Determine the mean customer waiting time when that many checkers are providing service.

(b) What is the mean customer waiting time if one more checker is added?

(c) The salary expense for each checker is $10 per hour. What number of checkers will minimize the total hourly queuing system cost—the number in (a) or in (b)? (Ignore service time, since no penalty applies for actual checkout time spent.)

19-11   *Computer exercise.*   Another WaySafe supermarket manager is analyzing her operations on Saturday mornings, when 6 full-service checkout stands are currently in operation. The arrival rate (Poisson process) to the stands is 1 customer per minute. The mean checkout time is 5 minutes per customer (assuming an exponential distribution) and is the same for all checkers. By analyzing the records used to obtain these data, the manager has determined that one-half of the customers buy 5 items or less. This group can be serviced in an average of 1 minute each (again, assuming an exponential distribution); it takes a mean of 9 minutes to serve the longer customers. The manager wants to know if she should convert one full-service checkout stand to serve customers who buy only 5 items or fewer.

(a) What is the expected waiting time per customer for the present operational setup?

(b) For the proposed operational setup, what is the expected waiting time for customers buying (1) 6 or more items and (2) 5 or fewer items, assuming that the latter customers can only go through the small-item checkout stand?

(c) If you were buying more than 5 items, which system would you prefer? Why?

(d) Which system would be more efficient if the cost of a (1) customer's waiting time is $.05 per minute and the cost of a (2) customer's waiting time is $.20 per minute?

19-12 Refer to Problem 19-2(a). Solve the problem when the service time is normally distributed with a mean of $1/\mu = 1$ minute and a standard deviation of $\sigma = .30$ minutes.

19-13 Refer to Problem 19-5. Solve the problem assuming that the standard deviation in service time is (1) $\sigma = 2$ minutes ($1/30$ hour) and (2) $\sigma = 5$ minutes ($1/12$ hour).

*19-14 A hospital emergency room can accommodate a maximum of $M = 5$ patients. The patients arrive at a rate of 4 per hour. The single staff physician can only treat 5 patients per hour. Any patient overflow is directed to another hospital.
(a) Determine the probability distribution for the number of patients either waiting for or receiving treatment at any given time.
(b) Determine the mean values of the number of patients in the emergency room; the number of patients waiting to see the doctor; the patient waiting time; and the patient time spent in the emergency room.
(c) Repeat the calculations in (b) assuming that there is no restriction on the number of patients to receive treatment.

*19-15 A machinist services $M = 5$ machines as they break down. Machines fail at a rate of 1 per day, and the machinist fixes them at a rate of 2 per day.
(a) Determine the probability distribution for the number of machines that will break down at any given time.
(b) Calculate L_q, L, W_q, and W.
(c) Repeat the calculations in (b) for a machinist who services a population of thousands of machines. Assume that machine failures and service times occur at the given rates.

*19-16 Refer to Problem 19-2(a). Solve the problem when the service time is constant at a rate of $\mu = 1$ customer per minute.

---

* These problems involve material in the appendix to the chapter.

20

Simulation

In the **analytic solution procedures** we have examined thus far, an algorithm provides a problem solution that can be mathematically proved to be optimal. In decision making under uncertainty, a solution obtained in this manner generally provides a maximum expected payoff or a minimum expected cost. All of these problems therefore involve variables whose values are determined by chance, so that probability distributions must be specified in advance.

We will now consider a **numerical solution procedure** that seeks optimal alternatives essentially through a trial-and-error process. This simulation technique may be applied to practically any decision problem that involves uncertainty. It is a problem solving approach that offers several advantages over traditional analytic methods. The most significant advantage of simulation is that it can provide answers for problems that are difficult, or even impossible, to solve in a purely mathematical way.

Simulation thoroughly evaluates each alternative by generating a series of values for each random variable at the frequencies indicated by their probability distributions. This is done by sampling from populations of possible values of the variables. The resulting quantities are combined in accordance with an underlying mathematical model to provide a particular value for the payoff measure. After a number of repetitions, a statistical pattern in the results can be discerned. Simulation is therefore a procedure that tries out each alternative "on paper" over and over again; in effect, it represents a sample from the future. As in most random sampling procedures, random numbers are used to generate the events and quantities involved, as if they were determined by spins of a roulette wheel. For this reason, the procedure has become known as **Monte Carlo simulation**.

20-1 The Nature of Simulation

A simulation only *represents* reality and may be used in decision-making situations, training, or a variety of other applications. Monte Carlo procedures employ very special kinds of simulations that must be distinguished from the simulations that are most familiar to us.

Other Kinds of Simulation

A simulation is often physical in nature, as epitomized by ground flight simulators. These modern pilot training devices duplicate flying conditions as closely as possible. There are several advantages to simulated flight. It exposes pilots to a multitude of conditions over a short period of time—experiences that would be extremely costly to duplicate in an actual aircraft. Hazardous situations that would never be created intentionally with real planes may be routinely duplicated in simulated flights. Such exposure has proved valuable in training pilots to cope with real emergencies.

Training applications involving nonphysical simulations of a similar nature are encountered with increasing frequency. For instance, the case method used by many business schools asks the student to simulate the decision process of an actual manager. Like the errors of the airline pilot trainees, mistakes on such cases are not damaging (except to the grade point average), and these cases provide a concentrated exposure to problems that few managers would otherwise experience in their careers. Game-type simulations in which students run hypothetical businesses in competition with one another are also becoming popular. The interaction of individual decisions in a simulated marketplace produces results that are useful in making later choices and that represent improvements in the decision-making process itself.

Physical simulations are helpful when decisions must be made about the design of buildings, cities, waterways, or aircraft. An architect's three-dimensional model of a design is a simulation; the simulated building provides insights that are impossible to glean from sketches alone. The U.S. Army Corps of Engineers has constructed a physical model of the San Francisco Bay that is helpful in evaluating proposals for such activities as dredging and filling in terms of their overall impact on tides and navigation. The flight characteristics of a proposed aircraft may be determined in advance through the simulated flight of a model inside a wind tunnel; the model's aerodynamic properties may lead to refinements in the final design itself.

The Features of Monte Carlo Simulation

Monte Carlo simulation differs from other kinds of simulation in that it is nonphysical in nature and often employs a mathematical model having optimization as the desired end. Thus, Monte Carlo simulation is concerned almost exclusively with decision making itself rather than with training decision makers. Since the procedure is applied to decisions made under uncertainty, the models are *stochastic* in nature. Because chance elements are involved, an alternative must be evaluated under a variety of randomly generated conditions. Although an architect usually makes just one mock-up of a design, a Monte Carlo simulation repeatedly reconstructs the situation in variant forms, according to the events and values that turn up each time. With a somewhat changed model, the same process must be begun again for every alternative. And, when the simulation is finished, all that remains is a history of what happened, which is best analyzed by statistical techniques.

Although Monte Carlo simulation is more widely used than other quantitative methods, it should not be confused with other types of simulation used in decision making that bear a superficial resemblance. For example, it is possible to simulate stock market trading strategies by using past data to make hypothetical trades. Such a simulation involves a tremendous amount of data and may require a computer. In this respect, a stock market simulation resembles a Monte Carlo simulation. However, a stock market simulation is essentially *deterministic* in nature, since previous market conditions are known and *certain*. In contrast, Monte Carlo simulation is a special procedure that is ordinarily used in conjunction with *uncertain* situations.

A variety of problems have been analyzed using Monte Carlo simulations. The oil-tanker port facility study described in Chapter 1 was analyzed using this procedure. Each design alternative was evaluated by more than 1,000 years of simulated operation to arrive at a statistically reliable estimate of its expected rate of return. Monte Carlo simulation has been used to establish baseball batting orders, select rocket combinations to use in launching satellites, and evaluate starting-time policies at golf courses. It has served in planning restaurant menus, in choosing a car, and in estimating how many tellers a bank should hire. It has determined optimal inventory policies for small retailers and large conglomerates. It has proved useful in production control in the manufacture of automobiles, bicycles, and submarines. Monte Carlo simulation has been used to evaluate queuing systems of all kinds—even those without first-come, first-served policies or exponentially distributed service times.

20-2 Concepts and Procedures: A Waiting Line Simulation

As an aid in our discussion of the concepts and procedures of Monte Carlo simulation, we will apply the technique to a simple waiting line situation.

ILLUSTRATION
A One-Man Barbershop

Sammy Lee, owner of a one-man barbershop, is contemplating adding a part-time assistant on Saturdays—the busiest day of the week. His daughter Samantha, who is studying quantitative methods at a distant university, has offered to perform a study to help her father make his decision. As a first step, Samantha wants to evaluate the characteristics of the present operation.

Samantha knows that customers arrive at Sammy's more or less randomly over time and that the time Sammy spends with a particular customer may vary substantially. To help in performing her final analysis she wants to establish applicable Saturday values for the following.

1. Mean arrival rate (λ)
2. Mean time between arrivals $(1/\lambda)$
3. Mean service rate (μ)
4. Mean service time $(1/\mu)$
5. Mean customer waiting time (W_q)
6. Mean customer time in the system (shop) (W)
7. Mean number of customers in the waiting line (L_q)
8. Mean number of customers in the system (shop) (L)
9. Server utilization factor (proportion of time the barber is busy with customers) (ρ)

Samantha knows the textbook formulas for computing these values, but she also knows that they depend on a series of crucial assumptions that may not apply in her father's case. Since she is too far away to observe what goes on at Sammy's shop directly, she will have to simulate the Saturday operations in order to estimate the preceding parameters.

Duplicating Reality

Any Monte Carlo simulation seeks to duplicate reality as closely as possible within practical limitations. Thus, Samantha wants to conduct a simulation that resembles in all important respects what she would find if she actually observed her father's shop in operation.

If Samantha were watching the true operation, what information would she need to find the desired parameter values and how should she arrange the data to obtain the target results?

The simplest solution is to maintain a log, as illustrated in Figure 20-1, identifying each customer and recording when he arrives, when he receives his haircut, and when he

FIGURE 20-1
Simple customer log for actual observations at a barbershop.

Customer	Clock Time at Arrival	Clock Time at Beginning of Service	Clock Time at End of Service
Mr. Jones	9:15	9:15	9:30
Mr. Smith	9:25	9:30	9:45
Mr. Green	9:30	9:45	10:00

FIGURE 20-2
Detailed customer log for actual observations at a barbershop.

Customer	Time Between Arrivals	Clock Time at Arrival	Clock Time at Beginning of Service	Service Time	Clock Time at End of Service	Waiting Time
Mr. Jones		9:15	9:15	15	9:30	0
Mr. Smith	10	9:25	9:30	15	9:45	5
Mr. Green	5	9:30	9:45	15	10:00	15

is finished. As we will see, such a log contains the minimum amount of information necessary to answer the questions.

However, by giving a little additional thought to the design of such a log, we can save some work later on. Items 2 and 4 on Samantha's list of parameters are the mean times between arrivals and for service, respectively. The data needed to compute these means exist in the original log, but, by adding two more columns, the bored log keeper can list the times between successive customer arrivals and the service time for each customer. Another new column can record how long each customer must wait before receiving service. Since a new customer's service cannot begin until the barber is finished with those ahead of him, waiting time is the elapsed clock time between his arrival and the end of service for the preceding customer (and thus the beginning of service for him). Figure 20-2 shows what this more detailed log may look like.

Of course, Samantha cannot be there, so she must use fictional customers. Her simulated log, discussed later, will be similar to the one in Figure 20-2. Because she is only interested in the queuing aspects of the barbershop, it is important that the arrival and service patterns of her fictional customers match those of the real ones. In this way, the interactions between the timing of various events in her simulation will be representative of those occurring in real life.

Probability Distributions

The essential inputs for Samantha's simulation are probability data regarding the patterns of customer arrivals and service. Since much of her analysis involves time, two probability distributions are sought: one for the time between successive customer arrivals and another for the service times of individual customers. Although the basic data for generating these distributions may best be determined by clocking customers during the actual operation of the shop, Sammy cannot afford to hire someone to do this. Samantha therefore has to apply the techniques presented in Chapter 4 to help her father establish subjective probabilities for these random variables.

Although both variables are continuous, Samantha determines the discrete approximations in Table 20-1 for the underlying probability distributions. Her hypothetical customers must therefore arrive randomly, and the frequency of interarrival times must be

TABLE 20-1
Probability Distributions for Times between Customer Arrivals and Customer Service Times

TIMES BETWEEN ARRIVALS		CUSTOMER SERVICE TIMES	
Time	Probability	Time	Probability
5 min	.10	5 min	.05
10	.15	10	.20
15	.25	15	.40
20	.25	20	.20
25	.15	25	.10
30	.10	30	.05
	1.00		1.00

consistent with the probabilities given in Table 20-1. The amount of time taken to cut any customer's hair should also be unpredictable and vary according to the respective probabilities.

Generating Events Using Random Numbers

A Monte Carlo simulation generates events so that they occur with long-run frequencies that are identical to their probabilities. This process is similar to a statistical study in which **random numbers** are used to select a sample from a population of values.

You may recall from an earlier study of statistics that random numbers have no particular pattern and could record the outcomes from successive spins of a wheel of fortune, when any digit between 0 and 9 is equally likely to occur. Appendix Table F contains a list of random numbers created by the RAND Corporation. For convenience, we will use the following partial listings taken from the first two columns of that table.

*12*651	*61*646
*81*769	*74*436
*36*737	*98*863
*82*861	*54*371
*21*325	*15*732
*74*146	*47*887
*90*759	*64*410
*55*683	*98*078
*79*686	*17*969
*70*333	*00*201

Notice that the random numbers listed here contain five digits. Since the probability values for the barbershop simulation are accurate to only two places, we may therefore ignore all but the first two digits and use only the italicized portion of each number.

It really does not matter how random numbers are picked from the table, as long as the values of earlier numbers do not influence the choice of future ones.

In simulating the operations of Sammy Lee's barbershop, each hypothetical customer may be considered to be a sample observation taken from the population of all future clients seeking a Saturday haircut. In traditional statistics, sample customers are randomly selected from a master list. But in a simulation, the customers are imaginary ones with all the essential characteristics of real customers, so that they must be created in such a way that they could have come from a list like the log in Figure 20-2 that has not been and may never be constructed under actual operation. Although they are used differently in simulation than in an ordinary sampling study, random numbers serve this purpose.

In the actual operation of a barbershop, the chance events—each customer's arrival and service times—occur randomly. These events are simulated by translating successive entries on the list of random numbers. Thus, a random number of 67 for the tenth customer could mean that he arrives 20 minutes after the ninth. *A separate random number is used for each variable.* Thus, the next random number on the list might be 19, which could represent a service time of 10 minutes for this customer.

Before the actual simulation begins, exactly which random numbers are to correspond to each event or uncertain quantity must be determined. The barbershop study requires two random number assignments—one for each of the time random variables. Consider the time between arrivals first.

Table 20-1 indicates that an interarrival time of 5 minutes occurs with a probability of .10. This outcome should result 10% of the time in a simulation. Of course, there is no reason why more or less than 10% of these 5-minute outcomes cannot occur, just as a sequence of coin tosses may result in more or less than 50% heads. But when a large number of cases are considered, the frequency of occurrence for any event should be very close to its probability. We let random numbers determine when a 5-minute outcome will occur. Since any possible number is equally likely to appear in any position on a list of random numbers, we want to assign exactly 10% of these so that they correspond to an interarrival time of 5 minutes.

Any 10% of the random numbers will suffice, but these numbers must be identified in advance. It's easiest if we assign the smallest 10% of them to represent 5 minutes. Thus, we will set any two digit random number between 01 and 10, inclusively, to correspond to a 5-minute interarrival time.

The next possible interarrival time is 10 minutes, which occurs with a probability of .15. Thus, the second 15% of the random numbers—those between 11 and 25—will be

TABLE 20-2
Random Number Assignment for Times between Arrivals
Using Cumulative Probabilities

TIME BETWEEN ARRIVALS	PROBABILITY	CUMULATIVE PROBABILITY	RANDOM NUMBERS
5 min	.10	.10	01–10
10	.15	.25	11–25
15	.25	.50	26–50
20	.25	.75	51–75
25	.15	.90	76–90
30	.10	1.00	91–00

TABLE 20-3
Random Number Assignment for Service Times

SERVICE TIME	PROBABILITY	CUMULATIVE PROBABILITY	RANDOM NUMBERS
5 min	.05	.05	01–05
10	.20	.25	06–25
15	.40	.65	26–65
20	.20	.85	66–85
25	.10	.95	86–95
30	.05	1.00	96–00

assigned to that event. To speed the process of assigning random numbers, it is helpful to construct a cumulative probability distribution like the one shown in Table 20-2. Each successive set of random numbers begins where the last set left off, ending with the value that is identical (except for the decimal point) to the respective cumulative probability. This approach guarantees that the proportion of random numbers assigned will always be identical to the probability for the outcome. In doing this, 00 is treated as 100.*

The same procedure is used to assign random numbers to service times in Table 20-3.

Setting Up the Simulation

Before starting her simulation, Samantha Lee must set it up so that she can create a hypothetical log. She begins by making up the *worksheet* in Figure 20-3. For convenience, each customer is given an identity number corresponding to the order of arrival. Notice that two additional columns [(1) and (5)] are required for the random numbers that

FIGURE 20-3
Worksheet for the one-man barbershop simulation.

Trial or Cust. No.	(1) Rand. No.	(2) Time Betw. Arriv.	(3) Clock Time at Arriv. [last (3) + (2)]	(4) Clock Time at Beg. of Serv. [(3) or last (7)]	(5) Rand. No.	(6) Serv. Time	(7) Clock Time at End of Serv. [(4) + (6)]	(8) Waiting Time [(4) − (3)]
1								
2								
3								

---
* An alternative procedure is to use 00 as the low value. The assignment would then be 00–09 for 5 minutes, 10–24 for 10 minutes, ..., 90–99 for 30 minutes.

determine the times between arrivals and the service times. The numbers in these columns may be entered in advance or one at a time as they are needed.

In general, a simulation is a series of **trials**, each of which is a repetition of the basic steps. In our example, the entries made in each customer row constitute a trial. The steps taken comprise a portion of the **simulation model**. In the barbershop simulation, the worksheet itself spells out that part of the overall model in which the trials are generated. Later, we will discuss the remaining parts of the particular model.

The simulation model is basically mathematical and may be defined in terms of algebraic expressions. It is often more convenient, however, to indicate the procedures of the model in a worksheet that clearly delineates each step. In large-scale simulations that must be run on a digital computer, the model is generally imbedded in the programming instructions.

Conducting the Simulation

We are now ready to conduct the simulation. The worksheet entries for one customer at a time appear in Table 20-4.

Samantha begins with the first customer, obtaining the random number 12 from the first list provided earlier. This appears in column (1) and corresponds to a time between arrivals of 10 minutes, which is entered in column (2). Since there is no prior customer, these minutes are simply added to the shop's 9:00 opening time, providing 9:10 as the clock time at arrival for customer number 1. This time is entered in column (3) and also in column (4) for the clock time at beginning of service, since Sammy is free to serve that customer immediately on his arrival. The next random number, 61, is read from the second list and entered in column (5). This corresponds to the service time of 15 minutes, which is placed in column (6). Adding the values in columns (4) and (6) yields a clock time of 9:25 when service ends, which is entered in column (7). Because this customer is served immediately, there is no waiting time.

The second customer is assigned the random number 81 and arrives at 9:35, 25 minutes after the first. Sammy Lee has finished with the preceding customer at 9:25, so service begins immediately at 9:35 with no waiting. The next random number, 74, corresponds to a 20-minute service time, so customer 2 is finished at 9:55.

Meanwhile, the third customer arrives 15 minutes after the second, at 9:50. Sammy is busy with customer 2 until 9:55, so customer 3's service cannot begin until then and he must wait 5 minutes. In general, the clock time at beginning of service is the *greatest* of the entries in columns (3) and (7).

The simulation continues until 20 customers have been monitored. It is now possible for Samantha to estimate the various parameters. This procedure constitutes the remaining portion of the simulation model.

Summing the values in column (2) and dividing by the number of customers, we calculate the first result as follows.

Estimated Mean Time between Arrivals

$$\frac{\text{Total time between arrivals}}{\text{Number of customers}} = \frac{345}{20} = 17.25 \text{ minutes per customer}$$

TABLE 20-4
Worksheet Entries for the Barbershop Simulation

TRIAL OR CUST. NO.	(1) RAND. NO.	(2) TIME BETW. ARRIV.	(3) CLOCK TIME AT ARRIV. [last (3) + (2)]	(4) CLOCK TIME AT BEG. OF SERV. [(3) or last (7)]	(5) RAND. NO.	(6) SERV. TIME	(7) CLOCK TIME AT END OF SERV. [(4) + (6)]	(8) WAITING TIME [(4) − (3)]
Open			9:00					
1	(12)	10	9:10	9:10	(61)	15	9:25	0
2	(81)	25	9:35	9:35	(74)	20	9:55	0
3	(36)	15	9:50	9:55	(98)	30	10:25	5
4	(82)	25	10:15	10:25	(54)	15	10:40	10
5	(21)	10	10:25	10:40	(15)	10	10:50	15
6	(74)	20	10:45	10:50	(47)	15	11:05	5
7	(90)	25	11:10	11:10	(64)	15	11:25	0
8	(55)	20	11:30	11:30	(98)	30	12:00	0
9	(79)	25	11:55	12:00	(17)	10	12:10	5
10	(70)	20	12:15	12:15	(00)	30	12:45	0
11	(14)	10	12:25	12:45	(53)	15	1:00	20
12	(59)	20	12:45	1:00	(08)	10	1:10	15
13	(62)	20	1:05	1:10	(62)	15	1:25	5
14	(57)	20	1:25	1:25	(97)	30	1:55	0
15	(15)	10	1:35	1:55	(90)	25	2:20	20
16	(18)	10	1:45	2:20	(23)	10	2:30	35
17	(74)	20	2:05	2:30	(68)	20	2:50	25
18	(11)	10	2:15	2:50	(16)	10	3:00	35
19	(41)	15	2:30	3:00	(17)	10	3:10	30
20	(32)	15	2:45	3:10	(91)	25	3:35	25
		345				360		250

Elapsed time = 3:35−9:00
= 6 hours and 35 minutes
= 395 minutes

The reciprocal of this result, in units of customers per minute provides the following.

Estimated Mean Arrival Rate

$$\frac{1}{\text{Mean time between arrivals}} = \frac{1}{17.25} = .058 \text{ customers per minute}$$
$$(3.48 \text{ customers per hour})$$

Summing the entries in column (6) and dividing by 20 customers, we calculate the following result.

Estimated Mean Service Time

$$\frac{\text{Total service time}}{\text{Number of customers}} = \frac{360}{20} = 18.00 \text{ minutes per customer}$$

And the reciprocal of this result provides the following.

Estimated Mean Service Rate

$$\frac{1}{\text{Mean service time}} = \frac{1}{18} = .056 \text{ customers per minute}$$
$$(3.36 \text{ customers per hour})$$

The true values of these parameters may be computed from the initial probability distributions, so that it is unnecessary to use these estimates. But some interesting points may be made by comparing the estimates to their true values (the expected values calculated in Table 20-5 using the initial probability distributions).

Notice that the true mean time between arrivals is 17.50 minutes per customer, which is quite close to the simulation result of 17.25. However, the true mean service time of 16.25 minutes per customer is considerably smaller than the simulated value of 18.00. We must keep in mind that a simulation is a sample result, and like any statistical estimate, it may be expected to contain sampling errors. In this particular simulation, the service times were longer than usual, reflecting the fact that abnormally large random numbers were used. This should not detract from the value of the simulation, however, since the service times actually observed on any particular Saturday may also tend to be longer than usual.

As in any sampling situation, the only protection against sampling error is to increase the precision or the reliability of the simulation estimates by conducting a sufficiently large number of trials. If 200 rather than 20 customers were evaluated, we would expect

TABLE 20-5
Expected Value Calculations to Determine True Parameter Values

POSSIBLE TIMES	PROBABILITY	TIME × PROBABILITY
Between arrivals:		
5 min	.10	.50 min
10	.15	1.50
15	.25	3.75
20	.25	5.00
25	.15	3.75
30	.10	3.00
	$1/\lambda$ = Mean time between arrivals = 17.50 min	
For service:		
5 min	.05	.25 min
10	.20	2.00
15	.40	6.00
20	.20	4.00
25	.10	2.50
30	.05	1.50
	$1/\mu$ = Mean service time = 16.25 min	

the estimated mean service time to be much closer to the true parameter value. Later we will consider the question of just how many trials ought to be used.

Samantha's other parameters must be estimated because they cannot be computed as easily as the simple expected values we just determined. Returning to Table 20-4, we divide the total of the column (8) values by the number of customers to determine the following.

Estimated Mean Customer Waiting Time

$$\frac{\text{Total waiting time}}{\text{Number of customers}} = \frac{250}{20} = 12.50 \text{ minutes}$$

Including the total of the column (6) service times in the numerator, we obtain the following expression.

Estimated Mean Customer Time Spent in the System

$$\frac{\text{Total waiting time} + \text{Total service time}}{\text{Number of customers}} = \frac{250 + 360}{20}$$

$$= 30.50 \text{ minutes}$$

This calculation reflects that a customer's time in the barbershop must be spent waiting for and then receiving service. This result is therefore equivalent to the sum of the mean waiting and service times.

$$12.50 + 18.00 = 30.50$$

The remaining parameter estimates require some thought. Consider the problem of finding the average number of customers waiting at any given time. This could be accomplished by taking every five-minute time interval in the simulation and determining how many customers are waiting in each one. A relative frequency distribution indicating the proportion of times 0, 1, 2, 3, or 4 persons were waiting could then be found, and their weighted average would provide the desired result. Fortunately, all of this extra work is unnecessary. Instead, we divide the total waiting time in column (8) by the simulation's **elapsed time**, or its duration from start to finish (calculated in Table 20-4 to be 395 minutes) to obtain the following result.

Estimated Mean Number of Customers Waiting

$$\frac{\text{Total waiting time}}{\text{Elapsed time}} = \frac{250}{395} = .63 \text{ customers}$$

It may seem a bit odd that customers result when we divide minutes by minutes, but this computation is the mathematical equivalent of the weighted average approach. We may view total waiting time as the product of the times when customers wait and the number of customers waiting, so that the numerator is in units of customer-minutes.

Similarly, the totals for columns (6) and (8) can be added and divided by elapsed time to provide the following.

Estimated Mean Number of Customers in the System

$$\frac{\text{Total service time} + \text{Total waiting time}}{\text{Elapsed time}} = \frac{360 + 250}{395}$$

$$= 1.54 \text{ customers}$$

This represents the average number of customers either waiting or receiving service at any point in time.

To find the proportion of time the barber is busy with a customer, we divide the total from column (6) by the elapsed time to obtain a value for the following.

Estimated Server Utilization Factor

$$\frac{\text{Total service time}}{\text{Elapsed time}} = \frac{360}{395} = .91$$

We see that Sammy Lee spends about 91% of the time that the shop is in operation on Saturday actually cutting hair. Another interpretation of .91 is that it represents the fraction of a customer who may be receiving service at any point in time. By subtracting this value from the estimated mean number of customers in the barbershop, we obtain the estimated mean number of customers who are waiting, or

$$1.54 - .91 = .63$$

Transient Simulation States

You may have wondered why Samantha Lee stopped her simulation abruptly with the twentieth customer at 3:35, in the middle of a busy period that started at about 2 P.M. Shouldn't she have continued her simulation until closing time?

All simulations must begin and end some time, and the number of trials is generally established in advance. In the barbershop example, this can lead to distortions near the beginning and the end of the simulation. Sammy Lee opened his shop at 9 A.M., and customers started trickling in at 9:10. No opening-time congestion, which may occur in reality, was possible. Also, no successful barber quits for the day when customers are still waiting. The middle of the simulation is the closest approximation of reality. Distortions encountered at the beginning and the end arise because the simulation is then in *transient states*. An analogy with the performance test on an automobile engine may be helpful. An engine exhibits different characteristics while warming up than it does when it has been running for a while. To realistically assess performance, only the results obtained after the engine has warmed up should be considered. Also, a slight sputtering or coughing the instant after the ignition switch is shut off should not be reflected in the performance rating.

The impact of transitional distortions can be minimized by conducting the simulation over a longer period of time. If Samantha uses 1,000 customers (so that 50 Saturdays are considered back-to-back), distortions at the beginning and the end may be safely ignored.

It is another matter entirely if the barbershop actually goes through transient states when it is in actual operation. This may happen if customers are lined up at the door when Sammy arrives or if he varies his closing time to accommodate stragglers. Also, arrivals may be more concentrated at 2 or 3 P.M. than at other times. And Sammy may slow down in the afternoon, thereby increasing the service times. The simulation model itself must be sufficiently complex to realistically reflect the varying characteristics of a system.

Decision Making with Simulation

Samantha Lee's simulation provides a variety of estimates for the key parameters that may be helpful in any further analysis. Remember that Sammy Lee's basic problem is deciding whether or not to hire a second barber to work on Saturdays. To evaluate this alternative, a second simulation must be performed that involves a somewhat more complex procedure (which is left as an exercise for the reader to determine). A similar set of estimated parameter values will be obtained in this later simulation and may then be compared with the initial ones.

The comparison of two or more simulations may be a demanding task, especially when several kinds of information are provided by each one. To a certain extent, such a comparison presents the same problems we encountered when we evaluated samples taken from several populations. The statistical aspects of simulation will be discussed in the next section.

20-3 The Statistical Aspects of Simulation

A simulation is completely analogous to a sampling study. Consider the similarities between estimating the mean customer waiting time and estimating a city's mean disposable family income. Each simulation trial provides one randomly chosen waiting time, whereas a randomly selected family yields a sample observation of income. In either case, planning is involved in setting up the study and in deciding how many observations to make. Although the data are collected differently, the results are qualitatively equivalent. Whether we are reporting results or deciding what to do, we must acknowledge and contend with potential sampling error. Thus, conclusions in either situation are in the nature of *statistical inferences*.

Required Number of Trials

As indicated earlier, the number of simulation trials determines the precision and reliability of the resulting estimate. This number plays the same role as the sample size does in traditional statistics. In the planning stage of the simulation, the number of trials must be treated as a variable, which we denote by n. Samantha Lee used $n = 20$ in her simulation, but how large should n be in estimating mean waiting time? In determining the answer, we will assume that no simulation data are available.

To simplify our discussion and ease the transition from traditional statistics, we will adopt conventional notation. Each individual waiting time may be represented by an X with the appropriate subscript, so that X_1 represents customer 1's waiting time, X_2 represents customer 2's waiting time, and so on. The arithmetic mean of these X values is denoted by $\bar{X}$. The standard deviation for the population of all future Saturday waiting times is σ. The mean waiting time for the population is denoted by W_q (instead of μ, which represents the true mean service rate in standard queuing formulas). W_q is the quantity to be estimated. The expected value of $\bar{X}$ is W_q, and from the central limit theorem we know that $\bar{X}$ is approximately normally distributed with

$$\text{Mean} = W_q \qquad \text{Standard deviation} = \frac{\sigma}{\sqrt{n}}$$

where σ is known in advance.

Of course, we do not know the value of σ. We must guess its value, and we use the subscript g to distinguish the guessed value of the standard deviation from its true value, so that

$$\sigma_g = \text{Guessed value for standard deviation}$$

A rule of thumb for finding σ_g is that it should equal one-sixth the difference between the largest and smallest conceivable values.*

$$\sigma_g = \frac{\text{Largest value} - \text{Smallest value}}{6}$$

Suppose that Sammy Lee occasionally keeps a Saturday customer waiting up to 60 minutes, but never any longer. The smallest waiting time is obviously zero, so that

$$\sigma_g = \frac{60 - 0}{6} = 10 \text{ minutes}$$

Before finding n, it is necessary to establish target levels for precision and reliability. These are

$d = $ Target precision level (maximum deviation from the true value)

$z = $ Normal deviate for the target reliability level

It should be emphasized that both of these levels are essential, since precision and reliability are competing ends. An overly precise estimate, such as $W_q = 2.343$ min $\pm .0005$, is almost totally unreliable. On the other hand, a very imprecise result, such as "W_q lies between 0 and 100 minutes," may be perfectly reliable—even if no simulation is conducted.

The target precision level d expresses the maximum deviation that may be tolerated between the estimate and its true value—either above or below it—in terms of the units

---

* If the individual waiting times were normally distributed, they would fall within $\pm 3\sigma$, or a range of 6σ, of the true mean about 99.7% of the time. Of course, some other distribution may apply, so the above procedure is not completely accurate.

involved (minutes, in the present example). The reliability expresses the probability that the target precision level will be met. Because such a probability is obtained from a normal curve centered at the true mean with standard deviation of $\sigma/\sqrt{n}$ (represented by $\sigma_g/\sqrt{n}$), for a specific d, z, and σ_g there is a unique n such that[†]

$$n = \frac{z^2 \sigma_g^2}{d^2}$$

Suppose that Samantha wishes to be precise to the nearest whole minute, so that $d = 1$, with a reliability of .95, so that the required normal deviate is $z = 1.96$. Plugging these values and $\sigma_g = 10$ into the preceding equation, we find that her required sample size is

$$n = \frac{(1.96)^2(10)^2}{(1)^2} = 384.16, \text{ or } 385$$

(Since n is always expressed in whole numbers, 384.16 is raised to 385.) By using only 20 customers, Samantha has *undersampled* and will not meet her target levels. Often, n values calculated in this manner are huge, so that hand simulations by necessity involve undersampling. (In computer simulations, the proper n can usually be applied at minimal cost.) Undersampling produces fuzzy results, which makes it difficult to compare the alternatives simulated.

The Confidence Interval Estimate

An **interval estimate** is often used to report data from a simulation, just as it is used to report ordinary sample data. When estimating a mean, two values are used to construct such an interval—the sample mean $\bar{X}$ and the **sample standard deviation**

$$s = \sqrt{\frac{\sum (X - \bar{X})^2}{n - 1}}$$

The latter statistic may be calculated from simulation data and serves as the estimator of the unknown value of σ. The n used here—and in any other statistical calculation involving data—must be the *actual* number of trials. In the barbershop simulation, $n = 20$ (not the desired level of 385 found earlier).

Ordinarily, some **confidence level**, such as 95% or 99%, is used to report the results. A normal deviate value z, such as 1.96 or 2.57, corresponds to the level chosen. For the large samples generally used in simulations, the following expression determines the **confidence interval estimate**.

$$\text{True mean} = \bar{X} \pm z \frac{s}{\sqrt{n}}$$

[†] A complete explanation and derivation of this equation is too lengthy to include here. See Lawrence L. Lapin, *Statistics for Modern Business Decisions*, 5th ed. (New York: Harcourt Brace Jovanovich, 1990), pp. 305–14, for a complete discussion.

Before computing the confidence interval for the mean customer waiting time, the sample standard deviation must be found. This is calculated in Table 20-6 to be $s = 12.4$ minutes. Samantha desires a 95% confidence level, so that $z = 1.96$. Plugging these values, along with $\bar{X} = 12.50$ and $n = 20$, into this equation we determine the confidence interval for the mean customer waiting time.

$$W_q = 12.50 \pm (1.96)\frac{12.4}{\sqrt{20}} = 12.50 \pm 5.43 \text{ minutes}$$

or,

$$7.07 \leq W_q \leq 17.93 \text{ minutes}$$

The proper interpretation of this result is: *If the 20-customer simulation were repeated over and over again, using different random numbers each time, then an interval constructed in this manner would contain the true mean waiting time in about 95 out of every 100 cases, but about 5 of such intervals would lie totally above or below the true value.*

Notice that this confidence interval is quite wide, reflecting the lack of precision due to undersampling.

TABLE 20-6
Calculations for the Sample Standard Deviation
of Customer Waiting Times

CUSTOMER i	WAITING TIME X_i	DEVIATION $(X_i - \bar{X})$	$(X_i - \bar{X})^2$
1	0	−12.50	156.25
2	0	−12.50	156.25
3	5	−7.50	56.25
4	10	−2.50	6.25
5	15	2.50	6.25
6	5	−7.50	56.25
7	0	−12.50	156.25
8	0	−12.50	156.25
9	5	−7.50	56.25
10	0	−12.50	156.25
11	20	7.50	56.25
12	15	2.50	6.25
13	5	−7.50	56.25
14	0	−12.50	156.25
15	20	7.50	56.25
16	35	22.50	506.25
17	25	12.50	156.25
18	35	22.50	506.25
19	30	17.50	306.25
20	25	12.50	156.25
	250	0.00	2,925.00

$$\bar{X} = \sum X/n = 250/20 = 12.50 \text{ min}$$

$$s = \sqrt{2{,}925.00/(20-1)} = \sqrt{153.95} = 12.4 \text{ min}$$

Further Statistical Considerations

We have barely scratched the statistical surface of simulation. Many other kinds of inferences may be made. For instance, Samantha Lee may want to compare the W values for one-man and two-man barbershops, which would bring another set of sample data into the picture. Various hypothesis testing procedures may be employed for this purpose. If several alternatives are to be simulated, an analysis of variance may be conducted. A detailed discussion of these procedures is beyond the scope of this book, but many good statistical references are provided in the bibliography at the back of the book.

However, there are further complications. Samantha wants to estimate nine parameters, and an elaborate report may consider inferences about them as well. Usually a simulation estimates only one parameter.

In some simulations, a probability or a proportion is estimated instead of a mean. For example, the optimal number of telephone information operators may be the smallest sized crew that provides a .95 probability of rendering service within 10 seconds. In simulating various alternatives, the true probability for a particular crew size could be estimated by the proportion of calls (trials) receiving service within 10 seconds. Although there is not enough space to describe them in this book, equivalent expressions can be used to find n and to compute confidence intervals for such quantities.

20-4 Simulation and PERT

In our discussion of PERT (Program Evaluation and Review Technique) in Chapter 18, we saw that much of the analysis ignores the uncertainties about activity times. Using only expected times, we can provide the project manager with a time–cost trade-off curve for deciding which activities, if any, should be crashed. Unfortunately, the project completion times obtained in this manner can seriously understate the true expected project completion times.

Consider the PERT network in Figure 20-4, which illustrates a project with five activities. Each activity is represented by an arrow, and the regular activity completion times appear on the respective arrows. The times in boldface for activities b and d are *certain* and cannot vary; the times for activities a, c, and e are *expected* times. Traditional

FIGURE 20-4
A PERT network illustrating a project with five activities.

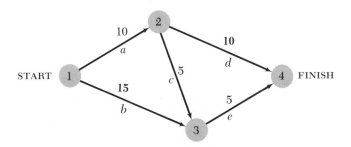

FIGURE 20-5
Cumulative probability distributions for PERT expected activity completion times.

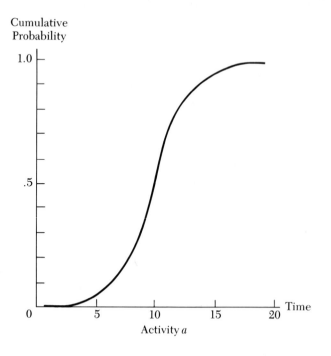

Activity *a*

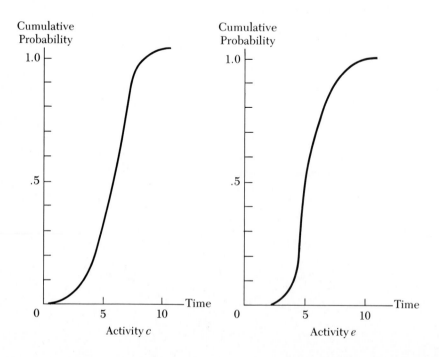

Activity *c*

Activity *e*

PERT analysis is based on the **critical path**, which is the longest duration activity sequence from start to finish. Given the times in this network, all paths (*a-d*, *a-c-e*, and *b-e*) are critical, and each path is expected to take 20 days.

The continuous probability distributions for the three expected activity completion times are represented in Figure 20-5 by cumulative probability graphs. The project will be simulated using random numbers to determine the times that will be obtained in each trial.

Using Random Numbers with Continuous Distributions

When a cumulative probability graph has been constructed for a continuous random variable (see Chapter 4 to find out how this is done), the graph itself may be used to determine which quantities correspond to the random numbers. As we saw in the barbershop simulation, random numbers can be assigned to trial variable values by establishing the *range* for the random numbers. The upper limit of that range is identical to the cumulative probability for the value, except for the decimal point. When the variable is continuous, cumulative probability serves the same purpose, except that only

FIGURE 20-6

Using a cumulative probability curve to assign random numbers to quantities.

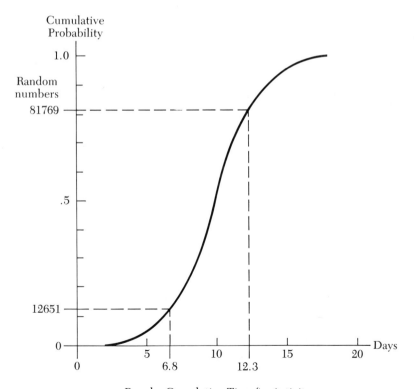

Regular Completion Time for Activity *a*

single quantities—not ranges—are involved. Because fractional activity times are possible, it is convenient to use all of the digits in each random number.

Figure 20-6 illustrates the procedure for generating completion times for activity *a*. Consider 12651 as the first random number; this corresponds to a cumulative probability of .12651, representing a height on the graph slightly below .13. From the curve, we can see that the time corresponding to this cumulative probability is roughly 6.8 days. Similarly, we may locate the cumulative probability corresponding to a second random number, 81769. The curve at that height represents a time of approximately 12.3 days. Since any random number between 00000 and 99999 is equally likely, each possible height on the curve is just as likely in each trial. Notice that the steepest portion of the curve occurs around 10 days, indicating that more possible random numbers will yield times falling near 10 than any other time. The curve is flatter near 5 days, so that fewer random numbers will lead to times near that level. The graphical procedure therefore generates times more frequently for the more typical levels and less frequently for the rarer levels. For a large number of trials, the frequencies can be expected to match the underlying probabilities exactly, which is just what a simulation is supposed to do.

TABLE 20-7
Worksheet and Results for the PERT Simulation

| | ACTIVITY TIMES (days) | | | | | | | | LONGEST | |
| | *a* | | *b* | *c* | | *d* | *e* | | (critical) | PROJECT |
TRIAL	Random Number	Time	Time	Random Number	Time	Time	Random Number	Time	PATH	DURATION
1	(12651)	6.8	15	(61646)	6.3	10	(11769)	4.2	*b-e*	19.2
2	(81769)	12.3	15	(74436)	6.8	10	(02630)	2.7	*a-d*	22.3
3	(36737)	9.4	15	(98863)	8.5	10	(77240)	6.2	*a-c-e*	24.1
4	(82861)	12.6	15	(54371)	6.2	10	(76610)	6.2	*a-c-e*	25.0
5	(21325)	7.8	15	(15732)	4.0	10	(24127)	4.6	*b-e*	19.6
6	(74146)	11.3	15	(47887)	6.0	10	(62463)	5.4	*a-c-e*	22.7
7	(90759)	13.9	15	(64410)	6.5	10	(54179)	5.1	*a-c-e*	25.5
8	(55683)	10.2	15	(98078)	8.3	10	(02238)	2.7	*a-c-e*	21.2
9	(79686)	12.0	15	(17969)	4.2	10	(76061)	6.2	*a-c-e*	22.4
10	(70333)	11.0	15	(00201)	.5	10	(86201)	6.9	*b-e*	21.9
11	(14042)	7.0	15	(53536)	6.1	10	(07779)	3.8	*b-e*	18.8
12	(59911)	10.3	15	(08256)	3.1	10	(06596)	3.6	*a-d*	20.3
13	(62368)	10.4	15	(62623)	6.4	10	(62742)	6.0	*a-c-e*	22.8
14	(57529)	10.2	15	(97751)	8.2	10	(54976)	5.4	*a-c-e*	23.8
15	(15469)	7.1	15	(90574)	7.5	10	(78033)	6.3	*b-e*	21.3
16	(18625)	7.6	15	(23674)	4.6	10	(53850)	5.1	*b-e*	20.1
17	(74626)	11.3	15	(68394)	6.7	10	(88562)	7.2	*a-c-e*	25.2
18	(11119)	6.4	15	(16519)	4.1	10	(27384)	4.7	*b-e*	19.7
19	(41101)	9.6	15	(17336)	4.2	10	(48951)	4.9	*b-e*	19.9
20	(32123)	9.0	15	(91576)	7.6	10	(84221)	6.7	*a-c-e*	23.3
Totals		196.2	300		115.8	200		103.9		439.1
Averages		9.81	15		5.79	10		5.20		21.96

The Simulation

The results of $n = 20$ trials for the PERT simulation are provided in the worksheet shown in Table 20-7. Each trial involved reading three random numbers onto the respective cumulative probability graphs for activities a, c, and e to determine the corresponding activity completion times. The path with the longest total time through the network was then determined, and the duration of that critical path established the project completion time for the particular trial.

The simulation provides some interesting results. Notice that the simulated mean project completion time of 21.96 days is almost two days *longer* than the 20-day completion time indicated using expected values alone. Since only 20 trials were used, we must rely on statistical analysis to tell us whether this difference is significant or the natural result of sampling error. However, studies have established that similar results are generally the case in PERT simulations with a larger number of trials. Also notice that if the mean simulation times for the various activities are considered, all three paths based on these averages are shorter than 21.96 days. This illustrates the tendency of traditional PERT procedures, which are based on average times and individual paths, to understate the mean completion time for the project as a whole. One explanation for this is that no particular path can really be considered singly, for there is some probability that any one of several paths will actually be the longest. Notice that all three paths turned out to be critical in at least one trial and that in no trial was there more than one critical path.

20-5 Simulating Inventory Policies

Simulation can also be used to evaluate alternative inventory policies. Figure 20-7 shows the log a retailer may use to record the actual operations of an inventory system for

FIGURE 20-7
Hypothetical log for the actual daily operation of an inventory system.

Day	Starting Inventory	Items Received	Items Demanded	Items Sold	Items Backordered	Items Ordered	Days for Order to Arrive	Holding and Shortage Costs	Ordering Cost
6/7	150	0	100	100	0	0	—	$1.50	—
6/8	50	0	75	50	25	500	2	3.00	$5.00
6/9	0	0	85	0	85	0	—	8.50	—
6/10	0	500	55	55	0	0	—	0.00	—
6/11	335	0	60	60	0	0	—	3.35	—

a single product. From this log format, a more detailed simulation worksheet may be developed to simulate various inventory policies, such as "order 500 items whenever any day starts with less than 60 units."

Daily demand is one random variable for which a probability distribution must be obtained. Some probability distribution would apply to the number of days until an order arrives, and another uncertainty may be reflected in the lead time it takes to receive the order. The values of both variables would apply to the number of days until an order arrives and would be generated with random numbers.

The log picture in Figure 20-7 indicates that all items demanded will be sold unless the inventory is depleted, in which case short items will be back-ordered and supplied when the next shipment arrives. Inventory holding costs are presumed to be $.01 per item held at the start of each day, which represents a daily proration of annual holding costs (usually expressed as a monetary amount per dollar value). A straight penalty of $.10 is assumed to apply for each item short, and the ordering cost is $5.00, regardless of how many items are ordered.

The same approach may be taken for more elaborate problems that involve several products, each having different demand and lead-time distributions. These products may compete for space and working capital, and their costs will differ. Some items may receive quantity discounts from the supplier. Shortage penalties may be more elaborate and may include an additional cost for each day the shortage lasts.

20-6 Simulation versus the Analytic Solution

Whenever possible, management scientists use simulation as a last resort. An analytic solution is preferable if it is valid and can be obtained with less work. One reason is that simulation involves a great deal of effort and expense, even when it is performed with the assistance of a computer. A separate simulation is required for each alternative, and hundreds or thousands of these may have to be performed. And after the simulations are finished, only statistical estimates—not true values—are available. It is not surprising that an algebraic expression providing the exact answer would be more desirable.

Simulation should be viewed in its proper perspective and used sparingly. But no one has categorized the situations in which it should and should not be used. We must never force a problem to fit a particular analytic solution simply to avoid the tedium of simulation, unless the assumptions underlying the model closely fit the problem. We illustrate the pitfalls of doing this by considering the barbershop illustration once again.

In Chapter 19, we saw that various formulas can be used to obtain the parameters of a single-channel queue. These formulas depend only on the mean arrival rate λ and the mean service rate μ. In the case of Sammy Lee's barbershop, the reciprocals of these values were computed earlier from the probability data.

$$1/\lambda = 17.50 \text{ minutes per customer}$$

$$1/\mu = 16.25 \text{ minutes per customer}$$

Thus,

$$\lambda = 1/17.50 = .057 \text{ customers per minute}$$

$$\mu = 1/16.25 = .062 \text{ customers per minute}$$

Plugging these values into the formula for the mean customer waiting time gives us

$$W_q = \frac{\lambda}{\mu(\mu - \lambda)} = \frac{.057}{.062(.062 - .057)} = 184 \text{ minutes}$$

which is more than ten times the value obtained in the simulation. Another queuing formula tells us that the mean arrival rate multiplied by W_q equals the mean number of customers waiting. Thus,

$$L_q = \lambda W_q = .057(184) = 10.5 \text{ customers}$$

which disagrees with the simulation results by the same factor.

Why are these discrepancies so great? The explanation is that the operation of Sammy Lee's barbershop does not agree with an underlying assumption of the queuing model—the often overlooked assumption that the arrival and service times must be *exponentially distributed.* The probability distributions used in the simulation do not even resemble the exponential distribution, which indicates that a time of zero is the most likely to occur.

The barbershop illustration was purposely picked to dramatize what may happen if an appropriate analytic solution procedure is blindly followed. Not all procedures work so poorly—even when their assumptions are not met exactly. The EOQ (economic order quantity) formulas used to design inventory policies are generally very successful in finding answers that are close to optimal in such cases. They are said to be *robust* with regard to a variety of violations in the underlying assumptions. It may not be worth the extra work to simulate inventory policies when a very good answer can be found much more simply by working a 30-second calculation.

In the quest for analytic solutions, the model itself can so distort reality that the mathematically developed conclusions are not valid and can even be misleading. This happened with PERT. Appendix 18-1 describes in detail a popular procedure for obtaining the probability distribution for the duration of that particular path identified as the "critical" one. The label "critical path" is something of a misnomer, since expected (average) activity completion times are traditionally used to identify this activity sequence. Earlier in this chapter, we saw why such an analysis based on average times understates the true mean *project* completion time.

The traditional PERT model provides a probability analysis for a variable nobody really cares about—namely, the length of a particular path that may or may not turn out to be the longest one. Project managers are more appropriately concerned with the time it will take to finish the entire project, which is a totally different variable. Analytic procedures cannot provide a probability analysis of this variable, except in very small networks. In conjunction with the PERT network, simulation is the more viable procedure to use to determine the characteristics of project completion times.

20-7 Simulation and the Computer

Monte Carlo simulation involves many repetitions of the same computational steps, which makes the digital computer an ideal tool for applying simulation. Once the computer program has been written, each alternative may be simulated and thousands of trials may be conducted at a relatively modest cost. Indeed, perhaps no other management science technique has been nurtured so dramatically by the advent of bigger and faster computers.

Simulation Programs and Languages

Simulation has become so integrated with the computer that special computer languages (similar to BASIC, COBOL, and FORTRAN) have been written just to perform simulations. One of these languages is SIMSCRIPT, which is based on FORTRAN. Instructions may be written in this language without a detailed knowledge of computers. A special program, called a *compiler*, then converts the SIMSCRIPT instructions into machine language. (Compilers exist for a variety of computers.)

Another popular simulation procedure applies the General Purpose System Simulator (GPSS), which is really a program developed by IBM for its computers. Versions are also available for use on computers from other manufacturers. GPSS is more efficient in some respects than SIMSCRIPT, but inferior in others. In choosing a simulation language, the overriding consideration is the system that happens to be available.

If no special simulation software is accessible, it is still possible to use ordinary programming languages, such as FORTRAN, to conduct a computer simulation. All the major languages are supplied with library routines that are useful in computer simulation. These routines are especially important in generating random numbers.

Random Number Generation

It would be terribly impractical to prepare random numbers ahead of time and feed them into the computer during a simulation. This would not only slow down the processing, but it may consume too much core memory. Besides, consider the awful job of compiling and entering these numbers and the fact that computer simulations may involve billions of random numbers—far too many to be taken from published lists.

The random numbers in a computer simulation are invariably generated by the computer itself as they are needed. This is usually done by providing a seed number, which is multiplied by one constant and divided by another value; the remainder term is then used as the random number. The next number is always found in this way from the last number. Of course, all such numbers can be predicted in advance, so that they are not really random at all.

Values generated in this way are called **pseudo-random numbers**. They may be used in simulations because *they look like true random numbers*. The generation of pseudo-random numbers yields a stream of numbers that exhibit all essential properties—nearly equal frequencies for all possible values, little serial correlation, and no abnormally long or short runs of any particular type of number.

The Disadvantages of Computer Simulation

Computer simulation does have some disadvantages. Paramount among these is the programming effort. Unless statistical reliability is very critical or a large number of alternatives must be considered, it is often easier in the long run to "crank it out by hand." The inherent characteristics of the digital computer may create a lot of extra work. For example, computers do not read graphs, necessitating the approximation of continuous probability distributions by constructing a table of typical values and their associated probabilities. Also, some computer models are pictorial in nature (similar to a PERT network), and it is especially demanding to write a special program that duplicates the human capacity to make visual inspections.

CASE

The Balloon Saloon

The Balloon Saloon is a boutique providing balloons for special occasions. Most of the business is with balloon bouquets for birthdays, anniversaries, promotions, and similar occasions. The proprietor, Mrs. H. E. Lium, wishes to establish the best combination of reorder point and order quantity for the more expensive and popular Mylar balloons. The following probability distributions are assumed to apply on any given day for Mylars.

NUMBER OF CUSTOMERS	PROBABILITY	DEMAND PER CUSTOMER	PROBABILITY
15	.05	1	.20
16	.10	2	.15
17	.15	3	.10
18	.15	4	.07
19	.10	5	.07
20	.10	6	.06
21	.10	7	.06
22	.08	8	.05
23	.07	9	.05
24	.06	10	.04
25	.04	11	.04
		12	.04
		13	.03
		14	.02
		15	.02

Lium pays $.50 per Mylar balloon, each selling for $1.25 when inflated with helium (which along other supplies costs $.25 per Mylar). Each dollar tied up in inventory costs Lium $.001 per day. She incurs a cost of approximately $10 to place, track, and process each balloon order—regardless of size. The following probability distributions are assumed to apply for each order. The supplier is rarely able to fill the entire order.

LEAD TIME DAYS	PROBABILITY	PROPORTION OF ORDER FILLED	PROBABILITY
2	.10	.75	.10
3	.15	.80	.20
4	.20	.85	.25
5	.20	.90	.30
6	.15	.95	.10
7	.10	1.00	.05
8	.10		

When the Balloon Saloon is out of Mylars, 70% of the customers will settle for rubber balloons, each bringing a markup of $.20. The remaining customers will leave without making a purchase. Additionally, Lium believes that the expected present value of future profits lost due to being out of Mylars is $.30 per balloon.

Questions

1. Set up a schedule of random number assignments for number of customers, demand per customer, lead time, proportion of order filled, and whether or not a customer leaves when out of stock.

2. Set up necessary simulation worksheets for determining the Mylar balloon profit for several days of operation.

3. Conduct a 20-day simulation, using a reorder point of 200 Mylar balloons and an order quantity of 500 Mylar balloons. Then, compute the total Mylar profit for the period. Assume that orders are placed at the beginning of the day, depending on the opening inventory, and that shipments arrive just before the store opens on the date indicated by the lead time. Assume also that the Mylar customer arriving just before stockout will accept any available quantity and fill his or her remaining demand with rubber balloons.

PROBLEMS

20-1 Consider the following probability distribution for the times between arrivals of cars stopping at a New Guernsey toll booth.

TIME	PROBABILITY
5 sec	.35
10	.23
15	.15
20	.11
25	.08
30	.05
35	.03

(a) Construct the cumulative probability distribution and determine a random number assignment suitable for simulation. (Use the first two digits of the random numbers.)
(b) Simulate the arrival of 20 cars and calculate the estimated mean time between arrivals.

20-2 For the probability distribution in Problem 20-1, perform the expected value calculation to find the true mean time between arrivals.

20-3 As part of a simulation to determine advertising response, you must create trial persons who fall into one of the following categories.

CATEGORY	PROBABILITY
Urban	.36
Suburban	.47
Rural	.17

Prepare a two-digit random number assignment to generate these events.

20-4 Consider the cumulative probability for demand provided in Figure 4-8 on page 114. Use the following random numbers to generate 20 demands.

99582	53390	46357	13244
18080	02321	05809	04898
30143	52687	19420	60061
46683	33761	47452	23551
48672	28736	84994	13071

What is the estimated mean demand?

20-5 A staff analyst for Big-E Corporation has developed a simulation model to estimate the mean annual rate of return for new projects. Separate simulations, each consisting of several investment lifetime trials, will be conducted for the various alternatives. The analyst wishes to determine how many trials to create for a particular case if the lifetime annual rate of return may fall between -20% and 40%. How many trials are required to estimate the mean rate of return to the nearest 1% when a reliability of 95% is desired?

20-6 The mean time required by automobile assemblers to hang a car door is to be estimated. Assuming that the guessed value of the standard deviation is 10 seconds, determine the required n under the following conditions.
(a) The desired reliability probability for being in error by no more than 1 second (in either direction) is .99.
(b) The desired reliability probability for being in error by no more than 1 second is .95.
(c) A reliability of .99 is desired, with a target precision of 2 seconds. How does the n you obtain here compare with your answer to (a)?

20-7 Construct a 95% confidence interval for the true means, given the following simulation results.
(a) $n = 100$; $\bar{X} = 100.53$ min; $s = 25.3$ min
(b) $n = 200$; $\bar{X} = 69.2$ in; $s = 1.08$ in
(c) $n = 350$; $\bar{X} = \$12.00$; $s = \$7.00$

20-8 Construct a 95% confidence interval estimate for the mean project completion time using the simulation results given in Table 20-7 (page 614) for the PERT illustration in the chapter.

20-9   Consider the alternative of adding a second barber to Sammy Lee's shop on Saturdays. This will attract more clients, so that customers will arrive closer together. Suppose that the following probabilities apply.

TIME BETWEEN ARRIVALS	PROBABILITY
5 min	.35
10	.25
15	.20
20	.10
25	.10

Also, suppose that the second barber has the same service time distribution as Sammy.
(a) Set up a worksheet for simulating the two-man barbershop. (*Hint:* Only one random number is needed for each customer's service time.)
(b) Assume that a customer will pick Sammy if both barbers are free and the first free barber otherwise. Conduct a 20-customer simulation with the random numbers used in Table 20-4 (page 603).
(c) Find the estimated mean customer waiting time.

20-10   Consider Sammy's barbershop again. Suppose that enough simulations were conducted to determine the following true mean waiting times.

$$W_q = 15 \text{ minutes for one barber}$$
$$W_q = 5 \text{ minutes for two barbers}$$

Also, suppose that Sammy suffers a loss of goodwill of $.05 for each minute that *each* customer spends waiting. The shop is open for 8 hours on Saturdays. Each customer brings in an average revenue of $4.00, and the second barber costs Sammy $5.00 per hour.

Using the probability data in the chapter and in Problem 20-9, compute Sammy's average Saturday earnings for one barber and for two barbers. What should Sammy do?

20-11   Suppose that the retailer in Section 20-5 experiences a daily demand for items according to the following probability distribution.

DEMAND	PROBABILITY
40	.04
50	.08
60	.15
70	.23
80	.20
90	.15
100	.10
110	.05

The following lead time distribution for filling an order applies.

LEAD TIME	PROBABILITY
1 day	.20
2	.25
3	.20
4	.15
5	.10
6	.10

(a) Simulate 25 days of operation to estimate the mean daily inventory cost, given an order quantity of 500, if an order is placed whenever a day's starting inventory falls below 60 items and the starting inventory is 150 items.

(b) Repeat your simulation given an order quantity of 1,000 and an order point of 100. Use the same random numbers you did in (a).

(c) Which of the two inventory policies appears to be less costly?

20-12 Although it is not an accepted practice, you can generate your own random numbers in a pinch by tossing a coin. For instance, a list of two-digit decimal numbers can be obtained by generating a list of seven-digit binary numbers from seven tosses of a coin. This is done by assigning a 0 to a tail and a 1 to a head and then converting the results of every seven tosses to a decimal number. For example, the sequence HTHHTTH yields the binary number 1011001. In decimals, this number may be expressed as the following sum.

$$1 \times 2^6 = 64$$
$$0 \times 2^5 = 0$$
$$1 \times 2^4 = 16$$
$$1 \times 2^3 = 8$$
$$0 \times 2^2 = 0$$
$$0 \times 2^1 = 0$$
$$1 \times 2^0 = \underline{1}$$
$$89$$

Any decimal values greater than 99 can be thrown away. Generate a list of ten two-digit random decimal numbers this way.

20-13 The dice game of "Craps" provides an interesting example of when not to simulate. The outcome is based on the values achieved from tossing two six-sided dice. One way to place a bet is to "play the field." Here, the bettor indicates that he or she wishes to make a bet with a complicated payoff, depending on which faces of the dice show. If a "field" number (defined by a sum value of 2 through 4 or 9 through 12) occurs, the player wins. If the roll of the dice yields any other total, the player loses. A field gamble is further complicated by varying payoffs: 1 to 1 for all field numbers except 2 or 12, 2 to 1 on a 2, and 3 to 1 on a 12. Winning bettors keep their original bet and are also paid their winnings. Losing players forfeit their wagers.

(a) For a bet of $1, use this information and the basic concepts of probability to determine the probability distribution for a gambler's net winnings.

(b) Suppose that a system player has an initial bankroll of $7. Beginning with a $1 bet, this player's strategy is to place successive field bets until winning once or losing the original $7. Either of these outcomes terminates the play. As long as money remains, the gambler will double the last wager lost.

Simulate 10 runs of this system to estimate the gambler's mean winnings per play. (To simplify things, you may roll dice rather than use random numbers.)

(c) Solve the problem in (b) analytically by determining the appropriate probability values and finding the gambler's expected winnings. Then, compare this to the simulated value you found in (b). (*Hint:* A tree diagram may be helpful.)

20-14 Big-E Corporation's computer microwave transmission network, which connects five cities, is provided in Figure 20-8. Each line represents a channel, and transmissions between two cities may be routed over any sequence of clear channels. The number above each line represents the probability for interference on that channel at any given moment. Management is contemplating adding more channels and wants to estimate the probability that San Francisco and New York communications will be completely blocked by interference at any given time.

Estimate this probability by simulating this system for 20 trials. (*Hint:* You may want to make 20 copies of the network before starting, so that the blocked channels for each trial can be clearly identified.)

FIGURE 20-8
Network for Problem 20-14.

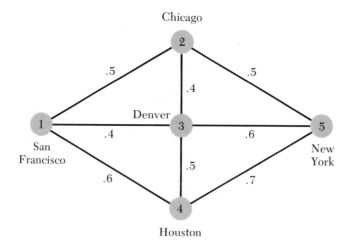

21

Basic Concepts of Decision Making

$\mathbb{T}$ he central focus of this book is on the use of quantitative methods in decision making. This chapter considers the structure of decisions in general. We make a basic distinction between decision making under *certainty* where no elements are left to chance, and decision making under *uncertainty*, where one or more random factors affect the outcome of a decision.

21-1 Certainty and Uncertainty in Decision Making

The least complex applications of decision theory are encountered when we make decisions under certain conditions. Perhaps the simplest example of *decision making under certainty* is selecting what clothes to wear. Although the possibilities are numerous, we all manage to make this choice quickly and with little effort. But not all decisions are this easy to make. Remember how hard it was to choose from among an assortment of candy bars when you were a child? And not all decisions made under certainty are as trivial as choosing the day's apparel.

When the outcomes are only partly determined by choice, the decision-making process takes on an added complexity. So that we can see what is involved in structuring a decision under uncertainty, we will consider the choice of whether to carry an umbrella or some other rain protection. Here, we are faced with two alternatives: carrying an ungainly item that can, in the event of rain, help to defer a cleaning bill or a cough, or challenging the elements with hands free and hoping not to be caught in the rain. Because the weather prediction may be inaccurate we are uncertain about whether it will rain. Yet faced with the needs of daily life, we must make a decision despite our uncertainty. This illustrates a common decision made under uncertainty: An action must be taken, even though its outcome is unknown and determined by chance.*

In this chapter, we will present a framework within which we can explain how and why particular choices are made. The decision that we must make in coping with the weather illustrates the essential features of making any decision under uncertainty. We choose to carry an umbrella when the chance of rain seems uncomfortably high, and we choose not to carry it when rain seems unlikely. But two people will make two different choices occasionally. Is there always one correct decision? If so, how can two persons make different choices? We begin to answer these questions by identifying several key elements common to all decisions and then structuring them in a convenient form for analysis.

21-2 Elements of Decisions

Every decision made under certainty exhibits two elements—**acts** and **outcomes**. The decision maker's choices are the acts. For example, when one must choose among three television programs in the 9 P.M. time slot, each program represents a potential act. The outcomes may be characterized in terms of the enjoyment we derive from each of the programs.

If the decision is made under uncertainty, a third element—**events**—exists. Continuing with our uncertainty about the rain, the acts are "carry an umbrella" and "leave the umbrella home." All decisions involve the selection of an act. But the outcomes resulting from each act are uncertain, because *an outcome is determined partly by choice and partly by chance.* For the act "carry an umbrella" there are two possible outcomes: (1) unnecessarily carting rain paraphernalia and (2) weathering a shower fully protected. For the other act, "leave the umbrella at home," the two outcomes are (1) getting wet unnecessarily and (2) remaining dry and unencumbered. Again, whether the first or second outcome occurs depends solely on the occurrence of rain. The outcome for any particular chosen act depends on which *event*, rain or no rain, occurs.

The Decision Table

To facilitate our analysis, we may summarize a decision problem by constructing a **decision table**, which indicates the relationship between pairs of decision elements. The decision table for the umbrella decision is provided in Table 21-1. Each row of the decision table corresponds to an event, and each column corresponds to an act. The outcomes appear as entries in the body of the table. There is a specific outcome for each act-event

---

* This class of decisions is often divided into two categories—decision making under *risk*, where outcome probabilities are known, and decision making under *uncertainty* where outcome probabilities are unknown. We will make no distinction here, but will assume that probabilities may always be found somehow—either objectively, through long-run frequency, or subjectively.

TABLE 21-1
Decision Table for the Umbrella Decision

	ACT	
EVENT	Carry Umbrella	Leave Umbrella Home
Rain	Stay dry	Get wet
No Rain	Carry unnecessary burden	Be dry and free

combination, reflecting the fact that the interplay between act and event determines the ultimate result.

Only the acts that the decision maker wishes to consider are included in this decision table. "Staying home" is another possible act, which we will exclude because it is not contemplated. The acts in Table 21-1 are mutually exclusive and collectively exhaustive, so that exactly one act will be chosen. The events in the table are also mutually exclusive and collectively exhaustive.

The Decision Tree Diagram

A decision problem may also be conveniently illustrated with a **decision tree diagram** like the one shown in Figure 21-1. It is especially convenient to portray decision problems

FIGURE 21-1
Decision tree diagram for the umbrella decision.

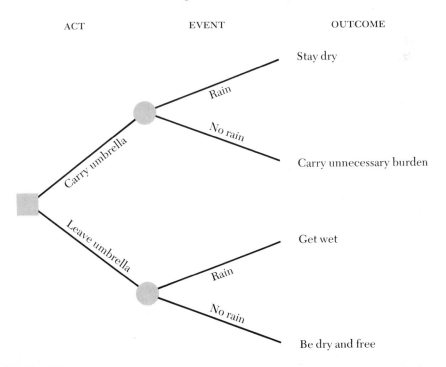

in the form of decision trees when choices must be made at different times over an extended period of time. The decision tree diagram is similar to the probability tree diagrams we used in Chapters 2 and 3. The choice of acts is shown as a fork with a separate branch for each act. The events are represented by separate branches in other forks. We distinguish between these two types of branching points, using squares for **act-fork nodes** and circles for **event-fork nodes**. A basic guideline for constructing a decision tree diagram is that the flow should be chronological from left to right. The acts are shown on the initial fork, because the decision must be made *before* the actual event is known. The events are therefore shown as branches in the second-stage forks. The outcome resulting from each act-event combination is shown as the end position of the corresponding path from the base of the tree.

21-3 Ranking the Alternatives and the Payoff Table

In this chapter, we will consider how the choice of an act should be determined. We all cope with rain and manage to make umbrella decisions. But if we analyze the decision-making process, we will be able to make better decisions under more complex circumstances. Our analysis will focus on two measures: one for *uncertainty* and one for the *comparative worth* or **payoff** of the outcomes to the decision maker.

For now, we will consider examples with outcomes that have obvious payoffs, such as dollars. Every outcome—that is, every act-event combination—has a payoff value. Since the payoffs that the decision maker actually receives after choosing a particular act are conditional on whichever event occurs, these payoffs are sometimes referred to as *conditional values*. These values may be conveniently arranged in a **payoff table**, or a *conditional value table*, as shown in Table 21-2 for a gambling decision. The decision is to choose one of two acts: "gamble" or "don't gamble." Regardless of the choice made, a coin will be tossed, which will result in one of two possible events: "head" or "tail." The possible outcomes correspond to the four act-event combinations. A wager of $1 will be made if the decision maker chooses to gamble, and net winnings will be the payoff measure.

Objectives and Payoff Values

In determining appropriate payoffs, we will assume that decision makers will choose to take actions that will bring them closest to their objectives. Each outcome must somehow be ranked in terms of how close it is to the decision maker's goal. The payoff table should provide a meaningful basis for comparison and enhance the decision maker's ability to make a good choice.

For example, if a business decision maker's goal is to achieve a high level of profits, then a natural payoff would be the profit for each outcome. Profit is a valid measure for a limited set of objectives, but it is by no means the top concern of all business managers. The goal of the founder of a successful corporation may be to maintain personal control

TABLE 21-2
Payoff Table for a Gambling Decision

	ACT	
EVENT	Gamble	Don't Gamble
Head	$1	$0
Tail	− 1	0

and the founder may consciously keep profits low so that the firm will not be attractive to other merger-minded entrepreneurs.

In general, decision making involves different kinds of goals, each requiring a distinct payoff measure. Decision makers with different goals may even select dissimilar measures for payoffs when considering the same set of alternatives. The following example illustrates this.

EXAMPLE

Finding the Way to San Francisco

Charles Snyder, Herman Brown, and Sylvia Gold wish to choose one of three routes from Los Angeles to San Francisco: (1) Interstate 5, which is a freeway nearly all the way and has a high minimum speed limit; (2) State Highways 118 and 33, which are fairly direct and have no minimum speed limit; and (3) State Highway 1, which winds along the Pacific coast and is slow and long but very beautiful. Mr. Snyder is a salesman who travels to San Francisco regularly; his goal is to reach his destination as quickly as possible. Mr. Brown is an economy "nut"; he wants to reach San Francisco as cheaply as possible. Ms. Gold is on vacation and loves to drive on hilly, winding, scenic roads; she wishes to select the route that provides the greatest driving pleasure.

The payoffs that each person would assign to the three routes appear in Table 21-3. Time savings is Mr. Snyder's payoff measure, so he chooses Interstate 5, which yields the

TABLE 21-3
Payoffs for the Alternative Routes Relevant to the Goals of Three Decision Makers

	PAYOFF MEASURE		
	MR. SNYDER	MR. BROWN	MS. GOLD
ALTERNATIVE ROUTE	Time Savings (hours)	Fuel Savings (gallons)	Enjoyment (subjective rating)
Interstate 5	4	3	1
Highways 118 & 33	3	7	3
Highway 1	0	0	10

greatest payoff of 4 hours. Mr. Brown likes to drive at a moderate speed to obtain maximum gasoline mileage, while taking the shortest route possible. His payoff measure is fuel savings (based on the amount of gasoline required on the most expensive route), so he chooses the back roads, State Highways 118 and 33, to save 7 gallons of gas. Ms. Gold has rated the routes in terms of points of interest, types of scenery, and number of hills and curves. This rating serves as her payoff measure, so her best route is scenic State Highway 1, which rates 10.

We conclude that *a payoff measure should be selected so that the payoff will rank outcomes by the degree to which they attain the decision maker's goals.* The goal dictates which payoff measures are valid.

ILLUSTRATION
Choosing a Movement for Tippi-Toes

As a detailed example of a business decision made under uncertainty, we will consider a hypothetical toy manufacturer who must choose among four prototype designs for Tippi-Toes, a dancing ballerina doll that does pirouettes and jetés. Each prototype represents a different technology for the moving parts, all powered by small, battery-operated motors. One prototype is a complete arrangement of gears and levers. The second is similar, with springs instead of levers. Another works on the principle of weights and pulleys. The movement of the fourth design is controlled pneumatically through a system of valves that open and close at the command of a small, solid-state computer housed in the head cavity. The dolls are identical in all functional aspects.

The choice of the movement design will be based solely on a comparison of the contributions to profits made by the four prototypes. The payoff table is provided in Table 21-4. The demand for Tippi-Toes is uncertain, but management feels that one of the following events will occur.

Light demand	(25,000 units)
Moderate demand	(100,000 units)
Heavy demand	(150,000 units)

The toy manufacturer in this example is considering only three possible events—here,

TABLE 21-4
Payoff Table for the Tippi-Toes Decision

EVENT (level of demand)	ACT (choice of movement)			
	Gears and Levers	Spring Action	Weights and Pulleys	Pneumatic
Light	$ 25,000	−$ 10,000	−$125,000	−$300,000
Moderate	400,000	440,000	400,000	300,000
Heavy	650,000	740,000	750,000	700,000

levels of demand—which greatly simplifies our analysis. Demand does not have to be precisely 25,000 or 100,000 units, however. The problem could be analyzed at several hundred thousand possible levels of demand—say, from 0 to 500,000 dolls. The techniques we will develop here may be applied to a more detailed situation. Due to the computational requirements, the demand probability distribution could be approximated to the nearest 100, 1,000, or 10,000 units.

Similarly, our example has only four alternatives. In the practical, business decision-making environment, the number of possible acts may be quite large. For instance, deciding what mix of toys to sell could easily involve trillions of alternatives. *The decision analysis should include only the alternatives that the decision maker wishes to consider.* When there is no compelling reason for choosing one of the alternatives, "doing nothing" should be an alternative. The search for attractive alternatives is essential to sound decision making. However, decision analysis cannot tell us what factors should and should not be considered, although it may be used to guide our selection.

21-4 Reducing the Number of Alternatives: Inadmissible Acts

Regardless of the decision-making process that we ultimately employ to help us make a choice, an initial screening may be made to determine if there are any acts that will never be chosen. To illustrate this, consider the payoffs in Table 21-4. An interesting feature is exhibited by the payoffs of the acts "weights and pulleys" and "pneumatic." No matter which demand event occurs, the weights-and-pulleys act results in a greater payoff. If a light demand occurs, for instance, the payoff for weights and pulleys is −$125,000, which is more favorable than the −$300,000 payoff for the pneumatic movement. A similar finding results if we compare these two acts for the other possible demand events. Because the weights-and-pulleys movement will always be a superior choice to the pneumatic movement, we say that the first act *dominates* the second act. One act dominates another when it achieves a better or an equal payoff, no matter which events occur, and when it is strictly better for one or more events.

In general, whenever an act is dominated by another one, it is *inadmissible*. Thus, the pneumatic movement is an **inadmissible act**. The toy manufacturer's decision may be simplified by eliminating pneumatic movement from further consideration. Removing the pneumatic act leaves us with the modified payoff table in Table 21-5.

TABLE 21-5
Modified Payoff Table for the Tippi-Toes Decision

EVENT (level of demand)	ACT (choice of movement)		
	Gears and Levers	Spring Action	Weights and Pulleys
Light	$ 25,000	−$ 10,000	−$125,000
Moderate	400,000	440,000	400,000
Heavy	650,000	740,000	750,000

A simple way to determine if an act is inadmissible is to see if every entry in a single column of the payoff table is greater than or equal to the corresponding entry in its column. It is easy to verify that this is not true for the entries in Table 21-5, so the remaining movement acts must be retained. The acts that remain are called **admissible acts**.

21-5 Maximizing Expected Payoff: The Bayes Decision Rule

How does a decision maker choose an act? When there is no uncertainty, the answer is straightforward: Select the act that yields the highest payoff (although finding this particular optimal act may be very difficult when there are many alternatives). But when the events are uncertain, the act that yields the greatest payoff for one event may yield a lower payoff than a competing act for some other event.

Suppose that our toy manufacturer accepts the following probabilities for the demand for Tippi-Toes.

Light demand	.10
Moderate demand	.70
Heavy demand	.20
	1.00

We calculate the expected payoff for each act in Table 21-6 by multiplying each payoff by the respective event probability and summing the products from each column. We find that the spring-action movement results in the maximum expected payoff of $455,000. Thus, using maximum expected payoff as a decision-making criterion, our toy manufacturer would select the spring-action movement for the Tippi-Toes doll.

The criterion of selecting the act with the **maximum expected payoff** is sometimes referred to as the **Bayes decision rule**. This rule takes into account all the information about

TABLE 21-6
Calculation of Expected Payoffs for the Tippi-Toes Decision

EVENT (level of demand)	PROBABILITY	ACT (choice of movement)					
		Gears and Levers		Spring Action		Weights and Pulleys	
		Payoff	Payoff × Probability	Payoff	Payoff × Probability	Payoff	Payoff × Probability
Light	.10	$ 25,000	$ 2,500	−$ 10,000	−$ 1,000	−$125,000	−$ 12,500
Moderate	.70	400,000	280,000	440,000	308,000	400,000	280,000
Heavy	.20	650,000	130,000	740,000	148,000	750,000	150,000
	Expected payoff		$412,500		$455,000		$417,500

the chances for the various payoffs. But we will see that it is not a perfect device and can lead to a choice that is not actually the most desirable. However, we will also see that this criterion is a suitable basis for decision making under uncertainty when the payoff values are selected with great care.

21-6 Decision Tree Analysis

The decisions under uncertainty encountered thus far may be portrayed in terms of a payoff table. But some problems are too complex to be presented in a table. Difficulties arise when the same events do not apply for all acts. For example, a contractor may have to choose between bidding on a construction job for a dam or on one for an airport, not having sufficient resources to bid on both. Regardless of the job chosen, there is some probability (which may differ for the two projects) that the contractor will win the job bid on. Separate sets of events and probabilities are required for each act.

Decisons must often be made at two or more points in time, with uncertain events occurring between decisions. Sometimes these problems may be analyzed in terms of a payoff table, but usually the earlier choice of the act will have a bearing on the type, quantity, and probabilities of later events. At best, this makes it cumbersome to attempt to force the decision into the limited confines of the rectangular arrangement of a payoff table.

The decision tree diagram described earlier allows us to meaningfully arrange the elements of a complex decision problem without the restrictions of a tabular format. A further advantage of the decision tree is that it serves as an excellent management communication tool, because the tree clearly delineates every potential course of action and all possible outcomes.

ILLUSTRATION
Ponderosa Record Company

The president of Ponderosa Record Company, a small independent recording studio, has just signed a contract with a four-person rock group, called the Fluid Mechanics. A tape has been cut, and Ponderosa must decide whether or not to market the recording. If the record is to be test marketed, then a 5,000-record run will be made and promoted regionally; this may result in a later decision to distribute an additional 45,000 records nationally, for which a second pressing run will have to be made. If immediate national marketing is chosen, a pressing run of 50,000 records will be made. Regardless of the test market results, the president may decide to enter the national market or decide not to enter it.

A Ponderosa record is either a complete success or a failure in its market. A recording is successful if all records that are pressed are sold; the sales of a failure are practically nil. Success in a regional market does not guarantee success nationally, but it is a fairly reliable predictor.

The Decision Tree Diagram

The structure of the Ponderosa decision problem is presented in the decision tree diagram in Figure 21-2. Decisions are to be made at two different points in time, or stages. The immediate choice is to select one of two acts: "test market" or "don't test market." These acts are shown as branches on the initial fork at node *a*. If test marketing is chosen, then the result to be achieved in the test marketplace is uncertain. This is reflected by an event fork at node *b*, where the branches represent favorable and unfavorable outcomes. Regardless of which event occurs, a choice must be made between two new acts: "market nationally" or "abort." These acts occur at a later stage and are represented by a pair of act forks. Each fork corresponds to the two different conditions under which this decision

FIGURE 21-2

Decision tree diagram for the Ponderosa decision.

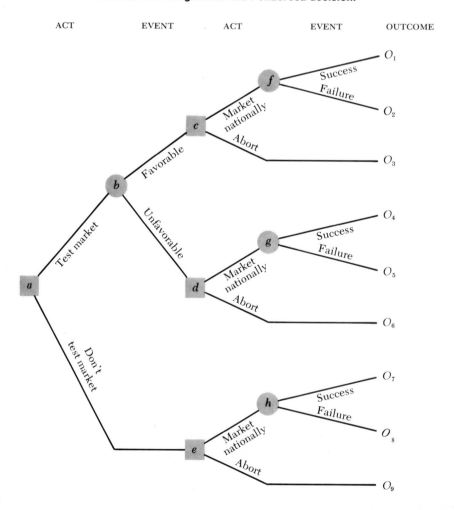

may be made: at node *c*, when the test marketing is favorable, and at node *d*, when it is unfavorable. If national marketing is chosen at either node *c* or node *d*, the success or failure of the recording still remains unknown, and the possible events are reflected on the decision tree as branches on the terminal event forks at nodes *f* and *g*.

If the initial choice at decision point *a* is "don't test market," then a further choice must be made at the act fork represented by decision point *e*: "market nationally" or "abort." As before, node *h* reflects the two uncertain events that will arise from the choice to market nationally. The "abort" path leading from node *e* contains a "dummy" branch—a diagrammatical convenience that allows event and act forks of similar form to appear at the same stage of the problem and permits all paths to terminate at a common stage. Thus, all "abort" acts are followed by a dummy branch.

Every path from the base of the decision tree leads to a terminal position corresponding to a decision outcome. Each possible combination of acts and events, or each path, has a distinct outcome. For instance, O_1 represents the following sequence of events and acts: "test market," "favorable," "market nationally," "success."

The first step in analyzing the decision problem is to obtain a payoff for each outcome.

Determining the Payoffs

The contract with the Fluid Mechanics calls for a $5,000 payment to the group if records are produced. Ponderosa arranges with a record manufacturer to make its pressings. For each pressing run, there is a $5,000 fixed cost plus a $.75 fee for each record. Record jackets, handling, and distribution cost an additional $.25 per record. The total variable cost per record is therefore $1.00. Using these figures, we calculate the immediate cast effect of each act in the decision tree in Figure 21-2. Some of these cash effects, or **partial cash flows**, are computed in Table 21-7.

The negative cash flows indicate expenditures. The partial cash flows in Table 21-7 appear on the respective branches extending from decision points *a* and *e* of the decision

TABLE 21-7
Some Partial Cash Flows Used to Determine Ponderosa's Payoffs

ACT		PARTIAL CASH FLOW	
Test market		−$ 5,000	(payment to group)
		− 5,000	(fixed cost of pressing)
		− 5,000	(variable costs of 5,000 records at $1.00)
	Total	−$15,000	
Don't test market		$0	
Market nationally		−$ 5,000	(payment to group)
(without test)		− 5,000	(fixed cost of pressing)
		− 50,000	(variable costs of 50,000 records at $1.00)
	Total	−$60,000	
Abort		$0	

tree in Figure 21-3. In a similar manner, we determine the partial cash flows for the acts at the forks at decision points *c* and *d*: −$50,000 to market nationally ($5,000 fixed pressing cost plus $1.00 each in variable costs for 45,000 records) and $0 to abort.

Ponderosa receives $2 for each record it sells through retail outlets. Since the events— "favorable" and "unfavorable" or "success" and "failure"—represent sales of all and no records, respectively, the partial cash flows may be obtained by multiplying the number of records sold by $2. The partial cash flows for the events at the fork at node *b* are therefore +$10,000 (for 5,000 records sold) and $0 (for no sales). The amounts for the events at nodes *f* and *g* are +$90,000 (for 45,000 records sold) and $0, whereas the amounts for the events at node *h* are +$100,000 and $0.

FIGURE 21-3

The Ponderosa decision tree diagram showing partial cash flows and probabilities on the branches, with net-cash-flow payoffs at the terminal positions.

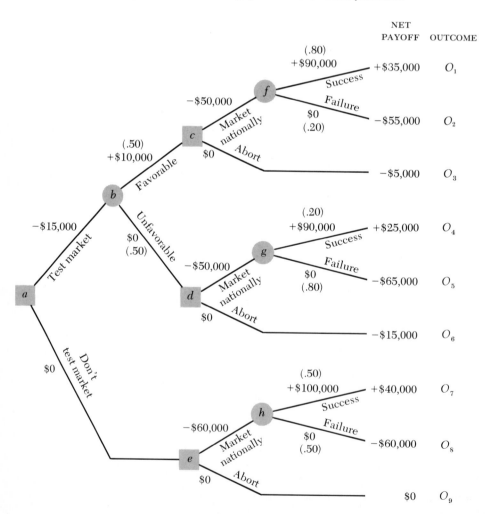

The payoff for each outcome may be obtained by adding the partial cash flows on the branches of the path leading to its terminal position. Thus, for O_1, we add the partial cash flows $-\$15,000$, $+\$10,000$, $-\$50,000$, and $+\$90,000$. The payoff for O_1 is therefore $+\$35,000$. The payoffs calculated for each outcome are shown at the respective terminal positions of the decision tree in Figure 21-3.

Assigning Event Probabilities

Ponderosa's management wishes to choose the act that will yield the maximum expected payoff. But before this choice can be made, probability values must be assigned to the events in the decision structure. Suppose that Ponderosa's president believes that the chance of favorably test marketing the recording is .50. The probability of unfavorably test marketing the recording is also .50. These probability values are placed in parentheses along the branches at node b in Figure 21-3. In assigning probability values to the success and failure events for national marketing, our decision maker is faced with three distinctly different situations. With no test marketing, the chance of national success is judged to be .50. A favorable test marketing indicates that a record appeals to the regional segment of the market, so the chance of national success in this case is judged to be a much higher .80; this is a *conditional probability*. Similarly, unfavorable test marketing is a likely indication of poor national appeal, so the conditional probability for success is judged to be .20 in this case. The following probability values are placed on the branches for the events at the remaining forks in the decision tree diagram: .80 for success and .20 for failure at node f; .20 for success and .80 for failure at node g; and .50 for success and .50 for failure at node h. (It is just coincidental that the probability for national marketing success after unfavorable test marketing is .20, which is also the probability for national marketing failure after favorable test marketing. Our decision maker could have selected another value, such as .10.)

Backward Induction

We are now ready to analyze Ponderosa's decision. Our decision maker wishes to select an initial or immediate act at decision point a. The first act that we will evaluate is "test market." What is the expected payoff for this act? Figure 21-3 shows us that six outcomes, O_1 through O_6, may result from this choice. How can we translate the corresponding payoffs into an expected value? We cannot do this until we specify the intervening acts that will be chosen at nodes c and d. In general, *it is impossible to evaluate an immediate act without first considering all later decisions that result from this choice.*

Thus, to find the expected payoff for the "test market" act, our decision maker must first decide whether to market nationally or to abort if (1) test marketing proves favorable or (2) test marketing proves unfavorable. This illustrates an essential feature of analyzing multistage decisions: *Evaluations must be made in reverse of their natural chronological sequence.* Before deciding whether to test market, our decision maker must decide what to do if the test marketing is favorable or if it is unfavorable. The procedure for making such evaluations is called **backward induction**.

We clarify this point by describing the procedure for our decision-making problem. For simplicity, the Ponderosa president's decision tree diagram is redrawn in Figure 21-4 without the partial cash flows.

Consider the act fork at decision point c. If the decision is to market nationally, then Ponderosa's president is faced with the event fork at node f. With a probability of .80 that marketing nationally will be a success, a net payoff of $+\$35,000$ will be achieved. The probability that marketing nationally will be a failure is .20, which leads to a net payoff of $-\$55,000$. The expected payoff for this event fork is calculated as

$$.80(+\$35,000) + .20(-\$55,000) = +\$17,000$$

The amount $+\$17,000$ is entered on the decision tree at node f, since this is the expected

FIGURE 21-4
The Ponderosa decision tree diagram, showing backward induction analysis.

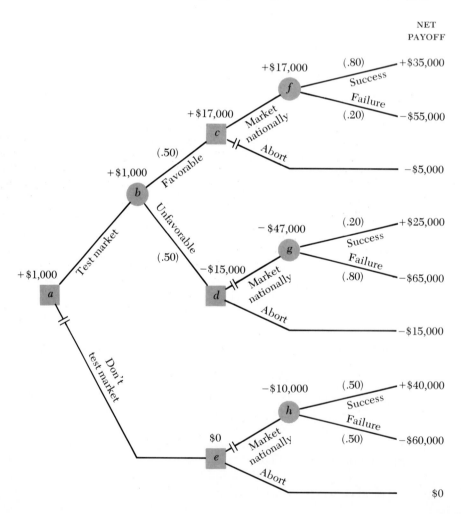

payoff for the act to market nationally. For convenience, we place the expected payoff for a sequence of acts or events above the applicable node.

The act to abort at decision point c will lead to a certain payoff of $-\$5,000$. Since the expected payoff for the act to market nationally ($+\$17,000$) is larger than $-\$5,000$, the choice to market nationally should be made over aborting. We may reflect this future choice by *pruning* the branch from the tree that corresponds to the act "abort" at decision point c. This act merits no further consideration, since if decision point c is reached, the president will choose to market nationally. That is, if the decision maker initially decides to test market and the results turn out to be favorable, the president will choose to market nationally. Thus, $+\$17,000$ is the expected payoff resulting from making the best choice at decision point c. We bring back the amount $+\$17,000$ and enter it on the diagram above the node at c.

As a rule of thumb in performing backward induction, ultimately all but one act will be eliminated at each decision point (except in the case of ties), so that all branches except those leading to the greatest expected payoff will be pruned. Only the *best single payoff* from the later stage is brought backward to the preceding decision point (square). *Branch pruning takes place only in act forks—never in event forks.* Instead, event forks (circles) involve an expected value calculation, so that an average payoff is always computed from the later stage values.

The available choices when test marketing results are unfavorable may be handled in the same way. First, we calculate the expected payoff at node g that arises from the act "market nationally," or

$$.20(+\$25,000) + .80(-\$65,000) = -\$47,000$$

We place this figure on the decision tree diagram above node g. Since the act "abort" leads to a payoff of $-\$15,000$, which is larger than $-\$47,000$, the branch for the act to market nationally is pruned from the tree. The best choice when test marketing fails is to abort. We therefore bring back and enter the amount $-\$15,000$ on the diagram above the node at decision point d.

In a similar fashion, the expected payoff of the event fork at node h, when the initial choice is to market nationally, is determined as follows.

$$.50(+\$40,000) + .50(-\$60,000) = -\$10,000$$

At decision point e, the act "abort" is superior to the act "market nationally," and the latter branch is pruned from the tree. Our decision maker must now compare the acts at decision point a. The expected payoff from the act "test market" is still to be determined. This is the expected payoff for the event fork at node b, which has two event branches. The branch corresponding to success leads to a portion of the tree with an expected payoff of $+\$17,000$. The other branch leads to a choice with an expected payoff of $-\$15,000$. We use these two amounts to calculate the expected payoff at node b.

$$.50(+\$17,000) + .50(-\$15,000) = +\$1,000$$

We enter the amount $+\$1,000$ on the diagram above node b.

Ponderosa's president is now in a position to compare the two acts at decision point *a*: "test market" and "don't test market." Since the expected payoff for test marketing (+$1,000) is higher than the expected payoff for not testing ($0), our decision maker should choose to test market. The expected payoff of $1,000 is brought back and placed above node *a*. The branch corresponding to "don't test market" is pruned, and our backward induction is complete.

A decision is indicated. Ponderosa's president should choose to test market the Fluid Mechanics' record. If the test marketing is favorable, then the president should market nationally; if the test marketing is unfavorable, then the president should abort the recording. This result is illustrated in Figure 21-4 by the unpruned branches that remain on the decision tree.

Additional Remarks

Choices that are made in later stages are not irrevocable, and this analysis does not preclude the fact that the decision maker's mind may change over time. Before the future decision must be made at node *c*, for instance, new information may be received that would indicate a need to revise the probability for national success downward. If there is bad publicity about one of the Fluid Mechanics, for example, the expected payoff for national marketing may be smaller than the expected payoff for aborting. Possible changes in conditions do not invalidate the original backward induction analysis. In our example, *the choice to test market is the best decision that may be made based on the currently available information.*

The decision tree structure is suitable for analyzing decisions that extend over a long time period. It indicates the best course of action for the *current* decision. As time progresses, however, some uncertainties may be reduced and new ones may arise. Acts previously identified as optimal may turn out to be obviously poor choices, and brand new candidates may be determined. The relevant portion of the decision tree may be updated and revised prior to each new immediate decision. But each such decision is analyzed in the same general manner, using the best information available at the time a choice must be made.

Although a decision tree is analyzed by moving backward in time, the analysis is really forward-looking because it indicates the optimal course of action to take when future decision points are reached. The dollar amount brought backward to each node represents the best payoff the decision maker can expect to achieve if that position is reached at a later time. Regardless of what events have occurred, the optimal course of action for future choices is still indicated by the original analysis.

21-7 Computer Applications of Decision Analysis

Computers are used more often to facilitate decision analysis. Although the methods of this chapter are not particularly computationally intensive, decision tree analysis is one of the more prominent areas where computers are used. Computers may be very helpful in graphically displaying the tree itself, a capability that may free investigators from artistic

FIGURE 21-5

QuickQuant report showing the decision tree analysis for the Ponderosa Record Company illustration.

```
==============================================================================
                          QuickQuant Report
                       DECISION TREE ANALYSIS
------------------------------------------------------------------------------
PROBLEM: Ponderosa Record Company                      Date: 02-10-1990
                                                              Larry

                                                       $35000.00
                                                        (.80)        \
                                                      +-----012-----:
                                                      :Success    013
                                                      :90000
                                                      :
                                          $17000.00:     -$55000.00
                                                \:(.20)          \
                                  +-----006-----E+-----013-----:
                                  :Mkt. Nat.  007 Failure    014
                                  :-50000          0
                                  :
                      $17000.00:                   -$5000.00
            (.5)            \:                             \
      +-----003-----A+--X--007-----D------014-----:
      :Favorable   004 Abort      008             015
      :10000            0
      :
      :                                           $25000.00
      :                                            (.20)       \
      :                                          +-----015-----:
      :                                          :Success    016
      :                                          :90000
      :                                          :
      :                      -$47000.00:     -$65000.00
      :                             \:(.80)          \
      :                      +--X--008-----E+-----016-----:
      :                      :Mkt. Nat.  009 Failure    017
      :                      :-50000          0
      :                      :
      $1000.00:    -$15000.00:                   -$15000.00
            \:(.5)          \:                           \
  +-----001-----E+-----004-----A+-----009-----D------017-----:
  :Test Mkt.  002 Unfavor.  005 Abort    010             018
  :-15000        0              0
  :
  :                                           $40000.00
  :                                            (.50)        \
  :                                          +-----018-----:
  :                                          :Success    019
  :                                          :100000
  :                                          :
  :                      -$10000.00:     -$60000.00
  :                             \:(.50)          \
  :                      +--X--010-----E+-----019-----:
  :                      :Mkt. Nat.  011 Failure    020
  :                      :-60000          0
  :                      :
  $1000.00:              $0.00:                   $0.00
        \:                   \:                          \
  A+--X--002-----D------005-----A+-----011-----D------020-----:
  001 Don't Test 003           006 Abort    012             021
      0                            0
------------------------------------------------------------------------------
```

feats. A computer can function both as a drafting instrument and as a number cruncher, performing the backward induction analysis.

QuickQuant, the personal computer software available to the users of this book, has a decision analysis segment that performs these functions. The tree is constructed one fork at a time at the computer, with the users specifying whether the branches are acts or events. From the keyboard all needed data for each branch are entered. The tree grows during the input session as additional forks and branches are created. The program allows the tree to be saved for later, and it may be edited and updated as required. Figure 21-5 shows the decision tree generated for the Ponderosa Record Company illustration. There the backward induction results are provided, with the inferior acts pruned.

QuickQuant may also be used to compute expected payoffs for the columns of the payoff table. These may be found using the probability segment of the program. The greatest computational needs, however, are encountered in Chapters 24 and 25. *Quick-Quant* provides all the needed values for the heavily computational-intensive procedures described in those chapters.

CASE

Gypsy Moth Eradication

A government official wishes to determine the most effective way to control tree damage from the gypsy moth. There are three methods for attacking the pest: (1) spray with DDT; (2) use a scent to lure and trap males, so that the remaining males must compete for mating with a much larger number of males that have been sterilized in a laboratory and then released; and (3) spray with a juvenile hormone that prevents the larvae from developing into adult moths.

The net improvement in current and future tree losses using DDT is lowest, because it is assumed that DDT will never completely eradicate the moth.

If the scent-lure program is instituted, the probability that it will leave a low number of native males is .5, with a .5 chance that it will leave a high number. Once the scent-lure results are known, a later choice must then be made either to spray with DDT or to release sterile males. The cost of the scent lures is $5 million and the cost of sterilization is an additional $5 million. But if this two-phase program is successful, the worth of present and future trees saved will be $30 million. If scent lures leave a small native male population, there is a 90% chance for success using sterile males; otherwise, there is only a 10% chance for success using sterile males. A failure results in no savings.

The juvenile hormone must be synthesized at a cost of $3 million. There is only a .20 probability that the resulting product will work. If it does, the worth of trees saved would be $50 million, because the gypsy moth would become extinct. If the hormone does not work, savings would be zero.

Should one of the esoteric eradication procedures be chosen and then fail, the official's contingency plan is to spray with DDT. The savings from successful implementation of the sterile male or juvenile hormone procedures reflect the value of environmental damage and other costs avoided by not having to use DDT.

To compare outcomes, the official proposes to use the net advantage (crop and environmental savings minus cost) relative to where she would be were she forced to spray with DDT.

Questions

1. Under the official's proposal, the selection of DDT without even trying the other procedures would lead to an outcome with zero payoff. Discuss the benefits of her proposed payoff measure.

2. Construct the official's decision tree diagram, using the proposed payoff measure.

3. What action will maximize the decision maker's expected payoff?

PROBLEMS

21-1 Willy B. Rich is deciding whether to spend his Christmas vacation skiing at a resort in Utah or surfing in Hawaii. He must commit himself to one of these alternatives in the early fall, since reservations have to be made months in advance. He really enjoys skiing more than surfing. Unfortunately, he cannot be certain about December snow conditions, and his ski trip will be ruined if there is poor snow. The trip to Hawaii would be a sure bet. But if he must go there when the snow is good elsewhere, his trip will be somewhat spoiled by regrets that he did not make arrangements to spend his vacation skiing.

(a) Construct Willy's decision table.

(b) Construct his decision tree diagram.

21-2 Peggy Jones, the founder of a computer programming services firm, wishes to expand the firm's activities into the manufacture of peripheral equipment. Funds must be raised to build and operate the necessary facilities. Three financing alternatives are available: (1) issue additional common stock, (2) sell bonds, and (3) issue nonvoting preferred stock. A common stock issue will provide a strong financial base for future expansion through borrowing, but it will considerably reduce Jones' percentage of ownership and control from its current 100%. New common stock will also divide future earnings into smaller amounts per share to existing shareholders. Bonds will allow existing shareholders to accrue all of the benefits of new earnings, but they will also increase the risk of forced liquidation if the new venture proves unsuccessful. Preferred stock will give its holders no claims on the firm's assets, but it will drastically reduce the rate of earnings participation on the part of existing common stockholders. Table 21-8 summarizes the forecast financial status of the firm if the manufacturing venture is successful.

For each of the following goals, suggest an appropriate payoff measure. Then, use this measure to identify the best and the worst alternative choices for financing in terms of the degree to which each *single* goal is met. Indicate any ties.

(a) Maintain a high percentage of control by Jones.

(b) Maximize the earnings of Jones' shares.

(c) Maximize the availability of short-term credit.

(d) Maximize the potential for cash dividends to Jones.

TABLE 21-8
Payoff Measures and Values for Problem 21-2

POSSIBLE PAYOFF MEASURE	FINANCING ALTERNATIVES		
	Additional Common Stock	Bonds	Preferred Stock
1. Earnings after taxes and preferred dividends	$5,000,000	$3,500,000	$4,000,000
2. Common shares outstanding	1,000,000	500,000	500,000
3. Earnings per common share	$5.00	$7.00	$8.00
4. Jones' percentage of common ownership	50	100	100
5. Emergency line of credit	$1,000,000	$400,000	$500,000
6. Earnings available for common dividends	$5,000,000	$2,000,000	$4,000,000
7. Maximum possible dividends per share of common stock	$5.00	$4.00	$8.00

21-3   Shirley Smart has final examinations in accounting and finance on Monday and only 10 hours of study time left. The following anticipated grades apply, depending on the exam format.

STUDY TIME (Hours)	MULTIPLE-CHOICE FORMAT		CASE FORMAT	
	Accounting	Finance	Accounting	Finance
0	C	B	B	C
5	C	B	A	B
10	B	A	A	A

Shirley plans to allocate her study time in one of the following ways.

PLAN	ACCOUNTING	FINANCE
1	0 hours	10 hours
2	5	5
3	10	0

Although a single exam format will apply for any course, Shirley is uncertain which one each professor will pick, so any combination of multiple-choice and case formats is possible.

Using her combined accounting and finance grade point average (GPA) as her payoff measure (A = 4 points, B = 3 points, C = 2 points), construct Shirley's payoff table.

21-4 The Aero Spad plant manager must choose a method for assembling parts. The size of the production run will depend on the number of units ordered, which is an uncertain quantity. The following quantities are believed to be equally likely: 4,000, 6,000, 8,000, and 10,000. The parts will be sold for $200 each, regardless of quantity ordered.

The following data apply to the three methods of production.

	METHOD A	METHOD B	METHOD C
Set-up cost	$200,000	$160,000	$100,000
Unit material cost	20	30	40
Unit labor cost	20	20	30

(a) Using total profit from the parts as the payoff measure, construct the manager's payoff table.

(b) Determine the expected payoff for each act. Which method will maximize expected profit?

21-5 Identify any inadmissible acts in the following payoff table.

	ACT				
EVENT	A_1	A_2	A_3	A_4	A_5
E_1	3	4	4	5	1
E_2	6	2	1	4	2
E_3	1	8	8	7	3

21-6 Consider the following payoff table for a graphical design decision.

TEXTURE EVENT	PROBABILITY	COLOR THEME ACT				
		Brown	Orange	Red	Green	Yellow
Full-tone	.2	100	110	50	120	90
Half-tone	.5	80	70	80	60	100
Mixed	.3	100	90	90	90	110

(a) Identify any inadmissible color choices.

(b) Compute the expected payoff for each admissible act. Which color theme should be chosen?

21-7 Refer to the payoffs for the Tippi-Toes decision in Table 21-6. Suppose that the development cost of the spring-action movement is $40,000 higher than before (regardless of demand) and that revenues generated by the doll when demand is heavy are $50,000 lower than before (regardless of movement chosen).

(a) Construct a new payoff table reflecting these revisions.

(b) Using the payoff table, compute the expected payoff for each act. Which movement should be chosen under the Bayes decision rule?

21-8 Recompute the expected payoffs for the Tippi-Toes decision in Table 21-5, assuming that the following demand event probabilities now apply.

Light demand	.20
Moderate demand	.50
Heavy demand	.30

According to the Bayes decision rule, which act should the toy manufacturer choose?

21-9 A new product is to be evaluated. The main decision to be made is whether or not to market the product, in which case it will be a success (probability = .40) or a failure. The net payoff for a successful product is $10 million; a failure would result in a −$5 million payoff. Construct a payoff for the decision, and then compute the expected payoffs. Should the product be marketed?

21-10 Suppose that the president of the Ponderosa Record Company uses the following probability values to analyze the decision about the Fluid Mechanics' recording.

$$\Pr[\text{national marketing success} \mid \text{favorable test marketing}] = .9$$

$$\Pr[\text{national marketing failure} \mid \text{unfavorable test marketing}] = .6$$

$$\Pr[\text{national marketing success}] = .7$$

$$\Pr[\text{favorable test marketing}] = .75$$

Repeat the Ponderosa decision tree analysis to determine the company's optimal marketing strategy. Assume that all payoffs remain unchanged.

21-11 The manager of Getting Oil's data processing operations personally interviews applicants for jobs as data-entry operators. Employees who are hired with no previous experience are placed in a one-month training program on a trial basis. Satisfactory employees are retained; all others are let go at the end of the month. Most of the people who have been let go in the past have been found to be lacking in aptitude. The manager is contemplating contracting the testing services of a personnel agency. For a fee the agency would administer a battery of aptitude tests. The manager has developed the decision tree in Figure 21-6 to help her make her hiring decisions. Perform backward induction analysis to determine the strategy or course of action that will maximize the manager's expected payoff.

21-12 Buzzy-B Toys must decide the course of action to follow in promoting a new whistling yo-yo. Initially, management must decide whether to market the yo-yo or to conduct a test marketing program. After test marketing the yo-yo, management must decide whether to abandon it or nationally distribute it.

A national success will increase profits by $500,000, and a failure will reduce profits by $100,000. Abandoning the product will not affect profits. The test marketing will cost Buzzy-B a further $10,000.

If no test marketing is conducted, the probability for a national success is judged to be .45. The assumed probability for a favorable test marketing result is .50. The conditional

FIGURE 21-6
Decision tree for Problem 21-11.

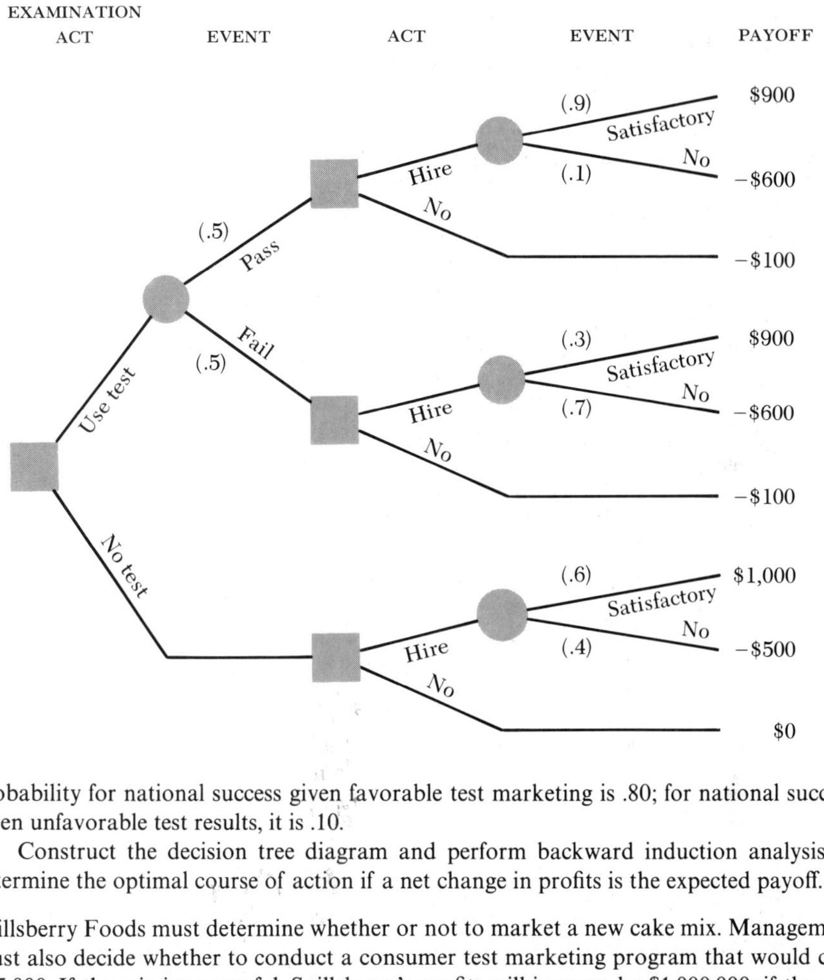

probability for national success given favorable test marketing is .80; for national success given unfavorable test results, it is .10.

Construct the decision tree diagram and perform backward induction analysis to determine the optimal course of action if a net change in profits is the expected payoff.

21-13 Spillsberry Foods must determine whether or not to market a new cake mix. Management must also decide whether to conduct a consumer test marketing program that would cost $25,000. If the mix is successful, Spillsberry's profits will increase by $1,000,000; if the mix fails, the company will lose $250,000. Not marketing the product will not affect profits. The cake mix is considered to have a 60% chance of success without testing. The assumed probability for a favorable test marketing result is 50%. Given a favorable test result, the chance of product success is judged to be 85%. However, if the test results are unfavorable, the probability for the product's success is judged to be only 35%.

Construct a decision tree diagram that may be used to determine the optimal course of action that will provide the greatest expected payoff. Include the choice of whether or not to use the test. Perform backward induction analysis to determine which course of action maximizes the expected payoff.

21-14 Fiber Synthetics' manager must decide whether to process a chemical order or to contract it out at a cost of $20,000. The final product batch will be sold for $40,000. In-house processing involves direct costs for raw materials of $4,000. The first step, costing $2,000, is chlorosulfanation, for which there is an 80% chance of getting a satisfactory intermediate chemical base. If the base is unsatisfactory, there will not be sufficient time to start a new batch, but there will still be a choice of turning down the order or contracting out the production. In the latter case, there is a 60% chance of being too late and having to dump the final product. The last stage of in-house processing may be a low-temperature one costing $10,000 or a high-temperature one costing $16,000. There is a 30% chance that the low-temperature process will fail, so that the resulting chemicals must be dumped; it would then be too late to go outside. The high-temperature procedure is certain to work.

(a) Using net cash flow (revenue minus costs) as the payoff measure, diagram the manager's decision tree.

(b) What action maximizes expected payoff?

21-15 Using the new product in Problem 21-9, the following two experiments have been proposed. (Both experiments cannot be used.)

> *Test market* at a cost of $1 million. Results will be "favorable" (probability = .48) or "unfavorable." Given a favorable result, the probability for product success is .75. Given an unfavorable result, the probability for product success is only .08.

> *Attitude survey* at a cost of $.5 million. Results will be "warm" (probability = .40) or "cold." Given a warm response, the probability for product success is .70. Given a cold response, the probability for success is only .20.

In addition to these choices, the main decision to market or not to market may be made without obtaining any further information.

Construct a decision tree diagram for this problem, indicating all of the probabilities and payoffs. Perform backward induction analysis to determine which course of action maximizes expected payoff. (Specify all choices that may then have to be made.)

21-16 *Computer exercise.* Enter the data for the Ponderosa Record Company decision into the computer. Then, determine the course of action that maximizes expected payoff for each of the following versions of the original problem. In each case, begin with the original data before making the required changes.

(a) Raise the cost of test marketing from $15,000 to $20,000

(b) Change the variable costs for records from $1.00 to $1.25

(c) Ponderosa is to receive $3 per record sold instead of $2

(d) Reduce the probability of national success given favorable test marketing from .8 to .75. Also, given unfavorable test marketing, reduce the probability of national failure from .8 to .75.

(e) Reduce the original tree to eliminate the abort choice after favorable test marketing and to remove the national marketing choice after unfavorable test results.

22

Decision Theory

$\mathbb{M}$odern analysis of decision making under uncertainty has its roots in the area of study called **statistical decision theory**. A primary focus of statistical decision theory is establishing systematic means for choosing an act, which is largely accomplished by using the payoff table introduced in Chapter 21. Various **decision-making criteria** may be employed in selecting the best act. The payoff measure itself is a key element in determining rules for decision making, and decision theory encompasses a variety of these measures.

We will begin our discussion of decision theory by examining some of the well-known criteria used in selecting a best act. Then, we will describe **opportunity loss**—a payoff measure that enables us to assess the worth of the *information* that is obtained about uncertain events. Indeed, we use the adjective *statistical* because sampling is a rich source of such information.

For various reasons, we will also see that the Bayes decision rule, which helps the decision maker select the act with the maximum expected payoff, is the favored criterion. The theoretical concepts of decision making largely expand on this rule, since this criterion makes use of all the information at the disposal of the decision maker. When the proper payoff measure is used, the Bayes decision rule always leads to the most desirable choice. The device that makes this possible is the **utility payoff**, which measures a decision maker's preference. **Utility theory** is a special field within the broader context of decision theory.

Although utility payoffs allow decision makers to make consistently optimal choices in the face of *risk*, they rest on a body of behavioral assumptions about which there is some disagreement. However, identical decisions may often be reached by another procedure described in this chapter which finds for each course of action a **certainty equivalent**. These quantities may be obtained by discounting the expected monetary payoff by a **risk premium**.

This chapter surveys decision theory. In later chapters, we will consider more specialized topics. Chapter 23 examines how experimental information may be systematically incorporated into decision making. Chapters 24 and 25 are more statistical in nature; there, specific probability distribution structures are melded with decision-making concepts. Chapter 26 describes utility theory and outlines the practical details of obtaining and using utility values. This topical grouping concludes in Chapter 27 with a discussion of **game theory**, where two or more persons independently determine outcomes, which helps to explain interactive decision making.

22-1 Decision Criteria

The Maximin Payoff Criterion

No decision-making theory is complete until the decision maker has considered the various rules that may be used in selecting the most desirable act. We will begin with the simplest criterion, the **maximin payoff criterion**—a procedure that guarantees that the decision maker can do no worse than achieve the best of the poorest outcomes possible. As an illustration, we will use the payoff table given in Table 22-1, which presents the toy manufacturer's choices of movement for the Tippi-Toes doll.

Suppose that our toy manufacturer wishes to choose an act that will ensure a favorable outcome no matter what happens. This may be accomplished by taking a pessimistic viewpoint—that is, by determining the *worst* outcome for each act, regardless of the event. For the gears-and-levers movement, the lowest possible payoff is $25,000 when light demand occurs. The lowest payoff for the spring-action movement is a negative amount, −$10,000, also obtained when demand is light. For the weights-and-pulleys movement, the lowest payoff is −$125,000, again when demand is light. By choosing the act that yields the largest lowest payoff, our decision maker can guarantee a minimum return that is the best of the poorest outcomes possible. In this case, a gears-and-levers movement for the doll will guarantee the toy manufacturer a payoff of at least $25,000.

The gears-and-levers movement is the act with the maximum of the minimum payoffs. A more concise statement would be to say that gears and levers is the **maximin payoff act**. To show how the maximin payoff can be determined in general, we reconstruct the payoff table for the Tippi-Toes decision in Table 22-2.

TABLE 22-1
Payoff Table for the Tippi-Toes Decision

EVENT (level of demand)	ACT (choice of movement)		
	Gears and Levers	*Spring Action*	*Weights and Pulleys*
Light	$ 25,000	−$ 10,000	−$125,000
Moderate	400,000	440,000	400,000
Heavy	650,000	740,000	750,000

TABLE 22-2

Determining the Maximin Payoff Act for the Tippi-Toes Decision

EVENT (level of demand)	ACT (choice of movement)		
	Gears and Levers	Spring Action	Weights and Pulleys
Light	$ 25,000	−$ 10,000	−$125,000
Moderate	400,000	440,000	400,000
Heavy	650,000	740,000	750,000
Column minimums	$ 25,000	−$ 10,000	−$125,000

Maximum of column minimums = $25,000

Maximin payoff act = Gears and levers

In most decision-making illustrations so far, we have used profit as the measure of payoff. As we noted in Chapter 21, a variety of measures may be used to rank outcomes. In business applications, *cost* is often used for this purpose when the goal is to minimize operational cost and when revenues are not subject to chance. We apply the maximin payoff criterion to a situation involving costs by reversing our rule and selecting the act with the minimum of the maximum costs. The comparable terminology for this rule would be *minimax cost*. This criterion is identical to the maximin profit in the sense that cost may be viewed as negative profit, so that what is minimized and maximized must be reversed. Either criterion leads to choosing the best of the poorest outcomes. To avoid confusion, we will always use maximin and minimax as adjectives connected to a noun such as profit or cost.

The suitability of the maximin payoff criterion depends on the nature of the decision to be made. Consider the decision problem in Table 22-3. In this situation, the maximin decision maker chooses A_1 over A_2. A_2 may be a better choice if the probability of E_2 is high enough, but the maximin decision maker is giving up an opportunity to gain $10,000 in order to avoid a possible loss of $1. To avoid losing $1, the decision maker chooses an act that will guarantee the maintenance of the status quo. We may, however, envision

TABLE 22-3

Determining the Maximin Payoff Act for Hypothetical Decision A

EVENT	ACT	
	A_1	A_2
E_1	$0	−$1
E_2	1	10,000
Column minimum	$0	−$1

Maximum of column minimums = $0

Maximin payoff act = A_1

TABLE 22-4

Payoff Table for Hypothetical Decision *B*

	ACT	
EVENT	B_1	B_2
E_1	$1	$10,000
E_2	−1	−10,000

circumstances in which A_1 *would* be the better choice. If our decision maker had only $1 and had to use it to pay a debt to a loan shark or lose his life, the payoffs would not realistically represent the true values that the decision maker assigned to them.

Consider the situation represented by the payoffs given in Table 22-4. Here, the maximin payoff act is B_1. This would be the better choice for a decision maker who could not tolerate a loss of $10,000, no matter how unlikely it was. Few people would risk losing their businesses by choosing an act that could lead to bankruptcy unless the odds were extremely small. But an individual who could survive a loss of $10,000 would find B_2 a superior choice if the probability of E_2 were substantially lower than E_1.

Our examples illustrate a key deficiency of the maximin payoff: It is an extremely conservative decision criterion and may lead to some very bad decisions. Any alternative with a slightly larger risk is rejected in favor of a comparatively risk-free alternative, which may be far less attractive. Taken to a ludicrous extreme, a maximin payoff policy would force any firm out of business. No inventories would be stocked, because there would always be a possibility of unsold items. No new products would be introduced, because management could never be certain of their success. No credit would be granted, because there would always be some customer who would not pay.

Another major deficiency of the maximin payoff criterion exists if the probabilities of the various events are known. The maximin payoff is primarily suited to decision problems with unknown probabilities that cannot be reasonably assessed. As our illustrations indicate, it is usually in the extreme cases—the person hounded by loan sharks or the business that could go bankrupt—that the maximin payoff criterion leads to the best decision.

The Maximum Likelihood Criterion

Another rule that serves as a model for decision-making behavior is the **maximum likelihood criterion**, which focuses on the most likely event, to the exclusion of all others. Table 22-5 illustrates this criterion for the Tippi-Toes toy manufacturer's decision.

For this decision, we see that the highest probability is .70 for a moderate demand. The maximum likelihood criterion tells us to ignore the light and heavy demand events completely—in effect, to assume that they will not occur. This rule then tells us to choose the best act assuming that a moderate demand will occur. In this example, the **maximum likelihood act** is to use the spring-action doll movement, which provides the greatest profit of $440,000 for a moderate demand.

TABLE 22-5
Determining the Maximum Likelihood Act for the Tippi-Toes Decision

EVENT (level of demand)	PROBABILITY	ACT (choice of movement)		
		Gears and Levers	Spring Action	Weights and Pulleys
Light	.10	$ 25,000	−$ 10,000	−$125,000
Moderate	.70	400,000	440,000	400,000
Heavy	.20	650,000	740,000	750,000

Most likely event = Moderate demand
Maximum row payoff = $440,000
Maximum likelihood act = Spring action

How suitable is the maximum likelihood criterion for decision making? Using it in this example does not permit us to consider the range of outcomes for the spring-action movement, from a $10,000 loss if a light demand occurs to a $740,000 profit if demand is heavy. We also ignore most of the other possible outcomes, including the best (selecting weights and pulleys when demand is heavy, which yields a $750,000 profit) and the worst (selecting weights and pulleys when demand is light, which leads to a $125,000 loss). In a sense, the maximum likelihood criterion would have us "play ostrich," ignoring much that might happen. Then why is it discussed here?

We describe this criterion primarily because it seems to be so prevalent in the decision-making behavior of individuals and businesses. It may also be used to explain certain anomalies that would otherwise be hard to rationalize. These quirks are epitomized by the so-called "hog cycle" in the raising and marketing of pigs, which is related to the more or less predictable two-year-long pork price movement from higher to lower levels and back to higher levels again. Hog farmers have been blamed for this, since they expand their herds when prices are high, so that one year later the supply of mature hogs is excessive and prices are driven downward; then when prices are low, these same farmers reduce their herds, cutting the supply of marketable hogs, and next year's prices consequently rise.

Why don't the farmers break this cycle? It doesn't seem rational to be consistently wrong in timing hog production. One explanation is that the hog farmers use the maximum likelihood criterion. In their minds, the most likely future market price is the current one—and we know that this has proved to be a very poor judgment. Given such a premise, the maximum likelihood act is to increase herd sizes when current prices are high and to decrease them when prices are low.

The Criterion of Insufficient Reason

Another criterion employed in decision-making problems is the **criterion of insufficient reason**. This criterion may be used when a decision maker has no information about the event probabilities. In this case, no event may be regarded as more likely than any other event, and all events are assigned equal probability values. Since the events are collectively exhaustive and mutually exclusive, the probability of each event must be

$$\frac{1}{\text{Number of events}}$$

Using these event probabilities, the act with the maximum expected payoff is chosen.

A major criticism of the criterion of insufficient reason is that, except in a few situations, some knowledge of the relative chances that events will occur is always available. When more realistic probabilities may be obtained, employing the Bayes decision rule will provide more valid results.

The Preferred Criterion: The Bayes Decision Rule

The three decision-making criteria just discussed have obvious inadequacies. *None of them incorporates all of the information available to the decision maker.* Maximin payoff totally ignores event probabilities. Although it is argued that this is a strength when probabilities cannot be easily determined, judgment may be used to arrive at acceptable probability values in all but a few circumstances.

The maximum likelihood criterion ignores all events but the most likely one, even if that event happens to be a lot less likely than the rest combined. (Out of 20 events, for instance, the most likely event may have a probability of .10, leaving a .90 probability that one of the other 19 events will occur.)

The criterion of insufficient reason essentially asks us to ignore judgments and "willy nilly" assume that all events are equally likely. According to this criterion, even such events as "war" and "peace," and "prosperity" and "depression," have equal probabilities.

The *Bayes decision rule* has become the central focus of statistical decision theory. This makes the greatest use of all available information and is the only criterion that allows us to extend decision theory to incorporate sampling or experimental information. The major deficiency of the Bayes decision rule occurs when alternatives involve different magnitudes of risk. To illustrate this point, we will consider the decision structure in Table 22-6. Acts C_1 and C_2 are equally attractive according to the maximum expected payoff criterion (Bayes decision rule). Yet most decision makers would clearly prefer C_2, because it avoids the rather large risk of a $1,000,000 loss.

TABLE 22-6
Payoff Table for Hypothetical Decision C

EVENT	PROBABILITY	ACT C_1		ACT C_2	
		Payoff	Payoff × Probability	Payoff	Payoff × Probability
E_1	.5	−$1,000,000	−$ 500,000	$250,000	$125,000
E_2	.5	2,000,000	1,000,000	750,000	375,000
	Expected payoff		$ 500,000		$500,000

The paradox here may be resolved not by choosing another criterion, but by reconsidering the values chosen for the payoffs. The theory of utility presented in Chapter 26 will allow us to establish payoffs at values that express their true worth to the decision maker.

22-2 The Bayes Decision Rule as the Favored Criterion

Decision theory is useful because it shows how we might uncover that course of action which is truly preferred by the decision maker. There is no fail-safe system for achieving this goal. All decision criteria have imperfections.

Of the several criteria presented in this chapter, the **Bayes decision rule**—select that act having maximum expected payoff—appears to be most suitable. One advantage is that it makes use of more information than the others. As we have seen, a criterion based on expected values uses all the available probability data and assigns the proper weight to every outcome. The other decision-making criteria employ fewer structural elements from the decision. Expected values also provide us with a gauge for evaluating additional sources of information that may be used in decision making.

Consistently applied to routine day-to-day decisions, each of which involves little risk, the Bayes decision rule should lead to the best overall results. For example, envision a buyer for the magazine department in a high-volume bookstore. If the buyer always selects that order quantity for each magazine that maximizes its expected profit, then over the long haul the buyer will tend to experience higher average profits from the dozens of titles than what would be achievable using any other set of choices. (This conclusion may be reached only by assuming that demand probabilities used are correct values. There is no way to guarantee that, although in Chapter 4 we saw how the best available expertise may be employed to find workable probability values.)

Maximizing expected payoff has wide acceptance because it so often picks the course of action preferred by the decision maker. But this is not always the case. When applied to *monetary* payoffs, the Bayes decision rule often leads to a less preferred choice.

Perhaps the best example of this occurs in casualty insurance decisions, where the choices are to buy or not to buy a policy. Most drivers have liability insurance for their cars, and most carry greater coverage than the legal minimum. We know that the policyholder's annual insurance costs exceed the expected loss from an accident. (This is because insurance companies must charge more than what they expect to pay in claims just to meet overhead costs and expenses.) But according to the Bayes decision rule, the best decision would be not to insure, because no insurance would have a greater expected monetary payoff (that is, the expected cost of no insurance is less than the cost of insurance). This course of action contradicts the true preference of most people.

Similar breakdowns of the Bayes decision rule occur whenever a person prefers a less risky alternative to one that involves considerable risk but actually has a greater expected monetary payoff. Since other decision-making criteria have serious defects, too, how should we objectively analyze decisions that involve great risk?

Fortunately, *decision theory accounts for attitudes toward risk by permitting an adjustment in the payoff values themselves.* This is accomplished by establishing a true-worth index called a *utility value* for every outcome. Thus, a decision may be analyzed using utilities instead of dollars or some other standard payoff measure.

In Chapter 26, we will describe the theory of utility and its application in great detail. One very important principle will be established there: *When the Bayes decision rule is applied to a decision-making problem with utility payoffs, it always indicates the most preferred course of action.* This makes that rule the theoretically perfect criterion for decision making, no matter how complex the decision happens to be.

22-3 Decision Making Using Certainty Equivalents

The key issue in evaluating any decision under uncertainty is finding a summary number that clearly indicates for each choice its worth to the decision maker. A little introspection may be all that is required.

Suppose, for example, that you find a lottery ticket selected for a special drawing with a grand prize of $10,000. You may sell your ticket to a broker for cash now or you may wait for tomorrow's drawing; your chance of winning the prize has been judged to be only 1%, and you will get nothing if you lose. Think hard about your answer to this question: What is the minimum amount of money you would take now from the broker for your ticket? Write this amount on a piece of paper.

Of course, there is no "right" answer, since the amount depends upon your attitudes, needs, and preferences. Many people would sell for about $100, although some would want more and a few would settle for less. Your minimum selling price is your **certainty equivalent** for the act of keeping the lottery ticket. Once you have this number, it should be easy to decide what to do with the lottery ticket.

Suppose that the broker offers $75. Your choice would be easy. If your minimum selling price is greater than $75, you should keep the ticket and wait for the drawing; if your minimum selling price is smaller than $75, you should sell; and if your selected amount is exactly $75, you should be indifferent between selling and keeping the ticket.

This example illustrates how good decision making involves a fundamental valuation of uncertainties. In generalizing this concept, we will make the following definition.

> DEFINITION: The **certainty equivalent** is that payoff amount that the decision maker would be willing to receive in exchange for undergoing the actual uncertainty, with its rewards and risks.

A certainty equivalent may be positive or negative. For example, imagine a decision regarding whether or not to insure your luggage against total loss while you make a long airplane trip. You may be willing to pay $5 for complete protection; your certainty equivalent for the act *not* to insure would then be −$5. If such insurance could be bought for $2, you would get it; were the premium $10, you would forgo it.

The certainty equivalent is a personal valuation, and need not be tied to an actual exchange. There may be no broker willing to buy your lottery ticket at any price, and there may be no luggage insurance available. Nevertheless, your certainty equivalents still exist; they reflect the certain amount you would be willing to exchange, were such an opportunity to be made available.

Decision Rule: Choose the Greatest Certainty Equivalent

The hypothetical lottery ticket illustrates how we may evaluate a decision using certainty equivalents. Applied to a single-stage decision, with a structure summarized by a payoff table, the first step would be to find a certainty equivalent for each act (column). The optimal choice would be to select that act having the greatest certainty equivalent.

As we have seen, some decisions require a more complex structural representation. These are best represented by a decision tree diagram. To find the best course of action in such decisions, the tree must be pruned at each decision point. This may be accomplished by finding a certainty equivalent for each act in the fork, pruning all branches but the one leading to the greatest certainty equivalent.

The justification for such an approach is compelling. By selecting that act having the greatest certainty equivalent, you are simply picking the biggest certain amount available. This cannot be the wrong thing to do (in the sense of doing what you most prefer). Of course, decision makers will want to establish their certainty equivalents in a *consistent* manner. That is the hard part.

Finding the Certainty Equivalent

You were able to pull "from thin air" your certainty equivalent for keeping the lottery ticket. This may be considerably harder for you to do in deciding what amount you would accept in lieu of the right (or obligation) to participate in a different kind of gamble, one involving the same upside potential ($+\$10,000$, if you win) but with a downside ($-\$1,000$, if you lose). Your certainty equivalent should depend on the probabilities for winning or losing. At a 10% chance of winning, you would value the gamble differently than if the odds were more favorable.

The less clear-cut uncertainties involve a mixture of positive and negative payoffs and probabilities that may be hard to relate to. As we have seen, the expected payoff calculation integrates all available information in a neat package. For uncertain situations with a limited range of payoffs, many people will assign a certainty equivalent which turns out to be close to the expected payoff.

To see how this works, consider the following gambles. The payoff amounts represent your net monetary change, and the lottery probabilities are given in parentheses.

LOTTERY A		LOTTERY B		COIN GAMBLE C		CARD DRAWING D	
Win	$+\$10$ (80%)	Win	$+\$100$ (60%)	Head	$+\$100$	Face	$+\$100$
Lose	$-\$10$ (20%)	Lose	$-\$50$ (40%)	Tail	$-\$100$	Other	$\$0$

Write on a piece of paper your certainty equivalents for each gamble. Then, compute the respective expected payoffs.*

---

* These are $6 for *A*, $40 for *B*, $0 for *C*, and $23.08 for *D*.

How do the two sets of amounts compare? You may want to revise some of your certainty equivalents. (Changing your mind is permissible in any evaluation involving these subjective values.)

Discrepancies between certainty equivalents and expected payoffs will ordinarily be substantial when the payoffs are large in magnitude or have great extremes. (To see this, just add a couple of zeroes to the payoffs in the above gambles, so that the outcomes involve thousands of dollars, and rethink your certainty equivalents.)

Experiments show that it is much easier for a person to arrive at a certainty equivalent for an act by first computing its expected payoff. That amount may then be adjusted up or down until the subject feels comfortable that the resulting figure is a satisfactory certainty equivalent. These experiments show that the most pronounced adjustments arise when there is a mixture of high-valued positive and negative payoffs, with the certainty equivalent for such risky acts ordinarily being smaller than the expected payoff.

This should be no surprise. Consider the amount you are paying for collision and comprehensive insurance for your car. If you have a fairly new car, you undoubtedly have such coverage. Now consider what you may expect to collect in claims against your policy. Whatever that amount is, your insurance company has already figured it out and has priced your insurance accordingly. They must be charging more than they expect to pay in claims, perhaps double or more. (Otherwise, how could they meet operating expenses and earn a profit?) And yet, you still buy that "overpriced" coverage and may continue to buy it even if your rates were suddenly increased. The maximum premium you would be *willing to pay* is your certainty equivalent for that car risk.

Lots of people have no collision or comprehensive coverage. But they drive old cars, and have little to lose if their car is stolen and totaled by a wild teenager. But even they would buy insurance if it were cheap enough.

The Risk Premium

The difference between the expected payoff and the certainty equivalent for any act is the **risk premium** for that act. For example, consider again the lost luggage risk discussed earlier. Suppose that it would cost you $300 to replace your baggage and contents, and that there is a 1% chance that you would lose everything. (For simplicity, we will ignore partial losses.) Your expected payoff from having no insurance would be

$$\text{Expected payoff} = (-\$300)(.01) + (\$0)(.99) = -\$3$$

Suppose that your certainty equivalent is $-$5$. (That is, the maximum you would be willing to pay for complete replacement insurance is $5.)

Your risk premium for the act of not insuring is computed as follows.

$$\text{Risk premium} = \text{Expected payoff} - \text{Certainty equivalent}$$

$$= -\$3 - (-\$5) = \$2$$

The $2 risk premium represents the amount you are willing to pay for insurance beyond what your expected loss would be. Generally, the more serious the risk, the greater would be the risk premium.

To further illustrate this concept, suppose you win as a door prize the privilege of engaging in a special lottery. If you participate, a fair coin will be tossed. Should a head appear, you will receive $1,000; if a tail is obtained, you must forfeit $500. (An easy-payment loan will be arranged if you do not have the $500.) One of your friends wants to buy the right to gamble. What would be your asking price (certainty equivalent for gambling)?

The expected payoff from gambling is

$$\text{Expected payoff} = (\$1,000)(.5) + (-\$500)(.50) = \$250$$

Shirley Smart said she would sell for $100, so that for her,

$$\text{Certainty equivalent} = \$100$$

and

$$\text{Risk premium} = \$250 - 100 = \$150 \quad \text{(Shirley Smart)}$$

This indicates that Shirley is considerably risk averse, willing to accept $150 less than her expected payoff to avoid the risk of gambling.

Willy B. Rich said he would take $200 for his rights. For him,

$$\text{Certainty equivalent} = \$200$$

and

$$\text{Risk premium} = \$250 - 200 = \$50 \quad \text{(Willy B. Rich)}$$

Willy has a higher certainty equivalent than Shirley does, and his risk premium is therefore smaller. He is less risk averse than she is.

As a positive quantity, the risk premium may be interpreted as the amount by which the subject would discount the expected payoff in arriving at his or her certainty equivalent. Sometimes a risk premium will turn out negative, which would be the case when a person is so attracted to the highest positive payoff that his certainty equivalent for the gamble exceeds the expected payoff. (The absolute value of a negative risk premium is the individual's "aspiration incentive"—that amount in excess of the expected payoff that must be received in exchange for the gamble.) Negative risk premiums are less common than positive values, and they are not ordinarily encountered in business decision making.

Discounting Expected Values by the Risk Premiums

For business decision making the direct approach is a clumsy way to arrive at certainty equivalents. A more workable alternative is to first compute, for each act, the expected value. The certainty equivalent for any act may be viewed as that act's *discounted* expected payoff, so that the certainty equivalent may be found by subtracting the appropriate risk premium from the expected payoff.

$$\text{Certainty equivalent} = \text{Expected payoff} - \text{Risk premium}$$

What makes this approach practical is that risk premiums are easily found. Since a single amount would be appropriate for a wide class of risks, a table of risk premiums may be established ahead of time. These may be applied as required to evaluate a series of decisions. The risk premium table may be periodically updated as circumstances change.

The selection of any act having uncertain payoff and possible loss involves risk. The seriousness of the risk may be gauged by two components: (1) the amount of loss (downside potential) and (2) the probability of loss. Experiments with people show that these two components are the primary determinants of the risk premium used in discounting expected payoff.

The entire adjustment is motivated by the loss and its likelihood. Subjects experiencing two gambles with the same downside will tend to have nearly the same risk premiums for both. For example, consider the following.

COIN TOSS A		COIN TOSS B	
Head	$0	Head	+$1,000
Tail	−$500	Tail	−$500

One subject arrived at a risk premium of $100 each for gambles A and B, even though his certainty equivalents (discounted expected payoffs) of course differed.

	A	B
Expected payoff	−$250	+$250
Less risk premium	100	100
Certainty equivalent	−$350	+$150

Raising the loss probability in any gamble would increase the risk and should therefore result in a higher risk premium. Similarly, a greater downside potential, reflected in a more extreme negative payoff amount, would increase the risk and, thus, the risk premium.

Not all uncertain situations involve risk. Risk is not present unless there is a downside and some probability of ending there. For example, a coin toss where "heads you win $100" and "tails you only win $50" has no risk. For most persons, the risk premium would be zero for such an ideal gamble. They would not discount the expected payoff at all, so that it would equal their certainty equivalent.

ILLUSTRATION
Ponderosa Record Company

The Ponderosa Record Company decision in Chapter 21 illustrates how certainty equivalents, obtained by discounting expected payoffs, may be used in evaluating decisions. A consultant begins this process by obtaining a few risk premiums. These are found by interviewing the president, having him provide assessments for a few relevant risks.

Recording Equipment   Ponderosa's recording equipment has a replacement value of $100,000. The president is asked what he would be willing to pay Lloyd's of London for full coverage against total loss of equipment due to flood, fire, or other natural disaster. To simplify this assessment, it is assumed that there is a 1% chance of such an occurrence in any given year. Because such a loss could wipe the company out, the president indicates a willingness to pay up to $2,500 for such a policy. The consultant then computes the expected payoff from not having such insurance as

$$\text{Expected payoff} = (\$0)(.99) + (-\$100,000)(.01) = -\$1,000$$

The certainty equivalent is $-\$2,500$, and the difference between these amounts provides the

$$\text{Risk premium} = -\$1,000 - (-\$2,500) = \$1,500 \quad \text{(equipment)}$$

Earthquake Damage   The decision maker owns a home valued at $200,000 that is fully insured against fire and flood, but not earthquake. The consultant brings up the idea of earthquake damage. He presents a scenario where a high-energy earthquake may cause such severe damage to his home and the neighborhood that its market value would be lost. The president is informed of one geologist who reported that an earthquake of that magnitude may be expected in his region once every thousand or so years. After some introspection, the president reluctantly agreed that he would feel comfortable with earthquake insurance and would pay up to $500 for full coverage. His certainty equivalent for that risk is $-\$500$. Using a probability of .001 for total loss of his home value, the following

$$\text{Expected payoff} = \$0(.999) + (-\$200,000)(.001) = -\$200$$

would apply to not having insurance for the year. The difference in the two amounts gives for this risk the president's

$$\text{Risk premium} = -\$200 - (-\$500) = \$300 \quad \text{(earthquake)}$$

Real Estate Partnership   The president confesses to the consultant the details of a regretted investment involving $50,000 placed in a real estate limited partnership. The partnership has spent its entire capital on an option to buy for resale a piece of land. If the city council approves the buyer's building permit application, the partnership will receive enough proceeds to return the president a profit of $100,000. If the permit is refused, the option will be worthless and the entire investment will be lost. Both of the above monetary amounts are after-tax figures. There has been much anti-growth agitation lately, and there is only a 50–50 chance that the permit will be approved. (These odds are far worse than those which applied when he joined the partnership.)

The consultant suggests that another partner may offer to buy the president's partnership share now for the original stake plus a negotiated amount. The president decides that he would take no less than his investment plus an after-tax equivalent of $15,000, which becomes his certainty equivalent for staying in the partnership. That act has an expected payoff of

$$(-\$50,000)(.50) + (\$100,000)(.50) = \$25,000$$

and the difference provides his

$$\text{Risk premium} = \$25,000 - 15,000 = \$10,000 \quad (\text{partnership})$$

Table of Risk Premiums   The amounts obtained above are highlighted in Table 22-7, which shows the risk premiums for a variety of losses and probabilities of loss. Since the seriousness of a risk increases as the loss magnitude rises, the risk premiums get larger as you move down each column. Likewise, the risk is higher as the probability for loss increases, so that in each row the risk premiums become progressively larger as you move from left to right.

Only the three "hard" numbers, highlighted in Table 22-7, were directly obtained from the subject. The remaining risk premiums are extrapolations that seem to fit into the president's risk premium "profile." After examining a rough draft of Table 22-7, the president changed only a few values from the consultant's original figures.

Decision Tree Analysis

The consultant reevaluated Ponderosa's decision tree, using certainty equivalents as the basis for selecting acts. Figure 22-1 shows the decision tree diagram. The backward induction begins at nodes f, g, and h. First the expected payoffs (EP) are computed. Then, from Table 22-7 the respective risk premiums (RP) are read. For node f the loss value is $55,000 (corresponding to the negative payoff amount); this figure is closest to $50,000 in the table, and the entry in that row under the .20 probability column gives $RP = \$4,000$. Thus, at f the certainty equivalent is

$$CE = EP - RP = \$17,000 - 4,000 = \$13,000 \quad (\text{node } f)$$

The event fork at node g represents a huge risk, with the closest tabled risk premium occurring in the $50,000 loss row and the .75 probability column, $RP = \$15,000$. For that

TABLE 22-7
Risk Premiums for the President of Ponderosa Record Company

NEAREST POSSIBLE LOSS	NEAREST PROBABILITY OF LOSS					
	.001	.01	.1	.20	.50	.75
$ 5,000	0	0	0	100	200	400
20,000	0	500	800	1,500	3,000	5,000
50,000	0	1,000	2,000	4,000	10,000	15,000
100,000	100	1,500	4,000	8,000	17,000	20,000
200,000	300	4,000	9,000	15,000	30,000	35,000

FIGURE 22-1

The Ponderosa decision tree diagram showing backward induction with
certainty equivalents computed by discounting expected payoffs.

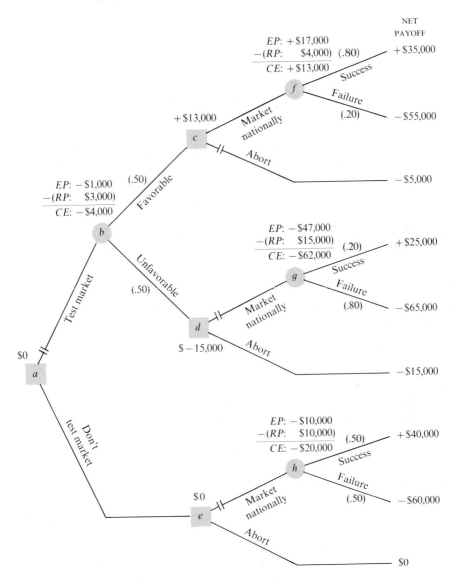

node, the certainty equivalent is

$$CE = -\$47,000 - 15,000 = -\$62,000 \quad (\text{node } g)$$

The event fork at node h represents a risk with an intensity lying between those of the
above two nodes; from the $50,000 loss row and the .50 probability column we find

$RP = \$10,000$. The certainty equivalent is

$$CE = -\$10,000 - 10,000 = -\$20,000 \quad \text{(node } h\text{)}$$

The act fork at c leads to f ($CE = \$13,000$) if Ponderosa Records markets nationally and leads to a certain payoff of $-\$5,000$ if the recording is aborted. The latter branch is pruned, and the greater amount is brought back to node c. At that point, marketing nationally has a certainty equivalent to the president of $13,000, and this figure is the best available valuation for that node. The tree is similarly pruned at node d, where abort is chosen for a certain payoff of $-\$15,000$ and at node e, where abort is also chosen for a certain payoff of \$0.

The valuation at node b requires first an expected value calculation, followed by a risk premium adjustment. In evaluating any event fork, *the evaluation is confined to the fork.*

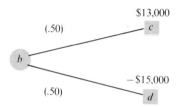

The values brought back are used to compute the expected payoff.

$$EP = \$13,000(.50) + (-\$15,000)(.50) = -\$1,000$$

In finding the risk premium from Table 22-7, the downside amount is \$15,000 (not \$65,000, which lies beyond the current fork). The nearest tabled loss is \$20,000, and the corresponding risk premium lies in that row in the .50 probability column, $RP = \$3,000$. Thus, the certainty equivalent at node b is

$$CE = -\$1,000 - 3,000 = -\$4,000 \quad \text{(node } b\text{)}$$

This amount, resulting from test marketing the recording, is worse than the \$0 at node e from not testing and then aborting. The president should choose the latter.

This result differs from the conclusion reached in Chapter 21, where an evaluation based on undiscounted expected payoffs leads to the choice to test market, followed by a choice to market nationally only if that proves favorable. Although messier, the above analysis should indicate the action most preferred (which is the best that any decision analysis can possibly do).

22-4 Opportunity Loss and the Expected Value of Perfect Information

Is it worthwhile to buy information that may help us choose the best act? Information is usually not free. Resources, for example, are required to take a sample or to administer a test. In this section, we will attempt to place a value on such information. To do this, we will introduce the concept of opportunity loss.

Opportunity Loss

Suppose that we view each possible outcome in terms of a measure that expresses the difference between the payoff for the chosen act and the best payoff that could have been achieved. This measure, referred to as an **opportunity loss**, is defined as the amount of payoff that is forgone by not selecting the act that has the greatest payoff for the event that actually occurs.

Table 22-8 shows how the opportunity losses are obtained for the payoffs for the toy manufacturer's decision. To calculate the opportunity losses, the maximum payoff for each row is determined. Each payoff is then subtracted from its respective row maximum.

The **opportunity loss table** for the Tippi-Toes decision appears in Table 22-9. All opportunity loss values are non-negative, since they measure how much worse off the decision maker is made by choosing some act other than the best act for the event that occurs. Let us consider the meaning of the opportunity loss values. For example, suppose that the gears-and-levers movement is chosen and that a light demand occurs. The opportunity loss is zero, because we see from Table 22-8 that no better payoff than $25,000 (the row maximum) could have been achieved if another act had been chosen. But if the gears-and-levers movement is chosen and a heavy demand occurs, the opportunity loss is $100,000, because the weights-and-pulleys movement has the greatest payoff for a heavy demand ($750,000). Since the gears-and-levers movement has a payoff of only $650,000, the payoff difference $750,000 − $650,000 = $100,000 represents the additional payoff forgone by not selecting the act with the greatest payoff. It should be emphasized that the $100,000 opportunity loss is not a loss in the accounting sense because a net positive contribution of $650,000 to profits is obtained. Instead, the opportunity to achieve an additional $100,000 has been missed. We might say that should demand prove to be heavy, the decision maker would have $100,000 worth of *regret* by not choosing weights and pulleys instead of gears and levers.

TABLE 22-8
Determining the Opportunity Losses for the Tippi-Toes Decision

EVENT (level of demand)	PAYOFF			ROW MAXIMUM
	Gears and Levers	Spring Action	Weights and Pulleys	
Light	$ 25,000	−$ 10,000	−$125,000	$ 25,000
Moderate	400,000	440,000	400,000	440,000
Heavy	650,000	740,000	750,000	750,000
	Row maximum − Payoff = Opportunity loss (thousands of dollars)			
Light	25 − 25 = 0	25 − (− 10) = 35	25 − (− 125) = 150	
Moderate	440 − 400 = 40	440 − 440 = 0	440 − 400 = 40	
Heavy	750 − 650 = 100	750 − 740 = 10	750 − 750 = 0	

TABLE 22-9
Opportunity Loss Table for the Tippi-Toes Decision

EVENT (level of demand)	ACT (choice of movement)		
	Gears and Levers	Spring Action	Weights and Pulleys
Light	$ 0	$35,000	$150,000
Moderate	40,000	0	40,000
Heavy	100,000	10,000	0

The Bayes Decision Rule and Opportunity Loss

We calculate the expected opportunity loss for each act and then select the act that has the minimum loss. This is done in Table 22-10 for the Tippi-Toes decision. The minimum expected opportunity loss is $5,500 for the spring-action movement, which is the **minimum expected opportunity loss act** in this example.

In Chapter 21, we saw that the spring-action movement was also the maximum expected payoff act and was therefore the best choice according to the Bayes decision rule. Our new criterion leads us to the same choice. It can be mathematically established that this will always be so. Since either criterion will always lead to the same choice, we can say that the *Bayes decision rule is to select the act that has the maximum expected payoff or the minimum expected opportunity loss.*

The Expected Value of Perfect Information

Up to this point, our toy manufacturer has selected an act without the benefit of any information except that acquired through experience with other toys. But it is possible to secure better information about next season's demand by test marketing, by taking opinion and attitude surveys, or by obtaining inside information concerning competitors' plans. How much should the decision maker be willing to pay for additional information?

TABLE 22-10
Calculation of Expected Opportunity Losses for the Tippi-Toes Decision

EVENT (level of demand)	PROBABILITY	ACT (choice of movement)					
		Gears and Levers		Spring Action		Weights and Pulleys	
		Loss	Loss × Probability	Loss	Loss × Probability	Loss	Loss × Probability
Light	.10	$ 0	$ 0	$35,000	$3,500	$150,000	$15,000
Moderate	.70	40,000	28,000	0	0	40,000	28,000
Heavy	.20	100,000	20,000	10,000	2,000	0	0
Expected opportunity loss			$48,000		$5,500		$43,000

It is helpful to know the payoff that may be expected from securing improved information about the events. We will consider the extreme case when the decision maker may acquire **perfect information**, so that the decision will be made *under certainty*. This is because with perfect information, the decision maker can guarantee the selection of the act that yields the greatest payoff for whatever event actually occurs. Because we wish to investigate the worth of such information *before* it is obtained, we will determine the expected payoff once perfect information is obtained. That quantity is called the **expected payoff under certainty** (with perfect information).

To calculate the expected payoff under certainty, we determine the highest payoff for each event. This is illustrated for the Tippi-Toes decision in Table 22-11. The maximum payoff for each demand level is determined by finding the largest payoff in each row. Thus, for a light demand, we find that choosing the gears-and-levers movement yields the largest payoff ($25,000). If perfect information indicated that light demand was certain to occur, our decision maker would choose this movement. Similarly, $440,000 is the maximum payoff possible for moderate demand, and this amount may be achieved only if the spring-action movement is chosen. Likewise, $750,000 is the maximum possible payoff when a heavy demand occurs, and this amount corresponds to a choice of the weights-and-pulleys movement. The last column of Table 22-11 shows the products of the maximum payoffs and their respective event probabilities. Summing these, we obtain $460,500 as the expected payoff under certainty (with perfect information). This figure represents the average payoff if the toy manufacturer were faced with the same situation repeatedly and always selected the act that yielded the best payoff for the event indicated by the perfect information. Keep in mind that the $460,500 represents the expected payoff viewed from some point in time *before* the information becomes available. *After* the information has been obtained, exactly one of the payoffs, $25,000, $440,000, or $750,000, is bound to occur. When the information is actually obtained, the payoff is a certainty.

We now answer the question regarding the worth of perfect information to the decision maker. As we have seen, the Bayes decision rule leads to the choice of the particular act that maximizes the expected payoff without regard to any additional information. Since this is the best act that our decision maker can select without any new information and since the expected payoff under certainty is the average payoff that may be anticipated with the best possible information, the worth of perfect information to the decision maker is expressed by the difference between these two amounts. We call the

TABLE 22-11

Calculation of the Expected Payoff under Certainty for the Tippi-Toes Decision

EVENT (level of demand)	PROBABILITY	ACT			UNDER CERTAINTY		
		Gears and Levers	Spring Action	Weights and Pulleys	Maximum Payoff	Chosen Act	Payoff × Probability
Light	.10	$ 25,000	−$ 10,000	−$125,000	$ 25,000	G&L	$ 2,500
Moderate	.70	400,000	440,000	400,000	440,000	SA	308,000
Heavy	.20	650,000	740,000	750,000	750,000	W&P	150,000
						Expected payoff under certainty =	$460,500

resulting number the **expected value of perfect information**, which is conveniently represented by the abbreviation EVPI and may be expressed as

$$EVPI = \text{Expected payoff under certainty}$$
$$- \text{Maximum expected payoff (with no information)}$$

For the toy manufacturer's decision, we obtain the EVPI by subtracting the maximum expected payoff of $455,000 (calculated in Table 21-6 on page 632) from the expected payoff under certainty of $460,500:

$$EVPI = \$460,500 - \$455,000 = \$5,500$$

In this case, the EVPI represents the greatest amount of money that the decision maker would be willing to pay to obtain perfect information about what the demand will be. Stated differently, $5,500 is the increase in the decision maker's expected payoff that may be attributed to perfect knowledge of demand. Both $455,000 and $460,500 are meaningless values *after* the perfect information is obtained. Thus, the EVPI of $5,500 may be interpreted only *before* the perfect information has become known.

EVPI and Opportunity Loss

Note that $5,500 is the same amount as the minimum expected opportunity loss calculated in Table 22-10. Thus, we see that *the expected value of perfect information is equal to the expected opportunity loss for the optimal act.*

Therefore, we calculate the expected value of perfect information by calculating the expected opportunity losses. The minimum loss is then the EVPI. Table 22-12 summarizes the relationships among expected payoff, expected opportunity loss, and expected value of perfect information for the toy manufacturer's decision. Note that for any act, the sum of the expected payoff and the expected opportunity loss is equal to the expected payoff under certainty (with perfect information).

Since perfect information is nonexistent in most real-world decision making, why are we interested in the EVPI? Our answer is that it helps us to establish a limit on the worth

TABLE 22-12
Relationships among Expected Payoff, Expected Opportunity Loss, and EVPI for the Tippi-Toes Decision

	GEARS AND LEVERS	SPRING ACTION	WEIGHTS AND PULLEYS
Expected payoff	$412,500	$455,000	$417,500
Expected opportunity loss	48,000	5,500	43,000
Expected payoff under certainty (with perfect information)	$460,500	$460,500	$460,500
Expected value of perfect information (EVPI) = $5,500		↑ Optimal act	

of less-than-perfect information. For example, if a marketing research study aimed at predicting demand costs $6,000, which exceeds the EVPI by $500, the study should not be conducted, regardless of its quality. We will investigate the concepts involved in decision making with experimental information further in Chapter 23.

22-5 Decision Making Using Strategies

One important aspect of decision making is the use of information that may be helpful in making a choice. In establishing an employment policy based on a screening test, an applicant's score is the basis for hiring or rejecting that person. Regardless of the score achieved, a person who is hired will ultimately perform satisfactorily or not. When receiving components for assembly, manufacturers generally take a random sample to decide whether to accept or reject a shipment; the actual quality of the entire shipment will be known only after this decision has been made. As a further example, consider the choice between adding a new product to the line or abandoning it. This decision may be based on the results of a marketing research study; the success or failure of the new product will be known only after it has actually been marketed.

All of these situations are decisions with two points of uncertainty. The first uncertainty is the kind of information obtained—the screening test score, the number of defective sample items, or the results of the marketing research study. The second uncertainty concerns the ultimate outcome—the new employee's performance, the quality of the shipment, the new product's performance. Between these points in time, a decision has to be made. The chosen act depends on which particular event has just occurred.

It is possible to determine the best acts to select for each informational event in advance. The resulting decision rule is called a **strategy**. The ultimate decision is what particular strategy to select. We will show how this is done by means of a case illustration that involves sampling and inspection.

ILLUSTRATION
The Cannery Inspector

A cannery inspector monitors tests for mercury contamination levels before authorizing shipments of canned tuna. The procedure is to randomly select two crates of canned fish from a shipment and determine the parts per million of mercury. The number of these crates R exceeding government contamination guidelines is determined. The inspector may then approve (A) or disapprove (D) the shipment. If approved, the shipment is sent to distributors who perform more detailed testing to determine whether the average mercury levels of the entire shipment are excessive (E) or tolerable (T). An excessively contaminated shipment is returned to the cannery. If the company inspector originally disapproves a shipment, the production batch is sent to the rendering department to be converted into pet food. At this time, it is determined whether the entire shipment actually contains excessive average levels of mercury.

The decision tree diagram for the cannery inspector's decision is provided in Figure 22-2. Eight strategies, S_1 through S_8, are identified in Table 22-13. A strategy must specify which act—"approve" or "disapprove"—should be chosen for each possible test result. From Table 22-13, we see that strategy S_1 is a decision rule specifying that the shipment must be approved no matter what the number of excessively contaminated crates R happens to be. Strategy S_2 specifies approval if $R = 0$ or $R = 1$, but disapproval if $R = 2$. Eight strategies are possible because there are 2 choices for each of the 3 events and therefore $2^3 = 8$ distinct decision rules.

As portrayed with the decision tree diagram, a strategy will be a particular pruned version of the tree. There are 8 distinct ways to prune the cannery inspector's tree, as

FIGURE 22-2

Decision tree diagram for the cannery inspector illustration.

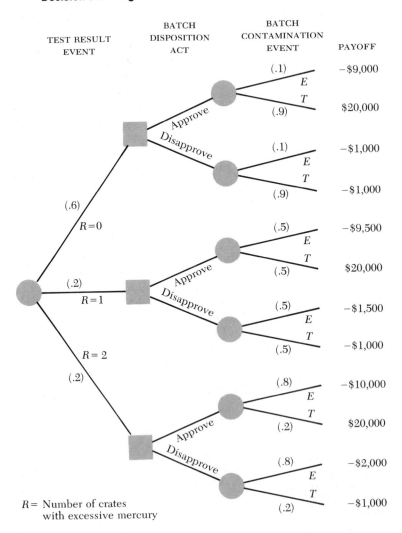

TABLE 22-13
Strategies for the Cannery Inspector's Decision

TEST RESULT EVENT	STRATEGY							
	S_1	S_2	S_3	S_4	S_5	S_6	S_7	S_8
$R = 0$	A	A	A	D	A	D	D	D
$R = 1$	A	A	D	A	D	A	D	D
$R = 2$	A	D	A	A	D	D	A	D

shown in Figure 22-3. Only one of these versions will result from backward induction analysis.

A table may be constructed to indicate the payoff for each strategy-event combination. Such a payoff table, shown in Table 22-14, is identical in form to the payoff table for a single-stage decision, except that strategies are used in place of acts. Another difference is that there are uncertainties at two stages in the cannery decision: (1) how many excessively contaminated crates will be found in the sample and (2) whether the contamination level of the entire production batch will be found to be excessive or tolerable on the average. The six joint events are of the form $R = 0$ *and E*, $R = 2$ *and T*. The payoff values given in the table are the same as the payoff values on the decision tree in Figure 22-2 and correspond to the joint event that occurs for the specified strategy. Thus, if the joint event $R = 2$ *and E* occurs when S_1 is used, the payoff is -10 thousand dollars, since the inspector approves the shipment whenever $R = 2$, according to this particular strategy. If the inspector uses S_2, the same event indicates disapproval, and because the shipment contains excessive mercury, the payoff is -2 thousand dollars.

This strategy-selection decision may be analyzed by applying any of the various decision-making criteria we encountered earlier and then treating each strategy in the same way that an act is treated in a single-stage decision structure. However, we will continue to maximize expected payoff.

TABLE 22-14
Payoff Table for the Cannery Inspector's Decision Using Strategies
(payoffs in thousands of dollars)

JOINT EVENT	STRATEGY							
	S_1	S_2	S_3	S_4	S_5	S_6	S_7	S_8
$R = 0$ and E	-9	-9	-9	-1	-9	-1	-1	-1
$R = 0$ and T	20	20	20	-1	20	-1	-1	-1
$R = 1$ and E	-9.5	-9.5	-1.5	-9.5	-1.5	-9.5	-1.5	-1.5
$R = 1$ and T	20	20	-1	20	-1	20	-1	-1
$R = 2$ and E	-10	-2	-10	-10	-2	-2	-10	-2
$R = 2$ and T	20	-1	20	20	-1	-1	20	-1

FIGURE 22-3

Pruned decision tree diagram illustrating the eight strategies for the cannery inspector's decision given in Table 22-13.

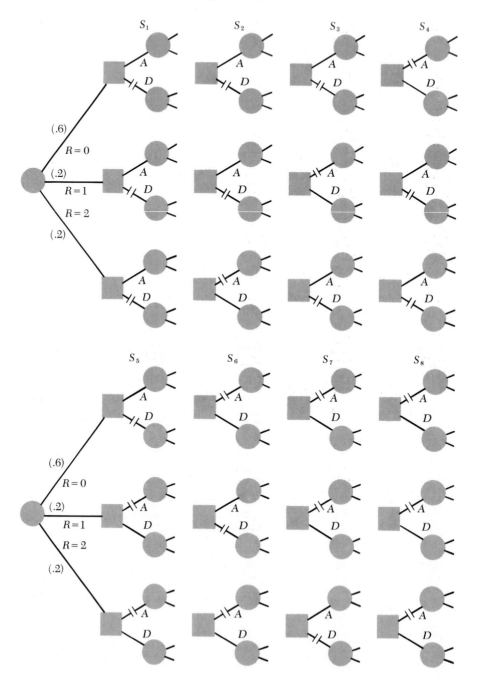

Extensive and Normal Form Analysis

The cannery strategy-selection decision may be analyzed using the Bayes decision rule and maximizing expected payoff either by (1) backward induction on the decision tree or (2) direct computation from the values given in the payoff table to determine the strategy with the maximum expected payoff. *The two approaches will provide identical results.* When a decision tree is used, the procedure is called an **extensive form analysis**. When the analysis is based on the payoff table, it is referred to as **normal form analysis**.

Figure 22-4 illustrates extensive form analysis. The probability value determined for each event is shown on the corresponding branch of the decision tree. Backward induction indicates that the best procedure is to approve the shipment when $R = 0$ or $R = 1$ and to disapprove the shipment when $R = 2$. Referring to Table 22-13, we see that this corresponds to strategy S_2.

The results of the normal form analysis for the cannery inspector's decision are shown in Table 22-15. Although similar calculations had to be made for each, there is room enough to illustrate only those for strategy S_2, which has the maximum expected payoff of 10.95 thousand dollars. This is the same result we obtained in extensive form analysis ($10,950). Fortunately, extensive form analysis requires that we prune the tree for just one strategy. This makes decision tree analysis superior to payoff table analysis in terms of computational efficiency. In backward induction, only the maximum expected payoffs need to be brought back to the earlier branching point. It is not even necessary to catalog the various strategies.

Extensive form analysis using a decision tree is often the only possible approach, because the problem structure cannot be forced into the rectangular format of a payoff table. This is especially true of multistage problems that have two or more decision points, such as the Ponderosa Record Company problem diagrammed in Figure 22-1 (page 663). Only problems that result in a symmetrical decision tree like the one in Figure 22-2 may be analyzed either way in terms of expected payoff.

TABLE 22-15
Results of Normal Form Analysis for the Cannery Inspector's Decision Using Strategies, Showing the Expected Payoff Calculations for Strategy S_2 (payoffs in thousands of dollars)

(1) FIRST-STAGE EVENT PROBABILITY	(2) SECOND-STAGE EVENT PROBABILITY	(3) JOINT PROBABILITY (1) × (2)	(4) PAYOFF FOR S_2	(5) PAYOFF × JOINT PROBABILITY (3) × (4)
$\Pr[R = 0] = .6$	$\Pr[E \mid R = 0] = .1$	.06	−9	−.54
$\Pr[R = 0] = .6$	$\Pr[T \mid R = 0] = .9$	.54	20	10.80
$\Pr[R = 1] = .2$	$\Pr[E \mid R = 1] = .5$	.10	−9.5	−.95
$\Pr[R = 1] = .2$	$\Pr[T \mid R = 1] = .5$	.10	20	2.00
$\Pr[R = 2] = .2$	$\Pr[E \mid R = 2] = .8$	.16	−2	−.32
$\Pr[R = 2] = .2$	$\Pr[T \mid R = 2] = .2$	.04	−1	−.04
				Expected payoff = 10.95

Strategy	S_1	S_2	S_3	S_4	S_5	S_6	S_7	S_8
Expected Payoff	10.51	10.95	9.21	−.35	9.65	.09	−1.65	−1.21

FIGURE 22-4

Extensive form analysis of the cannery inspector's decision using the decision tree diagram.

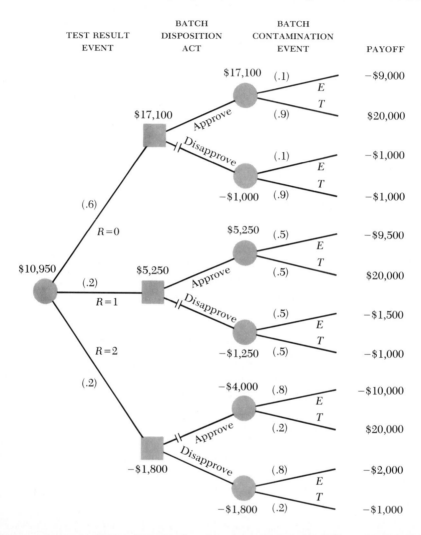

| TEST RESULT EVENT | BATCH DISPOSITION ACT | BATCH CONTAMINATION EVENT | PAYOFF |

CASE

SoftWhereHaus

Klaus DeBugger is the founder of SoftWhereHaus, a start-up software publishing company. The company's major product is the securities evaluation package, *Opt-a-Miser*. Version 1.0 of this program has been a moderate success. A variety of enhancements are contemplated for version 2.0, the release of which could be a vital boost to SoftWhereHaus' future.

Unfortunately, Exploiteers Inc. has developed a competing package called *Max-a-Myser*. DeBugger claims that this package has the "look and feel" of *Opt-a-Miser*, substantially violating SoftWhereHaus' copyright. He is contemplating retaliatory action.

DeBugger's immediate choices are (1) to negotiate with the help of a mediator (whose fee is $10,000), (2) to litigate (requiring a $20,000 non-refundable attorney retainer), or (3) to ignore Exploiteers. Ultimately, SoftWhereHaus will either sell the program rights to GrossHaus for an amount dependent on what prior events transpire or keep the program and develop version 2.0 (at a cost of $20,000). Version 2.0 of *Opt-a-Miser* may be assumed to result in a success (culminating in enhanced profits having a present value of $200,000) or in a weak marketplace reception (yielding only $20,000).

Negotiation may bring about a favorable or unfavorable settlement. With a favorable outcome (50% chance), SoftWhereHaus may sell program ownership for $75,000; and, releasing instead version 2.0 will provide a 70% chance of success. An unfavorable negotiation result will drastically reduce the selling price to $20,000 and will lower the success probability of version 2.0 to .25.

Litigation may have three results: positive (40% chance), neutral (30% chance), or negative (30% chance). The following data apply in that case.

	LITIGATION RESULT		
	Positive	*Neutral*	*Negative*
V-2.0 success probability	.8	.5	.15
Proceeds from sale	$100,000	$50,000	$15,000

Ignoring Exploiteers will of course involve no unusual cash expenditure. In that case, there would be a 50–50 chance for version-2.0 success versus a weak reception, and GrossHaus will give DeBugger $50,000 to gain ownership of the unrevised *Opt-a-Miser*.

Questions

1. Construct Klaus DeBugger's decision tree diagram, placing all partial cash flows and probabilities alongside their respective branches. Then, determine, for each outcome, the net cash flow.

2. Consider the *litigation case* only.
   (a) Identify DeBugger's possible strategies.
   (b) Construct a payoff table using the above strategies as acts and the joint events for litigation result and the success probability that would apply for a version-2.0 release.

(c) Determine the following.
   (1) Maximin strategy
   (2) Maximum likelihood strategy
   (3) Maximum expected payoff strategy.
(d) Determine DeBugger's EVPI. How might this number help DeBugger in his evaluation? What kinds of predictive information might DeBugger find helpful in evaluating his litigation strategies?
(e) Construct DeBugger's opportunity loss table. Which strategy minimizes expected opportunity loss?

3. Perform backward induction using the tree in Question 1. What course of action maximizes DeBugger's expected net cash flow?

4. Although less so than most people, Klaus DeBugger is nevertheless risk averse. This is evidenced by his willingness to buy casualty insurance at various amounts exceeding the expected claim size. The following table applies.

GREATEST POSSIBLE LOSS	DOWNSIDE RISK PREMIUM COMPONENT						
	Pr[Loss]						
	.15	.20	.25	.30	.50	.70	.85
$10,000	300	400	600	650	800	1,000	2,000
20,000	1,100	1,200	1,400	1,500	2,000	3,000	5,000

The above amounts must be subtracted from expected payoffs to arrive at Klaus' certainty equivalents.

But Klaus also expresses the need to make *upside* adjustments by *further* discounting. The following apply.

GREATEST POSSIBLE GAIN	UPSIDE RISK PREMIUM COMPONENT						
	Pr[Gain]						
	.15	.20	.25	.30	.50	.70	.85
$ 25,000	200	100	0	0	0	0	0
50,000	800	500	400	300	200	100	0
75,000	1,100	700	500	400	300	200	100
100,000	1,300	1,000	700	500	300	200	100
125,000	1,500	1,200	900	600	400	300	200
150,000	2,000	1,300	1,100	800	600	400	200
175,000	2,500	1,500	1,300	1,000	800	500	400
200,000	3,000	2,000	1,500	1,200	1,000	700	500

DeBugger's risk premium is the sum of the two components.

Risk premium = Downside component + Upside component

Using the nearest applicable tabled values, determine Klaus DeBugger's (1) expected payoff, (2) risk premium, and (3) certainty equivalent for each of the following gambles (probabilities in parentheses).

	(a)	(b)	(c)	(d)
Win	$100,000 (.30)	$50,000 (.50)	$200,000 (.30)	$20,000 (.90)
Lose	−$20,000 (.70)	$20,000 (.50)	−$20,000 (.70)	−$20,000 (.10)

5. Klaus DeBugger's certainty equivalents are determined by the rules in Question 4. Perform a second backward induction analysis of his decision tree to determine which course of action maximizes his certainty equivalent.

PROBLEMS

22-1 Refer to the Tippi-Toes decision in Table 22-1. Suppose that reduction in the development cost of the gears-and-levers movement allows a $50,000 increase in all payoffs for that act. In addition, an upward revision of unit sales when demand is heavy results in a further $100,000 increase in all payoffs for that event. Finally, the following revised probabilities now apply to the demand levels: light, .50; moderate, .30; and heavy, .20.
(a) Construct the new Tippi-Toes payoff table.
(b) Determine the maximin payoff act.
(c) Determine the maximum likelihood act.
(d) Calculate the expected payoffs. According to the Bayes decision rule, which act should be chosen?

22-2 (*Continuation of Problem 22-1*):
(a) Calculate the EVPI for the modified Tippi-Toes decision.
(b) Construct the opportunity loss table and compute the expected opportunity losses.

22-3 You have decided to participate in a gamble that offers the following monetary payoffs.

	ACT	
EVENT	Choose Red	Choose Black
Red	$1	−$2
Black	−1	100

(a) Which act is the maximin payoff act?
(b) Supposing that the probability of red is .99, calculate the expected payoffs for each act. Which act is better according to the Bayes decision rule? Which act would you choose?

(c) Supposing that the probability of red is .5, calculate the expected payoffs for each act. Which act has the maximum expected payoff? Which act would you choose?

(d) In view of your answers to (b) and (c), what is your opinion of the maximin payoff decision criterion in this case?

22-4 Rich Sod is a farmer who intends to sign a contract to provide a cannery with his entire crop. Rich must choose to produce one of the following five vegetables: corn, tomatoes, beets, asparagus, or cauliflower. Rich will plant his entire 1,000 acres with the selected crop. The yields of these vegetables will be affected by the weather to varying degrees. The following table indicates the approximate productivities for each vegetable in dry, moderate, and damp weather and also lists the price per bushel that the cannery has offered for each crop.

WEATHER	APPROXIMATE YIELD (bushels per acre)				
	Corn	Tomatoes	Beets	Asparagus	Cauliflower
Dry	20	10	15	30	40
Moderate	35	20	20	25	40
Damp	40	10	30	20	40
Price per bushel	$1.00	$2.00	$1.50	$1.00	$.50

(a) Construct the payoff table for the farmer's decision. For the payoff measure, use the approximate total cash receipts when the crop is sold.

(b) Identify any inadmissible acts and eliminate them from the payoff table.

(c) Which act is the maximin payoff act?

(d) Suppose that the following probabilities have been assigned to the types of weather. Calculate the expected payoff for each act. Then, identify the act that has the maximum expected payoff.

WEATHER	PROBABILITY
Dry	.3
Moderate	.5
Damp	.2

22-5 Refer to the risk premiums for the president of Ponderosa Record company in Table 22-7. For each of the following situations, determine (1) the expected payoff, (2) his risk premium, and (3) his certainty equivalent.

(a)		(b)		(c)		(d)	
PROB.	PAYOFF	PROB.	PAYOFF	PROB.	PAYOFF	PROB.	PAYOFF
.90	+$50,000	.99	+$20,000	.50	+$10,000	.25	+$300,000
.10	−$100,000	.01	−$50,000	.50	−$5,000	.75	−$100,000

22-6   A news dealer must decide how many copies of *Snappy Almanac* to stock in December. He will not stock less than the lowest possible demand or more than the highest possible demand. Each magazine costs him $.50 and sells for $1.00. At the end of the month the unsold magazines are thrown away. Three levels of monthly demand are equally likely: 10, 11, and 12. If demand exceeds stock, sales will equal stock.

(a) Using December profit as the payoff measure, construct the news dealer's payoff table.

(b) According to the maximin criterion, how many copies should he stock?

(c) Which number of copies will provide the greatest expected payoff?

22-7   Use the payoff table below to construct an opportunity loss table.

EVENT	PROBABILITY	ACT				
		A_1	A_2	A_3	A_4	A_5
E_1	.2	10	20	10	15	20
E_2	.2	-5	10	-5	10	-5
E_3	.6	15	5	10	10	10

Compute the expected opportunity loss for each act. Which act yields the lowest expected opportunity loss?

22-8   Answer the following questions based on the payoff table below.

EVENT	PROBABILITY	ACT		
		A_1	A_2	A_3
E_1	.3	10	20	30
E_2	.5	40	-10	20
E_3	.2	20	50	20

(a) What is the maximum expected payoff? To which act does this payoff correspond?

(b) What is the expected payoff under certainty (with perfect information)?

(c) Using your answers to (a) and (b), calculate the expected value of perfect information.

(d) What is the minimum expected opportunity loss?

(e) What do you notice about your answers to (c) and (d)?

22-9   A product manager for Gimble and Proctor wishes to determine whether or not to market BriDent toothpaste. The present value of all future profits from a successful toothpaste is $1,000,000, whereas failure of the brand would result in a net loss of $500,000. Not marketing the toothpaste would not affect profits. The manager has judged that BriDent would have a 50–50 chance of success.

(a) Construct the payoff table for this decision.

(b) Which act will maximize the expected payoff?

(c) Compute the decision maker's EVPI. What is the minimum expected opportunity loss?

22-10 B. F. Retread, a tire manufacturer, wishes to select one of three feasible prototype designs for a new longer-wearing radial tire. The costs of making the tires are given below.

TIRE	FIXED COST	VARIABLE COST PER UNIT
A	$ 60,000	$30
B	90,000	20
C	120,000	15

There are three levels of unit sales: 4,000 units, 7,000 units, and 10,000 units; the respective probabilities are .30, .50, and .20. The selling price will be $75 per tire.

(a) Construct the payoff table using total profit as the payoff measure.

(b) Determine the expected payoff for each act. According to the Bayes decision rule, which is the best act?

(c) Calculate the EVPI.

(d) Complete the opportunity loss table and compute the expected opportunity losses.

22-11 Rod Shafter is an oil wildcatter deciding whether to drill on a leased site. His judgment leads him to conclude that there is a 50–50 chance of oil. If Shafter drills and strikes oil, his profit will be $200,000. But if the well turns out to be dry, his net loss will be $100,000.

(a) According to the Bayes decision rule, should the wildcatter drill or abandon the site?

(b) What is the wildcatter's EVPI?

(c) A seismologist offers to conduct a highly reliable seismic survey. The results could help the wildcatter make his decision. What is the most that the wildcatter would consider paying for such seismic information?

22-12 Refer to the Buzzy-B Toys decision in Problem 21-12. Suppose that the following risk premiums apply.

NEAREST POSSIBLE LOSS	NEAREST PROBABILITY OF LOSS			
	.10	.20	.50	.90
$ 10,000	$ 100	$ 200	$ 1,000	$ 3,000
50,000	1,000	3,000	10,000	25,000
100,000	3,000	10,000	25,000	50,000

Construct the decision tree diagram and perform backward induction analysis using certainty equivalents obtained by discounting the expected payoffs.

22-13 Refer to the Spillsberry Foods decision in Problem 21-13. Suppose that the following risk premiums apply.

NEAREST POSSIBLE LOSS	NEAREST PROBABILITY OF LOSS		
	.10	.40	.60
$ 25,000	$ 1,000	$ 3,000	$ 5,000
100,000	5,000	10,000	15,000
250,000	10,000	25,000	40,000

Construct the decision tree diagram and perform backward induction analysis using certainty equivalents obtained by discounting the expected payoffs.

22-14 Suppose that the following probabilities apply to the cannery illustration in Section 22-5.

TEST RESULT	PROBABILITY	CONDITIONAL PROBABILITIES	
$R = 0$	.4	.2 (E)	.8 (T)
$R = 1$	.3	.6 (E)	.4 (T)
$R = 2$	.3	.9 (E)	.1 (T)

(a) Conduct a new extensive form analysis (using a corrected decision tree) to determine the strategy that maximizes expected payoff.
(b) Conduct a new normal form analysis (using corrected joint probabilities) to select the strategy that maximizes expected payoff.

22-15 A dispatcher classifies each truckload of apricots purchased by Yellow Giant under contract from local orchards as underripe, ripe, or overripe. She must then decide whether a particular truckload will be used for dried apricots (D) or for apricot preserves (P). A truckload of apricots used for preserves yields a profit of $6,000 if the fruit has a high sugar content, but only $4,000 if the sugar content is low (because costly extra sugar must be added). Regardless of sugar content, a truckload of dried apricots yields a profit of $5,000. In either case, the actual sugar content can be determined only during final processing.

The probabilities are .3 for an underripe truckload, .5 for a ripe one, and .2 for an overripe one. The following probabilities for sugar content have been established for given levels of ripeness.

SUGAR CONTENT	UNDERRIPE	RIPE	OVERRIPE
Low	.9	.4	.2
High	.1	.6	.8
	1.0	1.0	1.0

(a) Construct the dispatcher's decision tree diagram and perform an extensive form analysis to determine the maximum expected payoff strategy for disposing of a truckload of apricots.
(b) List the possible strategies for disposing of a truckload of apricots. Perform a normal form analysis to select the strategy that yields the greatest expected profit.

22-16 Suppose that the manager in Problem 22-9 wishes to implement a consumer testing program at a cost of $50,000. Consumer testing will be either favorable (a 40% chance) or unfavorable. Given a favorable test result, the chance of product success is judged to be 80%. For an unfavorable test result, the toothpaste's success probability is judged to be only 30%.

(a) Assuming that testing is used, construct a decision tree diagram. Then, perform backward induction analysis to determine the optimal strategy to employ in using the test results.
(b) Identify the basic strategies involving the use of the results of the consumer testing program. Construct a payoff table with these strategies as the choices and the joint market outcomes and test results as the events. Then, conduct a normal form analysis to determine which strategy maximizes expected payoff.

23

Decision Making Using Experimental Information

We usually associate the term *experiment* with a test or an investigation. All experiments have one feature in common: *They provide information.* This information may serve to realign uncertainty. Information obtained by observing a solar eclipse can support hypotheses regarding the effect of the sun's gravity on stellar light rays. The way in which a person responds to your questions may help you decide whether you want him or her for a friend. *An experiment helps us make better decisions under uncertainty.*

However, most experiments are not conclusive. Any test may camouflage the truth. For instance, some potentially good employees will flunk well-designed employment screening tests, and some incompetents will pass them. Another good example is the seismic survey, which provides geological information about deep underground rock structures and is used to explore for oil deposits. Unfortunately, a seismic survey may deny the presence of oil in a field that is already producing oil and may confirm the presence of oil under a site that has already proved to be dry. Still, such imperfect experiments may be valuable. An unfavorable test result may increase the chance of rejecting a poor prospect—a job applicant or a drilling site—and a favorable test result may enhance the likelihood of selecting a good prospect.

In this chapter, we will incorporate experimentation into the framework of our decision-making analysis. The information we obtain will affect the probabilities of the events that determine the consequences of each act. We revise the probabilities of these events upward or downward, depending on the evidence we obtain. Thus, a geologist will increase the probability of oil if the seismic survey analysis is favorable and will lower this probability if the survey is unfavorable.

The seismic survey epitomizes the role of experimental information in decision making. In business situations, several other classic sources of such information are commonly employed. A marketing research study serves to realign uncertainty regarding the degree of success that a new product will achieve in the marketplace. An aptitude test is often used to help predict a job applicant's future success or failure if he or she is hired—a decision that involves considerable uncertainty. A sampling study is frequently employed to facilitate quality control decisions related to how satisfactorily items are produced or how many defective items are arriving from a supplier.

23-1 Stages for Analyzing Decisions Using Experiments

Four stages are involved in analyzing decisions under uncertainty.

1. **Prior Analysis**   In this evaluation stage, the decision maker identifies the decision structure, selects a payoff measure, and determines prior probabilities. The decision maker then computes the expected payoff for each act and the expected value of perfect information, or EVPI. If the latter is small, no further investigation is required, and the main decision should be made. Otherwise, the next stage commences.

2. **Preposterior Analysis**   At this point in the evaluation, the decision maker looks for sources of information to predict the events in the decision structure. Only those sources that have low cost (in relation to the EVPI) and that have a history of reliable predictions need be evaluated. That evaluation (to be described shortly) includes both probability and decision tree analyses.

3. **Posterior Analysis**   When the source of experimental information has been chosen, the decision maker will revise probabilities, with one set of values coinciding with each result possible. The main decision is made after the experiment, according to how the actual result relates to the actions prescribed here.

4. **Future Analysis**   It is common for one evaluation to raise further questions. Later decisions might have to be made that would involve some of the same uncertainties. In some cases, posterior probability values for events in the present investigation will serve as the prior probabilities for those or similar events in a future investigation. Data from ongoing evaluations should be collected in a data base to be used in future decisions.

The following example illustrates the four stages just described.

TABLE 23-1
Payoff Table for the Oil Wildcatting Decision

| EVENT | PRIOR PROBABILITY | ACT | |
		Drill	Abandon
Oil	.50	$150,000	$0
Dry	.50	−100,000	0

ILLUSTRATION
The Oil Wildcatter

An oil wildcatter must decide whether or not to drill an oil well. His payoff table is provided in Table 23-1.

The subjective probabilities of .50 for oil and .50 for dry are the wildcatter's **prior probabilities** and are based on personal judgment formed during preliminary investigations. The payoffs result from the assumption that an oil-bearing leasehold will be sold for $250,000 and that the drilling will cost $100,000. The probability values are the culmination of the wildcatter's efforts in studying rock samples and correlating other evidence. Each bit of experimental information has refined the wildcatter's judgment. Dramatic shifts in probabilities may be expected to follow a high-reliability experiment, such as a seismic survey.

23-2 Prior Analysis of the Decision

Using the data in the payoff table, the wildcatter could make the main decision of whether to drill or to abandon—simply by applying the Bayes decision rule. The expected payoffs are

$$(\$150,000)(.50) + (-\$100,000)(.50) = \$25,000$$

for drill and $0 for abandon. If he wants to maximize expected payoff, he should choose to drill.

Another course of action would be to seek out some kind of experimental information, postponing the main decision until a result is achieved from that investigation.

The Role of EVPI

Before we look at any specific source of predictive data, consider the hypothetical case when perfect information is available. A perfect predictor will indicate, without error, either that there is oil or that the site is dry. Should the decision maker have that information, he would pick the better act for each case.

TABLE 23-2
Perfect Information Evaluation for the Oil Wildcatting Decision

EVENT	PROBABILITY	ACT		WITH PERFECT INFORMATION		
		Drill	Abandon	Maximum Payoff	Chosen Act	Payoff × Probability
Oil	.50	$150,000	$0	$150,000	Drill	$75,000
Dry	.50	− 100,000	0	0	Abandon	0
						$75,000

Expected payoff under certainty (with perfect information) = $75,000
EVPI = Expected payoff with perfect information − Maximum expected payoff (with no information)
    = $75,000 − $25,000 = $50,000

Table 23-2 shows the calculations for the oil wildcatter's expected value of perfect information. The practical significance of EVPI = $50,000 is what it implies regarding less-than-perfect information. Any imperfectly reliable predictor must have a worth to the decision maker of some amount less than the EVPI, which sets the threshold.

The EVPI may be a helpful screening device. If any information were to cost more than the EVPI, that source of data should be rejected out of hand—regardless of its purported quality. For instance, if the wildcatter were offered a highly reliable seismic survey for a fee of $105,000, it would be turned down without a second thought.

The absolute level of the EVPI is itself a useful number. Imagine a decision where the computed value of EVPI is $50. It could hardly be worth the time and effort to consider further predictive information when the maximum benefit (in terms of expected payoff) is so small. The main decision under such circumstances should be made immediately on the basis of present knowledge alone. On the other hand, a large value, such as EVPI = $1,000,000, suggests that a great deal of effort should be devoted to the search for potential sources of predictive information.

23-3 Preposterior and Posterior Analysis

For a fee of $30,000, a consulting firm will perform a complete seismic survey of the subterranean structure of the lease site. Two predictive results are assumed: favorable or unfavorable. Figure 23-1 shows the oil wildcatter's decision tree diagram, with an initial act fork for the decision to order the seismic survey or not. Notice that if the seismic survey is ordered the main decision will not be made until after its results have become known. The payoff values are the original ones, less the $30,000 cost of the survey for the applicable outcomes. Notice that there are no site status event forks following the abandon acts—reflecting the fact that oil and dry never become known unless drilling is done. (Although potentially misleading, it would not be improper to include those missing forks in the tree.)

Preposterior analysis is concerned largely with the decision about whether or not to take the seismic. Imbedded in that evaluation is the posterior analysis of what should actually be done for each possible finding, assuming that the seismic survey will be taken.

FIGURE 23-1

Decision tree diagram for the wildcatting decision (incomplete).

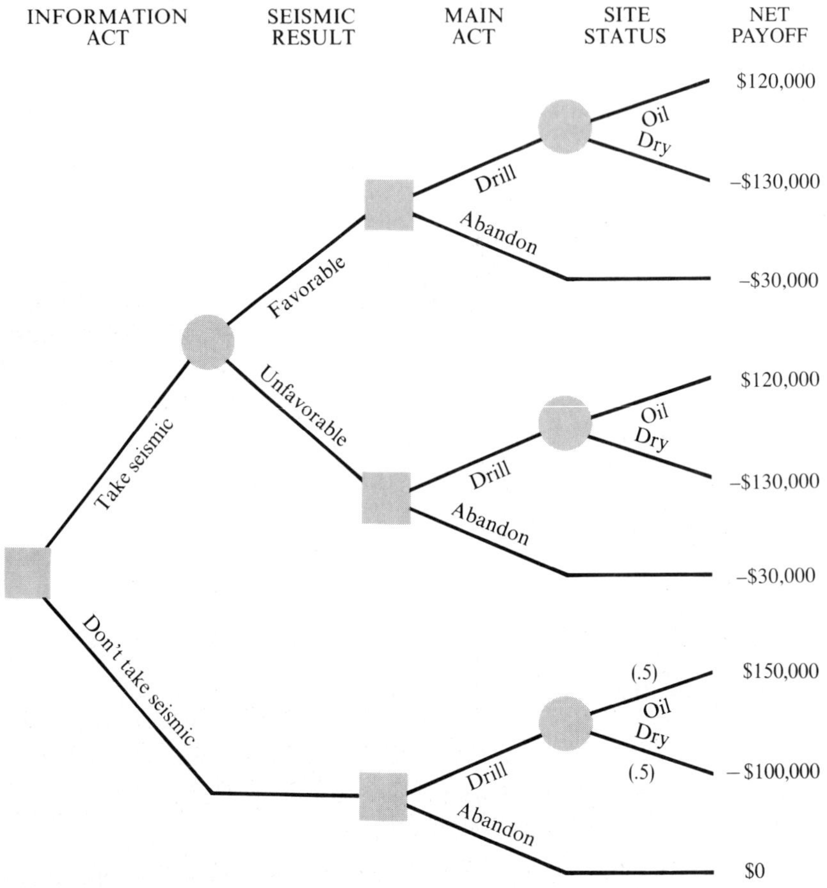

INFORMATION ACT	SEISMIC RESULT	MAIN ACT	SITE STATUS	NET PAYOFF

Probability Evaluations

The decision maker usually makes some kind of judgment about the uncertain events, which may be expressed as a set of *prior probabilities* for the respective events. Occasionally, such a judgment must be quantified in terms of *subjective probabilities*, because the events in question frequently arise from nonrepeatable circumstances. At other times, the prior probabilities may be *objective* in nature. In accordance with the information obtained from the experiment, the event uncertainties are realigned to obtain **posterior probabilities**. Figure 23-2 presents the sequence of steps in this procedure— exactly the one originally proposed by Thomas Bayes. (Bayes' Theorem was discussed in Chapter 2.)

As a first step, the wildcatter must *exercise judgment* regarding the likelihood of striking oil. Since no two unproved drilling sites are very similar, no historical frequency is available. The wildcatter has therefore established subjective probability values. Letting O

FIGURE 23-2

Steps for performing the probability portion of the decision analysis using experimental information.

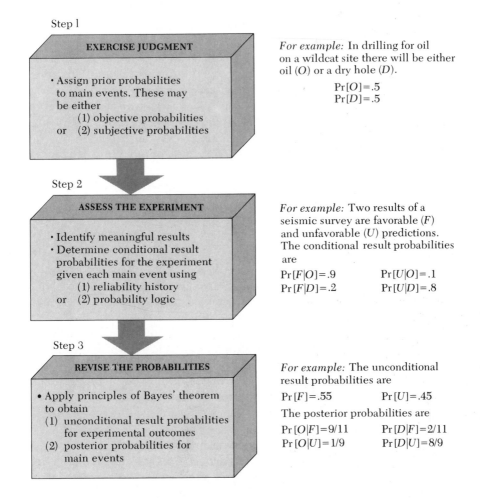

Step 1

EXERCISE JUDGMENT

· Assign prior probabilities to main events. These may be either
    (1) objective probabilities
or (2) subjective probabilities

For example: In drilling for oil on a wildcat site there will be either oil (O) or a dry hole (D).

$$\Pr[O]=.5$$
$$\Pr[D]=.5$$

Step 2

ASSESS THE EXPERIMENT

· Identify meaningful results
· Determine conditional result probabilities for the experiment given each main event using
    (1) reliability history
or (2) probability logic

For example: Two results of a seismic survey are favorable (F) and unfavorable (U) predictions. The conditional result probabilities are

$\Pr[F|O]=.9$ $\Pr[U|O]=.1$
$\Pr[F|D]=.2$ $\Pr[U|D]=.8$

Step 3

REVISE THE PROBABILITIES

· Apply principles of Bayes' theorem to obtain
  (1) unconditional result probabilities for experimental outcomes
  (2) posterior probabilities for main events

For example: The unconditional result probabilities are

$\Pr[F]=.55$ $\Pr[U]=.45$

The posterior probabilities are

$\Pr[O|F]=9/11$ $\Pr[D|F]=2/11$
$\Pr[O|U]=1/9$ $\Pr[D|U]=8/9$

represent oil and D represent a dry hole, the prior probabilities for the basic events are

$$\Pr[O] = .5 \qquad \Pr[D] = .5$$

The next step the wildcatter takes is to *assess the experiment*—the seismic survey, in this case. He begins by contemplating what results would be meaningful to him. Although the seismic output might be highly complex and varied, we will assume, for simplicity, that the geologist's analysis may lead to only two meaningful results: a favorable (F) prediction for oil or an unfavorable one (U). It is necessary to obtain **conditional result probabilities** for the respective seismic outcomes given each possible basic event. Ordinarily, the conditional result probabilities for the experiment may be obtained objectively, either by estimation based on historical frequencies or by application of the underlying logic of probability. Thus, we may refer to these values as "logical-historical" probabilities to distinguish them from the several other types of probabilities that we will encounter.

In our present example, the geologist has recorded the "batting average" for the procedure. Historical records show that on 90% of all fields known to produce oil, the survey's prediction of oil has been favorable; that is, 90% of all similar seismic survey data have provided favorable oil predictions when oil did exist. (Of course, such a percentage should not be biased by the fact that the seismic survey result may have affected the earlier decisions to drill on those sites. It is best to obtain a reliability figure by conducting a special test of the tester itself, which might be done by taking special seismic measurements on sites that are already producing oil.) Similarly, by taking simulated readings on known dry holes, the geologist has also determined that the survey is only 80% reliable in making an unfavorable prediction when no oil is present. The appropriate conditional result probabilities are

$$\Pr[F|O] = .90 \quad \text{and} \quad \Pr[U|O] = .10$$
$$\Pr[F|D] = .20 \quad \text{and} \quad \Pr[U|D] = .80$$

These are **historical probabilities** and may be regarded as statistical estimates of the underlying values, since they are based on limited samples of drilling sites. (Note that the conditional probability for a favorable result given oil is greater than the probability for an unfavorable prediction given a dry hole. There is no reason why a test must be equally discerning in both directions.)

In other situations conditional result probabilities for an informational experiment may be obtained more directly without relying on historical frequencies. This would be true, for example, in assessing a quality control sample. The precise probability distribution for the sample result may be determined through logical deduction, based only on the principles of probability and the type of events that characterize the sampled population. In Chapter 24, we will see how such **logical probabilities** may be determined using the binomial distribution.

The final step toward incorporating experimental information into the probability portion of decision analysis is to *revise the probabilities*. This revision ordinarily results in two kinds of probability values that are applicable at different stages of uncertainty: The *posterior probabilities* apply to the main events, and the **unconditional result probabilities** apply to the experimental outcomes themselves. Although the underlying concepts of Bayes' Theorem are used to arrive at these values, there is a more streamlined procedure that proves more convenient when using probability tree diagrams to analyze a decision.

Using Probability Trees

The probability tree diagram in Figure 23-3(a) depicts the **actual chronology** of events in our illustration. The first fork represents the events for the site status: oil or dry. The second stage forks represent the seismic survey results. This particular arrangement follows the sequence in which the events actually occur: first, nature determined (several

FIGURE 23-3
Probability tree diagrams for the wildcatter's event chronologies using a seismic survey.

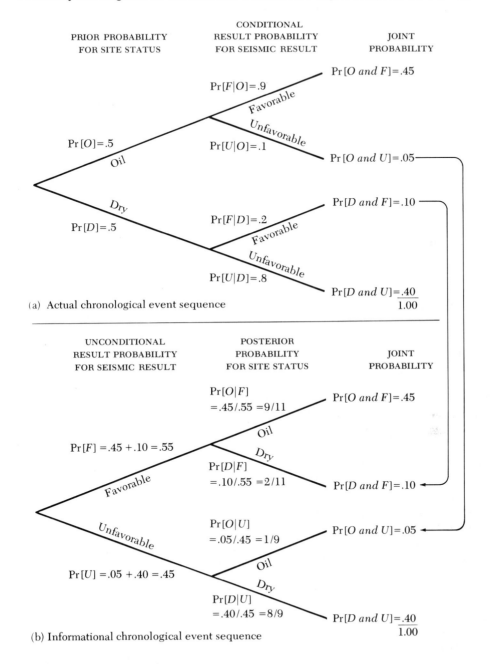

(a) Actual chronological event sequence

(b) Informational chronological event sequence

million years ago) whether this site would cover an oil field; second, our geologist conducts a seismic test today. The actual chronology also adheres to the manner in which the probability data were initially obtained. The wildcatter has directly assessed the probabilities for the site-status events, and the geologist has indicated the reliabilities for the survey. Thus, the values given earlier for the prior probabilities for oil and dry and the conditional result probabilities are placed on the corresponding branches in the probability tree in Figure 23-3(a).

The probability tree diagram in Figure 23-3(b) represents the **informational chronology**. This is the sequence in which the decision maker finds out what events occur. First, the wildcatter obtains the result for the seismic survey, which is portrayed by the initial event fork. Then, if he chooses to drill, he ultimately determines whether or not the site covers an oil field. This is the sequence of events as they would appear on a decision tree (which will be discussed later). But this particular chronology does not correspond directly to the initial probability data. Additional work is required to obtain the probability values shown on the tree diagram in Figure 23-3(b).

We begin by multiplying the branch probabilities together on each path in the tree diagram in Figure 23-3(a) to obtain the corresponding joint probability values. The same numbers apply regardless of the chronology, so the joint probabilities may be transferred to tree diagram (b). This must be done with care, since the in-between joint outcomes are not listed in the same order in (b) as they are in (a), because the analogous paths (event sequences) differ between the diagrams. For example, in diagram (a) we obtain the joint probability for oil and an unfavorable seismic result

$$\Pr[O \text{ and } U] = \Pr[O] \times [\Pr[U \mid O] = .5 \times .1 = .05$$

This is the second joint probability in diagram (a) and corresponds to the third end position in diagram (b).

Next, we work entirely in diagram (b). First, we compute the unconditional result probabilities at the first stage. Here, we use the addition law to obtain

$$\Pr[F] = \Pr[O \text{ and } F] + \Pr[D \text{ and } F] = .45 + .10 = .55$$

$$\Pr[U] = \Pr[O \text{ and } U] + \Pr[D \text{ and } U] = .05 + .40 = .45$$

These values are placed on the applicable branches at the first stage. Finally, the posterior probabilities for the second-stage events are computed using the basic property of conditional probability.

$$\Pr[A \mid B] = \frac{\Pr[A \text{ and } B]}{\Pr[B]}$$

Thus, we determine the posterior probability for oil, given a favorable seismic survey result, to be

$$\Pr[O \mid F] = \frac{\Pr[O \text{ and } F]}{\Pr[F]} = \frac{.45}{.55} = \frac{9}{11}$$

This value is placed on the second-stage branch for oil that is preceded by the earlier branch for a favorable result. Each of the other posterior probabilities shown in diagram (b) is found by dividing the respective end-position joint probability by the probability on the preceding branch.

Probabilities must be revised in this manner whenever experimental information is used in decision making. This happens because we ordinarily obtain our probabilities in the reverse chronology from the chronology required to analyze the problem.

Decision Tree Analysis

The completed oil wildcatter's decision tree diagram is shown in Figure 23-4. Performing backward induction, we see that the decision maker would take the seismic.

FIGURE 23-4
Complete decision tree diagram with backward induction for the wildcatting decision.

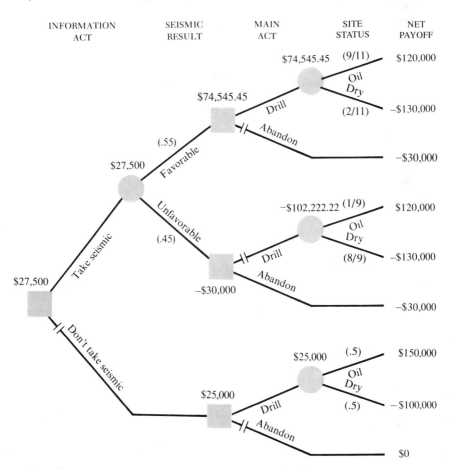

He should prune the abandon branch and drill if a favorable seismic result were obtained and would do the opposite in the case of an unfavorable prediction. Even though drilling will lead to identical payoffs for either seismic result, the posterior probabilities for oil and dry are different for the favorable and unfavorable predictions. The expected payoff from drilling is $74,545.45 for a favorable seismic result, but it is a negative value (−$102,222.22) for an unfavorable result. The wildcatter's expected payoff for the optimal strategy is $27,500.

Obviously Nonoptimal Strategies

In the simpler decision structures, it may be convenient to streamline the decision tree diagram. We conclude that the wildcatter would prune the same branches in the seismic portion for almost any plausible payoffs that might apply. Since he is paying $30,000 for

FIGURE 23-5

The simplified decision tree diagram for wildcatting decision with obviously nonoptimal strategies excluded.

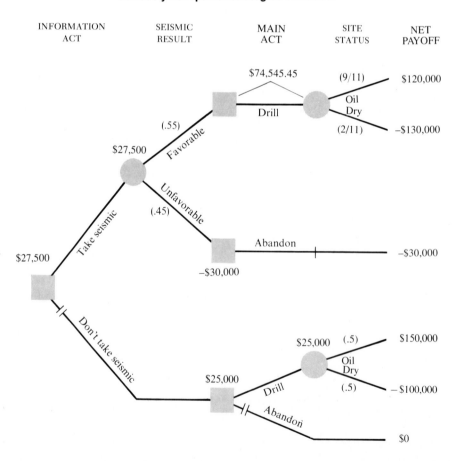

the seismic survey and this experiment provides fairly reliable predictions, the wildcatter should choose acts that are consistent with the information obtained. But the tree in Figure 23-4 allows for three other strategies: (1) drill regardless of the result (prune both abandon branches); (2) abandon in either case (prune the two drill branches); or (3) do the opposite of what is predicted (prune the drill branch if the seismic result is favorable, and prune the abandon branch if it is unfavorable). The last strategy is ridiculous and would never be considered. The other two strategies are inferior to two actions not shown on the present trees—drilling or abandoing without benefit of seismic results—since the $30,000 cost could be saved in either case by not even using the seismic. Such inferior strategies are *obviously nonoptimal strategies.*

Figure 23-5 illustrates how the wildcatter's decision tree diagram could have been drawn to exclude the obviously nonoptimal strategies. This representation may help to simplify an otherwise complex decision tree. However, for expository convenience we will always use the complete decision tree diagram. When more than two acts or experimental results are involved, it is not easy to determine which strategies are obviously nonoptimal.

23-4 Preposterior Analysis: Valuing and Deciding about Experimental Information

We have seen that the EVPI may be useful as a filter to eliminate very expensive sources of predictive information. And, when the EVPI is large, it signals that an improved decision may be achieved if the main decision is deferred until potential sources of experimental information have been examined. At the other extreme, EVPI may be so obviously tiny that little would be gained from such an evaluation, and the main decision should be made without delay.

Candidate sources of predictive information may be measured in an analgous fashion to the theoretically perfect (but almost never actually available) forecast. To illustrate how less-than-perfect information may be so valued, we will examine the oil wildcatter's decision using an alternative approach.

We begin with a fresh decision tree analysis of just the seismic survey portion, shown in Figure 23-6. (Again, for simplicity, the obviously nonoptimal strategies, abandoning no mater what, and so on, have been prepruned from the tree.) Under this alternative analysis, the outcomes are quantified in terms of *gross* payoffs that do not reflect the cost of the experimental information. The $30,000 survey cost has therefore been added back into the payoff column. (That amount will be accounted for at a later stage of the evaluation.)

The Expected Value of Experimental Information: EVEI

Backward induction prunes the new smaller tree exactly as before, with an ultimate expected payoff of $57,500. This quantity is referred to as the **expected payoff with experimental information**. The expected payoff advantage of having that information may

FIGURE 23-6
The alternative decision tree analysis for wildcatting decision using a seismic survey.

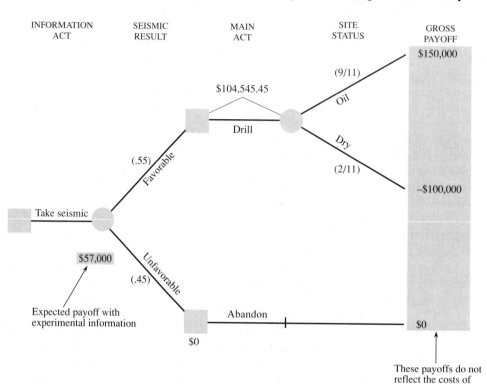

be found by subtracting the maximum expected payoff (with no information), found earlier to be $25,000 (from drilling) for the oil wildcatter. This difference is the **expected value of experimental information**, or EVEI.

EVEI = Expected payoff with experimental information (from tree)

— Maximum expected payoff (with no information)

For the oil wildcatter's seismic survey, we compute

EVEI(seismic) = $57,500 − $25,000 = $32,500

The above quantity indicates that the decision maker would experience a $32,500 advantage in expected payoff by first taking a seismic survey, followed by the indicated choices, over deciding (drilling) without benefit of that experimental information. This amount is totally analogous to the earlier EVPI figure of $50,000. The EVEI must be smaller than the EVPI, however, because an actual experiment is not 100% reliable (as a perfect predictor would be).

The Expected Net Gain of Experimenting: ENGE

Although the EVEI is analogous to EVPI, it cannot be used as the final yardstick because it does not incorporate the *cost* of the experiment. (And, we have never bothered to consider a cost for perfect information, which is strictly hypothetical.) The net advantage from predictive information must reflect its cost. Subtracting the cost from EVEI, we obtain the **expected net gain of experimenting**, or ENGE.

$$ENGE = EVEI - Cost$$

The seismic survey will cost $30,000, and thus has an expected net gain of

$$ENGE(seismic) = \$32,500 - \$30,000 = \$2,500$$

This amount conveys the net expected payoff advantage from using a seismic survey—and then taking the best action indicated for the results achieved—over choosing the best main act without that information.

Using ENGE to Choose Alternative Experiments

A decision maker may have several candidate experiments helpful in predicting the main events. The ENGE may be determined for each, resulting in a value that reflects the respective experiment's reliability and cost. Since the ENGE's will summarize, in a consistent manner, the worth of each source of information, those values may be used in choosing among the possible experiments.

This may be demonstrated by continuing with our oil wildcatter's decision. Suppose that a second experiment may be employed as an alternative to the seismic survey. This involves an aerial mapping of the lease site with a magnetic anomaly detector, a procedure that has proven successful in helping to pinpoint promising drilling locations.

For simplicity, we assume that just three outcomes are possible: generally positive readings, neutral findings, and an overall negative result. Previous experience with this procedure has shown that it will give a positive result with .70 probability in similar fields known to have oil; for those same sites it will give a neutral result 20% of the time and a negative one 10% of the time. Also, in regions known to have no oil it predicts negative 60% of the time, neutral 30%, and positive 10%. Using the same prior probabilities as before, Figure 23-7 provides the probability trees for the actual and informational chronologies.

The probabilities for the informational chronology with the magnetic anomaly detection are entered onto the decision tree in Figure 23-8. (Since there are three experimental results, the nonoptimality of some strategies is not clear-cut, and all act forks are portrayed in complete form.) As with the last tree, gross payoffs are used, and the cost of the procedure is not reflected. A backward induction analysis indicates that the wildcatter should drill if a positive reading is achieved, will achieve tying expected payoffs if it is neutral, and should abandon the lease site if the results are negative. Magnetic anomaly detection provides an expected payoff with experimental information of $47,500, the amount brought back to the initial event node.

FIGURE 23-7

Probability tree diagrams for the wildcatter's event chronologies using a Magnetic anomaly detector.

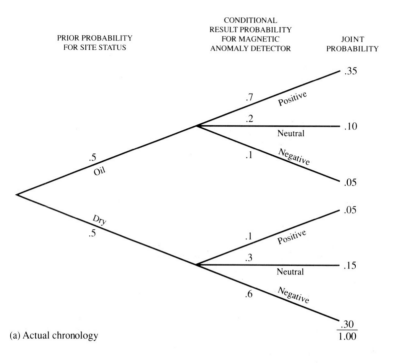

(a) Actual chronology

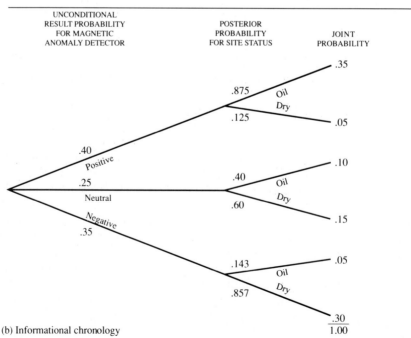

(b) Informational chronology

FIGURE 23-8

The alternative decision tree analysis for wildcatting decision using a Magnetic anomaly detector.

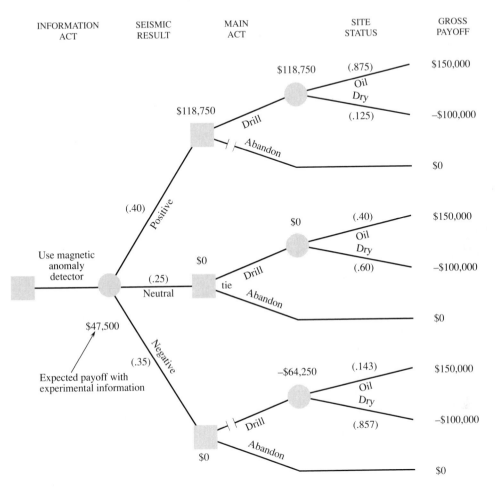

Subtracting the maximum expected payoff when no information is used, we have

$$\text{EVEI (magnetic)} = \$47,500 - \$25,000 = \$22,500$$

This amount is smaller than the counterpart found for the seismic, reflecting the lower reliability of magnetic anomaly detection. But the complete analysis must consider cost as well. The surveyor will do the job for $22,000—quite a bit less than the cost of the seismic survey. But that is not low enough to justify the procedure, since we compute the expected net gain to be

$$\text{ENGE (magnetic)} = \$22,500 - \$22,000 = \$500$$

which is worse than what may be achieved using the original seismic survey. The oil wildcatter will maximize expected payoff by using the seismic survey in preference to magnetic anomaly detection.

23-5 Future Analysis

The future analysis stage may or may not come into play. In the context of the wildcatter's decision, a future analysis may only be made once the seismic result is known. Should it turn out favorably, the wildcatter might want to defer the main decision whether or not to drill until after considering a second test, for example, based on finding magnetic anomalies. The posterior probabilities of 9/11 for oil and 2/11 for dry would serve as the prior probabilities in such an evaluation.

CASE

Comp-u-Com

Comp-u-Com is a telecommunications equipment manufacturing company specializing in computer-telephone interfacing. Management is deciding what items to introduce in the company product mix in the coming season. One possibility is a high-speed modem intended for home use. If successful, the new product is expected to increase Comp-u-Com's profits by $200,000. If unsuccessful, the modem's introduction cost of $100,000 will be lost.

On a trial basis, the company has in the past employed an outside panel of experts to screen new products. In evaluating that arrangement for a six-month trial period, Comp-u-Com found that the panel approved 7 out of 11 products that later proved to be successful. The panel disapproved 5 out of 7 products that had been introduced anyway and eventually failed.

A high-tech marketing research firm proposes, instead, to give a market prognostication. For similar products, the firm's batting average has been 90% in making favorable forecasts for items that later prove to be successful and 95% in making unfavorable predictions for devices that later fail in the marketplace.

Management judges the new modem very positively, assigning a 40% chance that it will be a successful new product.

Questions

1. The decision has not yet been made to employ the panel.
   (a) If the main modem decision were to be made now, which act would maximize expected payoff?
   (b) What is the upper limit on what management would pay for highly reliable information predicting the success or failure of the modem?
2. For the modem events and the panel results, construct the probability trees for the actual and informational chronologies.

3. Using gross payoffs, determine the expected payoff with panel evaluation. Then, determine, for the panel evaluation, the EVEI and ENGE. The panel cost is assumed to be $10,000.

4. Construct the probability trees for the actual and informational chronologies for the high-tech marketing research experiment.

5. The high-tech marketing research firm will make its prognostication for $20,000. Using gross payoffs, construct a decision tree diagram for this experiment and perform a backward induction analysis to determine the expected payoff using this information. Compute the EVEI and ENGE.

6. What should Comp-u-Com do to maximize expected payoff?

CASE

Hoopla Hoops

The marketing manager of Ace Widgets must choose one of three models to feature in the new product sweepstakes: Dooper Super, Double Dipper, or Triple Dipple. The following manufacturing cost and price data apply.

| | | UNIT COST | | |
ITEM	SET UP	Labor	Material	PRICE
Dooper Super	$45,000	$2.00	$3.00	$10.00
Double Dipper	60,000	1.80	2.90	11.00
Triple Dipple	65,000	1.50	2.50	10.60

Once production has been set up, the unit costs apply regardless of volume. Production volume will be linked to market demand, so that no unsold items will be made. For planning purposes, the manager assumes that the demand will be at one of the following levels: 10,000 (.3 probability), 15,000 (.4), or 20,000 (.3).

A marketing research study may be used. Either a positive or a negative result is possible. Based on past tests, the following conditional result probabilities apply.

| GIVEN DEMAND | CONDITIONAL PROBABILITY | |
	Positive	Negative
10,000	.5	.5
15,000	.6	.4
20,000	.8	.2

Questions

1. Assuming that no marketing research study will be taken, which model should Hoopla feature to maximize expected contribution?

2. Determine the expected value of perfect information. Discuss whether or not Hoopla should seek further experimental information on the demand for the new product.

3. Consider the marketing research study. Construct the probability trees for the actual and informational chronologies.

4. (a) Construct a complete decision tree diagram for Hoopla Hoops showing all possible choices that might be made. Ignore any cost for the study.
   (b) Compute (1) the EVEI and (2) ENGE when the marketing research has a cost of $20.

5. Suppose that a demand forecast experiment may be substituted for the marketing research study. The following probabilities apply.

GIVEN DEMAND	CONDITIONAL PROBABILITY		
	Weak	Moderate	Strong
10,000	.6	.3	.1
15,000	.3	.5	.2
20,000	.1	.2	.7

Construct the probability trees for the actual and informational chronologies.

6. (a) Construct a complete decision tree diagram for Hoopla Hoops showing all possible choices that might be made. Ignore any cost for the experiment.
   (b) Compute (1) the EVEI and (2) ENGE when the demand forecast experiment has a cost of $50.

7. Time will only permit Hoopla to use one source of information. To maximize expected payoff, should Hoopla request the marketing research study or the demand forecast experiment?

PROBLEMS

23-1 Oil wildcatter Rich Wells has assigned a .40 probability to striking oil on his property. He orders a seismic survey that has proved only 80% reliable in the past. Given oil, it predicts favorably 80% of the time; given no oil, it augurs unfavorably with a frequency of .8.

Construct probability trees for the actual and informational chronologies, and indicate the appropriate probability values for each branch and end position.

23-2 Inscrutable Smith places two coins in a box. The coins are identical in all respects, except that one is two-headed. Without looking, you select one coin from the box and lay it on the table.
(a) What is the prior probability that you will select the two-headed coin?
(b) As a source of predictive information about the selected coin, you may examine the showing face. Construct the probability tree diagram for the actual chronology of events.
(c) After you have examined the showing face of the coin, you may then turn it over to see what is on the other side. Construct the probability tree diagram for the informational chronology.
(d) If a head shows before you turn the coin over, what is the posterior probability that you selected the two-headed coin?

23-3 Refer to Problem 2-26 (page 46). Solve the weather forecasting problem by constructing probability trees for the actual and informational chronologies.

23-4 Refer to Problem 2-28 (page 47). Solve the deodorant marketing problem by constructing probability trees for the actual and informational chronologies.

23-5 Refer to Problem 2-24 (page 46). Solve the movie reviewer's prediction problem by constructing the probability trees for the actual and informational chronologies.

23-6 Refer to Problem 2-29 (page 47). Solve the employment screening test problem by constructing the probability trees for the actual and informational chronologies.

23-7 A box contains two pairs of dice. One pair is a fair one. The other pair consists of one die cube with a three on every side and one die cube with a four on every side. A pair is to be selected at random and tossed. You will only be able to see the top showing faces and not the sides. The main events of interest pertain to the crookedness or fairness of the tossed dice. (Both dice in the tossed pair will fall into the same category.) In each of the following cases, construct probability trees for the actual and informational chronologies.
(a) The experimental result is finding out whether or not a seven-sum (three and four, two and five, one and six) occurs.
(b) The experimental result is finding out whether or not a three-four combination occurs, which has a greater predictive worth than the result in (a).

23-8 Consider, again, the oil wildcatter in Section 23-4. Suppose that, for an additional $10,000, a special computer run can enhance the magnetic anomaly detection results. The new procedure will provide the following conditional result probabilities.

RESULT	GIVEN OIL	GIVEN NO OIL
Positive	.90	.05
Neutral	.07	.20
Negative	.03	.75

(a) Construct the new probability trees for the informational and actual chronologies.
(b) Compute the new EVEI and ENGE for enhanced magnetic anomaly detection.
(c) In terms of the expected payoff advantage, is the enhancement worth the added cost? Of the two original ones and the new one, which source of experimental information would now be best for the oil wildcatter to use?

23-9 The exploration manager for Crockpot Domes must decide whether to drill on a parcel of leased land or to abandon the lease. As an aid in making this choice, the manager must first decide whether to pay $30,000 for a seismic survey, which will confirm or deny the presence of the anticlinal structure necessary for oil. She has judged the prior probability for oil to be .30. For oil-producing fields of similar geology, her experience has shown that the chance of a confirming seismic is .9, but for dry holes with approximately the same characteristics, the probability that a seismic survey will deny oil has been established at only .7. Drilling costs have been firmly established at $200,000. If oil is struck, the manager's company plans to sell the lease for $500,000.

(a) What is the manager's EVPI for the basic decision, using profit as the payoff measure? Comparing this value to the cost of the seismic survey, can you conclude definitely that no survey should be made?

(b) Construct the manager's decision tree diagram, and determine the appropriate net payoffs.

(c) Determine the revised probabilities for the informational chronology and place these values on the corresponding branches of your decision tree diagram.

(d) Perform backward induction analysis to determine the course of action that will provide the maximum expected profit.

23-10 Refer to the decision in Problem 23-9 and to your answers.

(a) Construct the manager's prepruned decision tree diagram assuming that the seismic is used. Then, using gross payoffs, determine the expected payoff with experimental information.

(b) Compute the EVEI and ENGE. Does using the seismic have an expected payoff advantage over making the main decision with no experimental information?

23-11 The following payoff table of marketing choices for a new film has been determined by the management of Twentieth Century Folks.

BOX OFFICE RESULT EVENTS	Distribute As "A" Feature	Sell to TV Network	Distribute As "B" Feature
Success	$5,000,000	$1,000,000	$3,000,000
Failure	−2,000,000	1,000,000	−1,000,000

The prior probability for a box office success has been judged to be .3. The studio plans a series of sneak previews. Historically, 70% of all the studio's successful films have received favorable previews and 80% of all the studio's box office failures have received unfavorable previews.

(a) Construct the probability trees for the actual and informational chronologies.

(b) Construct a table indicating all of the studio's possible strategies contingent on results of the sneak preview.

(c) Construct a decision tree diagram for the studio's decision, assuming that the film will definitely be previewed at no cost.

(d) Perform backward induction analysis. What is the optimal course of action? To which strategy in (b) does this correspond?

23-12 Refer to Problem 23-11 and to your answers. Suppose that a special version of the film must be used in the sneak preview.

(a) Assuming that the same probabilities apply as before, compute the EVEI.

(b) If the new film costs $100,000 to make, compute the ENGE.

(c) For an additional $100,000, a special statistical analysis may be done following the sneak preview results. That analysis will result in an overall favorable or unfavorable rating. But each of the percentages given in Problem 23-11 will be 15 points higher. Construct the new probability trees for the actual and informational chronologies.

(d) Determine the expected payoff with the enhanced experiment in (c).

(e) Compute the EVEI and ENGE for the enhanced experiment in (c). Would the extra $100,000 be justified?

23-13 The makers of Quicker Oats oatmeal have packaged this product in cylindrical containers for 50 years. Management believes that the cylindrical container is inseparable from the product's image. But consumer tastes change, and the new marketing vice-president wonders if younger people will regard the round box as old-fashioned and unappealing. The vice-president wishes to analyze whether or not to package Quicker Oats in a rectangular box that will save significantly on transportation costs by eliminating dead space in the packing cartons. It is also believed that the change can actually expand Quicker Oats' market by uplifting the product's image. But previous study has shown that a small segment of the existing market buys the oatmeal primarily for the round box; these customers would be lost if the package were changed. The following payoff table has been established for the present net worth of retaining the old box versus using the new box.

NATIONAL MARKET RESPONSE TO NEW BOX EVENTS	ACT	
	Retain Old Box	Use New Box
Weak (W)	$0	− $2,000,000
Moderate (M)	0	0
Strong (S)	0	3,000,000

As prior probabilities for the new box response events, the marketing vice-president arrived at the following estimates: $\Pr[W] = .20$; $\Pr[M] = .30$; $\Pr[S] = .50$. The new box is to be test marketed for six months in a "barometer" city. Three outcomes are possible: decreased sales (D), unchanged sales (U), and increased sales (I). Historical experience with other products has established the following conditional result probabilities.

$$\Pr[D|W] = .8 \qquad \Pr[D|M] = .2 \qquad \Pr[D|S] = 0$$
$$\Pr[U|W] = .2 \qquad \Pr[U|M] = .4 \qquad \Pr[U|S] = .1$$
$$\Pr[I|W] = 0 \qquad \Pr[I|M] = .4 \qquad \Pr[I|S] = .9$$

(a) Construct the probability tree diagrams for the actual and informational chronologies.

(b) Construct the Quicker Oats decision tree diagram, assuming that the new box will be test marketed.

(c) Perform backward induction. Then indicate the maximum expected net payoff act for each test outcome. What is the optimal strategy?

23-14 Refer to Problem 23-13 and to your answers.

(a) Using the given prior probabilities for the national response, determine the expected payoff for retaining the old box and for using the new box. Which act maximizes expected payoff?

(b) Determine Quicker Oat's EVPI.

(c) Compute the EVEI for the test marketing.

(d) Suppose that the test marketing costs $100,000. Compute the ENGE. Does Quicker Oats actually maximize expected net payoff by using test marketing?

23-15 Portentous Prospector must decide how to dispose of a particular gas lease, which may be sold now for $20,000 or drilled on at a cost of $100,000. The drilling events and their prior probabilities are dry (D) at .6, low-pressure gas (L) at .3, and high-pressure gas (H) at .1. The lease will be abandoned for no receipts if D, it will be sold for $300,000 if L, and it will be sold for $500,000 if H.

(a) Which act—sell or drill—will maximize Prospector's expected profit?

(b) Determine the Prospector's EVPI?

(c) For a cost of $10,000 a 90% reliable seismic survey can predict gas favorably (F) with a probability of .90 if there is gas or unfavorably (U) with a probability of .90 if the site is dry, but it cannot measure pressure. Construct probability trees for the actual and informational chronologies, using the three gas events.

(d) Perform a decision tree analysis to determine what course of action will maximize Prospector's expected net profit.

23-16 Refer to the decision in Problem 23-15 and to your answers.

(a) Construct the Prospector's decision tree diagram assuming that the seismic is used. (Eliminate obviously non-optimal strategies.) Then, using gross payoffs, determine the expected payoff with experimental information.

(b) Compute the EVEI and ENGE. Does using the seismic have an expected payoff advantage over making the main decision with no experimental information?

23-17 Lucky Jones must decide whether to participate in a card game offered by Inscrutable Smith. For the price of $5, Jones will draw a card from an ordinary deck of playing cards. If the card is a king, Smith is to pay Jones $60 (so that Jones wins $55). But if the card is not a king, Jones will receive nothing for the $5. Smith, eager for action, offers Jones an additional enticement. For $3, Jones can draw a card without looking at it. Smith will then tell Jones whether or not the card is a face card. If Jones wishes to continue, an additional payment of $5 must be made for the game to proceed.

(a) Construct a decision tree diagram showing the structure of Jones' decision.

(b) Determine the probabilities for the events and the total profits for the end positions.

(c) What course of action will provide Jones with the greatest expected payoff?

23-18 The decision tree diagram in Figure 23-9 has been constructed by a marketing manager who wishes to determine how to introduce Wee Tee's. The manager judges that the prior probability for marketing success is .40.

(a) From a consumer survey costing $30,000, the manager obtains an 80% reliable indication to the Wee Tee's impact in the marketplace. Thus, the probability for a favorable survey result given market success is .80, and the probability for an unfavorable result given market failure is .80. Determine the posterior probabilities for the market events and the unconditional result probabilities for the survey events.

(b) A sales program costing $50,000 might be conducted in a test region. The results are judged to be 95% reliable. Determine the posterior and unconditional result probabilities.

(c) Using the information given in the problem statement and your answers to (a) and (b), perform backward induction to find the manager's optimal course of action. (The payoffs in Figure 23-9 include the cost of experimenting.)

FIGURE 23-9
Wee Tee's decision tree diagram for Problem 23-18.

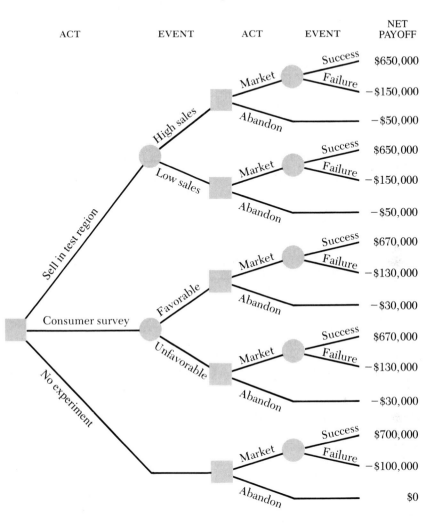

24

Bayesian Analysis of Decisions Using Sample Information

$\mathbb{I}$n Chapter 23, we considered the general problem of using experimental information in decision making. We will now consider a decision, commonly encountered in business situations, that involves just *two acts*. The experiment is taking a **random sample** from a population whose characteristics will affect the ultimate payoffs. The decision maker's choice depends on the particular sample result obtained.

Two types of populations are encountered in these sampling experiments. The **qualitative population** is composed of units that may be classified into categories. Examples are persons who may be categorized by occupation (blue-collar, professional), sex (male, female), or preference (preferring a product, disliking a product); and production items that may be classified in terms of quality (satisfactory, unsatisfactory), weight (below the limit, above the limit), or color (light, medium, dark). The **quantitative population** associates a numerical value with each unit. For example, people may be measured in terms of income levels, aptitude test scores, or years of experience; and items may be assigned numerical values to indicate weight, volume, or quantity of an ingredient.

A sample from a qualitative population tells us how many sample units fall into a particular category, and this number reflects the prevalence of that attribute in the population, which in turn affects the payoff associated with the incidence of the attribute.

For example, in deciding how to dispose of a supplier's shipment, a receiving inspector may discover that 12 of the items out of a random sample of 100 are defective, indicating that there is a high probability that the entire shipment is bad and that returning it might maximize expected payoff. The payoffs in such a problem are often expressed in terms of the proportion P of the population having the key attribute (for example, the proportion of defective items in the entire shipment). As in most decision making using experiments, the value of P itself and the number of defectives that will turn up in the sample are both uncertain. Probabilities for the number of defectives may be determined by using the binomial distribution.

A sample taken from a quantitative population provides a similar basis for action, such as accepting or rejecting a machine setting in a chemical process. Here, the mean quantity of a particular ingredient in each gallon may be the determining factor in establishing the payoff. The population mean μ measures the central quantity of the ingredient in all gallons made under that setting. The true value of μ is uncertain. A second area of uncertainty involves the quantities in the sample itself; here, the sample mean $\bar{X}$ may serve as the basis for decision making.

In this chapter, we will consider how to integrate sample information into the basic decision-making structure. As in Chapter 23, the procedure involves prior probabilities for P or μ, which must be revised to coincide with possible sample results to provide posterior probabilities for these population parameters. Backward induction with revised probabilities then provides the optimal decision rule, based on the sample statistic that is obtained. The analysis may be expanded to consider how many sample observations must be made.

24-1 Decision Making with the Proportion

We begin our discussion of Bayesian sampling with procedures based on the proportion. There are surprising features. First, good decision making might be reached without sampling at all; that is because sampling may be very expensive in relation to the value of perfect information. Second, a great deal of information may be gleaned from very small sample sizes.

Application to Acceptance Sampling

ILLUSTRATION
Disk Drive Quality

A quality assurance manager for a computer OEM (original equipment manufacturer) wishes to establish a procedure for determining whether to accept or reject shipments of hard disk drives. Each drive unit in an accepted shipment will be directly installed, untested, in computer housings. Should an installed unit later prove to be defective, the computer must be disassembled and a new disk drive installed, at great expense. This expense may be avoided if the manager instead rejects the shipment and then routes all disk drive units to an inspection facility to be tested prior to assembly.

The manager is primarily concerned with the proportion P of defective units in each shipment. Should P be small, then it may be cheaper to accept the shipment and install untested disk drives. But for a large P it may be considerably less expensive to reject the shipment and test all incoming drives before installation. Of course, the value of P for any given shipment is an uncertain quantity.

The payoff measure for this decision is based on $50 value added to the final product per installed disk drive, which establishes a basic value of $50,000 for a 1,000-unit shipment. The net payoff is found by subtracting any relevant costs. Replacing a defective drive already installed in a computer costs $100, so that for the entire shipment the cost of accepting is $100P(1,000) = $100,000P$. The cost of 100% testing of the disk drives (in rejected shipments) is $20 per unit. Because the supplier gives full credit for returned units, the total cost of rejecting a shipment is $20(1,000) = $20,000$, so that the net payoff is $50,000 - $20,000 = $30,000$.

The manager's payoffs may be expressed algebraically as

$$\text{Payoff} = \begin{cases} \$50{,}000 - \$100{,}000P & \text{for accept} \\ \$30{,}000 & \text{for reject} \end{cases}$$

Using the above, the payoff table is constructed in Table 24-1 applicable to each shipment containing 1,000 disk drives. Five possible levels are provided for P, with subjective prior probabilities based on previous experience with the supplier and the manager's judgment. The analysis is simplified by considering P to the nearest whole 5%. (The same procedures would apply if we considered $P = .01, .02, \ldots, .27$.)

Prior Analysis of the Decision

The expected payoff for accept is $32,500, which is greater than the $30,000 payoff achieved by reject. This indicates that without pursuing any further experimental information the manager should accept each shipment, replacing only those disk drives that are found to be defective after they are installed.

However, the expected value of perfect information is

$$\text{EVPI} = \$34{,}000 - \$32{,}500 = \$1{,}500$$

TABLE 24-1
Payoff Table for Disk Drive Decision

PROPORTION DEFECTIVE EVENT	PROBABILITY	ACT		PAYOFF WITH PERFECT INFORMATION
		Accept	*Reject*	
$P = .05$	.10	$45,000	$30,000	$45,000
$P = .10$	.15	40,000	30,000	40,000
$P = .15$	.20	35,000	30,000	35,000
$P = .20$	.25	30,000	30,000	30,000
$P = .25$	.30	25,000	30,000	30,000
	Expected payoff	$32,500	$30,000	$34,000

which indicates that considerable potential savings may be achieved by sampling each incoming shipment and testing randomly selected disk drives.

Posterior Analysis Using Sample Information

If a sample is used, the manager will not decide what to do with a shipment until after obtaining the sample results. If the sample contains a high number of defectives, the manager should reject the shipment. The shipment should be accepted if the sample contains a low number of defectives.

The choice of sample size, and the question of whether to sample at all, will be considered shortly. For now, suppose that the manager will use a sample of $n = 2$ items. The decision tree diagram in Figure 24-1 applies. Notice that there are three possible levels

FIGURE 24-1
One of several decision trees for acceptance sampling of disk drives.

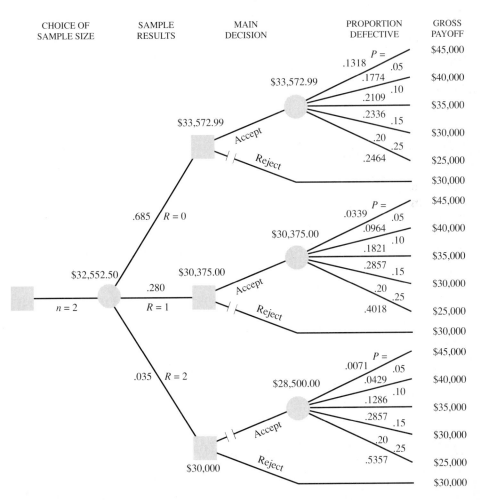

TABLE 24-2

Binomial Conditional Result Probabilities
for
the Number of Defective Disk Drives
($n = 2$)

P	r	$\Pr[R = r] = \dfrac{n!}{r!(n-r)!} P^r (1-P)^{n-r}$
.05	0	$1(.05)^0(.95)^2 = .9025$
.05	1	$2(.05)^1(.95)^i = .0950$
.05	2	$1(.05)^2(.95)^0 = .0025$
		1.0000
.10	0	$1(.10)^0(.90)^2 = .8100$
.10	1	$2(.10)^1(.90)^1 = .1800$
.10	2	$1(.10)^2(.90)^0 = .0100$
		1.0000
.15	0	$1(.15)^0(.85)^2 = .7225$
.15	1	$2(.15)^1(.85)^1 = .2550$
.15	2	$1(.15)^2(.85)^0 = .0225$
		1.0000
.20	0	$1(.20)^0(.80)^2 = .6400$
.20	1	$2(.20)^1(.80)^1 = .3200$
.20	2	$1(.20)^2(.80)^0 = .0400$
		1.0000
.25	0	$1(.25)^0(.75)^2 = .5625$
.25	1	$2(.25)^1(.75)^1 = .3750$
.25	2	$1(.25)^2(.75)^0 = .0625$
		1.0000

for the number of defectives R found in the sample. In each case, an act fork follows with accept and reject as the choices. The event forks in the final stage each have five branches, one for each P event. The final payoffs were determined from the above expression. For brevity, there is no event fork following reject, because the payoffs will be the same regardless of the level for P. The probability values are found using the same basic procedure as in Chapter 23.

The conditional result probabilities are obtained using the following binomial formula.*

$$\Pr[R = r] = \frac{n!}{r!(n-r)!} P^r (1-P)^{n-r}$$

---

* The binomial serves only as an approximation when sampling from a finite population. The true sampling distribution for R in those cases is the hypergeometric, which should be used instead when the population size N is small.

The result probabilities follow logically from the given *n* and the assumed level for *P*. Table 24-2 shows the calculations using the above to determine the conditional result probabilities for the number of sample defectives *R*. The values obtained appear on the second-stage branches in the probability tree for the actual chronology in Figure 24-2.

Each level of *P* corresponds to a *different population* and therefore requires a separate set of binomial probabilities. In calculating these values, *it is important not to confuse the level of P with its prior probability.* For example, in calculating the conditional result probabilities for the number of defectives in the sample when $P = .05$, we use .05 as the trial success probability *P*; we do not use .10, which is the prior probability of the event and is applied in a later step of the analysis.

FIGURE 24-2
Probability tree for actual chronology in disk drive acceptance sampling.

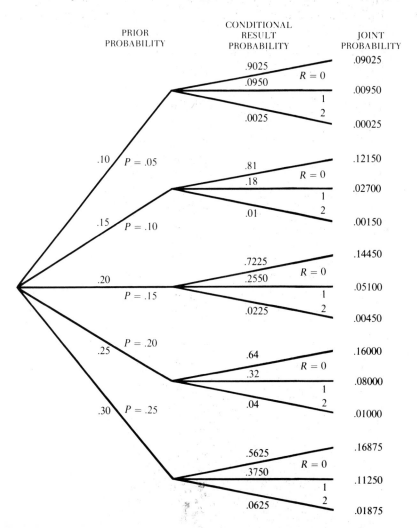

The joint probabilities are then computed, as in Chapter 23, by multiplying the probabilities on the respective branches. These are transferred to their proper location in the probability tree for the informational chronology in Figure 24-3. In making the computations, *the events should not be confused with their probabilities.* Remember that $P = .05$ and $P = .10$ are the *events* and represent possible levels for the number of defectives in the population. (Because these equations are events, it makes no sense to combine the values of P arithmetically. Since they should not be added together, they certainly do not have to add up to 1.) The prior probabilities .10, .15,... are the multipliers. Thus, the top joint probability in Figure 24-2 is

$$\Pr[P = .05 \text{ and } R = 0] = .10 \times .9025 = .09025$$

and the other joint probabilities are calculated in the same way.

Figure 24-3 shows the probability tree for the informational chronology. Shown there are the unconditional result probabilities found for R and the posterior probabilities

FIGURE 24-3

Probability tree for informational chronology in disk drive acceptance sampling.

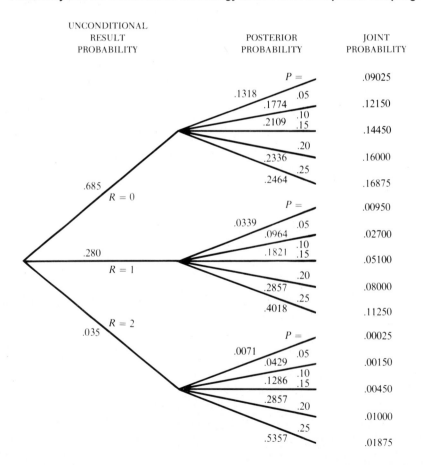

established for P for each given level of R. These are the probabilities that were transferred to the manager's original decision tree diagram in Figure 24-1.

Backward induction with the decision tree (page 709) indicates that when $n = 2$, the maximum expected payoff for $R = 0$ is \$33,572.99. The result corresponds to choosing the act *accept*. When $R = 1$, the same act provides a maximum expected payoff of \$30,375.00. For $R = 2$, the payoff \$30,000 for reject is greater than the expected payoff for accept, so that reject is the selected act.

The Decision Rule and Critical Value

The result of the backward induction may be summarized in terms of the following **decision rule**.

$$\text{Accept} \quad \text{if } R \leq 1$$

$$\text{Reject} \quad \text{if } R > 1$$

The greatest level for R at which accept is the better choice is called the **critical value**, which we denote by C. In quality assurance applications, this is ordinarily called the **acceptance number**. In the present evaluation $C = 1$. Here, C represents the maximum number of sample defectives for which accepting a shipment is the act maximizing expected payoff.

The expected payoff in using a sample of $n = 2$ disk drives is \$32,552.50. That amount is greater than the expected payoff of \$32,500 found in Table 24-1 for accept. This suggests that sampling shipments first may be better than accepting them without inspection. Should the cost be low enough, sampling would be superior. But, by itself, the decision tree analysis cannot settle this issue, since the cost of sampling was not reflected. We next consider a systematic evaluation of the sampling issue.

24-2 Valuing Sample Information

We are now ready to quantify sample information itself in terms of expected payoff. The decision tree analysis in Figure 24-1 for the disk drive acceptance sampling illustration provides a maximum expected payoff of \$32,552.50 when the sample size is $n = 2$. We refer to this quantity as the expected payoff with sample information. It is based on gross payoffs, and does not reflect the cost of sampling. Of course, sampling costs must ultimately be considered. Thus far, our analysis may be classified as *posterior* (oriented toward actions after sampling). We still have to consider the more basic decision of whether or not to sample in the first place, and, if we sample, how large a sample to take. To answer these questions, we must move into the area of *preposterior* analysis (where the vantage is before sampling).

The Expected Value of Sample Information

Recall that the EVPI establishes the worth of perfect information and represents the expected payoff advantage that perfect information would have over making the best choice with no information at all. It is computed from the following difference.

EVPI = Expected payoff with perfect information (under certainty)

      − Maximum expected payoff (with no information)

Earlier, we computed the quality assurance manager's EVPI to be

$$EVPI = \$34{,}000 - \$32{,}500 = \$1{,}500$$

The following measure is similar to the EVPI, but it expresses the worth of the information contained in the sample. The expected value of sample information is calculated as

EVSI = Expected payoff with sample information

      − Maximum expected payoff (with no information)

This is analogous to EVEI introduced in Chapter 23, with S (for sample) replacing E (for experimental). (Indeed, a sample is just a special type of experiment that results in predictive information.) The EVSI expresses the net advantage, in terms of gross expected payoff, of having sample results over having no information at all.

To illustrate, we continue with the disk drive acceptance sampling illustration. From the decision tree in Figure 24-1, we read the expected payoff of $32,552.50 from using a sample of size $n = 2$ and accepting only those shipments having $C = 1$ defective or fewer. That amount is the manager's expected payoff with imperfect sample information. (The $32,552.50 plays the same role in establishing EVSI that the $34,000 does in obtaining EVPI.) Subtracting the maximum expected payoff (with no information) found earlier, we have

$$EVSI = \$32{,}552.50 - \$32{,}500 = \$52.50$$

This amount represents how much better off the quality assurance manager would be on the average if he had the $n = 2$ sample result instead of no information at all. The EVSI is totally analogous to the EVPI, but it applies to less reliable information gleaned from the sample. Like the EVPI, the EVSI establishes an upper limit on the amount a decision maker should pay to obtain the sample results.

The Expected Net Gain of Sampling

Preposterior analysis often begins (as in this illustration) with *gross* payoffs rather than net payoffs, and sampling costs must therefore be integrated at a later stage. (One reason for waiting to include the sampling costs is that it is sometimes easier to minimize expected opportunity loss than it is to maximize expected payoff. It is more convenient to include sampling costs at the end when such an approach is used.)

In terms of gross annual savings, the manager is better off by the EVSI of $52.50 if he obtains the sample results and then applies the optimal decision rule with $C = 1$. Thus, the manager should be willing to pay up to $52.50 for the sample but should not sample at a higher cost. *As long as the cost of sampling is less than the EVSI, the decision maker is better off with the sample than without it.*

How large should n be? This question is ordinarily a matter of economics. We could compute EVSI for several levels of n, subtracting the sampling costs in each case. Each resulting value would then represent the **expected net gain of sampling** or ENGS. Treating n as a variable, the expected net gain of sampling is expressed as

$$ENGS(n) = EVSI(n) - Cost(n)$$

(The above is analogous to ENGE found in Chapter 23.) Continuing with our illustration, when $n = 2$,

$$ENGS(2) = EVSI(2) - Cost(2)$$

Using a cost per inspected item of $20, we have

$$ENGS(2) = \$52.50 - 2(\$20) = \$12.50$$

Comparable figures could be obtained for other sizes of n, and the **optimal sample size** would be the one with the greatest expected net gain.

Depending on the payoffs and on the prior probability distribution for P, the Bayesian procedure may indicate that no sample should be used. In some cases the optimal n is no larger than 5 or 10 observations. Such small sample sizes are unheard of in traditional statistics.

Preposterior Analysis of Sample Information

Since in the present illustration it is better to sample than not, the analysis may be continued into the preposterior stage. There, an optimal sample size is established. To find that n, the preceding analysis must be duplicated for each candidate n. In each case, a new set of probability trees and probability values must be found (as in Figures 24-2 and 24-3) and then a fresh backward induction analysis must be performed (as in Figure 24-1) to compute the expected payoff and to find the applicable acceptance number.

The ensuing computational task may be formidable, and is a chore properly relegated to a computer. The personal computer software package *QuickQuant*, available to users of this book, will make the necessary computations. Figure 24-4 shows a portion of the *QuickQuant* report when $n = 3$ and binomial probabilities are again used. There, Act 1 represents accept and Act 2 signifies reject. (As an exercise, you may sketch the two probability trees and the decision tree diagram, placing numbers from the printout onto the respective branches.) A detailed discussion of how to use the program is given in Section 24-4.

For supplied parameters, *QuickQuant* will do all necessary computations needed for a preposterior analysis. It can accommodate sample sizes up to $n = 100$. Runs may be made with either binomial or hypergeometric probabilities for R; the probabilities are determined automatically within the program.

FIGURE 24-4

Portion of a *QuickQuant* report showing actual and informational binomial probabilities and decision tree analysis results for disk drive acceptance sampling when *n* = 3.

```
==============================================================================
                              QuickQuant Report
              SPECIAL REPORTS FOR DECISION MAKING WITH PROPORTION
------------------------------------------------------------------------------
PROBLEM: Disk Drive Quality (Using Binomial)                 Date: 04-08-1990

        DECISION MAKING WITH PROPORTION--ACTUAL PROBABILITY CHRONOLOGY

    Sample    Level for      Prior     Sample  Cond. Result     Joint
    Size      Proportion  Probability  Result  Probability   Probability
    ----------------------------------------------------------------------
    n=3       P=.050       0.100000    R=0      0.857375      0.085737
                                       R=1      0.135375      0.013538
                                       R=2      0.007125      0.000713
                                       R=3      0.000125      0.000013
    n=3       P=.100       0.150000    R=0      0.729000      0.109350
                                       R=1      0.243000      0.036450
                                       R=2      0.027000      0.004050
                                       R=3      0.001000      0.000150
    n=3       P=.150       0.200000    R=0      0.614125      0.122825
                                       R=1      0.325125      0.065025
                                       R=2      0.057375      0.011475
                                       R=3      0.003375      0.000675
    n=3       P=.200       0.250000    R=0      0.512000      0.128000
                                       R=1      0.384000      0.096000
                                       R=2      0.096000      0.024000
                                       R=3      0.008000      0.002000
    n=3       P=.250       0.300000    R=0      0.421875      0.126563
                                       R=1      0.421875      0.126563
                                       R=2      0.140625      0.042188
                                       R=3      0.015625      0.004688

     DECISION MAKING WITH PROPORTION--INFORMATIONAL PROBABILITY CHRONOLOGY

      Sample    Sample   Unconditional   Level of     Posterior
      Size      Result    Probability    Proportion  Probability
      ------------------------------------------------------------
      n=3       R=0       0.572475        P=.050      0.149766
                                          P=.100      0.191013
                                          P=.150      0.214551
                                          P=.200      0.223591
                                          P=.250      0.221079
      n=3       R=1       0.337575        P=.050      0.040102
                                          P=.100      0.107976
                                          P=.150      0.192624
                                          P=.200      0.284381
                                          P=.250      0.374917
      n=3       R=2       0.082425        P=.050      0.008644
                                          P=.100      0.049136
                                          P=.150      0.139218
                                          P=.200      0.291174
                                          P=.250      0.511829
      n=3       R=3       0.007525        P=.050      0.001661
                                          P=.100      0.019934
                                          P=.150      0.089701
                                          P=.200      0.265781
                                          P=.250      0.622924

        DECISION MAKING WITH PROPORTION--DECISION TREE SUMMARY

   Sample   Critical   Expected  Sample    EXPECTED PAYOFFS        Best
   Size     Value      Payoff    Result    Act 1        Act 2      Act
   -------------------------------------------------------------------------
   n=3      C=1        $32620.75 R=0      $34123.98   $30000.00  Act 1
                                 R=1      $30769.83   $30000.00  Act 1
                                 R=2      $28757.96   $30000.00  Act 2
                                 R=3      $27558.14   $30000.00  Act 2
   -------------------------------------------------------------------------
```

Table 24-3 shows a partial listing of the *QuickQuant* results for the disk drive acceptance sampling illustration. (These data appear in a modified format from the actual computer report, a more detailed example of which is provided later.) Notice that the sample sizes $n = 2$ through $n = 7$ all provide the same acceptance number, $C = 1$. The best sample size in that group is $n = 6$, having the highest ENGS(n). The second grouping

TABLE 24-3
Partial Summary of Sample Size Evaluations for Disk Drive Acceptance Sampling

SAMPLE SIZE n	USING BINOMIAL PROBABILITIES FOR R				USING HYPERGEOMETRIC PROBABILITIES FOR R			
	EVSI(n)	Cost(n)	ENGS(n)	C	EVSI(n)	Cost(n)	ENGS(n)	C
1	$32,500.00	$ 20.00	$ −20.00	0	$32,500.00	$ 20.00	$− 20.00	0
2	32,552.50	40.00	12.50	1	32,552.55	40.00	12.55	1
3	32,620.75	60.00	60.75	1	32,621.11	60.00	61.11	1
4	32,683.58	80.00	103.58	1	32,684.48	80.00	104.48	1
5	32,729.91	100.00	129.91	1	32,731.46	100.00	131.46	1
6	32,755.02	120.00	135.02	1	32,757.20	120.00	137.20	1
7	32,758.05	140.00	118.05	1	32,760.74	140.00	120.74	1
8	32,811.15	160.00	151.15	2	32,812.85	160.00	152.85	2
9	32,866.14	180.00	186.14	2	32,868.76	180.00	188.76	2
10	32,909.27	200.00	209.27	2	32,912.85	200.00	212.85	2
11	32,938.82	220.00	218.82	2	32,943.29	220.00	223.29	2
12	32,954.15	240.00	214.14	2	32,959.39	240.00	219.39	2
13	32,955.47	260.00	195.47	2	32,961.32	260.00	201.32	2
16	33,069.30	320.00	249.30	3	33,075.83	320.00	255.83	3
17	33,088.93	340.00	248.93	3	33,096.36	340.00	256.36	3
22*	33,189.39	440.00	249.39	4	33,198.80	440.00	258.80	4
27	33,268.55	540.00	228.55	5	33,279.79	540.00	239.79	5
32	33,333.37	640.00	193.37	6	33,346.37	640.00	206.37	6
37	33,387.93	740.00	147.93	7	33,402.61	740.00	162.61	7
42	33,434.82	840.00	94.82	8	33,451.08	840.00	111.08	8
47	33,475.69	940.00	35.69	9	33,493.49	940.00	53.49	9
53	33,526.12	1,060.00	− 33.88	10	33,546.11	1,060.00	− 13.89	10
58	33,557.81	1,160.00	− 102.19	11	33,579.19	1,160.00	− 80.81	11
63	33,586.23	1,260.00	− 173.77	12	33,608.91	1,260.00	− 151.09	12
68	33,611.93	1,360.00	− 248.07	13	33,635.86	1,360.00	− 224.14	13
74	33,645.07	1,480.00	− 334.93	14	33,670.57	1,480.00	− 309.43	14
79	33,666.09	1,580.00	− 413.91	15	33,692.68	1,580.00	− 387.32	15
84	33,685.39	1,680.00	− 494.61	16	33,713.02	1,680.00	− 466.98	16
89	33,703.13	1,780.00	− 576.88	17	33,731.73	1,780.00	− 548.27	17
94	33,720.33	1,880.00	− 659.67	17	33,749.10	1,880.00	− 630.90	18
95	33,726.22	1,900.00	− 673.78	18	33,755.85	1,900.00	− 644.15	18
100	33,741.17	2,000.00	− 758.83	19	33,771.72	2,000.00	− 728.28	19

includes $n = 8$ through $n = 13$, all with $C = 2$ as the acceptance number. In this second group, $n = 11$ provides the greatest expected net gain. The boldface rows in the remainder of Table 24-3 list the payoff information for the best sample size in each successive C-level group.

Since each shipment involves $N = 1,000$ units and sampling is done without replacement, the *hypergeometric* distribution represents the true probabilities for R. Using these, Figure 24-5 was constructed. The graph in Figure 24-5(a) plots EVSI(n) against

FIGURE 24-5

Graphs for disk drive acceptance sampling showing how EVSI(n) and ENGS(n) relate to sample size, sampling cost and EVPI (based on hypergeometric probabilities).

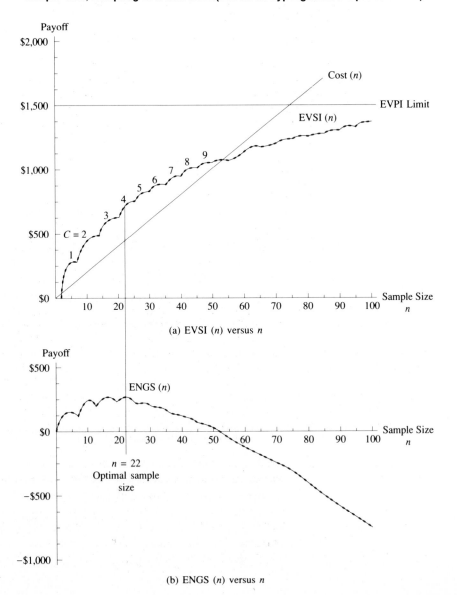

(a) EVSI (n) versus n

(b) ENGS (n) versus n

sample size for all n's from 1 to 100. Notice the cusping effect for those n's that share a common acceptance number C. Notice also that EVSI(n) gets steadily higher as n becomes greater, approaching a threshold level of $1,500 (the EVPI). (Indeed, as n becomes arbitrarily large, sample data become perfect information, so that in the limiting case EVSI(n) converges to EVPI.) But the best choice for n lies at a much lower level. Reflecting the cost of sampling, ENGS(n) is used to find the best n.

Figure 24-5(b) plots ENGS(n) against sample size. That graph shows that each cusp achieves a local maximum for the n's within each group. The global maximum is $258.79, occurring at $n = 22$. The greatest expected payoff overall is achieved when ENGS(n) is maximized, so that $n = 22$ is the *optimal sample size*.

Payoff Functions in Decision Making

Decision making with sample information ordinarily involves *two acts*. This reflects the general thrust of statistical decision making, where there are two actions.

Accept the null hypothesis

Reject the null hypothesis

(Hypothesis testing is briefly reviewed in Section 24-5.) The payoffs for the two acts may be characterized as *functions* of P.

Figure 24-6 shows the commonly encountered situations and how the statistical decision rule fits in. Figure 24-6(a) portrays the payoff functions as lines. For low levels of P, Act 1 provides greater payoffs. Act 2 is the better choice for high P levels. That payoff ranking is reflected in the statistical decision rule, which requires choosing Act 1 when the number of sample successes R is $\leq$ the critical value C and Act 2 when $R > C$.

Figure 24-6(b) graphs the linear payoff functions when Act 1 dominates Act 2. In such a case, EVPI $= 0$ and there is no advantage from sampling (Why?). Figure 24-6(c) illustrates the case when payoff functions are nonlinear. This case ordinarily results in the same type of decision rule as those found with linear payoffs. Decisions involving linear payoff functions may be analyzed using the simple geometry of lines to achieve computational advantages. Nonlinear payoff functions may be more cumbersome and will ordinarily require evaluation in terms of payoff tables.

24-3 Decision Making with the Sample Mean

A completely analogous procedure to decision making using binomial probabilities applies when samples are taken from quantitative populations.

ILLUSTRATION
A Computer Memory Device Decision

To illustrate decision making based on the sample mean, we will consider the decision of a computer center manager regarding the kind of peripheral memory storage device to

FIGURE 24-6
Payoff functions encountered in decision making with proportion.

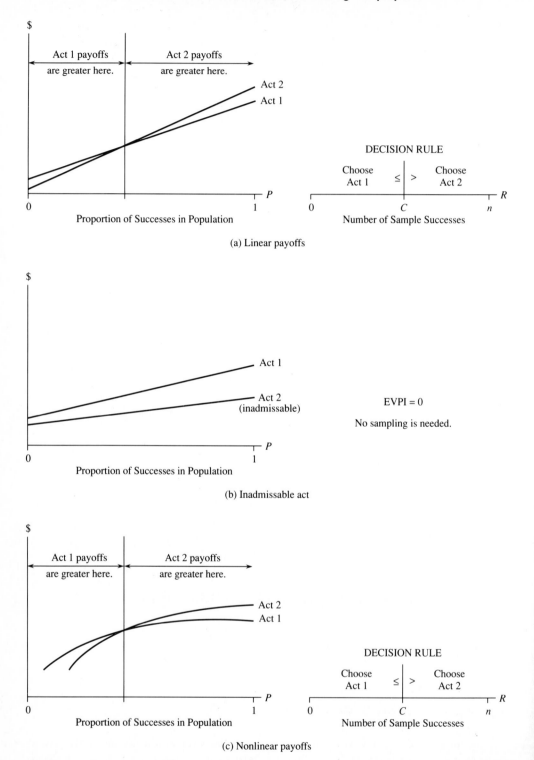

(a) Linear payoffs

(b) Inadmissable act

(c) Nonlinear payoffs

use in the computer system. The two proposed units are based on laser technology, and both units will operate more efficiently than the current memory storage device. One alternative is based on photographic principles and requires special film for storing the data. The other alternative employs holography—a process in which a three-dimensional image is retrieved from a special wafer. A photographic memory unit costs less to lease than a holographic unit, but it is slower and therefore more costly to operate. The storage capacities and reliabilities of the two units are identical.

The annual savings from using either alternative unit depends on the daily volume of peripheral memory access. Although the actual number of bits stored or retrieved varies daily, the mean daily access level may be used to establish an average annual access savings for each alternative. When this savings is added to the fixed lease cost, the result-ing mean total annual savings serves as the payoff measure for this decision. This payoff depends on the mean daily gigabits (billion bits) accessed μ, which represents the average volume over all days.

The computer center manager is uncertain about the value of μ, since historical data on the density of peripheral memory traffic are incomplete.

Prior Analysis

Figure 24-7 presents the manager's decision structure when no sample information is available. Notice that different payoff values for mean annual savings are obtained for each type of unit and μ combination. Using prior probabilities of .5 for $\mu = 2$ and .5 for

FIGURE 24-7
The computer center manager's decision structure when no sample is used.

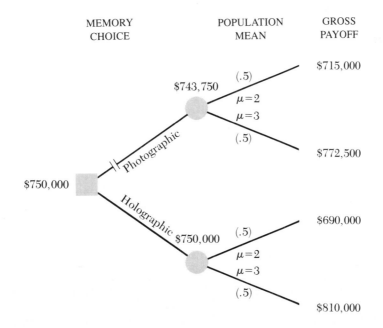

$\mu = 3$, we find that the holographic memory unit provides the greatest expected payoff of $750,000 in mean annual savings.

The attractiveness of deferring the main decision until after experimentation through sampling is roughly gauged by the EVPI. With a perfect predictor, the chosen payoffs would be $715,000 (for photographic) when $\mu = 2$ and $810,000 (for holographic) when $\mu = 3$. The expected payoff with perfect information is thus,

$$\$715,000(.50) + \$810,000(.50) = \$762,500$$

Subtracting the $750,000 maximum expected payoff with no information found earlier, we have

$$\text{EVPI} = \$762,500 - \$750,000 = \$12,500$$

This amount is big enough to justify further analysis of sample information, from which a considerable expected payoff advantage may be achieved.

Posterior Analysis

We will now consider the manager's analysis using sample data. The manager believes that for an extra few hundred dollars per day she can determine the precise level of peripheral memory access on sample days by adding a special accounting program to the software system. Any sampling cost arises from the slower processing that will result. Suppose that a sample of $n = 9$ days is to be used.

Since the sample data will be used to predict mean daily access levels, it is appropriate to summarize the sampling results in terms of the sample mean memory access level, which is computed from

$$\bar{X} = \frac{X_1 + X_2 + \cdots + X_n}{n}$$

where $X_1, X_2, \ldots, X_n$ are the observed levels for individual sample days. A large $\bar{X}$ will lend credence to the greater population mean value of $\mu = 3$ gigabits per day, and a small $\bar{X}$ will support $\mu = 2$. But since the sample results are not yet known, the actual value of $\bar{X}$ is uncertain. In Chapter 3, we investigated the properties of the sample mean. For large n, the sample mean is approximately normally distributed (under appropriate conditions that are assumed to apply here) with a mean of μ.

There will be a separate normal curve for $\bar{X}$ for each level of μ, as shown in Figure 24-8. Recall, from Chapter 3, that the standard deviation for the $\bar{X}$ normal curve is related to the population standard deviation σ_I (where the subscript emphasizes that the measure summarizes *individual* differences) by the following transformation.

$$\sigma_{\bar{X}} = \frac{\sigma_I}{\sqrt{n}}$$

FIGURE 24-8

Normal distribution for $\bar{X}$ used in establishing approximate conditional result probabilities.

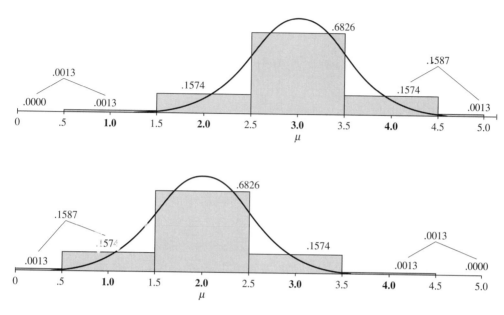

Sample Mean $\bar{X}$

In the present illustration, it is assumed that $\sigma_I = 1.5$ gigabit per day, so that when $n = 9$,

$$\sigma_{\bar{X}} = \frac{1.5}{\sqrt{9}} = .5 \text{ gigabit per day}$$

The procedure for evaluating a decision with the mean parallels that for a decision with the proportion. Conditional result probabilities for $\bar{X}$ must be found for the actual chronology. These must be obtained from the respective normal distribution through an approximation procedure that begins with dividing the possible levels for $\bar{X}$ into intervals.

Table 24-4 shows how this is done using six intervals for each case. Each non-zero interval probability is represented in Figure 24-8 by a rectangle. Interval midpoints are used to represent all possible $\bar{X}$'s falling in the respective interval. To simplify the ensuing tree evaluations, the extreme cases for each normal curve tail are grouped into one category. This leaves four representative levels for $\bar{X}$ in each case. (Of course, the accuracy of the procedure will improve with a greater number of intervals.)

The approximate conditional result probabilities for $\bar{X}$ are used in the tree for the actual chronology in Figure 24-9(a). The probabilities for the informational chronology in Figure 24-9(b) are obtained in the usual manner.

The manager's decision tree diagram using sample information is provided in Figure 24-10. The revised probabilities used there are obtained from Figure 24-9. Backward induction in Figure 24-10 indicates that the maximum expected annual savings

TABLE 24-4

Interval Probabilities for Sample Mean in Computer Memory Device Decision

INTERVAL FOR $\bar{X}$	$\mu = 2.0$				$\mu = 3.0$		
	Normal Deviate z	Cumulative Probability	Interval Probability		Normal Deviate z	Cumulative Probability	Interval Probability
< .5	−3.00	.5 − .4987 = .0013	.0013		−5.00	.0000	.0000
.5–1.5	−1.00	.5 − .3413 = .1587	.1574		−3.00	.0013	.0013
1.5–2.5	1.00	.5 + .3413 = .8413	.6826		−1.00	.1587	.1574
2.5–3.5	3.00	.5 + .4987 = .9987	.1574		1.00	.8413	.6826
3.5–4.5	5.00	1.0000	.0013		3.00	.9987	.1574
>4.5	∞	1.0000	.0000		∞	1.0000	.0013

will be achieved by selecting the photographic memory unit for $\bar{X} = 1$ or $\bar{X} = 2$ and the holographic peripheral storage unit for $\bar{X} = 3$ or $\bar{X} = 4$. We express this result in terms of the decision rule

$$\text{Select photographic unit} \quad \text{if } \bar{X} \le C$$
$$\text{Select holographic unit} \quad \text{if } \bar{X} > C$$

where $C = 2$ gigabits per day. The manager would thus select the photographic unit if $\bar{X} = 1.53$ or 1.95 and the holographic unit if $\bar{X} = 3.13$ or 2.04.

The amount $757,540.66 is the expected payoff with sample information. Subtracting from this the maximum expected payoff of $750,000 found earlier for using a holographic memory without getting sample information, we obtain

$$\text{EVSI}(9) = \$757,540.66 - \$750,000 = \$7,540.66$$

The extra software required to monitor memory during testing will slow down the computer, resulting in extra daily costs of $100. The cost of sampling for nine days would then be $900. The expected net gain of sampling is thus,

$$\text{ENGS}(9) = \text{EVSI}(9) - \text{Cost}(9) = \$7,540.66 - \$900 = \$6,640.66$$

Preposterior Analysis

The sample size used above may not provide a maximum level for ENGS(n). A complete preposterior analysis would consider other levels for n, some of which may be considerably better. Each n will involve its own set of conditional result probabilities for $\bar{X}$. Finding those probabilities would be a formidable task, since for each n, distinct normal curves apply, the standard deviations of which become smaller as n becomes larger. All of these must be approximated by a few representative values of $\bar{X}$, and the respective probability trees for the actual chronology must have a branch for each $\bar{X}$ in every fork that follows a μ branch.

FIGURE 24-9

Revised probability trees for the computer center manager's decision.

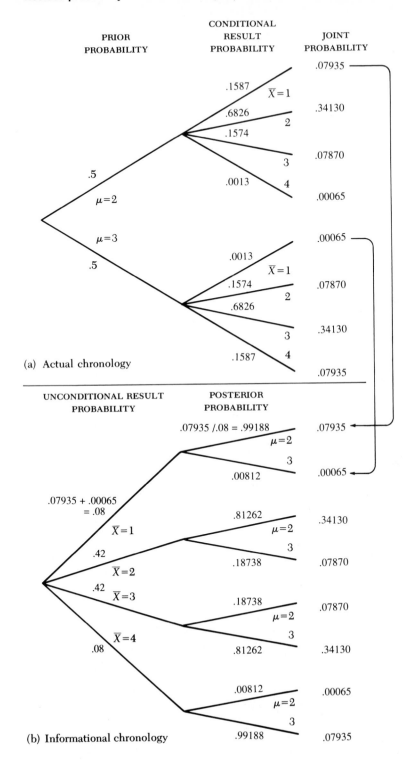

	CONDITIONAL	
PRIOR	RESULT	JOINT
PROBABILITY	PROBABILITY	PROBABILITY

.07935

.1587 $\bar{X}=1$

.6826 .34130
2

.1574

.07870
3

.5 .0013 4

$\mu=2$ .00065

$\mu=3$ .00065

.0013
.5 $\bar{X}=1$

.1574 .07870
2

.6826

.34130
3

.1587 4
(a) Actual chronology .07935

| UNCONDITIONAL RESULT | POSTERIOR |
| PROBABILITY | PROBABILITY |

.07935 /.08 = .99188 .07935
$\mu=2$

3
.00812 .00065

.07935 + .00065
= .08 .81262 .34130
$\bar{X}=1$ $\mu=2$
.42 3
$\bar{X}=2$ .18738 .07870
.42
$\bar{X}=3$ .18738 .07870
$\mu=2$
$\bar{X}=4$ 3
.08 .81262 .34130

.00812 .00065
$\mu=2$
3
(b) Informational chronology .99188 .07935

725

FIGURE 24-10

The computer center manager's decision structure using a sample of size n = 9.

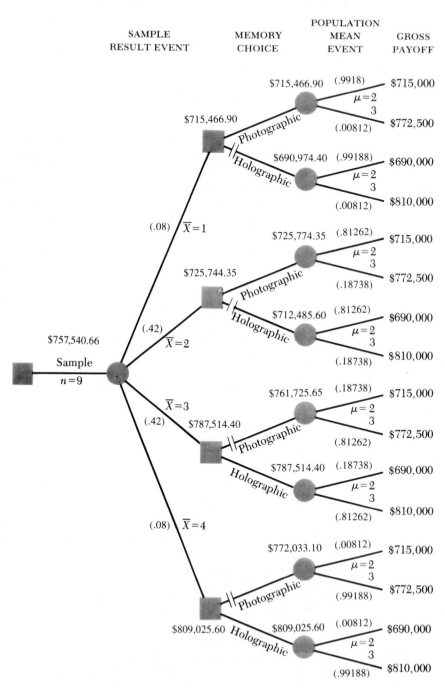

This job defies human patience and is best done with computer assistance. Even computers will get bogged down when there are many levels of μ and when a large number of intervals are involved. An alternative procedure, described in Chapter 25, is ordinarily used in those cases.

24-4 Computer Evaluations of Decision Making with the Proportion

QuickQuant may be used to evaluate decision situations having either linear or nonlinear payoffs. The program allows data entry in two modes, a *tabular* or a *functional* form. When the data are nonlinear the tabular form must be used.

Tabular Data Input

The simplest data input mode is the tabular one, which is based on the payoff table. The method is illustrated next with a decision involving product design.

ILLUSTRATION
A Product Design Decision

A soft drink manufacturer is evaluating a potential restoration of a historical design for its bottles. The choices are the standard cylindrical container and a revived "aerodynamic" shape. The key parameter is the proportion P of persons in the target market who prefer the aerodynamic bottle. Based on a complicated formula involving production costs and on potential market share during follow-on test marketing, the payoffs in Table 24-5 apply.

A *QuickQuant* run begins with prior analysis, in which the expected payoffs are computed for each act and the EVPI determined. Upon examining these values, the user may request preposterior analysis. In the present example this will involve an evaluation of sample size and the determination of critical values for R. Here, R is the number of sample persons who prefer the aerodynamic design. The program requires that Act 1 always be the choice which yields the greater payoff when P is small. In the present

TABLE 24-5
Payoff Table for Bottle Design Decision

PROPORTION PREFERRING AERODYNAMIC SHAPE	PRIOR PROBABILITY	ACT 1 CYLINDRICAL	ACT 2 AERODYNAMIC
$P = .4$	.10	$50,000	$-15,000
$P = .5$	.23	42,000	28,000
$P = .6$	.38	35,000	41,000
$P = .7$	.29	30,000	50,000

illustration, Act 1 is to choose the cylindrical design, while Act 2 is to select the aero-dynamic design.

Figure 24-11 shows the first portion of the *QuickQuant* report. The greatest expected payoff is achieved with Act 1 (cylindrical design). The EVPI is $8,080, which suggests that further experimental information might be valuable. This may be true even though sampling is expensive, with a $100 cost per sample observation. (That cost was entered into the computer with the payoff data.) *QuickQuant* was requested to perform the preposterior analysis.

Using a beginning sample size of $n = 1$ and a maximum of $n = 30$, the *QuickQuant* run continues. The binomial distribution was selected, since the population size is well into the millions. Figure 24-12 shows the report generated. There, we see that the optimal sample size is $n = 17$ with $C = 9$, which provides the maximum ENGS of $3,343.33. The following decision rule will be used.

Choose cylindrical (Act 1)   if $R \leq 9$

Choose aerodynamic (Act 2)   if $R > 9$

FIGURE 24-11
QuickQuant report for prior analysis of bottle shape decision.

```
==================================================================
                       QuickQuant Report
               DECISION MAKING WITH PROPORTION
------------------------------------------------------------------
PROBLEM: Bottle Shape Decision                  Date: 04-08-1990
                                                          Larry

       PROBLEM PARAMETERS FOR DECISION WITH PROPORTION

            Maximum n =   30   Beginning n =   1
            Maximum number of P levels =   4
            Population size =   1E+20
            Cost per Sample Observation =   100

               PRIOR PROBABILITY DISTRIBUTION

                 P Level        Probability
                 ----------------------------
                  .400             0.1000
                  .500             0.2300
                  .600             0.3800
                  .700             0.2900

                       PAYOFF TABLE

             P Level          Act 1            Act 2
             ------------------------------------------
               .400          50000.00         -15000.00
               .500          42000.00          28000.00
               .600          35000.00          41000.00
               .700          30000.00          50000.00

        DECISION MAKING WITH PROPORTION--PRIOR ANALYSIS

                      Act 1              Act 2
     Expected Payoffs:    $36660.00         $35020.00
     Best Act = Act 1
     Expected Value of Perfect Information =    $8080.00
------------------------------------------------------------------
```

FIGURE 24-12

Abbreviated *QuickQuant* report for the preposterior analysis of bottle shape decision.

```
===============================================================
                        QuickQuant Report
                 DECISION MAKING WITH PROPORTION
---------------------------------------------------------------
PROBLEM: Bottle Shape Decision (Using Binomial)        Date: 04-08-1990
                                                              Larry

         DECISION MAKING WITH PROPORTION--SUMMARY ANALYSIS

                                                          Critical
   Sample                                                  Value
    Size
     n        EVSI(n)          Cost(n)          ENGS(n)      C
   --------------------------------------------------------------
     1       $37,878.00        $100.00        $1,118.00      0
     3       $38,786.64        $300.00        $1,826.64      1
     4       $39,352.27        $400.00        $2,292.27      2
     6       $39,946.37        $600.00        $2,686.37      3
     8       $40,390.09        $800.00        $2,930.09      4
    10       $40,737.57      $1,000.00        $3,077.57      5
    11       $40,925.53      $1,100.00        $3,165.53      6
    13       $41,239.96      $1,300.00        $3,279.96      7
    15       $41,494.28      $1,500.00        $3,334.28      8
    17*      $41,703.33      $1,700.00        $3,343.33      9
    18       $41,780.09      $1,800.00        $3,320.09     10
    20       $41,982.66      $2,000.00        $3,291.29     11
    22       $42,151.29      $2,200.00        $3,291.29     12
    24       $42,292.83      $2,400.00        $3,232.83     13
    25       $42,321.57      $2,500.00        $3,161.57     14
    27       $42,463.39      $2,700.00        $3,103.39     15
    29       $42,583.52      $2,900.00        $3,023.52     16
   --------------------------------------------------------------
```

Functional Input for Linear Payoffs

The earlier disk drive quality decision was kept simple to convey essential concepts. But there are several unrealistic elements. First, the original analysis (pages 707–15) presupposes that defective units found in the sample will be reinspected when a shipment is rejected (in which case, a 100% inspection will be made). To avoid wasted effort, a good quality assurance plan would mandate that already-inspected items instead be set aside; the resulting cost savings were not reflected in the original evaluation. Second, those items found defective in a sample will not be installed, as suggested earlier. Not installing known defectives should provide considerable downstream savings of costs that would otherwise arise when those computers with defective components must eventually be rebuilt. Third, the variable cost of inspecting with a thousand items (in a rejected lot) should be lower than with a handful of sample items. There may be differences in fixed inspection costs as well.

QuickQuant can accommodate an analysis with a general linear payoff function involving, for each act, a constant term and coefficients for P, n, and R. Some or all of these may differ between Act 1 (accept) and Act 2 (reject). To illustrate, suppose that the variable cost of inspection is $25 when done on a sampling basis, but only $20 in high volumes (the case with rejected shipments). Furthermore, there is a set-up expense (fixed cost) of $500 for inspecting rejected shipments, regardless of size. There are cost savings for early detection of defective disk drives of $100 (avoided rebuilding expenses). The revised payoff function is thus,

$$\text{Payoff} = \begin{cases} \$50,000 - \$100,000P + \$100R - \$25n & \text{if accept (Act 1)} \\ \$50,000 - \$20(1,000) - \$500 - \$5n & \\ \quad\quad\quad\quad\text{or} & \\ \$29,500 + 0P + 0R - \$5n & \text{if reject (Act 2)} \end{cases}$$

The $50,000 constant term (called the intercept) for accept (Act 1) is the same as before. The counterpart for reject (Act 2) is now $29,500, reflecting both the fixed and variable costs of 100% inspection for the rejected shipments. The coefficients for P, are $-\$100,000$ and 0, as in the original evaluation. Reflecting the savings from early detection of bad disk drives, the coefficients of R apply only to those defectives found in the sample. For reject (Act 2), that coefficient is 0, reflecting that any defective disk drives would have been removed anyway, so that early detection would yield no savings. But, for accept (Act 1), the coefficient of R is $+\$100$. Finally, the coefficients for n are $-\$25$ for accept (Act 1) and $-\$5$ for reject (Act 2). The latter applies because there would then only be a $5 net cost per sample unit, reflecting the small-scale inspection cost of $25 per item, less the $20 saved by not reinspecting each sample item during the follow-on large-scale 100% inspection.

A second *QuickQuant* run was performed using the modified payoffs. The printout in Figure 24-13 shows the *QuickQuant* report. There, we see that the optimal sample size for the modifed evaluation is $n = 42$ with $C = 8$. When sampling costs differ between Acts 1 and 2, *QuickQuant* performs backward induction using *net* payoffs, so that the report in Figure 24-13 lists values for the *net* payoffs with sample information, rather than EVSI, which is not very useful when sampling costs differ between acts. In those cases, *QuickQuant* computes the expected net gain of sampling from the following difference.

$\text{ENGS}(n) = $ Expected *net* payoff with sample information

$\quad\quad\quad - $ Maximum expected payoff (with no information)

For example, by subtracting the original $32,500 maximum expected payoff for accepting disk drives without sampling from the expected net payoff with sample information of $32,841.28 when $n = 42$, we have

$$\text{ENGS}(42) = \$32,841.28 - \$32,500 = \$341.28$$

The following decision rule applies to this modified decision.

$$\text{Accept the lot (Act 1)} \quad \text{if } R \leq 8$$
$$\text{Reject the lot (Act 2)} \quad \text{if } R > 8$$

24-5 Decision Theory and Traditional Statistics

To complete our discussion of decision making using sample information, a few comments should be made about the procedure presented here and the traditional

FIGURE 24-13

Abbreviated *QuickQuant* printout for the modified disk drive acceptance sampling illustration, using hypergeometric probabilities for *R*.

```
================================================================================
                              QuickQuant Report
                        DECISION MAKING WITH PROPORTION
--------------------------------------------------------------------------------
PROBLEM: Disk Drive Quality (Using Hypergeometric)          Date: 04-08-1990
                                                                   Larry

            PROBLEM PARAMETERS FOR DECISION WITH PROPORTION

                Maximum n =  10    Beginning n =  1
                Maximum number of P levels =  5
                Population size =  1000

                Coefficients of Act 1 Line:
                    Intercept =  50000
                    Coefficient of P = -100000
                    Coefficient of R =  100
                    Coefficient of n = -25

                Coefficients of Act 2 Line:
                    Intercept =  29500
                    Coefficient of P =  0
                    Coefficient of R =  0
                    Coefficient of n = -5

                PRIOR PROBABILITY DISTRIBUTION

                    P Level    Probability
                    -----------------------
                     .050        0.1000
                     .100        0.1500
                     .150        0.2000
                     .200        0.2500
                     .250        0.3000

            DECISION MAKING WITH PROPORTION--PRIOR ANALYSIS

                        Act 1          Act 2
        Expected Payoffs:   $32500.00     $29500.00
        Best Act = Act 1
        Expected Value of Perfect Information =      $1350.00

            DECISION MAKING WITH PROPORTION--SUMMARY ANALYSIS

        Sample      Net Expected Payoff               Critical
        Size            with                           Value
          n         Sample Information    ENGS(n)         C
        ------------------------------------------------------------
           4          $32,556.00          $56.00          1
          10          $32,660.64         $160.64          2
          16          $32,733.00         $233.00          3
          21          $32,782.20         $282.20          4
          26          $32,812.88         $312.88          5
          31          $32,830.71         $330.71          6
          37          $32,839.77         $339.77          7
          42*         $32,841.28         $341.28          8
          47          $32,836.91         $336.91          9
          52          $32,827.88         $327.88         10
          57          $32,814.98         $314.98         11
          62          $32,798.90         $298.90         12
          66          $32,780.50         $280.50         13
          71          $32,759.82         $259.82         14
          76          $32,737.17         $237.17         15
          81          $32,712.74         $212.74         16
          87          $32,684.82         $184.82         17
          92          $32,657.07         $157.07         18
          97          $32,628.16         $128.16         19
        ------------------------------------------------------------
```

statistical approach. In the above disk drive evaluation, the critical value is $C = 8$. Traditional statistics also finds a critical value, but the process is totally different.

Hypothesis-Testing Concepts Reviewed

In traditional statistics, the basic uncertainty is couched in special terminology. The main events are expressed as *hypotheses*. Each decision has two kinds of hypotheses. One is referred to as the **null hypothesis** (originally used to represent "no change"), and the other is the complementary **alternative hypothesis**. In the language of classical statistics, the following hypotheses would apply to disk drive acceptance sampling.

Null hypothesis: $\quad\quad P = .10\quad$ (The lot is good.)

Alternative hypothesis: $P > .10\quad$ (The lot is poor.)

The decision rule we formulated earlier may be expressed in terms of these hypotheses. For disk drive acceptance sampling, they take the form

Accept the null hypothesis   if $R \leq C$

Reject the null hypothesis   if $R > C$

Traditional statistics focuses on the worst outcomes of the decision. These are called *errors* and are of two types. The **Type I error** occurs when the null hypothesis is rejected when it is actually true; the **Type II error** occurs when the null hypothesis is accepted when it is actually false. For the disk drive acceptance sampling inspection problem, these errors are

Type I error: Reject the lot when it is good.

Type II error: Accept the lot when it is poor.

The decision structure for traditional statistical analysis is presented in Table 24-6. The main events themselves are not assigned probabilities. Rather, the controlling factors in establishing the decision rule (the value of C) are the probabilities for the two kinds of errors.

$\alpha = \Pr[\text{Type I error}] \;=\; \Pr[\text{Reject the null hypothesis when it is true.}]$

$\beta = \Pr[\text{Type II error}] = \Pr[\text{Accept the null hypothesis when it is false.}]$

These probabilities are usually established in advance of sampling and are actually conditional probabilities (for which the status of the null hypothesis—true or false—is the given event). Conventionally, the Greek letters α (alpha) and β (beta) are used to represent the error probabilities. In the disk drive acceptance sampling, α represents the probability for rejecting a good lot, which is sometimes referred to as the **producer's risk**, and β is the probability for accepting a poor lot, or the **consumer's risk**.

Both types of errors are undesirable, but obviously neither error may be avoided entirely. Traditional statistics is concerned with selecting the sample size n and the

TABLE 24-6
Decision Table for the Traditional Statistical Decision

	ACT	
EVENT	*Accept Null Hypothesis* (Accept the lot.)	*Reject Null Hypothesis* (Reject the lot.)
Null Hypothesis True (Lot is good.)	*Correct Decision*	*Type I Error* Probability = α (Reject a good lot.)
Null Hypothesis False (Lot is poor.)	*Type II Error* Probability = β (Accept a poor lot.)	*Correct Decision*

decision rule (the value of C) that will achieve an acceptable balance between α and β. If n is fixed, one error probability may be reduced only by increasing the probability for the other error. Because the sample size itself is often dictated by economic or other considerations, it is usually possible to control only one error completely.

Generally, the null and alternative hypotheses are formulated in such a way that the Type I error is more serious. The tolerable probability for this error is specified at a level such as $\alpha = .001$, $\alpha = .05$, or $\alpha = .10$. A value of C is then chosen that guarantees that this level of α is not exceeded.

To illustrate, we will return to the disk drive acceptance sampling problem. Suppose that $\alpha = .01$, so that C must be the smallest value such that

$$\text{Pr[Rejecting the null hypothesis when it is true.]} \leq \alpha$$

or

$$\Pr[R > C \,|\, P = .10] \leq .01$$

To find C, the binomial (or hypergeometric) probabilities must be determined. These may be computed directly, found from tables, approximated, or determined with computer assistance. Using the same sample size $n = 42$ as in the preceding illustration, exact hypergeometric probabilities in Figure 24-14 were obtained with a separate computer run using the *QuickQuant* probability segment. The critical value will be that possible level for R having a cumulative probability closest to, but not falling below, $1 - \alpha = .99$. The number fitting the bill is $R = 9$, for which

$$P[R \leq 9 \,|\, P = .10] = .99389$$

so that

$$\Pr[R > 9] = 1 - .99389 = .00611$$

The traditional hypothesis testing approach provides $C = 9$, a slightly different value than found earlier. The achieved Type I error probability is thus,

$$\Pr[\text{Reject } H_0 \,|\, H_0 \text{ true}] = \Pr[R > 9 \,|\, P = .10] = .00611$$

How good is the decision rule with $C = 9$? As we have seen, traditional statistics is also concerned with the Type II error. A second *QuickQuant* run using $P = .15$ provides

FIGURE 24-14

Portion of *QuickQuant* report showing hypergeometric probabilities for disk drive quality decision.

```
=================================================================================
                              QuickQuant Report
                  HYPERGEOMETRIC PROBABILITY DISTRIBUTION
---------------------------------------------------------------------------------
PROBLEM: Disk Drive Quality                                    Date: 04-11-1990
                                                                        Larry

              Parameters: n = 42   P = .1   N =  1000

              Number of                     Cumulative
              Successes    Probability      Probability
                 r          Pr[R=r]          Pr[R<=r]
              ------------------------------------------------
                 0          0.010849         0.010849
                 1          0.053044         0.063893
                 2          0.125178         0.189071
                 3          0.189973         0.379044
                 4          0.208430         0.587474
                 5          0.176212         0.763686
                 6          0.119480         0.883166
                 7          0.066775         0.949941
                 8          0.031373         0.981314
                 9          0.012576         0.993890
                10          0.004351         0.998241
              ------------------------------------------------
```

the report in Figure 24-15. There, we see that there is a considerable chance that such a poor quality lot will be accepted.

$$\beta = P[R \le 9 \,|\, P = .15] = .915943$$

A β probability may be found for any specified level for P. An examination of these might be helpful in making a final choice of C.

Traditional statistics will often provide different decision rules than those found using the Bayesian approach, even when the sample sizes are the same, which will not usually be the case.

Contrasting the Two Approaches

Why do decision theory and traditional statistical analysis lead to different decision rules? This is because of the differences between these two procedures.

1. The decision-theory procedure considers the payoffs from every possible outcome. Payoffs are not explicitly considered in hypothesis testing, although they may influence the choice of α.

2. Prior probabilities are applied directly in the decision-theory approach. Like payoffs, prior probabilities ought to play some role in establishing α.

3. Hypothesis testing proceeds directly from the prescribed α to the decision rule. Decision-theory analysis arrives at the optimal decision rule by means of the Bayes decision rule, using the appropriate posterior probabilities and the payoffs for each outcome. The resulting decision maximizes expected payoff.

FIGURE 24-15

Portion of second *QuickQuant* report showing hypergeometric probabilities for disk drive quality decision.

```
================================================================================
                              QuickQuant Report
                    HYPERGEOMETRIC PROBABILITY DISTRIBUTION
--------------------------------------------------------------------------------
PROBLEM: Disk Drive Quality                              Date: 04-11-1990
                                                                   Larry

            Parameters: n = 42  P = .15  N =  1000

            Number of                    Cumulative
            Successes      Probability   Probability
               r            Pr[R=r]       Pr[R<=r]
            ---------------------------------------------
               0           0.000928      0.000928
               1           0.007227      0.008155
               2           0.027252      0.035407
               3           0.066310      0.101717
               4           0.117043      0.218760
               5           0.159742      0.378502
               6           0.175474      0.553976
               7           0.159449      0.713425
               8           0.122249      0.835674
               9           0.080269      0.915943
              10           0.045659      0.961602
--------------------------------------------------------------------------------
```

Which procedure is preferable? Decision theory is plagued by subjective prior probabilities, which are considered by many to be the weakest link in its analytical chain. Many statisticians deny the existence of subjective probabilities, thereby relegating much of statistical decision theory to the ash heap. A major feature that makes traditional hypothesis testing procedures more universally accepted is that no prior probabilities are required at all. *But the uncertainties regarding the population parameter still exist,* and traditional statistical procedures must also involve some sort of subjective assessment of these uncertainties when desired error probabilities are being established. In hypothesis testing, everything hinges on the prescribed significance level α (and also on β when there is the freedom or the capability to prescribe β). Unless α is carefully determined, inferior decisions are bound to occur. Decision theory permits the consistent and systematic treatment of chance and payoffs as well as attitude toward risk. In addition, decision theory does not burden the decision maker by requiring him or her to do everything at once by choosing a single number—"an α for all seasons."

When the outcomes do not have a natural numerical payoff measure or when the decision maker is risk-seeking or risk-averse, then the strengths of decision-theory analysis rest on a foundation of utility values. As we will see in Chapter 26, obtaining utilities requires a set of assumptions about attitudes, which are obtained by means of an elaborate procedure. Although any difficulties involved in employing utilities may be avoided by traditional statistics, α embodies everything, so that even more care must be exercised in choosing the appropriate target value.

The final and perhaps the most significant advantage of decision theory is that *it considers whether or not a sample should even be used.* We have seen that a greater expected payoff may be achieved by deciding what to do immediately, without incurring the expense of a sample. Traditional statistics never satisfactorily copes with this question.

In addition, the choice of proper sample size is too often an *ad hoc* process in traditional statistics. (A sample size of 30 may be used, for example, because the Student *t* table stops at 30 degrees of freedom.) Decision theory explicitly considers the costs of the various sample sizes.

At this point you might wonder why classical hypothesis testing is used at all. Although classical hypothesis testing has roots in biological and medical studies, its use has been expanded into all areas of science. Traditional statistics permeates our society— used in the social sciences, in education, in government, and even in business.

Traditional statistics prevails in public arena decision making, where there is little room for anything subjective. Indeed, science epitomizes objectivity. Therefore, any use of subjective prior probabilities is unacceptable; they only create controversy and destroy credibility. Also, public decision making involves societal issues and human lives. In such a decision-making environment the very notion of a payoff value may be at best controversial, perhaps even irrelevant.

The Bayesian statistics of this chapter coexist side-by-side with classical hypothesis testing. Factors that determine the appropriate procedure to use include the type of application, who is making the decision, and who will see the analysis. The Bayesian approach is best suited to private decision making, where the decision maker alone is held accountable for the outcome and no controversy need ever arise from using subjective probabilities and the selection of payoffs. The classical approach works best in public.

A pharmaceutical house may use both types of statistics. Experiments done with new drugs in order to gain government approvals involve public issues and must be strictly based on classical hypothesis testing. But decisions regarding what types of new drugs to develop and market may be done in private, where Bayesian statistics should be more beneficial.

24-6 Additional Remarks

In this chapter, we have learned to analyze decision making using sampling. By employing the procedures described here, we exercise judgment about the population characteristics by assigning prior probabilities to the possible values of the decision parameter P or μ. The benefits and costs of sampling may be systematically evaluated in a way that explicitly accounts for the payoffs for every outcome. This makes it possible even to consider the question of whether or not to sample in the first place. The principles of decision theory permit a more thorough analysis to be made than traditional statistics provides.

The procedures presented in this chapter have drawbacks. The main difficulties arise from the nature of decision tree analysis itself. Because the possible number of sample results and population parameters may be huge, many problems are too large to fit conveniently on a tree. Some problems require such a large amount of computational effort that a computer is needed to evaluate them.

But decision tree analysis presents a more fundamental problem. It is an inherently *discrete* procedure, since each event must be represented by a separate branch. Many problems involve *continuous* random variables. For example, P and μ may range over a continuous spectrum of possible values. Also, the sample mean $\bar{X}$ is often a continuous variable that is generally represented by the normal distribution. In Chapter 25, we will consider the case in which the normal curve serves as the prior distribution for μ. Nevertheless, it is still possible to apply decision tree analysis to these problem situations by approximating the continuous distributions. Methods for doing this with a few typical values representing the entire range of the continuous variable were described in Chapter 4.

CASE

Charismatic Chimeras

Three-dimensional puzzles are the specialty products of Charismatic Chimeras. The company must decide whether or not to introduce the Snuggler Puzzler as the replacement for its Cozy Cubit. But there is some uncertainty about the proportion P of the market that will actually prefer the new product. The marketing vice-president assumes that P is normally distributed, believing it to be a 50–50 proposition that P will lie at or above .70. She also feels that it is equally as likely for P to fall in the limits .65 to .75 as outside that range. She knows that the payoff for introducing the Snuggler Puzzler is $-\$100,000$, plus or minus $\$20,000$ for each percentage point by which P exceeds .60. At a cost of $\$100$ per observation, it is possible to tell whether or not a Cozy Cubit fan prefers the Snuggler Puzzler.

A related decision must be made by the operations vice-president whether to manufacture the Snuggler Puzzlers in-house or to have them made under contract. The major uncertainty pertains to the mean unit direct cost of production μ. The breakeven level is $\$10$ per unit. The vice-president believes that there is a 50–50 chance that μ will lie at or below $\$9$ per unit, with an even proposition that μ lies between $\$7.50$ and $\$10.50$ rather than higher or lower. As with P, a normal curve applies.

Questions

1. Determine the expected value and standard deviation of the subjective prior probability distribution for P. Using the following intervals, determine the applicable probabilities.

CLASS INTERVAL
below .55
.55–.65
.65–.75
.75–.85
above .85

2. Using $P = .50$, $P = .60$, $P = .70$, $P = .80$, and $P = .90$ as the main events, construct a payoff table for the marketing vice-president's product decision.

Using your interval probabilities from Question 1 as the respective main event probabilities, determine the expected payoff for each act.

3. Using your answer to Question 2, compute the EVPI. Does a cost of $100 per sample observation seem reasonable?

4. Determine the expected net gain of sampling when $n = 3$.

5. Determine the expected value and standard deviation for the subjective prior probability distribution for the mean unit direct cost of production μ. Then, using the following intervals, determine the applicable probabilities.

CLASS INTERVAL
below $6
$6–$8
$8–$10
$10–$12
above $12

6. A production run of 20,000 Snuggler Puzzlers will be made. A contractor will do them for $12 each. The fixed cost of in-house manufacturing is $40,000. Each unit will provide a net revenue of $20. Use $\mu = \$5$, $\mu = \$7$, $\mu = \$9$, $\mu = \$11$, and $\mu = \$13$ as the main events and construct a payoff table for the operations vice-president's production decision. Using the respective interval probabilities from Question 5 for the event probabilities, determine the expected payoff for each act.

7. Determine the EVPI for the production decision. Do you think sample information would even be appropriate here?

PROBLEMS

24-1   The president of Admiral Mills believes that the proportion of children P who will like Crunchy Munchy has the following probability distribution.

POSSIBLE PROPORTION P	PROBABILITY
1/4	1/3
1/2	1/3
3/4	1/3
	1

The president must decide whether to market Crunchy Munchy now or to abandon the product. If the cereal is marketed, there will be a $50,000 loss if $P = 1/4$, a $100,000 gain if $P = 1/2$ and a $200,000 profit if $P = 3/4$.

(a) Perform the prior analysis to determine which act maximizes expected payoff.

(b) Determine the EVPI.

24-2 (*Continuation of Problem 24-1*): The president wishes to conduct a preposterior analysis. A portion of this evaluation considers a sample of three children who have been chosen at random, given Crunchy Munchy, and then asked if they like it.

(a) (1) Construct the actual chronological probability tree diagram for the outcomes. Let the values of P represent the events of the branches in the first-stage fork and let the number of children found to like Crunchy Munchy represent the events of the second-stage branches. Use the binomial distribution.

(2) Enter the above probabilities for the possible P values on the appropriate branches. Then, use the binomial formula to determine the probabilities for the branches in the remaining forks, and enter them on your diagram.

(3) Determine the joint probabilities for each end position.

(4) Construct the probability tree diagram for the informational chronology, reversing the event sequences so that the branches of the first fork represent the number of children who like Crunchy Munchy, followed by forks for the values of P. Determine the probabilities for the events represented by each branch.

(5) If all three children like Crunchy Munchy, what are the posterior probabilities for P?

(b) (1) Construct the president's decision tree diagram using gross payoffs to obtain the expected payoff with sample information. What is the critical value at or below which it is best to abandon the product?

(2) Determine EVSI (3).

(3) Each sample observation costs $100. Determine ENGS (3).

24-3 High Crock, the brewmaster and part owner of High & Higher Distilleries, has discovered a new fermentation process for malt ale that reclaims corn mash from whiskey vats to begin fermentation. Get, the marketing manager and joint owner of High & Higher, is excited about the revolutionary ale and has assigned the prior probabilities of $Pr[P = .10] = .20$, $Pr[P = .20] = .50$, and $Pr[P = .30] = .30$ to the proportion P of the market segment he feels will buy the new beer. Get must decide whether to market the new ale or to abandon it. A 10% market share will result in losses of $500,000, 20% is the breakeven level, and 30% will bring $500,000 in present value of future profits.

(a) Perform the prior analysis to determine which act maximizes expected payoff.

(b) Determine the EVPI.

24-4 (*Continuation of Problem 24-3*): Get wishes to conduct a preposterior analysis. A portion of this evaluation considers a sample of $n = 3$ connoisseurs who will be chosen at random to test the new ale. For each person, it will be determined whether or not they would buy the new ale.

(a) Construct the actual chronological probability tree diagram, using the prior probabilities assigned by the marketing manager and the applicable binomial, conditional result probabilities obtained from Appendix Table A.

(b) Using the probabilities generated in the actual chronology, construct the probability tree diagram for the informational chronology. Indicate the unconditional result, posterior, and joint probabilities.

(c) (1) Construct Get's decision tree diagram using gross payoffs to obtain the expected payoff with sample information. What is the critical value at or below which it is best to abandon the new ale?

(2) Determine EVSI (3).

(3) Each sample observation costs $100. Determine ENGS (3).

24-5   Stella Deal asks two politicians what they believe to be the true proportion P of voters favoring their party's candidate. The respective replies are .40 and .50. Stella's judgment leads her to assign equal chances that either politician is correct. A random sample of $n = 100$ registered voters will be chosen, and the number R preferring the candidate will be found. The following results are of interest: $R < 40$; $40 \le R \le 50$; $R > 50$.
  (a) Construct the actual chronological probability tree diagram, using the sample results in the second stage. (Appendix Table A provides the conditional result probabilities.)
  (b) Construct the probability tree diagram for the informational chronology.
  (c) Determine the posterior probability that $P = .40$, given each of the following results.
    (1) $R < 40$ (2) $40 \le R \le 50$ (3) $R > 50$

24-6   Suppose that the prior probabilities for the proportion P of CornChox buyers favoring a new package design are $\Pr[P = .4] = .5$ and $\Pr[P = .6] = .5$. Also suppose that if the new design is used, the present value of future profits will decrease by $10,000 when $P = .4$ and increase by $10,000 when $P = .6$. It must be decided whether to use the new design or keep the old one.
  (a) Compute the expected payoffs for each act. Which one is best?
  (b) Determine the EVPI.

24-7   (Continuation of Problem 24-6): A company marketing researcher wishes to conduct a preposterior analysis. Sampling is very costly, $500 an observation to determine for a test subject whether or not he or she likes the new product design. For (a) $n = 1$ and (b) $n = 2$, answer the following.
    (1) Using the binomial distribution, construct the probability tree diagrams for the actual and informational chronologies.
    (2) Using gross payoffs, construct the decision tree. Then, perform backward induction analysis to determine the critical value at or below which the old design should be retained.
    (3) Find the expected payoff with sample information and compute EVSI (n).
    (4) Determine ENGS (n).
  (c) Does sampling provide a greater expected payoff than not sampling? Which of the two sample sizes is best?

24-8   Consider the disk drive acceptance sampling illustration in the chapter. For a sample size of $n = 4$, answer the following.
  (a) Construct the probability tree diagrams for the actual and informational chronologies. (Use the binomial distribution.)
  (b) Construct the decision tree diagram for this sample size. What is the acceptance number?

24-9   Comp-u-Quick must select the optimal sample size to use in determining whether to accept or reject incoming shipments of black boxes. The following payoffs apply to the various assumed levels of the proportion defective.

		ACT	
PROPORTION DEFECTIVE	PRIOR PROBABILITY	Accept	Reject
$P = .05$	.3	$100	$-$100
$P = .10$	.4	0	0
$P = .20$	.3	-100	100

The following expected payoffs with sample information (ignoring the cost of sampling) have been obtained.

SAMPLE SIZE	EXPECTED PAYOFF
$n = 1$	$ 9.00
$n = 2$	15.70
$n = 3$	20.50
$n = 4$	24.22

(a) Calculate the expected payoff using sample information when $n = 5$. What acceptance number applies to the number of sample defectives R? (Use the binomial distribution.)
(b) Assuming that each sample observation costs $3, determine ENGS($n$) for $n = 1$ through $n = 5$. What is the optimal sample size?

24-10 The quality control manager for the computer manufacturer in the text is faced with a similar evaluation regarding a second supplier for the same disk drives. That supplier has a better reputation than the first, with prior probabilities for the proportion of defectives in a 1,000-unit shipment of .20 for $P = .10$ and .80 for $P = .20$. The payoffs are the same for both suppliers.

(a) Compute the expected payoffs for accepting and rejecting shipments without sampling. Which act maximizes expected payoff?
(b) Compute the manager's EVPI. Does it appear that sampling might be beneficial in this case?
(c) Suppose that a sample size of $n = 10$ is used. Construct the probability tree diagrams for the actual and informational chronologies. (Use the binomial distribution.)
(d) For $n = 10$, find the acceptance number and expected payoff. Would the inspector be better off using $n = 10$ or no sample at all?

24-11 Consider a slight modification in the computer-memory device decision discussed in this chapter. Suppose that the following prior probabilities for the mean memory access levels apply.

$$\mu = 2 \text{ gigabits per day: } .6$$
$$\mu = 3 \text{ gigabits per day: } .4$$

Determine the new probabilities for the actual and informational chronologies in Figure 24-9 (page 725), assuming that the same conditional result probabilities apply.

24-12 The marketing manager of Blitz Beer must determine whether or not to sponsor Blitz Day with the Gotham City Hellcats. She is uncertain what the effect of the promotion will be in terms of the mean increase in daily sales volume that would result during the 100-day baseball season. The cost of sponsorship is $10,000, and each can of Blitz has a marginal cost of $.20 and sells for $.40. Two levels are judged equally likely for the mean increase in sales for the season: $\mu = 490$ and $\mu = 530$ cans per day.

(a) Construct the manager's payoff table.
(b) If the manager wishes to maximize expected payoff, what action should she take?

(c) Further experimental information may be desired before making a final decision. Calculate the EVPI. Would a sample from the underlying population—assuming it is cheap enough—be helpful in reaching this decision? Explain.

24-13 Sonic Phonics is considering modifying the components in a quadraphonic speaker system to boost its effective power. The ultimate result depends on the mean signal-to-noise ratio μ, an unknown quantity for which the following subjective probability distribution applies.

MEAN SIGNAL-TO-NOISE RATIO	PROBABILITY
$\mu = 90$	.20
$\mu = 100$	.40
$\mu = 110$	.40

Unfortunately, the modified system may result in a poorer overall performance rating than the system's current 30 points, rising or dropping .25 point for each unit that μ falls above or below 100.

The following approximate probabilities apply for the level of the sample mean $\bar{X}$ when $n = 5$.

POSSIBLE SAMPLE MEAN	GIVEN LEVEL OF POPULATION MEAN		
	$\mu = 90$	$\mu = 100$	$\mu = 110$
$\bar{X} = 85$	.40	.10	.10
$\bar{X} = 95$	.30	.40	.20
$\bar{X} = 105$	.20	.40	.30
$\bar{X} = 115$	.10	.10	.40
	1.00	1.00	1.00

(a) Assuming that no sample is used, construct Sonic Phonics' payoff table. In order to maximize expected final system rating points, should the system be modified?
(b) Construct the probability trees for the actual and informational chronologies.
(c) Ignoring the cost of collecting the sample, construct Sonic Phonics' decision tree diagram when the sample is used. Find the level of the acceptance number C, representing the largest level for the sample mean at which the present system will provide the greatest expected rating payoff.

24-14 In evaluating a new electronic scanning cash register, the facilities planner for WaySafe Markets judges that the mean $30-purchase customer checkout time with the new device is equally likely to be either (1) $\mu = 3.0$ or (2) $\mu = 4.0$ minutes. In either case, individual checkout times have a standard deviation of $\sigma_I = 2$ minutes. A sample of $n = 25$ customers will be monitored.

(a) The sampling distribution for $\bar{X}$ is normally distributed, with mean μ and standard deviation $\sigma_{\bar{X}} = \sigma_I/\sqrt{n}$. Determine, for each μ, the following conditional result probabilities for $\bar{X}$.

CLASS INTERVAL $\bar{X}$	NORMAL DEVIATE AT UPPER LIMIT	APPROXIMATE CUMULATIVE PROBABILITY	INTERVAL MIDPOINT $\bar{X}$	INTERVAL PROBABILITY
.75–under 1.25				
1.25–under 1.75				
1.75–under 2.25				
2.25–under 2.75				
2.75–under 3.25				
3.25–under 3.75				
3.75–under 4.25				
4.25–under 4.75				
4.75–under 5.25				
5.25–under 5.75				
5.75–under 6.25				

(b) Construct the probability tree diagrams for the actual and informational chronologies, using $\bar{X}$ branches for each interval midpoint.

24-15 Suppose that the peripheral memory device decision problem in this chapter is modified so that the following prior probabilities for the mean memory access levels apply.

$$\mu = 2 \text{ gigabits per day:} \quad .3$$
$$\mu = 3 \text{ gigabits per day:} \quad .7$$

The decision tree diagram in Figure 24-16 now applies.
(a) Perform backward induction.
(b) What is the value of C that will maximize expected payoff? Formulate the optimal decision rule.
(c) Calculate the EVSI.
(d) Determine the expected net gain of sampling for a sample costing $900.

24-16 The chemical processing for Anomaly perfume yields a mean of μ grams of active ingredient for every liter of gland extract processed. Due to variations in the raw material and in the control settings, the true population mean for any particular batch is unknown until processing is complete. From past history, the plant superintendent judges that the following prior probabilities for μ apply.

POSSIBLE MEAN μ	PROBABILITY
25 g	.3
30	.4
35	.3

The plant superintendent must decide whether or not to adjust the control settings in processing a batch of Anomaly. Suppose that the following payoff table applies.

FIGURE 24-16
Decision tree diagram for Problem 24-15.

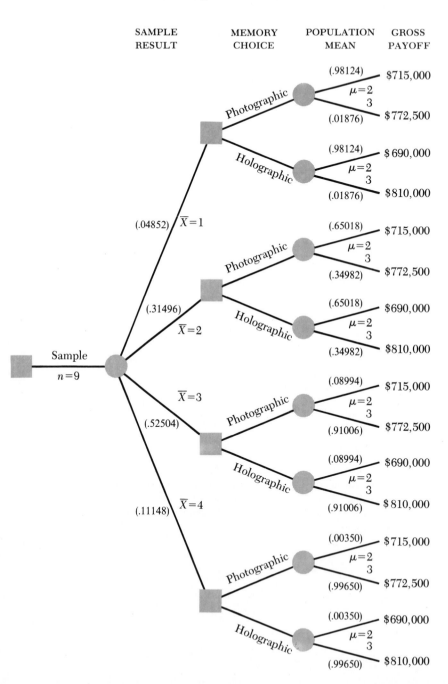

	ACT	
POPULATION MEAN μ	Adjust	Leave Alone
25 g	$ 500	− $500
30	0	0
35	− 1,000	500

(a) Assuming that no sample is taken, what course of action will maximize the expected payoff?
(b) Calculate the plant superintendent's EVPI. Would he use a sample to facilitate his decision if it cost $400? (Answer yes, no, or maybe.) If it cost $200? Explain.

24-17   Refer to Problem 24-16. Suppose that the plant superintendent will base the decision for control settings on a sample. The sample will consist of $n = 3$ liters of gland extract, for each of which the precise amount of resulting active gland ingredient will be determined after processing. The sample mean will then be calculated from these readings. Suppose that the following approximate conditional result probabilities apply.

	PROBABILITIES FOR $\bar{X}$		
$\bar{X}$	$\mu = 25$ g	$\mu = 30$ g	$\mu = 35$ g
25 g	.7	.2	.2
30	.2	.6	.3
35	.1	.2	.5

(a) Construct the probability tree diagram for the actual chronology.
(b) Using the probabilities that you found in (a), construct the probability tree diagram for the informational chronology and to compute the unconditional result and posterior probabilites for μ.

24-18   Refer to Problems 24-16 and 24-17 and to your answers.
(a) Construct the plant superintendent's decision tree diagram, assuming that he is committed to taking a sample. Use gross payoff figures.
(b) Perform backward induction to determine the value of C (for accepting the need for adjustment) that will maximize expected gross payoff. Formulate the optimal decision rule.
(c) Calculate the EVSI.
(d) Suppose that a sample of $n = 3$ liters costs $50. Calculate the superintendent's expected net gain of sampling.

24-19   Refer to the disk drive quality discussion on pages 730–34. Suppose that α is changed to .05. Determine the new critical value.

24-20   Refer, again, to the disk drive quality discussion.
(a) Suppose that $n = 20$ is used instead and that $\alpha = .05$. Using binomial probabilities as an approximation to the true ones, determine the critical value.
(b) Determine the Type II error probabilities applicable to your answer to (a) when (1) $P = .20$ and (2) $P = .30$.

24-21 A market researcher wishes to determine whether to accept the null hypothesis regarding the proportion P of Appleton smokers who will switch to a new mentholated version, Mapleton. Her null hypothesis is that $P = .1$. She takes a random sample of 100 current Appleton smokers, who will be contacted in six months to see if they have switched. The researcher wishes to protect against the Type I error with a probability of $\alpha = .005$. Using Appendix Table A, determine the smallest acceptance number C such that the probability that the number of switchers will exceed this number is less than or equal to the desired α. Then, formulate the researcher's decision rule.

24-22 Referring to Problem 24-21, suppose that the following prior probabilities are obtained for P.

P	PROBABILITY
.05	1/3
.10	1/3
.15	1/3
	———
	1

The following conditional result probabilities for the number of switchers R apply.

	$P = .05$	$P = .10$	$P = .15$
$R \le 17$	1.0000	`.9900	.7633
$R = 18$	0	.0054	.0739
$R \ge 19$	0	.0046	.1628

The decision maker's payoffs, including the cost of sampling, are

	ACCEPT NULL HYPOTHESIS	REJECT NULL HYPOTHESIS
$P = .05$	$10,000	− $2,000
$P = .10$	5,000	0
$P = .15$	−2,000	4,000

(a) Determine the posterior probability distribution for P, given each of the sample result events above. Then, find the unconditional result probabilities.

(b) Construct the market researcher's decision tree diagram. Enter the probabilities that you found in (a) on the appropriate branches, and place the payoffs along the respective end positions.

(c) Should the decision maker accept or reject the null hypothesis if $R = 18$? Compare this result with your result in Problem 24-21.

24-23 *Computer exercise.* Refer to Problems 24-1 and 24-2. Find the optimal sample size.

24-24 *Computer exercise.* Refer to Problems 24-3 and 24-4. Find the optimal sample size.

24-25 *Computer exercise.* Suppose that the OEM illustrated in the chapter also receives *hard* disk drives in shipments of 500 units each. The installed components add $200 in value to the final product.

Replacement of installed defective drives costs $400, and the cost of prior inspection and testing is $35. Accepted shipments will be untested and installed directly, while rejected ones will receive 100% testing prior to installation, at a cost of $10 each. Other costs for rejecting a shipment of hard disk drives are $11,500.

(a) Express the payoff function for accepting and rejecting in terms of the proportion of defectives P in the shipment.

(b) The following subjective prior probability distribution applies for one supplier.

PROPORTION DEFECTIVE	PROBABILITY
$P = .03$	.08
$P = .06$	.37
$P = .09$	.41
$P = .12$	.14

Find the optimal sample size and decision rule for disposing of incoming shipments. Use *binomial* conditional result probabilities.

24-26 *Computer exercise.* Repeat Problem 24-25 using *hypergeometric* conditional result probabilities.

24-27 *Computer exercise.* NewScents has just been introduced. Its proportional present market share is uncertain. The following probabilities apply.

SHARE	PROBABILITY
.20	.05
.25	.13
.30	.17
.35	.27
.40	.16
.45	.13
.50	.09

The choices are whether or not to conduct a special promotion. The profit gain from the promotion declines with market share of the millions of potential buyers. Starting at $40,000, it drops $1,000 for each percentage point that market share falls above 0%.

A sample will have a fixed cost of $100 and a variable cost of $10 per observation. Only if the promotion is used, follow-on testing will be worth $20 for every potential buyer identified in the sample, while non-buyers found will yield nothing.

(a) Assuming that no sample is used, determine the expected payoffs, identify the best act, and calculate the EVPI.

(b) Assuming that sampling will be used, find the optimal sample size and critical value.

24-28 *Computer exercise.* An advertising agency must decide between a feminine slanted commercial for BriDent toothpaste and another with a masculine orientation. The ultimate payoff from the spot will depend on the proportion of female buyers, not presently known. The following payoffs and probabilities are assumed to apply.

FEMALE PROPORTION	PROBABILITY	MASCULINE	FEMININE
$P = .47$	.05	$180,000	$ 50,000
$P = .48$	.10	140,000	80,000
$P = .49$	.17	130,000	120,000
$P = .50$	.29	125,000	150,000
$P = .51$	.14	122,500	190,000
$P = .52$	.11	120,000	230,000
$P = .53$	.09	119,000	240,000
$P = .54$	.05	118,000	260,000

(a) Determine the expected payoffs, identify the best act, and calculate the EVPI.

(b) A sample of buyers may be selected and the person's sex established. The cost of sampling is $1 per observation. Find, for each n from 1 to 100, EVSI(n), Cost(n), ENGS(n), and C.

(c) What do you notice that is unusual about this problem?

CHAPTER

25

Decision Making Using the Normal Distribution

In Chapter 24, we saw how sampling may be used to obtain experimental information to facilitate decision making. There, we applied sampling to situations involving two acts with payoffs determined by the value of an uncertain population parameter, such as the mean μ or the proportion P. Our earlier discussion of decision making using the mean considered only discrete probability distributions, which apply when the number of possible values for the population mean or the sample mean is limited. But in most situations, both μ and $\bar{X}$ may be any point in a continuous range of values. In such cases, it is more realistic to analyze the decision in terms of continuous probability distributions.

In describing the procedures for doing this, we will expand the computer center manager's decision described in Chapter 24. Recall that a choice must be made between two peripheral memory storage units based on laser technology. One alternative is photographic in nature; the other employs the principles of holographic imagery. Our earlier analysis was based on only two values of the population mean of memory access levels μ, expressed in gigabits per day. There, we used prior probabilities of .5 for $\mu = 2$ and .5 for $\mu = 3$. We will now treat the unknown μ as a random variable with a *continuous prior probability distribution*, reflecting the possibility that μ may assume many other levels. For any given level of μ, we will also assume that there is a *continuous conditional probability distribution* for the possible values of $\bar{X}$, instead of the four whole numbers used earlier.

In both cases, the particular distributions are members of the *normal distribution* family. Although a variety of other prior distributions might be used for μ, we know from the central limit theorem (discussed in Chapter 3) that $\bar{X}$ tends to be normally distributed and that this is the only appropriate distribution to use.*

25-1 Structure of Decision Making with the Normal Distribution

In this chapter, we will assume that μ is a random variable having prior probabilities obtainable from the normal curve. Recall, from Chapter 3, that any particular normal curve may be specified entirely by its mean and standard deviation (or variance). These parameters are denoted by μ_0 and σ_0, where the subscript zeros indicate that these are the initial, prior values and are not based on sampling information. Here, μ_0 is the expected value of the unknown population mean. This is the central value, and we will refer to μ_0 as the **prior expected mean**. The **prior standard deviation** σ_0 summarizes the variability in possible levels of μ.

The values of μ_0 and σ_0 must be based largely on judgment, when no historical data are directly related to μ. Or, μ_0 and σ_0 might be obtained from previous experience. For example, μ might represent the mean ingredient yield in several successive batches of a raw material used in chemical processing, and records might have been kept of the mean yield that each batch achieved. Chapter 4 describes how subjective prior probability distributions may be obtained.

We will illustrate the structure of decision making with the normal curve using the computer memory device decision in Chapter 24.

Computer Memory Device Decision

Recall, from Chapter 24, the decision by the computer center manager regarding which peripheral memory device to lease, the photographic one or the holographic one. The evaluation is based on the annual cost savings over the existing system. The photographic memory will save $600,000 in base costs, while the holographic will save $450,000. Additionally, there will be further operating cost savings, depending on the overall mean daily level of memory access. For the photographic memory, the additional savings amount to $57,500 for each gigabit (billion bits), while the holographic memory yields $120,000 in further cost reductions.

Of course, the daily memory traffic is anticipated to fluctuate considerably, with individual daily figures such as 2,245,000,000 or 5,907,550,000 bits conceivable. The level of memory access could be as low as .5 gigabit (500,000,000 bits) or as high as 20 gigabits

---

* The necessary conditions are that the population variance be finite and known and that the samples be large and independently selected.

(20,000,000,000 bits). The center manager is uncertain about the mean value μ of this population of individual daily memory access levels.

The manager assumes that μ is normally distributed. Using the procedures in Chapter 4, he selected 2.50 gigabits per day as the 50–50 point for mean daily memory access level. Thus, the center of the prior normal curve for μ is $\mu_0 = 2.50$. He also found it to be "even money" that μ would fall inside the interval 2.40–2.60 versus outside. From this he arrived at the standard deviation $\sigma_0 = .15$ for the prior subjective probability distribution for μ.

25-2 Decision Making Using Opportunity Losses

In Chapter 24, we saw how we might evaluate this decision using the payoff table in Table 25-1. As events, representative levels for μ are listed.

Linear Payoff Functions and the Breakeven Mean

The population mean is a continuous variable, so that the payoffs may be computed for an infinite number of levels for μ. In such cases, it is ordinarily more convenient to express the payoffs as *linear functions of μ*.

Figure 25-1 shows the essential relationship between payoff and opportunity loss for the computer memory device decision. The gross payoffs for the two memory units may be expressed in terms of the unknown mean daily access level as

$$\text{Gross payoff} = \begin{cases} \$600,000 + \$ \ 57,500 \ \mu & \text{for photographic} \\ \$450,000 + \$120,000 \ \mu & \text{for holographic} \end{cases}$$

TABLE 25-1
Payoff Table for Computer Memory Device Decision

MEAN DAILY MEMORY ACCESS LEVELS μ	MEMORY DEVICE CHOICES	
	Photographic	*Holographic*
1.90	$709,250	$678,000
2.00	715,000	690,000
2.10	720,750	702,000
2.20	726,500	714,000
2.30	732,250	726,000
2.40	738,000	738,000
2.50	743,750	750,000
2.60	749,500	762,000
2.70	755,250	774,000
2.80	761,000	786,000
2.90	766,750	798,000
3.00	772,500	810,000
3.10	778,250	822,000

FIGURE 25-1
Linear payoff functions for memory device decision.

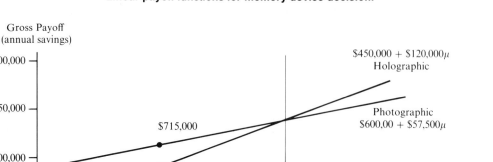

These payoffs are plotted as two lines in the graph in Figure 25-1. The height of the respective lines at any level μ may be determined from the preceding equations. The slope of the photographic-unit payoff line is $57,500$, and the slope of the steeper holographic-unit payoff line is $120,000$. The two lines cross at that value of μ where the gross payoff is identical under each act. This value is referred to as the **breakeven mean** and is denoted as μ_b. The breakeven mean is found by setting the two payoff expressions equal to each other and solving for μ_b. In this case,

$$\$600,000 + \$57,500 \, \mu_b = \$450,000 + \$120,000 \, \mu_b$$

so that

$$(\$120,000 - \$57,500) \, \mu_b = \$600,000 - \$450,000$$

$$\$62,500 \, \mu_b = \$150,000$$

and

$$\mu_b = \$150,000/\$62,500 = 2.4 \text{ gigabits per day}$$

For values of μ less than $\mu_b = 2.4$, the photographic memory yields the greatest annual savings; for means greater than μ_b, the holographic unit is preferable. At $\mu = \mu_b$, the annual savings is $738,000 using either alternative.

Finding Opportunity Losses

Until this point, we have been able to analyze decisions by maximizing expected payoff—a procedure sometimes referred to as the *Bayes decision rule*. We have established that an equivalent criterion is to minimize expected opportunity loss. For two-action problems involving continuous probability distributions, it is more convenient to focus on opportunity losses as a basis for decision making.

The opportunity losses may be found for any row in Table 25-1 by first identifying the maximum payoff with the event for that row and subtracting every payoff in the row from that amount. The opportunity loss for picking the photographic memory when $\mu = 2.00$ is zero, since that act provides the maximum payoff in the $\mu = 2.00$ row. The opportunity loss for picking the holographic memory when $\mu = 2.00$ is the following difference in payoffs from that same row.

$$\$715,000 - 690,000 = \$25,000$$

Duplicating this for each row of the payoff table, the complete listing of opportunity losses for the computer memory device decision were found, as shown in Table 25-2.

The opportunity losses may also be plotted as a graph, shown in Figure 25-2. We see that the photographic unit is the better choice when the true population mean lies below the breakeven level μ_b. Thus, whenever $\mu \leq \mu_b$, choosing the photographic unit will result in zero opportunity loss, which is represented by the horizontal line segment to the left of μ_b. If the true mean exceeds the breakeven level, the opportunity losses for the photographic unit rise, as represented by the upward-sloping line segment beginning at μ_b. The reverse holds for the holographic unit. For true population means above μ_b, the holographic alternative is better and its opportunity losses must be zero, as represented by the dashed horizontal line segment to the right of μ_b. To the left of μ_b, the opportunity losses for the holographic unit are represented by the downward-sloping dashed line segment falling toward μ_b. The heights of points lying on the V-shaped portion represent the difference in savings between the best and worst acts at each level of μ. The V is symmetrical, and the two rising line segments have identical slopes (with opposite signs) of a magnitude equal to the difference between the slopes of the two payoff lines: $\$120,000 - \$57,500 = \$62,500$.

TABLE 25-2
Opportunity Loss Table for Computer Memory
Device Decision

MEAN DAILY MEMORY ACCESS LEVELS μ	MEMORY DEVICE CHOICES	
	Photographic	*Holographic*
1.90	$ 0	$31,250
2.00	0	25,000
2.10	0	18,750
2.20	0	12,500
2.30	0	6,250
2.40	0	0
2.50	6,250	0
2.60	12,500	0
2.70	18,750	0
2.80	25,000	0
2.90	31,250	0
3.00	37,500	0
3.10	43,750	0

FIGURE 25-2
Opportunity loss functions for memory device decision.

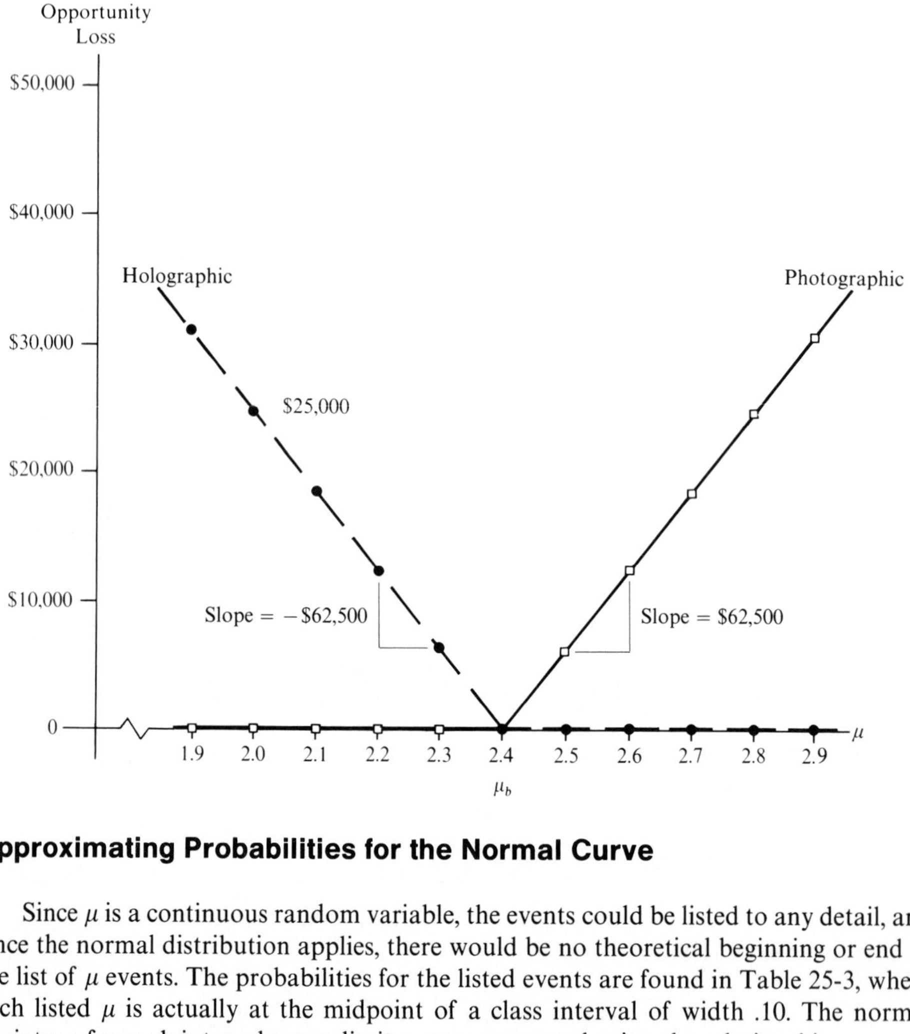

Approximating Probabilities for the Normal Curve

Since μ is a continuous random variable, the events could be listed to any detail, and since the normal distribution applies, there would be no theoretical beginning or end to the list of μ events. The probabilities for the listed events are found in Table 25-3, where each listed μ is actually at the midpoint of a class interval of width .10. The normal deviates z for each interval upper limit μ were computed using the relationship

$$z = \frac{\mu - \mu_0}{\sigma_0}$$

These probabilities may be used to compute expected values.

Finding Expected Opportunity Losses

The expected opportunity loss for each act may be computed by multiplying each value in the respective loss column of Table 25-2 by the probability values in column (5) of Table 25-3.

TABLE 25-3

Prior Probabilities for μ Intervals in Memory Device Decision

(1) INTERVAL FOR μ	(2) NORMAL DEVIATE z	(3) CUMULATIVE PROBABILITY	(4) MIDPOINT μ	(5) INTERVAL PROBABILITY
1.85–under 1.95	−3.67	.0001	1.90	.0001
1.95–under 2.05	−3.00	.0013	2.00	.0012
2.05–under 2.15	−2.33	.0099	2.10	.0086
2.15–under 2.25	−1.67	.0475	2.20	.0376
2.25–under 2.35	−1.00	.1587	2.30	.1112
2.35–under 2.45	−.33	.3707	2.40	.2120
2.45–under 2.55	.33	.6293	2.50	.2586
2.55–under 2.65	1.00	.8413	2.60	.2120
2.65–under 2.75	1.67	.9525	2.70	.1112
2.75–under 2.85	2.33	.9901	2.80	.0376
2.85–under 2.95	3.00	.9987	2.90	.0086
2.95–under 3.05	3.67	.9999	3.00	.0012
3.05–under 3.15	4.33	1.0000	3.10	.0001

Figure 25-3 shows the relationship between these values when the prior normal curve for μ is superimposed on the loss function for the holographic-unit choice. That act provides the following *approximate* value.

$$\text{Expected opportunity loss} = \$1,360 \quad \text{(holographic)}$$

The analogous interrelationship is shown in Figure 25-4 for the photographic-unit choice.

FIGURE 25-3

Illustration of how expected opportunity loss may be computed using loss function and prior normal curve for μ.

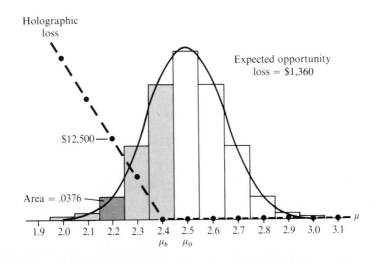

FIGURE 25-4

Illustration of how expected opportunity loss may be computed using loss function and prior normal curve for μ.

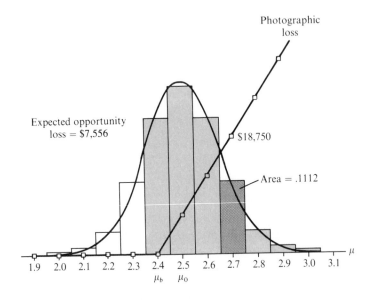

That act provides

$$\text{Expected opportunity loss} = \$7,556 \quad \text{(photographic)}$$

The main decision might be made right now. The Bayes decision rule indicates that the holographic memory device should be chosen. This act not only minimizes expected opportunity loss, but it must also maximize expected payoff. Rather than commit himself to the main decision, the computer center manager wanted to explore the possibility of using *sample information*. The decision maker needs to determine if it might be worthwhile to pursue such information.

EVPI: Minimum Expected Opportunity Loss

The expected value of perfect information is useful in gauging the potential worth of less-than-perfect sample information. We should compute the EVPI before deciding about a sample. Recall, from Chapter 22, that the following applies.

$$\text{EVPI} = \text{Expected opportunity loss for best act}$$

Thus, the expected opportunity loss for the best act equals the needed value.

We next introduce a streamlined procedure that the manager could have used in reaching the same conclusion. The following procedure would ordinarily be used in evaluating any decision having a structure similar to his.

25-3 Streamlined Prior Analysis without Sample Information

The streamlined procedure begins with some preliminaries. First is the definition of the population for which the mean μ is unknown and pivotal in establishing payoffs. The next step is to identify the linear payoff function for each act. From these the breakeven level μ_b is obtained. Figure 25-5 shows the general situation. Note that μ_b divides the range for μ into one segment where Act 1 has greater payoffs and one where Act 2 is better. The final preliminary step is to establish the expected value μ_0 and standard deviation σ_0 for the prior normal distribution for μ.

Identifying the Act Having Minimum Expected Opportunity Loss

Figure 25-6 relates the opportunity losses to the probabilities for μ by superimposing the normal curve for μ onto the respective opportunity loss graphs for the two acts involved. Figure 25-6(a) shows the possible arrangements when the expected mean μ_0 lies below the breakeven level. If $\mu_0 < \mu_b$, it is easy to see that the expected opportunity loss for Act 1 will be smaller than the expected opportunity loss for Act 2, since most of the area under the normal curve is concentrated in the range of μ where Act 1 has zero opportunity loss. (Remember that the *area* under the normal curve provides the probability.) The

FIGURE 25-5
Identifying better acts.

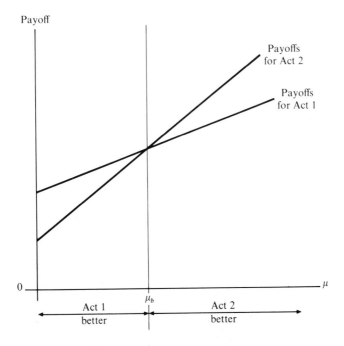

FIGURE 25-6
Prior normal curves for μ with loss functions superimposed.

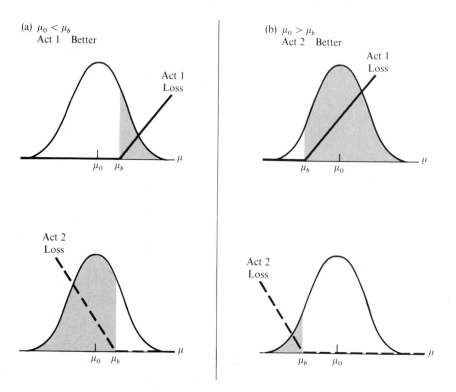

(a) $\mu_0 < \mu_b$
   Act 1   Better

Act 1
Loss

μ_0 μ_b

Act 2
Loss

μ_0 μ_b

(b) $\mu_0 > \mu_b$
   Act 2   Better

Act 1
Loss

μ_b μ_0

Act 2
Loss

μ_b μ_0

positive opportunity losses for Act 1, represented by the rising solid line segment, occur for unlikely levels of μ that are covered by the upper tail of the normal curve. On the other hand, the falling portion of the line for Act 2 occurs over the most likely range of μ values, so the expected opportunity loss is greater for that act.

The reverse situation is shown in Figure 25-6(b), where $\mu_0 > \mu_b$ and the expected opportunity loss for Act 2 is smaller.

From these graphs, we conclude that the *optimal act having the minimum expected opportunity loss is the one with zero opportunity losses that lie on the same side of the breakeven level as the expected mean.* In our present example, Act 1 is optimal when $\mu_0 < \mu_b$, whereas Act 2 is optimal when $\mu_0 > \mu_b$. *If the expected mean coincides with the breakeven level, then the two alternatives are equally attractive.*

The Normal Loss Function

It is unnecessary to go to the trouble of first approximating the normal curve by intervals and then multiplying by opportunity losses calculated in a table. Those calculations have largely been done when the loss lines have slope one and the prior normal curve has unit standard deviation. The resulting values describe the **normal loss function** $L(D)$ tabled in Appendix Table C. There $L(D)$ is given for any standard deviation distance D separating μ_0 and μ_b.

Figure 25-7 shows some cases from six different decision problems. The losses are only tabled for the best act (with μ_0 lying on its good side of breakeven). The expected opportunity losses and $L(D)$ get smaller as D becomes greater. (That is reflected by a smaller tail area under the normal curve covering μ's that involve nonzero opportunity loss.)

The $L(D)$ values from Appendix Table C equal the respective opportunity loss when the loss function has unit slope and the normal curve for μ has unit standard deviation. To compute an expected value, we must ordinarily adjust the tabled value to account for other levels in slope and standard deviation.

FIGURE 25-7

Various cases encountered in decision making using the normal distribution.

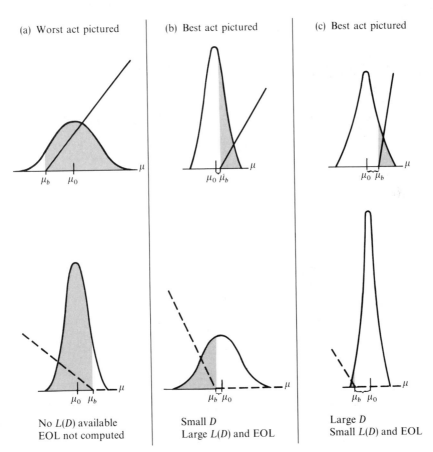

(a) Worst act pictured

(b) Best act pictured

(c) Best act pictured

No $L(D)$ available
EOL not computed

Small D
Large $L(D)$ and EOL

Large D
Small $L(D)$ and EOL

Finding the EVPI

As noted, it is not actually necessary to compute the expected opportunity loss to make the main decision, but rather to establish the worth of perfect information, since

$$EVPI = \text{Expected opportunity loss for best act}$$

Thus, the expected opportunity loss for the best act equals the needed value.

Under the streamlined procedure, the expected opportunity loss for the best act is the EVPI, which may be computed from

$$EVPI = |\text{slope}|\sigma_0 L(D_0)$$

Three constants must be specified: (1) the absolute value of the **slope** of the opportunity loss line; (2) the standard deviation of the prior probability distribution for μ; and (3) the **standardized distance**

$$D_0 = \frac{|\mu_b - \mu_0|}{\sigma_0}$$

which expresses the separation between μ_b and μ_0 in units of standard deviation. (The numerator must always be positive, so absolute values are used.)

Returning to the computer memory device decision, we may use this streamlined procedure to find the EVPI. We have already seen that the holographic memory unit would be the better choice. Referring to Figure 25-2, we see that the holographic loss line has a slope of $-\$62,500$, so that $|\text{slope}| = \$62,500$. Using the same values as before, $\mu_0 = 2.5$, $\sigma_0 = .15$, and $\mu_b = 2.4$, the standardized distance separating the expected mean from the breakeven level is

$$D_0 = \frac{|\mu_b - \mu_0|}{\sigma_0} = \frac{|2.4 - 2.5|}{.15} = .67$$

Referring to Appendix Table C, we find that for $D_0 = .67$

$$L(D_0) = L(.67) = .1503$$

and the expected value of perfect information is

$$\begin{aligned} EVPI &= \$62,500(.15)L(.67) \\ &= \$62,500(.15)(.1503) \\ &= \$1,409 \end{aligned}$$

The above amount is also the expected opportunity loss for the holographic-unit choice. This is a more precise value than the approximate one obtained earlier. The greater accuracy is due to the L table (which was constructed with many more, narrower μ intervals.)

This tells us that a perfect prediction for μ is worth only $1,409. This is the upper limit on the amount the decision maker might be willing to pay for less-than-perfect sample information. (This value differs from the EVPI of $12,500 calculated in Chapter 24. The discrepancy is due to the change in the prior probability distribution; our earlier example involved only two levels of μ, each with a probability of .5.)

ILLUSTRATION
ATM Transaction Times

The Million Bank has successfully reduced its personnel by using automated teller machines (ATMs). An engineering firm is deciding whether or not to contract with the bank to develop a second-generation machine. Although nobody knows what the mean cash-withdrawal time μ will be for the new machine, the engineers will receive an incentive of $100,000 for each second that μ falls below the current overall ATM average of 20 seconds, but must forfeit from a performance bond the same amount for each second that μ goes beyond that time. All of the firm's direct costs will be reimbursed by the Million Bank.

The firm's payoff function for taking the contract is

$$\text{Payoff} = 100,000(20 - \mu)$$
$$= \$2,000,000 - 100,000\mu \quad \text{(accept contract)}$$

The above plots on the graph in Figure 25-8 as a downward-slanting line with intercept $2,000,000 and slope $= -\$100,000$. The alternative is to refuse the contract, which involves the following neutral payoff function.

$$\text{Payoff} = \$0 \quad \text{(refuse contract)}$$

This appears on the same graph in Figure 25-8 as a horizontal line lying directly on the μ axis. As with the computer memory device decision, the breakeven level for the mean is that level for μ where the two payoff lines cross, here $\mu_b = 20$ seconds.

The owner feels that a normal distribution would be appropriate for generating probabilities for the unknown μ. He also believes that the state-of-art for the needed mechanisms has advanced to the point where it is "even money" that his firm will create a design which will yield a mean time at or below 15 seconds. Thus, the center of his prior normal curve is $\mu_0 = 15$. His judgment also leads to a standard deviation of $\sigma_0 = 2$ seconds for the subjective normal curve.

If the main decision were to be made without getting any further information, the owner would maximize his firm's expected profit (and minimize the expected opportunity loss) by accepting the contract. This is because μ_0 falls on that side of breakeven where accepting the contract yields greater payoffs.

However, it may be advantageous to do some further investigating before making the main decision. The potential worth of such information may be gauged by reference to the EVPI.

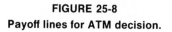

FIGURE 25-8
Payoff lines for ATM decision.

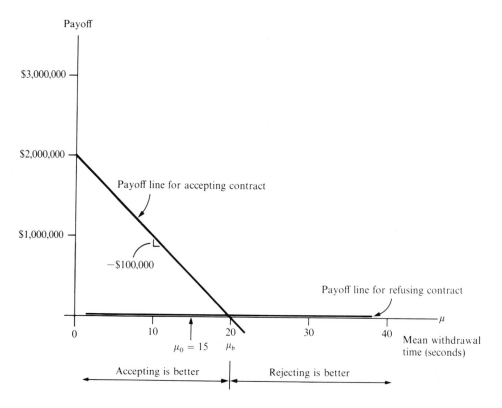

Accepting the contract, the better act, has an opportunity loss function with a rising line segment above μ_b. The slope of this portion is found by subtracting the slope $0 of the payoff line for refusing the contract from the slope $-$100,000$ of the payoff line for accepting the contract. The absolute value of this difference is the constant needed in computing EVPI, so that

$$|\text{slope}| = |-\$100,000 - 0| = \$100,000$$

The standardized distance separating the breakeven level of μ from its expected value is

$$D_0 = \frac{|20 - 15|}{2} = 2.50$$

so that from Appendix Table C, $L(2.50) = .002004$ and

$$\text{EVPI} = \$100,000(2)(.002004) = \$400.80$$

This amount is so relatively small that the owner decided that there would be little benefit from any further investigation. He signed the contract.

25-4 Decision Structure When Sampling Is Considered

The structure for the computer memory device decision using sample information is provided by the decision tree diagram in Figure 25-9. Here, the initial choice of whether or not to use sample information is made. If no sample is taken, the prior probability distribution for μ applies. If sampling is chosen, the sample size must be selected, the

FIGURE 25-9

The structure of the computer memory device decision when a prior normal probability distribution applies to the population mean.

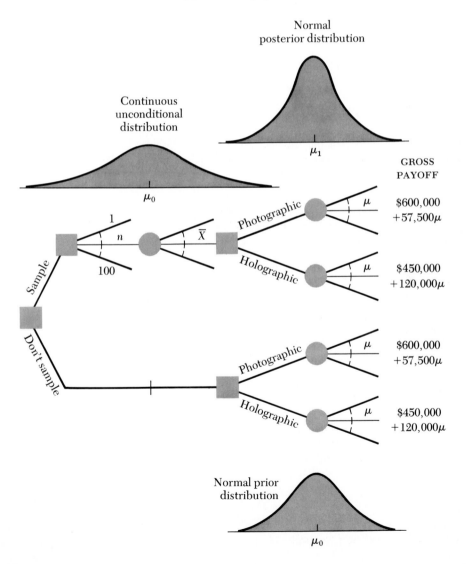

sample data collected, and the sample mean calculated. Based on the value achieved for $\bar{X}$, either the photographic or the holographic memory unit is chosen. With sampling, the posterior probability distribution applies to the population mean μ. The event forks for the values of $\bar{X}$ and μ have many branches, since each variable is continuous. In each case, probability values may be obtained only by finding the appropriate areas under the respective normal curves.

The probability distributions provided in the upper portion of the decision tree represent the informational chronology. This event sequence is the reverse of the order in which probability information is generally presented.

Since our probability distributions are continuous, it is not easy to obtain the revised versions needed to construct the decision tree. The backward induction required to determine the optimal decision rule, which specifies the action to take for each possible sample result, is also complicated. We must therefore depart from decision tree analysis and revert to *normal form analysis*, which itself must now be dressed in unfamiliar clothing.

25-5 Decisions Regarding the Sample: Preposterior Analysis

We are now ready to consider the decision of whether or not to take a sample from the population of individual values. This will also involve choice of the sample size n. Once that has been decided, the sample observations will be made and from these the sample mean $\bar{X}$ then computed.

Designating as Act 1 that choice that is better when $\mu_0 < \mu_b$ and Act 2 as the better one for $\mu_0 > \mu_b$, a decision rule of the following form will be used in making the final choice.

$$\frac{\text{Choose Act 1} \quad \leq \mid > \quad \text{Choose Act 2}}{C} \quad \bar{X}$$

The rationale is that a low value for $\bar{X}$ is evidence favoring a smaller level for μ, in which case Act 1 would be the better choice. And, a high value for $\bar{X}$ favors a greater μ, the case when Act 2 is better. In Section 25-6, we will see how to find the point of demarcation C. But first, we must determine how large the sample size n must be.

The Population Frequency Distribution

In all decisions having the applicable structure, the sample is drawn from the population of X individual values, the mean μ of which is uncertain. It is not necessary to know anything regarding the form of the frequency distribution, and its frequency curve may have a shape that is non-normal. A good guess must be made of the value for the population standard deviation, denoted as σ_I (where I reminds us that the distribution applies to *individual* population values).

In the computer memory device decision, the manager examined past data and compared his operation to similar systems. He established an educated guess for the population standard deviation of $\sigma_I = .5$ gigabit per day. (This is smaller than the value used in Chapter 24.) Of course, the mean μ of that population remains unknown. This is the major uncertainty.

We should take extra caution not to confuse σ_I, really an index summarizing the variability in *individual population values*, with σ_0, a parameter summarizing the variability in *possible means* μ of that population.

Probabilities for $\bar{X}$

Once values have been assumed for the parameters μ and σ_I of the underlying population, probabilities may be found for the possible levels of the sample mean. These will reflect the chosen sample size n. The central limit theorem tells us $\bar{X}$ has a probability distribution (sometimes referred to as the sampling distribution) closely approximated by a normal curve when n is large. This curve is centered on μ and has a standard deviation of

$$\sigma_{\bar{X}} = \frac{\sigma_I}{\sqrt{n}}$$

(The above quantity is sometimes referred to as the standard error of $\bar{X}$.)

Continuing with the memory device decision, if the manager were to use a sample of size $n = 25$, then

$$\sigma_{\bar{X}} = \frac{.5}{\sqrt{25}} = .1$$

A different value would be achieved for each possible n.

The sampling distribution for $\bar{X}$ is represented by a *second* normal curve, distinct from the prior normal curve for μ discussed earlier in the chapter. The $\bar{X}$ curve is centered on μ (which is unknown). Its standard deviation depends both on σ_I and on the sample size n that will be used. Since n is not fixed and may be chosen by the decision maker, the particular normal curve for $\bar{X}$ is not set until the final choice is made for the sample size.

Figure 25-10 illustrates how the possible normal curves for $\bar{X}$ become more compact as n gets larger. The sample mean in a taller, thinner curve (achieved by increasing the level for n) will tend to be closer in value to μ. Thus, as n is raised it will become more likely that a value will be computed for $\bar{X}$ that falls close to its μ target.

In effect, large sample sizes provide greater informational content, which should be reflected in the value of that information. As in Chapter 24, we may quantify a sample's potential worth in terms of the **expected value of sample information**, EVSI.

The Expected Value of Sample Information

Recall, from Chapter 24, that EVSI should approach EVPI as greater reliability is achieved from increasing the sample size. This is illustrated in Figure 25-11.

FIGURE 25-10

Sampling distributions (normal curves) for $\bar{X}$ at various sample sizes.

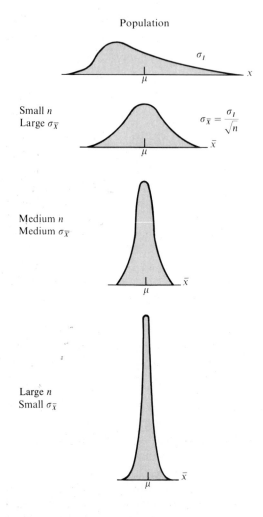

The unit normal loss function may be used in an analogous fashion in computing EVSI. The following expression applies.

$$\text{EVSI}(n) = |\text{slope}|\sqrt{v_n}\,\sigma_0 L(D_n)$$

The above is similar to the expression for EVPI. New is the added term involving v_n and a modified distance D_n. A different value for EVSI is achieved for each possible level for n. The new term is the **variance fraction**.

$$v_n = \frac{\sigma_0^2}{\sigma_0^2 + \sigma_{\bar{X}}^2} = \frac{\sigma_0^2}{\sigma_0^2 + \sigma_I^2/n}$$

The above fraction provides a modified variance $v_n\sigma_0^2$ that is smaller than that of the prior

FIGURE 25-11
Relationship between EVSI(n) and sample size.

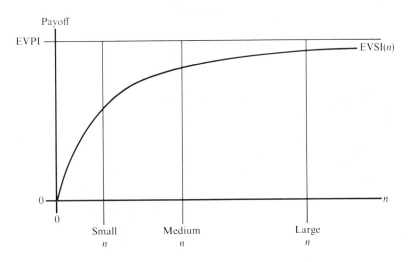

probability distribution for μ. The modified standard deviation is used in expressing the distance between μ_b and μ_0.

$$D_n = \frac{|\mu_b - \mu_0|}{\sqrt{v_n}\,\sigma_0}$$

Both v_n and D_n will change as n is changed. As n becomes larger, $\sigma_{\bar{x}}$ gets smaller; this makes the denominator for v_n shrink, and the v_n fraction becomes closer to 1 in value. That, in turn, gives a value for D_n which approaches D_0. Thus, EVSI(n) must approach the level of EVPI as n increases. (In the theoretical case when the sample size is so great it is in effect a *census*, sample information would be perfect information.)

For the computer memory device decision, $\mu_b = 2.4$, $\mu_0 = 2.5$, $\sigma_0 = .15$, $|\text{slope}| = \$62,500$, and $\sigma_{\bar{x}} = .1$ when $n = 25$. The variance fraction is

$$v_n = \frac{(.15)^2}{(.15)^2 + (.1)^2} = .692$$

and the standardized distance is

$$D_n = \frac{|2.4 - 2.5|}{\sqrt{.692}\,(.15)} = .80$$

so that, from Appendix Table C

$$L(D_n) = L(.80) = .1202$$

and

$$\text{EVSI}(25) = \$62,500\sqrt{.692}\,(.15)(.1202) = \$938$$

TABLE 25-4
The Expected Net Gain of Sampling Computed for Several Sample Sizes

n	$\sigma_{\bar{x}} = \sigma_I/\sqrt{n}$	V_n	D_n	$L(D_n)$	EVSI(n)	Cost(n)	ENGS(n)
10	.1581	.4737	.97	.08819	$ 569	$100	$469
15.	.1291	.5745	.88	.1042	740	150	590
20	.1118	.6429	.83	.1140	857	200	657
25	.1000	.6923	.80	.1202	938	250	688
28	.0945	.7159	.79	.1223	970	280	690
29	.0928	.7230	.78	.1245	992	290	702
30	.0913	.7297	.78	.1245	997	300	697
40	.0791	.7826	.75	.1312	1,088	400	688
50	.0707	.8182	.74	.1334	1,131	500	631
60	.0645	.8438	.73	.1358	1,169	600	569

The above indicates that $938 is the true worth of a sample of $n = 25$ to the decision maker. As long as the sampling cost is less than this amount, the computer center manager will be better off with the sample information than without it.

The Decision to Sample and Finding the Optimal n

Now suppose that the computer center manager has established the cost of sampling at $10 per day. With $n = 25$, the sampling cost would be $250. Since this amount is smaller than EVSI(25), *the manager should definitely make a decision based on a sample of some size* rather than choose an act without any information at all. The question remaining is: How large should n be?

We answer this question by finding the **expected net gain from sampling** for various sample sizes, which is computed

$$\text{ENGS}(n) = \text{EVSI}(n) - \text{Cost}(n)$$

The optimal sample size is the one with the greatest ENGS(n) *value.* By trial and error, trying various values of n, we determine the appropriate sample size. Table 25-4 provides the ENGS(n) values for a few sample sizes. Notice that the expected net gain increases until $n = 29$, after which it decreases. Thus, $n = 29$, for which ENGS(29) = $702, is the optimal sample size.

25-6 Posterior Analysis for a Given Sample Size

Once the sample size has been determined, the next step is to collect the sample data. The computed value for $\bar{X}$ will then be compared to the critical value C and the act selected for which $\bar{X}$ lies on the best side. The sample information also provides the basis for revising the prior probability distribution for μ.

Although the mathematical justifications are beyond the scope of this book, the concepts of Bayes' theorem may be extended to continuous normal curves in establishing the **posterior probability distribution for** μ. Like the prior probability distribution, a normal curve applies. We use the subscript 1 to distinguish the parameters of the posterior probability distribution. The center of the normal curve is denoted by μ_1 and its standard deviation by σ_1.

Figure 25-12 helps to explain this process. The non-normal population of individual daily access levels is provided at the top of the figure. Although the standard deviation of individual daily access levels is presumed to be $\sigma_I = .5$, the population center is unknown. This unknown mean μ is the entire focus of our analysis. The sample mean of n random daily observations $\bar{X}$ is to be computed. Since its value is presently unknown, statistical theory tells us that the tall, solid normal curve in the lower portion of Figure 25-12 provides the probabilities for $\bar{X}$. This is a conditional curve, since it is presumed to be centered on the prior expected mean μ_0. The flatter, solid normal curve represents the prior probabilities for the value of the unknown μ and is also centered on μ_0.

When it is actually computed, the sample mean value may fall anywhere in the vicinity of μ_0. Depending on the location of the sample mean, the appropriate posterior normal curve for μ (represented here by the dashed curve centered on μ_1) is obtained. The center of the posterior normal curve will always lie between μ_0 and the computed $\bar{X}$.

Posterior Expected Value of μ

The **posterior expected mean** μ_1 of the posterior probability distribution is computed by taking a *weighted average* of μ_0 and $\bar{X}$.

$$\mu_1 = \frac{I_0 \mu_0 + I_S \bar{X}}{I_0 + I_S}$$

The weights are the following indexes.

Index for prior information: $I_0 = 1/\sigma_0^2$

Index for sample information: $I_S = 1/\sigma_{\bar{X}}^2$

In averaging μ_0 and $\bar{X}$, proportional weight is given to prior judgment and to the sample results. The indexes are the reciprocals of the respective variances.

Returning to the computer memory device decision, where $\mu_0 = 2.5$ gigabits per day and $\sigma_0 = .15$, suppose that the optimal sample size is used. Thus, $n = 29$ days will be monitored by a special program and the individual daily access levels will be determined precisely for each. Using $\sigma_I = .5$ gigabit per day, the standard error for $\bar{X}$ is

$$\sigma_{\bar{X}} = \frac{.5}{\sqrt{29}} = .093$$

The above values give

$$I_0 = 1/\sigma_0^2 = 1/(.15)^2 = 44.44$$
$$I_S = 1/\sigma_{\bar{X}}^2 = 1/(.093)^2 = 115.62$$

We cannot compute μ_1 until the sample data have been collected.

FIGURE 25-12

Distributions involved in posterior analysis with sampling (not drawn to scale).

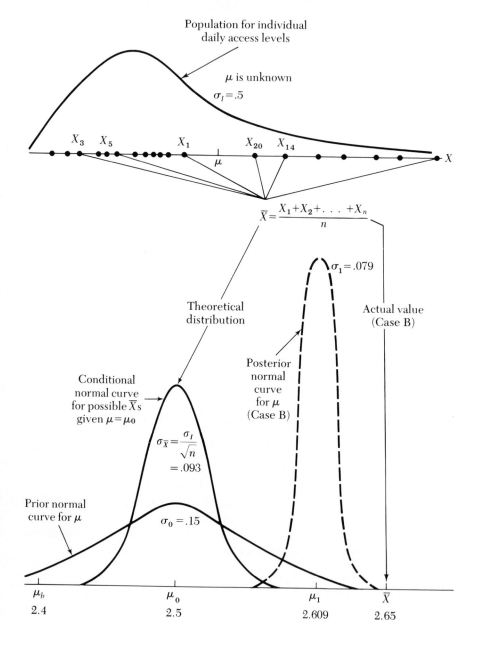

Population for individual
daily access levels

μ is unknown

$\sigma_I = .5$

X_3 X_5 X_1 X_{20} X_{14}

μ

X

$$\bar{X} = \frac{X_1 + X_2 + \ldots + X_n}{n}$$

$\sigma_1 = .079$

Theoretical
distribution

Actual value
(Case B)

Posterior
normal
curve
for μ
(Case B)

Conditional
normal curve
for possible $\bar{X}$s
given $\mu = \mu_0$

$$\sigma_{\bar{X}} = \frac{\sigma_I}{\sqrt{n}}$$
$$= .093$$

Prior normal
curve for μ

$\sigma_0 = .15$

μ_b μ_0 μ_1 $\bar{X}$
2.4   2.5   2.609   2.65

The resulting value for μ_1 must lie *between* the prior value of $\mu_0 = 2.5$ and the *computed value* for $\bar{X}$. Since $I_S = 115.62$ is greater than $I_0 = 44.44$, greater weight will be given to $\bar{X}$, and μ_1 must lie closer to that computed value. Consider the following possibilities.

CASE A	CASE B

CASE A

$\bar{X} = 2.2$

$\mu_1 = \dfrac{44.44(2.5) + 115.62(2.2)}{44.44 + 115.62}$

$= 2.283$

CASE B

$\bar{X} = 2.65$

$\mu_1 = \dfrac{44.44(2.5) + 115.62(2.65)}{44.44 + 115.62}$

$= 2.608$

The Decision Rule and Critical Value for the Sample Mean

We now consider the problem of finding the appropriate decision rule to apply to the posterior analysis. This involves selecting the critical value of C that minimizes the expected opportunity loss according to the decision rule

$$\text{Select Act 1} \quad \text{if } \bar{X} \leq C$$

$$\text{Select Act 2} \quad \text{if } \bar{X} > C$$

where, as before, Act 1 is the better choice when μ_0 falls below μ_b and Act 2 is the better choice when μ_0 exceeds μ_b.

The value of C is the point of demarcation between those levels of $\bar{X}$ where Act 1 is the better choice and those levels of $\bar{X}$ where Act 2 is better. This is the level of $\bar{X}$ where the expected opportunity losses are identical under either act. Both acts are equally attractive when the expected mean is equal to the breakeven level. After sampling, the posterior expected mean applies, so that the point of demarcation must be the value of $\bar{X}$ that provides a posterior expected mean where

$$\mu_1 = \mu_b$$

Thus, we substitute C for $\bar{X}$ in the earlier expression for μ_1 and set this expression equal to μ_b.

Solving algebraically for C, an expression may be derived. The following equation is obtained and may be used in computing the critical value.

$$C = \frac{(I_0 + I_S)\mu_b - I_0\mu_0}{I_S}$$

The above expression may be used to compute the critical value for any problem where μ_0, μ_b, and the informational indexes are given.

Consider once more the computer memory device decision. Substituting $\mu_b = 2.4$, $\mu_0 = 2.5$, $I_0 = 44.44$, and $I_S = 115.62$ into the above expression, we obtain

$$C = \frac{(44.44 + 115.62)(2.4) - 44.44(2.5)}{115.62} = 2.36$$

The decision rule for a sample of size $n = 29$ is therefore

Select photographic unit   if $\bar{X} \leq 2.36$

Select holographic unit   if $\bar{X} > 2.36$

Thus, if the manager decides to sample with $n = 29$ and $\bar{X}$ turns out to be larger than $C = 2.36$ (say, $\bar{X} = 2.65$), then the holographic memory unit should be chosen. But, if a smaller mean is found (say, $\bar{X} = 2.2$), then the photographic unit would instead be chosen.

It may seem perplexing that $C = 2.36$ is a value smaller than $\mu_b = 2.4$. But C represents that level for $\bar{X}$ below which the sample result is extreme enough to force the main decision the other way from that suggested during prior analysis. C will therefore always lie on the opposite side of μ_b from μ_0.

Posterior Variance and Standard Deviation for μ

The **posterior variance** (standard deviation) for the posterior probability distribution for μ may be computed from

$$\sigma_1^2 = \left(\frac{\sigma_{\bar{X}}^2}{\sigma_0^2 + \sigma_{\bar{X}}^2} \right) \sigma_0^2$$

The above states that σ_1^2 must be a fraction of σ_0^2, with the fraction becoming smaller as n gets larger ($\sigma_{\bar{X}}$ gets smaller). Also, if we rearrange terms, the following expression may be obtained from the above.

$$\sigma_1^2 = \left(\frac{\sigma_0^2}{\sigma_0^2 + \sigma_{\bar{X}}^2} \right) \sigma_{\bar{X}}^2$$

You see that σ_1^2 is also just a fraction of $\sigma_{\bar{X}}^2$. Thus, σ_1 must be smaller than either σ_0 or $\sigma_{\bar{X}}$.

Continuing with the computer memory device decision, the following results are obtained.

$$\sigma_1^2 = \left(\frac{(.093)^2}{(.15)^2 + (.093)^2} \right)(.15)^2 = .0062$$

$$\sigma_1 = \sqrt{.0062} = .079$$

Notice that the posterior standard deviation for μ is smaller than both $\sigma_0 = .15$ and $\sigma_{\bar{X}} = .093$. This illustrates an essential feature of *information theory*.

Concepts from Information Theory

As I_0 and I_S are defined, a smaller variance (standard deviation) gives a larger index value, reflecting greater informational content. Thus, a larger n gives a more reliable sample having a smaller $\sigma_{\bar{X}}$ and a bigger I_S. Likewise, an expert with greater knowledge about μ should provide a subjective prior probability distribution having a smaller σ_0 and a greater I_0.

Information theory postulates that the informational content indexes are additive, so that

$$\text{Posterior information} = \text{Prior information} + \text{Sample information}$$

$$I_1 = I_0 + I_S$$

where I_1 denotes the index of the content of information posterior to (after) sampling. In fact, it may be established mathematically that

$$1/\sigma_1^2 = 1/\sigma_0^2 + 1/\sigma_{\bar{X}}^2$$

so that the index for the information available posterior to sampling is

$$I_1 = 1/\sigma_1^2$$

For the computer memory device decision the index for posterior information is

$$I_1 = 1/\sigma_1^2 = 1/.0062 = 161$$

or, equivalently,

$$I_1 = I_0 + I_S = 44.44 + 115.62 = 161$$

which exceeds both original informational indexes. Altogether, more is known regarding μ after the sampling experiment than before, but the earlier judgment still has an effect too.

25-7 A Summary of the Procedures

Before concluding, it will be helpful to summarize the concepts and procedures examined in this chapter. The various time frames involved are shown in Figure 25-13, where decision making using the normal distribution is separated into four stages.

We begin with **prior analysis**, during which the prior distribution for the unknown μ is obtained, generally through judgment. During this stage, payoffs are determined as linear functions of μ, leading directly to a breakeven analysis. The main decision might be made in this stage by comparing the mean μ_0 of the prior distribution to the breakeven level μ_b. Whether or not we stop at this stage depends on how worthwhile any further information

FIGURE 25-13

**A summary of the relationship between the concepts and procedures for
decision making using the normal distribution.**

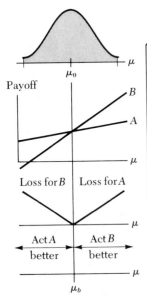

PRIOR ANALYSIS

- Exercise judgment to get prior probability distribution for μ.
- Establish variability of individual members in population.
- Determine breakeven level of mean.
- FINAL DECISION—compare μ_0 to μ_b to find maximum expected payoff act.
- Calculate EVPI to gauge the worth of further information.

APPLICABLE VARIABLES AND PARAMETERS

μ_0 = Prior expected value of μ

σ_0 = Prior standard deviation of μ

σ_I = Standard deviation of individual values

μ_b = Breakeven level for mean

It may not be desirable to go any farther.

The final decision will be made during prior analysis, unless sampling is done. In that case, the optimal act will be chosen during posterior analysis.

PREPOSTERIOR ANALYSIS

- Evaluate various sample sizes.
- Compute preliminary parameters.
- Calculate EVSI (n).
- Calculate ENGS (n).
- Pick best sample size.

n = Trial sample size

$\sigma_{\bar{X}}$ = Standard deviation of possible sample means

n = Chosen sample size

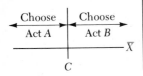

POSTERIOR ANALYSIS

- Formulate the decision rule.
- Collect the sample data.
- FINAL DECISION—compare $\bar{X}$ to C.

$\bar{X}$ = Computed value of the sample mean

The final stage is optional.

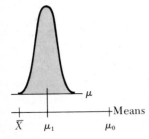

FUTURE ANALYSIS

- Determine the posterior probability distribution for μ.

μ_1 = Posterior expected value of μ

σ_1 = Posterior standard deviation of μ

about μ happens to be. This is roughly gauged by the EVPI, and further investigation is warranted only if the EVPI is great enough to justify the extra bother of evaluating the sample information. (Clearly, an EVPI of only $10 would not justify any further analysis; even an EVPI of $100 is apt to be smaller than the cost of a modest sampling study.)

If it might be worthwhile to obtain further information, then **preposterior analysis** follows. Here, the question is primarily whether or not to sample, and if sampling is chosen, what sample size n to take. The evaluation is computationally lengthy, involving calculations of various EVSI's and sampling costs for several values of n, so that the size with the greatest expected net gain from sampling may be determined.

The next stage involves **posterior analysis**. Here, the decision rule is established, the sample is collected, and the actual sample mean $\bar{X}$ is calculated. Depending on the value obtained for $\bar{X}$, the choice of the act for the main decision is indicated.

An *optional* fourth stage completes the procedure. Here, **future analysis** is concerned with the posterior probability distribution for μ. *This distribution is not required to make the main decision*, although it may serve as the starting point for future decisions involving μ. (This fact was not obvious in our earlier discussions, where we had to investigate the characteristics of the posterior distribution for μ to explain the procedures involved in posterior and preposterior analyses.)

Most students of this material suffer from a mild form of "symbol shock"—and for good reason! We have introduced four different standard deviations and five means. Moreover, $\bar{X}$ appears as a subscript to another symbol. Unfortunately, this Greek

TABLE 25-5

Glossary of Statistical Symbols for Decision Making Using the Normal Distribution

---

MEANS

μ *The mean of the underlying population.* The value of μ is the main uncertainty. Payoffs depend on the level of μ. Although probabilities for μ may be revised, we will never know the true value of μ.

μ_b *The breakeven level for μ.* This is a known value, representing the level of μ where the payoff lines cross.

μ_0 *The expected or central value of the prior normal probability distribution for μ.* Largely *a matter of judgment*, this quantity is the decision analyst's 50–50 point for where μ might fall.

μ_1 *The expected or central value of the posterior normal probability distribution for μ.* This quantity is a weighted average of μ_0 and the computed sample mean $\bar{X}$, and it may be calculated only after obtaining sample results. This quantity provides the decision analyst with a revised 50–50 point for μ.

$\bar{X}$ *The sample mean.* The computed value of $\bar{X}$ determines which act will be chosen.

STANDARD DEVIATIONS

σ_0 *The standard deviation of the prior normal probability distribution for μ.* Largely *judgmental*, this value summarizes (or indexes) the magnitude of the decision analyst's uncertainty about the value of μ.

σ_1 *The standard deviation of the posterior normal probability distribution for μ.* Based on both earlier judgment and actual sample results, this value also expresses the magnitude of uncertainty about the value of μ (but after revision in accordance with sample results).

σ_I *The standard deviation of the population of individual values.* This is an index of the extent of individual differences. Like μ itself, σ_I is ordinarily unknown, and we must make an "educated guess" or use a "ballpark figure" for its value.

$\sigma_{\bar{X}}$ *The standard error (deviation) of $\bar{X}$.* This tells us how tightly $\bar{X}$ values will cluster about μ. It is computed by dividing the population standard deviation σ_I by $\sqrt{n}$.

"alphabet soup" is unavoidable. Table 25-5 provides a glossary to help you keep track of these symbols. It may also help to mention a few of the pitfalls commonly encountered in applying the various analyses.

1. **Remember that some expressions involve the standard deviation σ and that others involve the variance σ^2.** Be sure to take the square root of the variance to obtain the corresponding standard deviation when it is needed, and to square the standard deviation to obtain the variance.

2. **Prior analysis compares μ_b and μ_0, whereas posterior analysis compares $\bar{X}$ and C. Only one of these comparisons is ultimately used in making the main decision.**

3. **Do not confuse σ_0 with σ_1.** The former expresses variability in μ itself and gauges how close to μ_0 we judge that μ lies. The standard deviation σ_1 pertains to individual population values. Ordinarily, σ_0 and σ_1 are not equal. (In a decision involving human heights, σ_0 might be $\frac{1}{4}$ inch, reflecting our lack of precision in predicting the population mean, and σ_1 might be $2\frac{1}{2}$ inch, expressing variability from person to person.)

4. **Keep in mind that μ remains unknown.** There will be no population census, and the value of μ will be uncertain throughout the entire analysis. On the other hand, μ_0 and μ_1 are the expected values of μ at the beginning and the end of the analysis, respectively. The value of μ_0 is known throughout, but μ_1 is uncertain throughout most of the analysis and may only be calculated last. The value of $\bar{X}$ is also uncertain until after the sample has been collected.

25-8 Additional Remarks

The special difficulties encountered when dealing with several different normal curves have forced us to depart from our usual decision tree analysis. If we approximated the various continuous probability distributions by discrete tables (using typical values for μ and $\bar{X}$), then we could apply the methods presented in Chapter 24 to reach nearly identical conclusions to those we achieved using the procedures discussed in this chapter. But it is more convenient to focus on opportunity losses and to use normal form analysis when the prior probability distribution for μ may be represented by the normal curve and the sample observations themselves range over a continuous scale (so that the probabilities for $\bar{X}$ are represented by another normal curve).

But what do we do if the prior probability distribution for μ is not a normal curve? An amazing fact, established by Robert Schlaifer, who originally proposed the procedures examined in this chapter,* is that *for practically any other type of prior probability distribution, the posterior probability distribution for μ will still very closely approximate a normal curve.* Thus, what form applies to the prior distribution for μ really makes very little difference.

---

* Much of the material in Schlaifer's books, *Probability and Statistics for Business Decisions* (New York: McGraw-Hill, 1959; reprint, Melbourne, Fla.: Kreiger, 1983) and *Introduction to Statistics for Business Decisions* (New York: McGraw-Hill, 1961; reprint, Melbourne, Fla.: Kreiger, 1982), carefully develops the concepts discussed in this chapter.

Another nice feature of the present approach to decision making using sample information is that it is simpler than applying decision tree analysis with approximate probability distributions, which involves a tremendous number of computations that are unnecessary here. The present procedure entirely avoids the problem of finding the unconditional result probabilities for $\bar{X}$. The nature of the opportunity loss lines permits us to evaluate the two-action problem through a breakeven analysis that considers only the central value of μ and the nature of its prior probability distribution.

There are limitations to the procedures presented here, however. For instance, they cannot be used when the payoffs cannot be graphed as straight lines or when more than two basic actions are contemplated. We have presented a special-purpose tool that applies only to limited situations. Fortunately, many practical business decision-making applications fall into this category.

25-9 Computer-Assisted Analysis

The streamlined procedure discussed in this chapter requires extensive calculations, especially when the sample size has not yet been decided. To avoid the arithmetic problems and the potential for error, the necessary calculations might be delegated to the computer. It would be easy to employ a spreadsheet program to this end, with one problem serving as the template for subsequent ones needing only changes to input parameters. Lotus 1-2-3 would work well at this task. It still would be necessary, however, to make keyboard entries for the necessary $L(D)$ values, which would have to be pulled from Appendix Table C.

That task is automatically performed by the *QuickQuant* software package available to users of this book. Once you supply the requested payoff function parameters and levels for the prior expected mean and standard deviation, the program will compute the breakeven mean, indicate the act having maximum expected payoff, and supply the EVPI. For any stipulated sample size or ranges of n, *QuickQuant* will compute EVSI(n), ENGS(n), and the corresponding critical value. It will even find the optimal sample size. For the computed level of the sample mean, the program will also compute the posterior expected mean and standard deviation. Complete operating instructions are provided in the Appendix of this book.

CASE

Pickwick Pipe Shoppes

Rod Tamper is the marketing director for Pickwick Pipe Shoppes, a chain of franchises specializing in tobacco products. Rod is evaluating the second-phase expansion of the Gentrytown Mall as a possible site for a new store. The proposed site lies on the main concourse, just beyond a barricade that will be removed in a few months. The major uncertainty is the amount of foot traffic that will pass the store front. Although historically mall traffic varies by time of day and day of week, peaking on Saturday afternoons, and fluctuating seasonally as well, the sales potential of a new store may be gauged closely by the mean number of customers passing the store front in the Saturday afternoon rush during non-Christmas selling periods.

Rod acknowledges uncertainty regarding the mean level, judging it just as likely to lie at or below 1,000 per hour as above that level. He furthermore thinks that it is just as likely for the mean to fall between 900 and 1,100 per hour as outside that interval.

Another major uncertain quantity is the percentage of the traffic flow that will stop in the store and eventually make a purchase. Previous experience with other malls leads Rod to conclude that the following probabilities apply: .23 for .5%; .28 for .6%; .17 for .7%; .15 for .8%; .11 for .9%; and .06 for 1.0%. Also uncertain is the average transaction amount, which he judges to be equally likely to be $5 or $6. Annual sales for stores in Rod's franchises are expected to be about 3,000 times hourly sales during non-Christmas Saturday afternoons.

The annual operating costs for the proposed store are $30,000 plus 50% of sales for cost of goods. Additionally, Rod expects new stores to make a $20,000 operating profit in the first year.

To help in his evaluation, Rod hires students to count customers passing specific spots in the open portion of the mall. The cost for this service is $10 per hour.

Questions

1. Determine the expected value and standard deviation for the subjective prior probability distribution for the mean level μ of Saturday afternoon foot traffic.

2. Compute the expected percentage of passing persons who will stop at the new store.

3. The following levels for μ are possible: (a) $\mu = 800$, (b) $\mu = 1,100$, and (c) $\mu = 1,200$. In each case, answer the following.
   (1) Compute the expected annual revenue for the new store.
   (2) Find the expected annual profit.
   (3) Would Rod find the new store to meet his profit goal?

4. Treating μ as an unknown variable, express Rod's expected payoff as a function of μ. Find the breakeven level for μ that yields an expected profit of exactly $20,000. Assuming that Rod wishes to maximize expected payoff, would he build the proposed store?

5. Determine the EVPI. Does there seem to be the potential for improvement in expected payoff by deferring the main decision until after collecting sample information?

6. Individual hourly traffic levels in Rod's other mall stores on Saturday afternoons have a standard deviation of 650 persons. Assuming that this value applies for the new store site, answer the following.

(a) Compute the expected net gain from sampling when (1) $n = 25$ and (2) $n = 100$.

(b) Which of the two sample sizes provides the greater expected payoff?

7. Suppose a sample of $n = 25$ hourly foot traffic counts will be obtained. Express Rod's decision rule.

PROBLEMS

25-1   In each of the following situations, the prior probability distribution for the population mean is represented by the normal curve.

	(a)	(b)	(c)	(d)
Mean	50	100	60	40
Standard deviation	10	10	20	10
Breakeven level	55	90	62	38
Slope	$1,000	$5,000	$5,000	$10,000

Below the breakeven level for the mean, Act 1 is more profitable; beyond the breakeven level, Act 2 is better. In each case, (1) indicate which act is better and (2) calculate the EVPI.

25-2   Sonic Phonics specializes in stereo headphones. It is considering adding a new stereo helmet receiver for motorcyclists, but the owner is uncertain about the mean annual sales volume per outlet in the retail chain it supplies. He believes that the mean is normally distributed, with a mean of 60 and a standard deviation of 10 helmets per store. Altogether, 100 stores are involved. The helmet will have a product life of about one year, after which it is believed that the novelty will wear off. Production set-up costs will be $50,000. Each helmet will have a variable cost of $30 and will sell for a retail price of $40.

(a) Assume that the total increase in profits is to be maximized. In terms of the mean number of helmets sold per store, determine an expression for the payoff for making the helmet. For not making the helmet. What is the breakeven level?

(b) Should Sonic Phonics make the helmet?

(c) Calculate the EVPI.

25-3   The marketing manager of Blitz Beer must determine whether or not to sponsor Blitz Day with the Gotham City Hellcats. She is uncertain what the effect of the promotion will be in terms of the mean increase in daily sales volume that would result during the 100-day baseball season. The cost of sponsorship is $10,000, and each can of Blitz has a marginal cost of $.20 and sells for $.40.

(a) Assuming that change in profit is to be maximized, express the payoff function for the two alternatives in terms of the mean daily increase in cans sold.

(b) Suppose that Blitz Day will result in a mean increase that is judged to be normally distributed with a mean of 600 and a standard deviation of 50 cans per day. Should the brewer sponsor the event?

(c) What is the EVPI? Do you think it is worthwhile to obtain further information? Can a sample from the underlying population even be helpful in making this decision? Explain.

25-4   Sonic Phonics is considering modifying the components in its quadraphonic speaker system to boost its effective power. The ultimate result depends upon the mean signal-to-noise ratio μ. The latter index is unknown, although its prior probability distribution has been judged to be normally distributed with a mean of 100 and a standard deviation of 10. Unfortunately, the modified system may result in a poorer overall performance rating than the current system's 30 points, rising or dropping .25 points for each unit that μ lies above or below 90.
   (a) Assuming that system performance rating is to be maximized, what is the breakeven level for the mean signal-to-noise ratio?
   (b) Should Sonic Phonics modify its quadraphonic speakers?
   (c) Calculate the EVPI.

25-5   Reconsider the illustration in the chapter of choosing between photographic and holographic peripheral memory storage units. Suppose that the following annual savings payoff function applies, where the access portion depends on the unknown mean access level of μ gigabits per day.

$$\text{Payoff} = \begin{cases} \$500,000 + \$ 65,000\mu & \text{for photographic} \\ \$330,000 + \$150,000\mu & \text{for holographic} \end{cases}$$

   (a) Find the breakeven level for the population mean.
   (b) Which unit maximizes annual savings when the prior expected mean is $\mu_0 = 2.5$ gigabits per day?

25-6   (*Continuation of Problem 25-5*): Suppose that the prior probability distribution for the population mean access level has an expected value of 2.3 gigabits per day and a standard deviation of .75 and that the population of individual daily access levels has a standard deviation of 3.5 gigabits per day.
   (a) Calculate the EVPI.
   (b) If a random sample of $n = 16$ days is chosen, find the optimal value of C that will maximize expected annual savings.
   (c) Suppose that the sample mean turns out to be 1.75 gigabits per day. Determine the mean and the standard deviation of the posterior probability distribution for μ. Which memory unit will be chosen?
   (d) Use your results from (c) to find the probability that the mean daily access level lies above the breakeven level.

25-7   (*Continuation of Problem 25-5*): The sample size has not been chosen, but the cost of each daily observation is now $500. Use the constants provided earlier to calculate the expected net gain from sampling for the indicated sample sizes.
   (a) 4
   (b) 9
   (c) 100
   (d) Which one of the above sample sizes is best? Formulate the optimal decision rule for the corresponding sample mean.

25-8   The first stage of a chemical process yields a mean of μ grams of active ingredient for every liter of raw material processed. Due to variations in the raw material and in the control settings, the true population mean for any particular batch is unknown until processing is complete. The plant superintendent believes that μ is normally distributed with a mean of 30 g and a standard deviation of 2 g. The amount of variation in individual liters within a batch is summarized by a standard deviation of 6 g.

The plant superintendent will use the active ingredient in either a high-pressure or a low-pressure final-stage process. Each process provides an identical final product. The ultimate profit from each alternative is partly determined by μ. The following payoff function applies.

$$\text{Payoff} = \begin{cases} \$10,000 + \$300\mu & \text{for high-pressure process} \\ \$13,100 + \$200\mu & \text{for low-pressure process} \end{cases}$$

(a) Determine the breakeven level of μ. Will the high-pressure or the low-pressure process yield the greater expected profit?

(b) Calculate the value of the slope of the opportunity loss lines and the superintendent's EVPI.

25-9 (*Continuation of Problem 25-8*): For a cost of $1 per liter, the superintendent determines the actual yield of active ingredient per liter.

(a) Calculate the EVSI for (1) $n = 4$; (2) $n = 9$; (3) $n = 16$.

(b) Calculate ENGS(n) for each of the sample sizes in (a). Which sample size is the best?

(c) Determine the optimal decision rule for the optimal sample size you found in (b). Which process should be used if (1) $\bar{X} = 30$ g? (2) $\bar{X} = 32$ g? (3) $\bar{X} = 33$ g?

25-10 A decision must be made between two procedures. The following function expresses the payoff in terms of an unknown population mean.

$$\text{Payoff} = \begin{cases} -\$500 + \$10\mu & \text{for } A \\ \$1000 - \$5\mu & \text{for } B \end{cases}$$

The normal prior distribution for the mean has expected value of 110 with a standard deviation of 10. Individual observations may be made of the underlying population, which has a standard deviation of 30.

(a) Determine the breakeven level for the mean. Based on the prior distribution only, which alternative maximizes expected payoff?

(b) Calculate the EVPI.

(c) A sample of size $n = 9$ will be used in helping to make the decision. What are the EVSI and ENGS if each observation costs $.10?

(d) Find the decision rule involving the sample mean $\bar{X}$.

(e) Suppose that a sample mean of $\bar{X} = 96$ is obtained. What procedure should be chosen?

(f) For a sample result of $\bar{X} = 96$, determine the applicable mean and standard deviation for the posterior normal distribution for μ. Then, find the applicable probability that μ exceeds its breakeven level.

25-11 A facilities planner for Waysafe Market is evaluating a new electronic scanning cash register. The planner is uncertain about the mean time μ that the new equipment will take to check out a typical customer with 2 sacks of groceries. Experience with present automatic registers yields a standard deviation for individual checkout times of $\sigma_I = 1$ minute, and this value is assumed to apply to the new system. It is the planner's judgment that μ has a prior normal probability distribution with a mean of $\mu_0 = 3$ minutes and a standard deviation of $\sigma_0 = .20$ minute.

(a) Determine the probability that (1) $\mu \geq 3.5$ and (2) $\mu \leq 2.75$.

A random sample of new system checkout times is to be obtained for further study.

(b) Assuming that $n = 100$ typical customers' checkout times will be obtained, calculate $\sigma_{\bar{X}}$ and determine the following conditional result probabilities

(1) $\bar{X} \leq 2.75$ minutes, given $\mu = 2.90$

(2) $\bar{X} > 3.25$ minutes, given $\mu = 3.10$

(3) $\bar{X}$ lies between 2.85 and 3.15 minutes, given $\mu = 3.00$

(c) Calculate the standard deviation σ_1 of the posterior probability distribution for μ. This should be smaller than its prior probability distribution counterpart.

(d) Suppose that the sample results yield a computed value of $\bar{X} = 3.20$ minutes. Compute the expected value μ_1 of the posterior probability distribution for μ. In revising the probability distribution for μ, which source of information—prior judgment or the sample results—has been given the greater weight?

(e) According to the prior probability distribution for μ, there is a .50 probability that the true population mean checkout time will be $\mu \le 3.00$ minutes. For future study, the posterior probability distribution will apply. Determine the new probability that μ will fall at or below 3 minutes.

25-12 Yokum University's president knows that the population standard deviation in height of his male students is 2.5 in. He is uncertain about the mean height, which he characterizes as having a prior normal probability distribution with a mean of 69.5 in. and a standard deviation of .25 in. He wishes to decide whether or not to gamble with the president of Near Miss, whose men are known to be an average of 69 in. tall. The terms are that Yokum will get (give up) 100,000 druthers or fraction for each inch or fraction that the mean height of Yokum men exceeds (lies below) the Near Miss mean.

(a) Calculate the EVSI when a sample of $n = 100$ Yokum men are measured.

(b) Suppose that $n = 25$ Yokum men are measured in the sample. Find the level of $\bar{X}(C)$ that would make Yokum's president indifferent between gambling and not gambling.

(c) A sample of $n = 25$ Yokum men has a mean of $\bar{X} = 69.2$ in. Find the mean and the standard deviation of the posterior probability distribution for the mean height of Yokum men. Then, determine the probability that Yokum men are actually shorter than Near Miss men on the average.

25-13 *Computer exercise.* Two configurations are possible for rigging test equipment to monitor a chemical process. The payoff depends on the mean batch pressure μ (in pounds per square inch). The following applies.

$$\text{Payoff} = \begin{cases} -\$10,000 + 50\mu & \text{for configuration } A \\ -\$20,000 + 60\mu & \text{for configuration } B \end{cases}$$

The level of μ is uncertain, and this quantity is judged to be normally distributed with prior expected mean 1,010 psi and standard deviation 25 psi. Individual batch pressures have standard deviation assumed to be 50 psi.

(a) If the main decision were to be made now, which configuration would maximize expected payoff?

(b) Compute the EVPI.

(c) Sample observations cost $.50 per test batch. Find the optimal sample size and corresponding decision rule.

(d) Suppose that $\bar{X} = 987.5$.

(1) Applying your answer to (c), what configuration should be selected in order to maximize expected payoff?

(2) Determine the parameters of the posterior normal distribution for μ.

(3) Determine the probability that μ falls below the original breakeven level.

26

Decision Making with Utility

The goal of this chapter is to broaden the scope of decision theory through the introduction of a new payoff measure. We have seen that a good payoff measure should rank all possible outcomes in terms of how well they meet the decision maker's goals. This is often an easy task when there is no uncertainty. But the presence of uncertainty may severely complicate the issue when the possible outcomes from a decision are extreme. Such decisions contain elements of *risk*. Because people usually have different attitudes toward risk, two persons faced with an identical decision may actually prefer different courses of action.

The crucial role that attitude plays in any decision is illustrated by the divergent behavior of different persons faced with the same decision. The *umbrella situation* nicely demonstrates this point. *How can we explain why everyone does not carry an umbrella when we do?* To a certain extent, we say that all individuals are not equally adept at selecting and exercising appropriate decision criteria. But this is only one possible explanation. With much justification, however, we conclude that the difference in behavior may also be explained by differing attitudes toward the consequences. Some people may enjoy getting wet, but others may view it as an invitation to pneumonia and possibly the first step to a premature grave. Some people think it is chic to carry rain paraphernalia when it's not raining; others would rather lug around a ball and chain. Even if we find two persons who have identical attitudes toward the decision consequences, they may still make opposite decisions because they may not have made identical *judgments* regarding the chance of rain.

In this chapter, we will discuss utility as an alternative expression of payoff that reflects a person's attitudes. We will begin by examining the rationale for buying insurance. A brief historical discussion of utility and the underlying assumptions of a theory of utility will then be presented. Finally, a procedure will be introduced that may be used to determine utility values. The utility function so obtained provides a basis for our discussion of some basic attitudes toward risk.

26-1 Attitudes, Preferences, and Utility

In Chapter 22, we examined several procedures and criteria that help decision makers to make choices in the presence of uncertainty. In all cases, the payoff value of each outcome is required to analyze the decision. As we have seen, not all outcomes have an obvious numerical payoff. In this section, we will see how payoffs may be determined in such cases. Later in the chapter, we will develop methods of quantifying such consequences as reduced share of the market, loss of corporate control, and antitrust suits. Even when numerical payoffs may be naturally determined, we have seen that it may be unrealistic to select the act with the maximum expected payoff. In some cases, an extremely risky act fares better under the Bayes decision rule than an obviously preferred act. As noted in Chapter 22, this difficulty is not the fault of the Bayes criterion, but is caused by payoff values that do not reflect their true worth to the decision maker.

The Decision to Buy Insurance

The inadequacy of using such obvious measures as dollar cost or profit to indicate payoffs may be vividly illustrated by evaluating an individual's decision of whether or not to buy fire insurance. Spiro Pyrophobis wishes to decide whether to buy a fire insurance policy for his home. Our decision maker's payoffs will be expressed in terms of his out-of-pocket costs, which we will represent by negative numbers. Our question is: Will the Bayes decision rule lead to the choice of the act that is actually preferred?

In answering this question, we will use the hypothetical payoff table provided in Table 26-1. Here, we have greatly simplified the decision. The acts are to buy or not to

TABLE 26-1
Payoff Table for the Decision to Buy Fire Insurance

		ACT			
		Buy Insurance		*Don't Buy Insurance*	
EVENT	PROBABILITY	*Payoff*	*Payoff × Probability*	*Payoff*	*Payoff × Probability*
Fire	.002	−$100	−$ .20	−$40,000	−$80.00
No fire	.998	− 100	−99.80	0	0
Expected payoff			−$100.00		−$80.00

buy an annual policy with a $100 premium charge. If there is a fire, we will assume that Spiro's home and all its contents, valued at $40,000, will be completely destroyed.

Insurance actuaries have established that historically 2 out of every 1,000 homes in the category of Spiro's home burn down each year. The probability that Spiro's home will burn down is therefore set at $2/1,000 = .002$. Thus, the complementary event—no fire— has a probability of $1 - .002 = .998$. We use these probability values to calculate the expected payoffs for each act in Table 26-1. The maximum expected payoff is $-\$80$, which corresponds to the act "don't buy insurance" and is larger than the $-\$100$ payoff from buying fire insurance.

In this example, the *Bayes decision rule indicates that it is optimal to buy no insurance.* Insurance policy premiums are higher than the expected claim size, which is equivalent to the policyholder's expected dollar loss, so that the insurance company can pay wages and achieve profits. Thus, buying insurance may be considered an unfair gamble, where the payoff is not in the buyer's favor. Individuals can expect to pay more in insurance premiums than they will collect in claims,* and they feel fortunate if they never have to file a claim. Yet most persons faced with this decision choose to buy fire insurance. Loss of a home, which composes the major portion of a lifetime's savings for many people, is a dreadful prospect. The expenditure of an annual premium, although not exactly appealing, buys a feeling of security that seems to outweigh the difference between the expected payoffs.

The Bayes decision rule selects the *less preferred act.* Does this mean that it is an invalid criterion? Rather than answer no immediately, let us consider the payoffs used. The true worth of the outcomes is not reflected by the dollar payoffs. A policyholder is willing to pay more than the expected dollar loss to achieve "peace of mind." We say that the policyholder derives greater **utility** from having insurance. If dollar losses are valued on a scale of true worth or utility, then each additional dollar loss will make our decision maker feel disproportionately worse off. Thus, a 10% reduction in wealth may be more than twice as bad as a 5% reduction. The same is usually true for gains in dollar wealth; the second increase may not increase the decision maker's sense of well being as much as the first. In the parlance of economics, *the policyholder's marginal utility for money is decreasing.* Each successive dollar gain buys a smaller increase in utility; each additional dollar loss reduces utility by a greater amount than before.

Thus, we may question the validity of using dollars as our payoff measure. Instead, it might be preferable to measure the payoff of an outcome in terms of its worth or utility.

26-2 Numerical Utility Values

We wish to obtain *numerical utility values* that express the true worth of the payoffs that correspond to decision outcomes. We refer to such numbers as **utilities**. Much investigation has been made of the true worth of monetary payoffs. The early eighteenth-century mathematician Daniel Bernoulli—a pioneer in developing a measure of utility—

---

* This is not true of life insurance, which is ordinarily a form of savings.

proposed that *the true worth of an individual's wealth is the logarithm of the amount of money possessed*. Thus, a graphical relationship between utility and money would have the basic shape of the curve in Figure 26-1. Note that although the slope of this curve is always positive, it decreases as the amount of money increases, reflecting the assumption of decreasing marginal utility for money.

The Saint Petersburg Paradox

A gambling game called the **Saint Petersburg Paradox** led Bernoulli to his conclusion. In the game, a balanced coin is fairly tossed until the first head appears. The gambler's winnings are based on the number of tosses that are made before the game ends. If a head appears on the first toss, the player wins $2. If not, the "kitty" is doubled to $4—the reward if a head appears on the second toss. If a tail occurs on the second toss, the kitty is doubled again. The pot is doubled after every coin toss that results in a tail. The winnings are $2 raised to the power of the number of tosses until and including the first head. This procedure will be more interesting if you pause to think about what amount you would be willing to pay for the privilege of playing this game.

The probability that $n + 1$ tosses will occur before payment is the probability that there is a run of n tails and that the $(n + 1)$st toss is a head, or $(1/2)^{n+1}$. The payoff for $n + 1$ tosses is 2^{n+1}. We calculate the player's expected receipts from the sum

$$\$2(1/2) + \$2^2(1/2)^2 + \$2^3(1/2)^3 + \cdots = \$1 + \$1 + \$1 + \cdots = \$\infty$$

Since the number of $1's in this sum is unlimited, the *expected receipts from a play of this game are infinite*! Whatever amount you were willing to pay to play must have been a finite amount and therefore less than the expected receipts. Thus, the expected payoff for this gamble is also infinite, no matter what price is paid to play.

FIGURE 26-1
Bernoulli's utility function for money.

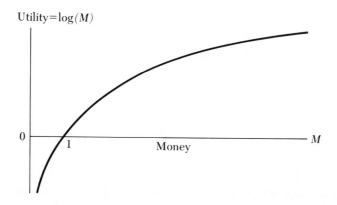

Few people are willing to pay more than $10 to play this game, and even at this price, a player would win only 1 out of 8 games on the average. A player paying $500 would show a profit in only 1 out of every 256 gambles on the average. The natural reticence of players to pay very much for this gamble led Bernoulli to his conclusion about the utility for money. In general, we say that a person who prefers not to participate in a gamble in which the expected receipts exceed the price to play has a **decreasing marginal utility** for money.

The Validity of Logarithmic Values

Via different paths of reasoning, other early mathematicians arrived at conclusions similar to Bernoulli's—that the marginal utility for money is decreasing—and proposed other utility curves with the same basic shape. A major fault of these early works is that they do not account for individual differences in the assignment of worth. A more modern treatment of utility in the abstract sense was advanced by John von Neumann and Oskar Morgenstern in 1947 in their book *Theory of Games and Economic Behavior*. There, they proposed that a utility curve may be tailored for any individual, provided certain assumptions about the individual's preferences hold. These assumptions provide several valid, basic shapes for the utility curve, including curves similar to Bernoulli's. We will investigate some of these utility curves later in the chapter.

Outcomes without a Natural Payoff Measure

Until now, the outcomes of our examples have had a *natural* numerical payoff measure, such as dollar profits, gallons of gasoline, or time saved. But we have noted that some decisions have no numerical outcomes. As decision makers, we should be able to assess the relative worth of such an outcome.

In the case of most decisions, it is possible to determine preferences, although this is not always an easy task. Indeed, value judgments may be the most difficult step in analyzing a decision. Consider the student selecting a school from several top universities, the child choosing a candy bar, the single person contemplating getting married and forgoing the carefree life, the tired corporate founder pondering merger and retirement versus retaining control and delegating operating responsibility, or the innocent person choosing between pleading guilty to manslaughter or facing trial for murder. If we assume that we have the capability of ranking the consequences in order of preference, we extend the notion of utility so that numerical payoffs may be made for the most intangible outcomes.

26-3 The Assumptions of Utility Theory

The fundamental proposition of the modern treatment of utility is that it is possible to obtain a numerical expression for an individual's preferences. We rank a set of outcomes by preference and then assign utility values that convey these preferences. The largest utility number is assigned to the most preferred outcome, the next largest number is assigned to the second most preferred outcome, and so forth. Suppose, for instance, that you are contemplating a menu. If you prefer New York steak to baked halibut and you wish to assign utility values to the entrees in accordance with your preferences, the utility for steak will be 5, or $u(\text{steak}) = 5$, and $u(\text{halibut})$ will be some number smaller than 5.

Before we describe how specific utility numbers may be obtained, we will discuss some of the assumptions underlying the theory of utility. Various assumptions have been made about the determination of utilities.* All of them have one feature in common—that the values obtained pertain only to a *single individual* who behaves *consistently* in accordance with his or her own tastes.

Preference Ranking   The first assumption of utility theory is that a person can determine for any pair of outcomes O_1 and O_2 whether he or she prefers O_1 to O_2, prefers O_2 to O_1, or regards both equally. This assumption is particularly advantageous when we consider monetary values, because then we assume that more money is always better than less. But we have seen that it may be very difficult to rank preferences when qualitative alternatives are considered. Can a person always determine a preference for or establish an indifference toward outcomes? If not, then utilities cannot be found for these outcomes.

Transitivity of Preference   The second assumption of utility theory is that if A is preferred to B and B is preferred to C, then A must be preferred to C. This property is called **transitivity of preference** and reflects an individual's consistency. Again, when we are dealing with monetary outcomes, we usually assume transitivity.

The Assumption of Continuity   The third assumption of utility theory is that of **continuity**, which tells us that the individual considers some *gamble* having the best and worst outcomes as rewards to be equally preferable to some middle or in-between outcome. To illustrate continuity, we will consider the following example.

Homer Briant owns a small hardware store in a deteriorating neighborhood and is contemplating a move. Because Homer is still young and has no special skills, he will not consider leaving the hardware business. A move cannot be guaranteed to be successful, since relocating will involve the maximum extension of his credit and there will be no time for a gradual buildup of business. Therefore, moving will either improve Homer's present business or be disastrous. Thus, Homer is faced with one of the following outcomes.

Most preferred O_3 Increasing sales (if move is a success)

O_2 Decreasing sales (if Homer stays)

Least preferred O_1 Imminent bankruptcy (if the move is a failure)

Whether a move will be a success depends largely on luck or chance. Our assumption of continuity presumes that there is some probability value for a successful move that will make Homer indifferent between staying and moving. Figure 26-2 presents the decision

---

* The assumptions discussed in this book are simplifications of the original axioms postulated by von Neumann and Morgenstern.

FIGURE 26-2

Decision tree diagram for Homer Briant's decision.

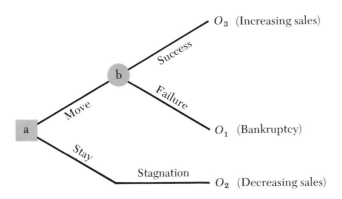

tree diagram for this decision. The fork at node b represents a gamble between O_3 and O_1 resulting from the act "move." Continuity may be justified by observing that if the value of Pr[success] is close to 1, so that a move will almost certainly be a success, Homer will prefer the gamble of moving to staying. But if Pr[success] is close to 0, making bankruptcy a near certainty, Homer will prefer to stay in his present location. Thus, there must be a success probability somewhere between 0 and 1 beyond which Homer's preference will pass from O_2 to the gamble. This value for Pr[success] makes the gamble as equally attractive as O_2.

Continuity is a crucial assumption of utility theory, but it may be hard to accept, especially if the outcomes include the ultimate one—death. Suppose that you are allowed to participate in a lottery that offers you $100 if you win and death if you lose. Is there any probability for winning that would make you indifferent between the status quo and playing? A natural response is that this is not a very meaningful gamble, so we will recast the situation. Suppose that you are informed by a reliable source that you can drive your car one mile down the road and someone will be passing out $100 bills, one to a person. There are no gimmicks, and you will not be inconvenienced by a mob of people. Would you go? If you answer yes, then consider your chances of getting killed in an automobile accident on your journey. For the past several years, approximately 50,000 persons have been killed in such accidents in the United States annually. So although it is quite small, the probability that your rather untimely death will occur while you are collecting your $100 is not zero. Going to get your $100 is a gamble having death as a possible outcome, and you prefer the gamble to the status quo. Now suppose that we increase the chance of death. To reach your benefactor, you must cross a condemned bridge. Would you still go? Probably not, because the chance of death would be significantly higher. Somewhere in between these two extremes lies a probability for safely getting your $100 and a complementary probability for death that would make you indifferent between the status quo and the gamble.

The Assumption of Substitutability   A fourth assumption of utility theory allows us to revise a gamble by *substituting* one outcome for another outcome that is equally well regarded. The premise is that the individual will be indifferent between the original and the revised gambles. The **substitutability** assumption may be illustrated by means of an example.

A husband and wife cannot agree on how to spend Saturday night. In desperation, they decide to gamble by tossing a coin to determine the kind of entertainment they will select. If a head occurs, they will spend the evening at the opera (her preference), and if a tail occurs, they will go to a basketball game. Suppose that the wife changes her mind and wants to go to a dance instead. The husband dislikes dancing just as much as the opera, so he would be indifferent between tossing for the opera or basketball and a revised gamble between dancing and basketball. This will hold regardless of the odds, providing that the chance of going to the basketball game remains the same for the original and the revised gambles.

The principle of substitutability also holds if we treat a gamble as an outcome. For any outcome, we substitute an *equivalent gamble* with two other outcomes as rewards that is equally as well regarded as the outcome the gamble replaces. For example, suppose that the wife insists on a movie instead. She wants to see a romance story, but he feels that as compensation for being dragged to a movie, they should see an adventure film. Suppose that the husband is indifferent between an opera or a coin toss to determine which of the two movies to see. The second coin toss is an equivalent gamble to the opera outcome.

FIGURE 26-3

An illustration of the assumption of substitutability. The single-stage gamble at *A* and the two-stage gamble at *B* are equally well regarded.

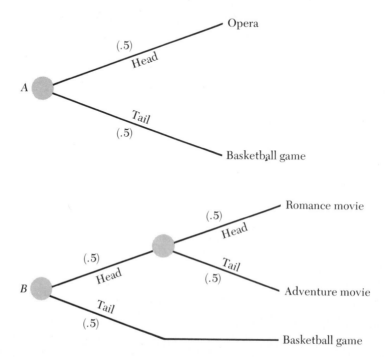

Thus, the husband should be indifferent between the single- and the two-stage gambles in Figure 26-3.

The Assumption of Increasing Preference   The final assumption of utility theory concerns any pair of gambles with identical outcomes. The gamble that has the greater probability for the more desirable outcome must be preferred. Thus, the preference for gambles between the same two outcomes *increases* as the probability for attaining the better outcome increases. The plausibility of **increasing preference** should be apparent. Suppose that when a coin is tossed, you are paid $100 if a head occurs and nothing if a tail occurs. The probability for winning $100 is 1/2. It should be obvious that this gamble would be decidedly inferior to a gamble with the same outcomes and a probability for winning greater than 1/2.

26-4 Assigning Utility Values

Utility numbers must be assigned to outcomes in such a way that the outcome for which a person has a greater preference receives the greater value. The resulting values gauge that person's relative preferences. Any numbers satisfying these requirements will be suitable as utilities, and their absolute magnitudes may be arbitrarily set.

To lay the foundation for the methodology used in finding utility values, we again view the uncertain situation as a gamble.

Gambles and Expected Utility

We are presently concerned with making choices under uncertainty. Thus, the payoffs for decision acts are unknown, and each act may be viewed as a gamble with uncertain rewards. To evaluate such decisions, we must extend the concept of utility to gambles.

Recall that the Bayes decision rule involves comparisons between the expected payoffs of acts or strategies, so that the "optimal" choice has the maximum expected payoff. But the major difficulty with this criterion, as we have seen, is that the indicated course of action may be less attractive than some other action. For example, the Bayes decision rule tells us not to buy fire insurance when most people feel that insurance is desirable. We wish to overcome this obstacle by using utilities in place of dollar payoffs. We therefore require that the expected utility payoffs provide a valid means of comparing actions so that the action having the greatest expected utility is actually preferred to the alternative actions. Thus, buying fire insurance should have greater expected utility than not buying it.

But we can go one step further. Suppose that the most preferred action has the greatest expected utility, the next most preferred action has the next greatest utility, and so forth. Then expected utility would express preference ranking, and the *expected utility values would themselves be utilities*. Each utility value would express the worth of a *gamble* between outcomes obtained by averaging the utility values of the outcomes, using their respective probabilities as weights. This may be stated more precisely as a property of utility theory.

PROPERTY: In any gamble between outcome A and outcome B, with probabilities of q for A and $1 - q$ for B

$$u(\text{gamble}) = qu(A) + (1 - q)u(B)$$

Thus, the utility for a gamble between two outcomes is equal to the expected utility for the gamble. When acts having uncertain outcomes are viewed as gambles, the utility for an act is equal to the expected utility for its outcomes. *When payoffs are measured in terms of utilities, the Bayes decision rule will indicate that the act having the maximum expected utility is optimal*, so that this criterion may always be used to select the most preferred act or strategy.

We are now ready to assign utility values to outcomes. Figure 26-4 outlines this procedure. The numbers are obtained from a series of gambles between a pair of outcomes.

The Reference Lottery

The process begins with a preference ranking of all the outcomes to be considered. The most preferred and the least preferred outcomes are determined, and a gamble between these outcomes establishes the individual's utilities. We call this a **reference lottery**. It has two events: "win," which corresponds to achieving the best outcome, and "lose," which corresponds to attaining the worst outcome. Such a gamble is purely *hypothetical* and only provides a framework for assessing utility. The events "win" and "lose" do not relate to any events in the actual decision structure and are used to divorce the reference lottery from actual similar gambles. *The probability for winning the hypothetical reference lottery is a variable*, denoted by q, which changes according to the attitudes of the decision maker.

The initial assignment of utility values to the best and worst outcomes is *completely arbitrary*. It does not matter what values are chosen; assigning different values to these arbitrary utilities will result in different utility scales. This is similar to temperature measurement, in which two different and quite arbitrary values are used to define the Fahrenheit and Celsius scales. The choices of $32°$ Fahrenheit and $0°$ Celsius for the freezing point of water and of $212°F$ and $100°C$ for its boiling point, result in quite different values on these two scales for any particular temperature.

FIGURE 26-4
The procedure for assigning values to a set of outcomes.

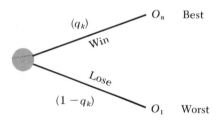

Obtaining Utility Values

Once the extreme utility values are determined, the decision maker may use the reference lottery to obtain utilities for the intermediate outcomes. This is accomplished by varying the "win" probability q until the decision maker establishes a value of q that serves as a *point of indifference* between achieving that outcome for certain and letting the reward be determined by the reference lottery. That particular value of q makes the reference lottery a gamble that is equivalent to the intermediate outcome so evaluated. We have seen that the assumption of continuity makes this possible.

Again, we add meaning to this procedure by considering its similarities to temperature measurement.

The decision maker's subjective evaluation is analogous to designing a thermometer. A thermometer is designed by determining a core diameter that will permit a substance such as mercury to rise to various levels within its tubular cavity. For each level of heat, there is a corresponding height to which the mercury must rise. On the Celsius scale, the $100°$ mark corresponds to the mercury's height when the thermometer is placed in boiling water. Various levels of heat between the freezing and boiling points of water correspond to marks at prescribed heights above the zero mark, allowing heat to be measured in relative degrees. Similarly, the values of q established to make the decision maker indifferent between respective intermediate outcomes and the reference lottery serve to measure his or her relative preferences. The indifference values of q are like the markings on a thermometer, and the different outcome preferences are analogous to different levels of heat. These values of q are established through introspection and have no more to do with the actual chance of winning than the design of a thermometer is related to tomorrow's temperature.

Once an indifference value of q has been established for an outcome, its utility value may be determined by calculating the expected value of the reference lottery using that value of q. Letting O_1 and O_n represent the least and the most preferred outcomes, we then find the utility of an outcome O_k of intermediate preference from

$$u(O_k) = q_k u(O_n) + (1 - q_k)u(O_1)$$

Here, q_k is the value of q that makes the decision maker *indifferent* between the certain achievement of O_k and taking a chance with the reference lottery. The utility value $u(O_k)$ is analogous to a numerical degree value beside a marking on a thermometer.

To illustrate, we will continue with Homer Briant's contemplated business relocation. Homer has ranked his preferences for the outcomes of increasing sales (O_3), decreasing sales (O_2), and bankruptcy (O_1), and the reference lottery is shown in Figure 26-5. Suppose that the utility values of the extreme outcomes are arbitrarily set at 10 and -5, so that

$$u(O_3) = 10 \qquad u(O_1) = -5$$

Now assume that Homer contemplates the reference lottery in terms of 100 marbles in a box, some labeled W for "win" and the rest labeled L for "lose." A marble is to be selected at random. If it is a W, then Homer will be guaranteed outcome O_3 (increasing sales), but if it is an L, he will go bankrupt for certain, achieving outcome O_1. Homer is then asked what

FIGURE 26-5
The reference lottery for Homer Briant's decision.

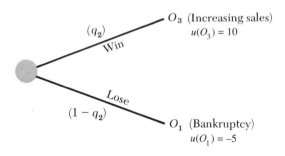

number of W marbles would make him indifferent between facing declining sales (outcome O_2) or taking his chances with the lottery. After considerable thought, Homer replies that 75 W marbles would make him regard O_2 and the reference lottery equally well. This establishes a reference lottery win probability of q_2 that makes it an equivalent gamble to outcome O_2.

$$q_2 = 75/100 = .75$$

This probability may then be used to calculate the utility of declining sales.

$$u(O_2) = q_2 u(O_3) + (1 - q_2)u(O_1)$$
$$= .75(10) + .25(-5)$$
$$= 6.25$$

Attitude versus Judgment

It must be emphasized that the value $q_2 = .75$ is merely a device used to establish indifference. *The selected probability for winning the lottery has nothing to do with the chance that the most favorable outcome will occur.* In setting $q_2 = .75$, the decision maker is expressing an *attitude* toward one outcome in terms of the rewards of a hypothetical gamble. This value was obtained through introspection in an attempt to balance tastes and aspirations between remaining in a declining business or gambling to improve it. Homer is assumed to be capable of switching from introspection to dispassionate *judgment* when asked later what he thinks the actual chance is that moving his business will be a success. To arrive at the probability of success, our decision maker must use his experience and knowledge of such factors as the history of failures by relocated businesses, prevailing economic conditions, and possible competitor reactions.

Suppose that Homer judges his chance of success after moving to be 1/2. We now analyze his decision problem by applying the Bayes decision rule, using utilities as payoff values. The decision tree diagram is shown in Figure 26-6. The expected utility payoff for the event fork at b is 2.5, which is the utility achieved by moving. Since this value is smaller

FIGURE 26-6

Homer Briant's decision tree diagram showing backward induction analysis with utility payoffs.

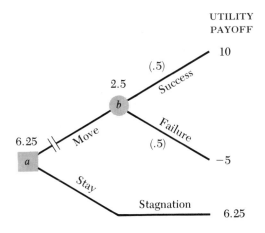

than the 6.25 utility achieved by remaining in his present location, Homer Briant should not move. Thus, we prune the branch corresponding to the act "move" and bring the 6.25 utility payoff back to node *a*.

Utility and the Bayes Decision Rule

This example illustrates why the Bayes decision rule is valid when utility payoffs are used. The utility for a gamble is the expected value of the utilities assigned to its rewards. Since any act with uncertain outcomes may be viewed as a gamble, the act that provides the greatest utility—and therefore the one that must be preferred—is the act with the maximum expected utility payoff. The Bayes decision rule may therefore be viewed as an extension of utility theory, and the criterion serves only to translate the decision maker's preferences into a choice of act. Homer Briant decides to stay because this act provides the greater utility—which may only be the case, our theory states, if remaining in the present location is the preferred act. *In arriving at a choice, both the decision maker's attitudes toward the consequences and judgment regarding the chances of the events are considered and integrated.* The choice indicated by the Bayes criterion is optimal because it is preferred above all others.

If some other success probability (say, .90), had been determined, Homer would relocate, because doing so would have the higher utility: .9(10) + .1(−5) = 8.5. This might be the case, for example, if Homer learned that his major would-be competitor had just been taken over by his incompetent son. Changing event probabilities reflects only the decision maker's judgment regarding the factors that influence their occurrence. Only the *expected* utilities of uncertain *acts* may be affected by the revision of event probabilities. Regardless of the chance of the success of the relocation, the decision maker's utilities for the ultimate *outcomes* must remain unchanged. Only a change of taste or attitude, which might be caused by a death in the family or by a change in personal finances, can justify revising the ultimate outcome utilities.

26-5 The Utility for Money

Applying the Utility Function in Decision Analysis

The reference lottery may be used to construct a **utility function** for money. To do this, the best outcome is selected so that it is no smaller than the greatest possible payoff, and the worst outcome is selected so that it is no larger than the lowest possible payoff. Monetary outcomes offer some special advantages. A monetary amount may be measured on a continuous scale, so that the utility function itself will be continuous. This suggests that it may be determined by finding an appropriate smoothed curve relating money values to their utilities. To do this, only a few key dollar amounts and some knowledge of the curve's general shape are required. The curve obtained by connecting the points can then serve as an approximation of the utility function.

Such a curve is shown in Figure 26-7 for the Ponderosa Record Company decision in Chapter 21. This utility curve has been derived according to the procedures just described by applying a reference lottery and using a few key monetary amounts as the outcomes. The reference lottery that is used ranges from $+\$100,000$ (win) to $-\$75,000$ (lose), which, for ease of evaluation, are more extreme than any possible payoff. Arbitrary utility values of $u(+\$100,000) = 1$ and $u(-\$75,000) = 0$ have been set for simplicity.

FIGURE 26-7
The utility function for the president of the Ponderosa Record Company.

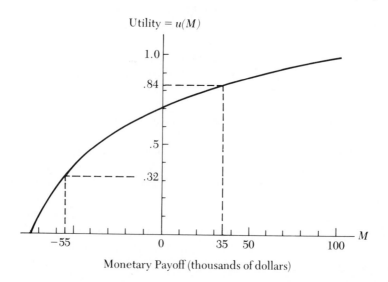

Monetary Payoff (thousands of dollars)

In practice, a utility function is found empirically by personally interviewing the decision maker. Ordinarily, the function will be described graphically by reading the utilities directly from the curve rather than by using a mathematical equation.

We use the utility curve in Figure 26-7 to analyze the Ponderosa president's decision problem. The original decision tree diagram is reconstructed in Figure 26-8. The utilities corresponding to each monetary payoff have been obtained from the utility curve and added to the tree. For instance, the utilities for the monetary payoffs $35,000 and − $55,000 are .84 and .32, respectively.

Backward induction is then performed using utilities instead of dollars. Here, we find that the optimal choice is "don't test market" and "abort." The two alternatives that

FIGURE 26-8

The Ponderosa decision tree diagram showing backward induction analysis with utility payoffs.

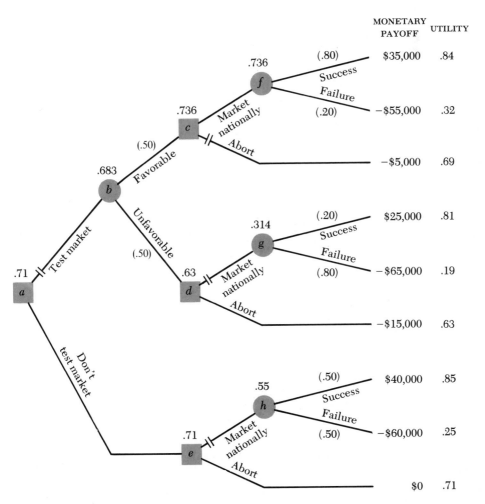

involve marketing the record are too risky. Recall that we reached a different conclusion in Chapter 21 when expected monetary values were used. But since utility values express the true worth of monetary outcomes, our latest solution is the valid one.

Certainty Equivalents and Utilities

In Chapter 22, we encountered **certainty equivalents**, payoff amounts that the decision maker would be willing to accept in lieu of undergoing the uncertainty. There, a cumbersome procedure is described for finding certainty equivalents. That involves discounting expected payoffs by the risk premium amount, a method requiring tabulation of risk premiums. These are not only hard to find, but only a few amounts may be listed from the infinite number of possibilities.

A backward induction using utility payoffs is more streamlined and consistent than one using certainty equivalents. And working with expected utilities will accomplish precisely the same thing. This is because any utility amount has a matching dollar amount, found by reading the utility graph in reverse order.

Consider the Ponderosa decision tree in Figure 26-8. Take the utility value of .736 at node f and read the corresponding M from the utility curve in Figure 26-7. This corresponds to about $+\$11,000$ on the monetary scale; that amount may be interpreted as the decision maker's certainty equivalent for node f. Each utility value above the nodes in the decision tree may be converted into a unique certainty equivalent by reading the corresponding monetary value from the utility function graph.

Doing this will provide nearly the same values found in Chapter 22 for the Ponderosa decision in Figure 22-1 (page 663). The utility-generated certainty equivalents differ slightly from those, because of the approximations taken in establishing the risk premiums used in Chapter 22.

The backward induction itself in Figure 26-8 was conducted wholly with utility values, the expected values computed directly, without any adjustments in the values obtained. Certainty equivalents would not be used in pruning the tree, and are not needed at all to complete the decision analysis. The role of the certainty equivalent is to help in communicating the results. (Ponderosa's president would relate to $11,000 more easily than to .736, the utility of that amount.) The decision analyst might prevent some unnecessary controversy by converting all expected utilities to their certainty equivalent amounts before showing the pruned tree to the decision maker.

Utility and the Decision to Buy Insurance

Earlier, we showed how the Bayes decision rule will ordinarily indicate that the greatest expected *monetary* payoff is achieved by not buying casualty insurance. But when *utility* payoffs are employed, that same procedure reaches the opposite conclusion: *Utility is maximized by buying the insurance.* This confirms the choices most of us have made in determining our own insurance needs.

To illustrate, we will return to our first insurance example. Suppose that Spiro Pyrophobis values the dollar changes in his assets according to the utility function in Figure 26-9. There we read the following values.

$$u(-\$40,000) = -200$$

$$u(\$0) = 0$$

$$u(-\$100) = -.25$$

Each act is a gamble. Buying insurance is a gamble having two identical outcomes in terms of dollar expenditure of $-\$100$, since the same amount applies whether or not there is a fire. Buying no insurance is a gamble having cash outcomes of $-\$40,000$ if there is a

FIGURE 26-9
Utility function for Spiro Pyrophobis.

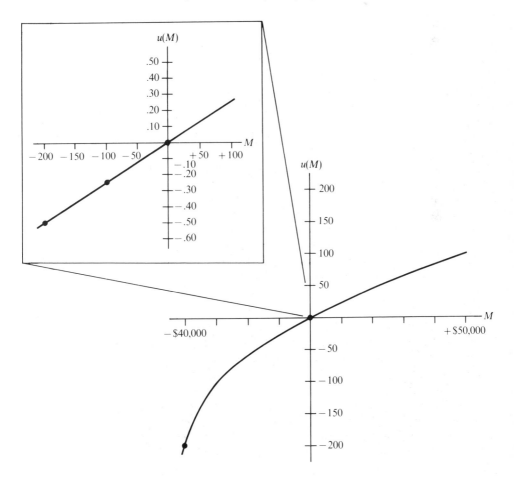

fire and $0 if there is no fire. The utilities for the respective acts are therefore the expected utilities for the corresponding gambles. We see from Table 26-2 that the expected utilities are −.25 for buying insurance and −.40 for not buying insurance. Since buying insurance has the higher utility, it must be preferred by the decision maker. Stated differently, the act "buy insurance" has the maximum expected utility payoff, so the Bayes decision rule indicates that this act is the optimal choice.

Thus, when we use utilities as payoff values, the Bayes decision rule indicates the "proper" result. However, this does not permit us to conclude that whenever utilities are used as payoffs, this criterion will lead to a decision to buy insurance. The choice depends on the relationship between the chance of fire and the price of the insurance policy. Suppose, for example, that the price of Spiro's policy is raised to $200, so that Figure 26-9 provides

$$u(-\$200) = -.50$$

The expected utility for buying insurance must therefore be −.50, so that if the probability for fire remains the same, the act "don't buy insurance" will have a utility of −.40, which is greater than −.50, making "don't buy insurance" the preferred act. This is the opposite outcome from our earlier decision. The insurance has become too expensive to be attractive.

Many people faced with the same circumstances would buy insurance even if the premium were raised to $1,000 or more. *Their tastes would be different and this would be reflected by the different utility values that they would assign to each outcome.* Premium prices may partly explain the prevalence of fire insurance coverage and the paucity of protection against natural disasters, such as earthquakes, tornados, and floods. One reason why people do not generally buy insurance policies to cover natural disasters is the high premium required by insurance companies for such coverage (if it is offered at all) in relation to the probabilities for occurrence (which are difficult to obtain actuarily for such rare phenomena).

TABLE 26-2
Determination of Utilities for Outcomes of the Fire Insurance Decision and Calculation of Expected Utilities

(1) EVENT	(2) PROBABILITY	(3) CASH CHANGE M	(4) UTILITY	(5) UTILITY × PROBABILITY
		Buy Insurance		
Fire	.002	−$100	−.25	−.0005
No fire	.998	−100	−.25	−.2495
				Expected utility = −.2500
		Don't Buy Insurance		
Fire	.002	−$40,000	−200	−.40
No fire	.998	0	0	0
				Expected utility = −.40

26-6 Constructing the Utility Function

A person's utility function is easily constructed from the information gleaned in a short interview. The following example, involving two MBA students, illustrates how this may be done.

The Interview Method

Guy Sharpe asks a few questions of Shirley Smart. Each involves a series of hypothetical win-lose gambles, with various dollar rewards; each time Shirley is asked to establish a win probability that would make her indifferent between the choices of gambling or accepting an intermediate amount. A range of monetary outcomes is used that Shirley, still a student, can relate to; the highest amount is $+$10,000$, with $-$5,000$ as the lowest. These two amounts serve as the outcomes of the initial reference lottery.

The interview proceeds as follows.

Guy Suppose that you are offered a gamble in which you will receive $+$10,000$ if you win and must forfeit $5,000 if you lose, so that losing results in a change in your net worth of $-$5,000$. For simplicity, let's keep this discussion on an "after-tax" basis.

Shirley That part is easy. I'm presently in the zero tax bracket. But where will I get the $5,000 if I lose?

Guy A special student loan will be arranged, and you can pay it back for five years after graduation. Interest will be prime plus 2%. Let's begin. You have signed a contract obligating you to participate in the gamble and to take the consequences.

Shirley Boy, am I glad this is not for real.

Guy You'll change your mind fast. *You get to pick the win probability!* Before we begin, I want to define the starting utility values. One utility value is arbitrarily given to each outcome of the gamble (reference lottery). These will define your utility scale. Under this scale, a change in your net worth of $+$10,000$ will have a utility of 100, and your utility for $-$5,000$ will be 0.

$$u(+\$10,000) = 100 \qquad u(-\$5,000) = 0$$

Shirley Why don't you use a negative value for the utility of 0?

Guy We could. But I make mistakes mixing positives and negatives. It really makes no difference. I also like the Fahrenheit temperature scale, which rarely goes negative in our city. It's hard to relate to the Celsius scale, with negatives throughout most of the winter. Our utility scale is totally arbitrary and has nothing to do with how you feel about risk, any more than our comfort is affected by where the marks are printed on our thermometer. I will be happy to change the utility benchmarks if you want.

Shirley I like your temperature scale analogy. I'm ready. Let's proceed.

Guy I'm going to plot the two values defining the "Shirley scale" as two points on a graph (see Figure 26-10). These points will lie on a curve that represents your utility function. We need only a few points to provide a detailed graphical description of your utility function. To help us keep track of things, I am going to designate our first reference lottery as gamble A (where you get $+$10,000$ if you win and $-$5,000$ if you lose).

FIGURE 26-10
Shirley Smart's utility function.

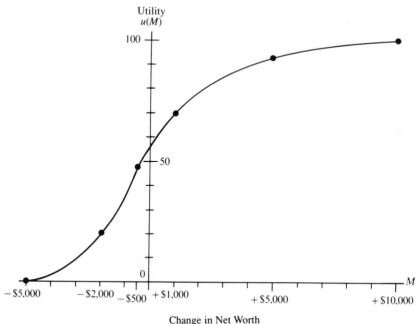

Change in Net Worth

Shirley I think I'm going to enjoy this.

Guy Now, suppose that you may exchange your contract for +$1,000. If the gamble *A* probabilities were 50–50, would you do it?

Shirley Of course I would take the thousand. What have I got to lose by doing that?

Guy A crack at the $10,000 gain. Let's adjust the odds a bit. Suppose that the probabilities are now .90 for winning and .10 for losing. Would you still take the +$1,000, or would you keep the gamble contract?

Shirley Oh, I see. Golly, I think I would gamble. My expected payoff would be huge, and if I lose, I'll only have to pay $100 a month for a few years. I'd definitely gamble.

Guy I hate to shatter the illusion, but I want to change the probabilities. I'm trying to find your point of indifference. Suppose that we reduce the win probability to .60 (increasing the lose probability to .40). How do you feel about the gamble now?

Shirley Awful! I'll take the thousand dollars and run.

Guy All right, let's raise the odds a bit. Suppose that the win probability is now .70. Would you gamble or take the thousand?

Shirley Wow, this is tough! I really would like the thousand, but the gamble is terribly appealing. I really don't know which I would take.

Guy Good. We have established your indifference win probability at $q = .70$. We now have a new point for your utility function graph. Your utility for the latest gamble is its expected utility.

$$u(\text{gamble } A \mid q = .70) = .70u(+\$10,000) + .30u(-\$5,000)$$

$$= .70(100) + .30(0) = 70$$

And, since you are indifferent between $+\$1,000$ and the gamble, they must have the same utility. Thus,

$$u(+\$1,000) = u(\text{gamble } A \mid q = .70) = 70$$

Shirley Amazing.

Guy Although we could stay with gamble A for the remainder of our interview, things would get a little stale. It will also be easier on you if we narrow the payoff range a little bit. Let's change the gamble to a new reference lottery involving $+\$10,000$ if you win and $+\$1,000$ if you lose. This is gamble B.

Shirley I'll take it. But who's dumb enough to offer me such a deal?

Guy You're jumping the gun. First of all, I have not told you the probability for winning. Secondly, you must remember that we are playing "let's pretend." We won't worry about whether or not the gamble will ever take place. If you prefer, think of me as emcee Monty Hall and imagine yourself as a contestant on "Let's Make a Deal."

Shirley As a kid, that was one of my favorite programs. I hope I don't win a goat. Fire away, Monty.

Guy Now, suppose that you may trade your rights to gamble B for a certain $+\$5,000$. The outcome will be determined by the toss of a coin.

Shirley I'll take the five thousand. Although the ten thousand looks mighty appealing, I wouldn't feel that much more comfortable with that than I would with five thousand.

Guy All right, now let's improve the gamble. The win probability is now .70. Do you still prefer not to gamble?

Shirley Yes, but we're close. Raise the win probability to .75 and I'll gamble.

Guy Your indifference win probability here is $q = .75$. We have another data point for your utility function. Using the utility value of 70 established earlier for $+\$1,000$, and using your latest indifference probability of .75, the following applies.

$$u(+\$5,000) = u(\text{gamble } B \mid q = .75) = .75u(+\$10,000) + .25u(+\$1,000)$$

$$= .75(100) + .25(70)$$

$$= 92.5$$

Shirley I guess I said that.

Guy Now, Shirley, I'm sure you would prefer a goat to the following reference lottery, which we will label gamble C. If you lose, you end up with $-\$5,000$. If you win, you only get $+\$1,000$ this time. Suppose that you have to pay to get out of this one, and the price for doing so is $\$500$, so that you are looking at a change in your net worth of $-\$500$ if you don't gamble. Furthermore, the outcome will be determined by a coin toss.

Shirley I'll pay to get out of that one.

Guy   Let's raise the odds a bit. Suppose that there is a 60 percent chance of winning. What would you do?

Shirley   I would still pay.

Guy   Okay, let me raise the win probability to .65.

Shirley   I would be indifferent if the probability for winning were .70.

Guy   Using $q = .70$, we now add one more point to our graph. Your utility for $-\$500$ is calculated as follows.

$$u(-\$500) = u(\text{gamble } C \mid q = .70) = .70u(+\$1,000) + .30u(-\$5,000)$$

$$= .70(70) + .30(0)$$

$$= 49$$

We need one more point to completely specify your utility function. Consider gamble C one more time, but in comparison to being $2,000 in the hole.

Shirley   We've gone from bad to worse. I cannot even fathom such a situation.

Guy   Well, you have a well-used car, which I guess would cost you about $2,000 to replace.

Shirley   That's right.

Guy   Okay. Imagine that you will lose your car if you don't take gamble C.

Shirley   I can't imagine how I could ever get into such a situation.

Guy   Well, you signed a contract to participate in gamble C, and now the ante has been raised.

Shirley   This is awful. All right, proceed.

Guy   You've already indicated indifference between gamble C and $-\$500$ with a win probability of .70. Suppose that the odds are lowered to 50–50. Would you give up your car or gamble?

Shirley   Being five thousand down is not much worse than being without a car. I would gamble, hoping to get out of the mess and be a thousand ahead.

Guy   What if the win probability were only .10?

Shirley   I would give up my car. The chance of getting out of hock would be too low. I think if you split the difference, giving me a win probability half way between those values, I might be indifferent. But I feel emotionally drained by all of this introspection. I don't think I can do another one of these gambles.

Guy   Relax. We're finished playing "Let's Make a Deal." Using an indifference win probability of $q = .30$, you have established the following utility for $-\$2,000$.

$$u(-\$2,000) = u(\text{gamble } C \mid q = .30) = .30u(+\$1,000) + .70u(-\$5,000)$$

$$= .30(70) + .70(0)$$

$$= 21$$

Implementing the Utility Function

Guy Sharpe completed Shirley Smart's utility graph, as shown in Figure 26-10. Shirley can use this curve in any personal decision analysis in which the payoffs fall between $-\$5,000$ and $+\$10,000$. A fresh utility function would be required for evaluating a decision with more extreme payoffs or if Shirley's attitudes change because of a new job or lifestyle change. Utility functions must be revised over time.

Shirley's curve has an interesting shape. The shape of the utility function reflects the underlying attitude toward risk. Section 26-7 discusses shapes commonly encountered.

Utility functions are totally empirical. Only a few well spread out graphed points (three or four, plus the main reference lottery values) are required. As the above interview shows, it can be exasperating to get these points. The interviewer needs some skill, and the subjects must have patience and a willingness to let their minds be probed.

The intimacy of the interview process can inhibit implementation of utility functions in decision analysis, especially in organizations. A junior decision analyst should not expect to use this method on senior executives. An outside consultant would be in a stronger position to interview those decision makers.

This could be the major reason why there is not an extensive history of utility being applied in business decision making. Nevertheless, utility theory has compelling advantages. And, as we shall see, the theory is useful in generally qualifying decision analysis.

26-7 Attitudes Toward Risk and the Shape of the Utility Curve

The utility function for money may be used as the basis for describing an individual's attitudes toward risk. Three basic attitudes have been characterized. The polar cases are the **risk averter**, who will accept only favorable gambles, and the **risk seeker**, who will pay a premium for the privilege of participating in a gamble. Between these two extremes lies the **risk-neutral individual**, who considers the face value of money to be its true worth. The utility functions for each basic attitude appear in Figure 26-11. Each function has a particular shape, corresponding to the decision maker's fundamental outlook. All three utility functions show that utility increases with monetary gains. This reflects the underlying assumption of utility theory that utility increases with preference, which is combined with the additional assumption that more money will always increase an individual's well-being, so that the outcomes with greater payoffs are preferred. (This

FIGURE 26-11
Utility functions for basic attitudes toward risk.

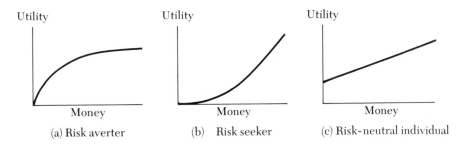

(a) Risk averter   (b)   Risk seeker   (c) Risk-neutral individual

assumption may not be strictly true, but with the exception of eccentrics, most people behave in a manner that supports it.)

The Risk Averter

Throughout most of their lives, people are typically risk averters. These individuals buy plenty of casualty insurance. They avoid actions that involve high risks (chances of large monetary losses). Only gambles with high expected payoffs will be attractive to them. A risk averter's utility drops more and more severely as losses become larger, and the utilities for positive amounts do not grow as fast with monetary gains. The risk averter's marginal utility for money diminishes as the rewards increase, so that the risk averter's utility curve, shown in Figure 26-11(a), exhibits a decreasing positive slope as the level of monetary payoff becomes larger. Such a curve is *concave* when viewed from below.

The Risk Seeker

The risk seeker's behavior is the opposite of the risk averter's behavior. Many of us are risk seekers at some stage of our lives. This attitude is epitomized by the "high roller," who may behave recklessly and who is motivated by the possibility of achieving the maximum reward in any gamble. The risk seeker will prefer *some* gambles with negative expected monetary payoffs to maintaining the status quo. The greater the maximum reward, the more the risk seeker's behavior will diverge from the risk averter's behavior. The risk seeker is typically self-insured, believing that the risk is superior to forgoing money spent on premiums. The risk seeker's marginal utility for money is increasing: Each additional dollar provides a disproportionately greater sense of well-being. The loss of one more dollar is felt only slightly more severely for large absolute levels of loss than for small ones. Thus, the slope of the risk seeker's utility curve, shown in Figure 26-11(b), increases as the monetary change improves. This curve is *convex* when viewed from below.

The Risk-Neutral Individual

Our third characterization of attitude toward risk is the risk-neutral individual, who prizes money at its face value. The utility function for such an individual is a straight line, as shown in Figure 26-11(c). His or her utility for a gamble is equal to the utility for the expected monetary payoff. Risk-neutral individuals buy no casualty insurance, since the premium charge is greater than the expected loss. Risk-neutral behavior is epitomized by individuals who are enormously wealthy. The decisions of large corporations are often based on the Bayes decision rule applied directly to monetary payoffs, reflecting that increments in dollar assets are valued at their face amount.

In general, risk neutrality holds only over a limited range of money values. For example, many large firms do not carry casualty insurance, but almost all giant corporations will insure against extremely large losses—airlines buy hijacking insurance, for example. The same holds for individuals. Many risk-averse persons are risk-neutral when the stakes are small. The player in the World Series office pool falls into this category; losses are hardly noticeable, and winnings permit the individual to indulge in some luxury. (Small gambles may add spice to a person's life—they are a form of entertainment. Thus, a person might play poker with more skillful players, where the expected payoff would be negative, just for the fun of it.) That people are risk-neutral for small risks is illustrated by their car insurance purchases. Many generally risk-averse people carry deductible comprehensive coverage when they first purchase an automobile, and they usually keep only the liability coverage when their car gets old. Again, this reflects risk neutrality over a limited range of monetary outcomes. This behavior does not contradict the curve shapes in Figure 26-11(a) and (b), because each curve can be approximated by a straight line segment throughout a narrow monetary interval.

Composite Attitudes toward Risk

Many people may be both risk averters and risk seekers, depending on the range of monetary values being considered. To an entrepreneur founding a business, the risks are very high—a lifetime's savings, plenty of hard work, burned career bridges, a heavy burden of debt, and a significant chance of bankruptcy. Those who embark on the hard road of self-employment may often be viewed as risk seekers. They are motivated primarily by the rewards—monetary and otherwise—of being their own boss. Once entrepreneurs become established and are viewed by peers as future pillars of the community, their attitudes toward risk will have evolved to a point where they may be characterized as risk averters. They are much more conservative (now there is something to conserve), and probably no venture imaginable could persuade them to risk everything they own to further their wealth.

We conceive of an individual's attitudes varying between risk seeking and risk aversion over time. Usually a risk seeker has some definite goal or **aspiration level**, which may be achieved by obtaining a specific amount of money. A young sports enthusiast might be willing to participate in an unfair gamble if winning would provide sufficient cash for a down payment on a first motorcycle. The young professional may speculate in volatile stocks to try to earn enough money for a down payment on a fashionable home. To these risk seekers, losing is not much worse than maintaining the status quo. But once the goal is achieved, the risk seeker's outlook changes, and with a sated appetite, the risk seeker becomes a risk averter until some new goal enters the horizon.

A hybrid-shaped utility function might also occur for persons having few assets. For them, losing $5,000 may not be materially worse than losing a couple of thousand. Shirley Smart's utility function in Figure 26-12 illustrates this commonly encountered shape. Somewhere around −$1,000, her utility function goes from convex to concave, and she moves from a risk-seeking posture to one of risk aversion for possible changes in her net worth above that level.

Regardless of the shape of a person's utility function, he or she will always find his or her preferred course of action by maximizing expected utility.

FIGURE 26-12
Shirley Smart's utility function illustrating simultaneous risk-seeking and risk-averse attitudes, depending on ranges of monetary outcomes.

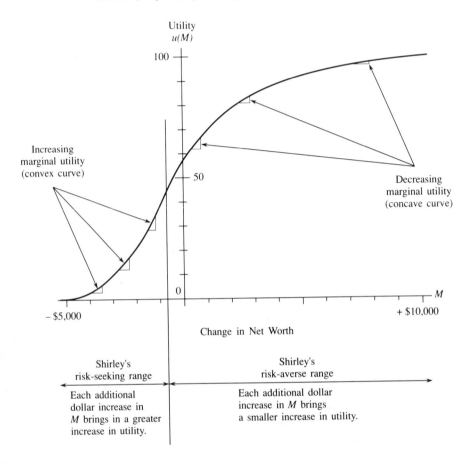

26-8 Attitudes Toward Risk and Valuation in Decision Making

The shape of a person's utility function fundamentally affects the relationships between utilities, expected payoffs, certainty equivalents, and risk premiums. We are ready to explore in detail those relationships, which are distinctly different, depending on the individual's underlying attitude toward risk.

The Risk Averter

When all possible monetary outcomes fall in the decision maker's range of risk aversion, the following properties hold.

1. Expected payoffs (*EP*) are greater than their counterpart certainty equivalents (*CE*).
2. Expected utilities will be less than the utility of the respective expected monetary payoff.
3. Risk premiums (*RP* = *EP* − *CE*) are *positive*.

Figure 26-13 illustrates the above for Shirley Smart when evaluating gamble *A* for which there is a 50–50 chance for experiencing a change in her net worth by −$500 or +$2,000. Shirley's expected payoff for this gamble is

$$EP = .50(-\$500) + .50(\$2,000) = \$750 \quad \text{(Gamble } A\text{)}$$

Her utility curve provides respective utilities of 49 and 78 for the gamble payoffs. Her expected utility for the gamble is thus,

$$\text{Expected utility} = .50u(-\$500) + .50u(\$2,000)$$
$$= .50(49) + .50(78)$$
$$= 63.5 \quad \text{(gamble } A\text{)}$$

The certainty equivalent for any gamble is that monetary amount such that

$$u(CE) = \text{Expected utility}$$

FIGURE 26-13
Illustration of the relationship between expected payoff, expected utility, certainty equivalent, and risk premium when Shirley Smart is *risk averse*.

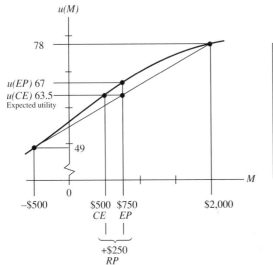

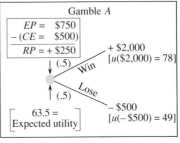

Shirley Smart's utility curve achieves a height of 63.5 at $M = \$500$, so that

$$u(\$500) = 63.5$$

This establishes her certainty equivalent for the gamble.

$$CE = \$500 \quad \text{(gamble } A\text{)}$$

Shirley's risk premium for the gamble is found by subtracting the certainty equivalent from the expected payoff.

$$RP = EP - CE = \$750 - \$500 = \$250$$

We may view Shirley's certainty equivalent valuation of the gamble as the discounted expected payoff,

$$CE = EP - RP = \$750 - \$250 = \$500$$

A similar result would apply to any gamble having outcomes falling in her risk-averse range.

Although the utility curve directly provides CE's, these amounts will always equal that amount reached by discounting an individual's expected payoff by the amount of the risk premium (which will vary with the magnitude of the risk). As long as all monetary payoffs lie within the risk averse range, the above procedure should provide *positive* RP's—even when all possibilities involve positive monetary payoffs.

To illustrate, consider gamble B, involving a coin toss that determines which of two positive payoffs will occur. A head provides Shirley with $5,000 [$u(\$5,000) = 92.5$] and a tail yields her only $1,000 [$u(\$1,000) = 70$]. Her expected utility is 81.25, which corresponds to a certainty equivalent of about $2,500. The expected payoff is $3,000, and Shirley's risk premium is

$$RP = EP - CE = \$3,000 - \$2,500 = \$500 \quad \text{(gamble } B\text{)}$$

Even though we would not ordinarily consider such a win-win situation as having risk, Shirley would still be willing to accept a discounted certain amount in lieu of gambling.

The Risk Seeker

When all possible monetary outcomes fall in the decision maker's risk-seeking range, the following properties hold.

1. Expected payoffs (EP) are less than their counterpart certainty equivalents (CE).
2. Expected utilities will be greater than the utility of the respective expected monetary payoff.
3. Risk premiums ($RP = EP - CE$) are *negative*.

Figure 26-14 illustrates the above for Shirley Smart when evaluating gamble C for which there is a 50–50 chance for experiencing a change in her net worth by $-\$4,000$ or $-\$1,000$. Shirley's expected payoff for this gamble is

$$EP = .50(-\$4,000) + .50(-\$1,000) = -\$2,500 \quad \text{(gamble } C\text{)}$$

Her utility curve provides respective utilities of 3 and 37 for the gamble payoffs. Her expected utility for the gamble is thus,

$$\text{Expected utility} = .50u(-\$4,000) + .50u(-\$1,000)$$

$$= .50(3) + .50(37)$$

$$= 20 \quad \text{(gamble } C\text{)}$$

Shirley's utility curve achieves a height of 20 at about $M = -\$1,800$, so that her certainty equivalent for the gamble is

$$CE = -\$1,800 \quad \text{(gamble } C\text{)}$$

Shirley's risk premium for the gamble is

$$RP = EP - CE = -\$2,500 - (-\$1,800) = -\$700$$

FIGURE 26-14

Illustration of the relationship between expected payoff, expected utility, certainty equivalent, and risk premium when Shirley Smart is *risk seeking*.

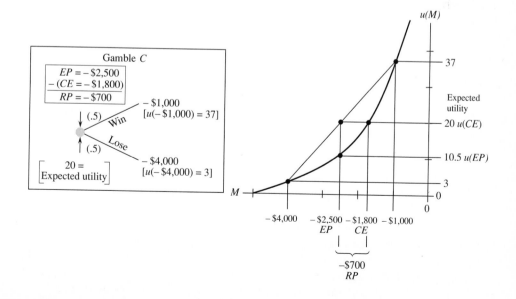

Here, Shirley's certainty equivalent valuation of the gamble implies that she would be indifferent between gambling and paying $1,800 to relieve herself of the obligation to do so. In effect, her *CE* may be reached by *adding* +$700 to the expected payoff.

$$CE = EP - RP = -\$2,500 - (-\$700) = -\$2,500 + \$700 = -\$1,800$$

Any gamble having monetary payoffs in Shirley's risk-seeking range will involve a similar negative risk premium.

This of course does not mean that Shirley likes gamble *C*. She would be willing to pay up to $1,800 not to have to undergo it. But that amount is $700 greater than the −$2,500 payoff she would expect by remaining with the gamble. In effect, her *valuation* of terrible gamble *C* is skewed in the opposite direction (vis-a-vis the expected payoff) to that which applies to favorable gambles *A* and *B*.

The Risk-Neutral Individual

The Ponderosa Record Company example shows how the decision maker's course of action can differ tremendously if he maximizes expected monetary payoff (as in Chapter 21) from what he would do by maximizing his expected utility. This is true when the decision maker is risk seeking or risk averse. That is not the case, however, for the risk-neutral person, whose payoff function graphs as a straight line. Such an individual will have an expected utility equal to the utility of the expected payoff. Risk-neutral persons will have certainty equivalents equal to their expected payoffs. In effect, their utility functions become superfluous.

Decision Making with a Narrow Payoff Range

Paradoxically, regardless of shape, all utility functions are best approximated by a line segment over a narrow range of monetary outcomes. To see that this is so, look at Figure 26-10 and consider the shape of Shirley Smart's utility function from −$2,500 to −$2,000, from +$500 to +$1,000, or from +$8,000 to +$9,000. She would, in effect, be almost risk neutral over any of these intervals.

To verify this, let's compute her expected utility for a coin-toss gamble with payoffs of +$500 and +$1,000. Reading her curve in Figure 26-10, we have $u(+\$500) = 65$ and $u(+\$1,000) = 70$. Thus,

$$u(\text{coin toss}) = .50(65) + .50(70) = 67.5$$

Next, we find Shirley's expected monetary payoff from the gamble to be

$$.50(+\$500) + .50(+\$1,000) = \$750$$

Shirley's curve provides a utility value very close to 67.5 for getting $750. In effect, the utility of the gamble is nearly equal to the utility of the gamble's expected monetary payoff. She is almost risk neutral over the gamble's range of monetary outcomes.

Since Shirley is nearly risk neutral over the narrow range of payoffs, her utility function would not really be needed to identify her most preferred course of action. This would be true of any decision where the possible payoffs are all close together. The original Bayes decision rule, maximize monetary payoff directly, would nicely find for her what action to take in those cases.

But how narrow must the monetary range be before the discrepancies between maximizing expected utility and maximizing expected monetary payoff matter? That depends on the individual and the particular utility function shape. And this partly depends on the individual's overall level of assets.

A teenager might feel comfortable with any gambling situation of $\pm\$5$, while a college student's utility function might be linear over $\pm\$100$. A young professional person might have a linear utility function over any change in net worth of $\pm\$1,000$, while for a small business entrepreneur this might be $\pm\$2,000$, and for an established professional, perhaps $\pm\$5,000$ might be appropriate. For a corporate officer, we might find that linearity could be assumed over any range of bottom-line impact within $\pm\$10,000$. For a chief executive, maybe $\pm\$1$ million would work.

Utility theory is important because it permits us to do a better job at decision analysis, by explicitly incorporating risk attitude, but it implies much more than that.

Ratifying the Bayes Decision Rule and the Delegation of Authority

Utility theory implies that an individual always does the preferred thing when he or she maximizes utility. That will be achieved in any decision under uncertainty when *expected* utility is maximized. If we somehow do that, we will end up with a perfect tool for decision making.

Thus, *utility theory ratifies the original Bayes decision rule*, as long as the payoffs are limited to a *narrow range*. We need to know nothing about its shape; it will always be a straight line over a narrow monetary range. Maximizing expected monetary payoff in effect maximizes expected utility. And, since doing that maximizes utility itself, it will also indicate the preferred action. Using Bayes decision rule would, in those cases with original monetary payoffs, always lead to the best choice.

This allows managers to delegate routine decisions (ones having narrow monetary consequences) to others, with the prescription that expected payoff always be maximized. Only the decisions having extreme outcomes need to be evaluated with special care regarding attitude toward risk. Utility theory provides the rationale for delegation of decision-making authority.

CASE

Wendy Storm's Career Plans

Wendy Storm is a senior marketing major who must decide whether to go to graduate school for an MBA or to accept a full-time traveling sales position. Her major uncertainty about the MBA is whether she will successfully complete the program; she judges her chances of completion at .70. If she finishes the MBA, Wendy will apply for a consulting position, which she believes she will then get with a probability of .80; otherwise, she will take a position in corporate sales. Should Wendy not complete the MBA, she will have no recourse but to assume a traveling sales position—a year later than if she had gone to work immediately after graduation. Wendy believes there is a 50–50 chance she can move from a traveling job to corporate sales within one year after starting.

Listed in decreasing order of preference, the following outcomes apply to Wendy's decision.

> MBA plus consulting
> MBA plus corporate sales
> Corporate sales, no graduate school
> Corporate sales, unfinished MBA
> Traveling sales position, early start
> Traveling sales position, late start

Wendy arbitrarily assigns a utility value of 1,000 to the outcome "MBA plus consulting" and a utility value of 100 to "traveling sales position, late start." She would be indifferent between "MBA plus corporate sales" and a 50–50 gamble yielding those two outcomes. Using this same reference lottery, she would be indifferent between it and "corporate sales, no graduate school" if the probability for achieving the best outcome were .40. The stigma of failure would so taint the outcome, "corporate sales, unfinished MBA," that she would reduce her indifference probability to .20 for winning the reference lottery in exchange. Finally, she would be indifferent between the gamble and "traveling sales position, early start" if the probability of the best outcome were only .10.

Questions

1. Find Wendy's utility for the listed outcomes.
2. Construct Wendy's decision tree diagram, using utility payoffs.
3. What should Wendy do?
4. Interview a colleague who plays the role of Wendy Storm. Establish her utility function over the range of net change in her net worth from −$5,000 to +$10,000. Plot the results on a graph.
5. Determine from your graph "Wendy Storm's" (1) expected utility and (2) certainty equivalent for each of the following situations.
   (a) Fair coin toss: −$500 if tails and +$1,000 if heads.
   (b) Lottery: +$5,000 if won (probability .10) and $0 if lost.
   (c) Investment: +$10,000 if success (probability .20) and −$2,000 if failure.

PROBLEMS

26-1 Suppose that you are offered a gamble by Ms. I. M. Honest, a representative of a foundation studying human behavior. A fair coin is to be tossed. If a head occurs, you will receive $10,000 from Ms. Honest. But if a tail results, you must pay her foundation $5,000. If you do *not* have $5,000, a loan will be arranged, which must be repaid over a five-year period at $150 per month but may be deferred until you have graduated from school.
(a) Calculate your expected profit from participating in this gamble.
(b) Would you be willing to accept Ms. Honest's offer? Does your answer indicate that your marginal utility for money is decreasing?

26-2 Mr. Smith has offered you a gamble similar to that of Ms. Honest in Problem 26-1. If a head occurs, he will hand you $1.00. But if a tail results you must pay Mr. Smith $.50.
(a) Calculate your expected profit from participating in this gamble.
(b) Would you be willing to accept Mr. Smith's offer?

26-3 A homeowner whose house is valued at $40,000 is offered tornado insurance at an annual premium of $500. Suppose that there are just two mutually exclusive outcomes—complete damage or no damage from a tornado—and that the probability of damage from a tornado is .0001.
(a) Construct the homeowner's payoff table for the decision of whether or not to buy tornado insurance.
(b) Calculate the decision maker's expected monetary payoff for each act. Which act has the maximum expected payoff?
(c) Suppose that the homeowner decides not to buy tornado insurance. Does this contradict the decreasing marginal utility for money? Explain.

26-4 Actor Nathan Summers enjoys wearing costumes in front of audiences. Nathan likes dressing up like a little old lady the most and hates to dress up like an animal. Somewhere in between lies his preference for wearing a cowboy outfit. Assigning a utility of 10 to being a lady and a utility of -5 to being an animal, what is Nathan's utility for playing a cowboy if he is indifferent between this outcome and a coin toss determining which of the other two roles he will play?

26-5 Ty Kune, a potential entrepreneur, is faced with the following outcomes.

O_3 Successfully established in his own business
O_2 Maintaining present employee status
O_1 Personal bankruptcy

Ty would be indifferent between remaining on his present job and opening a restaurant when the probability is q_2 for success and $1 - q_2$ for bankruptcy.
(a) At age 22, Ty finds that $q_2 = .50$ makes him indifferent. If he arbitrarily sets $u(O_3) = 200$ and $u(O_1) = -100$, calculate Ty's utility value for keeping his present job (and not going into business for himself).
(b) At age 30 Ty's outlook has changed drastically, and $q_2 = .90$ now applies. Find $u(O_2)$ again when $u(O_3) = 200$ and $u(O_1) = -100$.
(c) Undergoing a midlife crisis at age 40, Ty revises his indifference probability to .20. Preferring big numbers, he arbitrarily establishes $u(O_3) = 10,000$ and $u(O_1) = 0$. Calculate Ty's utility for remaining on somebody else's payroll.

26-6   You may achieve the following outcomes (no rights are transferable).

- 100 new record albums of your choice
- A grade of C on the next examination covering utility
- A year's assignment to Timbuktu, Mali
- Confinement to an airport during a three-day storm
- A month of free telephone calls to anywhere

(a) Rank these outcomes in descending order of preference, designating them $O_5, O_4, O_3,$ O_2, and O_1.

(b) Let the utilities be $u(O_5) = 100$ for the best outcome and $u(O_1) = 0$ for the worst outcome. Consider a box containing 1,000 marbles, some of which are labeled "win" and the remainder of which are labeled "lose." If a "win" marble is selected at random from the box, you will achieve O_5. If a "lose" marble is chosen, you will attain O_1. Determine how many marbles of each type would make you indifferent between gambling or achieving O_2. Determine the same for O_3 and O_4.

(c) The corresponding probabilities for winning q_k may be determined by dividing the respective number of "win" marbles by 1,000. Use these probabilities to calculate $u(O_4)$, $u(O_3)$, and $u(O_2)$.

26-7   Willy B. Rich wants his utility curve constructed for the change M in his net worth over the range from $-\$10,000$ to $+\$20,000$. He arbitrarily sets the respective utilities at 0 and 100. In response to queries regarding hypothetical gambles involving these amounts, Willy establishes the following equivalences.

EQUIVALENT AMOUNT	PROBABILITY FOR WINNING $20,000
$-\$5,000$	.60
0	.80
$+10,000$	.95

(a) Calculate his utilities for the above monetary amounts.

(b) On graph paper, sketch Willy's utility function.

(c) From your curve read Willy's utilities for the following changes in net worth.
    (1) $-\$2,000$ (2) $+\$2,000$ (3) $+\$5,000$

26-8   Suppose that Alvin Black's attitude toward risk is generally averse. For each of the following 50–50 gambling propositions, indicate whether Alvin (1) would be willing, (2) might desire, or (3) would be unwilling to participate. Explain.
(a) $10,000 versus $0   (d) $500 versus $-\$600$
(b) $10,000 versus $-\$1,000$ (e) $20,000 versus $10,000
(c) $15,000 versus $-\$10,000$

26-9   Lucille Brown is risk-neutral. Would she buy comprehensive coverage for her automobile if she agreed with company actuaries regarding the probability distribution for future claim sizes? Explain.

26-10 Victor White is a risk seeker. Does this necessarily imply that he will never buy casualty insurance? Explain.

26-11 Refer to Shirley Smart's utility function in Figure 26-10 (page 802). Shirley is faced with the following gambles.

(1) GAMBLE V		(2) GAMBLE W		(3) GAMBLE Y		(4) GAMBLE Z	
Prob.	Payoff	Prob.	Payoff	Prob.	Payoff	Prob.	Payoff
.90	+$5,000	.50	+$1,000	.75	+$4,000	.20	+$10,000
.10	−$5,000	.50	−$1,000	.25	−$1,000	.80	−$ 2,000

(a) Calculate Shirley's expected utilities for each gamble.
(b) Find Shirley's certainty equivalent for each gamble.
(c) Compute Shirley's expected monetary payoff for each gamble.
(d) For each gamble, subtract your answer to (b) from that for (c), to find Shirley's risk premium.

26-12 Conduct an interview with another person and construct a graph for the individual's utility function. Use changes in net worth ranging from a low of −$5,000 to a high of +$10,000. You may use any arbitrary utility scale. Ignore any tax implications.

26-13 A contractor must determine whether to buy or rent the equipment required to do a job up for bid. Because of lead-time requirements, he must decide whether to obtain the equipment before he knows if he has been awarded the contract. If he buys the equipment, the contract will result in $120,000 net profit after equipment resale returns, but if he loses the job, then the equipment will have to be sold at a $40,000 loss. By renting, his profit from the contract (if he wins it) will be only $50,000, but there will be no loss of money if the job is not won. The contractor's chances of winning are 50–50, and his utility function is $u(M) = \sqrt{M + 40,000}$.
(a) Construct the contractor's payoff table using profit as the payoff measure.
(b) Calculate the expected profit for each act. According to the Bayes decision rule, what act should the contractor select?
(c) Construct the contractor's payoff table using utilities as the payoff measure.
(d) Calculate the expected utility payoff for each act. Which act provides the maximum expected utility?
(e) Which act should the decision maker choose? Explain.

26-14 Suppose that the Ponderosa Record Company's utility function for money is $u(M) = [(M + 65,000)/10,000]^2$.
(a) Redraw Figure 26-8 (page 797), and calculate the utility for each end position.
(b) Perform backward induction analysis using the new utilities you have calculated. What strategy is optimal?
(c) On a piece of graph paper, plot the utilities you calculated in (a) as a function of monetary payoffs M. Sketch a curve through the points. Of what attitude toward risk is the shape of your curve indicative?

26-15 An insurance policy would cost Hermie Hawks $1,000 per year to protect his home from tornado damage. Assume that any actual tornado damage to Hermie's house, valued at

$100,000, would be totally destructive and that the probability that a tornado will hit his house during the year is .0025.

(a) If Hermie is risk neutral, what would his optimal decision be regarding buying tornado insurance? Show your computations.

(b) How much above its expected claim size is the insurance company charging Hermie for its combined overhead and profit on the proposed policy?

(c) Hermie's utility function for any change in his monetary position for any amount M is

$$u(M) = 10,000 - (M/1,000)^2$$

What action should Hermie take to maximize his expected utility?

(d) What annual insurance premium charge would make Hermie indifferent between buying or not buying tornado insurance?

26-16   J. P. Tidewasser has just undergone the first traumatic phase of determining his utility function for a range of money values. By his response to a series of gambles, it has been established that he is indifferent between making the 50–50 gambles on the left and receiving the certain amounts of money shown on the right.

REWARDS OF GAMBLE		EQUIVALENT AMOUNT
+$30,000	−$10,000	$ 0
+ 30,000	0	+ 10,000
0	− 10,000	− 7,000
+ 10,000	− 7,000	1,000

(a) If J. P. sets $u(\$30,000) = 1$ and $u(-\$10,000) = 0$, determine his utility for $0.

(b) Calculate J. P.'s utilities for +$10,000 and −$7,000.

(c) Calculate J. P.'s utility for +$1,000. What, if any, inconsistencies do you notice between this and your previous answers?

26-17   Hoopla Hoops is a retail boutique catering to current crazes. The owner must decide whether or not to stock a batch of Water Wheelies. Each item costs $2 and sells for $4. Unsold items cannot be returned to the supplier, who sells them in batches of 500. The following probability distribution is assumed to apply for the anticipated demand for Water Wheelies.

DEMAND	PROBABILITY
100	.05
200	.10
300	.15
400	.20
500	.20
600	.15
700	.10
800	.05
	1.00

Consider demand to mean the potential for sales. No more than what is demanded may be sold; but if demand exceeds on-hand inventory, then not all of the demand may be fulfilled.

(a) Calculate the expected demand. If you assume that the expected demand will actually occur, what profit corresponds to this amount? Use the utility curve shown in Figure 26-15 to determine the corresponding utility value.

FIGURE 26-15
Utility function for Problems 26-17 and 26-18.

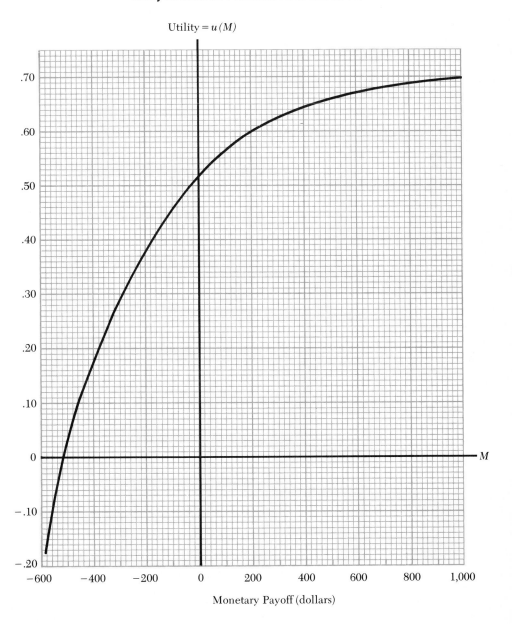

Utility = $u(M)$

Monetary Payoff (dollars)

(b) Calculate the expected profit from stocking 500 Water Wheelies. Does this differ from the amount you found in (a)? Explain this. Determine the utility for the expected profit.

(c) Calculate the expected utility for stocking 500 Water Wheelies. (First, calculate the profit for each level of possible demand; then, find the utility for each level; finally, apply the probability weights.) Which act—stocking or not stocking Water Wheelies—provides the greatest expected utility?

26-18 Consider the plight of the decision maker in Problem 21-11 (page 646). She must interview dozens of candidates annually for data entry jobs. Losses of her recoverable training expenses may therefore be significant. Suppose that she has constructed the utility function shown in Figure 26-15.

(a) Redraw Figure 21-6 (page 647).

(b) For the monetary payoff value for each end position, determine the decision maker's approximate utility value from the curve in Figure 26-15.

(c) Perform backward induction analysis using utilities as payoffs. Which strategy is optimal?

Games and
Interactive Decisions

Until now, we have discussed decision-making situations in which choices are made by only one person. Such decision problems fall into two broad categories, depending on whether conditions are certain or uncertain. We have seen that when decisions are made under uncertainty, the ultimate outcome is determined jointly by the particular act that is chosen and by whatever uncertain event occurs. Uncertain events are generated randomly and could be called *nature's choices*. We could therefore view decision making under uncertainty as an **interactive decision making** process with two participants—the decision maker and nature.

27-1 Interactive Decision Making and Game Theory

In this chapter, we will be concerned with interactive decision making involving more than one person. The outcomes of such decision problems, sometimes referred to as **games**, are determined by whatever combination of actions results from the independent choices of several individual decision makers. Many important business decisions involve the interaction between two or more participants. Interaction often occurs in the pricing of products, where a firm's ultimate sales are determined not only by the price levels it selects but also by the prices its competitors set. The interaction between several decision makers is also necessary in operational applications. Television provides a good example. In recent years, TV networks have found that program success is largely dependent on what the competition presents in the same time slot; the outcomes of one network's programming decisions have therefore been increasingly influenced by the corresponding decisions made by other networks. Even financial planning involves interactive decision making. The success of a business tax strategy depends greatly on the position taken by the Internal Revenue Service regarding the expenses that may be disallowed.

When two or more persons collectively determine the outcomes, decision-making analysis takes on an added complexity. Good decision making requires not only the evaluation of personal alternatives but also the investigation of the opponent's or competitor's possible choices. A certain amount of second-guessing and role playing is required. Interactive decision making may be compared to a parlor game, such as chess, *Monopoly*, or bridge. To establish a winning strategy, successful players must be able to put themselves in their opponents' positions and try to anticipate their actions. The need to consider another person's goals and choices distinguishes interactive decision making from ordinary decisions under uncertainty, in which the only opponent is nature, who chooses randomly. It is obviously pointless to rationalize why nature chooses a particular event or how the occurrence of that event might be influenced by our actions. (We exclude decisions about how to influence the environment or weather.)

Within the past 40 years, an analytical framework for interactive decision making based on investigations of game situations has been developed. This effort was pioneered by John von Neumann and Oskar Morgenstern and culminated in 1947 with the publication of their book *Theory of Games and Economic Behavior*. As an area of academic study, **game theory** provides a series of mathematical models that may be quite useful in explaining interactive decision-making concepts. But as a practical tool, game theory is severely limited in scope. As we will see, the situations that may be analyzed by game theory must be extremely simple. For instance, most parlor games, such as chess, have not yet been thoroughly analyzed mathematically and may never be; even computerized systems cannot beat a competent human in chess, much less Bobby Fischer. And chess is orders of magnitude less complex than many interactive decisions encountered in business. Although game-theory principles may be applied directly to make optimal decisions in certain special situations, the primary value of game theory is the conceptual framework it provides that permits us to explain interactive decision making.

The simplest game to analyze involves two players, each of whom must make exactly one choice from his or her own set of alternatives. The game's outcome depends only on the particular pair of acts selected. Each player receives a numerical payoff, depending on the outcome that the players determine collectively.

An Example from the Battle of the Bismarck Sea

A vivid illustration of such a game situation may be taken from the Battle of the Bismarck Sea during World War II.

In the critical stages of the struggle for New Guinea, intelligence reports indicated that the Japanese would move a troop and supply convoy from the port of Rabaul at the eastern tip of New Britain to Lae, which lies just west of New Britain on New Guinea. It could travel either north of New Britain, where poor visibility was almost certain, or south of the island, where the weather would be clear; in either case, the trip would take three days. General Kenney had the choice of concentrating the bulk of his reconnaissance aircraft on one route or the other. Once sighted, the convoy could be bombed until its arrival at Lae. In days of bombing time, Kenney's staff estimated the following outcomes for the various choices.*

The decision may be summarized by the payoff table in Figure 27-1. Which routes should the two opponents have chosen? By going north, the Japanese commander would be no worse off than if he took the southern route; the northern route also provided the best of the worst possible exposures to bombing. General Kenney's choice was also clear; by concentrating his forces in the north, he could guarantee having two full bombing days. As it turned out, both commanders selected the northern alternative. As we shall see, their choices were consistent with the principles of game theory.

27-2 Two-Person Zero-Sum Games

Another detailed example will help to clarify the principles of game theory. Consider the case of Ms. Gray and Mr. Flannel—two bored rail commuters who while away the mind-numbing hours by playing several games of Color-Bland daily. To play this game each player writes a color on a slip of paper. Patriotically, each participant may choose red, white, or blue. Depending on the colors chosen, varying numbers of pennies are exchanged. The payoff amounts used by Gray and Flannel are determined before playing each game of Color-Bland by a formula based on how many cars of the respective colors are seen by each person between stations (Gray looks out the left side; Flannel, the right). Between Dullstone and Blahsburg, Figure 27-2 is constructed. The amounts shown are what Gray receives from Flannel (a negative figure represents a payment to Flannel).

Color-Bland is the simplest type of game we could encounter. One player's gain is matched by a corresponding loss to the opponent. Flannel's payoff table would contain the same amounts as in Gray's payoff table with the signs reversed. For instance, if both

FIGURE 27-1
Decisions for the Battle of Bismarck Sea.

	JAPANESE STRATEGIES	
KENNEY'S STRATEGIES	Northern Route	Southern Route
Northern Route	2	2
Southern Route	1	3

---

* This example was developed by O. G. Haywood, Jr., and is quoted from R. Duncan Luce and Howard Raiffa, *Games and Decisions* (New York: John Wiley & Sons, 1958) pp. 64–65.

FIGURE 27-2
Gray's Color-Bland payoff table (amounts in cents).

FLANNEL'S ACTS

		Red	White	Blue
GRAY'S ACTS	Red	−3	2	5
	White	−2	1	6
	Blue	−3	−3	−7

players select red, Gray's payoff is −3 and Flannel's is +3, because Gray pays Flannel 3 cents; if both players choose white, Flannel pays Gray 1 cent, so that Gray's payoff is +1 and Flannel's is −1. Since the payoffs for either player provide all the essential information, only one player's payoff table is required to evaluate the decisions. By convention, the payoff table for the player listed at the left is constructed. Regardless of the outcome, Flannel's payoff will always be the negative of Gray's, so that the respective payoffs of the two players sum to zero. For this reason, Color-Bland is referred to as a **two-person zero-sum game**.

Analyzing the Decision: The Minimax Principle

Now we will consider the respective acts that Gray and Flannel should choose. Our clue as to how these choices should be made may be taken from the Battle of the Bismarck Sea example, in which each opposing commander selected the act for which the worst outcome was best. Such a decision-making criterion is referred to as the **minimax principle**. In two-person zero-sum games, the minimax principle always leads to the most preferred choices for both players.

Returning to the Color-Bland game, consider Flannel's choices. His losses or payments to Gray are represented in Figure 27-3 by the quantities in the respective *column* for each of Flannel's color-choice acts. We will assume that Flannel wants to minimize his long-run losses from playing the game and keep his payments to Gray as small as possible. Flannel should therefore focus on the *circled* numbers in Figure 27-3. These are the *column maximums* that represent the greatest payments Flannel might have to make to Gray. The smallest of these losses is −2, which occurs when Flannel chooses red and Gray picks white. Regardless of what color Gray selects, Flannel can do no worse than lose −2 cents (receive 2 cents) by choosing red. Flannel's choice of red is his **minimax loss act**, since this column amount is the minimum of the maximum possible payments that might be made to his opponent.

The possible payoffs to Gray for each of her color-choice acts are provided in the corresponding *rows* of the payoff table. We will assume that Gray views the game similarly and wishes to maximize her receipts from Flannel. Since the payoffs given in Figure 27-3 are what Gray receives, she is concerned with the *boxed* quantities, which represent the *row minimums*. Gray can do no worse than receive one of these values, and the best of them occurs when she chooses white; this choice provides a payoff of −2 when

FIGURE 27-3

Gray's Color-Bland payoff table showing minimax analysis.

FLANNEL'S ACTS

		Red	White	Blue	Row minimum
		Red	White	Blue	
GRAY'S ACTS	Red	-2	4	5	$-2 \leftarrow$ Maximin payoff
	White	0	-3	6	-3
	Blue	-5	1	-6	-6
Column maximum		0	4	6	

↑
Minimax loss

Flannel chooses red. We refer to Gray's choice of white as her **maximin payoff act**, because this row contains the maximum of Gray's minimum possible payoffs from her opponent.

If the payoffs had originally been given from Flannel's point of view, all of the signs in Figure 27-3 would be reversed and the numbers would represent payments to Flannel. A choice of white by Gray would then be the act resulting in the smallest of her greatest possible payments to Flannel, so that Gray's choice of white would also be her minimax loss act. Because one player's loss is always another player's gain, a feature of zero-sum games is that *one player's minimax loss act must be identical to the same player's maximin payoff act*. Thus, Flannel's choice of red is the same act that maximizes his own minimum potential gains.

For this particular Color-Bland game, Gray should choose white and Flannel should select red. Both participants would thereby be acting in accordance with the minimax principle of minimizing their maximum losses to the other player. It is easy to see why no other criterion should be used for this game.

By choosing his minimax loss act (red), Flannel guarantees himself a gain of at least 2 cents (a loss of -2 cents), regardless of the color that Gray picks. There is no advantage in Flannel choosing another color such as blue, which has a potentially larger gain of 7 cents (a loss of -7 cents) when Gray also chooses blue. That amount cannot be guaranteed, since Gray could reverse the take by picking red or white. Similarly, Gray can guarantee herself a payoff of at least -2 cents by choosing her maximin payoff act (white). Flannel can make her outcome worse if she chooses any other color. In following the minimax principle, neither player can sabotage the plans of the opponent without placing himself or herself in a worse position unnecessarily.

Saddle Points and the Value of the Game

Notice that in Figure 27-3 the quantity -2 in the white row and red column is both boxed and circled. It is both the minimum of the column maximums and the maximum of the row minimums. We refer to this value as a **saddle point**, since it is the minimum value in its row and the maximum quantity in its column. Games with saddle points exhibit special features.

Even if the game is played repeatedly, no participant can advantageously deviate from the minimax principle for very long. Each player will always choose the same act — the one that provides the minimax loss to the other player and, at the same time, the maximin payoff to himself or herself. The two acts so obtained are referred to as the **equilibrium act-pair**. As long as either player continues to choose one of these acts, it is of no advantage to the other player to choose any other act.

When a saddle point is present, it is easy to find the **value of the game**. This quantity is the payoff amount in the saddle-point position. For the preceding Color-Bland game,

$$\text{Value of the game} = -2 \text{ cents} \quad (\text{to Gray})$$

The value of the game is always expressed from the point of view of the participant whose receipts appear in the payoff table (and whose acts are listed on the left). In this example, the value to Gray is -2 cents, since that would be her payoff when both Gray and Flannel observe the minimax criterion.

Other Features of Two-Person Zero-Sum Games

The game-theory examples we have considered thus far have involved competitive situations in which each player has the same kind and number of acts to choose from. This may not always be the case, however. One player may have more acts than the other, as the payoff table in Figure 27-4 indicates. There, player A has only three possible choices, and player B has five. Opponents may also have different types of choices. In Color-Bland, one player might pick green, yellow, or orange, and the other might select red, white, or blue. In some competitive situations, the opponents' alternatives are not remotely similar. For example, a firm in a regulated industry may be considering alternative *price levels* for a particular product at the same time government officials are determining *allowable rates of return* on invested capital. The company's future financial position obviously depends on its pricing choice and the rate of return selected by the government. Although it would

FIGURE 27-4
A payoff table for a game involving more choices for one player.

PLAYER B'S ACTS

		B_1	B_2	B_3	B_4	B_5
PLAYER A'S ACTS	A_1	1	2	4	5	0
	A_2	3	3	4	5	4
	A_3	4	③	5	5	6

be hard to put such a situation into a game framework, analogous disparities in types of player choices exist in simple games, too.

The game in Figure 27-4 exhibits a saddle point, when player A chooses act A_3 and player B selects act B_2. This game has another saddle point, which is left as an exercise for the reader to find. When a game has several saddle points, all of the corresponding payoff quantities must be identical and each payoff must equal the value of the game.

More perplexing are games *without a saddle point*. We will now consider how such a game should be played.

27-3 Mixed Strategies in Games without a Saddle Point

Suppose that the bored commuters continue to play from Blahsburg to Gotham City and that en route their car counts result in the new game of Color-Bland summarized in Figure 27-5. This game does not have a saddle point, since no payoff is both largest in its column and smallest in its row. Gray's maximin payoff act is to choose red, and Flannel's minimax loss act is also to select red.

Should each player apply the minimax criterion? First consider Gray, who thinks that Flannel will pick red and may choose to play white instead, thereby achieving the better payoff of zero for herself. Anticipating Gray's plan, Flannel will switch to white to give Gray a worse payoff. But Gray knows what Flannel is guessing, and can choose red to his white, dramatically improving her outcome. However, Flannel (no dummy) knows that Gray knows what he should be guessing, and he can choose red to her red. Knowing all of this, Gray could pick white instead of red, in which case the second-guessing will begin all over again.

There is no single act that one player can choose that will guarantee either player the best of the worst outcomes. Since this game does not have a saddle point, there is no equilibrium act-pair.

FIGURE 27-5
Gray's new payoff table.

		FLANNEL'S ACTS			
		Red	White	Blue	Row minimum
GRAY'S ACTS	Red	$\boxed{-3}$	$\bigcirc 2$	5	-3
	White	$\boxed{-2}$	1	$\bigcirc 6$	-2 ← Maximin payoff
	Blue	-3	-3	$\boxed{-7}$	-7
Column maximum		-2	2	6	

Minimax loss (under -2)

The Mixed Strategy

The goal of game theory is to remove all guesswork on the part of the players by indicating an optimal course of action for each player. When there is a saddle point, a player can choose an act based on the predictability of his or her opponent. In games without saddle points, paradoxically, the guesswork may be eliminated only by *removing* all elements of predictability. And the only way for a player to confuse an opponent is to not know himself what act he will choose. This may be accomplished if each player selects his or her act randomly. Even if such a game is played the same way repeatedly, the random selection of acts will provide no pattern for prediction and there will be no way for either player to take undue advantage of the other.

Thus, in the latest version of Color-Bland, Gray and Flannel each roll a six-sided die to select their colors. For instance, Gray chooses red if the die toss results in a 1 or a 2, white if she rolls a 3 or a 4, and blue if she rolls a 5 or a 6. Since each die has six equally likely faces, each potential color act will have a probability of $1/3$, so that the following decision rule applies for Gray's mixed strategy.

GRAY CHOOSES ACT	WITH PROBABILITY
Red	$P_R = 1/3$
White	$P_W = 1/3$
Blue	$P_B = 1/3$

Such a rule is referred to as a **mixed strategy**, because any one of several acts may be chosen.

In games with a saddle point, each player will choose only one act. When a single act is selected, it is sometimes referred to as a *pure strategy*. This is a special case of mixed strategy in which the selected act has a probability of 1 and all other acts have a probability of zero.

Similarly, Flannel can apply his decision rule so that he picks red if his die toss results in a 1, white if a 2, 3, 4, or 5 is rolled, and blue if a 6 is rolled. Flannel's mixed strategy would then be

FLANNEL CHOOSES ACT	WITH PROBABILITY
Red	$Q_R = 1/6$
White	$Q_W = 4/6$
Blue	$Q_B = 1/6$

Notice that Flannel's probabilities differ from Gray's probabilities. By convention, we will use subscripted P's to denote the probabilities for the player whose payoffs appear in the payoff table (and whose acts are listed on the left) and subscripted Q's to represent the probabilities for the other player. The symbols are necessary because each player must select an optimal mixed strategy and the P and Q values must therefore be treated as variables.

Since uncertainty is now present, each player must evaluate his or her strategy in terms of expected payoff or expected loss. The calculations for obtaining Gray's expected payoff appear in Table 27-1.

First, the original amounts in each row of the payoff table are multiplied by the probability that Gray will choose the act in that row. The products are then summed one column at a time, so that the resulting subtotals provide Gray's expected payoffs *given* Flannel's color choice. Since Flannel's acts are also chosen randomly, the final step is to multiply each subtotal by Flannel's corresponding probability Q for that color-choice act and then to sum the resulting products. Under the initial strategies, Gray's expected payoff is 1/3 cent. This means that after repeatedly playing this version of Color-Bland, Gray would expect to achieve an average payoff of 1/3 cent.

But this amount is deceptive, because it reflects Gray's expected winnings if and only if Flannel plays this particular mixed strategy. However, Flannel can dramatically worsen Gray's situation by simply changing his strategy. For instance, if Flannel makes a color-choice of red, Gray's expected payoff becomes $-7/3$ cents (a worse payoff by nearly 3 cents). As we have seen in earlier games, a player should assume the worst from an opponent. Gray might be able to improve her situation by changing strategies. What is her best mixed strategy? We will suppose that *Gray's goal is to maximize her expected payoff, regardless of the strategy Flannel chooses.* The *minimax theorem,* proved by von Neumann, tells us that it is possible for Gray to achieve this goal. An identical conclusion applies to Flannel as well, who may minimize his maximum expected loss (payment) to Gray through the judicious selection of his own strategy—again, regardless of how Gray plays the game.

TABLE 27-1

Gray's Expected Payoff Calculations When Both Players Use Initial Mixed Strategies

GRAY'S ACTS	GRAY'S PROBABILITIES	$P \times$ PAYOFF FLANNEL'S ACTS		
		Red	White	Blue
Red	$P_R = 1/3$	$-2/3$	4/3	5/3
White	$P_W = 1/3$	0	$-3/3$	6/3
Blue	$P_B = 1/3$	$-5/3$	1/3	$-6/3$
	Subtotals	$-7/3$	2/3	5/3
	Flannel's probabilities	$Q_R = 1/6$	$Q_W = 4/6$	$Q_B = 1/6$
	$Q \times$ Subtotal	$-7/18$	8/18	5/18
		Expected payoff $= -7/18 + 8/18 + 5/18$		
		$= 6/18 = 1/3$		

Before we see how the players can determine their optimal strategies, we will introduce a shortcut procedure that permits us to simplify the required mathematics considerably.

The Elimination of Inadmissible Acts

In Chapter 21, we saw how some acts in a decision problem may be eliminated at the outset before any further analysis is required. This simplifies the decision structure because it permits a smaller number of acts to be considered. Acts that are eliminated at the outset of a decision problem are called **inadmissible acts**, because they will never be chosen. We extend this concept to games. *If a player has an act that is inferior to another act, regardless of what choice the opponent makes, then that act is inadmissible.*

Consider the latest Color-Bland game. For convenience, the payoffs are repeated in Figure 27-6. It is easy to see that Gray would never choose blue, since that act provides smaller payoffs than red does for each of Flannel's color choices. Gray's red act *dominates* her blue act, making blue inadmissible. Gray would never choose blue under any circumstances, and its row may be crossed out of the payoff table. Ignoring Gray's blue row, we see that Flannel's blue color-choice act provides greater payoffs to Gray than a choice of either red or white does, no matter what action Gray takes. Flannel's red and white both dominate his blue, which is therefore inadmissible. Flannel's blue column may also be crossed out of the payoff table. The remaining rows and columns are all admissible, so that the reduced payoff table must be analyzed further.

Notice that the blue column does not become inadmissible until the blue row is eliminated, because the −6 in the blue–blue position is smaller than either the blue–white payoff of 1 or the blue–red payoff of −5, making blue a better choice for Flannel than red or white if Gray actually makes a blunder and picks blue. Thus, we see that whenever a row (or column) is crossed out, all columns (or rows) remaining in the payoff table must be reevaluated.

In games with saddle points, the successive elimination of inadmissible acts eventually enables us to cross out all rows and columns except those representing equilibrium act-pairs. In some games, it is possible for an entry to be both the minimum value in its row *and* the maximum value in its column and still lie in the row or column of an inadmissible act. Although such an entry is technically a saddle point, it cannot

FIGURE 27-6
Gray's payoff table with the inadmissible acts eliminated.

FLANNEL'S ACTS

GRAY'S ACTS		Red	White	Blue	
	Red	−2	4	5	
	White	0	−3	6	
	Blue	−5	1	−6	Inadmissible

Inadmissible

correspond to an equilibrium act-pair. In a game with several saddle points, there may be ties (but not necessarily so) for equilibrium act-pairs. Before concluding that ties exist, *be sure to check all saddle points to see if any lie in inadmissible rows or columns.*

27-4 Optimal Mixed Strategies for Zero-Sum Games

We are now left with the 2×2 Color-Bland game in Figure 27-7, where each player can choose from only two acts. We must now find the act probabilities for each player. To simplify this procedure, we observe that all P and all Q values must sum to 1 and that P_B and Q_B are now zero. It therefore follows that

$$P_W = 1 - P_R \qquad Q_W = 1 - Q_R$$

so that only two quantities, P_R and Q_R, are unknown.

We begin by evaluating Gray's possible strategies. Her expected payoff depends on Flannel's color choices and may be calculated for any value of P_R using the payoffs in the applicable column of the payoff table. Gray's expected payoffs may be expressed as

$$-2P_R + 0(1 - P_R) = -2P_R \qquad \text{(if Flannel picks red)}$$
$$4P_R - 3(1 - P_R) = -3 + 7P_R \qquad \text{(if Flannel picks white)}$$

The Graphical Solution

The procedure and rationale for finding the respective optimal mixed strategies for Gray and Flannel are easy to explain graphically. Figure 27-8 shows how Gray's expected payoffs vary for each possible level of P_R, which can range from zero to 1.

First, we will consider the case in which Flannel picks red, so that only the first column of the payoff table applies. If Gray applies $P_R = 0$, she will be certain to choose white and her expected payoff of 0 will be obtained from the bottom cell in the red column of Figure 27-7; this provides the point at the origin in the graph. At the other extreme, Gray might apply $P_R = 1$, in which case her expected payoff will be -2, which appears in the top cell in the red column of her payoff table; this corresponds to a second point at the bottom of the graph on the right side. The straight line connecting these two

FIGURE 27-7
Gray's Color-Bland payoffs reduced to a 2 × 2 game.

			FLANNEL'S ACTS	
			Q_R	$1 - Q_R$
			Red	White
GRAY'S	P_R	Red	-2	4
ACTS	$1 - P_R$	White	0	-3

points provides Gray's expected payoffs for all levels of P_R between zero and 1, assuming that Flannel chooses red.

If Flannel chooses white instead, then the expected payoffs of -3 when $P_R = 0$ and 4 when $P_R = 1$ appear in the white column of Gray's payoff table. The line connecting the two corresponding points on the graph provides Gray's expected payoffs for all levels of P_R between zero and 1.

What value of P_R should Gray select? Remember that she wants to guarantee herself the largest expected payoff, regardless of what action her opponents takes. We must therefore consider how Flannel would behave if he knew Gray's P_R value. Notice that the two expected payoff lines in Figure 27-8 cross at $P_R = 1/3$. Suppose that Gray picks a smaller red probability, such as 1/4. Knowing this, Flannel will choose white, because that act will provide Gray with the lower expected payoff line. On the other hand, if Gray applies a P_R value greater than 1/3, such as 2/3, then Flannel will select red, which corresponds to the lower expected payoff line in this case. Flannel can effectively limit Gray's expected payoffs to those points on the heavy line segments meeting at $P_R = 1/3$. Gray receives her greatest expected payoff where these lines cross. Applying $P_R =$

FIGURE 27-8

A graphical representation of Gray's optimal mixed strategy.

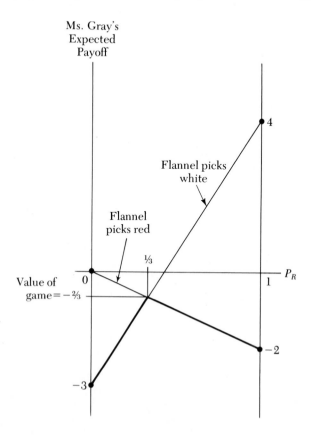

1/3, Gray will receive the same expected payoff, regardless of the act Flannel chooses.

$$-2P_R = -2(1/3) = -2/3 \quad \text{(if Flannel picks red)}$$
$$-3 + 7P_R = -3 + 7(1/3) = -2/3 \quad \text{(if Flannel picks white)}$$

Unfortunately for Gray, this particular Color-Bland game is not in her favor. But by employing a mixed strategy with $P_R = 1/3$ and $P_W = 1 - P_R = 2/3$, she can make the best of a bad situation. This is Gray's optimal mixed strategy.

We must still determine Flannel's optimal mixed strategy. This is tantamount to finding the best level of Q_R. Using the applicable rows in the payoff table, we express Flannel's expected payoffs in terms of this unknown quantity as

$$-2Q_R + 4(1 - Q_R) = 4 - 6Q_R \quad \text{(if Gray picks red)}$$
$$0Q_R - 3(1 - Q_R) = -3 + 3Q_R \quad \text{(if Gray picks white)}$$

Figure 27-9 presents the corresponding graph, in which separate lines are plotted (as

FIGURE 27-9
A graphical representation of Flannel's optimal mixed strategy.

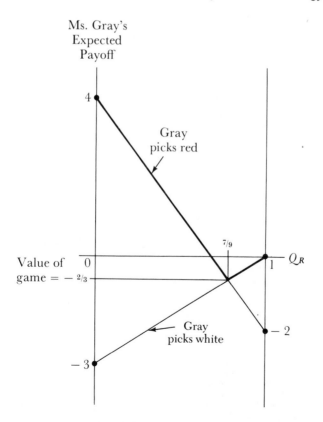

before) for each of Gray's possible color choices. Flannel wants to minimize Gray's expected payoff (his expected loss). By knowing Flannel's level of Q_R, Gray can effectively limit the game's outcome to the points on the heavy line segments. The minimum expected payoff that Flannel can obtain occurs when $Q_R = 7/9$, where the two lines cross.

Flannel's optimal mixed strategy is to apply $Q_R = 7/9$ and $Q_W = 1 - Q_R = 2/9$, which leads to the same expected payoff regardless of Gray's choice.

$$4 - 6(7/9) = -2/3 \quad \text{(if Gray picks red)}$$

$$-3 + 3(7/9) = -2/3 \quad \text{(if Gray picks white)}$$

Notice that by following this strategy, Flannel is guaranteed a minimum expected payoff that is equal to Gray's maximum expected payoff.

For any zero-sum game involving mixed strategies, the value of the game is the maximum expected payoff that can be guaranteed, and this amount is also the minimum expected loss that can be assured. For the present Color-Bland game,

$$\text{Value of the game} = -2/3 \text{ cents}$$

The Algebraic Solution

The graphical analysis provides the key for finding a player's mixed strategy in a 2×2 game. It always corresponds to the point at which the two payoff lines cross—and that happens to be the point where the expected payoff is identical for both opponents' acts. We may solve the game algebraically by setting the two expected value equations equal to each other and solving for the unknown probability.

For Gray, the expected payoffs are $-2P_R$ (if Flannel picks red) and $-3 + 7P_R$ (if Flannel picks white). Thus, the optimal level of P_R occurs when

$$-2P_R = -3 + 7P_R$$

$$-9P_R = -3$$

and

$$P_R = 3/9 = 1/3$$

As before, $P_W = 1 - P_R = 2/3$, and the value of the game is $-2/3$.

For Flannel, the expected payoffs are $4 - 6Q_R$ (if Gray picks red) and $-3 + 3Q_R$ (if Gray picks white), so that Q_R must satisfy

$$4 - 6Q_R = -3 + 3Q_R$$

$$-9Q_R = -7$$

and thus,

$$Q_R = 7/9$$

and $Q_W = 1 - Q_R = 2/9$.

Solving 3 × 2 and Larger Games: Salary Negotiations

The procedures just discussed may be applied to games in which one of the players has more than two acts from which to choose. An algebraic solution to such a game is more complex than the solution to the 2×2 game. However, we can easily extend the graphical method to find the optimal mixed strategy for each player as long as one of the players selects only two acts.

As a change of pace, we will consider an illustration of a conflict in which one party's gain is the other party's loss. Union and management bargaining over a labor contract, where each side can adopt a variety of stances and ploys, provides a good example of such a conflict. We will consider the case of a star baseball player who is seeking a salary increase from the owner of the Gotham City Robins. He is considering one of the three negotiating approaches shown in Figure 27-10 which also indicates the assumed percentage salary increases. These payoffs are partly determined by the stance chosen by the owner.

Investigation of the payoff table does not show a saddle point, so mixed strategies must be determined. Since there are no inadmissible acts, we must find three probabilities, P_1, P_2, and P_3, for the baseball star's acts and two probabilities, Q_1 and Q_2, for the owner's choices.

First, we consider the owner's problem. She has only two acts and only one variable Q_1, since the probability for her second act is $Q_2 = 1 - Q_1$. The owner wants to pick a level of Q_1 that will keep the star's expected percentage increase as small as possible. The graph in Figure 27-11 shows the expected payoff lines for each of the ballplayer's choices; the heavy segments indicate the largest levels he can achieve for various levels of Q_1. The lowest point on these line segments occurs at the intersection of the S_2 and S_3 lines, which corresponds to the Q_1 level the owner should use.

To find Q_1, first we determine the expected payoff expressions, assuming that one of these acts will be chosen by the ballplayer. Using only the payoffs in the S_2 and S_3 rows of

FIGURE 27-10

Baseball star's negotiation for a percentage salary increase.

			OWNER'S ACTS	
			Q_1	$Q_2 = 1 - Q_1$
			O_1 Benevolent	O_2 Stingy
	P_1	S_1 Go fishing	30	10
BASEBALL STAR'S ACTS	P_2	S_2 Firm stand	25	15
	P_3	S_3 Hat in hand	10	25

FIGURE 27-11
A graphical representation of the baseball team owner's optimal mixed strategy.

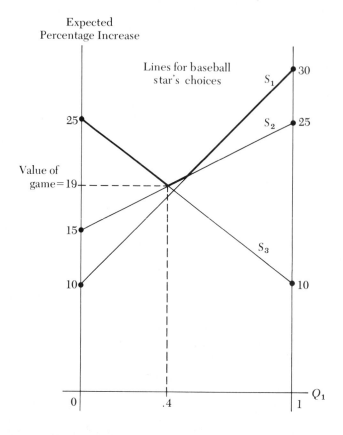

FIGURE 27-11

A graphical representation of the baseball team owner's optimal mixed strategy.

Figure 27-10, we find that the following expressions apply.

$$25Q_1 + 15(1 - Q_1) = 15 + 10Q_1 \quad \text{(if ballplayer picks } S_2)$$
$$10Q_1 + 25(1 - Q_1) = 25 - 15Q_1 \quad \text{(if ballplayer picks } S_3)$$

Since these expressions represent the equations for the S_2 and S_3 lines in the graph, the Q_1 value where the lines intersect is found by setting the equations equal to each other and solving for the unknown value.

$$15 + 10Q_1 = 25 - 15Q_1$$
$$25Q_1 = 10$$
$$Q_1 = 10/25 = .4$$

The value of the game may then be found by substituting $Q_1 = .4$ into either expected payoff expression. Choosing the expression for S_2

$$\text{Value of the game} = 15 + 10(.4) = 19\%$$

Thus, the owner of the Robins can guarantee a minimum expected salary increase of 19% to her star by following a mixed strategy of assigning a probability of $Q_1 = .4$ to being benevolent (O_1) and a probability of $Q_2 = 1 - Q_1 = .6$ to being stingy (O_2).

But we have yet to establish the ballplayer's mixed strategy. Figure 27-11 shows that he would never choose S_1, since the owner could then guarantee a lower expected payoff when using $Q_1 = .4$. Thus, the player must consider a mixed strategy between S_2 and S_3 only and set $P_1 = 0$. This means that $P_2 + P_3 = 1$, so that $P_3 = 1 - P_2$. Using the S_2 and S_3 rows of the payoff table, we determine the ballplayer's expected payoffs for each of the owner's possible acts.

$$25P_2 + 10P_3 = 25P_2 + 10(1 - P_2)$$
$$= 10 + 15P_2 \quad \text{(if owner picks } O_1)$$

and

$$15P_2 + 25P_3 = 15P_2 + 25(1 - P_2)$$
$$= 25 - 10P_2 \quad \text{(if owner picks } O_2)$$

Setting these expressions equal to each other, we solve for the unknown P_2.

$$10 + 15P_2 = 25 - 10P_2$$
$$25P_2 = 15$$
$$P_2 = 15/25 = .6$$

Thus, the ballplayer's optimal mixed strategy is not to go fishing by choosing S_1 $(P_1 = 0)$, to take a firm stand (S_2) with a probability of $P_2 = .6$, and to plead with "hat in hand" (S_3) with a probability of $P_3 = 1 - P_2 = .4$. To verify this, we compute his expected payoff using either of the above expressions to see if his expected percentage increase is identical to the minimum expected value found earlier for the owner's strategy. Plugging $P_2 = .6$ into the first expression gives us

$$10 + 15(.6) = 19\%$$

which is identical to the value of the game established earlier.

When both players of a game have a choice of more than two acts, a more involved procedure based on linear programming principles is required to find the mixed strategies.

27-5 Non-Zero-Sum and Other Games

The two-person zero-sum game is easiest to analyze. A wide variety of other games have been studied, but unlike two-person zero-sum games, these more complex situations often have no pat solutions that are acceptable to all players.

Two-Person Non-Zero-Sum Games

A two-person **non-zero-sum game** occurs when one player's gain does not necessarily equal the other player's loss. This may be the case in games similar to those described earlier in this chapter when the particular payoff measure does not reflect the true worth of an outcome. In playing Color-Bland for example, Gray may derive much greater satisfaction from beating Flannel than the payoffs indicate, and losing a little bit may be just as undesirable to Gray as losing a lot. Flannel may have analogous feelings as well. A player's ego might be the dominant factor in evaluating a simple parlor game. Rather than points or monetary values, personal utility values would therefore serve as a more accurate way of ranking outcomes in such cases.

The essential feature of non-zero-sum games is not the way in which the true payoff values are determined but the requirement that the respective payoffs achieved by the two players do not sum to zero for at least one act-pair. This feature can severely complicate the analysis.

The Prisoner's Dilemma

A classical example of a non-zero-sum game is provided by the following "prisoner's dilemma."

> Two suspects are taken into custody and separated. The district attorney is certain that they are guilty of a specific crime, but he does not have adequate evidence to convict them at a trial. He points out to each prisoner that each has two alternatives: to confess to the crime the police are sure they have done, or not to confess. If they both do not confess, then the district attorney states he will book them on some very minor, trumped-up charge, such as petty larceny and illegal possession of a weapon, and they will both receive minor punishments. If they confess, they will be prosecuted, but he will recommend less than the most severe sentence. But if one confesses and the other does not, then the confessor will receive lenient treatment for turning state's evidence, whereas the latter will get "the book" slapped at him.*

The outcomes in Figure 27-12 might apply to this example. Regardless of the numerical utility payoff values assigned to the various outcomes, the essential characteristic is that when one suspect confesses and the other does not, materially different payoffs result. Consider just the outcomes for prisoner *A*.

	B Does Not Confess	B Confesses
A Does Not Confess	1 year	10 years
A Confesses	3 months	8 years

---

* R. Duncan Luce and Howard Raiffa, *Games and Decisions* (New York: John Wiley & Sons, 1958) p. 95.

FIGURE 27-12
Possible outcomes for the prisoner's dilemma.

PRISONER *B*'S ACTS

		Not Confess	Confess
PRISONER *A*'S ACTS	Not Confess	1 year each	10 years for *A* and 3 months for *B*
	Confess	3 months for *A* and 10 years for *B*	8 years each

It is easy to see that confessing is superior to not confessing for *A*, regardless of what *B* does. Not confessing is therefore an inadmissible act for *A*, and it would not be rational to choose it. A similar conclusion applies to prisoner *B*.

Thus, if both prisoners behave rationally, both will confess and receive eight-year sentences as their reward. The paradox here is that *if both prisoners behave irrationally instead, the positions of both prisoners will be significantly improved.* If neither prisoner confesses, then each will receive a light sentence of one year apiece.

The joint confessions may be regarded as an equilibrium act-pair, just as in a zero-sum game. As long as the prisoners are not allowed to cooperate, confessing is the minimax loss act for both suspects. If they are allowed to *cooperate* and enter a binding agreement, then it is clearly in the best interests for both prisoners not to confess and for each to receive a one-year sentence.

Similar interactive decision-making situations are sometimes encountered in business. For instance, two small firms, each dominant in a separate region, might consider whether or not to market in each other's territory. As long as neither firm invades the other's region, both firms will continue to earn satisfactory profits. But if one firm begins to invade the other's territory when the second firm has not planned to expand also, then the second firm could be eliminated. If both firms try to expand simultaneously, each firm may survive but achieve a lower profit level than before. If the companies are not allowed to cooperate, the only rational outcome is for both firms to engage in damaging expansion—just like the joint confessions in the prisoner's dilemma. Clearly, if they are allowed to cooperate, both firms will choose to maintain the status quo.

Unlike the simpler zero-sum games in which it is never advantageous for a player to disclose his or her planned action, different solutions may arise in non-zero-sum games when disclosure and cooperation is allowed than when the game is strictly competitive. A variety of special situations arise in the study of non-zero-sum games. The prisoner's dilemma provides us with just one example. These other forms have been analyzed with varying degrees of success. In general, the non-zero-sum game is much more difficult to solve, and even when solutions are obtained, they are often not completely satisfactory.

Games with Several Players

In this chapter, we have considered games that involve only two persons. When three or more parties participate in a game, the situation may be too complex to be solved satisfactorily. The variety added by a third or a fourth person is staggering. Two or more players may gang up on the others, making collusions and partnerships of varying kinds and degrees possible. Multiplayer games are even less amenable to solution than the two-person non-zero-sum game.

27-6 Additional Remarks

Game theory, as we have seen, serves primarily as a model for explaining interactive decision making. In simpler situations, it may even be used to determine the best course of action. Its applicability to real-world problems is therefore quite limited. Even when it may be applied, the practicality of its results are criticized. It is hard to imagine a board chairman or an army general letting the final decision to a problem be determined by a role of the dice. Nor would we expect two bored commuters to solve a linear program to determine the probabilities to three decimal places for choosing a color to play—just to win a few pennies.

But successful and meaningful results may sometimes be achieved by exercising game-theory principles. Interactive decision making is highly complex, and game theory may provide good approximations for analyzing an otherwise intractable problem. For instance, the prisoner's dilemma may be used as a model to explain oligopolistic behavior or a farmer's crop-planting decision. Another approximation is provided by the mixed strategy. Although game theory presumes that one player knows the other player's acts and outcomes precisely, this is rarely true in the real world. Paradoxically, this fact makes the concept of mixed strategies more relevant. We do not actually have to toss a pair of dice to give an action the element of unpredictability that is required in a formal mixed strategy.

Game analysis serves as a microcosm for all quantitative methods, which share its strengths and imperfections to varying degrees. Almost all mathematical models developed to solve practical problems are imperfect approximations to reality, but even the simplest models may help to organize problem evaluation and to cull out a myriad of poor solutions. At the very least, game theory provides us with a point of departure from which to investigate the most difficult type of decision making, and, as such, it is a very valuable management-science tool.

CASE

Avery's versus Blomberg

Avery's is a small chain of neighborhood department stores located in a suburban county. C. P. Blomberg is a similar establishment situated in an adjacent county. Both chains are financially strong enough to expand, and the only viable manner in which this may be accomplished is for each chain to open stores in the other's county. The following expected payoff tables provide the anticipated average profit levels over the next five years for the various courses of action.

AVERY'S PROFITS

	Blomberg Doesn't Expand	Blomberg Expands
Avery's Doesn't Expand	$300,000	−$100,000
Avery's Expands	500,000	100,000

BLOMBERG'S PROFITS

	Blomberg Doesn't Expand	Blomberg Expands
Avery's Doesn't Expand	$200,000	$400,000
Avery's Expands	−200,000	50,000

Questions

1. Is this situation a zero-sum game? Explain.
2. Find the equilibrium act-pair, if there is one.
3. If the two chains are prohibited by state antitrust laws from cooperating, what course of action would each store take?
4. If the two stores can cooperate, what course of action would each prefer?

PROBLEMS

27-1 Find the saddle point (or points) in each of the following two-person zero-sum games.

(a)

	B_1	B_2
A_1	3	−1
A_2	4	3

(b)

	B_1	B_2	B_3
A_1	4	4	10
A_2	2	3	1
A_3	6	5	7

(c)

	B_1	B_2
A_1	0	8
A_2	0	6
A_3	−2	4

(d)

	B_1	B_2	B_3
A_1	5	3	3
A_2	6	2	4

27-2   Find the inadmissible acts in the following game.

	B_1	B_2	B_3	B_4	B_5
A_1	3	2	4	3	4
A_2	2	3	3	2	3
A_3	2	3	-5	4	1
A_4	3	0	4	3	5

27-3   For the following game, determine the minimax course of action for player X and for player Y. What is the value of the game?

	Y_1	Y_2
X_1	2	0
X_2	3	2

27-4   Consider the following game (payoffs are profits to player A). P is the probability that player A will choose act A_1 and Q is the probability that player B will choose act B_1.

		Q	$1-Q$
		B_1	B_2
P	A_1	5	-4
$1-P$	A_2	-4	3

(a) Construct a graph that locates the optimal P that player A should apply, regardless of the action B takes.

(b) Determine the optimal P for player A algebraically. Then, find the value of the game.

(c) Find player B's optimal mixed strategy.

(d) Find player A's expected payoff from the P you determined in (b) if player B chooses probability $Q = 1/5$ instead of applying his or her optimal mixed strategy. Is this different from the value of the game you found in (b)? Explain.

(e) Find player A's expected payoff when B chooses the Q you determined in (c) and A selects $P = 1/4$. Is this different from the value of the game you found in (b)? Explain.

(f) Find player A's expected payoff when B chooses the Q given in (d) and A selects $P = 1/4$. Is this different from the value of the game you found in (b)? Explain.

27-5   Consider the following game.

	B_1	B_2	B_3
A_1	2	7	4
A_2	5	1	5
A_3	3	4	4

(a) Eliminate any inadmissible acts.
(b) Find player B's optimal mixed strategy.
(c) What act would player A never choose?
(d) Find player A's optimal mixed strategy and the value of the game.

27-6 Compass Point is a game played by two people. Each player has a small wheel with a pointer that must be set at north, east, south, or west. One player is designated "northeast-adjacent" and receives 2 points if two adjacent compass points (for example, north and west) are chosen. The other player is designated "southwest-opposite" and receives 4 points when two opposite directions (north–south or east–west) are chosen. If both players pick the same direction, then 5 points are awarded to the player whose designation includes that direction (that is, 5 points to the northeast-adjacent player if both players choose north or both pick east).
(a) Construct the payoff table representing the points awarded to the northeast-adjacent player.
(b) Eliminate any inadmissible acts.
(c) Does this game have an equilibrium act-pair? If so, identify it.
(d) Find the optimal course of action for each player and the value of the game.

27-7 The Amalgamated Coffin Workers of Transylvania are negotiating with Dracula Enterprises over how many new converts must be housed in the coming year. The union wishes to make as few coffins as possible, whereas Dracula wants to maximize the number of coffins. The following payoff table represents the number of coffins expected to be made for the various combinations of union and management acts.

		UNION'S ACTS		
		Tranquil	Strike	Wooden Stake Sabotage
DRACULA'S ACTS	Tranquil	15	8	10
	Lock-in	10	12	15
	Bite Union Leaders	10	10	15

Find the optimal course of action for each of the participants and the value of the game.

27-8 The tennis coaches for Old Ivy College and Slippery Rock University must each determine which of their leading men and women players to pair in a mixed-doubles match. Although men and women have never played together before at either school, a record has been kept of the number of sets won in previous all-male and all-female matches at both schools. Both coaches feel that the difference in past sets won represents a player's relative advantage or disadvantage against a particular opponent. The following tables represent the net number of sets won by the Old Ivy players.

		SLIPPERY ROCK WOMEN	
		Ann	Belva
OLD IVY WOMEN	Cheryl	5	−3
	Sandra	−4	2

		SLIPPERY ROCK MEN	
		Harry	Larry
OLD IVY MEN	Fred	−3	8
	Ted	0	4

(a) Assuming that the relative advantage a particular mixed-doubles team has over its opponents may be expressed by adding the respective historical net winnings of the corresponding all-male and all-female matches, determine the net advantages to Old Ivy of each possible combination of mixed-doubles teams.

(b) Suppose that each coach must determine who will play before finding out who the opponents will be. Assuming that the net advantage of each possible team combination expresses the payoff for a zero-sum game, eliminate the inadmissible teams.

(c) Using the reduced payoff table you constructed in (b), determine the minimax action for each coach. Which school has the advantage? How many sets of tennis does it equal?

27-9   It is possible to treat single-person decision making under uncertainty as a game with nature as the second participant and the uncertain events as nature's choices. Consider the following payoff table regarding a new product that may be produced in-house or whose patent may be sold to another manufacturer for a fixed fee plus a royalty on future sales.

	PRODUCT EVENTS	
ACTS	*Success*	*Failure*
Make	$100,000	− $50,000
Sell Patent	15,000	10,000

(a) Using the minimax principle of game theory, find the manufacturer's optimal course of action. What is the corresponding payoff level?

(b) Suppose that the manufacturer judges that there is a 50–50 chance of product success. According to the Bayes decision rule, which course of action should the manufacturer take? What is the corresponding expected payoff?

(c) Using the probability information given in (b), calculate the manufacturer's expected payoff for the action indicated in (a).

(d) Does the minimax principle maximize the manufacturer's expected payoff as it would in a two-person game? Explain.

27-10   Two opposing political parties are nominating candidates for governor in separate conventions that are being held simultaneously. The following probabilities apply for the respective party winning the election for the indicated nominee pair.

DEMOCRATIC NOMINEE	REPUBLICAN NOMINEE	PROBABILITY FOR DEMOCRAT WINNING	PROBABILITY FOR REPUBLICAN WINNING
Muck	Raker	.75	.25
Muck	Slinger	.25	.75
Mudd	Raker	.30	.70
Mudd	Slinger	.60	.40

Assume that each party wishes to maximize its probability for winning the election.

(a) If the Republican's win probability is subtracted from the Democrat's, the resulting difference may be used as the Democrat's payoff measure, so that a zero-sum game applies. Construct the appropriate payoff table.

(b) Apply the minimax criterion to find the optimal action for each party.

27-11 The zero-sum game is a special case of the *constant-sum game*, and the same principles may be used to analyze both games. For example, in playing Color-Bland against Ms. Gray, the chauvinistic but chivalrous Mr. Flannel may give her a handicap by increasing each of her regular payoffs by 5 cents. Consider the following game without a handicap.

FLANNEL'S ACTS

		Red	White	Blue
	Red	−2	4	−3
GRAY'S	White	1	2	−4
ACTS	Blue	1	1	1

(a) Solve this game to find the minimax courses of action for the two players. What is the value of the game?

(b) Construct Gray's payoff table with the 5-cent handicap included. Then, solve the game. Are the optimal courses of action the same? Compare the value of the handicapped game to the value of the game in (a). What is the difference in these amounts?

CHAPTER

28

Dynamic
Programming

Often decision making involves several choices that must be made at different times. For example, in automobile production planning, monthly decisions may be made regarding how many cars of various models should be produced in each assembly plant. Successful planning requires that enough cars be available to satisfy the highly seasonal and varying monthly demands, that this be achieved at a minimum cost, and that very few cars remain unsold at the start of the new model year. In meeting monthly demands while minimizing total annual production costs, more units will be produced in certain months than in others. But there should not be much variation in month-to-month production, since this might necessitate excessive overtime costs in some periods and inefficient use of labor in others.

We may view each month's production level as a separate decision. Each earlier choice, however, affects the freedom of choice in later months. And the annual profit or cost is determined collectively from the individual monthly decisions.

A variety of similar situations involving sequential decision making may be evaluated by **dynamic programming**—a quantitative method that is similar in scope to linear programming. The goal of both procedures is the efficient allocation of resources. Thus, either programming approach is designed to determine the variable values that minimize cost, maximize profit, or optimize any one of a variety of other kinds of payoffs. Dynamic programming differs from the other allocation models described in this book in that it considers decision making *over time*. We use the word *dynamic* because *time* is explicitly incorporated into the model.

This does not mean that decision making over time may only be evaluated by a dynamic programming model. In Chapter 15, we saw how the transportation method of linear programming may be used to establish several successive monthly production levels. But in automobile production planning, linear programming would simultaneously consider all 12 monthly production levels. Dynamic programming simplifies matters considerably, since it allows us to view each month *separately*. Unlike linear programming, dynamic programming may consider a variety of relationships between variables—including nonlinear ones.

The main advantage of dynamic programming is its *computational efficiency*. Suppose that we are faced with a situation involving a sequence of 4 decisions, each having 10 alternatives. Evaluating such a problem by a trial-and-error method would be an onerous chore, since $10^4 = 10,000$ possible choices would have to be considered in order to locate the optimal decision. Using dynamic programming, we reduce the number of evaluations to $4 \times 10 = 40$. The savings in effort realized by using dynamic programming rather than complete enumeration may be extremely great when decision problems have many decision points.

A classic explanation of dynamic programming concepts is provided by the **stagecoach problem**.*

28-1 Basic Concepts: The Stagecoach Problem

Following the advice of Horace Greeley to "go West, young man," Tom Wysaker is selecting a stagecoach route from New York to San Francisco. His possible choices are shown in Figure 28-1. Each westward leg of Tom's journey begins with a decision to take a particular stagecoach line (represented by an arrow). Successive decision points are therefore called **stages**. Regardless of the overall route chosen, a total of five stages are involved in the trip to California. Each stagecoach line begins in one state (or territory) and ends in another. Thus, each successive decision-point square represents a beginning **state** for the subsequent journey leg. Picking a stagecoach line in one state is tantamount to choosing the state from which the next stagecoach will depart. The stagecoach problem highlights the essential features of any dynamic programming problem. Each successive decision point is a stage, which is usually numbered 1, 2, 3, . . . , for convenience. All stages begin in some kind of state, which instead of a place could be a set of circumstances, a number, or a collection of quantities. The state at any stage is determined by only two factors: the preceding state and the decision made at the prior state.

The Best Policy: The Principle of Optimality

A nineteenth-century stagecoach trip across North America is fraught with hazards ranging from Indians and robbers to floods, forest fires, and buffalo stampedes. Tom Wysaker's overriding goal is therefore to get to San Francisco in one piece. Since he is no

---

* This problem was originally described by Harvey M. Wagner. Our example differs in many ways from the version in his book, *Principles of Operations Research*, 2nd ed. (Englewood Cliffs, N.J.: Prentice-Hall, 1975).

FIGURE 28-1

A routing network for the stagecoach problem.

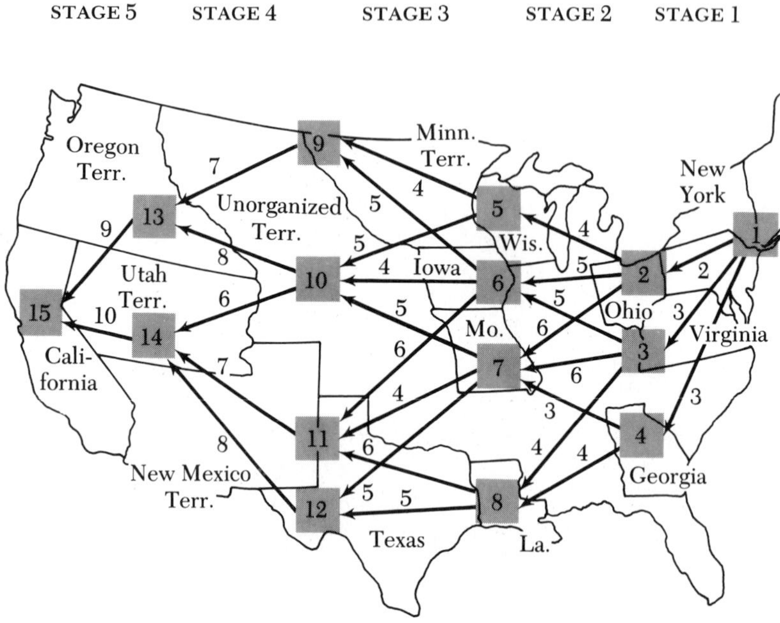

expert in evaluating risks, Tom relies on life insurance companies for help. They have provided rates for $10,000 of coverage for one trip on the various stagecoaches; these charges are indicated along the arrows in Figure 28-1. Assuming that the probability of being killed is directly proportional to the total premium charge, Tom wants to pick the route (the 5-stagecoach sequence) with the minimum life insurance policy cost.

In a multistage decision problem analyzed by dynamic programming, a particular sequence of alternatives is called a **policy**. The optimal policy is the sequence of alternatives that achieves the decision maker's goal.

The fundamental precept of dynamic programming is the **principle of optimality**, which tells us that

> The optimal policy must be one such that, regardless of how a particular state is reached, all later choices proceeding from that state must be optimal.

As we will see, the principle of optimality allows us to find the best policy by evaluating one stage at a time. Thus, dynamic programming procedures start with the *last* stage and work from stage to stage *backward* in time.

Mathematical Formulation of the Problem

In his final stage, Tom Wysaker will be in one of the two states, 13 or 14, preceding his destination. In either case, he has a single choice—to take the final stagecoach to San

Francisco, which will bring him to state 15. His policy cost includes a charge of $9 if Tom ends his journey on stage 5 from state 13 and a cost of $10 if he ends his journey from state 14.

It is convenient to express mathematically the cost of or the payoff for the optimal policy of going from one stage to the end. This representation is provided by the **cost function**

$$f_n(s) = \text{Cost, entering from state } s, \text{ of using an optimal policy}$$
$$\text{from stage } n \text{ to the end}$$

Since Tom Wysaker's last leg is stage 5, the following values of the cost function apply at that stage.

$$f_5(13) = \$\ 9 \quad \text{(to state 15)}$$
$$f_5(14) = \$10 \quad \text{(to state 15)}$$

In applications with another objective, such as maximizing profit or optimizing some other payoff measure, $f_n(s)$ is the profit or the payoff function.

The objective of any dynamic program is to find the value of the cost function for the initial state at stage 1 and the corresponding optimal choices. To achieve this for the stagecoach problem, further notation is required. We represent the cost of taking a particular stagecoach line that connects two states by

$$c_{sj} = \text{Cost of going from state } s \text{ to state } j$$

The cost at stage n of the optimal policy from any given state to the end is therefore

$$f_n(s) = \text{Minimum } [c_{sj} + f_{n+1}(j)]$$

Notice that the cost function for an earlier stage is evaluated using the values from the succeeding stage, since the procedure works backward in time. This expression is called a **recursive relationship**. It provides the optimal choice at stage n for the given optimal policy at stage $n + 1$ and applies to every stage except the last one, for which the starting values are generally available directly.

In the stagecoach problem, all possible values of $f_n(s)$ are found for successively smaller stages n, beginning with the f_5 values. The recursive relationship is last applied to determine $f_1(1)$. The minimum cost of the optimal policy is equal to $f_1(1)$. The optimal policy is identified by tracing back through the steps taken to determine the corresponding sequence of states. (Several policies might be optimal due to ties.)

Solving the Problem

We begin solving the problem in the final stage, using the values $f_5(13) = \$9$ and $f_5(14) = \$10$, and move backward to stage $n = 4$. Suppose that stage 4 begins in state 9; a stagecoach leaving from there only goes to state 13, where the insurance cost (from

Figure 28-1) is $c_{9,13} = \$7$. Thus,

$$f_4(9) = c_{9,13} + f_5(13)$$
$$= \$7 + \$9 = \$16 \quad \text{(to state 13)}$$

Stage 4 may also begin in state 10. Since this state is connected to two states, 13 and 14, we must evaluate two sums.

$$c_{10,13} + f_5(13) = \$8 + \$\ 9 = \$17 \quad \text{(to state 13)}$$
$$c_{10,14} + f_5(14) = \$6 + \$10 = \$16 \quad \text{(to state 14)}$$

The cost function for departing from state 10 is the smaller of these sums.

$$f_4(10) = \text{Minimum } (\$17, \$16) = \$16 \quad \text{(to state 14)}$$

We see that if stage 4 starts in state 10, it will be cheaper to go from there to state 14 rather than to state 13. Regardless of how state 10 is reached, it will always be better to go from there to state 14. This doesn't mean that Tom Wysaker must ever enter state 10. But if his optimal policy brings him there, then that same policy must lead him to state 14— not to state 13. This illustrates the principle of optimality. Since we are evaluating the problem backward, we cannot know the state that it will ultimately be best to start from at stage 4 until we are finished. It might be state 9, 10, 11, or 12. But we determine the best course of action for each of these possibilities. Only when all the stages have been evaluated can the pieces be put together to form the final picture. To achieve the answer, it is necessary to save enough information to use in future evaluations of the earlier stages.

Two types of data must be stored. Since the recursive relationship determines the levels of $f_n(s)$, the values of this function must somehow be recorded so that they may be used in the evaluation of the next stage. It is also important at any stage to note the corresponding optimal decisions, so that the complete optimal policy may be identified

FIGURE 28-2
Evaluation of stage 4 for the stagecoach problem.

STAGE 4

Possible Choices

s	j	$c_{sj} + f_5(j)$		Minimum $= f_4(s)$	Optimal Decision
		13	14		
Entering State	9	$16	—	$16	to state 13
	10	17	$16	16	to state 14
	11	—	17	17	to state 14
	12	—	18	18	to state 14

once the procedure is finished. Usually, this can all be accomplished by constructing a table for each of the earlier stages. The cost function for each possible entering state for stage 4 is computed and recorded for later use in Figure 28-2. The final column indicates the optimal decision for each starting state.

Our evaluation of stage 4 is completed by considering the other two possible starting states, which have minimum costs to the journey's end of

$$f_4(11) = \$7 + \$10 = \$17 \quad \text{(to state 14)}$$
$$f_4(12) = \$8 + \$10 = \$18 \quad \text{(to state 14)}$$

The evaluations of stages 3, 2, and 1 are similar. The results are provided in Figure 28-3.

FIGURE 28-3
Evaluations of earlier stages for the stagecoach problem.

STAGE 3

Possible Choices

	j	$c_{sj} + f_4(j)$					
s		9	10	11	12	Minimum $= f_3(s)$	Optimal Decision
Entering State	5	$20	$21	—	—	$20	to state 9
	6	21	20	$23	—	20	to state 10
	7	—	21	21	$23	21	to state 10 or 11
	8	—	—	23	23	23	to state 11 or 12

STAGE 2

Possible Choices

	j	$c_{sj} + f_3(j)$					
s		5	6	7	8	Minimum $= f_2(s)$	Optimal Decision
Entering State	2	$24	$25	$27	—	$24	to state 5
	3	—	25	27	$27	25	to state 6
	4	—	—	24	27	24	to state 7

STAGE 1

Possible Choices

	j	$c_{sj} + f_2(j)$				
s		2	3	4	Minimum $= f_1(s)$	Optimal Decision
Entering State	1	$26	$28	$27	$26	to state 2

We see that stage 1 involves a minimum cost of $26 if Tom Wysaker's first choice is the optimal one of proceeding to state 2 on his first stagecoach trip. By following the optimal policy, the first leg of Tom's journey will take him from state 1 to state 2, where he will catch the second stagecoach. The evaluation of stage 2 indicates that Tom's optimal decision on leaving state 2 is to go to state 5. Taking the stagecoach on that line will bring Tom to the third leg of his trip. The evaluation of stage 3 indicates that Tom will minimize his overall life insurance cost by proceeding from state 5 to state 9. Figure 28-2 indicates that stage 4 proceeds from there to state 13 at the minimum cost for the remainder of the journey. The fifth stagecoach may then be taken from state 13 to Tom's final destination, state 15 (California).

This optimal policy is expressed by the sequence of states 1-2-5-9-13-15. It is easy to verify from Figure 28-1 that the total cost for a life insurance policy over this route is indeed $26 (the sum of the costs on the corresponding arrows).

Alternative Solution Approaches

To the uninitiated, this procedure may seem overly elaborate. After all, there are only 27 possible routes (which may be verified by counting). Wouldn't it be simpler just to sum the costs along each route and then select the lowest one?

This naive approach might actually be a simpler way to solve a small problem. But imagine trying to evaluate a similar route-selection situation involving 10 stages, each having 10 states, which could result in $10^{10} = 10$ billion separate policies. The complete

FIGURE 28-4
A graphical network analysis of the stagecoach problem.

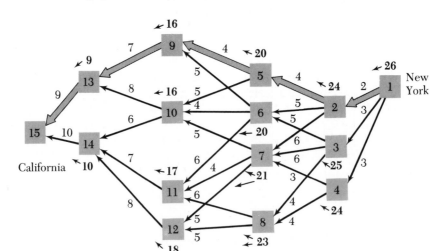

Optimal Policy: 1-2-5-9-13

enumeration of all of these policies would involve about 100 million times as many evaluations as dynamic programming.

But can't dynamic programming be applied without employing all the elaborate mathematics? Yes, sometimes this is convenient, depending on the structure of the problem. For instance, the required bookkeeping could be kept on the routing network itself by writing above each node the smallest cost expended to reach the destination from that state and somehow flagging the corresponding decision.

Figure 28-4 illustrates such a graphical *network analysis* of the stagecoach problem (which has been evaluated in a similar manner to the backward pass through a PERT network). The boldface numbers are the minimum policy costs for the remaining portion of the stagecoach trip. They are identical to the cost function values given in the earlier mathematical evaluation and were found in essentially the same way; working from left to right, the next boldface number is the smallest sum of the preceding one plus the policy cost between the two states. The little arrows indicate the optimal choice for each state by pointing in the direction in which the minimum cost was obtained. Starting in New York, these flag arrows indicate the optimal policy for the stagecoach journey.

For many small problems, a graphical approach may require the least amount of work to determine the solution. But a graphical analysis is not always possible due to either the sheer size or the complex nature of a problem.

Another approach to solving problems of modest size is to perform a **decision tree analysis**. Figure 28-5 provides the decision tree diagram for the stagecoach problem. Each box on the tree represents a decision point, and each possible choice is designated by a separate branch. There may be several possible decision points at each stage, depending on the choices made in earlier stages; all decision points at a common stage are aligned vertically. There are two numbers on each branch: the identity of the chosen state and (in parentheses) the policy cost of that particular leg of the journey. For instance, stage 1 departures from state 1 leave for states 2, 3, or 4. The costs of these legs are shown on the first three branches as (2), (3), and (3). Each possible policy is represented by a path, or sequence of branches, through the tree. Altogether, there are 27 such paths.

The analysis is performed through a process of **backward induction** similar to the one we used in Chapter 21. The process begins with the decision points in stage 5. The respective policy costs from a particular stage to the end of the journey are represented by the boldface numbers above the boxes. These values are found by adding the succeeding boldface value and the cost on the connecting branch. The minimum sum is then entered above the box for the decision point being evaluated. All branches with greater sums correspond to inferior choices and are pruned from the tree. The optimal solution is represented by the sequence of unpruned branches. Again, we see that the path 1-2-5-9-13-15 represents the optimal policy, at a cost of $26.

Like network analysis, decision tree analysis involves essentially the same steps as the mathematical procedure. The cost function values of $f_n(s)$ are the boldface numbers in Figures 28-4 and 28-5. Although we avoid expressing the underlying recursive relationship mathematically, it is still present regardless of how a dynamic programming problem is solved. Large problems may require an elaborate set of calculations and may best be solved with a computer. The tabular arrangement used in Figures 28-2 and 28-3 lends itself to computer applications.

FIGURE 28-5
A decision tree analysis of the stagecoach problem.

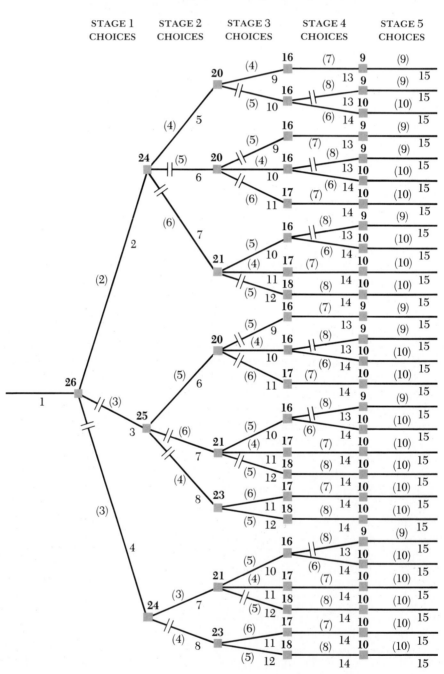

28-2 Types of Dynamic Programs

Dynamic programs exist in a variety of forms. The formulation of each problem is unique, but all problems are similar to the stagecoach problem in that only one stage needs to be evaluated at a time. The principle of optimality guarantees that the optimal policy will be found eventually after evaluating all possible entering states for each stage. Dynamic programs fall into several categories.

One classification is in terms of the problem objective and the corresponding recursive relationship. In the stagecoach problem, the objective is to minimize cost, and the cost function for a stage is obtained by adding the cost of a journey leg to the cost function value of the succeeding stage and selecting the minimum sum. In the next section, we will consider the objective of maximizing payoff, so that payoffs are added together and the greatest sum constitutes the value of the payoff function. A later example involves a problem in which the reliability of a system is maximized by finding the smallest failure probability; each evaluation involves the *product* of failure probabilities.

It is possible to treat a variety of constraints in a dynamic programming problem. The knapsack problem, described in the next section, involves choosing various items in amounts such that their collective weight does not exceed a specific limit. When several constraints exist, a multidimensional formulation exists. Advanced dynamic programming techniques allow such problems to be solved by a one-dimensional procedure.

All of the problems considered in this chapter fall into the discrete category, since the possible choices and states are limited to a finite number of values. It is possible to extend dynamic programming principles to analyze problems involving continuous variables, so that the number of states or variable values can be infinite. Another important dichotomy is deterministic (no uncertainty) versus stochastic problems. Stochastic problems deal with uncertainty about the state that will result from a particular choice and are analyzed by dynamic programming in a manner similar to decision tree analysis.

Unlike linear programming, this solution procedure is difficult to summarize in a concise way that will tell us how to solve all of the problems that are represented as dynamic programs. Each case is different. Our discussion of dynamic programming of necessity must be limited to a few examples. By studying them, we learn how dynamic programming may be applied to other situations.

28-3 Maximizing Payoff: A Knapsack Problem

Our second example of dynamic programming involves deciding how many items of various types should be transported via a method with limited carrying capacity. Each item consumes a portion of this capacity and will yield a specific unit payoff when unloaded at the destination.

In our illustration, a smuggler is faced with the dilemma of determining which of the various items listed in Table 28-1—and how many of each—to carry in a knapsack. The smuggler plans a cross-country ski trip into Transylvania, where possession of these items is either forbidden or incurs large import duties. Past experience shows that a maximum of

TABLE 28-1
Items for the Smuggler's Knapsack

TYPE OF CONTRABAND ITEM	PAYOFF	WEIGHT
n	v_n	w_n
(1) Bundle of cigars	$104	2 lbs
(2) Gold ingot	42	1
(3) Bundle of ermine pelts	212	4
(4) Jug of perfume	270	5
(5) Radio transmitter	165	3

10 pounds of contraband may safely be carried on any trip. The weight of each item and the payoff on reaching Transylvania are also given in Table 28-1.

This example falls into the broad category of the **knapsack problem**.

Formulation of the Problem

The smuggler's problem is to select numbers of the various items to carry in such a way that total payoff will be maximized. We let

$$x_n = \text{Number of items of type } n \text{ to carry}$$
$$N = \text{Number of item types considered}$$
$$v_n = \text{Payoff of one type } n \text{ item}$$
$$w_n = \text{Weight of one type } n \text{ item}$$
$$W = \text{Total weight limitation}$$

The products $v_n x_n$ and $w_n x_n$ express the payoff and weight, respectively, for carrying x_n items of type n. The sum of these terms over all item types will provide the total payoff and weight. Thus, the objective is to find the values of x_n that

$$\text{Maximize} \sum_{n=1}^{N} v_n x_n$$

$$\text{Subject to} \sum_{n=1}^{N} w_n x_n \leq W$$

where x_n may be any integer between zero and the largest amount of item n that does not exceed the total weight limitation. In our illustration, $N = 5$ and $W = 10$ pounds.

Suppose that the smuggler tries to solve this problem without using dynamic programming. One approach is to identify the item type with the greatest return per pound, which happens to be item (5), radio transmitters, at $55 per pound. The smuggler can pack the greatest possible number of transmitters without exceeding the 10-pound limit. Since each transmitter weighs 3 pounds, the smuggler can pack 3 of them and 1 pound will still remain to be filled. All other items, with the exception of a single gold ingot, are too heavy to take up the remaining knapsack capacity. Thus, the smuggler may carry $x_5 = 3$ transmitters and $x_2 = 1$ gold ingot. The total payoff for this policy would be $537. As we will see, the smuggler can actually improve the value of the items in the knapsack through a systematic evaluation.

The Dynamic Programming Solution

This problem may be solved as a dynamic program in a similar manner to the way in which we solved the stagecoach problem. A straightforward approach is to determine the number of items of each type by selecting them one at a time. We may treat each item type as a separate stage in which a decision must be made about the number of items to be included in the smuggler's knapsack. It is convenient to use the unassigned knapsack capacity as the starting state for each stage. As in the stagecoach analysis, we will begin our evaluation by working backward from item 5.

Analogous to the function in the stagecoach problem, the payoff function $f_n(s)$ will represent the payoff when starting in state s and using the optimal policy from stage n to the end. In other words, when s pounds remain in the knapsack for the inclusion of item of type n and beyond, $f_n(s)$ represents that portion of the total payoff obtained just from these items.

The payoff function for stage 5, representing the possible payoffs in radio transmitters, is expressed by

$$f_5(s) = \text{Maximum } v_5 x_5$$

where

$$w_5 x_5 \leq s$$

Thus, $f_5(s)$ is the maximum possible payoff for the number of radio transmitters packed. That quantity is x_5, which cannot exceed the unassigned weight capacity of s pounds. The payoff value and the corresponding optimal decision for each possible state are listed in Figure 28-6. Notice that x_5 can assume a value of at most 3, but that a smaller maximum level may apply, depending on the remaining knapsack capacity level s. At this stage, $v_5 = 165$ and the maximum level of s is 10.

The recursive relationship for this problem is

$$f_n(s) = \text{maximum } [v_n x_n + f_{n+1}(s - w_n x_n)]$$

The quantity x_n represents the amount of item n placed in the knapsack. This amount will add $v_n x_n$ to the total payoff and will take up $w_n x_n$ pounds of the weight remaining for assignment to later items. The payoff for the optimal policy from the later stage corresponds to this remaining capacity state in the amount of $s - w_n x_n$ pounds. Thus, x_n must be chosen to maximize the sum of the present item type payoff and the payoff function values for all future items.

Figure 28-7 shows the payoff function values for the various stages. To see how these values were obtained, consider stage 4, where $s = 8$. This indicates that there are 8 pounds

FIGURE 28-6

Last-stage evaluation for the number of radio transmitters for the knapsack problem.

STAGE 5

Possible Choices

	x_5		$165x_5$				
s	0	1	2	3	Maximum $= f_5(s)$	Optimal Decision
0	$0	—	--	—	$ 0	$x_5 = 0$
1	0	—	—	—	0	$x_5 = 0$
2	0	—	—	—	0	$x_5 = 0$
3	0	$165	—	—	165	$x_5 = 1$
4	0	165	—	—	165	$x_5 = 1$
5	0	165	—	—	165	$x_5 = 1$
→6	0	165	$330	—	330	$x_5 = 2^*$
7	0	165	330	—	330	$x_5 = 2$
8	0	165	330	—	330	$x_5 = 2$
9	0	165	330	$495	495	$x_5 = 3$
10	0	165	330	495	495	$x_5 = 3$

Entering State (rows 0, 1 labeled)

FIGURE 28-7

Evaluations of earlier stages for the knapsack problem.

STAGE 4

Possible Choices

	x_4		$270x_4 + f_5(s - 5x_4)$				
s	0	1	2	Maximum $= f_4(s)$	Optimal Decision
0	$ 0	—	—	$ 0	$x_4 = 0$
1	0	—	—	0	$x_4 = 0$
2	0	—	—	0	$x_4 = 0$
3	165	—	—	165	$x_4 = 0$
4	165	—	—	165	$x_4 = 0$
5	165	$270	—	270	$x_4 = 1$
→6	330	270	—	330	$x_4 = 0^*$
7	330	270	—	330	$x_4 = 0$
8	330	435	—	435	$x_4 = 1$
9	495	435	—	495	$x_4 = 0$
10	495	435	$540	540	$x_4 = 2$

Entering State (rows 0, 1 labeled)

FIGURE 28-7 (continued).

STAGE 3

Possible Choices

x_3	$212x_3 + f_4(s - 4x_3)$			Maximum $= f_3(s)$	Optimal Decision
s	0	1	2		
Entering 0	$ 0	—	—	$ 0	$x_3 = 0$
State 1	0	—	—	0	$x_3 = 0$
2	0	—	—	0	$\dot{x}_3 = 0$
3	165	—	—	165	$x_3 = 0$
4	165	$212	—	212	$x_3 = 1$
5	270	212	—	270	$x_3 = 0$
6	330	212	—	330	$x_3 = 0$
7	330	377	—	377	$x_3 = 1$
8	435	377	$424	435	$x_3 = 0$
9	495	482	424	495	$x_3 = 0$
→10	540	542	424	542	$x_3 = 1^*$

STAGE 2

Possible Choices

x_2	$42x_2 + f_3(s - 1x_2)$											Maximum $= f_2(s)$	Optimal Decision
s	0	1	2	3	4	5	6	7	8	9	10		
Entering 0	$ 0	—	—	—	—	—	—	—	—	—	—	$ 0	$x_2 = 0$
State 1	0	$ 42	—	—	—	—	—	—	—	—	—	42	$x_2 = 1$
2	0	42	$ 84	—	—	—	—	—	—	—	—	84	$x_2 = 2$
3	165	42	84	$126	—	—	—	—	—	—	—	165	$x_2 = 0$
4	212	207	84	126	$168	—	—	—	—	—	—	212	$x_2 = 0$
5	270	254	249	126	168	$210	—	—	—	—	—	270	$x_2 = 0$
6	330	312	296	291	168	210	$252	—	—	—	—	330	$x_2 = 0$
7	377	372	354	338	333	210	252	$294	—	—	—	377	$x_2 = 0$
8	435	419	414	396	380	375	252	294	$336	—	—	435	$x_2 = 0$
9	495	477	461	456	438	422	417	294	336	$378	—	495	$x_2 = 0$
→10	542	537	519	503	498	480	464	459	336	378	$420	542	$x_2 = 0^*$

STAGE 1

Possible Choices

x_1	$104x_1 + f_2(s - 2x_1)$						Maximum $= f_1(s)$	Optimal Decision
s	0	1	2	3	4	5		
Entering 10	$542	$539	$538	$524	$500	$520	$542	$x_1 = 0^*$
State								

of unfilled capacity at the start of stage 4, where the number of perfume jugs to include must be decided. The given values $v_4 = \$270$ and $w_4 = 5$ pounds apply to this item.

Suppose that no jug of perfume is packed, so that $x_4 = 0$. This leaves $8 - 0 = 8$ pounds for stage 5, radio transmitters. Figure 28-6 indicates a payoff of $f_5(8) = \$330$ when 8 pounds remain at that stage. The applicable payoff at stage 4 when $s = 8$ and $x_4 = 0$ is

$$v_4 x_4 + f_5(8 - w_4 x_4) = 270 x_4 + f_5(8 - 5 x_4)$$

$$= 0 + f_5(8) = \$330 \quad \text{(when } x_4 = 0)$$

Now suppose that $x_4 = 1$ jug of perfume is packed. This leaves $8 - 5(1) = 3$ pounds of remaining knapsack capacity and, from Figure 28-6, $f_5(3) = \$165$. Thus,

$$270 x_4 + f_5(8 - 5 x_4) = \$270(1) + f_5(3)$$

$$= \$270 + \$165 = \$435 \quad \text{(when } x_4 = 1)$$

We do not consider the case when $x_5 = 2$ jugs are placed in the knapsack. This amount is infeasible, since it would take up more than the available 8 pounds.

The payoff function at stage 4 when $s = 8$ pounds is the maximum of these two amounts, or

$$f_4(8) = \text{Maximum } [\$330, \$435] = \$435 \quad \text{(when } x_4 = 1)$$

The optimal decision on reaching state $s = 8$ in stage 4 is to pack $x_4 = 1$ jug of perfume. The same procedure applies for other levels of s.

Similar evaluations were made successively at each of the earlier stages, as shown in Figure 28-7. The last evaluation is for stage 1, where the maximum possible payoff is found to be

$$f_1(10) = \$542 \quad \text{(when } x_1 = 0)$$

(Only one state, $s = 10$, is considered for this stage, since the problem begins with an empty knapsack.)

This amount corresponds to the following optimal policy.

$$x_1 = 0 \quad \text{(bundle of cigars)}$$
$$x_2 = 0 \quad \text{(gold ingot)}$$
$$x_3 = 1 \quad \text{(bundle of ermine pelts)}$$
$$x_4 = 0 \quad \text{(jug of perfume)}$$
$$x_5 = 2 \quad \text{(radio transmitters)}$$

This optimal policy was found by tracing back through the evaluation tables. The results of this procedure are shown in Figures 28-6 and 28-7, by the arrow for the entering state and the asterisk for the optimal item amount. Starting in stage 1, we see that $x_1 = 0$

is the optimal decision, so no cigars are packed. This leaves 10 pounds for the second item type, so that $s = 10$ is the starting state for stage 2. There, the optimal decision is $x_2 = 0$, and no gold ingots are packed. Thus, 10 pounds remain for the third item type, and the $s = 10$ row for the stage-3 evaluation leads to the optimal choice of $x_3 = 1$ bundle of ermine pelts. Since each bundle weighs 4 pounds, only 6 pounds of knapsack capacity remain. Reading across the $s = 6$ row in the stage-4 evaluation, we see that $x_4 = 0$ jug of perfume is the optimal choice, so that 6 pounds of knapsack capacity still remain. Finally, we proceed to the stage-5 evaluation in Figure 28-6 where the $s = 6$ row indicates the optimal choice of $x_5 = 2$ radio transmitters.

Applications of the Knapsack Problem

The knapsack problem may be expanded to consider additional constraints. Thus, it might be applied to a variety of cargo-loading problems, where the volume of the items must be considered in addition to their weight. The same concepts could be extended to a multiproduct inventory decision involving floor space or budgetary restrictions. The problem of provisioning space parts to inaccessible places—for, say, oil exploration in Alaska or scientific expeditions in the Antarctic—is structured similarly to the smuggler's knapsack problem.

The knapsack problem has even been used to analyze capital budgeting decisions. For each alternative project, the projected rate of return on invested capital usually constitutes the payoff measure. Since the actual return is generally subject to chance, the variation in possible returns provides a measure of risk. The objective in solving this type of problem is to select projects in such a way that the total return is maximized without exceeding tolerable limits on risk while remaining within the overall budget.

When several constraints are involved in a knapsack-type problem, special mathematical difficulties arise. A discussion of these difficulties is beyond the scope of this book. The detailed solutions to more advanced dynamic programming problems are provided in many of the references listed in the bibliography at the back of the book.

28-4 Maximizing a System Reliability

Many important problems in the area of reliability may be solved using a variety of quantitative methods. Consider the decisions faced by the designers of an interplanetary space probe with a variety of component systems (guidance, propulsion, television, reception, transmission, and so on). Unless all systems function throughout the entire mission, it will be a complete failure. Various components must be carefully designed to satisfy overall payload constraints and still be capable of surviving in a hostile space environment. One interesting question concerns the power supply for the various system components.

Suppose that a particular probe is designed to carry exactly five power cells, each of which must be located physically within one of three electronic systems. If one system's power should fail, it will be powered on an auxiliary basis by the cells of the remaining systems. The probability that any particular system will experience a power failure depends on the number of cells originally assigned to it. Table 28-2 provides the estimated power-failure probabilities for a particular space probe.

Since almost any power failure would result from environmental factors rather than excessive use, any overloading effect on a cell due to auxiliary use may be ignored. The failure events for the respective systems may therefore be treated as if they were independent.

The design engineers must determine how many power cells should be assigned to each system to maximize overall system reliability. This may be accomplished by minimizing the probability that all systems will suffer a power failure.

The Dynamic Program

The dynamic programming formulation begins with the specification of the states and stages. We may view each decision about the number of power cells for a system as a stage. The number of power cells chosen for one system limits the amount of cells available for the next system, so that the entering state s for a particular stage must be the number of cells as yet unassigned. The decision variables may be expressed as x_1, x_2, and x_3 and represent the number of cells assigned at the respective stage to the corresponding system. It is convenient to denote the probability for a power failure in the nth system, or stage, symbolically in terms of the corresponding variable by $p_n(x_n)$.

Because system failures are independent, the multiplication law tells us that the product of these individual probabilities provides the probability that all systems will suffer a power failure. The problem is therefore to find the variable values that

$$\text{Minimize} \quad p_1(x_1)p_2(x_2)p_3(x_3)$$
$$\text{Subject to} \quad x_1 + x_2 + x_3 = 5$$
$$\text{where} \quad x_1, x_2, x_3 \geq 1$$

The constraint indicates that all five power cells must be assigned. No system may operate on auxiliary power at the outset, so that variable values of zero are impossible.

TABLE 28-2
Power-Failure Probabilities for a Space Probe System

NUMBER OF POWER CELLS	PROBABILITY OF SYSTEM POWER FAILURE		
	System 1	System 2	System 3
1	.50	.60	.40
2	.15	.20	.25
3	.04	.10	.10
4	.02	.05	.05
5	.01	.02	.01

The function $f_n(s)$ for this problem expresses the smallest probability, entering with state s, that the nth and all higher systems will fail. In the case of system 3,

$$f_3(s) = \text{minimum } p_3(x_3)$$

is the starting state, and the recursive relationship is

$$f_n(s) = \text{minimum } [p_n(x_n)f_{n+1}(s - x_n)]$$

Solving the Dynamic Program

The evaluations of the reliability problem are provided in Figure 28-8. Notice that stage 3 cannot be entered from states $s = 4$ or $s = 5$, since at least one power cell a piece

FIGURE 28-8
Evaluations of the reliability problem.

STAGE 3

Possible Choices

x_3		$p_3(x_3)$				
s	1	2	3	Minimum $= f_3(s)$	Optimal Decision
Entering →1	.40	—	—	.40	$x_3 = 1^*$
State 2	.40	.25	—	.25	$x_3 = 2$
3	.40	.25	.10	.10	$x_3 = 3$

STAGE 2

Possible Choices

x_2		$p_2(x_2)f_3(s - x_2)$				
s	1	2	3	Minimum $= f_2(s)$	Optimal Decision
Entering →2	.24	—	—	.24	$x_2 = 1^*$
State 3	:15	.08	—	.08	$x_2 = 2$
4	.06	.05	.04	.04	$x_2 = 3$

STAGE 1

Possible Choices

x_1		$p_1(x_1)f_2(s - x_1)$				
s	1	2	3	Minimum $= f_1(s)$	Optimal Decision
Entering 5	.02	.012	.0096	.0096	$x_1 = 3^*$
State					

must be assigned in stage 1 and in stage 2. Likewise, the minimum cell requirements for each system do not permit stage 2 to be entered from states $s = 1$ or $s = 5$. Thus, no more than three cells may be assigned in any stage.

The stage-3 function values are obtained directly from the given data. It may be helpful to illustrate how the values are obtained for stage 2. Consider entering stage 2 with $s = 4$ power cells to be assigned. If $x_2 = 1$ power cell is assigned to system 2, then $s - x_2 = 4 - 1 = 3$ cells will be available for system 3. The failure probability for systems 2 and 3 combined will then be

$$p_2(x_2)f_3(s - x_2) = p_2(1)f_3(3)$$

$$= .60(.10) = .06 \quad \text{(when } x_2 = 1\text{)}$$

since $p_2(1) = .60$ is the given failure probability for system 2 when only one cell is assigned to it. Likewise, when $x_2 = 2$, the failure probability is

$$p_2(x_2)f_3(s - x_2) = p_2(2)f_3(2)$$

$$= .20(.25) = .05 \quad \text{(when } x_2 = 2\text{)}$$

and when $x_2 = 3$, the failure probability is

$$p_2(x_2)f_3(s - x_2) = p_2(3)f_3(1)$$

$$= .10(.40) = .04 \quad \text{(when } x_2 = 3\text{)}$$

The minimum failure probability for systems 2 and 3, when stage 2 is entered with $s = 4$, is therefore

$$f_2(4) = \text{Minimum } (.06, .05, .04) = .04 \quad \text{(when } x_2 = 3\text{)}$$

The values of $f_2(s)$ when $s = 2$ or $s = 3$ are calculated in a similar manner.

Notice that stage 1 has only one entering state of $s = 5$, since all of the cells are yet to be assigned when system 1 is considered.

We see that $f_1(5) = .0096$ is the smallest probability for total power failure. The corresponding optimal policy is to make the following power cell assignments.

$$x_1 = 3 \text{ to system 1}$$

$$x_2 = 1 \text{ to system 2}$$

$$x_3 = 1 \text{ to system 3}$$

28-5 Optimizing Multi-Period Inventories and Production

In Chapter 14, we solved a problem about production and inventory decisions regarding skis made in a Juarez plant and sold from a Phoenix warehouse. That particular problem was expressed as a linear program and solved by using the transportation method.

TABLE 28-3
Demands for Pairs of Skis

MONTH	DEMAND
n	d_n
(1) August	100
(2) September	200
(3) October	300
(4) November	400

Recall that linear programs require that all underlying relationships be expressed mathematically by straight lines or planes in higher dimensions. We will now reconsider the ski manufacturing and distribution problem in a more general form, so that a linear programming formulation no longer applies. This new problem will be solved as a dynamic programming problem.

Table 28-3 provides the monthly demands d_n for skis during the winter season. Virtually all direct labor is casual and temporary, so that any number of skis up to the plant capacity of 400 pairs may be produced each month. The direct labor cost is $40 per pair. The Juarez plant is completely shut down during months when there is no production, and supervisory personnel are given an unpaid holiday to save a further $2,000 in monthly payroll costs. Demands may be filled either from current production or from inventory. Each ski held in inventory at the beginning of the month costs the company $5. Our problem is to determine the monthly production levels $x_1, x_2, x_3,$ and x_4 in such a way that total cost is minimized. The production quantities may be 0, 100, 200, 300, or 400 pairs. Each month is a separate problem stage with some beginning inventory level as its entering state. Stage 1 (August) has a beginning inventory level of $s = 0$. Since no skis can be saved until the next season, stage 4 (November) must end with zero inventory.

The Dynamic Program

The combined monthly production and inventory cost for the ski manufacturer depends on the beginning inventory s and on the production quantity x_n. This cost may be determined from

$$c(s, x_n) = \begin{cases} 5s + 2{,}000 + 40x_n & \text{if } x_n > 0 \\ 5s & \text{if } x_n = 0 \end{cases}$$

Regardless of the production level, there will be an inventory cost of $5s$ dollars. Since $2,000 in supervisory costs are incurred only for nonzero production levels, two separate cost expressions apply, depending on whether or not $x_n = 0$.

Because the fixed supervisory cost is incurred for only some of the possible variable values, a linear program cannot be used to solve this problem.* The dynamic

---

* Our illustration could actually be formulated as an *integer program* involving a set of variables assigned a value of either zero or 1 to represent the presence or absence of the fixed monthly supervisory cost.

programming procedure applies when the variable cost of making skis changes with the level of production; in this case, a nonlinear relationship exists between costs and quantities.

In any given month, the beginning inventory plus the production level determines how many units are available to satisfy that month's demand. All demands must be met. A month's ending inventory serves as the beginning inventory for the next month and is the sum of the available quantities minus the demand. Beginning with s pairs of skis, the number of pairs on hand at the end of the month n is

$$s + x_n - d_n$$

which is also the beginning inventory for month $n + 1$.

The last month must end with no inventory, so that

$$s + x_4 - d_4 = 0$$

or

$$x_4 = d_4 - s$$

where s is that month's beginning inventory. Since $d_4 = 400$ and x_4 may fall anywhere between 0 and 400, then s may equal 0, 100, 200, 300 or 400 when $n = 4$.

The cost function $f_n(s)$ represents the minimum remaining cost of entering from state s and following an optimal policy from stage n to the end. For the last stage,

$$f_4(s) = c(s, x_4) = c(s, d_4 - s)$$

so that when $s = d_4 = 400$ (so that $x_4 = 0$)

$$f_4(400) = 5(400) = \$2{,}000$$

If s is less than $d_4 = 400$, then the cost function is

$$f_4(s) = 5s + 2{,}000 + 40(400 - s)$$

For instance, when $s = 300$

$$f_4(300) = 5(300) + 2{,}000 + 40(400 - 300)$$
$$= 1{,}500 + 2{,}000 + 4{,}000$$
$$= \$7{,}500$$

which corresponds to a production level of $x_4 = 100$ units.

The recursive relationship is

$$f_n(s) = \text{minimum } [c(s, x_n) + f_{n+1}(s + x_n - d_n)]$$

FIGURE 28-9
Evaluations of the ski manufacturing problem.

STAGE 4

	s	$f_4(s)$	Optimal Choice
Entering	→0	$18,000	$x_4 = 400$*
State	100	14,500	$x_4 = 300$
	200	11,000	$x_4 = 200$
	300	7,500	$x_4 = 100$
	400	2,000	$x_4 = 0$

STAGE 3

Possible Choices

		\multicolumn{5}{c}{$c(s, x_3) + f_4(s + x_3 - 300)$}	Minimum	Optimal
	x_3						$= f_3(s)$	Choice
	s	0	100	200	300	400		
Entering	→0	—	—	—	$32,000	$32,500	$32,000	$x_3 = 300$*
State	100	—	—	$28,500	29,000	29,500	28,500	$x_3 = 200$
	200	—	$25,000	25,500	26,000	26,500	25,000	$x_3 = 100$
	300	$19,500	22,000	22,500	23,000	21,500	19,500	$x_3 = 0$
	400	16,500	19,000	19,500	18,000	—	16,500	$x_3 = 0$
	500	13,500	16,000	14,500	—	—	13,500	$x_3 = 0$

STAGE 2

Possible Choices

		\multicolumn{5}{c}{$c(s, x_2) + f_3(s + x_2 - 200)$}	Minimum	Optimal
	x_2						$= f_2(s)$	Choice
	s	0	100	200	300	400		
Entering	0	—	—	$42,000	$42,500	$43,000	$42,000	$x_2 = 200$
State	100	—	$38,500	39,000	39,500	38,000	38,000	$x_2 = 400$
	→200	$33,000	35,500	36,000	34,500	35,500	33,000	$x_2 = 0$*
	300	30,000	32,500	31,000	32,000	33,000	30,000	$x_2 = 0$

STAGE 1

Possible Choices

		\multicolumn{5}{c}{$c(s, x_1) + f_2(s + x_1 - 100)$}	Minimum	Optimal
	x_1						$= f_1(s)$	Choice
	s	0	100	200	300	400		
Entering	0	—	$48,000	$48,000	$47,000	$48,000	$47,000	$x_1 = 300$*
State								

which represents the smallest sum of the month n cost and the minimum cost for beginning month $n + 1$ with a starting inventory of $s + x_n - d_n$.

Solving the Dynamic Program

Figure 28-9 provides the evaluations of the four stages for this problem. Notice that in stage 3, the production level plus the starting inventory must be at least the 300 units demanded in the third month, so that x_3 must be at least 300 when $s = 0$ and 200 when $s = 100$. Also, no more than 400 units may be carried over to stage 4, so that x_3 cannot exceed 300 when $s = 400$ and 200 when $s = 500$. The maximum inventory level for entering stage 3 is $s = 500$, which reflects the maximum possible production of 400 each in stages 1 and 2, less the demands of 100 and 200 pairs for those months. Similar restrictions apply at stage 2, where $s = 300$ is the largest possible beginning inventory.

The value of the cost function for stage 1, $f_1(0) = \$47,000$, corresponds to the following optimal policy.

$$x_1 = 300 \text{ pairs}$$
$$x_2 = \quad 0$$
$$x_3 = 300$$
$$x_4 = 400$$

Thus, the Juarez plant will have a beginning inventory only at stage 2 (September), which is exactly enough to satisfy that month's demand of 200 units. The plant should be shut down in September and should produce in the other months.

28-6 Probabilistic Dynamic Programming

The examples we have considered so far are deterministic, since they do not involve uncertainty. Dynamic programming may also be used to solve problems in which the state resulting from a particular choice is uncertain. This uncertainty is expressed in terms of the probabilities that a particular state will occur. In Chapter 21, we saw that the usual decision criterion for making choices under uncertainty is the Bayes decision rule. Whether this leads to *maximizing* expected payoff or *minimizing* expected cost, the principle of optimality still applies, and a stage-by-stage evaluation of the decision as a dynamic programming problem will lead to the optimal policy. The procedure is very similar to the backward induction used in decision tree analysis that we encountered in earlier chapters. Further discussion of this topic is beyond the scope of this book, but additional information may be obtained from many of the references listed in the bibliography in the back of the book.

28-7 Advantages and Use of Computers

Dynamic programming is a very useful quantitative method that may be applied to a wide variety of multi-stage decision problems occurring over time or when choices may be made sequentially. At times, it can serve as an alternative to linear programming, although dynamic programming may also be used to solve integer and nonlinear programming problems. Situations suited to this procedure are similar in structure from stage to stage, so that a single recursive relationship holds for all stages. The principle of optimality indicates that the optimal policy may be found by evaluating a stage at a time and finding the best choice for every possible starting state.

The main advantage of dynamic programming is its computational efficiency. The procedure is often used in conjunction with a digital computer, and the simple mathematical formulation and tabular arrangement make it especially easy to write a computer program for conducting individual evaluations. Even when dynamic programming problems are moderately large, a computer solution is desirable—if only to eliminate computational errors, which magnify in impact as the earlier stages are reached.

Certain dynamic programming problems share a common form, so that it would be unnecessary to write special computer programs to solve them. The *QuickQuant* software package available to users of this textbook will solve stagecoach, knapsack, and inventory problems. Once you supply the requested parameter values, the program will find the optimal policy. Special instructions for using *QuickQuant* are included in the Appendix of this textbook. Figure 28-10 shows the *QuickQuant* report obtained for the smuggler's knapsack problem.

FIGURE 28-10

***QuickQuant* report showing the computer solution to the smuggler's knapsack problem.**

```
==============================================================================
                            QuickQuant Report
              DYNAMIC PROGRAMMING EVALUATION--KNAPSACK PROBLEM
------------------------------------------------------------------------------
PROBLEM: Smuggler's Knapsack                          Date: 03-03-1990
                                                                Larry


                         PROBLEM PARAMETERS

                      Number of Items = 5
                      Available Capacity = 10

                   SOLUTION TO KNAPSACK PROBLEM

                   Optimal Policy--Payoff = 542

         Item        Value        Weight        Quantity
          n           vn            wn             xn
         ------------------------------------------------
          1          104.00          2             0
          2           42.00          1             0
          3          212.00          4             1
          4          270.00          5             0
          5          165.00          3             2

------------------------------------------------------------------------------
```

CASE

Partnership Limiters

Partnership Limiters is an investment service which places its clients in a variety of limited partnership investments. Each investment package comprises a grouping of investments of approximately the same duration and degree of risk. The following is a listing of one set of comparable limited partnership investments.

LIMITED PARTNERSHIP	SIZE OF INVESTMENT UNITS	EXPECTED NET PRESENT VALUE
(1) Business Park	$50,000	$84,000
(2) High Towers	20,000	35,000
(3) Computer Rental	15,000	27,000
(4) Mobile Home Sites	10,000	30,000
(5) Crossroads Mall	9,000	17,000
(6) Kaanapoli	8,000	21,000
(7) Dune Lagoon	6,000	14,000
(8) Boxcars	5,000	13,000
(9) Movie Package	4,000	11,000
(10) Geopet	3,000	7,000

One client will join in several of the above partnerships. He has $110,000 to invest. Any number of units, constrained only by available funds, may be chosen from each deal. The client wants to maximize his total expected net present value.

Questions

1. Formulate the problem as a dynamic program.
2. Find, for the client, the optimal number of units of the respective partnerships to invest in.

PROBLEMS

28-1   Modify the stagecoach problem in Figure 28-1 by raising the insurance costs $2 for each journey leg beginning in an even-numbered state and reducing insurance costs $1 for each journey leg beginning in an odd-numbered state. Then, solve the modified problem in each of the following ways.
(a) network analysis
(b) decision tree analysis
(c) the standard manner, providing a separate evaluation table for each stage

28-2 The following evaluation results have been obtained for a knapsack problem involving a capacity of 10 pounds.

STATE s	STAGE 1 $f_1(s)$	x_1	STAGE 2 $f_2(s)$	x_2	STAGE 3 $f_3(s)$	x_3	STAGE 4 $f_4(s)$	x_4
0	—	—	$60	2	$26	0	$10	0
1	—	—	63	2	27	0	12	0
2	—	—	65	1	29	0	12	0
3	—	—	67	3	30	1	12	1
4	—	—	68	2	32	1	14	1
5	—	—	68	2	34	1	14	1
6	—	—	70	3	36	2	15	1
7	—	—	72	4	38	1	16	1
8	—	—	73	3	40	2	17	2
9	—	—	73	4	41	3	18	2
10	$100	2	75	4	41	3	20	2

Items 1 and 2 weigh 1 pound each, item 3 weighs 2 pounds, and item 4 weighs 3 pounds. Find the optimal policy. How many pounds will be carried in the knapsack?

28-3 Suppose that we modify the problem in Section 28-3 slightly, so that the smuggler's knapsack can carry no more than 9 pounds.
(a) Use dynamic programming procedures to find $f_1(9)$.
(b) Trace through your evaluation tables to determine the optimal policy.

28-4 Modify the ski manufacturing problem in Section 28-5 by raising September demand to 300 and reducing November demand to 300. Find the optimal production quantities for each month.

28-5 The following contraband items may be carried in a knapsack.

ITEM	PAYOFF	WEIGHT
(1) Silicon chips	$300	1 oz
(2) Eagle feathers	400	2
(3) Poppy seeds	500	3
(4) Emeralds	700	4

The contents cannot exceed 16 ounces. Determine the items and quantities to be carried.

28-6 The Ace Widget Company is planning its manufacturing operations for the next five months. The following demands apply.

January	200
February	300
March	300
April	200
May	400

Each item held in inventory from one month to the next incurs a $1 carrying charge. There are 200 unsold items remaining at the end of December. The widgets are to be redesigned for June, so that no ending inventory is desired. A maximum of 400 units may be manufactured in any given month. Total production costs are

0 units	$ 0
100 units	1,000
200 units	1,300
300 units	1,450
400 units	1,525

Determine the minimum-cost production plan.

28-7 A construction superintendent must assign additional dump trucks to various excavation sites so that total cost is minimized. Only five trucks are available. The following costs apply.

NUMBER OF TRUCKS	EXCAVATION SITE		
	1	2	3
0	$11,000	$15,000	$20,000
1	10,000	14,000	18,000
2	9,000	13,250	17,500
3	8,500	12,750	17,250
4	8,000	12,500	17,000
5	7,500	12,000	16,750

Determine the optimal number of additional trucks that should be assigned to each site.

28-8 Traveling salesman Hoppy Scott must visit five cities, making exactly one stop in each. The following airfares apply.

From \ To	A	B	C	D	E
A	—	$100	$ 60	$130	$ 70
B	$100	—	50	80	110
C	60	50	—	90	120
D	130	80	90	—	40
E	70	110	120	40	—

Hoppy must visit city A first, and may arrive in the remaining cities in any order. It does not matter in which city the trip ends.

Use dynamic programming to determine the sequence of cities that will minimize Hoppy's total airfare.

28-9 Resolve the space probe power cell assignment problem in Section 28-4, assuming that there is no longer a minimum requirement that one or more power cells must be located within each system.

28-10 Refer to the assignment of brats to daily chores in Problem 15-4 (page 477). Use dynamic programming to solve that problem so that total working time is minimized.

28-11 Fly Me Airlines must determine how many planes of various types to order for next year. The following data apply.

AIRCRAFT	MEAN PROFIT PER PASSENGER-MILE	MEAN NUMBER OF PASSENGERS CARRIED	PRICE
(1) CD-10	$.02	200	$20 million
(2) L-1111	.03	150	25
(3) B-7070	.01	100	10
(4) Tupolev 100	.02	150	15

The aircraft fleet expansion budget is $75 million. The company must spend some or all of these funds in such a way that the mean profit per 1,000-mile trip is maximized. How many planes of each type should Fly Me order?

28-12 Shirley Smart must take five final examinations. She has 60 hours of study time available, and her expected grade in each course will depend on how she allocates her time. The following data apply.

COURSE	EXPECTED GRADE FOR HOURS OF STUDY TIME			
	5	10	15	20
Accounting	C	C	B	A
Finance	B	B	B	A
Marketing	B	A	A	A
Quantitative methods	D	C	B	A
Statistics	C	C	C	B

Shirley wishes to maximize her expected total grade points. For each course, 4 points are given for an A, 3 for a B, 2 for a C, and 1 for a D. Determine how Shirley should budget her study time.

28-13 *Computer exercise.* A production planner for the Make-Wave Corp. is scheduling fabrication of Water Wheelies. In any month when there is non-zero production, there will be a fixed cost of $5,000. The per-unit variable cost is $1.50. The cost of holding items in inventory is $.25 per unit per month. Up to 10,000 units may be produced in any given month. The following monthly demands apply.

MONTH	DEMAND
January	1,000
February	2,000
March	3,000
April	5,000
May	12,000
June	17,000
July	8,000
August	4,000
September	3,000
October	2,000
November	1,000
December	1,000

(a) Determine the monthly production quantities that will minimize total Water Wheelies cost.

(b) For $1,000 per month, new equipment may be leased that will lower the per-unit variable cost to $1.00. The lease cost applies only when items are being manufactured in the current month. Determine (1) the new optimal production quantities and (2) whether Make-Wave should lease the equipment.

29

Decision Making with Markov Processes

Much decision making is concerned with establishing continuing policies for the various operational aspects of a business or organization. Business functions such as marketing, production, and finance involve uncertainties of a recurring nature. In this chapter, we describe a procedure based on the structure of these uncertainties that can sometimes help to select an operating policy.

29-1 The Markov Process

The particular situations we will consider here are broadly categorized as **Markov processes**, after the Russian mathematician who helped to pioneer modern probability theory. Several features distinguish a Markov process from more general uncertain situations. The basic process structure is best described in terms of a **system**. Examples of such systems include the marketplace for a product and its competing brands, the machinery used to manufacture that product, and the billing, credit, and collection procedures involved in converting accounts receivable from the product's sales into cash. At any given time, the respective systems may be in one of several possible **states**. In marketing applications, these states may be expressed in terms of the brand that a customer is presently using. In production, that state of concern may be the number of machines in working order. A customer's financial transaction can fall into one of the following states: cash sale, credit sale, or uncollectable funds.

The Characteristics of a Markov Process

The main distinguishing feature of a Markov process is that is is concerned with the *probabilities* for being in various states at any given time and for moving from one state to another. A Markov process essentially has no memory, so that the probability for moving from one state to another state does not depend on previous occurrences. This feature is sometimes called the *Markovian property*. For example, consider a smoker who is a potential buyer of Lucky Strike cigarettes. Suppose that we view brand switching as a Markov process. If this assumption is valid, the Markovian property tells us that this person will change from Camel to Lucky Strike with a *constant probability*, such as 1/10 (determined by marketing research), when making a subsequent cigarette purchase— regardless of whether he or she has been a loyal Camel smoker for decades or has recently switched to Camel from Pall Mall. A further characteristic of a Markov process is that the *long-run probability* of being in a particular state will be constant over time and will hold regardless of the state probabilities that applied in the beginning. This tells us that the long-run probability that any particular smoker will buy Lucky Strike on the next purchase, which sales experience might show to be a value such as 1/20, must be *constant* over time.

The implications from assuming that a Markov process applies to cigarette pur- chases may seem a bit unrealistic. After all, brands come and go. Once Camel, Lucky Strike, Pall Mall, and Viceroy were leading sellers; today, none of them are leaders (and some may be gone forever). How can we realistically assume that today's favorite brand will not suffer the same fate? The answer is that we cannot. What is ignored is that the various probabilities in a Markov process may be changed through *outside action*. For example, advertising and promotion can cause more or fewer persons than before to switch to or from a particular brand. The possibility of such action adds the element of decision making to a Markov process.

State and Transition Probabilities

To further illustrate the concepts of a Markov process, we will expand on the problem of brand switching. Suppose that three brands *A*, *B*, and *C* all satisfy the same need and may be readily substituted for each other. The product is a convenience item (such as toothpaste or cigarettes) that is bought frequently. Any user is said to be in one of the states *A*, *B*, or *C*, depending on the brand he or she is presently using. Thus, each buyer will be faced from time to time with a buying decision that may result in a change from one state (brand) to another. We will assume that this decision will be made periodically, so that changes will occur over time. We will also assume that the number of states (brand choices) is finite. Our example therefore falls into the class of situations called *Markov chains*, which are distinguished from more general Markov processes in which states may be continuous (for example, a physical dimension or the level of bulk inventory).

A marketing research study based on detailed interviews with a sample of several hundred users has determined the frequency at which buyers as a whole have either remained with their present brand or changed brands. These data provide the **transition probabilities** given in Figure 29-1. Such a table is sometimes referred to as the **transition matrix**.

The number in the top left-hand corner reflects the research result that 90% of the users of brand A were found to retain that brand on a subsequent purchase. This led to the conclusion that the probability is .90 for moving from state A to state A on the next purchase. Likewise, the probability is .05 for moving from state A to state B, and the same value applies to switching from A to C. These transition probabilities are *conditional probabilities* for entering the state listed on the top given the starting state on the left. As such, the values in each row must sum to 1.

In establishing their advertising policies, the producers of the various brands are concerned not with the transition probabilities but with their relative shares of the market. More specifically, each producer wishes to determine the probability that any particular customer will purchase its brand. We refer to such a value as a **state probability**. Such a number is an unconditional probability, and its value may change over time. For convenience, we represent the state probability for state i at period n symbolically as

$$p_i(n) = \Pr[\text{state } i \text{ occurs in period } n]$$

Suppose that further marketing research data shows that brand A currently captures 45% of the market; brand B, 35%; and brand C, 20%. These values apply in the initial period of our investigation. Our interpretation of these numbers is that any particular randomly chosen user of the product will have the following state probabilities in the initial period $n = 0$.

$$p_A(0) = .45$$
$$p_B(0) = .35$$
$$p_C(0) = .20$$

FIGURE 29-1
Transition matrix for the buyers of three brands.

From State \ To	State		
	A	B	C
A	.90	.05	.05
B	.10	.80	.10
C	.10	.15	.75

How State Probabilities Change Over Time

The product manufacturers are concerned with how permanent these market shares are and how they might change from period to period. We determine such changes by looking at the state probabilities in successive periods. As we have noted, a Markov process should have long-run probabilities that are constant over time. Before that equilibrium situation is reached, the process should be given some time to settle down.

Assuming that each customer will make the next brand choice in accordance with the transition probabilities given earlier, we determine the state probabilities that apply in period $n = 1$ after the buyers have made their initial purchases.

Consider state A. To find the probability that brand A will be chosen, we assume that this choice will be made by retaining brand A or by switching from either brand B or C to A. The joint probabilities for these results may be determined by multiplying the respective transition probabilities in column A of the transition matrix by the corresponding state probabilities. Summing these products, we obtain the new state probability for A.

OLD STATE PROBABILITY	×	TRANSITION PROBABILITY	=	NEW STATE PROBABILITY
.45	×	.90	=	.4050
.35	×	.10	=	.0350
.20	×	.10	=	.0200
		$p_A(1)$	=	.4600

Similar calculations provide the other new state probabilities.

$$.45 \times .05 = .0225 \qquad .45 \times .05 = .0225$$
$$.35 \times .80 = .2800 \qquad .35 \times .10 = .0350$$
$$.20 \times .15 = .0300 \qquad .20 \times .75 = .1500$$
$$p_B(1) = .3325 \qquad p_C(1) = .2075$$

Notice that the state probabilities for period 1 have changed, indicating that more people will be buying brands A and C than before and that brand B's share of the market will drop. We use the state probabilities for period 1 in the same manner as before to find the applicable state probabilities for period 2.

$$.4600 \times .90 = .41400 \qquad .4600 \times .05 = .02300 \qquad .4600 \times .05 = .02300$$
$$.3325 \times .10 = .03325 \qquad .3325 \times .80 = .26600 \qquad .3325 \times .10 = .03325$$
$$.2075 \times .10 = .02075 \qquad .2075 \times .15 = .03113 \qquad .2075 \times .75 = .15563$$
$$p_A(2) = .46800 \qquad p_B(2) = .32013 \qquad p_C(2) = .21188$$

We see that the state probabilities have changed further, although not by as much as

TABLE 29-1
State Probabilities for Selected Periods

	$n = 0$	$n = 5$	$n = 10$	$n = 15$	$n = 20$	$n = 25$	$n = 30$
$p_A(n)$	.45	.48371	.49466	.49824	.49942	.49982	.49994
$p_B(n)$	.35	.30023	.28970	.28693	.28610	.28584	.28575
$p_C(n)$	.20	.21616	.21564	.21483	.21448	.21434	.21431

before. Using our latest results, we find the state probabilities for period 3.

$$.46800 \times .90 = .42120 \qquad .46800 \times .05 = .02340 \qquad .46800 \times .05 = .02340$$

$$.32013 \times .10 = .03201 \qquad .32013 \times .80 = .25610 \qquad .32013 \times .10 = .03201$$

$$\underline{.21188 \times .10 = .02119} \qquad \underline{.21188 \times .15 = .03178} \qquad \underline{.21188 \times .75 = .15891}$$

$$p_A(3) = .47440 \qquad\qquad p_B(3) = .31128 \qquad\qquad p_C(3) = .21432$$

Continuing in this manner, we find further changes in the state probabilities. Table 29-1 shows the results for increments of five periods. Notice that the successive changes are smaller. This suggests that the state probabilities may be converging toward a set of constants and that they will eventually remain unchanged. At that point, the process reaches a **steady state** and will remain the same until outside actions change the transition probabilities.

Once a steady state has been reached, the state probabilities for a Markov process are constant from period to period. These values are referred to as **steady-state probabilities**. From Table 29-1, we see that in our illustration the steady-state probabilities are approximately .500 for brand A, .286 for brand B, and .214 for brand C. These probabilities represent the long-run shares of the market for each brand.

29-2 The Calculation of Steady-State Probabilities

A considerable amount of work was required to evaluate this problem for $n = 30$ time periods. It is possible to take a shortcut and to find the steady-state probabilities algebraically. In doing this, we use the fact that *when the process is in a steady state, the probability for leaving any particular state must equal the probability for entering that state.* We therefore ignore the time period n and represent the steady-state probability for state i by p_i. As we have seen, the probability for entering a particular state is found by multiplying the state probability by the respective quantities in the applicable *column* of the transition matrix. In our example, the fact just stated provides the following relationships.

$$p_A = .90p_A + .10p_B + .10p_C$$

$$p_B = .05p_A + .80p_B + .15p_C$$

$$p_C = .05p_A + .10p_B + .75p_C$$

And the following restriction applies.

$$p_A + p_B + p_C = 1$$

The steady-state probabilities must satisfy these equations. (Although there are more equations than unknowns, any one of the first three equations is redundant, due to the fact that the transition probabilities for any starting state must sum to 1.)

We solve these equations simultaneously to determine the steady-state probabilities exactly. Solving the first equation for p_A gives us

$$p_A - .9p_A = .1p_B + .1p_C$$
$$.1p_A = .1p_B + .1p_C$$

and

$$p_A = p_B + p_C$$

Since all of the probabilities must sum to 1, using $p_B + p_C$ for p_A gives us

$$(p_B + p_C) + p_B + p_C = 1$$

or

$$2p_B + 2p_C = 1$$

Thus,

$$p_B = .5 - p_C$$

and

$$p_A = (.5 - p_C) + p_C = .5$$

Substituting $p_A = .5$ and $p_B = .5 - p_C$ into the second equation, we find

$$.5 - p_C = .05(.5) + .80(.5 - p_C) + .15p_C$$
$$-.35p_C = -.075$$

and

$$p_C = \frac{-.075}{-.35} = \frac{3}{14} = .21429$$

Thus,

$$p_B = .5 - \frac{3}{14} = \frac{7}{14} - \frac{3}{14}$$

$$= \frac{4}{14} = .28571$$

and the complete set of steady-state probabilities is

$$p_A = .50000 \qquad p_B = .28571 \qquad p_C = .21429$$

which agrees closely with the probabilities given in Figure 29-2 for $n = 30$.

FIGURE 29-2

Transition matrices and steady-state probabilities for alternative advertising and promotional policies.

POLICY 1

From State \ To	State		
	A	B	C
A	.95	.025	.025
B	.10	.800	.100
C	.10	.150	.750

$$p_A = 14/21 \qquad p_B = 4/21 \qquad p_C = 3/21$$
$$= .667 \qquad\qquad = .190 \qquad\qquad = .143$$

POLICY 2

From State \ To	State		
	A	B	C
A	.90	.05	.05
B	.15	.75	.10
C	.10	.15	.75

$$p_A = 19/34 \qquad p_B = 8/34 \qquad p_C = 7/34$$
$$= .559 \qquad\qquad = .235 \qquad\qquad = .206$$

POLICY 3

From State \ To	State		
	A	B	C
A	.90	.05	.05
B	.10	.80	.10
C	.15	.15	.70

$$p_A = 6/11 \qquad p_B = 3/11 \qquad p_C = 2/11$$
$$= .545 \qquad\qquad = .273 \qquad\qquad = .182$$

29-3 Decision Making with a Markov Process

We have now set the stage for a decision analysis. Suppose that the manufacturer of product A wishes to consider three different advertising and promotional policies. Policy 1 will increase brand A loyalty through a coupon-redemption plan. Policy 2 involves a series of ads aimed at capturing some of the brand B market, and policy 3 involves a series of ads aimed at capturing some of the brand C market. Each policy will modify the Markov process, and each change will result in a different transition matrix.

The transition matrices for these three policies are provided in Figure 29-2. The transition probabilities in each matrix are determined by the policy itself, and they are

TABLE 29-2
Evaluation of Three Alternative Advertising and Promotional Policies for Brand *A*

	MARKET SHARE p_A	EXPECTED TOTAL GROSS PROFIT $\$10,000,000p_A$	EXPECTED IMPROVEMENT	ADDED COST OF POLICY	EXPECTED NET PAYOFF
No change	.500	$5,000,000	—	—	—
Policy 1	14/21 (.667)	6,666,667	$1,666,667	$1,500,000	$166,667
Policy 2	19/34 (.559)	5,588,235	588,235	400,000	188,235
Policy 3	6/11 (.545)	5,454,540	454,540	300,000	154,540

assumed to apply only if the particular policy is actually put into operation. The applicable steady-state probabilities corresponding to the respective transition matrices are also provided in Figure 29-2. These values were obtained algebraically in the same manner as before, using the entries from the respective transition matrices.

Which policy is best? Altogether, 10,000,000 units of all brands are projected to be sold while the various campaigns are in effect. The manufacturer of brand *A* achieves a gross profit of $1 on each item sold. The expected total gross profit for brand *A* is therefore $10,000,000 × p_A. This is computed in Table 29-2 for each policy. We now establish each policy's expected improvement over the status quo. Subtracting the costs of the various plans, we determine the expected net payoffs for the policies shown in Table 29-2. Policy 2 appears to be the best choice, even though it captures a smaller market share than policy 1.

A further illustration involving the establishment of an optimal maintenance policy will help us to understand how to analyze decision making using Markov processes.

29-4 Finding an Optimal Maintenance Policy

Questions of equipment maintenance occur in almost all businesses, including households. When should routine maintenance—such as cleaning a typewriter, lubricating a car, or replacing the bearings in a milling machine—be conducted? Most machines will function a long time without care, but as we well know from personal experience, such neglect may be costly in the end and may result in major overhaul or even junking the equipment.

We view the problem of establishing a maintenance policy in terms of a Markov process in which the various operating conditions are the states. An optimal decision rule or policy is sought that specifies the remedial action to be taken for each equipment state. Any difference between actions for a given state can be reflected in terms of the cost or payoff and the transition probabilities. Entire policies may be compared in terms of expected costs or payoffs calculated by using the applicable state probabilities obtained from the respective transition matrices.

As an illustration, consider a machine that is classified in one of the following states at the beginning of each day.

OPERATING CONDITION STATES
(1) Good operating condition
(2) Slightly out of adjustment
(3) Operating erratically
(4) Inoperable

Any one of the following actions may be taken to put the machine into operation at the corresponding cost.

ACTION	COST
(1) Do nothing	$ 0 (n)
(2) Do routine maintenance	100 (r)
(3) Adjust	300 (a)
(4) Adjust and do routine maintenance	350 (a & r)
(5) Overhaul	1,000 (o)

For each of the 4 states, any one of 5 actions may be taken, so that the number of possible distinct maintenance policies is $5^4 = 625$. Fortunately, management considers only a limited number of policies, since many of these policies are prohibitively costly or obviously unattractive. Further restrictions limit the possibilities. For instance, an inoperable machine must be overhauled before it can work again, and a machine that is in good operating condition or that only requires adjustment should not be overhauled.

The simplest policy is to do nothing until the machine is inoperable and then overhaul it. The transition matrix for this plan, referred to as policy 1, is given in Figure 29-3. Remember that the policy itself establishes the transition probabilities, so that these probabilities apply only if the policy is adopted. The transition probabilities reflect the daily change in state. They are obtained from testing a variety of actions under all operating conditions. The data indicate that doing nothing when the machine is in good

FIGURE 29-3
Transition matrix for policy 1: Do nothing until machine is inoperable.

From State	To State 1	2	3	4	Action	Cost	Steady-State Probability
1	.90	.06	.03	.01	n	$ 0	50/76 = .658
2	0	.80	.10	.10	n	0	15/76 = .197
3	0	0	.50	.50	n	0	6/76 = .079
4	1	0	0	0	o	1,000	5/76 = .066

operating condition (state 1) results in a .90 probability that that same state will occur on the second day. Smaller probabilities apply in row 1 for ending up in the other states; these values become progressively smaller as the degree of disrepair increases. If the machine is out of adjustment (state 2), it cannot be restored to good operating condition without human intervention; the probability for moving from state 2 to state 1 is therefore zero. The other row 2 probabilities indicate that it is most likely for the machine to remain out of adjustment (state 2) than to revert to erratic operation (state 3) or inoperability (state 4). Row 3 indicates that once the machine is operating erratically (state 3), there is a 50–50 chance that it will remain in that state or become inoperable (state 4). Finally, row 4 indicates that there is a probability of 1 moving from inoperability (state 4) to good operating condition (state 1), since the machine must then be overhauled.

The steady-state probabilities p_1, p_2, p_3, and p_4 may then be obtained for policy 1 in the usual manner by solving the following equations.

$$p_1 = .90p_1 + 1p_4$$

$$p_2 = .06p_1 + .80p_2$$

$$p_3 = .03p_1 + .10p_2 + .50p_3$$

$$p_4 = .01p_1 + .10p_2 + .50p_3$$

$$p_1 + p_2 + p_3 + p_4 = 1$$

The first equation tells us that

$$p_4 = .10p_1$$

and the second equation provides the result

$$p_2 = .30p_1$$

Substituting $.30p_1$ for p_2 in the third equation and solving for p_3, we obtain

$$p_3 = .03p_1 + .10(.30p_1) + .50p_3$$

or

$$.50p_3 = .03p_1 + .03p_1$$

so that

$$p_3 = .12p_1$$

Finally, substituting the preceding results into the last equation

$$p_1 + .30p_1 + .12p_1 + .10p_1 = 1$$

so that

$$1.52p_1 = 1$$

and

$$p_1 = 1/1.52 = 100/152 = 50/76$$

The other steady-state probability values follow from this result, so that

$$p_1 = 50/76 = .658$$

$$p_2 = 15/76 = .197$$

$$p_3 = 6/76 = .079$$

$$p_4 = 5/76 = .066$$

The applicable transition matrices for the four other policies to be considered by management are given in Figure 29-4. The transition probabilities in the *rows* of these matrices reflect the particular action indicated.

Policy 2 involves the routine maintenance for states 1, 2, and 3 and overhauling in state 4. The transition probabilities in rows 1, 2, and 3 differ from those for policy 1, reflecting the fact that routine maintenance reduces the chance of declining to a worse state of disrepair.

Policy 3 involves a different action for each state. Row 1 is the same as it is under policy 1, since the action taken from state 1 is doing nothing in either case. Row 2 applies when the machine is out of adjustment (state 2) and is adjusted under this policy, so that there is a .80 probability that the machine will return to good operating condition (state 1). The probabilities for achieving the inferior operating conditions from state 2 are substantially lower than before. Row 3, corresponding to an erratically operating machine, contains more favorable probabilities than it does under policy 2, since both adjustment and routine maintenance will be performed.

Policy 4 differs from policy 3 only in row 1, where routine maintenance is done. This action is identical to what is done in state 1 under policy 2. Policy 5 is the same as policy 4 except that when the machine is operating erratically (state 3); then an overhaul is made, and the row 3 transition probabilities indicate a certain return to good operating condition (state 1).

The steady-state probabilities under each policy appear to the right of the respective transition matrices. These probabilities may be used to determine the expected daily operating cost of each policy. The computations in Table 29-3 indicate the surprising result that policy 1—do nothing until the machine is inoperable and then overhaul it—minimizes expected daily cost at a steady-state average of only $66 per day. One explanation for this is that the steady-state probability for the machine becoming inoperable is only .066, so that it is unworkable only 66 out of every 1,000 days on the average. Routine maintenance and adjustment costs are just too high to warrant those actions while the machine will still work.

This policy is similar to the one that many Americans apply to automobile maintenance. We generally abuse our vehicles and—except for oil changes, lubrications, tune-ups, and the replacement of batteries, worn tires, and brake linings—we make repairs only after the car stops running. One explanation is that mechanical work is very expensive, often costing more than a worn-out and depreciated car is worth. However, airlines go to the other extreme in maintaining planes, replacing engines after several hundred hours of operation and performing extensive preventive maintenance, whether or not it is visibly needed. In the latter case, the cost of failure is huge in comparison to the relatively trivial costs of routine maintenance.

FIGURE 29-4
Transition matrices for the four remaining maintenance policies.

POLICY 2

From State \ To	State 1	2	3	4	Action	Cost	Steady-State Probability
1	.95	.03	.01	.01	r	$ 100	40/53 = .755
2	0	.85	.10	.05	r	100	8/53 = .151
3	0	0	.60	.40	r	100	3/53 = .057
4	1	0	0	0	o	1,000	2/53 = .038

POLICY 3

From State \ To	State 1	2	3	4	Action	Cost	Steady-State Probability
1	.90	.06	.03	.01	n	$ 0	450/554 = .812
2	.80	.10	.08	.02	a	300	30/554 = .054
3	0	0	.70	.30	a & r	350	53/554 = .096
4	1	0	0	0	o	1,000	21/554 = .038

POLICY 4

From State \ To	State 1	2	3	4	Action	Cost	Steady-State Probability
1	.95	.03	.01	.01	r	$ 100	900/989 = .910
2	.80	.10	.08	.02	a	300	30/989 = .030
3	0	0	.70	.30	a & r	350	38/989 = .038
4	1	0	0	0	o	1,000	21/989 = .021

POLICY 5

From State \ To	State 1	2	3	4	Action	Cost	Steady-State Probability
1	.95	.03	.01	.01	r	$ 100	1,500/1,585 = .946
2	.80	.10	.08	.02	a	300	50/1,585 = .032
3	1	0	0	0	o	1,000	19/1,585 = .012
4	1	0	0	0	o	1,000	16/1,585 = .010

TABLE 29-3
Expected Daily Cost Calculations for the Various Maintenance Policies

POLICY	STATE	STEADY-STATE PROBABILITY	ACTION	COST	COST × PROBABILITY
1	1	.658	n	$ 0	$ 0
	2	.197	n	0	0
	3	.079	n	0	0
	4	.066	o	1,000	66.00
					$66.00 = Expected cost
2	1	.755	r	100	75.50
	2	.151	r	100	15.10
	3	.057	r	100	5.70
	4	.038	o	1,000	38.00
					$134.30 = Expected cost
3	1	.812	n	0	0
	2	.054	a	300	16.20
	3	.096	a & r	350	33.60
	4	.038	o	1,000	38.00
					$87.80 = Expected cost
4	1	.910	r	100	91.00
	2	.030	a	300	9.00
	3	.038	a & r	350	13.30
	4	.021	o	1,000	21.00
					$134.30 = Expected cost
5	1	.946	r	100	94.60
	2	.032	a	300	9.60
	3	.012	o	1,000	12.00
	4	.010	o	1,000	10.00
					$126.20 = Expected cost

29-5 Additional Remarks

In this chapter, we have illustrated the underlying concepts of a Markov process. A class of decisions may be analyzed using the appropriate transition matrix for each alternative policy to find the steady-state probabilities. These probabilities are then combined with economic data to calculate the expected costs or payoffs, which may then be compared to determine the optimal policy.

The validity of this analysis is based on the steady-state behavior of the system under the various policies. Although the adoption of a new operating policy can result in a new transition matrix immediately, it generally takes a while for any Markov process to settle into the steady state. This is because the individual state probabilities usually differ from their long-run values. Until the equilibrium condition is reached, the system as a whole is in a **transient state**.

Thus, a complete analysis should consider what conditions apply in the transient state and how long the revised system takes to reach a steady state. If the changes are greater under some alternatives than others or if the durations of the transient phases differ, then these differences should also be considered when selecting the optimal policy.

Analyzing a decision in terms of a Markov process may be more valid in some applications than in others. For instance, this approach has been criticized when applied to brand switching, because the transient state may be quite lengthy in relation to the duration of the alternative advertising policies being evaluated. There is some question of whether a steady state is ever reached before the marketplace is perturbed by further competitive forces. Obviously, an analysis based wholly on steady-state behavior would be invalid if this were true. A more fundamental criticism of brand-switching applications pertains to the transition matrix itself. Competitors and shifting customer tastes may cause unanticipated changes in the transition probabilities, so that these values may be uncertain and even short-lived regardless of the marketing policy that a particular manufacturer adopts. The transition matrix that actually results might be viewed as the outcome of a complex interactive decision process involving several parties.

In other applications where outside forces are minimal and where policies are expected to operate under stable conditions for a long time, an analysis based on the Markov process may be the proper procedure. This is often the case in establishing equipment maintenance policies. The same basic approach has been employed with varying degrees of success in a wide variety of applications, including designing port facilities, planning political strategies, and establishing policies for releasing water from dams.

We have barely covered the theoretical aspects of Markov processes here. The processes themselves are special cases of more general stochastic processes. When the Markov process is combined with decision making, the resulting mathematical procedure falls into the broad category of a **Markovian decision model**. These models, in turn, may fit into a variety of categories described in this book. For instance, decisions involving a Markov process can be solved as linear programming problems. Others may be expressed as dynamic programs. Thus, the simplex method or a variety of other solution procedures may be used to establish an optimal policy for a particular situation. Although a detailed discussion of the theory of Markov processes and the more advanced models and procedures used with them in decision making is beyond the scope of this book, several references provided in the bibliography provide opportunities for further study of this rich topic.

29-6 Computer Applications

Finding the steady-state probabilities may be a formidable computational task. This is easily done with the assistance of a digital computer. The *QuickQuant* software package available to users of this textbook will determine these probability values for any transition matrix provided. Special instructions for using *QuickQuant* are included in the Appendix of this textbook. Figure 29-5 shows the *QuickQuant* report for the three brands discussed earlier in the chapter.

FIGURE 29-5

QuickQuant **report showing the computer solution to the three brands problem.**

```
============================================================================
                            QuickQuant Report
                         MARKOV PROCESS ANALYSIS
----------------------------------------------------------------------------
PROBLEM: Three Brands                              Date: 03-03-1990
                                                              Larry


        Transition Probability Matrix

       ---------------------------------------------
        : To
From :      1              2              3
       ---------------------------------------------
   1 : .9            .05            .05
   2 : .1            .8             .1
   3 : .1            .15            .75
       ---------------------------------------------


             Steady State
State        Probability
        ---------------------------
   1           0.5000
   2           0.2857
   3           0.2143


----------------------------------------------------------------------------
```

CASE

Puffin Plungers

Puffin Plungers is an oil exploration company evaluating two alternative plans for supplying an Arctic drilling platform with drill bits. The first policy is to keep just one working bit at the site and air-drop a replacement in when it breaks. The alternative policy is to keep two bits at the site and to send a replacement by boat only when one of them breaks; the boat will replace all broken bits. There is only a 10% chance that a drill bit will break on any given day; a bit cannot be replaced on the same day that it breaks. An air-drop takes place the next day, so no lost production occurs. A sea delivery takes one or more days and only one boat may be dispatched at a time. Each day's lost production represents $10,000 in lost future profits, and the two delivery modes have identical costs. A production loss occurs whenever a bit breaks, which is assumed to happen near the beginning of a working day. When replacements are made or deliveries are received, they occur just before the day's drilling begins. Depending on the delivery policy chosen, some or all of the following states apply at the beginning of any particular scheduled drilling day.

A: No good bits
B: One good bit; no break yesterday

C: One good bit; a break yesterday
D: Two good bits; last replacement was for one bit
E: Two good bits; last replacement was for two bits

Questions

1. Construct the transition matrices for the two policies.
2. Determine the steady-state probabilities for each policy.
3. Consider the air-drop policy. Each transition may involve a production cost (a loss). Determine the expected cost of starting in each state by summing the products of these costs with the corresponding probabilities in the applicable row of the transition matrix. Then, apply the steady-state probabilities to determine the expected daily policy cost.
4. Repeat the process in Question 3 for the sea-delivery policy.
5. Which policy minimizes expected daily cost?

PROBLEMS

29-1 A system may be in state 1 or state 2. The following transition matrix applies.

From \ To	1	2
1	1/3	2/3
2	3/4	1/4

Determine the steady-state probabilities.

29-2 A system may be in one of three states. The following transition matrix applies.

From \ To	A	B	C
A	1/2	0	1/2
B	1/4	1/4	1/2
C	1/3	1/3	1/3

(a) Suppose that in the initial period, the system will be in state A with certainty. Determine the values $p_A(5)$, $p_B(5)$, and $p_C(5)$.
(b) Determine the steady-state probabilities.

29-3 The following transition matrix applies to a system.

From \ To	1	2
1	.2	.8
2	.6	.4

(a) Determine the steady-state probabilities.
(b) Suppose that $p_1(0) = .4$ and $p_2(0) = .6$. Determine the successive state probabilities $p_1(n)$ and $p_2(n)$ for $n = 1, 2, 3,$ and 4. In what period does $p_1(n)$ lie within .001 of the steady-state probability for state 1?

29-4 Suppose that the brand A manufacturer discussed in Section 29-3 tries advertising policy 4, under which a 98% period-to-period retention applies to brand A, and there is only a 1% chance of switching either from A to B or from A to C. Under this policy, the transition probabilities for starting from the other brands remain at the policy 1 levels. Policy 4 will cost $3 million. If we assume that the goal of maximizing expected gross payoff is valid, would the manufacturer prefer this policy to the ones discussed in the chapter?

29-5 Reevaluate the maintenance decision discussed in Section 29-4 when the following costs apply.

$$
\begin{array}{rl}
\$\quad 0 & (n) \\
50 & (r) \\
150 & (a) \\
200 & (a \ \& \ r) \\
1{,}000 & (o)
\end{array}
$$

Which policy yields the minimum expected daily cost?

29-6 Consider a sixth possible policy for the machine maintenance decision described in Section 29-4. Under this policy, nothing is done until the machine begins to operate erratically (when it is adjusted and routine maintenance is performed) or until it is inoperable (when an overhaul is performed).
(a) Determine the applicable transition matrix. (This may be obtained by using the pertinent rows from policy 1 and policy 3 in Figures 29-3 and 29-4.)
(b) Determine the steady-state probabilities.
(c) What is the expected daily maintenance cost of this new policy? Is it better than all of the original five policies?

29-7 The following transition matrix applies for the buyers of two competing brands of exotic cigarettes.

From \ To	Casbah	Tangier	Other
Casbah	.90	.10	0
Tangier	.05	.90	.05
Other	.02	.03	.95

Assuming that market conditions will not change, what long-run percentage shares of the exotic market will Casbah and Tangier eventually achieve?

29-8   Whenever one state may be reached from another state sometime in a Markov process, the two states are said to *communicate*. If a state is never left, it is referred to as an *absorbing state*.

(a) What may be said regarding the steady-state probability for an absorbing state that communicates with all of the remaining states?

(b) A Hawaiian potato chip is reputed to have the following transition matrix for brand-switching in its market.

From \ To	Hawaiian Chip	Mainland Chip
Hawaiian Chip	1	0
Mainland Chip	.01	.99

If this matrix is valid, which chip will eventually have the entire market to itself? Verify your answer by computing the steady-state proportion of the market held by each chip. What kind of state is the buyer of Hawaiian chip in?

29-9   Each sales transaction at Ace Widgets falls into one of the following states.
(1) Cash received
(2) Account receivable
(3) Uncollectable funds
Suppose the following transition matrix applies to each successive month after a sale.

From \ To	1	2	3
1	1	0	0
2	.80	.19	.01
3	0	0	1

(a) If $p_1(0) = .9$, $p_2(0) = 0$, and $p_3(0) = .1$, find $p_1(1)$, $p_2(1)$, and $p_3(1)$. Do you notice anything unusual?

(b) What can you conclude regarding the steady-state probabilities with respect to the values of the initial state probabilities?

29-10   Republican Senator Herman Angel is running for reelection against a Democratic challenger, Representative Sheila Saint. The 10,000 voters of Pearly Gates may be categorized in one of five ways.

STATE	PERCENTAGE WHO VOTE FOR ANGEL
(1) Rabid Republican	99%
(2) Liberal Republican	95
(3) Fence sitter	50
(4) Straying Democrat	40
(5) Indelible Democrat	10

Angel forces are running a special campaign to attempt to move the voters into the more favorable categories. Without these special efforts, the following transition matrix currently applies to a day-to-day switch in voter sentiment.

From \ To	1	2	3	4	5
1	.95	.05	0	0	0
2	.10	.80	.10	0	0
3	0	.15	.70	.15	0
4	0	0	.20	.70	.10
5	0	0	0	.25	.75

(a) Election day is a long way off. If no special campaign is conducted, how many Pearly Gaters may be expected to vote for Angel?

(b) The special campaign will focus on making fence sitters more favorable to Republican sentiment. This will result in an identical transition matrix except for new row 3 transition probabilities of

$$0 \quad .40 \quad .50 \quad .10 \quad 0$$

Now, how many Pearly Gaters may be expected to vote for Angel?

Guide to QuickQuant

$\mathcal{Q}$uickQuant is a comprehensive software package available to adopters of this textbook. There are two versions of this program:

PC Version 2.0

MacIntosh Version 2.0

The PC version will operate on any IBM-PC or MS-DOS compatible computer with 256K RAM. The MacIntosh version will operate with any Mac Plus, SE, or MacIntosh II computer using System 6.0 or later software.

Important Features of *QuickQuant*

Although not essential for using this book, user-friendly *QuickQuant* can save time on elaborate (and messy) computations. Since *QuickQuant* was tailor-made for this textbook, readers can easily integrate the computer with the computationally intensive topics. Users of the program will appreciate its extensive capacity to print reports that match and support text material.

Hundreds of students have found *QuickQuant* easy to use and helpful in mastering the subject material of this textbook. The program has been extensively tested, reworked, debugged, and refined to make it as easy to use as a video game. It is so user-friendly that students can begin using *QuickQuant* immediately—without having to use a manual—as soon as the remaining pages in this Guide have been read.

Major Version 2.0 Improvements

Present *QuickQuant* users should be happy with the expanded applications, displays, and refinements in Version 2.0. Figure A-1 shows the present program modules, slightly regrouped to make diskette space for the new applications, which include the following:

- New Payoff Table Analysis
- New Decision Tree Segment
- Expansion of Inventory Models to Include Lost Sales Case
- Improved Bayesian Statistical Input and Output
- Expanded Forecasting Segment, Providing:
     Seasonal Exponential Smoothing
     Probabilities for Regression Evaluations
     Scatter Plots

Many changes should make the program easier to use. Notably, the PC screen displays have been redone to avoid difficulties experienced with certain monitors in handling colors. And, the MacIntosh version has an improved user interface that better reflects that system's superior ease of use.

FIGURE A-1

***QuickQuant* master menu for PC Version 2.0.**

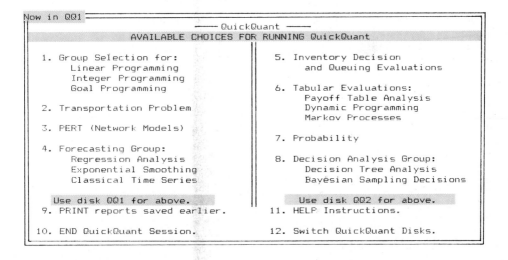

```
Now in QQ1
┌──────────────────────── QuickQuant ────────────────────────┐
│              AVAILABLE CHOICES FOR RUNNING QuickQuant        │
│                                                             │
│   1. Group Selection for:        5. Inventory Decision      │
│      Linear Programming             and Queuing Evaluations │
│      Integer Programming                                    │
│      Goal Programming            6. Tabular Evaluations:    │
│                                     Payoff Table Analysis   │
│   2. Transportation Problem         Dynamic Programming     │
│                                     Markov Processes        │
│   3. PERT (Network Models)                                  │
│                                  7. Probability             │
│   4. Forecasting Group:                                     │
│      Regression Analysis         8. Decision Analysis Group:│
│      Exponential Smoothing          Decision Tree Analysis  │
│      Classical Time Series          Bayesian Sampling Decisions │
│                                                             │
│    Use disk QQ1 for above.          Use disk QQ2 for above. │
│   9. PRINT reports saved earlier.  11. HELP Instructions.   │
│                                                             │
│  10. END QuickQuant Session.       12. Switch QuickQuant Disks. │
└─────────────────────────────────────────────────────────────┘
```

Running *QuickQuant*

The Diskettes   Your instructor should provide you with your own copies of the two *QuickQuant* program diskettes, QQ1 and QQ2. You should also have a blank *formatted* diskette on which you will store your personal data. For most PC setups, you will also need the DOS (disk operating system) diskette, which comes with the computer itself. The data disk is not absolutely essential, but it will be beneficial for saving long problems that may have to be fixed and run again. It will also allow you to store *QuickQuant* reports that need to be printed at a more convenient time. (Do not use the program disks for this purpose—they are too full.)

Getting Started with the PC   Most users of *QuickQuant* will have a computer with two floppy disk drives. In that case, after booting DOS you will place either the QQ1 or QQ2 diskette into drive A, where it will remain until you are finished. The data disk will be placed in drive B, where it too will remain for the duration.

Once DOS is booted and your QQ1 disk has been placed into drive A, you will see on screen the prompt

$$A > \_$$

Type **qq1** and press the Enter key. The disk drive will spin for a few seconds while the QQ1 master program is loaded. The master menu in Figure A-1 will then appear on screen. (An identical startup procedure will be used to start the QQ2 program from the other program disk.)

The Master Menu   There are three sections to the menu. The upper lefthand portion shows the program segments that may be accessed from the QQ1 disk. Choose **1** to run linear programs, integer programs, or goal programs. Select choice **2** to run transportation problems and choice **3** to conduct a PERT evaluation. Pick selection **4** for making forecast using regression, time-series analysis, or exponential smoothing.

The selections on the upper righthand side of the menu are activated from the QQ2 diskette. Grouped together as choice **5** are inventory decisions with queuing evaluations and as choice **6** are the tabular evaluations: payoff table analysis, dynamic programming, and Markov processes. Probability is a separate menu choice **7**, and group choice **8** is for decision analysis. In a floppy disk operating mode, the QQ2 diskette must be inserted into the drive, replacing the QQ1 diskette.

The bottom four master menu options (**9** through **12**) are common to both diskettes.

MacIntosh Version 2.0   *QuickQuant* takes advantage of the special MacIntosh user interface features. The individual program segments match those in Figure A-1 (with abbreviated file names). The desired program segment is booted by clicking on the selected file icon in the QQ1 or QQ2 diskettes. (These may be combined into a single folder on a hard disk system.) MacIntosh users do not need the master menu described above, and the chaining described below does not apply. Unlike the PC version, the program diskettes should have sufficient room for storing the problem data files and output files needed in a single *QuickQuant* session. But those files should be removed to another diskette for permanent storage.

Chaining in PC Applications   Master-menu selections 1 through 9 each activate an independent application program. *QuickQuant* is designed to *chain* from program to program. For example, to run a linear program, menu choice 1 causes the QQ1 program to boot the program named "Simplex." (You will not ordinarily have to use the application program names.) All application programs are separately executable because they are too big to share computer memory space. When you are finished with one application, that program will automatically direct the computer to reload QQ1 (or QQ2).

Note: *If you have only one floppy disk drive*, you will have to swap between the program disk and your data disk. Either the QQ1 or QQ2 program disk should be present in drive A, except when you are reading or writing to the data disk.

Adding Command.com to the PC Version Program Disks   So that *QuickQuant* can chain programs, it is necessary that you copy onto *each* QQ disk the command.com module from the DOS disk controlling the computer you are currently using. To copy that program, insert the DOS disk in drive A, the QQ1 (QQ2) disk in drive B, and type the following:

copy a:command.com b:

Press the Enter key, and the file will be copied from the DOS disk onto your program disk. (On a single-drive system, you will place the DOS disk in drive A, type **copy command.com**, next press Enter, and then follow the directions as they appear on the screen.)

Note: *If you switch computers* in a later session, you should repeat the above steps, because a different DOS may have a slightly different command.com program. (You may want to duplicate the QQ1 and QQ2 disks so that you will have a separate set for each computer you use.)

Warning: Sometimes chaining breaks down due to PC incompatability, an old DOS program, the wrong command.com, or some unknown reason. You will then have to boot each program segment separately. For example, to run a linear program, upon getting the **A >** prompt you will enter the application program directly by typing

simplex

and then pressing the Enter key.

Independent Application Program Modules   The following file names comprise the application programs:

On the QQ1 Diskette	On the QQ2 Diskette
simplex.exe	invenque.exe
transp.exe	tabular.exe
pert.exe	prob.exe
forecast.exe	decision.exe

PC users don't have to type the .exe file extension to run any of these application programs. You will most likely never need them at all. *QuickQuant* is designed to make smooth transitions between program segments. But should chaining fail, when you finish with one program you will be unceremoniously dumped back under DOS control. You may still print reports saved earlier on your data file by booting from scratch QQ1 or QQ2 and selecting menu choice 9.

MacIntosh Version   The same prefix names are used for the MacIntosh program modules. (The .exe suffix is not used.) There is no master menu, and you must click on the respective file icon to run an application.

PC Hard Disk Operation   The *QuickQuant* procedures for hard disk operations are considerably streamlined. You can install both program disks on drive C by creating a QQ directory. You can do this when you see the **C >** prompt by first typing

md c:qq

and then pressing Enter. Next, the files in the QQ1 and QQ2 diskettes must be copied into the QQ directory. This is accomplished by inserting each diskette into drive A and executing the following command:

copy a:*.* c:

Your data files will be automatically stored and read from the QQ directory, unless otherwise specified. Chaining will be automatic, and there is no need to copy the command.com file.

Running Problems with *QuickQuant*

Let's follow the experiences of Shirley Smart as she uses *QuickQuant* to solve the modified Redwood Furniture problem of Chapter 11. Shirley has completed all the preliminaries and is now ready to run the linear programming problem. She has booted QQ1, and upon seeing the master menu she selects choice 1. All goes well, and the corresponding application program is automatically loaded. After a few seconds Shirley sees the model choice menu in Figure A-2(a). She then picks selection 1 from the new menu, getting the problem running menu in Figure A-2(b).

MacIntosh Version   Although the illustrations that follow apply to the PC version of *QuickQuant*, the same sequence is followed with the MacIntosh version. Choices are made with the MacIntosh by selecting the appropriate item from the menu bar, clicking on that segment that applies. The item numbers and choices closely match those of the PC version. And, where the PC version often requests pressing the Home key to get a new screen, the MacIntosh version asks instead that the mouse be clicked.

FIGURE A-2
Menus for programming models using PC Version 2.0.

```
 ―― QuickQuant ――
          CHOICES FOR PROGRAMMING MODEL TYPE


     1. Linear Programming

     2. Integer Programming

     3. Goal Programming

     4. FINISHED--Return to main program.
```

(a) Programming model choice menu

```
 ―― QuickQuant ――
      CHOICES FOR RUNNING LINEAR, INTEGER, OR GOAL PROGRAMS


     1. Enter new problem--From keyboard.

     2. Enter new problem--From disk file.

     3. Revise current problem.

     4. Store current problem--Onto disk file.

     5. Run current problem.

     6. Display current problem on screen.

     7. FINISHED--Return to main program.
```

(b) Problem running menu

Shirley Smart's Linear Programming Session   The choices shown in the detailed third menu are typical of all the *QuickQuant* program segments. Choice 1 is for entering the problem data for the first time. Later, Shirley can pick choice 3 and make further modifications. Choice 4 stores the problem information on the data disk. That choice is ordinarily picked *before* processing data. If you want to work again in a later session with the same problem, you can retrieve it by selecting choice 2.

Suppose Shirley chooses number 1. A new screen appears, and Shirley is asked to name her problem, to specify how many variables and constraints the problem will have, to state whether the objective is to Maximize P or to Minimize C, and to name her variables.

The next screen then appears, and Shirley is instructed to enter her data by filling in the blanks—first for the objective, as shown in Figure A-3. *QuickQuant* allows Shirley to go back and fix her entries as she goes along, using the arrow keys to move the highlighter left, right, up, or down.

FIGURE A-3
Entering a new problem from the keyboard.

```
Type needed values where highlighted.   ENTER or ARROW keys move highlighter.
Entries become permanent when highlighter moves.   BACKSPACE erases mistakes
in unfinished entries. You can skip any spot or go back and retype entries.
DO NOT USE COMMAS.   NEW SCREENS appear as needed.   Press HOME when finished.
```

```
Objective Function for: Redwood Furniture

Maximize P =
            + 5 XTS         + 6 XTR   +_____ XTL   +_____ XCS
     +_____ XCA   +_____ XBS   +_____ XBT
```

After completing the objective, Shirley presses the Home key (or clicks the mouse). *QuickQuant* then brings a similar screen for the problem constraints. She fills in the blanks, erasing, fixing and backing up, as needed, until her input is perfect. Since the modified Redwood Furniture problem is so long, it takes two screens just to do the constraints. Pressing the Home key (clicking the mouse) one last time brings the finished linear program, the first screen of which is shown in Figure A-4, for one final verification.

QuickQuant automatically takes care of the auxiliary variables. It is not necessary to list among your variables the slacks, surpluses, or artificials, and you do not have to include these in your constraint data.

Pressing Home (clicking the mouse) again returns Shirley to the problem-running menu [Figure A-2(b)]. Since she has just spent many precious minutes entering the data, she doesn't want to do it again if something goes wrong. She picks choice 4, and *QuickQuant* saves her data under a file name selected for quick recognition in the future. Shirley then picks choice 5, and *QuickQuant* solves the linear program.

FIGURE A-4
***QuickQuant* screen showing completed input for Redwood Furniture problem.**

```
Problem: Redwood Furniture

Maximize P =
            + 5 XTS         + 6 XTR         + 7 XTL         + 6 XCS
            + 10 XCA        + 8 XBS         + 6 XBT

Subject to:
  C1:       + 20 XTS        + 30 XTR        + 40 XTL        + 15 XCS
            + 25 XCA        + 20 XBS        + 30 XBT                    ≤      3000

  C2:       + 4 XTS         + 5 XTR         + 6 XTL         + 8 XCS
            + 12 XCA        + 6 XBS         + 8 XBT                     ≤      1100

  C3:       + 2 XTS         + 2 XTR         + 2 XTL         + 3 XCS
            + 3 XCA         + 2 XBS         + 2 XBT                     ≤       250

  C4:       + 1 XTS         + 1 XTR         + 1 XTL         + 0 XCS
            + 0 XCA         + 0 XBS         + 0 XBT                     ≥        30
```

```
INSPECT this formulation in detail.   Note the locations of errors.   You may
make corrections by selecting option 3 when you get back to the menu.
Press HOME key when ready for the next screen.
```

FIGURE A-5

Final *QuickQuant* simplex tableau for Redwood Furniture problem.

```
        PROBLEM: Redwood Furniture                              Iteration:  8
UNIT P,C           5          6          7          6          10
```

	Basic	1	2	3	4	5	
	Mix	XTS	XTR	XTL	XCS	XCA	Solution
0	1S1	0	-10	0	0	0	135
0	2S2	0	-1	0	0	0	319
0	3S6	0	0	0	0	0	45
7	4XTL	0	1	1	0	0	15
10	5XCA	0	0	0	0	1	4
6	6XBT	0	0	0	0	0	32.5
5	7XTS	1	0	0	0	0	15
6	8XCS	0	0	0	1	0	16
8	9XBS	0	0	0	0	0	32.5
	Sac.	5	7	7	6	10	771
	Imp.	0	-1	0	0	0	--

```
FINISHED. ARROW keys move window. Press HOME key to get final report.
```

QuickQuant displays on screen the first simplex tableau. Shirley has the choice of seeing the subsequent tableau or skipping to the end. Her final simplex tableau is shown in Figure A-5. Not everything can be shown on the screen at once, and several columns are missing for the slacks, surpluses, and artificials. She can see the missing portion by pressing the arrow keys to move screen window, and she can even print the tableau by depressing the shift key and pressing the PrtSc key (command-shift-3 on the MacIntosh).

That screen-dumping process is slow, and it could take several passes to print out all the missing pieces. It can only be done while you process the data, and that type of output cannot be stored on disk for later printing. (Many printers will not faithfully copy all screen characters, and your printout borders may resemble the striping on a checkered taxicab!) For big problems, the final simplex spreadsheet may be assembled by cutting and pasting from several screen dumps.

Shirley depresses the Home key (clicks the mouse) one final time to bring to screen the *QuickQuant* report in Figure A-6. A second screen (not shown) provides the values of the slack and surplus variables. Should the problem be infeasible or unbounded, a message appears instead in the report box.

All *QuickQuant* segments end with an on-screen report, which may then be duplicated onto hard copy or saved on disk file. The output report will contain the date and your name. It will also have a segment that summarizes the problem data giving rise to the reported solution.

After viewing the screen report, Shirley presses any key. *QuickQuant* screens the message shown in Figure A-7, and Shirley decides how to dispose further the output.

Several *QuickQuant* segments involve further choices for additional processing. In the case of linear programming, Shirley is asked next whether she wants to see the dual and sensitivity analysis. If so, she gets additional screen reports. For each report, she gets to

FIGURE A-6

QuickQuant screen report for Redwood Furniture problem.

```
              ——— QuickQuant ———
           SOLUTION TO LINEAR PROGRAM

   PROBLEM: Redwood Furniture

               Original
               Variable          Value
               ------------------------------
                 XTS           15.00000
                 XTR            0.00000
                 XTL           15.00000
                 XCS           16.00000
                 XCA            4.00000
                 XBS           32.50000
                 XBT           32.50000

          Objective Value: P =     771.00000
```

decide whether to print a hard-copy version. After following her instructions, *QuickQuant* brings Shirley back to the problem-running menu [Figure A-2(b)].

Choice 3 allows Shirley to modify the existing problem, which remains in memory until she replaces it or leaves the current application program. You can use this option to fix an existing problem (should your linear program be infeasible or unbounded) or to explore various modifications. That choice brings to screen the modification menu in Figure A-8. The selections on this menu allow complete flexibility in modifying an existing problem by "recycling" old data with minimal work. Similar modification menus apply to all the *QuickQuant* applications.

Shirley plays with the problem for a while. She adds new variables and new constraints. She changes coefficients for constraints and the objective function. She reverses directions of inequalities. Each time she runs the new version. One change makes the problem infeasible; another results in an unbounded linear program.

FIGURE A-7

Selections for printing QuickQuant report—PC version only.

```
You have the following choices for the preceding report:

    1. PRINT the report now.

    2. SAVE the report on DISK FILE to be printed later.

    3. NEITHER of the above.


What is the number of your choice?
```

FIGURE A-8
QuickQuant problem modification menu.

```
                         —— QuickQuant ——
                CHOICES FOR MODIFYING CURRENT PROBLEM


    1. Revise costs or profits.        7. Delete a variable.

    2. Modify constraint coefficients.  8. Delete a constraint.

    3. Revise righthand sides.          9. Reverse objective.

    4. Switch constraint types.        10. Change a problem name.

    5. Add a new variable.             11. Change a variable name.

    6. Add a new constraint.

            12. Display revised problem on screen.

        FINISHED with Modifications:

            13. Return to program menu.
```

Since by now the original Redwood Furniture problem has been obliterated from memory, Shirley retrieves it from her data disk, runs it again, and prints a hard copy. She then returns to the programming-model-choice menu [Figure A-2(a)], where she selects integer programming (choice 2). She then sees how *QuickQuant* solves this same problem by the branch-and-bound method, which separately evaluates over 20 different linear programs.

Shirley ends the session by returning to the master menu [Figure A-1]. She plans a future *QuickQuant* excursion, exploring transportation problems and PERT.

Now you are ready for *your* first session with *QuickQuant*.

Interrupting *QuickQuant*

There may be occasions when you want to interrupt the program. If you want to do so because of an error in data entry or the wrong menu choice, it may be best to let the program run its course, fixing data through the edit menu choice or then reselecting the proper menu choice. Some *QuickQuant* segments, however, are time consuming, and waiting is impracticable. The program may usually be interrupted by pressing Control-Break on the PC or Command-Period on the MacIntosh. This cannot be done while filling in blanks during data entry. In those cases you must first terminate data entry by pressing Home with the PC or by clicking the mouse with the MacIntosh.

Such an interruption requires rebooting the necessary *QuickQuant* programs. You will lose all of the current data that was not stored on file. To minimize any great inconvenience, your best insurance is always to save large problems on a file before running them.

Important Features of MacIntosh Version

Most *QuickQuant* screens and main reports are indistinguishable between the PC and MacIntosh versions. The MacIntosh version has user interfacing with the look and feel expected with MacIntosh applications programs. The major menu choices are made using standard pull down menus, incorporating the mouse or command keys. Dialogue boxes are employed at the beginning of major program segments, and the usual file handling procedures apply.

There are some special cautions when using *QuickQuant* on the MacIntosh.

Screen-Saver Interruptions   If you have a screen saver program, any interruption of *QuickQuant* may make it impossible to bring back the original screen, and even the menu strip may disappear. You may still be able to continue where the program left off, but you may have to interrupt the program. As insurance, you should always save any large problem onto a file.

The recovery steps are listed below, in the sequence in which they should be applied. The first four may enable you to continue.

1. Jiggle the mouse.
2. Press the space bar.
3. Press enter.
4. Click the mouse.
5. Press command-period (which exits *QuickQuant*).

Printing *QuickQuant* reports   There are special requirements for printing *QuickQuant* reports. It is possible to print directly from *QuickQuant* only to an Imagewriter that is tied to the single computer. *If your MacIntosh is connected to a laser printer or shares a printer with other computers, you must leave* QuickQuant *to print.*

Many users must therefore save *QuickQuant* output onto a file. That file may be printed later using a word processing program such as *MacWrite*. In those cases, potential problems arise from the printing fonts and type sizes used.

QuickQuant reports are generated onscreen using a monospace font (Currier). Each character is the same width. The same computer code is used to write files to be printed onto hard copy. MacIntosh word processing programs ordinarily use default setting for proportionally spaced fonts (for example, Geneva). A printed *QuickQuant* report using a proportional font will have a jagged appearance, as in Figure A-9 for Shirley Smart's linear program.

After opening the *QuickQuant* report file from the word processing program, select the entire contents onto the desktop and change the typeface to Currier. This procedure will give the uniform appearance shown in Figure A-10. This report is still not suitable for printing, since the typeface is too large to permit all 80 columns to appear on a single line with a laser printer.

Figure A-11 shows the final form with the line wrap-arounds eliminated. This was accomplished by reducing the typesize from 12 to 10 points.

FIGURE A-9

MacWrite screen showing *QuickQuant* report with Geneva font that has proportional spacing.

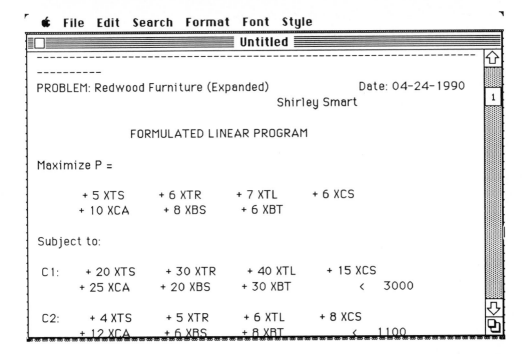

FIGURE A-10

MacWrite screen showing *QuickQuant* report converted to Currier font with monospacing.

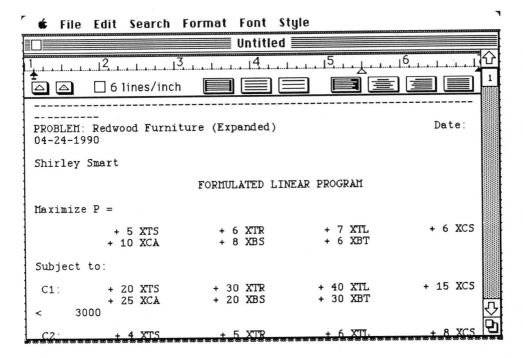

FIGURE A-11

MacWrite screen showing QuickQuant report with Currier font and 10 point type size.

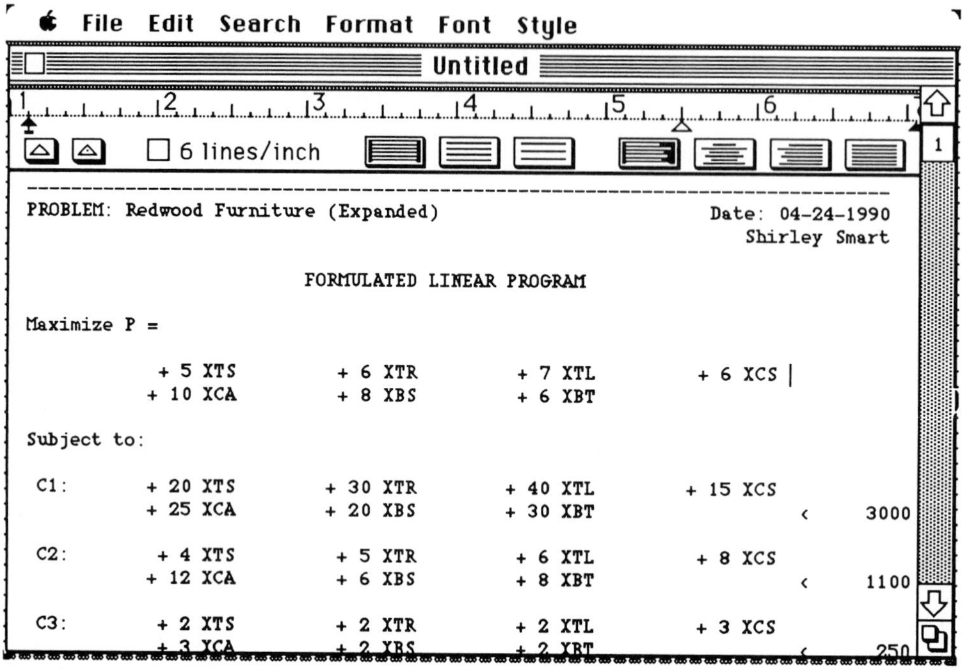

```
  File   Edit   Search   Format   Font   Style
═════════════════════════════════ Untitled ═══════════════════════════════
1.......,.2......,.3.......,4......,.5......,.6......,.
[△] [△]  □ 6 lines/inch   [▰] [▱] [≡]      [▰] [≡] [≡] [≡]    1
----------------------------------------------------------------------------
PROBLEM: Redwood Furniture (Expanded)              Date: 04-24-1990
                                                        Shirley Smart

                      FORMULATED LINEAR PROGRAM

Maximize P =

          + 5 XTS        + 6 XTR        + 7 XTL        + 6 XCS |
          + 10 XCA       + 8 XBS        + 6 XBT

Subject to:

  C1:     + 20 XTS       + 30 XTR       + 40 XTL       + 15 XCS
          + 25 XCA       + 20 XBS       + 30 XBT                <     3000

  C2:     + 4 XTS        + 5 XTR        + 6 XTL        + 8 XCS
          + 12 XCA       + 6 XBS        + 8 XBT                 <     1100

  C3:     + 2 XTS        + 2 XTR        + 2 XTL        + 3 XCS
          + 3 XCA        + 2 XBS        + 2 XBT                 <      250
```

Bibliography

Basic Concepts and Survey of Topics

Ackoff, R. L., and P. Rivett. *A Manager's Guide to Operations Research.* New York: John Wiley & Sons, 1963.

Baumol, W. J. *Economic Theory and Operations Analysis.* 4th ed. Englewood Cliffs, N.J.: Prentice-Hall, Inc., 1977.

Caywood, T. E., et al., "Guidelines for the Practice of Operations Research," *Operations Research,* September 1971, pp. 1127–48.

Churchman, C. W., R. L. Ackoff, and E. L. Arnoff. *Introduction to Operations Research.* New York: John Wiley & Sons, 1957.

Duckworth, W. E., et al. *A Guide to Operational Research.* 3rd ed. New York: Halsted Press, 1977.

Hillier, F. S., and G. J. Lieberman. *Introduction to Operations Research.* 4th ed. San Francisco: Holden-Day, 1986.

Miller, D. W., and M. K. Starr. *Executive Decisions and Operations Research.* 2nd ed. Englewood Cliffs, N.J.: Prentice-Hall, Inc., 1969.

———, and M. K. Starr. *The Structure of Human Decisions.* Englewood Cliffs, N.J.: Prentice-Hall, Inc., 1967.

Rivett, P. *Model Building for Decision Analysis.* New York: John Wiley & Sons, 1980.

Turban, E., "A Sample Survey of Operations-Research Activities at the Corporate Level," *Operations Research,* May–June 1972, pp. 708–721.

Wagner, H. M. *Principles of Operations Research with Applications to Managerial Decisions.* 2nd ed. Englewood Cliffs, N.J.: Prentice-Hall, Inc., 1975.

Winston, Wayne L. *Operations Research: Applications and Algorithms,* Duxbury Press, 1987.

Woolsey, R. E. D., "Operations Research and Management Science Today," *Operations Research,* May–June 1972, pp. 729–37.

Probability Concepts (Chapters 2–4)

Feller, W. *An Introduction to Probability Theory and Its Applications,* Vol. 1, 3rd ed. New York: John Wiley & Sons, 1968.

Hodges, J. L., Jr., and E. L. Lehmann. *Elements of Finite Probability.* San Francisco: Holden-Day, 1965.

Lapin, L. L. *Statistics for Modern Business Decisions.* 5th ed. San Diego: Harcourt Brace Jovanovich, 1990.

Laplace, Pierre Simon, Marquis de. *A Philosophical Essay on Probabilities.* New York: Dover Publications, 1951.

Lindgren, B. W., and G. W. McElrath, *Introduction to Probability and Statistics,* 4th ed. New York: Macmillan, 1978.

Mostellar, F., R. Rourke, and G. Thomas, Jr. *Probability and Statistics.* Reading, Mass.: Addison-Wesley, 1961.

Parzen, Emanuel. *Modern Probability Theory and Its Applications.* New York: John Wiley & Sons, 1960.

Forecasting (Chapter 5)

Box, G. E. P., and G. M. Jenkins. *Time Series Analysis: Forecasting and Control.* Rev. ed. San Francisco: Holden-Day, 1976.

Brown, R. G. *Smoothing, Forecasting, and Prediction.* Englewood Cliffs, N.J.: Prentice-Hall, Inc., 1963.

Chambers, J. C., S. K. Mullick, and D. D. Smith, "How to Choose the Right Forecasting Technique," *Harvard Business Review,* July–August 1971, pp. 45–74.

Gross, C., and R. Peterson. *Business Forecasting.* Boston: Houghton Mifflin, 1976.

Holt, C. C., F. Modigliani, J. F. Muth, and H. A. Simon. *Planning Production, Inventories, and Work Force.* Englewood Cliffs, N.J.: Prentice-Hall, Inc., 1960.

Lapin, L. L. *Statistics for Modern Business Decisions.* 5th ed. San Diego: Harcourt Brace Jovanovich, 1990.

Makridakis, S., and S. C. Wheelwright. *Forecasting: Methods and Applications.* New York: John Wiley & Sons, 1978.

———, *Interactive Forecasting: Univariate and Multivariate Methods.* 2nd ed. San Francisco: Holden-Day, 1978.

McLaughlin, R. L. *Time Series Forecasting.* Marketing Research Technique, Series No. 6, American Marketing Association, 1962.

Spencer, M. H., C. G. Clark, and P. W. Hoguet. *Business and Economic Forecasting: An Econometric Approach.* Homewood, Ill.: Richard D. Irwin, 1965.

Inventory Decisions (Chapters 6–7)

Arrow, K. J., S. Karlin, and H. Scarf. *Studies in the Mathematical Theory of Inventory and Production.* Stanford, Ca.: Stanford University Press, 1958.

Buffa, E. S., and J. G. Miller. *Production-Inventory Systems: Planning and Control.* 3rd ed. Homewood, Ill.: Richard D. Irwin, 1979.

Greene, J. H. *Production and Inventory Control Handbook.* New York: McGraw-Hill Book Co., 1970.

Hadley, G., and T. M. Whitin. *Analysis of Inventory Systems.* Englewood Cliffs, N.J.: Prentice-Hall, Inc., 1963.

Hillier, F. S., and G. J. Lieberman. *Introduction to Operations Research.* 4th ed. San Francisco: Holden-Day, 1986.

Holt, C. C., F. Modigliani, J. F. Muth, and H. A. Simon. *Planning Production, Inventories, and Work Force.* Englewood Cliffs, N.J.: Prentice-Hall, Inc., 1960.

Magee, J. R., and D. M. Boodman. *Production Planning and Inventory Control.* 2nd ed. New York: McGraw-Hill Book Co., 1967.

Starr, M. K., and D. W. Miller. *Inventory Control: Theory and Practice.* Englewood Cliffs, N.J.: Prentice-Hall, Inc., 1962.

Wagner, H. M. *Principles of Operations Research with Applications to Managerial Decisions.* 2nd ed. Englewood Cliffs, N.J.: Prentice-Hall, Inc., 1975.

———. *Statistical Management of Inventory Systems.* New York: John Wiley & Sons, 1962.

Whitin, T. M. *The Theory of Inventory Management.* Reprint of 1957 ed. Westport, Conn.: Greenwood Press, Inc.

Linear, Integer and Goal Programming (Chapters 8–17)

Dantzig, G. B. *Linear Programming and Extensions.* Princeton, N.J.: Princeton University Press, 1963.

Garvin, W. W. *Introduction to Linear Programming.* New York: McGraw-Hill Book Co., 1960.

Gass, S. I. *Linear Programming.* 4th ed. New York: McGraw-Hill Book Co., 1975.

Hillier, F. S., and G. J. Lieberman. *Introduction to Operations Research,* 4th ed. San Francisco: Holden-Day, 1986.

Kim, C. *Introduction to Linear Programming.* New York: Holt, Rinehart and Winston, Inc., 1971.

Kwak, N. K. *Mathematical Programming with Business Applications.* New York: McGraw-Hill Book Co., 1972.

Naylor, T. H., E. T. Byrne, and J. M. Vernon. *Introduction to Linear Programming: Methods and Cases.* Belmont, Ca.: Wadsworth Publishing Co., 1971.

Simonnard, M. *Linear Programming.* Englewood Cliffs, N.J.: Prentice-Hall, Inc., 1966.

Schniederjans, Marc J. *Linear Goal Programming,* Princeton: Petrocelli Books, 1984.

Wagner, H. M. *Principles of Operations Research with Applications to Managerial Decisions.* Englewood Cliffs, N.J.: Prentice-Hall, Inc., 1975.

Williams, H. *Model Building in Mathematical Programming,* 2nd ed. New York: Wiley, 1985.

Pert (Chapter 18)

Baker, B. N., and R. L. Ellis. *An Introduction to PERT/CPM.* Homewood, Ill.: Richard D. Irwin, 1964.

Evarts, H. E. *Introduction to PERT.* Boston: Allyn and Bacon, 1964.

Levin, R. I., and C. A. Kirkpatrick. *Planning and Control with PERT/CPM.* New York: McGraw-Hill Book Co., 1966.

Lockyer, K. G. *An Introduction to Critical Path Analysis,* New York: Beekman Pubs, 1969.

MacCrimmon, K. R., and C. A. Ryavec, "Analytical Study of the PERT Assumptions," *Operations Research,* January 1964, pp. 16–37.

Mande, C. *Applied Network Optimization.* Orlando, Fla.: Academic Press, 1979.

Moder, J. J., and C. R. Philips, *Project Management with CPM and PERT.* 2nd ed. New York: D. Van Nostrand, 1970.

Weist, J. D., and F. K. Levy. *A Management Guide to PERT/CPM: With Gert-PDM, DCPM and Other Networks.* 2nd ed. Englewood Cliffs, N.J.: Prentice-Hall, Inc., 1977.

Queues (Chapter 19)

Cooper, R. B. *Introduction to Queueing Theory,* 2nd ed. New York: Macmillan, 1981.

Cox, D. R., and W. L. Smith. *Queues.* London: Methuen & Co., Ltd., 1961.

Gross, D., and C. M. Harris, *Fundamentals of Queueing Theory,* 2nd ed. New York: Wiley-Interscience, 1985.

Hillier, F. S., and G. J. Lieberman. *Introduction to Operations Research.* 4th ed. San Francisco: Holden-Day, Inc., 1986.

Lee, A. M. *Applied Queueing Theory.* New York: St Martin's Press, 1966.

Morse, P. M. *Queues, Inventories, and Maintenance.* New York: John Wiley & Sons, 1958.

Newell, G. F. *Applications of Queueing Theory.* New York: Halsted Press, 1971.

Prabhu, N. U. *Queues and Inventories.* New York: John Wiley & Sons, 1965.

Saaty, T. L. *Elements of Queueing Theory.* New York: McGraw-Hill Book Co., 1961.

Wagner, H. M. *Principles of Operations Research with Applications to Managerial Decisions.* 2nd ed. Englewood Cliffs, N.J.: Prentice-Hall, Inc., 1975.

Simulation (Chapter 20)

Bonini, C. P. *Simulation of Information and Decision Systems in the Firm.* Englewood Cliffs, N.J.: Prentice-Hall, Inc., 1963.

Emshoff, J. R., and R. L. Sisson. *Design and Use of Computer Simulation Models.* New York: Macmillan, 1970.

Evans, G. W., G. F. Wallace, and G. L. Sutherland *Simulation Using Digital Computers.* Englewood Cliffs, N.J.: Prentice-Hall, Inc., 1967.

General Purpose Simulation System/360: Introductory User's Manual. White Plains, N.Y.: IBM Corporation, 1967.

Kleijnen, J. P. *Statistical Techniques in Simulation.* Parts 1 and 2. New York: Marcel Dekker, 1974, 1975.

Markowitz, H. M., "Simulating with SIMSCRIPT," *Management Science,* June 1966, pp. B-396–404.

Martin, F. F. *Computer Modeling and Simulation.* New York: John Wiley & Sons, 1968.

Meier, R. C., W. T. Newell, and H. J. Pazer. *Simulation in Business and Economics.* Englewood Cliffs, N.J.: Prentice-Hall, Inc., 1969.

Naylor, T. H., J. L. Balintfy, D. S. Burdick, and K. Hu. *Computer Simulation Technniques.* New York: John Wiley & Sons, 1966.

Pugh, A. L. *DYNAMO User's Manual,* 5th ed. Cambridge, Mass.: MIT Press, 1976.

Schmidt, J. W., and R. E. Taylor. *Simulation and Analysis of Industrial Systems.* Homewood, Ill.: Richard D. Irwin, 1970.

Tocher, K. D. *The Art of Simulation.* London: The English University Press, 1963.

Decision Theory and Utility (Chapters 21–26)

Aitchison, J. *Choice Against Chance: An Introduction to Statistical Decision Theory.* Reading, Mass.: Addison-Wesley, 1970.

Brown, R. V., A. S. Kahr, and C. Peterson. *Decision Analysis for the Manager.* New York: Holt, Rinehart and Winston, 1974.

Chernoff, H., and L. E. Moses. *Elementary Decision Theory.* New York: John Wiley & Sons, 1959.

Lapin, L. L. *Statistics for Modern Business Decisions.* 5th ed. San Diego: Harcourt Brace Jovanovich, 1990.

Luce, R. D., and H. Raiffa. *Games and Decisions: Introduction and Critical Survey.* New York: John Wiley & Sons, 1957.

Miller, D. W., and M. K. Starr. *Executive Decisions and Operations Research.* 2nd ed. Englewood Cliffs, N.J.: Prentice-Hall, Inc., 1969.

Morris, W. T. *Management Science: A Bayesian Introduction.* Englewood Cliffs, N.J.: Prentice-Hall, Inc., 1968.

Pratt, J. W., H. Raiffa, and R. Schlaifer. *Introduction to Statistical Decision Theory*. New York: McGraw-Hill Book Co., 1965.

Raiffa, H. *Decision Analysis: Introductory Lectures on Choices Under Uncertainty*. Reading, Mass.: Addison-Wesley, 1968.

Schlaifer, R. *Analysis of Decisions Under Uncertainty*. Reprint of 1969 ed. Melbourne, Fla.: Robert E. Krieger, 1978.

———. *Introduction to Statistics for Business Decisions*. New York: McGraw-Hill Book Co., 1961.

Games and Interactive Decisions (Chapter 27)

Davis, M. D. *Game Theory: A Nontechnical Introduction*. New York: Basic Books, Inc., 1973.

Karlin, S. *Mathematical Methods and Theory in Games, Programming and Economics*. Reading, Mass.: Addison-Wesley Publishing Co., Inc., 1959.

Luce, R. D., and H. Raiffa, *Games and Decisions: Introduction and Critical Survey*. New York: John Wiley & Sons, 1957.

May, F. B. *Introduction to Games of Strategy*. Boston: Allyn and Bacon, 1970.

McKinsey, J. C. C. *Introduction to the Theory of Games*. New York: McGraw-Hill Book Co., 1952.

Owen, G. *Game Theory*. 2nd ed. New York: Academic Press, 1982.

Rapoport, A. *Two Person Game Theory*. Ann Arbor: University of Michigan Press, 1966.

Vajda, S. *The Theory of Games and Linear Programming*. New York: Halsted Press, 1967.

Von Neumann, J., and O. Morgenstern. *Theory of Games and Economic Behavior*. Princeton, N.J.: Princeton University Press, 1953.

Williams, J. D. *The Compleat Strategist*. rev. ed. New York: McGraw-Hill Book Co., 1965.

Dynamic Programming (Chapter 28)

Bellman, R. E. *Adaptive Control Processes: A Guided Tour*. Princeton, N.J.: Princeton University Press, 1961.

———. *Dynamic Programming*. Princeton, N.J.: Princeton University Press, 1957.

———, and S. E. Dreyfus. *Applied Dynamic Programming*. Princeton, N.J.: Princeton University Press, 1962.

Hillier, F. S., and G. J. Lieberman. *Introduction to Operations Research*, 4th ed. San Francisco: Holden-Day, 1986.

Howard, R. A. *Dynamic Programming and Markov Processes*. Cambridge, Mass.: MIT Press, 1960.

Kaufman, A., and R. Cruon. *Dynamic Programming: Sequential Scientific Management*. New York: Academic Press, 1967.

Nemhauser, G. L. *Introduction to Dynamic Programming*. New York: John Wiley & Sons, 1966.

Wagner, H. M. *Principles of Operations Research with Applications to Managerial Decisions*. 2nd ed. Englewood Cliffs, N.J.: Prentice-Hall, Inc., 1975.

White, J. D. *Dynamic Programming*. San Francisco: Holden-Day, 1969.

Markov Processes (Chapter 29)

Derman, C. *Finite State Markovian Decision Processes*. New York: Academic Press, 1970.

Freedman, D. *Markov Chains*. San Francisco: Holden-Day, 1971.

Hillier, F. S., and G. J. Lieberman. *Introduction to Operations Research*. 4th ed. San Francisco: Holden-Day, 1986.

Howard, R. A. *Dynamic Programming and Markov Processes*. Cambridge, Mass.: MIT Press, 1960.

Kemeny, J. G., and J. L. Snell. *Finite Markov Chains.* New York: Springer-Verlag New York, Inc., 1976.

Martin, J. J. *Bayesian Decision Problems and Markov Chains.* Reprint of 1967 ed. Melbourne, Fla.: Robert E. Krieger, 1975.

Wagner, H. M. *Principles of Operations Research with Applications to Managerial Decisions.* 2nd ed. Englewood Cliffs, N.J.: Prentice-Hall, Inc., 1975.

Appendix Tables

TABLE A

Cumulative Values for the Binomial Probability Distribution

$$\Pr[R \leq r]$$

$n = 1$

P	.01	.05	.10	.20	.30	.40	.50
r							
0	0.9900	0.9500	0.9000	0.8000	0.7000	0.6000	0.5000
1	1.0000	1.0000	1.0000	1.0000	1.0000	1.0000	1.0000

$n = 2$

P	.01	.05	.10	.20	.30	.40	.50
r							
0	0.9801	0.9025	0.8100	0.6400	0.4900	0.3600	0.2500
1	0.9999	0.9975	0.9900	0.9600	0.9100	0.8400	0.7500
2	1.0000	1.0000	1.0000	1.0000	1.0000	1.0000	1.0000

$n = 3$

P	.01	.05	.10	.20	.30	.40	.50
r							
0	0.9703	0.8574	0.7290	0.5120	0.3430	0.2160	0.1250
1	0.9997	0.9927	0.9720	0.8960	0.7840	0.6480	0.5000
2	1.0000	0.9999	0.9990	0.9920	0.9730	0.9360	0.8750
3	1.0000	1.0000	1.0000	1.0000	1.0000	1.0000	1.0000

$n = 4$

P	.01	.05	.10	.20	.30	.40	.50
r							
0	0.9606	0.8145	0.6561	0.4096	0.2401	0.1296	0.0625
1	0.9994	0.9860	0.9477	0.8192	0.6517	0.4752	0.3125
2	1.0000	0.9995	0.9963	0.9728	0.9163	0.8208	0.6875
3	1.0000	1.0000	0.9999	0.9984	0.9919	0.9744	0.9375
4	1.0000	1.0000	1.0000	1.0000	1.0000	1.0000	1.0000

$n = 5$

P	.01	.05	.10	.20	.30	.40	.50
r							
0	0.9510	0.7738	0.5905	0.3277	0.1681	0.0778	0.0313
1	0.9990	0.9774	0.9185	0.7373	0.5282	0.3370	0.1875
2	1.0000	0.9988	0.9914	0.9421	0.8369	0.6826	0.5000
3	1.0000	1.0000	0.9995	0.9933	0.9692	0.9130	0.8125
4	1.0000	1.0000	1.0000	0.9997	0.9976	0.9898	0.9688
5				1.0000	1.0000	1.0000	1.0000

SOURCE: From *Management Science for Business Decisions* by Lawrence L. Lapin, copyright © 1980 by Harcourt Brace Jovanovich, Inc. Reproduced by permission of the publisher.

TABLE A (*continued*)

$$n = 10$$

P	.01	.05	.10	.20	.30	.40	.50
r							
0	0.9044	0.5987	0.3487	0.1074	0.0282	0.0060	0.0010
1	0.9957	0.9139	0.7361	0.3758	0.1493	0.0464	0.0107
2	˙0.9999	0.9885	0.9298	0.6778	0.3828	0.1673	0.0547
3	1.0000	0.9990	0.9872	0.8791	0.6496	0.3823	0.1719
4	1.0000	0.9999	0.9984	0.9672	0.8497	0.6331	0.3770
5	1.0000	1.0000	0.9999	0.9936	0.9526	0.8338	0.6230
6	1.0000	1.0000	1.0000	0.9991	0.9894	0.9452	0.8281
7				0.9999	0.9999	0.9877	0.9453
8				1.0000	1.0000	0.9983	0.9893
9						0.9999	0.9990
10						1.0000	1.0000

$$n = 20$$

P	.01	.05	.10	.20	.30	.40	.50
r							
0	0.8179	0.3585	0.1216	0.0115	0.0008	0.0000	0.0000
1	0.9831	0.7358	0.3917	0.0692	0.0076	0.0005	0.0000
2	0.9990	0.9245	0.6769	0.2061	0.0355	0.0036	0.0002
3	1.0000	0.9841	0.8670	0.4114	0.1071	0.0160	0.0013
4	1.0000	0.9974	0.9568	0.6296	0.2375	0.0510	0.0059
5	1.0000	0.9997	0.9887	0.8042	0.4164	0.1256	0.0207
6	1.0000	1.0000	0.9976	0.9133	0.6080	0.2500	0.0577
7	1.0000	1.0000	0.9996	0.9679	0.7723	0.4159	0.1316
8	1.0000	1.0000	0.9999	0.9900	0.8867	0.5956	0.2517
9	1.0000	1.0000	1.0000	0.9974	0.9520	0.7553	0.4119
10				0.9994	0.9829	0.8725	0.5881
11				0.9999	0.9949	0.9435	0.7483
12				1.0000	0.9987	0.9790	0.8684
13					0.9997	0.9935	0.9423
14					1.0000	0.9984	0.9793
15						0.9997	0.9941
16						1.0000	0.9987
17							0.9998
18							1.0000

TABLE A (*continued*)

$n = 50$

P	.01	.05	.10	.20	.30	.40	.50
r							
0	0.6050	0.0769	0.0052	0.0000	0.0000	0.0000	0.0000
1	0.9106	0.2794	0.0338	0.0002	0.0000	0.0000	0.0000
2	0.9862	0.5405	0.1117	0.0013	0.0000	0.0000	0.0000
3	0.9984	0.7604	0.2503	0.0057	0.0000	0.0000	0.0000
4	0.9999	0.8964	0.4312	0.0185	0.0002	0.0000	0.0000
5	1.0000	0.9622	0.6161	0.0480	0.0007	0.0000	0.0000
6	1.0000	0.9882	0.7702	0.1034	0.0025	0.0000	0.0000
7	1.0000	0.9968	0.8779	0.1904	0.0073	0.0001	0.0000
8	1.0000	0.9992	0.9421	0.3073	0.0183	0.0002	0.0000
9	1.0000	0.9998	0.9755	0.4437	0.0402	0.0008	0.0000
10	1.0000	1.0000	0.9906	0.5836	0.0789	0.0022	0.0000
11	1.0000	1.0000	0.9968	0.7107	0.1390	0.0057	0.0000
12	1.0000	1.0000	0.9990	0.8139	0.2229	0.0133	0.0002
13	1.0000	1.0000	0.9997	0.8894	0.3279	0.0280	0.0005
14	1.0000	1.0000	0.9999	0.9393	0.4468	0.0540	0.0013
15	1.0000	1.0000	1.0000	0.9692	0.5692	0.0955	0.0033
16				0.9856	0.6839	0.1561	0.0077
17				0.9937	0.7822	0.2369	0.0164
18				0.9975	0.8594	0.3356	0.0325
19				0.9991	0.9152	0.4465	0.0595
20				0.9997	0.9522	0.5610	0.1013
21				0.9999	0.9749	0.6701	0.1611
22				1.0000	0.9877	0.7660	0.2399
23					0.9944	0.8438	0.3359
24					0.9976	0.9022	0.4439
25					0.9991	0.9427	0.5561
26					0.9997	0.9686	0.6641
27					0.9999	0.9840	0.7601
28					1.0000	0.9924	0.8389
29						0.9966	0.8987
30						0.9986	0.9405
31						0.9995	0.9675
32						0.9998	0.9836
33						0.9999	0.9923
34						1.0000	0.9967
35							0.9987
36							0.9995
37							0.9998
38							1.0000

TABLE A (*continued*)

$$n = 100$$

P r	.01	.05	.10	.20	.30	.40	.50
0	0.3660	0.0059	0.0000	0.0000	0.0000	0.0000	0.0000
1	0.7358	0.0371	0.0003	0.0000	0.0000	0.0000	0.0000
2	0.9206	0.1183	0.0019	0.0000	0.0000	0.0000	0.0000
3	0.9816	0.2578	0.0078	0.0000	0.0000	0.0000	0.0000
4	0.9966	0.4360	0.0237	0.0000	0.0000	0.0000	0.0000
5	0.9995	0.6160	0.0576	0.0000	0.0000	0.0000	0.0000
6	0.9999	0.7660	0.1172	0.0001	0.0000	0.0000	0.0000
7	1.0000	0.8720	0.2061	0.0003	0.0000	0.0000	0.0000
8	1.0000	0.9369	0.3209	0.0009	0.0000	0.0000	0.0000
9	1.0000	0.9718	0.4513	0.0023	0.0000	0.0000	0.0000
10	1.0000	0.9885	0.5832	0.0057	0.0000	0.0000	0.0000
11	1.0000	0.9957	0.7030	0.0126	0.0000	0.0000	0.0000
12	1.0000	0.9985	0.8018	0.0253	0.0000	0.0000	0.0000
13	1.0000	0.9995	0.8761	0.0469	0.0001	0.0000	0.0000
14	1.0000	0.9999	0.9274	0.0804	0.0002	0.0000	0.0000
15	1.0000	1.0000	0.9601	0.1285	0.0004	0.0000	0.0000
16	1.0000	1.0000	0.9794	0.1923	0.0010	0.0000	0.0000
17	1.0000	1.0000	0.9900	0.2712	0.0022	0.0000	0.0000
18	1.0000	1.0000	0.9954	0.3621	0.0045	0.0000	0.0000
19	1.0000	1.0000	0.9980	0.4602	0.0089	0.0000	0.0000
20	1.0000	1.0000	0.9992	0.5595	0.0165	0.0000	0.0000
21	1.0000	1.0000	0.9997	0.6540	0.0288	0.0000	0.0000
22	1.0000	1.0000	0.9999	0.7389	0.0479	0.0001	0.0000
23	1.0000	1.0000	1.0000	0.8109	0.0755	0.0003	0.0000
24				0.8686	0.1136	0.0006	0.0000
25				0.9125	0.1631	0.0012	0.0000
26				0.9442	0.2244	0.0024	0.0000
27				0.9658	0.2964	0.0046	0.0000
28				0.9800	0.3768	0.0084	0.0000
29				0.9888	0.4623	0.0148	0.0000
30				0.9939	0.5491	0.0248	0.0000
31				0.9969	0.6331	0.0398	0.0001
32				0.9984	0.7107	0.0615	0.0002
33				0.9993	0.7793	0.0913	0.0004
34				0.9997	0.8371	0.1303	0.0009
35				0.9999	0.8839	0.1795	0.0018

TABLE A (*continued*)

$n = 100$

P r	.01	.05	.10	.20	.30	.40	.50
36				0.9999	0.9201	0.2386	0.0033
37				1.0000	0.9470	0.3068	0.0060
38					0.9660	0.3822	0.0105
39					0.9790	0.4621	0.0176
40					0.9875	0.5433	0.0284
41					0.9928	0.6225	0.0443
42					0.9960	0.6967	0.0666
43					0.9979	0.7635	0.0967
44					0.9989	0.8211	0.1356
45					0.9995	0.8689	0.1841
46					0.9997	0.9070	0.2421
47					0.9999	0.9362	0.3086
48					0.9999	0.9577	0.3822
49					1.0000	0.9729	0.4602
50						0.9832	0.5398
51						0.9900	0.6178
52						0.9942	0.6914
53						0.9968	0.7579
54						0.9983	0.8159
55						0.9991	0.8644
56						0.9996	0.9033
57						0.9998	0.9334
58						0.9999	0.9557
59						1.0000	0.9716
60							0.9824
61							0.9895
62							0.9940
63							0.9967
64							0.9982
65							0.9991
66							0.9996
67							0.9998
68							0.9999
69							1.0000

TABLE B

Areas Under the Standard Normal Curve

The following table provides the area between the mean and normal deviate value z.

Normal Deviate z	.00	.01	.02	.03	.04	.05	.06	.07	.08	.09
0.0	.0000	.0040	.0080	.0120	.0160	.0199	.0239	.0279	.0319	.0359
0.1	.0398	.0438	.0478	.0517	.0557	.0596	.0636	.0675	.0714	.0753
0.2	.0793	.0832	.0871	.0910	.0948	.0987	.1026	.1064	.1103	.1141
0.3	.1179	.1217	.1255	.1293	.1331	.1368	.1406	.1443	.1480	.1517
0.4	.1554	.1591	.1628	.1664	.1700	.1736	.1772	.1808	.1844	.1879
0.5	.1915	.1950	.1985	.2019	.2054	.2088	.2123	.2157	.2190	.2224
0.6	.2257	.2291	.2324	.2357	.2389	.2422	.2454	.2486	.2518	.2549
0.7	.2580	.2612	.2642	.2673	.2704	.2734	.2764	.2794	.2823	.2852
0.8	.2881	.2910	.2939	.2967	.2995	.3023	.3051	.3078	.3106	.3133
0.9	.3159	.3186	.3212	.3238	.3264	.3289	.3315	.3340	.3365	.3389
1.0	.3413	.3438	.3461	.3485	.3508	.3531	.3554	.3577	.3599	.3621
1.1	.3643	.3665	.3686	.3708	.3729	.3749	.3770	.3790	.3810	.3830
1.2	.3849	.3869	.3888	.3907	.3925	.3944	.3962	.3980	.3997	.4015
1.3	.4032	.4049	.4066	.4082	.4099	.4115	.4131	.4147	.4162	.4177
1.4	.4192	.4207	.4222	.4236	.4251	.4265	.4279	.4292	.4306	.4319
1.5	.4332	.4345	.4357	.4370	.4382	.4394	.4406	.4418	.4429	.4441
1.6	.4452	.4463	.4474	.4484	.4495	.4505	.4515	.4525	.4535	.4545
1.7	.4554	.4564	.4573	.4582	.4591	.4599	.4608	.4616	.4625	.4633
1.8	.4641	.4649	.4656	.4664	.4671	.4678	.4686	.4693	.4699	.4706
1.9	.4713	.4719	.4726	.4732	.4738	.4744	.4750	.4756	.4761	.4767
2.0	.4772	.4778	.4783	.4788	.4793	.4798	.4803	.4808	.4812	.4817
2.1	.4821	.4826	.4830	.4834	.4838	.4842	.4846	.4850	.4854	.4857
2.2	.4861	.4864	.4868	.4871	.4875	.4878	.4881	.4884	.4887	.4890
2.3	.4893	.4896	.4898	.4901	.4904	.4906	.4909	.4911	.4913	.4916
2.4	.4918	.4920	.4922	.4925	.4927	.4929	.4931	.4932	.4934	.4936
2.5	.4938	.4940	.4941	.4943	.4945	.4946	.4948	.4949	.4951	.4952
2.6	.4953	.4955	.4956	.4957	.4959	.4960	.4961	.4962	.4963	.4964
2.7	.4965	.4966	.4967	.4968	.4969	.4970	.4971	.4972	.4973	.4974
2.8	.4974	.4975	.4976	.4977	.4977	.4978	.4979	.4979	.4980	.4981
2.9	.4981	.4982	.4982	.4983	.4984	.4984	.4985	.4985	.4986	.4986
3.0	.49865	.4987	.4987	.4988	.4988	.4989	.4989	.4989	.4990	.4990
4.0	.49997									

SOURCE: From *Statistical Analysis for Decision Making* by Morris Hamburg, copyright © 1970 by Harcourt Brace Jovanovich, Inc. Reproduced by permission of the publisher.

TABLE C
Loss Function for Decision Making with the Normal Curve

$L(D)$

D	.00	.01	.02	.03	.04	.05	.06	.07	.08	.09
.0	.3989	.3940	.3890	.3841	.3793	.3744	.3697	.3649	.3602	.3556
.1	.3509	.3464	.3418	.3373	.3328	.3284	.3240	.3197	.3154	.3111
.2	.3069	.3027	.2986	.2944	.2904	.2863	.2824	.2784	.2745	.2706
.3	.2668	.2630	.2592	.2555	.2518	.2481	.2445	.2409	.2374	.2339
.4	.2304	.2270	.2236	.2203	.2169	.2137	.2104	.2072	.2040	.2009
.5	.1978	.1947	.1917	.1887	.1857	.1828	.1799	.1771	.1742	.1714
.6	.1687	.1659	.1633	.1606	.1580	.1554	.1528	.1503	.1478	.1453
.7	.1429	.1405	.1381	.1358	.1334	.1312	.1289	.1267	.1245	.1223
.8	.1202	.1181	.1160	.1140	.1120	.1100	.1080	.1061	.1042	.1023
.9	.1004	.09860	.09680	.09503	.09328	.09156	.08986	.08819	.08654	.08491
1.0	.08332	.08174	.08019	.07866	.07716	.07568	.07422	.07279	.07138	.06999
1.1	.06862	.06727	.06595	.06465	.06336	.06210	.06086	.05964	.05844	.05726
1.2	.05610	.05496	.05384	.05274	.05165	.05059	.04954	.04851	.04750	.04650
1.3	.04553	.04457	.04363	.04270	.04179	.04090	.04002	.03916	.03831	.03748
1.4	.03667	.03587	.03508	.03431	.03356	.03281	.03208	.03137	.03067	.02998
1.5	.02931	.02865	.02800	.02736	.02674	.02612	.02552	.02494	.02436	.02380
1.6	.02324	.02270	.02217	.02165	.02114	.02064	.02015	.01967	.01920	.01874
1.7	.01829	.01785	.01742	.01699	.01658	.01617	.01578	.01539	.01501	.01464
1.8	.01428	.01392	.01357	.01323	.01290	.01257	.01226	.01195	.01164	.01134
1.9	.01105	.01077	.01049	.01022	$.0^2 9957$	$.0^2 9698$	$.0^2 9445$	$.0^2 9198$	$.0^2 8957$	$.0^2 8721$
2.0	$.0^2 8491$	$.0^2 8266$	$.0^2 8046$	$.0^2 7832$	$.0^2 7623$	$.0^2 7418$	$.0^2 7219$	$.0^2 7024$	$.0^2 6835$	$.0^2 6649$
2.1	$.0^2 6468$	$.0^2 6292$	$.0^2 6120$	$.0^2 5952$	$.0^2 5788$	$.0^2 5628$	$.0^2 5472$	$.0^2 5320$	$.0^2 5172$	$.0^2 5028$
2.2	$.0^2 4887$	$.0^2 4750$	$.0^2 4616$	$.0^2 4486$	$.0^2 4358$	$.0^2 4235$	$.0^2 4114$	$.0^2 3996$	$.0^2 3882$	$.0^2 3770$
2.3	$.0^2 3662$	$.0^2 3556$	$.0^2 3453$	$.0^2 3352$	$.0^2 3255$	$.0^2 3159$	$.0^2 3067$	$.0^2 2977$	$.0^2 2889$	$.0^2 2804$
2.4	$.0^2 2720$	$.0^2 2640$	$.0^2 2561$	$.0^2 2484$	$.0^2 2410$	$.0^2 2337$	$.0^2 2267$	$.0^2 2199$	$.0^2 2132$	$.0^2 2067$

TABLE C (continued)

x										
2.5	$.0^{2}2004$	$.0^{2}1943$	$.0^{2}1883$	$.0^{2}1826$	$.0^{2}1769$	$.0^{2}1715$	$.0^{2}1662$	$.0^{2}1610$	$.0^{2}1560$	$.0^{2}1511$
2.6	$.0^{2}1464$	$.0^{2}1418$	$.0^{2}1373$	$.0^{2}1330$	$.0^{2}1288$	$.0^{2}1247$	$.0^{2}1207$	$.0^{2}1169$	$.0^{2}1132$	$.0^{2}1095$
2.7	$.0^{2}1060$	$.0^{2}1026$	$.0^{3}9928$	$.0^{3}9607$	$.0^{3}9295$	$.0^{3}8992$	$.0^{3}8699$	$.0^{3}8414$	$.0^{3}8138$	$.0^{3}7870$
2.8	$.0^{3}7611$	$.0^{3}7359$	$.0^{3}7115$	$.0^{3}6879$	$.0^{3}6650$	$.0^{3}6428$	$.0^{3}6213$	$.0^{3}6004$	$.0^{3}5802$	$.0^{3}5606$
2.9	$.0^{3}5417$	$.0^{3}5233$	$.0^{3}5055$	$.0^{3}4883$	$.0^{3}4716$	$.0^{3}4555$	$.0^{3}4398$	$.0^{3}4247$	$.0^{3}4101$	$.0^{3}3959$
3.0	$.0^{3}3822$	$.0^{3}3689$	$.0^{3}3560$	$.0^{3}3436$	$.0^{3}3316$	$.0^{3}3199$	$.0^{3}3087$	$.0^{3}2978$	$.0^{3}2873$	$.0^{3}2771$
3.1	$.0^{3}2673$	$.0^{3}2577$	$.0^{3}2485$	$.0^{3}2396$	$.0^{3}2311$	$.0^{3}2227$	$.0^{3}2147$	$.0^{3}2070$	$.0^{3}1995$	$.0^{3}1922$
3.2	$.0^{3}1852$	$.0^{3}1785$	$.0^{3}1720$	$.0^{3}1657$	$.0^{3}1596$	$.0^{3}1537$	$.0^{3}1480$	$.0^{3}1426$	$.0^{3}1373$	$.0^{3}1322$
3.3	$.0^{3}1273$	$.0^{3}1225$	$.0^{3}1179$	$.0^{3}1135$	$.0^{3}1093$	$.0^{3}1051$	$.0^{3}1012$	$.0^{4}9734$	$.0^{4}9365$	$.0^{4}9009$
3.4	$.0^{4}8666$	$.0^{4}8335$	$.0^{4}8016$	$.0^{4}7709$	$.0^{4}7413$	$.0^{4}7127$	$.0^{4}6852$	$.0^{4}6587$	$.0^{4}6331$	$.0^{4}6085$
3.5	$.0^{4}5848$	$.0^{4}5620$	$.0^{4}5400$	$.0^{4}5188$	$.0^{4}4984$	$.0^{4}4788$	$.0^{4}4599$	$.0^{4}4417$	$.0^{4}4242$	$.0^{4}4073$
3.6	$.0^{4}3911$	$.0^{4}3755$	$.0^{4}3605$	$.0^{4}3460$	$.0^{4}3321$	$.0^{4}3188$	$.0^{4}3059$	$.0^{4}2935$	$.0^{4}2816$	$.0^{4}2702$
3.7	$.0^{4}2592$	$.0^{4}2486$	$.0^{4}2385$	$.0^{4}2287$	$.0^{4}2193$	$.0^{4}2103$	$.0^{4}2016$	$.0^{4}1933$	$.0^{4}1853$	$.0^{4}1776$
3.8	$.0^{4}1702$	$.0^{4}1632$	$.0^{4}1563$	$.0^{4}1498$	$.0^{4}1435$	$.0^{4}1375$	$.0^{4}1317$	$.0^{4}1262$	$.0^{4}1208$	$.0^{4}1157$
3.9	$.0^{4}1108$	$.0^{4}1061$	$.0^{4}1016$	$.0^{5}9723$	$.0^{5}9307$	$.0^{5}8908$	$.0^{5}8525$	$.0^{5}8158$	$.0^{5}7806$	$.0^{5}7469$
4.0	$.0^{5}7145$	$.0^{5}6835$	$.0^{5}6538$	$.0^{5}6253$	$.0^{5}5980$	$.0^{5}5718$	$.0^{5}5468$	$.0^{5}5227$	$.0^{5}4997$	$.0^{5}4777$
4.1	$.0^{5}4566$	$.0^{5}4364$	$.0^{5}4170$	$.0^{5}3985$	$.0^{5}3807$	$.0^{5}3637$	$.0^{5}3475$	$.0^{5}3319$	$.0^{5}3170$	$.0^{5}3027$
4.2	$.0^{5}2891$	$.0^{5}2760$	$.0^{5}2635$	$.0^{5}2516$	$.0^{5}2402$	$.0^{5}2292$	$.0^{5}2188$	$.0^{5}2088$	$.0^{5}1992$	$.0^{5}1901$
4.3	$.0^{5}1814$	$.0^{5}1730$	$.0^{5}1650$	$.0^{5}1574$	$.0^{5}1501$	$.0^{5}1431$	$.0^{5}1365$	$.0^{5}1301$	$.0^{5}1241$	$.0^{5}1183$
4.4	$.0^{5}1127$	$.0^{5}1074$	$.0^{5}1024$	$.0^{6}9756$	$.0^{6}9296$	$.0^{6}8857$	$.0^{6}8437$	$.0^{6}8037$	$.0^{6}7655$	$.0^{6}7290$
4.5	$.0^{6}6942$	$.0^{6}6610$	$.0^{6}6294$	$.0^{6}5992$	$.0^{6}5704$	$.0^{6}5429$	$.0^{6}5167$	$.0^{6}4917$	$.0^{6}4679$	$.0^{6}4452$
4.6	$.0^{6}4236$	$.0^{6}4029$	$.0^{6}3833$	$.0^{6}3645$	$.0^{6}3467$	$.0^{6}3297$	$.0^{6}3135$	$.0^{6}2981$	$.0^{6}2834$	$.0^{6}2694$
4.7	$.0^{6}2560$	$.0^{6}2433$	$.0^{6}2313$	$.0^{6}2197$	$.0^{6}2088$	$.0^{6}1984$	$.0^{6}1884$	$.0^{6}1790$	$.0^{6}1700$	$.0^{6}1615$
4.8	$.0^{6}1533$	$.0^{6}1456$	$.0^{6}1382$	$.0^{6}1312$	$.0^{6}1246$	$.0^{6}1182$	$.0^{6}1122$	$.0^{6}1065$	$.0^{6}1011$	$.0^{7}9588$
4.9	$.0^{7}9096$	$.0^{7}8629$	$.0^{7}8185$	$.0^{7}7763$	$.0^{7}7362$	$.0^{7}6982$	$.0^{7}6620$	$.0^{7}6276$	$.0^{7}5950$	$.0^{7}5640$

SOURCE: From Robert O. Schlaifer, *Introduction to Statistics for Business Decisions.* New York: McGraw-Hill Book Co., 1961. Reproduced by permission of the copyright holder, the President and Fellows of Harvard College.

TABLE D
Exponential Functions

y	e^y	e^{-y}	y	e^y	e^{-y}
0.00	1.0000	1.000000	3.00	20.086	.049787
0.10	1.1052	.904837	3.10	22.198	.045049
0.20	1.2214	.818731	3.20	24.533	.040762
0.30	1.3499	.740818	3.30	27.113	.036883
0.40	1.4918	.670320	3.40	29.964	.033373
0.50	1.6487	.606531	3.50	33.115	.030197
0.60	1.8221	.548812	3.60	36.598	.027324
0.70	2.0138	.496585	3.70	40.447	.024724
0.80	2.2255	.449329	3.80	44.701	.022371
0.90	2.4596	.406570	3.90	49.402	.020242
1.00	2.7183	.367879	4.00	54.598	.018316
1.10	3.0042	.332871	4.10	60.340	.016573
1.20	3.3201	.301194	4.20	66.686	.014996
1.30	3.6693	.272532	4.30	73.700	.013569
1.40	4.0552	.246597	4.40	81.451	.012277
1.50	4.4817	.223130	4.50	90.017	.011109
1.60	4.9530	.201897	4.60	99.484	.010052
1.70	5.4739	.182684	4.70	109.95	.009095
1.80	6.0496	.165299	4.80	121.51	.008230
1.90	6.6859	.149569	4.90	134.29	.007447
2.00	7.3891	.135335	5.00	148.41	.006738
2.10	8.1662	.122456	5.10	164.02	.006097
2.20	9.0250	.110803	5.20	181.27	.005517
2.30	9.9742	.100259	5.30	200.34	.004992
2.40	11.023	.090718	5.40	221.41	.004517
2.50	12.182	.082085	5.50	244.69	.004087
2.60	13.464	.074274	5.60	270.43	.003698
2.70	14.880	.067206	5.70	298.87	.003346
2.80	16.445	.060810	5.80	330.30	.003028
2.90	18.174	.055023	5.90	365.04	.002739
3.00	20.086	.049787	6.00	403.43	.002479

TABLE E
Cumulative Probability Values for the Poisson Distribution

$$\Pr[X \le x]$$

λt	1.0	2.0	3.0	4.0	5.0	6.0	7.0	8.0	9.0	10.0
x										
0	0.3679	0.1353	0.0498	0.0183	0.0067	0.0025	0.0009	0.0003	0.0001	0.0000
1	0.7358	0.4060	0.1991	0.0916	0.0404	0.0174	0.0073	0.0030	0.0012	0.0005
2	0.9197	0.6767	0.4232	0.2381	0.1247	0.0620	0.0296	0.0138	0.0062	0.0028
3	0.9810	0.8571	0.6472	0.4335	0.2650	0.1512	0.0818	0.0424	0.0212	0.0103
4	0.9963	0.9473	0.8153	0.6288	0.4405	0.2851	0.1730	0.0996	0.0550	0.0293
5	0.9994	0.9834	0.9161	0.7851	0.6160	0.4457	0.3007	0.1912	0.1157	0.0671
6	0.9999	0.9955	0.9665	0.8893	0.7622	0.6063	0.4497	0.3134	0.2068	0.1301
7	1.0000	0.9989	0.9881	0.9489	0.8666	0.7440	0.5987	0.4530	0.3239	0.2202
8		0.9998	0.9962	0.9786	0.9319	0.8472	0.7291	0.5926	0.4557	0.3328
9		1.0000	0.9989	0.9919	0.9682	0.9161	0.8305	0.7166	0.5874	0.4579
10			0.9997	0.9972	0.9863	0.9574	0.9015	0.8159	0.7060	0.5830
11			0.9999	0.9991	0.9945	0.9799	0.9466	0.8881	0.8030	0.6968
12			1.0000	0.9997	0.9980	0.9912	0.9730	0.9362	0.8758	0.7916
13				0.9999	0.9993	0.9964	0.9872	0.9658	0.9262	0.8645
14				1.0000	0.9998	0.9986	0.9943	0.9827	0.9585	0.9165
15					0.9999	0.9995	0.9976	0.9918	0.9780	0.9513
16					1.0000	0.9998	0.9990	0.9963	0.9889	0.9730
17						0.9999	0.9996	0.9984	0.9947	0.9857
18						1.0000	0.9999	0.9993	0.9976	0.9928
19							0.9999	0.9997	0.9989	0.9965
20							1.0000	0.9999	0.9996	0.9984
21								1.0000	0.9998	0.9993
22									0.9999	0.9997
23									1.0000	0.9999
24										0.9999
25										1.0000

SOURCE: From *Management Science for Business Decisions* by Lawrence L. Lapin, copyright © 1980 by Harcourt Brace Jovanovich, Inc. Reproduced by permission of the publisher.

TABLE E (continued)

λt	11.0	12.0	13.0	14.0	15.0	16.0	17.0	18.0	19.0	20.0
x										
0	0.0000	0.0000	0.0000	0.0000	0.0000	0.0000	0.0	0.0	0.0	0.0
1	0.0002	0.0001	0.0000	0.0000	0.0000	0.0000	0.0000	0.0000	0.0000	0.0
2	0.0012	0.0005	0.0002	0.0001	0.0000	0.0000	0.0000	0.0000	0.0000	0.0000
3	0.0049	0.0023	0.0011	0.0005	0.0002	0.0001	0.0000	0.0000	0.0000	0.0000
4	0.0151	0.0076	0.0037	0.0018	0.0009	0.0004	0.0002	0.0001	0.0000	0.0000
5	0.0375	0.0203	0.0107	0.0055	0.0028	0.0014	0.0007	0.0003	0.0002	0.0001
6	0.0786	0.0458	0.0259	0.0142	0.0076	0.0040	0.0021	0.0010	0.0005	0.0003
7	0.1432	0.0895	0.0540	0.0316	0.0180	0.0100	0.0054	0.0029	0.0015	0.0008
8	0.2320	0.1550	0.0998	0.0621	0.0374	0.0220	0.0126	0.0071	0.0039	0.0021
9	0.3405	0.2424	0.1658	0.1094	0.0699	0.0433	0.0261	0.0154	0.0089	0.0050
10	0.4599	0.3472	0.2517	0.1757	0.1185	0.0774	0.0491	0.0304	0.0183	0.0108
11	0.5793	0.4616	0.3532	0.2600	0.1847	0.1270	0.0847	0.0549	0.0347	0.0214
12	0.6887	0.5760	0.4631	0.3585	0.2676	0.1931	0.1350	0.0917	0.0606	0.0390
13	0.7813	0.6815	0.5730	0.4644	0.3632	0.2745	0.2009	0.1426	0.0984	0.0661
14	0.8540	0.7720	0.6751	0.5704	0.4656	0.3675	0.2808	0.2081	0.1497	0.1049
15	0.9074	0.8444	0.7636	0.6694	0.5681	0.4667	0.3714	0.2866	0.2148	0.1565
16	0.9441	0.8987	0.8355	0.7559	0.6641	0.5660	0.4677	0.3750	0.2920	0.2211
17	0.9678	0.9370	0.8905	0.8272	0.7489	0.6593	0.5640	0.4686	0.3784	0.2970
18	0.9823	0.9626	0.9302	0.8826	0.8195	0.7423	0.6549	0.5622	0.4695	0.3814
19	0.9907	0.9787	0.9573	0.9235	0.8752	0.8122	0.7363	0.6509	0.5606	0.4703
20	0.9953	0.9884	0.9750	0.9521	0.9170	0.8682	0.8055	0.7307	0.6472	0.5591
21	0.9977	0.9939	0.9859	0.9711	0.9469	0.9108	0.8615	0.7991	0.7255	0.6437
22	0.9989	0.9969	0.9924	0.9833	0.9672	0.9418	0.9047	0.8551	0.7931	0.7206
23	0.9995	0.9985	0.9960	0.9907	0.9805	0.9633	0.9367	0.8989	0.8490	0.7875
24	0.9998	0.9993	0.9980	0.9950	0.9888	0.9777	0.9593	0.9317	0.8933	0.8432
25	0.9999	0.9997	0.9990	0.9974	0.9938	0.9869	0.9747	0.9554	0.9269	0.8878
26	1.0000	0.9999	0.9995	0.9987	0.9967	0.9925	0.9848	0.9718	0.9514	0.9221
27		0.9999	0.9998	0.9994	0.9983	0.9959	0.9912	0.9827	0.9687	0.9475
28		1.0000	0.9999	0.9997	0.9991	0.9978	0.9950	0.9897	0.9805	0.9657
29			1.0000	0.9999	0.9996	0.9989	0.9973	0.9940	0.9881	0.9782
30				0.9999	0.9998	0.9994	0.9985	0.9967	0.9930	0.9865
31				1.0000	0.9999	0.9997	0.9992	0.9982	0.9960	0.9919
32					0.9999	0.9999	0.9996	0.9990	0.9978	0.9953
33					1.0000	0.9999	0.9998	0.9995	0.9988	0.9973
34						1.0000	0.9999	0.9997	0:9994	0.9985
35							0.9999	0.9999	0.9997	0.9992
36							1.0000	0.9999	0.9998	0.9996
37								1.0000	0.9999	0.9998
38									1.0000	0.9999
39										0.9999
40										1.0000

TABLE F
Random Numbers

12651	61646	11769	75109	86996	97669	25757	32535	07122	76763
81769	74436	02630	72310	45049	18029	07469	42341	98173	79260
36737	98863	77240	76251	00654	64688	09343	70278	67331	98729
82861	54371	76610	94934	72748	44124	05610	53750	95938	01485
21325	15732	24127	37431	09723	63529	73977	95218	96074	42138
74146	47887	62463	23045	41490	07954	22597	60012	98866	90959
90759	64410	54179	66075	61051	75385	51378	08360	95946	95547
55683	98078	02238	91540	21219	17720	87817	41705	95785	12563
79686	17969	76061	83748	55920	83612	41540	86492	06447	60568
70333	00201	86201	69716	78185	62154	77930	67663	29529	75116
14042	53536	07779	04157	41172	36473	42123	43929	50533	33437
59911	08256	06596	48416	69770	68797	56080	14223	59199	30162
62368	62623	62742	14891	39247	52242	98832	69533	91174	57979
57529	97751	54976	48957	74599	08759	78494	52785	68526	64618
15469	90574	78033	66885	13936	42117	71831	22961	94225	31816
18625	23674	53850	32827	81647	80820	00420	63555	74489	80141
74626	68394	88562	70745	23701	45630	65891	58220	35442	60414
11119	16519	27384	90199	79210	76965	99546	30323	31664	22845
41101	17336	48951	53674	17880	45260	08575	49321	36191	17095
32123	91576	84221	78902	82010	30847	62329	63898	23268	74283
26091	68409	69704	82267	14751	13151	93115	01437	56945	89661
67680	79790	48462	59278	44185	29616	76531	19589	83139	28454
15184	19260	14073	07026	25264	08388	27182	22557	61501	67481
58010	45039	57181	10238	36874	28546	37444	80824	63981	39942
56425	53996	86245	32623	78858	08143	60377	42925	42815	11159
82630	84066	13592	60642	17904	99718	63432	88642	37858	25431
14927	40909	23900	48761	44860	92467	31742	87142	03607	32059
23740	22505	07489	85986	74420	21744	97711	36648	35620	97949
32990	97446	03711	63824	07953	85965	87089	11687	92414	67257
05310	24058	91946	78437	34365	82469	12430	84754	19354	72745
21839	39937	27534	88913	49055	19218	47712	67677	51889	70926
08833	42549	93981	94051	28382	83725	72643	64233	97252	17133
58336	11139	47479	00931	91560	95372	97642	33856	54825	55680
62032	91144	75478	47431	52726	30289	42411	91886	51818	78292
45171	30557	53116	04118	58301	24375	65609	85810	18620	49198
91611	62656	60128	35609	63698	78356	50682	22505	01692	36291
55472	63819	86314	49174	93582	73604	78614	78849	23096	72825
18573	09729	74091	53994	10970	86557	65661	41854	26037	53296
60866	02955	90288	82136	83644	94455	06560	78029	98768	71296
45043	55608	82767	60890	74646	79485	13619	98868	40857	19415
17831	09737	79473	75945	28394	79334	70577	38048	03607	06932
40137	03981	07585	18128	11178	32601	27994	05641	22600	86064
77776	31343	14576	97706	16039	47517	43300	59080	80392	63189
69605	44104	40103	95635	05635	81673	68657	09559	23510	95875
19916	52934	26499	09821	87331	80993	61299	36979	73599	35055
02606	58552	07678	56619	65325	30705	99582	53390	46357	13244
65183	73160	87131	35530	47946	09854	18080	02321	05809	04898
10740	98914	44916	11322	89717	88189	30143	52687	19420	60061
98642	89822	71691	51573	83666	61642	46683	33761	47542	23551
60139	25601	93663	25547	02654	94829	48672	28736	84994	13071

SOURCE: The Rand Corporation. *A Million Random Digits with 100,000 Normal Deviates* (New York: Free Press, 1955), excerpt from page 387. Copyright 1955 by The Rand Corporation. Used by permission.

TABLE G Four-Place Common Logarithms

N	0	1	2	3	4	5	6	7	8	9				Proportional Parts					
											1	2	3	4	5	6	7	8	9
10	0000	0043	0086	0128	0170	0212	0253	0294	0334	0374	4	8	12	17	21	25	29	33	37
11	0414	0453	0492	0531	0569	0607	0645	0682	0719	0755	4	8	11	15	19	23	26	30	34
12	0792	0828	0864	0899	0934	0969	1004	1038	1072	1106	3	7	10	14	17	21	24	28	31
13	1139	1173	1206	1239	1271	1303	1335	1367	1399	1430	3	6	10	13	16	19	23	26	29
14	1461	1492	1523	1553	1584	1614	1644	1673	1703	1732	3	6	9	12	15	18	21	24	27
15	1761	1790	1818	1847	1875	1903	1931	1959	1987	2014	3	6	8	11	14	17	20	22	25
16	2041	2068	2095	2122	2148	2175	2201	2227	2253	2279	3	5	8	11	13	16	18	21	24
17	2304	2330	2355	2380	2405	2430	2455	2480	2504	2529	2	5	7	10	12	15	17	20	22
18	2553	2577	2601	2625	2648	2672	2695	2718	2742	2765	2	5	7	9	12	14	16	19	21
19	2788	2810	2833	2856	2878	2900	2923	2945	2967	2989	2	4	7	9	11	13	16	18	20
20	3010	3032	3054	3075	3096	3118	3139	3160	3181	3201	2	4	6	8	11	13	15	17	19
21	3222	3243	3263	3284	3304	3324	3345	3365	3385	3404	2	4	6	8	10	12	14	16	18
22	3424	3444	3464	3483	3502	3522	3541	3560	3579	3598	2	4	6	8	10	12	14	15	17
23	3617	3636	3655	3674	3692	3711	3729	3747	3766	3784	2	4	6	7	9	11	13	15	17
24	3802	3820	3838	3856	3874	3892	3909	3927	3945	3962	2	4	5	7	9	11	12	14	16
25	3979	3997	4014	4031	4048	4065	4082	4099	4116	4133	2	3	5	7	9	10	12	14	15
26	4150	4166	4183	4200	4216	4232	4249	4265	4281	4298	2	3	5	7	8	10	11	13	15
27	4314	4330	4346	4362	4378	4393	4409	4425	4440	4456	2	3	5	6	8	9	11	13	14
28	4472	4487	4502	4518	4533	4548	4564	4579	4594	4609	2	3	5	6	8	9	11	12	14
29	4624	4639	4654	4669	4683	4698	4713	4728	4742	4757	1	3	4	6	7	9	10	12	13
30	4771	4786	4800	4814	4829	4843	4857	4871	4886	4900	1	3	4	6	7	9	10	11	13
31	4914	4928	4942	4955	4969	4983	4997	5011	5024	5038	1	3	4	6	7	8	10	11	12
32	5051	5065	5079	5092	5105	5119	5132	5145	5159	5172	1	3	4	5	7	8	9	11	12
33	5185	5198	5211	5224	5237	5250	5263	5276	5289	5302	1	3	4	5	6	8	9	10	12
34	5315	5328	5340	5353	5366	5378	5391	5403	5416	5428	1	3	4	5	6	8	9	10	11
35	5441	5453	5465	5478	5490	5502	5514	5527	5539	5551	1	2	4	5	6	7	9	10	11
36	5563	5575	5587	5599	5611	5623	5635	5647	5658	5670	1	2	4	5	6	7	8	10	11
37	5682	5694	5705	5717	5729	5740	5752	5763	5775	5786	1	2	3	5	6	7	8	9	10
38	5798	5809	5821	5832	5843	5855	5866	5877	5888	5899	1	2	3	5	6	7	8	9	10
39	5911	5922	5933	5944	5955	5966	5977	5988	5999	6010	1	2	3	4	5	7	8	9	10
40	6021	6031	6042	6053	6064	6075	6085	6096	6107	6117	1	2	3	4	5	6	8	9	10
41	6128	6138	6149	6160	6170	6180	6191	6201	6212	6222	1	2	3	4	5	6	7	8	9
42	6232	6243	6253	6263	6274	6284	6294	6304	6314	6325	1	2	3	4	5	6	7	8	9
43	6335	6345	6355	6365	6375	6385	6395	6405	6415	6425	1	2	3	4	5	6	7	8	9
44	6435	6444	6454	6464	6474	6484	6493	6503	6513	6522	1	2	3	4	5	6	7	8	9
45	6532	6542	6551	6561	6571	6580	6590	6599	6609	6618	1	2	3	4	5	6	7	8	9
46	6628	6637	6646	6656	6665	6675	6684	6693	6702	6712	1	2	3	4	5	6	7	7	8
47	6721	6730	6739	6749	6758	6767	6776	6785	6794	6803	1	2	3	4	5	5	6	7	8
48	6812	6821	6830	6839	6848	6857	6866	6875	6884	6893	1	2	3	4	4	5	6	7	8
49	6902	6911	6920	6928	6937	6946	6955	6964	6972	6981	1	2	3	4	4	5	6	7	8
50	6990	6998	7007	7016	7024	7033	7042	7050	7059	7067	1	2	3	3	4	5	6	7	8
51	7076	7084	7093	7101	7110	7118	7126	7135	7143	7152	1	2	3	3	4	5	6	7	8
52	7160	7168	7177	7185	7193	7202	7210	7218	7226	7235	1	2	2	3	4	5	6	7	7
53	7243	7251	7259	7267	7275	7284	7292	7300	7308	7316	1	2	2	3	4	5	6	6	7
54	7324	7332	7340	7348	7356	7364	7372	7380	7388	7396	1	2	2	3	4	5	6	6	7
N	0	1	2	3	4	5	6	7	8	9	1	2	3	4	5	6	7	8	9

TABLE G   (*continued*)

N	0	1	2	3	4	5	6	7	8	9	Proportional Parts								
											1	2	3	4	5	6	7	8	9
55	7404	7412	7419	7427	7435	7443	7451	7459	7466	7474	1	2	2	3	4	5	5	6	7
56	7482	7490	7497	7505	7513	7520	7528	7536	7543	7551	1	2	2	3	4	5	5	6	7
57	7559	7566	7574	7582	7589	7597	7604	7612	7619	7627	1	2	2	3	4	5	5	6	7
58	7634	7642	7649	7657	7664	7672	7679	7686	7694	7701	1	1	2	3	4	4	5	6	7
59	7709	7716	7723	7731	7738	7745	7752	7760	7767	7774	1	1	2	3	4	4	5	6	7
60	7782	7789	7796	7803	7810	7818	7825	7832	7839	7846	1	1	2	3	4	4	5	6	6
61	7853	7860	7868	7875	7882	7889	7896	7903	7910	7917	1	1	2	3	4	4	5	6	6
62	7924	7931	7938	7945	7952	7959	7966	7973	7980	7987	1	1	2	3	3	4	5	6	6
63	7993	8000	8007	8014	8021	8028	8035	8041	8048	8055	1	1	2	3	3	4	5	5	6
64	8062	8069	8075	8082	8089	8096	8102	8109	8116	8122	1	1	2	3	3	4	5	5	6
65	8129	8136	8142	8149	8156	8162	8169	8176	8182	8189	1	1	2	3	3	4	5	5	6
66	8195	8202	8209	8215	8222	8228	8235	8241	8248	8254	1	1	2	3	3	4	5	5	6
67	8261	8267	8274	8280	8287	8293	8299	8306	8312	8319	1	1	2	3	3	4	5	5	6
68	8325	8331	8338	8344	8351	8357	8363	8370	8376	8382	1	1	2	3	3	4	4	5	6
69	8388	8395	8401	8407	8414	8420	8426	8432	8439	8445	1	1	2	2	3	4	4	5	6
70	8451	8457	8463	8470	8476	8482	8488	8494	8500	8506	1	1	2	2	3	4	4	5	6
71	8513	8519	8525	8531	8537	8543	8549	8555	8561	8567	1	1	2	2	3	4	4	5	5
72	8573	8579	8585	8591	8597	8603	8609	8615	8621	8627	1	1	2	2	3	4	4	5	5
73	8633	8639	8645	8651	8657	8663	8669	8675	8681	8686	1	1	2	2	3	4	4	5	5
74	8692	8698	8704	8710	8716	8722	8727	8733	8739	8745	1	1	2	2	3	4	4	5	5
75	8751	8756	8762	8768	8774	8779	8785	8791	8797	8802	1	1	2	2	3	3	4	5	5
76	8808	8814	8820	8825	8831	8837	8842	8848	8854	8859	1	1	2	2	3	3	4	5	5
77	8865	8871	8876	8882	8887	8893	8899	8904	8910	8915	1	1	2	2	3	3	4	4	5
78	8921	8927	8932	8938	8943	8949	8954	8960	8965	8971	1	1	2	2	3	3	4	4	5
79	8976	8982	8987	8993	8998	9004	9009	9015	9020	9025	1	1	2	2	3	3	4	4	5
80	9031	9036	9042	9047	9053	9058	9063	9069	9074	9079	1	1	2	2	3	3	4	4	5
81	9085	9090	9096	9101	9106	9112	9117	9122	9128	9133	1	1	2	2	3	3	4	4	5
82	9138	9143	9149	9154	9159	9165	9170	9175	9180	9186	1	1	2	2	3	3	4	4	5
83	9191	9196	9201	9206	9212	9217	9222	9227	9232	9238	1	1	2	2	3	3	4	4	5
84	9243	9248	9253	9258	9263	9269	9274	9279	9284	9289	1	1	2	2	3	3	4	4	5
85	9294	9299	9304	9309	9315	9320	9325	9330	9335	9340	1	1	2	2	3	3	4	4	5
86	9345	9350	9355	9360	9365	9370	9375	9380	9385	9390	1	1	2	2	3	3	4	4	5
87	9395	9400	9405	9410	9415	9420	9425	9430	9435	9440	0	1	1	2	2	3	3	4	4
88	9445	9450	9455	9460	9465	9469	9474	9479	9484	9489	0	1	1	2	2	3	3	4	4
89	9494	9499	9504	9509	9513	9518	9523	9528	9533	9538	0	1	1	2	2	3	3	4	4
90	9542	9547	9552	9557	9562	9566	9571	9576	9581	9586	0	1	1	2	2	3	3	4	4
91	9590	9595	9600	9605	9609	9614	9619	9624	9628	9633	0	1	1	2	2	3	3	4	4
92	9638	9643	9647	9652	9657	9661	9666	9671	9675	9680	0	1	1	2	2	3	3	4	4
93	9685	9689	9694	9699	9703	9708	9713	9717	9722	9727	0	1	1	2	2	3	3	4	4
94	9731	9736	9741	9745	9750	9754	9759	9763	9768	9773	0	1	1	2	2	3	3	4	4
95	9777	9782	9786	9791	9795	9800	9805	9809	9814	9818	0	1	1	2	2	3	3	4	4
96	9823	9827	9832	9836	9841	9845	9850	9854	9859	9863	0	1	1	2	2	3	3	4	4
97	9868	9872	9877	9881	9886	9890	9894	9899	9903	9908	0	1	1	2	2	3	3	4	4
98	9912	9917	9921	9926	9930	9934	9939	9943	9948	9952	0	1	1	2	2	3	3	4	4
99	9956	9961	9965	9969	9974	9978	9983	9987	9991	9996	0	1	1	2	2	3	3	3	4
N	0	1	2	3	4	5	6	7	8	9	1	2	3	4	5	6	7	8	9

Answers to Selected Problems

2-1 (a) 1/5   (b) 1/10,000   (c) 1/4   (d) 2/3

2-3 (a) (1) .20 (2) .35 (3) .40 (4) .05
     (b) (1) .15 (2) .65 (3) .20
     (c) (1) .06 (2) .04 (3) .01

2-7 (a) .7   (b) .5   (c) .7   (d) .3   (e) .6

2-12 (a) .12   (b) .48   (c) .08   (d) .32

2-15 (a) .774   (b) .226

2-19 (a) $\Pr[\text{reject}] = .15$; $\Pr[\text{bad}] = .10$; $\Pr[\text{reject} \mid \text{bad}] = .95$ (b) .095

2-26 (a) .947   The greens should *not* be watered.   (b) .333

2-27 (a) .8   (b) .2

3-2 $(-\$1)(20/38) + \$1(18/38) = -\$0.053$
     After many wagers the gambler will lose an average of 5.3¢ per play.

3-7 (a) .72398   (b) .00051   (c) .25257

3-12 (a) Yes   (b) Yes   (c) No   (d) No   (e) No

3-15 (a) .25   (b) .50   (c) 5

3-18 (a) .0490   (b) .2262   (c) .6723   (d) .9687

3-20 (a) .0565   (b) .0710   (c) .8744   (d) .5956   (e) .2500   (f) .8534

3-23 (a) .4332   (b) .1915   (c) .2420   (d) .0062   (e) .0968   (f) .9861
     (g) .97585   (h) .0606

3-24 .9544

3-31 (a) .0774   (b) .9797   (c) .0286   (d) .6315

4-1 (a) No   (b) Yes   (c) Maybe

4-4 (a) 60 sec; 22.4 sec   (b) (1) .3472 (2) .0594 (3) .5000 (4) .8732

4-8 (a) .105   (b) .15   (c) .38   (d) .73

4-14 302

5-1 Winter $ 72,000   Spring $ 84,700
      Summer 121,000   Fall   179,685

5-9 (a) $\hat{Y} = 200.67 + 9.673X$ $(X = 0$ at 1981)
      (b) 297.40

5-12 (b) $\hat{Y} = 22.405 + 3.619X$

5-13 (a) 1,100   (b) 900   (c) 700

5-16 Winter   50.6   Spring 89.8
      Summer 150.9   Fall   108.7

5-17

Quarter	(a) Moving Average	(b) Percentage of Moving Average	Seasonal Index
1986 W			93.4
S			112.0
S	6.8	63.2	69.2
F	7.8	138.5	125.4
1987 W	8.7	89.7	93.4
S	9.4	112.8	112.0
S	10.3	67.0	69.2
F	11.6	116.4	125.4
1988 W	12.6	102.4	93.4
S	13.6	111.8	112.0
S	14.4	71.5	69.2
F	14.4	129.9	125.4
1989 W	14.3	97.2	93.4
S	14.1	102.1	112.0
S	13.9	73.4	69.2
F	14.3	121.0	125.4
1990 W	15.3	88.2	93.4
S	16.2	112.3	112.0
S			69.2
F			125.4

5-21 $\hat{Y} = -.5595 + .0817X_1 + 1.1605X_2$

6-1 $Q^* = 200$; order once every .2 year.

6-4 (a) $Q^* = 2,620, S^* = 2,544, T^* = .262$ year   Out of stock .029 of the time.
      (b) $763.23; smaller

6-11 (a) 158.1 tons   (b) .79 year   (c) .1581 year

6-15 (a) 632.5 acres   Fertilize every .127 year, or 7.9 times yearly.

7-2 Stock 150 boxes.

7-6 (a) 62   (b) $16.235   (c) $14.015

7-9 6,120 trees

7-14 (a) $\mu = 7.3$ pairs   (b) $r^* = 9, Q^* = 32$ (c) 1.7 pairs   (d) $68.21

7-18 $r^* = 67$ $Q^* = 406$

7-20 $r^* = 5,180$ gallons $Q^* = 10,760$ gallons

8-2 (a) $X_1 = 7.5, X_2 = 2.5$ (b) $X_1 = 1.5, X_2 = 1$ (c) $X_1 = -.5, X_2 = 2$
(d) $X_1 = -1.5, X_2 = 4.5$

8-3 $X_A = 2.4, X_B = 2.4, P = 26.4$

8-8 (b) There are two most attractive corners:
(1) $X_1 = 4, X_2 = 4, P = 24$ (2) $X_1 = 12, X_2 = 0, P = 24$
(c) $P = 24$ The point represents an optimal solution.

8-12 (a) Letting X_R = Quantity of regular models; X_D = Quantity of deluxe models

$$\begin{aligned}
\text{Maximize} \quad & P = 10X_R + 15X_D \\
\text{Subject to} \quad & 5X_R + 8X_D \le 80 \quad \text{(labor)} \\
& X_R + X_D \le 12 \quad \text{(frame)} \\
\text{where} \quad & X_R, X_D \ge 0
\end{aligned}$$

(b) $X_R = 5\frac{1}{3}, X_D = 6\frac{2}{3}, P = 153\frac{1}{3}$ dollars

8-14 4 forged bits, 6 machined bits, $P = 102$ dollars

9-1 Letting
X_F = quantity of fancy lamps
X_O = quantity of ornate lamps
X_P = quantity of plain lamps
X_R = quantity of rococco lamps

$$\begin{aligned}
\text{Maximize} \quad & P = 100X_F + 150X_O + 200X_P + 200X_R \\
\text{Subject to} \quad & 10X_F + 8X_O + 10X_P + 20X_R \le 1,000 \quad \text{(labor)} \\
& 2X_F + 3X_O + 1X_P + 1X_R \le 200 \quad \text{(machine)} \\
& 10X_F + 20X_O + 15X_P + 30X_R \le 5,000 \quad \text{(sheet metal)} \\
& \qquad\qquad - X_P + 2X_R \le 0 \quad \text{(quantity)} \\
\text{where} \quad & X_F, X_O, X_P, X_R \ge 0
\end{aligned}$$

9-7 Letting
X_H = pounds of hog bellies X_P = pounds of pork
X_T = pounds of tripe X_C = pounds of chicken
X_B = pounds of beef

$$\begin{aligned}
\text{Minimize} \quad & C = .30X_H + .20X_T + .70X_B + .60X_P + .45X_C \\
\text{Subject to} \quad & X_H + X_T \qquad\qquad\qquad\qquad\qquad\qquad \le .10 \quad \text{(restriction)} \\
& \qquad\qquad\qquad\qquad\qquad\qquad\quad X_C \le .25 \quad \text{(chicken)} \\
& \qquad\qquad\qquad X_B \qquad\qquad\qquad\qquad \ge .30 \quad \text{(beef)} \\
& 3X_H + 5X_T + 4X_B + 3X_P + 3X_C \ge 3 \quad \text{(protein)} \\
& 5X_H + 3X_T + 2X_B + 4X_P + 3X_C \le 4 \quad \text{(fat)} \\
& 6X_H + 4X_T + 5X_B + 9X_B + 4X_C \le 8 \quad \text{(water)} \\
\text{where} \quad & \text{all } Xs \ge 0
\end{aligned}$$

9-8 Letting
X_A = number of gallons of Ant-Can't
X_B = number of gallons of Boll-Toll
X_C = number of gallons of Caterpillar-Chiller

$$\begin{aligned}
\text{Maximize} \quad & P = 5X_A + 6X_B + 7X_C \\
\text{Subject to} \quad & .1X_A + .1X_B + .1X_C \le 1,000 \quad \text{(catalyst)} \\
& .1X_A \qquad\quad + .1X_C \le 1,000 \quad \text{(malathion)} \\
& \qquad\quad .2X_B + .2X_C \le 2,000 \quad \text{(parathion)} \\
& X_A - X_B \qquad\qquad \le 500 \quad \text{(quantity mix)} \\
\text{where} \quad & X_A, X_B, X_C \ge 0
\end{aligned}$$

9-11 Letting $\quad X_{ij}$ = Number of tombstones shipped from quarry i to mason j
$i = A$ or B
$j = C, D,$ or E

Minimize	$C = 10X_{AC} + 15X_{AD} + 8X_{AE} + 12X_{BC} + 9X_{BD} + 10X_{BE}$
Subject to	$X_{AC} + \quad X_{AD} + X_{AE} = 100 \quad$ (Abinger capacity)
	$X_{BC} + \quad X_{BD} + X_{BE} = 200 \quad$ (Barnesly capacity)
	$X_{AC} + X_{BC} = \quad 50 \quad$ (Cedrick's demand)
	$X_{AD} + X_{BD} = 150 \quad$ (Dunstan's demand)
	$X_{AE} + X_{BE} = 100 \quad$ (Eldred's demand)
where	all $Xs \geq \quad 0$

9-16 Letting $\quad X_B$ = Number of spots on KBAT
X_J = Number of spots on WJOK
X_R = Number of spots on WROB
X_P = Number of spots on KPOW

Maximize	$P = 300X_B + 120X_J + 150X_R + 400X_P$
Subject to	$100X_B + \quad 50X_J + \quad 75X_R + 150X_P \leq 10{,}000 \quad$ (funds)
	$X_B \qquad\qquad\qquad\qquad\qquad \leq \quad 30 \quad$ (availability on KBAT)
	$X_P \leq \quad 40 \quad$ (availability on KPOW)
	$.25X_B - .75X_J - .75X_R + .25X_P \leq \quad 0 \quad$ (golden oldie)
where	all variables $\geq \quad 0$

10-3 (a) *Sac.* $\quad 3 \quad 7 \quad 9 \quad -3 \qquad 23 \quad 75$
$\qquad$ *Imp.* $\quad 2 \quad 0 \quad 0 \qquad 10 \quad -15 \quad$ —
(b) X_4 is the entering variable; X_3 is the exiting variable.

10-5 (a, b)

UNIT PROFIT		3	2	1	0	0	
	Basic Mix	X_1	X_2	X_3	X_4	X_5	Sol.
0	X_4	0	2	1↓	1	0	10
0	X_5←	0	−3	②	0	1	15
3	X_1	1	1	0	0	0	20
	Sac.	3	3	0	0	0	60
	Imp.	0	−1	1	0	0	—

(c)

UNIT
PROFIT

		3	2	1	0	0	

	Basic Mix	X_1	X_2	X_3	X_4	X_5	Sol.
0	X_4	0	3.5	0	1	$-.5$	2.5
1	X_3	0	-1.5	1	0	.5	7.5
3	X_1	1	1	0	0	0	20
	Sac.	3	1.5	1	0	.5	67.5
	Imp.	0	.5	0	0	$-.5$	—

10-9 (a) $X_1 = 0$, $X_2 = 3$, $P = 9$

(b) Letting X_A, X_B, and X_C represent the respective slack variables.

Maximize $P = 2X_1 + 3X_2 + 0X_A + 0X_B + 0X_C$

Subject to
$$3X_1 + 2X_2 + 1X_A + 0X_B + 0X_C = 6 \quad \text{(resource } A)$$
$$1X_1 + 0X_2 + 0X_A + 1X_B + 0X_C = 5 \quad \text{(resource } B)$$
$$0X_1 + 1X_2 + 0X_A + 0X_B + 1X_C = 4 \quad \text{(resource } C)$$

where $\quad$ all $Xs \geq 0$

(c)

UNIT
PROFIT

		2	3	0	0	0	

	Basic Mix	X_1	X_2	X_A	X_B	X_C	Sol.
0	$X_A \leftarrow$	3	②↓	1	0	0	6
0	X_B	1	0	0	1	0	5
0	X_C	0	1	0	0	1	4
	Sac.	0	0	0	0	0	0
	Imp.	2	3	0	0	0	—

3	X_2	3/2	1	1/2	0	0	3
0	X_B	1	0	0	1	0	5
0	X_C	$-3/2$	0	$-1/2$	0	1	1
	Sac.	9/2	3	3/2	0	0	9
	Imp.	$-5/2$	0	$-3/2$	0	0	—

$$X_1 = 0 \qquad X_B = 5$$
$$X_2 = 3 \qquad X_C = 1$$
$$X_A = 0$$
$$P = 9$$

10-15 Letting S_W = quantity of unused wood

S_L = quantity of unused labor

UNIT PROFIT		20	15	15	0	0	
	Basic Mix	X_T	X_C	X_B	S_W	S_L	Sol.
0	$S_W \leftarrow$	⑩ ↓	3	10	1	0	100
0	S_L	5	5	5	0	1	60
	Sac.	0	0	0	0	0	0
	Imp.	20	15	15	0	0	—

20	X_T	1	.3 ↓	1	.1	0	10
0	$S_L \leftarrow$	0	③.⑤	0	−.5	1	10
	Sac.	20	6	20	2	0	200
	Imp.	0	9	−5	−2	0	—

20	X_T	1	0	1	1/7	−3/35	64/7
15	X_C	0	1	0	−1/7	2/7	20/7
	Sac.	20	15	20	5/7	18/7	1,580/7
	Imp.	0	0	−5	−5/7	−18/7	—

$$X_T = 64/7 \qquad S_W = 0$$
$$X_C = 20/7 \qquad S_L = 0$$
$$X_B = 0$$
$$P = 1,580/7$$

10-16 (c) Sammy should make 150 butterscotch, 0 cinnamon, and 100 peppermint apples, at a profit of $35.

10-17 ChipMont should make 285,714.3 chips each of the CPU and integrated types and no memory chips, at a profit of $185,714.30.

11-3 (a) $X_1 = 2.4$, $X_2 = 1.2$; $P = 5(2.4) + 6(1.2) = 19.2$

(b) X_R = unused quantity of resource

X_M = surplus beyond minimum mixture requirement

a_M = artificial variable for mixture constraint

Maximize $P = 5X_1 + 6X_2 + 0X_R + 0X_M - Ma_D$

Subject to $3X_1 + 4X_2 + 1X_R + 0X_M + 0a_M = 12$ (resource)

$2X_1 + 6X_2 + 0X_R - 1X_M + 1a_M = 12$ (mixture)

where   all variables ≥ 0

(c)

UNIT
PROFIT

		5	6	0	0	$-M$	
	Basic Mix	X_1	X_2	X_R	X_M	a_M	Sol.
0	X_R	3	4$\downarrow$	1	0	0	12
$-M$	$a_M \leftarrow$	2	⑥	0	-1	1	12
	Sac.	$-2M$	$-6M$	0	M	$-M$	$-12M$
	Imp.	$5+2M$	$6+6M$	0	$-M$	0	—
0	$X_R \leftarrow$	⑩/6 $\downarrow$	0	1	4/6	$-4/6$	4
6	X_2	2/6	1	0	$-1/6$	1/6	2
	Sac.	2	6	0	-1	1	12
	Imp.	3	0	0	1	$-M-1$	—
5	X_1	1	0	6/10	4/10	$-4/10$	12/5
6	X_2	0	1	$-2/10$	$-9/30$	9/30	6/5
	Sac.	5	6	18/10	6/30	$-6/30$	96/5
	Imp.	0	0	$-18/10$	$-6/30$	$-M+6/30$	—

$$X_1 = 12/5 = 2.4 \qquad X_R = X_M = 0$$
$$X_2 = 6/5 = 1.2$$
$$P = 96/5 = 19.2$$

11-5 (a) $X_A = 2$, $X_B = 4$; $P = 2.2$

(b) X_Y = surplus beyond restriction Y $\qquad a_Y$ = artificial variable for restriction Y
X_Z = surplus beyond restriction Z $\qquad a_Z$ = artificial variable for restriction Z

Minimize $\quad C = .5X_A + .3X_B + 0X_Y + 0X_Z + Ma_Y + Ma_Z$
Subject to $\quad 1X_A + 2X_B - 1X_Y + 0X_Z + 1a_Y + 0a_Z = 10 \quad (Y)$
$\qquad\qquad 2X_A + 1X_B + 0X_Y - 1X_Z + 0a_Y + 1a_Z = 8 \quad (Z)$
where $\qquad$ all variables ≥ 0

(c)

UNIT
COST

		.5	.3	0	0	M	M	
	Basic Mix	X_A	X_B	X_Y	X_Z	a_Y	a_Z	Sol.
M	$a_Y \leftarrow$	1	② $\downarrow$	-1	0	1	0	10
M	a_Z	2	1	0	-1	0	1	8
	Sac.	$3M$	$3M$	$-M$	$-M$	M	M	$18M$
	Imp.	$.5-3M$	$.3-3M$	M	M	0	0	—

.3	X_B	1/2↓	1	−1/2	0	1/2	0	5
M	a_Z←	(3/2)	0	2/2	−1	−1/2	1	3
	Sac.	.15 +1.5M	.3	−.15 +.5M	−M	.15 −.5M	M	1.5 +3M
	Imp.	.35 −1.5M	0	.15 −.5M	M	−.15 +1.5M	0	—

.3	X_B	0	1	−8/12	2/6	8/12	−2/6	4
.5	X_A	1	0	2/6	−2/3	−2/6	2/3	2
	Sac.	.5	.3	−4/120	−7/30	1/30	7/30	2.2
	Imp.	0	0	1/30	7/30	M −1/30	M −7/30	—

$$X_A = 2 \qquad X_B = 4 \qquad X_Y = 0 \qquad X_Z = 0 \qquad C = 2.2$$

11-9 (a) unbounded problem   (b) $X_1 = 0$, $X_2 = 10$, $X_3 = 0$; $P = 20$

11-13 Quicker Oats should spend the following amounts:

$100,000 for television
55,000 for radio
20,000 for magazines
25,000 for prizes

11-20 Using the variables X_E = number of tons from Eastern, X_N = number of tons from Northern, X_T = number of tons from Tom's Lucky, with X_L representing unused labor, X_R and X_C as surplus variables for the Northern requirement and copper constraints, the following linear program applies:

Maximize $P = 280X_E + 185X_N + 260X_T$
Subject to

$$
\begin{array}{rll}
1X_E + 2X_N + 2X_T \le & 300 & \text{(labor)} \\
1X_N \ge & 100 & \text{(requirement)} \\
50X_E + 20X_N + 25X_T \ge & 5{,}000 & \text{(copper)}
\end{array}
$$

where $X_E, X_N, X_T \ge 0$
The optimal solution is

$X_E = 100$ tons $X_L = 0$
$X_N = 100$ $X_R = 0$
$X_T = 0$ $X_C = 2{,}000$
            $P = \$46{,}500$

11-21 160 beef, 60 chicken, 80 fish; $C = 490$ dollars

12-1 Letting $U_A = A$ cost per unit
        $U_B = B$ cost per unit

Minimize $C = 16U_A + 24U_B$
Subject to $4U_A + 6U_B \ge 12$ (variable 1)
            $4U_A + 4U_B \ge 16$ (variable 2)
where $U_A, U_B \ge 0$

$U_A = 4$, $U_B = 0$, $C = 64$

12-2 (b) Letting U_L = cost per hour of labor
U_F = cost per frame
(c) $U_L = 5/3$, $U_F = 5/3$, $C = 460/3$ dollars

12-5 (a) $5/7$; $18/7 (b) $U_T = 0$, $U_C = 0$, $U_B = 5$ (c) $X_T = 64/7$, $X_C = 20/7$,
$X_B = 0$, $P = 1580/7$ dollars (d) Yes

12-13 (e) Rott should make no Baltics, 400/7 Gothics, and 300/7 chics, at a profit of $8,500/7.

13-1 (a)

	Lower Limit	Upper Limit
Wood	36	120
Labor	50	$166\frac{2}{3}$

	(b)	(c)
X_T	54/7	40/7
X_C	30/7	100/7
X_B	0	0
P	1,530/7	2,300/7

13-2 (a)

	Lower Limit	Upper Limit
Table	15	50
Chair	6	20
Bookcase	$-\infty$	20

13-5 (a)

Constraint	Lower Limit	Upper Limit
A	70	∞
B	40	72
C	$-\infty$	75
D	14.5	25

(b) Only X_A changes, to 130.
(c) $X_1 = 10$, $X_2 = 0$, $X_3 = 10$; $X_A = 40$, $X_B = 0$, $X_C = 30$; $P = 300$

13-6 (a)

Variable	Lower Limit	Upper Limit
X_1	$-\infty$	20
X_2	$-\infty$	30
X_3	12.5	∞

(b) 360

14-5   See completed schedule for ski distribution problem on p. 436.

14-6   (b)

To From	U	V	W
A	—	50	50
B	—	—	150
C	150	150	—

$$C = 4{,}350$$

14-11   Ship 100 tombstones to Eldred from Abinger, and ship 50 tombstones to Cedrick and 150 tombstones to Dunstan from Barnesly.

15-4

Brat	Chore
Fritz	Retrieve the Captain's pipe
Hans	Scare cannibals
Gert	Pen ostriches
Zelda	Chase hippos

15-9

Production	Used for Demand
August regular—25	August—25
August overtime—75 ⎫ September regular—100 ⎭	September—175
October regular—100 ⎫ October overtime—50 ⎭	October—150
November regular—100 ⎫ November overtime—50 ⎭	November—150
$C = \$27{,}875$	

16-1   (c) $X_1 = 2,\ X_2 = 3;\ P = 18$

16-4 $X_R = 6,\ X_D = 6;\ P = 150$ $X_R = 0,\ X_D = 10;\ P = 150$
$X_R = 3,\ X_D = 8;\ P = 150$

16-10 $X_T = 9,\ X_C = 3,\ X_B = 0;\ P = 225$

17-1   (a) $5\frac{1}{3}$ regulars, $6\frac{2}{3}$ deluxes, $P = 153\frac{1}{3}$
(b) 0 regulars, 10 deluxes, $R = 600$

14-5 Completed shipment schedule for Problem 14-5

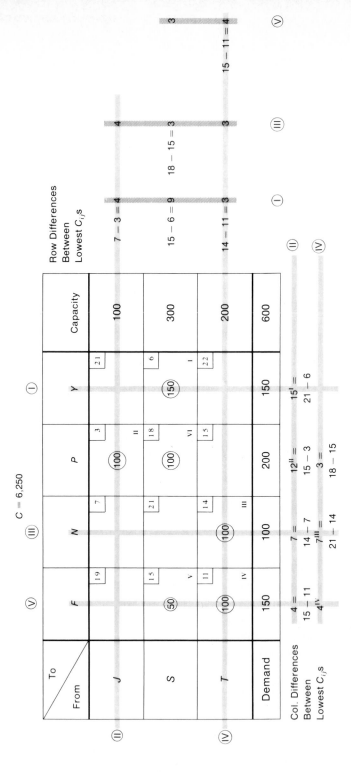

17-4 (b)

Original Variable	Value	Goal Deviation Variable	Value
X_E	49.88	Y_1^+	0.00
X_L	99.75	Y_1^-	0.00
X_R	276.18	Y_2^+	0.00
X_S	100.00	Y_2^-	166.57
X_M	7.61	Y_3^+	0.00
		Y_3^-	1,987.32
		Y_4^+	0.00
		Y_4^-	307.86

$$C = 641.0068$$

18-1 $a-c-e$

18-5 (b) $b-f-g-h$

18-8 (a) $a-c-d-f-i-j-k-m-n-o-p$ 32 months

18-17 (a)

Activity	Expected Time	Variance
a	6	.11
b	7	5.44
c	14	7.11
d	4	.11
e	17	.11

(b) $a-c-d$ (c) .7568

19-1

	(a)	(b)	(c)	(d)
L	4	2	.67	1.33
W	.20	.25	.34	3.33
L_q	3.2	1.33	.27	.76
W_q	.16	.17	.13	1.90
	.8	.67	.4	.57

19-4 (a) .20   (b) 66.67%; 2 hours

19-7 $34

19-8 (a) (1) .0923 hour   (2) .0606 hour   (b) (1) $28.38   (2) $21.82
One machinist clerk is cheapest.

19-10 (a) 5 checkers; 1.11 minutes   (b) .290 minute   (c) $56.66 for $S = 5$; $61.74   for $S = 6$

19-12 $L_q = .2725$, $L = .7725$, $W_q = .545$ minute, $W = 1.545$ minutes

19-14 (a)

n	P_n
0	.271
1	.217
2	.173
3	.139
4	.111
5	.089

(b) $L = 1.868$, $L_q = 1.139$, $W_q = .31$ hour, $W = .51$ hour   (c) $L = 4$, $L_q = 3.2$, $W_q = .8$ hour, $W = 1$ hour

19-15 (a)

n	P_n
0	.0367
1	.0918
2	.1835
3	.2753
4	.2753
5	.1376

(b) $L_q = 2.11$, $L = 3.07$, $W_q = 1.09$ days, $W = 1.59$ days   (c) $L_q = .5$, $L = 1$, $W_q = .5$ day, $W = 1$ day

19-16 $L_q = .25$, $L = .75$, $W_q = .5$ minute, $W = 1.5$ minutes

20-2 $1/\lambda = 13.05$ seconds

20-5 385

20-7 (a) $95.57 \le \mu \le 105.49$ minutes   (b) $69.05 \le \mu \le 69.35$ inches
(c) $\$11.27 \le \mu \le \$12.73$

20-10 $89.142 for one barber; $113.191 for two barbers. Hire the helper.

20-13 (a)

Net Winnings	Probability
$-\$1$	20/36
1	14/36
2	1/36
3	1/36

(c) $-\$.09$

21-5 A_3 and A_5

21-8 Spring-action movement

21-10 Test market. If that is successful, market nationally; if it is unsuccessful, abort.

21-11 Use no test and hire each candidate.

22-7

Event	Probability	Act				
		A_1	A_2	A_3	A_4	A_5
E_1	.2	10	0	10	5	0
E_2	.2	15	0	15	0	15
E_3	.6	0	10	5	5	5
Expected Opportunity Losses:		5	6	8	4	6

Act A_4 has the lowest expected opportunity loss.

22-8 (a) 27 for A_1 (b) 39   (c) 12   (d) 12   (e) They are the same values.

22-10 (a)

Sales Event	Probability	Tire Act A	B	C	Row Maximum
4,000	.30	$120,000	$130,000	$120,000	$130,000
7,000	.50	255,000	295,000	300,000	300,000
10,000	.20	390,000	460,000	480,000	480,000
Expected Payoffs:		241,500	278,500	282,000	285,000

(b) See above. Tire C is best.

(c) EVPI = $285,000 - 282,000 = $3,000

(d)

Sales Event	Probability	Tire Act A	B	C
4,000	.30	$10,000	$ 0	$10,000
7,000	.50	45,000	5,000	0
10,000	.20	90,000	20,000	0
Expected Opportunity Losses:		43,500	6,500	3,000

23-2 (a) 1/2   (d) 2/3

23-7 (a)

Result	Unconditional Probability	Posterior Probability Fair	Crooked
7	7/12	1/7	6/7
Not 7	5/12	1	0

23-11 (d) Distribute the film as an "A" feature if the results of the sneak preview are favorable, but sell to TV (T) if the results are unfavorable.

23-13 (c) The optimal strategy is to retain the old box if sales decrease and to use the new box otherwise.

24-2 (b)

Number of Children Liking	Proportion		
	$P = 1/4$	$P = 1/2$	$P = 3/4$
$R = 0$	.4219	.1250	.0156
$R = 1$	.4219	.3750	.1406
$R = 2$	.1406	.3750	.4219
$R = 3$	.0156	.1250	.4219
	1.0000	1.0000	1.0000

(e)

P	Posterior Probability
1/4	.02778
1/2	.22222
3/4	.75000
	1.00000

24-4 (c) (2) $21,559
(3) $21,259

24-6 (a) $0 for old and new designs
(b) $5,000

24-15 (b) $C = 1$ (c) $1,317.30 (d) $417.30

24-16 (a) Leave alone. (b) $300 He would not sample for a cost of $400, but he might sample if the cost is only $200.

24-18 (b) $C = 25g$ (c) $120.23 (d) $70.23

25-1

	(a)	(b)	(c)	(d)
(1)	Act 1	Act 2	Act 1	Act 2
(2)	$1,978	$4,166	$35,090	$30,690

25-2 (a) Payoff $= \begin{cases} -\$50,000 + \$1,000\,\mu & \text{for helmet} \\ \$\,0 & \text{for no helmet} \end{cases}$

$\mu_b = 50$ helmets per store
(b) Yes (c) $833.20

25-6 (a) $14,688
(b) 1.59 gigabits per day
(c) $\mu_1 = 2.07$; $\sigma_1 = .57$ Choose the holographic unit.
(d) .5478

26-3 (a)

	Acts	
Events	Policy	No Policy
Tornado	− $500	− $40,000
No tornado	− 500	0

(b) − $500 for a policy; − $4 for no policy (c) No

26-8 (a) Willing   (b,c) Might be willing   (d) Unwilling   (e) Willing

26-10 No

26-13 (a)

	Acts	
Events	Buy	Rent
Win contract	$120,000	$50,000
Lose contract	− 40,000	0

(b) $40,000 for buying; $25,000 for renting

(c)

	Acts	
Events	Buy	Rent
Win contract	400	300
Lose contract	0	200

(d) 200 for buying; 250 for renting   (e) Rent

26-16 (a) 1/2   (b) 3/4; 1/4   (c) 1/2   Inconsistent

27-2 A_3, A_4, B_3, B_4, B_5

27-4 (b) $P = 7/16$; Value of game $= -1/16$ (c) $Q = 7/16$ (d) Unchanged
(e) Unchanged   (f) 13/20; Yes

27-7

DRACULA		UNION	
Act	Probability	Act	Probability
Tranquil	2/9	Tranquil	4/9
Lock-in	7/9	Strike	5/9
Bite union leaders	0	Wooden stake sabotage	0
		$V =$ value of game $= 100/9$ coffins	

27-11 (a) Both players should choose blue; 1 cent.   (b) Yes; 5 cents.

28-1 (a,b,c) 1–2–5–9–13–15   cost = 24 dollars

28-3 (a) $495   (b) All items are zero except for radio transmitters, 3 of which will be carried.

28-6 Produce 400 units in February, March, and May, and make no units in the other months, at a cost of $5,075.

28-7 Assign two trucks to sites 1 and 2 and one truck to site 3, at a cost of $40,250.

28-11 The two best policies are: (1) to buy 3 CD-10s, 1 Tupolev 100, and none of the other models, or (2) to buy 5 Tupolev 100s.

29-1 $p_A = .5294, p_B = .4706$

29-3 (a) $p_1 = 3/7, p_2 = 4/7$ (b) In period 4

29-5 Policy 3

29-10 (a) 7,977   (b) 9,080.2

Index